JEFFREY WOLF GREEN EVOLU

EA Glossary

Compiled by Linda Jonson
and the School of Evolutionary Astrology

The EA Glossary is a well-researched, informative and illuminating compilation of key terms, topics and guiding principles used in Jeffrey Wolf Green's Evolutionary Astrology that affirms and expands upon the core EA paradigm taught in his books:

Pluto: The Evolutionary Journey of the Soul (Vol. 1)
Pluto: The Soul's Evolution through Relationships (Vol. 2)

Compiled from extracts from the message board of the School of Evolutionary Astrology from March 2009 to October 2013, the EA Glossary provides indispensable study material for resourceful EA students and discerning members of the astrological community, in essence serving as a compass to help navigate into the depths of Evolutionary Astrology.

THE SCHOOL OF EVOLUTIONARY ASTROLOGY

Website: www.schoolofevolutionaryastrology.com
Message board: www.schoolofevolutionaryastrology.com/forum/

Copyright © 2014   School of Evolutionary Astrology
All rights reserved.
ISBN-13:978-1497443402
ISBN-10:1497443407

JEFFREY WOLF GREEN EVOLUTIONARY ASTROLOGY

EA Glossary

TABLE OF CONTENTS

MAIN CHAPTERS

ASPECTS & PHASES	1	EVOLUTION	163
ASPECTS & PHASES (JWG)	16	GENERAL ASTROLOGY	174
ASTROLOGER/CLIENT RELATIONSHIP	31	GOD/GODDESS – SPIRITUAL PRACTICE	198
DAEMON SOUL	39	KARMA	227
EA ARCHETYPES		LOVE AND SEXUALITY	230
ARIES	42	LUCIFER	236
TAURUS	47	LUNAR NODES	242
GEMINI	52	MATRIARCHY AND PATRIARCHY	256
CANCER	61	NATURAL LAW	260
LEO	72	PLANETARY NODES	270
VIRGO	75	PLUTO	280
LIBRA	84	RELATIONSHIPS – SYNASTRY & COMPOSITE	304
SCORPIO	90	RETROGRADE ARCHETYPE	314
SAGITTARIUS	101	SKIPPED STEPS	320
CAPRICORN	111	SOUL	335
AQUARIUS	122	STAGES OF EVOLUTION	357
PISCES	131	TRANSITS	382
EA CHART INTERPRETATION	147		

TABLES AND FIGURES

TABLE 1 – Seven Soul Types	394	TABLE 8B – Asteroid Speeds	398
TABLE 2 – Stages of Evolution	394	TABLE 9 – Lilith Trinity	399
TABLE 3 – Chart Rectification – Questions to Ask	395	TABLE 10 – EA General Orbs	400
TABLE 4 – Planetary Nodes for Everyone	396	TABLE 11 – Key Planetary Pairs	400
TABLE 5 – EA Phases and Zodiacal Correlations	396	TABLE 12 – EA Archetypes	401
TABLE 6 – Astrological Ages and Sub-Ages	397	FIG 1 – Chakra Correlations Diagram	404
TABLE 7 – EA Phases, Aspects and Degrees	398	FIG 2 – EA Phases, Aspects and Degrees Chart	404
TABLE 8A – Planetary Speeds	398		

ASPECTS AND PHASES

Mathematical model	1	Polarities of the phases	9
Difference between phases and aspects	1	Current life Sun and angles	10
Phasal relationship – between two planets	1	Conjunction	10
Phasal relationship between two planets – examples	1	New phase conjunction of two planets – example	10
Phasal relationship – nodes	2	Example of new phase conjunction – Moon/Neptune	10
Phasal relationship – between the nodes and a planet	2	Balsamic conjunction of two planets – example	10
Phasal relationship – nodes in synastry	2	Septile	10
Phasal relationship – the conjunction	2	Sextile	10
Phasal relationship – Pluto polarity point	3	Square, semisquare, sesquiquadrate	11

iii

Topic	Page	Topic	Page
Phasal relationship – between the Sun and a planet	3	Sesquiquadrate – other names for	11
Phasal relationship – transits	3	Inconjunct: the most misunderstood aspect	11
Phasal relationship – nodes and planets, transiting and natal	3	Inconjunct, gibbous phase	11
Phasal relationship – between retrograde planets	3	Inconjunct, full phase	12
Yang to yin aspects	4	Inconjunct – between 2nd house (Taurus) and 7th house (Libra)	12
Phases correlating to zodiacal archetypes	4	Triseptile	13
Key turning points of aspects within a phase	4	Sesquiquadrate	13
TABLE 5 – EA Phases and Zodiacal Correlations	5	Sesquiquadrate, first quarter	13
Evolutionary timing cycles	6	Sesquiquadrate, full phase	13
Waxing and waning halves of the phasal cycle	6	Sesquiquadrate, disseminating phase	13
Stressful aspects	7	Interpretation of a phasal relationship aspect, eg conjunction	13
Culmination in the balsamic phase	7	FIG 2– EA Aspects, Phases and Degrees Chart	14
TABLE 7 – EA Aspects, Phases and Degrees	8	Opposition	14
Balsamic phases – in relationships	9	Transiting opposition, example	14
Pluto/Mars balsamic conjunction	9	Quintile	14
Comparison of balsamic and new phase aspects in composite	9	Yod	15
Transitional aspects (aspects occurring at the end of a phase)	9	Understanding phases, aspects and signs within a planetary configuration, eg yod	15

ASPECTS AND PHASES (JWG)

Topic	Page	Topic	Page
Introduction	16	First quarter phase biseptile	23
NEW PHASE	16	Relationship between biseptile and its polarity aspect	23
Action and reaction	16	First quarter phase trine	
New evolutionary cycle	16	GIBBOUS PHASE	23
Relationship between new phase and full phase	17	Relationship between gibbous phase and balsamic phase	24
New phase conjunction	17	Gibbous phase triseptile	25
Absolute conjunction to 10 deg of separation	18	FULL PHASE	25
Progressions	18	Gibbous phase opposition	25
Stelliums	18	Full phase opposition	26
New phase semi-sextile	18	Full phase triseptile	26
Relationship between new phase semi-sextile and full phase inconjunct	18	Full phase inconjunct	26
New phase novile	19	Full phase biquintile	26
Mutational aspects	19	Sesquiquadrate (full phase and disseminating phase)	26
CRESCENT PHASE	19	DISSEMINATING PHASE	26
Relationship between crescent phase and disseminating phase	19	Disseminating sesquiquadrate	26
Semisquare (mutational aspect – new phase and crescent phase)	20	Disseminating trine	27
Relationship between crescent semisquare and disseminating sesquiquadrate	20	Relationship between disseminating phase and crescent phase	27
Crescent phase septile	20	LAST QUARTER PHASE	27
Crescent phase sextile	21	Square (disseminating and last quarter)	27
Relationship between crescent phase and disseminating phase	21	Last quarter square	28
Crescent phase quintile	21	Last quarter quintile	28
Relationship between crescent phase quintile and disseminating phase	21	Last quarter sextile	29
Crescent phase square (crescent phase and first quarter phase)	21	Last quarter septile	29
Relationship between first quarter square and disseminating square	22	Semisquare (last quarter phase and balsamic phase – mutational aspect)	29
Relationship between crescent phase square and disseminating square	22	BALSAMIC PHASE	29
FIRST QUARTER PHASE	22	Last quarter phase semisquare	29
First quarter phase square	22	Balsamic phase semisquare	29
Crescent phase and first quarter phase square	23		

ASTROLOGER/CLIENT RELATIONSHIP

EA methodology	31	"The value is in the effort"	34
Adjust readings to the evolutionary stage of the client	31	Individual context of a Soul	35
Observation and correlation	31	Inductive/deductive knowledge	35
Clients asking their questions in advance	31	Karmic causes vs evolutionary necessity	35
Different approaches to client readings	31	Repeating themes	35
Answering the client's questions	32	True EA work is guided by Spirit	35
Beginning a session with a prayer, candle and crystal	33	Making predictions	36
Asking "Why?"	33	Hiding signature	36
Astrologer unearthing unresolved trauma	34	Advice to clients – an example	36
Very difficult chart dynamics	34	Looking into the Souls of others	36
Abuse as catalyst for evolution	34	Chart rectification	37
Use of intuition in readings	34	TABLE 3 – Chart rectification – questions to ask	38

DAEMON SOUL

Natural Laws	39	Daemon Soul from other star system	40
Totality of nature	39	Dominion over nature – distortion of Natural Laws	40
Observation and correlation of the Daemon nature	39	Sagittarius archetype	40
Devas, angels, fairies	39	Healing the Daemon nature within the Soul	40

ARIES – MARS – 1ST HOUSE

Aries keywords	42	Mars/Pluto in primary life	44
Aries, Mars, 1st house archetype	42	Mars retrograde	44
Pluto in the 1st house or Aries	42	Cardinal signs/houses	44
Pluto polarity point – 7th house or Libra	42	Aspects to Mars/Aries	45
Aries archetype	43	Mars transit	45
Mars, lower octave of Pluto	43	Mars transit – anger	45
Mars rulership	44	Mars – natal, transits & progressions	46
Mars/Pluto interface	44	War	46

TAURUS – VENUS – 2ND HOUSE

Taurus keywords	47	Taurus side of Venus Rx	50
Taurus, Venus, 2nd house archetype	47	Venus – past, present, future orientations	50
Pluto in the 2nd house or Taurus	47	Inner hearing	50
Pluto polarity point – 8th house or Scorpio	47	Voyeurism	50
Venus archetype	48	Life purpose	50
Venus double rulership – Taurus and Libra	49	Venus transit	51
Psychology of listening, inner and outer sides of Venus	50	Music	51

GEMINI – MERCURY – 3RD HOUSE

Gemini keywords	52	Mercury/Jupiter – balsamic conjunction	55
Gemini, Mercury, 3rd house archetype	52	Mercury/Jupiter – new phase conjunction	55
Pluto in the 3rd house or Gemini	52	Beliefs – unconscious, fragmented, disconnected contradictory	55
Pluto polarity point – 9th house or Sagittarius	53	Differences/nuances between Pluto 3rd house, Mercury in Scorpio, Scorpio ruling 3rd house	57
Mercury retrograde	53	Mercury function of the Soul in human form Q & A	57
Hearing	53	Maya of phenomenal appearance Q & A	58
Data, observation and correlation	53	Natural limit to the perception of the totality of the manifested Creation Q & A	58
How a planet, eg Mercury, manifests in each Evolutionary Stage – by Gonzalo Romero	54	Is the thought function a creative act? Q & A	58
Mercury and Jupiter correlations	55	Disillusionment and doubt, a personal experience	58
Crisis of belief, waning square Mercury/Jupiter	55	Information/knowledge/beliefs from life to life	60

CANCER – MOON – 4TH HOUSE

Cancer keywords	61	Spiritual bypass	66
Cancer, Moon, 4th house archetype	61	Emotional manipulation	68
Pluto in the 4th house or Cancer	61	Security needs – Cancer, Libra, Aries	68

Pluto polarity point – 10th house or Capricorn	62	Co-dependency	68
Moon/Cancer archetype – core dynamics	63	Conditioned gender assignment	68
Ego as vehicle of evolution	63	Gender switch	69
Wave/ocean analogy	63	Mother/father archetype	69
Familiarity and security	64	4th/10th houses – one size does not fit all	69
Water trinity – Cancer, Scorpio, Pisces	64	Progressed Moon	69
Cardinal signs/houses	64	South or North Node in Cancer – on an individual level	69
Emotional conditioning – the womb and early childhood development	64	South Node in Cancer, North Node in Capricorn – on a global level	70
Displaced emotions	65	Pluto's Nodes in Capricorn/Cancer	70
Evolution through the emotional body NEW	65	Moon/Neptune interface	70
Practices to work with the emotional body	65	What is that Cancer polarity? Reflections on Pluto in Capricorn – by Bradley Naragon	70

LEO – SUN – 5TH HOUSE

Leo keywords	72	Nodes of the Sun	73
Leo, Sun, 5th house archetype	72	North Node – and next life's Sun	73
Pluto in the 5th house or Leo	72	Children	74
Pluto polarity point – 11th house or Aquarius	73	Father	74
Sun	73	Creation	74
Sun/Pluto interface	73	Leo/Virgo interface	74
Polarity point of the Sun?	73		

VIRGO – MERCURY – 6TH HOUSE

Virgo keywords	75	JWG's method of eliminating LEARNED masochism (for children)	79
Virgo, Mercury, 6th house archetype	76	Synthesis of Virgo/Leo archetypes	79
Pluto in the 6th house or Virgo	76	Natural square Virgo/Sagittarius	80
Pluto polarity point – 12th house or Pisces	77	Conditioned and unconditioned Virgo	80
Natural guilt	77	Inductive and deductive thought	80
Man-made guilt and natural guilt	77	Life purpose	80
Guilt and atonement	77	Compensation	80
How to deal with natural guilt	77	Disillusionment and doubt, a personal experience	81
Perfection	78	Pluto in Virgo generation – Great Mother Goddess	82
Chart markers of masochism	78	"The Secret," thoughts changing reality	83
JWG's method of eliminating LEARNED masochism	78		

LIBRA – VENUS – 7TH HOUSE

Libra keywords	84	Inner Venus (2nd house)	87
Libra, Venus, 7th house archetype	84	Projection	87
Pluto in the 7th house or Libra	84	Projections, delusions, expectations	87
Pluto polarity point – 1st house or Aries	85	De facto God or Goddess	88
Venus double rulership – Libra and Taurus	85	Dance and music	88
Past, present, future orientations of a planet (eg Venus)	86	Venus transit	88
Psychology of listening	86	Neptune and higher octave Venus	88
Cardinal energy	86	Co-dependency	88
Venus retrograde	87	Giving away power in relationships	89
Venus in composite and synastry	87		

SCORPIO – PLUTO – 8TH HOUSE

Scorpio keywords	90		
Scorpio, Pluto, 8th house archetype	90	Pluto in the 8th house – example	96
Pluto in the 8th house or Scorpio	90	Pluto/Uranus interface	96
Pluto polarity point – 2nd house or Taurus	91	North Node in Scorpio, ruler Pluto	97
Where Pluto/Scorpio fits into the total structure of consciousness	91	South Node in Scorpio, ruler Pluto	97
Abandonment, betrayal, loss, violation of trust	91	Hate	97

Evolution through the emotional body	91	Early/sudden death	98
Practices to work with the emotional body	92	Death	98
Spiritual bypass	92	Suicide	98
Choice whether to evolve or not	95	Suicide and other archetypes (Capricorn, Aries, Virgo, Pisces, Taurus)	99

SAGITTARIUS – JUPITER – 9TH HOUSE

Sagittarius keywords	101	Sagittarius/Capricorn archetypes, and Natural Law	105
Sagittarius, Jupiter, 9th house archetype	101	Understanding the Sagittarius and Pisces archetypes within the Consensus state	106
Pluto in the 9th house or Sagittarius	101	Understanding the Sagittarius and Pisces archetypes within the Individuated state	106
Pluto polarity point – 3rd house or Gemini	102	Manifest and unmanifest creation	107
Compensation	102	Sagittarius, Jupiter, 9th house correlations	107
Resolutions for compensation	103	Crisis of belief – waning square Mercury/Jupiter	107
Compassion	103	Mercury/Jupiter – balsamic conjunction	107
False beliefs of the Soul	104	Mercury/Jupiter – phase conjunction	107
Data, observation and correlation	104	Beliefs – unconscious, fragmented, disconnected, contradictory	107
Intuition	104	Mercury and Jupiter correlations	109
Synthesizing truths via intuition	104	Information/knowledge/beliefs from life to life	109
Awareness inducing realizations	105	Disillusionment and doubt, a personal experience	109

CAPRICORN – SATURN – 10TH HOUSE

Capricorn keywords	111	Saturn retrograde	116
Capricorn, Saturn, 10th house archetype	111	Saturn, and Spiritual evolution	116
Pluto in the 10th house or Capricorn	111	Natural Law, and the Sagittarius/Capricorn archetypes	116
Pluto polarity point – 4th house or Cancer	112	Perversion of Natural Laws	117
Cardinal signs/houses	113	What does undistorted Capricorn look like?	117
Saturn correlations	113	Capricorn archetype as an expression of Love	117
Life purpose – work – career	113	Mother/father archetype	117
Time / timelessness	113	Saturn Return	118
Archetype of judgment (Capricorn) manifesting through Pisces	113	Need to access chaos	119
Gender switch	114	Conditions of birth, life and death	119
Transit of Saturn	114	Projected judgments	119
Pluto in Capricorn transit	114	Judgments	120
South Node of Pluto in Capricorn	115	Races of people on earth	120
Archetype of distortion	115	Earned guilt	120
Reflection	116	What is that Cancer polarity? Reflections on Pluto in Capricorn – by Bradley Naragon	121

AQUARIUS – URANUS – 11TH HOUSE

Aquarius keywords	122	Past life memories and long term memories	126
Aquarius, Uranus, 11th house archetype	122	Projections, delusions, expectations	126
Pluto in Aquarius or the 11th house	123	Behavioral contagion – collective delusion	127
Pluto polarity point – 5th house or Leo	123	Uranus/Pluto interface	127
Trauma	124	Number sequences and patterns occurring in consciousness	127
Repetitive thoughts	124	Judgment and projection	128
Thought complexes	124	Personal application of Uranus/Saturn to Pluto	128
Data, observation and correlation	124	Kundalini / root chakra	129
De-conditioning	125	Physiology of the brain	130
Objectification	125	Channeling	130
Collective unconscious / individuated unconscious	125	The breath	130
Individuated unconscious	125	South Node of Neptune in Aquarius	130
Unconscious beliefs	126		

PISCES – NEPTUNE – 12TH HOUSE

Pisces keywords	131	Perfection	138
Pisces, Neptune, 12th house archetype	131	Neptune correlations	139
Pluto in the 12th house or Pisces	131	Emphasized 12th house	139
Pluto polarity point – 6th house or Virgo	133	Inductive/deductive thought	139
The totality of consciousness	133	Neptunian emotions	139
Wave/ocean analogy	134	Evolution through the emotional body	140
Absolute totality of truth	134	Practices to work with the emotional body	140
Creation, manifest and unmanifest	135	Spiritual bypass	140
Soul and the veil of maya – Yogananda	135	Neptune and higher octave Venus	142
South Node of Neptune in Aquarius	135	Guilt	143
Natural Law that holds Creation together	136	Neptune retrograde	143
Hiding signature	136	Retrograde Venus into Pisces	143
Unconditional love	136	True channeling	143
Divine love	136	Psychics	143
Mercy	136	Pluto/Neptune, addictions	144
Collective unconscious / individuated nconscious	136	Neptune sextile Pluto	144
Projections, delusions, expectations	136	Guilt/atonement	144
Behavioral contagion – collective delusion	137	Disillusionment and doubt, a personal experience	144
Dreams	137	Man-made guilt and natural guilt	145
Dreams – sleep walking	137	Chart markers of masochism	146
Dreams – super-conscious dreams	137	Planetary pairs, Neptune and Moon	146
Dreams – under attack, aggression, danger, sexual assault, attack by evil?	137	Music and dance	146
Dreams – unresolved Soul trauma	138	Archetype of judgment (Capricorn) manifesting through Pisces	146
Soul correlates to Pluto (not Neptune)	138		

EA CHART INTERPRETATION

Primary evolutionary/karmic axis	147	Changing habits	154
Understanding EA as holistic and non-linear	147	Changing habits – example 10th house Pluto	154
EA methodology	148	Changing habits through the PPP, North Node, and North Node ruler	154
Natural Law of the trinity	148	Polarity points of the planets	154
Karmic causes / 'victimized' clients	148	Natural polarities	155
Karmic causes / evolutionary necessity	148	Natural polarities – retrograde planets	155
Determining the past evolutionary dynamics	149	Paradoxical charts	155
Past, present, future orientations of a planet	149	Paradoxical chart – Lunar Nodes example	156
House system and planetary method of chart interpretation	149	Paradoxical chart – example	156
Repeating themes	149	Same house, sign and planet combinations (eg Jupiter in Sagittarius in the 9th house)	157
Individualized context	149	Soul playing out both sides of a dynamic	157
Understanding the entire contents of the chart	150	Hiding signature	157
Inductive/deductive knowledge	150	Planet near a house cusp	157
Intuition and integrity	150	Unaspected planets	158
True EA work is guided by Spirit	150	Planets in opposition	158
How to Transcend Astrological Influences by Paramhansa Yogananda	150	Planet conjunct house cusp – mutation of archetypes	158
Porphyry house system	151	Understanding skipped steps	158
Correlation	151	Archetypes evolving into another	158
True Nodes, Mean Nodes	152	New evolutionary cycle	158
Synthesizing the layers	152	Original conjunction	159
House, sign and planet = one archetype	152	Transit event charts – original conjunction, 1st quarter square, etc.	159
Facilitator/ruler	152	Stationary planet or node	160
Ruler of Pluto polarity point	152	Singleton archetype	160

Soul correlates to Pluto, not Neptune	152	Chart patterns – bucket, bundle, locomotive, splash, splay, etc.	160
Progression of Pluto's evolution through the houses	152	Example of bowl chart pattern	160
Sun	152	Making predictions	160
Sun polarity point?	152	Unconscious guilt patterns	160
Mars	152	Parent/child relationships	160
Mars/Pluto phase – subsidiary/primary lives	153	Health/disease issues	160
Generational planets	153	Death, early/sudden	161
Understanding the individual context within a chart	153	Difficult aspects, fear of death	161
Soul's prior lives	153	Prediction of death	161
Asking "Why?"	153	Unknown birth time	161
One size does not fit all	153	Chart rectification	161
Chart weighted toward growth	154		

EVOLUTION

TABLE 2 – Stages of Evolution	163	Collective evolution, on a global scale	167
Natural law of evolution	163	Collective evolution – Pluto sextile Neptune	168
Evolution of the Soul	163	Advancing one's own evolution	168
Three reactions to evolutionary growth	164	Evolution via polarity points of the planets	169
Evolutionary signature	164	Progressive evolution	170
Evolution of consciousness	164	Natural Law of elimination	170
Evolutionary past	164	Natural evolution, evolving beyond that which has been developed	171
Natural Law of the Trinity	165	New evolutionary cycle, meaning of	171
Evolution through the emotional body	165	Evolutionary capacity	171
Practices to work with the emotional body	165	Rates of evolution	171
Changing old habits	165	Evolving the consensus	171
Reaching an evolutionary limit	166	Evolution and involution	172
Resistance – self-consistency – evolution	166	Advanced Souls attempting to change the world	172
Resistance – example	166	De-evolution	172
Progression of Pluto's evolution through the houses	166	When Souls go back to Source	172
Retrograde archetype and accelerated evolution	166		

GENERAL ASTROLOGY

AC-DC-MC-IC	174	Planet one degree or less from a house cusp	186
Ascendant	174	Planet at 0 deg or 30 deg of a sign	186
Transiting Pluto crossing the Ascendant	175	Decans - natural trinities within each sign	186
Nodes square angle	175	Signs on the houses	187
Example of Nodes square angle	175	"Culminating" archetype	187
ASTEROIDS	176	Planet conjunct a non-angular house cusp	187
TABLE 8B – Asteroid Speeds	176	Pluto, evolutionary progression through houses	187
Asteroid square Nodes	176	Two signs in a house	187
Asteroid – retrograde	176	INTERCEPTED SIGNS	188
Octave transformers	177	KEY PLANETARY PAIRS	189
Pallas	177	Synthesizing the archetypes	189
Psyche	177	Sun/Moon phase	189
CHART PATTERNS	178	Moon/Saturn	189
Bucket, bundle, bowl, locomotive, seesaw, splash	178	TABLE 11 – Key Planetary Pairs by JWG	190
CHIRON	178	Mars/Venus	190
Planetary Nodes of Chiron	179	Mercury/Jupiter	190
Chiron square Nodes	179	Jupiter/Saturn	190
Chiron transit	179	Saturn/Uranus	191
Chiron – masochism, guilt	180	Mars/Venus phase in relationship	191
Chiron in EA	181	LAYERS – HOUSE, PLANET, SIGN, ASPECTS	191
Chiron's influence in the chart	181	LILITH TRINITY	191
Rulership of Chiron	181	TABLE 9 – Lilith Trinity	192
Chiron conjunct North Node of Moon	181	Asteroid Lilith	192

DECANS	182	Black Moon Lilith	193
Decans and planetary ruler	182	Dark Moon Lilith	193
Natural trinities within each sign	182	Lilith trinity and the chakras	194
DEGREES AND ORBS	183	Octave transformers	194
Orbs – how long working on any given issue	183	MOTION OF THE NODES, MOON, PLANETS	195
TABLE 10 – EA General Orbs	183	MYSTIC RECTANGLE	195
Working with wider orbs	183	ORBS (See DEGREES AND ORBS)	183
Planet at 0-1 degrees	184	PLANETARY SPEEDS	196
Planet at 29 degrees	184	Table 8A – Planetary Speeds	196
Planet at 0 deg or 30 deg of a sign	184	PROGRESSED CHART	196
Degree of house cusp	184	RULERSHIPS	196
Pluto, culminating degree	184	SABIAN SYMBOLS	196
Critical degrees	184	SECONDARY PROGRESSIONS	196
ECLIPSES	184	SOLAR ARCS	196
FINAL DISPOSITOR	185	SOLAR-LUNAR RETURNS	197
HOUSE SYSTEM	185	TRUE NODES	197
HOUSES AND CUSPS	186	VERTEX AND ANTI-VERTEX	197
Degree of a house cusp	186		

GOD/GODDESS – SPIRITUAL PRACTICE

Natural God	198	Practices to work with the emotional body	211
Cycles of creation	198	Unconditional and conditional love	211
God's Will	199	Natural Law of free choice	212
Imperfection of the Creator	199	Deviation from Natural Law	212
Source, the ultimate projector	199	Dharma	212
Manifest and unmanifest creation	199		
Absolute totality of Truth	199	When Souls go back to Source	212
Aligning with God/ess	200	Death	213
Seeking God first	200	'1, 2' Meditation (Hong Sau), the way back home to the Creator	213
How to be happy?	200	Kundalini and Kriya yoga	215
How to Transcend Astrological Influences by Paramhansa Yogananda	200	Laya Yoga	216
God/Goddess enforcing evolution	201	Laya Yoga – Sounds specific to each chakra	216
Water trinity	201	The veil of maya	216
Ocean/wave analogy	201	South Node of Neptune in Aquarius	216
The third eye	202	Natural Law that holds creation together	217
Neptunian emotions	202	JWG's method of eliminating LEARNED masochism	217
Evolution through the emotional body	203	Jeffrey Wolf Green's Method of Eliminating LEARNED Masochism (for children)	218
Neptune and higher octave Venus	203	Archetypes correlating to the chakra system	218
EA paradigm	204	FIG 1 – Chakra correlations diagram	219
Soul	204	Spiritual nature of water signs	219
Stages of Samadhi	205	Can putting God first be the cause of skipped steps?	220
Guru/Avatar assignments	206	Disillusionment and doubt, a personal experience	220
Karma of an Avatar	206	How to deal with natural guilt	221
Soul of Jesus	206	Awareness of transcendent truths	221
Ramana Maharshi	206	Natural Law of separation	221
Yogananda	206	Exhausting separating desires	222
Co-creation with the Divine	206	Profound discontent	222
TABLE 1 – Seven Soul types	207	Perfection	222
Guru, teacher, shaman	207	Misconceptions about God	224
Guru/disciple relationship	207	Patriarchal standard of God-perfection	224
Martial arts	208	Dominion over nature	224
Guru/devotee crisis	208	Violation of Natural Law	225
Spiritual bypass	208	Inherent knowledge of right and wrong	225

The non-dual state	211	Archetype of judgment (Capricorn) manifesting through Pisces	225
Length of time it takes for liberation	212	A letter about the journey of human Souls – by Bradley Naragon	225
How far can one evolve in one lifetime?	212		

KARMA

What is karma?	227	Relationship karma	228
Karma or evolutionary necessity?	227	Karma through sexual exchange	228
Karmic signature	228	Cleansing karma	229
Karma in the birth chart	228	Agni ritual	229
Karma of skipped steps	228	Do Avatar's have karma?	229
Karma with parents	228	Yogananda	229

LOVE AND SEXUALTY

Love – conditional and unconditional	230	Sexual arousal with not actually having sex	232
Soul mates	230	Agni ritual	233
Loving feelings vs loving behaviors	230	Understanding sexuality through the EA paradigm	233
Love and control	231	Sex and sexuality	233
Patriarchal sexual reality	231	Gender and gender identity	233
Primary brain, sexual desires	232	Gender switch	233
Suppression of sexual desires	232	Signatures correlating to homosexuality and bisexuality	233
Neptune and higher octave Venus	232	Gender switch, bisexuality, homosexuality, duplicity	233
When sexuality is not a function of separating desires	232	Androgyny	234
Karma through sexual exchange	232	Dark Moon Lilith – fear and hatred of sexuality	235

LUCIFER

Lucifer – symbolizing God and Evil	236	Anger	238
Evil	236	Dreams – under attack, aggression, danger, sexual assault, attack by evil?	238
Making or breaking a contract with evil	236	Lucifer – connection to Leo	239
Contract with evil and the North Node/Pluto polarity point	237	Pluto transiting natal Lucifer	239
Contract with evil – Hitler	237	Transiting Lucifer/Bearer of Light in Capricorn	239
Lucifer Rx	238	Transiting South Node of Lucifer/Bearer of Light	240
Profound discontent, dark clouds, violation of Natural Law	238	Transiting Lucifer/Bearer of Light in Aquarius	241

LUNAR NODES

South Node	242	Pluto conjunct South Node	249
North Node	242	Pluto conjunct South Node, balsamic	250
North Node and Pluto polarity point	242	Pluto conjunct North Node, integrating the sign of the PPP	250
Mean motion of the Nodes	242	Pluto conjunct North Node – NO Pluto polarity point	250
True Nodes	242	Pluto conjunct North Node – what about the South Node?	250
Nodes at 29 degrees	242	Pluto conjunct North Node – and planet(s) aspecting South Node	251
Nodes at 0 degrees	242	Pluto conjunct North Node – amount of distance between Pluto and North Node	251
Nodes at 1 degree	243	North Node in the same sign as, but not conjunct, Pluto – is there a Pluto polarity point?	251
Nodes – direct	243	North Node in the same sign as, but not conjunct, Pluto, and in a different house to Pluto – is there a Pluto polarity point?	251
Nodes – stationary	243	Ruler of North Node conjunct Pluto – is there a Pluto polarity point?	251
Transiting Lunar Nodes, 'apparent' versus 'actual'	243	South Node Leo, ruled by the Sun	251
Transiting Lunar Nodes t-square natal planet	243	Sun conjunct North Node	251
Transiting Lunar Nodes t-square planet – in a death chart	243	Sun square Nodes, and planets conjunct the North Node	251
Transiting South Node of anything	243	Sun square Nodes, and NO planets conjunct the North Node	252

Conscious/unconscious patterns	243	Sun square Nodes, and nodal ruler conjunct the Sun	252
Nodes – calculation of phasal relationship	244	Sun square Nodes, nodal ruler conjunct the Sun – and orbs	252
Nodes in synastry – calculation of phasal relationship	244	Sun square Nodes, and North Node ruler conjunct the Sun	252
Calculation of phasal relationship – nodes and planets, transiting and natal	244	North Node – and next life's Sun	252
Nodal Axis, in the next life	244	Nodal rulers in any non-conjunction aspect to each other	252
Shifts from South Node to North Node, and Pluto to Pluto polarity point	244	Ruler of South Node conjunct Pluto	252
North Node Scorpio, ruled by Pluto	244	Ruler of South Node conjunct ruler of North Node (which is Pluto itself)	253
South Node Scorpio, ruled by Pluto	245	Ruler of South Node conjunct ruler of North Node, and both also conjunct South Node	253
South or North Node in Cancer – on a personal level	245	Ruler of South Node conjunct ruler of North Node	253
South Node in Cancer, North Node in Capricorn – on a global level	245	Ruler of South Node conjunct ruler of North Node, new phase	253
Planet conjunct South Node	245	Ruler of South Node conjunct South Node	254
Retrograde planet conjunct South Node	246	Ruler of North Node conjunct North Node	254
Planet conjunct North Node	246	Ruler of North Node conjunct South Node, and both conjunct Pluto	254
Retrograde planet conjunct North Node	246	Ruler of North Node conjunct South Node	254
Moon conjunct South Node, ruler of North Node conjunct Pluto	247	Role of North Node when a planet is conjunct South Node	254
Moon conjunct South Node, example	247	Nodal rulers in any non-conjunction aspect to each other	255
Pluto conjunct South Node, and second Saturn return	248		

MATRIARCHY AND PATRIARCHY

Transition from matriarchy to patriarchy	256	Natural Law, and the Sagittarius/Capricorn archetypes	258
Arcs within the Yugas	256	What does undistorted Capricorn look like?	258
Zarathustras	257	Extinction of the human race	258
Planetary Nodes Capricorn/Cancer	257	Biological parents	258
Patriarchy, and evolutionary states	257	Patriarchal standard of God-perfection	259
Modern culture vs indigenous culture	257	Patriarchal self-judgment	259
Matriarchal groups in recent times	258		

NATURAL LAWS

Leadership within Natural Law	260	Learned guilt vs natural guilt	265
Natural Law of giving, sharing and inclusion	260	Natural atonement – "I am sorry"	265
Knowledge vs belief	260	How to deal with natural guilt	265
Deviation – distortion – violation – perversion of Natural Law	260	Patriarchal standard of God-perfection	265
Forces of evil	261	Patriarchal self-judgment	266
Extinction of the human race	261	Law of attraction – "The Secret"	266
Biological parents	261	Anger	266
Natural Law of evolution of consciousness	262	Hate	266
Natural Law and command of the Natural Goddess	262	Fear of Natural Law	267
Natural Law of the trinity	262	Natural parenting	267
Natural Law of involution	262	Natural roles for men and women	268
Natural Laws of light, gravity, motion, magnetism, vibration, and heat	263	Male courting	268
Natural Law of free choice	263	Nature	268
Natural Law of separation	263	Daemon Soul	268
Natural Law of elimination	263	Consciousness of plants	268
Natural Law of love	264	Archetype of judgment (Capricorn) manifesting through Pisces	268
Natural Law of guilt	264		

PLANETARY NODES

Use and function of Planetary Nodes	270	Planet conjunct Planetary South Node	275
TABLE 4 – Planetary Nodes for everyone	271	Natal planets conjunct collective Nodes	275
SPREADSHEET – Annual Planetary Node Cycles Each Year	271	Planet square Planetary Nodes	275
Planetary Nodes – generational and individual context	272	Lunar Nodes square Planetary Nodes	276
Motion of Planetary Nodes	272	Planet conjunct its own South Node, and both square the Nodal Axis	276
Nodes of the Sun	272	Planet conjunct the South Node of another planet, and both square the Nodal Axis	276
Planetary South Node and North Node in the same sign	272	Sun conjunct another's Planetary South Node in synastry	276
Distinction between the North Node of Pluto and the Pluto polarity point	273	Planetary Nodes correlating to Astrological Ages	276
Planetary Nodes of Pluto in Capricorn/Cancer	273	The Great Cycles	277
Nodes of Pluto	274	Transiting Planetary Nodes	277
Nodes of Venus	275	Transiting South Node of anything	278
Nodes of Mars	275	South Node of Neptune in Aquarius	278

PLUTO

Primary evolutionary/karmic axis, "the bottom line"	280	Pluto polarity point (PPP)	292
Root structure of the chart	280	Pluto polarity point – ruler of	292
Evolution is set in motion by Pluto, the Soul	280	Pluto polarity point – planetary phases	292
Pluto paradigm	280	Pluto polarity point – Rx	293
Truth of the Pluto paradigm	281	Pluto polarity point – transiting	293
Layers – Pluto, nodes, rulers	281	Is there a Pluto polarity point? – North Node in the same sign as, but not conjunct, Pluto	293
Pluto, why it (and not other planets) represents the desires of the Soul	281	Is there a Pluto polarity point? – North Node in the same house as, but not conjunct, Pluto	293
Step by step approach to understanding the evolutionary dynamics	282	Is there a Pluto polarity point? – North Node in the same sign as, but not conjunct, Pluto, and in a different house to Pluto	293
EA question, "Why?"	283	Is there a Pluto polarity point? – Ruler of North Node conjunct Pluto	293
Pluto paradigm analysis, an example	283	Pluto polarity point – conjunct planet	293
Soul's desire nature – separating desires	283	Pluto polarity point – conjunct Sun	293
Resistance and cooperation	284	Pluto polarity point – conjunct Sun, gibbous and full phase	293
Evolution of natal Pluto itself	284	Pluto polarity point – square the Nodes	294
Individualized context	284	Pluto polarity point – conjunct Mars	294
Pluto, the sign of	284	Pluto conjunct North Node, integrating the sign of the PPP	294
Pluto rulership	284	Pluto – retrograde and direct	294
Pluto and Mars	285	Pluto Rx and PPP Rx	294
Pluto/Mars phase – subsidiary or primary life	285	Nodes of Pluto	295
Pluto square Nodes – skipped steps	286	Distinction between the North Node of Pluto and the Pluto polarity point	295
Pluto square Nodes 1st/7th houses – emotional paradox	287	Pluto on the cusp	296
Planet conjunct Pluto	287	Pluto culminating in a house	296
Sun conjunct Pluto	288	Pluto near a house cusp, and feeling that Pluto is in another house	297
Sun conjunct Pluto, South Node in Scorpio	288	Pluto in intercepted sign	297
Sun opposite Pluto	288	Pluto, evolutionary progression through the houses	297
Sun opposite Pluto - gibbous and full phase	288	Pluto in the 8th house	297
Pluto conjunct South Node, and second Saturn return	288	Significance of Scorpio and the 8th house in the Pluto paradigm	297
Pluto conjunct South Node	290	Differences/nuances between Pluto 3rd house, Mercury in Scorpio, Scorpio ruling 3rd – an example	298
Pluto conjunct South Node ruler	290	Pluto aspecting Sun	299
Pluto conjunct North Node – NO Pluto polarity point	291	Pluto/Uranus interface	299

Pluto conjunct North Node – what about the South Node?	291	Pluto/Neptune interface	299
Pluto conjunct North Node – and planet(s) aspecting South Node	291	Soul correlates to Pluto, not Neptune	300
Pluto conjunct North Node – amount of distance between Pluto and North Node	291	Pluto sextile Neptune – collective evolution	300
North Node in the same sign as, but not conjunct, Pluto – is there a Pluto polarity point?	291	Pluto generations	300
North Node in the same sign as, but not conjunct, Pluto, and in a different house to Pluto – is there a Pluto polarity point?	291	Transiting Pluto	300
Ruler of North Node conjunct Pluto – is there a Pluto polarity point?	292	Pluto transits – and the transiting Pluto polarity point	300
Pluto, ruler of Scorpio SOUTH Node	292	Pluto in Capricorn transit	301
Pluto, ruler of Scorpio NORTH Node	292	What is that Cancer polarity? Reflections on Pluto in Capricorn – by Bradley Naragon	302
Shifts from South Node to North Node, and Pluto to Pluto polarity point	292		

RELATIONSHIPS – SYNASTRY AND COMPOSITE

How to read synastry and composite charts	304	Shared affinities	308
Venus and Mars in synastry – example	304	Soul mates	308
Mars/Venus phase in relationship	304	Determining past life gender of a couple	308
Synastry – past life dynamics	304	Love – conditional and unconditional	308
Synastry – Pluto opposition by house	305	Culminating archetype in relationships	309
Synastry – how to calculate phasal relationship between the Nodes	305	Power dynamics in relationships	309
Synastry – nodal opposition	305	Past life connection with historical figures	309
Synastry – one person's planet square the other's Nodes	305	Scorpio archetype – abandonment, betrayal, violation of trust	310
Synastry – one person's Sun square the other's Nodes	306	Libra archetype – projection	310
Synastry – one person's Nodes square the other's Nodes	306	Projections, delusions, expectations	310
Synastry, nodal square – person A Venus conjunct North Node, person B Venus conjunct South Node	306	Libra archetype – de facto God or Goddess	311
Synastry – one person's planet conjunct the other's South Node	307	Venus archetype – natural inconjunct between Taurus and Libra	311
Synastry – one person's planet conjunct the other's North Node	307	Venus archetype – the psychology of "listening"	312
Synastry – with famous people	307	Venus archetype – past, present and future orientations	312
Composite – midpoint method	307	Venus retrograde	312
Composite and Progressed Composite charts	307	Venus in Virgo	313
Composite – skipped steps between two people	307	Higher octave of Venus – Neptune	313
Composite – transits, progressions and bi-wheel	307	Venus transit	313
Composite South Node Scorpio, North Node Taurus	307	Karmic relationships – Agni ritual	313
Understanding the WHY in relationships	307	Davison relationship chart	313
Resolving relationship dynamics	308		

RETROGRADE ARCHETYPE

Accelerated evolution	314	Venus retrograde	317
Individuation	314	Venus retrograde, example	318
Resistance	315	Saturn retrograde	318
Dissatisfaction	315	Neptune retrograde	318
Retrograde-type personality	315	Pluto retrograde, and evolutionary state	318
Retrograde archetype, and evolutionary state	315	Pluto retrograde 10th house, example	318
Retrograde archetype, and Consensus state	316	Transiting Pluto, retrograde and direct	318
Retrograde archetype, and Spiritual state	316	Asteroid – retrograde	319
Integrating the totality of a retrograde planet	316	Retrograde planet square the Nodes	319

Phasal relationship between retrograde planets	316	Retrograde planet conjunct North Node	319
Retrograde planet conjunct South Node	316	Oblique retrograde (retrograde planet aspecting non-retrograde planet)	319
Retrograde planet conjunct North Node	316	Retrograde archetype, and progressions	319
Mars retrograde	317	Stationary planet or node	319
Mercury retrograde	317		

SKIPPED STEPS

Planet square Nodes – skipped steps	320	Pluto square Nodes – emotional paradox	327
Planet square Nodes, 10 degree orb	320	Pluto square Nodes, South Node Scorpio, North Node Taurus	327
Planet (applying) just outside of orb of a square to the Nodes	321	Planet square Pluto	328
Planet (separating) just outside of orb of a square to the Nodes	321	Sun square Nodes	328
Flip flopping	321	Moon square Nodes	328
Rulers of the Nodes	321	Jupiter square Nodes	328
Determination of Resolution Node	321	Neptune square Nodes, example	328
Causes of skipped steps	321	Planetary Nodes square Lunar Nodes	330
Karma	321	Planet square Planetary Nodes (or square the midpoint of Planetary Nodes)	330
Three reactions to evolutionary growth	321	Outer planet square Planetary Nodes	330
Exactly what needs to be recovered?	322	Any planet square Planetary Nodes	331
How to recover the skipped steps?	322	Planet conjunct its own South Node, and both square the Nodal Axis	331
How to ascertain if the skipped steps have been resolved?	322	Planet conjunct the South Node of another planet, and both square the Nodal Axis	331
What is the "done" point in skipped steps?	322	Angles square Nodes	331
Making choices not to deal with skipped steps	322	Angles square Nodes, example	331
Appearance of earlier evolutionary stage	323	Semisquare to the Nodes	332
General themes	323	Retrograde planet square Nodes	332
Creating skipped steps in the current life	323	Asteroids or Black Moon Lilith square Nodes	332
Skipped steps, and the Pluto polarity point	324	Chiron square Nodes	332
Two planets square the Nodes	324	Other planets aspecting a planet square Nodes	332
Two planets square the Nodes forming a grand cross	324	Planet conjunct South Node when the South Node is the Resolution Node	333
Multiple planets square the Nodes	324	Planet conjunct North Node when the South Node is the Resolution Node	333
Multiple planets square the Nodes, forming a grand cross	324	Planet square South Node, Pluto square North Node, example	333
South Node resolution – why develop the past habitual patterns?	325	Ruler of both Nodes in same sign and house	333
South Node resolution, and planets conjunct the South Node	325	When the ruler of the Resolution Node is the skipped step planet	334
North Node resolution, and planet conjunct South Node	325	Mars/Pluto new conjunction square Nodes	334
Pluto square Nodes	325	Skipped steps – different sign on house cusp	334
Pluto square Nodes, and the Pluto polarity point	327	Examples of Avatars with skipped steps	334
Pluto polarity point square Nodes	327		

SOUL

Soul	335	Souls blocking their inherent nature	345
EA paradigm – the evolutionary journey of the Soul	336	Spiritual bypass	345
Dual desires within the Soul	337	The non-dual state	347
Soul memories of prior lives	337	Deepening the awareness of self as Soul	348
Past dynamics of the Soul	337	Looking into the Souls of others	348
Past life memories and long term memories	338	Special capacity to see past lives of any Soul	348
Future dynamics of a Soul	338	Soul projecting from within itself	349
Soul desires in the next lifetime	338	Life purpose of the Soul	349
Conditioning patterns created by the Soul	338	Soul evolving via polarity points of the planets	349
Evolution comes from the root of Pluto, the Soul	338	Split Soul – Same Soul – Twin Soul	350

Pluto, why it (and not other planets) represents the desires of the Soul	339	Same Soul – Obama/Lindbergh	350
How the Soul effects its evolution	339	Same Soul – Romney/Greely, Paul Ryan/Hans Fritze	351
When Souls goes back to Source	339	Same Soul – phasal relationship from one life to the next	351
Frequency of incarnation	340	Two or more Souls – walk-ins – Soul possession	351
Karmic 'script' of the Soul	340	Soul mates	352
Ocean/wave analogy	340	Soul – application of Uranus/Saturn to Pluto	352
Past life identity (name) of Soul	341	The nature of a question the Soul can ask	353
Seven Soul types	341	Soul types, and religion	353
TABLE 1 – Seven Soul Types	341	Soul worker	353
Soul type example, Daemon Soul	341	Souls from other planets/star systems, eg Pleiades	353
Unique individuality of Soul	342	Guilt within a Soul	354
Soul's gender	342	Natural guilt stays within the Soul forever	354
Awareness of Soul	342	Death – astral plane	354
Ego of the Soul	342	Suicide	354
FIG 1 – Chakra correlations diagram	343	Soul and the veil of maya – Yogananda	355
Ego identities created by the Soul	344	South Node of Neptune in Aquarius	355
Soul's memory of the ego	344	Natural Law that holds creation together	356
Soul's resistance to change	344		

STAGES OF EVOLUTION

TABLE 2 – Stages of Evolution	357	SPIRITUAL STATE	366
Percentages in the evolutionary states	357	1st stage Spiritual	367
Accurate determination of evolutionary stages	357	1st stage Spiritual manifestations	367
Natural archetype of evolutionary stages	358	1st stage Spiritual examples	369
Evolutionary sub-sub-stages	358	2nd stage Spiritual	369
Evolutionary stages – difference between appearance and reality	359	2nd stage Spiritual examples	371
How evolution occurs through each state	359	3rd stage Spiritual	371
Natural Law of the Trinity	359	Soul/ego from 3rd stage Spiritual perspective, what does it look like?	372
Dimly Evolved State	359	Spiritual state, and Saturn	372
CONSENSUS STATE	360	Ocean/wave analogy	372
1st stage Consensus	360	Sense of aloneness and alienation in the Spiritual state	373
2nd stage Consensus	360	Discrimination in the Spiritual state	374
3rd stage Consensus	360	Emotional complexes in the Spiritual state	374
Consensus, and Natural Laws	361	Awareness of Soul in the Spiritual state	374
Consensus, and patriarchy	361	Advancing one's own evolution in the Spiritual state	374
Rates of evolution	361	Evolutionary stage – baby and parents	375
Consensus, hating	361	Evolutionary state of children	375
Consensus state, and transcendental belief systems	361	Evolutionary state of twins	377
INDIVIDUATED STATE	362	Hiding signature	377
1st stage Individuated	362	Compensation	377
2nd stage Individuated	363	Evolutionary state and the retrograde archetype	378
Transition from 2nd stage to 3rd stage Individuated	363	Evolutionary state and Pluto retrograde	378
3rd stage Individuated	363	Client readings, adjust for evolutionary stage	378
3rd stage Individuated examples	363	How a planet, eg Mercury, manifests in each evolutionary stage – by Gonzalo Romero	378
3rd stage Individuated transition to 1st stage Spiritual	363	Illness and personal sacrifice	379
Souls on the 'spiritual path' but not necessarily in the Spiritual state	365	Countries	380
Individuated, hiding signatures	365	Advancement of evolutionary stages – exhaustion of separating desires	380
Compensation	365	Evolutionary states, changes in percentages	380
Understanding the Sagittarius and Pisces archetypes within the Individuated state	366	Evolutionary state, and the survival instinct	380

TRANSITS

Understanding transits	382	Transiting Lunar Nodes, 'apparent' and 'actual'	386
Karmic 'script' of the Soul	382	Transiting Lunar Nodes t-square natal planet	386
Phasal relationships – transiting to natal	382	Transiting Lunar Nodes t-square natal planet - in a death chart	386
Comparing transits to the natal chart	382	Transiting Planetary Nodes	386
Transits, activating other planets in the chart	382	Saturn Return	387
Transit creating a temporary planetary configuration, eg yod	382	Mid-life transits	388
Difficult transits	383	Uranus opposite Uranus	388
Making predictions	383	Neptune square Neptune	388
Mars transit	383	Pluto square Pluto	388
Mars transit – anger	384	Pluto crossing the Ascendant	388
Mars transit – example	384	Pluto transit – and the transiting Pluto polarity point	389
Venus transit	385	Pluto in Capricorn transit	340
Uranus transit	385	What is that Cancer polarity? Reflections on Pluto in Capricorn – by Bradley Naragon	391
Pluto transit – retrograde and direct	385	Original conjunction of Uranus/Pluto 1965	392
Transiting Pluto polarity point	385	Transit event charts – original conjunction, 1st quarter square, etc.	392
Chiron transit	385	Cardinal Grand Cross (2011 onwards)	393

ASPECTS AND PHASES

Mathematical model

Aspects need to be looked at in context – for example, you can have four kinds of possible squares, but very few of the traditional books teach this. Aspects need to be looked at with respect to the phase relationship in which you find them. In Pluto Vol. 1, the phases are intertwined in the interpretation of the aspects which are looked at from an evolutionary point of view, but they are not identified as such. The essence of astrology is a circle from 0 to 360 degrees. A basic way of looking at life is a circle or cycle. This simplistic mathematical model provides a way for astrologers to look at interpretation. There are a number of ways to divide this up depending upon the number of quotients used to divide it. Using the number 6 or 12 or 3 or 9, you can create different answers with respect to the division. Houses are, for instance, a relatively new phenomenon and not part of the origin of astrology per se. An excellent book on the history of astrology is called "The Origin of the Zodiac" by Gleadow. Excellent. For the purposes of aspects, we use the number 8, ie the lunation cycle. This will give us two quadrants in the first half and two in the second half. If we move in a clockwise direction, we come over to 360 degrees. Each phase equals 45 degrees. (The Chaldean Zodiac is based on 28 days, or a lunation cycle, and is more complex; we use a simpler method: 8 phases rather than 28.)

Difference between phases and aspects

The mathematical number which represents the distance between two planets represents the phasal relationship between those two planets. The phase determines how the relationship manifests; the aspect accentuates the phase. Since the zodiac correlates to what you call human consciousness projected into space, inner space and apparent outer space, the point is that consciousness is inclusive. Relative to its inclusion, it is exclusive, ie that which it cannot be. The phases correlate to the various dynamics within that consciousness and how it develops and evolves through time relative to what it can be vs. what it cannot be. Aspects mark key turning points in that evolutionary development or journey. Look upon them as turnstiles, if you will. Like revolving doors. The aspect moves you from one developmental stage to another in an accelerated fashion. Looking at this revolving door, the space on either side of it is relatively calm in comparison to the revolving door. One goes from a relatively calm and developed space to another space which is trying to be developed. The tension between past and future is the aspect. The metaphor includes the possibility of being caught in that revolving door and going backwards or getting caught in it – then they come here. Each aspect is going to have a certain RPM, if you will, or a certain rate of spin that is different than another aspect. (JWG)

Phasal relationship – between two planets

To determine phases always use the SLOWER MOVING of the two planets being considered as your baseline. Thus, if Venus were at say 10 deg Aries, and Mars were at 10 deg Cancer, Mars would be the slower moving of the two. So this would equal a last quarter phase. (Rad)

Count the number of degrees between the two planets. Go from the slower moving planet to the faster moving planet, counter-clockwise, that is, from left to right. The slower moving planet is the one that is farther away from the Sun, in the physical solar system. If you are working with Saturn in the 3rd house and Jupiter in the 10th, count the number of degrees between Saturn in the 3rd, through the 4th, 5th, etc. until you reach Jupiter in the 10th. Then determine the phase in which that number of degrees is located. (Steve)

Phasal relationship between two planets – examples

[Example: Venus/Mars balsamic conjunction] The phase between two planets has a range of archetypal manifestations that is dependent on the individual context, reality, of any given Soul. For some this example could certainly be experienced as a chronic disillusionment in regards to Mars/Venus issues. For others it could simply be an inner conflict of desiring to be alone altogether yet, karmically and evolutionarily, required to complete relationships with many Souls that it has prior connection to in some way. And so on. It all depends on the context. The phases between two planets exist for an entire lifetime, and serves as the FOUNDATION for the entire life.

The progression of the two planets can correlate to a change in the phase, ie balsamic Mars and Venus progressed to a new phase, but that does not mean that the balsamic phase stops. It remains to be the foundation for the life. The new phase progression would then mean that the Soul is creating within itself, in the current life, the types of experiences that will serve as the foundation for the next life when that Mars/Venus would indeed be in a new phase. You can see how this would then lend itself to not only feeling exhausted via the natal Mars/Venus being balsamic, exhausted from having to complete, but also disillusioned. It's like the proverbial 'grass is greener on the other side' where the progression into the new phase correlates to the green grass just on the other side of the fence, yet one is still stuck behind that fence and being forced to feed itself with what's under its feet. Yes, it can crane its neck and eat a little of that grass on the other side, the new phase, but must remain behind the fence. (Rad)

To have any planets in any kind of relationship to one another implies that prior to that particular relationship, they were building up to the point of being in that relationship. Aspects imply a process. When two planets (or luminaries such as the Sun or Moon, or any celestial body) are right next to one another (what we will call an exact conjunction, or combustion) it implies that prior to the conjunction they were in some other relationship with one another, one that naturally preceded the exact conjunction. For example: If you are walking into a room right now, what does this imply? It implies that prior to this walking into the room, you were just outside of the room. Now, let's say you are walking out of a room right now. What does this imply? It implies that prior to your walking out of the room you were inside of the room. We can think of aspects just like that. To have any two planets, or points in a chart in any particular relationship to one another, innately implies that that relationship is the next step of a long-spanned evolutionary journey.

Here is an astronomical example to illustrate this point: Everyone knows that there is a thing called a New Moon and a Full Moon. Astronomically what is actually taking place during those two events? On the New Moon, the Sun and the Moon are in the exact same place from the point of view of the Earth. On the Full Moon, the Sun and Moon are seen to be in opposite positions of the zodiac. We can call the "New Moon" the beginning of a lunar cycle as it symbolizes the point at which the Sun and Moon are in the same place. We can call the "Full Moon" the culmination of the entire lunar cycle as it is the greatest point of separation achieved during the entire lunar cycle. Now, based on that simple understanding, what can we say about the Full Moon? It implies that prior to the Moon being Full, it was on its way towards being Full. What can we say about the New Moon? That prior to the Moon being New, it was on its way towards being New. (Ari)

Phasal relationship – nodes
For planets, we always start with the SLOWER moving planet of the two planets or points being considered. And then in a clockwise direction determine the degrees of separation between the two. When using the nodes, because the mean motion is retrograde, the rule is reversed: using the slower moving point of the two you count in a counter-clockwise direction. When using the Sun the Sun is always the first point of reference. (Rad)

Phasal relationship – between the nodes and a planet
The Lunar Node's mean motion is retrograde. In that case you move CLOCKWISE (through the houses backwards) from the planet to the node. If Venus is in the 4th and the South Node is in the 11th, start with Venus in 4th, moving to the 11th. Count the number of degrees between Venus and the South Node. The number of degrees between Venus and the North Node would then be the number of degrees between Venus and South Node, plus 180. Then determine the phase in which that number of degrees is located. (Steve)

It has nothing to do with how fast or slow a planet is relative to the nodal movement. It's the same method for all planets regardless of speed. Going *clockwise*, you move from the planet to the node you want to determine the planet-to-node phase. Count the number of degrees. That's it. Doesn't matter if it's Sun or Moon or Pluto or Mercury, same method. (Steve)

Phasal relationship – nodes in synastry
Always use the natural zodiac as the frame of reference to calculate the phases of any two points. So in calculating the nodes in synastry that would mean to use the one person's node that preceded, naturally, the other person's node, ie South Node in Aries would precede the South Node in Cancer. Thus using that South Node in Aries as the baseline or start point. Yet, because the mean motion of the nodes is retrograde, we would then have to reverse the normal rules of the phases. If I had, say, Mars at 1 deg Aries, and another had their Mars at 1 deg Cancer, that would naturally be a first quarter square through natural progression of the signs. But the nodes are retrograde through mean motion. So even though we would still use the South Node of Aries as the baseline we would then see through the natural motion of the retrograde that the South Node of Cancer is MOVING TOWARDS that South Node in Aries. So it would then be a last quarter square or phase versus a first quarter square or phase if indeed the South Nodes were at 1 deg Aries and Cancer respectively. In this example that would then make the North Nodes at 1 deg Libra and 1 deg Capricorn. So, again, using the natural zodiac as our baseline we then see that Libra precedes Capricorn. With the mean motion of the nodes in mind that again means that the Capricorn node is moving towards the Libra node: another last quarter square or phase. (Rad)

Phasal relationship – the conjunction
The way to determine whether the conjunction between any two planets is beginning a cycle or completing one is to simply put your finger on the slower moving planet (or celestial body) and move counter-clockwise in the natural direction of the zodiac. If

you have to go all around the chart to reach the faster moving planet, then the conjunction between the two planets are completing a cycle (balsamic). If however your finger immediately, within the first 10 degrees, reaches the faster moving planet, then the conjunction between the two planets is just beginning a cycle (new phase). Moving beyond conjunctions: The above principle can be applied to any two planets that are positioned anywhere in the chart. Basically, all planets are in some sort of phasal relationship with one another. (Ari)

Phasal relationship – Pluto polarity point
The PPP is 180 degrees away from Pluto, thus its phase will always be the polarity of the phase between Pluto and the reference planet. Thus, figure the phase between Pluto and that planet, and then the polarity of that phase is the phase between that planet and the PPP. If Pluto to planet is new phase, the PPP is full phase, etc. (Steve)

Phasal relationship – between the Sun and a planet
When working with the Sun and a planet, the Sun is always the baseline, meaning you treat it as if it is the slower moving planet. Count the number of degrees between the two planets. Go from the Sun to the planet, counter-clockwise, that is, from left to right. (Steve)

The Sun is always considered the "slower moving planet" as in actuality it is not moving and is the point of integration for the entire chart. Therefore the same method would be used for determining the phasal relationship between the Sun and the Moon as well as the Sun and Pluto for example. (Ari)

Phasal relationship – transits
There are phasal relationships via transiting planets to natal ones. The natal one, whatever planet it is, is used as the baseline to determine the phase relative to transiting planets. For example, if the Moon is at 5 Gemini, and transiting Saturn is at 2 Gemini, then this would be a balsamic phase. If the transiting Saturn were at 8 then it would be a new phase. (Rad)

Phasal relationship – nodes and planets, transiting and natal

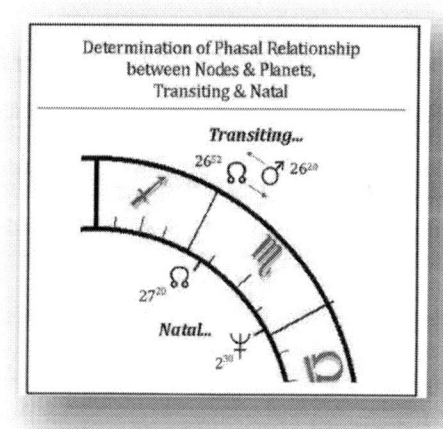

- ✓ Natal Neptune is in a **balsamic phase** with the natal North Node.
- ✓ Transiting Mars is in a **balsamic conjunction** with the transiting North Node.
- ✓ Transiting North Node is in a **new phase conjunction** with the natal North Node (a recent Nodal Return; a new cycle now beginning).
- ✓ Transiting North Node is in a **balsamic phase** in relation to natal Neptune.
- ✓ Transiting Mars is in a **balsamic conjunction** with the natal North Node (a cycle ending, with a new cycle beginning soon).
- ✓ Transiting Mars is in a **new phase** relative to Natal Neptune.

Phasal relationship – between retrograde planets
It could, for some reasons, be experienced somehow similar to a balsamic conjunction. While the new phase conjunction produces instinctual, unchecked action without egocentric awareness, the retrogradation of Mars will require the individual to listen to himself, his Soul or God, before taking action. This implies that action is required to operate not merely in an instinctual way. Mercury retrograde will require the Soul to discriminate about the type of information it collects from the environment in order to select information which serves its evolutionary intentions; otherwise, the Soul will be – as most likely has been in the past – mentally overwhelmed by indiscriminate information intake, and will experience confusion, leading to not knowing what to think, not knowing what to do. Thus, each planet in this new phase is requiring a deeper evolutionary response, which in turn is necessary because of what the prior response to each archetype has been – thus, a higher likelihood exists that the Soul may experience confusion in relation to these archetypes in the new cycle beginning – and also, they could serve as vehicles to grasp from within something deeper or more universal. (Gonzalo)

Yang to yin aspects
From taking action to the resolution of that action. And for those moving from yin to yang, from that which is existing to taking action in order for that which exists to evolve. (Rad)

EA places a lot of importance on phases. There are eight phases in a circle, which makes every 45 degrees the beginning of the next phase. Phases come in pairs, yang and yin, representing 90 degrees, a quarter of the totality. This is another reason cardinal is significant. Looking at houses and signs and aspects through the filter of phases sheds a lot of light on their significance, and the archetypes of the division of quadrants into thirds. Basically, cardinal initiates (the new), fixed grounds and stabilizes what was initiated in cardinal, and mutable is like the culmination of the previous two, mutating into whatever is coming next, the pattern repeating again starting in the cardinal sign/house that follows.

The 15 degree midpoint of each of the fixed signs/houses corresponds to the beginning of the yin phase in the cycle of phases, as each phase is 45 degrees. It's the midpoint between two adjacent cardinal points, in essence like the Full Moon point – half way through the current quarter of the cycle. In the system of 12 divisions, each quadrant has either yang-yin-yang or yin-yang-yin. That transition from yang to yin and back itself is not easy, because we *get used to* the way it has been. Yang is energy going OUT – yin requires the energy to reverse direction and go back to the center – like putting on the brakes when we have gotten used to stepping on the gas. And vice versa. After a long stretch in yin we are used to being inward, and it's an adjustment to start orienting outward again. Back and forth, back and forth – stretching us, working us.

I began seeing phases as mile markers, marking out points of completion and change along the archetypal journey around a circle of a cycle (actually, more like one revolution around a three dimensional spiral than completing a two dimensional circle). Each part of the circle (the journey) has its own archetypes. The beginning (conjunction) is the birth of a new chapter. All beginnings have Aries-like qualities – instinctual. So we start seeing these archetypes not just in charts but taking place in outer and inner life – in a person's life, in the shifting of the seasons in nature, in the creation, maturing and decay of cultures and civilizations – patterns, archetypes which are the ways the Divine principles behind all creation manifest in dualistic time-space reality – through these blueprints, the archetypes. Other astrologers, such as Dane Rudhyar, had written about cycles and phases before. But Jeffrey greatly deepened the concepts and applied them to all the planets and aspects, and all the spheres of life. (Steve)

Phases correlating to zodiacal archetypes
Each phase can be correlated to a specific archetype (Aries, Taurus, Gemini, etc.). The new phase is an Aries phase (self-discovery, initiation of actions in order for self-discovery to occur). In this phase we learn through action and reaction. The crescent phase is a Taurus phase in which the evolutionary intention started at the new phase conjunction must be rooted, so to speak, or consolidated through the act of internalization and also withdrawal. The person must now "slow down" in order to establish the evolutionary purpose/intention from within him or herself (give it personal meaning). The semisquare is the transitional aspect from the new phase into the crescent phase which creates the tension/stress within this aspect (the person does not want to slow down, or to feel restricted in the context of the freedom to initiate actions, yet this is what the evolutionary intention now requires). (Deva)

Jeffrey's answer was he had never taught the cycle of phases as a direct correlation to the 12 signs of the zodiac. They are two different systems. All of the archetypes of the zodiac are found in the cycle of phases, but not necessarily in the identical layout to the zodiac. All the archetypes are there because they are the totality of life in human form. But we can't make a literal one to one comparison, by numeric degrees, between the zodiac and the cycle of phases. In some cases the correlation is identical. But it is not identical in all. Example: Disseminating would correlate with half of Scorpio and all of Sagittarius in the zodiac. Yet disseminating by its nature corresponds to Capricorn. Last Quarter correlates with Capricorn and first half of Aquarius in the zodiac. Yet the function of Last Quarter is not Capricorn in nature, it is more Aquarian, completing and beginning to break away from what has come before. (Steve)

Key turning points of aspects within a phase
The typical orb given to a square is 20 degrees. For first quarter square, it starts at 80 degrees and ends at 100 degrees. Between 80 and 90 degrees leads to culmination of the old. As you move closer to exact aspect, you are having balsamic-like issues – culmination. Although we are talking about a first quarter square, even within that experience – first quarter square, it begins with the end of the old, the known – which is the nature of balsamic. As it reaches 90 degrees, then we start having a new phase-like flavor – Aries – instinctual. We are in something new, not known, we don't consciously know how to do it. Thus we fly by gut instinct – new, Aries. As the aspect moves closer to 100 degrees we have been working with it long enough that its new reality has established itself – we no longer feel we are flying blind. Have begun integrating the changes into our sense of self-identity, who I see myself as. Then it is no longer new and we are on our way towards the next transition point (aspect). That's why the most profound aspects tend to be conjunction, square, opposition. These represent the 90 degree turning points. Equate it to the seasons in a 12 month solar cycle. We are well aware each season requires an inward adjustment within ourselves, which takes time to acclimate. It is exactly like that.

That is why Jeffrey gave the sesquiquadrate and semisquare a lot of weight, because they are the midpoints of a square – 45 degrees. They correlate to the biquadrant points – 15 degrees of the fixed signs, Taurus, Leo, Scorpio, Aquarius. Think of it – the middle of fixed signs, where resistance would tend to be at its peak. At that point the phase shifts from a yang phase to a yin phase, forcing us to go within and assimilate what has been experienced in the yang phase that preceded. The aspects within those phases mark the key turning points. These are the archetypes of a cycle, repeated endlessly in life, from the microscopic to the galactic. When a square is between 80 and 90 degrees (prior to the exact square) the event of the square has not yet occurred. We sense change is coming. Most humans tend to resist change, because the effects of change are unknown and our sense of security comes from doing what we know. Yet we sense that what we know is coming to some sort of change. Thus an ending of reality as we have known it. Thus, typically, an unconscious resistance to the impending change.

TABLE 5   EA Phases and Zodiacal Correlations

NEW PHASE	Aries Yang	INITIATION BEGINNING	The beginning of a cycle. Action is instinctual. Absolute freedom is required. The question is, "Who am I?" The actions one takes brings feedback.
CRESCENT	Taurus Yin	INTERNALIZATION OF NEW PHASE, WITHDRAWAL, STRUGGLE	The feedback has been obtained. The need is to withdraw and to come to an understanding of who one is.
FIRST QUARTER	Gemini Yang	CHOICES TO BE MADE CRISIS IN ACTION	One now has an understanding of who one is. Now the question is, "What specific form do I take?" A time of intense activity. Building one's foundations in terms of who one is.
GIBBOUS	Virgo Yin	HUMBLING AND ADJUSTING	The old (egocentric) ways are no longer working. The need to re-evaluate. The realization that it is not about "me" anymore.
FULL PHASE	Libra Yang	ENTERING THE SOCIAL SPHERE, SOCIALIZATION	The dilemma is now in the full light of day. This is me vs what is required of me in the social sphere. Comparing and contrasting self to everyone else. The necessary feedback from significant others in one's life to begin the process of integrating oneself/one's sense of purpose into the social sphere.
DISSEMINATING	Capricorn Yin	TOTALITY OF SOCIETY, INTEGRATION OF PURPOSE	Fully integrating oneself/one's sense of purpose into the social sphere. What has been learned enters the mainstream.
LAST QUARTER	Aquarius Yang	BREAKING FREE OR REBELLING FROM ALL THAT HAS COME BEFORE IN THIS CYCLE, CRISIS IN BELIEF	Questioning the underlying beliefs that have underpinned all prior actions. Detaching from what one has created and the social sphere in which one has participated.
BALSAMIC	Pisces Yin	CULMINATION OF THE ENTIRE CYCLE, IT DISSOLVES BACK INTO FROM WHENCE IT CAME	Attunement to the Divine. Understanding oneself in the context of the Divine and the corresponding expansion of consciousness. Letting go of all that has come before that hinders this attunement. The beginnings of new imaginings for a new cycle.

All of those qualities, the hesitation towards what we know or feel is coming, are balsamic-like qualities. Endings, the need to complete what is unfinished. When the square is 90-100 degrees, the actual conjunction has now occurred. If we have been resisting we find ourselves dragged into something new, like it or not. The nature of new is it is unknown. We can feel insecure or uncertain on how to proceed. We find that what we have learned no longer applies in quite the same ways that we are used to. We have to operate a bit from instinct because we don't know how else to operate. All of those qualities, the sense we are in something new that we don't yet know how to navigate, are new phase-like qualities. When I say balsamic-like and new phase-like, it is more like the aspect contains the *flavor* of those things rather than being those things. Life consists of thousands of endings (deaths) and beginnings (births) repeated over and over. And every one of those death – rebirths (death-rebirth is a core archetype of Pluto) is a mini-experience of a culmination (balsamic) and beginning (new phase). When one is having an actual balsamic phase or new phase, those archetypes of endings and beginnings are heightened – at their extreme. But every moment in life contains tiny versions of those archetypes. (Steve)

Evolutionary timing cycles

There are natural archetypes and *timings* in life. I sometimes tell "create your own reality" advocates, let me see you grow tomatoes outdoors in Seattle in December. There are certain issues that can only reach culmination with the approach of aspects – natural timings. That's why there ARE aspects in the first place. In three-dimensional dualistic reality the Soul's evolutionary intentions play out over TIME. Time = Saturn (and there is some of the significance of Saturn Returns – passage into a new archetypal stage). What we can do with our free will is learn to COOPERATE with, work with, rather than resist, the evolutionary process. In *that* way we can speed up evolution. If the impulse to evolve is a wave, we can't make a wave come to shore any sooner than it's going to come. What we can do is, when the wave comes in, ride it as far as we can vs consciously resisting the wave, trying to hold back from its intents. Through developing inner resolve to let go, and go through whatever that wave is asking us to embrace, we can make maximum benefit of the natural timing of that wave. In that way we are speeding up evolution, through riding that wave as far as we can. As opposed to the majority who, when change appears, want it to be over, to get back to "normal" (ie old familiar ways) ASAP.

As we realize we can NEVER get back to the old, it is dead and gone, and that true security is just to ride the wave, then we are taking maximum advantage of the evolutionary timing cycles, which means maximizing evolution. Keep that bit about tomatoes in mind. That metaphor extends, because if I don't plant the tomatoes in the Spring and tend to them in Spring and Summer, there will not be much of a tomato crop. We tend those plants on faith – there is no guarantee we will ever see tomatoes. We put in the effort anyway because we feel the potential of fruition is worth the risk it might not happen. It's like that – you can put in the necessary effort BEFORE the aspect backs you into the corner and makes you put in the effort. Then the transition doesn't have to be catastrophic. But you are still not going to see tomatoes until tomato ripening season. You can speed it up a bit with some plastic, but you are still not going to have tomatoes in December. The natural process is subject to Natural Law. Aspects are manifestations of Natural Law, natural timing. (Steve)

Waxing and waning halves of the phasal cycle

Any aspect must be related to its part in the bigger picture of the whole phasal cycle which is based on the planets orbiting the Sun. The planets all orbit the Sun from different distances and at different speeds meaning each planet takes a different amount of time to orbit the Sun. As we know those planets closer to the Sun move faster while those further out move slower and take longer. This is reflected in their differing speeds of movement through the zodiac – in the chart one of the planets moving faster around the chart than the other. When looking at any two planets the outer planet will, on average, be moving more slowly around the zodiac than the other (more) inner planet, which is closer to the Sun. Therefore, in its journey around the Sun, the faster planet will always be overtaking the more slower moving (outer) planet. This means the alignment of the planets with each other is constantly changing – the two planets are in a cyclic relationship with each other which repeats over time – time and time again. This ongoing relationship between the two planets is shown by their phasal cycles. Whenever the faster inner planet catches up to the slower (more) outer planet – and they are at the same point in the chart – a new phasal cycle begins. As the faster moving planet then pulls away from the slower one the separation between them increases until they are exactly opposite each other in the chart (*waxing* part of cycle). Then the separation starts decreasing until the faster inner planet has caught up to the slower planet again and the cycle ends (*waning* part of cycle). This whole cycle is the phasal cycle.

Both the *waxing* and *waning* halves are each broken down into four equally sized phases, making eight phases in the whole cycle. Each phase is a 45 degree segment of the zodiac (chart), all adding up to 360. The end of each phase is a critical junction point, or gate, into the following phase. Between any two planets the conjunction and opposition mark the beginning and midway parts of the cycle, and all the other aspects will occur once in the waxing half, and once again in the waning half. Planets represent different energies we have to fulfill various different functions in our lives. We direct our energy into different functions required by the situations and circumstances we are involved in.

Just how we integrate inside us the energies used to fulfill these differing functions is shown firstly, in a general way, by the phase between the planets, and within that, more specifically by any aspect occurring between them – in the way that aspect manifests in that particular phase. When two planets start a new cycle their different energies completely combine into a single new energy – this seeds something new – an intention or purpose, related to the combination of those two energies. As the energies have totally combined it is not possible at first to really know what is happening, and the only approach to life that can be taken as far as those two functions (now a combined energy) is concerned, is an instinctual one. It's a subconscious sense of the new.

The whole waxing half of the cycle is about gaining more consciousness of this sense of new intention and purpose, the nature of which will be shown by the two different functions involved. Finding personal meaning for the new intention is necessary, so as to focus that energy in a direction as a purpose that will actualize and thus fulfill the intention. This involves gestating the energy, growing meaning for it inside first – lots of experimentation with things until the meaning becomes clear. Then developing the purpose as a personally identifiable thing to give it shape and form, at least for oneself. This can be very satisfying. However as the planets move through the waxing phase the personal identification with the new purpose has to be relinquished to allow further growth and interaction with others, regarding it, to happen.

Once this has been achieved the new purpose can be established in a social context which is necessary to validate it, and also infuse the process with the further energy required to bring the intention to full expansion. The waning half is about fully actualizing the new intention in a social context, which requires a full merging of one's purpose within the existing structure, rules, regulations, understanding and taboos etc. of the society in which this process is happening. This requires ever more expansion of consciousness as any remaining personal identification and attachment to the process/activity creates blocks and obstacles to its fulfillment, and eventual fruition within a collective context. But once this has happened, the purpose has been fulfilled externally (to oneself), and an even greater satisfaction is experienced.

However, since the purpose has now been fulfilled a loss of meaning starts to take over. Thus the process starts moving back inside where a deeper meaning for the original intention can be searched for – what was that all about? where do I go from here? and what does that really mean for me now? Also, the integration with society – that was required to fully establish the purpose externally and thus bringing satisfaction on that count – now also loses meaning – the integration was only for that specific purpose. For this reason, and also to get a better perspective, the person has to separate from the prevailing consensus views concerning their purpose, and see their intention from a more individualized point again, so they can then relate it to a larger sense of reality, whatever that may be to the person.

Through this final part of the cycle the person can now discover a more ultimate sense of meaning for the whole process, now that it has come to a culmination, completion. Of course it can take many lifetimes for two planets to complete a full phasal cycle. The particular phasal aspect that any two planets are in, in the chart, shows where the Soul has got to in its development of those energies/functions, firstly in the larger unfolding of their whole phasal cycle, but also the orb will show how relatively new or old any particular aspect is for the Soul. An aspect does actually have a basic generic meaning, but it operates very differently depending on whether it's in the waxing or waning half of the cycle. So that's the first thing to determine, and it will show you which phase it is in. (Upasika)

Stressful aspects

Phases and aspects are basically the same thing. Phases mark the progression of the passage through a cycle. Aspects are the gateways, like revolving doors, that transition us between one part of the cycle and the next. Remember the root issue is resistance, the human tendency to want to stay with what is safe and known. The stressful aspects force us to embrace change. We resist change, until we finally accept its necessity and move ahead – that is like going around and around in the revolving door until we make the decision to leave the safety of the doors and go out the door that leads to the next part of the journey. The revolving door is the aspect. The resolution is making the choice to exit the revolving door. That resolution could occur BEFORE the aspect, at the exact aspect, or after the exact aspect, depending on the person's relationship with self and their willingness to embrace the change. As the orb gets tighter, the issues become more conscious, the person is less able to ignore or repress them, thus stress/fear can be at a peak. Thus the intensity increases. That is why it increases. The change is going to happen, ready or not, willing or not. (Steve)

Culmination in the balsamic phase

In the balsamic phase the main archetype within it is CULMINATION. The culmination of the entire cycle that began at the new phase. The attunement to the Divine in this phase is a core archetype yet many, many Souls will not be consciously embracing it as such. For many, this archetype morphs into a state of total disillusionment that sets in motion the need to begin anew, the movement towards the new phase, or the sense of becoming totally worn out or exhausted due to an entire cycle coming to a place of culmination. Yet, because the two planets are in this balsamic state being 'forced' to live them out anyway even as they desire not to: the need to begin anew.

The intention in this is to create within the Soul's consciousness an active state of reflection that allows for a complete awareness of all the dynamics that have been responsible for the types of realities that the Soul has created because of those dynamics. Self-knowledge is the result, and intent. In this way the Soul then lays the groundwork for a positive culmination of those dynamics that then leads to the new phase down the line. Remember too there can be an 'exhaustion' for some Souls who have felt they have 'finished' with something, are done with it, yet are evolutionarily required to continue living these dynamics equaling circumstances via the two planets that are in this balsamic phase. (Rad)

It all goes back to the principle of a subconscious past, and what defines our sense of security. For almost all of us, security equates to what is known, consciously and subconsciously. When an archetype is culminating, it means patterns that have been in place a long time are coming to a head. The feelings are pretty familiar – that growing sense that something we have been really into, or defined ourselves by/as for a long time, no longer brings the satisfaction or meaning it once did. In other words, something is in the process of ending. Emotionally, endings are often a mixed experience – simultaneous excitement, fear, sense of loss or grief, and expectation of the new and what might be coming.

I describe it sometimes like winter – preceded by Fall, followed by Spring. If you live in a harsh climate, nothing much is happening in Winter. The outer can feel like death. This is gradually followed by a rebirth, the first green of spring slowly appears. At some point it is clearly no longer Winter, it is now Spring. But what is the difference between Dec 19th and Dec 24th – between March 19th and March 24th? We have changed a season within those few days, but to what degree can we feel that difference within? There is a subtle difference, on one side or the other, culminating or new, but close to that conjunction the difference is hard to consciously feel. Similarly, planets crossing a house cusp or changing signs. We are either "almost there" or "have now reached the new" – the difference between those in our outer lives may not be very significant. And yet, one or the other will be the dominant archetype. Balsamic phase (culminating) and new phase have their own inherent archetypes and thus are quite different. The way I look at it is – everything new, by definition, was preceded by something we now call "old" – a past. Thus there is subconscious memory of what came before, and our need for security and safety causes us at times to want to retreat back to what previously made us feel that way. Jeffrey made the point many times that life, and thus astrology, is not linear. Having Neptune in the 9th house by 4 minutes (just past the 8th house) does not necessarily imply that in the last life it was at the end of the 8th house. There are many ways an archetype can manifest in a chart. They might have had a stellium in late Pisces, or in the 12th house (perhaps in Scorpio), for example. They could have had a number of planets in late degrees, in stressful aspects to Neptune and Pluto. The point is, the past that the new has just released from is represented by subconscious habit patterns, behaviors, emotional patterns, orientations, interests – ways of looking at life. Those are what has culminated. That doesn't mean they are GONE – it just means the center of gravity within that consciousness has now shifted to the new, even if only a tiny amount.

The new phase and Aries represents a lot of freedom, and a need for that. At the same time, nothing is very clear – it's all new and instinctual. At times the person can feel they have no idea what they are doing or where they are going. When stressed, that does not cause one to feel secure. At such times the subconscious appeal of an unseen past that represented safety can at times be quite strong. The problem is the foot has outgrown the sneaker that represents safety. The person increasingly sees when trying to go back to the old that it's just not having the same effect it used to. Instead of feeling safe, they feel stifled – "been there, done that." Thus they wind up again thrown back on themselves – the old patterns are not working.

Gradually they learn through experience (new phase) that the only real solution is to embrace the unknown and "not knowing," out of which gradually come new answers, solutions, and directions. Gradually the hold of the past weakens, and the new directions start cutting new grooves in the brain. The grooves of old outmoded patterns gradually erode away. And gradually that old past loses its hold over the present. This is a cyclical process – the day will come when what is now new itself becomes that which is outmoded, no longer serving the growth needs – becomes itself the archetype that is now *culminating*, as life pushes the person forward towards an even newer new. Some of these cycles take a series of lives to complete. Most of us don't remember what came before this life – its influence on us is subconscious. Thus again affected by the influences of a forgotten past, without even realizing that. When planets are near or have crossed a cusp, the intent is to start letting go of, or to really release from, what has come before. (Steve)

TABLE 7   EA Phases, Aspects & Degrees

Phase	Aspect	Degrees	Phase	Aspect	Degrees
New	Conjunction	0	**Full**	Opposition	180
	Semi-Sextile	30		Tri-Septile	206
	Novile	40		Inconjunct	210
Crescent	Semisquare	45	**Disseminating**	Bi-Quintile	216
	Septile	51.25		Sesquiquadrate	225
	Sextile	60		Trine	240
	Quintile	72		Bi-Septile	257
First Quarter	Square	90	**Last Quarter**	Square	270
	Bi-Septile	102.5		Quintile	288
	Trine	120		Sextile	300
				Septile	308
Gibbous	Sesquiquadrate	135	**Balsamic**	Semisquare	315
	Bi-Quintile	144		Novile	320
	Inconjunct	150		Semi-Sextile	330
	Tri-septile	154		Conjunction	360

Balsamic phases – in relationships
First, one can't tell from just the birth charts alone [if a relationship is coming to an end]. One has to do the traditional astrology thing which is to observe and correlate the symbols to the observation. Thus, if I have a couple in front of me that feels from within themselves that their relationship is culminating, coming to an end, that they feel they have done all they can do with one another, this is the relevant observation to make based on their feedback. I then would look at their charts individually and combined. If I then observed in so doing a lot of planetary phases that are indeed culminating, as in balsamic phases, I could then confirm to them their own observation/feelings.

Conversely, if they made that observation about themselves and I looked into their charts and did not see a lot of planets in a balsamic phase then I would offer my view that I didn't feel that to be true. I would then explore with them why they felt this way and would point to the areas/dynamics within themselves as individuals, and how they came together in relationship, that still needed to be worked on together. If I did see planets in a balsamic relationship to one another I would also talk to them about the dynamics that are specific to those archetypes that are indeed culminating and why, and what the new seeds are for those dynamics to come: future lives. There is no one signature in EA that says, absolutely, that any relationship is totally over. (Rad)

Pluto/Mars balsamic conjunction
Pluto/Mars balsamic does correlate with the need to bring to closure, or culminate, an entire evolutionary cycle relative to how the desire nature was acted upon, or played out, prior to the life. The culmination of the old cycle does prepare the way for the new cycle to begin relative to the new phase. (Deva)

Comparison of balsamic and new phase aspects in composite
[Example: Venus/Pluto and Venus/Mars composite aspect] When the Venus/Pluto is *balsamic* it correlates to bringing an entire cycle to closure, culmination. Thus what is being culminated is the living, actual, reality for those two people. And because it has been in place for a very long time those two Souls will be very wary and weary of it. They will feel like they are like a living record that keeps repeating itself over and over: the old pants. The *new phase* of Venus/Mars means that the couple has come through the chute of culmination that has born all kinds of realizations of how to rebirth, renew, recreate their relationship in all kinds of new ways: the new pants. They will have the instinct to do just that. This will require lots of trial and error. If the couple has a positive intention within that trial and error it will lead to re-stabilizing their relationship later on in their evolutionary journey. That initial stabilization can take place at the semi-sextile aspect within the new phase. (Rad)

Transitional aspects (aspects occurring at the end of a phase)
In the DVD school, in the section on planetary phases, Jeff spoke about Swami Kriyananda's crescent phase Sun/Moon square. Quote, "He moved in that life from that last stage of the crescent to the first quarter." He clarified that of course the phase didn't change. The archetype of the phase in the natal chart is the active archetype for the entire incarnation. In regards to any aspect, if it is at a transitional point (ie a conjunction, opposition, semisquare, sesquisquare, or square occurring at the end of a phase), it implies that this particular lifetime is about doing what work is necessary in order to bring about a completion of that phase. This innately means the necessity to surrender to what needs to happen FIRST before moving forward in the way that's symbolized by the proceeding phase. When the appropriate actions, or non-actions are taken in this regard, then it seems that the rest of the life can have the quality of the next phase by way of things working out the way they are supposed to. Meaning, the work has been done, now everything can unfold on its own. (Ari)

The outside world is so very full of not me. The crescent phase truly requires a retreat from the outside world of interaction in order to deeply settle into one's own subjective inner reality. How could anyone or anything else be an accurate reflection of the RICHNESS that is waiting inside of the Soul? What are my values? What are the thoughts that wish to come forth from me? How can this truth express through me? I can only find this by settling deeply in my own space. The moment I appeal to the consensus views, perhaps from people who "know how the system works" (disseminating polarity) I dishonor myself, I dishonor the way I am meant to be. Building a nest and settling in it with absolute contentment and satisfaction is the point of the crescent phase. In this nest a highly unique and abundant development occurs; something that can only come from a self-honoring life of quiet solitude. (Ari)

Polarities of the phases
The phases, like the signs, do have their natural polarity. The phases also internalize the polarity points just as the signs do. For example, the balsamic phase and its polarity, the gibbous phase. All too often the balsamic phase creates an inner sense of emptiness, of diffuseness, of not being able to connect to anything, or make sense of anything. The gibbous phase, internalized, would then manifest as the person keeping busy all the time, the famous lists of things to do, of never doing the core of what needs to be done, all this in order to escape from the balsamic phase itself. (Rad)

Current life Sun and angles
(Q) How do we interpret the phase when it only applies to a current life intention, eg Sun/angle? (Cat)
(A) Yes, we consider the phase in these situations. The phase will correlate to how the current life intentions or purposes are intended to be acted upon by the Soul relative to aspects from other planets to the Sun, or the angles, that are then integrated by the Soul relative to the entire EA signature in the birth chart. (Rad)

Conjunction
The planets unite in function so that a new evolutionary purpose and cycle can begin in an instinctual way. The new cycle of purpose will be projected spontaneously, instinctively, without any egocentric awareness. It is pure, unchecked expression or action. Random experiences will be initiated in order to begin the process of self-discovery of this new evolutionary purpose. (JWG)

New phase conjunction of two planets – example
[Example: Mercury/Jupiter] The new phase of the two planets correlates with the beginning of a new evolutionary cycle of development wherein the Soul is desiring to expand upon its existing knowledge and/or beliefs about life itself, and the new ideas it will be attracted to for that purpose. (Rad)

Example of new phase conjunction – Moon/Neptune
This is a brand new cycle, and thus the Soul will create many new experiences for itself with the purpose of discovering its own emotional reality as linked with the truth of Love. This Soul will not have developed an awareness of appropriate boundaries, techniques, forms, etc. of service – rather the intent at this juncture is to discover how service through the emotional body can happen. This will produce many random experiences that will teach the Soul about who it is, and how it can serve others. For example, its own home and family will provide many experiences whereby it will discover more layers of the truth. (Ari)

Balsamic conjunction of two planets – example
[Example: Mercury/Jupiter] The balsamic conjunction of Mercury/Jupiter means that the Soul is in the evolutionary process of culminating all kinds of beliefs, and the ideas from those beliefs, that it has used in understanding the nature of its lives until now: this life. (Rad)

Septile
In septiles, the involvement of fate will typically be linked with Y's in the road. In other words, in the course of developing the intention, there will be certain points where the path will present two different options. One can go this way or one can go that way. Both directions will often appear equally valid in terms of how to go forward. Keyword is 'appear.' One of the paths is meant to be taken, the other is not. If one attempts to take the wrong path, fate will then come into play by presenting some event, circumstance, message, etc. in order to prevent one from straying too far from the correct path that is meant to be taken. The phase in which the septile is occurring will supply further detail about the nature of the process. (Stacie)

The seed point of intention of a new cycle is always at the original conjunction. Thus you go back to the most recent conjunction of the two planets prior to the current septile, the moment at which their relationship became new phase. That is the seed point of the upcoming cycle – very much like the New Moon (which is the monthly conjunction of Sun and Moon) where we are told one plants (or realizes) the intentions of the upcoming month. The septile is just a bit after half way between the New Moon/Phase and the First Quarter Moon/Phase. Thus it is referencing back to the New Moon/moment of conjunction. Fate intervenes to bring the focus back to the original INTENTION of the conjunction of the two planets. What this means is we all get pulled off track in Earth reality.

The septile represents fated events intended to realign us to the original intention/purpose of the new phase between those two planets, as indicated by the house and sign of the conjunction, the aspects made to other planets, and the meaning of those planets in relation to the natal evolutionary signature – Pluto and polarity, Nodes, rulers of Nodes. For a relevant current example, the essence of the 1960's was the conjunction of Pluto and Uranus in 1965. Life has been all over the place since then. Now with Uranus increasingly squaring Pluto it is going to pull us back to the evolutionary intent released in 1965 at the point of the original conjunction. Life's intentions will be to eliminate everything that has gotten in the way. The degree to which people open to that intention will determine the outer results that occur. (Steve)

Sextile
The process of consciously understanding the new evolutionary cycle and purpose occurs through contrast and comparison. The individual must isolate him or herself from the impact of the external environment in order to realize and discover from within that which is uniquely new and individualistic about him or herself. Action is now internalized as the individual effects self-contemplation in contrast to the external reality conditions. The individual can now understand the issues pertaining to the past, individually and

collectively, and, in so doing, understand what experiences, methods, or skills to use to foster the development of the new evolutionary purpose in an individual way. (JWG)

Square, semisquare, sesquiquadrate
The square family (squares and semi/sesquisquares) are crucial in phasal development, they are transitions from one phase to another. So they are always going to imply some sort of resistance and insecurity based on fear of the unknown (new phase). Nature herself is set up in this way. We have the four natural seasons (solstice and equinox points all 90 degrees from one another) and the four midpoints in between them. Earth based spiritualities have always recognized the sacredness of these eight points in the course of a solar year. (Ari)

Sesquiquadrate – other names for
Most of the time JWG used the word sesquiquadrate, but **sesquiquad** and **sesquisquare** mean the same aspect. It really doesn't matter it would seem which term is used. (Rad)

Inconjunct: the most misunderstood aspect
The Virgo inconjunct. The meaning, the definition, of the inconjunct is to realign your sense of personal identity or ego with a higher will or ego called God and until you do so you have a crisis equalling the inability to manifest what you sense is a possibility or purpose for your life. The nature of an inconjunct is to teach humility at an egocentric level. The way it teaches the humility is to experience a sense of powerlessness or a core sense of inferiority in which you don't feel you're quite ready or good enough to do what your higher mind is suggesting that you can do; and until the conscious linkage is made with a higher power (we can call that God), you are blocked. The Virgo inconjunct (150 degrees) creates a feeling of inferiority. It can equal the archetype of masochism, leading to the sacrificing of one's own ego to a larger whole. A larger whole can even mean a person's needs.
The Scorpio inconjunct (210 degrees). You've already had the sense of inner power, you already know you can do it, but where the adjustment occurs, where the humility occurs, is that social circumstances will conspire in such a way as to block you until you make this linkage, until you learn to listen to that social sphere in such a way as how to integrate it on THEIR terms, not yours. The nature of the inconjunction (either one), archetypically, is to create crisis. Crisis thus becomes the specific experience through which the individual comes to understand what the evolutionary lessons are. How does the Yod relate? You're just magnifying the archetype. That's why in old-time astrology it was called the Finger of God. (JWG)

Inconjunct, gibbous phase
To understand anything in astrology is to understand the individual context of any Soul. One size does not fit all. Thus, the inconjuncts do have their archetypal meaning, yet that meaning must be fit to the individual context of any Soul. In the gibbous phase inconjunct, Virgo, the Soul will inwardly feel that it has something special to do in order to help the environment in some way, of being of service to it in order to help it, yet will inwardly feel not ready, good enough, or perfect enough in order to actualize or fulfill it. Thus, the Soul will find a variety of rational reasons, excuses, of why it will not, cannot, do what it feels inwardly drawn to do. The very nature of this type of inconjunct, in the gibbous phase, is an archetype of self-improvement which implies a conscious awareness of that which needs to be improved for its own evolutionary reasons. Thus, this creates a psychological sense of lack, of that which is not 'perfected' and needs to be improved upon.
The inconjunct correlates to the need to become aware of a special purpose that the Soul is meant to fulfill, and the crisis in aligning with the appropriate actions necessary in order to fulfill that purpose. Thus it has a lot to do with "getting out of one's own way," "letting go and letting god" and "taking it one step at a time." Until the inconjunct is integrated, it can manifest as angst that there's something to do but "I just don't know how or what to do." Typically, this archetype also creates an awareness within the Soul of others who have, or are doing, the same or similar tasks or functions that it feels inwardly drawn to do itself. This awareness can then reinforce the inner sense of not being ready as the Soul compares itself to these others who are perceived to be more perfect or ready than the Soul itself. All this occurs in order for the Soul to know or remember that there is a larger force, or God, behind whatever the special task, function, or capacity is that the Soul is aware of within itself. Thus, the challenge for the Soul is to inwardly align, consciously, with that higher will, or God, so that whatever the task, capacity, or function is actualized via that conscious alignment. In essence, to realize that God is the doer, and that the path to 'perfection' occurs one step at a time.
I do remember Wolf saying that he had an exact inconjunct between his Mercury in Scorpio and Uranus in Gemini: a gibbous phase inconjunct. And his 1st house Mercury was inconjunct his 12th house Jupiter. He said that the first Pluto book, the entire paradigm of EA, was put into his Soul, consciousness, in a dream. The symbolism is perfect for this. And, of course, he was instructed or empowered to write this book for anyone who could benefit by it. Yet he kept making excuses, for four or five years, of why he could not write the book. All the excuses certainly sounded like rationale reasons of course. Among them was not having enough money to take off from his counselling work. He needed to keep working. One day a woman showed up and asked him how much he needed to get by in order to write the book. He told her how much that would be needed. She gave him the money. He had no more excuses. Yet the money would only last about two months. As it turned out, Wolf wrote the entire first Pluto book

in those two months: by hand. I remember him saying too that as he finally sat to write the book that the book literally wrote itself. That he was learning the material himself as it was being written. And that, at times, the material was coming into his consciousness so quickly that he would end up with his hand in knots because he could not keep up with it. Well of course the book got written in this way, and, as they say, the rest is history. It speaks for itself in terms of how this gibbous phase inconjunct manifested in his context. (Rad)

Inconjunct, full phase
To understand anything in astrology is to understand the individual context of any Soul. One size does not fit all. Thus, the inconjuncts do have their archetypal meaning, yet that meaning must be fit to the individual context of any Soul. What Wolf taught about the full phase, Scorpio, inconjunct is that the Soul will experience humility, blockage, from the external environment if the Soul attempts to IMPOSE itself on that environment relative to the two planets that are in this full phase inconjunct in their chart. The intention in that blockage is to force the Soul to objectify the nature of the environment that it is in order to understand what that environments needs. In essence it would be a change in the inner orientation from showing up in some environment with an inner attitude that said, "I am here to help" to "how can I help the environment that I find myself within?"

This underlying issue here is opening up to a larger will, not just coming from a place of one's own will. Until this inner adjustment is made the Soul will experience crisis in that it will experience blockage from the environment from being able to apply, actualize, fulfill, its own inner sense of being able to help the environment, of being of service to it, relative to the sense of purpose 'from on high' as symbolized in the two planets in this full phase inconjunct. The Soul is 'full of itself' in this full phase inconjunct, and wants to actualize or express whatever it is from 'on high' in the environments that it is in. It feels ready and able. (Rad)

The key here is for the Soul to allow the environment that it is in, relative to the function of the full phase inconjunct, to show the Soul what is needed from it relative to the function or capacity that the Soul has that can benefit that environment. So even if the Soul is not in any way consciously identifying with God as the 'doer'– letting go and letting God – by allowing the 'larger forces' of the environment itself to show the way this is a de facto manifestation of that. Everything the Soul does requires choices. Thus, the choices themselves correlate to an active effort on the part of the Soul. The Soul will develop the skills it needs in order to be of service in just the way that Source intends by taking one step at a time. And each step that is taken allows for the 'larger forces,' or God, to manifest through the Soul because of those actions. This is why I use the example of JWG writing the first Pluto book. By simply putting the pen on the paper the book began to write itself. (Rad)

The Scorpio inconjunct (210 degrees). You've already had the sense of inner power, you already know you can do it, but where the adjustment occurs, where the humility occurs, is that social circumstances will conspire in such a way as to block you until you make this linkage, until you learn to listen to that social sphere in such a way as how to integrate it on THEIR terms, not yours. The nature of the inconjunction (either one), archetypically, is to create crisis. Crisis thus becomes the specific experience through which the individual comes to understand what the evolutionary lessons are. How does the Yod relate? You're just magnifying the archetype. That's why in old-time astrology it was called the Finger of God. (JWG)

Inconjunct – between 2nd house (Taurus) and 7th house (Libra)
Jeffrey was the first astrologer to teach about Venus' correlation to the inner relationship that all people have with themselves. He taught why Venus had a double rulership for the signs Libra and Taurus. He said that Taurus and the 2nd house correlated to the inner relationship we all have with ourselves, and that the 7th house and Libra correlated to the types of outer relationships that we form with other people and why. He taught that the planet Venus, of itself, symbolized both the inner and outer relationships within the archetype of Venus itself. A simple example: if a person has, let's say, Venus in Virgo and their inner relationship to themself is one of intense criticism, all the things that are wrong with them, that it shouldn't then be surprising that that person would then 'attract,' Venus, others who are then critical of them: the inner reflecting the outer. And that which we attract is a reflection of the inner vibration within us where that inner vibration is a reflection of our inner relationship to ourselves. Or, for another example, let's say that Venus in Virgo person was inwardly experiencing a high degree of 'lack' in their lives which then leads to a sense of being 'empty' from within. That inner relationship to themselves could then manifest outwardly as needing, Venus, many other people in their lives in order to 'fill them up,' and needing others to give to them that which they felt they were lacking.

He talked about the natural inconjunct between the 2nd house, Taurus, and the 7th house, Libra. He taught that this is the natural 'crisis' that exists in all of us that involves the need to be self-reliant and fulfilling our own needs, and how our needs can be projected onto others in such a way as to become dependent on others for the very needs that we need to satisfy within ourselves. And how our projected needs onto others correlate to 'expectations' that we can set up with other people. So what happens when our expectations that are projected onto others do not occur? For most some kind of crisis will occur where the intent of the crisis is to force the person back upon themselves so that self-reliance in some way can be developed when those expectations have reached a point of excessive dependency on others. He taught about the need for the EA astrologer to understand the totality of the Venus archetype. Thus, to not only understand the sign that Venus is in but all the aspects that it is making to other planets, the North and South Nodes of Venus in terms of what the past, present, and future of the evolving Venus archetype is in all charts, and to fully grasp the signs on the 2nd and 7th houses as they condition those natural archetypes, and the reasons for that conditioning relative to the ongoing evolutionary intentions of the Soul, and, lastly, the location of the planetary rulers of those signs and the aspects that they are making for the same reasons. (Rad)

Triseptile
JWG did not use a 5 degree orb for inconjuncts. He used 3 degrees. And that is because of the triseptile aspect being so close to the inconjunct aspect. If your [example Mars/Pluto] aspect is exactly 154 degrees equaling a triseptile this would mean that your very last life was a primary one which has led to your current life being a refinement of that last life where such refinement is symbolized and reflected in the nature of the Gibbous phase triseptile. (Rad)

Sesquiquadrate
To me the buzzword for the sesquiquadrate is "adjustment." It is a Virgo-like aspect that involves crisis, analysis, and often paralysis resulting from over analysis, used to justify not acting. It is a gateway aspect because it represents the boundary between two phases, thus an inherent tendency to resist. We are crossing from a masculine phase to a feminine phase. It is a powerful aspect, because of that. The gibbous sesquiquadrate represents the 15 degree of Leo point, the disseminating the 15 degree of Scorpio: both of these are biquadrant points, mid-points of fixed signs. As such they are quite powerful. (Steve)

Sesquiquadrate, first quarter
The first quarter phase sesquiquadrate: being a transitional state to a new phase, has the balsamic quality of "completing" (this is true for all aspects that occur at the end of a phase). What's necessary is for the Soul to learn how to slow down, to curb whatever behaviors are overly excessive/do not allow further participation in society. When we're moving from the first quarter phase to the gibbous phase the archetypal theme is humility via inner withdrawn and reflection on what needs fixing. (Ari)

Sesquiquadrate, full phase
The sesquiquadrate that occurs within the full phase is again, completing a phase. The example JWG gave is Mercury/Pluto in a full phase sesquiquadrate. If the Soul realizes that becoming a psychologist would be an appropriate way to integrate its own unique purpose, then the Soul necessarily needs to understand what is required by society in order to do that (school, credentials, prerequisites, etc.). Again micromanaging. (Ari)

Sesquiquadrate, disseminating phase
The sesquiquadrate in the disseminating phase reflects the beginning of a complete immersion within society. The intent at this point is to continue to make whatever adjustments are necessary in order to fully participate in society in a way that meets the needs/realities of its society. Progressively through the disseminating phase, a Soul osmoses into its own consciousness a deeply penetrating awareness of its social reality, and how to participate within it in a way to fulfill its purpose. And so in the beginning of this phase, with the sesquiquadrate, there needs to be an immense degree of awareness channeled into understanding one's society and making the necessary adjustments based on that awareness. (Ari)

Interpretation of a phasal relationship aspect, eg conjunction
(Q) Which planet in the pair should the interpretation be based upon? Example:
Sun/Mercury = correlates to the thoughts, ideas, opinions and points of view the Soul uses to justify its life purpose.
(1) Sun/Mercury New Phase Conjunction – A new evolutionary cycle begins in which the individual instinctually initiates new experiences in order to explore new thoughts ideas, opinions and points of view in order to justify its life purpose.
(2) Sun/Mercury New Phase Conjunction – A new evolutionary cycle begins in which the individual instinctually initiates new experiences in order to develop a new life purpose which serves to justify his thoughts, ideas, opinions and point of view. (Cat)
(A) First, I would say both interpretations apply at the same time. In the example we are looking at the interface between the individual's sense of individual purpose for this lifetime that translates into how the individual creatively actualizes self (Sun), and the linear and analytic thought function (Mercury). Thus, on one hand, the individual 'instinctually initiates new experiences in order to explore new thoughts ideas, opinions and points of view in order to justify its life purpose.' The archetype implies the possibility that the sense of individual purpose may be linked with intellectual dynamics. The individual will instinctually project itself into its circumstantial reality in order to communicate with other people as a reflection of the individual's own subjective sense of self. The individual may also project itself into the environment in order to give names and classifications to phenomena from his/her own subjective point of view, and can be very creative in producing thought/ communication forms and very personal arrangements of reality at an intellectual level.
At the same time, 'the individual instinctually initiates new experiences in order to develop a new life purpose which serves to justify his thoughts, ideas, opinions and point of view.' The archetype implies that the individual will be collecting information that, in time, will serve not only to justify, but also to linearly understand what the personal purpose is, or to adjust or discriminate this

personal purpose, and the specific ways to creatively actualize this sense of purpose and special destiny. Sometimes this will imply the need to create crises (because Mercury 'carries' the energy of both Gemini and Virgo) on an instinctual spontaneous basis serving to induce the need for adjustment or discrimination of the personal purpose and the ways in which this needs to be actualized. Thus, both archetypes – Sun and Mercury – integrate in both ways. Also, I would say that there will be variations and one way may be more relevant than the other in each individual case, depending on the signature of the birth chart and the main evolutionary axis, in relation with the evolutionary condition of the individual. (Gonzalo)

FIG 2
EA Aspects, Phases & Degrees Chart

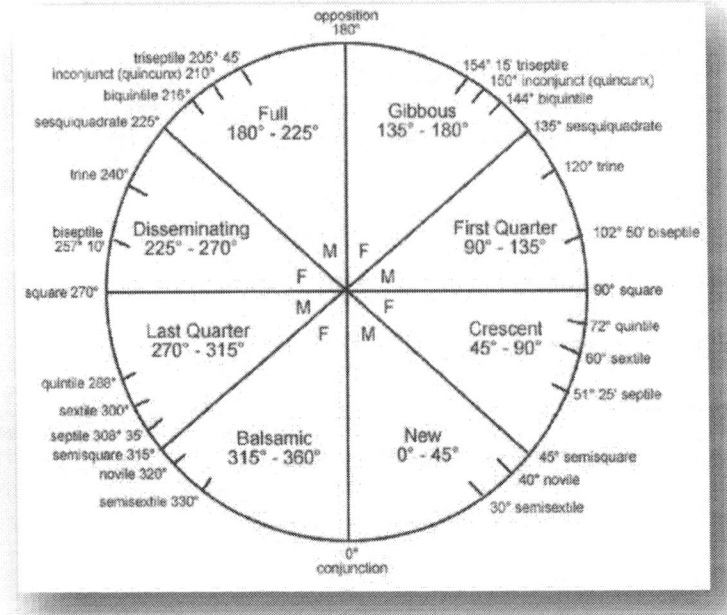

Opposition
An opposition symbolizes that something has reached an extreme, and must be brought back into a state of balance. In order to do this, we must "throw off" specific dynamics symbolized by the planets by house and sign that are creating an extremity. For example, if I have Venus/Pluto opposition, this dynamic would be specific to relationships in the context of the issues of equality, and reaching a balanced state of giving and receiving within relationships, and also the person's inner relationship with themselves. The opposition symbolizes that the person is throwing off extremes relative to his or her approach to relationships in general, and must also change his or her inner relationship with him or herself that created these types of relationships. (The nodal axis is included in this.) (Deva)

Any planets in opposition correlate with the evolutionary need to throw off something, to oppose it, in order for evolution to proceed via those dynamics. (Rad)

Transiting opposition, example
An opposition is an opportunity to throw off something and any opposition can be viewed as such, including say a transiting opposition of Mars opposing Pluto and so on. This can serve like a tuning fork for the Soul if they are getting off track at all, throwing off dynamics or forcing one into an experience that puts a spotlight on where things are out of balance. In a natal chart using your Mars and opposing a planet in your 1st house, can be a signature where your will/desires are opposing those of others. So you are learning to align your will, with the will of others and meeting people halfway. Depending on what that Mars is opposing, will explain what those opposing desires are about but certainly in the area of relationships.

For example, if that Mars is opposing Saturn, someone might continue to attract people that want to bulldoze them so the need here is to establish your own inner authority and platform of strength. To become very clear on what you need, yet still considering the needs of others and then making choices from there, ie not undermining your own needs. The opposition will continue happening through attracting more oppositions until you respond appropriately for your Soul's necessary growth and throw them off. Then when you are successful with throwing them off, those two planets making the opposition play out more like a conjunction – a powerful new beginning. So instead of feeling overwhelmed by a natal opposition or feeling fear around seeing one on its way through transit, take the Mars lead and use it as a vehicle to accelerate your evolution. (Kristin)

Quintile
The quintile in the crescent phase, which is yin and also relatively new, implies that the entirety of what has lead the Soul to where it is now needs to be furthered internalized to the point that it can pave the road for a new level of actualization that will begin in the crescent square. The analogy that comes to mind is the painter that is developing their skills for the first time. By the crescent phase quintile a unique style, or way of creatively actualizing through painting has emerged. This new style will then be the essencethat is carried forth in the next phase. During this phase the creative purpose can develop as best as it can if the Soul becomes highly internalized such that it can retreat within its creativity and fully flow with its inspiration. (Ari)

Yod

The yod or "finger of God" aspect pattern involves three planets or points, two of them are linked by a sextile and form inconjuncts to the third one – thus three aspects are involved: two inconjuncts and one sextile. Given that inconjuncts link signs which are not connected either by element, polarity (yin-yang) or modality or nature (cardinal, fixed, mutable) they correlate with crisis and/or need to adjust. Thus, the yod is also associated with dynamics involving crisis. An example of a natural yod is the relation between Aries/Virgo/Scorpio. (Gonzalo)

This is another very problematic pattern, the double inconjunct linked with the sextile. This was originally called a "Finger of God." This implies a feeling of destiny; a trusting of the intuition so that when you come to the "Y" in the road you would know which way to go. The deeper issue is that commonly people with this pattern experience tremendous frustration. The yod promotes a knowing, a vision, an awareness from on high that is not necessarily consciously defined. It is like a telephone line inconjunct to God and receiving messages that somehow seen utterly unrelated to your current circumstances or reality which then sets in motion this tremendous level of analysis in which you are now focusing on all the imperfections and lacks of your reality contrasted now with this vision from on high. So life always seems somehow less than right. It either leads to perpetual or transitory bitchiness, complaints, something's always wrong, or making crises where none need to exist. It can lead into negative self-concepts because, in their own evaluation, they cannot actualize the vision from on high. The inconjuncts focus on the issue of humility, personal and social limitations. The person is now analysing themselves mercilessly and now comparing themselves, full phase/gibbous phase, to the authority on high. Of course they are going to seem less than adequate. So they never feel quite ready to implement or actualize the vision from on high. It is always held in the head. It creates a really highly tuned electrical system because it is so tight. The midpoint in the sextile/opposition point of the focus of the yod is called the boomerang point. The boomerang point, of itself, is never activated unless there is a planet at that midpoint, thus creating an opposition. If there is, then there is a natural coming and going, coming and going. The planet on the ends of those two inconjuncts is doubly stressed but where that planet is manifesting by house and sign is exactly the area where this vision on high is meant to be expressed. That is the point. Through that function or area. So, the solution of the yod is to realize that the path to perfection simply occurs through action, one step at a time. Clearly, this kind of pattern is emphasizing the evolutionary necessity for humility from an egocentric point of view. What you are actually trying to do, from another point of view, is to shift the very center of gravity in your consciousness and that means in this kind of culture from the left brain to the right brain, from deductive logic to inductive logic, from empirical to intuitive. (JWG)

Understanding phases, aspects and signs within a planetary configuration, eg yod

[Example: Transiting yod configuration – Saturn, Pluto, and Jupiter at the apex] It is important to understand the archetypal meaning of the phase first. The various aspects within the totality of a phase correlate to the evolutionary progression through the phases. Firstly, by understanding the nature of the phases: the full phase relative to Jupiter and Saturn, and the gibbous phase relative to Pluto and Jupiter. Then the meaning of the archetypes of the inconjunct within the phasal context. Then add onto that the archetypes of the signs involved: Gemini, Scorpio, and Pluto. You can then apply this understanding to the collective as well as each individual: where this is taking place in their chart. (Rad)

ASPECTS AND PHASES (JWG)

Introduction

We will always talk about polarities, yin/yang, light/dark, male/female, because to understand any one phase, you have to understand its opposite – its natural polarity. For example, to truly understand Virgo, you have to understand Pisces; to truly understand Capricorn, you have to understand Cancer, etc. For example, most people think of Capricorn as crystallized in space, ie somehow without emotion relative to how Capricorn naturally projects itself. But, of course, underneath that Capricorn, and the very basis of how it projects itself, is Cancer. The essence of vulnerability. Why do you think Virgo needs crisis? Look at the polarity of Pisces. Virgo is going for a kind of reality that is not possible on earth – thus, crisis. In most cases, astrology is not taught this way, but it is very basic. The houses and signs in which you find planets in phase to each other tell you the kinds of experiences, inner and outer, that the person will gravitate to in order to fulfill the intent of the phase. The idea of phases and cycles is as ancient as astrology itself, back to Babylonian times. It was Dane Rudhyar who resurrected the idea in modern astrology.

Mercury and Venus never venture very far from the Sun and therefore do not go around the full circle, but within the balsamic and new phase relationships, there are degree relationships to which you can apply the evolutionary view. In a Mercury/Sun phase, you are dealing with the Mercury function as it is applied to the Sun, and Mercury means the ideas that we use to justify what we are doing at any level at which we participate. So it is either time to let go of some ideas or time to make new ones. Similarly with the Venus function. Here it can be as much as 48 degrees apart, the early part of crescent or the last part of last quarter. This concept is applied to planets only. Astrology of itself is nothing. There is no inherent meaning to Venus. It is just a chunk of matter in space. It is what we project onto it through correlations and observations that create the meanings. The aspects are described from an evolutionary point of view, from 0 to 360 degrees. Phases are determined by measuring the distance in degrees from the slower moving planet counterclockwise to the faster moving planet. Any two planets who are 45 degree or less arc in the new phase; any two planets that are from 45 to 90 degrees are in crescent phase, etc. The Sun is always considered the stationary point. The nodes are also used and because they fluctuate, one needs to look in the ephemeris and determine which is slower, the planet or the node.

NEW PHASE

So, in order to understand new phase, we have to understand full phase. The new phase is, of itself, just that: new. The keyword is **"instinctual."** Instinct is without forethought, a feeling or inclination (it is not intuition, however), an automatic reaction. Instinct is simply action without thought. So the instinct, in the new phase, correlates to the instinct to become. Is not life itself a continuous state of becoming? Becoming what? That which it is not. The instinct to become that which one is not equals action without forethought – the simple, instinctual urge to initiate action relative to one's need to become that which you individually are. The new phase is inherently yang, meaning energy moving out from center, projecting. If the energy was left unchecked in the new phase, it would simply blow out into space and in an utterly disintegrated fashion. The essence of the new phase is a brand new evolutionary cycle which demanded the initiation of experience to create reaction which then determines knowledge. In the new phase, the actions are relatively random, although the various aspects promote a narrowing of experience.

Action and reaction

Thus, the simple instinctual need to initiate action and through the inevitable reaction to the action, one develops knowledge. Does the baby know that the stove is hot before it touches it? It must create action in order to experience reaction, then it knows. Thus the knowledge that is gained in the new phase is determined through reaction to the action.

New evolutionary cycle

If we understand the nature of the circle from an evolutionary point of view because the phenomena of life and time and space evolves, it is not static, thank God, the new phase then means that any two planets in a new phase are embarking upon a new cycle of evolutionary development, that which has not come before. This implies that prior to this life a cycle has just ended that has been in place for beaucoup (many) lifetimes. It is a brand new phenomenon. There is not any conceptual superstructure to explain the reasons or why's behind the instinct to become. It does not have the conceptual equipment to explain why it wants to do what it wants to do. Thus, it needs independence and freedom to simply initiate whatever experiences are deemed necessary in order to discover the ongoing process of becoming through the reactions to the initiated experiences.

Relationship between new phase and full phase
The relationship between new phase and full phase entering into a relationship and withdrawing and is the need to participate in the world and the need to withdraw from it. **"Isolation and periodic participation."** The isolation is a way of reaffirming or re-establishing what one is, and thus, over time, progressively asserting through establishment of itself in society, its individuality in society.

However when we understand the full phase, its natural polarity, the keyword for the full phase is **"completion."** What is completed in the full phase is the evolutionary journey from the new phase through the crescent phase through the first quarter phase through the gibbous phase. Any two planets you find in a full phase relationship, evolutionarily speaking, prior to this life, have already come through these phases. Thus as the new phase planets and the individual who has these planets in this state interacts with life itself, it is instinctually and inherently going to be aware of other individuals, full phase, who have more of a conceptual ability to explain who and what they are and why they are there, why they are going to do what they are going to do, or what they have done. Through the natural temptation of this polarity to compare (the new phase is without conceptual ability to do so), there is going to be some degree of instinctual temptation to adopt the beliefs and/or value systems which are the basis of explanations in all people, in order to explain its own actions and thus be out of harmony with that inherent and emerging individuality implied in this new phase.

What commonly happens in this new phase/full phase phenomena is that the person fluctuates in extreme behavioral patterns – from one extreme of wanting to be absolutely alone and free, to the cyclic need to be overly engaged or involved in a relationship with people who seem to reflect what the individual is trying to become. This creates two very deep alternating behavioral patterns which seem apparently inconsistent. What this really touches upon is the nature of creation, the projection through time/space – the need to become what? If the creator was perfect in the beginning why create anything? The implication is that the creator was, in the beginning, imperfect. The instinctual energy is related to that separating desire and the need to go back to God. If we agree that creation and its distinct forms did not create itself, then what created it? And if that which is called the creation point, the source, the uncreated created, in Buddhist terms, and we observe things like imperfection – wherein lies the origin of imperfection? The inherent truth is in every part of creation, every molecule, every cell, every substance, every particle – so the instinct to become ultimately correlates to the creation projected, projection being an inherently masculine principle, and contraction or reception being an inherently feminine principle. So, in these two distinct phases, a mirror of this basic truth: on the one hand, needing to act, and in the process of acting in an environmental sense, instinctually comparing, relative to full phase, other individuals to itself creating retreat.

New phase conjunction
Example: Mercury conjunct Jupiter in Scorpio in the new phase. Would this not correlate to unformulated thought processes and/or belief systems coming into this life because the intent is to establish utterly new ones, that which has not come before? Would this not then demand a freedom of action to determine what my beliefs and/or thoughts are going to be through my actual experiences? Would it not tend to imply that my thoughts and/or beliefs would tend to grow and would not want to be static even though the fixed component of Scorpio would tend to want to make it so? Because we have two competing archetypes – fixed relative to new phase, would it not tend to suggest that I would come up with philosophical or intellectual systems that worked in my life for a time, fixed, only to become stagnated or outmoded, Scorpio, which would then generate the need to generate even more experiences, new phase, to evolve them? Would this not also suggest, with respect to full phase polarity, that at various points in my life I might become hypnotically, Scorpio, attracted to individuals, full phase, who represented or symbolized to me, Scorpio, a more well-thought out and formulated conceptual, abstract, intellectual system and feel the temptation, Scorpio, to adopt, full phase, such systems?

Yet, because they were not systems that were inwardly realized or developed by me through my own actions and as I attempt to deliver such thoughts or beliefs to another, thoughts or beliefs that were not developed through my own experience, would this not tend to promote for me, Scorpio, confrontations with individuals that could out-argue me because they could see that what I was saying was not based on actual experience? Would this not have the effect of creating the opposite behavior, Scorpio now saying, we will not use those words, but retreating into a stance of isolation, through a vindictive, instinctual response? For a time, I would feel quite righteous in my vindictive response and now I would instinctually console myself. One the other hand, as the individual is loyal, to itself, ie new phase, then as it simply instinctually communicated, Mercury/Jupiter/new phase, what came to it as it occurred without forethought, would that which was being communicated not have a spellbinding, mesmerizing, Scorpio, impact on the listener? What is now being instinctually communicated is new and that which is new is going to be challenging that which is not new, ie other people's prevailing opinions, ie Mercury/Jupiter. That itself could create a defensive response. This situation could also generate frustration. As one evolves in this life, one may become aware of a new way, and yet relative to the evolutionary necessity, of culminating that which has been. This is the common problem of the poet: How many truly understand the spirit of what the poet is trying to say?

Absolute conjunction to 10 deg of separation
In the new phase conjunction, we can have two planets that are absolutely conjunct or that have 10 degrees of separation. From a purely evolutionary point of view, these two are different from each other. We have evolved and there is a subtle difference. The number of degrees of separation from the absolute conjunction represents relative evolution of the principle. Once one has been through something, one gets used to it and begins to know how to respond to it.
Example: I have Mars at 0 degree Aries and Venus at 10 degrees Aries, as compared with Venus at 2 degrees Aries. The former is more evolved than the latter. Anything that came before that [absolute] conjunction is a balsamic conjunction, not a new phase conjunction, in the final stages of wrapping up countless lifetimes, having come through all of the phases and is balsamic and almost done.

Progressions
It is possible for a person to have both of these [balsamic and new conjunction] in one lifetime and that can be measured through progression. The progressions measure the evolution of the natal imprint. We evolve. We all have Aries, an Ascendant and a Mars function. These operate in all of our lives, no matter what is going on in the phases and aspects. This is an inherent dynamic in our consciousness that evolves and that natural principle is reflected through the Arian archetype that is in every chart in all cases.

Stelliums
Sometimes, when you see a stellium, five or six planets in the same sign, there is going to be a mixture in most cases of new phase and balsamic conjunctions. That is the real way to understand the nature of a stellium and why a person would have that amount of energy in one sign.

New phase semi-sextile
What we want to keep in mind here is that the new phase evolves through time. This is now how we start measuring aspects. If you have two planets in a semi-sextile relationship, 30 degrees, yet still in the new phase, this symbolism clearly suggests that the individual, prior to this life, has already had a couple of experiences – maybe a couple of lives, who knows – involving this new phase process. In other words it is not utterly new. Because it suggests that there has been something before, the semi-sextile tends to have the effect of checking the pure instinctual process of the new phase. Prior to the semi-sextile, there is the instinct for unchecked action, random-like, but through a process of action/reaction prior to this life, the individual has already begun to become somewhat aware instinctually, of course, but aware of what this new purpose is, evolutionarily speaking, and thus the knowledge implied allows the semi-sextile to have a checking action or narrowing of experience. There is still the need to initiate action. There is still the action/reaction process. There is still much which is unformulated and yet the person has more of a sense of undefined direction, ie to narrow the randomness. The person may have unconscious memories of coming through the conjunction because in any life 80% of your thoughts, beliefs, values, interpretation and perception patterns, self-relatedness patterns are determined by subconscious memories. This is itself, based on that which has come before. The memory is in the Soul and is the sum-total of all that which has come before.

If I have had two planets in a new phase condition prior to this life and I now find them in a semi-sextile relationship, this constitutes subconscious memories. This, of itself, narrows the experience field, not happily so however, because new phase wants to be instinctive. So the tension of the semi-sextile is a tension based on feeling checked or constrained. It is the tension, for example, between Aries/Taurus. That is a natural semi-sextile and I think most of us would agree that Aries of itself wants absolute freedom and the instinct in Taurus is to consolidate. This new phase condition creates an irritant. It is like the competing archetypes of water/fire. Water tends to have the effect of dampening the spirit of fire. So the semi-sextile is going to narrow, to focus, to stabilize, and to begin the process of forethought prior to action.

Relationship between new phase semi-sextile and full phase inconjunct
This is going to have a natural polarization in the full phase inconjunct. One of the meanings of the full phase inconjunct is to understand the meaning of the personal limitations as measured against the social environment. What you can and cannot be, what you can and cannot become, what you are and are not. This can correlate to a social function. You can see how this is mirrored in this new phase semi-sextile. It is the very first aspect to begin the checking of excessively willful egocentric expression – to begin the initial experience and, yes, humiliation, of limitation. When a baby is born, it knows no limitations, it demands all. The biological instinct in the parents is to provide all – it is utterly catered to. However, there does come a time in which that baby learns, semi-

sextile, new phase. Traditional books do not tell you the phase, and how a new phase semi-sextile is utterly different from a balsamic phase semi-sextile, and that how it manifests is determined by context.

New phase novile
The Novile is actually a very interesting aspect evolutionarily speaking. Some people claim that the novile is such a high octave aspect, that unless the person is sufficiently spiritually evolved, they cannot develop it. If this were true, why have it? Since in the west, dreams are somehow not linked with consciousness, it is important to know that dreams are conscious, not unconscious. Even a dream that you cannot remember, you know that you have had it and been conscious during it because you felt the effect. So, my bias tells me that noviles work for everyone. The key dynamic in a novile is gestation and it is this dynamic that tempts some people to argue for an essentially unconscious process, or, in other cases, you have to be highly evolved to be aware of it. Even for those in a consensus state, it is conscious. It can be something as simple as a twinge. Let's say that in contemplating two or three equally valid courses of action, one feels a twinge – that is the novile working. This will somehow orient the person to the proper experience. At the point of the novile the person is more accepting of the dynamics with respect to resignation.

Mutational aspects
As we evolve through the new phase there is more strength and courage gained to be that which you are or are becoming, to resist the full phase temptations which are experienced at its maximum in the semisquare which becomes a mutational aspect from new phase to crescent phase. This turnstile equals mutation from one orientation to a radically different orientation.

CRESCENT PHASE

We will define the crescent phase before we talk about the semisquare and talk about it in terms of its polarity, the disseminating phase. The keyword for crescent phase is **"struggle."** It is an inherently yin phase, whereas the new phase is inherently yang. Yang meaning energy moving out from center, projecting, and Yin meaning energy moving back to center, or retreating. In the crescent phase, energy is returning to center. If the energy was left unchecked in the new phase, it would simply blow out into space and in an utterly disintegrated fashion. Keep in mind that the essence of the new phase is a brand new evolutionary cycle which demanded the initiation of experience to create reaction which then determines knowledge. In the new phase, the actions are relatively random, although the various aspects promote a narrowing of experience. By the time the crescent phase happens, it is now time to withdraw from the excessive initiation of experience in order to consolidate and stabilize that which has been realized via the new phase, to establish it, to make it concrete, real, to give it roots. By giving it roots, allowing it to grow; yet still reflecting, however, on the individuality of the new cycle, new phase.

Relationship between crescent phase and disseminating phase
It is a struggle in that the polarity phase is disseminating. The disseminating phase, of itself, is the **"totality of society."** Everything that your culture or society is, is reflected in the disseminating phase, thus "status quo." So, what is the struggle? The struggle is to establish in a concrete way individuality as discovered in the new phase as contrasted with the status quo. Because this is still a relatively new development, the individual is shaky, still not quite certain, still comparing relative to the disseminating phase and thus the temptation to borrow and become a vicarious extension of ideas or values or lifestyles of external authority figures that tend to symbolize what the individual senses itself to be, without doing the necessary work to establish that on its own terms. Planets in a disseminating phase with each other would give you an idea of what the pull away from the crescent phase is all about.
Examples
– Let's say we have Mercury and Jupiter in Crescent phase and this individual is drawn to be a lawyer. The crescent phase in this case would be the need to establish its own unique way of communicating its own ideas relative to its inherent philosophical beliefs. Yet, relative to the disseminating phase, the temptation would be to compare itself with the established external authority figures in a cultural context and to borrow their way of presenting themselves, their way of communicating. Because it is a yin phase, there is a natural temptation to withdraw from conflict or confrontation. This makes its own kind of struggle.
– Let's say we have Venus and Mars in the Crescent phase. This is an individual who is meant to struggle to establish its own individual way of being in a relationship. Yet, if the polarity phase is disseminating, we have all kinds of cultural possibilities. It is tempting to just select one and decide that that is more reflective of what I am trying to do.
Another form of the struggle is when the individual does "x" amount of work on herself to determine who she is, her individuality, and just trying to maintain that without doing additional work. She reaches a degree of comfortability and says, "Ah, that's it! I'm fine now," without continuing the struggle of further development. So, what is required in this phase to actualize it? The relationship between new phase and full phase, entering into a relationship and withdrawing, and is the need to participate in the world and the need to withdraw from it. Isolation and periodic participation. The isolation is a way of reaffirming or re-establishing what one is, and thus, over time, progressively asserting through establishment of itself in society, its individuality in society.

Semisquare (mutational aspect – new phase and crescent phase)
So, we run into the semisquare and relative to orb issues we can have a new phase semisquare and a crescent phase semisquare. The new phase semisquare suggests that the person is in a relatively new state, new in the sense of moving into the crescent phase and there is a **"tremendous conflict or stress,"** semisquare. The habit pattern of the Soul is to experience non-restriction, to have energy moving out from center, to just be and to do and to act without restriction. The crescent phase semisquare which is now looming on the individual's horizon is saying, "Stop! Slow Down! Consolidate! Go within." It is reversing the very flow of what it is used to doing. This creates conflict for this person. Behavioral patterns of coming and going, situations of being out of harmony with oneself until it is brought under control are going to be prevalent. Happily, the semisquare does emphasize and intensify the **"creative energy to actualize individuality."** The new phase semisquare will not accept any external authority model which is attempting to determine what it is meant to be. Happily, it will put its middle finger in the air. So you can determine the degree of struggle relative to the orb issue, by how new or old the aspect is.

With respect to the crescent phase, we still have a Soul whose experience is to not feel restriction, and yet these restrictions have been encountered prior to this life and thus the individual has already begun the psychological battle and process of resolving itself, resigning itself to such restrictions. This means then, that in the actual crescent state that that conflict will not be as intense as it will be in the new phase semisquare. The exact 45 degrees is very intense because one is right on the fulcrum between the two. But, when it is actually in the crescent phase, the person has already succeeded in dealing with it. Until they have succeeded in dealing with it, you won't find that aspect. Also, of course, the crescent phase semisquare does give the individual the continuing power to establish its individuality, to root it. In the very nature of a stressful mathematical equation, semisquare, is a tendency to creatively induce stress, that stress equaling Soul development, personality, emotional, intellectual development – these developments equaling individuality, not status quo.

Relationship between crescent phase semisquare and disseminating phase sesquiquadrate
The polarity aspect is the 135 degree sesquiquad. The waning sesquiquad, relative to the disseminating pull, means that the individual now has a vision of its social purpose. The conflict is how to integrate it and here is the challenge, on society's terms. Until that is realized, the society perceives that individual as a threat to its own existence. So, with respect to this polarity, the individual can expect conflict, stress, and **"confrontation from external circumstances"** that the individual is creating. The intent of these confrontations and conflicts is to reaffirm the essential individuality with respect to the middle fingers in the air.

With respect to the crescent phase, we still have a Soul whose experience is to not feel restriction, and yet these restrictions have been encountered prior to this life and thus the individual has already begun the psychological battle and process of resolving itself, resigning itself to such restrictions. This means then, that in the actual crescent state that that conflict will not be as intense as it will be in the new phase semisquare. The exact 45 degrees is very intense because one is right on the fulcrum between the two. But, when it is actually in the crescent phase, the person has already succeeded in dealing with it. Until they have succeeded in dealing with it, you won't find that aspect. Also, of course, the crescent phase semisquare does give the individual the continuing power to establish its individuality, to root it. In the very nature of a stressful mathematical equation, semisquare, is a tendency to creatively induce stress, that stress equaling Soul development, personality, emotional, intellectual development – these developments equaling individuality, not status quo.

In the semisquare, there are memories of a cycle that preceded this life and before that the cycle that had come before the new phase conjunction, there are still sub-conscious memories of balsamic conditions. The fear that manifests in these two phases and particularly in this aspect is being trapped by a past that it cannot even conceptualize – an irrational fear. But that fear itself is used to further develop the individuality because of the determination not to be trapped by it.

Crescent phase septile
Now the sense of individuality which has been initially established in the new phase, by the time it gets to the Septile, it is linked with a conceptual sense or an instinctual sense, depending upon the planets, of a **special destiny**, something out of the ordinary. This aspect has been called an aspect of "fate." This is actually true, but let's agree on what we mean by "fate" first. What is fate? "A fickle finger." Fate is simply an event that is determined to happen, no matter what you do. Fate is usually a rather meaningful event in your life. Twenty percent of anybody's life is fated. Eighty percent is free choice. We all have fated events. Fate is normally linked with karmic consequence. (This is not a sacrifice. On a developmental basis, one of the main things with inconjuncts is the lesson of humility and this tends to imply sacrifice.) A Septile means that the Soul makes a program wherein throughout its life there will be, on a cyclic basis, the famous **"Y" in the road**, and at key points in one's life, fate prevails, meaning that circumstances will be manifested in which the very nature of the circumstances point out the right direction to go. The value of understanding the fated quality of this aspect would be that when you see a transiting planet affecting either one of these planets, you can expect something. In an opposition, the fated event that pointed to the turn in the road tends to oppose what the person thought was going to happen. Normally what happens is that the opposing force is stronger than the will of the individual so they tend, relative to fate, to take the right direction even though it opposes what they thought they wanted. Karma is different. When those karmic debts and/or fruitions come due, that equals a fated event. I use a 2 degree orb for a septile. One degree on either side. It doesn't

demand a transit to activate it. Transits will always activate it, but it doesn't need a transit to activate it. A classic example is myself. I have Uranus/North Node in a waning Septile to my natal Pluto and it is now in a last quarter phase. I had a very dim view of astrology, Uranus. At a key point in time, in a monastery, I was given a certain kind of message that revealed my long term future in astrology, like it or not. You don't have to like your destiny; it is a matter of cooperating with it, with any of it.

Crescent phase sextile

Now we move into a crescent phase Sextile. I use a 4½ to 5 degree maximum orb. It can be extremely helpful because it is non-stressful. It is very helpful from an evolutionary point of view to **integrate all that has come before**, ie from the new phase conjunction in this life and to permanently establish roots as to what the individual purpose was, already previously linked with special destiny in this life. Relative to orbital issues, a person is given many lives to get this done.

Relationship between crescent phase and disseminating phase

The temptation continues, the disseminating phase is ever on the horizon because the sextile does not, of itself, have creative stress and thus, it can be very "easy" to resist, especially in a yin phase, the actual establishment. This is why there is a larger orb involved, because one is given normally quite a few lifetimes to get it done, and it must be done before the quintile can be experienced, the keywords of which will be "creative transformation." The teaching in this aspect is to learn how the world works, disseminating, which can be easily grasped, sextile, and then to go ahead and **integrate one's individual purpose** linked with the two planets on the individual's own terms. That is where the conflict lies, the temptation to do it on society's terms.

Neptune in this aspect can mean that it can be easy for the person to resist the spiritualizing influence of Neptune. It means that people can take existing cultural forms and try to find their spirituality through that. That is one of the reasons that a while ago all the traditional religions were rejected in a large en masse way. On the other hand, it is just as responsible for all this modern stuff, channeling and so forth, the advent of so many "psychics." Astronomers are now beginning to agree that Pluto was originally a Moon of Neptune, but that it has now become a binary system in its own right. So with respect to Christian symbolism, the original sin, or in chauvinistic terms, man being cast out from God, here we have this symbolism of Pluto being thrown out from Neptune which could correlate to the ultimate archetype of divinity or the absolute. Pluto does have this binary system that does correlate to the dual desire principle and the evolution of the Soul. What it means in the beginning, of course, is that what is called God is imperfect. If God was perfect in the beginning, why create anything? The Hindus like to dismiss this as God's amusement. I think God needs more than simple amusement. If it was only for amusement, why create suffering?

Crescent phase quintile

Now we move to the Quintile. **"Creative transformation."** For example, Carl Jung. If you look at his overall birth pattern, it is called a quintile chart, a five-pointed star pattern. He took the existing psychology, Freudian, and creatively transformed it, Jungian. That is what this aspect wants to do. When you find it in the crescent phase, of course, it can be a struggle to establish it, basically an inability to believe in it because it is so new. This is not an uncommon aspect, but a lot of astrologers do not pay attention to it. For those who want to develop it, it can be a source of great enthusiasm about life, feeling good about things as you develop it because it is utterly new, like an adventure, unfolding every minute.

Relationship between crescent phase quintile and disseminating phase

The person is still comparing and contrasting this new vision with the status quo. Don't you think that in Jung's life he met with some status quo conflict with his ideas? If you find yourself an artist and you find this aspect, you will find your creations to be utterly unique. Frank Lloyd Wright and Velikovsky were both not easily accepted in their times. Velikovsky was not accepted by the scientific community, and his books were not allowed in the universities. One of his ideas was that Venus was originally a part of Jupiter that was cast into space through a massive collision. Based on this ideal he predicted the atmosphere that should be discovered on Venus and his idea was right, but at that point in time it was in direct contrast with what the scientists said was on Venus. Einstein said that you have violent opposition when genius interfaces with mediocrity.

Crescent phase square (crescent phase and first quarter phase)

Now we come to the crescent phase square which precedes the entering of the first quarter phase. This is an extremely difficult aspect to deal with. Equally hard is the disseminating square which precedes the last quarter square. The point is that what is looming on the individual's horizon is the vision of the first quarter. The first quarter is a yang phase energy, now moving out from center, action. In the first quarter it is going to be very important for the individual to actualize and establish concrete forms, actual lifestyle, that reflects what has been realized in the first two phases. So, here we have this dynamic tension between internalization in smaller environments and now the need to bring it out to the world. The keywords for the first quarter phase is **"crisis in action."** The initial crisis is experienced in the crescent phase square. You literally have a push-pull. The square itself is demanding action and externalization, the crescent phase is demanding internalization. Push-pull. The height of individual development is now at hand, tremendous creative stress to finally establish it.

Relationship between first quarter square and disseminating square
Here we have an absolute rebellion, because what is now the polarity point – the disseminating square. The disseminating square means that that person is leaving behind cultural definitions, cultural archetypes, normalcy, status quo. Its consciousness is philosophically mutating in that particular aspect. This is a Van Gogh aspect. The first struggle is to create an intellectual and/or philosophical superstructure in order to conceptualize or intellectualize and thus explain and/or communicate the actions contemplated because of the disseminating polarity. There is still the vision of society and how to establish its individual purpose in the context of the very society that the individual feels alienated from. As a result, this aspect can be very tough evolutionarily speaking to get through. The temptation is to rebel against all external authority. The fear is of being re-absorbed back into the very system that it wants to get out of. This aspect can promote the hyperculturally-alienated people of the world and based on cultural alienation, they never fully develop it. It can promote an ongoing, unceasing restlessness, a high degree of unpredictability of action. The positive side is that it is an aspect of leadership – the courage to confront the status quo, to do that which is new, to use the vision of how the status quo works upon itself. Yet, the status quo tends to feel utterly threatened by the new vision, the new way.

Relationship between crescent phase square and disseminating square
How many of you are familiar with Swami Kriyananda? Here is a man who established a spiritual community in Northern California in the midst of a red-neck population. What do you think his reception was? His Sun/Moon in a crescent phase square. From another point of view, he was perceived as a threat by the very organization that he was involved with, the Self-Realization Fellowship. His mission was to establish one of Yogananda's principles for living, a spiritual colony of plain living and high thinking. He designated Kriyananda to do so. By the time he wanted to actualize Yogananda's vision, around 1960, the prevailing powers that were in SRF perceived this and interpreted it in the wrong way. They perceived it as him somehow trying to make a power play. So he was cast out. Crescent phase square, natural polarity, disseminating. He was cast out by the prevailing status quo, SRF, because he was now challenging that status quo, relative to Yogananda's own vision. So between 1960 and 1961, in a typically crescent phase way, he was literally forced to walk in the wilderness of his own loneliness without understanding what happened. Utterly confused by it. But now look. Relative to struggle, he was the one who established it, he was the one who spent four to five years working on it and totally supporting it financially by actualizing his own Sun/Moon purpose, teaching Yoga. But it has come full circle, and it now supports Kriyananda. Karma – action equaling reaction.

FIRST QUARTER PHASE

First quarter phase square
Now we have the first quarter square – the keywords are **"crisis in action."** What it means is that the individual is striving to determine the actual form and/or lifestyle and/or how to actually make real this individual thing that was developed all the way back in the new phase conjunction. To actually act upon it and to establish it in the world in its own individual way. **Example:** If you have Mercury and Jupiter in first quarter phase square, it tends to suggest that that individual at minimum would be argumentative. It will attempt to confront the existing opinions or ideas or philosophies of another in order to establish its own knowledge of its own opinions through such confrontations and clashing. The person can even argue just to argue. The crisis in action is to determine the specific knowledge and opinions and language structure and philosophical conceptions that reflect its individuality. The polarity point, of course, would be last quarter phase, the words of which are **"crisis in consciousness."** This essentially means crisis in belief. What commonly happens in a first quarter phase, because you are still dealing with a relatively new issue here, after all it is only the third phase – is that the temptation is to borrow the philosophical superstructure of that which it feels drawn to.
Let's say that I am fond of pondering metaphysical issues, Mercury/Jupiter/first quarter phase. My mind and my intuition lead to metaphysical ponderings. The effort, of course, is to establish my own view of things, but because it is still relatively new, my temptation is to borrow from existing philosophical systems, for example, Zen. I want to use this as my philosophical justification to explain the nature of my own opinion. I use this as a roadmap to explain myself to myself and to anybody else. Let's say I have Mars/Venus in this situation. Am I going to happily conform to status quo ways of being in relationships? If I am a male, am I going to be attracted to being Rambo? If I am female, do I want to be Betty Crocker? The thing I want to do is to actualize concrete forms that reflect my individuality to which prevailing status quo offers me no clues. I tend to go through a variety of mates and/or experiences in order to find out what it is – essentially through a process of elimination, crisis in action. This crisis could be experienced as a partner who gives me flack like, you are not with me enough, and my first quarter phase saying, I want freedom. This can be a crisis. Maybe my Venus function is wanting the relationship and my Mars function is saying that I want my freedom. I am in a dynamic state of conflict, square. This is where you start filling in the blanks. What if I have Mars/Venus both in Capricorn, but in a new phase conjunction? Interesting symbolism. Does not Capricorn correlate to prevailing status quo, cultural norms, clues, the how you do it's? But what is my new phase telling me?

Crescent phase and first quarter phase square
We tend to use a 10 degree orb. That will give you 5 degrees for a crescent phase and 5 degrees for the first quarter phase. The crescent phase square is passive/aggressive whereas the first quarter square is downright aggressive. Just dwell on the archetype, because the manifestations are many. What if I have borrowed the philosophy to explain myself? If that philosophy has not been internally realized by me, do I really know it? What happens if I interface with someone who has inwardly realized Zen? Does this not now promote a conflict for me? As they question my knowledge?

First quarter phase biseptile
Here is the biseptile – 102 degrees and some odd minutes. This is the externalization of the crescent septile – that special destiny. Similarly, in the first quarter phase, there is a sense of social destiny being now linked with that first quarter phase. The person will be tempted to link what their individual directions are with the conceptual framework that this is something special, something that I am trying to do that is special. Linked with the concept of fate which the biseptile carries forth. If I am dealing with Mars/Venus as my example, then I am fated to experience varied key people throughout my life that will have an intimate connection to me, special lovers. People who themselves are outside the ordinary, the status quo, who have a sense of special destiny about them, people who encourage me to develop, people I encourage to develop themselves, at minimum, a mutual respect for independence. The frustration in this phase is not achieving or actualizing what the special something is sensed to be because of the fear of being reabsorbed back into the past pattern. Thus a person who retains a rebellious stance throughout life, never meaningfully integrating into the society. A fear of entrapment. One evolves through that by realizing that it is a fear because the individuality is guaranteed. That started in the square, and is not being carried forth.

Relationship between biseptile and its polarity aspect
The polarity aspect at about 248 degrees is characterized by a condition where a person has programmed into their Soul at key points in their life people who will come into their lives circumstantially who are more evolved than they are, those people now tending to operate as mentors and/or who understand in an utterly objective way who this person is and thus have very timely messages or communications and/or last quarter teachings for that individual. They come at a key moment. The neat thing in that aspect is that the individual will recognize such an individual when they do in fact appear. Thus the normal resistance to external authority will not take place. That is also connected to the thing called fate. The person with this biseptile will resist lesser authorities, but recognize the real authorities.

First quarter phase trine
The first quarter phase trine means that things have come to a temporary head with respect to evolutionary development. The person prior to this aspect has been struggling to actualize its own inherent individual expression of the two planets. It has come through many trials and tribulations. It has come through the need to instinctually assert itself and now it is time to develop it in the sense of total integration. The trine in the first quarter phase means that it is time to integrate this new evolutionary impulse within the ongoing daily context of the person's life. To have it a living reality every single day. Not something that is sought for or something to be held out as a carrot or a potential promise on yet another distant horizon, but to be established and lived out daily. The benefit of the trine in this arrangement is to have an understanding of all that has preceded it. To take the best of the past, ie to no longer fear it and to integrate it into the now, the best of both worlds. At best, this aspect demonstrates leadership, the courage to pioneer the new and knowing how to integrate it. That is the power of the trine. One the other hand, the characteristic of all non-stressful aspects is that the individual may reach a degree of comfortability and try to maintain just that and resist the impulse to change it. Thus, it maintains the status quo even if it is its own individual status quo. Does the trine between mutable planets have a better chance of resisting the change? Not at all. The very archetype of mutability is continuous growth. One of the great strengths of the mutable archetype is adaptability. That is why the human species is still on the planet because of its innate ability to adapt to an ever changing environment. The instinct and dynamic of mutability is adaptability. So the mutable connection is one that guarantees growth actually.

We now have another mutational aspect. The sesquisquare or sesquiquad between the first quarter phase and the gibbous phase – 135 degrees.

GIBBOUS PHASE

This is a transitional phase of itself. It is the transition between the subjective orientation and objective orientation – from individual development to social development, integrating the individual development into the social scheme of things. The gibbous phase is the transitional archetype between the two. The keyword for the gibbous phase is **"adjustment or self-analysis."** What happens here is that now that we have moved through the first quarter trine, the individual is full of himself, very Leonian, and it wants to display and project itself to all. It is the same archetype of the actor who has received an Academy Award and wants all to know.

And rightfully so in its own way. After all, it has been a hard-won journey all the way from that new phase conjunction. We get a few bennies in our life now and then, even in the midst of hardship. But, let's face it, most people in these kinds of societies feel threatened by another's accomplishments, by another's sense of well-beingness, by another being full of themselves and having a clear vision of what they are trying to accomplish. This kind of society, because of its religious ethics put such things down. There is nobody around here with pats on the back and congratulations for a journey hard-won. It's more the voice of, "Who in the hell do you think you are?" We meet this environmental feedback at the first quarter sesquiquadrate. The first quarter reaction is to throw the question back, and to fight back. This is where it is important to understand sociological context. At some point, whether we like it or not we have to acknowledge that we belong to that context. Envy and jealousy abound. Another culture might say, "More power to you." The first quarter sesquiquadrate is preparing the individual to integrate on society's terms, not on the individual's terms and therein lies the rub because at this juncture the person is full of themselves and does not want to bend to any one's will.

And so there is tremendous tension, sesquiquadrate, conflict. How do I accomplish the goals relative to the vision now that I am receiving this environmental feedback that feels like rejection? That is why we have these keywords in the gibbous phase of **"analysis and adjustment,"** because when you meet that environmental feedback in this sociological context, it will necessarily promote an existential and experiential crisis which will lead to analysis. Why has this happened? It is the search for knowledge. It is that search that progressively promotes the awareness of how that sociological context is put together. The problem in this kind of aspect is that once that awareness becomes known, the individual begins to feel very small and begins to feel overwhelmed by the sociological context. Then they begin to analyze all their own deficiencies, inferiorities, lacks and shortcomings and all the things they would necessarily have to accomplish, develop or adjust to make that vision reality. And all too often there is a shrinking from the task relative to another yin phase, the person is thrown in on them self and they are literally experiencing the desert of their own personality and Soul. Somehow where there was richness and fertility, there is now a barren inheritance and thus the person feels lonely as if they are living in an existential void. This promotes crisis. From a purely archetypical point of view, it is meant to induce humility meaning the person is full of them self and thus perhaps overly identified with their ego in the sense of being the center of the universe, too narcissistic. So this induces necessary ego-centric humility and thus the soul programs, via this aspect, the negative feedback as well as negative inner feedback as one analyzes oneself.

All of us go through this thing just by the sheer fact of having a 6th house cusp. This lesson begins at the midpoint of the 5th house, at those natural power points: 15 degrees Taurus, 15 degrees Leo, 15 degrees Scorpio, and 15 degrees Aquarius. The 135 degrees aspect is 15 degrees Leo as contrasted with 0 degrees Aries in the natural zodiac. Sri Yukteswar said that the Soul is born when the celestial rays are in mathematical harmony with its karma. The essence of astrology. Moses said that astrology is a symbolic language of God. The orb that I use is 3 degrees, 1-2 degrees on either side for the sesquiquadrate. I give the trine 10 degrees. I do not give the Sun or the Moon a wider orb. So, until the individual learns this lesson, they tend to remain in the first quarter because the tendency is to go back where the fertility and richness lies. If you are standing on the edge of a desert and in back of you plants are growing, which choice will you make? But, at some point, we have to march forward, as ever, like it or not. It's either march forward or get forced out. So the humility lesson and the need to acknowledge how the system works leads, in most cases, to seeking out the necessary training and activities and schools of higher learning that will give you the necessary certification to actualize the vision. This is another way of acknowledging humility.

Relationship between gibbous phase and balsamic phase

The polarity phase here is balsamic. The gibbous phase is now promoting the awareness of the nitty gritty details of one's mundane daily life on a moment to moment basis. I am sensing the balsamic polarity and I want to escape. I am tired of these routines. I am bored. The balsamic is the vision of the absolute, the timeless, divinity, the ultimate, the ideal. So now that I am living my life in this very mundane way, submitting myself to this sociological context, this polarity point progressively tempts me to escape, to compare my reality with an ideal reality that I cannot find, but only can sense. What if I have Mars/Venus in a gibbous phase? Are not my relationships going to seem less than adequate as measured against the undefined ideal? I will get bored with the normal tedious work I have to do in relationships to sustain it. This could make me irritable and critical and help me to take all the stupid little details and irritants and cause me to blow them out of all proportion. This could make me feel, Venus, that this is less than something I want, Mars. The school of life is now experienced through this relationship. Doubts, partner criticizes, I project. There could even be a refusal to accept any kind of relationship because of the sense of the ideal, timeless relationship. This gibbous phase is to realize that the path to perfection is not through analyzing and criticizing, but through doing. Imperfection is a natural law of the earth. Perfection is not here. Ultimately that gibbous phase Mars/Venus is teaching the person to seek a divine cosmic relationship within. With respect to what has come before, the person has all kinds of subconscious memories of freedom and independence and now they are being required to be in a relationship which demands work, so resentment and anger exist.

When we talk about the quincunx or inconjunct, we are talking about a sincere humility, a real humility, not a false humility. The problem with this kind of aspect relative to the balsamic phase polarity is that anytime you have two planets in a waxing inconjunct (it used to be called a "Finger of God"), the person senses some kind of mission from on high and yet, relative to the gibbous phase, feels less than adequate as a personal vessel or entity to actualize it. It is imperfect, not good enough, inadequate. It doesn't realize how to actualize it, how to get there. It is the sensing of it, but it is like going from A to B with a million directions in between, not a straight line, but lots of adjustments in between. At its worst, this aspect can promote the image of groveling in the dark. Sexually, a masochist, a need to feel inferiority. There was a church in New York, a masochistic church, and an astrological study was done of these people and it was found that in 75% of these people, the nodal axis was in the 6th and 12th houses conjuncting the Ascendant and Descendant. This was reported in Astrology Now in one of the original issues. In this aspect, there is a sensing from on high. What tends to happen because the person is feeling less than perfect, they generate all kinds of rational reasons and excuses which in effect undermines the actualization of that which is promised from on high. God wants to express through you in this aspect, but the problem is that if I am a 10-watt bulb and God is 10,000 watts, that is a waxing inconjunct speaking.

I, myself, have a 1 degree waxing inconjunct between an 8th house Uranus in Gemini and Mercury in Scorpio in the 1st house. When the Pluto book first came to me back in 1978 or 1979, I was overwhelmed, 10,000 watts, and there I was, a little bulb that was flickering, at best. So I kept generating all the rational reasons and excuses why I couldn't write the book: I didn't have the time. I wasn't ready. I didn't have the financial luxury. I had too many kids, etc. for many years. Of course, inwardly, I was feeling inadequate because it certainly wasn't a book that I had deduced or decided upon or analyzed or thought about – it simply presented itself from on high. But, you can run out of excuses. My final excuse was a monetary one, Scorpio. At the right time, a financial benefactor turns up and gives me the necessary money, non-repayable loan. So I didn't even have that excuse to take off. However, that financial gift would last me 60 days at most, so that clearly meant that the book was meant to be written in 60 days. So I stopped all my counseling and all my teaching and wrote it in 60 days. It turned out that it was something as simple as putting the pen on the paper – it wrote itself. My frustration was that my hand could not keep up. So, that was the school of life adjusting the dream to English all those years, the apprenticeship, because, of course, the dream was not in English, it was in Sanskrit. But, in the end, there was no excuse and it was very simple to do. The problem was an egocentric one. That is the dilemma of the gibbous phase. The way out is just to do it. There is nothing to think about. If you think about it you are lost. Perfection is realized by putting one foot in front of the other – one day at a time. A centipede is fine as long as it just walks. But what happens when it tries to figure out where the sixth foot is? Paralysis.

Gibbous phase triseptile

We now have a very interesting aspect called the triseptile. Because this aspect is the final aspect before the gibbous phase opposition, it promotes a clarification of the individual's self-concept. Essential humility.

Now we are moving into the objective realm with the opposition. All that has come before has been subjective and has been adjusted in the gibbous phase, humiliated in the gibbous phase, and now is thrust into the world of the social environment, not as an inferior, not as a superior, but as an equal. Before the gibbous phase, the person was full of themselves, thus superior. Gibbous phase has made them inferior. Now we reach a balance point in the full phase at least potentially.

FULL PHASE

The key words for the full phase are **"meaning and completion."** The individual has been completed. It is now time to completely establish it. It is time to release it, to share it, to relate it. It is time to be in relationship as an equal. The problem in the full phase with respect to the new phase, the polarity, is that it tends to compare oneself with others. To evaluate the individuality of oneself through contrast with others, to understand what your individuality is through comparison and contrast with the individuality of others their values, beliefs, and lifestyles. It is through contrast and comparison, counterpoint awareness that I become aware of my social identity, not my subjective identity, but my social identity. The need in the full phase is to initiate a diversity of relationships with a diversity of types which symbolize and represent a diversity of values, beliefs, lifestyles and through contrast and comparison, understanding myself. The problem, of course, relative to the new phase, the polarity, is to overly engage in relationships. My social identity is new, it is not well established, that won't happen until the disseminating phase. Thus, my social identity is relatively insecure. When I go too far afield, ie too many relationships, too many comparisons, too many contrasts, I lose sight of my social identity and my temptation becomes to become that which I am not in order to feel socially secure. When this happens, the new phase polarity kicks in, ie the need to withdraw from social relationships, to recover the centeredness of my subjectivity, to rally around my own subjectivity, my subjective identity, my individual identity, not my social identity. This is an overload. Like mainlining too many people. For all of those who have a dominant Libra archetype in your nature, you know exactly what I am talking about. So, when you have recovered, then you need to return to the social sphere. So the person keeps going back and forth until the person learns how to remain centered within their own identity which is now integrated at a social level. The meaning of the opposition, then, is to teach this lesson. You have two opposing forces.

Gibbous phase opposition

To describe the difference between an opposition in the gibbous phase and in a full phase, we will use Pluto opposed Jupiter as our comparison. In the gibbous phase, Pluto opposed Jupiter would translate into deferring to other people's presentations and ideas, the gibbous phase again is one of humility, self-analysis, yin, withdrawal and thus they would defer. The other would be seen as potentially more powerful, more dominant, more well-formulated conceptually speaking than how the individual is evaluating itself. If the person attempted to oppose the individual that they are in conversation with, they would tend to draw criticism from the person. The other person would tend to point out the loopholes, the weak links in their own intellectual arguments. Thus the person could be made to feel inferior.

Full phase opposition
To contrast this, let's look at a full phase opposition of Pluto and Jupiter. Now this person is driving the other person into the dirt. It is like a reaction because of the social insecurity. The positive scenario would be that this person would treat others as equals, not needing to put others down in order to feel socially secure.

Full phase triseptile
So, we come to the waning triseptile, cooperation with social and collective need in a realized state. **"Cooperation"** is the key.

Full phase inconjunct
The full phase inconjunct or quincunx is a very interesting aspect because in contrast with the gibbous phase inconjunct which has more of a Virgo dynamic to it, this one contains the vibration of Scorpio. This now has everything to do with social limitations as contrasted with subjective or individual limitations. The waning inconjunct induces social humility and purification. This is the aspect that all Seth people hate. In Seth philosophy, you are taught that you can be anything that you want, create your reality at will. However, it may be karmically, evolutionarily, destiny-wise impossible for you to be president of the US due to social limitations. All Souls, all spirits are free, there are no limitations, no container, no boundaries. But then you put that Soul in something as limited as the human body and place it on something like the Earth – time/space limitations. This is hard for the Soul or spirit to accept. Until the lesson is learned in this aspect, confrontations will come your way. That is what the aspect is for – inner and outer confrontations.

Full phase biquintile
Biquintile is contrast of capacities against those of others. If I go to an astrology convention, this aspect tells me who I am, that my special capacity is contrasting with another's capacity. Thus the uniqueness of my social function becomes clear.

Sesquiquadrate (full phase and disseminating phase)
Sesquisquare 225 degrees. This one is now taking place between the full phase and the disseminating phase.

DISSEMINATING PHASE

The disseminating phase correlates to the totality of the sociological cultural system in which you find yourself. In our time, everything that America is correlates to the disseminating phase. All possible lifestyles, beliefs, values and all that which is impossible – disseminating phase. It is the highest degree of socialization, the absolute need to disseminate your purpose which was initiated all the way back at the new phase conjunction. Not just amongst friends and close relationships, but in a full blown integration within the world – job or career. When you pass the inconjunct, you become aware of what you are and what you can do and you go out and do it.

From an evolutionary point of view, the disseminating phase is to establish social contracts, stabilities, laws, regulations, norms and having lots of people live together in a non-anarchistic state. We all have that need. Spoken like a true Marxist. Marxism is a very attractive philosophy until you understand it. Marxism's ultimate carrot is to promote a social system that has no rules, regulations, leaders, government. Everything being self-run through conscious individual choice. To do that which is necessary without instruction or guidance or dictums. That is Marxism's ultimate vision. But no political utopian philosophy, which Marxism is, has ever succeeded, and never will. This is why Marxism gets stuck, stuck in communism and other authoritarian, dictatorial governments which try to impose that ultimate Marxist vision which is not possible. Ideally Marxism is a completely socially equitable system. A more practical form of Marxism and/or communism is socialism as expressed in various governments in which it works – Sweden, Denmark, and Holland. This is why capitalists hate communism, because communism is social equitability, social equality, an even distribution of wealth. It won't work because of human nature. The Mars function, the 1st house function, the Aries function. You can validate that by driving on the freeway. Do you not see the Mars principle alive and well? How many people do you see when they want to change lanes back off versus speed up?

Disseminating sesquiquadrate
The problem is that the sesquisquadrate is the last initiation, the last social ritual, social rite toward that goal [full blown integration within the world]. You have realized the you are meant to be a stockbroker and you have a powerful vision of wanting to be a

stockbroker. In this aspect, you have a powerful vision of how to do it in a unique way, in a way that will actually change the social system that you are about to participate in, now being the world of a stockbroker. At the full phase sesquisquadrate, until you learn the ways and the means of the stock brokering world, all their little happy rituals, all the things that they do, the consensus of the stockbroker world. Until you learn that, you will be rejected in the sesquisquadrate full phase. You will be perceived as willful and as threatening to the established status quo. The security is now found through consensus and disseminating phase. The challenge is to acknowledge how that system is working, how the consensus is working, not in the way of becoming it, but in a way of making it work for you. That is the enlightened approach. The problem in most cases is the becoming – that is the easier path. It creates and leads to less social and individual stress, does it not? That's the voice that says, "If you can't beat them, join them." The challenge is to join them without them knowing that you haven't really joined. After all, if things are left in the consensus state forever, it is just going to crystallize and die off. We have to have new blood. That is what this aspect is for, new input, new visions. The key word for disseminating phase is just that – to disseminate, to share, to give.

Disseminating trine

Now we move into a disseminating trine. At this point that consensus system will not perceive it as a threat. You have already learned to make it work to your advantage in such a way as to not be perceived as a threat, or you have given in and become it. In either case, you can integrate, establish, actualize, disseminate, give and do all the things that that trine promises, but you are still going to have this crescent phase polarity. If the disseminating correlates to the complexity of your society, can't this lead to a feeling of social weariness, of overload? You can get tired of all the crap that is going on, all the scandals, all the bullshit, and now the banks want to charge you for depositing money in their bank. See first, you are paying them money to put your money in their bank. It's ludicrous! You will find other banks following suite in a lemming-like way.

Relationship between disseminating phase and crescent phase

This crescent phase polarity, in our times and in our society, means the wistful desire to get out of the system, to withdraw, simplify, isolate, to pull the covers over the head. A national survey recently showed that most people don't want to know about all the crap, they want their soap operas. They don't want to watch the trials. That's why we have all these sitcoms. Dead on arrival. That's why we have Reagan being elected in this country, for nobody is paying attention. Crescent phase is also what we call vacations when contrasted with the disseminating phase – time out. The temptation can be so strong with some people, to simplify and withdraw and to minimize the complexity in the disseminating phase, that some people will try to totally become that crescent phase. My point is that the disseminating phase, of itself, on balance, needs complexity, it needs to socially interact. It doesn't need consistent isolation, but periodic isolation.

Now we move into the disseminating square which is a very difficult aspect – the Van Gogh aspect.

LAST QUARTER PHASE

The key words for this are **"crisis in consciousness"** (these are Rudhyar's words) which essentially means **"crisis in belief."** What are you going to believe in? You have just now evolved out of consensus, out of social systems. You are now mutating into a consciousness which now needs to establish new beliefs, new ideas, to look at reality differently, the bottom line being that what you believe determines your values. Your values determine how you live your life, how you are relating to yourself as well as to someone else. Values determine lifestyles relative to beliefs. So if you are having a crisis in consciousness/beliefs, you are having a crisis in lifestyle and identity.

Square (disseminating and last quarter)

This square is kicking off the first quarter square but also the opposition and the conjunction points – the primary vertical/horizontal of the natural circle. So it is massive tension, the temptation to go backwards where familiarity lies, the known, the controlled. The fear is moving into an unknown that you cannot define, but can only sense. The pull is toward the balsamic so that the disseminating square begins to highlight this tension. Van Gogh felt alienated from the very system that he was trying to integrate his paintings within. So he did, crescent phase polarity. He hung out in his little place. This massive inner conflict of belief, is it not self-torture? He had a square between the Sun/Moon. The archetype of the Sun/Moon is self-actualization, how you actualize your purpose on a daily basis. I tend to describe this as the mutation between Scorpio and Sagittarius and/or Capricorn to Aquarius. The temptation that most people feel at that last quarter square junction especially when it is still in the disseminating phase is to go backwards rather than forwards. For example, if you found Mars/Venus in a disseminating square, the temptation in most people would be to adopt cultural norms with respect to learning how to and being in relationships. They take social clues as the clues, because that constitutes familiarity and thus security. Yet you are still going to have this dynamic tension, square, between that Mars and Venus. This is moving into this "crisis in consciousness" which now equals "crisis in belief" relative to how to be in relationships. The person is beginning to move beyond the status quo or cultural norms as clues. Yet they don't, at this point in time, know how to consciously define that which they are trying to move into. Since they can't define what they are moving into, the temptation is to simply go with what "works." Thus they end up manifesting frustration.

In general, if a person adopts that behavioral compensation, roughly around the first Saturn Return, they will reach a major degree of crisis if the person is at all conscious, meaning not asleep. If they are asleep, it won't make any difference, sort of like the nudge against the elephant, but the elephant remains in place. If you throw a pebble against an elephant, is it going to move? However, for some who are in some way awake, this will equal a developmental crisis around the first Saturn Return, a relationship crisis, a behavioral crisis. What the person is trying to evolve into is a radically different kind of relationship in which that partner is going to be like them self, ie actually challenging and questioning, square, the nature of cultural norms himself in all value systems, all cultural moral imperatives. They are going to need a partner who, like themselves, is now challenging these things and thus, the most immediate new need is to find a partner who is now going to have a degree them self now challenging these things and thus, to find a partner who is now going to have a degree of philosophical sympatico which will then allow for the emotional sympatico in this case, it is a matter of what comes first. Thus, they march off together to establish with courage their own norms.

Last quarter square
This will finally evolve into the last quarter square itself. This particular aspect tends to produce two extremes, either individuals who rabidly defend the past in a William Buckley-like way (what an arrogant creep, eh?) or utterly challenge the past. Cults are a phenomenon of all times and places, not just this one. The deeper issue in the Uranus/Neptune square generation (taking place from Cancer to Libra) is a group of people who are born to parents or a culture, in either case your early family or early environment, which does not have a lot of cultural or family support for their inherent individuality. This sets in motion identity and/or emotional confusion because they are going to be exposed to cultural or parental norms that have no relationship to that individuality. This, of course, forces the child in on itself. It makes it confused. It doesn't know why it is happening and creates all kinds of displaced child-like emotions that are dragged into adulthood which become the basis of overt or covert emotional projections onto the adult partner, the adult partner itself now reflecting the parent who didn't understand and the adult relationship collapses.
The point here is that you have a whole bunch of people, Uranus in Cancer, who are learning how to be utterly self-secure, learning how to liberate, Uranus, from emotional dependencies. That is why it dictates such conditions. But of course the child does not have the conceptual equipment to understand it that way – it just knows that its needs are not being met. Any child will rightfully feel that it has a right to have its needs met, after all it is a child. We are only children once, aren't we? So it creates an identity confusion. A bunch of folks in that generation beyond this have gender confusion, because it is a generation that is actually trying to liberate from the restrictions of just purely male and female. They are actually trying to seek a degree of actualized androgyny – the unification of the genders. This can create gender confusion in these people. All they know is that they are not either Betty Crocker or Marlboro Man. So, unless there is cultural or family support, it can turn out gay people in an increasing percentage. Or, in other cases, people who simply refuse to be in relationships, who would rather go it alone, Cancer. The issue of relationship, Neptune in Libra, is just too confusing, too emotionally messy and the Uranus part in Cancer says, "I'd rather not deal with that!" Yet they still have very viable emotional needs that must be met in their relationships. When you put all this in a last quarter square, you can see how all this, ie crisis in belief, crisis in consciousness, now in identity, manifests.
From a purely evolutionary point of view, there is a whole generation that is meant to learn how to parent in different ways because what has preceded this is a bunch of parents who have said, "Do it my way, be a vicarious extension of me." There is a whole ethic in this country where the children are not supposed to talk, just do what I say. That is a prevailing ethic. Now all of a sudden, here comes this generation who is meant to learn how to parent in a radically different way, ie parents who must learn how to encourage the unique individuality of the child, not to make them carbon copies of themselves. So unless the child has that kind of parent, they will rebel against their parent. So, at this evolutionary gate, until the individual learns to adopt and embrace beliefs that are unique to its own identity, it will remain at this gate. Any two planets that you find in this kind of situation remain there until they succeed. That means breaking through cultural norms. The square creates the necessary tension or stress to do so. That is the point. Even if it is the Second Saturn return. If you have Pluto in Cancer, even if you are in a consensus state with a last quarter aspect, that shows that at least those two functions in you are trying to individuate to some extent and yet within the context of the herd state.

Last quarter quintile
We said with the quintile, the two keywords that can apply here are **"creative transformation."** A person in the herd state with this aspect could be a welder with Mercury quintile Jupiter last quarter. This person could find himself inwardly inspired, who knows from what origin, to evolve welding, new techniques, to creatively transform the existing knowledge called welding and feeling inwardly inspired to do so. Of course, the consensus state person may not yet be able to conceptualize the cosmic other, but nonetheless, they will feel the inspiration, and at some point, wonder, "Where did this thought come from?" It is certainly not going to be a thought based on deductive analysis. Thus he transforms not only himself, but also the system of the welding world in which he finds himself. At some point somebody had to evolve helioarc welding – maybe it was somebody who had this quintile aspect.

Who knows? This aspect is a very creative aspect – the spirit of uniqueness, invention, innovativeness is here no matter what evolutionary station the person finds himself in.

Last quarter sextile
Alright, Sextile. **"Productive purpose and understanding of the role in society."** Again, the herd state person may not define it this way. They would simply find themselves fulfilling a role that transcends or is beyond or outside of the status quo of welding. It doesn't mean that the person needs to conceptualize it in this way with fancy words, they may just be it. As the person evolves, then the intuitive awareness of how to conceptualize it, to explain it comes with that turf, ie as the person evolves. The transition between the past and the future can be easily made or easily resisted at this evolutionary juncture. Again, the problem with non-stressful aspects is that they can reach a certain level of growth that the phase dictates and then reach a degree of comfortability with it and then attempt to maintain their own status quo because of that and resist future impulses to go forward. **Example:** Jupiter quintile Pluto, at minimum the person is going to throw atomic bombs at prevailing consensus belief systems. There is going to be an evolutionary necessity to transcend sectarian views. That is the expansiveness of Jupiter experiencing the sectarianism's limitations, Pluto.

Last quarter septile
Septile. This special purpose is beyond an individual issue. It is a socialized issue. A social function in which the individual finds the purpose relative to the function itself. Again, in my own case, Uranus in septile aspect to Pluto. One of the hatreds I have carried through many lives now is astrology and it finally came to a head in this life – and much to my own horror, Pluto, I had to fulfill this socialized role, Uranus. I was quite content to live in the monastery. So this special event, the "Y" in the road, comes through a teacher in the monastery, "You can't have this opinion of astrology without studying what you have the opinion about." Certainly makes sense. Since I have to respect the demand, Pluto, I went out and bought a book, read two pages and had a great vision. I would say the hatred is gone. I still feel the limitations, but it certainly has been a vehicle for me to accomplish much of what my Soul has intended, a number of which is finding a language which makes sense to most people and to accomplish the deeper tasks of helping people to free themselves from their own conditioning to empower people to be themselves. I get satisfaction in the sense of cooperating with God's will by simply fulfilling the function. When the rare client has the courage to apply the advice, that's excitement. The universe is excited at that point.

Semisquare (last quarter phase and balsamic phase – mutational aspect)
Semisquare – again a mutational aspect, we are now leaving behind the last quarter phase and moving into the balsamic.

BALSAMIC PHASE

The keywords are **"absolute, infinite, the timeless,"** that which goes beyond time and space. There is an impulse in every single human being to transcend, the sense in every single human being that there is more to reality than meets the eye. Every human being has that knowledge; it is the conflict in every human being between ideals and reality. When one moves into the balsamic phase, it means that one is beginning to complete an entire cycle which has preceded it, it is a culmination issue, a yin phase. The temptation in the yin phase is to completely withdraw, to retreat, to recluse from all that which has come before. Yet, relative to culmination, you have to complete, to tie up all the loose ends that have come before so that the new evolutionary cycle that you are preparing for can be born cleanly, without residual effect from the past. So we have a push-pull here. On the one hand the individual in itself wants to retreat and yet, relative to the necessity for completing, must come out of itself and engage in the normal circumstances which will constitute anybody's life. So it is a push-pull. This, from a purely archetypical point of view, demonstrates or symbolizes the final merging of divine will. That is the archetype.

Last quarter phase semisquare
So when we come into this semisquare, it is an incredible irritant. When you find it still in the last quarter phase, there are still all kinds of external obligations, duties and demands, roles to play, that must be fulfilled. And yet the person always inwardly senses a kind of feeling of a distant horizon that they are trying to get to. A horizon that has no obligations and duties, only freedom. So there is inner conflict.

Balsamic phase semisquare
In the balsamic semisquare, the key is to follow those contrasting rhythms and to do both the new and the old when the impulse manifests. Then the person will be in absolute harmony with themselves and thus, there will be no conflict. The problem in this semisquare is the sensing of new seeds for they are not conceptualized or defined. They don't have words to put on them. They are just sensed. The person wants to have the experiential freedom to initiate that which they need to initiate to find out about it.

It is the vision of the poet who sees the future and yet people of the existing moment don't want to see it. The person is considered strange, balmy, outside of the status quo and nobody can relate to them. They are trying to move into a timeless form. What would be a timeless form of relationship for example, just monogamy? Just one to one? Is that a timeless form of relationship?

Example: What if you have Mars/Venus in a balsamic state? Your quest is for a timeless ideal relationship. That which reflects timelessness, that which is natural, not conditioned. Is monogamy, a one-to-one relationship, that which is most natural to the species? What is the natural and actual instinct in the species? The answer is that there are no absolutes. So, if you take Mars/Venus in the balsamic phase, it means that that individual is seeking an entirely different kind of relationship, a relationship with the divine first and foremost and learning how to see the divine in their partner, first and foremost, thus effecting unconditional love, not conditional love. In this state, you are in a timeless relationship. Relative to cultural context, it doesn't matter if you find yourself as an American Indian 200 years ago and find yourself with one man/two women or more. Everything reflects cultural necessity in the end. So if it is most efficient to live in that relationship model, then that is what happens. If it is most efficient to live in a monogamous model, one-to-one, relative to cultural necessity, that is what happens. If it is most efficient to live in a harem state, that is what happens. Efficient for who? The culture. Not the individual, but the culture. The point being that in those cultures, they had many children, so it took lots of people to raise them. In those times, survival itself was important. Simple food gathering was the norm. Biologically speaking, man, stronger physically, was more evolved to hunt down the animal for food. It's not that the woman can't do it, it is just more efficient for the man to do it. So it comes down to cultural efficiency, cultural necessity. The balsamic is trying to reach these kinds of understandings. If you have Mars/Venus in a balsamic phase, it simply means, relative to culmination, that you are destined to meet many people throughout your life with whom you have had prior live dealings, people with whom you are culminating or finishing relationships with. It means that the older you become in this life, if that is your condition, that you will begin to meet new people, people who you will not be allowed to be in an intimate relationship with, but with whom you will establish seeds that will grow into future lifetimes together.

So, given the backdrop of the balsamic phase, there is a temptation to withdraw from the nitty gritty details, gibbous phase polarity, of any of our lives. There is also a degree of psychological compensation, ie many people who experience balsamic planets don't know how to live with them. It makes them feel inwardly too strange. So what do they do, they effect compensation to the gibbous polarity and attempt to live life as most people live it. For example, if you are in a culture that places a major premium on possession gathering, that is what the person will become in an overemphasized way. They would be even more into the collecting of possessions. If you are in a culture that advocates sexual promiscuity, and you have this Mars/Venus balsamic, and your natural inclination is to withdraw to find the cosmic lover, yet you are feeling strange about that because you can't conceptualize it this way, don't you see how the gibbous polarity interacts now? The person overdoes it. And this will finally degenerate into a gibbous phase crisis and now the person must analyze what they have been doing. In the Mars/Venus balsamic, we are dealing with different types of relationships, not just intimacy. It is just that we are trying to culminate a certain type of way of being in relationship with someone and to evolve into new ways. (JWG)

ASTROLOGER/CLIENT RELATIONSHIP

EA methodology
The methodology of EA, and thus its 'rules,' is what it is. And it has been tested for many, many years now through correlations and observations to tens of thousands of Souls. Of course to understand where any given Soul is in their evolutionary journey, because of the Natural Law of free choice, requires observing their actual reality given the parameters of the evolutionary paradigm that is called Evolutionary Astrology. (Rad)

Adjust readings to the evolutionary stage of the client
In terms of how to best use language during readings, it is very important to determine, of course, what is most important to the client (why the reading in the first place), and take note of the kind of language they use, and adjust to whatever level (stage of evolution) of reality the client is at. Another good technique I use that is taught by my father is to look at Pluto's polarity point in the natal chart, and to use simple language that reflects the core evolutionary intentions for that Soul based on the understanding of what the polarity point symbolizes (guide the person in that direction). My main point is that based on the interaction with the client and understanding core dynamics within the chart, we can adjust our own language and approach to the reading to reflect the client's level of reality and orientation. (Deva)

Observation and correlation
So many in astrology, and many other disciplines, feel within themselves that they have to be in an inner position of 'authority' relative to the work that they do: because of doing the work itself. So they adopt an inner attitude that they 'know all,' and present themselves this way. Typically, in the world of astrology, a person comes to an astrologer and the astrologer feels within themselves that they must know all about the person from the moment they sit down. Thus, the person comes in, sits down, and the astrologer begins immediately reciting a variety of descriptions about the person in front of them, where these descriptions themselves have been learned from this or that book, this or that teacher. What JWG taught was the very opposite. He taught that one of the very best ways to learn astrology was through observation and correlation. Thus, when a person comes in to learn about themselves through astrology to sit with them at first, and actually ask questions about their life. Or to have the person present questions to the astrologer where the very nature of the questions would correlate to that person's actual reality, and the nature of their individual evolutionary conditions. This then allows for the astrologer to actually orientate their consciousness, and intuition, to the person's actual reality. The very essence of this approach is one of LISTENING first to the person's actual reality, and then based on that listening gained through observation orientating the symbols in their chart to that observation gained through the listening. (Rad)

Clients asking their questions in advance
One of the ways that JWG suggested going about doing consultations is to have the client ask their questions in advance. The point is that by doing so the very nature of the questions will help you 'correlate' to the evolutionary condition of any given Soul. This then helps the astrologer orientate them self to the actual reality of each client. Beyond that correlation and observation is also meant to be employed as an ongoing focus for the astrologer as he or she interacts with every client over time. In this way each astrologer then can learn about the nature of the astrological symbols on an ongoing basis. (Rad)

Different approaches to client readings
For the astrologer who is learning their work, who does not have a lot of water under the bridge, so to speak, it then comes down to how the astrologer presents them self to the person. And that means acknowledging to the person that they are in the process of learning, and thus they are not an 'authority' wherein everything they see or say is the gospel truth. In the beginning it is necessary to use words like, 'this signature suggests this or that: do you find or feel that is true?' This way then encourages a dialogue between the astrologer and the person where the dialogues themselves present an ongoing vehicle in which the astrologer is continuing to observe and correlate. Thus the astrologer is continuing to learn. This process will naturally deepen not only the

astrologer's capacity through the knowledge gained, but their own intuition as well. JWG shared many times that in the beginning of his work that he worked for 'free' for over five years. And wherever he lived in the world he would put out signs that said, in essence, 'free readings.' And he did so on purpose for the reasons above. In this way there will always come a time in which the would-be astrologer would then feel 'ready' to do their work on a more professional basis. And, in this way, they will have learned a great deal that will not only prepare them for the work, but also learn how NOT TO HARM PEOPLE. (Rad)

The most unexpected aspect of doing readings for people for me has been this whole psychic/astrologer thing. I do sometimes have dreams about clients before they arrive to me, but in a way the last thing I want to do is read through everyone. Sometimes the stuff I pick up about the clients they are not ready to deal with. I have learned to intuit to say to some prospective clients that I am not a psychic and I do ask questions about their lives. It has been a great learning experience for me. I have actually had to turn a client or two down as they just wanted someone to tell them what to do and ultimately I don't feel comfortable with that. It's a good thing to know when you start seeing clients that this stuff does happen. I let the client guide the reading. (Pam)

To me it's exactly the right way to do this work. I have had many clients too over the years that just wanted me to talk without any interaction with them. Their attitude being something akin to going to a gambling place and putting their money in the slot, and pulling the handle. "Hey, I am here, have paid you money, now do your thing." I quickly have shown them the way out. (Rad)

What I do is take quite a lot of time working with each chart I am to read based on the questions the Soul has asked. I ask them beforehand what their concerns are. Sometimes this is not easy because of the expectation of many Souls to be passive in the face of astrology, which many times is a projection of their desire not to be responsible for the situation. I always check through questions how the clients feel about what I tell them. And I check how they feel at the end of the session, and many times I also write to them or call them some time after the session to know how they have felt, and if they need any clarification or have any further questions. If you are there for the right reasons, then God is with you, helping you in your work. It is necessary to have faith. Another point I think helps me to avoid causing harm is that I normally want people to feel good about the reading. I want them to feel encouraged, and supported. So normally I will not tell them anything that will make them feel bad, unless it is necessary and they have asked the relevant question. In such case I will be even more careful with what I say. (Gonzalo)

I realized that some of the best times and most valuable for others have been the 'off the cuff' informal discussions. The actual set-up for readings and expectations I had put on myself were being counter-productive and blocking my own intuition and capacity to listen and connect with people. I am now at a donation level for readings and consider this all to be like 'internship rates' so to speak. What this has allowed me to do is really relax, take the pressure off myself and really find out what they want to know and how I can help. I had concern of the reading being 'worth it,' spent so much time preparing – another reason a part of me didn't want to do it. Then I would have an overwhelming amount of information for a session. So, I have changed to mainly just sitting with the chart for a couple hours. I've dropped a lot of the progressions, returns, midpoints, arcs and really try to know the core meaning of the birth chart – through E(A) Also, I've begun to include the planetary nodes, which I will never do without again. (Bradley)

I try to be a really good listener and see what they are saying from their own point of view. I try to draw out of them what the solution is, for many times they seem to know it intuitively. Lately, since learning from EA, I always suggest patience with their own self as it is a process. I don't mention astrological symbols, since no-one asks for that. I am reading books on counseling technique and process right now, since I am certain that my intuitive skills need improvement and refinement. I am praying that if it is appropriate for my path, I learn how to be of positive help to others. I try to support their self-image and try not to undermine their own sense of stability. Trust that God'dess will speak through you if you don't have your own agenda, and sincerely want to help. (Stephen)

I view my work as a spiritual service (not a business) to others who wish to learn about the Soul and evolution. I feel it is right to accept a donation. (Linda)

When we strive to be a clean channel while doing a reading, sometimes we have to deliver messages the client may not like hearing. Sometimes the person opens right away. Sometimes they come back later thanking you for having the courage to speak the truth. Sometimes they never open up and project back that you are a deluded fraud. One of the greatest values I've gotten from working with EA is a deeper understanding of why we have to go through so many things we experience as difficult or painful. That in the long run they are for our benefit, being the most expedient ways to get us to the inner places we yearn to go. This makes it easier to emotionally accept what at times must be dealt with. (Steve)

Answering the client's questions

I have learnt the hard way that it needs a great deal of skill/care to get it right! I learnt to always ask at the beginning what they are expecting, and try to stick to that. Also I always check my synastry with them, just in case we have any 'history' from previous lives that I should be consciously aware of. And if someone asks as they often do, "Oh, I'm just curious, you just tell me what you see," I get them to do the talking at the beginning and tell me A LOT (more than usual) about themselves, so I can more easily gauge what might be appropriate to tell them. I feel sometimes people come for help, with their resistance but also despite their resistance, and sometimes it's a blessing for them to hear what they need, and not what they want. As gently as possible, but with persistent firmness so that their resistance is gently, gradually swept aside. If it's clear that that's what they really want. I find it takes deep trust in oneself that you've read the situation right, deep trust in EA, compassion for the other – to be safe it's often easier to say you can't help – and courage to follow through. It was very rewarding when a couple later got back to me, and said how quite a long time afterwards they'd had a deep insight into their block against feeling xyz – a core issue we struggled to talk about because they weren't always comfortable but I had persisted – and how much better it felt that they weren't trapped inside that feeling anymore. That is when I silently bless EA that it helps me to help others, and that I can trust it. There is no other way I could have done that. And other times, clearly what a person absolutely most needs is complete and total safety, and nothing else would be right. (Upasika)

In the end, we have to be careful but we can't always avoid answering people's questions. Sometimes we might go "Oops, maybe I shouldn't have said that." When we do have those experiences, it's because we needed to! It's all for a reason and every mistake has a purpose. (Cat)

When I had my reading with JWG in the early 90's his approach was simply, "What do you want to know?" At one point I asked what my life was just before this one and he asked, "Do you really want to know?" and I said, "Yes." Then he asked again with a sigh and a smile, "Are you sure you want to know?" Clearly he saw the trauma but at that point it was my decision and I said, "Yes." It was revealing and tough for him to relate it to me because he had to 'see' it but it was my choice at that point and it lead into other topics that I wouldn't have asked about otherwise. I think as an astrologer if you see something that may be traumatic for the client to hear just let them know that you see something that they may not want to hear and then if they choose to hear it at that point then it is their choice. It's the astrologers choice how to present it in the gentlest way possible. Readings are a two way street. (Sunyata)

Summarising all these descriptions of learnings given by everyone so far – for anyone just starting to give readings I'd recommend the rule of thumb that's emerged here: "Don't give any more than what the client asks for, and even then tread carefully." Make sure they are actually ready to hear what they have asked for, that they are presently capable of taking responsibility for their actions and thus this decision. But if you are sure they are, then it is their responsibility, and you can safely tell them whatever it is that they have asked. That said, it does take experience to really know all this in a reliable way, so be initially conservative in your assessments (for as long as it takes) until you have found your own way that you can rely upon. It's over time that this feeling for what your own way is/will be arises. Everyone comes to their way in their own timeframe, via their own pathway – astrology is Uranian after all. (Upasika)

One more thing I would say about this is that when someone comes along and says, "I am just curious, tell me anything you see" that, at that point, the EA astrologer should inform such a person that is not what the EA astrologer does. Thus, look elsewhere. (Rad)

As a client and a practitioner of therapy, bodywork, astrology, etc., helping professions are just that, we are here to assist others in their process, sometimes slowly, sometimes quickly. When I have had readings or sessions with healers, astrologers, etc. who want me to move faster than I am ready, or forcefully provide information, it just doesn't help. That said, I am open to honest and sometimes painful assessments that I need to hear to move on, or take responsibility for my Soul, my life. Clients usually call based on referral from my website or friend. In the initial conversation I give an overview of my work, including its comprehensive and evolutionary perspectives. This has certainly turned numerous prospective clients away, but it also provides a sorting that proves beneficial to both myself and prospective clients. My own evolutionary signature and body-mind is geared to help others go deep and to evolve with compassion. Those who are not ready for progressive and evolutionary themes, whether they be consensus or further along, usually go elsewhere within a short period of time when I stay true to my offerings and Soul work. It's called a practice for good reason, we are practicing and thus learning. Mistakes are inevitable, and some seem more painful than others. And I'm very grateful for the mature practitioners who have taught me and personally helped me know myself and my Soul better. They are the ones I have gleaned the most help and support from. (Wendy)

Beginning a session with a prayer, candle and crystal

I have recently begun the practice of starting each session with a prayer that I recite out loud, so that the client can hear it as well. It generally goes something like this: "I now dedicate this space in service for this Soul ___. I intend and ask that my words are only an expression of the truth that is most relevant and helpful for this Soul ___ at this time. I devote all that is shared and experienced here in this session for the highest good only. And so it is."

I light a candle to focus that prayer. I also follow JWG's advice to keep a crystal between me and my client. I find that offering that intention and then letting go allows me to be just completely present and to trust whatever is wanting to come through me. I have also learned to take pauses during the readings to go inside and reflect on my words whenever I don't feel totally certain about what to say or do. Very often I'm called to just be present with the client, to perhaps do some "off the chart" work for a time before getting back into sharing information. (Ari)

Asking "Why?"

To step back and objectify for oneself [or for a client] just why one needed to create whatever trauma [or experience] in the first place. This leads to self-knowledge of a liberating nature, and that knowledge can then be used to radically change oneself. (Rad)

Astrologer unearthing unresolved trauma
This is so very important to all counsellors including astrologers. For myself what I have LEARNED to do over a great length of time is to ask the client exactly the questions that they have for the astrological reading, and then sticking to those questions. In the course of answering certain questions that are linked to unresolved trauma(s) I will always go very slowly and make sure the client wished to proceed at every step. If the client says 'enough' then of course I stop right then and there. I have found this approach works in almost every single case of counselling clients. (Rad)

I learned a valuable lesson from a highly experienced EA member that basically we are here to help others, not to make things worse for clients by being overly concerned with our performance. To tread lightly, let the Higher Power guide, and be of service so that the little pointers we make can work for clients by adding insight and understanding into the dynamics unfolding for them. (Linda)

Very difficult chart dynamics
[Example: Female client with very difficult chart dynamics] In cases like these it is very important to simply follow the lead of the client, and to only go where they want to go. It is not our job as EA people to force into anyone's consciousness that which they are not prepared to receive. The issue for this woman is to simply answer the questions she is asking you. If in the course of interacting with her in the context of her questions, and the answers that you have for her, this naturally leads to deeper questions as to the 'why' of something in her nature, it becomes necessary to pose Socratic-type questions that have the answers contained within them. By posing such questions, and leaving them as questions, if she then wants to privately ponder those questions honestly then the answers will occur within her in her own natural time. There are deep, deep reasons and causes that have led to her own desire to create the box of control that has led to just wanting life to be ok, NORMAL! The box has been created as a form of Soul survival that can allow her to carry on in the ways that she does. This is also one of the great reasons that God/ess has placed a veil within the consciousness of most that does not allow them to see the past lives that they have lived. If most could do that they simply could not carry on with the business of the current life that they are living. So we must be very, very aware of this Natural Law so as to not transgress it in a way that could harm another. (Rad)

Abuse as catalyst for evolution
(Q) Does the type of abuse a Soul experiences in the current life, always stem from an abuse that they portrayed in a previous life? (Wendy)
(A) No. (Rad)
(Q) Is it also true to say that the abuse a soul experiences in this life (a re-live possibly) is purely a catalyst for evolution, and not necessarily that the Soul was not the abuser in the past?
(A) That's right.

Use of intuition in readings
We have to observe our tendency to make these things overly complex. The underlying principles are very simple. They don't need to be run through the left brain grinder very much. The key is to let the intuition grasp in an instant the essence of an EA principle – to know without knowing how I know. Then to deal with the principles in a top/down way instead of a bottom/up way. Grasp the simplicity, the essence, of the principle. Then learning to apply the simple principle to the myriad complexity of manifest diversity, keeping the simplicity in mind as we do so, to not get lost in the details. The left brain will never feel it has ingested enough detail, correctness, no matter how much is taken in. At a certain point one has to learn to say "enough" and just apply what has already been taken in. Interestingly enough, the deeper insights and realizations come from applying what has been taken in rather than being overly concerned with getting every nuance just right before trying it all. Part of this earth reality really is trial and error – not only will we make mistakes (that are not really mistakes) along the way, there is no way to avoid doing so. We get better at it by putting what we are learning to work and skinning our knees at times in the process, not by trying to absorb every nuance before trying. (Steve)

"The value is in the effort"
Many people feel they don't want to lead anyone astray and so want to perfect it before trying. To which I say, anyone that is coming to any of us, on the Soul level knows what they are getting into, including coming to someone who is not a total master and may not be 99.93% accurate. The value is in the effort, and the purity of intention is what really matters, more than conveying every last detail 100% accurately to a client. We evolve as we practice. Just let yourself run with instincts and insights. If your pre-existing tendencies are to do that left-brained question thing, that is not bad but it has its limits. After a while it becomes the excuse for never being ready – one more thing I must be certain of before I am good enough. At a certain point one must realize, ready or not, I am who I am and I know what I know (and I don't know what I don't know). That's as good as we can do. We have been CONDITIONED to think it's all so complex. Thus major goals of Uranian de-conditioning are to strip away, break open, these

thoughts/beliefs of complexity we have taken on over time. The manifests are complex. The principles are very very simple. That is our real work, truly, to remind people of their underlying simplicity, and how the path back to really knowing and feeling one's self is to embrace that and gradually let go of everything else. (Steve)

Individual context of a Soul

Each Soul is its own individual context through which to understand the nature of any given aspect within the natal chart. As a result, there is no one answer to any given aspect when one remembers that archetypes correlate to an entire spectrum that exists within an archetype. Understanding the individual context thus allows the EA astrologer to know exactly where any given Soul is within the total spectrum of specific archetypes. When this is then properly understood then knowing how to proceed in evolutionary terms simply occurs. (Rad)

Inductive/deductive knowledge

With the revelation of repeating themes, it is here that the transition from deductive logic to inductive understanding will occur. The more regularly you put this exercise into practice, the more quickly this shift will occur until it eventually becomes automatic. It is not a development you want to rush. It is important to allow this to happen in its own natural time, because your deductive efforts will serve as your long term foundation. Once the inductive orientation becomes relatively automatic, the foundation established through the deductive development will make a real difference in the accuracy of the inductive information that comes to you in terms of the big picture you will see. (Stacie)

Think of it this way. Inductive knowledge is as easy to misinterpret as it is to mix up facts and data. If you get your facts solid in the beginning, the information that will be supplied to your intuition from that point on will be grounded and will have solid integrity, which of course will minimize errors in grasping the chart in total. The other thing to do is be aware of any expectations you may have toward your own process. (Stacie)

Karmic causes vs evolutionary necessity

These concepts (karmic causes, evolutionary necessity) are easy to misapply and can create a lot of trouble and misunderstanding. I think it's important we don't lose sight of the fact that these ARE distinct dynamics, otherwise what reason would Wolf have for attempting to teach about their distinctions? Wolf has said that determining evolutionary necessity is simple to determine in the birth chart: it is reflected in every symbol that's connected to Pluto in the natal signature. He also made it clear that being able to determine karmic causes is NOT easy, and that there is no 'technique' that can be taught for making this determination.

The issue I think, is that they are so CLOSELY linked, so non-linear, and so nuanced, that it takes an extremely developed capacity to be able to KNOW which is which. And even when karmic causes are accurately identified, one must have an absolute purity of intention and sensitivity/Soul attunement when attempting to communicate something like karmic causes to another, because the individual may not be ready on an inner basis to hear or resolve the content. To impose this kind of information upon someone who isn't actually ready to deal with it creates the risk of generating the exact *opposite* effect that EA was brought forth to serve, as does imposing this kind of information when it has not been correctly interpreted in the first place.

As I understand it, those who have the developed capacity/clarity to accurately identify actual karmic causes from evolutionary necessity will convey it on the basis of receiving the specific inner direction to do just that. So when it comes to the practical application of EA for most of us, I agree that it's better to come from the simple standpoint of acknowledging that *any* emphasized dynamic in the Soul/birth chart simply reflects the outcome of experiences and choices made therein, relative to intention, relative to evolutionary capacity, and that the existing dynamics are exactly what the Soul needs for continuing on with its evolutionary growth. (Stacie)

Repeating themes

First, combine both the house method and the method of planetary interpretation. From each method you will have specific information about all of the relevant points in the chart. Then examine all the information you've gathered through those methods, looking specifically for REPEATING THEMES. It is through focusing on the repeating themes in any chart that the story reflected in that chart will begin to reveal itself. (Stacie)

True EA work is guided by Spirit

True EA work is guided by Spirit. If your intent is to understand the Soul as deeply as you can such that you can offer the messages they are ready and needing to hear, those messages will be made known to you from within. This is a timeless phenomenon. The understanding you are meant to have with any given chart will come to you at the moment it is needed, and that is something that is best embraced by trust in the inner teacher. (Stacie)

Making predictions
Most of our life is about free choice relative to the 'parameters' of one's life where those parameters are defined by the nature of the EA paradigm in each chart: individual context. And of course those parameters are reflections of choices/desires that the Soul has already made in prior lives, relative to past life evolutionary intentions. And that in turn has set up the parameters/intentions for the current life, and the choices to be made. Once one understands those parameters, and the intention for the whole life within them, then one can 'predict' when various issues, dynamics, and circumstances will occur in the future of one's life. And that of course is determined by the nature of the transits and progressions in one's life at any point in time. One cannot 'predict' the choices any Soul will make in the face of those future circumstances, dynamics, and issues because of the Natural Law of free choice. Yet an EA astrologer can understand what the natural tendencies are for any given Soul given their prior life choices, or the choices made in the current life. One of the best things for any EA astrologer to do when working with clients, and the future for them, is to point out the WHY of future circumstances, dynamics, and issues and then to provide the insight as to what the consequences would be given this or that choice. The consequences of the choices can be rightly 'predicted.' (Rad)

Hiding signature
A phenomena called masking or hiding – a Soul that creates an outer reality in which it operates, and has itself convinced it is, at a level below its actual state of Spiritual evolution. (This is often associated with the Pisces archetype – hiding.) Reasons for this can vary but quite commonly include intense traumas that have occurred in past lives relative to its actual state of Spiritual awareness, it being perceived as different, outside the mainstream, challenging or threatening to the existing order. And in the present life that Soul says to itself, "who needs more of that? I'm just going to act like I'm 'supposed to,' and convince myself that I'm not really as different as I feel I am." And it will live that way, perhaps for a really long time. Such Souls are identified when doing readings for them because on the outside they are living very conventional lives, yet the degree of depth and insight they exhibit goes well beyond the nature of the outer life, even the physical appearance – dress, manner of speaking, etc., they have adopted. (Steve)

Advice to clients – an example
[Example: Judgment and projection] Judgment as an archetype correlates with Capricorn, Saturn, and the 10th house, not Pisces or any other sign, house, or planet. The archetype of judgment is natural to consciousness for that is one of the ways that Souls learn about the nature of life. The archetype of judgment of course manifests through all the houses, signs, and planets relative to the archetypes of each, yet judgment as such is the 10th house, Capricorn, and Saturn. JWG often taught about this and one of the main things he taught was that first judgment is natural to consciousness but the real issue is THE CONTENT TO BE USED TO FORM OR MAKE JUDGMENTS. Is that content rooted in all the Natural Laws that were set in motion by the Creator, or is the content rooted in man-made laws, rules, regulations, taboos, norms, etc? Projection, as an archetype within consciousness, correlates to Aquarius, the 11th house, and Uranus. When linked with Capricorn, the 10th house, or Saturn this then can correlate to our projected judgments upon others, and our own inner projected judgments upon our self.

[In terms of speaking to a client] I would approach it by explaining to them why people do these things in the first place. One of the core reasons that people do this in the first place is to avoid or deny taking any responsibility in their own actions. In so doing such people then need to create scapegoats in order to blame others for that which they are responsible for. These people always need to feel 'victimized' by something, or someone, in order to psychologically function. So, in essence, my advice is for those who are the recipients of this [judgment/projection] is to stand back and see it for what it is, to not take it on or 'believe' in any way that that which is being projected upon them is true. That it is essential to stand back and OBJECTIFY the very nature of the situation and persons involved: to detach from it even as it can of course really hurt. Beyond that general advice of course it is necessary to know the specifics of each situation in which this sort of thing happens. Those specific then, of themselves, will dictate the natural and right way to proceed. (Rad)

Looking into the Souls of others
One of the reasons Wolf "got the job" to bring EA forth around the planet is because his Soul is of a level of evolution at which it sees directly into the Souls of others, discerning their actual natures, life lessons, past and future. He did not need a birth chart to see someone's evolutionary signature. He is not the only person with that capacity. But it is a very low percentage of humans (probably 5% or less). This is a potential capacity in all Souls, to see much more of the totality of what is in front of them. Unless the person reading the chart has the capacity to peer directly into the Soul, you cannot know with absolute certainty the actual nature of a physical condition. This person could then refine and tweak the system, to get the conclusions reached from the chart to match the conclusions reached from peering directly into a person's Soul.

A major point of the development of EA was to create a way that those of us who cannot directly see into the Soul (most of us) can see the workings and intentions of the Soul through the birth chart, by understanding the EA system. Wolf called this a gift to humanity from Yogananda's guru Sri Yukteswar, who he called a galactic astrologer. The Soul is beyond time and space. It's a matter of tuning in to the unique vibration of that particular Soul. Souls who have that capacity, those who have aligned themselves with doing God/Goddess intent, do not abuse that capability. They know by what feels right when they are "supposed to" look into a

Soul, and when they are violating Natural Law by doing so. A pure impulse would be to simply desire to align self ever more with doing God/Goddess intent. Then that ability, the desire to be able to see into the past of the Souls in front of it, would either manifest over time, or not. The knowing would be, if it appears, a gift given to assist with the God/dess intended work. If it does not, it is simply not part of what is intended for the present time (or lifetime).

Another way this is explained in the east is "phenomena, phenomena, phenomena," which means, these powers, skills, abilities are not the end goal in themselves. When looked at in those ways, they become yet another separating desire that must be released from. The idea is to focus on the root, not the manifestation. The goal is to align the sense of self-identification with the Soul not personality. As that is progressively accomplished, possibly over thousands of years, the rest simply happens. You can't isolate it to specific practices in a single lifetime. If you are doing these practices with an end in mind, to attain an ability like past life viewing, you have an agenda, a desired outcome. What happens if you've done the practices intently for 60 years, your life is ending, and the ability has not appeared? We have to be prepared to spend 10, 20, 30 lifetimes if necessary. Not seeking an ability, but seeking to align ourselves ever more with Soul and divine intent. That is much closer to the way things really work. (Steve)

As I understand it, this capacity is really a function of evolution/expansion of consciousness itself, and one that is the development of intuition as Yogananda described it in the Gita. One can be "aligned with doing God/Goddess intent" and still not have that capacity. As far as Wolf originally explained it (and I understand it), this can BEGIN to happen sometime in 1st stage Spiritual, and then this increases as one's consciousness expands, to the point that someone like Krishna, Jesus, Yogananda, could see ALL the lifetimes of the Souls they helped. Within this, of course, effort must be made to expand one's consciousness, which results, then, in increasing degrees of this capacity; ie, from seeing one or two pertinent lifetimes, to being able to see all, but only, those lifetimes that are pertinent to the current life, to ALL lifetimes that the Avatars can see. Still, as always, the underlying "condition" for any capacity is simply to desire God first, to seek God first, then one develops/is given the capacities necessary for their own evolution and their particular "mission" on behalf of and as defined by God'dess. (Adina)

Chart rectification

What you can do when the birth time is unknown is rectify the chart. That means to back into the birth time through various methods. Typically this is done through finding out what and when have been the major events in the life and using various astrological timing techniques to position the Ascendant. You can search Google for 'rectify birth chart' to get information on some of the traditional techniques. Jeffrey taught a different technique, which is to determine which house the natal Pluto is in. He prepared a series of questions you ask the client to determine which house they feel is their bottom line (Pluto is the bottom line). The way I do this is I've observed often people can't narrow it to one since they identify with several house attributes, since they have a Nodal Axis, perhaps a stellium in a house/sign, etc. So I ask them to determine which one(s) they identify with the most, and then ask them, of those selected, which one feels like the real bottom line, the underlying cause (Pluto) that the others then sit on top of. Usually they can come up with one bottom line house. Then I construct a chart with Pluto in that house on the birth date. That narrows the birth time down to a 2 hour period (12 houses, 24 hours in a day). Then I move the time around to see what planets shift from house to house, trying to get something closer within the 2 hour period. This requires asking questions – if the Moon is either in the 4th or 5th house, I'd ask Moon/Cancer-like questions to see if they feel more Leo-like (special, pyramid reality) or Cancer (insecure/ watery/ emotional). (Lucius)

TABLE 3 – Chart Rectification – Questions to Ask by Pluto House

House	Questions
1st	Do you feel you have a special destiny to achieve, meaning something out of the ordinary? The related question, Do you have an inner resistance to completing yourself in relationship? (Why? There has been a whole prior life background of essential independence.) You could also ask the Pluto polarity point questions.
2nd	Do you feel that you are fundamentally self-contained? Do you feel that you are fundamentally able to identify and meet your own needs?
3rd	Do you feel that you have a fundamental curiosity to understand the nature of life, that curiosity primarily manifesting at an intellectual level? As an example, Do you feel you have a compulsion to read many, many books, and yet your tendency being to read three or four pages in each book and not the whole book? Do you feel that your mind is simply a roller coaster brain of competing perspectives, the roller coaster or roll x-carts generating competing perspectives? The polarity point question would be, Do you feel that you are trying to find that one philosophical system that puts it all together for you?
4th	Do you feel that you are born with fundamental insecurity at a compulsive level? Do you feel that you had parents that were unable to understand the nature of your emotional needs, and therefore the nature of nurturing accordingly? Do you feel that you have a problem identifying with traditional gender role assignment? Do you feel in your intimate relationships that at times you have problems with what we can call pathological jealousy that is quite different than normal jealousy? Pathological jealousy is demonstrated in O.J. Simpson, meaning a person that can never let go.
5th	Do you feel that you are the center of your own universe? Do you unconsciously expect all things to revolve around you? Do you feel you have a bottomless pit in terms of the need to receive positive feedback for whatever your efforts may be?
6th	Do you feel that you have a problem with a core feeling of fundamental inadequacy? An inner feeling that you are not good enough to do what your higher mind suggests is possible to do? This becomes the basis of compulsive excuse-making, which sounds like rational reasons. Do you feel you have a problem with priority confusions? Do you feel you have a compulsion to make crisis out of thin air? Do you feel the emphasis in your consciousness is left brain analytical thought processes? Do you feel that you are plagued by personal doubt? Do you feel that you are your own worst enemy?
7th	Do you have a compulsive need to be needed? Do you feel you have a lesson in terms of learning when to give and when not to give, and more importantly, how to receive? Do you feel you have problems in co-dependency in relationship? Do you feel you have problems in projection in relationship? (either one or both partners compulsively projecting their subjective reality on one another)
8th	Do you feel you are born with fundamental emotional fears of betrayal, emotional fears of loss, emotional fears of abandonment, impacting on your ability to trust? Do you feel that you crawled out of the womb asking "why?" ie do you feel that you psychoanalyze yourself to the point of tears, and psychoanalyze everyone else to the point of tears? Do you feel that you are an inherently suspicious person? Do you feel that you have an awareness of larger forces in the universe that you cannot control?
9th	Do you feel that you have been asking giant questions for lifetimes, why life, why death, how do I fit into the cosmos? Do you have an element in your consciousness that just knows what it knows without knowing how it knows it? Meaning, do you feel the strength of your Soul is intuitive? Are you born with a fundamental restlessness? For an Individuated or Spiritual person the question becomes, Do you feel that you have a core alienation from society? Do you feel that you have a need to understand yourself in cosmological terms?
10th	Do you feel that you are born with a core sense of guilt that you can no longer define? Do you feel that you have a tremendous standard of inner judgment, which equals becoming your own worst enemy? Do you feel you have a fundamental fear of losing control? Do you have a need to be recognized by society? A related question in the Individuated and Spiritual state, Are you having problems in gender assignment (consensusly defined)? Was there a power problem with one or both parents?
11th	Were you born with a fundamental feeling of being inherently different than most other people? A related question, Not knowing quite where to fit, in society's terms? Do you feel you are born with an inherent capacity to innovate? Do you feel you are born with major lessons in terms of who is a friend and who is not? Do you have a consciousness that is naturally constructed to promote social orders that are more equitable for all concerned, meaning natural humanitarian? That will exist even in the consensus state. Lyndon Johnson had an 11th house Pluto, Bill Clinton has an 11th house Pluto.
12th	Fundamental question, Is your deepest fear falling into the great, great inner abyss? Do you feel you are born with a core of ideals that are continually frustrated? Were you born with no clear sense of boundaries between where you start and something else starts around you? Do you have a fundamental fear of going crazy or insane? Do you have an inner feeling of being in a prison, in which there is no way out?

DAEMON SOUL

Daemon is actually a Latin word that the Christians, removing themselves from what Christ actually taught, perverted into the word Demon. According to old Latin dictionaries the word Daemon means Souls that are utterly unified with Nature and all of its Natural Laws, especially the world of animals and plants, and because of this total union with Nature they become 'messengers of God.' This is why the Christians who became so far removed from the teachings of the original Jesus created cosmologies of Hell that were symbolized by all kinds of weird animals. All natural Daemon Souls feel a fundamental alienation from most other humans. They are 'home' in nature and naturally aligned with all the 'devas' of nature that many call angels, fairies, and the like. Devas are Souls/consciousness that are within nature, but veiled from the eyes of most. They also inhabit the life force within various plants. The nervous systems of plants and animals are almost identical to humans. Daemon Souls are naturally alone, and enjoy being alone in Nature. Another word that can relate to Daemon is Shaman. (Rad)

Natural Laws
Daemon Souls, shamans, have evolved their state of consciousness to be in total unity within the consciousness of what many call Gaia: the total state, consciousness, of Nature manifesting in a variety of forms. In this unified consciousness the Daemon/Shaman Soul is thus aware of all the Natural Laws that exist in the time/space reality we call Earth. Being aligned and unified with these Natural Laws they are thus able to be in conscious relationships with the different states of consciousness as manifested in the various forms on Earth. The Daemon/Shaman Soul evolves, over time, into to this total state of awareness. (Rad)

Totality of nature
The 'totality of nature' is reflected in the natural mutable archetype of Gemini, Virgo, Sagittarius, Pisces which is clearly intrinsic to the nature of the Daemon Soul: "fusion of human consciousness with the totality of nature." (Stacie)

Observation and correlation of the Daemon nature
The Daemon Soul, and all Soul types, can only be known thru observation and correlation and then be backed up and/or revealed through the birth chart. (Adina)

Jeffrey Wolf Green always taught that you can't tell whether someone is a Daemon Soul just by looking at an astrology chart, any more than you can tell whether a person is male or female, or what their evolutionary stage is, by looking at a chart. A Daemon Soul orients to nature because it finds it naturally resonates with nature, sees nature as an externalization of its own inner nature, because that is the way that Soul was created. Similarly for the other Soul types. We desire resonance with experiences and others, including location and planet, that vibrate with our natures. I don't think there is an explanation beyond it's just the way it is. Desire is the root cause of everything we do, and the nature of a Soul's desires has a lot to do with the natural Soul type of that Soul. (Steve)

Many things in EA can only be intuited through observation and correlation. A Daemon Soul cannot be determined through the chart alone. Also, sometimes, a person/Soul can feel a deep connection to and love for nature and the specific kingdoms within nature, have the markers in the chart, and still not be a Daemon Soul. The Daemon Soul type I think is especially relevant given what is happening on the planet right now, and especially the oil gusher in the Gulf. While many, many of us will be feeling the pain of nature, the Daemon Souls in particular will be linked to and feeling it in exquisitely excruciating ways. And the more highly evolved the Daemon Soul is, the more intense and deep those feelings will be. (Adina)

Devas, angels, fairies
Daemon Souls are 'home' in nature and naturally aligned with all the 'devas' of nature that many call angels, fairies, and the like. Devas are Souls/consciousness that are within nature, but veiled from the eyes of most. They also inhabit the life force within various plants. The nervous systems of plants and animals are almost identical to humans. (Rad)

Daemon Soul from other star system
(Q) If a Soul is from a particular star system, are the previous lives associated only with special 'missions' to Earth, and does the Daemon Soul have fewer lifetimes on Earth, and do they accumulate karma differently? (Wendy)
(A) First the totality of the Daemon archetype is Sagittarius, Virgo, Gemini, Pisces. In other words ONE of the archetypes within those signs: these signs also of course correlate to many other archetypes that are specific to these signs. No, it is not associated with only special 'missions' to Earth. The Daemon Soul can have as many lifetimes on this planet as any other the purposes and reasons of which are of course unique to the nature of such Souls. And, no, the karma they accumulate is rooted in the natural law of cause and affect like all other Souls on this planet. (Rad)

Dominion over nature – distortion of Natural Laws
Humans' separation from each other via distorted belief systems, as well as separation from other life forms on the planet (not separation from God'dess) includes the idea that humans are "superior" to other life forms, ie plants, animals, etc., instead of simply different from and interdependent. The idea of this kind of separateness – the DISTORTION of it – goes back to the Old Testament when humans were given "dominion over" nature. And that dominion over has created the destruction OF nature. Since the entire system IS interdependent, then we can see why humans' extinction is looming ahead of us. (Adina)

Sagittarius archetype
Astrology is about correlation and observation. Sagittarius, Jupiter, and the 9th house correlate to the phenomena of a Daemon Soul, BUT that does not mean every time you see a Sun in Sagittarius, or a Moon, or a 9th house Pluto, or a South Node in Sagittarius or the 9th house, or a planet conjunct the Galactic Center at 28 deg Sagittarius, etc., etc., etc., that this correlates in all cases to a Daemon Soul. It doesn't. When a Daemon type Soul is observed and known for sure through such observation then of course the Sagittarius archetype will be in place in some way. The core of any Daemon Soul is rooted in the fact that their orientation to phenomenal reality is rooted in Nature, being in Nature, their 'home' is in Nature: the entire world of animals, and plants that are within the totality of Nature itself. An evolved Daemon Soul has the consciousness wherein it is in 'communication' with Nature itself in a variety of ways. Daemon Souls are all right brain based Souls: intuitive and non-linear. Even when a Daemon Soul is compensating for its actual nature for a variety of reasons that could have taken place in its prior lives this core orientation to Nature, animals, and plants will still be in place. Souls that emanate from Sirius, and incarnate on Earth, are indeed Daemon Souls. (Rad)

Healing the Daemon nature within the Soul
How to work/heal the daemon nature within the Soul, the tremendous amount of unresolved trauma that most daemon Souls are born with that must be healed in order to actualize/re-align with the individual's natural nature. The core issue is that because of the fundamental sense of alienation from the majority of society, and also the continual experience of being misunderstood/experiencing many projections and wounding judgments from those in the mainstream of society the Soul is afraid of/hides his or her actual nature from the majority through the act of compensation. In other words, the Soul attempts to deny or avoid the feelings of alienation and also of unresolved trauma by creating a life style that appears on the surface as "normal." At some point, however, the Soul must come out of this hiding and heal the unresolved trauma by actualizing his or her natural nature no matter how many judgments and projections he or she comes across. The point within this is that those with Daemon natures have their own journey in the context of healing and actualizing that which is natural and true within their Soul, and when counseling such people it is important to remain sensitive to the trauma that has been suffered, and encourage the other to recover his or her actual nature in whatever way is deemed necessary. (Deva)
In terms of working with those with a Daemon nature, it is important to understand that these Souls will feel very alienated from society because of his/her core orientation (feeling more at home within nature, and being able to "tune into" animals and plants, and also being able to work in a healing fashion with nature in a way most cannot). In other words, there are commonly a lot of misunderstandings/projections from others upon those with Daemon natures because of this core orientation. Many can feel confusion and disillusionment because of this experience, and some will choose to live in isolation from most others. Communing with nature and animals serves as a necessary healing of the deep wounds that can occur in these areas. These Souls can be incredible healers because of their intrinsic hypersensitivity, and again can tune into nature (plants and animals) and also other people who they sense are in pain. Also, because of this intrinsic hypersensitivity it is important to emphasize the thought that they must also have strategies to not be overwhelmed by that sensitivity. For example, if a person with a Daemon nature is working with people in a healing way, it is a good idea to suggest taking time away from any interaction with people in order to recharge their batteries and "unload" from the healing work (what was absorbed through osmosis from others during this time). (Deva)
The best way or practice specific for Daemon Souls to help realign with their natural Soul expression, as a way of shedding the alienation and traumatic lives experienced here of course is to get into Nature as much as possible and then remember how to breathe with the wind, or the natural inhale and exhale of Nature/Gaia itself. When the breath is thus harmonized this will naturally allow the consciousness to expand, and progressively embrace the universal. In this way the natural capacity of the Daemon Soul

to become aware, and attuned with, the various spirits or devas within Nature then exists in such a way as a natural communion takes place in which a variety of knowledge is then transmitted. Within this of course to be around as many animals as possible, and the ones which the Daemon Soul has a natural affinity for. Each animal of course has its own Soul and thus by unifying the consciousness of the Daemon Soul with the consciousness/Soul of animals another form of direct transmission takes place in which knowledge of different types occurs. So too with the entire world of plants. Daemon Souls have an affinity for all animals. Of course each Daemon Soul is different in their own ways and, as a result, have more of an affinity for this animal or that.

The other day I was around a Daemon Soul in which I observed this person sitting in the middle of some plants and flowers, focused on a bumble bee that was in the throes of dying. This person simply picked the bee up and put it in the middle of his palm and let the bee die right there. He told me the bee did not want to die alone. (Rad)

ARIES – MARS – 1st HOUSE

Aries keywords

Separation	War	Primal	Narcissism
Anxiety of separation	Loner	Spontaneous enthusiasm	Self-interest
Anger / Rage	Self	Initiative	Warrior
Desires	Violence	Initiation	Pioneer
Desire nature	Sexual instinct	Expression of will	Sexual violence
Identity	Impatience (anger at limitations)	Super-human	Destroyer
Freedom	Intolerance for weakness	Zarathustra	Paranoia
Independence	Instinct	Special destiny	

Aries, Mars, 1st house archetype

Aries is Fire, Yang (male), and Cardinal. Natural home is the 1st house, ruled by Mars. Yang (male) energy represents the desire to separate. It is energy moving out from the center. Yin (female) energy represents the desire to return to the center. Aries represents the original anxiety of separation from the womb. Mars is the agent on the subjective, egoic level the Soul uses to carry out its desires. It's tied to the primal brain. The sign that is on the 1st house, the house sign that Aries is in, the house and sign that Mars is in, all represent the types of desires we are aware of to connect with our evolutionary requirements. Ascendant, Mars, Aries, 1st house correlate to the phenomenon of becoming – we are all in a perpetual state of becoming. This is why Aries requires freedom to act upon the core desires and can tolerate no restrictions. The 1st house naturally opposes the 7th house (Libra, relationships). The emotional paradox – too much isolation vs. too much social interaction with loss of sense of self. We understand who we are by comparing and contrasting ourselves to others. Ascendant is NOT the persona – Aries is instinctive, nothing instinctive is constructed. The 7th house Descendant is the actual constructed personality, how others see us. Pluto related to Mars represents the sexual instinct in all organisms, as well as all that is primal in nature – breathing, eating, excreting, etc. (JWG's Pluto Vol. 1 and the School's course)
[Recommended Reading: Jeffrey Wolf Green's Pluto Vol. 1 – The Evolutionary Journey of the Soul]

Pluto in the 1st house or Aries

Pluto in 1st house – new evolutionary cycle, feeling of special destiny (as do all Cardinal signs/houses). They REQUIRE freedom and independence to explore the new and relatively undefined new cycle. This is the underlying cause of the famous Arian self-centeredness. They must be free to act on any impulse that comes to them because it is through experience that they come to know who they are. The conflict – Aries wants total freedom – Pluto seeks security. This can result in a cyclic identity crisis, frustration and anger which can be projected upon others or events that are seen as the cause of the problem. Most of these people have difficulties in relationships involving confrontations they experienced in early life. They must experience the sense of being attacked or attacking or being misunderstood or misunderstanding. These confrontations are necessary to promote lessons of equality, giving, and listening, to become aware of the needs of others before their own. They need to learn to balance their need for freedom with their need for relationship. They must learn to balance the need for time alone with the need to be with others. They tend to be intense individualists, strong willed, magnetic, bull headed, courageous, leadership abilities, can be hard to know deeply. (JWG's Pluto Vol. 1 and the School's course)

Pluto polarity point – 7th house or Libra

The identity crisis kicks off the need for inter-relationship with others. The process of self-discovery requires this. These people will be instinctively attracted to or repelled by others. The attractions can be sexual or magnetic in nature. They may not always be sexualized but they can often be experienced in that way. The resonance creates a feeling in each that there is something that they can learn about themselves through interaction with the other. The duration of these attractions may be long or short. (JWG's Pluto Vol. 1 and the School's Course)

Aries archetype

The innocence of Pisces carries over to Aries, but all its universal aspects have been stripped away to leave just a core innocence of self. Aries is the sign that is the most aware of itself, and this awareness is very concentrated. The increased awareness of itself means it is largely unaware of much else other than itself. This might normally be pretty depressing, except Aries core innocence protects it from that, and instead it is happy to be what it is, as any innocent self is naturally happy within itself – it's built in. However, while Aries is happy to be, the increased awareness of itself does produce an equally acute awareness of "all that isn't Aries." It's not that Aries is much concerned about "all that isn't Aries" – no, it's naturally centered in itself and simply happy in being that way. But Aries has an active and keen intelligence, and being aware that there is an awfully big amount of "all that isn't Aries" it feels at a subconscious level something not being quite right with everything ("everything" – the deep Soul memory carried over from Pisces of Oneness). It's simple happiness at being able to just be itself is disturbed (usually at a subconscious level) by the contrast presented in the way it intuitively perceives its life situation – as that of being just a "dot" (self) within the universe ("all that isn't Aries"). The Aries situation is being naturally happy due to its inherently totally simple and uncluttered nature, yet never being able to relax into that happiness because it's obviously incomplete. And Aries immediately senses that that doesn't "add up." And the "pain" of separation arises then and there immediately and directly from this intuitive knowing, and this becomes the underlying shadow of Aries – its subconscious insecurity and lack of confidence, self-doubt, in total – a deep hidden anxiety. And Aries' increased sense of itself makes sure this anxiety is carried wherever Aries goes. This leads Aries into its search, the driving need to explore and discover more and more of and about itself, with all the attendant needs of absolute freedom, self-focus, no limitations or interference from others whatsoever, and absolutely no demands from anyone else – to maximize its chances of succeeding in its quest. (Upasika)

Mars, corresponding to separating and returning desires like Pluto, as I understand it, on one level Mars is just the fuel. Through Aries there is the impulse to be in CONSTANT motion. To where is this motion leading the Soul? That's where the impulses in Aries can serve EITHER the separating desires of the Soul or the desire to return. (Ari)

ALL desire originates in the Soul for its evolutionary requirements. All paths lead to God'ess – even this very impulse begins in Aries – since there is a beginning to every intention. An interesting relationship to note is that between natal Mars and Pluto, and the phase that they are in. JWG taught that generally each evolutionary intention is played out over 8 lifetimes (or 8 primary phases). Each life will project an evolutionary progression describing how far along the Soul has come in working through the original intention. In the last phases, the resistance could be less, and the conscious awareness could be higher as compared to the initial lifetimes. (Linda)

Mars, lower octave of Pluto

Mars is the lower octave of Pluto, and correlates, in each life, how our desires emanating from our Soul become conscious in each life. As these desires become conscious Mars correlates to how we instinctively act upon, act out, those desires. There is also the natural 1st house that is a natural Aries house. Whatever the sign is on our Ascendant also correlates to how our desires become conscious, and are acted out. The sign Aries will also be on a house cusp somewhere. This too correlates to how the various desires within the Soul become conscious, and are acted out. Within this we also have a South Node of Mars that will be in a house and sign somewhere. This too correlates to the progressive evolution of the Soul as new desires occur within the Soul. Yet it must be understood that all of these desires come from the Soul, and that these desires manifest or occur as a direct result of the core evolutionary intentions, desires, that the Soul has from life to life. And that core, ongoing evolutionary intention from life to life, is of course symbolized in the main karmic/evolutionary axis within the birth chart itself: the natal Pluto, its polarity point, the North and South Nodes of the Moon, and the location of their planetary rulers. (Rad)

Mars is the lower octave of Pluto, and symbolizes how we will consciously act out the desires symbolized by Pluto. Mars symbolizes our conscious desire nature. The point within this is that Pluto in the birth chart will determine the core specific past patterns of behavior that are creating limitations and represent emotional security for the Soul. We will unconsciously resist growth by attempting to maintain these past patterns (separating desires). Pluto's polarity point symbolizes the current evolutionary intentions for the life, and the types of desires that the Soul will have to break free from the past patterns of behavior that are inhibiting further growth. Mars is the conscious desire nature we have that reflects how we will act out, or act upon, these desires symbolized by Pluto and to actualize the current evolutionary intentions for this life (Pluto's polarity point). (Deva)

Mars is Aries energy, instinctual, and is the carrier, the vehicle, by which the Soul (Pluto) transmits its intentions, desires, into human awareness at an instinctual subconscious level – primal urges. (Steve)

The current position, the natal position, of Mars correlates to how to move forwards in this life in order to evolve beyond where the Soul left off with the existing desires from past lifetimes. It is essential to remember that all desires emanate from the Soul. And that the root of such desires to evolve, the ongoing evolutionary journey of the Soul, is of course all symbolized by the natal position of Pluto, and its polarity point. Mars, as an archetype, is the lower octave of Pluto that instinctually acts out, acts upon, those desires emanating from the Soul itself. (Rad)

Mars rulership
In Evolutionary Astrology, Mars is the ruler of Aries, Ascendant, and the 1st house. So when you see the Nodes in Scorpio that does not mean that it has a co-ruler with Pluto. Mars, the 1st house, and Aries all correlate to how the desires of the Soul get instinctually acted upon via the current life ego, Moon, and the subjective consciousness therein. (Rad)

Mars/Pluto interface
Being a lower octave of Pluto, Mars will express on an ongoing external basis the dual desire nature of the Soul: the desire to separate and the desire to return to the Source. Aries, Mars, the 1st house, correlate with the desire and need to separate in order to create a sense of being a distinct individual, which in turn will induce a crisis because of the natural inconjunct between Aries and Scorpio – the Soul. This crisis is rooted in the dual desires of the Soul, which allows the ego perception (Cancer, 4th house, Moon) of being totally separate from anything else, yet needing to integrate back to where it emanated from – the Soul. Via Mars, the Soul will instinctively produce actions creating the experiences the Soul – Pluto – needs to actualize its intentions, to externally create what it desires. In turn, by means of actualizing its desires, and creating that which the Soul desires, the Soul will be able to discover what it is that it has desired: that which was unconscious will become apparent.

Thus, Mars will allow the Soul to evolve, because the externalization of desires, the surfacing of Soul desires through created experiences, is necessary for the process of exhausting and eliminating its separating desires. When Mars is in aspect to Pluto, the function of acting out desires is subject to metamorphic change: instinctual creation of experiences – Mars – strongly fueled by the desire nature of the Soul – Pluto. The individual will create experiences directly expressing its desires, be they desires of separation or desires to return. The individual will face its unconscious desire nature because he will have the power to externally or consciously create that which he desires: his desires will produce an effect. This effect will allow conscious awareness of the desire nature of the individual, and a metamorphosis of how the individual is acting out his desires. This dynamic exists in all people – it is the basis of evolution of human consciousness – whether or not Mars is in aspect to Pluto, though it will be emphasized when these aspects exist. (Gonzalo)

[Mars is implicated with Pluto] when there are aspects to it from Pluto, or aspects to the South Node, its planetary ruler, or aspects to that planetary ruler. (Rad)

Mars/Pluto in primary life
Pluto and Mars indicating a primary lifetime means more evolutionary work is intended in that life. Since the end intention of evolutionary work is to deepen the awareness of self as Soul, to the extent the intended lessons are learned, that can deepen the knowing of self as Soul. It is more possible or probable in a primary life only because the intention of that life is to make that Soul do certain necessary work. Whether primary or secondary life, a Soul is still in the evolutionary station it is in. The issue is how much evolutionary advancement is intended. There are other indicators of that besides Mars/Pluto, including the number of aspects Pluto makes to other planets, number of planets in the birth chart that are retrograde. (Steve)

Mars retrograde
Retrograde is always the R words – redo, renew, review. A person could be born before Mars turns retrograde and it would be direct in natal and go retrograde by progression during their life. Or they could be born with Mars retrograde and Mars goes direct by progression during their life. Or they could be born with Mars retrograde by progression for the entire life. These are going to be distinct conditions for that Soul. Some of it undoubtedly relates to where that Soul was prior to the present life. (Steve)

The intent of the retrograde as an archetype is to re-live, redo, repeat. And the intention within that, the reason for that, is to INDIVIDUATE. Any retrograde planet either by birth, or going retrograde in the context of a lifetime, is not only to repeat, re-live, and redo, which can have many reasons, but one of the core reasons is to individuate. It accelerates the evolutionary process of individuation. Thus the Soul desires to withdraw from ANY external circumstance or condition that is attempting to define, through expectations, how the archetype of the planet that is retrograde, at birth, progression, or transit, how that archetype (planet) is 'meant' to be actualized or lived out. And that is because the Soul is desiring to individuate its function which, in turn, allows for an acceleration of the Soul's development because of the effort to individuate. In its own way it ignites a deep feeling in the Soul that says 'not this, not that, so what is it?' (Rad)

Cardinal signs/houses
Cardinal houses are intense because they represent major shifts or turning points – the natural squares-oppositions-conjunctions in the chart. The cardinal signs/houses contain their own paradoxes. Cardinal is an instinctual need to initiate change. Our sense of security is based on sameness, not on change. Thus the very nature of cardinal insures that at certain points we are going to freak out a bit, because all the change we have been instinctually creating results in a loss of familiarity and known–ness. This, at key points, results in the loss of an emotional sense of safety/security, leading to a desire to STOP, to want to go inward to emotionally regroup – to ground and stabilize the new realities we have been initiating. This is an inherent and necessary part of the cardinal

archetype. It's especially pronounced in Cancer, but applies to all cardinal signs/houses – two steps forward, one step back. The natural need to regroup and reground after taking two steps into new directions. After a period of timeout, the cardinal instinct to initiate change again takes over, and we are back pursuing the next step forward again. (Steve)

Aspects to Mars/Aries
The cardinal cross is generally a challenge to Aries to face its separation square on, a kind of either/or situation, eg work with society or not (Capricorn), open to nurturing or not (Cancer), connect with others or not (Libra). The trines encourage Aries to use its natural openness to the new to easily grow from its position to be more than what it is – being creative within its freedom (Leo), moving from self-interest into understanding nature (Sagittarius). The sextiles provide a platform for Aries, an opportunity, to see itself as part of something more valuable than it could ever achieve by itself on its own – learning about people and situations (Gemini) and being part of a group with all the richness that can provide (Aquarius). The quincunxes are possibly the hardest for Aries as they require patience (in very short supply in Aries) to deal with them, working diligently with that very sense of separation that Aries carries so anxiously in its shadow. By slowing down and completing everything it starts, conscientiousness, paying attention to its body not just the energy it has for its desires, serving others instead of itself (Virgo), and sacrificing its freedom (one of the hardest things for an Aries) for the depth of intimacy that commitment can bring, examining its desires and their worth and ultimately allowing itself to be transformed by something or someone (Scorpio).

The semisextile to Taurus kick starts Aries into "all that isn't Aries," through the way Aries listens to and values itself, which it needs to do as part of the process of operating in the world as it pursues its desires. But the opposition (Libra), being the polarity point, is the key natural growth point. The instinctive awareness of self and its separating desires that defines Aries is absolutely necessary as a basis on which all the other signs grow from – each following sign has this core self already absorbed into it, and is developing the consciousness of that self in ever more involved and sophisticated ways, eventually leading to the relative totality of experience that is Pisces – then back again to Aries for a new cycle on an elevated level, on and on with the wheel of life and death, perpetuated by separating desires, until they finally are no more. (Upasika)

Mars transit
Mars is the leading edge of evolutionary growth, or change. It gives the evolutionary dynamics in the chart a constant forward motion, or momentum. It is the lower octave of Pluto, or how we consciously act out the desires that emanate from Pluto. Mars correlates with the beginning of a brand new evolutionary cycle, and the need to initiate, or put into motion, actions that will allow this new cycle to begin. Mars transits symbolize the need to put into motion necessary life changes relative to the beginning of a new part or cycle within our life that will allow the current evolutionary/karmic dynamics to be actualized. Mars correlates with instinctual behavior, and learns on an action-reaction basis. When experiencing Mars transits there will be an increasing need for freedom and independence to initiate the necessary actions, or direction, that will allow the new evolutionary cycle to move forward. It is important to understand that the new evolutionary cycle is not consciously known, or understood by the individual because it is so new. In other words, Mars/Aries/1st house correlates with the process of self-discovery, and again, the need for freedom and independence to discover what the new evolutionary cycle is about.

Mars also correlates with anger. Anger can be linked with many things, but one critical dynamic that is linked with anger is not wanting to have personal freedom restricted in any way. When experiencing Mars transits, anger at personal limitations or any external restrictions to initiating the new cycle that the individual feels is necessary at that time of the transit can manifest. It is important to understand that anger can be projected into external situations that are perceived as the cause of the limitations instead of understanding that the increasing desire to change existing life circumstances is a reflection of the desire to create forward momentum in evolutionary growth, and to use anger in a constructive way to create the necessary changes that must be made at this time. A Pluto, Saturn, Jupiter or Uranus transit to Mars will have a deeper impact than transiting Mars to these planets because of the length of the transit itself (Mars moves fast in the sky). (Deva)

Mars transit – anger
My main point about Mars and anger is that anger that is projected upon others, or the environment as the source of personal limitations typically creates a negative and destructive outcome (personal degeneration) during Mars transits because the person does not understand that the limitations/restrictions are actually a reflection of the need to move forward in life, and that it is an inner limitation that is creating the restriction towards further growth. When this anger is used constructively, or in a positive way, the person can respond to a Mars transit in a way to grow past whatever personal limitation is creating a block towards putting into motion a new evolutionary cycle. Anger that is triggered at this time that is linked with not wanting personal freedom or independence to be limited can be used to create a new way of responding to external circumstances that are limited, or confining in some way to change those situations instead of just blowing up on another person, or blaming the outer circumstance. Anger can be used to initiate the new cycle of becoming that correlates with Mars instead of creating situations of personal degeneration or self-implosion.

Just as a simple example: I recently had a Mars return (natal Mars in Capricorn/9th house), and I found myself feeling so much repressed anger coming to the surface that needed to be released that I become very impatient and also intolerant in ways that were inappropriate. The point within this is that there was also a desire to release this kind of anger, and to use it in a way to be free from my own inner dynamics of emotional repression that were the cause of my intense anger at that time. I had to learn to respond to certain situations that triggered this anger in a new way that allowed personal growth to occur (not reacting in an instinctual way to the triggers of the past that created personal degeneration). Mars also correlates with fears of all sorts, and during these transits our fears can come to the surface. Mars transits offer an opportunity to break free from these fears. (Deva)

Mars – natal, transits and progressions
The natal Mars/Pluto phase and of course house and sign position correlates to how the evolutionary intentions within the birth chart will be acted upon in a consistent manner. Mars transits/progressions reflect critical times in the Soul's journey that trigger, or ignite, these core dynamics relative to the specific nature of the transit/progression. (Deva)

War
This area shows up so much in regression work. In reality if anyone has been incarnating in say the last 4,000 years much of the history of humanity has been one of warring. In my view we are all working through the collective wounds of war. It seems to me that warriors go through a long karmic history with war with a few distinct phases that can play out through a series of lifetimes. A turning point lifetime seems to be one of disillusionment, where the warrior or soldier sees into the stupidity of repeated killing. From that point onwards it seems the Soul works to uplift or purify all of the ingrained warrior skills through several lifetimes essentially setting the person on a path of becoming a spiritual warrior. (Patricia)

It may also be useful to consider that there is an entire Soul type that correlates with the naval chakra, Souls who in essence reflect the nature of this chakra, Pluto/Mars. Spiritualization of these Souls would naturally embrace paths that allow them to harness and spiritualize the 'physical edge' that is intrinsic to their nature/Soul structure. See Chapter 6 in Autobiography of a Yogi, The Tiger Swami. (Stacie)

TAURUS – VENUS – 2nd HOUSE

Taurus keywords

Survival	Self-sufficiency	Starvation	Cautious
Fertility	Security	Poverty	Literal
Procreation	Isolated	Give up	Materialist
Preservation	Withdrawal	Suppress emotions	Possessions
Self as Resource	Stagnation	Shut down	Landowner
Inner resources	Personal worth	Stubborn	Farmer
Values	Personal value	Hoarding	Thief
Beauty	Self-esteem	The Body	Carpenter
Prostitution	Patience	Pleasure	Shepherd

Taurus, Venus, 2nd house archetype

Yin / fixed / earth / rules 2nd house / ruled by Venus. Taurus brings the Arian energies back to Earth, grounds, centers, stabilizes. Taurus represents the biological instinct for survival. Whatever it takes to survive correlates to your values, which creates your meaning, which leads to your beliefs and philosophy. In Aries we experience evolutionary becoming. The types of desires associated with that lead to what we value. Taurus rules the procreation instinct, closely linked to the biological instinct for survival. Life must go on. The sign on the 2nd house, the location and aspects of the 2nd house ruler, Venus and its aspects, the house that Taurus is on correlate to our values and meaning, and sexual values. Taurus represents self-reliance, self-sufficiency, self-containment, self-sustainment. Yet again we have an inconjunct (150 degree aspect) to the 7th house, the need to be in relationship with others. When we get too isolated, it begins a crisis in our lives and we feel the need to be with others. When we get too close to others and begin losing the sense of our own individuality, we feel the need to withdraw and re-establish the sense of our own self – this is Taurus. (from JWG's Pluto Vol. 1 and the School's course)

[Recommended Reading: Jeffrey Wolf Green's Pluto Vol. 1 – The Evolutionary Journey of the Soul]

Pluto in the 2nd house or Taurus

These people tend to have an extra strong survival instinct and sexual nature. They have needed to withdraw into themselves in past lives to develop their own value systems. They have a tendency to over isolate, to get cut off from the greater life, to stay content in their own small space that gives them the sense of controlling a piece of life. This can create a sense of laziness or inertia. The sense of survival can lead to a desire for over accumulation of STUFF. Money, possessions, fancy homes, cars, fine food, wines, the good life. A very sensually oriented and fulfilling life. Some of these people have not learned how to sustain themselves in the world financially, yet they still have the desire for the good life. They are good at getting other people to supply it for them. Marrying into money, house sitting in fine homes, vicariously living the good life through associating with affluent people, etc. A small minority of them will use devious or illegal means to acquire other people's wealth or resources. They can be sexually or emotionally manipulative, to get what they want. (JWG's Pluto Vol. 1 and the School's Course)

Pluto polarity point – 8th house or Scorpio

This will lead the person into confrontations that will reveal the limits in their value systems, that will shake them out of isolation. Those with wealth will gradually discover that material abundance does not necessarily equate with happiness or a sense of security. The 8th house teaches that there is more to life than material values. Those who've lived beyond their means will receive financial shocks to bring them to these realizations. They will have to open up to others, merge with others (the 8th house/Scorpio principle) from which they will discover the ways in which they have limited themselves through being overly isolated and having values and a sense of life that is too fixed. Their personal limitations will be confronted. The 8th house also represents major metamorphosis, and through opening up they will begin to experience life transformation. These people tend to change slowly, creating the possibility of cataclysmic change, an 8th house Pluto archetype. As they open up and begin learning their lessons, they can be very good at pointing out others' limitations to them and helping them through the growth process. They learn how to merge with others without becoming dependent on those they merge with. Common qualities include stubborn, defensive, stable, inner strength, patience, perseverance, slow to change, quietly powerful and intense, need to link to that which is powerful, need to possess what they own. Can also promote self-reliance in others and realize they actually own nothing. (JWG's Pluto Vol. 1 and the School's Course)

Venus archetype

Venus correlates with our inner relationship with ourselves, and also the external relationships we form as a reflection of our inner relationship. Venus is co-ruled by the signs of Taurus and Libra. Taurus reflects our inner relationship with ourselves, and the inner side, or inner nature, of Venus. Libra reflects the relationships we attract and initiate with other people (outer or external side of Venus). Venus correlates with our values which are a determinate to who we form relationships with and whom not, and also the needs we have within relationships. When we have not learned to meet our own needs they become projected onto our partner and others in general within relationships. There is a natural inconjunct between the Taurus and Libra archetypes which correlates with the crisis (inconjunct) that occurs when we project too many needs onto another within relationships and are then thrown back onto ourselves in order to learn self-reliance. Venus correlates with extremities, and how we will go about balancing or uniting discordant aspects of ourselves. Again, the need is to learn to identify what our specific needs are within relationships and meet those from within ourselves in order to attract relationships that are balanced, equal, and based on mutual independence. The natal placement of Venus in the birth chart correlates with the person's pre-existing relationship patterns, and the values and needs an individual will have within relationships.

Venus also correlates to the nature of our "inner dialogue" with ourselves (Taurus side of Venus) and how we can all project this inner dialogue onto others. In other words, if I have Venus in Scorpio I will naturally be listening to others from a "bottom line" psychological standpoint ("where is this person coming from, can I relate to this or not?"). The Venus in Scorpio person may also come into relationships with unconscious fears of abandonment, betrayal, and loss, and unconsciously project these fears onto the other by listening to their partner in a defensive manner, and also project that the other person has ulterior motives or agendas which the other in fact does not have. The point within this is that Venus correlates with the psychology of listening (Libra side of Venus), and when we listen to others based on our own subjective inner dialogue we do not truly hear what they are communicating. Remember that the archetype of Libra correlates with the need to learn to listen to others from their reality, not our own, in order to truly understand what the other is communicating. (Deva)

Taurus and Libra are both ruled by Venus – the inner relationship, our self-worth, values and meaning in life – and are considered to be the Taurus side of the Venus function. Feelings, not emotions (that would be Moon), are also part of the Taurus/Venus associations. I generally feel that the earth signs, frequently in astrology, and perhaps in spiritual pursuits, get either little attention or the negative attributes are emphasized. I think that this is the general state after millennia of dualistic patriarchal nonsense – the projections onto to the earth, the body, the feminine has to do with a dismissive attitude to these archetypes (EA is thankfully free of this attitude!). How essential can our instinct to survive be? I don't think it should be dismissed too lightly – but again I think the degradation of the body and what we can be compelled to do to survive isn't always an easy subject but it is definitely spiritual. One correlation with Taurus is our inner relationship, our relationship with ourselves. Whatever this inner relationship is will be pervasive in our lives. I think that much of the 'visualization' movement ultimately is rooted in this archetype. Many of us are fairly unconscious how we view our own selves, our basic feeling of self-worth, values, meaning – this then creates lives that are lived unconsciously via projections, perceived needs, desires and situations wherein we don't see that we've created this from the inside out – unfulfilling jobs, abusive relationships, people's reactions and projections, etc.

If I have subconscious assumptions that I don't deserve to be treated equally in relationships, to be treated with respect and love, or that I don't even deserve to be able to meet my own needs (survive) in a manner that reflects who I am– what does that say about my inner relationship? I think many people are operating under the duress of a negative relationship with themselves. In this type of extrovert society there is practically zero emphasis on the inner relationship. Even most of the 'creative visualization' has as its focus the 'presto' magic of getting something you want versus seeing the underlying values and needs you either have or perceive to need as why you find yourself in the reality you do. The focus is frequently entirely outside – but, we all have that inner relationship – it doesn't go away simply because it's not focused upon – unfortunately, it is merely projected unconsciously. The universe has a way of throwing you back within yourself if the balance of inner/outer becomes too distorted. I think that the nature of our outer relationships can reflect this – help us to recognize unconscious assumptions about ourselves. This is profoundly how the outer reflects the inner. The balance can be distorted either way – introversion at the expense of relationship, transformation, participation – and being cognizant of other's reality and needs is the 'frog in the well' dynamic. A person wants to stay in their safe place where there is no need for others, for compromise – one could be rather vicious in maintaining their survival however they can (versus barely surviving with the minimal) simply not have to be bothered with the threatening outside world.

Using the fixed cross one can see how most people are operating with a huge disconnect between their inner relationship, values (Taurus) with personal sense of love, acceptance and creativity (Leo) – how we look to transform ourselves via relationships, intimacies (Scorpio), and the larger social context, ability to be objective, and the nature of projections (Aquarius) – how much projections are a part of how we value ourselves and what we think we need to survive or what we lack and how we'll go about obtaining it. The nature of desires itself is partially rooted in this archetype (also Scorpio) – what we perceive we don't have we want – this can be true of material or non-material desires. I think this is interesting in the context of the opposition to Scorpio and the sextile to Cancer and Pisces – our inner value and meaning, and perceived strengths and weakness – and it's connection to our ego, self-image and the ego structure we create to obtain our desires, the transformation we undergo within our Soul structure and the possible illusions/delusions we encounter that if seen properly helps connect us to a greater reality. (Lucius)

Venus double rulership – Taurus and Libra

Jeffrey was the first astrologer to teach about Venus' correlation to the inner relationship that all people have with themselves. He taught why Venus had a double rulership for the signs Libra and Taurus. He said that Taurus and the 2nd house correlated to the inner relationship we all have with ourselves, and that the 7th house and Libra correlated to the types of outer relationships that we form with other people and why. He taught that the planet Venus, of itself, symbolized both the inner and outer relationships within the archetype of Venus itself. A simple example: if a person has, let's say, Venus in Virgo and their inner relationship to themself is one of intense criticism, all the things that are wrong with them, that it shouldn't then be surprising that that person would then 'attract,' Venus, others who are then critical of them: the inner reflecting the outer. And that which we attract is a reflection of the inner vibration within us where that inner vibration is a reflection of our inner relationship to ourselves. Or, for another example, let's say that Venus in Virgo person was inwardly experiencing a high degree of 'lack' in their lives which then leads to a sense of being 'empty' from within. That inner relationship to themselves could then manifest outwardly as needing, Venus, many other people in their lives in order to 'fill them up,' and needing others to give to them that which they felt they were lacking.

He talked about the natural inconjunct between the 2nd house, Taurus, and the 7th house, Libra. He taught that this is the natural 'crisis' that exists in all of us that involves the need to be self-reliant and fulfilling our own needs, and how our needs can be projected onto others in such a way as to become dependent on others for the very needs that we need to satisfy within ourselves. And how our projected needs onto others correlate to 'expectations' that we can set up with other people. So what happens when our expectations that are projected onto others do not occur? For most some kind of crisis will occur where the intent of the crisis is to force the person back upon themselves so that self-reliance in some way can be developed when those expectations have reached a point of excessive dependency on others. He taught about the need for the EA astrologer to understand the totality of the Venus archetype. Thus, to not only understand the sign that Venus is in but all the aspects that it is making to other planets, the North and South Nodes of Venus in terms of what the past, present, and future of the evolving Venus archetype is in all charts, and to fully grasp the signs on the 2nd and 7th houses as they condition those natural archetypes, and the reasons for that conditioning relative to the ongoing evolutionary intentions of the Soul, and, lastly, the location of the planetary rulers of those signs and the aspects that they are making for the same reasons. (Rad)

Venus correlates with our inner relationship with ourselves, and also the external relationships we form as a reflection of our inner relationship. Venus is co-ruled by the signs of Taurus and Libra. Taurus reflects our inner relationship with ourselves, and the inner side, or inner nature, of Venus. Libra reflects the relationships we attract and initiate with other people (outer or external side of Venus). Venus correlates with our values which are a determinate to who we form relationships with and whom not, and also the needs we have within relationships. When we have not learned to meet our own needs they become projected onto our partner and others in general within relationships. There is a natural inconjunct between the Taurus and Libra archetypes which correlates with the crisis (inconjunct) that occurs when we project too many needs onto another within relationships and are then thrown back onto ourselves in order to learn self-reliance. Venus correlates with extremities, and how we will go about balancing or uniting discordant aspects of ourselves. Again, the need is to learn to identify what our specific needs are within relationships and meet those from within ourselves in order to attract relationships that are balanced, equal, and based on mutual independence. The natal placement of Venus in the birth chart correlates with the person's pre-existing relationship patterns, and the values and needs an individual will have within relationships.

Venus also correlates to the nature of our "inner dialogue" with ourselves (Taurus side of Venus) and how we can all project this inner dialogue onto others. In other words, if I have Venus in Scorpio I will naturally be listening to others from a "bottom line" psychological standpoint ("where is this person coming from, can I relate to this or not?"). The Venus in Scorpio person may also come into relationships with unconscious fears of abandonment, betrayal, and loss, and unconsciously project these fears onto the other by listening to their partner in a defensive manner, and also project that the other person has ulterior motives or agendas which the other in fact does not have. The point within this is that Venus correlates with the psychology of listening (Libra side of Venus), and when we listen to others based on our own subjective inner dialogue we do not truly hear what they are communicating. Remember that the archetype of Libra correlates with the need to learn to listen to others from their reality, not our own, in order to truly understand what the other is communicating. (Deva)

Psychology of listening, inner and outer sides of Venus

Venus correlates to the psychology of listening. Via the Taurus side of Venus our inner dialogue with our self is all too often projected (Libra side of Venus) onto others in our relationships. Example, Venus in Virgo, the person could project the inner critical relationship/inner dialogue on to the other in the form of "hearing" the other criticize or undermine them when this is not the case (the other may be trying to give helpful advice for example). The point is that via the Libra side of Venus we must learn to objectively hear and listen to others from their reality so we do not project in this way, and truly hear what is being said. (Deva)

Since Pisces is the polarity of Virgo, the Soul with Venus in Virgo is always comparing themselves to perfection and often feeling the LACK to greater degrees. The Venus in Virgo can be so self-critical that this criticism can then be transferred to the partner, ie not just the self-judgment trips or hearing another incorrectly but also focusing on the partner's inadequacies versus their strengths, ie focusing on their lacks too. It is impossible to love another (7th house) unconditionally until and unless one can learn to love themselves (2nd house) unconditionally first, which is the evolutionary intent with a Venus in Virgo, ie the polarity of Virgo being PISCES (unconditional LOVE). (Kristin)

Taurus side of Venus Rx

Venus Rx indicates that the Soul is defined through the Taurus side of Venus (establishing a primary relationship within him or herself first) instead of the Libra side as most folks are (initiation of relationships with others which is the externalized side of Venus). (Deva)

Venus – past, present, future orientations

The present life Venus is conditioned by all the past "self and other" relationship tendencies and patterns that have preceded it. The South Node of Venus represents directly the way the Venus functions were handled in the past. The South Node of the Moon represents the Soul's past personality structures and emotional habits/patterns. Both of these are alive within the present life Venus function, subconsciously coloring it. Yet that Venus also contains the possibility of changing the past, in the present moment (the only moment in which anything can be changed). The intended directions for that Venus to evolve are indicated in the North Node of Venus, the Lunar North Node ruler, the Lunar North Node, and the Polarity Point of Pluto, in that order, from top to bottom. We try to mentally separate the past and the present and the future, to see them as different things. But in reality it's all the same, and it can't be separated. That is why EA says you work the North Node, learn new ways of doing things, and then evolve your South Node function by integrating these new ways into your old ways of doing the South Node. The end result is the entire structure, Soul and personality, evolve. We can't really separate our internal Venus functions from our Mars functions, from our Moon functions, from our Saturn functions. We are complex beings that have all of these inner drives, desires, motivations, orientations. In reality they are all mixed together within us. We use astrology to gain objectivity by assigning this function to this planet and that function to that planet, but past a certain point those are constructs, not complete reality. In reality we are the sum total of all of them, and that includes our past and future also. EVERYTHING has something to do with the past. The imprint of the past is contained within the present Venus and every other planet too. (Steve)

Inner hearing

The issue of pre-existing needs relative to Venus: Venus in reference to the 2nd house correlates to one's survival issues. The second house is a fixed energy momentum. Inner Venus, correlating to the 2nd house archetype, corresponds to the psychology of inner hearing. Put this together and you have the psychology of inner hearing relative to how one is resonating inwardly with survival issues that have become fixed or rooted within one's consciousness or inner hearing. Note also that the archetype of the 2nd house is opposed by the fixed 8th house: this sign/house polarity suggests resonating with that which is rooted or embedded in the (pre-existing and evolving) psychology of the Soul. That which pre-exists also energizes the principle of magnetic attractions of resources – that which one has (previously) evaluated is essential to survival – at all the levels – emotional, psychological, biological, physical, material, and spiritual. The planetary nodes, etc. fill in the rest of the story. (Rose)

Voyeurism

Vicariousness is a reflection of laziness. And laziness correlates with Taurus. Thus, vicarious relationships leading to things like voyeurism. This is also self-evident in the charts of Yoko and Lennon to the extreme point of both of them creating a voyeurism for the world, Lennon's Uranus in Taurus in his 2nd, ruled by his Moon is Aquarius in his 10th. They literally invited the world into their bedroom. Yoko has her Vesta and Chiron in Taurus in her 8th, ruled by her Venus in Aquarius in her 5th, which of course is John's Moon. So the 'bed in' they both created lead to a form of world voyeurism. (Rad)

Life purpose

Every Soul, relative to its evolutionary conditions, has a true life purpose that is consistent with its ongoing evolutionary needs. The entire paradigm of the 10th, Saturn, Capricorn, 2nd, Taurus, Venus, the 6th, Mercury, and Virgo correlate to life purpose as expressed through the agency of one's work, or career. When the Soul begins to evolve into the Spiritual State then the Soul is inwardly and progressively attuned to the consciousness we call the Source, or God/ess. As such, these Souls will desire to do work that they feel inwardly called to do from that Source. The inner degree of awareness, evolution, within the Spiritual stage will correspond to not only the nature of what that is, but also that the nature of that work in every way is being consciously directed by that Source. The Souls who have reached the point in evolution in which the center of gravity has finally shifted from the subjective ego that the Soul creates to the Soul itself. At that point there no longer is any 'personal identification' with that work other than consciously cooperating with the inner directions from the Source to do that work. (Rad)

Venus transit

Venus through transit reflects the ongoing evolution of our inner relationship with ourselves, and our outer relationships. The awareness of new and changing needs occurs through Venus transits. The transits of Venus also reflect the specific inner and outer relationship patterns we are working on at that moment in time relative to the house and sign it occupies in our natal chart. We can simply "outgrow" a current relationship we are in ("I do not feel I need this anymore"), or feel that it has reached a natural point of separation (no more growth is occurring for either person). We have all experienced times in our lives when we have exhausted the specific needs that were the basis of a relationship, and become aware of deeper aspects of ourselves that now need to be nourished, or nurtured, so to speak. In my view, it reflects that we are deepening our inner relationship with ourselves and this growth creates a natural evolution of our needs within relationships. We must then make the necessary inner and our changes in our life to accommodate these changing needs. In general, Venus transits to the outer planets such as Jupiter, Uranus, Saturn, and Pluto will induce the deepest levels of change relative to the dynamics already described. (Deva)

Music

Music is a Venus/Neptune archetype. (Rad)

GEMINI – MERCURY – 3rd HOUSE

Gemini keywords

Communication	Scattered	Short-term memory	Instability
Learning	Superficial	Fluctuating viewpoint	Ever changing
Writing	Literal	Rationalization	Teacher
Speaking	Cynic	Siblings / Twins	Scribe
Thinking / Left Brain	Liar / Lies	Relatives	Short journeys
Information	Trickster	Logic	Trader / Merchant
Duality	Opinion	Intellectual doubt	

Gemini, Mercury, 3rd house archetype

Yang / mutable / air / rules 3rd house / ruler is Mercury. The world of appearances, shapes, and form simply is – it just exists. A desk doesn't call itself a desk. Desk is a label, a symbol that we humans attach to the object so we can classify, identify, and categorize it, and distinguish it from all other objects, names, and forms. The function of Gemini/Mercury is to give names and classifications to that which is, to create an intellectual system of organization that allows us to logically order things. Gemini relates to our need to know the physical laws of our world so we can understand how it works. This is tied to our need for security. Naming and classifying things helps us to explain the nature of Creation. Out of this logical organization we are then able to communicate what we have found to ourselves, through our inner thinking process, and to others. Gemini being a male sign, the energy flows out from the center with no inherent limits. The inherent desire is to know as much as possible, intellectually, to understand the nature of life through the brain. This can be pictured as series of progressively expanding concentric circles. Gemini/Mercury represents the left brain functions.

The natural polarity to the 3rd house (Gemini/Mercury) is the 9th house (Sagittarius/Jupiter), representing the right brain. Sagittarius represents Truth and Natural Law; Gemini represents our opinions about those truths. Gemini is subjective, personal. We take in our overall view about what is true in life for each of us through Jupiter/Sagittarius, and create names, classifications, and opinions about those truths through Gemini/Mercury. The sign on the 3rd house, the location of the planetary ruler of that sign and the aspects that it makes to other planets, the house and sign that Mercury is in and the aspects it makes to other planets correlate to the nature of your thought within yourself and how you communicate your thoughts. Gemini allows us to communicate the values and meanings we have developed from our 2nd house experiences. They also correlate to the type of mental structure the Soul intends for this life. (JWG's Pluto Vol. 1 and the School's Course)

[Recommended Reading: Jeffrey Wolf Green's Pluto Vol. 1 – The Evolutionary Journey of the Soul]

Pluto in the 3rd house or Gemini

People with Pluto in the 3rd house have had a past life emphasis on developing mind and intellect. They have been busy collecting information, facts, and data. They have defined themselves through attempting to understand their relationship within the scheme of things. These people have desired to experience many circumstances and situations. Their intellectual curiosity has allowed them to build on who they thought they were and who they think they are now. There is a desire to accumulate endless facts and information about the world in an attempt to rationally explain their relationship to the environment. The past desire has not been to understand the deeper meaning of the collected facts but upon facts that are verifiable through the senses.

The emotional security of 3rd house Pluto people is tied to their ability to logically order their environment and their relationship to their environment. They know themselves through their environment. There is a built-in paradox in this approach. On one hand, there is a ceaseless desire to collect more information. On the other, there is a desire for emotional security based on having an intellectual construct of the ordering of reality. The problem is that the new information being taken in inevitably leads to an undermining of the intellectual constructs that the security has been based on. They learn that the intellectual reality that they have constructed their emotional reality upon is limited. New facts have appeared that point out the shortcomings in the constructs. They must be reformulated. This causes an emotional crisis over loss of security. However, Gemini is a mutable sign, which means that change is relatively easy. The extent of the crisis depends on the extent to which the person has identified with the constructs that are now being shown as limited and needing revision. These crises occur when no more evolutionary growth is possible within the confines of the currently accepted intellectual constructs.

These people have a deep restlessness due to their need to continually take in new information. They need relationships with others to process themselves, to release the build-up of mental energy. They also take in new information from their interactions with others. Through these interactions they have a constant need to adjust their ideas, which requires more and more facts to explain everything in ever-greater detail. They feel they will never know enough facts. Too many facts that logically collect in too many inter-related ways means there is no holistic way to tie everything together. They can feel there is no center through which they can create a composite picture. Everything will be seen as being relative. The center is always moving. They seek to find one fact that they can call their own. Yet all of this is necessary. The center IS the movement itself. The movement is needed to eliminate the intellectual limits that appear as they attempt to hold onto a perspective in an attempt to feel secure. The cycles of intellectual expansion and then the meltdowns as the sense of security dissolves when new facts undermine the constructs are required to lead the Soul to the realization that there is only so much that the mind can ever know. (JWG's Pluto Vol. 1 and the School's Course)

Pluto polarity point – 9th house or Sagittarius

The intent is to develop the right brain and intuitive nature. The left brain intellectual nature is already highly developed, from past life activities. They need to learn the deeper meaning of the facts that they have been collecting – the universal laws that lie behind and beneath outer reality. The 9th house relates to the Natural Laws through which Creation has been created, the underlying truths. It is only through this understanding, and intuitive thinking, that they will come to the composite and holistic view that they have been seeking through the endless fact collecting. In order to learn how to do that, they need to learn how to quiet their minds. The best way for most to do that is to align with one philosophical or metaphysical system that they connect with on a gut level. There is an issue here in remembering the relativity of all things; that one's preferred philosophical system is not inherently THE way, THE answer, for all, but merely for that one person, that all truths are relative, and relevant and necessary for those who believe them. Until that point, these people can be argumentative, attempting to convince. Or, not truly listening to another, waiting merely for a moment in the conversation where they can again make their own points. They need to learn to determine the truths in life that are relevant to THEM, and then to discriminate when taking in information, taking in only that which is relevant to what they are intuitively drawn to. When they learn the 9th house lessons, they will have natural communicative gifts that can affect and transform other people's intellectual constructs through their interactions with those people. They will have mastered the ideas of what is true and what is opinion. They will be able to relate random facts to the central common principle between them. They can penetrate to the bottom essence of any issue that is raised. Common characteristics: deep, penetrating mind, intelligent, curious with a need to control the direction of the curiosity, recognize the weak link in arguments, can uncover facts, logical yet defensive when other's ideas threaten their own intellectual order. (JWG's Pluto Vol. 1 and the School's Course)

Mercury retrograde

Mercury Rx actually points to the Jupiter function (right brain leading the left brain). (Deva)

Mercury, when going retrograde, for a period of time in the Soul's life, GENERALLY means focusing on information that the Soul is interested in, and no more. (Rad)

Hearing

The anatomy of the ears, hearing, is Mercury. The psychology of hearing is Venus. Visuals are a manifestation of thought complexes within the brain. The thought complexes themselves are Uranian and Mercurial, and the visuals of thought complexes are the archetypes of Neptune/Moon/and Pluto. (Rad)

Data, observation and correlation

The right brain is said to be intuitive/conceptual/abstract, and the left brain is said to be linear, rational, and empirical. Astrologically this would be the difference, again, between Sagittarius and Gemini. That which manifests through the right brain is that part in all of us which is plugged into the totality of manifested creation. The manifested or projected creation is Uranus. The plug in the socket, so to speak, is Jupiter. Jupiter intuits, and makes consciously available to the individual, the projected creation of Uranus. The intuitions of Jupiter translate into abstract or conceptual thought involving principles. Mercury is plugged into Uranus by way of Jupiter. Mercury translates into linear or applied thought that is specific and reflective of the nature of each individual. Thus, Uranus projects through Jupiter to the existing channels of Mercury in order to make new connections; thoughts. (JWG)

(Q) If I am looking at a bird making certain sounds before a storm, the observation of the phenomena itself is **Aquarius**, the correlation to *what* those sounds mean implies a synthesis of various observed data, which is **Sagittarius**. The data itself that I am observing and synthesizing implies classifications and names that I have associated with that phenomenal reality, which is **Gemini**. (Ari)
(A) Yes (Rad)

Uranus also correlates, in complete detail, to all the memories of this and other lives. This is why it is called the higher octave of Mercury. Most of us can't remember in explicit detail what we did two days ago. So my question is, where do all these memories go? Mercury correlates to what you can consciously recall in the form of memories, or that which you have learned or been taught. But Uranus correlates to all the memories and knowledge that have ever come before; that which you can not necessarily recall consciously. (JWG)

(Q) Is it true to say that observation (Aquarius) does not depend on mental classifications (Gemini)? In other words, can creation be observed without any mental constructs being associated with that observed creation?
(A) Sure (Rad)

How a planet, eg Mercury, manifests in each evolutionary stage – by Gonzalo Romero
[The examples are just examples, and don't intend to be exhaustive or comprehensive of all possible manifestations. This methodology can be further refined.]
First, we know the evolutionary stages are conditioned by archetypes. Consensus is conditioned by Saturn, Individuated is conditioned by Uranus, and Spiritual is conditioned by Neptune. That is, Capricorn, Aquarius, and Pisces within the natural zodiac. We just have to apply this to each archetype, first in general terms, let's say, Mercury, and then in an individual case, let's say Mercury in the 2nd house Virgo. In general terms, each archetype, eg Mercury, is conditioned in each evolutionary stage by Saturn/Capricorn, Uranus/Aquarius, and Neptune/Pisces.
Thus, within Consensus, Mercury is conditioned by the relationships within the zodiac of Gemini with Capricorn. Further, it is conditioned by the relationship between Virgo and Capricorn. Within the zodiac, an inherent inconjunct exists between Gemini and Capricorn. Very simply, this aspect reflects that, within Consensus, the thought and language forms are required to adjust – inconjunct – to the prevailing intellectual orientations defining the consensus of society. If the individual's thought forms fail to adjust to such requirement, a crisis – inconjunct – will be delivered upon the individual, a crisis of validation of these thought orientations, etc. At the same time, thought forms that are validated by Consensus, and that support Consensus, will be integrated within social functioning. Thus, the thought forms at this evolutionary stage need to support, be submissive, and serve, or be an extension of the intellectual constructions of Consensus – Virgo trine Capricorn. The individual thought orientation is expected to serve established authority from a position of inferiority, and if such position is assumed, the though forms of the individual will be accepted, validated and supported by social authority.
Now the same Mercury within the Individuated state. A natural trine exists between Gemini and Aquarius. Here we can see the tremendous development of neuronal connections required for people to start thinking in their own, personal ways, ie beyond Consensus, and the role within Individuation of transcultural thought forms, revolutionary ideologies, etc. Further, we can see the role of group associations with like-minded individuals that will support and encourage the emerging thought forms that allow the separation from Consensus, and then becoming a minority. With Virgo being inconjunct Aquarius, the thought forms intend to change society or to help society improve or become better, and the individual will experience diverse crises of alienation, exclusion, or persecution, because the new thought forms are at odds with Consensus.
Within the Spiritual state, that Gemini is square Pisces. Thus, an inherent crisis in consciousness/action because the individual desires to know the Whole, not just a part, the individual wants to experience the Unknown, instead of dealing with the known, and wants to relate to the unconditioned, absolute and timeless, instead of referring to the relative, time/space conditioned reality. Thus, the desire to de-condition thought forms, and define new thought forms that reflect the new purpose at the intellectual level. With Virgo being naturally opposite Pisces, the intellect is humbled because of the Soul's desire to know the Unknown, and because of the dynamic of contrast and comparison (opposition) with something so much larger. The individual will desire and need to define – Gemini square Pisces – new thought forms that serve to relate to a reality that is perceived in a new way, and that are adequate to be of service to the Source.
These are general archetypes that condition the Mercury function at each stage. Then we apply the archetypes to the individual Mercury in the birth chart, ie Mercury in 2nd house Virgo, keeping in mind the general archetypes.
Within Consensus, the trine between Virgo and Capricorn correlates with thought forms that intend to serve society in society's terms, or that are submissive to authority, or that are approved or validated by authority, etc. The natural trine between 2nd house and 10th house correlates to thought forms that support Consensus value associations, and that serve Consensus to survive, and to expand. These thought orientations will allow the individual to make money in an easy way (this is a possibility among others). In some cases, if the individual at this stage is more focused on serving society and helping society to survive, versus its own self-

interest, some individuals with Mercury in Virgo in the 2nd may be able to only survive, or not to survive, through their intellectual function. We can see this as a manifestation of the trine between Virgo and Capricorn, and further, as a manifestation of the Gemini/Capricorn inconjunct: groups in power are not interested in the survival of all society, but instead are merely concerned in their own self-interest. Thus, the helping professions within Consensus don't make much money unless they also serve wealthy people to become more wealthy, or sustain the existing power structures or ideologies. As an example, we can see the difference between the authoritative role of a medical doctor within the health system, versus the role of a nursing assistant which is more focused on providing regular care.

Within Individuated, the intellectual isolation will first create crisis (2nd house square 11th house, Virgo inconjunct Aquarius) because the individual will tend to be slow to change its way of thinking. Duplicity, if it exists, will be exposed. Further along the road, isolation will serve the individual to define thought forms that are highly personal and highly elaborate in nature, which embrace increasing connections with overall reality, even if this will be occurring from a personal point of view. Thus, a very systematic and consistent approach to understanding reality, which, though, will be difficult to integrate socially, or beyond the scope of like-minded Souls. In some cases, the individual's intellectual orientation will evolve through independent thinking, ie withdrawing almost totally from social interaction. In other cases, the individual will indeed develop deep intellectual connections with groups of like-minded individuals (the 2nd house/11th house square, and the Gemini/Aquarius trine). The ideas of the individual may serve to support or define the intellectual framework of groups rebelling against Consensus. Crises in survival or sustainment can also occur because of intellectual isolation. Also, because the individual can be perceived by Consensus as an embodiment of revolutionary ideas which threaten the existing order (the 2nd house/11th house square, and the 2nd house/10th house trine).

Within the Spiritual state, the 2nd house sextile to the 12th house, and the Virgo/Pisces opposition, in relation with the Gemini/Pisces square, reflects a crisis in intellectual organization because of a transition between perception of the conditioned and the unconditioned. This impacts in how the individual relates to self, other people, and overall reality. This can be seen in Mercury being Mercury in the 2nd house Virgo, but also reflects the interface between the last quarter sextile, versus the crescent phase sextile, both between Gemini and Pisces. On the one hand, a need to withdraw from interaction in order to discover from within the new thought forms reflecting new value associations rooted in progressive perception of the Spiritual. On the other hand, the need to have this new orientation applied through new roles at a social level. (Gonzalo)

Mercury and Jupiter correlations

An opinion is a specific idea, ideas correlating with Mercury, Gemini, and the 3rd house, that reflects an interpretation of any given phenomena. A cosmology is a combination of many ideas that, when combined, create an entire system of beliefs (Jupiter, Sagittarius, and the 9th house). (Rad)

Crisis of belief, waning square Mercury/Jupiter

The crisis of belief or crisis in consciousness would correlate to the fact that the Soul has already learned a variety of ways to philosophically and intellectually understand its reality. It has created a great philosophical and intellectual system that has been put together by empirical facts that have been learned over many lifetimes. And it has done so in order to actualize the underlying evolutionary intentions, whatever they have been. The Soul at this evolutionary juncture has now reached a place in its evolution that those existing intellectual and philosophical ways of understanding its overall reality are breaking down, and losing their meaning. Thus, all the existing ideas, Mercury, that have served as an empirical way of organizing its reality leading to the Soul's philosophical way of understanding life, must now begin the process of dissolving. This then creates the crisis of belief, or crisis in consciousness. (Rad)

Mercury/Jupiter – balsamic conjunction

The balsamic conjunction of Mercury/Jupiter means that the Soul is in the evolutionary process of culminating all kinds of beliefs, and the ideas from those beliefs, that it has used in understanding the nature of its lives until now: this life. (Rad)

Mercury/Jupiter – new phase conjunction

The new phase of the two planets correlates with the beginning of a new evolutionary cycle of development wherein the Soul is desiring to expand upon its existing knowledge and/or beliefs about life itself, and the new ideas it will be attracted to for that purpose. (Rad)

Beliefs – unconscious, fragmented, disconnected, contradictory

Knowledge that the Soul has been able to assimilate or realize in prior lifetimes will be reflected in the Jupiter natal archetype. Jupiter itself correlates with the Soul desires to expand beyond what the Soul already knows, and beyond the immediacy of circumstances in order to know the truth of anything, including personal truth, the nature of the phenomena themselves, and the nature of the whole truth or 'the Truth' which is the basis of all the rest. The nature of truth itself is non-conceptual. However, aspects of the truth, and aspects of the phenomena themselves, even though not linearly ordered, are not merely 'chaotic.' They manifest 'emergent' patterns which then serve as the basis for the creation of concepts, which can be linearly arranged serving for different types of descriptions. These concepts, arrangements and descriptions are a function of the Mercury archetype. From the point of view of how we can relate to phenomena, or to the nature of truth, perhaps the main intention of these Mercury concepts and descriptions is to direct the 'observer' in some direction allowing to directly experience that which is pointed at through the nature of words. Though, when such direct experience does not occur and the observer does not realize the nature of the phenomena, the left brain thought function can continue to operate within the scope of the linear connections language used in the description: a reflection of the nature of the mind. This can lead to confusion between 'map and territory,' and between the observer and the observed.

Because 'knowledge' provides a relative security for the Soul, the Soul can desire to think it 'knows' that which it does not know. Thus, we have the phenomenon of beliefs, ie the Soul can believe whatever it wants to believe. The dynamic of believing means that whatever belief the Soul has operates within consciousness 'as if' it were real. That which is believed is given the value of an experienced truth. Given that beliefs filter the direct impact of reality, any Soul can have different types of desires that are a reason for any beliefs, and no other, or not just 'not knowing.' In the dynamic of beliefs, the Soul relies on linguistic descriptions. As a simple example, someone can believe, "God is the Father, the Son, and the Holy Spirit." A Christian can believe this, and some 'Christians' have killed other people to defend this 'truth,' even having no direct experience of what such 'dogma' could refer to.

Souls can have many types of beliefs which are formulated in linguistic terms, and which form a system. Souls can learn any belief system from books. Even, if a Soul chooses to consistently apply some Mercury 'instructions' this can lead the Soul to directly realize whatever aspect of reality the instruction points at, beyond the linguistic form itself. Here there's a direct natural connection and collaboration between the Jupiter and Mercury functions, right and left brains.

However, beliefs are not necessarily dependent on Mercury thought forms, and they can be based directly on experience. The nature of Jupiter is inherently experiential. As an example, let's say a Soul experiences abandonment, rejection and abuse during early childhood, which have the effect of inducing intense insecurity for the Soul. This can lead the Soul to 'believe' that life or people in general are dangerous or hostile. Given that early experiences are internalized, the Soul can believe in some cases it deserves rejection and abuse because of something being inherently wrong or evil in its own nature (this could be the case with Jupiter 4th house Scorpio, ruled by Pluto in Virgo conjunct Mars in Virgo being the ruler of the 9th house). These beliefs can at some point become expressed by means of Mercury linguistic propositions. Though, they can also exist as such beliefs without manifesting through words. These types of beliefs as in the example don't necessarily form a 'system.' (Gonzalo)

(Q) Are there unconscious beliefs? (Gonzalo)
(A) Yes. These types of beliefs have been formulated in prior lifetimes which then reside, in most cases, in the individuated unconscious of the Soul: Uranus, Aquarius, and the 11th house. (Rad)

(Q) If beliefs can be unconscious, and further, if we can have beliefs which don't form a system, can a Soul have fragmented beliefs, disconnected beliefs, or contradictory beliefs?
(A) Yes.

In the Jupiter Scorpio example with Jupiter being in the 4th house, the Soul can have a simultaneous unconscious belief that people in general are giving, honest and wise or defined by natural law and that life, as a result, is nurturing and secure. This would originate in prior lifetimes in which the Soul were born through families or mother figures which were defined by these natural orientations. At the same time, these 'disconnected' unconscious beliefs could relate to aspects of the individual personality or psyche (4th house, Scorpio) which have been unintegrated in the past and/or present lifetime, which have created the necessary experiences for integration to occur. In the example, the 'extremes' in these types of experiences that have led to co-existing and unintegrated generalizations of truth, could have manifested in past lives where the Soul embraced belief systems based on duality, such as Manichaeism, implying good and evil, black and white, as definite states instead as evolving states. This could have occurred as a result of alienation (Jupiter) from its own emotional life and its own psychological dynamics, resulting in desires to compensate and/or the creation of polarization and distortions of the self-image. Based on the example, beliefs are conditioned by the types of direct experience the Soul has been attracted to in order to expand or evolve beyond its pre-existing understanding or pre-existing beliefs. Thus, the natal Jupiter archetype (in relation to the evolutionary axis and the overall natal signature) reflects:

* Pre-existing beliefs or understanding, and prior belief systems that have been promoting the Soul's expansion of awareness
* Types of past lives experiences which have directly induced the prior understanding and beliefs
* Types of experiences the Soul will continue to gravitate to in order to learn more about the nature of reality in a way consistent with the Soul intentions to expand its awareness
* Nature of belief systems the Soul can gravitate to in order to promote these lessons.

In an effort to make a clear distinction between Jupiter and Mercury functions: Mercury correlates with the construction of a world of objects through linear arrangement of phenomenal reality from the observer's relative point of view. It correlates with the thought and language forms that result from this linear arrangement or construction. Further, it relates to the types of information the Soul needs to find, by means of such linear arrangements of thought and language and the resulting communication patterns, and how they have occurred in past and present lifetimes. Mercury reflects the impact of information taken from whatever environment-observation, communication, opinions, books, etc. including information and opinions about beliefs, knowledge, the nature of phenomena, and truth. A same proposition or statement could be either an opinion or a belief, depending on how invested the Soul is in such statement. Some Souls seem to simply believe in whatever opinions. An intention of the Mercury archetype would be to create distinctions between what the Soul knows, and what it does not know, and the natal Mercury archetype, in relation with the evolutionary axis and the overall natal signature would reflect the types of information the Soul needs to find in order to feed the Jupiter intention of 'knowing' what it needs to know in order to expand and evolve its understanding. (Gonzalo)

(Q) However, in some cases a Soul could be directed to some types of 'books' based on the natal Jupiter archetype. In the example, the Scorpio Mercury could be attracted to psychological written material in order to promote the intention of psychological/emotional self-knowledge. In such case would the natal Mercury intend to make this intention more specific, ie what type of information within the field of psychology will allow the Soul to understand or learn what it needs to learn? – Where and how it needs to find this type of information? – What type of intellectual approach is needed for this to occur? (Gonzalo)
(A) Yes. For example we could put that Mercury in Scorpio in the 4th house. One of the fields within psychology that such a Soul could be attracted to is called 'emotional anatomy.' (Rad)

Differences/nuances between Pluto 3rd house, Mercury in Scorpio, Scorpio ruling 3rd
The way that the linear mind works, how it is put together, would be the same: Scorpio. The core issue and differences then would be based on the following: With Scorpio on the 3rd house cusp where then is the natal Pluto? What aspects to other planets is it making? With Mercury in Scorpio what natal house is it in? What aspects to other planets is it making? With Pluto in the 3rd house where is the sign Scorpio in the natal chart? And what aspects is that Pluto making to other planets? All of these differences of the various possibilities correlate then to what the actual CONTENT is within that Scorpio linear mind. Within these key differences the underlying issue, from the point of view of Evolutionary Astrology, is what is the evolutionary state of the Soul. Understanding that evolutionary state then is its own determinate of what that content is when we remember that a sign or a house correlates to a total spectrum within each archetype. The underlying evolutionary state of any given Soul then is the determinate of where within that total spectrum of an archetype that the Soul will be orientated to. From the point of view of Evolutionary Astrology it is very important to make these individual determinations for one size does indeed not fit all. The specific nature of the content within the linear mind defined by Scorpio reflects the specific ongoing evolutionary needs of any given Soul. (Rad)

Mercury function of the Soul in human form
(Q) The Mercury function within consciousness provides the individual with an arrangement of the phenomenal world which allows the individual to operate in midst of his/her individual reality in an ordered and linear way. The variety of possible arrangements is almost unlimited, because phenomena can be ordered in many different ways. Further, socialization will induce a relative uniformity among these possible arrangements, so that communication between individuals can be possible. Is the variety of possible arrangements, however, limited or conditioned by some inherent structure of the manifested Creation? (Gonzalo)
(A) The inherent structure here would be the structure of the human body and the consciousness/Soul that inhabits it, and the fact that such human form is then limited by the structure of the earth itself relative to the perception of phenomenal possibilities. On the other hand one of the inherent structures of the manifested creation is the structure of 'consciousness' itself within which exists intelligence: what the great Yogananda called 'lifetrons' which are at the level of sub-atomic particles that permeate the totality of the manifested Creation. It is this underlying fact of the manifested creation that gives rise to the impulse within consciousness now limited by the form that it finds itself in, human/earth, that desires or attempts to transcend the limitations themselves as bound by the time/space continuum of its consciousness/Soul, place of being: inhabiting = earth for us. Thus, the natural relationship between the linear 'mind' or consciousness and the non-linear 'mind' or consciousness that then creates abstractions as consciousness/Soul considers the causative factors for that which is perceived in the essentially phenomenal world of its perceptions. In essence to transcend its perceived limitations caused by the nature of the form that consciousness/intelligence is inhabiting. (Rad)

(Q) Let's say I die, so will not be looking at my desk any longer. Raw idealism of philosophical nature would affirm that my desk would then disappear, because it existed only in my perception. I understand, on the contrary, that my desk will continue to exist and will even look quite similar after my passing, ie will continue to be perceived by my wife and children in a way very similar to how I perceived it, except for some detail perhaps which only I noted. Hence, there is a collective perception which keeps the

common world in place, in which the individual consciousness's interact with the phenomenal reality and provide a shape and order to the phenomena, an order which reflects the nature or structure of this collective subjectivity. OK, so let's now say that all the human beings die in a moment. Will the known human world of things disappear? Would it still exist, though having an utterly different appearance? (Gonzalo)
(A) It would still exist because it existed in the first place. The phenomenal appearance would be the same although if some other life form came along after the fact of the humans not being in the place that it inhabited anymore. This other life form could very well decide within its own consciousness/intelligence the naming of the phenomenal forms, left behind by the disappeared human life form, to be different. So the desk could very well be named something else as this other life form organized its perception of phenomenal reality differently. (Rad)

Maya of phenomenal appearance
(Q) Is there some basic structure, Maya, within the manifested Creation, which conditions the potential ways in which the phenomenal reality can be perceived by sentient beings? Is this structure, Maya (which I thought correlated to Mercury, because of the relation with duality), held in place by some conscious beings such as some type of angels, through some act of 'perception' or rather, of thought? (Gonzalo)
(A) Maya to me correlates with Neptune, Pisces, and the 12th house that is part of the natural mutable cross between Gemini, Virgo, and Sagittarius – Mercury, Neptune, Jupiter, where Maya is understood as the illusion of the phenomenal appearance, even though the illusions of phenomenal appearance if 'real' in the sense that it does exist yet this existence is only a 'symptom' of the Cause of the phenomenal appearance in the first place. And this phenomenal appearance of the manifested Creation is then 'perceived' differently relative to the specific nature of the forms through which consciousness/intelligence/Soul manifests, the very nature of the form by which the nature of the form itself is the causative factor in how the phenomenal appearance is perceived. (Rad)

Natural limit to the perception of the totality of the manifested Creation
(Q) Would this imply that the final return of the manifested Creation into the Creator will occur only once all the individual sentient beings return to the Source, a point where the manifested Creation would become an empty place, so to speak, where the final act of return would be the moment in which these 'angels' stop holding the Creation with their thought, and then withdraw into God themselves? (Gonzalo)
(A) Essentially yes, but here again lies the natural limit to the perception of the totality of the manifested Creation, ie what is the CAUSE OF GOD? – AND WHAT IS THAT CAUSE? – and so on. This is why the 'big bang' theory is so utterly ridiculous, as in the perceived universe is continuing to 'expand' – really? – into what? – and what is it expanding into? – what is that? – and when it retracts itself, into what? – where is that exactly? – and what is that extraction point within? – what is the within? And so forth. The limit of consciousness/intelligence/Soul in human form CANNOT KNOW. So what does that then mean in terms of the actual totality of the consciousness that we want to call 'god?' (Rad)

Is the thought function a creative act?
(Q) Another related question concerns the role of Mercury within individual consciousness. I had the insight that I had created for myself the deep need to really 'think' about the reasons of my frustration and rage, in order to linearly 'create' a 'net,' allowing to contain this frustration and rage, in order to avoid causing damage to my family (my Mars/Mercury/Moon conjunction). The feeling was of literally weaving a net that would hold the anger. The questions are: is the thought function a 'creative' act, ie are we, when thinking, creating things which didn't exist before the thinking? Are we co-creators of Maya? (Gonzalo)
(A) Yes, and yes. And yet by the nature of the form the consciousness/intelligence/Soul is in here: human form. It then becomes 'predictable,' because of the nature of the form, that the natural thought functions of that form are universal to the form itself. And we are co-creators of Maya only because 'we' are all manifestations of the original source of Maya: what we call god. (Rad)

Disillusionment and doubt, a personal experience

(Q) I have been undergoing massive disillusionment within my own spiritual life and within my relationship to Spirit itself. I have noticed as a reaction to this, I have become extremely cautious and guarded about interpreting *anything* in directly spiritual terms anymore. It is as JWG frequently said, disillusionment can be one of the most bitter and difficult experiences that any of us can have, and I can say from direct experience that this is UTTERLY true. And because that experience is so hard and so painful, the last thing I personally want to do – and I'm sure the same is often true for others – is delude myself again and walk right back into it. This also connects to the Virgo archetype: transition. In my own case, I recognize that I am manifesting an extreme response to the disillusionment that has had to occur in myself – and one of the serious, unfortunate effects is that it has cut me off from my own lifeblood. That is something I just have to work out for myself, I know. But I do have this question correlating to disillusionment and doubt. How does one go through massive disillusionment and not get caught up in the debilitating psychology of doubt? If something has been regarded in one's heart of hearts as 'real' – and that something has also been providing the basis for ultimate meaning – it is a complete shock to consciousness when the illusions are exposed and the meaning within it is finally seen as an embellishment of one's own making. So the question becomes, how does one recover one's confidence in interpreting spiritual reality, ie what is a real manifestation of Spirit vs what is imagined or 'hoped,' following a major disillusioning of consciousness? – particularly when there is no immediate resource available to confirm or clarify the accuracy of one's interpretation? (Stacie)

(A) The actual archetype that specifically correlates with being disillusioned is Neptune, Pisces, 12th house, that can then trigger its natural polarity of the Virgo, 6th house, and Mercury that manifests as doubt. With Neptune now transiting Pisces, and it has been squaring the transiting nodal axis that was in Gemini/Sagittarius, this experience of disillusionment leading to doubt has been happening to many, many people. And necessarily so because the intention with Neptune in Pisces is to know or learn about that which is true, and that which is not. While those transiting Nodes were in Gemini/Sagittarius this then focuses on the difference between beliefs that are projected as ultimate meaning, that which is true from the point of view of pure beliefs, and that which is true from the point of view of INNER KNOWING. Inner knowing does not correlate with beliefs because what is known is experienced within the interior of the Soul itself as a by-product of desire to know that which is true, and that which is not. Inner knowing of that which is universally true occurs of course through various practices, Virgo, that are all aimed and shallowing or stopping the breath. As that occurs the Soul is then able to penetrate the inner realms of consciousness itself: Neptune correlates with the phenomena of consciousness. As it progressively penetrates these inner realms of consciousness a variety of natural truths that correlate with the nature and cause of consciousness itself become KNOWN. And this knowing, again, is not a function of beliefs because, as these inner truths are known, there is nothing to literally believe and everything to know. And because these inner truths are simply known there then becomes nothing to doubt. The knowing is a function of actual experience, and those experiences are universal to any Soul who so desires to know these inner truths that correlate with the nature of consciousness. Because they are in fact universal it then serves as a way of knowing that which is true, versus that which is make-believe.

When this is the baseline within the Soul's consciousness, the point of personal Soul knowing and integration, this then serves as the vehicle through which, and because of, the Soul then 'interprets' the nature of any given phenomenal reality. The dynamic or archetype of interpretation specially correlates to Sagittarius, Jupiter, and the 9th house. As the Soul interprets the nature of any external phenomenal reality relative to this inner baseline the MEANING of whatever external phenomenal reality is then projected upon that phenomenal reality. As the Soul does this it will then automatically create a way of intellectually organizing all of phenomenal reality that reflects the core inner baseline of the inner knowing of the nature of consciousness itself. This natural process of intellectually organizing phenomenal reality correlates to Gemini: how the nature of thoughts that occur as a function of the inner knowing are connected to create a larger whole that is organized. All of this then correlates to the nature of various 'spiritual' cosmologies that humans have manifested going back to its own origins on this Earth that are then called 'religions.' This is then exactly where the conflict between pure beliefs versus actual knowing can occur because many who do desire to know the Origin of all things, the Origin of consciousness itself, indeed the Origin of themselves, align themselves with whatever spiritual cosmology without actually doing what is necessary to know for themselves that which is true.

Thus, by attaching themselves to whatever cosmology then leads to their personal belief system that is of course used to interpret whatever phenomenal reality. When a Soul does this, without actually doing that which is necessary to inwardly know, these beliefs are then projected upon phenomenal reality so that when phenomenal reality manifests in ways that cause conflict with the projected beliefs the result is then doubt: doubting the nature of the projected beliefs themselves that have been born, again, from whatever spiritual cosmology they have latched onto relative to the pure desire to Know. This conflict caused by projected beliefs initially creates the disillusionment of those beliefs that then triggers the doubt. It should be said too that a Soul who does not do their own actual inner knowing but simply latches onto whatever spiritual cosmology can also create 'beliefs' about themselves and/or others that are also delusional or illusionary. Thus, when certain types of inner or outer events take place that defeat those projected inner beliefs about themselves or others that same experience of being disillusioned takes place that then leads to doubt: doubt about oneself, or doubt about another(s). In essence this correlates to self-deception, and/ or being deceived by others.

To recover one's confidence in interpreting phenomenal reality, or as you say 'spiritual' reality, is to go deeply within the interior of one's own consciousness with the pure desire to KNOW. To know the actual truth of anything. To do so always starts with some sort of natural practice that aims at stilling the breath, of shallowing it to the point that it NATURALLY STOPS. If one does this while at the same time holding the nature of whatever one is wanting to know about within their consciousness there will come a moment, a time, in which the answer simply OCCURS WITHIN CONSCIOUSNESS OF ITS OWN VOLITION: like a bubble manifesting from the depths of the sea onto the surface of the sea itself. And a Soul can do this repeatedly in such a way that the truth of what one is wanting to know about can be repeated as many times as the Soul needs it to be repeated so that the lingering doubt simply dissolves. The point here is that if that which is true relative to what one is asking about is indeed true it will repeat itself over and over for as many times that the Soul needs it to. In this way confidence is regained. (Rad)

Information/knowledge/beliefs from life to life

(Q) Any Soul can read the same spiritual books many times, life after life. This doesn't mean the spiritual knowledge contained in the books is realized, until it is realized, ie assimilated. After each life ends, the Soul forgets the knowledge forms contained in these books. Later, the Soul desires will lead the Soul to the same types of books in a next lifetime. These knowledge forms are Mercury. Once they are assimilated, they become Jupiter, and the Soul will not need to read these books again, because they are already part of what the Soul knows. Is this correct? (Gonzalo)

(A) Yes. But also remember that Jupiter correlates with the nature of 'beliefs' in any given life, and Mercury will correlate to the information taken in to not only create beliefs, but to reinforce those beliefs. Of course what one 'believes' does not necessarily correlate with what is actually true from the point of view of all the Natural Laws and truths reflected in those laws as set in motion by the Creator Of All Things. Humans can literally make themselves 'believe' anything which, to me, is one of the greatest problems human beings have. Many people 'believe' that the Earth is less than 10,000 years old and that humans co-mingled with the dinosaurs for example. And that belief then correlates to what is 'true' for them even though it is not actually true. This is why the 12th house naturally squares the 9th house: the necessity of a Soul to be disillusioned from anything that is not actually true which then leads, at some point to that which is true. So the Soul in fact can carry forwards into future lives the nature of 'beliefs' and the information necessary that 'informs' those beliefs. In terms of a Soul 'knowing' that which is true, realizing that from within, that knowing of that truth(s) will in fact be carried forwards as you have rightly stated. (Rad)

(Q) Is it possible for a Soul to remember knowledge forms or 'information' from prior lifetimes which, though, have not been assimilated? Can Uranus/Mercury memory contain un-integrated knowledge forms of intellectual nature, ie Mercury, from past lifetimes?

(A) No.

(Q) Will you clarify this Rad? I would expect that since Mercury is detailed information and Uranus symbolizes the long-term memories of the Soul, that there would be the possibility for such a recall when these archetypes are synthesized either natally or by transit, ie remembering how to identify various things that were never learned about in this life, the nature of such things just being empty information. For example, the ability to identify certain herbs that one may have learned to identity in a past life based on physical characteristics which implies observation of empirical data (Mercury) but not necessarily the intuitive holistic understanding of the herbs (Jupiter). (Ari)

(A) If that information about the herb had been internally integrated and used on oneself or others that information could be remembered: sustained. Conversely, if that information about the herb had simply been read about, or heard through word of mouth, without actually being internally integrated and/or used on oneself or others, then it will not be retained.

CANCER – MOON – 4th HOUSE

Cancer keywords

Ego	Security	Inner	Emotions
Womb	Protection	Nurturing	Self-image
Childhood Environment	Mother	Protection	Touchy
Children	Family	Neglect	Subjective
Home	Clan	Helpless	Gender Roles
Roots	Ancestors	Needs	Housewife/husband

Cancer, Moon, 4th house archetype

Water / yin / cardinal / 4th house / ruled by the Moon. Cancer represents the Ego. In Aries I experienced my instinctive, becoming nature. In Taurus I developed my values and sense of meaning. In Gemini I learned about and classified the outer reality within which I function. And in Cancer I give myself personal form, name, and identity – who I am, and how I think. I acknowledge myself as distinct from all other beings. I become consciously aware of myself as a subjective self. THIS is who I am. An Ego is necessary. An Ego is a vortex of energy within consciousness, the lens in the projector through which the movie of the Soul can be seen. The point is not to LOSE one's ego, but rather to re-identify one's ego. Most of us are almost completely identified with Who I Am as a separate and unique ego that has a name and a form; that was born and will die. The goal of evolution, over great lengths of time, is to cause us to re-identify Who I Am with the CAUSE of the Ego, with that which created the ego in the first place – the Soul, rather than with the Ego itself. The ego is self-image – how we see ourselves inwardly, not how others see us. That is related to the Ascendant and the Descendant.

The 4th house is naturally square to both the 1st house – Aries – and the 7th house – Libra. Libra represents extremes, and in Aries we have the extreme of the Ego identifying itself as a separate being, with no connection to any other being. This can cause the ego, through Mars, to dominate and to impose its will on others. The sign on the 4th house, the planetary ruler of the 4th house, the location of Cancer and the aspects it makes, the location of the Moon and the aspects it makes point out the structure of the personality and self-image, and the nature of the emotional dynamics. The Moon correlates to the nature of our early childhood environment and parental conditions, which the child imprints wholesale. This thoroughly shapes the sense of self. The evolutionary issue becomes, "Why did the Soul pick that environment? What were the evolutionary necessities it was attempting to deal with?" The Moon connects to emotional reality. Feelings are a Venus function. They are the immediate reaction to existing stimulus. Emotions are a reaction to our feelings. How often do we react in a less than ideal way to something that triggers us, even though our feelings and our beliefs can understand and even agree with what has happened. Yet our emotions are our reaction to those feelings. Cancer represents our need for security, particularly the security of home and family. Yet its ultimate teaching is that the only true security is within us, in our relationship to God or the Cosmos, not to anything external. Everything in our society teaches us that security is outside of my self, in things and in others. Yet ultimately everything outside of myself can and probably will be eventually removed from my life. Over-identification with anything external tends to lead to a life crisis in which it is suddenly removed from my life. The point of this is to remind me that the only real security is internal. You can determine a person's ability to adapt to change by looking at the sign on the 4th house, and the house and sign that the Moon is in. If you see mostly fixed signs (Taurus, Leo, Scorpio, Aquarius), the person may have a problem adapting to change. (JWG's Pluto Vol. 1 and the School's Course) [Recommended Reading: Jeffrey Wolf Green's Pluto Vol. 1 – The Evolutionary Journey of the Soul]

Pluto in the 4th house or Cancer

As a cardinal sign, it indicates that a new cycle is beginning (as do Aries, Libra, and Capricorn). The lesson here has been learning that security is internal and not found in parents, job, lover, home, etc. They have been learning how to create their own emotional security from within. Since this is a new cycle, most of them have not yet finished learning this lesson. So most are born into difficult family situations. One or both parents do not give the child what any child needs. Thus their emotional needs are unfulfilled. This forces the child back in on its own self, and they realize early on that they are going to have to learn to fulfill their own needs or those needs are not going to be fulfilled. Because of the nature of the Moon and the 4th house, these lessons are all within the emotional structure of the child. This is a very difficult environment for a child. Most of these people have had a series of past lives in similar conditions. Often they have prior life unresolved karma with one or both of the parents. They are born with subconscious memories of these prior encounters. Although they are not conscious of them, these past emotional patterns color the interaction between both the parent and the child. They will feel unappreciated, misunderstood, and/or insufficiently nurtured. This situation creates intense emotional needs and intense emotions. They have an unconscious expectation that the parents should meet these needs. The child's experience may be very different than the parent's experience of the same situation.

They arrive with an inherent insecurity, and it creates a situation that no amount of nurturing can ever completely fill their need. Sometimes the parent has a legitimate reason for the situation, such as work requirements, etc. Yet the child does not understand this and only feels that the parent is not meeting its needs. This feeling triggers the past life memories, and they trigger the intense emotional states. In effect, the feelings and emotions the child experiences are not even from the present life experience but are unresolved feelings carried in from the past. This can also manifest in some cases as a parent who totally dominates the child's life and does not allow the child to grow up. The parent is relating only to his or her own emotional needs, not to the child's. Or the parent can be cruel or abusive. The effect is the same – the child is thrown back upon itself as the only way to get its needs met. Because the child cannot generally process these intense emotions, they are often repressed. They appear in adult life as displaced emotions, bursting forth in relationships and romances in situations that trigger the old feelings. In effect they will still be attempting to get their unresolved childhood emotional needs met through others. They project this need, and the expectation that others should fulfill the need, onto others.

In romances they draw partners with psychological make-ups similar to one or both of the parents. The unconscious need is again to resolve the old stuff and have their emotional needs met. Because the nature of the partner is similar to the nature of the parent(s), the needs are still not met, and once again they are thrown back in on themselves. Needless to say, they may not be very happy about this state of affairs, which can have an effect on the relationship. Gradually they begin to understand WHY this keeps happening. They begin to learn how to supply their own emotional needs and internal security. Until then they often attempt to emotionally manipulate others into fulfilling their childlike needs. Some have a deep fear of emotional vulnerability. All have sensitive and touchy emotions. Some resort to stuffing their emotions and living in denial of them to avoid the pain of continual removal of emotional dependencies. Those who have repressed emotions tend to draw people to them whom they can emotionally dominate, typically people in need of some form of emotional healing. They attempt to make themselves indispensable in the person's life, both as a way to create emotional security for themselves, and as a way to feel 'better than' someone else. They can take out the repressed anger and rage they feel towards the parent(s) on the partners or other people in their lives. Through being dominant they maintain their relationship and feel secure. Yet still their deepest needs for nurturing are unfulfilled because the partner is too wounded to fulfill those needs.

All 4th house Pluto people experience a wide range of emotions in an intense way – everything is deeply felt. The moods are often triggered from an external experience. These swings can be as confusing to the person as they are to those who experience them. These intense states are, in fact, necessary, because they lead to self-knowledge and ultimately inner security. If they attempt to understand WHY these things are happening, it can lead to deep understanding of emotional dynamics. They have two distinct emotional cycles. In one they are withdrawn and want to be left alone. In the other they become animated and outwardly directed. The two cycles are inconsistent and can change at any moment. They need people around them who understand that they fluctuate between these two cycles, and that both are necessary. 4th and 10th house Pluto often relates to recent gender switch, in this or a very recent lifetime. Because the gender assignment is so new, many of them feel insecurity in their current gender. It may not feel quite natural. There are many emotional and hormonal differences between being a male and being a female, and the past life thought patterns and emotions would be associated with the other gender. These people are learning to know and trust themselves so they can know and trust others. A few born with 4th house Pluto will already have learned to be inwardly secure and will not be subject to most of these conditions. (JWG's Pluto Vol. 1 and the School's Course)

Pluto polarity point –10th house or Capricorn
The intent here is learning to accept responsibility for one's actions, emotional maturity, how to integrate one's personality into society. These learnings will occur through work and career. Through this they can get out of victim mode and realize that the conditions of their childhood were necessary for their evolution, that even the lack of nurturing from the parental figures was required. Thus, blame will dissolve and there will be a greater acceptance of the larger view of life and evolution. Through establishing them self in the work arena they will gradually gain control over the emotional swings. The moods will still come and go but they will be less extreme. Their emotional empathy for others helps others to understand their own natures. They will be encouraging others to accept responsibility for their own actions and lives, help them minimize their emotional dependencies, and help them to understand the nature of their emotional blocks. Common 4th house Pluto characteristics: emotionally intense and demanding, cycles of depression and optimism, can be emotionally manipulative, insecure, defensive, intensely loyal, need to control their space, easily threatened, potentially cruel mean or vindictive in negative cycles and empathetic, sympathetic, and nurturing in positive cycles. (JWG's Pluto Vol. 1 and the School's Course)

Moon/Cancer archetype – core dynamics

The natal Moon in the birth chart symbolizes the current self-image of the Soul, and the conscious emotional security patterns of the Soul (Pluto is the unconscious emotional security patterns of the Soul). The South Node of the Moon reflects the prior egocentric structure of the Soul, and the North Node symbolizes the evolving egocentric structure of the Soul. The transition from the past to the future, then, is integrated on a consciousness basis by the natal Moon. The Moon represents our inner home, or how we are living within ourselves, on a day to day, minute to minute basis. It also symbolizes our ability to nurture ourselves in the ways that we need. The Moon also symbolizes the anima/animus dynamic within the Soul (or inner male and female), and the ability to integrate both genders within our self over a great length of evolutionary time.

The Moon symbolizes the nature of the early childhood environment, and the nurturing that was (or was not received). If the child was not nurtured in the ways that they needed, then displaced emotions will follow into adult life. The issue of culturally conditioned gender assignments are also critical to understand (Capricorn polarity point). The example that my father uses that helped clarify this issue for me was the woman with an Aries Moon, and the man with a Pisces Moon: both cannot relate to themselves as the traditional "Betty Crocker" or "Marlboro Man" that are presented as the socially accepted ways of behavior for men and women. Yet, we have all been subjected to the wounding judgments from others when we do not conform to these social norms, and conformity then commonly takes place.

That is why the issue of internalizing emotional security is so essential (we can then withstand such judgments) and actualize a natural masculinity and femininity within ourselves. Again, the impact of the early childhood environment is critical to understand because of the effect to the self-image. Was the father a "traditional male," and reinforced the culturally accepted ways of being to his child who could not truly relate to such behavior? What was the mother's ability to nurture her child's unique individuality, and so on? These are core dynamics of the Moon/Cancer archetype. In the natal chart, the Moon by house, sign and aspect will correlate to how these core dynamics are played out, and the specific self-image of the Soul. (Deva)

Coming into human form, the Soul will manifest what is known as the ego. The ego correlates astrologically to the Moon. The ego, too, is pure energy. We cannot open the brain and find it. Unlike the energy of the Soul, which is sustained from life to life until the final merging with The Source occurs, the energy of the ego in any life is dissolved after that physical life ends. The analogy of the wave and the ocean again serves to illustrate this point. The ocean can be equated with the Soul, and the wave can be equated with the ego. Of course the ocean (Soul) is manifesting the waves (ego), life after life. And just as the waves can rise and fall, in any given life that the Soul creates the ocean is sustained. In other words, the egos that the Soul manifests in each life rise from birth, but finally dissolve back into the ocean (Soul) upon the completion of that life. Its energy are not destroyed, but simply absorbed back into the energy that created it in the first place. The ego created by the Soul thus allows for the individualizing aspect of the Soul in each life. (JWG)

Ego as vehicle of evolution

In each life the ego is created by the Soul in such a way as to serve as the vehicle through which the evolutionary intentions of the Soul in that life can occur. Each ego that the Soul creates is oriented to reality in such a way that the very nature of the orientation serves as the vehicle through which the life lessons can occur and be understood by the Soul. In each life, the ego allows for a self-image of the Soul to occur, relative to the individualizing aspect of the Soul. An analogy to a movie projector will illustrate the point. If I have a movie projector loaded with a reel of film, and a screen in front of the projector, and I turn on the machine, generating light from it, I will have no distinct image on the screen unless I also have a lens in the projector. Without the lens, what manifests from the projector is simply diffuse light. Thus the lens serves as a vehicle, through which the images on the film can be focused and given distinct shape and form. In the very same way, the ego that the Soul generates in each life allows for a vehicle, or lens, through which the inherent images that exist with the Soul can take form. This Natural Law of consciousness is thus the cause that allows for individual self-perception and the word "I" itself.

The Soul, Pluto, also correlates to the genetic code – RNA and DNA, chromosomes, and enzymes. In each life the Soul IS THE DETERMINANT FOR THE ENTIRE GENETIC CODE OF THE LIFE, HUMAN FORM, THAT IT IS BEING BORN INTO. Each life that the Soul chooses is a continuation of that which has come before, where each new life taken correlates to the ongoing evolutionary lessons or intentions of that Soul. Thus, the body type, which includes which race to be born into; the appearance of it; the culture to be born into; the parents of origin; the specific and individual nature of the emotions, feelings, psychology, desires; and so on, correlate to the Soul's intentions, reflected in the genetic code in total, in each life. This is all then given individual form in each life via the egocentric structure (Moon) that the Soul creates in that life. Thus any person can then say things like, "this is who I am," "this is what I need," "this is what I am feeling," "this is what I am trying to learn," and so on: the individualizing aspect of the ego that the Soul creates in each life. (JWG)

Wave/ocean analogy

The ego/personality does NOT CREATE ITSELF, NO DIFFERENT THAN A WAVE ON THE OCEAN DOES NOT CREATE ITSELF. The ego/personality in any given life, for any of us, is created by the Soul as a reflection of the Soul's ongoing evolutionary intentions and requirements. The difference, again, is in the center of gravity within the consciousness of any of us. Is that center of gravity in the Soul, or is it in the ego/personality? (Rad)

Like the vast majority of we humans, you [Jana] are looking at this from the perspective that "you" are the ego Jana, and that this Jana is distinct from all the other egos "your Soul" has ever created, and that Jana is also separate from the Soul who created Jana. Reality is who you are has never been Jana the ego. You have always been the Soul who created Jana the ego. Whether you experience that or not, it is still true. We can believe we are separate (and we do) but that doesn't make it so. It's not so much the ego "will identify increasingly more with Soul" as the ego will increasingly realize it never was who it thought it was in the first place, a separate ego. It will see that all along it has always been only the Soul. When the ego Jana identifies as Soul, it will realize it is one and the same as all the other egos that this Soul has ever created. They have all been steps along the way in the evolution of that Soul.

Within that Soul all the memories from every ego/lifetime that Soul has ever experienced are stored. The metaphor of the wave and the ocean explains this. There are many waves on top of the ocean. Each wave separates from the ocean at some point, and ultimately "dies" when it crashes on a beach and rejoins the ocean. Jana believes she is a wave, distinct from all the other waves, when in reality she and all the other waves are only the ocean. The ocean represents the Soul, the waves represent the egos the Souls created. As soon as a wave rejoins the ocean there is no issue of each individual wave having to remember it is the ocean – there is no more wave, only ocean. To match the metaphor, the ocean contains the memory of every wave it has ever created, and all that each wave ever experienced. (Steve)

Familiarity and security

The Moon represents what is known, safe and familiar, what causes us to feel secure. Thus the tendency, down through all those past lives, the emotional nature, Moon, of what has caused us to feel secure. Generally the same from life to life to life with only small changes. That being the root of why we find it difficult to release from the past, to change in the present. Because the past represents feelings of security, as it is KNOWN. Even if what is known is dysfunctional, it is still known, familiar. The present calls us to step into what is NOT known, which tends to feel insecure, not known. (Steve)

Water trinity – Cancer, Scorpio, Pisces

Cancer is one of the archetypes of the subjective ego that the Soul creates in any given life, and is part of the natural trinity of Pisces and Scorpio. In combination these correlate to the evolution of the Soul in general, and how that evolution is reflected in the subjective ego, Cancer, in each life. In the end this is about remembering our origins: God/ess. And, thus, aligning, consciously, our Soul/will with that Origin. In so doing the subjective ego simply reflects that. So it's a matter of aligning our Soul, and the will within it, to the will of the Creator, the origin of the Soul in the first place. (Rad)

Cardinal signs/houses

Cardinal houses are intense because they represent major shifts or turning points – the natural squares-oppositions-conjunctions in the chart. The cardinal signs/houses contain their own paradoxes. Cardinal is an instinctual need to initiate change. Our sense of security is based on sameness, not on change. Thus the very nature of cardinal insures that at certain points we are going to freak out a bit, because all the change we have been instinctually creating results in a loss of familiarity and known–ness. This, at key points, results in the loss of an emotional sense of safety/security, leading to a desire to STOP, to want to go inward to emotionally regroup – to ground and stabilize the new realities we have been initiating. This is an inherent and necessary part of the cardinal archetype. It's especially pronounced in Cancer, but applies to all cardinal signs/houses – two steps forward, one step back. The natural need to regroup and reground after taking two steps into new directions. After a period of timeout, the cardinal instinct to initiate change again takes over, and we are back pursuing the next step forward again. (Steve)

Emotional conditioning – the womb and early childhood development

The Moon, Cancer, 4th house archetype essentially correlates to our self-awareness in the body on a basic emotional level. That is the so-called 'ego.' It is how we emotionally identify ourselves, how we feel as 'me' as a being that knows it exists, and we know that as 'I.' This can never originate from the 'father' simply because it comes out of the womb of a woman, Moon, Cancer, 4th house. In the physical development of the embryo, it already has emotions that are part of the foundation of the 'ego.' The emotional conditioning starts in the womb and creates the basis on which the new baby will develop its emotional relatedness to the 'world' around it including everything and everyone outside of itself. It does not matter who will provide for the baby once it's born – from the point of view of the baby all that matters is if the needs will be met or not. These needs are Moon, Cancer 4th house. HOW those needs will be provided for is 10th house, Saturn, Capricorn, by both parents. (In our world there usually are two, in different ancient times there was no nuclear family nor one particular father figure, rather a group of people, the biological mother was backed up by several so-called 'mother and father' figures who delivered the care all together).

The Moon will always correlate to both the womb and the concrete early life experiences as well as to the mother and the individual emotional perception of itself. Why? Because the separation from the mother's emotions, perceptions, feelings etc. does not happen all at once, there is a period starting at the womb while it is all intermingled. From the baby's point of view the mother is simply 'part of itself,' part of its existence and relative to him/her they are 'one.' The baby feels everything the mother feels etc. etc. so there is no real separation. After birth this separation starts, but it takes a long while until the new born baby goes through the transition of separating itself as an individual being from its mother AND its overall environment. At first it all feels just like 'one,' it all feels like 'itself.' How it 'feels' is always the Moon. The particular birth and the early family environment is the 4th house, and so are the Soul's current life lessons about its own evolutionary self-related or egocentric development and lessons.

Cancer on the other hand wherever it falls in the chart and whatever may fall into it is the indicator of HOW the Soul has been trying to develop these self-related lessons and how it attempted and will still attempt to develop its own egocentric emotional security. Moon will always rule Cancer so we can see the correlation as how any current womb and early childhood environment will set forth the continuation of the ongoing lesson from the point of view of the self as an incarnated emotional being. The only thing that is gender-related is the mother in order to give birth: it has to have a womb for that. But anything else is totally open – for example today there are surrogate mothers who are neither biologically related to nor give any nurturing to the child, yet still there will be a womb experience which will be the foundation of the yet-to-be-born child's emotional conditioning for life. So point being, the polarity, Saturn, Capricorn 10th house will always DEFINE the time and space circumstances (including but not exclusive to the social circumstances), in other words there must always be REALITY SETTINGS within which everything will take place. That reality indeed has been defined for a long time by male figures due to the patriarchal order, ie we usually have an identified father who according to patriarchal tradition was the 'bread winner' etc. etc. But in essence we need to have a setting of reality within which we can exist (or not!) within the world and our mother, family, caretakers etc. are part of that reality in some ways. So these two will always interact and one cannot exist without the other. (Lia)

Displaced emotions

In relation to the emotional dynamics in the Cancer archetype, Jeffrey talked about displacement of emotions as part of this archetype. When we have displaced or disowned parts of our self they show up in our outer world, through other people. Since so much of our ego security self is formed in the current life through mirroring, first with mother, then others, it is important to look at what shows up in one's life as a mirror. For example, if we have disowned an inner child self that feels unloved and forlorn – others will step into our orb and energy field and play out that disowned part back to us – and treat us as if we are unlovable. The personal work then becomes to re-own that vulnerable child self through Cancer nurturing, and through the polarity point of Capricorn, re-parent that part of the self.

It does seem also to be part of this archetype that rather than the displaced emotional neediness that can manifest from unconscious emotions, that healthy containment and mirroring is needed to start to unravel and heal the emotional complex. So finding those 'sources of love' that don't simply replay the unconscious karmic and current life parental dynamics but provide a new model, while pointing one to self-reliance and non-dependency is essential. (Patricia)

Evolution through the emotional body

EA teaches that processing life experiences through the emotional body is evolutionary precisely because it enables the Soul to fully EXPERIENCE whatever experiences are the natural consequence of its desires and choices. If the Soul does not fully EXPERIENCE that which its choices have generated, then it will not truly know in a deep way the consequences of those desires and choices, and will not be able to integrate and learn from these experiences, and thus to make new choices and evolve. Evolution is a natural process of the universe – we can trust it to happen and we do not have to 'make' it happen, so much as let it happen. As Jeffrey taught, the Water Trinity shows involution in that Spirit/Neptune differentiates to Soul/Scorpio differentiates to Ego/Cancer; and also shows that evolution occurs naturally in the natural direction of the zodiac of the shift in conscious identification from Ego/Cancer to Soul/Scorpio to Spirit/Pisces. I find in my work that when people are able to experience their experience through the emotional body (Cancer/Moon), such a full experience naturally eventually leads them (over a period of minutes or lifetimes) to a desire to understand and transform the deeper unconscious patterns and/or Soul history (both Scorpio/Pluto) that has led to the given emotional experience. I don't need to try to push this inquiry in any way, it is the natural result of deeply experienced emotion, it is just what happens when we get out of the way and feel. And then I have also found that when people start to work at this deeper level, then also very naturally begin (again, whether in this lifetime or later) to experience their own encounters with Source (Pisces/Neptune), however this may manifest as appropriate to their perceptual capacities. The water naturally returns to the sea. So to me it is not so much about energy releasing or other particular things as much as it is about having a natural experience that leads to new understanding and choices (and thus new experiences) that eventually exhaust separating desires and leave only the desire to return to Source. In general bypassing the emotional body is essentially resisting evolution, which Souls at any stage in consciousness can do. (Jason)

Practices to work with the emotional body

[Example: Various practices within Dzogchen and Tibetan Buddhism] These practices are not only unnecessary but in fact confuse those who try to practice them. They take what is inherently simple and complicates that. This happens because such practices are not in alignment with Natural Laws: they are essentially invented by individuals who have been conditioned by man-made laws, the patriarchy, that are then trying to harness the Natural Laws in unnatural ways. Personally, I won't have anything to do with them. To me the practices to be used are life itself. To have the knowledge of emotions is simply to experience them within a consciousness that becomes one with whatever emotion is existing relative to a cause that has ignited it in the first place. And, within this, to have a desire, conscious intention, to understand the nature of whatever emotion: its cause, and the reasons for that cause. Within this, the inherent knowledge that then exists in whatever emotion the consciousness becomes one with. Over time of course a state of total self-knowledge defined by the emotional body will take place. A book that came up that appears relevant to all this is "The Spiritual Anatomy of Emotion: How Feelings Link the Brain, the Body, and the Sixth Sense" [Paperback] by Michael (A) Jawer (Author), Marc S. Micozzi (Author), Larry Dossey (Foreword). (Rad)

Spiritual bypass

As I understand it, EA teaches that processing life experiences through the emotional body is evolutionary precisely because it enables the Soul to fully EXPERIENCE whatever experiences are the natural consequence of its desires and choices. If the Soul does not fully EXPERIENCE that which its choices have generated, then it will not truly know in a deep way the consequences of those desires and choices, and will not be able to integrate and learn from these experiences, and thus to make new choices and evolve. In some sense spiritual bypass is a kind of delaying tactic – the Soul resisting coming to terms with the natural consequences of its own desires and choices (though at the ego level this can simply look like a person avoiding painful emotions using Jesus or altered states or "ascension" or whatever). In this way the Soul keeps itself in a kind of evolutionary limbo in that it cannot truly exhaust separating desires since it is ever delayed from truly feeling what those desires have resulted in, and therefore must repeat them (in a sense wilfully failing to learn from history). You can see how this can correlate with skipped steps in some Souls.

Spiritual bypass to me also relates to the control orientation most of us carry and to the lack of trust in natural law that has been learned on this planet. Evolution is a natural process of the universe – we can trust it to happen and we do not have to "make" it happen, so much as let it happen. As Jeffrey taught, the Water Trinity shows involution in that Spirit/Neptune differentiates to Soul/Scorpio differentiates to Ego/Cancer; and also shows that evolution occurs naturally in the natural direction of the zodiac of the shift in conscious identification from Ego/Cancer to Soul/Scorpio to Spirit/Pisces. I find in my work that when people are able to experience their experience through the emotional body (Cancer/Moon), such a full experience naturally eventually leads them (over a period of minutes or lifetimes) to a desire to understand and transform the deeper unconscious patterns and/or Soul history (both Scorpio/Pluto) that has led to the given emotional experience. I don't need to try to push this inquiry in any way, it is the natural result of deeply experienced emotion, it is just what happens when we get out of the way and feel. And then I have also found that when people start to work at this deeper level, then also very naturally begin (again, whether in this lifetime or later) to experience their own encounters with Source (Pisces/Neptune), however this may manifest as appropriate to their perceptual capacities. The water naturally returns to the sea. So to me it is not so much about energy releasing or other particular things as much as it is about having a natural experience that leads to new understanding and choices (and thus new experiences) that eventually exhaust separating desires and leave only the desire to return to Source.

If we stay with the Water Trinity, then spiritual bypassing can be seen as an attempt to "bypass" the emotions (Cancer) and critically the step of self-confrontation and transformation (Scorpio) – after all that is really hard. But of course natural law doesn't work that way and what I would say is actually happening is that the Soul is actually going in the involutionary (clockwise) direction on the wheel, trying to escape to a regressive experience of preconsciousness rather like the womb (Pisces), so as not to feel the pain of emotion (Cancer). In therapy this is sometimes called the "flight into health." To me it exemplifies the issue of trines in that as Jeffrey taught they can make it "easy" to be conscious and cooperative with evolution but they can also make it "easy" to resist it. Regarding evolutionary states and spiritual bypass, I have personally encountered bypass in all three of the main stages. At Consensus stages I often see it as "religious bypass" – people avoiding emotions by logging into pre-digested and pat religious answers (eg I don't want to feel grief about Sandy Hook, so I'll just blame it on schools not having Christian prayer every morning; or we don't want to feel the pain of Katrina so let's just blame it on the gays). At Individuated stages I often see it as "science bypass" or "political bypass" – people avoiding emotions by logging into political causes or sophisticated explanations of the aspects of experience they are avoiding. "Psychology bypass" also happens and a lot of insight-oriented psychotherapy does this, avoiding direct experience of emotions by explaining them. And then in the Spiritual stages and the later Individuated stages I often see it as the kind of "spiritual bypass" where people prefer to log in to particular states of consciousness or metaphysical frameworks and log out of the direct and lived experience of their emotions. But to me in general bypassing the emotional body is essentially resisting evolution, which Souls at any stage in consciousness can do.

Regarding whether the kind of mental/head-based quality that typifies the specific bypass (of preferring to dwell in primordial states), means that such individuals may be in the Individuated states vs Spiritual states, I would say that could be occurring in a Spiritual or an Individuated Soul. The difference would have to be discerned by understanding the nature of the Soul's motivation for its practice in the first place. I have seen some practitioners of these paths and techniques who are (mostly) seeking to reinforce their own sense of themselves and their specialness and ability to "achieve" and use spiritual practice as the vehicle for this (Individuated); and I have seen some who are (mostly) truly seeking to unite themselves with Source (Spiritual). And at both of these levels, I have seen Souls periodically fall into the trap of using these paths to dissociate from their emotions, or even live an entire lifetime in that kind of resistance.

Considering how to help Souls in this dynamic, as mentioned we are in the territory of Pisces/Neptune, and as EA teaches this archetype is about Source and spiritual realization, but at the same time also the process by which we "deify" all sorts of people and things and states of consciousness as if they themselves are Source or are spiritual realization, and then we experience eventual disillusionment when this turns out not to be true. In this context for me it has rarely worked to point out to people they that are in spiritual bypass; those rose-coloured glasses are pretty sticky and if you get Virgo/Mercury discerning and analytical they get even more Pisces/Neptune cloudy and ascending. Unless they are somehow really ready to hear it and to experience it as real, it is just a mental thing to say it, like telling an active addict that he or she has an addiction.

What I do find helpful in many situations is to assist the person in fully experiencing whatever they are experiencing, to feel what it is like to be where they are. In this case of bypass, to feel what it is like to view or use access to this primordial state as the "answer." What does that feel like, what is the impact of that in life? After all, the desire to prematurely transcend and resist the evolutionary process is itself also a desire that the Soul has created and wants to experience. Assisting the Soul to fully experience the full experience that is a consequence of that desire (whether it is the 'high' states, the frequent interpersonal isolation that results, the tendency to judge the 'unenlightened,' the pressure to maintain one's 'enlightenment,' whatever the full experience is), and eventually it will naturally include the experience of disillusionment, and the felt sense of disillusionment – feeling it, not just being told it by someone else – the disappointment, the grief, the anger – is what naturally leads the Soul to truly release the desire for bypass and move on to whatever is next for it. Just realizing it cognitively or because someone points it out typically means that although today's bypass strategy may be dropped, the desire will still exist in the Soul to do it and it will find another way to bypass (kind of like switching addictions from one substance/behavior to another when the deeper desires driving the addiction have not been addressed and released, only deferred). (Jason)

All that Jason has shared about this is exactly right. We need to remember/understand that the Pisces, Cancer, Scorpio trinity, the Source, the Soul, and the ego it manifests, all emanate from the Water archetype. Water is of course pure emotion. The non-dual state, the desire for, is itself an emotional delusion that is impossible to achieve, or arrive at, relative to consciousness in the Soul in a human form. A Soul relative to certain 'spiritual' methodologies can indeed arrive at some sort of 'transcendental' state but that state always, cause and effect, snaps back to a 'normal' state of consciousness. Even in these naturally transcendental states or 'cosmic consciousness' the very essence of such a consciousness or state is EMOTIONAL: the emotion or feeling within that state of consciousness as it 'perceives' the various realities of those states. That perception leads to an emotional state as it 'reacts' to the nature of the perception itself. The need of all of our Souls to directly feel the nature of our emotions as they relate to any possible experience created by the Soul for its own evolutionary needs is the bottom line truth. For those who are able to create within themselves the various degrees of cosmic consciousness all of them will report being in a temporary state of ecstasy. Ecstasy of course is an experience of pure emotion.

When Souls align themselves with various religious and/or spiritual teachings that teach it is important, necessary even, to control or repress the emotions in order for 'x' spiritual state to be realized these Souls are reacting to the nature of their own emotional lives. In essence, they are running from those emotional lives for their own reasons but all reasons that lead to this running lead to repressing the very nature of the emotions themselves. In so doing they are repressing that which is NATURAL AND NECESSARY FOR THE SOUL TO EXPERIENCE for its own evolutionary reasons. If we accept that God/ess is the origin of all things then wherein lies the origin of emotions? And for what reasons? So for Souls who do orientate to these teachings that require repression, to 'transcend' them which means repressing them, the very act of repression then magnifies and distorts those natural emotions within the consciousness of those that do so. When anything that is natural is repressed for whatever reasons ANGER IS THE DIRECT RESULT: a natural inner anger. When this occurs all too often the Soul then feels itself to be a victim of life, a victim even to their own emotions which continue to live on, to exist, despite the repression. When this natural anger is then linked to the created consciousness of feeling to be a victim first to itself, then to others, this becomes the causative basis of lashing out at anyone the Souls feels 'victimized' by. In a 'religious' and/or 'spiritual' context this then is the cause of all the horror stories we are all too familiar with: the priest abusing boys, the 'guru' who is having intercourse with some devote, and so on.

As JWG and others have taught the liberation of the Soul does indeed take place through and because of the emotional body for the reasons that Jason [above] had correctly pointed out. A story that I just remembered about this is the story of one of Yogananda's chief disciples, a women who was essential for Yogananda and his work. She developed a terminal medical condition in which Yogananda interceded upon by way of asking God/ess to keep her alive because of the critical nature of her tasks helping his work. She lived ten years longer as a result. And upon her final transition, upon the moment of the very last breath, her final words were: "TOO MUCH JOY." (Rad)

The disciple that Rad is referencing in this post is Sri Gyanamata and the book is called "God Alone: Life and Letters of a Saint." This is a wonderful book which I highly recommend as it gives great perspective about how to emotionally heal and grow without any "spiritual bypass." (Deva)

Since deep emotional processing is the heart of the work I do, what I have found is that we simply cannot easily move through our own emotional defenses. Spiritual systems that are 'transcendent' in nature often collude with the already dissociative defence in place. Yes it is quite easy for already dissociated, fragmented psyches (ie all of us) to access "other/higher worlds" since so many of our parts already reside there!! The difficult part is unlocking the trauma that caused the fragmentation in the first place and then real Soul retrieval can happen. Re-living, ie descending into the original terror, wound, fear, horror, pain (fill in the blank) opens up not only the complex formed around such an event, but the defences that were crystallized also. These defences involved ALL levels of the being, etheric/physical body, emotional body, mental body and spiritual body. ALL these bodies need to become congruent in order for full integration to happen and each one can hold their own separate defence. One body is not superior to another despite what patriarchal bias tells us. Personally I trust the veracity and truth of emotion before I trust the machinations of head, my personal bias. Sharing a quote from R.D. Laing: "When our personal worlds are rediscovered and allowed to reconstitute themselves, we first discover a shambles. Bodies half-dead; genitals dissociated from heart; heart severed from head; heads dissociated from genitals... Without inner unity, with just enough sense of continuity to clutch at identity: the current idolatry. Torn, body, mind and spirit, by inner contradictions, pulled in different directions, Man cut off from his own mind, cut off equally from his own body – a half-crazed creature in a mad world."

I perceive that we compensate for all these contradictions and dissociations largely with our mental prowess, using it to repress the true reality that lies underneath. This is why, collectively, we are so mentally defended because under those defences lies a much different, initially terrifying inner world, where our compensated identity is threatened to come apart, but when one has the courage to go there the reward is integration and coherence. (Patricia)

Emotional manipulation
I would only say IN GENERAL that because the Cancerian emotional dynamics (Moon dynamic) can relate back to very infant-like emotions, when we are in the grip of those, others can feel we are being manipulative. Simply because when you are a baby and cry to get attention for a need to be met, it is expected (by healthy parents), but as an adult it can be seen as being emotionally manipulative. So I wouldn't discount that emotional manipulation is a function of displaced emotions within this archetype, ie in ALL of us since we all have a Moon, a 4th house and Cancer archetype somewhere in our charts. (Patricia)

Security needs – Cancer, Libra, Capricorn, Aries
Cancer is naturally square Libra. Cancer of course is the archetype in which we learn to become secure within ourselves. When that inner security in not evolved into then the 'needs' for security are then projected onto our external relationships. This can be friends or intimate others that then creates a 'co-dependent' relationship. The natural square from Cancer to Libra correlates to co-dependency (ie the relationship between internal security and the relationships in our life). (Rad)

Cancer represents the need for emotional security. The person desires to feel secure. Libra represents our relationship with "the other." The intent in Cancer is to learn to feel secure within self. When that has not been achieved, the desire to feel secure is then projected onto "the other" (Libra), believing it is "the other" who is causing me to feel secure when in reality the feelings of security are coming from within myself, and only appear to be coming from "the other." When this insecurity/projection dynamic is mutual between two partners, they only feel secure when they are with each other – which is the definition of co-dependency. The evolutionary intent is to trigger the Libra polarity of Aries. Aries, like Libra, squares Cancer – the intent being to find the solution to Cancer's insecurity within Aries – myself. As this is learned, the Libran co-dependent tendencies can evolve. (Steve)

Saturn (Capricorn) correlates to the structural nature of our consciousness which means that whatever house and sign that our Saturn is in conditions and defines every other archetype, planet, within our consciousness. Saturn correlates with what is called 'reality' in general, and what constitutes 'reality' as defined by the consensus of any given group of people at any point in time. Saturn correlates to the natural function that all within a group have in order to sustain the needs of that group. Thus, what has come to be called 'careers' or 'work' within a given group or society. Saturn correlates with the very phenomena of time and space and, as a result, finitude. Saturn correlates to gravity and thus mass. In combination Saturn thus correlates to form. Relative to a consensus of people Saturn correlates with laws, customs, and norms that the group is expected to conform to for the group to maintain stability. Thus, it correlates to man-made laws. Because of its correlation to time, and that which is finite, Saturn also correlates with aging and thus emotional/psychological maturation. (Rad)

Co-dependency
Cancer is naturally square Libra. Cancer of course is the archetype in which we learn to become secure within ourselves. When that inner security in not evolved into then the 'needs' for security are then projected onto our external relationships. This can be friends or intimate others that then creates a 'co-dependent' relationship. The natural square from Cancer to Libra correlates to co-dependency (ie the relationship between internal security and the relationships in our life). (Rad)

Conditioned gender assignment
The issue of culturally conditioned gender assignments are also critical to understand (Capricorn polarity point). The example that my father uses that helped clarify this issue for me was that women with an Aries Moon, and men with a Pisces Moon: both cannot relate to themselves as the traditional "Betty Crocker" or "Marlboro Man" that are presented as the socially accepted ways of behavior for men and women. Yet, we have all been subjected to the wounding judgments from others when we do not conform to these social norms, and conformity then commonly takes place. That is why the issue of internalizing emotional security is so essential (we can then withstand such judgments) and actualize a natural masculinity and femininity within ourselves. Again, the impact of the early childhood environment is critical to understand because of the effect to the self-image. Was the father a "traditional male," and reinforced the culturally accepted ways of being to his child who could not truly relate to such behavior?

What was the mother's ability to nurture her child's unique individuality, and so on. These are core dynamics of the Moon/Cancer archetype. In the natal chart, the Moon by house, sign and aspect will correlate to how these core dynamics are played out, and the specific self-image of the Soul. (Deva)

Gender switch
There can be many possible signatures that correlate to gender switches, not just Pluto and the Nodes. But that does not mean that just any planet, by itself, in the 4th or 10th correlates to gender switching. It is common to find gender-switch signatures and homosexuality/bisexuality signatures in the same chart. (Rad)

There is no way astrologically, or otherwise, to determine gender switch. It's an entirely individual, each Soul, issue that is dependent on many, many factors and variables. (Rad)

Mother/father archetype
The 4th/10th dynamic/archetype of parents – mother/father – is really, in the end, a cultural issue and related to different times in history. For example some cultures going back in time had the men nurse the babies: they were called 'brood males.' They developed the capacity to even produce milk through their breasts. And these males then served as the parent that did the daily upbringing and supplied the child's daily needs, etc. In other words, from the point of view of the patriarchal form of reality the 'roles' were reversed. So what it comes down to is the issue of 'gender assignment' which is a function of the 4th/10th, Cancer/Capricorn archetypes. And the gender assignment is a function of whatever culture/time in history that we could look at: what is then 'expected' by way of norms for what it means to be a male or female and the 'roles' therein. On the other hand the 4th house and Cancer will always correlate to the early upbringing of any child all the time, and the general environment that the child grows up within. This will also include the emotional environment and the types of emotional experiences that the child has as a result relative to the parents' own reality, and what they are able to provide. The 10th house will always correlate to the type of culture that a child is born into and thus all the social taboos, laws, norms, expectations that serve as the conditioning to that child's sense of 'reality.' So of course it's possible for a child to have parents that PROVIDE BOTH ROLES, it's possible for a child to have a mother who primarily does the daily emotional needs of the child while the father provides for the material needs of the child/family/mother, and it's possible for a SINGLE PARENT to do both. So, in the end, the 4th/10th, Capricorn/Cancer is not the black and white of one equaling the father, and the other being the mother. (Rad)

4th/10th houses – one size does not fit all
The 4th house, Cancer, Moon will correlate to the parental figure – mother OR father – who predominantly served in the role of nurturing emotional security, emotional bonding/proximity, emotional/personal relating, etc. in the upbringing. 10th house, Saturn, Capricorn correlates to the parental figure – mother or father – who most reflected the role of authority, sociological responsibility, emulation of emotional maturity in the context of relating, etc. Traditionally the 4th house has been considered to represent the mother and the 10th house the father. But as we know, one size does not fit all. Just because a woman's physiology permits her to give birth to a baby does not mean that her inner nature is going to be oriented to emotional bonding, nurturing, etc. over expressing/actualizing a role of authority, emotional maturation, sociological focus, etc. within the family structure. And of course, vice versa for males. Both roles archetypically serve a vital function in the imprinting and ongoing development of our consciousness, and those roles are fully interchangeable – so as we like to say around here, observation/correlation. (Stacie)

Progressed Moon
Knowing the natal chart and meaning of Moon within the Pluto paradigm, only then through this lens look at the Progressed Moon and consider the current progressed sign of the Moon and see what natal house this activates, and aspects within the natal chart when placed there. Then, additionally, consider the house and aspects within the progressed chart itself. After understanding this to the best of your current ability, to add even more timing and detail, then look at the recent Lunar Return charts around any time period in question and apply all this back to understanding of the above. Within the Lunar Return chart interpretation itself, the Moon's house placement in the Lunar Return chart plus aspects at the moment of the Return to complete the timing of all issues stemming from and through the emotional body. Within this whole process, also keep in mind the meaning of the transiting Nodes through the natal chart. (Bradley)

South or North Node in Cancer – on an individual level
The 'interpretation' when the South or North Nodes of the Moon are in Cancer is totally dependent on the individual context, reality, of each Soul. The symbols of Cancer, the Moon, and the 4th house correlate to a total archetype within which there is a spectrum that symbolizes that total archetype. The evolutionary condition, the four natural stages of the Soul's evolution, must first be taken into consideration in order to begin to understand where any given Soul is at within that spectrum. Within that the nature of the country, society, or tribe in which the Soul chooses to be born must also be considered because they all correlate to the nature of the 'imprinting,' or conditioning of consciousness, that each type of society is defined by. Within this we must also

consider the nature of the specific family structure that the Soul chooses to be born into that, of itself, influences wherein that total spectrum of the Cancer archetype is orientated to. Then, after these considerations, the specific nature of the Soul's past life history, dynamics, that are seen through the EA paradigm must be fully grasped in order to understand that Soul's individual context: their reality. When all of this is put together then the specific reasons as to why the Soul is choosing to have the North or South Nodes in Cancer can be rightly understood. In other words, there is no one 'cookbook' answer that fits all. (Rad)

South Node in Cancer, North Node in Capricorn – on a global level
On a global level with the South Node in Cancer, North Node in Capricorn, this correlates in general to the structural nature of our world at every level of reality that is rapidly changing. And, of course, how those structural changes are affecting every one of us on the planet: our individual reality, identity, sense of personal security, and of course our families. Each country, Capricorn, of course also has its own individual context defined by the nature of its governments, its economies, its demographics, and its laws. All of us of course live in whatever countries that we do. So the changing structural nature of reality in general at every level then affects each country relative to its own context. And within each country are all the individual citizens and their families that are then affected by the structural changes not only within their own country, but the world itself. For the millions of Souls that will be born while the transiting Nodal Axis is in Cancer/Capricorn they will be 'imprinted,' in general, by this high state of psychological/emotional anxiety based on the structural nature of the changes in the world as a whole, and their country of birth specifically. So the question then becomes from an EA point of view WHY? And each Soul will have their own unique answer. (Rad)

Pluto's Nodes in Capricorn/Cancer
Jeffrey said many times that the South Node of Pluto in Capricorn related back to the time period when the transition from matriarchy to patriarchy was already underway, and thus all Souls on Earth today have a natural connection to those times, or at least the energies of those times, even if they were not in human form on Earth at that time. Something interesting is that in 2018 transiting Pluto will be conjunct its own South Node of Pluto. We could consider what that means in terms of opening up the current version of the lessons from those times. Keeping in mind Cancer/Capricorn relate to gender role assignment, and the upcoming period we are entering is associated with the beginning of the return of the Goddess. Clearly the male-dominated present orientation is leading to the environmental devastation of the planet. Uranus enters Taurus in 2018/2019, and survival will necessitate radical change. Also, here in USA, we are having a US Pluto return in 2021/2022 at 27 deg Capricorn. Capricorn squares Libra (extremes) and we will have pushed everything to the maximum extremes, being forced to change from no other options remaining. (Steve)

Moon/Neptune interface
Neptune correlates to the transcendent impulse of the Soul. It implies the necessity for a Soul to surrender to the all encompassing truth that is. In that process its beliefs and ideas about what reality is are disillusioned. The Moon correlates to the ego, the human identity that the Soul creates as a focusing agent for its evolutionary journey. It implies the necessity to become emotionally secure and intimate with one's own self in such a way that a Soul can adopt to the changes that occur in life, on a moment to moment basis. The evolutionary intention behind Neptune/Moon aspects is for the Soul to consciously realize itself (Moon) as the Truth (Neptune). This places a Soul in a deeply vulnerable position whereby it is necessary to develop a relationship to home, to what provides security and safety on a subjective, personal level, that is also a direct experience of universal Love. This leads a Soul to understand the unity of all beings, as children of God. Transcendence occurs through serving God through the emotional body. (Ari)

What is that Cancer Polarity? Reflections on Pluto in Capricorn – by Bradley Naragon
Yesterday, I considered how appropriate the word 'streamlining' is to describe the Pluto in Capricorn phenomena, especially in a capitalistic competitive society and economy. Seemingly, at every turn and stop, organizations, institutions, and businesses are 'tightening' up operations. Paper towels are now half the size they used to be and I think the toilet paper went from 2 ply to 1.5 ply. Seriously, with Mars in Capricorn and the recent conjunction to Pluto, now more than ever 'getting organized' is the aim and drive. Keeping the ducks in a row is not intrinsically a bad thing. As the South Node transits Taurus, the question of "Will this survive?" is more appropriate than ever. What is desired to survive is all based on one's values. Many people still greatly value the form capitalism exists in. Many people have gained their own wealth and survived and thrived because the current model is a patriarchal system set up for some to win and many to lose. As a result, I now see so clearly the compulsions of what it means to just "do the Pluto Capricorn" without its Cancer polarity. It's a funny phenomenon – more than ever we need every single 'i' dotted and 't' crossed or we risk not having access to what we need. The compulsion to create even more policies and create more 'red tape' and hoops to jump through is ever so real with Pluto in Capricorn. We are lucky when we actually get to talk to a human. Yet, when we do, will they be so restricted in their role that they only reflect back to us what we can and cannot do based on current policies? Where has the human gone? Cancer, oh, Cancer, under all these layers of armor we put on to survive in this work, there is a human being underneath there with emotions and feelings.

Recently, I was helping rewrite a returns policy for business. It really came down to going the 'hard ball route' and being really tight and limiting or creating what some called a 'wishy-washy' policy that supported actually allowing some room for the exceptions; to still allow wiggle room of being human. No room for exceptions is the shadow side of Pluto in Capricorn. This is Pluto Capricorn without its Cancer polarity. You either do or you don't meet criteria and then need to go through all the process to get what you want/need IF you can even access it. Recently, a friend was hit by a car. She had major medical surgery. The man who hit her was genuinely sincere and wished to do the right thing. Yet, she was strongly advised by others to get a lawyer to represent her case OR the insurance company would try to limit the amount they had to pay out. With Pluto in Capricorn, the need for the Cancer polarity is SO MUCH MORE OBVIOUS. Who are these people and how do they live with themselves – removing financial support in a time of personal crisis based on "what's the best business decision." Granted, much of this already has existed. The USA, beginning with the top down Capitalistic model (natal Pluto Capricorn), has always had such ruthless motives visibly and invisibly operative. Rad and Steve have shown us this correlation time again here on this message board. Now that we have Pluto in Capricorn, every product seems to be shrinking in size or offering, or going up in price. With the South Node [currently] in Taurus followed by Pluto in the "Taurus decan" of Capricorn, how will people survive? Will the decisions that we face embrace the empathetic nurturing principle?

What is the best business decision? To include the Cancer polarity means to value helping others over the bottom line equation of profit margin. Before that person hangs up the phone on you, do they step out of just being in the position of their job and acknowledge the reality you face? Even to hear someone say, "I'm sorry that is happening to you," would give some hope of this polarity expressing itself. Do we meet the former or do we hear, "That's the way it is and I cannot help you"? May our hearts remain open and full of compassion in these difficult times. (Bradley)

LEO – SUN – 5th HOUSE

Leo keywords

Creative Self-Actualization	Grandiose	Being noticed	Gambler
Ruler King/Queen	Subjective awareness	Special recognition	Actor/ress
Power	Artist	Fame	Risk taker
Arts	Inflation – positive/negative	Romance	Affairs – Adultery
Drama	Involvement	Creativity	Mistress
Integration	Approval	Child Prodigy	Children
Purpose	Exhibitionism	Artist	Inner Child
Full of self	Applause		

Leo, Sun, 5th house archetype

Yang / fixed / fire / rules 5th house / Ruler is Sun. Leo and the Sun represents creative self-actualization. The Sun represents the integrative principle, how we go about integrating things, self-actualizing our purpose. The Sun's sign, house, and the aspects that it makes correlate to how we integrate and give purpose to our life. We tend to learn through crisis (Virgo). The Sun represents how I give purpose to, and integrate, these crises into my nature. Leo represents the principle of creativity, how we give a sense of purpose and meaning relative to our evolutionary intention. Leo is intentionally narcissistic. We must become full of self, realize the power and possibilities of self, before we can disseminate self in the world. However this is egocentric power and self, and can lead to delusions of grandeur. Again, this is a necessary stage in consciousness. To integrate the Sun, Leo must embrace the Aquarius polarity. Leo is the center of its own Universe. It has an attitude of, 'Here I am, integrate me' vs. Aquarius' awareness of what the overall social system needs from me. Too much Leo can lead to the starving artist syndrome, social isolation. Leo is naturally square to the 2nd and 8th houses, seat of the sexual instinct, and with its natural connection to creativity, is connected to children. Parents with too much Leo orientation tend to see their children as extensions of themselves rather than as individuals in their own right. (JWG's Pluto Vol. 1 and the School's Course)

[Recommended Reading: Jeffrey Wolf Green's Pluto Vol. 1 – The Evolutionary Journey of the Soul]

Pluto in the 5th house or Leo

As a natural Fire house, Pluto in the 5th people will feel they have a special destiny to fulfill. 5th house Pluto people need to actualize this special destiny. In the 5th house, the purpose has already been formed. They will feel it deeply. They have been learning to take charge of their lives, seize destiny, and shape it with their wills. They are born with the feeling of specialness, and need to be recognized. This need is so intense it can become a bottomless pit. They can feel the universe revolves around them, just as the Sun is the center of our solar system. They are SUPPOSED to feel this way, for they are here to creatively actualize and be in charge of their purpose. Depending on the rest of the person's chart, this can manifest in a noisy or a quiet way. The focus in this position is on the creative principle. Creativity can be expressed in many ways in life, using the unique abilities of the person. It requires an intense inner focus and determination to shape the destiny with the strength of will. The South Node and its planetary ruler will show how this has been achieved in the past. An issue with this placement is these people tend to see themselves as the source of their creativity because the subjective impulse is at its peak in Leo. This orientation contains a built-in limitation that they do not tend to see. In its worst cases this can be a God complex. Many 5th house Pluto's had past lives where they were recognized as special in some way. They have unconscious memories of this special treatment and can unintentionally expect to again be treated and acknowledged in this way. Some will manipulate people and situations to receive the desired recognition. In some cases this can even be achieved by playing the victim to draw attention to them.

Many will create a pyramid reality with themselves at the top. The need for power and recognition is an underlying theme. If they're not getting the recognition they need in their marriage, they may create a love affair in which they get the acknowledgement that they need. If they are discovered, this can cause the necessary emotional blows that force them to realize what they have done, and the reasons why. They can manipulate people to get their own emotional needs met, sweet talking a person into an affair, for example, and then abandoning the affair when it no longer serves their purpose. They also tend to try to shape and control the lives of others around them, including their children. They unintentionally project the force of their own self-actualization and purpose onto those around them. This can range from trying to totally control the lives of others, to encouraging the development of those around them because they value that quality. Their encouragement tends to be from the perspective of their own self, not really seeing the other person and what they truly need. They can be very giving and generous yet the generosity usually serves some personal need. It is hard for them to understand this, because within their own frame of reference they think they are being quite giving. Others may create emotional scenes or confrontations trying to point out what is going on. These scenes serve to undermine the 5th house Pluto pyramid reality structure. These people tend to have very strong willed children. The resulting battle of wills leads them to the lessons of objectivity. (JWG's Pluto Vol. 1 and the School's Course)

Pluto polarity point – 11th house or Aquarius
The intent is to develop an objective focus, learning to link their special destiny to something socially relevant. They must learn to link their special purpose to a socially useful or relevant function. Many will find fulfilling their purpose is blocked as part of forcing the need to embrace 11th house polarity. The social structure itself will be the blocking force. This can lead to frustration and anger as society appears to not acknowledge the person as special. Even if they fulfill part of their purpose, they may not get the recognition they require for it. Being forced to the sidelines forces the lesson of learning objectivity. It also detaches them from the pyramid structure of their inner reality. Through this they may learn how to link their purpose to society's needs. They will learn that others are just as special as they are. Through learning their lessons they will realize they are channels of universal creativity and not the source of that which they create. Common Leo characteristics: strength of will, dignity, creative, loving and giving, narcissistic, magnetic, powerful and intense, can be demanding, suspicious of yet needing flattery, protective of those who are close to them. (JWG's Pluto Vol. 1 and the School's Course)

Sun
The Sun is the current life integration point for the entire evolutionary paradigm in each chart. It gives it purpose, meaning, and the way of ACTUALIZING those intentions. (Rad)

Sun/Pluto interface
[The Sun in aspect to Pluto implying past life dynamics]….would be the one exception to the general rule about the Sun. Yet because the Sun does correlate to how the Soul gives the overall EA intentions for its life a purpose and way of integrating those intentions, the Sun, in this exception must then be understood in a two-fold way. One is that it does correlate to the prior modes of actualization of the Soul's intentions, South Node. This can then mean that the Soul can be stuck in its own past in the current life. If so, this of course would not allow for any evolution to occur for the Soul. Thus, the critical importance of the North Node, the location of its planetary ruler, and, of course Pluto's polarity point serve the Soul's intent to re-actualize that existing past in new ways so that the Soul can continue to evolve. (Rad)

Polarity point of the Sun?
The Sun has no polarity point. All is integrated relative to its sign and house in the birth chart. It does not evolve in the same way as all the other factors in the birth chart. The Sun can evolve from within the total archetypal spectrum of the sign and house that it is in natally as the Soul itself evolves relative to its intentions in any given life. (Rad)

Nodes of the Sun
The Nodes of the Sun are not used in Evolutionary Astrology. The present 'moment' only occurs because there is a past and future. Without a past or future there is no moment. (Rad)

North Node – and next life's Sun
In terms of the next life Sun being the sign of the present life North Node, it was stated [by JWG] that is often the case, but not always. Why Sun as past life North Node sign? The North Node is the future of our Moon, our personality, our sense of self. The Sun symbolizes actualization. This life's North Node, the evolutionary *potentials*, the direction to move in to break the hold of the past, would find expression in the next life as Sun, the intent being to directly *actualize* (Sun) those potentials, as life purpose (Sun). Thus the intention to turn potential into reality. (Steve)
There was a point in time that Wolf said the North Node in one's chart would become the Sun in the next life. As his work evolved he came to realize that this is not always true. (Rad)

Children
Children in one's birth chart are symbolized by the 5th house, the location of its planetary ruler, and aspects that it is making to other planets. The location of the sign Leo in the chart, and thus the location of its ruler, the Sun, and the aspects that it is making to other planets. There used to be a technique too that some astrologers used in terms of first, second, and third child, etc. And that was to use the 5th house, etc. as the first child, the 7th house, etc., as the second, the 9th house, etc., as the third, and so on. (Rad)

Father
Father is symbolized by the 5th house, the location of its planetary ruler, then aspects that it is making to other planets. The location of the sign Leo in the chart, and thus the location of its ruler, the Sun, and the aspects that it is making to other planets. It is a natural male archetype, and is ruled by the Sun. Meaning that in patriarchal reality the Father is considered the 'center' of the household upon which all is supposed to 'revolve:' planets revolving around the Sun. Within this, "Man was Created in God's own 'self-image.'" And of course, this is the Patriarchal 'Father' who has Created everything, including 'his' children. And, remember, that astrology itself, what is practiced to this day, was primarily born after the patriarchal takeover was completed long ago. (Rad)

Creation
(Q) Doesn't the Leo archetype correlate with putting together and fusing (Leo-Scorpio, Sun-Pluto?) different internal and external elements to create something unique by giving them a personal role or meaning, in order to obtain acclaim? In art, this creative process can involve elements which don't have any inherent connection among them, as in the bricolage. Their connection in this type of work of art is created by personal will. It produces something larger not by means of induction, but by means of creation, ie deduction, going from the causes to the effects. The world does not become more simple or understandable, quite on the contrary, it becomes fuller with phenomena. Thus the correlation of Leo with excess, but also with that which is fanciful or whimsy, or arbitrary. And further, with children and the way children play. So, I would think that there is a correlation between Leo and this type of synthesis. Is the above correct? (Gonzalo)
A Yes, in the way you have decided to put those archetypes together. But that is only one way to put together those archetypes. Yet, in the end, it still comes back to the same point: the Source of Creation itself and all of its dimensions and apparent complexities. The Sun itself does not exist in a vacuum by itself. It is but a manifestation of the total Creation that is part of the fabric or structure of that total Creation. (Rad)

Leo/Virgo interface
In terms of synthesizing the Virgo/Leo archetypes, generally speaking, it is good to remember that the Leo archetype correlates with creative self-actualization, and the need to actualize the Soul's special destiny. Leo is full of what it is, so to speak, and feels a sense of special destiny and purpose (as do all fire signs) that must now be actualized. The distortion of this archetype is one of over self-focus (narcissism) and being overly identified with one's creative purpose from an egocentric point of view. Delusions of self-grandeur correlate with this archetype. Typically, there is a deep insecurity within the Leo archetype that creates a bottomless pit in terms of how much external recognition and feedback the person feels they need. In other words, Leo also correlates to the need to be acknowledged as special, and because of the underlying insecurity in this archetype the need for this type of feedback, or acknowledgement can become never ending.
The Virgo archetype comes right after Leo, and correlates with the need for self-improvement and adjustment. This will be linked with any patterns of over self-focus and self-inflation that manifests in the Leo archetype. In essence, we are analyzing our egos in this archetype. While Leo is full of what it is, Virgo is becoming aware of all of its short comings and lacks (of what we are not). In a general sense then, the Virgo archetype can create a natural humility within a person who also has Leo in the chart because the person, potentially, will be able to discern delusions of grandeur and purify an overly self-absorbed focus in life. The person could also adjust the dynamic of the need for constant positive feedback from others, and recognize the special talents and capacities of others. When the Leo/Virgo archetype works together, the person could also effect self-improvement by creatively actualizing a special purpose that is linked with healing and serving others. Leo will now be linked with the need for self-improvement and service to the whole in some way, and through the act of service a natural humility can manifest. (Deva)

VIRGO – MERCURY – 6th HOUSE

Virgo keywords

Inferiority	Discipline	Lack	Healing
Service	Shame	Self-improvement	Craftsman
Servant / Slave	Perfection	Health	Reality
Apprentice	Place in Society	Critical	Discernment
Humility – Humiliation	Self-Improvement	Guilt	Nun
Victim	Existential Void	Masochism	Virgin
Persecuted	Aloneness	Crisis	Sadomasochism
Self-Sacrifice / Martyr	Inadequacy	Nurse / Medicine	

Virgo, Mercury, 6th house archetype

Earth / yin / mutable / rules 6th house / ruled by Mercury. Virgo is a transitional archetype, the boundary between subjective, self-orientation and objective, social orientation. Aries to Leo is the build-up of the subjective self, culminating in Leo with its tendency to grandiosity. Aries to Leo represents superiority. Virgo represents inferiority. Libra represents equality. The way to Libran equality from Leonian superiority is through Virgo and inferiority. If Leo is a pyramid with the ego on top, Virgo flips that pyramid upside down and puts the ego on the bottom. Virgo is about learning to be of service to the larger whole, not just to self. The method Virgo employs to bring about this transformation is to humiliate the ego, to tear it down. Virgo makes us aware that other people and social systems are around us. It enforces introspection, creates an awareness of lack, imperfection, and inadequacy. Shows us what we need to do to improve. The polarity to Virgo is Pisces, representing ultimate ideals. Virgo is aware that the ultimate something exists. It also knows that it has not yet evolved into an understanding of that ultimate something. Since Virgo is ruled by Mercury and is a yin energy, the process is mental and inward – introspection and analysis. This creates feelings of emptiness. The sign on the 6th house, location of Mercury and the ruler of the 6th house, and location of Virgo indicate the type of critical self-analysis, how much the criticism is emphasized, and how much of an impact it has on the person – is it inhibitive? The intent is to induce a sense of inferiority which humiliates the ego through developing the self-awareness of what it is not relative to what it wishes to be. Under the present conditioning patterns, we are all subject to the Garden of Eden Myth. This is based on the idea that there is a fundamental split between spirit and flesh; that spirit is good and flesh is bad. Adam was told by God to keep focused on God. But Eve tempted him and Adam got distracted and responded to the temptation, turned away from God, and they were consequently kicked out of the Garden. Eve felt guilt about her role in this, and felt the need to atone for what she had done. Guilt plus atonement equals the psychology of masochism. Adam felt guilt for what he had done, and he was angry about it. He blamed Eve for his fall. Guilt plus anger equals the psychology of sadism.

Because the underlying cause of this sadomasochistic distortion of life is the religious foundations of the culture, and because there is a collective unconscious which we are all tuned into, like it or not, we are all affected by this cultural conditioning. This manifests in both subtle ways such as women getting paid less to do the same job that a man is doing, to S & M sexual activities. The culture as a whole is in utter denial of its sadistic and masochistic underpinnings. Jesus' sacrifice of his own life has been set up as a cultural standard yet it in itself was a masochistic act. Notice that in the Garden of Eden myth, neither takes responsibility for their actions. Adam blames Eve for MAKING him be tempted, and Eve blames herself for causing Adam to be tempted. Adam does not take responsibility for his actions, and Eve accepts the blame for what Adam did. Thus there is an underlying victimization, and this plays out in our culturally accepted co-dependent and domination-submission relationship patterns. There are three possible thought patterns in the psychology of masochism:

1. I deserve pain, punishment, crisis, suffering, and denial, and I don't know why.
2. For my needs to be met I must somehow hurt first.
3. I'm essentially worthless while intellectually knowing better.

Virgo learns about the nature of its reality through crisis. Crisis leads to analysis, which leads to reflection. This is why Virgo endlessly analyses. At some point, analysis and crisis will produce self-knowledge, through pain. They are perpetually engaged in self-undermining activities – doing for others and not doing for self what they know they should do for self, and making rational reasons (that are actually excuses) why this is so. They have the ability to see spirit and potential, without grasping the actual reality of anything. Masochists learn through disillusionment, one of the most difficult emotional experiences of all, yet a necessary step. Leo was full of self and knew everything. In Virgo the awareness grows that what was thought to be true before is not true. There is a sense that there is a deeper, more cosmic reality, yet that reality is not yet known or experienced. In place of the Leonian sense of self is a deep emptiness. The ego has been shown to be an illusion, the balloon has been popped; the deeper reality is sensed but not yet known. Virgo compensates for this inner emptiness by always being busy. There is always something to do, and someone who needs my help. There is never time for me, or to tend to my needs – the masochistic principle in action. Virgo needs to embrace the Pisces polarity by developing a regular spiritual practice of a nature that speaks to the person, and to learn to discriminate between what is reality and what is illusion. (JWG's Pluto Vol. 1 and the School's Course)
[Recommended Reading: Jeffrey Wolf Green's Pluto Vol. 1 – The Evolutionary Journey of the Soul]

Pluto in the 6th house or Virgo

These people have been learning to serve society or individuals. They have been learning humility, self-doubt, discrimination, purification, and self-improvement. They develop these qualities through intense self-analysis. Virgo as an archetype symbolizes how individuals within a society learn to fulfill a function within the society. This requires sacrificing their personal wishes to the needs of the society. They have had to develop the skills needed to perform the work or service. Here they are learning about what they are NOT – learning humility, and a purification of self-glorification. They have a laser-like mind, which exposes any part of them that is not 'right.' This leads to introspection, which leads to purging the parts of them that are no longer aligned with the evolutionary direction. They will have inner feelings of what must change, reflecting an inner standard of that which is seen as right or perfect. That which is not right will be linked to egocentric, 1st to 5th house orientations. That which is perceived as perfect will be linked to 7th through 12th house orientations. Many have subconscious memories of prior mistakes and things not 'done right.' Guilt is tightly connected with those memories. There will be a desire to atone for the guilt. Serving others is one way to atone for the guilt. They will over-analyze and put themselves down. They become compulsively focused on imperfection.

They are never ready or good enough for what is at hand. Or, they do not deserve any more than they have. They create excuses why they are not doing what they know they should do, and then create more guilt around the inaction cycle. Often the guilt has existed for lifetimes. This can actually create states of perpetual crisis. Some will project this blame outwardly onto others. Crisis is necessary for these people. The post-crisis analysis can lead the person to self-awareness. In a negative reaction cycle, the person will tear themself down over and over, creating a state of inner paralysis. They need to learn to keep acting, to not paralyze. Atonement occurs through action. Through stripping themselves bare, they experience the imperfections and flaws in life. This produces the feeling that something is missing. They can be critical of everyone and everything, in addition to being critical of self. The criticisms are based on the illusive internal standards of perfection, and the places where self and life fall short of them. The feelings of aloneness can become overbearing and they can fill up their lives with endless activities. They can become workaholics. Those who criticize others draw people who criticize them into their own lives, adding to their sense of isolation and meaninglessness. They may feel persecuted. The key to resolving these issues is to become aware of why they are occurring in the first place. They subconsciously create situations where they must be of service to others. They are also susceptible to illness, to force the confrontations with that which must be acknowledged. (JWG's Pluto Vol. 1 and the School's Course)

Pluto polarity point – 12th house or Pisces

The intent is simplification, dissolving old barriers that prevent the understanding of the individual's self-concept. It shows the person that they are part of a larger force, a realization that begins to fill the existential hole left by the popping of the Leo balloon of ego. Many will deny a cosmic connection, dismissing it as impractical or irrational. There is a tendency to embrace spirituality during a crisis and to abandon it when the crisis ends, until the next crisis. Pisces facilitates the development of the holistic, intuitive approach to life, to counter Mercury's left brained logical orientation. Becoming aware of the connection to Divinity fosters self-forgiveness, and appreciation of the imperfections in others. The holistic view helps develop inner peace that puts the worrying mind at rest. They come to see the work function that is best aligned with their true purpose rather than working any old job. These people are natural karma yogis, serving God through the work and service that they perform. Those who resist can live lives of pain, illness, and a sense of being imprisoned. Those who follow the intent will surrender to the spirit and transform. They will be quite humble and serve anyone who truly needs their help. Those who go from resistance to surrender and back again will alternate between times of great clarity and times of crisis and discouragement. These people have keen minds, are self-effacing, willing to help others, naturally timid, self-conscious, critical or forgiving of others depending on the circumstances, always busy, dealing with endless crises, good organizational skills. (JWG's Pluto Vol. 1 and the School's Course)

Natural guilt
When guilt occurs to a Soul that is natural then the very nature of that guilt, the events that have caused it, will stay within the Soul forever. It does this so that the Soul will never repeat the causes or actions that lead to the natural guilt. On the other hand, any guilt that is within the Soul that is not natural can and will be expelled from the Soul at some point. Thus when dealing with clients it is very important to understand this critical difference which then dictates how a client is to be dealt with relative to a therapeutic approach. (Rad)

Man-made guilt and natural guilt
From my own personal experience, in relation to what JWG explained to me years ago, this technique helps eliminate LEARNED guilt, not natural guilt. Even in Natural Law we can experience natural guilt. But, at this point in our history we're just beginning to learn how to distinguish between natural guilt and the guilt we can feel by comparing ourselves to a "perfect" God. I think it boils down to a simple (Pisces) process of asking in any of these situations just WHAT the basis of the guilt is, ie whether it's rooted in man-made laws or Natural Laws. And as one asks that question more and more, I think we can start to weed out the source of any guilt. Even with the natural guilt, we need to remember that as Wolf used to put it, "God has goofed up, so why wouldn't WE goof up?" And another (Piscean) question: "How can anything perfect create something Imperfect?" It's really a shift in this understanding of "perfection" that I think helps in our understanding of Natural Law, and ultimately the forgiveness for both ourselves and others. (Adina)

There are really TWO BASIC types of guilt: man-made guilt (learned) based on religious, philosophical, psychological, etc. beliefs, and natural guilt (earned), based on our actions that are out of alignment with Natural Laws. I think for the most part the majority of the learned guilt DOES go back to what we think is "right" and "wrong" based on man-made religions. In general, EARNED guilt will be reflected in the symbols of Saturn/Capricorn/10th house, while the LEARNED guilt is more likely to come through the symbols of Virgo/Pisces and their respective rulers and houses. These, of course, are just two places to START looking for patterns of guilt. Some of figuring this out within ourselves will unfold as we evolve and realign with Natural Laws, but much can also be gleaned now if we simply reflect on the reasons for ANY kind of guilt we feel and then the SOURCE of those reasons. For example, if I beat my child to the point he needs to be hospitalized, I know (even if it's only deep down within and not necessarily conscious) that I have done something inherently wrong. On the other hand, if I get a divorce and feel guilty because whatever church says it's a "sin" to get divorced, then I've taken on an unnecessary guilt based on some humans' ideas about what is right and wrong. Even in countries where religion has been banned, the old USSR, for example, I could be found "guilty" of and punished for not bowing to the emperor because that's one of the laws of the country. However, to not bow to another human being isn't intrinsically "wrong;" it's only "wrong" because it's a man-made rule, and therefore actual guilt is unnecessary. (Adina)

Guilt and atonement
The EA paradigm is only reflecting, symbolizing, life in its totality. Of itself it causes nothing. Each Soul is unique to itself. The choices each Soul makes, and the reasons for those choices, is also unique to each Soul. Relative to the archetype of atonement linked with guilt each Soul reacts, and thus makes choices, differently. The natural process leading any Soul to finally be free of needing to atone for whatever guilt, natural or unnatural, is different for all Souls. And, of course, much depends on the very nature of the causative factors for the guilt in the first place: the extent and extremity of it. If any given Soul were responsible, say, for the deaths of a great many people due to its negligence, how long would it take for such a Soul to stop atoning for this fact? If it were you, how long do you think that might be? If it were someone else, how long do you think it may take for that person to be free of atoning for such guilt? There is just no way to know. Each Soul is different. The key issue here is whether the guilt is natural or not. When guilt occurs to a Soul that is natural then the very nature of that guilt, the events that have caused it, will stay within the Soul forever. It does this so that the Soul will never repeat the causes or actions that lead to the natural guilt. On the other hand, any guilt that is within the Soul that is not natural can and will be expelled from the Soul at some point. Thus when dealing with clients it is very important to understand this critical difference which then dictates how a client is to be dealt with relative to a therapeutic approach. (Rad)

How to deal with natural guilt
The best way to deal with it is to orientate to Soul to create conditions in its life that were the very causes that lead to the natural guilt in the first place, and then to do all that is possible to do the naturally right things in the face of those conditions. Everybody has natural guilt in varying degrees in their Soul. No Soul is 'perfect.' (Rad)

I was deeply struck when I first saw this, years ago in the movie Gandhi. More and more I understand why. It is such an example of this principle. During that fast, toward the end of the Gandhi movie, a devout Hindu came to Gandhi and said, "I am going to hell." Gandhi asked, "Why?" He said he had killed a Muslim boy during the violence that sprang up as the country was being divided into India and Pakistan. Gandhi replied, "I know a way out of hell. Find a child whose parents were killed in the violence and raise it. Only make sure it is a Muslim child and raise it as a Muslim." Think of the implications of a devout Hindu raising a child as a Muslim, and the effect that would have on the Hindu man's natural guilt, and also the effect on the child's Soul, whose parents had been murdered by Hindus. (Steve)

Another way one can make up for transgressions is, as one's life gradually changes, to remind other sincere Souls who struggle with a similar inner darkness that there is indeed a way out. This human life is often hard. But there is ALWAYS a path back to God/Goddess for sincere Souls ready to take the necessary steps, which start with owning where we have been. (Steve)

Perfection

To start, it's important that you (and anyone) follow the truth you know and find within yourself. As is implied in what you wrote about the nature of Neptune, all of our human truths are relative truths. One thing I found not addressed in what you wrote is you referred much to Source (Neptune) and also somewhat to personality (Cancer), but did not mention Soul/Pluto/Scorpio/8th house at all. I happen to have Pluto in the 8th house, and so am wired to be attuned to the reality of Soul. I'm not suggesting anything you said is wrong. I am just attempting to add a few pieces to what you wrote. The Soul is the *bridge* between the human and 'Neptune.' The Soul CREATES the human being, for its own evolutionary purposes, just as Neptune creates the Souls for *its* evolutionary purposes. That is why the focal point of everything in EA is Pluto, the Soul, and not Neptune, which is not really knowable in human form. Our work is to evolve our Souls, through the vehicle of our human natures. We CAN know our Soul, as opposed to knowing Neptune, and we are here as Steve and Heidi BECAUSE of our Souls – that is the point of our human evolutionary journey. In relation to Soul and the Soul's human journey, what I said about perfection and imperfection is quite relevant.

I have heard discussions about whether what EA calls imperfect is in the greater picture in fact perfect even though it is experienced as imperfect. I find these are discussions over the meaning of words. To me they miss the greater point that the words, limited as they must be, are trying to make. They are a *metaphor*. Day to day reality is very few (if any) humans are having an ongoing life they would describe as perfect. That is not debatable. And the patriarchal teachings of Divine Perfection cause many of these people to compare themselves to the unattainable patriarchal ideal of Divine Perfection vs their obvious human imperfection. As a result they judge themselves as inadequate, unworthy, less than, not good enough. And THAT is the cause of most of the masochistic patterns in people that I have encountered.

This begins with my own life history. My life changed radically after first encountering the EA perspective of God as an imperfect force seeking its own perfection. I felt more liberated and validated than I ever had in my life. And now that I am inwardly allowed to counsel others, somehow or other I attract many many people who have that issue (isn't that odd...). Almost everyone I have ever counselled on these issues, people with a similar conditioned orientation to feeling inadequate as a result of not measuring up to the ideal they'd been taught was the goal, has felt liberation on realizing what these words about imperfection vs perfection imply in their life. Why would a perfect God create imperfect creations – what is the point? How can I be more perfect than that which created me? Many times I have seen eyes light up – "You mean I am just okay as I am?" Patterns of many lifetimes begin cracking open before our eyes. That is both my personal experience, and the experience of many people I have counselled.

I also want to say that whether you call it imperfection or perfection, it's a METAPHOR, a *symbol*. If we are saying the same thing but using different words and tripping over each other's definitions of words, then please, throw my metaphor out and use whatever works for you and your clients. The metaphor's intent is to make people AWARE of the causes of their masochism, and to create a way to break those patterns. I have experienced it very effectively doing that. The last thing it's intended for is to create new masochism. If using that metaphor would create additional masochism for you or your clients, for God's sake, don't use it! (Steve)

Chart markers of masochism

While there ARE many masochists because of the Christian conditioning of a PERFECT God of the last 2,000 years, not everyone is a masochist. Chart markers of masochism can include the Nodal Axis in 6th/12th or Virgo/Pisces, Pluto in Virgo, Mars in Virgo, a stellium of planets in Virgo or Pisces or the 6th or 12th houses, etc. But even those alone do not necessarily indicate masochism. Again, we have to play astrological detective and employ observation and correlation of the person's thoughts and behaviors in order to determine this for sure, ie one would also have to display masochistic behaviors. Typically, if the chart reveals some of these placements AND you see a Soul who is not actualizing their evolutionary intentions, that could indicate a masochist. (Adina)

JWG's method of eliminating LEARNED masochism

From my own personal experience, in relation to what JWG explained to me years ago, this technique helps eliminate LEARNED guilt, not natural guilt. Even in Natural Law we can experience natural guilt. But, at this point in our history we're just beginning to learn how to distinguish between natural guilt and the guilt we can feel by comparing ourselves to a "perfect" God. I think it boils down to a simple (Pisces) process of asking in any of these situations just WHAT the basis of the guilt is, ie whether it's rooted in man-made laws or Natural Laws. And as one asks that question more and more, I think we can start to weed out the source of any guilt. Even with the natural guilt, we need to remember that as Wolf used to put it, "God has goofed up, so why wouldn't WE goof up?" And another (Piscean) question: "How can anything perfect create something Imperfect?" It's really a shift in this understanding of "perfection" that I think helps in our understanding of Natural Law, and ultimately the forgiveness for both ourselves and others. (Adina)

This is a very simple technique, and it's absolutely free (except for the price of a cassette tape).

(1) Take a sheet of notebook paper and fold it down the middle. On the left side, list every negative message you've ever received from whatever person at any time. Take at least a week to do this – longer if necessary, AND use as many pieces of paper as necessary. (I think I had six pages, and I wrote on them front and back.) If you're like most of us who've done this, you'll find that many of the negative messages have been coming from yourself. Example: "Mary, you're just no good for anything."

(2) Once you're sure you've written down all the negative messages, then on the right side of the paper, across from each of the negative messages, write a positive, counteractive message. Example: Mary's response to above. "No. That's only their opinion of me. It's not a fact. I am good for lots of things, and can, in fact, do many things very well." (Notice that even if we start with a negative, the majority of the message is said in positive language.)

(3) Once you have all your positive/counteractive messages written down, take a 90-minute tape and record each of the messages in your own voice, saying them like you really MEAN them. You may find this difficult at first because the statements don't FEEL right to you. But be the best actor you can be and read each one with positive conviction. You need to fill only one side of the tape. Since you will be playing this as you go to sleep, if you have difficulty falling asleep right away, or the sound of voices keeps you awake, then leave about the first 20 minutes of the tape blank before you start to record your messages. The remaining 25 minutes of the tape will be more than enough to accomplish your purpose.

(4) Each night for the next four to six months (minimum of four) when you go to bed, try to place your tape recorder as close to your right side as possible, turn on your tape (if you sleep with a partner, use ear phones) and go to sleep. The messages will enter through your right ear and, thus, affect the left brain. (According to Jeffrey this is a shamanic technique.) This is different from saying affirmations when you're awake because when you're asleep the left brain can't argue or discount the information. It's absolutely CRUCIAL to do this EVERY NIGHT for the four to six months – do not skip even one night. If you miss a night, the "chain" of positive reinforcement in your brain is broken, and you have to start all over again.

Another thing to keep in mind is that since this simple practice radically changes your consciousness, freeing you from what can be thousands of years of guilt and not feeling ready enough or good enough, Lucifer will do its darnedest to make sure this shift doesn't happen. Incredibly stupid things can happen. It actually took me 16 months to get through a full six months without interruption. I don't want anyone to dwell on that part, but do be AWARE and take appropriate precautions. For example, make sure you have new batteries (if necessary) on a regular basis, etc. After a week or so, you'll start to notice that with each day you'll feel a little 'lighter,' a little bit stronger, and a little bit happier or more content. You'll start to feel empowered and like you ARE ready enough and/or good enough to take on something you want to do. Since there's strength in numbers, if you plan to do this and are open to sharing that you ARE doing it (no need to give details of the messages, etc.), then perhaps you could set up an email support group. This is an amazing technique to rid oneself of the learned masochism, and I wish any and all of you who try this the greatest success and a new lease on life. (Adina)

JWG's Method of Eliminating LEARNED Masochism (for children)
To determine what behaviors indicate masochism in the child, read Pluto Vol. 2 in which Wolf went into detail about the sado-masochistic archetypes. In relation to children not being "steeped" in it yet, masochism will be reflected in a chart because it began BEFORE this lifetime, since the chart reflects the past, as experienced in the present, which leads to the future. When it's a young child, Wolf advocated the parents whispering the counteractive methods (for this and other conditions) in the child's right ear every night after the child had fallen asleep, and to do this for the four months, although sometimes the results start to appear much sooner. (Adina)

Synthesis of Virgo/Leo archetypes
In terms of synthesizing the Virgo/Leo archetypes, generally speaking, it is good to remember that the Leo archetype correlates with creative self-actualization, and the need to actualize the Soul's special destiny. Leo is full of what it is, so to speak, and feels a sense of special destiny and purpose (as do all fire signs) that must now be actualized. The distortion of this archetype is one of over self-focus (narcissism) and being overly identified with one's creative purpose from an egocentric point of view. Delusions of self-grandeur correlate with this archetype. Typically, there is a deep insecurity within the Leo archetype that creates a bottomless pit in terms of how much external recognition and feedback the person feels they need. In other words, Leo also correlates to the need to be acknowledged as special, and because of the underlying insecurity in this archetype the need for this type of feedback, or acknowledgement can become never ending.

The Virgo archetype comes right after Leo, and correlates with the need for self-improvement and adjustment. This will be linked with any patterns of over self-focus and self-inflation that manifests in the Leo archetype. In essence, we are analyzing our egos in this archetype. While Leo is full of what it is, Virgo is becoming aware of all of our short-comings and lacks (of what we are not). In a general sense then, the Virgo archetype can create a natural humility within a person who also has Leo in the chart because the person, potentially, will be able to discern delusions of grandeur and purify an overly self-absorbed focus in life. The person could also adjust the dynamic of the need for constant positive feedback from others, and recognizing the special talents and capacities of others. When the Virgo/Leo archetype work together, the person could also effect self-improvement by creatively actualizing a special purpose that is linked with healing and serving others. Leo will now be linked with the need for self-improvement and service to the whole in some way, and through the act of service a natural humility can manifest. (Deva)

Natural square Virgo/Sagittarius
Note also the natural square between Virgo and Sagittarius. Guilt about Natural Law. In this state of consciousness, a Soul perceives itself to be innately flawed and actually deserving of constant suffering based on its perceived nature as a sinner. The body itself is a sin. Immediately after eating the fruit, Adam and Eve covered up their nakedness with fig leaves. Suddenly they ate from the tree of knowledge of good and bad and they had "knowledge." Now sexuality was an act of "knowing." Now the body was something to be covered up. The natural isness of life was no longer experienced as they began to impose their ideas *about* nature upon nature. (Ari)

Conditioned and unconditioned Virgo
There is nothing perfect. Yet we have bought into the idea that unless I do something perfectly it is not good enough, and I am not good enough. These things are the conditioned Virgo. The natural or unconditioned Virgo is the acceptance of imperfection. You are still aware of what you (Virgo) lack, and what you need to improve. But instead of beating self up about one's failings, you realize that you are supposed to be where you find yourself. My intention is to self-improve (Virgo). It is not a failing that I am imperfect, but part of the intended plan. Intentions count – I strive to self-improve step-by-step (Virgo), little by little. A key natural Virgo archetype is The Value is in the Effort. Over time effort leads to change and self-improvement. That is a huge difference from the conditioned guilt-ridden masochistic patriarchal Virgo. Self-deprecation based on "I am worthless," or inadequate is something else altogether – masochism. That is pathology, not humility. (Steve)

Inductive and deductive thought
Inductive thought is Pisces, Neptune, and the 12th house. Thus, it's opposite, deductive thought, is Virgo, the 6th house, and Mercury. (Rad)
With the revelation of repeating themes, it is here that the transition from deductive logic to inductive understanding will occur. The more regularly you put this exercise into practice, the more quickly this shift will occur until it eventually becomes automatic. It is not a development you want to rush. It is important to allow this to happen in its own natural time, because your deductive efforts will serve as your long term foundation. Once the inductive orientation becomes relatively automatic, the foundation established through the deductive development will make a real difference in the accuracy of the inductive information that comes to you in terms of the big picture you will see. Think of it this way. Inductive knowledge is as easy to misinterpret as it is to mix up facts and data. If you get your facts solid in the beginning, the information that will be supplied to your intuition from that point on will be grounded and will have solid integrity, which of course will minimize errors in grasping the chart in total. The other thing to do is be aware of any expectations you may have toward your own process. True EA work is guided by Spirit. If your intent is to understand the Soul as deeply as you can such that you can offer the messages they are ready and needing to hear, those messages will be made known to you from within. This is a timeless phenomenon. The understanding you are meant to have with any given chart will come to you at the moment it is needed, and that is something that is best embraced by trust in the inner teacher. (Stacie)

Life purpose
Every Soul, relative to its evolutionary conditions, has a true life purpose that is consistent with its ongoing evolutionary needs. The entire paradigm of the 10th, Saturn, Capricorn, 2nd, Taurus, Venus, the 6th, Mercury, and Virgo correlate to life purpose as expressed through the agency of one's work, or career. When the Soul begins to evolve into the Spiritual State then the Soul is inwardly and progressively attuned to the consciousness we call the Source, or God/ess. As such, these Souls will desire to do work that they feel inwardly called to do from that Source. The inner degree of awareness, evolution, within the Spiritual stage will correspond to not only the nature of what that is, but also that the nature of that work in every way is being consciously directed by that Source. The Souls who have reached the point in evolution in which the center of gravity has finally shifted from the subjective ego that the Soul creates to the Soul itself. At that point there no longer is any 'personal identification' with that work other than consciously cooperating with the inner directions from the Source to do that work. (Rad)

Compensation
People in the beginnings of 1st stage Individuated do in fact feel very different than the Consensus folks/state through which they have just evolved and yet because it is relatively new it of course creates a deep sense of insecurity and anxiety in terms of fully acting upon this individuating impulse. As a result of that fear such folks 'compensate' by way of trying to counteract this inner sense of insecurity and anxiety by creating the external appearance of normalcy including the very structures of their life, including many 'friends' that come out of that very consensus, 'normal' type jobs, etc., thus creating a living lie because of the act of compensation. All of us can 'compensate' in areas of our life relative to where we feel most insecure or powerless. (JWG)

Compensation can show up in someone in any evolutionary stage where the person is not operating fully aligned with Natural Law. The gist of compensation is (as an example) if a person feels inadequate and bad about themselves inside (Virgo-like) they may cultivate an outer persona that seems really self-confident and almost full of self (Leo-like). It works the other way around also, a person with a big ego presenting themselves as humble and serving. Compensation is a form of AVOIDING rebalancing. Because it comes out of denial, where the person believes (Jupiter) that the way they are showing up IS the truth, when in fact it is a way of avoiding looking at (Virgo, denial) the actual reality, and pretending to be something other than what they really are. That is not my definition of rebalancing. If they OWNED the underlying condition and then practiced coming from a polarity to work towards balancing it, that I'd describe as rebalancing. Denial can never be a path to equilibrium.

I'm not sure I'd call compensation a natural phenomenon. It's more like a survival mechanism. A person feels so wounded inside they can't show up as what and where they really are – they pretend (fooling themselves) to be more than or less than what they actually are. That is to survive. If aligned with Natural Law, a person would just accept wherever they found themselves to be – why would they need to compensate? There's a big difference between being aware you feel highly inadequate, accepting that you do and showing up anyway with acceptance of your inadequacies (humility), and showing up acting like you are confident and self-assured, an adopted persona, when that is not at all where the person is within themselves. In other words, compensation is more making a condition even more out of balance than it is rebalancing a condition. The thought is one that Jeffrey used to say, that where Jupiter is transiting it has gifts to bring you. But you have to be willing to give something up before you can receive the gifts. The "something" is not some random something that you pick out yourself. Rather it is something that has become outmoded in the life and needs to be let go of. I'd say it's not a conscious process – Jupiter is intuition – one would just know what the something needs to be. No letting go, no gifts. (Steve)

Disillusionment and doubt, a personal experience

(Q) I have been undergoing massive disillusionment within my own spiritual life and within my relationship to Spirit itself. I have noticed as a reaction to this, I have become extremely cautious and guarded about interpreting *anything* in directly spiritual terms anymore. It is as JWG frequently said, disillusionment can be one of the most bitter and difficult experiences that any of us can have, and I can say from direct experience that this is UTTERLY true. And because that experience is so hard and so painful, the last thing I personally want to do – and I'm sure the same is often true for others – is delude myself again and walk right back into it. This also connects to the Virgo archetype: transition. In my own case, I recognize that I am manifesting an extreme response to the disillusionment that has had to occur in myself – and one of the serious, unfortunate effects is that it has cut me off from my own lifeblood. That is something I just have to work out for myself, I know. But I do have this question correlating to disillusionment and doubt. How does one go through massive disillusionment and not get caught up in the debilitating psychology of doubt? If something has been regarded in one's heart of hearts as 'real' – and that something has also been providing the basis for ultimate meaning – it is a complete shock to consciousness when the illusions are exposed and the meaning within it is finally seen as an embellishment of one's own making. So the question becomes, how does one recover one's confidence in interpreting spiritual reality, ie what is a real manifestation of Spirit vs what is imagined or 'hoped,' following a major disillusioning of consciousness? – particularly when there is no immediate resource available to confirm or clarify the accuracy of one's interpretation? (Stacie)

(A) The actual archetype that specifically correlates with being disillusioned is Neptune, Pisces, 12th house, that can then trigger its natural polarity of the Virgo, 6th house, and Mercury that manifests as doubt. With Neptune now transiting Pisces, and it has been squaring the transiting nodal axis that was in Gemini/Sagittarius, this experience of disillusionment leading to doubt has been happening to many, many people. And necessarily so because the intention with Neptune in Pisces is to know or learn about that which is true, and that which is not. While those transiting Nodes were in Gemini/Sagittarius this then focuses on the difference between beliefs that are projected as ultimate meaning, that which is true from the point of view of pure beliefs, and that which is true from the point of view of INNER KNOWING. Inner knowing does not correlate with beliefs because what is known is experienced within the interior of the Soul itself as a by-product of desire to know that which is true, and that which is not. Inner knowing of that which is universally true occurs of course through various practices, Virgo, that are all aimed and shallowing or stopping the breath. As that occurs the Soul is then able to penetrate the inner realms of consciousness itself: Neptune correlates with the phenomena of consciousness. As it progressively penetrates these inner realms of consciousness a variety of natural truths that correlate with the nature and cause of consciousness itself become KNOWN. And this knowing, again, is not a function of beliefs because, as these inner truths are known, there is nothing to literally believe and everything to know. And because these inner truths are simply known there then becomes nothing to doubt. The knowing is a function of actual experience, and those experiences are universal to any Soul who so desires to know these inner truths that correlate with the nature of consciousness. Because they are in fact universal it then serves as a way of knowing that which is true, versus that which is make-believe.

When this is the baseline within the Soul's consciousness, the point of personal Soul knowing and integration, this then serves as the vehicle through which, and because of, the Soul then 'interprets' the nature of any given phenomenal reality. The dynamic or archetype of interpretation specially correlates to Sagittarius, Jupiter, and the 9th house. As the Soul interprets the nature of any external phenomenal reality relative to this inner baseline the MEANING of whatever external phenomenal reality is then projected upon that phenomenal reality. As the Soul does this it will then automatically create a way of intellectually organizing all of phenomenal reality that reflects the core inner baseline of the inner knowing of the nature of consciousness itself. This natural process of intellectually organizing phenomenal reality correlates to Gemini: how the nature of thoughts that occur as a function of the inner knowing are connected to create a larger whole that is organized. All of this then correlates to the nature of various 'spiritual' cosmologies that humans have manifested going back to its own origins on this Earth that are then called 'religions.' This is then exactly where the conflict between pure beliefs versus actual knowing can occur because many who do desire to know the Origin of all things, the Origin of consciousness itself, indeed the Origin of themselves, align themselves with whatever spiritual cosmology without actually doing what is necessary to know for themselves that which is true.

Thus, by attaching themselves to whatever cosmology then leads to their personal belief system that is of course used to interpret whatever phenomenal reality. When a Soul does this, without actually doing that which is necessary to inwardly know, these beliefs are then projected upon phenomenal reality so that when phenomenal reality manifests in ways that cause conflict with the projected beliefs the result is then doubt: doubting the nature of the projected beliefs themselves that have been born, again, from whatever spiritual cosmology they have latched onto relative to the pure desire to Know. This conflict caused by projected beliefs initially creates the disillusionment of those beliefs that then triggers the doubt. It should be said too that a Soul who does not do their own actual inner knowing but simply latches onto whatever spiritual cosmology can also create 'beliefs' about themselves and/or others that are also delusional or illusionary. Thus, when certain types of inner or outer events take place that defeat those projected inner beliefs about themselves or others that same experience of being disillusioned takes place that then leads to doubt: doubt about oneself, or doubt about another(s). In essence this correlates to self-deception, and/ or being deceived by others.

To recover one's confidence in interpreting phenomenal reality, or as you say 'spiritual' reality, is to go deeply within the interior of one's own consciousness with the pure desire to KNOW. To know the actual truth of anything. To do so always starts with some sort of natural practice that aims at stilling the breath, of shallowing it to the point that it NATURALLY STOPS. If one does this while at the same time holding the nature of whatever one is wanting to know about within their consciousness there will come a moment, a time, in which the answer simply OCCURS WITHIN CONSCIOUSNESS OF ITS OWN VOLITION: like a bubble manifesting from the depths of the sea onto the surface of the sea itself. And a Soul can do this repeatedly in such a way that the truth of what one is wanting to know about can be repeated as many times as the Soul needs it to be repeated so that the lingering doubt simply dissolves. The point here is that if that which is true relative to what one is asking about is indeed true it will repeat itself over and over for as many times that the Soul needs it to. In this way confidence is regained. (Rad)

Pluto in Virgo generation – Great Mother Goddess

To reclaim our sacred inheritance, we have to meet our Plutonian Souls face to face otherwise we stay hidden in the shadow of Virgo. Traditionally, Virgo has been linked to the planet Mercury, also the ruler of Gemini. Gemini and Mercury represent the masculine and the ethers, yet Virgo is intrinsically feminine. And although she is mentally oriented like Gemini, she is so through her devotion and embodiment of the Sacred and Divine bodymind. In modern culture, the term "virgin" is misunderstood and portrays virginity as an untouched maiden, pure and chaste, appealing to a sexually dysfunctional culture cut off from the wild, embodied, and self-contained feminine. No wonder Virgo has been wound up so tight and placed within the realms of the mind – she has been stripped of her body and earthly essence. The Virgo archetype developed into a self-focused, self-anointing signature to survive the stifling effects of patriarchal rule. Defining the essence of Virgo from her repressed history only continues to feed the dualistic shroud the feminine principle has been wearing for centuries, Madonna or whore. The feminine Virgo archetype split off from her sexuality to survive patriarchal rule, and the consort Scorpio became the "prostitute." "When denied her sexual devotion to others (Scorpio) she turns her energy inward (Virgo) to realize the divine union within herself." (George)

In pre-Hellenic cultures the Great Mother Goddess was revered and the true meaning of "virgin" stood for unmarried women who devoted themselves to the sacred hearth and fire of ancient feminine rites. These vestal virgins were women who embodied the mysteries of the Kundalini fire, bestowing their mysteries through sacred sexual acts of union as a means to embody and create divinity (divine birth, Jesus) and to spiritually awaken their consorts and communities. During the rise of patriarchal culture in the Greek and Roman empires, also noted by Demetra George, vestal virgins were enshrined and vowed to chastity as a means to dismiss matriarchal lines and Goddess worship. Any virgin who strayed from her duty received severe whippings and was sentenced to a slow agonizing death by subterranean crypt. From this perspective we can easily grasp and understand the ancient and sacred depth the Virgoan archetype carries. This archetype remembers the pre-Hellenic cultures.

Thanks to the movement of the Moon's nodes through the Pisces/Virgo axis in 2006 and 2007, the sacred feminine was unveiled and awakened in the collective mind, unleashing Virgo the Magdalene from the underworld. (Virgo is associated with Persephone, Demeter, the Virgin Mary, Mary Magdalene and Mercury, Ceres, Vesta and Chiron). Virgo wants to perfect, craft, polish, and continually renew and develop towards self-improvement. She achieves this through noticing every nuance and every microscopic detail of her surroundings and her body. She is the Mrs Spock of the zodiac, observing any blemish, any non-essential or unnecessary factor that may distract her from her goal, the art of sacred devotion and healing. Her critical nature serves as the refining element needed to discern what actually deserves her sacred attention. Collectively and personally, it has not been an easy journey for the Virgo archetype up until now. Hidden in the shadow of patriarchal repression her characteristics become extremely self-critical, thus she seeks constant atonement for the unruly guilt complex she carries, believing she is lacking somehow. The Course in

Miracles would say this is all of us who have not awakened to who we truly are – the light of God. In astrological language, this refers to Pisces, the polarity of Virgo.

Virgo is a mutable sign (changeable), therefore she needs to be mindful as she is easily swayed by outer influences and authorities as she learns to determine her own ground. If she (or the Soul) doesn't know who she willingly (and unconsciously) sacrifices herself. She is a giver and wants to tend to the needs of others, living out her ancient path of service, therefore, she must be discerning about who and what she nurtures, or she will become devoted to an addiction or outside force (person, place or thing). Virgo is so precise, though, she sees right through deceptive influences if she is taught to honor her perceptions and trust her gifts. She needs validation of her wisdom more than ever, especially since outer culture (excessive masculine) has dishonored her role for so long. If our wounds (Pluto in Virgo generation) are not dealt with directly, we will perpetuate the illusion of separation from our Highest Self, our God source. When the Virgo archetype remains in constant guilt (shadow of Virgo) she is only lacking what the collective has not acknowledged in her and what she has not discerned within herself – her own sacredness and her sacred place on Earth. Because the feminine principle has been barren and misunderstood for so long, she is thirsty for sustenance, and only true sustenance will suffice us now. Virgo knows the difference. Remember, she is highly perceptive and acutely accurate. She will strip herself bare of the nurturance she so needs to stay hidden from the ruling patriarchy that has repressed her in the past, rather than outwardly risk captivity and death again. (Wendy)

"The Secret," thoughts changing reality

"The Secret" wasn't any "secret" and, to me, it's just the New Age version of Christian guilt. You're not getting wealthy, healthy, the new job, whatever it is we want – because we don't BELIEVE enough – we don't PRAY hard enough. We don't envision already having what we want, or we don't use enough emotion, you're not TRYing HARD enough, etc., etc., etc., ad nauseum – just reinforcing the person's guilt and/or deep sadness because they haven't been able to manifest whatever it is they want. Think of what this does to the person whose karma/evolutionary necessity demand that they NOT have whatever it is they're trying to manifest – more guilt, more anger, more feelings of helplessness and hopelessness. The underlying premise that we need to and can change our thoughts to change our reality is valid but it, too, somehow got distorted by tying it to man-made beliefs about what life is "supposed to look like/be." And again, it's getting back to the natural god, the natural way of doing things, and the way things naturally are that will actually bring us to our own inner state of balance and grace. Sometimes we're going to get eaten by the lion, and sometimes we're going to be the one feasting on the filet. The bottom line that JWG always went back to were the words of Jesus to seek God first, put God first, and what you need will be given to you. And that seeking needs to be sincere and consistent. Such a simple concept; and yet if we're honest with ourselves, it's much harder to pull off. But as JWG also said many times, "The value is in the effort." (Adina)

LIBRA – VENUS - 7th HOUSE

Libra keywords

The "other"	Listening	Choices	Damaged trust
Social	Extremes	Flirt	Intimacy
Objective awareness	Polarity	Beauty	Casanova
Relationships	Denial	Surface – Shallow	Philanderer
Comparison	Mask	Half-truths	Idealism
Others' needs	Relativity	Boundary-less	Appearance
Projection	Relatedness	Social grace	
Pleasing others	Co-dependency	Partner	

Libra, Venus, 7th house archetype

Air / yang / cardinal / 7th house / ruled by Venus. This is where we embrace the world of the social other, the shift from subjective to objective consciousness. There is an impulse to initiate all kinds of relationships with all types of people, to experience diversity. Libra connects with the other air signs, Gemini and Aquarius, to learn about the relativity of values and beliefs. Libra represents the principle of relativity. It breaks up the Leo viewpoint that my way is the only way, and teaches relativity, that all are equal, and that each person's views are valid. Through contrast and comparison with others, we evaluate our distinct individuality. In Libra we become aware of the needs of others, we learn to truly listen to others and to give them what they need, based on their own reality rather than our idea of what they need – that is the Leo style of giving. Libra actually represents extremes, the polarities of each person's life. The lesson of Libra is to learn balance. The balance is learned gradually through experiencing all sorts of extremes and gradually learning how to center self. Libra is not the marriage house. If it were, we would be married to everyone. Scorpio is the marriage house because marriage involves sex. Libra teaches us about the diversity of types. Out of this diversity we begin to learn discrimination, deciding which types, and who, we want to spend the majority of our time around. Libra can correlate to mental illness, as it is naturally inconjunct to Pisces and square to Cancer. This can create split or fractured personalities, multiple personalities, etc. (JWG's Pluto Vol. 1 and the School's Course)
[Recommended Reading: Jeffrey Wolf Green's Pluto Vol. 1 – The Evolutionary Journey of the Soul]

Pluto in the 7th house or Libra

The 7th is a cardinal house, indicating a new evolutionary cycle is underway. To experience the intent of this cycle 7th house Pluto people have been involved in a variety of relationships. Through this comes exposure to different value and belief systems of all kinds. Through this process these people come to understand who they are through comparing self with the others they are in relationship with. A fundamental issue is how to be in relationships. They will have felt in the past, and will continue to feel, a fundamental need to be in relationships. This is due to the desire to complete self through the relations with others, and to unite self with others. They need to be in relationships to feel fulfilled and complete. Most have not yet learned how to be in relationship on an equal basis. They may become involved in too many relationships and take in too many differing points of view. They can lose their sense of who they are in this process. They can become dependent on the advice and opinions of others to help them determine who they are or what they should be doing with their lives. When in this state, they can't relate to themselves without relating to others. They do not like being alone. They will become attracted to powerful people who appear to be stable and have the ability to guide the 7th house person. They become dependent on the partner. They can become dominated to the extent that they feel the other person's needs and desires are actually their own. They have become an extension of the other person's ego. In other cases, due to the polarities of extremity, they can become the dominating partner. They can attract those who will become dependent on them, giving a false sense of power and control over others.

They generally have karma with a variety of people. This creates situations where one or the other leaves the relationship, without the other person desiring this outcome, or they become mutually dependent on each other. The imbalances in relationships create confrontations to force the person to examine the relationship; to learn how to give to others and have one's own needs met through that. Because the impulse is new, most of them have not yet mastered the ability to live this way. This leads to conditional love, 'I will love you when you <whatever>.' This comes from projecting expectations onto partners, or having partners project expectations on the 7th house Pluto person. They are learning how to give and receive love. As this has not been mastered, situations may arise where they cannot accept what comes their way, or the partner may not recognize the love they are trying to offer. This is necessary so they can learn to relate in a way of equality and balance. It also teaches them what their relationship needs are, who they are because of relationships, and to develop social values of how people should relate to each other. They enforce the lesson of minimizing dependency. They will finally realize they need to be needed, and will see how this need controls the dynamics of their relationships. They will learn when and what to give and when and what not to give. (JWG's Pluto Vol. 1 and the School's Course)

Pluto polarity point – 1st house or Aries

The intent is for the person to learn how to initiate their own life directions without being dependent on advice from others. A parallel lesson is not to interfere in anyone else's decisions. They need to learn HOW to live alone, though they do not need to live alone. They need to learn to balance their need to be with others with their need to be alone. They need to learn to conduct relationships in a new way, and to select partners who will actualize their own lives through their own means. They will learn how to truly give to others and thus realize the balance of relationships. They will become among the most giving of people, able to identify the reality of the people with whom they interact. They will give these people what they need, and will not give them what they do not need. They will learn to be in relationship in a non-dependent way, and will encourage independence in their mate. They will learn to not lose themselves in relationships, and to remain balanced in life's external situations. They will learn to appreciate the diversity of humanity, and to recognize their own individuality because of it. They give others the courage to be themselves. Commonly these people have a compulsive need to be in relationship to feel complete, the need to dominate or be dominated, the need to be needed, the need to be liked, they will have a hypnotic effect on others, the need to give or receive advice. (JWG's Pluto Vol. 1 and the School's Course)

Venus double rulership – Libra and Taurus

Jeffrey was the first astrologer to teach about Venus' correlation to the inner relationship that all people have with themselves. He taught why Venus had a double rulership for the signs Libra and Taurus. He said that Taurus and the 2nd house correlated to the inner relationship we all have with ourselves, and that the 7th house and Libra correlated to the types of outer relationships that we form with other people and why. He taught that the planet Venus, of itself, symbolized both the inner and outer relationships within the archetype of Venus itself. A simple example: if a person has, let's say, Venus in Virgo and their inner relationship to themself is one of intense criticism, all the things that are wrong with them, that it shouldn't then be surprising that that person would then 'attract,' Venus, others who are then critical of them: the inner reflecting the outer. And that which we attract is a reflection of the inner vibration within us where that inner vibration is a reflection of our inner relationship to ourselves. Or, for another example, let's say that Venus in Virgo person was inwardly experiencing a high degree of 'lack' in their lives which then leads to a sense of being 'empty' from within. That inner relationship to themselves could then manifest outwardly as needing, Venus, many other people in their lives in order to 'fill them up,' and needing others to give to them that which they felt they were lacking.

He talked about the natural inconjunct between the 2nd house, Taurus, and the 7th house, Libra. He taught that this is the natural 'crisis' that exists in all of us that involves the need to be self-reliant and fulfilling our own needs, and how our needs can be projected onto others in such a way as to become dependent on others for the very needs that we need to satisfy within ourselves. And how our projected needs onto others correlate to 'expectations' that we can set up with other people. So what happens when our expectations that are projected onto others do not occur? For most some kind of crisis will occur where the intent of the crisis is to force the person back upon themselves so that self-reliance in some way can be developed when those expectations have reached a point of excessive dependency on others. He taught about the need for the EA astrologer to understand the totality of the Venus archetype. Thus, to not only understand the sign that Venus is in but all the aspects that it is making to other planets, the North and South Nodes of Venus in terms of what the past, present, and future of the evolving Venus archetype is in all charts, and to fully grasp the signs on the 2nd and 7th houses as they condition those natural archetypes, and the reasons for that conditioning relative to the ongoing evolutionary intentions of the Soul, and, lastly, the location of the planetary rulers of those signs and the aspects that they are making for the same reasons. (Rad)

Venus correlates with our inner relationship with ourselves, and also the external relationships we form as a reflection of our inner relationship. Venus is co-ruled by the signs of Taurus and Libra. Taurus reflects our inner relationship with ourselves, and the inner side, or inner nature, of Venus. Libra reflects the relationships we attract and initiate with other people (outer or external side of Venus). Venus correlates with our values which are a determinate to who we form relationships with and whom not, and also the needs we have within relationships. When we have not learned to meet our own needs they become projected onto our partner and others in general within relationships. There is a natural inconjunct between the Taurus and Libra archetypes which correlates with the crisis (inconjunct) that occurs when we project too many needs onto another within relationships and are then thrown back onto ourselves in order to learn self-reliance. Venus correlates with extremities, and how we will go about balancing or uniting discordant aspects of ourselves. Again, the need is to learn to identify what our specific needs are within relationships and meet those from within ourselves in order to attract relationships that are balanced, equal, and based on mutual independence. The natal placement of Venus in the birth chart correlates with the person's pre-existing relationship patterns, and the values and needs an individual will have within relationships.

Venus also correlates to the nature of our "inner dialogue" with ourselves (Taurus side of Venus) and how we can all project this inner dialogue onto others. In other words, if I have Venus in Scorpio I will naturally be listening to others from a "bottom line" psychological standpoint ("where is this person coming from, can I relate to this or not?"). The Venus in Scorpio person may also come into relationships with unconscious fears of abandonment, betrayal, and loss, and unconsciously project these fears onto the other by listening to their partner in a defensive manner, and also project that the other person has ulterior motives or agendas which the other in fact does not have. The point within this is that Venus correlates with the psychology of listening (Libra side of Venus), and when we listen to others based on our own subjective inner dialogue we do not truly hear what they are communicating. Remember that the archetype of Libra correlates with the need to learn to listen to others from their reality, not our own, in order to truly understand what the other is communicating. (Deva)

Past, present, future orientations of a planet (eg Venus)

The present life Venus is conditioned by all the past "self and other" relationship tendencies and patterns that have preceded it. The South Node of Venus represents directly the way the Venus functions were handled in the past. The South Node of the Moon represents the Soul's past personality structures and emotional habits/patterns. Both of these are alive within the present life Venus function, subconsciously coloring it. Yet that Venus also contains the possibility of changing the past, in the present moment (the only moment in which anything can be changed). The intended directions for that Venus to evolve are indicated in the North Node of Venus, the Lunar North Node ruler, the Lunar North Node, and the Polarity Point of Pluto, in that order, from top to bottom. We try to mentally separate the past and the present and the future, to see them as different things. But in reality it's all the same, and it can't be separated. That is why EA says you work the North Node, learn new ways of doing things, and then evolve your South Node function by integrating these new ways into your old ways of doing the South Node. The end result is the entire structure, Soul and personality, evolve. We can't really separate our internal Venus functions from our Mars functions, from our Moon functions, from our Saturn functions. We are complex beings that have all of these inner drives, desires, motivations, orientations. In reality they are all mixed together within us. We use astrology to gain objectivity by assigning this function to this planet and that function to that planet, but past a certain point those are constructs, not complete reality. In reality we are the sum total of all of them, and that includes our past and future also. EVERYTHING has something to do with the past. The imprint of the past is contained within the present Venus and every other planet too. (Steve)

Psychology of listening

Venus correlates to the psychology of listening. Via the Taurus side of Venus our inner dialogue with our self is all too often projected (Libra side of Venus) onto others in our relationships. Example, Venus in Virgo, the person could project the inner critical relationship/inner dialogue onto the other in the form of "hearing" the other criticize or undermine them when this is not the case (the other may be trying to give helpful advice for example). The point is that via the Libra side of Venus we must learn to objectively hear and listen to others from their reality so we do not project in this way, and truly hear what is being said. (Deva)

Since Pisces is the polarity of Virgo, the Soul with Venus in Virgo is always comparing themselves to perfection and often feeling the LACK to greater degrees. The Venus in Virgo can be so self-critical that this criticism can then be transferred to the partner, ie not just the self-judgment trips or hearing another incorrectly but also focusing on the partner's inadequacies versus their strengths, ie focusing on their lacks too. It is impossible to love another (7th house) unconditionally until and unless one can learn to love themselves (2nd house) unconditionally first, which is the evolutionary intent with a Venus in Virgo, ie the polarity of Virgo being PISCES (unconditional LOVE). (Kristin)

Cardinal energy

Libra brings so many options, and at a time of transition, the ego is easily confused about which way to go, how to proceed. Cardinal energy is so instinctive, so the Soul may 'cast a wide net,' trying to see what fits (Libra), and the blocks we experience thus help us narrow down our options so as to lead us in the appropriate direction. (Lesley)

Cardinal houses are intense because they represent major shifts or turning points – the natural squares-oppositions-conjunctions in the chart. The cardinal signs/houses contain their own paradoxes. Cardinal is an instinctual need to initiate change. Our sense of security is based on sameness, not on change. Thus the very nature of cardinal insures that at certain points we are going to freak out a bit, because all the change we have been instinctually creating results in a loss of familiarity and known-ness. This, at key points, results in the loss of an emotional sense of safety/security, leading to a desire to STOP, to want to go inward to emotionally regroup – to ground and stabilize the new realities we have been initiating. This is an inherent and necessary part of the cardinal archetype. It's especially pronounced in Cancer, but applies to all cardinal signs/houses – two steps forward, one step back. The natural need to regroup and reground after taking two steps into new directions. After a period of timeout, the cardinal instinct to initiate change again takes over, and we are back pursuing the next step forward again. (Steve)

Venus retrograde
When the planet Venus is retrograde in the sky, you may be able to feel the nature of this archetype intimately, especially the inner side of Venus as it works to help you reconnect with yourself and through extension Spirit. It is a time where your Soul is getting in touch with what holds the most meaning and value. A time to reflect about whether you are getting your essential needs (inner side of Venus) met and a time when your Soul is in the process of making changes to support those values. (Kristin)
Venus Rx indicates that the Soul is defined through the Taurus side of Venus (establishing a primary relationship within him or herself first) instead of the Libra side as most folks are (initiation of relationships with others which is the externalized side of Venus). (Deva)

Venus in composite and synastry
The composite chart reflects the two people as a single unit, or a combined person. In other words, the composite chart reflects the core evolutionary lessons that two people have desired to work on together as a couple or unit (for example, in the composite chart the couple may have Venus square Pluto). Synastry charts reflect the dynamics that exist between two people as separate beings, or between the two people as individuals (for example, person A might have Venus square person B's Mars. In this case person A will always manifest the Venus role, and person B will manifest the Mars role). You cannot interpret the composite chart without first understanding each person's natal chart, and the synastry charts. You could apply the core meaning of Mars and Venus in the natal chart in the composite as long as you adjust that meaning to reflect that it symbolizes the couple's mutual desires (Mars)/relationship patterns (Venus) as a single unit so to speak. (Deva)

Inner Venus (2nd house)
The issue of pre-existing needs relative to Venus: Venus in reference to the 2nd house correlates to one's survival issues. The 2nd house is a fixed energy momentum. Inner Venus, correlating to the 2nd house archetype, corresponds to the psychology of inner hearing. Put this together and you have the psychology of inner hearing relative to how one is resonating inwardly with survival issues that have become fixed or rooted within one's consciousness or inner hearing. Note also that the archetype of the 2nd house is opposed by the fixed 8th house: this sign/house polarity suggests resonating with that which is rooted or embedded in the (pre-existing and evolving) psychology of the Soul. That which pre-exists also energizes the principle of magnetic attractions of resources – that which one has (previously) evaluated is essential to survival – at all the levels – emotional, psychological, biological, physical, material, and spiritual. The planetary nodes, etc. fill in the rest of the story. (Rose)

Projection
Unless any reality is 'objectively' understood for what it is, whatever that reality is, then the Soul will project what they think that reality is into any situation that is not objectively understood. Projecting onto someone else what we think they need can be associated with Libra because Libra is naturally linked to Aquarius and Gemini through its own natural triad. (Rad)

Projections, delusions, expectations
Astrologically speaking, Aquarius is the archetype that correlates with projections (from our own unconscious). These projections can be based on past traumas (ie this reminds me of my ex-partner, old friend, parents, etc.) which are then cast onto the person who you are involved with now. These projections can also be based on the person's own unconscious inner dynamics/structure that are then cast onto others. In other words, the person projects what is inside themselves onto others. Aquarius correlates to the individuated unconscious and also to the dynamic of trauma. The projections that can surface within this archetype can be linked with the need to objectify and hopefully release what is stored/unresolved within the unconscious. [The situation you are describing] also sounds like dynamics that are linked with unconscious expectations that get projected upon others within relationships.
Astrologically speaking, expectations are linked with the archetype of Libra. Libra correlates with the nature of our expectations within relationships and our ability (or inability) to reach a balanced state of giving and receiving within relationships. Libra correlates with extremities, and the need to reach a state of balance relative to such extremities. Delusion/fantasy correlates with the archetype of Pisces. Pisces symbolizes the need for ultimate meaning, and to bring to closure an entire cycle of evolution in order to prepare for a new cycle which begins in the Aries archetype. When ultimate meaning is 'projected' externally within a relationship it is all too easy to fall into fantasies and delusions (infatuation) about the other person regardless of how much actual contact there has been.
The core point within this is that these types of projections and delusions are based on a need for ultimate meaning/fulfilment within life which we try to find in a variety of external sources. (There is a natural inconjunction between the Libra/Pisces archetypes

which reflects the crisis of disillusionment that so many of us have experienced because of this dynamic in which our expectations/need for ultimate meaning are not met.) Pisces also correlates to the need to meet the need for ultimate meaning through creating a relationship with the Divine. Pluto Vol. 2 goes into a wonderful in-depth description of the connection between the Taurus, Libra, and Pisces archetypes and how these archetypes correlate with the need in all of us to progressively internalize (Taurus) our need for ultimate meaning through union with Spirit/the Divine (Pisces) and to reach a state of balance within our relationships (Libra). (Deva)

Projection, in general, correlates to Uranus, the 11th house, and Aquarius. Delusions, in general, correlate with Pisces, the 12th house, and Neptune. Delusions manifest from within the consciousness of any given Soul that can then be projected outwardly into the overall environment in such a way as to condition the very nature of that environment relative to the nature of the delusion itself. There are many possible causes including one's own essential needs within a relationship that the other seems to correlate to, past life connections in which something was not finished, resolved, or is intended to pick up again in the current life, the inner creation of 'fantasy' type ideas about the 'perfect' partner that the other seems to correlate to, etc. etc. etc. All of this correlates, obviously, to delusions if none of it is true: actual. The correlations are above, and those archetypes would be active relative to the transits or progressions at the time that this occurs. (Rad)

De facto God or Goddess

The EA term is "making the partner the de facto God or Goddess." That is, we experience a taste of divinity THROUGH the partner. We become confused (Neptune) and think what we are feeling is coming from the partner, not realizing it is actually coming from within us. We then project (Libra) on the partner that they are the source of the good feelings we experience, when they are actually our own 12th house Return to Source yearnings. No human can ever consistently live up to these projections. As the interactions proceed we tend to start feeling let down by the partner's imperfections and tend to start criticizing the partner's faults as we start experiencing them more where they really are at, which is always less than the potential we saw within them. And yet, we also remember how wonderful we feel at those moments when we reach a momentary peak with that partner. All that becomes the root of co-dependence. In relationships EA describes this as the natural yod between the 12th, 2nd, and 7th houses. That brilliant material is covered in Pluto Vol. 2. (Steve)

Dance and music

Dance correlates with Venus, and its higher octave Neptune. Relative to Neptune this then means ecstatic dance that can lead to a temporary trance state in which spontaneous realizations about the nature of things in general, and the Source of all Things, can take place. Music is a Venus/Neptune archetype. (Rad)

Venus transit

Venus through transit reflects the ongoing evolution of our inner relationship with ourselves, and our outer relationships. The awareness of new and changing needs occurs through Venus transits. The transits of Venus also reflect the specific inner and outer relationship patterns we are working on at that moment in time relative to the house and sign it occupies in our natal chart. We can simply "outgrow" a current relationship we are in ("I do not feel I need this anymore"), or feel that it has reached a natural point of separation (no more growth is occurring for either person). We have all experienced times in our lives when we have exhausted the specific needs that were the basis of a relationship, and become aware of deeper aspects of ourselves that now need to be nourished, or nurtured, so to speak. In my view, it reflects that we are deepening our inner relationship with ourselves and this growth creates a natural evolution of our needs within relationships. We must then make the necessary inner and outer changes in our life to accommodate these changing needs. In general, Venus transits to the outer planets such as Jupiter, Uranus, Saturn, and Pluto will induce the deepest levels of change relative to the dynamics already described. (Deva)

Neptune and higher octave Venus

Neptune is the higher octave of Venus. Venus corresponds to the heart chakra. My intuition is that this does not mean that Neptune correlates to the heart chakra itself, but rather that the heart chakra and the crown have some sort of octave resonance to one another which is the manifestation of Source unity consciousness through the denser, interpersonal feeling center of the heart. (Ari)

A simple example: Neptune would correlate to unconditional love, whereas Venus would or can correlate to conditional love and the reasons for that conditional love. (Rad)

Co-dependency

Cancer is naturally square Libra. Cancer of course is the archetype in which we learn to become secure within ourselves. When that inner security in not evolved into then the 'needs' for security are then projected onto our external relationships. This can be friends or intimate others that then creates a 'co-dependent' relationship. The natural square from Cancer to Libra correlates to co-dependency (ie the relationship between internal security and the relationships in our life). (Rad)

Giving away power in relationships

Some of it comes down to better choice-making in the Libra person picking potential partners, of looking deeper before getting overly involved, to see if the potential partner has the capacity to go where they would like to go. Ideally that capacity is quite developed BEFORE entering the relationship. The old pattern would most likely be this is not the case, and the temptation to give in to temptation, yet again, would be quite strong. If one of the Libra person's core issues is giving their power away, they will want the kind of partner who won't let them do that, bottom line. That takes a pretty spiritually mature person who keeps pointing them back to themselves. (Steve)

SCORPIO – PLUTO – 8th HOUSE

Scorpio keywords

Commitment	Shared resources	Metamorphosis	Priest / Priestess
Fear of entrapment	Resourcefulness	Alchemy	Egypt
Spy	Power – Powerlessness	Taboo	Intensity
Betrayal	Magic – Curses	Covert	Fascination
Compulsions	Corrupt power	Secret	Macabre
Obsessions	Manipulation	Darkness	Psychological
Fear of Vulnerability	Loss	Sexual violence	Violence
Fear of Intimacy	Abandonment	Phobia	Evil
Sex	Merging	Paranoia	Destruction

Scorpio, Pluto, 8th house archetype

Yin / fixed / water / rules 8th house / ruler is Pluto. Scorpio/Pluto correlates to the Soul itself. The archetype here is metamorphosis linked with evolution. A metamorphosis is caterpillar to butterfly; a different, unrecognizable outcome as opposed to gradual transformation. Scorpio rules genetics and thus metamorphosis is related to mutation, out of which comes evolution. It represents the psychology of consciousness, awareness of motivations and intentions, compulsions and obsessions. It is the deepest unconscious sense of security. The need for security is a causal factor in the tendencies for obsessions and compulsions. Scorpio correlates with sexual law. The law of sexuality is much vaster and deeper than we generally realize. It is the vehicle through which the Soul learns that it co-creates physical reality with God. Karma is exchanged between people through the osmosing of sexual fluids. Celibacy is a natural condition for only 2% of the people on Earth. In all others the sexual impulse, when not expressed is repressed, where it becomes distorted. Scorpio is the seat of marriage, of sexual union, of commitment. A related archetype is fear of entrapment. Scorpio also rules the colon and intestine, the seat of toxins in the body leading to shortened life span. It also rules virus and bacteria, and the law of karma. The nature of Scorpio is penetration, not only sexually but also psychologically – to penetrate to the depths of their own motives, intentions, etc. (JWG's Pluto Vol. 1 and the School's Course)

[Recommended Reading: Jeffrey Wolf Green's Pluto Vol. 1 – The Evolutionary Journey of the Soul]

Pluto in the 8th house or Scorpio

Scorpio is the archetype through which we come face to face with who we are, and who we are not, and cannot be. Each of us is unique. Each of us experiences life in our own unique way. Because the evolutionary impulse is to evolve, 8th house people desire to transform their limitations by forming relationships to things that symbolize what they feel they need in order to evolve beyond those limitations. This implies that something exists that they are not, or do not already have. This leads to experiences of power and of powerlessness. The evolutionary impulse has required that they experience their limitations while simultaneously metamorphosing them. They cannot just say it's fine the way it is. They have become aware of universal forces beyond the limitations of their own individuality. They are required to merge with other sources of power to move beyond their limitations. They have learned how to absorb within themselves the power of whatever symbols of power they formed a relationship to. They become that which they have formed a relationship to. The nature of what symbolizes power to them depends on what they perceive is needed to move beyond existing limitations. These can include death, sex, ritual, taboos, relationships, money, status, a system of knowledge (astrology, religion, philosophy), etc. An intrinsic problem here is compulsion.

The experiences of power and powerlessness produce cyclical internal and external confrontations. They lead to a continual death-rebirth of the person's awareness. This correlates to reincarnation, the progressive need to eliminate all desires preventing a direct merging with God. Because of the Soul's dual desire nature, there is also a need to stabilize the current boundaries. This creates intense conflict between the Soul's dual desires, to separate and to merge back. The stabilized boundaries eventually become limitations to the ongoing need to move beyond limitation, necessitating a further confrontational crisis resulting in the removal of the current boundaries, which creates the desire to stabilize the new boundaries, etc. etc. The desire to merge back is the stronger of the two desires. The extent of disruption the person experiences through this process will depend on their degree of resistance to the impulse.

Scorpio is the archetype through which humanity psychoanalyzes itself. The confrontation and crisis force this necessary analysis. "Why am I like this? Why do I function this way? Why, why, why?" People with this placement want to know the bottom line of any situation. They are natural psychologists. Because they have been dealing with inner confrontation for many lifetimes, they have a well-developed awareness of their own motivations, intentions, desires, and emotional patterns. In the negative state, people with this placement may manipulate others, to be in power positions. They do this by making others dependent on them. They focus on the weakest point in the other person and put it down. This is due to their own subconscious fear of having their authority undermined. In the positive state, they can help others see and understand how and why they are the way that they are, and to help them purge negative patterns that prevent growth. They will give power TO others rather than using power to control them.

Pluto in the 8th house demands direct experience – "prove it to me". Through direct experience they merge with the transformative symbol they have selected and BECOME the symbol. The 8th house also demands that the individual make choices about whom to be involved with, whom to commit to in relationship. They are learning to choose from among a variety of people another who resonates with their own needs, desires, karma, etc. In the 7th house we learn what we need from relationship. In the 8th house we already know this and are learning to make appropriate choices. At the core level they seek relationship with either someone who symbolizes something that the individual desires, or with someone who is looking to them as the symbol of transformation that person wants in their own life. Various degrees of use and manipulation will occur in either case, leading to emotional dependence. The need to unite with symbols creates the need for sexual union in this type of relationship, as the sexual experience creates the necessary penetration and merging of the Souls. We take in, and take on, those with whom we have sexually merged. An exchange of karma takes place through the exchange of sexual fluids, and through the merging of the physical, emotional, and etheric bodies. The inherent 8th house problem is using or manipulating others to get one's own needs met. Because the needs keep changing, typically they maintain the relationship only as long as it fulfills the current need. After that, from the 8th house person's perspective, the relationship has become stagnant. On the other hand there is a conflicting desire for commitment. This can manifest as attractions to other people that would threaten the existing relationship if followed. These temptations are powerful because they symbolize change vs. the perceived stagnation in the existing relationship. Resistance to the impulse can repress the temptation into the subconscious. Yet the need to transform the stagnation they are experiencing is real. The temptations become stronger. Sometimes these people will manipulate and maintain a relationship for as long as their need lasts, and then move on. Often they use sex to get what they need. Sometimes sex is the reason for the involvement, though they don't admit that to themselves. Because of unresolved issues left from past life encounters of this nature, the people they are attracted to will be those they've been involved with in past lives. The attractions can be compulsive. There is often irrational behavior, from a this-life perspective. The source is past life experiences of abandonment, betrayal, or violations of emotional trust that subconsciously 'bleed through' into this life. Others adapt the strategy of maintaining a situation to the bitter end, resisting all temptations to change it. This produces emotional withdrawal, and can lead to near-catatonic ways of coping with their own life. The root of this is the need to learn commitment. It occurs with one with whom there have been past life difficulties or leavings. Through this determination to stay they are fulfilling the past life karma.

In either of these strategies, when one person finally leaves, negative behavior can result since one or both may feel they have totally emotionally invested self in the relationship. The recommended strategy is to choose partners who are willing to change and evolve. The essence of "Soul Mates" is to promote the spiritual development of each person because of the relationship. Confrontations and growth occur but they promote growth rather than degenerate into negative or vindictive behaviors. Many of these people have had a series of very upsetting prior lives, either through karmic necessity, or through too much emotional dependence. If the individual had patterns of abusing sex to get what they wanted, they may find they are the recipients of similar behavior. Most of these people come into this life with a defensiveness and suspicion of other people's motives and intentions. It can take a very long time for such a person to truly trust another. (JWG's Pluto Vol. 1 and the School's Course)

Pluto polarity point – 2nd house or Taurus

The intent is to learn self-reliance and to identify one's own values and resources in order to sustain self. They are learning to minimize compulsive dependence on anything outside of self. They are learning to look within and to use self as the symbol of transformation with which to merge. They must progressively simplify their lives. They need isolation from the external environment, so they can look within. They will learn to identify who they are vs. the parts of self that are actually other people with whom they've been karmically linked. The linkage is associated with the osmosis effect of sexuality, and the uniting of self with others. Through discovering the core of self, they will learn how to participate in committed, growing relationships in non-dependent and non-compulsive ways. They will thus attract self-sustaining people, and transmute the karma of manipulation because the need for growth will no longer be dependent on anything outside of self.

They will learn when to be involved and when not to be involved. They will eliminate misuses of power and sex. They will dance to their own tune. They will encourage others to strip away the layers of conditioning that dictate their behaviors. They will encourage others to realize their essence, and to sustain themselves. Their ability to penetrate to the essence will let them solve life's mysteries to better understand self and others. Common characteristics: intense, core of power, can be fixed or stubborn, dislike superficiality, can be vindictive, strong likes and dislikes, magnetic, transforming effect on those around them, can see things in black and white, motivate others, "why?, why, why?", can be emotionally manipulative, cycles of emotional withdrawal, secretive. (JWG's Pluto Vol. 1 and the School's Course)
[For more information on Pluto: *See* chapters PLUTO and SOUL]

Where Pluto/Scorpio fits into the total structure of consciousness
The zodiac, its houses and signs, correlate to the total structure of consciousness in human form. The planets within the zodiac correlate to bringing that consciousness to life, and thus setting in motion consciousness itself. The planets within the zodiac are the unique structural nature of that consciousness from life to life. They are the gasoline within the tank. This is why we start with Pluto, the Nodes, the location of their planetary rulers, and all the aspects to other planets that they are making. This is the core and foundation upon which the Soul structure and its evolutionary background, and its evolutionary development, is understood. Wherever the sign Scorpio is, by house, will contribute to this foundation because the signs on the houses correlate to how consciousness is orientated to phenomenal reality. And that current life orientation to phenomenal reality reflects the evolutionary needs of the Soul in this life. Planets that are in Scorpio, or the 8th house, correlate to the Soul's intention, in this life, to metamorphose the existing development and limitations implied in the archetypes of the planets themselves. The sign on the 8th house is an archetype in which this same Soul intention to metamorphose the existing development of that archetype within consciousness exists. (Rad)

Abandonment, betrayal, loss, violation of trust
Pluto rules Scorpio. Core Scorpio archetypes/fears are abandonment, betrayal, and violation of emotional trust. These are going to appear wherever Pluto and Scorpio appear in the chart. Of course each person will experience them in their own way, based on their past and present. The nature of the fears is determined by the house and sign that Pluto is in. For example, if it's in the 5th, there could be fears of losing children. In the 8th, partners and/or money. In the 12th, fears of being abandoned by God/Goddess. In the 2nd of losing money/resources. (That is NOT a definitive list of all the possible fears that could occur by house – it's a short list to illustrate the flavor of what I mean.) In most cases these fears are based on actual events that have occurred in this and previous lives, often subconscious – forgotten – which explains the compulsive nature of Pluto/Scorpio. They are memories in the Soul, yet not consciously remembered. The significance of them causes the fears to repeat over and over – compulsion, fears or behaviors that seem to have no logical sense yet are completely logical when looked at from the Soul's long term memory of past events. Also take into account the number of aspects Pluto is making to other planets in the chart. Anything aspecting Pluto acquires Plutonian qualities. Also consider aspects made to the Pluto polarity point, and the South and North Nodes of Pluto.
As to the reasons for abandonment, I look at Pluto as a cosmic garbage collector – anything that has outlived its useful time as an agent of growth in a life, Pluto eventually takes away. We all have many things in our life we don't really want taken away. We sometimes hold onto them tightly. So experiences arise that force us to let go – abandonment, betrayal, violation of trust. In a strong Pluto chart – 8th house Pluto, 8th house stellium, stellium in Scorpio, lots of planets aspecting Pluto, etc., the person is so used to having things just disappear from their life, the experience becomes second nature. They come to expect that to occur, which can make it a self-fulfilling prophecy. Expecting it or not, it still hurts at times. It's easy to get sick of those experiences of loss and just try to hold on to something until the bitter end. Ultimately Pluto will win and whatever is being held onto will, once again, be removed. The root of this, in most cases, is the need to become self-reliant and self-contained – the polarity of Scorpio/8th is Taurus/2nd. To focus on the inner rather than getting overly immersed in relationship with others, the outer. Abandonment is a very effective tool towards those realizations, while certainly being a harsh teacher at times. (Steve)

Evolution through the emotional body
EA teaches that processing life experiences through the emotional body is evolutionary precisely because it enables the Soul to fully EXPERIENCE whatever experiences are the natural consequence of its desires and choices. If the Soul does not fully EXPERIENCE that which its choices have generated, then it will not truly know in a deep way the consequences of those desires and choices, and will not be able to integrate and learn from these experiences, and thus to make new choices and evolve. Evolution is a natural process of the universe – we can trust it to happen and we do not have to 'make' it happen, so much as let it happen. As Jeffrey taught, the Water Trinity shows involution in that Spirit/Neptune differentiates to Soul/Scorpio differentiates to Ego/Cancer; and also shows that evolution occurs naturally in the natural direction of the zodiac of the shift in conscious identification from Ego/Cancer to Soul/Scorpio to Spirit/Pisces. I find in my work that when people are able to experience their experience through the emotional body (Cancer/Moon), such a full experience naturally eventually leads them (over a period of minutes or lifetimes) to a desire to understand and transform the deeper unconscious patterns and/or Soul history (both Scorpio/Pluto) that has led to

the given emotional experience. I don't need to try to push this inquiry in any way, it is the natural result of deeply experienced emotion, it is just what happens when we get out of the way and feel. And then I have also found that when people start to work at this deeper level, then also very naturally begin (again, whether in this lifetime or later) to experience their own encounters with Source (Pisces/Neptune), however this may manifest as appropriate to their perceptual capacities. The water naturally returns to the sea. So to me it is not so much about energy releasing or other particular things as much as it is about having a natural experience that leads to new understanding and choices (and thus new experiences) that eventually exhaust separating desires and leave only the desire to return to Source. In general bypassing the emotional body is essentially resisting evolution, which Souls at any stage in consciousness can do. (Jason)

Practices to work with the emotional body

[Example: Various practices within Dzogchen and Tibetan Buddhism] These practices are not only unnecessary but in fact confuse those who try to practice them. They take what is inherently simple and complicates that. This happens because such practices are not in alignment with Natural Laws: they are essentially invented by individuals who have been conditioned by man-made laws, the patriarchy, that are then trying to harness the Natural Laws in unnatural ways. Personally, I won't have anything to do with them. To me the practices to be used are life itself. To have the knowledge of emotions is simply to experience them within a consciousness that becomes one with whatever emotion is existing relative to a cause that has ignited it in the first place. And, within this, to have a desire, conscious intention, to understand the nature of whatever emotion: its cause, and the reasons for that cause. Within this, the inherent knowledge that then exists in whatever emotion the consciousness becomes one with. Over time of course a state of total self-knowledge defined by the emotional body will take place. A book that came up that appears relevant to all this is "The Spiritual Anatomy of Emotion: How Feelings Link the Brain, the Body, and the Sixth Sense" [Paperback] by Michael (A) Jawer (Author), Marc S. Micozzi (Author), Larry Dossey (Foreword). (Rad)

Spiritual bypass

As I understand it, EA teaches that processing life experiences through the emotional body is evolutionary precisely because it enables the Soul to fully EXPERIENCE whatever experiences are the natural consequence of its desires and choices. If the Soul does not fully EXPERIENCE that which its choices have generated, then it will not truly know in a deep way the consequences of those desires and choices, and will not be able to integrate and learn from these experiences, and thus to make new choices and evolve. In some sense spiritual bypass is a kind of delaying tactic – the Soul resisting coming to terms with the natural consequences of its own desires and choices (though at the ego level this can simply look like a person avoiding painful emotions using Jesus or altered states or "ascension" or whatever). In this way the Soul keeps itself in a kind of evolutionary limbo in that it cannot truly exhaust separating desires since it is ever delayed from truly feeling what those desires have resulted in, and therefore must repeat them (in a sense wilfully failing to learn from history). You can see how this can correlate with skipped steps in some Souls.

Spiritual bypass to me also relates to the control orientation most of us carry and to the lack of trust in natural law that has been learned on this planet. Evolution is a natural process of the universe – we can trust it to happen and we do not have to "make" it happen, so much as let it happen. As Jeffrey taught, the Water Trinity shows involution in that Spirit/Neptune differentiates to Soul/Scorpio differentiates to Ego/Cancer; and also shows that evolution occurs naturally in the natural direction of the zodiac of the shift in conscious identification from Ego/Cancer to Soul/Scorpio to Spirit/Pisces. I find in my work that when people are able to experience their experience through the emotional body (Cancer/Moon), such a full experience naturally eventually leads them (over a period of minutes or lifetimes) to a desire to understand and transform the deeper unconscious patterns and/or Soul history (both Scorpio/Pluto) that has led to the given emotional experience. I don't need to try to push this inquiry in any way, it is the natural result of deeply experienced emotion, it is just what happens when we get out of the way and feel. And then I have also found that when people start to work at this deeper level, then also very naturally begin (again, whether in this lifetime or later) to experience their own encounters with Source (Pisces/Neptune), however this may manifest as appropriate to their perceptual capacities. The water naturally returns to the sea. So to me it is not so much about energy releasing or other particular things as much as it is about having a natural experience that leads to new understanding and choices (and thus new experiences) that eventually exhaust separating desires and leave only the desire to return to Source.

If we stay with the Water Trinity, then spiritual bypassing can be seen as an attempt to "bypass" the emotions (Cancer) and critically the step of self-confrontation and transformation (Scorpio) – after all that is really hard. But of course natural law doesn't work that way and what I would say is actually happening is that the Soul is actually going in the involutionary (clockwise) direction on the wheel, trying to escape to a regressive experience of preconsciousness rather like the womb (Pisces), so as not to feel the pain of emotion (Cancer). In therapy this is sometimes called the "flight into health." To me it exemplifies the issue of trines in that as Jeffrey taught they can make it "easy" to be conscious and cooperative with evolution but they can also make it "easy" to resist it. Regarding evolutionary states and spiritual bypass, I have personally encountered bypass in all three of the main stages. At Consensus stages I often see it as "religious bypass" – people avoiding emotions by logging into pre-digested and pat religious answers (eg I don't want to feel grief about Sandy Hook, so I'll just blame it on schools not having Christian prayer every morning; or we don't want to feel the pain of Katrina so let's just blame it on the gays). At Individuated stages I often see it as "science bypass" or "political bypass" – people avoiding emotions by logging into political causes or sophisticated explanations of the aspects of experience they are avoiding. "Psychology bypass" also happens and a lot of insight-oriented psychotherapy does this, avoiding direct experience of emotions by explaining them. And then in the Spiritual stages and the later Individuated stages I often see it as the kind of "spiritual bypass" where people prefer to log in to particular states of consciousness or metaphysical frameworks and log out of the direct and lived experience of their emotions. But to me in general bypassing the emotional body is essentially resisting evolution, which Souls at any stage in consciousness can do.

Regarding whether the kind of mental/head-based quality that typifies the specific bypass (of preferring to dwell in primordial states), means that such individuals may be in the Individuated states vs Spiritual states, I would say that could be occurring in a Spiritual or an Individuated Soul. The difference would have to be discerned by understanding the nature of the Soul's motivation for its practice in the first place. I have seen some practitioners of these paths and techniques who are (mostly) seeking to reinforce their own sense of themselves and their specialness and ability to "achieve" and use spiritual practice as the vehicle for this (Individuated); and I have seen some who are (mostly) truly seeking to unite themselves with Source (Spiritual). And at both of these levels, I have seen Souls periodically fall into the trap of using these paths to dissociate from their emotions, or even live an entire lifetime in that kind of resistance.

Considering how to help Souls in this dynamic, as mentioned we are in the territory of Pisces/Neptune, and as EA teaches this archetype is about Source and spiritual realization, but at the same time also the process by which we "deify" all sorts of people and things and states of consciousness as if they themselves are Source or are spiritual realization, and then we experience eventual disillusionment when this turns out not to be true. In this context for me it has rarely worked to point out to people they that are in spiritual bypass; those rose-coloured glasses are pretty sticky and if you get Virgo/Mercury discerning and analytical they get even more Pisces/Neptune cloudy and ascending. Unless they are somehow really ready to hear it and to experience it as real, it is just a mental thing to say it, like telling an active addict that he or she has an addiction.

What I do find helpful in many situations is to assist the person in fully experiencing whatever they are experiencing, to feel what it is like to be where they are. In this case of bypass, to feel what it is like to view or use access to this primordial state as the "answer." What does that feel like, what is the impact of that in life? After all, the desire to prematurely transcend and resist the evolutionary process is itself also a desire that the Soul has created and wants to experience. Assisting the Soul to fully experience the full experience that is a consequence of that desire (whether it is the 'high' states, the frequent interpersonal isolation that results, the tendency to judge the 'unenlightened,' the pressure to maintain one's 'enlightenment,' whatever the full experience is), and eventually it will naturally include the experience of disillusionment, and the felt sense of disillusionment – feeling it, not just being told it by someone else – the disappointment, the grief, the anger – is what naturally leads the Soul to truly release the desire for bypass and move on to whatever is next for it. Just realizing it cognitively or because someone points it out typically means that although today's bypass strategy may be dropped, the desire will still exist in the Soul to do it and it will find another way to bypass (kind of like switching addictions from one substance/behavior to another when the deeper desires driving the addiction have not been addressed and released, only deferred). (Jason)

All that you [Jason] have said/shared about this is exactly right. We need to remember/understand that the Pisces, Cancer, Scorpio trinity, the Source, the Soul, and the ego it manifests, all emanate from the Water archetype. Water is of course pure emotion. The non-dual state, the desire for, is itself an emotional delusion that is impossible to achieve, or arrive at, relative to consciousness in the Soul in a human form. A Soul relative to certain 'spiritual' methodologies can indeed arrive at some sort of 'transcendental' state but that state always, cause and effect, snaps back to a 'normal' state of consciousness. Even in these naturally transcendental states or 'cosmic consciousness' the very essence of such a consciousness or state is EMOTIONAL: the emotion or feeling within that state of consciousness as it 'perceives' the various realities of those states. That perception leads to an emotional state as it 'reacts' to the nature of the perception itself. The need of all of our Souls to directly feel the nature of our emotions as they relate to any possible experience created by the Soul for its own evolutionary needs is the bottom line truth. For those who are able to create within themselves the various degrees of cosmic consciousness all of them will report being in a temporary state of ecstasy. Ecstasy of course is an experience of pure emotion.

When Souls align themselves with various religious and/or spiritual teachings that teach it is important, necessary even, to control or repress the emotions in order for 'x' spiritual state to be realized these Souls are reacting to the nature of their own emotional lives. In essence, they are running from those emotional lives for their own reasons but all reasons that lead to this running lead to repressing the very nature of the emotions themselves. In so doing they are repressing that which is NATURAL AND NECESSARY FOR THE SOUL TO EXPERIENCE for its own evolutionary reasons. If we accept that God/ess is the origin of all things then wherein lies the origin of emotions? And for what reasons? So for Souls who do orientate to these teachings that require repression, to 'transcend' them which means repressing them, the very act of repression then magnifies and distorts those natural emotions within the consciousness of those that do so. When anything that is natural is repressed for whatever reasons ANGER IS THE DIRECT RESULT: a natural inner anger. When this occurs all too often the Soul then feels itself to be a victim of life, a victim even to their own emotions which continue to live on, to exist, despite the repression. When this natural anger is then linked to the created consciousness of feeling to be a victim first to itself, then to others, this becomes the causative basis of lashing out at anyone the Souls feels 'victimized' by. In a 'religious' and/or 'spiritual' context this then is the cause of all the horror stories we are all too familiar with: the priest abusing boys, the 'guru' who is having intercourse with some devote, and so on.

As JWG and others have taught the liberation of the Soul does indeed take place through and because of the emotional body for the reasons that Jason [above] had correctly pointed out. A story that I just remembered about this is the story of one of Yogananda's chief disciples, a women who was essential for Yogananda and his work. She developed a terminal medical condition in which Yogananda interceded upon by way of asking God/ess to keep her alive because of the critical nature of her tasks helping his work. She lived ten years longer as a result. And upon her final transition, upon the moment of the very last breath, her final words were: "TOO MUCH JOY." (Rad)

The disciple that Rad is referencing in this post is Sri Gyanamata and the book is called "God Alone: Life and Letters of a Saint." This is a wonderful book which I highly recommend as it gives great perspective about how to emotionally heal and grow without any "spiritual bypass." (Deva)

Since deep emotional processing is the heart of the work I do, what I have found is that we simply cannot easily move through our own emotional defenses. Spiritual systems that are 'transcendent' in nature often collude with the already dissociative defence in place. Yes it is quite easy for already dissociated, fragmented psyches (ie all of us) to access "other/higher worlds" since so many of our parts already reside there!! The difficult part is unlocking the trauma that caused the fragmentation in the first place and then real Soul retrieval can happen. Re-living, ie descending into the original terror, wound, fear, horror, pain (fill in the blank) opens up not only the complex formed around such an event, but the defences that were crystallized also. These defences involved ALL levels of the being, etheric/physical body, emotional body, mental body and spiritual body. ALL these bodies need to become congruent in order for full integration to happen and each one can hold their own separate defence. One body is not superior to another despite what patriarchal bias tells us. Personally I trust the veracity and truth of emotion before I trust the machinations of head, my personal bias. Sharing a quote from R.D. Laing:

"When our personal worlds are rediscovered and allowed to reconstitute themselves, we first discover a shambles. Bodies half-dead; genitals dissociated from heart; heart severed from head; heads dissociated from genitals... Without inner unity, with just enough sense of continuity to clutch at identity: the current idolatry. Torn, body, mind and spirit, by inner contradictions, pulled in different directions, Man cut off from his own mind, cut off equally from his own body – a half-crazed creature in a mad world."

I perceive that we compensate for all these contradictions and dissociations largely with our mental prowess, using it to repress the true reality that lies underneath. This is why, collectively, we are so mentally defended because under those defences lies a much different, initially terrifying inner world, where our compensated identity is threatened to come apart, but when one has the courage to go there the reward is integration and coherence. (Patricia)

Choice whether to evolve or not

As always with any placement - there are no innate "benefits" or otherwise since the chart itself is a reflection of the soul's karmic and evolutionary dynamics and everything that happens in a person's life comes from that inner condition. Within the 8th house the dynamic of choice is emphasized. Choice relating to whether or not to evolve. Taking in the entire context, planets or signs on the 8th house, including the planetary ruler of that sign on the 8th house and aspects to that planetary ruler will correlate with how the soul can resist or cooperate with evolution according to the needs of the current life. What karmic dynamics are implied – what kind of evolutionary purpose does that point to in the current life? (Ari)

Anyone with an emphasized 8th house or Scorpio is going to have an inherent deep desire to EVOLVE as the 8th house and Scorpio and Pluto correlate to the Soul itself. Evolving requires facing many things about one's self, and life overall, that are not always easy to face and accept. As a result, a person may have developed a deep habit of resisting intended evolution, trying to get away, avoid, this type of experience. That is when all of the negative qualities of Scorpio can manifest. If the person makes the decision to accept they are here to work, to grow, and cooperates with the sometimes difficult experiences that arise in the life, they are going to actualize the positive tendencies of Scorpio. Obsession and compulsion are typically caused by subconscious memories within the Soul that the ego/personality is not at present remembering. The Soul is seeking to understand what has happened to it along its journey, and why, to resolve those issues, so it focuses on them. The difficult growth experiences that come along are often necessary to blast the personality open so it can expand to a greater depth of conscious recognition and remembrance. They may not be easy at times but they are very effective. Scorpio/8th house has little time for superficiality or pleasantries. It wants to get right to the point. Whether that is seen as good or not depends on one's values. It is neither. It is simply the way the Scorpio energy tends to manifest. Suicide is an extreme example of Scorpio energy. It's not especially common so keep that correlation in perspective. Scorpio is the place where we can come face to face with our Soul, and the limits of the individual Soul/personality. At its worst it can be black magic and ruthless domination and control over others – sucking the power out of others and into self. At its finest it can be a near-complete merging with another, the mutual experience of two Souls feeling almost as one, deeply developed self-awareness of the Soul. Which way it goes depends on the choices one makes. (Steve)

We'd always have to ask 'why' would there be trauma or obsession – everything in the end points back to the desire nature of the Soul. And so if something horrible happens, why is that? The point is to come back to ourselves and ask ourselves what this is showing us about ourselves. So we can become conscious of our desires for that which is not absolute. This leads to regeneration – which is evolution. Out with the old, in with the new – we vibrate closer and closer to Source. We can also continually resist such self-awareness and not grow – this will naturally attract more cataclysmic/challenging events into our life – and if resistance to growth continues that will breed a natural psychology of victimization. And victims are the scariest and most fragile people out there. This is ultimately where the possibility of evil comes in. There are truly two polarities to the Scorpio/8th house/Pluto archetype – all dependent on choice. One is the growing closeness to Source. The other is growing resistance/separation from Source. An emphasized 8th house reflects where the Soul has in some way reached a limitation in their growth relative to their separating desires. And thus the OPPORTUNITY based on choice to evolve and move beyond those limitations. (Ari)

Pluto in the 8th house – example

[Example: Pluto Sagittarius 8th, South Node Taurus 1st, Jupiter Scorpio 7th, 3rd stage Individuated] The Pluto in Sagittarius in the 8th, the river of the Soul, has desired to understand the WHY'S of life itself, the causes and effects of anything, human psychology in its fullest dimensions, its own psychology and the causes of it, and Natural Laws of Creation itself, how people in general interpret the phenomena of life in all of its forms and dimensions, what motivates people and why, and the sexual realities and the reasons for those realities in human nature, and so on. One of the tributary streams that feeds this Soul river, with Jupiter in Scorpio in the 7th, would correlate with the cultural anthropology of humans in diverse cultures, tribes, and societies that the Soul would contemplate in order to understand the core desires as manifesting in the 8th house Pluto. This contemplation would be fuelled by reading a variety of materials, travelling to many places, and observing the diversity of peoples. The South Node being in Taurus in the 1st creates and egocentric structure in which the Soul keeps itself distant and independent from people in general. This symbolism correlates to a banyan tree that remains rooted in one place for thousands of years while the panorama of time passes it by. The banyan tree, the egocentric structure, thus is secure within its own inner isolation as it observes and learns by all that which passes it by.

On a very selective basis the Soul through its 1st house Taurus egocentric structure would engage others in relationship, the tributary stream of the Jupiter in Scorpio in the 7th relative to Pluto in Sagittarius in the 8th house, that were inwardly evaluated to be of use by the Soul for its evolutionary intentions: needs. In turn, this would set in motion very intense and deep philosophical and psychological type discussions in which the core desires of the Soul were being met. In the above example this would then place the evolving egocentric structure, one of the core evolutionary intentions, in the 7th house: North Node in the 7th in Scorpio. This would then mean, that as a next step in the Soul's evolution, that it now must learn how to jump out of its cocoon of self isolation: South Node in Taurus in the 1st. Rather than observing in such isolation in the ways that it has before, it must now learn how to FULLY ENGAGE, emotionally and psychologically, with others. The Soul intends to learn how to be in relationships with others in general in this way, and learn how to commit to being with a partner on a one to one basis. It is thus learning how to unite a core psychological and emotional paradox, the core paradox manifesting from the Soul. And that is the paradox of needing total independence and freedom relative to committing to others in general, and a partner specifically. (Rad)

Pluto/Uranus interface

A natal placement of some kind of connection between the Uranian and Plutonian archetypes is a life-long issue. There are reasons when the Soul is manifesting with that symbolism. Uranus in Scorpio or in the 8th house in itself (without any transit activation) is very intense. The Uranian archetype will have the Scorpionic intensity – trying to look for the bottom-line. Generally speaking, in one way or another, the liberation (inherent in the Uranian archetype) is directly intended to affect the deepest levels – the Soul level. This also signifies the fact that past traumas (Uranus) had already affected the Soul level in some way. The healing/liberation are intended to happen on that very level. Not only have deepest trust issues (Scorpio/8th house) been violated in general, but also very INTENSE deepest level shock and trauma have happened in ways that have blown apart the Soul's previous security base – the deepest Soul level security structure. Therefore there is an intention to heal that level. The previous limitation relates to those security structures which need to be reformulated in the most intense and most accelerated way. As for the repetitive messages and what to trust and what not to trust, the issue may correlate to the fact that on the deepest, unconscious level trust has been violated and that caused immense trauma in the past.

The Uranus/Pluto interface, in some ways, correlates to a HIGHLY traumatized SOUL. Keeping this symbolism in mind, the result is more than likely to manifest some level of GENERAL unconscious fear and distrust, even towards one's own perceptions from within, ie when the Soul trusted something or someone in the past the Soul experienced intense trauma (not an isolated experience). So for the Soul, it is natural to react to this unconscious content (Uranus) in a distrustful way (Scorpio). This can create some intense inner confusion and being stuck periodically. One of the evolutionary needs with this kind of symbol is to apply DETACHMENT and OBJECTIVITY instead of being lost in the intense inwardly experienced emotional turmoil. Can I trust something? What if I misread the signals from within? So whatever the issue may be, understanding the fact that the emotional body has been wounded in the DEEPEST POSSIBLE WAY is something that needs to be kept in mind.

In the higher evolutionary states another interesting phenomenon may occur: the content of the unconscious memories of the Soul can come to the surface of consciousness in a relatively easy way. And, together with the Uranian impulse, the Soul is simply able to "dump" the emotional content it carries onto the Uranian vehicle. Uranus also correlates to the subconscious which is just below our Saturnian current life egocentric consciousness. In a simplified symbolic way, Pluto/Scorpio is the core deep down, and the egocentric consciousness (Saturn) is high up and normally they are not directly connected. The Uranian archetype is the BRIDGE between them. The Uranian archetype does touch in some ways the Saturnian current life ego-level consciousness and at the same time is connected to the depth of the Soul. So on that bridge, the content of the unconscious Soul – with all the imprints, including many many past lives, and all kinds of information, BOTH past and present, relatively speaking – can "connect" more easily between these two points (Soul and egocentric consciousness) than without this kind of symbolism. Of course all this is dependent upon many other factors: first of all the evolutionary state of the Soul's overall consciousness, then the whole chart which will then explain why that configuration and why the Soul needed it, what happened, what it intends to liberate from and how. There can be infinite scenarios of course. The above is a very general (and far from complete) description of the functions, archetypically speaking, which are connected in some ways within consciousness, when these two symbols are directly connected in a chart. (Lia)

North Node in Scorpio, ruler Pluto
These symbols mean that such a Soul has been intensely resisting change/evolution in the most recent prior lives. The South Node being in Taurus would correlate to a 'frog in the well' in that the Soul has felt highly secure within the bottom of the well, and resisted jumping out of it in order to expose itself to the totality of the environment that surrounds the well. Jumping out of that well correlates to deep fears because it can no longer control its space or reality as defined in the bottom of the well. Thus, in these symbols the Soul will be continually confronted with its past, and the dynamics that are the cause of that past: the North Node in Scorpio ruled by the natal Pluto. The polarity point of the Pluto, the bottom line in the current life evolutionary intentions, will serve as a vehicle through which the Soul is given the opportunity to make new choices, changes, relative to re-experiencing its past, and the dynamics that correlate with that past. The house placement of the North Node in Scorpio also serves to create opportunities of the Soul to make new choices relative to re-experiencing its past as symbolized not only in the house and sign of the natal Pluto, but, of course, the South Node by house, and the location of its planetary ruler by sign, house, and aspects to it. So you can see that the key here is indeed the polarity point of Pluto. The Soul has chosen to re-experience its past because it has felt secure within that past, and the dynamics that correlate to that past. That past is symbolized by not only the North Node, the South Node, and its planetary ruler, but also the natal Pluto by house and sign. And yet it is these very symbols that also correlate to evolving beyond that past by making new choices in the face of that past. And those new choices start with the polarity point of Pluto. By making those new choices in this way it then has the effect of evolving the North Node, South Node and its planetary ruler, but also of course the natal Pluto itself. (Rad)

South Node in Scorpio, ruler Pluto
The significance is that Souls who have this symbol have overly identified with their sense of security, emotional /psychological/ sexual, in specific and fixed ways and that over-identification has caused the Soul to stop evolving due to the compulsiveness of it, the fixity of it. Thus, the Soul, by its own design, has created in most recent prior lives a series of lives of intense loss of those dynamics that have been overly identified with. This has been necessary in order for the Soul to continue with its evolution. Thus, the North Node being in Taurus and the total evolutionary change within the Soul in terms of its own inner relationship with itself. In so changing, the Soul is thus changing its own inner magnetism which, in turn, allows for an attraction of these exact types of circumstances (relative to both the dynamics that are symbolized by the South Node in Scorpio, and the North Node in Taurus) that allows the Soul to continue to grow and evolve. (Rad)

Hate
Hate correlates with Scorpio, the 8th house, and Pluto. It is a natural emotion. If the hate is being triggered because of conditions and/or events, there are many ways to deal with it, not just one way. All depends on the actual nature of such events and/or conditions. If such events and/or conditions are rooted in violations of Natural Laws then one can be pretty hard pressed to be free of it in meditation although, of course, it is possible. The guilt reaction to hate, itself, can be caused by many factors, not just one. It does not mean that things like rape, murder, etc. are natural at all. Hate is an emotion from within consciousness, the Soul that can be triggered by various external phenomena. What any given Soul does because of the emotion of hate, or anger which is another natural emotion, is up to that Soul. In patriarchal realities this can of course lead to things like murder and so on. Patriarchal realities are for the most part total distortions and perversions of Natural Laws. Thus, when a natural emotion like hate or anger is triggered within a Soul it can then manifest through these distorted realities in horrible ways like murder and so on. Hate is not a desire. It is an emotion that can be triggered by phenomenal events, or it can be triggered even as hate towards oneself by way of judging oneself against various standards that trigger the self-hate. One can see where the sign Scorpio is in any given chart, where Pluto is and/or Scorpio planets, and the sign on the 8th house cusp and the location of its planetary ruler by way of its own house, sign, and aspects to it that can all act as triggers for inner or outer hate. For example, if one had Gemini on the 8th house cusp one could feel 'jealous' of another's intellectual abilities that could then lead to 'hating' that person.

Nature is not human centered, indeed, and yet they are part of the totality of Nature. The fact that hatred can manifest in humans, as well as animals, has nothing to do whether a consciousness is distorted or not: the fact is it manifests and exists. Hatred does manifest in certain animals such as chimpanzees and other forms of the monkey kingdom for example. Humans are in fact part of the totality of Nature and humans have the emotion of hate within them which is simply an intensification of anger. Hate manifests from anger. It is a natural emotion, not one born simply of distortions. When hate is projected on another, humans or chimpanzees, that other can then become an enemy. In humans and chimpanzees an enemy can be attacked and killed because of the hate. Chimpanzees can not only kill other chimpanzees because of being enemies, but they can also kill humans. They can even kill humans who want to own them as pets. When these things happen it has nothing to do with 'abstractions.' Ask any human when they are in the emotion of hate if they feel they are in an abstract state, or, in fact, in an emotional state. (Rad)

Early/sudden death
There are many possible symbols for early and/or sudden death. Mars in the 11th, Mars conjunct the North or South Node, Mars in opposition or square Uranus, Uranus in the 1st, Uranus in the 8th house, the South Node in the 11th, Mars squaring the Nodes, Uranus squaring the Nodes, and the South Node in Aries are some of them. (Rad)

Death
An excellent book is *"On Death and Dying"* by Elisabeth Kubler-Ross. Of course Yogananda also explained in many of his teachings the actual transition from physical death of the body of the astral realm of the Soul. In his autobiography there is a chapter on the 'resurrection' of his own guru, Yukteswar, which could not be more graphic in actual detail. I also remember a chapter in Yukteswar's book, *"The Holy Science,"* where he describes step by step the transition of the Soul from physical death to the astral plane. (Rad)

Suicide
(Q) Do people who have taken their own life usually incarnate fairly soon after their death? I think I heard it on one of JWG's lecture tapes. (Henrik)
(A) Yes, that is what he taught, and also for those who have early life endings such a Soul will typically be reborn pretty quickly. (Rad)
(Q) Does the experience of "astral hell" leave an impression in the life that follows, for example, as having traumatic dreams or experiencing PTSD from birth? (JJ)
(A) It leaves an 'impression' within the Soul: a Soul memory. Upon returning into another life after this the resulting ego created by the Soul will not have a conscious memory of this in most cases. However, the memory within the Soul can manifest as specific types of dreams of that experience of being in the 'astral hell.' That same Soul memory can indeed create a form of PTSD relative to the ego created in the life following being in the astral hell. This is intentional so that the Soul does not commit suicide again. (Rad)
(Q) Does the act of unsuccessfully attempting suicide, one or more times, have an effect in the present life that makes it more difficult to move through what they are trying to avoid? I ask this because some times after someone tries to commit suicide, they may finally deal with the issue and move forward. Are there still negative consequences in this life or in the astral plane from making the attempt?
(A) This would depend on what you mean by 'negative consequences.' If you mean unsuccessful attempts lead to the 'astral hell' the answer is no. On the other hand the inner causes that have led to such attempts can create ongoing psychological difficulties if in fact the Soul has not made any efforts to resolve those existing causes: the reasons why, and then doing something constructive about them. An example of such psychological difficulties would be the degenerating psychology of futility that can permeate the Soul's entire reality. Or the psychology of a permeating sadness or grief that can impair the Soul in a variety of ways.
(Q) In the next life after a suicide, will suicidal thoughts tend to arise again when the Soul is faced with similar but intensified circumstances that they avoided in the life in which they committed suicide?
(A) Yes.
(Q) What is the purpose at a Soul level of having the circumstances be intensified in the next life? It seems like that could perpetuate the choice of suicide again in the next life.
(A) This is a karmic condition that the Soul itself is responsible for creating where the natural law of karma is ignited because of this natural law against suicide. The purpose of the intensified circumstances is to actually empower the Soul to make other choices that lead to its evolution BECAUSE OF THOSE INTENSIFIED CONDITIONS.
(Q) I am trying to check my understanding of the process of how the intensified conditions would empower the Soul to make other choices. Is it that the inner dynamics that created the conditions would become more clear to the Soul because the intensity of the conditions, and perhaps the consequent suffering, would provoke an inner questioning regarding "why these dynamics?" and also make it more difficult to avoid facing the dynamics?
(A) Yes. And remember that all Souls upon exiting any given life 'reviews' that life right after the life is exited. The intention in such a review of course is to learn in hindsight via the review many things related to that life. In the case of suicide this also applies BIG TIME. Thus, these types of 'lessons' are ingrained within the Soul upon its next birth in such a way that by recreating the conditions in its previous life in which the suicide took place this then has the effect of triggering those lessons learned in the review. Thus, acting upon those lessons relative to recreating those conditions empowers the Soul to evolve.

(Q) Of the four ways that Pluto effects evolution, in the case of a previous suicide, would the Soul come to understand the limiting dynamics most probably through cataclysm or stagnation, or could all of the ways that Pluto effects evolution be active in the discovery of limiting dynamics and the practical steps to take to move forwards? My understanding is that resistance to growth would be more likely to result in stagnation or cataclysm as a means of evolution; so until the Soul started to consciously desire and embrace their evolution, that would continue to be the primary means of evolution.

(A) Each Soul is unique to itself. Thus, the choices made by any given Soul reflect that individuality. Because of this all the four natural ways that Pluto affects its evolutionary necessities exits.

(Q) And in these kinds of charts would there be at least one or more stressful aspects involving Pluto, planets in Scorpio or the 8th house?

(A) These are some of the signatures, but there are also more.

Suicide and other archetypes (Capricorn, Aries, Virgo, Pisces, Taurus)

The whole archetype of 8th house, Scorpio and Pluto is where anyone/Soul meets their limits, what they can and cannot be. What they are and what they are not. It is where one experiences their power and their powerlessness. The suicide link is all about that limit – limit of power – when the Soul has experienced total powerlessness over lifetimes, the CHOICE MAKING that then comes as a response to those events – one path could be suicide, one path could be seeking power – the pendulum swings.

I've been revisiting the archetypes as they connect to suicide. So, it has been clear Scorpio/8th Pluto is the main archetype that is highlighted with suicide. Certainly, there is a lot of psychological "stuff" that will be tapes running through the consciousness of anyone who has or is seriously considering or desiring to commit suicide. When reflecting on the rest of the archetypes in this light, what came to me was:

Capricorn/10th/Saturn – can connect with a sense of futility, deep sorrow, and defeat. Impossible hurdles to jump. "It's just not worth it anymore" – it is one possible manifestation. You can see how this psychology will often tie into suicide. So, we would look at planets in Capricorn or the 10th house, planetary South Nodes in the 10th house, Saturn and its aspects, etc.

Aries/1st/Mars – the natural inconjunct of Aries to Scorpio correlates to the crisis of aligning individual desire with Soul desire. On a conscious level, this crisis can manifest as the anger and frustration of feeling powerlessness in acting upon one's desires. When we are talking about the desire to kill oneself, this is the destructive side of this archetype in a negative manifestation. To take such action upon oneself, would require a great amount of courage. There have been more unsuccessful attempts than not. So, within the psychology of suicidal thoughts, we look to this archetype and consider where is their anger, frustration, and what desires have not been acted upon and why.

Virgo/6th/Mercury – the psychological manifestation of this archetype of someone who is suicidal could be seen linked to negative self-image(self-image specifically ties to Moon/Cancer/4th). We could see somewhere in the chart symbols that correlate to the tapes running through the consciousness which JWG taught about – "I desire pain and suffering" or "I am not worthy" or "I have screwed up, carry deep guilt, and need to atone for this" or "I will never be good enough" etc. So, if you combine this consciousness with the futility of the Capricorn/10th/Saturn archetype, at some point someone feels they do not have the energy to carry on, that they cannot make right what they have done. Or, they could have the anger response combined with futility. It can be both simultaneously – anger and low self-esteem.

Pisces/12th/Neptune – reaching the place of even considering suicide reflects the Soul is in a deep state of delusion. The so called 'reality' of this world has taken full weight and gravity in the consciousness. This archetype, in its link to denial, avoidance, confusion and delusion all come up with someone at the point of suicide. In an ultimate sense, the trials and tribulations of Soul evolution through incarnations have led into a consciousness which is blinded to the real purpose for being alive.

Taurus/2nd/Venus – the polarity Scorpio directly correlates with death (and birth). In polarity, in EA, Taurus is survival. To end one's life could involve Venus, 2nd house, and Taurus; what we'd be looking for is an archetypal combination that suggests the opposite of survival. For example, a close friend committed suicide as Pluto was exactly conjunct his natal Venus.

Just a note of clarification in mental review of what I last wrote. I realized it can be confusing to the archetypes in written word and not fully clarified – as I see I did this with Virgo. First, the whole phenomena of how many suicides presently is going to be linked both with 'Age of Patriarchy' – which is a distortion of the Capricorn/10th/Saturn archetype and then presently we are in the 'Sub-Age of Virgo' relative to the Pisces Age. Jeff spoke of this present age and his efforts to aid in the collective purging of the archetype of sadomasochism from the collective consciousness. This is really relevant because we are looking at these archetypes in light of suicide being prevalent phenomena that links to the ages and times we are in. So, just to say, these sides of the archetypes are present distortions linked with the past and present; not the pure archetypes and have not and will not always manifest as such. So, in light of this, I realize that my description of the Virgo archetype was lacking in clarity due to wording. Specifically, the dual manifestations just from this archetype in distorted forms would be the spectrum of sadomasochistic pathology. I was sensing that heavier on the masochistic side would be more common in suicide, however surely there is a blend, as I have seen it myself. Then, when I said self-esteem in the Virgo section and earlier tied it to self-image – all this would suggest a combination may be happening in some suicide cases (and I'm not saying all) where this distorted manifestation of the Virgo archetype is then linked to self-image or self-esteem. This, respectively is the Moon and Venus, 4th and 2nd, Cancer and Taurus side of Venus – and this could be the ruler of the South Node in the 6th house; Mercury in gibbous inconjunct to South Node or Moon; Moon gibbous inconjunct to Venus; Venus Mars gibbous phase; Virgo on 2nd, Venus in 6th, South Node Venus in 6th, etc. The observation and correlation will need to happen. (Bradley)

SAGITTARIUS – JUPITER – 9th HOUSE

Sagittarius keywords

Adaptability	Intuition	Explorer	Half-truth
Beliefs	Honesty	Inspiration	Silver-tongue devil
Dogmatic	Long Journeys	Restless	Charmer
Philosophy	Pilgrimage	Wanderlust	Guru
Wisdom	Multicultural	Zealous faith	Teacher
Meaning	Foreigners	Missionary	Natural Law
Expansion	Immigrants	Priest	Shaman
Trust	Ideals / Ideas	Convert	Alienation
Faith	Nomad	Sales	
Truth	Homeless	Freedom	

Sagittarius, Jupiter, 9th house archetype

Yang / mutable / fire / rules 9th house / ruler is Jupiter. Sagittarius is a mutable sign (Gemini, Virgo, Sagittarius, Pisces) – mutability means adaptability – can adapt to the necessities of the survival instinct relatively rapidly. Sagittarius is the awareness that we are linked to something larger than the planet – related to philosophical thinking. Truth is relative within the creation – there must be a basis to explain that that exists, because it exists. Sagittarius/Jupiter connects to the right brain. It represents intuition, which functions in a non-linear way. Sagittarius connects to the function of belief systems. One's belief system determines how one interprets reality. Interpretations are not universally true. Your interpretation of reality correlates to your attitude towards living. Sagittarius/Gemini relate to the transmigration of ideas – globalization, the spread of Eastern and Western thought throughout the world. Sagittarius has a fundamental restlessness, a need to explore and to embrace totality. There is a tendency towards generalizations, to feel your beliefs are for all. There is a tendency to want to convince and convert. When others are converted this creates emotional security for the person because the conversion 'proves' that their beliefs are true. There is a tendency to orient towards a portion of the total truth (Pisces) but to see the portion of the truth as the total truth – the blind man and the elephant. Sagittarius correlates to Natural Law – truth is self-evident within nature, it has nothing to do with man's opinions. Through Pisces, all of manifested creation is interrelated and is equal to itself. Humans are not superior to animals, for example. Sagittarius also relates to humor, following the life and death archetype of Scorpio, the ability to laugh at self and at life's absurdities. (JWG's Pluto Vol. 1 and the School's Course)

[Recommended Reading: Jeffrey Wolf Green's Pluto Vol. 1 – The Evolutionary Journey of the Soul]

Pluto in the 9th house or Sagittarius

People with Pluto in the 9th house have had the evolutionary need to understand life and self in a metaphysical, philosophical, or religious context. This is the archetype through which humanity needs to explain its connection to the universe and world we live in. In the 8th house we sensed this connection. In the 9th the connection is known. Being a fire house, these people have the feeling of a special destiny. In this placement it is linked to their relationship to the metaphysical, philosophical, or religious principles that explain their connection to the universe and the world. They understand that the universe exists, beyond the labels and classifications we humans place on parts of it. They want to understand the truths that explain the world and universe. These people need freedom to go after the experiences they need to discover the knowledge that explains these larger forces.

Many are born as natural loners. Many have incarnated in diverse cultures all over the planet. Many will leave a country or society in which they feel their search for the truth is being stifled. Many will feel alienated from their own society. This is because their search for the truth runs into the limits of the consensus belief systems of the culture they find themselves in. The alienation tends to lead to external and thus internal confrontations. The confrontations reinforce the sense of alienation. Since many have incarnated in a series of different cultures, the current culture beliefs will seem alien since the subconscious memories are rooted in other cultures whose values and belief systems may be fundamentally different than those of the present cultures. This alienation is required by evolutionary necessity to understand the truths that lie beneath any culture's consensus values and beliefs. The alienation forces the elimination of the barriers that prevent the direct understanding they are seeking. Many of these people will feel rootless and will consider themselves world citizens.

Others will gravitate to a different philosophical or cultural tradition that feels more aligned with their own subconscious memories. Still others will have been reborn in a culture whose beliefs are aligned with their inner sense of truth – for them the sense of alienation will be much less. There is a concentrated development of the intuition, the ability to know something without arriving at the knowing through conscious reasoning. Since they know they are part of a larger Universe, they have tapped into the forces behind this world. Through this focus they become aware of the laws and principles behind those forces. The nature of human belief systems is determined by geographic location and individual and collective development. The underlying principles are the same for all cultures but are conceptualized and expressed in a diversity of cultural and individual ways. 9th house people interpret these principles according to their own state of evolution and karma. Their need to develop intuition in order to know truth creates problems related to the dual desire nature of the Soul. The separating desire results in over-identification with a specific philosophy or religion, based on the needs for security. This need gives rise for the society or the individual to defend against other cultural or individual interpretations of these same principles. They will either try to impose their view on others, or to withdraw.

Because the Soul's sense of security is based on the belief that its interpretation of reality is the 'right' one, any sense that another interpretation could also be correct threatens the philosophical basis upon which the sense of security has been constructed. Thus there is the need to convert others, to prove the rightness of one's own philosophy. This need to convert is called teaching but is actually indoctrination. The localized interpretation of truth is presented in a generalized way as truth that applies to all. Individuals coming from this perspective will consider others who have conflicting philosophies to be 'wrong.' True teaching is when what is being taught is presented as one expression or interpretation of truth and that individuals must experience and decide what their own truth is.

A problem related to intuition development is that the person may not know how to communicate what they are intuiting through linear, rational language. They become aware of principles and information that are not products of their education or reasoning process. Many do not understand why they know what they know. They simply know it. Many of these people have had many lives in the East where the languages have totally different structures than those of the West. In Oriental languages, some characters represent concepts rather than facts or objects. 9th house people think in concepts – finding words to explain intuited concepts creates problems, especially during childhood. This can reinforce the natural sense of alienation, promote withdrawal from the culture, and begin a lifelong search for a philosophy that feels natural. This may involve much travel, reading, or simply drifting through life. (JWG's Pluto Vol. 1 and the School's Course)

Pluto polarity point – 3rd house or Gemini

The intention for this life is that these people learn that their version of reality is relative, that the paths to truth are many, and that each person must discover their own truth. This will occur through confrontations with others or through cultural alienation. Their inner sense of security is linked to the beliefs they have identified with. The confrontations and challenges to these beliefs that they experience will challenge their sense of security, which is the evolutionary intention. They can be quite resistant to other points of view. They can be argumentative as they attempt to convert others to their viewpoint through exposing the weaknesses in the other person's perspectives. Yet they are destined to draw to them people who are as powerful or more powerful, who will point out the weaknesses in their perspective. They will also encounter others who don't understand what they are trying to communicate which will force them to learn to communicate in ways that others can understand. They will gradually come to realize the underlying unity of all paths. They will learn how to take in diverse facts and, using their intuitive abilities, synthesize them into deeper understandings. They will become less defensive and more understanding of the relativity of truth expressed through different peoples and cultures. They will lose the need to try to convert and replace it with sharing and teaching rather than indoctrination. Many have a natural wisdom and are natural teachers. But until they learn the relativity of all truths they will be blocked from being able to effectively teach. In the negative cases they can remain aloof and isolated from those who don't share their beliefs. Those who understand the true significance of this archetype will work to understand the evolutionary lessons that are at hand. They can help others transform their vision of the nature of reality. Common characteristics: sense of alienation, intuitive conceptual thinkers, can be fixed in beliefs, need to convert, value honesty, can be loners, philosophical, laugh at self, help others to laugh at self, storytellers with tendency to exaggerate, tend to be natural and not cosmopolitan. (JWG's Pluto Vol. 1 and the School's Course)

Compensation

Compensation as a dynamic in astrology correlates to Jupiter, Sagittarius, and the 9th house.

People in the beginnings of the 1st stage Individuated do in fact feel very different than the Consensus folks/state through which they have just evolved and yet because it is relatively new it of course creates a deep sense of insecurity and anxiety in terms of fully acting upon this individuating impulse. As a result of that fear such folks 'compensate' by way of trying to counteract this inner sense of insecurity and anxiety by creating the external appearance of normalcy including the very structures of their life, including many 'friends' that come out of that very consensus, 'normal' type jobs, etc., thus creating a living lie because of the act of compensation. All of us can 'compensate' in areas of our life relative to where we feel most insecure or powerless. (JWG)

Compensation can show up in someone in any evolutionary stage where the person is not operating fully aligned with Natural Law. The gist of compensation is (as an example) if a person feels inadequate and bad about themselves inside (Virgo-like) they may cultivate an outer persona that seems really self-confident and almost full of self (Leo-like). It works the other way around also, a person with a big ego presenting themselves as humble and serving. Compensation is a form of AVOIDING rebalancing. Because it comes out of denial, where the person believes (Jupiter) that the way they are showing up IS the truth, when in fact it is a way of avoiding looking at (Virgo, denial) the actual reality, and pretending to be something other than what they really are. That is not my definition of rebalancing. If they OWNED the underlying condition and then practiced coming from a polarity to work towards balancing it, that I'd describe that as rebalancing. Denial can never be a path to equilibrium. I'm not sure I'd call compensation a natural phenomenon. It's more like a survival mechanism.

A person feels so wounded inside they can't show up as what and where they really are – they pretend (fooling themselves) to be more than or less than what they actually are. That is to survive. If aligned with Natural Law, a person would just accept wherever they found themselves to be – why would they need to compensate? There's a big difference between being aware you feel highly inadequate, accepting that you do and showing up anyway with acceptance of your inadequacies (humility), and showing up acting like you are confident and self-assured, an adopted persona, when that is not at all where the person is within themselves. In other words, compensation is more making a condition even more out of balance than it is rebalancing a condition. The thought is one that Jeffrey used to say, that where Jupiter is transiting it has gifts to bring you. But you have to be willing to give something up before you can receive the gifts. The "something" is not some random something that you pick out yourself. Rather it is something that has become outmoded in the life and needs to be let go of. I'd say it's not a conscious process – Jupiter is intuition – one would just know what the something needs to be. No letting go, no gifts. (Steve)

Resolutions for compensation

The resolution in all charts in which compensation has taken place, is to first desire to undo the compensation which means to acknowledge that it has taken place in the first place. Once that occurs then the next step is to determine the causes, reasons, why that has happened. Once the reasons and causes have been determined to then determine the natural ways to undo that compensation in such a way as to utterly redesign the life in order to reflect who the Soul actually is. This of course requires great, great courage. The specific causes of what led to the compensation is different in every case as are the ways to undo it in order to redesign the life. Each birth chart in which this is symbolized tells the unique story for each. (Rad)

Compassion

Compassion correlates to the archetypes of Sagittarius, Jupiter, and the 9th house. The essence of compassion is UNDERSTANDING. This is the direct correlation to Sagittarius, etc., as related to Natural Laws. (Rad)

Compassion would be an application of Natural Laws. Natural Law of evolution, and self-evolution, would give the understanding of what is possible and what is not possible to realize or to resolve individually given one's own or the other's evolution. It would imply the idea of natural limits of what can be done for others, and what cannot be done for others because of their own need to resolve by themselves, to find their own way, even if they seem to be on a wrong path. Thus, it would imply the Natural Law of free will. Compassion would imply the Natural Law of interrelatedness, including how individual evolution contributes to the evolution of others, and then, the idea of evolution of all Souls. The Natural Law of inclusion and sharing would further require helping others. And from here, self-compassion would imply knowing that, despite the errors and imperfections, the Soul will find its way to evolve. Thus, compassion would provide the correct attitude to bear with one's own limitations and the limitations of others. Correlated with Sagittarius, these understandings would operate intuitively. (Gonzalo)

My thoughts on this are that Love is inherent in the fabric of creation (Pisces), the way that God/Goddess created everything. We are free to align ourselves with it or ignore its very existence. Compassion is wisdom (Sagittarius). Compassion (in human life anyway) is Love Applied. Compassion takes effort. It equates for me to the old Native saying about not judging anyone until you have walked a mile in their moccasins. It is the quality of empathy, not sympathy but empathy. The developed capacity to understand another from the inside out, what their inner reality is like, what their struggles and hopes and errors are, how they try, where they are stuck. To see all that and make no judgments, accepting they are where they are. Pointing out, if they so desire, what their next steps might be, with no personal agenda and no judgment, simply trying to do what is right. Depending on where they are, what is right and what is compassionate may not look and feel like what we think love is – sometimes compassion is smacking someone on the head so to speak – not from anger or frustration, but because what is right (in some cases) is to try to deliver a blow to the patterns they repeat that are the source of the misery they seek to be free of – to attempt to get their attention.

So many of us remain in denial of our own patterns, repeating them again and again. Compassion can appear in many external forms and guises. But no matter how it appears it always comes from an inherent selflessness, a simple desire to understand and to serve. Obviously this is a tall order for most humans, to consistently come from such a place. This is why it takes a really long time to truly develop. And it's why compassion is a quality we generally associate with very evolved Souls. They have walked the same roads, made the same mistakes, and somehow found their way through them. Thus they know what the other person is experiencing, from the inside out, from personal experience. On my wall is a saying, "There is no saint without a past and no sinner without a future." That, to me, is Life's compassion. (Steve)

False beliefs of the Soul
The operative word here is BELIEFS. People can conjure up anything and make themselves believe it. Once they do that then the nature of whatever those 'beliefs' are become the determinant of how they interpret the nature of actual (natural) reality. They become the basis of what they come to value, and what they come to value then becomes the basis of the MEANING for their lives. In combination this then becomes the causative factor in judgments: internal and external. This is very important for all of us to understand for in NATURAL LAWS, the actual laws that have been set in motion by what we call God'ess, does not require BELIEFS whatsoever. It does require knowledge, TO KNOW, what has actually been created by what we call God'ess. To know is very different that believing anything. When Jesus said, for example, 'When thy eye is single one's whole body is full of light,' this does not require believing that. This natural truth or law can indeed be experienced within oneself by simply shallowing and suspending the breath. At that point the Soul KNOWS this truth. It does not believe it, because it knows it. (Rad)

Data, observation and correlation
The right brain is said to be intuitive/conceptual/abstract, and the left brain is said to be linear, rational, and empirical. Astrologically this would be the difference, again, between Sagittarius and Gemini. That which manifests through the right brain is that part in all of us which is plugged into the totality of manifested creation. The manifested or projected creation is Uranus. The plug in the socket, so to speak, is Jupiter. Jupiter intuits, and makes consciously available to the individual, the projected creation of Uranus. The intuitions of Jupiter translate into abstract or conceptual thought involving principles. Mercury is plugged into Uranus by way of Jupiter. Mercury translates into linear or applied thought that is specific and reflective of the nature of each individual. Thus, Uranus projects through Jupiter to the existing channels of Mercury in order to make new connections; thoughts. (JWG)
(Q) If I am looking at a bird making certain sounds before a storm, the observation of the phenomena itself is **Aquarius**, the correlation to *what* those sounds mean implies a synthesis of various observed data, which is **Sagittarius**. The data itself that I am observing and synthesizing implies classifications and names that I have associated with that phenomenal reality, which is **Gemini**. (Ari)
(A) Yes (Rad)
Uranus also correlates, in complete detail, to all the memories of this and other lives. This is why it is called the higher octave of Mercury. Most of us can't remember in explicit detail what we did two days ago. So my question is, where do all these memories go? Mercury correlates to what you can consciously recall in the form of memories, or that which you have learned or been taught. But Uranus correlates to all the memories and knowledge that have ever come before; that which you can not necessarily recall consciously. (JWG)
(Q) Is it true to say that observation (Aquarius) does not depend on mental classifications (Gemini)? In other words, can creation be observed without any mental constructs being associated with that observed creation?
(A) Sure (Rad)
The observation part is of course Uranus, Aquarius, and the 11th house whereas the correlation part is Sagittarius, the 9th house, and Jupiter. (Rad)

Intuition
As far as intuition goes, ANY of us can be "wrong" intuitively. Although we ALL have intuition (because it comes from the Source, God, Goddess), there are different degrees of evolution OF that intuition, degrees that are actually reflected in the different evolutionary stages. There is, for example, a HUGE difference between the intuition of an avatar such as Yogananda, and the intuition of, say, George Bush. PLUS, anywhere along the way, as we develop our intuition of thousands of lifetimes, we can still "hear" our own intuitive insights inaccurately if the ego gets in the way. Like anything else in the EA paradigm, intuition is not a one-size-fits-all phenomenon either. (Adina)

Synthesizing truths via intuition
Pisces, Neptune, and the 12th house correlate to Ultimate and TOTAL truth. Yet consciousness in human form cannot know the absolute totality of the Truth: it is limited by the nature of the form. For example, what is the origin of God itself? And that Origin, and that Origin, and so on. Thus, the Soul and its consciousness within human form can only induce through its intuition a limited part of that total truth. And because it can only intuit through such induction limited truths of an ultimate nature this becomes the

basis of what APPEARS to be conflicting truths. These conflicting truths of an apparent nature thus become the basis of conflicting ideas leading to a variety of philosophies and/or religions. In turn this becomes the basis of doubt due to the nature of these apparent conflicts. Doubt thus becomes the cause of asking ever more or deeper questions about the nature of the Creation in the first place.

Sagittarius, the 9th house, and Jupiter attempts to synthesize via intuition the unity of these apparent conflicting truths, and the ideas that these various truths create. Yet, in the end, consciousness, embodied in human form that is called the Soul, can only realize, understand, or intuit via synthesis a limited amount of the Total Truth that is inductively sensed within the archetype of Pisces, Neptune, and the 12th house. This is why even within the idea systems we call astronomy, astrophysics, and the like that the greatest of the greats in those systems, like Einstein, Steven Hawkins, etc. come to the same conclusion about the nature and origins of the Creation. And they all call that God. (Rad)

Awareness inducing realizations

Sagittarius, Jupiter, and the 9th house correlate to our awareness that the Earth that we live upon is connected to a much larger whole that we call the universe. This awareness 'induces' realizations of a non-linear or abstract nature about the nature of the universe that the Earth is part of. This then includes what appears to be 'outside' of ourselves. This awareness thus induces how the whole of the universe, including Earth, is interconnected or related to one another. This then becomes the basis of understanding and knowing through intuition what we call the Natural Laws of the Creation that explains this interconnectedness: to understand the 'whole' truth. When this natural component of our consciousness is then linked with Pisces, Neptune, and the 12th house it then attempts to induce realizations as to the nature of the manifested Creation in the first place: that which is responsible for the Creation of the whole that we call the universe. Thus the 'transcendent' truths of Creation itself.

This awareness is then that which is responsible for desiring to KNOW those transcendent truths. In turn this desire to know these transcendent truths induces, through intuition, the natural truths or ways of doing so. To do so is then the basis or cause of intuitively knowing that such transcendent truths can only be known from WITHIN oneself: Pisces, Neptune, and the 12th house. This then becomes the basis and origin of natural methods or techniques that will allow for an 'induction' of that transcendent knowing. When those natural methods or techniques are employed by our consciousness this then leads to a 'transcendent state' within our consciousness in which the perception, knowing through direct perception, of the transcendent or comic laws of Creation occurs. And that knowing is 'induced' within our consciousness because of consciousness being in a cosmic or transcendent state. And this induction is based on what is perceived from WITHIN our consciousness that can then be applied to what we perceive by way of the Creation in its externalized forms: Earth, the universe itself. (Rad)

Sagittarius/Capricorn archetypes, and Natural Law

The Sagittarius archetype correlates with the need to become aware of our connection to the universe in a metaphysical/cosmological context. This underlying need gives rise to the nature of all sorts of belief systems (and also religions) that attempt to explain our connection to the universe. This is where the issue of interpretation comes into play (our belief system is the determinate to how any of us will interpret life itself). The point within this is that, by the sheer fact that Creation exists, there must be intrinsic Natural Laws that govern and explain the nature of Creation (Natural Laws that are self-evident in nature). These Natural Laws, of course, have nothing to do with man-made religions and the laws that are taught in such religions. The intent within the Sagittarius archetype is to align with Natural Law in order to evolve and grow past limited beliefs that are based on man-made laws (the Sagittarius archetype also symbolizes growth and expansion). This is why the Sagittarius archetype correlates with Natural Law.

The Capricorn archetype, then, symbolizes how those beliefs will become crystallized, or given a structure to operate through. In other words, we feel the consequences, or effects, of our beliefs through the Capricorn archetype. Like my father so often taught, we do not need any religion to tell us it is wrong to put a baby on the freeway, we naturally know it is wrong to do so. In the archetype of Capricorn, then, we have the issue of judgments and also conditioned verses natural guilt. Man-made laws, in general, manifest distorted justifications for actions that inherently violate Natural Laws (there are both subtle and extreme forms of this), but on an inner level we all feel what is inherently right and wrong. In the Capricorn archetype we internalize the standard of behavior that is deemed "right and wrong" and we form judgments of ourselves and others accordingly. Again, this is based on the belief system we have formed/aligned with in the Sagittarius archetype. This describes, in a general sense, the interaction of the Sagittarius and Capricorn archetypes. (Deva)

From the point of view of Natural Law, we can say: In Sagittarius our core beliefs are the determinant for how we interpret life in the first place. If our beliefs are contrary to Natural Law, then we will interpret life according to the distortion of our beliefs. Based on those core beliefs and consequential interpretation of life, we establish and act upon various ethics and standards and rules that crystallize those beliefs into a social construct. If our beliefs (Sagittarius) are a distortion of Natural Law, then our behavior and the way we set up our lives (Capricorn) based on those beliefs will also reflect that distortion. (Ari)

Understanding the Sagittarius and Pisces archetypes within the Consensus state
(Q) Would you please help me understand the Sagittarius and Pisces archetypes within the Consensus state? Especially Souls who don't believe in any religion, and who are living in a society lacking in belief systems or metaphysical information. How would they evolve, generally speaking, if they are not into metaphysical, philosophical or religious information? (Wei)
(A) At first the EA astrologer must ask why such Souls choose to be born into such conditions in the first place. Every Soul has their own reasons of course, and those reasons are reflected/symbolized by the specific EA paradigm in each chart. Within the Consensus state any Soul will accept the Consensus beliefs and philosophical orientation of any culture, society, or tribe at birth. As a result it does not matter whether they are Sagittarius, Pisces, or any other sign. Remember the nature of the consensus state is to CONFORM. (Rad)

Understanding the Sagittarius and Pisces archetypes within the Individuated state
(Q) Would you please help me understand the Sagittarius and Pisces archetypes within the Individuated state? Especially Souls who don't believe in any religion, and who are living in a society lacking in belief systems or metaphysical information. How would they evolve, generally speaking, if they are not into metaphysical, philosophical or religious information? (Wei)
(A) At first the EA astrologer must ask why such Souls choose to be born into such conditions in the first place. Every Soul has their own reasons of course, and those reasons are reflected/symbolized by the specific EA paradigm in each chart. In the Individuated state Sagittarius will inwardly experience a growing sense of alienation from the consensus of whatever society, tribe, or culture they are born into relative to the beliefs and philosophical orientation within them: the society at birth. Pisces will experience a fundamental sense of disillusionment relative to those beliefs, etc. Remember one of the core archetypes of Pisces is one of meaning, or ultimate meaning. Thus, the disillusionment is one of a sense of underlying meaninglessness relative to the society, etc., of birth. In the Individuated state itself these experiences of alienation and disillusionment do not automatically lead to seeking out replacement beliefs, philosophies, or cosmologies. In essence, such Souls can simply remain inwardly defined by this alienation and/or disillusionment without any replacement that would correlate to regaining a sense of meaning and/or not feeling as alienated. This would especially be so in the types of cultures or societies that do not offer any such replacements. Consequently such Souls can try to fill the inner void created by the alienation and disillusionment with any manner of external escapes in order to try to fill in that void. The manner/types of external escapes will be all the ways that exist within the structure of the culture, society, or tribe at birth. For some Souls in such conditions they will in fact desire, and make the effort, to understand exactly why they do feel this alienation and/or disillusionment. When this is the case they will do all that they can do, relative to the structure of the society, etc., of birth, in order to understand this inner question of why.

I remember a story that JWG shared with me long ago wherein he was invited to lecture in the country now called the Czech Republic. This was shortly after the big revolution there in which the people there kicked out the old Soviet Union from having total control of their culture. The old Soviet Union and those who ruled within it of course were all atheists who attempted to impose that atheism on the Czech culture. The Czech culture before the Soviet takeover of their country had a long tradition of religion and the spirituality within those religions. The Soviet control was such that no one was permitted to read anything along religious or spiritual lines. They could not take classes or attend any kind of lecture that was about this at all. So even within the consensus because of this Soviet imposition there was in fact a deep disillusionment and alienation from the atheistic philosophy being imposed because of the nature of the Czech culture: its long history before the Soviet invasion.

JWG was asked to lecture in Prague shortly after their revolution and kicking out the Soviets. His original book on Pluto somehow managed to go to many countries in the world including countries that were behind the Iron Curtain of those times. Thus, there were people in that country who knew of his work which, in the end, is about returning Home: the origins of all of our Souls. They could not offer him any money due to the hard economic times there at that time yet really sincerely asked him to come anyway. He could not say no. This little group that asked him to come was so poor that they could not even advertise his lectures. All they could do was put up hand-made posters around Prague advertising his lecture: The Evolutionary Journey of the Soul. As a result they did not expect very many to attend the lecture. Yet on the day of that lecture over 300 hundred people showed up in a 14th century library where the talk was held. No one knew English. Thus he spoke for hours, one sentence at a time that was being translated into Czech. It was the nature of the lecture that rang the inner bells of all those Souls that came to hear him, bells that were rung relative to their own long cultural history. This went on for hours, long after the allotted speaking time. Of all the places JWG lectured in his time he told me this was one of the most significant and meaningful experience of them all.

This reflects your questions, Wei. It is desire itself that is the determinant of anything the Soul creates for itself including being born into cultures, societies, or tribes whose existing consensus beliefs or philosophies are devoid of higher meaning. And it is desire that is the causative factor for any Soul to, no matter where they are born, that leads to the higher meaning, or ultimate understanding, of why we even have life in the first place: where did it all come from and why. There was one other part to that story that also demonstrates what a Soul can do when it so desires. The man who asked JWG to come to Prague desired to become a Catholic priest. Yet the Soviets repressed all religion. This man's desire was so strong that he would take himself deep underground into a specific building and shelter himself from making any sounds. Then he would read the Bible. (Rad)

Manifest and unmanifest creation
Pisces correlates with the totality of Creation that includes the manifested = known, and the unmanifested = unknown. Sagittarius correlates with the Natural Laws within the manifested Creation that can be understood by the Soul in human form as well as knowing what cannot be known: the unmanifested. God realization is limited to the manifested Creation. It can never be linked to the unmanifested = unknown because, after all, the unmanifested is not yet known because it is not manifested in the first place. What Souls in the human form can know is linked to the interfacing between the known = manifested and the unmanifested = unknown. That interfacing point between the manifested and the unmanifested is the point of Creation as Souls in human form can know it. This limitation is sustained until the Soul evolves beyond its causal body. At that evolutionary point in time, Capricorn, the Soul can then have a progressive knowledge of the unmanifested creation equaling the totality of what we call God/ess itself. (Rad)

Sagittarius, Jupiter, 9th house correlations
Synchronicity, Conscience, Atheism, Distorted sense of right and wrong. (Rad)

Crisis of belief – waning square Mercury/Jupiter
The crisis of belief or consciousness would correlate to the fact that the Soul has already learned a variety of ways to philosophically and intellectually understand its reality. It has created a great philosophical and intellectual system that has been put together by empirical facts that have been learned over many lifetimes. And it has done so in order to actualize the underlying evolutionary intentions, whatever they have been. The Soul at this evolutionary juncture has now reached a place in its evolution that those existing intellectual and philosophical ways of understanding its overall reality are breaking down, and losing their meaning. Thus, all the existing ideas, Mercury, that have served as an empirical way of organizing its reality leading to the Soul's philosophical way of understanding life, must now begin the process of dissolving. This then creates the crisis of belief, or crisis in consciousness. (Rad)

Mercury/Jupiter – balsamic conjunction
The balsamic conjunction of Mercury/Jupiter means that the Soul is in the evolutionary process of culminating all kinds of beliefs, and the ideas from those beliefs, that it has used in understanding the nature of its lives until now: this life. (Rad)

Mercury/Jupiter – new phase conjunction
The new phase of the two planets correlates with the beginning of a new evolutionary cycle of development wherein the Soul is desiring to expand upon its existing knowledge and/or beliefs about life itself, and the new ideas it will be attracted to for that purpose. (Rad)

Beliefs – unconscious, fragmented, disconnected, contradictory
Knowledge that the Soul has been able to assimilate or realize in prior lifetimes will be reflected in the Jupiter natal archetype. Jupiter itself correlates with the Soul desires to expand beyond what the Soul already knows, and beyond the immediacy of circumstances in order to know the truth of anything, including personal truth, the nature of the phenomena themselves, and the nature of the whole truth or 'the Truth' which is the basis of all the rest. The nature of truth itself is non-conceptual. However, aspects of the truth, and aspects of the phenomena themselves, even though not linearly ordered, are not merely 'chaotic.' They manifest 'emergent' patterns which then serve as the basis for the creation of concepts, which can be linearly arranged serving for different types of descriptions. These concepts, arrangements and descriptions are a function of the Mercury archetype. From the point of view of how we can relate to phenomena, or to the nature of truth, perhaps the main intention of these Mercury concepts and descriptions is to direct the 'observer' in some direction allowing to directly experience that which is pointed at through the nature of words. Though, when such direct experience does not occur and the observer does not realize the nature of the phenomena, the left brain thought function can continue to operate within the scope of the linear connections language used in the description: a reflection of the nature of the mind. This can lead to confusion between 'map and territory,' and between the observer and the observed.

Because 'knowledge' provides a relative security for the Soul, the Soul can desire to think it 'knows' that which it does not know. Thus, we have the phenomenon of beliefs, ie the Soul can believe whatever it wants to believe. The dynamic of believing means that whatever belief the Soul has operates within consciousness 'as if' it were real. That which is believed is given the value of an experienced truth. Given that beliefs filter the direct impact of reality, any Soul can have different types of desires that are a reason for any beliefs, and no other, or not just 'not knowing.' In the dynamic of beliefs, the Soul relies on linguistic descriptions. As a simple example, someone can believe, "God is the Father, the Son, and the Holy Spirit." A Christian can believe this, and some 'Christians' have killed other people to defend this 'truth,' even having no direct experience of what such 'dogma' could refer to. Souls can have many types of beliefs which are formulated in linguistic terms, and which form a system. Souls can learn any belief system from books. Even, if a Soul chooses to consistently apply some Mercury 'instructions' this can lead the Soul to directly realize whatever aspect of reality the instruction points at, beyond the linguistic form itself. Here there's a direct natural connection and collaboration between the Jupiter and Mercury functions, right and left brains.

However, beliefs are not necessarily dependent on Mercury thought forms, and they can be based directly on experience. The nature of Jupiter is inherently experiential. As an example, let's say a Soul experiences abandonment, rejection and abuse during early childhood, which have the effect of inducing intense insecurity for the Soul. This can lead the Soul to 'believe' that life or people in general are dangerous or hostile. Given that early experiences are internalized, the Soul can believe in some cases it deserves rejection and abuse because of something being inherently wrong or evil in its own nature (this could be the case with Jupiter 4th house Scorpio, ruled by Pluto in Virgo conjunct Mars in Virgo being the ruler of the 9th house). These beliefs can at some point become expressed by means of Mercury linguistic propositions. Though, they can also exist as such beliefs without manifesting through words. These types of beliefs as in the example don't necessarily form a 'system.' (Gonzalo)

(Q) Are there unconscious beliefs?

(A) Yes. These types of beliefs have been formulated in prior lifetimes which then reside, in most cases, in the individuated unconscious of the Soul: Uranus, Aquarius, and the 11th house. (Rad)

(Q) If beliefs can be unconscious, and further, if we can have beliefs which don't form a system, can a Soul have fragmented beliefs, disconnected beliefs, or contradictory beliefs?

(A) Yes.

In the Jupiter Scorpio example with Jupiter being in the 4th house, the Soul can have a simultaneous unconscious belief that people in general are giving, honest and wise or defined by natural law and that life, as a result, is nurturing and secure. This would originate in prior lifetimes in which the Soul were born through families or mother figures which were defined by these natural orientations. At the same time, these 'disconnected' unconscious beliefs could relate to aspects of the individual personality or psyche (4th house, Scorpio) which have been unintegrated in the past and/or present lifetime, which have created the necessary experiences for integration to occur. In the example, the 'extremes' in these types of experiences that have led to co-existing and unintegrated generalizations of truth, could have manifested in past lives where the Soul embraced belief systems based on duality, such as Manichaeism, implying good and evil, black and white, as definite states instead as evolving states. This could have occurred as a result of alienation (Jupiter) from its own emotional life and its own psychological dynamics, resulting in desires to compensate and/or the creation of polarization and distortions of the self-image. Based on the example, beliefs are conditioned by the types of direct experience the Soul has been attracted to in order to expand or evolve beyond its pre-existing understanding or pre-existing beliefs. Thus, the natal Jupiter archetype (in relation to the evolutionary axis and the overall natal signature) reflects:

* Pre-existing beliefs or understanding, and prior belief systems that have been promoting the Soul's expansion of awareness
* Types of past lives experiences which have directly induced the prior understanding and beliefs
* Types of experiences the Soul will continue to gravitate to in order to learn more about the nature of reality in a way consistent with the Soul intentions to expand its awareness
* Nature of belief systems the Soul can gravitate to in order to promote these lessons.

In an effort to make a clear distinction between Jupiter and Mercury functions: Mercury correlates with the construction of a world of objects through linear arrangement of phenomenal reality from the observer's relative point of view. It correlates with the thought and language forms that result from this linear arrangement or construction. Further, it relates to the types of information the Soul needs to find, by means of such linear arrangements of thought and language and the resulting communication patterns, and how they have occurred in past and present lifetimes. Mercury reflects the impact of information taken from whatever environment-observation, communication, opinions, books, etc. including information and opinions about beliefs, knowledge, the nature of phenomena, and truth. A same proposition or statement could be either an opinion or a belief, depending on how invested the Soul is in such statement. Some Souls seem to simply believe in whatever opinions. An intention of the Mercury archetype would be to create distinctions between what the Soul knows, and what it does not know, and the natal Mercury archetype, in relation with the evolutionary axis and the overall natal signature would reflect the types of information the Soul needs to find in order to feed the Jupiter intention of 'knowing' what it needs to know in order to expand and evolve its understanding. (Gonzalo)

(Q) However, in some cases a Soul could be directed to some types of 'books' based on the natal Jupiter archetype. In the example, the Scorpio Mercury could be attracted to psychological written material in order to promote the intention of psychological/emotional self-knowledge. In such case would the natal Mercury intend to make this intention more specific, ie what type of information within the field of psychology will allow the Soul to understand or learn what it needs to learn? – Where and how it needs to find this type of information? – What type of intellectual approach is needed for this to occur? (Gonzalo)

(A) Yes. For example we could put that Mercury in Scorpio in the 4th house. One of the fields within psychology that such a Soul could be attracted to is called 'emotional anatomy.' (Rad)

Mercury and Jupiter correlations

An opinion is a specific idea, ideas correlating with Mercury, Gemini, and the 3rd house, that reflects an interpretation of any given phenomena. A cosmology is a combination of many ideas that, when combined, create an entire system of beliefs (Jupiter, Sagittarius, and the 9th house). (Rad)

Information/knowledge/beliefs from life to life

(Q) Any Soul can read the same spiritual books many times, life after life. This doesn't mean the spiritual knowledge contained in the books is realized, until it is realized, ie assimilated. After each life ends, the Soul forgets the knowledge forms contained in these books. Later, the Soul desires will lead the Soul to the same types of books in a next lifetime. These knowledge forms are Mercury. Once they are assimilated, they become Jupiter, and the Soul will not need to read these books again, because they are already part of what the Soul knows. Is this correct? (Gonzalo)

(A) Yes. But also remember that Jupiter correlates with the nature of 'beliefs' in any given life, and Mercury will correlate to the information taken in to not only create beliefs, but to reinforce those beliefs. Of course what one 'believes' does not necessarily correlate with what is actually true from the point of view of all the Natural Laws and truths reflected in those laws as set in motion by the Creator Of All Things. Humans can literally make themselves 'believe' anything which, to me, is one of the greatest problems human beings have. Many people 'believe' that the Earth is less than 10,000 years old and that humans co-mingled with the dinosaurs for example. And that belief then correlates to what is 'true' for them even though it is not actually true. This is why the 12th house naturally squares the 9th house: the necessity of a Soul to be disillusioned from anything that is not actually true which then leads, at some point to that which is true. So the Soul in fact can carry forwards into future lives the nature of 'beliefs' and the information necessary that 'informs' those beliefs. In terms of a Soul 'knowing' that which is true, realizing that from within, that knowing of that truth(s) will in fact be carried forwards as you have rightly stated. (Rad)

(Q) Is it possible for a Soul to remember knowledge forms or 'information' from prior lifetimes which, though, have not been assimilated? Can Uranus/Mercury memory contain un-integrated knowledge forms of intellectual nature, ie Mercury, from past lifetimes?

(A) No.

(Q) Will you clarify this Rad? I would expect that since Mercury is detailed information and Uranus symbolizes the long-term memories of the Soul, that there would be the possibility for such a recall when these archetypes are synthesized either natally or by transit, ie remembering how to identify various things that were never learned about in this life, the nature of such things just being empty information. For example, the ability to identify certain herbs that one may have learned to identity in a past life based on physical characteristics which implies observation of empirical data (Mercury) but not necessarily the intuitive holistic understanding of the herbs (Jupiter). (Ari)

(A) If that information about the herb had been internally integrated and used on oneself or others that information could be remembered: sustained. Conversely, if that information about the herb had simply been read about, or heard through word of mouth, without actually being internally integrated and/or used on oneself or others, then it will not be retained. (Rad)

Disillusionment and doubt, a personal experience

(Q) I have been undergoing massive disillusionment within my own spiritual life and within my relationship to Spirit itself. I have noticed as a reaction to this, I have become extremely cautious and guarded about interpreting *anything* in directly spiritual terms anymore. It is as JWG frequently said, disillusionment can be one of the most bitter and difficult experiences that any of us can have, and I can say from direct experience that this is UTTERLY true. And because that experience is so hard and so painful, the last thing I personally want to do – and I'm sure the same is often true for others – is delude myself again and walk right back into it. This also connects to the Virgo archetype: transition. In my own case, I recognize that I am manifesting an extreme response to the disillusionment that has had to occur in myself – and one of the serious, unfortunate effects is that it has cut me off from my own lifeblood. That is something I just have to work out for myself, I know. But I do have this question correlating to disillusionment and doubt. How does one go through massive disillusionment and not get caught up in the debilitating psychology of doubt? If something has been regarded in one's heart of hearts as 'real' – and that something has also been providing the basis for ultimate meaning – it is a complete shock to consciousness when the illusions are exposed and the meaning within it is finally seen as an embellishment of one's own making. So the question becomes, how does one recover one's confidence in interpreting spiritual reality, ie what is a real manifestation of Spirit vs what is imagined or 'hoped,' following a major disillusioning of consciousness? – particularly when there is no immediate resource available to confirm or clarify the accuracy of one's interpretation? (Stacie)

(A) The actual archetype that specifically correlates with being disillusioned is Neptune, Pisces, 12th house, that can then trigger its natural polarity of the Virgo, 6th house, and Mercury that manifests as doubt. With Neptune now transiting Pisces, and it has been squaring the transiting nodal axis that was in Gemini/Sagittarius, this experience of disillusionment leading to doubt has been happening to many, many people. And necessarily so because the intention with Neptune in Pisces is to know or learn about that which is true, and that which is not. While those transiting Nodes were in Gemini/Sagittarius this then focuses on the difference between beliefs that are projected as ultimate meaning, that which is true from the point of view of pure beliefs, and that which is true from the point of view of INNER KNOWING. Inner knowing does not correlate with beliefs because what is known is experienced within the interior of the Soul itself as a by-product of desire to know that which is true, and that which is not. Inner knowing of that which is universally true occurs of course through various practices, Virgo, that are all aimed and shallowing or stopping the breath. As that occurs the Soul is then able to penetrate the inner realms of consciousness itself: Neptune correlates with the phenomena of consciousness. As it progressively penetrates these inner realms of consciousness a variety of natural truths that correlate with the nature and cause of consciousness itself become KNOWN. And this knowing, again, is not a function of beliefs because, as these inner truths are known, there is nothing to literally believe and everything to know. And because these inner truths are simply known there then becomes nothing to doubt. The knowing is a function of actual experience, and those experiences are universal to any Soul who so desires to know these inner truths that correlate with the nature of consciousness. Because they are in fact universal it then serves as a way of knowing that which is true, versus that which is make-believe.

When this is the baseline within the Soul's consciousness, the point of personal Soul knowing and integration, this then serves as the vehicle through which, and because of, the Soul then 'interprets' the nature of any given phenomenal reality. The dynamic or archetype of interpretation specially correlates to Sagittarius, Jupiter, and the 9th house. As the Soul interprets the nature of any external phenomenal reality relative to this inner baseline the MEANING of whatever external phenomenal reality is then projected upon that phenomenal reality. As the Soul does this it will then automatically create a way of intellectually organizing all of phenomenal reality that reflects the core inner baseline of the inner knowing of the nature of consciousness itself. This natural process of intellectually organizing phenomenal reality correlates to Gemini: how the nature of thoughts that occur as a function of the inner knowing are connected to create a larger whole that is organized. All of this then correlates to the nature of various 'spiritual' cosmologies that humans have manifested going back to its own origins on this Earth that are then called 'religions.' This is then exactly where the conflict between pure beliefs versus actual knowing can occur because many who do desire to know the Origin of all things, the Origin of consciousness itself, indeed the Origin of themselves, align themselves with whatever spiritual cosmology without actually doing what is necessary to know for themselves that which is true.

Thus, by attaching themselves to whatever cosmology then leads to their personal belief system that is of course used to interpret whatever phenomenal reality. When a Soul does this, without actually doing that which is necessary to inwardly know, these beliefs are then projected upon phenomenal reality so that when phenomenal reality manifests in ways that cause conflict with the projected beliefs the result is then doubt: doubting the nature of the projected beliefs themselves that have been born, again, from whatever spiritual cosmology they have latched onto relative to the pure desire to Know. This conflict caused by projected beliefs initially creates the disillusionment of those beliefs that then triggers the doubt. It should be said too that a Soul who does not do their own actual inner knowing but simply latches onto whatever spiritual cosmology can also create 'beliefs' about themselves and/or others that are also delusional or illusionary. Thus, when certain types of inner or outer events take place that defeat those projected inner beliefs about themselves or others that same experience of being disillusioned takes place that then leads to doubt: doubt about oneself, or doubt about another(s). In essence this correlates to self-deception, and/ or being deceived by others.

To recover one's confidence in interpreting phenomenal reality, or as you say 'spiritual' reality, is to go deeply within the interior of one's own consciousness with the pure desire to KNOW. To know the actual truth of anything. To do so always starts with some sort of natural practice that aims at stilling the breath, of shallowing it to the point that it NATURALLY STOPS. If one does this while at the same time holding the nature of whatever one is wanting to know about within their consciousness there will come a moment, a time, in which the answer simply OCCURS WITHIN CONSCIOUSNESS OF ITS OWN VOLITION: like a bubble manifesting from the depths of the sea onto the surface of the sea itself. And a Soul can do this repeatedly in such a way that the truth of what one is wanting to know about can be repeated as many times as the Soul needs it to be repeated so that the lingering doubt simply dissolves. The point here is that if that which is true relative to what one is asking about is indeed true it will repeat itself over and over for as many times that the Soul needs it to. In this way confidence is regained. (Rad)

CAPRICORN – SATURN – 10th HOUSE

Capricorn keywords

Social position	Punishment	Man-made law	Patriotism
Authority	Discipline	Ancestral	Politics
Judgment	Totalitarian	Tradition	Responsibility
Judge	Fear	Guilt	Depression
Maturity	Rigid	Self-defeat	Burden
Old age	Paralysis	Futility	"Fall from Grace"
Repression	Conformity	Boundaries	Conditioning by family/society
Oppression	Suicide	Structure / Form	
Grief	Isolation	Nationalism	

Capricorn, Saturn, 10th house archetype

Yin / cardinal / earth / rules 10th house / ruler is Saturn. In its highest manifestation Saturn represents time and space, cause and effect (karma), and allows for emotional maturation. It is about accepting responsibility for one's actions. It represents maturation, caused by an awareness of mortality, that there is a limited amount of time within which to fulfill the intended work of a lifetime. The first Saturn square at age 7 starts this process – the imprinting of the consensus reality begins at that age. Capricorn represents the desire for social position and status. Fueled through Leo this can lead to delusions of grandeur where the end justifies the means. Social groupings must have organized contracts so people can live together. This becomes the basis of consensus thought and turns into the pressure to conform. Capricorn represents boundaries and borders. It becomes nationalism and turns into 'I'm better than you' perspectives.

Capricorn represents repression and suppression. That which is natural to a person that falls outside of the consensus standards of the society tends to be repressed, where it becomes distorted. Capricorn is square Aries. Aries represents the sexual impulse. The square can creates a suppression of the natural sexual instincts relative to current cultural conditionings as defined by consensus society, conditioned by the nature of the prevailing religions. The repressed natural sexual impulses become distorted. Depression is associated with Capricorn. Depression causes a state of reflection that is necessary at times to the unfolding of consciousness. Depression causes us to become aware of what is within us that is no longer working and needs to change. Capricorn represents how you are going to establish your sense of personal authority (Leo) in the context of the society you live in. The need to establish personal authority is basic. When done rightly you receive recognition for it. (JWG's Pluto Vol. 1 and the School's Course)
[Recommended Reading: Jeffrey Wolf Green's Pluto Vol. 1 – The Evolutionary Journey of the Soul]

Pluto in the 10th house or Capricorn

As a cardinal house, Pluto in the 10th represents the beginning of a new cycle. This can apply to countries as well as people. These people have been learning how to establish their authority within a society. Societies must have laws, customs, and taboos to which people must conform so that society can function in a stable way. These may evolve naturally over time, may be established by a consensus of society's members, or may be imposed by those in power. A society represents collective authority that dictates how individuals are expected to conduct themselves. Each nation has a philosophical tradition (9th house) upon which its laws and customs are formulated. In the 10th house the philosophies become institutionalized. Individuals with 10th house Pluto have been learning how to integrate their own philosophy/identity into the framework of the society. This is the progressive socialization that began in Libra. Countries have borders, and individuals have a position or function within society.

These people are learning how to define their individuality though their social function. To do this they must learn how the society functions. They have been learning about discipline, self-determination, and submission to higher authority. Learning how to link their own individuality to a social purpose brings lessons in maturity. Each nation has its own vibration created through its laws and customs. Each is born in the nation that reflects the Soul's karmic and evolutionary needs. The 4th house described the early childhood environment. The 10th house describes our extended family environment – the *culture in which we grow up. Much of our sense of social identity is conditioned by the nation in which we grow up. These people have an evolutionary need to become socially responsible. They are born in the country that best reflects the way to learn these lessons.

A majority of these people have desired positions of social power or status. Many have held these positions in past lives. These people have used Pluto's ability to penetrate to the essence to learn how the social system works. Many have learned to manipulate the system to their advantage, to realize their ambitions of getting to the top. They need to be in control rather than allowing society to control them. They are aware of power and powerlessness. The nature of the society determines the ways through which social position is achieved. If the society is corrupt the person will use corrupt means to achieve power. Their thought will be that 'this is just the way it works' and they will feel no personal responsibility. This leads to two possible problems. Becoming overly identified with career, position, or status; and manipulating and using others. Both can lead to abuse of power, especially if their sense of emotional security is tied to the position they hold.

When the position (representing the sense of security) is threatened, individuals can use any means available to try to sustain power. This applies to nations as well as to individuals. These people need to learn to be responsible for their actions. People with past life patterns of manipulation will come into this life with subconscious guilt patterns. The issue of standards of conduct is intensified in Capricorn. Abuse of power is ultimately not right no matter how much it is rationalized. Those with the past life guilt patterns will find a strong inhibiting effect in this lifetime. They are punishing themselves and attempting to atone. Many do not know why they find themselves in this condition. They may feel that fate or society is keeping their doors closed. Others do this to themselves. This forces reflection through which they gradually become aware of the hidden dynamic that is the source of this pattern. It can bring on depression and a sense of powerlessness and futility.

They often draw to themselves parents who are stern, and who impose rigid rights and wrongs on the children. Or a parent who leaves, or won't take on the responsibilities of parenting. Often they themselves have been very judgmental in past lives. Another primary lesson is self-discipline and self-determination – identifying one's abilities and goals, and actualizing them. The need is to identify one's societal function, and to actualize it. This requires discipline and commitment. Many have not yet learned this lesson because it is a new impulse. Their pre-existing patterns still revolve around the need to identify with a career as a sense of identity and security. Many have settled for less in past lives, because they did not learn the necessary procedures, or because they did not make the necessary effort. Some with these prior-life experiences will have cycles of pessimism, depression, bitterness, and jealousy of those in authority positions. They may feel guilty through the inner awareness of the failure to use their potential, or they may project the guilt outward and blame society. The parents often reinforce the guilt by judging the children's shortcomings against their own standards. Those who have mastered the lessons have held meaningful social positions in past lives. They actualize the intended social function with relative ease since they have already learned the necessary lessons. These people often have a positive impact within their specific work area or on the society as a whole.

Those who have learned to operate with timeless standards of conduct can be inspirational to others. They will have natural leadership qualities and be the embodiment of self-determination. They will not use devious means and know they are responsible for their own actions. They tend to feel contempt for those who shortcut the process and are not afraid to confront them, thus exposing others to their own motivations, influencing them to a higher standard of conduct. The 10th house is where we realize our own mortality, and with time and space. 10th house people are highly aware that there is a limited time frame within which to fulfill the destiny. This causes maturity – it enforces the awareness of timing; that the structural organization of reality evolves over time. That which is outmoded or crystallized must change. A negative understanding of this principle can lead to attitudes of 'what's the point.' In most cases gender switch is associated with 10th house Pluto people. It usually signals that a state of imbalance has been reached that requires a gender switch so that necessary evolutionary growth can continue. The hormonal shift can create emotional moods and feelings that are difficult to relate to or to control. The need is to become aware of that which produces the moods rather than to be a victim of them. (JWG's Pluto Vol. 1 and the School's Course)

Pluto polarity point – 4th house or Cancer

The person must learn to develop internal security and sense of identity not bound up in the social position or role. They are also learning emotional lessons. They commonly receive shocks delivered by parents, children, or spouse. For example, the death of a parent, or having judgmental parents. The necessity is for self-examination. The shocks force deep self-examination. This helps them understand the nature and basis of their emotions, and to create the necessary sense of inner security not tied to social function. Problems experienced through their own children can force self-examination as never before. Sometimes they may neglect their own children due to career obligations and never get to know them. This can produce guilt, leading to self-examination. Sometimes the desired social position is denied to enforce the lessons. Other times this can happen due to previous abuses of power. Being held down again forces the self-examination.

The reflection gradually causes them to form a new self-image not dependent on career or anything external. They begin to develop an attitude that even if they lose everything, they will still be okay. As they develop these attitudes, the roadblocks to the social position will be released. They can then achieve the social recognition they desire. They learn to balance work time with private time. They learn that their values are subjective, and apply to them alone. They learn to not judge others. They learn to fulfill their ambitions in non-manipulative ways and encourage others to do the same. They learn to become responsible parents. Common characteristics: cycles of emotional withdrawal, need for recognition/power, good organizers, natural leaders, understanding of how systems work, ambitious, serious, pragmatic, anxiety-prone, may have cycles of depression, autocratic, hypocritical. (JWG's Pluto Vol. 1 and the School's Course)

Cardinal signs/houses
Cardinal houses are intense because they represent major shifts or turning points – the natural squares-oppositions-conjunctions in the chart. The cardinal signs/houses contain their own paradoxes. Cardinal is an instinctual need to initiate change. Our sense of security is based on sameness, not on change. Thus the very nature of cardinal insures that at certain points we are going to freak out a bit, because all the change we have been instinctually creating results in a loss of familiarity and known-ness. This, at key points, results in the loss of an emotional sense of safety/security, leading to a desire to STOP, to want to go inward to emotionally regroup – to ground and stabilize the new realities we have been initiating. This is an inherent and necessary part of the cardinal archetype. It's especially pronounced in Cancer, but applies to all cardinal signs/houses – two steps forward, one step back. The natural need to regroup and reground after taking two steps into new directions. After a period of timeout, the cardinal instinct to initiate change again takes over, and we are back pursuing the next step forward again. (Steve)

Saturn correlations
Saturn correlates to the structural nature of our consciousness which means that whatever house and sign that our Saturn is in conditions and defines every other archetype, planet, within our consciousness. Saturn correlates with what is called 'reality' in general, and what constitutes 'reality' as defined by the consensus of any given group of people at any point in time. Saturn correlates to the natural function that all within a group have in order to sustain the needs of that group. Thus, what has come to be called 'careers' or 'work' within a given group or society. Saturn correlates with the very phenomena of time and space and, as a result, finitude. Saturn correlates to gravity and thus mass. In combination Saturn thus correlates to form. Relative to a consensus of people Saturn correlates with laws, customs, and norms that the group is expected to conform to for the group to maintain stability. Thus, it correlates to man-made laws. Because of its correlation to time, and that which is finite, Saturn also correlates with aging and thus emotional/psychological maturation. (Rad)

Life purpose – work – career
Every Soul, relative to its evolutionary conditions, has a true life purpose that is consistent with its ongoing evolutionary needs. The entire paradigm of the 10th, Saturn, Capricorn, 2nd, Taurus, Venus, the 6th, Mercury, and Virgo correlate to life purpose as expressed through the agency of one's work, or career. When the Soul begins to evolve into the Spiritual State then the Soul is inwardly and progressively attuned to the consciousness we call the Source, or God/ess. As such, these Souls will desire to do work that they feel inwardly called to do from that Source. The inner degree of awareness, evolution, within the Spiritual stage will correspond to not only the nature of what that is, but also that the nature of that work in every way is being consciously directed by that Source. The Souls who have reached the point in evolution in which the center of gravity has finally shifted from the subjective ego that the Soul creates to the Soul itself. At that point there no longer is any 'personal identification' with that work other than consciously cooperating with the inner directions from the Source to do that work. (Rad)

Time / timelessness
Time is Capricorn, the 10th house and Saturn. Timelessness is Neptune, Pisces, and the 12th house. Relative to varying degrees of 'cosmic consciousness' where the phenomena of consciousness itself is Pisces, Neptune, and the 12th house consciousness in human form can expand and evolve to the point of perceiving and experiencing the interface between that which has been Created and SET IN MOTION, and that in which this Creation emanates from that which is formless and timeless. In this way the experience of Creation is perceived and known. (Rad)

Archetype of judgment (Capricorn) manifesting through Pisces
What JWG taught is that judgment as an archetype in human consciousness is natural, and that the archetype of judgment in and of itself is Capricorn, the 10th house, and Saturn. He taught that the issue is not the right or wrongness of judgment as such, BUT THE CONTENT USED TO MAKE JUDGMENTS IN THE FIRST PLACE. Is that content rooted in Natural Laws, or is that content merely a collection of all kinds of man-made laws that have nothing to do with Natural Laws. When the archetype of judgment that emanates from the 10th house, Capricorn, or Saturn manifests through the 12th house, Neptune, or Pisces that then can correlate with the judgments made about spiritual disciplines, practices, the 'rights and wrongs' of spiritual life, of various gods and goddesses, and, of course, one's own relationship to all things spiritual. He taught a lot about all the artificial man-made rules and laws concerning spiritual life, all the 'should be's' so to speak. And how any Soul who enters spiritual life where the nature of that spiritual life has been created and defined by man-made laws that the judgments made either through one's own inner judgment of itself, or judgments made and projected upon others and oneself, that this commonly leads to not being good enough as measured against

these man-made spiritual doctrines. This is why he talked and taught so much about the difference between these man-created, patriarchal, spiritual disciplines and their 'teachings' versus what natural spirituality is, what the Natural Laws are, and thus to change the very nature of the CONTENT used to make the judgments in the first place. (Rad)

Gender switch
There can be many possible signatures that correlate to gender switches, not just Pluto and the Nodes. But that does not mean that just any planet, by itself, in the 4th or 10th correlates to gender switching. It is common to find gender-switch signatures and homosexuality/bisexuality signatures in the same chart. (Rad)

There is no way astrologically, or otherwise, to determine gender switch. It's an entirely individual, each Soul, issue that is dependent on many, many factors and variables. (Rad)

Transit of Saturn
Capricorn/Saturn, when implicated through transit/progression, always induces reflection on our prior choices that have created the present reality (Saturn/Capricorn) in which we currently live. The purpose of the reflection and introspection (which the West wants to label "depression" in many cases) is to acknowledge and take responsibility for all of the issues and dynamics within that have created what is now being experienced as our limits or blocks in life – the life circumstances that no longer fit, but now feel constraining or limiting (Saturn/Capricorn). Following reflection regarding what has not worked for us up to this point, the Cardinal energy of Capricorn enables us to create a whole new reality based upon the new evolutionary cycle trying to be born. At this time, anything new that is initiated by the ego that is not relevant to the Soul's growth will be blocked in some way. It is Capricorn/Saturn's way of keeping us 'on course' for the next step, the next phase, in our lives and in our Soul's ongoing evolutionary path. It is the personal responsibility (Capricorn) taken for all prior actions and choices that enables an inner security (Cancer) while navigating the new evolutionary cycle that Cardinal energy always ushers in.

Once we see that we do in fact create our own reality, and all of our life circumstances, there is a tremendous sense of freedom (Aries square) that comes, and this makes available to the Soul a new and dynamic energy, so that it may begin to create again, and create anew. Libra factoring in is that new people will be brought into the life/reality as new choices and decisions are made and acted upon. Libra correlates with trial-and-error: a process of elimination that helps us ultimately arrive at a reality (Capricorn) that is relevant to and reflective of our inherent and true identity (Cancer). Libra brings so many options, and at a time of transition, the ego is easily confused about which way to go, how to proceed. Cardinal energy is so instinctive, so the Soul may, at a time like this, 'cast a wide net,' trying to see what fits (Libra), and the blocks we experience thus help us narrow down our options so as to lead us in the appropriate direction. (Lesley)

Pluto in Capricorn transit
The positive aspects of Pluto in Sagittarius were the foundation of new beliefs and cosmologies. That was followed by Pluto in Capricorn. Those new beliefs then have to be anchored and structured. Outer forms created then reflected those new beliefs. Yet we are caught in the struggle between the old and the new. Those who prospered under the old are using every trick to retain their control – a dark side of Pluto in Capricorn. The very systems and structures we have to live under are the problem itself (or at least a manifestation of the real problem, which is the very idea of me advancing myself at your expense). That is why those structures have to crumble. As structures crumble people experience real pain. And we are not exempt from experiencing some of that pain. Times of vast change are always uncertain and create insecurity. But they are also the only times during which great change CAN occur. So here we go again. Pluto in Capricorn also brings the Saturnian elements of facing reality, getting real, getting grounded, looking at our delusions and seeing them for what they are. It can bring on depression and futility too.

But the positive side of that is that when false hopes and beliefs are dashed on the rocks it opens the way for realistic hopes and beliefs to enter – what is POSSIBLE versus what I call magical thinking. We have to lower our grand ideals and deal with what is possible, rather than utopian dreams that are just not realistic given present context. Collectively we are in dire straits, and a lot of options that could have been possible if action had been taken decades ago when they were proposed are no longer possible. Pluto in Capricorn is also consequences – the consequences of our previous actions. So we are seeing that too. We are not going to get out of this with a story book ending. The best possible thing anyone can do is come to terms with that emotionally. That in itself can take time. Once you come to terms with that, what is possible, we can start acting in ways that are realistic and aligned with what is possible. A lot of that seems to be positioning self for personal survival through difficult times. Part of the intent of the discussions on these topics is to talk about what is possible, what can people realistically do, given the actual circumstances. (Steve)

Since JWG wrote Chapter 11 in Pluto Vol. 2, many collective choices have been made. Human activities have affected Gaia to the point that some of the damage is no longer reversible. And, every time there is an international climate summit, the proposals for what will be done are about a quarter of the minimum needed to really change things, and instead of being put into place immediately, they are phased in for 10 to 20 years in the future. And by the time 10 to 20 years has gone by, next to nothing has actually changed, and another international conference is held, with the same basic results. Unfortunately the handwriting is now on the wall. Global temperatures and wind and precipitation patterns are rapidly shifting. This is going to affect the world's major food producing regions. The number of people on the planet is at an all-time high and rapidly growing. We will be seeing vast shortages of food and fresh water. This will be exacerbated by the new global corporate reality, which sees these scarcities as opportunities to reap vast new fortunes, at the expense of people's lives.

Look at what Wall Street is getting away with in the USA, for example. We are not entering a fun era on earth. In my opinion the only thing that is up to free choice at this point is the extent of the upcoming difficulties. There is no longer any way we will avoid all of it – we have gone too far. What we will see, as this unfolds, are the dual influences of patriarchy and matriarchy – those who want to advance their own interests through exploiting the suffering at the expense of others, and those who want to band together and help their fellow humans and other species through the hardships, as much as possible. These two approaches to human life will increasingly be colliding. People will be forced off the fence through circumstantial necessity. Everyone will have to choose their approach. We must wait and see to find which approach prevails. The answer to that is still up in the air. This is not intended to scare, but to suggest people look closely at what is going on, the directions things are going in, and start thinking about where and how to prepare for the coming changes. Again, not from a place of fear but from a place of awakeness. There will be many opportunities to evolve spiritually through the difficulties. (Steve)

One of the consequences of 'global warming,' caused by human activities that violate Natural Laws, is that the warming climate causes an acceleration of the Natural Law of mutation where mutation is a consequence of the survival instinct in all forms of life. Thus, the forms of life that are called bacteria, viruses, and fungus have begun this acceleration of mutations in order to survive. This will continue to accelerate at such a pace that the humans' capacity to keep designing new drugs to counteract this will not be able to keep up with the accelerated pace of the evolving/ mutating viruses, bacteria, and fungus. This will create, progressively, pan epidemics that will have the effect of killing a tremendous amount of people all over the globe. This in combination, as Steve pointed out, with increasing scarcity of fresh water sources, the dehydration of increasing amounts of land affecting food production, will cause cataclysmic circumstances for an ever increasing amount of human beings on this planet.

With Pluto in Capricorn, in the context of now, the EARTH REALITY of now, the very nature of the structural reality at every level will be metamorphosed through varying degrees of cataclysms. And those cataclysms will occur as a consequence of CHOICES THAT HAVE ALREADY BEEN MADE, AND WILL CONTINUE TO BE MADE IN OUR COLLECTIVE FUTURE. The essence of those choices comes down to the fact that the Natural Law, set in motion by the Creator, of 'giving, sharing, and inclusion' has been perversely altered to 'exclusion and self-interest.' It is this perversion, at a root level, that has been, and will remain to be, the cause of all kinds of cataclysmic events for whole groupings of people that has already occurred, and will be occurring. The transit of Pluto through Capricorn will move over its own South Node, as well as the South Nodes of Saturn and Jupiter. It is intended to create increasingly glaring and shocking events, events that can have cataclysmic consequences due to choices made, in order to get the attention of human beings so that other choices, choices in alignment with the Natural Laws of God/ess, can be made. And those choices either way will determine, Capricorn, how all of us will be able to live our personal lives, Cancer, on this planet: Earth. Our home. (Rad)

South Node of Pluto in Capricorn

Jeffrey said many times that the South Node of Pluto in Capricorn related back to the time period when the transition from matriarchy to patriarchy was already underway, and thus all Souls on Earth today have a natural connection to those times, or at least the energies of those times, even if they were not in human form on Earth at that time. Something interesting is that in 2018 transiting Pluto will be conjunct its own South Node of Pluto in Capricorn. We could consider what that means in terms of opening up the current version of the lessons from those times. Keeping in mind Cancer/Capricorn relate to gender role assignment, and the upcoming period we are entering is associated with the beginning of the return of the Goddess. Clearly the male-dominated present orientation is leading to the environmental devastation of the planet. Uranus enters Taurus in 2018/2019, and survival will necessitate radical change. Also, here in USA, we are having a US Pluto return in 2021/2022 at 27 deg Capricorn. Capricorn squares Libra (extremes) and we will have pushed everything to the maximum extremes, being forced to change from no other options remaining. (Steve)

Archetype of distortion

I just wanted to confirm that from an EA point of view, the archetype of distortion does indeed correlate with Capricorn. Distortion is the natural result when any natural impulse becomes repressed over time. The natural impulse to give, share, and include – the core principle underlying all Natural Laws – became progressively repressed when the patriarchy started to take over. This led over time to the progressive distortion OF that natural impulse, and the distorted RESULT that we now see manifest is the impulse to put one's own self-interest above, and at the expense of, the interests of all others – and to exclude all those who are not seen as a direct means to one's desired end. This distorted impulse of self-interest and exclusion is now what underlies the superstructure of rules, protocols, and norms that now dominate the entire reality of the planet – ie man-made law. Just as repression of what is natural leads to distortion, distortion itself progressively leads to delusion if effort is not made to effect realignment to what is natural (natural trine from Virgo to Capricorn, natural sextile from Capricorn to Pisces). And this is exactly what humanity's distorted man-made laws have become: a delusional replacement of the Natural Laws Goddess designed/created to govern the entire living universe itself. (Stacie)

Reflection

Generally speaking the reasons for a predominant need to reflect within the birth chart have been caused in lives just previous to the current life in which the dynamics of denial have been predominant. Thus, the need to create a consciousness in the current life that purposefully, the intent of the Soul, reflects upon the past in order to gain self-knowledge no matter how difficult and/or painful that may be. In evolutionary terms this is essential in order for the evolution of the Soul to proceed. And one of the intentions in creating such a consciousness includes becoming aware of why the need for the previous denials manifested. Reflection and memory recovery are related because when a consciousness is reflective the energy within that consciousness turns inward. With the energy of the consciousness turned inwards this creates a natural pressure within that consciousness that then induces memory. (Rad)

Saturn retrograde

When Saturn is retrograde the Soul will naturally rebel from anyone or anything telling it how to be, or what to do, or what to think, of what 'reality' is actually about as defined and assumed to be real by the consensus of the society that it is born into. It will rebel even from the parental authority if that authority is imposed for no other reason than to impose it. Saturn retrograde needs to determine its own reality, its own authority, and integrate itself into society in its own way that honors what it feels to be its inherent individuality. With Saturn retrograde and correlating to the structural nature of consciousness this then means that every other archetype, planet, within that consciousness is also being defined via this overall retrograde archetype even if other planets themselves are not retrograde. With Saturn retrograde it's like pointing an arrow towards Uranus. (Rad)

Saturn, and spiritual evolution

Saturn, like all planets, absolutely correlates with spiritual evolution. As Saturn is about the nature and structure of our current reality at any given time, I believe that the task (Saturn!) regarding Saturn/Capricorn, for all of us 1st stage Spiritual Souls, is to deepen our spiritual reality, through disciplines (Saturn) like yoga, proper lifestyle (which means appropriate relationships, Libra; proper nourishment for the body, Cancer; proper understanding and directing of the desire nature, Aries). Like all planets, the way Saturn manifests in our lives can be evolved over the lifetime, based on a strengthening and deepening of the one desire to know God, and return Home. Saturn helps us manifest a spiritual reality on Earth within our own lives, when our desire nature (Aries) and emotional body (Cancer) are in alignment with that purpose, so that a Soul becomes a 'concrete' (Saturn!) example for others along the same path. (Yogananda was a Capricorn, with a 10th house Pluto/Neptune conjunction!) Saturn/Capricorn energy helps all of us become better creators, in the end, no matter where we fall on the spectrum. (Lesley)

Natural Law, and the Sagittarius/Capricorn archetypes

The Sagittarius archetype correlates with the need to become aware of our connection to the universe in a metaphysical/cosmological context. This underlying need gives rise to the nature of all sorts of belief systems (and also religions) that attempt to explain our connection to the universe. This is where the issue of interpretation comes into play (our belief system is the determinate to how any of us will interpret life itself). The point within this is that, by the sheer fact that Creation exists, there must be intrinsic Natural Laws that govern and explain the nature of Creation (Natural Laws that are self-evident in nature). These Natural Laws, of course, have nothing to do with man-made religions and the laws that are taught in such religions. The intent within the Sagittarius archetype is to align with Natural Law in order to evolve and grow past limited beliefs that are based on man-made laws (the Sagittarius archetype also symbolizes growth and expansion). This is why the Sagittarius archetype correlates with Natural Law.

The Capricorn archetype, then, symbolizes how those beliefs will become crystallized, or given a structure to operate through. In other words, we feel the consequences, or effects, of our beliefs through the Capricorn archetype. Like my father so often taught, we do not need any religion to tell us it is wrong to put a baby on the freeway, we naturally know it is wrong to do so. In the archetype of Capricorn, then, we have the issue of judgments and also conditioned verses natural guilt. Man-made laws, in general, manifest distorted justifications for actions that inherently violate Natural Laws (there are both subtle and extreme forms of this), but on an inner level we all feel what is inherently right and wrong. In the Capricorn archetype we internalize the standard of behavior that is deemed "right and wrong" and we form judgments of ourselves and others accordingly. Again, this is based on the belief system we have formed/aligned with in the Sagittarius archetype. This describes, in a general sense, the interaction of the Sagittarius and Capricorn archetypes. (Deva)

From the point of view of Natural Law, we can say: In Sagittarius our core beliefs are the determinant for how we interpret life in the first place. If our beliefs are contrary to Natural Law, then we will interpret life according to the distortion of our beliefs. Based on those core beliefs and consequential interpretation of life, we establish and act upon various ethics and standards and rules that crystallize those beliefs into a social construct. If our beliefs (Sagittarius) are a distortion of Natural Law, then our behavior and the way we set up our lives (Capricorn) based on those beliefs will also reflect that distortion. (Ari)

Perversion of Natural Laws
In Natural Law, Saturn, Capricorn, and the 10th house all correlate to the total structure of Natural Laws as manifesting in the time/space reality that we call Earth. On the other hand, they also correlate to the total perversion of those Natural Laws where those perversions have been caused by men through time. And, thus, what we call the patriarchy. So ever since the patriarchy began to emerge way back in the past this progressive perversion has in fact defined the vast majority, the consensus evolutionary stage, right up until this moment in time. (Rad)

What does undistorted Capricorn look like?
It looks like the natural structure of all Natural Laws inwardly realized, and applied. It looks like all humans living and being defined by those Natural Laws in terms of the reality that they live. This includes the natural roles between women and men. It includes natural parenting. It includes the vital principle of sharing, giving, and inclusion. It includes all knowledge being inwardly realized, versus having to 'believe' anything. It includes living in a STATE OF BALANCE WITHIN ALL OF CREATION AS MANIFESTED ON THIS EARTH: TO NOT DOMINATE OR CONTROL ANYTHING. (Rad)

Capricorn archetype as an expression of Love
In the totality of creation, there are natural structures set in place by the creator. An example of this would be the spiritual reality of angels, devas, nature spirits, etc. Also all the various saints and spiritual guides that serve a unique function and role in creation, and this includes the natural wisdom of any Soul who has lived a full life in alignment with Natural Law. One thing that Capricorn teaches is the appropriateness of time and space. Different "rules" operate at different size scales. The only law that does not change is the law of Love. Love is the guiding motivation of creation itself. I feel in essence, the Capricorn archetype reveals how we are meant to appropriately structure our existence in alignment with Natural Law, which is an expression of Love, as human beings here on earth. (Ari)

Mother/father archetype
The 4th house, Cancer, Moon will correlate to the parental figure – mother OR father – who predominantly served in the role of nurturing emotional security, emotional bonding/proximity, emotional/personal relating, etc. in the upbringing. 10th house, Saturn, Capricorn correlates to the parental figure – mother or father – who most reflected the role of authority, sociological responsibility, emulation of emotional maturity in the context of relating, etc. Traditionally 4th house has been considered to represent the mother and the 10th house the father. But as we know, one size does not fit all. Just because a woman's physiology permits her to give birth to a baby does not mean that her inner nature is going to be oriented to emotional bonding, nurturing, etc. over expressing/actualizing a role of authority, emotional maturation, sociological focus, etc. within the family structure. And of course, vice versa for males. Both roles archetypically serve a vital function in the imprinting and ongoing development of our consciousness, and those roles are fully interchangeable – so as we like to say around here, observation/correlation. (Stacie)

The 4th/10th dynamic/archetype of parents – mother/father – is really, in the end, a cultural issue and related to different times in history. For example some cultures going back in time had the men nurse the babies: they were called 'brood males.' They developed the capacity to even produce milk through their breasts. And these males then served as the parent that did the daily upbringing and supplied the child's daily needs, etc. In other words, from the point of view of the patriarchal form of reality the 'roles' were reversed. So what it comes down to is the issue of 'gender assignment' which is a function of the 4th/10th, Cancer/Capricorn archetypes. And the gender assignment is a function of whatever culture/time in history that we could look at: what is then 'expected' by way of norms for what it means to be a male or female and the 'roles' therein.

On the other hand the 4th house and Cancer will always correlate to the early upbringing of any child all the time, and the general environment that the child grows up within. This will also include the emotional environment and the types of emotional experiences that the child has as a result relative to the parents' own reality, and what they are able to provide. The 10th house will always correlate to the type of culture that a child is born into and thus all the social taboos, laws, norms, expectations that serve as the conditioning to that child's sense of 'reality.' So of course it's possible for a child to have parents that PROVIDE BOTH ROLES, it's possible for a child to have a mother who primarily does the daily emotional needs of the child while the father provides for the material needs of the child/family/mother, and it's possible for a SINGLE PARENT to do both. So, in the end, the 4th/10th, Capricorn/Cancer is not the black and white of one equaling the father, and the other being the mother. (Rad)

The Moon, Cancer, 4th house archetype essentially correlates to our self-awareness in the body on a basic emotional level. That is the so-called 'ego.' It is how we emotionally identify ourselves, how we feel as 'me' as a being that knows it exists, and we know that as 'I.' This can never originate from the 'father' simply because it comes out of the womb of a woman, Moon, Cancer, 4th house. In the physical development of the embryo, it already has emotions that are part of the foundation of the 'ego.' The emotional conditioning starts in the womb and creates the basis on which the new baby will develop its emotional relatedness to the 'world' around it including everything and everyone outside of itself. It does not matter who will provide for the baby once it's born – from the point of view of the baby all that matters is if the needs will be met or not. These needs are Moon, Cancer 4th house. HOW those needs will be provided for is 10th house, Saturn, Capricorn, by both parents. (In our world there usually are two, in different ancient times there was no nuclear family nor one particular father figure, rather a group of people, the biological mother was backed up by several so-called 'mother and father' figures who delivered the care all together).

The Moon will always correlate to both the womb and the concrete early life experiences as well as to the mother and the individual emotional perception of itself. Why? Because the separation from the mother's emotions, perceptions, feelings etc. does not happen all at once, there is a period starting at the womb while it is all intermingled. From the baby's point of view the mother is simply 'part of itself,' part of its existence and relative to him/her they are 'one.' The baby feels everything the mother feels etc. etc. so there is no real separation. After birth this separation starts, but it takes a long while until the new born baby goes through the transition of separating itself as an individual being from its mother AND its overall environment. At first it all feels just like 'one,' it all feels like 'itself.' How it 'feels' is always the Moon. The particular birth and the early family environment is the 4th house, and so are the Soul's current life lessons about its own evolutionary self-related or egocentric development and lessons.

Cancer on the other hand wherever it falls in the chart and whatever may fall into it is the indicator of HOW the Soul has been trying to develop these self-related lessons and how it attempted and will still attempt to develop its own egocentric emotional security. Moon will always rule Cancer so we can see the correlation as how any current womb and early childhood environment will set forth the continuation of the ongoing lesson from the point of view of the self as an incarnated emotional being. The only thing that is gender-related is the mother in order to give birth: it has to have a womb for that. But anything else is totally open – for example today there are surrogate mothers who are neither biologically related to nor give any nurturing to the child, yet still there will be a womb experience which will be the foundation of the yet-to-be-born child's emotional conditioning for life. So point being, the polarity, Saturn, Capricorn 10th house will always DEFINE the time and space circumstances (including but not exclusive to the social circumstances), in other words there must always be REALITY SETTINGS within which everything will take place. That reality indeed has been defined for a long time by male figures due to the patriarchal order, ie we usually have an identified father who according to patriarchal tradition was the 'bread winner' etc. etc. But in essence we need to have a setting of reality within which we can exist (or not!) within the world and our mother, family, caretakers etc. are part of that reality in some ways. So these two will always interact and one cannot exist without the other. (Lia)

Father

EA, as well as the vast majority of traditional astrology, correlates the father with Saturn, Capricorn, and the 10th house. Remember astrology is a natural science which simply means a science born of correlation and observation: not theories or hypothesis. Because of this humans have been observing and correlating within the realm of astrology for thousands of years. As a result, this archetype of the father correlates to Saturn, Capricorn, and the 10th house. (Rad)

Saturn Return

A major part of Saturn Returns to me is a maturation factor. They naturally divide a lifetime into segments. Saturn also represents Time itself, and maturation is a timing process. The first is childhood and the transition into adulthood. The second is the transition from adulthood into what we might call elderhood, if the person has been paying attention. The focus becomes more reflective (Saturn) and inward, tying all the pieces of a lifetime together. The start of a winding down process. A desire to give something back for all one has received is common. Some make it to the third Saturn Return. There from my understanding the focus increasingly moves to planning the next lifetime. As always, the great majority of us have a lot of resistance to these natural transitions. My experience is most don't really start growing up until 32 or 33, when life no longer tolerates their acting like children. Thus the period from 28/29 to 32/33 is a transition time. Similarly for the mid-life crisis which is Uranus opposition to itself followed by Saturn's opposition to itself in the midpoint of the first Saturn Return period. Another adjustment that is frequently resisted for a period of years. On the other hand, for those who have been paying attention the Saturn Return can be another Saturn archetype, fruition, the natural timing of release. Jeffrey used to talk of how he got his first astrology job on the very day of his first Saturn Return. One way I visualize it is, an act in the play is ending. A natural time to move on. (Steve)

JWG used to teach that the majority of Souls come into any given life by acting out their past in a variety of ways where that past is not only the past of the current life leading to the first Saturn Return, but the past history of the Soul itself which of course is symbolized by the EA paradigm in any chart. Because of this most Souls do not make the choices early in their life that reflect the core EA intentions for the life being lived. This is why the first Saturn Return for most can be such a difficult time because many Souls begin to realize that their life to date, the choices made, have not been in accordance with the underlying intentions for the current life. Thus, the first Saturn Return gives the Soul the opportunity to make the necessary adjustments that will reflect the underlying intentions for the current life. The keyword here is 'opportunity.' Even though such an opportunity exists at that time many Souls do not make those choices to adjust their life anyway because of the nature of their existing 'reality,' Saturn, at that time: the structural nature of the reality that has been created to date.

For those that do make the necessary adjustments to their reality that do honor the underlying intentions for the current life then this can lead to an acceleration of those Souls' ongoing evolution through time. For those that don't, the evolutionary intentions will be actualized in a very slow, minimal way in a variety of ways. This can occur through the internalization of the Soul's consciousness via that common frustration that Souls feel at the time of the Saturn Return: "If I had only done this or that, or gee I would really like to be doing that,' and so on. These internalizations of the consciousness at that time that leads to these sorts of inner realizations do serve as 'seed thoughts,' desires, that will become active at some time in the future for such Souls. For the Souls who have made the choices earlier in their life, prior to the first Saturn Return, that reflects the EA intentions for the life, then the first Saturn Return can serve as the timing for actualizing what the Soul has been preparing itself for. JWG was informed at 24, his second Jupiter return, as to the nature of the life he was to lead. And that included becoming an astrologer. From 24 right up to the time of his first Saturn Return he did learn astrology in his own way, and did charts for free so as to learn as much as he could through observation and correlation. To the very day his Saturn Return occurred he was offered a job as being an astrologer for a brand new astrology bookstore in Seattle, W(A) (Rad)

Need to access chaos
The core issue of the Capricorn archetype and the need to access chaos is the need to experience vulnerability (Cancer polarity point). The Capricorn archetype in its distorted form manifests as emotional repression, and also a fear of vulnerability. As a consequence there are repressed emotional needs that must be accessed at some point in order for "true emotional maturity" to manifest through this archetype. By "accessing chaos," or simply allowing oneself to be vulnerable and, ultimately, learn to nurture these repressed needs from within oneself (Cancer polarity point) the true wisdom and strength of the Capricorn archetype can be expressed. There is no specific definition of chaos used in EA (just the usual meaning of the word). All too often those with a dominate Capricorn signature attempt to control their environment and their emotions because of the fear of vulnerability. In other words, the person always has to be (or at least appear to be) "in control." In this sense, the need to access chaos means to release this pattern of emotional repression and control, and in this way access their true sensitivity and emotional nature. (Deva)

Conditions of birth, life and death
The 'conditions' that any given Soul creates for its life, in any life, are the conditions that the Soul needs in order to further its own ongoing evolutionary intentions: whatever those conditions are. And those conditions of course affect the Soul: intentionally so. It is the very 'effect' of whatever those conditions are that serve to advance the Soul's evolutionary intentions. All Souls are 'affected' by the conditions of its lives. Even the most evolved of all Souls start off as children. And the conditions of their births that they have chosen 'affect' them as they would any child. For example the great Yogananda chose to come through a mother who loved him dearly, and he loved her dearly, yet she died when he was very young: four or five years of age. For him at that age this was total trauma. Yet, at that age, he determined within himself, since his earthly mother was no longer present, to find his 'Divine Mother.' And so at that age he took himself into an attic space in his home and sat there with the determination not to budge from that spot until the Divine Mother revealed herself to him from within. And She did. Yogananda had a 10th house Pluto conjunct Neptune which were both in opposition to his Venus in the 4th. The perfect symbolism for the 'conditions' of his childhood, and how those conditions affected his own ongoing evolutionary journey. (Rad)

Projected judgments
Judgment as an archetype correlates with Capricorn, Saturn, and the 10th house, not Pisces or any other sign, house, or planet. The archetype of judgment is natural to consciousness for that is one of the ways that Souls learn about the nature of life. The archetype of judgment of course manifests through all the houses, signs, and planets relative to the archetypes of each, yet judgment as such is the 10th house, Capricorn, and Saturn. JWG often taught about this and one of the main things he taught was that first judgment is natural to consciousness but the real issue is THE CONTENT TO BE USED TO FORM OR MAKE JUDGMENTS. Is that content rooted in all the Natural Laws that were set in motion by the Creator, or is the content rooted in man-made laws, rules, regulations, taboos, norms, etc? Projection, as an archetype within consciousness, correlates to Aquarius, the 11th house, and Uranus. When linked with Capricorn, the 10th house, or Saturn this then can correlate to our projected judgments upon others, and our own inner projected judgments upon our self.

[In terms of speaking to a client] I would approach it by explaining to them why people do these things in the first place. One of the core reasons that people do this in the first place is to avoid or deny taking any responsibility in their own actions. In so doing such people then need to create scapegoats in order to blame others for that which they are responsible for. These people always need to feel 'victimized' by something, or someone, in order to psychologically function. So, in essence, my advice is for those who are the recipients of this [judgment/projection] is to stand back and see it for what it is, to not take it on or 'believe' in any way that that which is being projected upon them is true. That it is essential to stand back and OBJECTIFY the very nature of the situation and persons involved: to detach from it even as it can of course really hurt. Beyond that general advice of course it is necessary to know the specifics of each situation in which this sort of thing happens. Those specifics then, of themselves, will dictate the natural and right way to proceed. (Rad)

Judgments

(Q) Is Capricorn judging its self and others through its Sagittarian belief system? (Sunyata)

(A) Judgments are natural to consciousness. It is through the dynamic of judgments that we learn about life in every way. The issue is not judgments as such but the content being accessed that becomes the basis of the judgments themselves. Is that content, the structural nature of the Soul's reality, a composite of man-made beliefs that have nothing to do with the Natural Laws set in motion by Creator of all things, or is it in fact judgments that are made relative to those Natural Laws? A simple example of a Natural Law that correlates to natural judgments is if someone placed their baby on the autobahn. The Soul simply knows this to be wrong: a natural judgment emanating from the principles of Natural Laws. So almost all Souls on Earth, because of around 8,000 years now of man-made laws that are not rooted in Natural Laws, have been externally and inwardly judged according to those man-made laws. As the Soul progressively evolves it will, at some point, need to throw off all man-made laws equalling judgments and then to allow the consciousness within it to be realigned with all the Natural Laws that are already part or inherent to the consciousness of all Souls on this Earth anyway. The Soul judges itself from within relative to all Natural Laws and/or all the artificial man-made laws. It does so by 'objectifying' itself: Aquarius. Aquarius follows the natural progression from Capricorn. In an utterly objective state the Soul is then detached from its own emotional body which then allows for the objective state to be inwardly accessed. In this state the Soul then makes its judgments. Of course all Souls can also be subjected to the external judgments of others, of societies themselves. The basis of these external judgments are the same: either judgments that are a composite of all the man-made laws and/or Natural Laws. Those that are making such judgments of others are themselves 'objectifying' that other and then applying their judgments according to the very nature of their own structural reality. This then becomes one of the causes of others 'projecting' their own structural reality upon another manifesting as the judgments of others.

Sagittarius correlates with the totality of all the Natural Laws set in motion by the Creator relative to the act of Creation itself. Capricorn correlates to the totality of all man-made beliefs that correlate to the creation of laws, rules, customs, norms, taboos that are a function of those man-made beliefs. Of course because of the Natural Law of relationships that means, since about 8,000 years now, an interaction between Sagittarius and Capricorn wherein some of the Natural Laws remain rooted within the man-made laws, and some of the man-made laws/beliefs interact with the Natural Laws in such a way as to either distort those Natural Laws and or repress/suppress completely. This then becomes the basis of 'religions' and philosophies manifesting as beliefs versus the KNOWLEDGE that is inherent with all Natural Laws. Humans do not require, relative to Natural Laws, any religion whatsoever in order to know the Nature of the manifested Creation in the first place. That knowledge simply exists as a function of the manifested Creation in the first place. So it then simply becomes a matter of the Soul within any consciousness of 'attuning' itself to that inherent knowledge. This is done through the Natural Law of the breath within all humans that itself is a function of the Natural Laws of cause and effect. One of the deepest and sadist of all things is the fact that human beings can literally make themselves 'believe' in anything. Beliefs are then used to develop all the thoughts and rationalizations necessary in order to justify the nature of one's actions according to those beliefs: judgments made because of those beliefs. It is because of this sad fact that we now have the nature of our world, of Earth, as it is right now. (Rad)

Races of people on earth

Pluto now in Capricorn correlates to the nature of 'races' of people on Earth, nationalities with skin colors within that degenerates into finding 'scapegoats,' the collisions of the different 'status' of peoples in life: the poor, the rich, the middle class, the powerful versus those with no power, all will now be confronted in an accelerated way. We must remember to consider the natural squares from Capricorn to Libra and Aries that correlates to the undercurrents within all of this: the need for balance and equality so that a new way can be discovered for the whole of the human race which of course will necessitate an entirely new/old self-image for the entire race: Cancer the natural polarity of Capricorn. Failing all this, what will be the consequences? (Rad)

Earned guilt

There are really TWO BASIC types of guilt: man-made guilt (learned) based on religious, philosophical, psychological, etc. beliefs, and natural guilt (earned), based on our actions that are out of alignment with Natural Laws. I think for the most part the majority of the learned guilt DOES go back to what we think is "right" and "wrong" based on man-made religions. In general, EARNED guilt will be reflected in the symbols of Saturn/Capricorn/10th house, while the LEARNED guilt is more likely to come through the symbols of Virgo/Pisces and their respective rulers and houses. These, of course, are just two places to START looking for patterns of guilt. Some of figuring this out within ourselves will unfold as we evolve and realign with Natural Laws, but much can also be gleaned now if we simply reflect on the reasons for ANY kind of guilt we feel and then the SOURCE of those reasons. For example, if I beat my child to the point he needs hospitalized, I know (even if it's only deep down within and not necessarily conscious) that I have done something inherently wrong. On the other hand, if I get a divorce and feel guilty because whatever church says it's a "sin" to get divorced, then I've taken on an unnecessary guilt based on some humans' ideas about what is right and wrong. Even in countries where religion has been banned, the old USSR, for example, I could be found "guilty" of and punished for not bowing to the emperor because that's one of the laws of the country. However, to not bow to another human being isn't intrinsically "wrong," it's only "wrong" because it's a man-made rule, and therefore actual guilt is unnecessary. (Adina)

What is that Cancer Polarity? Reflections on Pluto in Capricorn – by Bradley Naragon

Yesterday, I considered how appropriate the word 'streamlining' is to describe the Pluto in Capricorn phenomena, especially in a capitalistic competitive society and economy. Seemingly, at every turn and stop, organizations, institutions, and businesses are 'tightening' up operations. Paper towels are now half the size they used to be and I think the toilet paper went from 2 ply to 1.5 ply. Seriously, with Mars in Capricorn and the recent conjunction to Pluto, now more than ever 'getting organized' is the aim and drive. Keeping the ducks in a row is not intrinsically a bad thing. As the South Node transits Taurus, the question of "Will this survive?" is more appropriate than ever. What is desired to survive is all based on one's values. Many people still greatly value the form capitalism exists in. Many people have gained their own wealth and survived and thrived because the current model is a patriarchal system set up for some to win and many to lose. As a result, I now see so clearly the compulsions of what it means to just "do the Pluto Capricorn" without its Cancer polarity. It's a funny phenomenon – more than ever we need every single 'i' dotted and 't' crossed or we risk not having access to what we need. The compulsion to create even more policies and create more 'red tape' and hoops to jump through is ever so real with Pluto in Capricorn. We are lucky when we actually get to talk to a human. Yet, when we do, will they be so restricted in their role that they only reflect back to us what we can and cannot do based on current policies? Where has the human gone? Cancer, oh, Cancer, under all these layers of armor we put on to survive in this work, there is a human being underneath there with emotions and feelings.

Recently, I was helping rewrite a returns policy for business. It really came down to going the 'hard ball route' and being really tight and limiting or creating what some called a 'wishy-washy' policy that supported actually allowing some room for the exceptions; to still allow wiggle room of being human. No room for exceptions is the shadow side of Pluto in Capricorn. This is Pluto Capricorn without its Cancer polarity. You either do or you don't meet criteria and then need to go through all the process to get what you want/need IF you can even access it. Recently, a friend was hit by a car. She had major medical surgery. The man who hit her was genuinely sincere and wished to do the right thing. Yet, she was strongly advised by others to get a lawyer to represent her case OR the insurance company would try to limit the amount they had to pay out. With Pluto in Capricorn, the need for the Cancer polarity is SO MUCH MORE OBVIOUS. Who are these people and how do they live with themselves – removing financial support in a time of personal crisis based on "what's the best business decision." Granted, much of this already has existed. The USA, beginning with the top down Capitalistic model (natal Pluto Capricorn), has always had such ruthless motives visibly and invisibly operative. Rad and Steve have shown us this correlation time again here on this message board. Now that we have Pluto in Capricorn, every product seems to be shrinking in size or offering, or going up in price. With the South Node [currently] in Taurus followed by Pluto in the "Taurus decan" of Capricorn, how will people survive? Will the decisions that we face embrace the empathetic nurturing principle?

What is the best business decision? To include the Cancer polarity means to value helping others over the bottom line equation of profit margin. Before that person hangs up the phone on you, do they step out of just being in the position of their job and acknowledge the reality you face? Even to hear someone say, "I'm sorry that is happening to you," would give some hope of this polarity expressing itself. Do we meet the former or do we hear, "That's the way it is and I cannot help you"? May our hearts remain open and full of compassion in these difficult times. (Bradley)

AQUARIUS – URANUS – 11th HOUSE

Aquarius keywords

Liberation from conditioning	Alienation	Trauma	Prometheus
Individuality	Hopes / Ideals	Mass trauma	Revolutionary
Individuation	Long-term memory	Splitting	Ostracized
Rebellion	Anarchist	Unique	Cast out
Like-minded groups	Tribe	Shocking	Astral plane
Group hysteria	Community	Projection	Telepathic
Secret societies	Fragmentation	Hyper-activity	Objective awareness

Aquarius, Uranus, 11th house archetype

Yang / fixed / earth / 11th house / ruler is Uranus. Aquarius/Uranus represents liberation from conditioning patterns – parental, societal, past life memories. Uranus represents the subconscious or individuated unconscious mind. When you repress something, it goes into the subconscious mind – Uranus. It represents rebellion against the known and the limitations of society. This is necessary for evolution to proceed. The majority of people conform to society's standards (Capricorn). People conform because of the feeling of security that conforming provides. This is a strategy for dealing with Cancerian insecurity. Uranus/Aquarius frees us from the need to find security through conforming to someone else's, or society's, values and standards. It takes a great deal of courage to develop one's individuality, to become a group of one. This allows you to create a lifestyle that reflects one's totality. The ultimate sense of Cancerian security is found within, in the inner living Universe, not without through acceptance by the society. People who demonstrate the courage to individuate change the nature of their attraction function (Venus) and begin attracting like-minded Souls. The location of Uranus and Aquarius in the birth chart shows the ways in which the Soul intends to liberate in this lifetime. For example, Uranus in the 8th house (Scorpio) wants to liberate through seeing through all feelings of betrayal, emotional violations, etc. Uranus in the 4th house (Cancer) wants to liberate through seeing through all forms of insecurity, etc.

Uranus rules electricity, electronics, and computers. God uses the medium of electricity to project the creation. In human consciousness, the brain is an electrical device. Uranus/Aquarius correlate with the synapses in the brain, the radio receiver that is tuned into God's station. Capricorn represents time and space, and the perception of time. The perception of time is related to the metabolic rate. Metabolism is regulated by the thyroid, which is regulated by iodine. The thyroid and iodine, since they ultimately regulate the sense of time, correlate to Capricorn, which rules time. Anything transited by Uranus is accelerated. There is a fundamental experience over the last 10 or 15 years, a sense that time is speeding up. Uranus is electrical – it creates dehydration when it accelerates something. Iodine is being dehydrated, which affects the thyroid, which changes the sensation of time. Within the human brain, Uranus correlates with dendrites. These are related to the evolution of the brain. Every time we have a new intuitive realization, dendrites are being created.

Both Uranus, which rules Aquarius, and Neptune, which rules Pisces, have been transiting in Aquarius for a number of years now. We are transitioning from the Piscean Age to the Aquarian age, and Uranus/Aquarius are the symbols of liberation from the known. Interesting coincidence? The speed-up in time is related to a rapid increase in evolution in the human brain. Many people are experiencing a consciousness full of random, sporadic, incomplete thoughts that they feel they are not in control of. These seem to appear by themselves. There are major disruptions in sleep cycles – people are wide awake at 3 am and ready for sleep at 2 pm, with no predictability or constancy. Sleep is regulated by the pineal gland, ruled by Neptune, through the production of melatonin. The brain is on the threshold of a rapid development of more of its potential. To know God, pay attention to the nature of the thoughts that appear in your consciousness on their own. These are non-analytical thoughts. They may even be incomplete thoughts. Out of these will come your future. The intention is to have a less conditioned future. Many of these thoughts are of a collective nature and represent the collective future directions of humanity. There are seed people here today who are receiving these thoughts and acting on them, well ahead of the consensus of society which perceives these thoughts as too radical.

[Recommended Reading: Jeffrey Wolf Green's Pluto Vol. 1 – The Evolutionary Journey of the Soul]

Pluto in Aquarius or the 11th house

Pluto in the 11th is learning to break free from all conditionings experienced in the early years. There are three strategies for responding to this intent. Some have been leaving behind the conditionings from this and past lifetimes. They reject anything that tries to define them or to tell them who to be and how to act. They have been pulling away from the mainstream society. They have been gaining objectivity by learning to view themselves outside of the confines of time and space. They feel disconnected from identification with nation or culture. They are learning to sever the attachments that limit growth or new ways of discovering themselves. They are learning how to identify the inner pieces that are no longer of value to them. Through this they come to see how each piece influences every other piece, and thus influences the whole structure. They observe self to see why they are as they are and to eliminate that which holds back further growth. Because of their need to explore new approaches, they are quite innovative. Their innovation can be perceived as threatening by the consensus, and as a result they may feel rejected or threatened by the consensus. This is because innovation creates insecurity within the consensus, as the source of that which produces the experience of security is progressively challenged. Society considers the proposed innovations too radical. These people have a need to challenge society's values, and even their lifestyles may be considered too radical as they challenge beliefs, customs, and taboos.

Some of these people will synthesize the traditions of more than one culture, applying them in a new way, in relation to the existing society. In extreme cases they may drop out of the society altogether. If they feel they have no meaningful role to play, or that the society will not allow them to integrate their vision into it, they can become anti-social. Some will work to bring down the system they feel alienated from. There is a need to learn objectivity and detachment. This can occur through intense, crisis-like experiences. These people tend to be quite rigid in their thinking (Aquarius is a fixed sign), and the nature of their ideas may cause confrontational encounters with people who are closer to the consensus perspective. The confrontations will cause the person to examine their ideas, to see if they have become too fixed or attached to them. If this is the case, and the ideas are limiting growth, the person will eventually make the necessary adjustments. With the compulsive Plutonian influence, the attachment to these ideas can be quite strong, however. If they resist too much, society will eventually isolate the individual. The isolation will force the person to examine what they are doing that brought on the isolation, which leads to objective awareness, which is the point. These archetypes allow each of us to understand that which is unique about ourselves. We experience our uniqueness through comparing and contrasting ourselves with others, and through bonding with like-minded individuals. This is how sub-groups are formed within society. We become objectively aware of our uniqueness in relation to sub-group, society, and the planet as a whole. We learn how one part influences all other parts. Change occurs when enough like-minded people bond together to force change within outmoded structures of the society, which are kept in place through the need for security based on consistency in relation to the past.

Some 11th house people fear change and fear being different. Some of these people rebel by rebelling against their need to rebel and be unique. They repress the inner need to liberate from past conditioning. Saturn, the co-ruler of Aquarius, along with Uranus, is expressing here. All 11th house Pluto people are born with a deep sense of being different. Those who fear this fact have a deep need to compensate. They will feel compelled to try to fit in. They try to do what everyone else is doing, no matter what it is. These people become dependent on their peer group for their sense of meaning and identity. Despite their best efforts to conform, they STILL feel fundamentally different. This will eventually bring about the Plutonian question of 'Why?' The third group also fears being different. They manifest this fear by becoming totally rooted in the past. They become social dinosaurs. They fear any change because it is perceived as upsetting to the old ways, undermining the established order from which they are trying to receive their sense of identity. They try to bring the outmoded visions from the past into the present and future as solutions for today's changing world. This is an out-picturing of their inner reality, in which they are resisting the impulse to change and flow with life. They also form bonds with like-minded people, and they develop detachment from the mainstream culture within their sub-groups. They wind up feeling that time is passing them by. Various combinations of these three groups underlay all subgroups with a society. When negatively expressed, one or more groups may try to limit another group or groups to retain power and to insure personal security. This impulse promotes rigidity and attachment rather than the detachment that is the evolutionary intent. This can occur between individuals as well as between groups. All 11th house Pluto people have a need to link their individual purpose to a group or socialized purpose. These people can be natural leaders. Many instinctively understand group dynamics. Because they are innovative by nature, they can be visionaries who work towards social progress. (JWG's Pluto Vol. 1 and the School's Course)

Pluto polarity point – 5th house or Leo

The intent is that they learn to take charge of their own destinies. They tend to think up future possibilities and then not act on them. This is a reflex reaction to the need to break free from the past. In this life they are learning to put their ideas into action. Accomplishing this requires that they learn to minimize their security needs and their pattern of needing others to tell them that it is okay for them to do what they feel to do. They must learn to take the initiative and not wait for everyone else to be acting before they act. Those who have been rejected by the consensus society must learn to develop their own purpose and link it to a socially useful need. They will not evolve through standing outside of society being eternal social critics. They must learn that their power is in the fact that they ARE different, and that it is okay to be different; in fact, it's even NECESSARY. Through learning to self-actualize they can become effective leaders. They all have the ability to be instruments of change. They need to become detached from their cherished ideals when those ideals are not appropriate to what they are currently dealing with. They must learn to impersonally change that which needs to be changed. These people can all experience shocks through friendships. Having the rug pulled out from under them enforces the need to take charge of their own lives. Generally these people will only have a few close friends at any one time in life. Common qualities: behavior can vary from anti-social to following the crowd to defending tradition; feeling of being different; obsessive-compulsive thought patterns, innovative, creative, unique, good friend, cycles of detachment and self-focus, sudden/erratic behavior, iconoclastic, hard to know, aloof. (JWG's Pluto Vol. 1 and the School's Course)

Trauma
Trauma as a dynamic in astrology correlates to Uranus, the 11th house, and Aquarius.

Repetitive thoughts
The Uranian archetype/function in consciousness being activated by important TRANSITS, produces repetitive abstract thoughts/awareness which are relevant to the nature of one's approaching future. These awarenesses occur spontaneously, of themselves, and NOT the result of effort or premeditated thought. And this, combined with sustained repetition over a length of time, are the indicators of the content being credible and appropriate to act upon when the time to act arrives, versus delusional thoughts for instance, which can manifest in a similar way, but will not demonstrate the sustained repetition over time. For this reason it is necessary to observe these kinds of Uranian thought patterns in as detached a way as possible over a period of time, and take action only when the natural rhythm of the archetypal pattern indicates it is right to do so, ie when the time to act arrives, the repeating messages/thoughts will occur (again, of themselves) with progressively brief intervals between them – more frequently – like a drumbeat – and though often seemingly disjointed or disconnected from the existing reality, will contain the specific information needed with respect to preparing for the abstract future which approaches. (Stacie)

At key evolutionary junctures in the Soul's life in which the Soul intends to liberate from its past, to embrace and act upon the thought forms that correlate to its own master blueprint for the entire life, the Soul will ignite thought forms to the current life ego, conscious awareness, that have a repetitive nature to them. In essence these thought forms that correlate to the Soul's next evolutionary steps will repeat over and over in order to get the attention by way of the ego that the Soul has created in the current life. It is these repetitive messages that the Soul, by way of the ego created, needs to act upon in order to evolve: to liberate from the past that binds it. These repetitive messages are just that: repetitive versus thought forms, ideas, that appear at random and have no repetitive occurrence. (Rad)

Thought complexes
The anatomy of the ears, hearing, is Mercury. The psychology of hearing is Venus. Visuals are a manifestation of thought complexes within the brain. The thought complexes themselves are Uranian and Mercurial, and the visuals of thought complexes are the archetypes of Neptune/Moon/and Pluto. (Rad)

Data, observation and correlation
The right brain is said to be intuitive/conceptual/abstract, and the left brain is said to be linear, rational, and empirical. Astrologically this would be the difference, again, between Sagittarius and Gemini. That which manifests through the right brain is that part in all of us which is plugged into the totality of manifested creation. The manifested or projected creation is Uranus. The plug in the socket, so to speak, is Jupiter. Jupiter intuits, and makes consciously available to the individual, the projected creation of Uranus. The intuitions of Jupiter translate into abstract or conceptual thought involving principles. Mercury is plugged into Uranus by way of Jupiter. Mercury translates into linear or applied thought that is specific and reflective of the nature of each individual. Thus, Uranus projects through Jupiter to the existing channels of Mercury in order to make new connections; thoughts. (JWG)

(Q) If I am looking at a bird making certain sounds before a storm, the observation of the phenomena itself is **Aquarius**, the correlation to *what* those sounds mean implies a synthesis of various observed data, which is **Sagittarius**. The data itself that I am observing and synthesizing implies classifications and names that I have associated with that phenomenal reality, which is **Gemini**. (Ari)

(A) Yes (Rad)

Uranus also correlates, in complete detail, to all the memories of this and other lives. This is why it is called the higher octave of Mercury. Most of us can't remember in explicit detail what we did two days ago. So my question is, where do all these memories go? Mercury correlates to what you can consciously recall in the form of memories, or that which you have learned or been taught. But Uranus correlates to all the memories and knowledge that have ever come before; that which you can not necessarily recall consciously. (JWG)

(Q) Is it true to say that observation (Aquarius) does not depend on mental classifications (Gemini)? In other words, can creation be observed without any mental constructs being associated with that observed creation?

(A) Sure (Rad)

The observation part is of course Uranus, Aquarius, and the 11th house whereas the correlation part is Sagittarius, the 9th house, and Jupiter. (Rad)

De-conditioning

The Individuated stage is inherently a Uranian phase, the nature of the archetype, to throw off the Consensus (Saturn) need to conform (Saturn) – to de-condition in other words. Evolutionary stage is simply the result of millions of choices one has made. De-condition really means to change how one sees one's self – self-image = Moon. We are totally attached to images of who I am that are not at all who I am. De-conditioning means to release these limited perspectives. The process goes on and on. Emptying is a necessary precursor. But the natural outcome of emptying is a gradual refilling, into the next level, which we then perceive as so far beyond the previous one. But the day or lifetime will come when even the new "this is so far beyond where I was before" itself will have to be emptied as it too has become too limited. That process never ends as there is always more that we are than we believe we are. So it's a continual opening, integrating (also a Uranian function), and then eventual releasing. It's been described as peeling the layers of an onion. (Steve)

Objectification

One of the core archetypes of the 11th house, Aquarius, and Uranus is one of objectification. To objectify the nature of anything independent of any subjective state of consciousness that can then project upon the objective nature of anything: to understand and see something for what it actually is independent of subjective interpretation of that which is of itself. As a result of this archetype the entire dimension of what we call 'science' is a reflection of this archetype. Astrology is nothing more than a natural science where any natural science is rooted in correlation and observation: like Darwin. (Rad)

To step back and objectify for oneself just why one needed to create whatever trauma [or experience] in the first place. This leads to self-knowledge of a liberating nature, and that knowledge can then be used to radically change oneself. (Rad)

Collective unconscious / individuated unconscious

The archetype of the 'individuated unconscious' correlating to Uranus, Aquarius, and the 11th house is different than the 'collective unconscious' correlating to Pisces, Neptune and the 12th house which applies to the entire species of humans. The individuated unconscious correlates to content within the Soul that is unique to that Soul. (Rad)

Individuated unconscious

The individual Soul contains all that correlates to the totality of its dynamics for all the lives it has ever lived which, of course, have all been caused by the nature of the dual desires within it. Thus, all the memories of all those lives exist within it. The consciousness within the Soul have different dynamics that allow for a knowledge of the Soul as manifested through the egocentric structure that the Soul creates from life to life. The dynamics that allow the egocentric structure within the Soul to know about its prior lives/memories correlate specifically to Uranus, the 11th house, and Aquarius. These archetypes correlate to the 'long term memories' that the egocentric structure within the Soul can access. In Jungian terms this is called the 'individuated' unconscious where individuated means memories that are unique to each individual. Long term memories exist with the current life of any Soul, and those memories also correlate to the past life memories of any Soul that can be accessed by the egocentric structure in a few ways. One of course is through hypnosis which can also create false memories as well as accurate ones. Another is simply based on the natural evolution of the Soul wherein at a certain point its past life memories can be accessed within itself relative to the egocentric structure created. Meditation is a good example of this process.

The archetype of the 'individuated unconscious' correlating to Uranus, Aquarius, and the 11th house is different than the 'collective unconscious' which applies to the entire species of humans. The individuated unconscious correlates to content within the Soul that is unique to that Soul. This content includes all the 'long term memories' that apply to not only this life, but the memories that correlate to the prior lifetimes that the Soul has lived that apply to the current life. The individuated unconscious also correlates to the evolutionary intentions of the Soul in the current life manifesting through this individuated unconscious. Those intentions correlate, so to speak, to a 'master blueprint' for the entire life. This master blueprint that correlates to the Soul's evolutionary intentions for the entire life manifests as 'thought forms' that percolate into the conscious awareness of the current life ego at key evolutionary stages of the Soul's development in the current life. In combination this then creates an interfacing of all the long term memories of the Soul's past that serve to bind the Soul to its past in any given moment of the current life, and the thought forms that manifest from the Soul by way of the current life ego that serve to actualize the evolutionary intentions for the current life. Thus, for a Soul to act upon, actualize, those thought forms that correlate to the Soul's evolutionary intentions for the current life is to 'liberate' from the past that binds the Soul to its past: freedom from the known.

This interfacing between these two archetypes of course occurs in the MOMENT: the past and the future interfacing in each moment of our lives. The past correlates for all humans to a known quantity. Thus familiarity and security. The future as manifested in these thought forms correlate to an unknown: thus insecurity. Most humans do not, cannot, psychologically embrace insecurity as a way of living their lives. Most make choices to recreate their pasts in various ways in order to maintain their sense of personal security. At key evolutionary junctures in the Soul's life in which the Soul intends to liberate from its past, to embrace and act upon the thought forms that correlate to its own master blueprint for the entire life, the Soul will then ignite these thought forms to the current life ego, conscious awareness, that have a repetitive nature to them. In essence these thought forms that correlate to the Soul's next evolutionary steps will repeat over and over in order to get the attention by way of the ego that the Soul has created in the current life. It is these repetitive messages that the Soul, by way of the ego created, needs to act upon in order to evolve: to liberate from the past that binds it. These repetitive messages are just that: repetitive versus thought forms, ideas, that appear at random and have no repetitive occurrence. (Rad)

Unconscious beliefs
(Q) Are there unconscious beliefs? (Gonzalo)
(A) Yes. These types of beliefs have been formulated in prior lifetimes which then reside, in most cases, in the individuated unconscious of the Soul: Uranus, Aquarius, and the 11th house. (Rad)

Past life memories and long term memories
The individual Soul contains all that correlates to the totality of its dynamics for all the lives it has ever lived which, of course, have all been caused by the nature of the dual desires within it. Thus, all the memories of all those lives exist within it. The consciousness within the Soul have different dynamics that allow for a knowledge of the Soul as manifested through the egocentric structure that the Soul creates from life to life. The dynamics that allow the egocentric structure within the Soul to know about its prior lives/memories correlate specifically to Uranus, the 11th house, and Aquarius. These archetypes correlate to the 'long term memories' that the egocentric structure within the Soul can access. In Jungian terms this is called the 'individuated' unconscious where individuated means memories that are unique to each individual. Long term memories exist with the current life of any Soul, and those memories also correlate to the past life memories of any Soul that can be accessed by the egocentric structure in a few ways. One of course is through hypnosis which can also create false memories as well as accurate ones. Another is simply based on the natural evolution of the Soul wherein at a certain point its past life memories can be accessed within itself relative to the egocentric structure created. Meditation is a good example of this process. (Rad)

Projections, delusions, expectations
Astrologically speaking, Aquarius is the archetype that correlates with projections (from our own unconscious). These projections can be based on past traumas (ie this reminds me of my ex-partner, old friend, parents, etc.) which are then cast onto the person who you are involved with now. These projections can also be based on the person's own unconscious inner dynamics/structure that are then cast onto others. In other words, the person projects what is inside themselves onto others. Aquarius correlates to the individuated unconscious and also to the dynamic of trauma. The projections that can surface within this archetype can be linked with the need to objectify and hopefully release what is stored/unresolved within the unconscious. [The situation you are describing] also sounds like dynamics that are linked with unconscious expectations that get projected upon others within relationships.

Astrologically speaking, expectations are linked with the archetype of Libra. Libra correlates with the nature of our expectations within relationships and our ability (or inability) to reach a balanced state of giving and receiving within relationships. Libra correlates with extremities, and the need to reach a state of balance relative to such extremities. Delusion/fantasy correlates with the archetype of Pisces. Pisces symbolizes the need for ultimate meaning, and to bring to closure an entire cycle of evolution in order to prepare for a new cycle which begins in the Aries archetype. When ultimate meaning is 'projected' externally within a relationship it is all too easy to fall into fantasies and delusions (infatuation) about the other person regardless of how much actual contact there has been.

The core point within this is that these types of projections and delusions are based on a need for ultimate meaning/fulfilment within life which we try to find in a variety of external sources. (There is a natural inconjunction between the Libra/Pisces archetypes which reflects the crisis of disillusionment that so many of us have experienced because of this dynamic in which our expectations/need for ultimate meaning are not met.) Pisces also correlates to the need to meet the need for ultimate meaning through creating a relationship with the Divine. Pluto Vol. 2 goes into a wonderful in-depth description of the connection between the Taurus, Libra, and Pisces archetypes and how these archetypes correlate with the need in all of us to progressively internalize (Taurus) our need for ultimate meaning through union with Spirit/the Divine (Pisces) and to reach a state of balance within our relationships (Libra). (Deva)

Projection, in general, correlates to Uranus, the 11th house, and Aquarius. Delusions, in general, correlate with Pisces, the 12th house, and Neptune. Delusions manifest from within the consciousness of any given Soul that can then be projected outwardly into the overall environment in such a way as to condition the very nature of that environment relative to the nature of the delusion itself. There are many possible causes including one's own essential needs within a relationship that the other seems to correlate to, past life connections in which something was not finished, resolved, or is intended to pick up again in the current life, the inner creation of 'fantasy' type ideas about the 'perfect' partner that the other seems to correlate to, etc. etc. etc. All of this correlates, obviously, to delusions if none of it is true: actual. The correlations are above, and those archetypes would be active relative to the transits or progressions at the time that this occurs. (Rad)

Behavioral contagion – collective delusion
This occurs when the nature of the delusions involved become projected in such a way that others who 'need' to BELIEVE in them manifest in sub-groupings – Aquarius 11th house, Uranus – within the whole of a society – Neptune, Pisces, the 12th house – relative to a 'behavioral contagion' that takes place with those sub-groupings who need to believe in the nature of the collective delusion within those sub-groupings. The phenomena of behavioral contagion specifically correlates to Uranus, Aquarius, and the 11th house. (Rad)

Uranus/Pluto interface
A natal placement of some kind of connection between the Uranian and Plutonian archetypes is a life-long issue. There are reasons when the Soul is manifesting with that symbolism. Uranus in Scorpio or in the 8th house in itself (without any transit activation) is very intense. The Uranian archetype will have the Scorpionic intensity – trying to look for the bottom-line. Generally speaking, in one way or another, the liberation (inherent in the Uranian archetype) is directly intended to affect the deepest levels – the Soul level. This also signifies the fact that past traumas (Uranus) had already affected the Soul level in some way. The healing/liberation are intended to happen on that very level. Not only have deepest trust issues (Scorpio/8th house) been violated in general, but also very INTENSE deepest level shock and trauma have happened in ways that have blown apart the Soul's previous security base – the deepest Soul level security structure. Therefore there is an intention to heal that level. The previous limitation relates to those security structures which need to be reformulated in the most intense and most accelerated way. As for the repetitive messages and what to trust and what not to trust, the issue may correlate to the fact that on the deepest, unconscious level trust has been violated and that caused immense trauma in the past.

The Uranus/Pluto interface, in some ways, correlates to a HIGHLY traumatized SOUL. Keeping this symbolism in mind, the result is more than likely to manifest some level of GENERAL unconscious fear and distrust, even towards one's own perceptions from within, ie when the Soul trusted something or someone in the past the Soul experienced intense trauma (not an isolated experience). So for the Soul, it is natural to react to this unconscious content (Uranus) in a distrustful way (Scorpio). This can create some intense inner confusion and being stuck periodically. One of the evolutionary needs with this kind of symbol is to apply DETACHMENT and OBJECTIVITY instead of being lost in the intense inwardly experienced emotional turmoil. Can I trust something? What if I misread the signals from within? So whatever the issue may be, understanding the fact that the emotional body has been wounded in the DEEPEST POSSIBLE WAY is something that needs to be kept in mind.

In the higher evolutionary states another interesting phenomenon may occur: the content of the unconscious memories of the Soul can come to the surface of consciousness in a relatively easy way. And, together with the Uranian impulse, the Soul is simply able to "dump" the emotional content it carries onto the Uranian vehicle. Uranus also correlates to the subconscious which is just below our Saturnian current life egocentric consciousness. In a simplified symbolic way, Pluto/Scorpio is the core deep down, and the egocentric consciousness (Saturn) is high up and normally they are not directly connected. The Uranian archetype is the BRIDGE between them. The Uranian archetype does touch in some ways the Saturnian current life ego-level consciousness and at the same time is connected to the depth of the Soul.

So on that bridge, the content of the unconscious Soul – with all the imprints, including many many past lives, and all kinds of information, BOTH past and present, relatively speaking – can "connect" more easily between these two points (Soul and egocentric consciousness) than without this kind of symbolism. Of course all this is dependent upon many other factors: first of all the evolutionary state of the Soul's overall consciousness, then the whole chart which will then explain why that configuration and why the Soul needed it, what happened, what it intends to liberate from and how. There can be infinite scenarios of course. The above is a very general (and far from complete) description of the functions, archetypically speaking, which are connected in some ways within consciousness, when these two symbols are directly connected in a chart. (Lia)

Number sequences and patterns occurring in consciousness
This is a Uranian phenomenon/archetype. And this sort of thing will happen to Souls who have deeply pondered upon the 'nature of things' in other lives so that the very way that they had been thinking or pondering has come forwards into the current consciousness of the life being lived in these fragmented forms. The repetitive nature of them is the archetype of Uranus itself as well as the apparent disconnect from the context of the current life being lived unless that context correlates with a Soul who is continuing its inner pondering as to the 'nature of things.' In rarer cases this can also correlate to a Soul who in other lifetimes has had direct experiences from 'beings' from other star systems that are much more evolved than our own in which such beings have attempted to 'transmit,' Uranus, various knowledge into the human consciousness in order to help it evolve. And, typically, that which has been transmitted is in the form of numbers equaling mathematics in various ways and/or 'patterns' which correlate to the structural nature of Creation itself that are intended to promote spontaneous realizations about 'the nature of things.' For the

humans who have been the recipient of such transmissions in other lifetimes they will have this transmitted knowledge deep within their Soul memories of course. And, because of this, the spontaneous and repetitive manifestations of fragmented memories of that transmitted knowledge manifest. Regarding the Soul fully integrating the transmissions from other lifetimes in the current life, for some the answer is yes, and for others those transmissions will continue into other lives because of the Soul's perplexity of what these symbols actually mean. (Rad)

Judgment and projection
Judgment as an archetype correlates with Capricorn, Saturn, and the 10th house, not Pisces or any other sign, house, or planet. The archetype of judgment is natural to consciousness for that is one of the ways that Souls learn about the nature of life. The archetype of judgment of course manifests through all the houses, signs, and planets relative to the archetypes of each, yet judgment as such is the 10th house, Capricorn, and Saturn. JWG often taught about this and one of the main things he taught was that first judgment is natural to consciousness but the real issue is THE CONTENT TO BE USED TO FORM OR MAKE JUDGMENTS. Is that content rooted in all the Natural Laws that were set in motion by the Creator, or is the content rooted in man-made laws, rules, regulations, taboos, norms, etc? Projection, as an archetype within consciousness, correlates to Aquarius, the 11th house, and Uranus. When linked with Capricorn, the 10th house, or Saturn this then can correlate to our projected judgments upon others, and our own inner projected judgments upon our self.

[In terms of speaking to a client] I would approach it by explaining to them why people do these things in the first place. One of the core reasons that people do this in the first place is to avoid or deny taking any responsibility in their own actions. In so doing such people then need to create scapegoats in order to blame others for that which they are responsible for. These people always need to feel 'victimized' by something, or someone, in order to psychologically function. So, in essence, my advice is for those who are the recipients of this [judgment/projection] is to stand back and see it for what it is, to not take on or 'believe' in any way that that which is being projected upon them is true. That it is essential to stand back and OBJECTIFY the very nature of the situation and persons involved: to detach from it even as it can of course really hurt. Beyond that general advice of course it is necessary to know the specifics of each situation in which this sort of thing happens. Those specifics then, of themselves, will dictate the natural and right way to proceed. (Rad)

Personal application of Uranus/Saturn to Pluto
The core role of the archetype of Uranus, relative to the Soul and Pluto, is to quicken or accelerate the evolution of the Soul itself. The archetype of Uranus correlates to the memories within the Soul that correlate to its prior lifetimes, as well as core blueprint, knowledge, that symbolizes its evolutionary future when that future is understood in the context of its past: Saturn. Thus, each Soul's history and future is unique to itself, yet, at the same time, all Souls of course share in the ultimate evolutionary future which is to return HOME to its origin: God, Neptune. The past is always defining the present moment as well as the future itself. The future and the past interface in each moment in time: the now. The Soul's evolutionary past is thus the determinant of its own unique moment, or life. In any given life of the Soul that past is familiar and known, thus secure. This is of course why most Souls evolve very slowly because that past is a known quantity. To move into any given moment that is completely free from that past is to create, for most Souls, a state of complete psychological and emotional insecurity. Thus, most Souls desire to stay connected to their past in order to feel psychologically secure and stable. Yet the Soul must evolve of course.

The next step in its evolution is symbolized by the EA paradigm that is the basis of the evolutionary journey of the Soul. Uranus correlates with the desire to quicken the evolutionary journey of the Soul, to accelerate it: 'to be free from the known.' To be free from the known is to emotionally and psychologically detach from the totality of all the lives that the Soul has lived which have brought it to its current lifetime. In this detachment the Soul is then able to observe itself in such a way as to be able to objectify all the inner dynamics within it that have been responsible for all that it has ever been and done. This objectification thus allows for a total knowledge of the Soul itself in such a way that the Soul by way of Uranus can then be free of that past because of the objectified knowledge of it. In this consciousness of detachment the Soul is then able by way of Uranus to determine what desires exist within it that it must act upon, desires to act upon, and the desires within it that no longer need to be acted upon: to liberate from them in this way. In this way the Soul is thus able to quicken or accelerate its evolution because it is no longer being conditioned by its past to the extent that that past is holding the Soul back from actualizing its next steps in evolution in the fastest or quickest way possible.

The polarity point of Pluto in any chart will be actualized to some extent by all Souls. Most Souls, as JWG taught, only make the most minimal efforts to do so because of the pull of their past: the familiar and the known. The natural first quarter square from the 8th and Scorpio to the 11th and Aquarius thus correlates to the 'crisis in action' relative to what paths to follow that allow for the quickest possible way for the Soul to evolve. The relationship of Uranus and Pluto is a generational one. It has a personal application in that the phase correlates to a variety of Uranian dynamics and archetypes that the Soul has been using for its ongoing evolutionary purposes that is then linked or understood in the context of the core EA paradigm, and how that core paradigm has been manifesting relative to the phase of Mars and Pluto. Freedom from the Known relative to Uranus correlates with the existing totality of any given Soul's reality: the entire past leading to the present life. It is a natural instinct, thus desire, within all of our Souls. As such it is operative in all Souls all the time. This is symbolized by Uranus. The totality of the Soul's reality, past and present, is of course Pluto itself.

Saturn correlates to the necessary structural reality of the Soul's consciousness in any given life where the nature of that structured consciousness is necessary so as to define the evolutionary impulse of the Soul from life to life in such a way that the Soul can then define the ongoing evolutionary impulse for itself in TIME. Thus, this structural definition of the evolutionary impulse by Saturn allows the Soul to integrate it in the context of the type of 'realities' that are necessary for that impulse to manifest in the way that the Soul so intends. The reality that the Soul thus creates relative to Saturn correlates with sequential lifetimes that all live: from life to life. And each life that the Soul creates through Saturn of course is given a subjective ego, Moon, the natural polarity of Saturn, so that the Soul can then focus itself as a subjective identity in each of these lives.

All of these lives in total, and as they are added to, correlates with the 'known' because they have been lived. Uranus is the archetype within our consciousness that desires to be 'free from the known:' to liberate from it. It is this archetypal desire, impulse, that then leads to Neptune and the root desire in all our Souls, Pluto, to go Home: to return back to the Origins Of All Things. All of this correlates to the inherent structure of consciousness in human form that we all share. Where Uranus is located by sign and house in any given chart, in any given life, correlates, among other things, to where, how, and why the 'quickening' evolutionary impulse that is rooted in the ultimate archetype of 'freedom from the known' is intended to manifest in any given life designed by the Soul itself. And this natural quickening impulse of course has its CONTEXT, the reasons for it, in all the lives that have preceded the current life. It is that preexisting context that thus correlates with the desire to 'be free from the known' where that known is the preexisting context itself. So, in essence, Uranus correlates with not only the ultimate impulse to be free, to go home to our Maker, but also the desire and impulse to accelerate our evolution in any given life relative to the preexisting context as defined or symbolized by the natal placement by house and sign of Uranus in any given life. (Rad)

As far as Uranus, I'd like to highlight a few other Uranian correlations – fracturing, trauma, and integration. One of the reasons we have such difficulty seeing the totality of this and trying to grasp the totality by reassembling the parts is because of the severe fracturing/fragmentation that has occurred in many many Souls. A major part of the de-conditioning process is realizing one's own fracturing, and going through the ongoing process of re-integrating self. It's like Humpty Dumpty who had a great fall and fractured into pieces that couldn't be put back together again. Except they can be put back together over time, step by step. And, the ongoing evolutionary process requires they must, little by little, over time through self-acceptance and patience. That is why we must de-condition, to see the greater totality of who we are and how we got to the place we now are. As that process proceeds, one finds the answers to the questions within self. You do see the parts. You don't quite know how to assemble them into a whole. That's because that's not something you do – it appears in flashes of intuition, of seeing the whole assembled, greater than its parts, beyond what can be perceived through left brain analysis. The value in pondering these questions is it keeps them active in your consciousness. That leads to the inevitable flashes of intuition. Those flashes are signs that the reintegration process is occurring. (Steve)

Kundalini / root chakra

Triple rulership, three layers. The outer layer correlates with Saturn, the middle layer with Uranus, and the nucleus with Pluto. Now most people think somehow that the root chakra and/or Kundalini is specifically linked with sexuality. This is a false thought. Kundalini has no specific relationship to sexuality. What you have here is the situation where, because the nucleus is Pluto, we correlate this with the specific action of Kundalini. However, the outer layer of this chakra is Saturn, and that means the ignition of Kundalini is latent in most people. Why? They are living, Saturn, in a consensus state, which in and of itself, psychologically speaking, prohibits the ignition of Kundalini. So the Kundalini gland, which is just on the other side of this chakra, remains latent or dormant, Saturn, in most. Now when that is the fact, this gland remains locked, retentive. This chakra specifically then correlates to the quality and condition of the lower extremities, the function of the nerves, the muscles, the circulation patterns, and also the quality and function of the anal canal. For example, in cultures like this (Saturn being the outer layer, or ruler), people typically develop hemorrhoids. Now why does that occur? Because there is not a free flow of movement of feces, and the person has to create internalized pressure to eliminate, which becomes the causal factor in hemorrhoids.

How does this connect to the idea of Saturn? You see how this is working! When the Soul decides to make a conscious act to evolve, that is to move away from the consensus, right then and there, the middle layer, Uranus is stimulated, meaning liberation from the consensus. And on that basis, this chakra begins to quicken, Uranus, meaning it is beginning to vibrate differently. This now becomes analogous to fissure lines in the crust of the earth. And what is coming through these fissure lines? Possibly lava. Lava here correlates with Kundalini. Meaning, as this chakra begins to quicken and vibrate differently, it is the quickening and vibrational action that causes the Kundalini to be ignited. And when Kundalini is ignited, it can create any manner of physical symptoms that cannot be diagnosed by any allopathic doctor. Why? The initial intention of Kundalini is to penetrate (Pluto) to the nucleus of every cell that needs to be either healed or alchemically changed. In the context of purging toxins, for example, from the nucleus of the cell, relative to Kundalini, the typical symptomology is either feeling intense heat in that area, or intense cold, for no apparent reason. In extreme cases, it will create transitory paralysis in those areas. Kundalini is a remarkable physiological substance. (JWG)

The natural first quarter square between Scorpio and Aquarius, in essence, is the natural dynamic tension within the structural nature of consciousness for all Souls on this Earth. (Rad)

Physiology of the brain
The physiology of the brain in general is a combination of Pluto/Uranus, Scorpio/Aquarius, 8th house/11th house. There are specific physiologies within this that have different planetary/sign/house correlations, ie melatonin correlates with Neptune/Pisces and the 12th house. Thought is Uranus and Mercury. The brain itself, in general, is Uranus. (Rad)

Channeling
Channeling as a 'phenomenon' is Aquarius. However, within Aquarius only the consciousness of the individual ego is sustained. And because of this the 'messages' that are then 'channeled' get mixed up with that ego: its own subjective reality. Which then explains why so many 'channeled' messages conflict from one channeler to the next. "True" channeling, again, then is the linkage between Aquarius and Pisces where Pisces follows Aquarius. In that true channeling state there is no subjective ego to mix things up with. (Rad)

JWG taught that 'channeling' in general is an 11th house, Aquarius, and Uranus archetype but that most who claim to 'channel' are in fact 'channeling' their own individuated unconscious and/or subconscious. We need to remember that the individuated unconscious in all of us correlates to our own 'long term' memory that connects to not only this life, but the individual memories of our own past lifetimes. This is why he also taught that so many of these 'channeling' messages from so many seem to conflict with one another. And it's also why so many of the 'channeled' messages simply don't come true at all, as in Clare Prophet's case and many others. JWG said true channeling does occur but is very, very rare because the ego within the consciousness of those that can truly channel becomes displaced during the channeling itself. And he used the analogy of a 10,000 watt bulb coming through a 5 watt bulb which then causes the entire system of the one who is truly channeling to burn out more quickly than normal. Thus, true channeling is then a Pisces, Neptune, and 12th house archetype. (Rad)

The breath
The archetypes for breathing or the breath is Uranus, Aquarius, and the 11th house.

South Node of Neptune in Aquarius
(Q) In relation with the South Node of Neptune being in Aquarius (reflecting the original matriarchal roots of the current desires in all Souls to spiritualize consciousness), and the connection of natal Neptune with the Aquarius Age, in the context of the current transition between the Pisces Age into the next Aquarius Age, would imply that the root of these desires (ie the past of the Soul) is also symbolic of the future ways for the Souls to spiritualize consciousness (ie ways which will be in place for these Souls in the next Age). Is this correct? (Gonzalo)
(A) Yes. (Rad)
(Q) For me this is interesting to consider because it confirms that the current time frame is defined by a potential for accelerated evolution of Souls because it implies that the past is becoming the future now. Thus, the work on resolution of issues from past lifetimes related to the spiritual roots of the Soul and, at the same time, work on the resolution of issues pertaining to the future of the Soul – ie the past and the future are contained and concentrated within the current time. Is this correct?
(A) Yes. And what this will mean of course is if the original spiritual root will manifest again or not which itself is linked with the survival of the species. Within Aquarius is the triad of Libra and Gemini. Libra correlates with the Natural Law of giving, sharing, and inclusion. This is how humans were defined relative to groups of humans, Aquarius, for the balance of humans' existence on our planet. In relatively recent times this Natural Law of course has become perverted to self-interest and exclusion which then causes one group of humans, or one human, then trying to compete with other groups, or a human, relative to the survival instinct itself. In turn this leads to dominance and submission. If this is not corrected by going back to the original root, or past, and bringing that forwards into the future, then the extinction of the species is guaranteed.

PISCES – NEPTUNE – 12th HOUSE

Pisces keywords

Disillusionment	Psychic	Wounded	Musician
Victim	Astral glamour	Suffering	Loss / erosion
Persecuted	Addiction	Innocence	Isolation
Martyr	Escape	The Fool	Confusion
Savior	Hopeless	Suicide	Dreamer
Illusions	Helpless	Lost identity	Dissociation
Priest	Weak boundaries	Masochist	Disbelief
Alcoholism	Surrender	Fantasy	Drugs
Mystic	Subconscious	Naïve	Guilt (individual)
Medium	Transcendence	Poet	Guilt (collective)

Pisces, Neptune, 12th house archetype

Yin / mutable / water / 12th house / ruler is Neptune. Pisces represents consciousness itself. Consciousness is like water – it has no form, it takes the form of whatever form is contained within it. Our perceptions of reality are conditioned through the form the consciousness is in. God permeates all consciousness. All forms of consciousness have the impulse to experience the transcendent reality. This is the impulse that stimulates the principle of evolution. Pisces ignites the desire to return to God. Scorpio demands proof. Pisces has blind faith. The location of Pisces and Neptune in the birth chart indicates the natural way for the person to spiritualize their life. These, plus planets in the 12th house, and the aspects they make, are the likely source of the types of disillusionment we will experience in our lives. The collective unconscious is content of consciousness that pertains to the entire human species. It resides within each human body. The collective conscious is the totality of all thoughts and vibrations existing at any moment in time, on the conscious level. We each tune into these through Neptune, and osmose them into ourselves through Scorpio. The impact of totality alters our perceptions and personal realities. There are three kinds of consciousness – racial (Caucasian, Oriental, African, etc.), national, and regional (South or Northwest of the US). (JWG's Pluto Vol. 1 and the School's Course)

[Recommended Reading: Jeffrey Wolf Green's Pluto Vol. 1 – The Evolutionary Journey of the Soul]

Pluto in the 12th house or Pisces

12th house Pluto people have the evolutionary intent to align themselves with a transcendental belief system to realize the unity of all of Creation, and to experience their individuality as an extension of the source of Creation. Pisces and the 12th house are the composite of all other houses, signs, and planets. It represents the totality of life, and reality in this and all other planes of existence. It is also the archetype in which the Source of all is sensed and must be consciously developed and realized by the individual. These people have an emphasized desire to dissolve all the barriers that prevent merging their power into the cosmic whole, to realize the ultimate Source of power. The barriers can be of any nature. There has been a need to realize values, beliefs, and knowledge that transcend time and space and that are culturally based. The 12th house correlates to Infinity. The culmination of the 12th house experience results in a merging of the Ego with the Source.

These people come into life with a sense of standing on a precipice. Behind them is the known world, including the past. In front of them is the darkness of infinity. Standing on the precipice they must decide what to do – go forward; go backwards; or remain on the precipice, paralyzed from moving. Within this person, the essence of identifying with self as Ego is being dissolved. Most of these people resist the pull to surrender to the Source. The resistance triggers confusion, disorientation, and alienation. They have unconscious fears of losing control of their lives. Most will latch onto anything that makes them feel they are in control of their lives. Yet due to the transcendental pull, they have the inner sense that whatever they identify with is not who they really are. Something is missing and they can't put their finger on what it is. There is a cycle of these behaviors, and at those times this sense becomes more dominant. While this is occurring, many will over-identify with a single element of self, trying to create a sense of identity over the inner sense of confusion.

Some of these people will adopt the values of groups within the whole as an attempt to create an identity. They give this great power in their life. This process produces compulsion because they have this one aspect that is known and familiar. Change threatens the loss of control they fear. But the transcendental impulse will cause change to occur because the intent is not to hold on but to evolve. This leads to cyclic meltdowns as that which is not real dissolves out of the life. This brings on disorientation, leading to questions like, 'Is this really me?' and 'there's more than this.' This causes the feeling of being out of control or of losing control. And nothing replaces that which is dissolving. In these cycles, nothing means anything, and they have no power to make their life mean anything. Some try to recreate old and familiar patterns, to give themselves something to relate to. In the end, these also will dissolve.

Many will eventually experience a metamorphosis where a new realization emerges from the Soul. This appears to occur by itself. This is actually divine inspiration, though many would not acknowledge that. This process is to teach them that they are a connected part of the whole. The process teaches them about the areas in which they limit their identification with the whole. They must shift their sense of identification to the whole. They must learn to step off the precipice into the future, not stand on the precipice or look backwards towards the past. They are learning faith – faith that the fear of surrendering to the higher power is an ego delusion. They learn through the cyclic disintegration process, willingly or unwillingly. Faith produces the awareness that, somehow, something has made the difficulties all right.

Many have denied the evolutionary impulse to merge with the Source. They create endless illusions trying to find the meaning they are seeking. They project the desire for the Source onto the latest separating desire, firmly believing that when they achieve that which they desire they will finally have found that meaning they have long sought. They give their dreams and fantasies tremendous power. The Pluto process in the 12th house teaches the person that they are a co-creator of reality with the Source. The power to actualize the dreams is linked to visualization and belief. If they believe enough, through visualization and affirmation the dream will come to manifest. The fantasies teach the person the nature of their illusions and delusions. These dreams are very real to the person, whether they are in their minds or manifested in three-dimensional reality. Even if the person has succeeded in manifesting the dream, it is still an illusion, because even though physically manifested, they are still separating desires, not the transcendental reality that is the evolutionary intent.

Chasing dreams can last many lifetimes because the types of fantasy are limited only by the person's imagination. At some eventual point they will have exhausted all of their dreams and fantasies, and a deep weariness will descend upon them. Disillusioned, they will finally turn to God. On that day they will know that life truly is 'but a dream.' At this point they can become Divinely inspired with the nature of their true identity and mission. Resistance to the merging can manifest in other ways as well. They can deny that anything is wrong at all. At a suitable karmic or evolutionary point, the cracks will appear in the wall of fantasy, through unconscious self-undermining activity, or through confrontations from which they will discover that the external reality they created is not what they thought it was. This leads to the cycle of disintegration and disillusionment, which will eventually end when the necessary knowledge appears in their consciousness. The extent of this clarity causes the person to consider that perhaps some other Power is operating in their life.

These people are born with a deep sense of right and wrong, which is reflected in a sense of idealized conduct. These people judge self, and others, in relation to this idealized sense. They judge negatively when the human behavior does not live up to the ideal. Many have a sense of being persecuted because of their sense that they are unable to do the right thing. Many will persecute or judge others based on this same principle. Many have drawn lifetimes of persecution upon self in an attempt to atone for that which they feel they have not done correctly. They then project this inner reality upon others. Some are born with a sense of victimization or martyrdom. Some will avoid reality through drugs, alcohol, or other avoiding activities.

These people generally have desired to erode the egocentric illusion of power. Many have had a God complex in a past life and have abused power. They experience a few lifetimes of persecution to compensate. If they do not realize the reason the present life is as it is, they will blame everything and everyone for their fate, to justify their victim-oriented behaviors. Others will manifest this as attempting to help everyone, whether or not anyone wants their help. This type will judge no one, as if judging is to be avoided altogether. 12th house Pluto people need to learn what judgment really means, and how to exercise proper judgment. The lesson is that ultimately judgment is based on intention, not on outcome. They must learn to look at their own and others' intentions, and judge accordingly. INNER judgment is necessary because it becomes the vehicle to get closer to the ideal of right conduct.

The key is self-forgiveness, and then forgiveness of others. The resolve to improve is the ultimate standard to judge by. They must use a standard of judgment when considering others, for not judging at all leaves them open to adopting the incorrect behaviors of others since they have no sense of what is appropriate or inappropriate, relative to their own intention. Many of these people have a deep fear of the unknown. Many of them cannot face self alone. Many experience the pull towards the All as a black hole that threatens to consume them. This can lead to mental conditions including paranoia, schizophrenia, and phobias. In less extreme cases, nightmares, sleep walking, can't be alone, always talking, intense escape or avoidance patterns, and denial of anything they don't want to hear or experience. Some experience visions or 'visits.' The intent of all of this is to remove the barriers leading to the direct transcendental experience. Again, the way out of all of that is through developing a transcendental belief system of a nature that appeals to the individual.

Many psychics, channels, and mediums have this placement. Others plunge into the abyss in faith and are almost entirely focused upon the Source. A few will have total cosmic experiences. Some of these will have repressed other areas of the human nature that actually need to be developed. Others will not understand why they are here. Some of these have spent many lives in other planetary systems, or else out of the body. This type is often frustrated with their inability to express how they feel. Others have had lifetimes of withdrawal from the world, in monasteries, prisons, in the wilderness, etc. All of these people have highly stimulated pineal glands. This gland secretes melatonin, which affects the state of consciousness. Over the long term, melatonin dissolves the boundaries between egocentric consciousness and the source. It is secreted at night, in the dark, and plays a role in the sleep cycle. Because of the stimulated pineal gland, these people can become very sensitive to impurities, such as food impurities, which can have adverse medical effects upon the body. In past lives these people have been learning to balance the need for alone time with the need for external activity. Too much of either can cause various kinds of emotional distortions. It is easy for them to lose awareness of self, and thus of their need for this balance. Losing touch is a product of the dissolution process, over-identifying with an aspect of self, or a fantasy being chased. There are three possible reactions to this placement:

(1) Some reject the evolutionary desire and turn their backs on the abyss, retreating to the known world – the past. They latch onto something familiar and deny any source outside of self. They become very ego-oriented. This will manifest situations of increasing powerlessness, such as physical disabilities, physical confinement, or being blocked from exercising any power at all. That is because the intention is to embrace the cosmic reality, not the ego reality, and the intention is being resisted. The difficult experiences are necessary to try to force the person to look in the intended directions.

(2) Others stand on the precipice, moving back or forward only a few steps at a time. They are aware there is a Source they are connected with, but they are too afraid to step too far into it. They are both attracted and repelled by the Source. Some only acknowledge spirituality when they are in crisis. This type tends to do human service work. They will experience periods of meaninglessness, futility, or disillusionment with the intent to force the person in the intended direction. Many gifted creative people fall in this category.

(3) The third group have taken the plunge and allowed the old egocentric limitations to be dissolved. They are reborn as pure channels through which the Source operates. They do what they are asked or intended to do. They are being freed from the necessity of returning to Earth.

The second group is by far the most common. It is also possible to have combinations of two or three of these group characteristics in a single person, at different points in their life.

These people must learn to let go of everything concerning their past to prepare for a new evolutionary cycle that will be represented by Pluto in the 1st house. This process goes round and round until all of our separating desires are fulfilled, and the karma that those desires generate has been released. (JWG's Pluto Vol. 1 and the School's Course)

Pluto polarity point – 6th house or Virgo

These people must develop specific techniques to learn to analyze themselves. Through this they will learn how and why they are the way they are, and how and why they work the way they do. They will gradually see how all parts are connected to other parts, and how each part influences the expression of every other part. Because of the need to connect to a transcendental belief system, they must develop their natural meditative state through specific techniques that bring a sharper focus to their living connection to the Source. They will consciously examine the inner dynamics that need adjustment, elimination, or purification because of the blockages they create. They must commit themselves to a form of work that is practical and useful to others. They must be involved in human service. They cannot isolate in self-centered pursuits. This relates to the Eastern concept of Karma Yoga, serving God through right work.

In addition to benefiting others, the work itself becomes a path towards self-realization. The attitude, the effort, is what matters, far more than the scale of the actual work. Work is necessary because it grounds the undefined energies of the 12th house Pluto. The work causes a focusing of self, and serves as a mirror where they can experience their inner states. They are also learning to see reality as it is, rather than in an illusive, delusive way. They typically must experiences cycles of deep crisis. The crisis forces them to deal with what is. Many have an unconscious compulsion to create crisis. Often they are not aware of this pattern, and cannot understand why crisis keeps occurring in their lives. Those who have abused power or over-identified with ego may have to accept what they consider to be menial work assignments. They will feel they are being held back by life. The intent here is to learn humility. Common characteristics: deeply private, deeply sensitive, take things to heart, shy at a core level, ultra-emotional, extremely giving in a silent way, deep and unresolved fears, dreaminess, powerful dreams, natural psychic. (JWG's Pluto Vol. 1 and the School's Course)

The totality of consciousness

The totality of Consciousness correlates with Neptune/Pisces, and the 12th house. And within that totality of Consciousness lies its total potential: of what can be realized. Virgo of course is the natural polarity of Pisces. That correlates, archetypically, to LACK where lack is in reference to the total potential that has yet to be realized. Immutable consciousness simply means energy, as Jeffrey pointed out, and that energy cannot be destroyed: it can only change form. It is inherently full of potential to be realized which is the causative factor for the evolution of the Soul: consciousness. Until that full potential of consciousness is realized the Soul necessarily experiences LACK because LACK infers or reflects THE DESIRE FOR MORE than we currently have. The desire for more infers DISSATISFACTION which is the evolutionary determinant for that which will correlate to total SATISFACTION. Total satisfaction correlates with the desire to return to the SOURCE of consciousness and/or the Soul which is held as potential within the Soul and the consciousness within it. Thus, the sense of lack IS ESSENTIAL FOR IT PROMOTES THE ONGOING EVOLUTION OF THE SOUL IN ORDER TO REALIZE IT'S TOTAL POTENTIAL WHICH, IN THE END, IS TO CONSCIOUSLY UNITE ITSELF WITH ITS SOURCE: GOD/ESS. (Rad)

Wave/ocean analogy
Neptune can be both the Wave and the Ocean depending ON THE POINT OF VIEW of consciousness itself as encased in the human form. If we remember the natural trinity between Pisces/Neptune, Scorpio/Pluto, and Moon/Cancer – God, Soul, Ego – then of course it's possible for the ego within a given Soul to be 'intoxicated' – Neptune – with itself via the Ego that it creates. Thus, its relationship to itself is separative in nature relative to the totality of the Creation that it is inter-related with. Thus, from its point of view, it has become deluded – Neptune – within the wave: ego. Other Souls of course, relative to evolution, have their center of gravity – Saturn – within the ocean and know that their Soul and its ego are simply part of the totality of Creation itself that is co-equal in nature. Thus, their inner Neptune, is within the Ocean.

In the wave/ocean analogy the sense of identity depends on the evolutionary condition of the Soul. For most that identity lies in the wave: the ego that feels, perceives and thinks that it is separate from everything else. From the vantage point of the wave then everything else, the boats, ripples, whatever else correlates to the totality of its life circumstances become simply props in its personal play. For Souls who have evolved progressively into the Spiritual state the center of gravity within their consciousness progressively shifts from the ego to the Soul itself. As such their sense of identity is the Soul, the ocean, upon which the wave of its ego has been created for whatever ongoing evolutionary purposes it has. A Soul in that condition thus experiences simultaneously its distinct egocentric personal identity while at the same time its timeless Soul identity.

What it all comes down to is how something is perceived including our own sense of 'identity.' From the point of view of consciousness the issue, in the end, is where the center of gravity is within in. Gravity has a natural correlation to Saturn, Capricorn, and the 10th house. Saturn, etc., also correlates to the structural nature of anything. Thus, the structural nature of consciousness. It also has a natural correlation to the boundary of anything. Thus, it correlates to the natural boundary between our subjective awareness and the consciousness therein, and the progressive levels of the unconscious as in the individuated unconsciousness, Uranus, and the collective unconsciousness/consciousness which is Neptune. Deep within the unconscious is the Soul. Consciousness, as such, emanates from the primary brain. Within the subjective consciousness in all of us is the egocentric structure that the Soul creates in each life to facilitate its evolutionary intentions and progressions.

The ego is the Moon, Cancer, and the 4th house, and is, of course, the natural polarity of Capricorn, the 10th, and Saturn. For most individuals, given the natural evolutionary stages, the sense of identity is their own ego. Thus, the PERCEPTION of being separate from everything else. Thus, the WAVE on the ocean where the wave correlates to the subjective ego within the consciousness of the individual. So if the center of gravity within the individual is their ego then their sense of identity is then defined by the wave: their ego. Yet, as evolution proceeds, the center of gravity within an individual's consciousness shifts to the Soul itself: the OCEAN. The natural boundary of Saturn relative to the structural nature of consciousness dissolves in such a way that the PERCEPTION OF IDENTITY changes from the wave to the ocean. As a result the individual is then perceiving, is consciously aware of, its timeless identity called their individual Soul and the egocentric structures it creates from life to life AT THE SAME TIME. In other words the Soul is aware of and perceives the continuation of its ongoing lifetimes from life to life at the same time. The center of gravity is the Ocean, the Soul. As a result they do not perceive themselves as separate from anything, but, in fact, inter-related to everything. (Rad)

Absolute totality of truth
Pisces, Neptune, and the 12th house correlate to Ultimate and TOTAL truth. Yet consciousness in human form cannot know the absolute totality of the Truth: it is limited by the nature of the form. For example, what is the origin of God itself? And that Origin, and that Origin, and so on. Thus, the Soul and its consciousness within human form can only induce through its intuition a limited part of that total truth. And because it can only intuit through such induction limited truths of an ultimate nature this becomes the basis of what APPEARS to be conflicting truths. These conflicting truths of an apparent nature thus become the basis of conflicting ideas leading to a variety of philosophies and/or religions. In turn this becomes the basis of doubt due to the nature of these apparent conflicts. Doubt thus becomes the cause of asking ever more or deeper questions about the nature of the Creation in the first place. Sagittarius, the 9th house, and Jupiter attempts to synthesize via intuition the unity of these apparent conflicting truths, and the ideas that these various truths create. Yet, in the end, consciousness, embodied in human form that is called the Soul, can only realize, understand, or intuit via synthesis a limited amount of the Total Truth that is inductively sensed within the archetype

of Pisces, Neptune, and the 12th house. This is why even within the idea systems we call astronomy, astrophysics, and the like that the greatest of the greats in those systems, like Einstein, Steven Hawkins, etc. come to the same conclusion about the nature and origins of the Creation. And they all call that God. (Rad)

Creation, manifest and unmanifest
Pisces correlates with the totality of Creation that includes the manifested = known, and the unmanifested = unknown. Sagittarius correlates with the Natural Laws within the manifested Creation that can be understood by the Soul in human form as well as knowing what cannot be known: the unmanifested. God realization is limited to the manifested Creation. It can never be linked to the unmanifested = unknown because, after all, the unmanifested is not yet known because it is not manifested in the first place. What Souls in the human form can know is linked to the interfacing between the known = manifested and the unmanifested = unknown. That interfacing point between the manifested and the unmanifested is the point of Creation as Souls in human form can know it. This limitation is sustained until the Soul evolves beyond its causal body. At that evolutionary point in time, Capricorn, the Soul can then have a progressive knowledge of the unmanifested creation equaling the totality of what we call God/ess itself. (Rad)

Soul and the veil of maya – Yogananda
"Every human being is essentially a Soul, covered with a veil of maya. Through evolution and self-effort, each human makes a little hole in the veil; in time, one makes the hole bigger and bigger. As the opening enlarges, the consciousness expands; the Soul becomes more manifest. When the veil is completely torn away, the Soul is fully manifest in him/her. That woman/man has become a master – master of their self and of maya." (Yogananda)

South Node of Neptune in Aquarius
(Q) In relation with the South Node of Neptune being in Aquarius (reflecting the original matriarchal roots of the current desires in all Souls to spiritualize consciousness), and the connection of natal Neptune with the Aquarius Age, in the context of the current transition between the Pisces Age into the next Aquarius Age, would imply that the root of these desires (ie the past of the Soul) is also symbolic of the future ways for the Souls to spiritualize consciousness (ie ways which will be in place for these Souls in the next Age). Is this correct? (Gonzalo)
(A) Yes. (Rad)
(Q) For me this is interesting to consider because it confirms that the current time frame is defined by a potential for accelerated evolution of Souls because it implies that the past is becoming the future now. Thus, the work on resolution of issues from past lifetimes related to the spiritual roots of the Soul and, at the same time, work on the resolution of issues pertaining to the future of the Soul – ie the past and the future are contained and concentrated within the current time. Is this correct?
(A) Yes. And what this will mean of course is if the original spiritual root will manifest again or not which itself is linked with the survival of the species. Within Aquarius is the triad of Libra and Gemini. Libra correlates with the Natural Law of giving, sharing, and inclusion. This is how humans were defined relative to groups of humans, Aquarius, for the balance of humans' existence on our planet. In relatively recent times this Natural Law of course has become perverted to self-interest and exclusion which then causes one group of humans, or one human, then trying to compete with other groups, or a human, relative to the survival instinct itself. In turn this leads to dominance and submission. If this is not corrected by going back to the original root, or past, and bringing that forwards into the future, then the extinction of the species is guaranteed.
(Q) So, in a sense, over lifetimes of evolution, as the "hole enlarges" or more veils are removed and more illusions dissolved (lots of disillusionment), from this perspective relative to Neptune's South Node, would it be sound understanding to correlate this symbol to what *has held* (past tense) ultimate meaning in the individualized consciousness relative to how much that consciousness has evolved? (Bradley)
(A) Yes. You can also include into this the natural planetary ruler of the South Node of Neptune which for all of us is Aquarius and its natural ruler Uranus. You can include the aspects to this Uranus as well as aspects to the South Node of Neptune itself. (Rad)
(Q) So, the Soul's journey has a past. The consciousness within the Soul journey, relative to the sense of an evolutionary past and future, has a past. This past may not be as we perceive linear time; however in the sense that the consciousness does has a past, along the journey it continues to evolve further into the fullest potential of consciousness within the human form. Would the South Node of Neptune then correlate to earlier in the Soul's evolutionary journey the ways which it spiritualized?
(A) Yes.
(Q) And then, relative to the Soul's individual past, what held ultimate meaning within that Soul's consciousness and thus still resonates as such, coming through the 'now' as a way to naturally spiritualize. And that which still holds a sense of ultimate meaning within the consciousness expressing outwardly relative to the stage at which the consciousness has evolved along the journey thus far (aka the evolutionary stage of the Soul)?
(A) Yes.

Natural Law that holds creation together
(Q) The glue or Natural Law that holds the creation together would have to be perfect. Is there anything at all that is PERFECT about God? (Linda)

(A) The 'glue' that holds the manifested Creation together, including all that which we call Natural Laws such gravity, is the Source of that glue itself. Your use of the word 'perfect' is indeed relative to any given moment in time yet 'time' itself is ever evolving so that what can appear to be 'perfect' at one point in time becomes 'imperfect' from the point of view of another point in time. It is indeed the interaction of what we can call perfect relatively speaking and imperfect that is the essence of evolution itself that leads to a 'timeless' perfect which is when what we call God/ess becomes perfect within Itself. (Rad)

Hiding signature
A phenomena called masking or hiding – a Soul that creates an outer reality in which it operates, and has itself convinced it is, at a level below its actual state of Spiritual evolution. (This is often associated with the Pisces archetype – hiding.) Reasons for this can vary but quite commonly include intense traumas that have occurred in past lives relative to its actual state of Spiritual awareness, it being perceived as different, outside the mainstream, challenging or threatening to the existing order. And in the present life that Soul says to itself, "Who needs more of that? I'm just going to act like I'm 'supposed to,' and convince myself that I'm not really as different as I feel I am." And it will live that way, perhaps for a really long time. Such Souls are identified when doing readings for them because on the outside they are living very conventional lives, yet the degree of depth and insight they exhibit goes well beyond the nature of the outer life, even the physical appearance – dress, manner of speaking, etc., they have adopted. (Steve)

Unconditional love
JWG does talk about Christ's love, and the power that unconditional love has to transform ourselves and others. He says that "Christ's love is so deep that you will never get to the bottom of it." He also talks about unconditional love, which is very different than conditional love, and when we experience unconditional love from the Divine and others it does have the power to transform our lives. The 12th house/Neptune/Pisces archetype reflects the dynamic of unconditional love/connecting to the Divine in this way (Divine Love). (Deva)

Divine love
Divine Love correlates to Pisces, Neptune, and the 12th house. (Rad)

Mercy
Mercy is specific to Pisces, Neptune, and the 12th house. Mercy is just not a form of forgiveness, but also an act of compassionate giving. Mercy is indeed very much part of Natural Laws for the Ultimate Creator is that which emanates Love, forgiveness, compassion, and mercy. (Rad)

Collective unconscious / individuated unconscious
The archetype of the 'individuated unconscious' correlating to Uranus, Aquarius, and the 11th house is different than the 'collective unconscious' correlating to Pisces, Neptune and the 12th house which applies to the entire species of humans. The individuated unconscious correlates to content within the Soul that is unique to that Soul. (Rad)

Projections, delusions, expectations
Astrologically speaking, Aquarius is the archetype that correlates with projections (from our own unconscious). These projections can be based on past traumas (ie this reminds me of my ex-partner, old friend, parents, etc.) which are then cast onto the person who you are involved with now. These projections can also be based on the person's own unconscious inner dynamics/structure that are then cast onto others. In other words, the person projects what is inside themselves onto others. Aquarius correlates to the individuated unconscious and also to the dynamic of trauma. The projections that can surface within this archetype can be linked with the need to objectify and hopefully release what is stored/unresolved within the unconscious. [The situation you are describing] also sounds like dynamics that are linked with unconscious expectations that get projected upon others within relationships.

Astrologically speaking, expectations are linked with the archetype of Libra. Libra correlates with the nature of our expectations within relationships and our ability (or inability) to reach a balanced state of giving and receiving within relationships. Libra correlates with extremities, and the need to reach a state of balance relative to such extremities. Delusion/fantasy correlates with the archetype of Pisces. Pisces symbolizes the need for ultimate meaning, and to bring to closure an entire cycle of evolution in order to prepare for a new cycle which begins in the Aries archetype. When ultimate meaning is 'projected' externally within a relationship it is all too easy to fall into fantasies and delusions (infatuation) about the other person regardless of how much actual contact there has been.

The core point within this is that these types of projections and delusions are based on a need for ultimate meaning/fulfilment within life which we try to find in a variety of external sources. (There is a natural inconjunction between the Libra/Pisces archetypes which reflects the crisis of disillusionment that so many of us have experienced because of this dynamic in which our expectations/need for ultimate meaning are not met.) Pisces also correlates to the need to meet the need for ultimate meaning through creating a relationship with the Divine. Pluto Vol. 2 goes into a wonderful in-depth description of the connection between the Taurus, Libra, and Pisces archetypes and how these archetypes correlate with the need in all of us to progressively internalize (Taurus) our need for ultimate meaning through union with Spirit/the Divine (Pisces) and to reach a state of balance within our relationships (Libra). (Deva)

Projection, in general, correlates to Uranus, the 11th house, and Aquarius. Delusions, in general, correlate with Pisces, the 12th house, and Neptune. Delusions manifest from within the consciousness of any given Soul that can then be projected outwardly into the overall environment in such a way as to condition the very nature of that environment relative to the nature of the delusion itself. There are many possible causes including one's own essential needs within a relationship that the other seems to correlate to, past life connections in which something was not finished, resolved, or is intended to pick up again in the current life, the inner creation of 'fantasy' type ideas about the 'perfect' partner that the other seems to correlate to, etc. etc. etc. All of this correlates, obviously, to delusions if none of it is true: actual. The correlations are above, and those archetypes would be active relative to the transits or progressions at the time that this occurs. (Rad)

Behavioral contagion – collective delusion

This occurs when the nature of the delusions involved become projected in such a way that others who 'need' to BELIEVE in them manifest in sub-groupings – Aquarius 11th house, Uranus – within the whole of a society – Neptune, Pisces, the 12th house – relative to a 'behavioral contagion' that takes place with those sub-groupings who need to believe in the nature of the collective delusion within those sub-groupings. The phenomena of behavioral contagion specifically correlates to Uranus, Aquarius, and the 11th house. (Rad)

Dreams

Dreams in EA correlate with Pisces, the 12th house, and Neptune. JWG taught that there are mainly three kinds of dreams: past life dreams, super conscious dreams, and dreams that are nonsensical. Within this he taught when dreams have reoccurring themes for a period of time, sometimes a whole life span, they correlate to unresolved dynamics within the Soul that correlate with some kind of trauma in which the Soul is trying to work through relative to the nature of such dreams. (Rad)

Dreams – sleep walking

Dreams in EA correlate with Pisces, the 12th house, and Neptune. Sleep walking is typically associated with unresolved traumas from other lives that are being re-lived in some way by way of the dreams that lead to this phenomenon. When the eyes are closed this means that the Soul is actually detached from the physical body and is thus 'seeing' its surroundings in this way. When the Soul does not remember this sleep walking, or the dreams that are associated with that, it means that the nature of the trauma in another life or lives has been so intense and deep that the Soul simply fragmented and detached from the event that is linked with the nature of the trauma itself. Thus, no memory. Sleep walking is linked to past life dreams in which trauma has taken place, and is not resolved within the Soul. In a dream where you are of the opposite sex, this will typically correlate with memories from another life.

Dreams – super conscious dreams

Super conscious dreams occur when the Soul, during sleep, travels to the Astral realm or plane in which some key message or teaching is given to the Soul by some kind of entity there. Upon waking the Soul typically is met with a sense of joy combined with depression where the joy correlates to the nature of the super conscious dream itself, and the depression correlates with the awareness that the Soul is back in its current life body on Earth. And, typically, upon initially 'waking up' the Soul cannot instantly remember who it is in the current life, or where it is. It takes some moments for the Soul to remember these things.

(Q) What are the dynamics during a dream where consciousness suddenly realizes it is a dream because he/she recognizes a symbol which reveals it to be a dream, and believing the dream to be 'real,' with this conflict between waking and dreaming continuing until waking. Does it correlate to certain fear and trauma within the Soul? (Wei)

(A) Yes, this is typically caused by unresolved trauma of some kind in which the Soul is trying to relive/ resolve it by the nature of the dream itself. (Rad)

Dreams – under attack, aggression, danger, sexual assault, attack by evil?

What you are sharing and describing here does not, of itself, correlate with dreams wherein the cause of such dreams is Lucifer/evil. For example, this sort of dream can also be a past life dream that reflects and symbolizes an intense trauma caused by extreme violence as in a war scenario. The sexual assault could also be linked with such a scenario as in being raped. The sense of suffocation can be the memory of the moment of death in such a life and/or linked with the act of the sexual violence as in being restrained or suffocated during the rape. [Attack by evil?] It could be, but it is much more likely that such dreams are rooted in some deep, unresolved, trauma that the Soul then relives in various ways in order to try to remove some of the pressure with the Soul caused by the intense repression of the trauma itself.

(Q) I notice people who have this experience truly believe in spirit – they are more close to God so evil wants to attack them? Why would evil attack a Soul through a dream?

(A) This can be because Evil wants to take Souls away from God so can create dreams in order to scare the Soul: to get it to back off from its desire for God or spirit life. It is to scare them away, make them back off from the Spirit life and/or some very important inner realization that has the effect of accelerating the evolution of the Soul.

(Q) Can evil chase the Soul life after life?

(A) Evil would not be the cause of the same kind of reoccurring dream. The reoccurring dream is almost always caused by unresolved trauma from prior lives.

(Q) If one meets and recognises someone as really evil whom they are terrified of, can the Soul warn them in a dream?

(A) This can be very true, yes. If this is the case such a dream will manifest very shortly after meeting such a person. When this is the case the face of the person who has been recently met will manifest within the dream that then morphs or changes into an evil image of some kind.

(Q) Is there any way to stop these dreams? Or is the point just to stay with God and not be afraid of these dreams?

(A) Once the Soul can objectify the nature of such dreams caused by Evil, thus detaching and distancing itself from the fear associated with such dreams, the 'power' that Evil has to cause such dreams is dramatically reduced if not eliminated altogether. Once objectified the Soul is thus self-empowered in such a way that there really is no reason to be afraid of these dreams. They are understood for what they are.

Dreams – unresolved Soul trauma

(Q) Once the nature of the trauma is realized and why, can the trauma be reduced?

(A) Yes it can, in the sense of whatever those traumas having an intense 'hold' on the Soul because the nature of those traumas have not been inwardly resolved. But this process, depending on each Soul and the specific nature of what those traumas have been, can be quite long to begin to have that desired effect. The value IS ALWAYS IN THE EFFORT. So if the Soul persists in this, no matter what, then at some point in time this desired effect can begin to take place.

(Q) For months I have been trying to understand the trauma in past lives and I've taken responsibility for my actions.

(A) This is a very good approach Wei. The key in the whole deal is accepting the responsibility in one's own actions and/or the karmic/evolutionary need to have such traumatic experiences in the first place.

Soul correlates to Pluto (not Neptune)

EA and its paradigm symbolizes the individual journey of the Soul through time as it evolves back to its Source: God/ess. Even though Neptune symbolizes that Source it does not symbolize or reflect the individual journey of the Soul itself. EA is about understanding each individual Soul as it actually is: where it has been and why, where it is now and why, and where it is headed and why. The Soul correlates to Pluto. Neptune does not. (Rad)

Perfection

To start, it's important that anyone follow the truth you know and find within yourself. All of our human truths are relative truths. I happen to have Pluto in the 8th house, and so am wired to be attuned to the reality of Soul. The Soul is the *bridge* between the human and 'Neptune.' The Soul CREATES the human being, for its own evolutionary purposes, just as Neptune creates the Souls for *its* evolutionary purposes. That is why the focal point of everything in EA is Pluto, the Soul, and not Neptune, which is not really knowable in human form. Our work is to evolve our Souls, through the vehicle of our human natures. We CAN know our Soul, as opposed to knowing Neptune, and we are here as Steve and Heidi BECAUSE of our Souls – that is the point of our human evolutionary journey. In relation to Soul and the Soul's human journey, what I said about perfection and imperfection is quite relevant.

I have heard discussions about whether what EA calls imperfect is in the greater picture in fact perfect even though it is experienced as imperfect. I find these are discussions over the meaning of words. To me they miss the greater point that the words, limited as they must be, are trying to make. They are a *metaphor*. Day to day reality is very few (if any) humans are having an ongoing life they would describe as perfect. That is not debatable. And the patriarchal teachings of Divine Perfection cause many of these people to compare themselves to the unattainable patriarchal ideal of Divine Perfection vs their obvious human imperfection. As a result they judge themselves as inadequate, unworthy, less than, not good enough. And THAT is the cause of most of the masochistic patterns in people that I have encountered.

This begins with my own life history. My life changed radically after first encountering the EA perspective of God as an imperfect force seeking its own perfection. I felt more liberated and validated than I ever had in my life. And now that I am inwardly allowed to counsel others, somehow or other I attract many many people who have that issue (isn't that odd...). Almost everyone I have ever counselled on these issues, people with a similar conditioned orientation to feeling inadequate as a result of not measuring up to the ideal they'd been taught was the goal, has felt liberation on realizing what these words about imperfection vs perfection imply in their life. Why would a perfect God create imperfect creations – what is the point? How can I be more perfect than that which created me? Many times I have seen eyes light up – "You mean I am just okay as I am?" Patterns of many lifetimes begin cracking open before our eyes. That is both my personal experience, and the experience of many people I have counselled.

I also want to say that whether you call it imperfection or perfection, it's a METAPHOR, a *symbol*. If we are saying the same thing but using different words and tripping over each other's definitions of words, then please, throw my metaphor out and use whatever works for you and your clients. The metaphor's intent is to make people AWARE of the causes of their masochism, and to create a way to break those patterns. I have experienced it very effectively doing that. The last thing it's intended for is to create new masochism. If using that metaphor would create additional masochism for you or your clients, for God's sake, don't use it! (Steve)

Neptune correlations

Neptune correlates with the phenomena of consciousness itself. Consciousness in human form. It correlates to infinity and thus timelessness. Ultimate reality versus man-made realities. It correlates to the Source of all things and our natural relationship to the Source. It correlates to the ultimate meaning versus temporal meaning that we give things that ultimately have no meaning when measured against ultimate meaning. It correlates with transcendence and the need to transcend temporal reality. (Rad)

Emphasized 12th house

The emphasized 12th house will always reveal that whatever the ego consciousness has identified with relative to the past, be it spiritual or individual in nature, will reach a point where it simply needs to dissolve. There is certainly a potential for great disillusionment. Having one's whole sense of spiritual identity dissolve is certainly a major crisis. The relativity of how 'deep' the crisis is most reflected in the nature of the Soul and degree of embracing or resisting evolution. The packed 12th alone, as I understand it, will not reflect a deeper spiritual crisis than some other signature/emphasis may. So, a Soul could have been fully embracing growth in their past and less so in the 'present' – the amount one is resisting or embracing their own evolution is not constant on the overall journey, so depth of crisis is always linked to the current orientation to embracing or resisting evolution, regardless of evolutionary stage. (Bradley)

Inductive/deductive thought

Inductive thought is Pisces, Neptune, and the 12th house. Thus, it's opposite, deductive thought, is Virgo, the 6th house, and Mercury. (Rad)

Neptunian emotions

One of the core emotions that correlate with Neptune, Pisces, and the 12th house, and the Nodes of Neptune, and evolution is one of disillusionment. To be disillusioned means that the Soul had been creating a reality around 'something' in which a sense of ultimate meaning has been projected upon that something. In so projecting that sense of ultimate meaning into that 'something' when that something is not Goddess itself it means that that something has become a de facto Goddess. Thus, to be disillusioned from that something holding such ultimate meaning is then to be faced with a deep inner void when the disillusioning is occurring. The Natural Law behind this is to make the Soul ask the question of what in fact constitutes the REAL ultimate meaning for its life. And that then is intended to lead right back to the Source of the Soul itself: Goddess. Of course most Souls don't do that even though it's the intention. Most Souls will then try to find another 'something' to project that ultimate meaning into all over again. So round and round the Soul goes in this way until the Soul finally realizes what that ultimate meaning for life is, and to commit to this.

The most intense and difficult Neptunian emotion that manifests relative to disillusionment is one of hysteria. Another natural emotion specific to Neptune, etc., is one of empathy where empathy allows us to truly understand the emotional realities and needs of others. And within this emotion the DESIRE to help others in the ways that we naturally can without any other motive or agenda attached to it: to give to others what they actually need in the best ways that we can. This then allows the Soul to evolve because it is one of the Natural Laws and 'commands' of the natural Goddess to do so. The deepest degree of this Natural Law and the emotion of it is to ALWAYS PUT OTHERS FIRST no matter what the consequences may be to oneself: think of Jesus here for example of an ultimate manifestation of this. And remember he did have six planets in Pisces, and Neptune conjunct his South Node. His South Node of Neptune was in Capricorn which is ruled by his Saturn in Pisces. When a Soul has committed through desire to reuniting itself with its own Source, and has inwardly realized that Source, then the natural Neptunian emotion of ECSTASY will permeate the Soul when that direct union with the Source takes place. Once any Soul has such an experience it will serve as the very basis and cause of its ongoing evolutionary journey back to the Source itself.

A pure emotion that correlates to Neptune, Pisces, and the 12th house that very, very few people understand or know about: the pure emotion of the psychological dynamics of feeling 'duped, naive, stupid' that can lead to that psychology is one wherein the Soul ASSUMES THAT ALL SOULS SIMPLY WANT TO DO THE RIGHT THING, ASSUMES THAT ALL PEOPLE ARE WHOM THEY APPEAR TO BE, ASSUMES THAT ALL OTHER SOULS DO NOT DO HARMFUL OR BAD THINGS TO ITS OWN SELF. This archetype here is one of EMOTIONAL ASSUMPTIONS. These kinds of emotional assumptions emanate from the natural psychological purity or innocence contained within the Pisces, Neptune, 12th house archetype. And it is this kind of emotion that can then lead to feeling stupid, duped, naive, disillusioned and so on. For evolution to take place through the emotions, *all three* types of emotions pertaining to the "water trinity" (Pisces, Scorpio, Cancer) are activated. (Rad)

Evolution through the emotional body
EA teaches that processing life experiences through the emotional body is evolutionary precisely because it enables the Soul to fully EXPERIENCE whatever experiences are the natural consequence of its desires and choices. If the Soul does not fully EXPERIENCE that which its choices have generated, then it will not truly know in a deep way the consequences of those desires and choices, and will not be able to integrate and learn from these experiences, and thus to make new choices and evolve. Evolution is a natural process of the universe – we can trust it to happen and we do not have to 'make' it happen, so much as let it happen. As Jeffrey taught, the Water Trinity shows involution in that Spirit/Neptune differentiates to Soul/Scorpio differentiates to Ego/Cancer; and also shows that evolution occurs naturally in the natural direction of the zodiac of the shift in conscious identification from Ego/Cancer to Soul/Scorpio to Spirit/Pisces. I find in my work that when people are able to experience their experience through the emotional body (Cancer/Moon), such a full experience naturally eventually leads them (over a period of minutes or lifetimes) to a desire to understand and transform the deeper unconscious patterns and/or Soul history (both Scorpio/Pluto) that has led to the given emotional experience. I don't need to try to push this inquiry in any way, it is the natural result of deeply experienced emotion, it is just what happens when we get out of the way and feel. And then I have also found that when people start to work at this deeper level, then also very naturally begin (again, whether in this lifetime or later) to experience their own encounters with Source (Pisces/Neptune), however this may manifest as appropriate to their perceptual capacities. The water naturally returns to the sea. So to me it is not so much about energy releasing or other particular things as much as it is about having a natural experience that leads to new understanding and choices (and thus new experiences) that eventually exhaust separating desires and leave only the desire to return to Source. In general bypassing the emotional body is essentially resisting evolution, which Souls at any stage in consciousness can do. (Jason)

Practices to work with the emotional body
[Example: Various practices within Dzogchen and Tibetan Buddhism] These practices are not only unnecessary but in fact confuse those who try to practice them. They take what is inherently simple and complicates that. This happens because such practices are not in alignment with Natural Laws: they are essentially invented by individuals who have been conditioned by man-made laws, the patriarchy, that are then trying to harness the Natural Laws in unnatural ways. Personally, I won't have anything to do with them. To me the practices to be used are life itself. To have the knowledge of emotions is simply to experience them within a consciousness that becomes one with whatever emotion is existing relative to a cause that has ignited it in the first place. And, within this, to have a desire, conscious intention, to understand the nature of whatever emotion: its cause, and the reasons for that cause. Within this, the inherent knowledge that then exists in whatever emotion the consciousness becomes one with. Over time of course a state of total self-knowledge defined by the emotional body will take place. A book that came up that appears relevant to all this is "The Spiritual Anatomy of Emotion: How Feelings Link the Brain, the Body, and the Sixth Sense" [Paperback] by Michael (A) Jawer (Author), Marc S. Micozzi (Author), Larry Dossey (Foreword). (Rad)

Spiritual bypass
As I understand it, EA teaches that processing life experiences through the emotional body is evolutionary precisely because it enables the Soul to fully EXPERIENCE whatever experiences are the natural consequence of its desires and choices. If the Soul does not fully EXPERIENCE that which its choices have generated, then it will not truly know in a deep way the consequences of those desires and choices, and will not be able to integrate and learn from these experiences, and thus to make new choices and evolve. In some sense spiritual bypass is a kind of delaying tactic – the Soul resisting coming to terms with the natural consequences of its own desires and choices (though at the ego level this can simply look like a person avoiding painful emotions using Jesus or altered states or "ascension" or whatever). In this way the Soul keeps itself in a kind of evolutionary limbo in that it cannot truly exhaust separating desires since it is ever delayed from truly feeling what those desires have resulted in, and therefore must repeat them (in a sense wilfully failing to learn from history). You can see how this can correlate with skipped steps in some Souls.
Spiritual bypass to me also relates to the control orientation most of us carry and to the lack of trust in natural law that has been learned on this planet. Evolution is a natural process of the universe – we can trust it to happen and we do not have to "make" it happen, so much as let it happen. As Jeffrey taught, the Water Trinity shows involution in that Spirit/Neptune differentiates to Soul/Scorpio differentiates to Ego/Cancer; and also shows that evolution occurs naturally in the natural direction of the zodiac of

the shift in conscious identification from Ego/Cancer to Soul/Scorpio to Spirit/Pisces. I find in my work that when people are able to experience their experience through the emotional body (Cancer/Moon), such a full experience naturally eventually leads them (over a period of minutes or lifetimes) to a desire to understand and transform the deeper unconscious patterns and/or Soul history (both Scorpio/Pluto) that has led to the given emotional experience. I don't need to try to push this inquiry in any way, it is the natural result of deeply experienced emotion, it is just what happens when we get out of the way and feel. And then I have also found that when people start to work at this deeper level, then also very naturally begin (again, whether in this lifetime or later) to experience their own encounters with Source (Pisces/Neptune), however this may manifest as appropriate to their perceptual capacities. The water naturally returns to the sea. So to me it is not so much about energy releasing or other particular things as much as it is about having a natural experience that leads to new understanding and choices (and thus new experiences) that eventually exhaust separating desires and leave only the desire to return to Source.

If we stay with the Water Trinity, then spiritual bypassing can be seen as an attempt to "bypass" the emotions (Cancer) and critically the step of self-confrontation and transformation (Scorpio) – after all that is really hard. But of course natural law doesn't work that way and what I would say is actually happening is that the Soul is actually going in the involutionary (clockwise) direction on the wheel, trying to escape to a regressive experience of preconsciousness rather like the womb (Pisces), so as not to feel the pain of emotion (Cancer). In therapy this is sometimes called the "flight into health." To me it exemplifies the issue of trines in that as Jeffrey taught they can make it "easy" to be conscious and cooperative with evolution but they can also make it "easy" to resist it. Regarding evolutionary states and spiritual bypass, I have personally encountered bypass in all three of the main stages. At Consensus stages I often see it as "religious bypass" – people avoiding emotions by logging into pre-digested and pat religious answers (eg I don't want to feel grief about Sandy Hook, so I'll just blame it on schools not having Christian prayer every morning; or we don't want to feel the pain of Katrina so let's just blame it on the gays). At Individuated stages I often see it as "science bypass" or "political bypass" – people avoiding emotions by logging into political causes or sophisticated explanations of the aspects of experience they are avoiding. "Psychology bypass" also happens and a lot of insight-oriented psychotherapy does this, avoiding direct experience of emotions by explaining them. And then in the Spiritual stages and the later Individuated stages I often see it as the kind of "spiritual bypass" where people prefer to log in to particular states of consciousness or metaphysical frameworks and log out of the direct and lived experience of their emotions. But to me in general bypassing the emotional body is essentially resisting evolution, which Souls at any stage in consciousness can do.

Regarding whether the kind of mental/head-based quality that typifies the specific bypass (of preferring to dwell in primordial states), means that such individuals may be in the Individuated states vs Spiritual states, I would say that could be occurring in a Spiritual or an Individuated Soul. The difference would have to be discerned by understanding the nature of the Soul's motivation for its practice in the first place. I have seen some practitioners of these paths and techniques who are (mostly) seeking to reinforce their own sense of themselves and their specialness and ability to "achieve" and use spiritual practice as the vehicle for this (Individuated); and I have seen some who are (mostly) truly seeking to unite themselves with Source (Spiritual). And at both of these levels, I have seen Souls periodically fall into the trap of using these paths to dissociate from their emotions, or even live an entire lifetime in that kind of resistance.

Considering how to help Souls in this dynamic, as mentioned we are in the territory of Pisces/Neptune, and as EA teaches this archetype is about Source and spiritual realization, but at the same time also the process by which we "deify" all sorts of people and things and states of consciousness as if they themselves are Source or are spiritual realization, and then we experience eventual disillusionment when this turns out not to be true. In this context for me it has rarely worked to point out to people they that are in spiritual bypass; those rose-coloured glasses are pretty sticky and if you get Virgo/Mercury discerning and analytical they get even more Pisces/Neptune cloudy and ascending. Unless they are somehow really ready to hear it and to experience it as real, it is just a mental thing to say it, like telling an active addict that he or she has an addiction.

What I do find helpful in many situations is to assist the person in fully experiencing whatever they are experiencing, to feel what it is like to be where they are. In this case of bypass, to feel what it is like to view or use access to this primordial state as the "answer." What does that feel like, what is the impact of that in life? After all, the desire to prematurely transcend and resist the evolutionary process is itself also a desire that the Soul has created and wants to experience. Assisting the Soul to fully experience the full experience that is a consequence of that desire (whether it is the 'high' states, the frequent interpersonal isolation that results, the tendency to judge the 'unenlightened,' the pressure to maintain one's 'enlightenment,' whatever the full experience is), and eventually it will naturally include the experience of disillusionment, and the felt sense of disillusionment – feeling it, not just being told it by someone else – the disappointment, the grief, the anger – is what naturally leads the Soul to truly release the desire for bypass and move on to whatever is next for it. Just realizing it cognitively or because someone points it out typically means that although today's bypass strategy may be dropped, the desire will still exist in the Soul to do it and it will find another way to bypass (kind of like switching addictions from one substance/behavior to another when the deeper desires driving the addiction have not been addressed and released, only deferred). (Jason)

All that you [Jason] have said/shared about this is exactly right. We need to remember/understand that the Pisces, Cancer, Scorpio trinity, the Source, the Soul, and the ego it manifests, all emanate from the Water archetype. Water is of course pure emotion. The non-dual state, the desire for, is itself an emotional delusion that is impossible to achieve, or arrive at, relative to consciousness in the Soul in a human form. A Soul relative to certain 'spiritual' methodologies can indeed arrive at some sort of 'transcendental' state but that state always, cause and effect, snaps back to a 'normal' state of consciousness. Even in these naturally transcendental states or 'cosmic consciousness' the very essence of such a consciousness or state is EMOTIONAL: the emotion or feeling within that state of consciousness as it 'perceives' the various realities of those states. That perception leads to an emotional state as it 'reacts' to the nature of the perception itself. The need of all of our Souls to directly feel the nature of our emotions as they relate to any possible experience created by the Soul for its own evolutionary needs is the bottom line truth. For those who are able to create within themselves the various degrees of cosmic consciousness all of them will report being in a temporary state of ecstasy. Ecstasy of course is an experience of pure emotion.

When Souls align themselves with various religious and/or spiritual teachings that teach it is important, necessary even, to control or repress the emotions in order for 'x' spiritual state to be realized these Souls are reacting to the nature of their own emotional lives. In essence, they are running from those emotional lives for their own reasons but all reasons that lead to this running lead to repressing the very nature of the emotions themselves. In so doing they are repressing that which is NATURAL AND NECESSARY FOR THE SOUL TO EXPERIENCE for its own evolutionary reasons. If we accept that God/ess is the origin of all things then wherein lies the origin of emotions? And for what reasons? So for Souls who do orientate to these teachings that require repression, to 'transcend' them which means repressing them, the very act of repression then magnifies and distorts those natural emotions within the consciousness of those that do so. When anything that is natural is repressed for whatever reasons ANGER IS THE DIRECT RESULT: a natural inner anger. When this occurs all too often the Soul then feels itself to be a victim of life, a victim even to their own emotions which continue to live on, to exist, despite the repression. When this natural anger is then linked to the created consciousness of feeling to be a victim first to itself, then to others, this becomes the causative basis of lashing out at anyone the Souls feels 'victimized' by. In a 'religious' and/or 'spiritual' context this then is the cause of all the horror stories we are all too familiar with: the priest abusing boys, the 'guru' who is having intercourse with some devote, and so on.

As JWG and others have taught the liberation of the Soul does indeed take place through and because of the emotional body for the reasons that Jason [above] had correctly pointed out. A story that I just remembered about this is the story of one of Yogananda's chief disciples, a women who was essential for Yogananda and his work. She developed a terminal medical condition in which Yogananda interceded upon by way of asking God/ess to keep her alive because of the critical nature of her tasks helping his work. She lived ten years longer as a result. And upon her final transition, upon the moment of the very last breath, her final words were: "TOO MUCH JOY." (Rad)

The disciple that Rad is referencing in this post is Sri Gyanamata and the book is called "God Alone: Life and Letters of a Saint." This is a wonderful book which I highly recommend as it gives great perspective about how to emotionally heal and grow without any "spiritual bypass." (Deva)

Since deep emotional processing is the heart of the work I do, what I have found is that we simply cannot easily move through our own emotional defenses. Spiritual systems that are 'transcendent' in nature often collude with the already dissociative defence in place. Yes it is quite easy for already dissociated, fragmented psyches (ie all of us) to access "other/higher worlds" since so many of our parts already reside there!! The difficult part is unlocking the trauma that caused the fragmentation in the first place and then real Soul retrieval can happen. Re-living, ie descending into the original terror, wound, fear, horror, pain (fill in the blank) opens up not only the complex formed around such an event, but the defences that were crystallized also. These defences involved ALL levels of the being, etheric/physical body, emotional body, mental body and spiritual body. ALL these bodies need to become congruent in order for full integration to happen and each one can hold their own separate defence. One body is not superior to another despite what patriarchal bias tells us. Personally I trust the veracity and truth of emotion before I trust the machinations of head, my personal bias. Sharing a quote from R.D. Laing:

"When our personal worlds are rediscovered and allowed to reconstitute themselves, we first discover a shambles. Bodies half-dead; genitals dissociated from heart; heart severed from head; heads dissociated from genitals... Without inner unity, with just enough sense of continuity to clutch at identity: the current idolatry. Torn, body, mind and spirit, by inner contradictions, pulled in different directions, Man cut off from his own mind, cut off equally from his own body – a half-crazed creature in a mad world."

I perceive that we compensate for all these contradictions and dissociations largely with our mental prowess, using it to repress the true reality that lies underneath. This is why, collectively, we are so mentally defended because under those defences lies a much different, initially terrifying inner world, where our compensated identity is threatened to come apart, but when one has the courage to go there the reward is integration and coherence. (Patricia)

Neptune and higher octave Venus

Neptune is the higher octave of Venus. Venus corresponds to the heart chakra. My intuition is that this does not mean that Neptune correlates to the heart chakra itself, but rather that the heart chakra and the crown have some sort of octave resonance to one another which is the manifestation of Source unity consciousness through the denser, interpersonal feeling center of the heart. (Ari)

A simple example: Neptune would correlate to unconditional love, whereas Venus would or can correlate to conditional love and the reasons for that conditional love. (Rad)

Guilt

There are really TWO BASIC types of guilt: man-made guilt (learned) based on religious, philosophical, psychological, etc. beliefs, and natural guilt (earned), based on our actions that are out of alignment with Natural Laws. I think for the most part the majority of the learned guilt DOES go back to what we think is "right" and "wrong" based on man-made religions. In general, EARNED guilt will be reflected in the symbols of Saturn/Capricorn/10th house, while the LEARNED guilt is more likely to come through the symbols of Virgo/Pisces and their respective rulers and houses. These, of course, are just two places to START looking for patterns of guilt. Some of figuring this out within ourselves will unfold as we evolve and realign with Natural Laws, but much can also be gleaned now if we simply reflect on the reasons for ANY kind of guilt we feel and then the SOURCE of those reasons. For example, if I beat my child to the point he needs to be hospitalized, I know (even if it's only deep down within and not necessarily conscious) that I have done something inherently wrong. On the other hand, if I get a divorce and feel guilty because whatever church says it's a "sin" to get divorced, then I've taken on an unnecessary guilt based on some humans' ideas about what is right and wrong. Even in countries where religion has been banned, the old USSR, for example, I could be found "guilty" of and punished for not bowing to the emperor because that's one of the laws of the country. However, to not bow to another human being isn't intrinsically "wrong;" it's only "wrong" because it's a man-made rule, and therefore actual guilt is unnecessary. (Adina)

Neptune Retrograde

When Neptune is retrograde it points to Pluto itself: our Soul. When Neptune is retrograde there is an accelerated evolutionary desire, need, to throw off all things that are of a delusive nature: that which is not actually 'real' yet what we have considered real before the delusion or illusion was finally understood. Thus, it emphasizes the process of disillusionment leading to that which is actually real from an ultimate point of view. Relative to uniting our consciousness, Soul, with that which has created us in the first place, the Neptune retrograde will necessarily do so in its own way. When Neptune is retrograde is does point to Pluto in that this symbolizes a Soul who intends to pierce the bubble of its own illusions, delusions, and all that has been given false meaning, an ultimate meaning in many ways, that has confused the Soul as to what the Ultimate Reality is really about: God/ess. (Rad)

Retrograde Venus into Pisces

Venus is the lower octave of Neptune and Neptune is the ruler of Pisces, so as Venus slows down and slowly stations at the last degree of Pisces, many Souls are searching beyond what holds earthly meaning and to what holds ULTIMATE meaning, which can only really be found within – God/Goddess (Pisces/Neptune). This can also be a time when relationships (outer side of Venus) that are not matching what we need are ending, a time of culmination, Venus in Pisces; and also a time for healing the past, old wounds in relationships that have injured our inner relationship with ourselves, things being cleared. So when Venus moves direct and back into Aries, we can be stronger in our self and more clear about our desires and needs (Venus in Aries) and as a result how to move forward with others. As our inner relationship with our self changes, our vibration also shifts and this will then alter the nature of whom and what we attract. (Kristin)

True channeling

Channeling as a 'phenomenon' is Aquarius. However, within Aquarius only the consciousness of the individual ego is sustained. And because of this the 'messages' that are then 'channeled' get mixed up with that ego: its own subjective reality. Which then explains why so many 'channeled' messages conflict from one channeler to the next. "True" channeling, again, then is the linkage between Aquarius and Pisces where Pisces follows Aquarius. In that true channeling state there is no subjective ego to mix things up with. (Rad)

JWG taught that 'channeling' in general is an 11th house, Aquarius, and Uranus archetype but that most who claim to 'channel' are in fact 'channeling' their own individuated unconscious and/or subconscious. We need to remember that the individuated unconscious in all of us correlates to our own 'long term' memory that connects to not only this life, but the individual memories of our own past lifetimes. This is why he also taught that so many of these 'channeling' messages from so many seem to conflict with one another. And it's also why so many of the 'channeled' messages simply don't come true at all, as in Clare Prophet's case and many others. JWG said true channeling does occur but is very, very rare because the ego within the consciousness of those that can truly channel becomes displaced during the channeling itself. And he used the analogy of a 10,000 watt bulb coming through a 5 watt bulb which then causes the entire system of the one who is truly channeling to burn out more quickly than normal. Thus, true channeling is then a Pisces, Neptune, and 12th house archetype. (Rad)

Psychics

Clients have been greatly confused by all kinds of 'psychics' who claim to be far more than they actually are. Sorry to say but this is the nature of reality we live in at this very segment of time. The Aquarian Age is just rising. People try to accelerate their consciousness but in reality those who haven't really done some real work on that before may end up in personal delusions. Why? Uranus' role in the chart is trying to accelerate consciousness, in order to bring the Soul closer to Neptune. Yet, when it is based on misunderstandings, personal delusions of some kind may happen either partially, in fragmented ways or sometimes even fully.

People who think they are far ahead than where they actually are. This is also true to in general to the Individuated state of consciousness for the same reason (Uranus acceleration issues). Some bits of consciousness are ahead and some bits are far behind – fragmented – and the result is a misunderstanding. (Lia)

Pluto/Neptune, addictions
For starters, Pluto relates to compulsion/repetition, the root of which is unconscious memories and desires within the Soul. An addiction is repetitive, so certainly there can be a Pluto component. Something is compulsive because the reasons for the attraction to it are below the threshold of awareness – emanating from the Soul, thus repeated and repeated seeking resolution, without understanding where the compulsion is coming from in the first place. Pisces/Neptune relates to delusion/escapism, and is definitely associated with addictions. If you take it deeper, the deepest craving in any of us is to return to Source, to experience Divinity, that which is the only thing that can truly fill all our desires and places of lack. Addictions are a counterfeit way, an attempt at a shortcut method, of fulfilling those desires – what we become addicted to makes us feel that very deep sense of pleasure and satisfaction, at least initially. The feelings themselves are real. The issue is we identify the source of what we are feeling as whatever it is that appears to be letting us feel that way, a drug, alcohol, or deep love of/from another person. That is a mis-identification, and that becomes the root of the addiction. Through the repetition complex (Pluto) we keep repeating the experience of taking the substance, or connecting with the person, hoping that this time we will once again feel the way it made us feel in the beginning. Somehow it never does. Yet we get in a loop and keep repeating the experience. In terms of the Nodes, we are conscious of the pulls of the Nodes because those are part of our sense of self, self-image. That relates to the "familiar feels secure" principle. So we repeat old patterns and habits. Pluto's compulsions lie beneath that level of awareness, in the unconscious. Both are operative. (Steve)

Neptune sextile Pluto
The Pluto/Neptune aspect can serve as collective inspiration or collective delusion within any generation on a personal and collective level. (Deva)
When everyone on a planet shares an aspect, that is an example of intended collective evolution. Something shared by all humans, each in their own way of course, and generationally through the shifting of the signs the planets are in. When an aspect exists for a really long time, it indicates the necessity of learning important collective lessons. Also, consider that at times one or the other or both of those planets will be retrograde, further reinforcing the intention of really getting the evolutionary lessons. (Steve)

Guilt/atonement

The EA paradigm is only reflecting, symbolizing, life in its totality. Of itself it causes nothing. Each Soul is unique to itself. The choices each Soul makes, and the reasons for those choices, is also unique to each Soul. Relative to the archetype of atonement linked with guilt each Soul reacts, and thus makes choices, differently. The natural process leading any Soul to finally be free of needing to atone for whatever guilt, natural or unnatural, is different for all Souls. And, of course, much depends on the very nature of the causative factors for the guilt in the first place: the extent and extremity of it. If any given Soul were responsible, say, for the deaths of a great many people due to its negligence how long would it take for such a Soul to stop atoning for this fact? If it were you, how long do you think that might be? If it were someone else, how long do you think it may take for that person to be free of atoning for such a guilt? There is just no way to know. Each Soul is different. The key issue here is whether the guilt is natural or not. When guilt occurs to a Soul that is natural then the very nature of that guilt, the events that have caused it, will stay within the Soul forever. It does this so that the Soul will never repeat the causes or actions that lead to the natural guilt. On the other hand, any guilt that is within the Soul that is not natural can and will be expelled from the Soul at some point. Thus when dealing with clients it is very important to understand this critical difference which then dictates how a client is to be dealt with relative to a therapeutic approach. (Rad)

Disillusionment and doubt, a personal experience
(Q) I have been undergoing massive disillusionment within my own spiritual life and within my relationship to Spirit itself. I have noticed as a reaction to this, I have become extremely cautious and guarded about interpreting *anything* in directly spiritual terms anymore. It is as JWG frequently said, disillusionment can be one of the most bitter and difficult experiences that any of us can have, and I can say from direct experience that this is UTTERLY true. And because that experience is so hard and so painful, the last thing I personally want to do – and I'm sure the same is often true for others – is delude myself again and walk right back into it. This also connects to the Virgo archetype: transition. In my own case, I recognize that I am manifesting an extreme response to the disillusionment that has had to occur in myself – and one of the serious, unfortunate effects is that it has cut me off from my own lifeblood. That is something I just have to work out for myself, I know. But I do have this question correlating to disillusionment and doubt. How does one go through massive disillusionment and not get caught up in the debilitating psychology of doubt? If something has been regarded in one's heart of hearts as 'real' – and that something has also been providing the basis for ultimate

meaning – it is a complete shock to consciousness when the illusions are exposed and the meaning within it is finally seen as an embellishment of one's own making. So the question becomes, how does one recover one's confidence in interpreting spiritual reality, ie what is a real manifestation of Spirit vs what is imagined or 'hoped,' following a major disillusioning of consciousness? – particularly when there is no immediate resource available to confirm or clarify the accuracy of one's interpretation? (Stacie)

(A) The actual archetype that specifically correlates with being disillusioned is Neptune, Pisces, 12th house, that can then trigger its natural polarity of the Virgo, 6th house, and Mercury that manifests as doubt. With Neptune now transiting Pisces, and it has been squaring the transiting nodal axis that was in Gemini/Sagittarius, this experience of disillusionment leading to doubt has been happening to many, many people. And necessarily so because the intention with Neptune in Pisces is to know or learn about that which is true, and that which is not. While those transiting Nodes were in Gemini/Sagittarius this then focuses on the difference between beliefs that are projected as ultimate meaning, that which is true from the point of view of pure beliefs, and that which is true from the point of view of INNER KNOWING. Inner knowing does not correlate with beliefs because what is known is experienced within the interior of the Soul itself as a by-product of desire to know that which is true, and that which is not. Inner knowing of that which is universally true occurs of course through various practices, Virgo, that are all aimed and shallowing or stopping the breath. As that occurs the Soul is then able to penetrate the inner realms of consciousness itself: Neptune correlates with the phenomena of consciousness. As it progressively penetrates these inner realms of consciousness a variety of natural truths that correlate with the nature and cause of consciousness itself become KNOWN. And this knowing, again, is not a function of beliefs because, as these inner truths are known, there is nothing to literally believe and everything to know. And because these inner truths are simply known there then becomes nothing to doubt. The knowing is a function of actual experience, and those experiences are universal to any Soul who so desires to know these inner truths that correlate with the nature of consciousness. Because they are in fact universal it then serves as a way of knowing that which is true, versus that which is make-believe.

When this is the baseline within the Soul's consciousness, the point of personal Soul knowing and integration, this then serves as the vehicle through which, and because of, the Soul then 'interprets' the nature of any given phenomenal reality. The dynamic or archetype of interpretation specially correlates to Sagittarius, Jupiter, and the 9th house. As the Soul interprets the nature of any external phenomenal reality relative to this inner baseline the MEANING of whatever external phenomenal reality is then projected upon that phenomenal reality. As the Soul does this it will then automatically create a way of intellectually organizing all of phenomenal reality that reflects the core inner baseline of the inner knowing of the nature of consciousness itself. This natural process of intellectually organizing phenomenal reality correlates to Gemini: how the nature of thoughts that occur as a function of the inner knowing are connected to create a larger whole that is organized. All of this then correlates to the nature of various 'spiritual' cosmologies that humans have manifested going back to its own origins on this Earth that are then called 'religions.' This is then exactly where the conflict between pure beliefs versus actual knowing can occur because many who do desire to know the Origin of all things, the Origin of consciousness itself, indeed the Origin of themselves, align themselves with whatever spiritual cosmology without actually doing what is necessary to know for themselves that which is true.

Thus, by attaching themselves to whatever cosmology then leads to their personal belief system that is of course used to interpret whatever phenomenal reality. When a Soul does this, without actually doing that which is necessary to inwardly know, these beliefs are then projected upon phenomenal reality so that when phenomenal reality manifests in ways that cause conflict with the projected beliefs the result is then doubt: doubting the nature of the projected beliefs themselves that have been born, again, from whatever spiritual cosmology they have latched onto relative to the pure desire to Know. This conflict caused by projected beliefs initially creates the disillusionment of those beliefs that then triggers the doubt. It should be said too that a Soul who does not do their own actual inner knowing but simply latches onto whatever spiritual cosmology can also create 'beliefs' about themselves and/or others that are also delusional or illusionary. Thus, when certain types of inner or outer events take place that defeat those projected inner beliefs about themselves or others that same experience of being disillusioned takes place that then leads to doubt: doubt about oneself, or doubt about another(s). In essence this correlates to self-deception, and/ or being deceived by others.

To recover one's confidence in interpreting phenomenal reality, or as you say 'spiritual' reality, is to go deeply within the interior of one's own consciousness with the pure desire to KNOW. To know the actual truth of anything. To do so always starts with some sort of natural practice that aims at stilling the breath, of shallowing it to the point that it NATURALLY STOPS. If one does this while at the same time holding the nature of whatever one is wanting to know about within their consciousness there will come a moment, a time, in which the answer simply OCCURS WITHIN CONSCIOUSNESS OF ITS OWN VOLITION: like a bubble manifesting from the depths of the sea onto the surface of the sea itself. And a Soul can do this repeatedly in such a way that the truth of what one is wanting to know about can be repeated as many times as the Soul needs it to be repeated so that the lingering doubt simply dissolves. The point here is that if that which is true relative to what one is asking about is indeed true it will repeat itself over and over for as many times that the Soul needs it to. In this way confidence is regained. (Rad)

Man-made guilt and natural guilt

From my own personal experience, in relation to what JWG explained to me years ago, this technique helps eliminate LEARNED guilt, not natural guilt. Even in Natural Law we can experience natural guilt. But, at this point in our history we're just beginning to learn how to distinguish between natural guilt and the guilt we can feel by comparing ourselves to a "perfect" God. I think it boils down to a simple (Pisces) process of asking in any of these situations just WHAT the basis of the guilt is, ie whether it's rooted in man-made laws or Natural Laws. And as one asks that question more and more, I think we can start to weed out the source of any guilt. Even with the natural guilt, we need to remember that as Wolf used to put it, "God has goofed up, so why wouldn't WE goof up?" And another (Piscean) question: "How can anything perfect create something Imperfect?" It's really a shift in this understanding of "perfection" that I think helps in our understanding of Natural Law, and ultimately the forgiveness for both ourselves and others. (Adina)

There are really TWO BASIC types of guilt: man-made guilt (learned) based on religious, philosophical, psychological, etc. beliefs, and natural guilt (earned), based on our actions that are out of alignment with Natural Laws. I think for the most part the majority of the learned guilt DOES go back to what we think is "right" and "wrong" based on man-made religions. In general, EARNED guilt will be reflected in the symbols of Saturn/Capricorn/10th house, while the LEARNED guilt is more likely to come through the symbols of Virgo/Pisces and their respective rulers and houses. These, of course, are just two places to START looking for patterns of guilt. Some of figuring this out within ourselves will unfold as we evolve and realign with Natural Laws, but much can also be gleaned now if we simply reflect on the reasons for ANY kind of guilt we feel and then the SOURCE of those reasons. For example, if I beat my child to the point he needs to be hospitalized, I know (even if it's only deep down within and not necessarily conscious) that I have done something inherently wrong. On the other hand, if I get a divorce and feel guilty because whatever church says it's a "sin" to get divorced, then I've taken on an unnecessary guilt based on some humans' ideas about what is right and wrong. Even in countries where religion has been banned, the old USSR, for example, I could be found "guilty" of and punished for not bowing to the emperor because that's one of the laws of the country. However, to not bow to another human being isn't intrinsically "wrong;" it's only "wrong" because it's a man-made rule, and therefore actual guilt is unnecessary. (Adina)

Chart markers of masochism
While there ARE many masochists because of the Christian conditioning of a PERFECT God of the last 2,000 years, not everyone is a masochist. Chart markers of masochism can include the Nodal Axis in 6th/12th or Virgo/Pisces, Pluto in Virgo, Mars in Virgo, a stellium of planets in Virgo or Pisces or the 6th or 12th houses, etc. But even those alone do not necessarily indicate masochism. Again, we have to play astrological detective and employ observation and correlation of the person's thoughts and behaviors in order to determine this for sure, ie one would also have to display masochistic behaviors. Typically, if the chart reveals some of these placements AND you see a Soul who is not actualizing their evolutionary intentions, that could indicate a masochist. (Adina)

Planetary pairs, Neptune and Moon
Neptune correlates to the transcendent impulse of the Soul. It implies the necessity for a Soul to surrender to the all-encompassing truth that is. In that process its beliefs and ideas about what reality is are disillusioned. The Moon correlates to the ego, the human identity that the Soul creates as a focusing agent for its evolutionary journey. It implies the necessity to become emotionally secure and intimate with one's own self in such a way that a Soul can adopt to the changes that occur in life, on a moment to moment basis. The evolutionary intention behind Neptune/Moon aspects is for the Soul to consciously realize itself (Moon) as the Truth (Neptune). This places a Soul in a deeply vulnerable position whereby it is necessary to develop a relationship to home, to what provides security and safety on a subjective, personal level that is also a direct experience of universal Love. This leads a Soul to understand the unity of all beings, as children of God. Transcendence occurs through serving God through the emotional body. (Ari)

Music and dance
Music is a Venus/Neptune archetype. Dance correlates with Venus, and its higher octave Neptune. Relative to Neptune this then means ecstatic dance that can lead to a temporary trance state in which spontaneous realizations about the nature of things in general, and the Source of all Things, can take place. (Rad)

Archetype of judgment (Capricorn) manifesting through Pisces
What JWG taught is that judgment as an archetype in human consciousness is natural, and that the archetype of judgment in and of itself is Capricorn, the 10th house, and Saturn. He taught that the issue is not the right or wrongness of judgment as such, BUT THE CONTENT USED TO MAKE JUDGMENTS IN THE FIRST PLACE. Is that content rooted in Natural Laws, or is that content merely a collection of all kinds of man-made laws that have nothing to do with Natural Laws. When the archetype of judgment that emanates from the 10th house, Capricorn, or Saturn manifests through the 12th house, Neptune, or Pisces that then can correlate with the judgments made about spiritual disciplines, practices, the 'rights and wrongs' of spiritual life, of various gods and goddesses, and, of course, one's own relationship to all things spiritual. He taught a lot about all the artificial man-made rules and laws concerning spiritual life, all the 'should be's' so to speak. And how any Soul who enters spiritual life where the nature of that spiritual life has been created and defined by man-made laws that the judgments made either through one's own inner judgment of itself, or judgments made and projected upon others and oneself, that this commonly leads to not being good enough as measured against these man-made spiritual doctrines. This is why he talked and taught so much about the difference between these man-created, patriarchal, spiritual disciplines and their 'teachings' versus what natural spirituality is, what the Natural Laws are, and thus to change the very nature of the CONTENT used to make the judgments in the first place. (Rad)

EA CHART INTERPRETATION

Primary evolutionary/karmic axis

The entire EA paradigm of natal Pluto, the location of the South Node of the Moon, the location of its own planetary ruler by house, sign, and aspects to other planets, Pluto's polarity point, the location of the North Node of the Moon by its own house and sign, and the location of its planetary ruler by its own house, sign, and aspects to it correlates to the primary evolutionary/karmic axis, the bottom line, for the Soul's ongoing evolution from life to life for any of us. It's like a foundation upon which a house is built. Relative to that foundation the REST of the entire birth chart is then properly understood relative to THAT CONTEXT. Everything else is referred to that context, that primary evolutionary/karmic axis. (Rad)

Pluto and its Nodes, planetary rulers, aspects to these from other planets, correlate to the root structure within any birth chart. And from that root all else, the South Nodes of the Moon, their planetary rulers, aspects to these points, are 'birthed' from that root. It's like a tree that has branches where the root produces the trunk of the tree, and the trunk then produces branches with leaves. This core root and its branches within the birth chart are treated EQUALLY for it is the very structure of the chart itself. If we understand this root structure within the birth chart and relate it to the Natural Law of cause and effect then we can understand that core structure within the birth chart at once. It will, of itself, induce inductive logic. And from there we can then understand the origins and causes of all the specific leaves [lives] manifesting from the branches, eg why is this Mars in Gemini squaring Mercury in Pisces? (Rad)

This means then that ...
- Pluto (sign/house)
- Pluto's Nodes (sign/house)
- Pluto's nodal rulers (sign/house)
- aspects from all of the above to other planets (and their signs/houses - and if more info is required, also their Nodes) ... are the fundamental root of any chart. From there, the sign/house of the Moon's Nodes, Moon's nodal rulers, and Pluto's polarity point are brought in. Then aspects from all these to other planets (and their signs/houses). Also at this level a planet's nodes can be examined if more info was required. Then progression to examination of any other part of the chart that thus becomes implicated out of this. (Realising of course that every part of the chart has a part in the whole person/event and so eventually needs to be included in a totally complete analysis.) (Upasika)

Where Pluto/Scorpio fits into the total structure of consciousness

The zodiac, its houses and signs, correlate to the total structure of consciousness in human form. The planets within the zodiac correlate to bringing that consciousness to life, and thus setting in motion consciousness itself. The planets within the zodiac are the unique structural nature of that consciousness from life to life. They are the gasoline within the tank. This is why we start with Pluto, the Nodes, the location of their planetary rulers, and all the aspects to other planets that they are making. This is the core and foundation upon which the Soul structure and its evolutionary background, and its evolutionary development, is understood. Wherever the sign Scorpio is, by house, will contribute to this foundation because the signs on the houses correlate to how consciousness is orientated to phenomenal reality. And that current life orientation to phenomenal reality reflects the evolutionary needs of the Soul in this life. Planets that are in Scorpio, or the 8th house, correlate to the Soul's intention, in this life, to metamorphose the existing development and limitations implied in the archetypes of the planets themselves. The sign on the 8th house is an archetype in which this same Soul intention to metamorphose the existing development of that archetype within consciousness exists. (Rad)

Understanding EA as holistic and non-linear

It has been taught by JWG and others on this message board, the various dynamics in one life symbolized by the entire EA paradigm are reflected in the next, and the next, in a variety of ways that are not linear. They are instead holistic and must be understood in this way. A simple example: in the chart a person had Pluto in Virgo in one life that turned up as a 6th house Pluto in the next. The Venus in Pisces in the first life turned into a balsamic conjunction with Mars in Cancer and in opposition to Neptune. And so on and so forth. This is how we must learn to see and understand E(A) It is not linear, it is holistic. (Rad)

EA methodology

The methodology of EA, and thus its 'rules,' is what it is. And it has been tested for many, many years now through correlations and observation to tens of thousands of Souls. Of course to understand where any given Soul is in their evolutionary journey, because of the Natural Law of free choice, requires observing their actual reality given the parameters of the evolutionary paradigm that is called Evolutionary Astrology. (Rad)

Natural Law of the trinity

The Natural Law of the trinity does apply to E(A) Very simply when one combines with another one, we have three. A simple example would be sperm and ovum. When they combine they produce a brand new organism. And of course the number three is the root number for all advanced math. It is in the union, combining, of the singular one's that then produces three. Union thus becomes the causative factor, or determinant, of evolution itself: genetic evolution through the RNA and DNA of all living organisms. Through this Natural Law we then can see, via the EA paradigm, and existing state of evolution as symbolized in the natal position of Pluto, it's polarity point that is then united with, which in turn allows for an evolution of the existing state of evolution relative to the natal position of that Pluto. Same thing is applied to the existing South Node of the Moon, it's North Node, that thus evolves the South Node itself. (Rad)

Karmic causes / 'victimized' clients

JWG used to teach that all Souls are responsible for the lives that they create from life to life. From that point of view he would then say that 'there are no victims.' He would also teach the utter importance of working with clients who have felt victimized in the sense of not hammering them over the head with words like, "there are no victims, you are responsible for what you have felt victimized by." He would also teach that everything is relative, even the feelings of being victimized. For example, say a woman gets brutally raped. And from the current life point of view that woman had done nothing that could be interpreted or perceived as her being responsible for the rape. So, from this life's point of view, this woman could easily and rightly be perceived as being a victim of that rape. Yet, if one could see the totality of that woman's prior lives, the reasons or causes for the current life could be seen. And those reasons are not just the simplistic stuff like she had raped someone in another life and, therefore, that's the reason that she created the rape in the current life: karma. That may, indeed, be one possible cause, but from the point of view of any given Soul's individual past life context, there can be an incredible amount of reasons or causes that have led to the current life rape.

The various evolutionary conditions have nothing to do with the idea and perception of victimization. This is a cultural/religious issue that spans all evolutionary conditions depending on the nature of the culture/religion that the Soul decided to be born into in any given life. And, thus, a function of conditioning depending on that culture/religion. In other words, there are, and have been, many other cultures/ways of understanding life that had no idea or conception of being a victim at all because, in those cultures/ways of understanding life, all Souls are responsible for what they create. This of course references the NATURAL LAW of cause and effect. Yet it is critical when working with clients, or ourselves, who have been victimized from the point of view of their, our, current life to exercise great compassion and understanding. One of the things that JWG taught when working with victimized clients is to ask them if they wanted to know the prior life causes that exist within them self that are in fact responsible for the current life circumstances that have led to the event in which they have felt victimized. And, if that answer is yes, then to gently do so. And, if not, to help that client deal with the effects of the event in which they have felt victimized by. (Rad)

Karmic causes / evolutionary necessity

These concepts (karmic causes/evolutionary necessity) are easy to misapply and can create a lot of trouble and misunderstanding. I think it's important we don't lose sight of the fact that these ARE distinct dynamics, otherwise what reason would Wolf have for attempting to teach about their distinctions? Wolf has said that determining evolutionary necessity is simple to determine in the birth chart: it is reflected in every symbol that's connected to Pluto in the natal signature. He also made it clear that being able to determine karmic causes is NOT easy, and that there is no 'technique' that can be taught for making this determination.

The issue I think, is that they are so CLOSELY linked, so non-linear, and so nuanced, that it takes an extremely developed capacity to be able to KNOW which is which. And even when karmic causes are accurately identified, one must have an absolute purity of intention and sensitivity/Soul attunement when attempting to communicate something like karmic causes to another, because the individual may not be ready on an inner basis to hear or resolve the content. To impose this kind of information upon someone who isn't actually ready to deal with it creates the risk of generating the exact *opposite* effect that EA was brought forth to serve, as does imposing this kind of information when it has not been correctly interpreted in the first place.

As I understand it, those who have the developed capacity/clarity to accurately identify actual karmic causes from evolutionary necessity will convey it on the basis of receiving the specific inner direction to do just that. So when it comes to the practical application of EA for most of us, I agree that it's better to come from the simple standpoint of acknowledging that *any* emphasized dynamic in the Soul/birth chart simply reflects the outcome of experiences and choices made therein, relative to intention, relative to evolutionary capacity, and that the existing dynamics are exactly what the Soul needs for continuing on with its evolutionary growth. (Stacie)

Determining the past evolutionary dynamics
In interpreting a chart, start with Pluto, the underlying evolutionary desires, before jumping further to the Nodes and other factors. In order to have a foundation and a clearer understanding it is best to follow these simple rules. Regarding Pluto, the Soul, what kind of desire nature lead to the present, via the past? Then and only then can you consider how it manifested via what kind of egocentric nature the Soul created (South Node). So how was this done? From there the ruler of the South Node as the facilitator of that kind of egocentric consciousness via which the Soul operated. These are the steps to uncover the secret of the Soul – that's the miracle of EA – it is able to uncover that. Follow this order in chart interpretation and you'll get closer to the whole picture. Then once you have determined at least the major evolutionary dynamics of the past – where the Soul actually comes from – you will understand more clearly the "whys" of the current evolutionary lessons, symbolized by Pluto's polarity and the North Node and then the North Node's ruler. Only in this way can you understand why, for example, any planet may conjunct the North Node and for what reason. The reason for any present condition always lies in the past. Without understanding that past we don't understand the present and that may lead to misunderstanding and misinterpretation. The future of course is just as much connected to the present (and the choices the Soul makes) as the present is to the past. It is all continuous and interconnected – one step leads to the next. (Lia)

Past, present, future orientations of a planet
[Example: Venus] The present life Venus is conditioned by all the past "self and other" relationship tendencies and patterns that have preceded it. The South Node of Venus represents directly the way the Venus functions were handled in the past. The South Node of the Moon represents the Soul's past personality structures and emotional habits/patterns. Both of these are alive within the present life Venus function, subconsciously coloring it. Yet that Venus also contains the possibility of changing the past, in the present moment (the only moment in which anything can be changed). The intended directions for that Venus to evolve are indicated in the North Node of Venus, the Lunar North Node ruler, the Lunar North Node, and the Polarity Point of Pluto, in that order, from top to bottom. We try to mentally separate the past and the present and the future, to see them as different things. But in reality it's all the same, and it can't be separated. That is why EA says you work the North Node, learn new ways of doing things, and then evolve your South Node function by integrating these new ways into your old ways of doing the South Node. The end result is the entire structure, Soul and personality, evolve. We can't really separate our internal Venus functions from our Mars functions, from our Moon functions, from our Saturn functions. We are complex beings that have all of these inner drives, desires, motivations, orientations. In reality they are all mixed together within us. We use astrology to gain objectivity by assigning this function to this planet and that function to that planet, but past a certain point those are constructs, not complete reality. In reality we are the sum total of all of them, and that includes our past and future also. EVERYTHING has something to do with the past. The imprint of the past is contained within the present Venus and every other planet too. (Steve)

House system and planetary method of chart interpretation
Both systems are founded upon the Pluto methodology. The house system analyzes the specific and individualized application, or expression, of the houses in a birth chart by analyzing the planetary rulers of the sign on each house cusp. The planetary method is a linear, step by step process in which a specific order, or sequence, is followed, based on all the planets in the birth chart. When the two methods are used in combination, we arrive at an incredibly in-depth interpretation of any birth chart. (Deva)
[For further information, see chapter 8, *Pluto and Your Karmic Mission* by Deva Green.]

Repeating themes
First, combine both the house method and the method of planetary interpretation. From each method you will have specific information about all of the relevant points in the chart. Then examine all the information you've gathered through those methods, looking specifically for REPEATING THEMES. It is through focusing on the repeating themes in any chart that the story reflected in that chart will begin to reveal itself. (Stacie)

Individualized context
To understand any one symbol in a birth chart one must understand the totality of that birth chart in order to understand the individual context that then allows for an understanding of any one symbol within it. One cannot make generalized statements about any one symbol that applies to all. The individual context is essential to understanding anything, and that starts with the EA paradigm itself, the evolutionary condition of the Soul, and the socio-cultural place of birth. (Rad)

Understanding the entire context of the chart
In order to understand any one symbol in a birth chart, or synastry charts, one must understand the entire context of the whole chart(s) first. If I take one ingredient out of a pie that has 20, it would be impossible for me to know what that pie actually is. The same principle applies to astrological charts. (Rad)

Inductive/deductive knowledge
With the revelation of repeating themes, it is here that the transition from deductive logic to inductive understanding will occur. The more regularly you put this exercise into practice, the more quickly this shift will occur until it eventually becomes automatic. It is not a development you want to rush. It is important to allow this to happen in its own natural time, because your deductive efforts will serve as your long term foundation. Once the inductive orientation becomes relatively automatic, the foundation established through the deductive development will make a real difference in the accuracy of the inductive information that comes to you in terms of the big picture you will see. (Stacie)

Intuition and integrity
Think of it this way. Inductive knowledge is as easy to misinterpret as it is to mix up facts and data. If you get your facts solid in the beginning, the information that will be supplied to your intuition from that point on will be grounded and will have solid integrity, which of course will minimize errors in grasping the chart in total. The other thing to do is be aware of any expectations you may have toward your own process. (Stacie)

True EA work is guided by Spirit
True EA work is guided by Spirit. If your intent is to understand the Soul as deeply as you can such that you can offer the messages they are ready and needing to hear, those messages will be made known to you from within. This is a timeless phenomenon. The understanding you are meant to have with any given chart will come to you at the moment it is needed, and that is something that is best embraced by trust in the inner teacher. (Stacie)

How to Transcend Astrological Influences by Paramhansa Yogananda
Astrology is a very deep subject, but most people consider it a kind of superstitious guide to material progress. If you use astrology only for guidance in material matters, you will be doing its teachings an injustice. Astrology is too vast, both mathematically and philosophically, to be rightly grasped except by people of profound understanding. In ancient times, astrology was seen primarily as a guide to spiritual development. To use astrology for material purposes was considered a lower application of what is essentially a divine science. Astrology is the study of man's response to planetary stimuli. All parts of creation are linked together and interchange their influences. No matter what your environment, the surrounding rays of the earth and universe will have an impact upon you. Astrology was intended to assist you on your inner journey, by helping you become more aware of the interrelationships between the objective universe and the inner aspects of yourself. The relation of the stars to the human body and mind is very subtle. There is a correlation between the six centers (chakras) in the spine, which become twelve by polarity, and the twelve signs of the zodiac. Millions of volts of electrical current are lodged in these spinal centers. If your body and your mind are very strong, you will be impervious to the evil vibrations from the stars when they begin to shed their rays upon you. But if your body and mind are weak through transgressions of wrong eating, wrong thinking, bad character, and bad company, then the stellar rays will have the power to affect you.

How the stars affect us The stars influence your life only in accordance with patterns that you yourself established in the past. A child is born on that day and at that hour when the celestial rays are in mathematical harmony with his individual karma (past actions). The astrological configurations serve only as symbols of karmic influences, which you have set into motion in the past. The stars and planets themselves can no more choose how they will affect you than you can select your own karmic destiny. The message boldly blazoned across the heavens at the moment of birth was not meant to emphasize fate, the result of past good and evil, but to arouse your will to escape from this universal bondage. What you have done, you can undo. You can overcome whatever effects are now prevalent in your life because you created them by your own actions in the first place, and because you have inner spiritual resources which are not subject to planetary pressure. The best way, therefore, to improve your lot is deliberately to act in such a way as to counteract the evil effects of past deeds. Especially if this course of action springs from inner attunement with God, or is adopted under the wise guidance of one who knows God, it will serve as an antidote to all baneful actions of the past.

Avoid passive dependence on astrology Superstition means to seek guidance from effects, in ignorance of their causes. Many people look to the heavens for signs instead of choosing the wiser path of seeking guidance in their Souls, from God. Some people refuse to do anything for themselves until the planetary positions are favorable. While it is not unwise to initiate worthwhile undertakings at astrologically auspicious times, it merely affirms your passive dependence on fate to wait for a shift in the planets' positions before making important changes in your life. Anything you do with deep faith in God will blossom under better influences than you could hope to find by consulting the heavens for favorable aspects. Do not wait for changes in astrological influences to change your destiny. Look, rather, to Him who made the heavens and the earth and who alone can grant you eternal freedom. The lawful effects of your karma may seem irrevocable, but the effects of past actions can be changed by seeking God. Unless you remember that, you cannot spiritualize astrology.

How to spiritualize astrology While studying astrology in a reasonable way, you must always remember that God's influence is the supreme influence. All human ills arise from some transgression of universal law. The scriptures point out that man must satisfy the laws of nature, while not discrediting the divine omnipotence. You should always say, "Lord, I trust in Thee, and know Thou canst help me, but I too will do my best to undo any wrong I have done." You have been given the free choice and intelligence, as a child of God, to surmount the difficulties of life. You are made in the image of God, not in the image of the stars. Strive unceasingly, from a center of inner calmness, to surmount every material, mental, and spiritual difficulty. Cooperate with His will by offering up to Him all the strength of your human will. If you can hold onto your happiness during all the difficulties in your life, then you will begin to rise above the influence of the stars. If you can retain your smile in spite of repeated challenges, that is a sign of the awakening of the consciousness of divinity within you. Through all such actions, you are changing your body and mind and how they are affecting the twelve centers in your spine. As a result of these changes, the stars will begin to smile upon you. By communing with God, you will reinforce the power of the twelve spinal centers, which will then act in cooperation with the twelve signs of the zodiac. The deeper your communion with God, the more you will automatically harmonize the influences of all planetary forces and transcend the evil effects of the powerful, but distant, planets. In these ways, you can spiritualize astrology. Seek help, therefore, not from the stars and planets, but from Almighty God. God is harmony; and if you attune yourself to Him, you will never perform any action amiss. Your activities will be correctly and naturally timed to accord with astrological law. After deep prayer and meditation you are in touch with His divine consciousness; there is no greater power than that inward protection. By plunging deeply into your own divine nature, you will discover those deeper levels within yourself that enable you to rise above all karmic realities.

The masters go beyond astrology Some people study astrology to ascertain the influence of their karma through the medium of planets, thus trying to counteract evil influences by astrological foreknowledge. But the great masters go beyond astrology. The man of realization does not choose any auspicious hour to perform noble deeds or initiate new wholesome ventures. He acts, moves, and sleeps under the one influence of God. He consults God instead of the stars for guidance. Although there is a certain vibratory influence of stars upon all human lives, a man of infinite will power tuned in with God, uses his free will to change his circumstances. He marches on, influenced only by the Sun of all Suns, the Almighty Spirit. To him, from the depths of his determination and faith, all things are possible. He burns the seeds of difficulties in the fire of wisdom, consults only God for guidance, and performs all of his actions according to divine guidance. Superstitious awe of astrology makes one an automaton, slavishly dependent on mechanical guidance. The wise man defeats his planets – which is to say, his past – by transferring his allegiance from the creation to the Creator. The more he realizes his unity with Spirit, the less he can be dominated by matter. The Soul is ever-free; it is deathless because birthless. It cannot be regimented by stars. If you live by astrology or anything else you will be bound by it. Depend wholly and solely on God. Live by God alone. Then nothing can hurt you.

Follow the way to inner freedom In karma's realm, karma rules supreme. Yet all human beings have the power to withdraw to another realm altogether. You cannot change the outer astrological influences, but you can do a great deal to change the way you receive them, inwardly. Instead of accepting fatalistically the decrees of karma, follow the inner way to freedom. Meditate daily. Commune deeply with God. Learn from Him, through the silent voice of intuition, the way out of Soul-degrading serfdom to bad habits. Ultimately, by ever deeper meditation, you will reach a point where you receive your influences from God alone.

Porphyry house system

The Porphyry house system is the preferred system for Evolutionary Astrology because it reflects the law of the trinity. The prime number in this system is 3. It was developed by a Christian mystic named Porphyry in the 4th Century AD. (Rad)

The recommended house system for EA is Porphyry. Porphyry is a very old house system that takes the space within each of the four quadrants and divides it into three equal sections. '3' is very important in EA, representing the trinity of past, present, and future, the essence of the Soul's evolutionary journey. (Steve)

Wolf said that he tried the various house systems out. He then settled on the Porphyry house system by using the astrological necessity of correlation and observation. He also said that he finally settled on it, not only because of trial and error, but also because of its evolutionary nature: meaning the root number used in its division is THREE. He said in the 4th century there was a Christian mystic named Porphyry who came up with this system. (Rad)

Correlation

A correspondence or connection between things.

True Nodes, Mean Nodes
EA uses the True Node, not Mean Node. (Rad)

EA astrologers have been taught to use True Nodes, as that is what actually exists in the sky. (Steve)

Mean is a mathematical smoothing of the actual movement of the Nodes, which is retrograde 90% of the time and direct 10% of the time. In EA we use True Nodes, because this is the actual movement of the Nodes. Mean is a mathematical abstraction that never exists in the sky. Yet it is frequently used in conventional astrology. (Steve)

Synthesizing the layers
In EA analysis the house always comes first as the foundation for any given symbol, and then relative to that archetypal foundation all is then added or built upon that foundation. (Rad)

In EA we are taught to start with the house, this representing the deepest expression of the energies in that part of the chart. Example: 10th house is inherently Saturnian so anything in the 10th house will operate in a Saturnian way. The sign on the house cusp represents the next level up. The art of EA is to synthesize how the natural house energy filtered through a layer of the sign on the cusp operates. If Pluto is in that house, add in another layer. What does the natural house energy filtered through a layer of the sign on the cusp expressing itself in a Scorpionic (Pluto) way operate like? Starting with the evolutionary state, the social conditioning patterns, and the evolutionary signature (Pluto, nodes, nodal rulers), you quickly have a detailed picture of how that Soul/ego is structured, from the core out. (Steve)

House, sign and planet = one archetype
In EA we look at houses, signs, and planets as the same – 1st house, Aries, Mars all the same. The Soul combines them in different ways to deliver the important messages to itself through the vehicle of you, in more than one way. It's fine while learning EA to concentrate on just the houses or signs as long as you keep in mind they are all really the same. There's only so much the brain can assimilate at once, and segmenting it is a valid approach for some students. (Steve)

Facilitator/ruler
"The ruler facilitating the process" applies to all Nodes in all charts. Another description of facilitating the process is "actualizing itself through." (Steve)

Ruler of Pluto polarity point
Although Wolf did not write about the planetary ruler of the polarity point for Pluto he did teach it for many years in his lectures. Just like the Nodes have their planetary rulers, by house and sign, that operate as the facilitators to the actualization of the Nodes themselves, so too with the location of the planetary ruler of Pluto's polarity point. (Rad)

Soul correlates to Pluto, not Neptune
EA and its paradigm symbolizes the individual journey of the Soul through time as it evolves back to its Source: God/ess. Even though Neptune symbolizes that Source it does not symbolize or reflect the individual journey of the Soul itself. EA is about understanding each individual Soul as it actually is: where it has been and why, where it is now and why, and where it is headed and why. The Soul correlates to Pluto. Neptune does not. (Rad)

Progression of Pluto's evolution through the houses
Pluto does NOT naturally evolve in progression through lifetimes from, example, the 10th house to an 11th house, then a 12th house, etc. (Rad)

Sun
The Sun is the current life integration point for the entire evolutionary paradigm in each chart. It gives it purpose, meaning, and the way of ACTUALIZING those intentions. (Rad)

Sun, polarity point?
The Sun has no polarity point. All is integrated relative to its sign and house in the birth chart. It does not evolve in the same way as all the other factors in the birth chart. The Sun can evolve from within the total archetypal spectrum of the sign and house that it is in natally as the Soul itself evolves relative to its intentions in any given life. (Rad)

Mars
Mars, Aries, the 1st house, and the Nodes of Mars all correlate to how the desires that emanate from the Soul are instinctually acted out. [This does not include cardinal signs, planets at early cardinal degrees, or conjunctions in the chart]. (Rad)

Mars/Pluto phase – subsidiary/primary lives

The Mars/Pluto phase in a subsidiary life is a life in which the Soul is working out its intentions in a variety of indirect ways. (Cat) [Mars in aspect to other planets is the "variety of indirect ways" that the Soul is currently working out its desires through Mars...] This is analogous to entering a room and seeing another door on the opposite side of that room, yet to get to that door there is a variety of debris that must be removed before the door can be gotten to, and then walked through. In a primary life, it would mean entering that same room, seeing that door on the other side, and moving directly towards it without any debris being in that room to move through. (Rad)

Generational planets

Jeffrey used to teach, especially relevant for outer planets, is that the sign of the planet is a generational signature. Since the nature of separating desires is to individuate ourselves from the generation, to discover our own uniqueness, the house the planet is in is how we individuate the generational impulse. Thus that is analyzed before the generational impulse (the sign Pluto is in) because that is how I am going to actualize, manifest that generational impulse. That is also the intent of the Pluto polarity point, to individuate myself from the generational impulse. (Steve)

Understanding the individual context within a chart

Each Soul is its own individual context through which to understand the nature of any given aspect within the natal chart. As a result, there is no one answer to any given aspect when one remembers that archetypes correlate to an entire spectrum that exists within an archetype. Understanding the individual context thus allows the EA astrologer to know exactly where any given Soul is within the total spectrum of specific archetypes. When this is then properly understood then knowing how to proceed in evolutionary terms simply occurs. (Rad)

In EA we never assume anything about any given Soul. The EA of Jeffrey Wolf Green developed a very specific paradigm through which to understand the evolutionary nature, and its ongoing evolution, of any given Soul. Each Soul has its own individual context that has been created by the desires within it that have been acted upon that then allows for the understanding of the uniqueness of each and every Soul being considered by the EA astrologer. There are so many possible EA signatures, relative to this paradigm, that it is necessary, essential, to study and understand this paradigm. (Rad)

Soul's prior lives

The Soul of course contains all the prior lives that it has ever lived. However, in any given life, the Soul does indeed only draw upon those prior lives which are directly linked to the current and ongoing evolutionary purposes that it has. The South Node of Pluto by house and sign does not correlate to ALL of the Soul's prior lives. A total and comprehensive understanding of the entire chart which would include the employment of geodetic equivalents which are linked to the Ages and their sub-ages would be necessary in order to understand where any given Soul was during the [patriarchal] transition.

(Q) Would the South Node of Pluto be the ultimate bottom line in which the house would correlate to a deeper level of unconscious security patterns than that of the natal Pluto?

(A) No. It would be equal to the natal Pluto itself. (Rad)

Asking "Why?"

To step back and objectify for oneself just why one needed to create whatever trauma [or experience] in the first place. This leads to self-knowledge of a liberating nature, and that knowledge can then be used to radically change oneself. (Rad)

One of the great dimensions of Evolutionary Astrology is to be able to answer the question WHY. So much of astrology is really a DESCRIPTIVE astrology without providing any insights into the why of anything. Describing something is very different than understanding something. (Rad)

The only reason why anyone would ever get sick, is the same reason why anyone would ever be born, die, feel pain, laugh, etc. Sickness, dis-ease etc. only exist as a part of the maya of this reality that we created for our evolution. A Soul never gets sick – at the core, it is always, only in a state of DESIRE. The nature of that desire is what manifests the physical reality that it will experience. When a Soul experiences anything at all – it can ask, in neutrality, "why?" I feel that "why" can take a Soul as far as it wants to go. Now I get why JWG emphasizes that Pluto folks ask "why" about everything "why life, why death" – those are really good questions. (Ari)

One size does not fit all

[Example: Cancer/Capricorn] The 4th house, Cancer, Moon will correlate to the parental figure – mother OR father – who predominantly served in the role of nurturing emotional security, emotional bonding/proximity, emotional/personal relating, etc. in the upbringing. 10th house, Saturn, Capricorn correlates to the parental figure – mother or father – who most reflected the role of authority, sociological responsibility, emulation of emotional maturity in the context of relating, etc. Traditionally the 4th house has been considered to represent the mother and the 10th house the father. But as we know, one size does not fit all. Just because a woman's physiology permits her to give birth to a baby does not mean that her inner nature is going to be oriented to emotional bonding, nurturing, etc. over expressing/actualizing a role of authority, emotional maturation, sociological focus, etc. within the family structure. And of course, vice versa for males. Both roles archetypically serve a vital function in the imprinting and ongoing development of our consciousness, and those roles are fully interchangeable – so as we like to say around here, observation/ correlation. (Stacie)

Chart weighted toward growth
The great gift with a chart heavily weighted towards growth is there is nothing you have to do to relinquish control. Life (Pluto) will simply make it impossible at key times for anything else to occur. Like good little humans we often resist until the bitter end, but in the end whatever is being resisted is removed from the life (Pluto) and the intention of relinquishing control is accomplished. And here you thought you were having a hard life – it's all been for your benefit, to accomplish the Soul's evolutionary intentions. That is why, once we realize this, we learn to try to cooperate with, rather than resist, the intentions, as they appear in our life as we move along. Even when they are difficult or painful. That helps accelerate the process of relinquishing control, once we have learned to trust that it is for our benefit, it is on our side, it is not there to try to mess up our lives no matter what it may feel like. (Steve)

Changing habits
The first step in changing a behavior is becoming aware you are in it – because then when you find yourself going into that pattern again, you can say, "wait, here I am in this pattern again," and make a different choice. It literally is changing an old habit. Like changing any habit, it takes time, effort, determination. These habits go straight to the Soul, so they are even more entrenched. But the point is YOU CAN CHANGE THEM, you are not trapped, no matter how deep they appear to be. *Desire* is the root determinant – you make up your mind you are going to change. Even when you catch yourself making the same choice in a situation where you could have made a new choice, you do not get down on yourself, you simply reaffirm that you are in the process of changing a deep pattern, and you keep at it. Step by step, inch by inch. Through determination you move forward. Because it's aligned to the evolutionary intentions, there are a lot of unseen forces at work to assist your moving in these directions.

Changing habits – example 10th house Pluto
Another issue is, at times you simply are going to feel overwhelmed with change, and unable to move forward at that moment. This too is part of the process. Especially with [example: 10th house Pluto], there needs to be an honoring of your emotional states, and their limitations. You cannot force your way through the process, cannot have complete control over it. It takes on a life of its own, over time, becomes the basis of new habits is a new way of living and of looking at life. There are moments, times, when you NEED to go back to the safety of the known, if only for a short while, just to keep yourself sane. This is okay and necessary – just do it consciously – "I need to do this right now," and remain aware when it is time to get back to moving forward again. In a sense this process is like growing a new baby in your womb (4th house PPP) that gradually takes on a life of its own. In this case that new baby will gradually replace your old existing sense of who you are altogether. It will integrate and incorporate these new perspectives, ways, into the totality of your own self-image (4th house). Words like organic, holistic, inclusive – it is a natural process that gradually engulfs you.

Changing habits through the PPP, North Node, and North Node ruler
Through this process the intentions of the PPP, the North Node, the North Node ruler simply unfold, because at the baseline you have inwardly committed yourself to the evolutionary intentions. You start the process by discerning what the chart symbols mean, what areas of life they reference, but as you increasingly move into that process as a way of life, it just unfolds by itself. This all starts by embracing the process in the first place and saying "yes" to it. The rest just happens. (Steve)

Polarity points of the planets
The nature of Life is that it evolves. It is ingrained. The way that life evolves is by going to its polarity point. It is not Pluto alone that has a polarity point. In his Pluto Vol. 2 Relationships book, Jeffrey detailed in the chapters about Mars and Venus what moving towards the polarity of the sign that Mars and Venus are in looks like. The same principle applies to all the planets and symbols in our charts. It's just the way life works. If it makes more sense to you, you could visualize it as it is the polarity point that is moving forward through the zodiac over time in its evolutionary track. Since the planet must be 180 degrees apart from its polarity point, the planet is getting dragged forward by its advancing polarity point. This is also indicated in progressed charts, which show how the evolutionary intentions are unfolding OVER TIME. Thus the polarity point progresses also.

It does come down to the desire nature. At a certain point we get sick of something we previously loved. The feeling becomes, "been there done that." This too is part of how life is constructed. (The EA material on the Cycles of Phases and Aspects is very relevant to this.) The Soul is not working on only one separating desire in a lifetime. The chart is a map of our desire nature. When you see grand crosses or a lot of squares or oppositions or a number of skipped steps, you are typically looking at the map of a Soul with conflicting simultaneous desires, wanting to go in multiple incompatible directions at the same time. The Pluto polarity point is the most significant polarity point as it tracks the evolution of the Soul itself. (Steve)

Wolf taught in the school that every sign carries its polarity – or ELEMENTS of its polarity – within it. What we may object to MOST in our lives will reveal itself THROUGH the polarity sign of whatever planet we consider in its natal position in our chart. An example I remember clearly was a former astrology teacher who was an Aquarius, and she had an incredible dislike for Leos. She was the only one who couldn't see how she herself was manifesting the Leo archetype, because she was too busy telling us that Aquarius was the BEST sign! (Adina)

Natural polarities

All signs have their natural polarity within them. And it is this inner polarity within the sign that allows for an evolution to occur within that sign. Like we can have the Pluto in Libra on the North Node of Libra and there is no polarity to develop there, yet within Libra there is its natural polarity: Aries. In NO conditions within the birth chart does any polarity point apply other than the polarity point of Pluto that needs to be consciously embraced, desire, for the evolution of the Soul to continue. And the one exception to that as Wolf taught is when the natal Pluto is conjunct the North Node. Even then there is a natural polarity within the sign that Pluto is in natally that NATURALLY is evolved towards via the Natural Law of polarities. And it is this natural polarity within the sign of a natal Pluto that then correlates to the evolution of an entire generation on Earth, and why any given generation is on Earth at any point in time.

Every sign has a natural polarity within it that serves as the evolution within that sign because of its natural polarity. Thus, as the Soul evolves, makes a choice to evolve, which is symbolized by its opposite house and sign, and in the case of Pluto conjunct the North Node, by sign, and the location of the planetary ruler of that North Node, the aspects that it is making, this then CAUSES the rest of the entire birth chart to also evolve. It's automatic. So all those natural polarities that exist within the signs that the planets are in, in any birth chart, automatically are evolved towards. It is a function of evolution. The degree of evolution is dependent of course on the choices that the Soul makes in any given life relative to its core evolutionary signature which is symbolized by natal Pluto, the South Node and its planetary ruler, the polarity point of Pluto, and the North Node and its planetary ruler.

Every natal planet in a sign also has a natural polarity point by house, ie Mars in Scorpio in the 7th house would have a natural polarity of not only Taurus within Scorpio, but the 1st house as the polarity to the 7th. These natural polarity points by house are also automatically evolved towards once the Soul has made a choice to evolve which, again, is symbolized by the main EA paradigm. It is because these natural polarities within the signs and houses that naturally evolve, once the Soul has made a choice to evolve, that JWG never really taught about them. He did so because they do in fact naturally evolve in this way. He did this intentionally so as not to create such an overwhelming amount of evolutionary procedures that could potentially confuse students, but of course overwhelm any given client. It is enough to know the core EA paradigm, how it works, and how to apply it to one's life. The rest of these natural evolutionary points take care of themselves. Over his long career JWG only once, to my knowledge, taught about these other polarity points of the planets, and the houses they are in. And that is in a long workshop he held in Holland called "From Karma to Dharma." (Rad)

Natural polarities – retrograde planets

Wolf taught that every sign has its natural polarity WITHIN IT. Those natural inner polarity points of any sign evolve within the context of the sign as the ongoing evolutionary journey of the Soul occurs. IT JUST NATURALLY HAPPENS. When a planet is retrograde in a sign Wolf taught that such a Soul has focused, prior to the current life, upon that inner polarity of the sign in order to actualize the archetype of the planet that is in that sign. So, for example, if Mars is retrograde in Libra this would mean that the Soul has desired, focused, on evolving the Mars archetype within the natural Aries polarity that exists relative to Libra. Thus, that Mars archetype in Libra is essentially actualizing the whole of the Libra archetype through its natural polarity: Aries. And this polarity would then be the lead point of how the Mars in Libra entered into, the orientation to, relationships. If Mars were not retrograde then the Mars in Libra would enter relationships, the orientation to, in the typical Libra way: co-dependent. This lead point would then be progressively evolved towards the natural polarity of Aries as the Soul's life unfolded over an entire lifetime. (Rad)

Paradoxical charts

The first thing to do is to understand why this paradoxical pattern has been determined by the Soul in the first place. In general when the chart is opposite, ie Libra ascendant, resulting house cusps all being in opposition to their natural placements, the individual must learn how to integrate and synthesize the oppositional nature of their own inner conflicts, ie Libra Ascendant has a primary desire to complete itself in relationship yet at the same time just as strong a desire for almost total freedom and independence. So the question becomes why is this from an evolutionary point of view? All too often such a signature means that in prior times, the most recent prior lives, the person had been fitting themselves into other people's reality, to live through them or others, to always give without a lot of receiving, to be so highly attuned to other people's needs that they lost sight of their own. So when that has been the case the meaning of the paradoxical symbols this time correlates to learning how to let others FIT THEIR REALITY versus the other way around. (JWG)

The root cause of everything is desire. Souls create human forms for themselves to experience and work through their desires. In most cases the cause of paradoxical charts is going to boil down to having conflicting desires within the Soul itself, and by extension, in the human form. I refer to it as an intense desire to want it to be Summer and Winter, or day and night, or male and female, or married and single, at the same time. Obviously in earth reality that is not going to occur. And yet the desire for it to occur, in a paradoxical chart, exists. When Pluto is involved it becomes compulsive. The Soul is trying to teach itself something by setting up this situation. What the something is will be unique to each Soul. But as general themes they can include (among many others) things like coming face to face with the inherent limits (Pluto) in the human form; learning to accept them and to develop strategies to deal with the desire for two simultaneous opposites that is impossible to fulfill since both can never simultaneously occur. We can learn to experience one of the opposites some of the time and the others at other times – having to accept that this is as good as it can get in human form on Earth as far as experiencing simultaneous opposing desires.

EA looks at the house position of any planet, not just Pluto, first. Because the house energies are the core bottom line energy for life realms ruled by that house. Whether or not there are planets in the house, everyone has a 3rd house or 8th house, etc. and those energies affect our human lives, planet or no planet. The way EA looks at it, the sign on the house cusp, or the planets within the house, represent a coating or veneer over the house energy. That is, anything related to the 1st house will always have an Aries energy. If I have Sagittarius on the 1st house cusp, it is Aries energy filtered through Sagittarius – there is a de facto trine in that set-up. But what if I have Pisces on the 1st house? Aries energy filtered through Pisces is not an easy fit. Why would a Soul set that situation up for itself?

If I have Pluto in Sagittarius in the 3rd house, to give an example, I have a de facto Pluto in Gemini, and yet the opposing Sagittarius energies are also part of the filter. That is a de facto opposition. So we have to look at what we know about the nature of oppositions – the why behind them. We are dealing with Libra-like stuff here, opposition – duality and the need to learn to synthesize opposites, to move from the extremes of swinging from one pole to the other, to develop moderation and cohesiveness (balance), to understand the value that both sides of that seeming paradox add to the process. Libra – to learn to listen deeply to the gifts both opposites bring to the totality – the relativity of all things on one hand – Gemini – and seeing from the top down, the whole, the inherent simplicity behind the apparent diversity – Sagittarius. (Steve)

Paradoxes in the psyche are a crucible for growth. I see Pluto's placement in Libra in the 1st house for example as an inherent conflict between say, war and peace, or the expression of personal will vs cooperation, self vs others. The Soul has experienced extremities of both and holds that external conflict now, internally – so as to find a third way – an integration. A way to frame a paradoxical signature in a chart is to understand that what might normally be experienced as an external conflict is internalized in the makeup of the psyche or Soul (especially when it is Pluto) depending upon what the signature is. Another example might be Pluto in Cancer in the 10th.

Most of us experience the duality or polarity of male-ness and female-ness, we see it all around us and engage in melding these polar opposites often by entering into relationship with them, being parented by them (mother and father) or by inner exploration of our own (anima/animus). Bringing a resolution to the intrinsic polarity of male and female may simply not be a pressing evolutionary intention. BUT the person with this signature as a paradox already has that conflict internalized. It then becomes a personal need, an evolutionary drive to reconcile something about the opposite archetypes within oneself. Many Libra ascendant charts are paradoxical charts. Ever wonder why? Libra itself being an archetype of extremity, polarity, splitting to find balance, internal conflict. (Patricia)

What I intuitively understand, in terms of determining "why" a chart will manifest in such a paradoxical way, is to simply look at where the planetary energies manifest themselves based on the karmic signatures of the chart. Combined, and understood within the complete EA paradigm, along with EA state, we can understand the specific cause for the paradox. (Ari)

Paradoxical chart – Lunar Nodes example

In the case of the South Node and North Node being in a paradoxical sign/house combo, there are still two different nodal rulers somewhere in the chart – one which points to the past and one which points to the future. In combination with Pluto and its polarity point, this is how we can ultimately understand the story of WHY the paradoxical chart to begin with. (Ari)

Paradoxical chart – example

A chart where house rulers are in the signs that are opposite to the natural rulers of those houses. The general rule of thumb is to help the person understand what the nature and causes are of the underlying paradoxes within them, and then to help them determine a way of resolving those paradoxes. Simple example: Pluto in Leo in the 11th house, South Node Cancer in the 10th, North Node Capricorn in the 4th, ruler of South Node Moon in Scorpio 2nd, ruler of North Node Saturn in Scorpio 2nd in the chart: deep, natural fear of loss and abandonment which has happened in many lives through misapplication of trust which, in turn, has caused the individual to emotionally and psychologically isolate themselves from others as a way of compensating for that, which in turn has caused them to feel very alone within the world, which then causes a deep need to connect with and/or be in at least one committed relationship of like mind, yet not knowing how to get there or make that happen because of the fears of abandonment, etc. A paradox.

The resolution in this case is to choose another who is not only of like mind, but one who is utterly self-reliant at the POINT OF ATTRACTION. The one who is self-reliant, self-empowered, etc. will not have a double agenda which could lead to a recreation of the past life dynamics leading to another misapplication of the trust which then leads to being used all over again. The underlying nature and causes of the paradox can be caused by any number of reasons. Each chart has its own unique signature. In the case of charts that do symbolize the core of paradoxes the symbols, in each chart, are the causes of those paradoxes. (Rad)

Same house, sign and planet combinations (eg Jupiter in Sagittarius in the 9th house)

I'll share what feel intuitive to me about this question. Something to think about: Jeff Green has taught that opposite sign house combinations are naturally paradoxical (like Gemini on the 9th) since it is a synthesis of two polar archetypes. It thus symbolizes the need for the Soul to learn balance in the current life. It has a very Libra energy to it. In the same way I think of same house sign combinations (Sagittarius on the 9th) as being very emphasized and single focused. All the meaning of Sagittarius would apply in a more direct way. It has a very Aries energy to it. Why is it that way? We'd really have to look at the chart and start with the core EA paradigm. It can mean many things, but the implication of it being very direct is clear. The strong focus of any archetype ultimately symbolizes something within the Soul – and there is a reason for it. Another thing to think about to exemplify this in a tangible way. Think of anyone you know who is a Leo Sun. Without intellectualizing it, can you see how they ARE a Leo? And of course there are many ways to be a Leo. That right there is a double Leo signature – and it would be more Leo'esqu if their Sun was in the 5th house. Same for Pluto in the 8th house for example. I know at least a few Pluto in Scorpio in the 8th house Souls. There are layers upon layers of meaning in that signature, but it is different for each Soul. Lastly I feel called to share with you that for me, the more information I receive from my clients the better I am able to interpret their charts as it illuminates the real living life context for the signatures. My intuition kicks in and I tend to see a lot more of the Soul story through the chart in ways that my linear mind simply would not have been able to grasp on its own. (Ari)

I would see the triple combination of an archetype as a triple-whammy – meaning that the triple dose of that archetype makes it very highly emphasized – perhaps correlating to natural gifts in that archetype. Using the example of Jupiter in Sagittarius in the 9th house (and reading that within the entire EA paradigm of the chart) one can look to see (or ask) if the client has a natural affinity with Natural Laws? Does the Soul feel quite alienated from others and their society in general? Could the Soul be a natural teacher type? A Daemon Soul? Questions like that. (Linda)

Soul playing out both sides of a dynamic

In EA we never assume anything about any given Soul. The EA of Jeffrey Wolf Green developed a very specific paradigm through which to understand the evolutionary nature, and its ongoing evolution, of any given Soul. Each Soul has its own individual context that has been created by the desires with it that have been acted upon that then allows for the understanding of the uniqueness of each and every Soul being considered by the EA astrologer. It is in the understanding of this specific EA paradigm in which the EA astrologer can then know and understand when any given Soul have played out both sides of any given coin. There are so many possible EA signatures, relative to this paradigm, that it is necessary, essential, to study and understand this paradigm in order to know who is who. (Rad)

Hiding signature

A phenomena called masking or hiding – a Soul that creates an outer reality in which it operates, and has itself convinced it is, at a level below its actual state of Spiritual evolution. (This is often associated with the Pisces archetype – hiding.) Reasons for this can vary but quite commonly include intense traumas that have occurred in past lives relative to its actual state of Spiritual awareness, it being perceived as different, outside the mainstream, challenging or threatening to the existing order. And in the present life that Soul says to itself, "who needs more of that? I'm just going to act like I'm 'supposed to,' and convince myself that I'm not really as different as I feel I am." And it will live that way, perhaps for a really long time. Such Souls are identified when doing readings for them because on the outside they are living very conventional lives, yet the degree of depth and insight they exhibit goes well beyond the nature of the outer life, even the physical appearance – dress, manner of speaking, etc., they have adopted. (Steve)

Planet near a house cusp

When one has an accurate birth time, the natal chart is a map of the present evolutionary condition and intentions of that Soul. All planet locations in the chart are in essence selected by the Soul, Pluto, as they reflect (as in, indicate) where that Soul is at, where it left off in the previous life, where it intends to go in this life. When a planet is near the beginning or end of a house it means that a new phase of evolution, relative to the archetypes of that planet and house, is at hand. When it is near the beginning, that new phase has just begun. When it is near the end it is approaching culmination. It all comes down to, we are where we are. We are not where we wish to be, no matter how strongly we desire or even believe we are there. We are where we are. And it is through accepting and embracing *where we are* that we best speed up the process of becoming what we wish to be. Again, being near the end of something is not the same as having completed it, no matter how much we yearn to be done with it and on with the next thing. The point to remember is *we are where we are*. That is what the birth chart indicates. Whether we want to believe what it is telling us is another matter altogether! (Steve)

Unaspected planets
A planet with no aspects to it operates in a Uranian like way: meaning it is free to act in the ways, manifest in the ways, that it feels drawn to act and manifest that is not being 'conditioned' by any other planet(s) by way of no aspects to them. Thus, such a planet can act to help a Soul accelerate its evolutionary journey because it is operating as an independent evolutionary force that is not bound by any other planet, archetype. Thus, it serves as a 'liberating' archetype from existing conditions within the Soul. From the point of view of EA it is then necessary to determine why the Soul has chosen to be born with a planet that has no other aspects to other planets. There is always a reason for anything. "Unaspected" means no aspects whatsoever. Which is why such a thing is very rare. It is the same idea as a 'void of course' Moon. (Rad)

Planets in opposition
Any planets in opposition correlate with the evolutionary need to throw off something, to oppose it, in order for evolution to proceed via those dynamics. (Rad)

Planet conjunct house cusp – mutation of archetypes
[Example: Planet conjunct a non-angular house cusp.] The individual will exhibit psychological/behavioral dynamics of both of the archetypes. In the case where the planet is before the actual house cusp in question the bottom line in those dynamics will be the actual house that the planet is in while moving towards the archetypal dynamics of the house that it is moving towards. In the case where the planet is already in the house by one degree or less the bottom line dynamics will be that house with an 'overlay' of the dynamics/behaviors of the house that has just been left behind. (Rad)

Understanding skipped steps
The causes of skipped steps are usually caused by traumas. But they can also be caused by guilt about something and the consequent 'need' to avoid or deny that guilt, and the reasons for it. This itself implies 'judgments' that the Soul has about itself that can be 'out-pictured' in the reality it creates: the circumstances of the life and the people in it. This can have the effect of reinforcing the guilt caused by such judgments. It then becomes important to understand the two causes of guilt: either man-made due to man-made rules, rights and wrongs, moralities, and the like, or natural guilt that is rooted in violations of Natural Laws. Avoidance and denial are the operative dynamics in skipped steps. So the EA astrologer has thus to play the role of 'detective' in order to understand what is causing that denial/avoidance. Those reasons will be contained within the symbols of the skipped step signature in all charts. Skipped steps can also occur as a function of 'spiritual' teachings that the Soul is attempting to embrace that has specific doctrines about what 'spiritual life' is all about, and meant to be. All too often such man-made doctrines attempt to inhibit or suppress natural human dynamics. This form of adherence to such doctrines can then cause 'skipped steps' relative to the natural human dynamics that are being repressed because of the nature of the spiritual doctrine being adhered to. (Rad)

For more information, *See* chapters on LUNAR NODES, SKIPPED STEPS.

Archetypes evolving into another
Traditional astrology never presented the archetypes as one evolving into another. Traditional astrology, as well as Evolutionary Astrology, has specific signs, houses, and planets that all correlate specifically to the totality of human consciousness. It has never been presented as one evolving into another, but that each of the various archetypes, ie Aries, Venus, Saturn, Virgo, the 9th house etc. etc. all correlate to specific archetypes within that totality. (Rad)
Astrology is Observation and Correlation – correlating natural phenomena to their effects on human life. All of the archetypes exist simultaneously within creation – their sum total is the essence of what EA calls Natural Law. It equates to the experience of being human on Earth. Thus they are not evolving into each other because they all already exist. Without all 12 already existing there could not be human life as we know it. Not because astrology makes our life. Because astrology SYMBOLIZES our lives, as they actually exist. Life is not linear. It is not going around a wheel sign by sign and then at the end turning around and retracing its steps in the opposite direction. Do you know anyone who would describe their life as working that way? If no human is experiencing life in that way, how can that be how astrology works? Thus the idea that there is a linear progression of evolution from sign to sign and back again is proven false by comparing it to the actual living reality of humans. (Steve)

New evolutionary cycle
It's just the next act in the unfolding evolutionary journey. All things end at some point, and new things arise that ultimately replace them. The bottom line on everything is still desire. At some point we are dealing with the desire nature of that which created us. (Steve)

In its simplest form this refers to the *qualities* (ways of behavior) of the houses: cardinal (the angular houses – 1st, 4th, 7th and 10th), fixed (2nd, 5th, 8th and 11th), and mutable (3rd, 6th, 9th and 12th). In the case of the angular houses, of course, it is to initiate change. They reveal what our Soul has determined needs to come to closure before we start something new. Within that new beginning, a natural ending to something is implied. The fixed quality allows us to stabilize our ways of being and thinking to give us a sense of security, and the mutable reflects our natural need to adapt and change at different points in our evolutionary journey. These qualities then reflect how the four *elements* of fire (1st, 5th and 9th houses), earth (2nd, 6th and 10th houses), air (3rd, 7th and 11th houses), and water (4th, 8th and 12th houses) are expressed. (Adina)

Original conjunction

For a relevant current example, the essence of the 1960's was the conjunction of Pluto and Uranus in 1965. Life has been all over the place since then. Now with Uranus increasingly squaring Pluto it is going to pull us back to the evolutionary intent released in 1965 at the point of the original conjunction. Life's intentions will be to eliminate everything that has gotten in the way. The degree to which people open to that intention will determine the outer results that occur. (Steve)

Transit event charts – original conjunction, 1st quarter square, etc.

[Example: Transiting Uranus square transiting Pluto] The specific 'rules' are these: upon the first conjunction this sets in motion the archetypal intention for the first Uranus/Pluto square. The second conjunction takes place while one or both are retrograde which is a time to reflect upon what the first conjunction has set in motion. And then upon the third conjunction the archetypal intent is to take action, real action, upon what the first conjunctions intent was/is that is deeply revealed upon the second conjunction. In the context of world events there is of course the general archetypal intentions for the entire world that is then made specific to the individualized context of each country/society. (Rad)

The specific rules [above] are also applied to the 1st quarter square as well as subsequent phasal aspects between the two transiting planets. (Linda)

[Example: Pluto transit through Capricorn] Event charts start with an understanding of the existing reality of any given country and/or society upon which the evolutionary intentions of evolving that reality is reflected, symbolized, by the transiting planets being considered. From an EA point of view this should always start with the transiting position of Pluto because this correlates to the natural law of evolution itself. Thus, the two primary ways in which the evolutionary intentions and/or necessity manifests: either through cataclysmic events or slow yet progressive change. As we have learned from JWG the determinant in how the evolutionary intentions is the degree of resistance to that evolutionary intention. When resistance reaches a point of preventing the EA intention this then manifests as cataclysmic events. So it is then necessary to understand the evolutionary intention of what Pluto transiting, now, Capricorn correlates to which, in essence, boils down to the existing structural nature of any country, indeed the world, that are the determinants of the 'reality' that each country, and the world, is currently experiencing.

The bottom line intention of the Pluto transit through Capricorn is to evolve any existing structure within the reality of any given country that is thwarting or preventing the necessary evolutionary needs of that country. Within this bottom line we then look to the other planets that correlate with a collective of people: Uranus, Neptune, and Saturn. The archetypes that each planet is energizing relative to the signs that they are transiting is then linked or added to the bottom line of the sign that Pluto is transiting. Within this to incorporate the signs that the transiting Lunar Nodes are moving through that symbolize the archetypes that the collective in any country is experiencing by way of the 'lead points' within that collective consciousness that serve as the specific triggers to events that are all part of the larger evolutionary intentions as symbolized by the outer planets starting with Pluto.

An example of all this is reflected in the Rio Tinto Mine in Australia. Here is a statement that reflects all the above: "Australia is riding an unprecedented wave of resources investment due to booming demand from Asia, with hundreds of billions of dollars' worth of resource projects in the pipeline." Here you see the leading edge of the Lunar Nodes in Taurus/Scorpio: an unprecedented wave of resources, Taurus, because of the booming demand, Scorpio, from Asia that will lead to all the money returned to Australia based on that investment. And, of course, all the competing interests of the various groups, Uranus in Aries, within Australia that have led to the confrontations with the Australian government, Pluto in Capricorn, that reflects the existing structural reality, that have and are impacting on what the Australian government perceives as its evolutionary needs in order to grow. Within these groups of competing interests the Neptune transit in Pisces manifests and that can range from utter disillusionment and bitter outrage to a kind of euphoria for those that this investment will benefit. And, of course, the underlying archetype of the Neptune in Pisces is whether all the reasons that have been used by the Australian government to justify this are delusional or inspired by actual reality. Saturn in Scorpio is currently conjunct the transiting North Node which then correlates with the specific timing, Saturn, correlating with time as does Capricorn, to this decision that lead to the various confrontations within the competing groups that are defined by their own structural reality. (Rad)

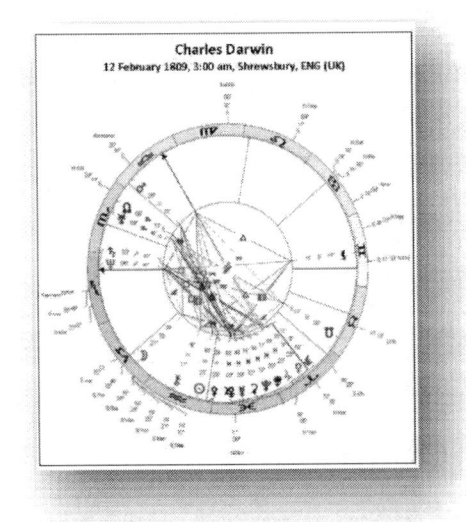

Chart patterns – bucket, bundle, locomotive, splash, splay, etc.
EA does use chart patterns and always from the perspective of EA: why whatever the pattern is that the Soul has chosen in any given life. (Rad)
[Left: example of bowl chart pattern]

Stationary planet or node
A stationing anything, planet or node, is a magnifying force. (Rad)

Singleton archetype
All archetypes are part of every life we live. Even if the sign of the 'singleton' archetype was not on a house cusp and the corresponding house was totally empty, we still would have some sign on the house of this archetype, a ruler of that house, and the linked planet archetype somewhere in the chart. Also, there is a South Node of this planet archetype. So, my understanding is looking at all of this also in light of everything the core evolutionary signature is telling us. Somewhere in the picture which the chart is painting, we will see how this archetype manifests in the current life dynamics. The story of how the singleton archetype in question interweaves with the totality of the Soul's experience is, of course unique to each Soul. The WHY behind each case of one lonely/singleton/emphasized archetype is impossible to say or conclude without understanding the whole chart in context of the Soul's reality. (Bradley)

Making predictions
Most of our life is about free choice relative to the 'parameters' of one's life where those parameters are defined by the nature of the EA paradigm in each chart: individual context. And of course those parameters are reflections of choices/desires that the Soul has already made in prior lives, relative to past life evolutionary intentions. And that in turn has set up the parameters/intentions for the current life, and the choices to be made. Once one understands those parameters, and the intention for the whole life within them, then one can 'predict' when various issues, dynamics, and circumstances will occur in the future of one's life. And that of course is determined by the nature of the transits and progressions in one's life at any point in time. One cannot 'predict' the choices any Soul will make in the face of those future circumstances, dynamics, and issues because of the Natural Law of free choice. Yet an EA astrologer can understand what the natural tendencies are for any given Soul given their prior life choices, or the choices made in the current life. One of the best things for any EA astrologer to do when working with clients, and the future for them, is to point out the WHY of future circumstances, dynamics, and issues and then to provide the insight as to what the consequences would be given this or that choice. The consequences of the choices can be rightly 'predicted.' (Rad)

Unconscious guilt patterns
A subtle filter that is very common in the western world (if not all over this planet), that the natural intention of life is to be long and healthy, that if they really have it together spiritually and health wise, everyone should be able to heal all conditions and live long with good health. I'd say that is more of an ideal than a complete reality. Let me add that I sometimes see clients who have internalized deep guilt over their inability to heal all of their conditions, despite their best efforts, because of belief in this subtle filter. All we can do is the best we can do. Past a certain point it is no longer up to us as human beings. Helping people to become aware of and to release from unconscious guilt patterns stemming from beliefs like this is one of the most valuable services an EA astrologer can do for clients and friends. (Steve)

Parent/child relationships
Take the interpretations given in Pluto Vol. 2, which are geared for intimate couples, and phrase the same principles in terms appropriate for parent-child relationships. Another valuable thing to do is look at the synastry chart of parent/child and see how the parent is going to appear to the child, through the filter of the child's chart, and vice versa, how the child is going to appear to the parent, through the filter of the parent's chart. These can be very different than the way the parent and the child appear to themselves. (Steve)

Health/disease issues
Both the house position and the sign that [the planet] is in can correlate to health issues that are associated with the nature of the house or the sign. And, at times, a condition that is archetypical to the nature of the house can indeed trigger a condition that is archetypical to the sign, and visa versa. (Rad)

Death, early/sudden
There are many possible symbols for early and/or sudden death. Mars in the 11th, Mars conjunct the North or South Node, Mars in opposition or square Uranus, Uranus in the 1st, Uranus in the 8th, the South Node in the 11th, Mars squaring the Nodes, Uranus squaring the Nodes, and the South Node in Aries are some of them. (Rad)

Difficult aspects, fear of death
Quite frequently when we make major changes all our fears rush to the surface, because shaking the roots of what is secure to us is scary!! Feeling very vulnerable is normal. For example, Jupiter/Uranus opposite Saturn is exactly that kind of transit. Most of the time when we make big changes, it is our Soul prompting us to do so and answering the Soul's call can feel threatening to our 'small' selves. Your energy is better spent praying/talking to the universe asking for clarity and support during your transition. (Patricia)

Abuse as catalyst for evolution
(Q) Does the type of abuse a soul experiences in the current life, always stem from an abuse that they portrayed in a previous life?
(A) No.
(Q) Is it also true to say that the abuse a soul experiences in this life (a re-live possibly) is purely a catalyst for evolution, and not necessarily that the soul was not the abuser in the past?
(A) That's right. (Rad)

Prediction of death
No astrologer who knows what they are doing will predict [death] based on symbols in a chart your plane will crash. Nothing in astrology is that specific. Archetypes are symbols. Symbols manifest symbolically, not literally. There are thousands of ways that a Jupiter/Uranus conjunction opposed Saturn could manifest. That is why specific predictions are wrong 90% of the time. A good way to approach this is to remember that your motivation and desire is to follow your Soul's intentions. Thus, anything that happens, including a plane crash, is part of your Soul's intentions, and ultimately brings you closer to God/Goddess. So there is nothing to fear, including death. You will not die until you are intended to die, and you are not going to avoid dying when it is your moment to die no matter what you do. Those are the parameters we live in while encased in human form, like it or not. Accepting them makes the whole process smoother. (Steve)

Unknown birth time
Just knowing the sign of the South Node and the sign of its ruler already says a lot – and aspects will indicate further information. The key is to only say what is certain, not to make up a story. The signs correlate to the specific domains of consciousness that have been at play in a Soul's evolutionary journey, and the activity in each sign is facilitated by the ruler of that sign. I find that simple, short and meaningful readings are possible. And if the client has questions or is seeking clarity on anything, often even without a birth time I can provide valuable perspective. (Ari)

Pluto represents the Soul. The Soul is the underlying cause of EVERYTHING related to a human being, including its past, that past represented astrologically by the South Node. The Soul is the bottom line, the CAUSE behind all the other qualities one relates to. It's the thing that puts all the other qualities in perspective. It is the reason we are attracted to those qualities rather than others. The Soul bottom line is not going to change as life goes on. However, it does EVOLVE. This relates to the Pluto evolutionary signature, where we say that Pluto actualizes itself through the South Node. The South Node is of the Moon, Moon is conscious, Moon is self-image. We are aware of our self-image, thus may identify with those qualities. Pluto is mostly unconscious, the underlying desires that lead to developing the human personality/self-image. Pluto is the yearnings within the Soul. Those yearnings lead to the personality structure, thus are the underlying cause of that personality structure. That is the bottom line.

You can't know for certain if the chart is accurate with *any* rectification process. For that matter, you can't know for certain if many birth times you are given are accurate. I see an out of proportion number of birth times of, eg, 7:00 or 3:30 (rounded times). I've been given birth times that came from the person's mother, and they discover 2 years later that mom had been off by 6 hours and 13 minutes! The key with EA work is keeping in mind that what we are really doing is READING THE PERSON'S SOUL, not just the piece of paper that is their birth chart. And much of that is intuitive, not logical. It's important to grasp that because of the way the EA system is constructed, and because the person self-selected what they most identify with, you will not be misleading the person and they will receive what you offer as valuable. In essence, you are doing the best you can possibly do under the circumstances of no birth time. (Steve)

Chart rectification
What you can do when the birth time is unknown is rectify the chart. That means to back into the birth time through various methods. Typically this is done through finding out what and when have been the major events in the life and using various astrological timing techniques to position the Ascendant. You can search Google for 'rectify birth chart' to get information on some

of the traditional techniques. Jeffrey taught a different technique, which is to determine which house the natal Pluto is in. He prepared a series of questions you ask the client to determine which house they feel is their bottom line (Pluto is the bottom line). The way I do this is I've observed often people can't narrow it to one since they identify with several house attributes, since they have a Nodal Axis, perhaps a stellium in a house/sign, etc. So I ask them to determine which one(s) they identify with the most, and then ask them, of those selected, which one feels like the real bottom line, the underlying cause (Pluto) that the others then sit on top of. Usually they can come up with one bottom line house. Then I construct a chart with Pluto in that house on the birth date. That narrows the birth time down to a 2 hour period (12 houses, 24 hours in a day). Then I move the time around to see what planets shift from house to house, trying to get something closer within the 2 hour period. This requires asking questions – if the Moon is either in the 4th or 5th house, I'd ask Moon/Cancer-like questions to see if they feel more Leo-like (special, pyramid reality) or Cancer (insecure/watery/emotional). (Lucius)

TABLE 3 – Chart rectification – Questions to Ask by Pluto house (*See* ASTROLOGER/CLIENT RELATIONSHIP)

EVOLUTION

TABLE 2 Stages of Evolution

CONSENSUS	INDIVIDUATED	SPIRITUAL
1ˢᵗ stage Consensus	*1ˢᵗ stage Individuated*	*1ˢᵗ stage Spiritual*
– beginning – established – culminating	– beginning – established – culminating	– beginning – established – culminating
2ⁿᵈ stage Consensus	*2ⁿᵈ stage Individuated*	*2ⁿᵈ stage Spiritual*
– beginning – established – culminating	– beginning – established – culminating	– beginning – established – culminating
3ʳᵈ stage Consensus	*3ʳᵈ stage Individuated*	*3ʳᵈ stage Spiritual*
– beginning – established – culminating	– beginning – established – culminating	– beginning – established – final liberation

Natural Law of evolution

Pluto correlates to the Soul itself, and within that, the Natural Law of evolution. It correlates to what the desires of the Soul have been that has led to the current life, and the desires that correlate to its ongoing evolutionary needs. This is contained within Pluto, the Soul, itself. All the other planets in a current life birth chart are thus created by the Soul for its ongoing evolutionary needs that are reflected in its desires. The current life birth planets have their own North and South Nodes. It is the South Nodes of these planets that correlate to the past life dynamics that the Soul has created for itself that have led to the current life, and the position of whatever planet IN THIS LIFE that symbolizes the current life's evolutionary needs. The current life position brings the past forwards through it: the South Node coming through the current position of the planet itself. The North Node of the planet in turn correlates to the ongoing evolutionary journey of the Soul as it continues to evolve through each of the archetypes of all the planets. The cause of that evolution is the Soul, not any of the other planets themselves. The natural polarity point of the natal Pluto is the bottom line evolutionary intent for the Soul in each life. It is the primary cause that causes the North Nodes of all the other planets to actualize according to that primary evolutionary intention. The natal planet, in the current life, birth chart, serves to integrate the past and the future in each moment FOR THE ENTIRE LIFE. (Rad)

Evolution of the Soul

The Soul evolves through purging separating desires. Separating desires are any desires that are not in harmony, or alignment with, the current evolutionary intentions for the life and rooted in the need to maintain the past (old patterns of behavior that are inhibiting further growth). We evolve through the evolutionary states as we exhaust our separating desires (it is a natural process). Pluto by house and sign in the natal chart will correlate to the specific past patterns of emotional security that must be transmuted in this life. Pluto's polarity point symbolizes the current evolutionary intentions for this life, and how to transmute the past patterns of behavior symbolized by Pluto. Remember that there are two coexisting, antithetical desires within the Soul – one to return and one to separate. We have a choice to cooperate or resist these evolutionary intentions. We can look at the natal chart and by using just Pluto and its polarity point we can determine how resistance or cooperation with the current evolutionary intentions will manifest. For example, if a person has a Pluto in the 5th house, and is compulsively acting upon desires that are rooted in the need to be recognized as special or important, that is excessively self-centered, and does not link the need for creative self-actualization in a way that reflects the need of others/humanity then resistance to the current evolutionary intentions symbolized by the 11th house polarity point is evident. Pluto itself symbolizes the dual desires within the Soul (one to return and one to separate).

Mars is the lower octave of Pluto, and symbolizes how we will consciously act out the desires symbolized by Pluto. Mars symbolizes our conscious desire nature. The point within this is that Pluto in the birth chart will determine the core specific past patterns of behavior that are creating limitations and represent emotional security for the Soul. We will unconsciously resist growth by attempting to maintain these past patterns (separating desires). Pluto's polarity point symbolizes the current evolutionary intentions for the life, and the types of desires that the Soul will have to break free from the past patterns of behavior that are inhibiting further growth. Mars is the conscious desire nature we have that reflects how we will act out, or act upon, these desires symbolized by Pluto and to actualize the current evolutionary intentions for this life (Pluto's polarity point). (Deva)

Three reactions to evolutionary growth

There are three reactions/responses to our evolutionary growth needs:
(1) to totally resist – which is not common;
(2) to cooperate in some ways yet not in others (this is by far the most common choice);
(3) totally go for it (this is also not a common choice).
Somebody being in a total state of non-growth or resistance is rare. (If skipped steps are not worked on, growth cannot occur.) (Deva)

Evolutionary signature

On a practical level, the first step is to become conscious of one's evolutionary signature (or karmic signature) – to understand the signatures of the past, and the evolutionary intentions for this lifetime. For example, Pluto square Nodes evolutionary signature would be a significant part of that. Then we have to ACCEPT this signature – beyond understanding it intellectually, to emotionally embrace it. The point is, quite often there are parts of this we don't like, or wish would be other than they are – don't want to embrace, don't even want to admit to. The process starts speeding up as we accept, "Here is where I am, today, and here is where I'm intended to be heading." Then one makes an inner choice, decision, to *cooperate with* this unfolding process. Knowing that at times it's not going to feel comfortable, it's not going to feel like what we want to do or where we want to go – that is part of the process, comes with the territory. We have to accept that also. (Steve)

Evolution of consciousness

The totality of Consciousness correlates with Neptune/Pisces, and the 12th house. And within that totality of Consciousness lies its total potential: of what can be realized. Virgo of course is the natural polarity of Pisces. That correlates, archetypally, to LACK where lack is in reference to the total potential that has yet to be realized. Immutable consciousness simply means energy, as Jeffrey pointed out, and that energy cannot be destroyed: it can only change form. It is inherently full of potential to be realized which is the causative factor for the evolution of the Soul: consciousness. Until that full potential of consciousness is realized the Soul necessarily experiences LACK because LACK infers or reflects THE DESIRE FOR MORE than we currently have. The desire for more infers DISSATISFACTION which is the evolutionary determinant for that which will correlate to total SATISFACTION. Total satisfaction correlates with the desire to return to the SOURCE of consciousness and/or the Soul which is held as potential within the Soul and the consciousness within it. Thus, the sense of lack IS ESSENTIAL FOR IT PROMOTES THE ONGOING EVOLUTION OF THE SOUL IN ORDER TO REALIZE IT'S TOTAL POTENTIAL WHICH, IN THE END, IS TO CONSCIOUSLY UNITE ITSELF WITH ITS SOURCE: GOD/ESS. (Rad)

Evolutionary past

It's really important to keep in mind we have a mainly invisible incredibly long past that we project into every 'new' moment. And we are shaped by that past – our very conception of 'me' is mainly based on our individual past, filtered through the conditions and experiences of the present lifetime. So even if the two people have a very similar evolutionary stage they're still going to breathe life into the very similar script in very different ways. We really are, every one of us, truly unique. That is simultaneously a great gift, and also the source of a lot of our human sense of aloneness. (Steve)

Natural Law of the Trinity

The Natural Law of the trinity does apply to E(A) Very simply when one combines with another one we have three. A simple example would be sperm and ovum. When they combine they produce a brand new organism. And of course the number three is the root number for all advanced math. It is in the union, combining, of the singular one's that then produces three. Union thus becomes the causative factor, or determinant, of evolution itself: genetic evolution through the RNA and DNA of all living organisms. Through this Natural Law we then can see, via the EA paradigm, an existing state of evolution as symbolized in the natal position of Pluto, its polarity point that is then united with, which in turn allows for an evolution of the existing state of evolution relative to the natal position of that Pluto. Same thing as applied to the existing South Node of the Moon, its North Node, that thus evolves the South Node itself. (Rad)

The natural evolutionary progression always involves the Natural Law of the trinity. The natal position of, for example, Pluto operates from birth relative to how the Soul comes into the current life from where it has been: there is a natural polarity point to this that symbolizes the core evolutionary intent. As the Soul moves, evolves, towards that intent it then simultaneously EVOLVES the orientation of the natal position of Pluto itself. Thus, the Natural Law of the trinity. We must remember that any house or sign is an entire archetype: a full spectrum within itself. As evolution proceeds within any archetype the various orientations within that spectrum are embraced as a result. (Rad)

Evolution through the emotional body

EA teaches that processing life experiences through the emotional body is evolutionary precisely because it enables the Soul to fully EXPERIENCE whatever experiences are the natural consequence of its desires and choices. If the Soul does not fully EXPERIENCE that which its choices have generated, then it will not truly know in a deep way the consequences of those desires and choices, and will not be able to integrate and learn from these experiences, and thus to make new choices and evolve. Evolution is a natural process of the universe – we can trust it to happen and we do not have to 'make' it happen, so much as let it happen. As Jeffrey taught, the Water Trinity shows involution in that Spirit/Neptune differentiates to Soul/Scorpio differentiates to Ego/Cancer; and also shows that evolution occurs naturally in the natural direction of the zodiac of the shift in conscious identification from Ego/Cancer to Soul/Scorpio to Spirit/Pisces. I find in my work that when people are able to experience their experience through the emotional body (Cancer/Moon), such a full experience naturally eventually leads them (over a period of minutes or lifetimes) to a desire to understand and transform the deeper unconscious patterns and/or Soul history (both Scorpio/Pluto) that has led to the given emotional experience. I don't need to try to push this inquiry in any way, it is the natural result of deeply experienced emotion, it is just what happens when we get out of the way and feel. And then I have also found that when people start to work at this deeper level, then also very naturally begin (again, whether in this lifetime or later) to experience their own encounters with Source (Pisces/Neptune), however this may manifest as appropriate to their perceptual capacities. The water naturally returns to the sea. So to me it is not so much about energy releasing or other particular things as much as it is about having a natural experience that leads to new understanding and choices (and thus new experiences) that eventually exhaust separating desires and leave only the desire to return to Source. In general bypassing the emotional body is essentially resisting evolution, which Souls at any stage in consciousness can do. (Jason)

Practices to work with the emotional body

[Example: Various practices within Dzogchen and Tibetan Buddhism] These practices are not only unnecessary but in fact confuse those who try to practice them. They take what is inherently simple and complicates that. This happens because such practices are not in alignment with Natural Laws: they are essentially invented by individuals who have been conditioned by man-made laws, the patriarchy, that are then trying to harness the Natural Laws in unnatural ways. Personally, I won't have anything to do with them. To me the practices to be used are life itself. To have the knowledge of emotions is simply to experience them within a consciousness that becomes one with whatever emotion is existing relative to a cause that has ignited it in the first place. And, within this, to have a desire, conscious intention, to understand the nature of whatever emotion: its cause, and the reasons for that cause. Within this, the inherent knowledge that then exists in whatever emotion the consciousness becomes one with. Over time of course a state of total self-knowledge defined by the emotional body will take place. A book that came up that appears relevant to all this is "The Spiritual Anatomy of Emotion: How Feelings Link the Brain, the Body, and the Sixth Sense" [Paperback] by Michael (A) Jawer (Author), Marc S. Micozzi (Author), Larry Dossey (Foreword). (Rad)

Changing old habits

The first step in changing a behavior is becoming aware you are in it - because then when you find yourself going into that pattern again, you can say "Wait, here I am in this pattern again," and make a different choice. It literally is changing an old habit. Like changing any habit, it takes time, effort, determination. These habits go straight to the Soul, so they are even more entrenched. But the point is YOU CAN CHANGE THEM, you are not trapped, no matter how deep they appear to be. *Desire* is the root determinant – you make up your mind you are going to change. Even when you catch yourself making the same choice in a situation where you could have made a new choice, you do not get down or down on yourself, you simply reaffirm that you are in the process of changing a deep pattern, and you keep at it. Step by step, inch by inch. Through determination you move forward. Because it's aligned to the evolutionary intentions, there are a lot of unseen forces at work to assist your moving in these directions. Another issue is, at times you simply are going to feel overwhelmed with change, and unable to move forward at that moment. This too is part of the process. Especially with 10th house Pluto, there needs to be an honoring of your emotional states, and their limitations. You cannot force your way through the process, cannot have complete control over it. It takes on a life of its own, over time, becomes the basis of new habits, a new way of living and of looking at life. There are moments, times, when you NEED to go back to the safety of the known, if only for a short while, just to keep yourself sane. This is OK and necessary – just do it consciously – "I need to do this right now," and remain aware when it is time to get back to moving forward again. In a sense this process is like growing a new baby in your womb (4th house PPP) that gradually takes on a life of its own. In this case that new baby will gradually replace your old existing sense of who you are altogether. It will integrate and incorporate these new perspectives, ways, into the totality of your own self-image (4th house). Words like organic, holistic, inclusive – it is a natural process that gradually engulfs you. Through this process the intentions of the PPP, the North Node, the North Node ruler simply unfold, because at the baseline you have inwardly committed yourself to the evolutionary intentions. You start the process by discerning what the chart symbols mean, what areas of life they reference, but as you increasingly move into that process as a way of life, it just unfolds by itself. This all starts by embracing the process in the first place and saying "yes" to it. The rest just happens. (Steve)

Reaching an evolutionary limit
When the Soul has reached a limit evolutionary speaking, and inwardly feels that growth is needed yet that need is met with fear and insecurity can create a lot of trouble and pain because the evolutionary pressure to transform becomes overwhelming. The common problem is that the cause of the stagnation is not consciously known by the Soul. The Soul is only aware of the problem, and the overwhelming feeling of not getting anywhere. This is exactly where the birth chart is so helpful. The overwhelming desire to change and grow commonly has to reach a very intense point in order to induce the necessary changes because of the high degree of emotional security that is linked with the past ways of being/with the past in general (ie the need to be self-consistent). It is like an inner death, and the re-birth cannot be felt or integrated until the death happens. This internal conflict reflects the dual desires within the Soul (one to return and one to separate). (Deva)

Resistance – self-consistency – evolution
The Soul creates egocentric structures in each life that is orientated to phenomenal reality in such a way that reflects the ongoing evolutionary intentions, desires, of the Soul. The resistance to change is rooted in the need for security where security is a function of being self-consistent. Self-consistency is a function of the past that defines each present moment. The 'future' is an 'unknown' from the point of view of the past equaling the present 'moment.' As such it is inherently perceived by the Soul as something insecure because it is not a known fact. As a result of this most Souls then 'project' their past into the future in order to feel secure: self-consistent. As a result this is why most Souls keep repeating their pasts over and over, making only minimal change in each life in order to grow at all: evolve. And yet all Souls must evolve. And they evolve as a function of desire for it is the dual desire nature of the Soul, as created by God/ess, that dictates this evolution. As a result we then have a 'future' because of the determinant of evolution: the dual desires inherent to all Souls. As Souls naturally evolve they do come to a place in which their sense of personal identification is no longer within the egos that they create from life to life. Rather the Soul comes to a place where the sense of personal identification is that with which created the Souls in the first place: God/ess. Once this happens the entire sense of what constitutes security utterly changes. And it changes to being in the hands of its origin: God/ess. Once this happens then the 'resistance' to change, to evolve, simply ends. (Rad)

Resistance – example
For example, if a person has a Pluto in the 5th house, and is compulsively acting upon desires that are rooted in the need to be recognized as special or important, that is excessively self-centered, and does not link the need for creative self-actualization in a way that reflects the need of others/humanity then resistance to the current evolutionary intentions symbolized by the 11th house polarity point is evident. (Deva)

Progression of Pluto's evolution through the houses
Pluto does NOT naturally evolve in progression through lifetimes from, example, the 10th house to an 11th house, then a 12th house, etc. (Rad)

Retrograde archetype and accelerated evolution
Dissatisfaction is a Plutonian experience. Dissatisfaction facilitates evolutionary need. Retrograde emphasizes the sense of dissatisfaction, which then facilitates the evolutionary needs. When a person says, "There is something else possible." No matter what the evolutionary level is. (JWG Quote: Retrograde function is non-static, never rests, is in a perpetual, cyclical state of growing, is always dissatisfied.) If dissatisfaction is a Plutonian experience, and the retrograde function is always dissatisfied, doesn't that make

the retrograde function inherently Plutonian? And Pluto does correlate with resistance. The more retrograde planets, the more resistance. That is why it is generally difficult for a retrograde personality (defined by Jeffrey as someone with four or more retrograde planets) to make the necessary changes, while at the same time there is a deep knowing of the NECESSITY of making those changes. The Soul has intentionally painted itself into a corner. (Steve)

In ALL Souls, not just those with retrogrades, individuation is necessary for evolution to continue. The process of evolution IS the progressive individuation of the Soul, until that Soul finally realizes in full who it truly is, not intellectually but experientially. Until then the individuation process is the progressive stripping away of all conditioned senses of "me" that have accumulated over many lifetimes, until finally all that's left is the experience of the true "me." That process takes many lives. The difference in a chart with retrogrades is the individuation process is heightened, emphasized – because there has been resistance to that process in the past. So the Soul through retrograde has set up conditions that will force it to emphasize its own individuation, as a way of overcoming its own conditioned resistance to that process. Other symbols emphasizing the individuation process include a lot of 11th house or Aquarius, Uranus aspecting many planets, etc. (Steve)

Retrograde (Rx) symbolizes that the specific areas within consciousness indicated by the house and sign position of the planet that is Rx is being relived, or repeated, in order to be fully resolved. When the issues are resolved then the Soul can grow by leaps and bounds. The analogy that is used in the Pluto material is peeling away at the layers of an onion to arrive at its core. As such, those that resolve the necessary issues related to a planet that is Rx will feel a deep sense of being released from those issues, coming into alignment with his or her natural individuality/identity in the context of "peeling away at the onion." The retrograde archetype accelerates a Soul's evolution no matter what evolutionary condition they have evolved too, even in the consensus state, because the archetype of retrograde correlates to 'individuation' as Carl Jung used that word: to individuate from any external conditioning factor that attempts to define for an individual how any given phenomena is 'meant' to be defined and lived out. The retrograde archetype is meant to induce a natural rebellion from those external conditioning pressures wherever they come from. And the intent of the rebellion is to arrive at a place of individuation. As a result it accelerates the evolutionary pace of the Soul by way of the planets that are retrograde in their birth charts. (Deva)

Accelerated evolution occurs when energy reaches a critical mass or peak momentum, which for many is more readily facilitated through the crisis or the cataclysmic experience. Anytime you have an intensification of experience, you are in a state of accelerated evolution. (Rose)

To understand the totality of a retrograde planet or planets in terms of not only the individuation process that accelerates the Soul's evolution, but also in terms of that which is being relived for karmic and evolutionary reasons, which are themselves DETERMINED relative to the underlying primary evolutionary/karmic axis, one first focuses on the actual nature of the planet(s) that are retrograde, the sign and house location of that natal planet that is retrograde, the location by sign/house that that planet naturally rules (ie Venus naturally rules Libra and Taurus), aspects to that planet that is retrograde because those archetypal dynamics of other planets that are aspecting the retrograde planet all contribute to the total context of that which is being relived and individuated, and, lastly, the location by house and sign of the planetary nodes of the planet(s) that are retrograde. Understanding and integrating the totality of this will then lead the EA astrologer to a comprehensive understanding of the retrograde planet(s) for any Soul's individual context that is always established by understanding the main evolutionary/karmic foundation of each birth chart as symbolized by the EA paradigm of Pluto, its polarity point, the location of the North and South Nodes of the Moon, and the location of their planetary rulers. (Rad)

Retrograde is a need to review/redo/renew because things need to change to allow evolution to proceed. Pluto symbolizes our Soul. Our Soul is the root principle/reason/cause/core of why we are all here in the first place. Pluto equates with resistance. This means, at our core every one of us has an inherent resistance. Anything that is at a core permeates through everything that manifests out of that core. The whole process is learning to accept that inherent resistance and not be completely limited and defined by it. The resistance to the forward movement will also still be present, thus there can be a real struggle within the Soul between its desire to evolve and its tendency to resist the evolutionary intentions. This can result in the feeling of painting self into a corner where there is no way out other than to do what is intended. The more retrograde planets in the chart, the more resistance has occurred in the past. Seven retrograde planets at times would not be a lot of fun as the two opposing forces to evolve and resistance to evolving would have quite a tug of war at times. The intention is to bust the pattern of resistance open once and for all, to release the log jam. If the person finally "gets it" and starts cooperating with the evolutionary intentions, as a result of this pressure/intensity, the progress can be rapid. If they continue with resistance as the primary response, the life may not be a lot of fun. The retrograde function adds a Uranian flavor to the planetary function – it is going to do what it does in its own unique way and not be so concerned with what others think about it. (Steve)

Collective evolution, on a global scale

Let's look at this realistically, releasing any wishful or "magical" thinking. There is no number or percentage of people that when reached is going to save the day. What is necessary to change things is CHANGE IN ACTUAL HUMAN BEHAVIORS on a collective level. What is coming is not a cosmic punishment for violating divine laws, but simply natural consequences. Natural Laws are the rules by which creation was created. When we live aligned with them we get a certain kind of result. When we collectively violate them, we can get away with it for a certain length of time. But a point comes when we have pushed things so far away that it starts changing the nature of that reality. And there are consequences when that occurs. Right now we have a political party in the country that is the biggest consumer of resources on earth whose political strategy includes denying there even are any problems ("Al Gore made all of this up so he could get rich." "The changes in climate have nothing to do with human behavior and are natural." "How can there be global warming when the winters are getting colder?" etc. etc.) Each time there is a global climate conference, the leading nations agree to do about 20% of the minimum necessary to slow these issues down, and set a date for achieving that 20% that is yet another 10 to 20 years in the future. And when the 10 to 20 years have gone by, the actual results achieved are about 20% of the 20% that was promised (20% of 20% is four percent). Then the UN yet again declares these crises are getting worse. Another conference is held where again not enough is agreed on, and the agreed on date of completion is again 10 to 20 years in the future, and the same thing happens again. Thus it is all talk and so far has not changed.

Until it turns into action on a global level the course we are on cannot change. Anecdotes about a few hundred people over here doing this and some windmills being built over there make us feel good, and hopeful. But the scale of such activities is about one percent (if that) of the minimum necessary to actually reverse the course of consequences that are building, in the available time left before those consequences take on a life of their own (which is already beginning to occur). These climate changes are natural phenomenon. As they continue they will permanently alter the physical reality of the world we have known. They change things humans can't reverse. Weather patterns – more heat and less rain in the largest food growing areas on the planet. Alterations in the path of the Atlantic Ocean Gulf Stream, which is what keeps northern Europe from being like frozen northern Canadian tundra – they are both on the same latitude. The increasing release of methane from newly unfrozen tundra areas now melting in the summer for the first time in hundreds of thousands of years. Methane has 10 times the greenhouse effect of carbon dioxide (methane exploding is what set off the oil leak in the Gulf of Mexico). The change that occurs is the more methane that's released the warmer things get. And the warmer things get, the more methane is released. That process takes on a life of its own. How do you stop the release of the gas from hundreds of thousands of acres?

No number of Souls praying for balance and harmony is going to stop that process. The only thing that is going to change things is vast numbers of humans/countries CHANGING THEIR DAILY BEHAVIORS. World economics are run by capitalism, which demands profit be maximized in every single circumstance. Thus reality is next to no countries have agreed to make the necessary changes. Billions of people in third world countries at this time, rather than deciding to reduce their resource use, are deciding they want to use even more. Positive spiritual God-loving humans are not going to be given a blanket pass to escape all these consequences. We are part of the collective process, no matter how much we have spent our life rebelling against the very decisions that are leading to these ends. Of course it is good that millions are starting to recognize this, make personal changes, praying for different outcomes, etc. Millions of people is a lot of people. But there are billions who are not at all thinking in those ways. Until billions start moving in the necessary directions, millions is just not going to be enough. That is just reality. I realize this is not what we want to hear. It is shocking and depressing. But I ask you or anyone to show me any grounded realistic ways that are going to lead to worldwide very rapid global change in collective behaviors. What signs do you see of this going on? Not a few people here and a small corporation there, but on a mass level?

The mind does not want to embrace what is going on and has to be made to do so. We are not going to be saved by benevolent aliens bringing new technologies to turn things around. Millions of "good humans" are not going to be transported to a peaceful planet or etheric plane that vibrates on a higher frequency, because of their inherent goodness. This is not personal. We collectively created this mess, and now we will increasingly experience the consequences. Our collective outcome does not look very good. Sanity and personal survival require us GETTING USED TO that as actual reality, and then making personal changes to adapt as best as is possible to where things seem to be going. That to me, is why it is wise to get educated to the economic and political realities that are going on around us. Yes, they are boring and painful and callous and cruel. But they are affecting everything. Seeing actual reality helps dispel wishful and "magical" thinking. On a brighter note, while the percentage of people who will face these realities is low, it is still millions of people. As we ourselves start facing this as reality we will inevitably and naturally meet others of like mind, leading to new connections. And those connections may well play a role in our long term personal survival. (Steve)

Collective evolution – Pluto sextile Neptune

The Pluto/Neptune aspect can serve as collective inspiration or collective delusion within any generation on a personal and collective level. (Deva)

When everyone on a planet shares an aspect, that is an example of intended collective evolution. Something shared by all humans, each in their own way of course, and generationally through the shifting of the signs the planets are in. When an aspect exists for a really long time, it indicates the necessity of learning important collective lessons. Also, consider that at times one or the other or both of those planets will be retrograde, further reinforcing the intention of really getting the evolutionary lessons. (Steve)

Advancing one's own evolution

A Spiritual state individual's burning desire to know the Divine will accelerate their evolutionary journey. If you find yourself on a large boat that appears to be sinking: even if you feel you may eventually drown, you still do everything you possibly can to try to help. Reality is accepting the boat may still sink. But you do all you can anyway, because it's the right thing to do. That is what EA means when it says the value is in the effort, not in the outcome. You are one Soul out of seven billion humans on this planet. So to the extent one Soul out of seven billion affects the human collective, yes you are advancing the collective evolution with your burning desire to know the divine. But the point of your burning desire is not to advance the collective evolution but to advance your own evolution. Advancing the collective is something that just happens from your personal efforts. Of course you have the desire to help. But the only person you can really change is yourself. You can support others in their evolutionary journey, but it's up to them to take the steps. (Steve)

Evolution via polarity points of the planets

The nature of Life is that it evolves. It is ingrained. The way that life evolves is by going to its polarity point. It is not Pluto alone that has a polarity point. In his Pluto Volume 2 Relationships book, Jeffrey detailed in the chapters about Mars and Venus what moving towards the polarity of the sign that Mars and Venus are in looks like. The same principle applies to all the planets and symbols in our charts. It's just the way life works. If it makes more sense to you, you could visualize it as it is the polarity point that is moving forward through the zodiac over time in its evolutionary track. Since the planet must be 180 degrees apart from its polarity point, the planet is getting dragged forward by its advancing polarity point. This is also indicated in progressed charts, which show how the evolutionary intentions are unfolding OVER TIME. Thus the polarity point progresses also. It does come down to desire nature. At a certain point we get sick of something we previously loved. The feeling becomes "been there done that." This too is part of how life is constructed. (The EA material on the Cycles of Phases and Aspects is very relevant to this.) The Soul is not working on only one separating desire in a lifetime. The chart is a map of our desire nature. When you see grand crosses or a lot of squares or oppositions or a number of skipped steps, you are typically looking at the map of a Soul with conflicting simultaneous desires, wanting to go in multiple incompatible directions at the same time. The Pluto polarity point is the most significant polarity point as it tracks the evolution of the Soul itself. (Steve)

In NO conditions within the birth chart does any polarity point apply other than the polarity point of Pluto that needs to be consciously embraced, desire, for the evolution of the Soul to continue. And the one exception to that as Wolf taught is when the natal Pluto is conjunct the North Node. Even then there is a natural polarity within the sign that Pluto is in natally that NATURALLY is evolved towards via the Natural Law of polarities. And it is this natural polarity within the sign of a natal Pluto that then correlates to the evolution of an entire generation on Earth, and why any given generation is on Earth at any point in time. Every sign has a natural polarity within it that serves as the evolution within that sign because of its natural polarity. Thus, as the Soul evolves, makes a choice to evolve, which is symbolized by its opposite house and sign, and in the case of Pluto conjunct the North Node, by sign, and the location of the planetary ruler of that North Node, the aspects that it is making, this then CAUSES the rest of the entire birth chart to also evolve. It's automatic. So all those natural polarities that exist within the signs that the planets are in, in any birth chart, automatically are evolved towards. It is a function of evolution. The degree of evolution is dependent of course on the choices that the Soul makes in any given life relative to its core evolutionary signature which is symbolized by natal Pluto, the South Node and its planetary ruler, the polarity point of Pluto, and the North Node and its planetary ruler.

Every natal planet in a sign also has a natural polarity point by house, ie Mars in Scorpio in the 7th house would have a natural polarity of not only Taurus within Scorpio, but the 1st house as the polarity to the 7th. These natural polarity points by house are also automatically evolved towards once the Soul has made a choice to evolve which, again, is symbolized by the main EA paradigm. It is because these natural polarities within the signs and houses that naturally evolve, once the Soul has made a choice to evolve, that JWG never really taught about them. He did so because they do in fact naturally evolve in this way. He did this intentionally so as not to create such an overwhelming amount of evolutionary procedures that could potentially confuse students, but of course overwhelm any given client. It is enough to know the core EA paradigm, how it works, and how to apply it to one's life. The rest of these natural evolutionary points take care of themselves. Over his long career JWG only once, to my knowledge, taught about these other polarity points of the planets, and the houses they are in. And that is in a long workshop he held in Holland called "From Karma to Dharma." (Rad)

Wolf taught that every sign has its natural polarity WITHIN IT. Those natural inner polarity points of any sign evolve within the context of the sign as the ongoing evolutionary journey of the Soul occurs. IT JUST NATURALLY HAPPENS. When a planet is retrograde in a sign Wolf taught that such a Soul has focused, prior to the current life, upon that inner polarity of the sign in order to actualize the archetype of the planet that is in that sign. So, for example, if Mars is retrograde in Libra this would mean that that Soul has desired, focused, on evolving the Mars archetype within the natural Aries polarity that exits relative to Libra. Thus, that Mars archetype in Libra is essentially actualizing the whole of the Libra archetype through its natural polarity: Aries. And this polarity would then be the lead point of how the Mars in Libra entered into, the orientation to, relationships. If Mars were not retrograde then the Mars in Libra would enter relationships, the orientation to, in the typical Libra way: co-dependent. This lead point would then be progressively evolved towards the natural polarity of Aries as the Soul's life unfolded over an entire lifetime. (Rad)

Progressive evolution

(Q) I always pictured the evolutionary path in terms of getting to a point, staying there for as long as it is necessary to learn the lessons of that place (since these lessons are the reason why it was necessary to get to that point in the first place) and then somehow refusing to move forward along the evolutionary journey because that place has become all too familiar. I always thought that it is only at this time that the need to move towards the polarity point comes into action, as in only after having overstayed somewhere. I totally understand why outmoded patterns need to be left behind, by moving towards the polarity point, but is there such a thing as patterns that have not yet become outmoded?

(A) I think the issue you are having in trying to understand this is your feeling that when you arrive at a new place you are supposed to be there and this means that everything stands still until it becomes outmoded and you are no longer supposed to be there. That perspective is overlooking some realities of life. I will give you the example of spring turning to summer. (I am using a northern hemisphere example. If you are in the southern hemisphere change my dates by 6 months.) Most of us, I suspect, wouldn't mind if it stayed late June and early July about three times longer than it does. None the less it doesn't. Evolution is progressive, day by day. Before you know it, it is late July and then early August. The days are getting shorter. The very seasonal change, day by day, itself is moving us forward, because the environment beneath our feet is changing before our eyes. The change from today to tomorrow, and tomorrow to the following day, is almost imperceptible. But if you take the daily change that occurs over 6 or 8 weeks, it is quite perceptible. Nothing in life ever stays the same. The ascendant moves one degree every four minutes. From what I see, the moon moves one degree about every hour and 30 to 40 minutes. They appear to be constant but they are not.

What you refer to is beautifully described in the EA material on the cycles of phases and aspects. That every circle/cycle has its own inherent meanings, reasons and evolutionary intents. And these progressively play out over the course of the cycle, moment by moment, not all at once. (That is why there IS a cycle. Otherwise it would all happen at the same time.) Even the seasons really are the phases of the Sun at the Aries point and its phasal relationship to the transiting Sun. That is why to me it makes a great example, because we can correlate astro theory with physical events we have all experienced lifelong. The same principle we can recognize at work in that example also applies to all the inner cycles going on within us. There are archetypes associated with all the points along the circle, the natural steps or behavioral tendencies that are going to occur when cycles reach certain points. The patterns of resistance and cooperation are built into the archetypes. (Of course we have choice over whether we will resist or cooperate. But most of us, until we start figuring this out from inside ourselves, that we can then make new choices, operate instinctually by repeating our pre-existing patterns, based on very familiar past decisions.)

As you start looking at it this way, you start to realize that the idea that you are in something new and you are supposed to stay there until it becomes outmoded is in fact true. But it's not that everything is fine and then one day it is outmoded. The progress through the changes proceeds moment by moment, hour by hour, day by day, week by week, month by month, etc. At every moment, even from the beginning of the new phase of the cycle, there are things we need to release from. New Phase is experiential. Right away we are going to try some new things that we then decide aren't right or didn't work. So we stop doing those things right away, right in the new phase. Thus we are shedding even as we are learning something new. Through trial and error we (hopefully) get better at it and closer to the ideal. The intended times of major sheddings, at end points, culminations, are when a whole bunch has to get dropped at once. But in every moment we can be dropping something and initiating something else. Endless endings and beginnings, or Involution and Evolution, as Jeffrey used to put it. Something has to die, no matter how infinitesimal, before something new can be born. That is just how life works – that is what EA calls Natural Law, in action. Death-rebirth is the way of life. And death-rebirth is a core Pluto archetype, thus the evolution of the Soul through that process.

The whole thing is a PROCESS. Trying to hang on to the present is quite like trying to make time stop in early July for a month or two. We might like that but it's not going to happen. On the other hand, we can get away with pretending for a while that is happening. We can convince ourselves it is happening. But that doesn't mean it is. If I convince myself something is happening that isn't (it's still early July) sooner or later I am going to experience evidence in my life that is not what is happening. The more I dig in and believe it is happening when evidence is showing me it's not, the more painful the day of reckoning is going to be when the belief finally blows up in my face for good. That is usually about the time we start talking about how unfair and cruel life is, when what I passionately believed turns out to not be aligned with the way "reality" has unfolded. (Does this sound at all familiar in terms of how we live our lives about things other than believing I am making it stay early July for 6 weeks?) Does that mean there is something unfair in life, or that I have let myself believe that the way that life works is different than the way it actually works? (Steve)

Natural Law of elimination

The integration point between the dual natures of desires within all of our Souls is elimination. Eliminating, in the end, all separating desires to the exclusion of the only desire that can remain, and that desire of course is to reunite with that which is the Cause of Creation. The means for evolution to take place is based on this Natural Law of elimination within the Soul as reflected progressively in the egos that it creates from life to life. And the origin, the manifested creation, which we can call God or the Source of All Things is the cause of this to take place in the first place. (Rad)

Natural evolution, evolving beyond that which has been developed
At any point in time any Soul has an existing reality that has already been 'developed.' And from the point of that which has been developed we continue to evolve beyond that which has already been developed. This is natural evolution. And as we evolve upon that which has been developed as an ongoing natural evolutionary process we must continually integrate this natural evolutionary process within the existing reality that we have developed at all times. This is natural and continuous process of life itself for all forms within the manifested Creation. The natal Pluto in the birth chart correlates to that which we 'developed' or evolved into prior to the current life. Its polarity point correlates to this natural evolutionary process relative to its natal position that is evolving and being integrated all the time that allows for the ongoing evolution of the Soul. It is simply adding onto that which has already been actualized and developed at any point in time. (Rad)

New evolutionary cycle, meaning of
It's just the next act in the unfolding evolutionary journey. All things end at some point, and new things arise that ultimately replace them. The bottom line on everything is still desire. At some point we are dealing with the desire nature of that which created us. (Steve)
In its simplest form this refers to the *qualities* (ways of behavior) of the houses: cardinal (the angular houses – 1st, 4th, 7th and 10th), fixed (2nd, 5th, 8th and 11th), and mutable (3rd, 6th, 9th and 12th). In the case of the angular houses, of course, it is to initiate change. They reveal what our Soul has determined needs to come to closure before we start something new. Within that new beginning, a natural ending to something is implied. The fixed quality allows us to stabilize our ways of being and thinking to give us a sense of security, and the mutable reflects our natural need to adapt and change at different points in our evolutionary journey. These qualities then reflect how the four *elements* of fire (1st, 5th and 9th houses), earth (2nd, 6th and 10th houses), air (3rd, 7th and 11th houses), and water (4th, 8th and 12th houses) are expressed. (Adina)
The Soul has specific desires that correlate to its ongoing evolutionary development from life to life. When any given desire has been exhausted, no longer a desire, that correlates to a culmination cycle relative to that desire. When a new desire manifests within the Soul this will then correlate with a new evolutionary cycle in which the Soul will typically manifest many lifetimes to work it out in order to exhaust it: culminate it. This dance of desires, new ones that culminate at some point that then leads to yet other/new desires, is the very essence of Evolutionary Astrology wherein only ONE desire can finally remain in any Soul: to go home to its Maker. (Rad)
It simply means that the Soul has made a decision, desire, to work upon a variety of existing dynamics within it in a new way. The core EA paradigm reflects this. (Rad)

Evolutionary capacity
The evolutionary capacity or stage of development as understood in human form on this Earth is not dependent on how long a Soul has incarnated itself on this Earth. (Rad)

Rates of evolution
(Q) Do some Souls simply evolve at different rates and this has nothing to do with resistance? So kind of like different flowers flowering at different times despite having been planted at the same time?
(A) Exactly. (Rad)

Evolving the consensus
The issue is not so much the majority evolving out of consensus, as evolving the level that defines consensus. For a clear example, go back to the early 1950's and compare what was consensus in Tibet with what was consensus in China. Notice that in Tibet they aspired to enter monasteries, and in China they aspired to conquer. In cultures like Tibet and India, valuing spirituality was deeply embedded in the heart of the cultures, including consensus. These cultures were far from perfect – women were treated as third class, and the mass of people were far from enlightened. Nonetheless the consensus was taught there is a Soul, and a thing called liberation or enlightenment exists. That through their efforts over many lifetimes their Souls could eventually be freed from having to endlessly reappear in bodies on the wheel of life and death. That the reason they were here was to move at least a step or two closer towards that eventual liberation. That how they lived, the attitudes they held, how they treated others, had a great deal to do with achieving spiritual progress. These consensus values in those cultures led, for the most part, to them being peaceful nations that were not aggressive toward other countries (Pakistan being an exception in India's case). Contrast that with the consensus values about aggression in countries like China, Germany, US(A) There is a noticeable difference. No culture is perfect. Even in Tibet and India there are those with "me first" orientations. The issue is how does a culture view such people – do they let them run the country? Do they glamorize the achievements of those who advance themselves at the expense of others, defining that in their mass media as "success?" There will always be a consensus in all groupings. It simply means how the majority see things.
The shape of a bell curve is a natural form – the majority always fit within the largest area of the curve. The area at the edges of a bell curve on both sides, is always smaller. You could equate those at the extreme right side of the curve with the upper Individuated

and Spiritual states. In an evolving reality there must always be a leading edge (Uranus) who are demonstrating where the consensus has the potential to go. As example, not so long ago in the USA much of the consensus accepted the validity of humans owning other humans (slavery). Proponents even used bible quotations to justify this. Gradually, increasing numbers of people started feeling this was wrong. Over time it was becoming increasingly unacceptable to more and more. A really ugly war was fought, one outcome of which was slavery being outlawed. That is an example of consensus evolving. Even today there are some who in their heart of hearts would be fine with the return of slavery. And yes, newer forms of slavery involving children and sex workers have appeared. But these are not mainstream cultural policy, as was the original USA slavery. Thus an evolution. Unfortunately that evolution usually occurs far too slowly for people like most of us here on this board. Nonetheless it does happen. Also true is too often the hard-won progress is followed by periods of backlash that seem to wipe out much of the progress. That is the two steps forward, one step back principle (that EA associates with Cancer and emotional security) playing out. The nature of evolving realities requires any species (including human) to "evolve or perish." Many species HAVE perished because they did not or could not evolve rapidly enough. Meanwhile the Earth is still here. The jury is still out on whether the human species will collectively choose to evolve in time or become part of the dust pile of history. Continuing to do what we are now doing as a species is unsustainable. (Steve)

Evolution and involution
Soul consciousness evolves or grows in the human experience through desire. Desire is the leading edge of our evolution in that we are initiating new experiences through which we evolve. At a certain point, any particular desire which was the leading edge of our growth/evolution exhausts its potential for continuing to serve our path of evolutionary growth. This is where we experience involution – that which was brought forth from that desire, no longer serving us, now ceases to exist. Naturally, because of "its" familiarity and comfortability, there may be attachment, thus may be held onto so tightly that external events are necessary to create cataclysmic loss of that which is removed and no longer serving this purpose. On the other hand, letting go of what our desires created may be natural, like leaves falling from a tree. When the Soul's consciousness is truly united with source, there are no more desires which need to be acted upon for the sake of its continued evolution within the physical plane of existence. (Bradley)

Advanced Souls attempting to change the world
A certain phenomena that happened before the outbreak of WW2: Yogananda, among others that included very advanced Souls within the Astral Realm, tried to put their consciousness and wills together in order to prevent that war. This group was highly, highly evolved. Yogananda even tried to visit and talk with Hitler himself. This request was of course denied. The point is that despite these herculean efforts by these very advanced Souls the war did in fact happen which included the genocide of millions of Jews, Gypsies, and 'undesirables.' It is of course 'natural' for almost all Souls to need faith and hope in order to survive hard times. It's the nature of the human being. Without that almost any Soul will get reduced to a state of total futility, and a sense of defeat that leads to a state of hopelessness. Not too many are able to live that way. Thus, to have any sense of sanity and purpose when times become hard, and harder, the human Soul will attempt to counteract the sense of personal powerlessness, at the hands of those that are in power, by creating or inventing what they must in order to 'believe' that there must be a way out, or through, that hard time and the times ahead that can seem even harder. And we must remember, in terms of Jesus, that he did in fact end up on the Cross, and died there. Love was not enough. (Rad)

De-evolution
When JWG taught about this issue of de-evolution he always taught about this in the context of karmic causes that dictated such a forced de-evolution. Forced here means in relation to violating Natural Laws. As a result it is the magnitude of that which has led to the violation of Natural Laws that in proportion to that magnitude that then dictates the degree of the de-evolution itself. He commonly used the example of Hitler to illustrate this dynamic. De-evolution does not dictate, in and of itself, a return to the dimly evolved state. It can be in lesser states relative to where the Soul had evolved to. The Soul starts over yet progresses in a much speedier fashion than the normal evolutionary progression of a Soul through the evolutionary states. And at each step of evolving back to where they had previously been the Soul is 'tested' in such a way that whatever it is that the Soul had done to create the karma in the first place that dictated the de-evolution is not repeated in any way, shape, or form. If the Soul passes those tests, each time, then the speed of the evolutionary return to where it had previously been also increases. It is the choices by the Soul itself that dictate how rapid the return to the former evolutionary state takes. (Rad)

A classic case of karmically caused de-evolution would be Hitler: after he committed suicide his Soul rebirthed very quickly into, of all places, Poland. He came into a mother who took some of the drugs of that time, I forgot that name now, that proved to create horrible deformities and disabilities in the fetus. Thus, Hitler was born without arms or legs: just stumps. His face was a gnarled mess too. And it goes from there. (Rad)

When Souls go back to Source

(Q) When all Souls finish their evolution and finally go back to God, is that the end of human beings? (Wei)

(A) EA does not specifically teach about that other than once the Soul is free from all separating desires, and has only one desire left which is to go home to its Source, God, then it will finally lead such a Soul back into a state of absolute union with its Source: God. In the end your question really refers to the nature of the manifested Creation in the first place, and the natural evolution that takes place within that manifested Creation. The deepest root of all within the manifested Creation is consciousness and intelligence within that consciousness. And of course the Source of the manifested Creation is that intelligence and the consciousness within it. From the point of view of consciousness/intelligence in 'human form' we must remember that is but one form among countless other forms that also contains consciousness and intelligence. What is the nature of those forms and the intelligent consciousness within them? Do they also have what we call Souls? Who can know the answers to this? Saying all this only to illustrate the complexity of the manifested Creation much of which is unknowable from the natural limitation of the human form. And because of that natural limitation humans thus create philosophies and beliefs that attempt to explain or answer the types of questions you have brought up. Evolutionary Astrology is focused on the evolution of the Soul in human form, and the dual desires that are at its core, and how those desires directly correlate to the Soul's evolution through time and space. And, of course, those desires, like the Soul, emanate from the Source Of All Things. In the end, then, it's about the Soul reuniting with its Source by the elimination of all separating desires that keep it from such a reunion. The Soul in human form can then only know its Source by unifying its consciousness with the consciousness of the Source itself. Is that then the 'end of the human being?' To me the only way to answer this is that such a total union releases the Soul from being bound by the natural limitation of the human form. (Rad)

GENERAL ASTROLOGY

AC - DC - MC - IC

In order to understand what these specific symbols mean we must first understand the nature of the cardinal archetypes (1st/7th, 4th/10th houses). Let's start with the AC-DC first. In a general sense, the AC-DC will reflect how we project ourselves to others consciously (DC/7th house) and how we instinctually express ourselves within the environment (AC/1st house). It is important to understand that how others see us based on that instinctual expression is not always how we see ourselves. This is because this instinctual response is not a conscious action on our part. On the other hand the conscious projection of ourselves towards others (DC 7th house) is based on the instinctual nature of the AC/1st house. The example JWG gives of a person with Scorpio on the AC and Taurus on the DC helped clarify this for me. In this example, when a person with this AC-DC comes into the room they sit in the very back and do not speak to anyone. The point within this is that Taurus DC is projecting a persona of being self-contained and inwardly secure and stable to "offset" fears of abandonment, betrayal and loss reflected in the Scorpio AC. The instinctual expression of the Scorpio AC is often perceived as "intense" although the person does not see themselves in this light.

The IC/4th house reflects the person's self-image and emotional responses/orientation to the environment. The MC/10th reflects how the person is going to express their personal authority in society and also the nature of the current cultural conditioning upon the self-image (IC/4th house). Let's put Pisces on the 4th house cusp to follow through with this example. The person is going to have an innate sensitivity to the environment and to the emotions of others. Yet, if that person is a man who grew up in a conventional environment where this sensitivity was not understood or nurtured how will that person react to these emotions/self-image based on current cultural conditioning? Will he be able to inwardly relate to the traditional "Marlboro man" image? No. However, relative to the AC-DC the person would typically try to appear as the traditional "tough guy" and would not openly express this sensitivity to others or in the environment. With Virgo on the MC the person may be hyper-critical of himself for having this type of emotional nature and attempt to deny and suppress it. The intention is to align with a type of service/healing work that helps the innate sensitivity be expressed through a career/social position. The point within this is that from an evolutionary view the person is meant to become inwardly secure (IC/4th house) in the context of expressing this innate sensitivity to others and within their social work (MC/10th house). In this way the expression of the AC-DC will also change because the person will be deflecting or hiding this innate sensitivity from others. (Deva)

The four angles are the natural gateways to the four quadrants of the chart. Thus they are cardinal in nature, initiating action and change. These are the natural conjunction, square, and opposition points in the chart. Passing through them can be stressful, because they require release from the known, into what is presently unknown. So they are like evolutionary mile markers. If you look at the material about the phases, the natural archetypes of those key aspects, you will see much about what those four angles represent. Conjunction (AC), waxing square (IC), opposition (DC), waning square (MC), back to conjunction. They also correlate in Earth physical reality, with the beginning of each of the four seasons of the solar year. (Steve)

Ascendant

The ascendant is the cusp of the 1st house. Thus it's going to be the gateway into new experience, and in that life area the person will have a very 1st house-Aries-Mars-like orientation. Similarly, the MC is the gateway into the 10th house, and the person is going to have a 10th house-Saturn-Capricorn orientation to whatever sign/planets may be on the MC. A core EA principle is the house is always the deepest energy, the bottom-line level. The sign on the house represents what that bottom-line energy is going to be filtered through. Learning the range of possible ways that Aries energy filters through, say Virgo, on the cusp can actualize. You always start with Pluto, the Soul, by house and sign. Then the Nodes and their rulers. These three represent the evolutionary signature. When you have a grasp on that, then you interpret Aries (1st house) energy filtered through Virgo. To consider, WHY did this Soul choose Virgo rising in this life? The gist is, you can't pick out one or three chart elements and analyze them independently of the totality of the chart. Everything goes back to the archetypes of the 12 signs and can be seen as expressions of them in various forms. And the underlying evolutionary signature, starting with Pluto, is the foundation on which everything else in the chart is based. (Steve)

Transiting Pluto crossing the Ascendant
[Example: Capricorn ascendant] You can expect that the life that you have known up until that point, the person you have seen yourself as, will end. Seriously. I have Ascendant in early Sagittarius. I've been through this. That may sound scary. And it will feel that way at times. But I suggest to people having this transit that, as best they can, look at it as an exciting adventure. Because the natural time for a very long past is coming to an end. One is forced by life circumstance to break free from much of that past. Many things that used to work will simply stop working. Ascendant being in Capricorn, major changes to the structure of life will require adjustment. The more one is able to co-operate with this process, the more at peace with it they will feel. It is definitely an adjustment. The intention is for major changes in the life of that Soul, over time a whole new reality, directions, orientations forming. Jeffrey Wolf Green taught that the maximum pressure or difficulty in the life of a person with that transit occurs 18 to 20 months ahead of the exact aspect. (Note to others reading this: that statement was made only about Pluto crossing the ascendant, not about other Pluto aspects and not about other planets crossing the ascendant.) If you happen to have Jeffrey's book, Pluto Vol. 1, read the section towards the back of the book on Pluto transiting through the 1st house. Also read the long section 'Pluto in the 1st house' natally, towards the front of the book. Although you don't have Pluto in the 1st house natally, the 15 years (plus or minus) that Pluto will be transiting through your 1st house will have you feeling and driven very much like what you will read about Pluto in the 1st. The difference is that because it is not your natal signature, it will be an overlay ON TOP OF your natal Pluto/Nodes signature rather than being your core itself. You will be feeling Aries-like much of the time. And you are SUPPOSED to feel that way – that is the point of the transit. (Steve)

How you might feel about the process will be determined to an extent by the condition of Pluto in the natal chart. If you have many aspects from Pluto to other planets in your chart, especially to personal planets, you will be more used to Pluto type energy/experiences as a result, than if you have a lightly aspected Pluto. Also if Pluto and Mars in the natal chart are in a major or hard aspect (conjunction, opposition, trine, square, semisquare, sesquiquadrate, inconjunct, sextile) then you will also have probably had strong evolutionary type experiences in your life before as a result from this too. All this would add up to being a person who knows through previous experience the turmoil and often deep gut level, very disturbing effect Pluto energy can have on themselves when it is activated in one's life. So if this were the case, with Pluto crossing your Ascendant you might feel more prepared (internally) for the approaching tsunami in your life. In fact if all the above were true for you, and you are a positively inclined person, as the process unfolds and these deep changes start taking place, you may recognize the great blessing that this transit can be – it will bring a huge rollercoaster of energy into your life that makes great personal and world changes now possible. You might come to feel that, without this energy now available to you, you would otherwise never be able to make such changes and benefit from such profound and rapid growth.

There could be a feeling that the energy this transit brings into your life is a great gift, and not a drop of it is to be wasted, as once it's gone you will be left with only your "normal" energy and power, and there'll never be the exact same opportunity again, not one involving the conjunction to your Ascendant anyway. But if the natal chart is not a strong Pluto type chart, and you haven't had any major Pluto transits up to now, then this transit may be a very new and eye-opening time for you, where, for the first time you come up against the full impact of the evolutionary force of Pluto. If that is the case, hang on to your hat, take many deep breaths and be prepared to learn a huge amount about how Pluto energy renders the past ways of being and doing things, approaches to situations, inoperable and recreates something new in its place. Again if viewed positively, you'll probably come to view these changes as invaluable, although it may be much later in the piece that this really becomes apparent. Either way, big changes are inevitable. Also, as Pluto will be conjuncting your Ascendant at the same time it will be opposing your Descendant. Some of these changes are highly likely to affect all your relationships, some of them directly. (Upasika)

Nodes square angle
The MC, IC, AC and DC are CURRENT LIFE SYMBOLS DETERMINED BY THE MOMENT OF BIRTH that all correlate to the current evolutionary intentions of the Soul. Thus, when the Nodes square any of these points, there is a specific evolutionary reason for that. And if those reasons are not fulfilled THEN it will correlate to SKIPPED STEPS IN THE NEXT LIFE. So, for example, if this were the Nodes squaring the MC-IC axis this could show up in the next life as the Nodes squaring Saturn and/or the Moon. (Rad)

Example of Nodes square angle
[Example: South Node in Sagittarius in the 3rd, North Node in Gemini in the 9th, and both rulers in Sagittarius in the 4th house] Ongoing evolutionary and karmic issue of absolute honesty at all costs to counteract lives of lying, misrepresentation, exaggeration, even making yourself actually 'believe' in your own lies to the point where the lies became your truth, has been in place for many lives now. It is not new. With your Ascendant and Descendent both squaring your Nodal Axis this means that it is this life that your Soul is making a choice to deal with this once and for all. These symbols mean that your Soul desires to bring to the forefront of your consciousness this very issue of long standing in this life. And to make choices that lead to being as honest as you can be at all times, and then letting the chips fall where they may. The underlying teaching is that honesty may hurt at times but it will always lead to exactly the right situation, the right resolution of any situation within or without. And, if you don't do this, then it will become the basis of a skipped step next time around. (Rad)

ASTEROIDS

The asteroids correlate with various aspects and dimensions within our consciousness that are very relevant to study and understand. The work of Demetra George is the very best place to start that studying and fundamental understanding. (Rad)

All asteroids rotate around the Sun in an orbit between Mars and Jupiter and thus have solar years of a similar length, approximately four years. (Steve)

All of the bodies in the asteroid belt, where both Ceres and Lucifer are located, orbit at speeds slower than Mars and faster than Jupiter. However, not all asteroids are in the asteroid belt and therefore some of them move faster than Mars or slower than Jupiter. For example, Eros, a so-called "near-Earth asteroid," has an orbital period is 1.76 years, which means that it falls between Venus and Mars. So when working with phasal relationships to asteroids, it is important to either look up their orbital period (which is usually included on their entries in Wikipedia), or at least to know their basic location (asteroid belt, near Earth, etc.) to determine phasal relationships. Chiron is not an asteroid but a planetoid with "cometary qualities" that continues to defy astronomical categories. It has an orbital period of 50.76 years, making it faster than Saturn and slower than Uranus. (Jason)

TABLE 8B   Asteroid Speeds
from fastest to slowest (with orbital periods)

Mars	
Vesta	3.63 years
Asteroid Lilith (not Black Moon Lilith or Dark Moon Lilith)	4.36 years
Juno	4.37 years
Kassandra	4.38 years
Pandora	4.58 years
Ceres	4.6 years
Pallas	4.62 years
Lucifer	4.93 years
Amazone, Persephone	5.34 years
Jupiter	

Asteroid square Nodes
Any planet or asteroid squaring the Nodes correlates to a skipped step. Interpreting the nature of that skipped step depends entirely on the nature of the asteroid or, in the case of Chiron, comet. The reason why this is intuitive to me, is based on the nature of a square to the Nodes. Nodes correlate to the Soul's evolutionary journey including the past, and squares correlate to a crisis in action (first quarter) and crisis in consciousness (last quarter). A square leads to constructive integration. So based on that, anything creating such an aspect to the Nodes must imply that there are choices to be made in this life time in order for resolution to occur. (Ari)

The Resolution Node is always to the left with all bodies including asteroids. (Steve)

Asteroid – retrograde
(Q) While it is an overall evolutionary impulse to reclaim/integrate the undistorted archetypes, if a person had many retrogrades natally or by progression of the asteroid goddesses, would it be even more incumbent for that person to reclaim the undistorted archetype in this lifetime? (Brenda)

(A) It depends on the evolutionary state of the Soul itself. From the Individuated state onwards the answer would be yes, yet the recovery would be an ongoing evolutionary process that could be finally realized within the 1st state Spiritual. (Rad)

(Q) For a person dealing with this, would they perhaps be confronted with many crises and induce a more inward internalization until this is achieved?

(A) This depends, again, on the evolutionary state of the person and other evolutionary factors. This would be one of the ways until internal realization was achieved.

Octave transformers

The Asteroids act as octave transformers because they dwell BETWEEN the inner-conscious-rational-leftbrain-personal planets (Mercury, Venus, Mars) and the outer transpersonal-unconscious-rightbrain-spiritual planets (Uranus, Neptune, Pluto), and therefore are seen as "transformers in the archetypal circuitry" by raising lower octave vibrations to a higher octave. The role of the Asteroids is to re-awaken the FEMININE energy so that individuals and thus the collective become more whole. The incorporation of the conscious with the depths of the unconscious requires FEMININE perception, focus, insight, awareness, sensitivity, intuition, imagination, therefore the Asteroids form this necessary 'bridge.' A shift is occurring between the thinking-rational processes and becoming more in tune with the emotions. Individuals cannot give to the Collective a wholeness that they do not yet possess, therefore the Feminine needs to be fostered and nurtured in the evolution of consciousness as we come out of patriarchal conditioning. (Linda)

LOWER OCTAVE	OCTAVE TRANSFORMERS	HIGHER OCTAVE	PERSONAL DESIRE TO ACT FOR THE COLLECTIVE INTEREST
Mercury	**Pallas** *(feminine creative energy birthing new ideas)*	Uranus	Mercurial mind inspired and transformed by Uranian illuminations.
Venus	**Juno** *(sacred marriage, emotional truth)*	Neptune	Venus values and feelings raised by Neptunian compassion.
Mars	**Lilith** *(wisdom of the natural world, natural expression)*	Pluto	Mars personal desires acting for Plutonian individual/collective evolution.

Pallas

Pallas is of course an asteroid that correlates, among other dynamics, to one's awareness or consciousness being 'seeded' from thoughts or ideas that come from Souls in higher planes of existence such as the astral plane. Pallas correlates, among other correlations, to a consciousness/Soul being 'seeded' by thoughts/directions/realizations from 'on high,' so to speak. 'On high' would of course correlate to entities/consciousnesses from other realms such as the astral realm. This was certainly the case with Joan of Arc. However being consciously aware of these seeded thoughts does correlate to levels of personal evolution that are beyond the Consensus state in most cases. That does not mean that it does not happen in that state, but does mean that most in that state are not consciously aware of such seeding and/or simply ignore it because it's so far outside the 'mainstream.' Thus the internal or external judgments of being 'crazy,' or 'you're crazy,' and the like. It may interest you to know that Wolf's own Pallas was at 19 Capricorn conjunct the South Node of PLUTO! And that both that Pluto and Pallas were of course ruled by his Saturn in Leo conjunct PLUTO in his 9th house. It also squares his Neptune in the 11th. Let's remember that he shared with others the fact that all of the Pluto material, the very basis of Evolutionary Astrology that he pioneered, was put into him via dreams 'from on high.' (Rad)

Psyche

Psyche = Greek meaning of the word SOUL. In the myth this represents the search for the Soul mate union, under the auspices of divine union/energy. Psyche was the most beautiful mortal, people would flock to her. This made Venus jealous so she sends her son Eros with his bow and arrow to prick her while she is sleeping and cast a spell so that she will fall in love with a monster. Instead he is SO captivated by her beauty, he pricks himself and falls in love with her. In their heavenly castle he comes to her at night. Psyche holds a candle and a dagger in case it is the monster. The situation dissolves because she does not trust him, she doubts him and Psyche is sent back to Earth tattered and in rags, pregnant and alone and looking for Eros. She was then sent to Aphrodite in her desperate attempt to find Eros. She is told in order to be re-united with Eros she was to fulfil a series of tests and trials, each test more impossible than the next, even involving a descent into the underworld – tests that were setting her up to fail. However to everyone's surprise, especially Aphrodite, she succeeds and is transformed by the Gods into a Goddess and is allowed to marry Eros.

From my observations through synastry Psyche can connect to the Soul mate connection between two people and also potentially, as in the myth, to many trials that would have to be overcome in order to be together. Via the myth, this is a theme of the pursuit of love against all odds. It also represents the power of desire/love and when this energy is channelled in such a way, what a Soul can overcome. In a natal chart, this connects to Souls, depending of course the stage of evolution, with penetrating ability to connect and to understand others with a greater depth, carrying a psychic sense of sorts. For example Jeffrey Green has Psyche in Virgo in the 10th, a SOUL WORKER for the sick, he used his psychic lens to help others heal and evolve, those that did not have the capacity to see these things for themselves. He helped the emotionally, psychologically and physically sick, Virgo, via SOUL counselling. It can represent someone who is deeply involved in Soul work of any kind.

If this Psyche is conjunct Venus in someone's chart, and following the myth, this would be someone where finding true love and the one true Soul mate can be in high focus. If the Psyche/Venus conjunction is making supportive aspects perhaps that Soul mate is found. Also I could see this being a symbol for doing deep Soul work together in the world. Each individual signature is different of course but in general Psyche is about the SOUL and what may be necessary to endure, as witnessed in the myth, in order to fulfil the desires and evolutionary intentions of the Soul. (Kristin)

Asteroid Ephemerides:
http://serennu.com/astrology/ephemeris.php
http://www.true-node.com/eph1/

CHART PATTERNS

Bucket, bundle, bowl, locomotive, seesaw, splash, splay
EA does use chart patterns and always from the perspective of EA: why whatever the pattern is that the Soul has chosen in any given life. (Rad)

CHIRON

Chiron is not an asteroid. It is a cross between a planetoid and a comet. Chiron has an irregular elliptical orbit and takes 50 years to travel around the Sun. It is not an asteroid in any traditional definition of asteroid. (Steve)

Chiron is not an asteroid but a planetoid with "cometary qualities" that continues to defy astronomical categories. It has an orbital period of 50.76 years, making it faster than Saturn and slower than Uranus. (Jason)

Chiron is treated in EA as any other archetype is. It is approached and understood from the point of view of the Soul's evolution: past, present, and its future. Chiron has its own Nodal Axis, South and North Nodes, relative to its current life natal position by house and sign. So, in essence, it's a matter of first understanding the totality of what the archetype is for Chiron, then integrating that understanding in the individual context of any Soul's evolutionary journey as symbolized by the totality of its birth chart starting, of course, with the core foundation of Pluto's placement in the chart, the North and South Nodes of the Moon, and the location of their planetary rulers. Within this core, foundational, context the specific manifestation of how the Chiron archetype has been, is, and will be, can be properly understood. (Rad)

In brief, Pluto correlates to the big picture evolution, Chiron correlates to a specific and key piece of the evolutionary puzzle, so to speak. Within the Chiron signature are found intensified memory imprints. These memory imprints, which are centralized around a core theme as is indicated by the chart details, correlate to standout memories/experiences. These memory pools are formed from our peak experiences, in other words, our critical thresholds and turning points, and as such they are ones that hold a particularly "enlivened" energy charge. (Think of the frictional quincunx aspect – ignites intensified awareness, requires concentrated focus.) Chiron references our greatest wounding experiences (experienced from all angles, wounder, wounded one) and our greatest potential for healing of those wounds, which ultimately serves to transform the conceptualizations of separateness consciousness, and facilitates more holistic (holographic/ simultaneous) integration and healing.

In other words, the Chiron homeopathic process (like eventually cures like; within the wound lies the key) prompts the advance of healing potentials and healing resources not only for self, but for others too (applies to/includes environmental/circumstantial, and collective). To use the analogy of the centipede, Chiron can be like that one leg that necessitates specialized attention. Further sharing my premise/a proposition on how the archetype of Chiron fits into the evolutionary paradigm: Pluto corresponds to the Soul itself and its evolutionary journey, archetypal 8th house placement. Mars, the instinct to grow beyond oneself/the activation of the Soul's will in the contemporary lifetime, archetypal 1st house placement. The relationship between the two is represented by the quincunx (8th house/1st house aspect). This is a mobilization aspect based on the frictional (energizing) influence of the 150 crisis aspect – paradox/conflict, heightened awareness, focus, adjustment. Positioning mutational Chiron, correlating to the healing crisis, in the 6th house position, sets up the YOD configuration: Chiron in quincunx crisis aspect to the subjective will (Mars) calls for a critical adjustment to be made. As the Soul confronts/explores the myriad of experience (1st house archetype/Mars), it ignites creative opportunity (Chiron in an archetypal sextile to Pluto) to transform the core/key wounds of the Soul into essential Soul growth (Pluto.) (Rose)

Chiron more often than not is highly active in the charts of those suffering from some sort of unresolved issues from past lives manifesting in THIS life as a chronic illness forcing the individual to face the underlying issues, however not always (but sometimes) able to heal the actual wounds/illnesses, but able to change the relationship the individual has to the past and thus heal the stigmata. (Sol)

Planetary Nodes of Chiron

Solar Fire reveals that the calculations for Chiron start at 650 AD. At that time the Nodes of Chiron were in direct opposition to one another at 12 Libra for the North Node, 12 Aries for the South Node. And the calculations then stop because of the limitation in Solar Fire to the year 4500 AD. The nodal axis of Chiron is often in that inconjunct relationship to another, its norm actually, yet it does repeat the opposition pattern at times as well. The movement through the signs appears very, very slowly of course. In the large time frame between 650 AD and 4500 AD the movement remains pretty slow. One of the places in her/history that the Nodes of Chiron were in Libra/Aries that needs to be included would correlate to the her/history of Crete. This is one of the last places that men and women were able to live, relatively speaking, in accordance with Natural Laws including the Natural Laws of Masculinity and Femininity. For example, the men and women in that place treated themselves as equals to the point that even their physical appearances closely resembled one another in terms of dress and decorations on the body. If I remember right that was sustained until the 4th century AD. It was a place, like Minoa, where the Amazon type women were still prevalent. (Rad)

Chiron's Nodes occupying three different possible combinations (Aries/Scorpio, Aries/Libra, Taurus/Libra) is that they suggest three distinct collective memory pools or collective consciousness. Chiron itself I attribute to cellular memory imprints of an exceptional charge (energy momentum/field) – that is to say that the content is one of peak experiences. For the individual, these peak experiences/memory imprints, are the ones that draw added attention, in terms of their unfinished work (the homeopathic healing journey). Re the collective, the memory imprints of the collective experience is embedded regardless of an individual's actual experience, each individual will be attuned – that we all draw from the undifferentiated collective memories (non-specific to the individual but at the root of the collective Soul and therefore contained within the individual too). This concept really affirms that there is no degree of separation between any component of the creation – that at the core, we are all connected. It is no different than the collective attunement of other species, like ants. For now, Chiron is a tool that we are using by "drawing down" the psychic content of the collective, as well as our own individual healing journey (re what Chiron indicates through the natal chart).

Aries/Libra correspond to the era of ancient Greece and Rome (a time when the mythologies were re-fashioned) and Scorpio/Taurus to Egyptian times, and Minoan times, what else would be added in terms of significant epochs? My thoughts on Chiron's Taurus/Libra Nodes is that it describes the collective consciousness of signature times (intensified acceleration) when the goddess/feminine was progressively socialized. These Nodes reference Venus cycles, as I suggested above the transit of Venus in relationship to the Sun and Earth (the consciousness of matter) repeats in approximately 100 year cycles of the five sign placements. Of course Venus cycles are the root of the Mayan calendar, so perhaps this is how we can reference a larger cycle. For both the collective and the individual, Aries/Scorpio nodal axis is suggestive of the acceleration/experience of key new chapters/critical shaping of human evolution, perhaps a drastic "corner turn." Aries/Scorpio seems to infer violent times, war, human sacrifice, etc., accelerated genetic development too. This planetary nodal combination will reference the Mars chapters (the Egyptian reference). The Aries/Libra combination references the Greece/Rome transition and extreme masculine/feminine polarization. Chiron's influence refers to the exceptional experiences of a person's life, all the key and critical ones – the most wounding and traumatizing, the most healing and gifted moments too (birth and death passages too). Chiron in aspect corresponds to the animation of peak cellular memories. (Rose)

Chiron square Nodes

Any planet squaring the Nodes indicates the necessity to continue specific resolving re that planet. Chiron's influence refers to the exceptional experiences of a person's life, all the key and critical ones – the most wounding and traumatizing, the most healing and gifted moments too (birth and death passages too). Chiron in aspect corresponds to the animation of peak cellular memories. When Chiron is square to the Nodes, what is revisited are the most dynamic, significant, traumatizing, defining, critical, turning point experiences. Cellular memory is particularly "juiced up and alive," and so whatever the imprint (and especially when found squaring the Nodes), it is highly sensitized and primed for karmic recall/replay. There is a strong sense/feel of the fated-ness of the life's key circumstances, experiences, and relationships. When Chiron is animated, the experiences are always beyond the usual, ordinary, or average – they are peak, special, exceptional, extraordinary, etc. When Chiron is emphasized, the memory imprints are vivid within cellular memory – they remain present/prevalent – which typically translates into a chronic condition or theme. Chiron correlates to homeopathic process, and creating an effective evolution for oneself. Chiron often translates into a chronic physical condition which forces concentrated attention and thus serves as a primary catalyst. Even birthmarks, scars, or physical handicaps can be echoes of the past life traumas – whether residues (minor) or wounds (major) they represent cellular memory imprints translated into the manifested/the physical. (Rose)

Chiron transit

If the person has done their inner work prior to this point in time, an inner work that has allowed them to become aware of the dynamics that have caused the previous wounding relative to the natal Chiron, and then applied that awareness to a new [example: intimate possibility] then these sorts of transits can in fact correlate to a healing of those wounds relative to the person who has now come into their life. If not, then of course these same transits can create a scenario in which those pre-existing wounds manifest in even deeper ways relative to the new person coming into their life. If so, the intention of course is to create a circumstance in which those pre-existing wounds are finally addressed. I would be talking to them [the client] about the nature of the wounds as symbolized in the natal chart/Chiron. Why they came about and why: the dynamics involved. Then I would ask them if they were aware of all that, and, if so, if they had already made some choices that correlated to addressing those dynamics so that the wounds would not repeat themselves. This of course would include being able to be aware when those old dynamics were being stimulated relative to the nature of a new person/attraction coming into their life. And, if so, being able to talk about those wounds/dynamics with the new person in such a way as to objectively gauge whether that new person, by way of their own responses, was coming into the life to help heal those old wounds and/or if that person has come into their life to recreate those wounds so that they could finally be addressed. So I would be sharing with the client this type of information and empowering them to be able to know what is what. (Rad)

A Chiron transit will manifest based on prior choices and advances one has made. Of course usually it is a mix, in the wounding experience comes opportunity for healing, in the healing experience comes some relinquishing, acquiescing, or bittersweet recognition – it is a homeopathic experience. (Rose)

Chiron – masochism, guilt

JWG made a critical distinction relative to the archetype of masochism because it can have two distinct causes. One cause is what he, and others, call spiritual masochism wherein the Soul is consciously and with intent 'sacrificing' its Soul for the benefit of others no matter what the personal cost to the Soul may be. The other cause is of course rooted in the need to atone for a sense of guilt because the Soul feels within itself that it has done something wrong which then necessitates the need to atone for that guilt. In both of these forms of masochism the 'wounding' that correlates with Chiron is thus based on the Soul having no boundaries or limits relative to the desire to help or heal others in the ways that are consistent with the evolutionary condition of the Soul: that which is possible because of the evolutionary condition or state of the Soul.

When Chiron is manifesting itself though guilt and the need to atone for that guilt it is imperative, for those who are working with Chiron, to understand the difference between 'learned' guilt and natural guilt. Learned guilt occurs when a Soul is subjected to all kinds of projected judgments from others where the nature of those judgments are rooted in artificial or man-made laws that are temporal in nature. It can also occur by way of an inner self-judgment as the Soul measures or judges itself against these same man-made laws in which they forever come up short. In both cases this leads to the inner voice of 'there must be something wrong with me' in which the Soul then needs to 'atone' which then leads to the masochism inherent within Chiron. Natural guilt is a guilt that is rooted in that which is naturally right and wrong relative to all the Natural Laws that have been set in motion by the Creator in the first place. When a Soul transgresses these Natural Laws a state of natural guilt will occur. When this natural guilt manifests within the archetype of Chiron the need to atone for that natural guilt occurs. And that can then lead to the two forms of masochism that JWG taught.

When working with those who are manifesting psychological or pathological masochism relative to their Chiron it is imperative to help them understand the difference between learned guilt versus natural guilt. Natural guilt will always remain in the Soul because that is how the Soul learns to do what is inherently right and wrong according the Natural Laws set in motion by the Creator. Learned guilt is that which can be jettisoned from the Soul because, after all, this type of guilt IS NOT NATURAL. In this way a healing of the wounds that correlate with Chiron can occur. It is also imperative that one understands the difference between pathological or psychological masochism versus what Green called 'spiritual masochism.' Spiritual masochism is a conscious choice by the Soul to sacrifice whatever wounds may occur to it by way of a pure giving to others ON THEIR BEHALF, ON GOD'S BEHALF. When this is the case it just is. There is nothing to heal or to change. JWG was the only one to my knowledge that taught that Chiron can also correlate to the wounding of others that then leads to a necessary guilt, and the need to atone for it NATURALLY. (Rad)

On the flip side, Chiron will also correlate to the possibility and often the past karma of a Soul creating such guilt and wounding for others. The nature of that would stem from a core denial of one's inner reality/condition by way of projecting that outwards towards others. This is how this would play out in patriarchal times where there are such strong distorted notions of absolute perfection and its implied polarity of fatal imperfection. The reality of having triggered wounding for others in the past can also be a cause for the Chiron guilt – and thus the psychological need to atone for that guilt. The integration of the Chiron archetype in a healthy way seems to entail a process of step by step healing which directly necessitates doing that which brings up the most pain while so doing it. In so doing, the Soul can receive the feedback/criticism of its environment and make necessary adjustments. Thus the Soul learns to bridge a higher spiritual purpose into this world by consciously integrating that purpose in a way that is pragmatic and focused – all rooted in deep self-acceptance. This produces in the end a great degree of compassion and ability to serve others, even in the midst of seemingly painful inner or outer circumstances. This can only be done through the vehicle of being willing and comfortable with one's own pain so that the Chiron work can evolve into selfless service without any martyrdom associated with it. (Ari)

This is essentially correct yet 'martyrdom' can also be a function of a Soul who has made a conscious choice to sacrifice itself on behalf of others no matter what the personal cost may be to the Soul who has made such a choice: spiritual masochism. (Rad)

Chiron in EA

Chiron is treated in EA as any other archetype is. It is approached and understood from the point of view of the Soul's evolution: past, present, and its future. Chiron has its own nodal axis, South and North Nodes, relative to its current life natal position by house and sign. So, in essence, it's a matter of first understanding the totality of what the archetype is for Chiron, then integrating that understanding in the individual context of any Soul's evolutionary journey as symbolized by the totality of its birth chart starting, of course, with the core foundation of Pluto's placement in the chart, the North and South Nodes of the Moon, the location of their planetary rulers. Within this core, foundational, context the specific manifestation of how the Chiron archetype has been, is, and will be can be properly understood. (Rad)

"There is no coming to consciousness without pain" seems inevitably true, and this is where Chiron can be seen operating very clearly. Something has to start fermenting inside us for us to want to look for more in life, and to me it is Chiron that is this yeast. Through the agony and pain of our wounds, or the pain of frustration and helplessness when we cannot fulfil our desires, or the gradual hollow emptiness that can arise even when we do actually fulfil them – Chiron gradually leads us to the biggest wound of all, the wound of feeling separate and incomplete – the wound that is the ego itself. And the path is from unconsciousness to consciousness, from consensus to individuation to a spiritual gravity of consciousness – from Capricorn/Saturn (mortality) to Aquarius/Uranus to Pisces/Neptune (immortality). I see Chiron as a yeast working in all aspects of this progression, but is most active in the movement from consensus to individuated, and through individuated. As I think about it I can possibly see why Rose attributes Chiron to the mutable cross – Sagittarius, Gemini, Virgo, Pisces – as it is a key facilitator in the *process* of change, and amongst other things the mutable cross is all about fluidity and change. As well as Chiron having a strong affinity with Sagittarius and Virgo – most seem to agree on that. And Chiron also relates to peak experiences (of consciousness) too, so that pulls in Pisces, and also to the learning of the student, which is Gemini. (Upasika)

Chiron's influence in the chart

Chiron's influence is more dynamic in some charts than others. This will depend on the evolutionary development – whether it's been worked on for a long time and is losing the potency of the energy charge, or whether it's building or receding from a peak. Angularity, dynamic aspects, and tightness of orbs are telling in this regard. Transits and progressions are stimulating. (Rose)

Rulership of Chiron

One could certainly explore correlating Chiron to the 6th house and get a lot out of it, but I don't give Chiron a fixed rulership placement. I think of Chiron as correlating to the mutable cross (Gemini-Virgo-Sagittarius-Pisces), perhaps with an emphasis on the Virgo/Pisces polarity. Besides the teaching aspect, Chiron is a visitor or alien to our solar system, which fits aptly with the Sagittarius archetype. Because he is temporarily with us, I am not sure about assigning rulership or co-rulership. (Have we assigned Ceres a rulership yet?) For now, thinking in terms of affinities seems to me a more comfortable notion. (Rose)

I have always felt though that Chiron is a bigger player in the chart than the likes of Ceres etc. I do find though on a possible co-ruler front, that Chiron so far always works very symbiotically with the deep healing aspects of the Virgo archetype, which Mercury just doesn't quite seem to stretch to enough for me. I've noticed many events corresponding between them. (Upasika)

Chiron conjunct North Node of the Moon

When Chiron is conjunct the North Node it facilitates the evolutionary forward by creating an added alertness to the content of the North Node and thus provides ready access to the tool kit/content found there. It is a sensitized point, an alert point, a consciousness raising or "raised consciousness" signature. It can be thought of as a skeleton key, one that unlocks many doors. In Chiron's case, it facilitates a key learning, a specific experiential thread. Through saturation, the repetition or chronic process, Chiron puts intensified concentration and intensified evolutionary pressure on this chart signature. In a sense, Chiron/North Node (or South Node for that matter) holds a particularly magnetized energy charge. Because of this intensified or magnetized activation, one is drawn there. As such it is a signature that serves to accelerate growth and evolution. Chiron cultivates the North Node growth potential in a way that may be viewed as fate or destiny at play. This occurs because of the exceptional experience or talents that ignite a sense of déjà vu, the out of the ordinary or beyond one's control experiences that irrevocably alter one's life, or the experiences replayed with such frequency that the individual feels somewhat trapped or doomed to meet up with the learning over and over. Those with Chiron on the North Node can more readily find/access natural talents and resources that serve their own evolution or that can be used in a healing capacity/in healing service for others. These individuals may more readily find a calling in life, may feel that a path of service has been cut out for them (born to do this). Chiron experiences tend to be a mix of both healing and wounding. (Rose)

DECANS

Each sign has three signs within it that correlate to the Natural Law of the trinity. For example, Cancer also contains Scorpio and Pisces. Each sign has these natural trinities that correlate to the evolution within each sign. So, for example, if a planet is within the first ten degrees of a sign it correlates to just that sign alone. Thus, a planet within the first 10 degrees of Cancer is manifesting the archetype of Cancer alone. If that same planet is within the second 10 degrees then it is simultaneously manifesting Cancer and Scorpio. If that planet is within the last 10 degrees of Cancer, then it is manifesting all three signs of Cancer, Scorpio and Pisces. Each sign has a natural element that correlates with it. Cancer is water, thus the other signs that correlate with water: Scorpio, and Pisces. Aries is fire. So for Aries, the natural trinity is Leo and Sagittarius. And so on. The specific degree of a planet within a sign thus correlates to what decan within that sign that it is evolving within. It is like dimensions within dimensions. And, of course, each Soul has its own ongoing evolutionary intentions that correlate to why the planets are within whatever signs, and whatever degrees: the various dimensions. One of the great astrologers of all time, Dane Rudhyar wrote a book on the specific meanings for each degree, in each sign called the Sabian Symbols. In this book Rudhyar creates metaphorical meanings for all the degrees within the all the signs in the zodiac. (Rad)

Each sign has a natural trinity within it, ie Cancer has Cancer, Scorpio, and Pisces. All signs have their natural trinities. Thus, there is an evolution within the archetypes of all signs. Each sign has a natural division of 10 within it due to the natural trinity of three signs. Thus, the first ten degrees of any sign correlates with that sign. The next ten degrees incorporates that sign and the next within the trinity. And the last ten degrees the entire trinity that exists within any sign. So, for example, the first 10 degrees of Cancer would be pure Cancer, the next 10 would be Cancer and Scorpio, and the final 10 would be Cancer, Scorpio, and Pisces. (Rad)

Decans and planetary ruler

In EA decans are acknowledged because of the natural trinity that exists within any given sign and, thus, the evolution within a sign. Generally speaking the planetary ruler of any given sign is considered as the planetary ruler of the birth chart yet the natural planetary ruler of the decan within the sign can be considered as a secondary ruler as well. That secondary ruler would of course be operating WITHIN the primary ruler of the sign, and thus the birth chart. (Rad)

Decans – natural trinities within each sign

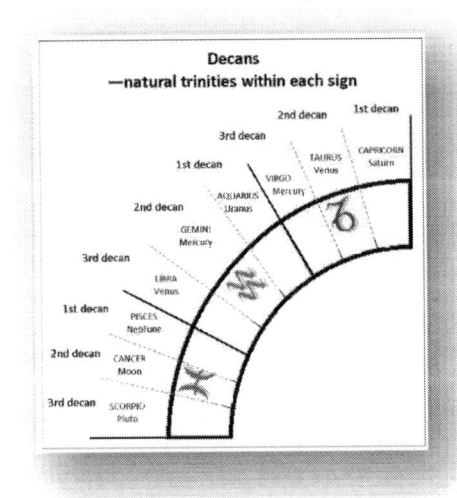

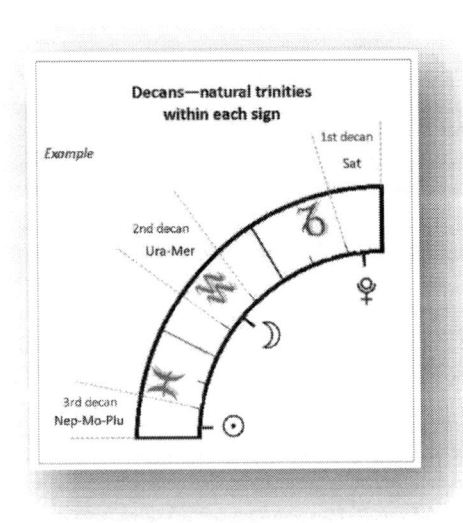

Every sign has a natural trinity within it, ie Aries has Aries, Leo, and Sagittarius. All signs have the natural trinities wherein the first ten degrees is specific to the natural planetary ruler of that sign, the next ten degrees correlates with the natural planetary ruler of the sign that is now combined with the planetary ruler of the sign of the next ten degrees, and the last ten degrees correlates to the natural planetary ruler of the sign now combined with the natural planetary ruler of the sign of that last ten degrees. In essence, there is a natural evolution with the signs, and any given symbol can of course be anywhere within a sign and its degrees. To know why any given symbol is in whatever sign and degree is to know the entire EA signature of any given Soul's individual evolutionary context. (Rad)

For example, if a Soul has a planet at 15 degrees of Sagittarius that will manifest, archetypically, as a combination of Sagittarius and Jupiter combined with Aries and Mars where the lead point is Sagittarius and Jupiter itself in which Aries and Mars are now adding to it. If a person has say Venus at 15 Sagittarius then that Venus is not only being conditioned by the archetypes of Sagittarius and Jupiter, but also the archetypes of Aries and Mars where Sagittarius and Jupiter are the baseline, the lead archetypes, in which the Aries and Mars are added onto. One does not then look to where the natal Mars is. The Aries/Mars archetypes within that 15 degree Venus in Sagittarius example simply means that it's an archetype within the Sagittarius archetype. Mars and Aries, archetypically, are the same. You don't want to link this with the actual placement of Mars but you do want to add the Aries/Mars archetype to the Jupiter/Sagittarius archetype in terms of understanding Venus at 15 Sagittarius in that example. (Rad)

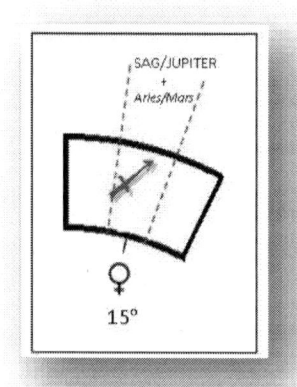

DEGREES AND ORBS

Orbs – how long one has been working on any given issue
The orbs simply correlate to how long a person has been working on any given issue, eg 10 degree orb relative to a square would mean that this would be the first lifetime for a person to work on whatever the two planets/archetypes/dynamics are. Conversely, for example, those same two planets could be in a 6 degree orb relative to the square, and this then suggests, in evolutionary terms, that the person has already been working on those evolutionary issues prior to the current life for at least several lifetimes. As such it is not 'new' to the person, there would be previous experience, and thus the orientation, and behavior, would be different than the person who had the 10 degree orb. (JWG)
Part of "how long the person has been working on any given issue" is that when looking at outer planet aspects like Mars/Pluto, a Soul may require more than one lifetime to progress through ONE crescent/first quarter Mars/Pluto square – 20 degrees. Thus, "how long the person has been working on the issue." Again resisting necessary changes is the underlying issue. Aspects occur WITHIN phases – they are the transition points, mile-markers along the journey through the phases. You can't separate them from phases. (Steve)

TABLE 10 – EA General Orbs				
Conjunction	10 degrees	Sextile	4 degrees
Opposition	10 degrees	Square	10 degrees
Inconjunct/Quincunx	5 degrees	Trine	10 degrees
Quintile	3 degrees	Bi-septile	2 degrees
Sesquiquadrate	5 degrees	Novile	2 degrees
Semi-sextile	3 degrees	Bi-quintile	3 degrees
Semisquare	3 degrees	Tri-septile	2 degrees
Septile	2 degrees		

Working with wider orbs
Aspects are considered as parts of phases, as evolutionary gates or markers to be specific. Thus we work with wider orbs because the orb is seen as part of the evolutionary transition. The closer the aspect is to exact, the stronger the effects will be felt (in most cases) although as always there are exceptions. There are people who are sensitive enough that they feel an upcoming Pluto transit at 12 or 13 degrees away, while others will be almost in exact aspect and tell you they don't feel much going on. EA uses orbs that are wider than many traditional astrologies do. For example, there are four types of squares (crescent, first quarter, disseminating, and last quarter). The meaning of each of those types of square is quite different. Thus it's necessary to understand the archetypes of the phases to truly be able to interpret the meaning of a square. (Steve)
When you are dealing with a sensitive tuned-in aware Soul, these energies can start affecting that Soul even outside of those guidelines – feeling a Pluto transit with a 12 degree orb, for example. It's an individual, case by case scenario. So some people would feel and be affected by sesquiquadrate at 3 degrees, others at 4, others at 5. None of those numbers are cast in stone and the only true answer. They were given as guidelines. The context around those numbers in the message board transcript was Jeffrey saying each astrologer had to determine for themselves what those orbs were, for them. And newer people saying they didn't have

the experience to determine those yet. So Jeffrey posted those lists, of what he used, as guidelines, not as literal truth. Every case is unique. Another, for example, might not really be affected by a Pluto square until an 8 degree orb had been reached. (Steve)

Planet at 0-1 degrees
0 or 1 degrees correlates to the very beginning of an evolutionary cycle. (Rad)

Planet at 29 degrees
29 degrees correlates to the very ending of an entire evolutionary cycle of development. (Rad)
In any chart, composite or otherwise, when Pluto, or any planet, is within a degree or two of the proceeding cusp this correlates, in evolutionary terms, to an evolutionary culmination of the whole archetype of the house of the actual Pluto, and relative to that culmination a new cycle of development is beginning – the proceeding house. (JWG)

Planet at 0 deg or 30 deg of a sign
Within any sign there of course are 30 degrees. When a symbol is at the zero degrees or within a degree or two of that, generally this correlates to a new evolutionary cycle of development relative to that symbol. Yet one must understand the entire EA paradigm, the whole chart, to know WHY that symbol is in a new evolutionary development. So too with a symbol at the end of that 30 degrees. This of course correlates to dynamics that are culminating. But, again, the need to know the entire EA paradigm and the rest of the chart is essential to know WHY that is. Within this to know why and what specifically is new or culminating is to know the entire EA context of any given Soul. Within this to know why and what specifically is new or culminating is to know the entire EA context of any given Soul. (Rad)

Degree of house cusp
This refers to the nature of the decans. The degrees within the decans that are within the signs correlates how far along in the evolutionary development the Soul is within the overall nature of the archetype of the sign itself. (Rad)

Pluto, culminating degree
In any chart, composite or otherwise, when Pluto, or any planet, is within a degree or two of the proceeding cusp this correlates, in evolutionary terms, to an evolutionary culmination of the whole archetype of the house of the actual Pluto, and relative to that culmination a new cycle of development is beginning... the proceeding house. (JWG)
There is always a long standing past. One of the core basics in life is that humans get attached to what they know. It comes to represent what feels safe and secure to us. That includes experiences that are quite dysfunctional – we get used to them and see them as normal, not dysfunctional, because they are the sorts of experiences many Souls have been having, over and over, for a long time. It takes much longer than one lifetime to learn all of the lessons of a single Pluto house. Jeffrey's words mean there have been a series of lives in which the Soul has been learning the lessons of that Pluto house. Thus those lessons, and that orientation to looking at life, have become very familiar. When Pluto is nearing the next house's cusp, that whole series of lives is drawing to a close. That is what "culminating" means. It implies that all necessary things – lessons, endings of outmoded habits and ways of looking at life, etc. – need to come to completion before the Soul can move on. Usually we put off to the end the parts of things we like the least. When an archetype is culminating the Soul will force itself to deal with all of that, through the medium of "you" – the personality. At the same time, the Soul in some ways has gotten tired of the present lessons as it has been engaged in for a series of lives. It feels, senses on the horizon, what is ahead. Something different and new. It experiences that promise as release and it will yearn for it. And yet, it is not there yet – it has to culminate what remains unfinished in the present Pluto house before it can truly move into that new. (Attempting to jump ahead prematurely can be one of the causes of skipped steps). (Steve)

Critical degrees
This theory is not used in E(A) (Rad)

ECLIPSES

Note that the effects of Eclipses are always strongest where they actually occur, and they will also be influential in corresponding geodetic (astro-mapping) regions. When a Lunar Eclipse occurs, our personal and private life journey can "pivot on a dime." The Lunar Eclipse is part of a 19 year Metonic cycle (the evolutionary mandate of an entire nodal cycle). We can be taken by surprise, but in reality, a Lunar Eclipse brings the already building undercurrents to the surface where we are forced to address them. It can reveal circumstances and relationship issues that we may have had a feeling about but have so far ignored, downplayed, avoided, etc. Eclipses can be positive catalysts. The Lunar Eclipse could bring life's circumstances to a long sought after mountain's peak and a potent time of circumstances ripening. Whatever is mobilized will spread with great force (and high volume/mass too). If possible, avoid travel for a few days either side of an Eclipse. Generally the orbs should be tight for an Eclipse – 1 to 1½ deg – perhaps you could consider 2 degrees. Astrologers look at the type of Eclipse and the duration.

The Metonic cycle repeats nearly exactly every 19 years and represents a Saros cycle plus one lunar year. Because it occurs on the same calendar date, the earth's shadow will be in nearly the same location relative to the background stars. It is a nodal return cycle, but more importantly, Metonic Eclipses will have the same luminary positions as their predecessors. Again, the actual Eclipse dates can produce events, but they are also launch-points; Eclipses hold influence over a duration of time. A Metonic Eclipse will complete an entire cycle of ego (Moon, Lunar Eclipse) consciousness and integration (Sun, Solar Eclipse) as it pertains to whatever planet is ignited. It refers to a completion of consciousness, an important time of restructuring. As this viewing and reassessment occurs, the Eclipse catalyst also prompts the creation of new programming at the Soul level. The Eclipse finds the Soul poised at an important threshold, one that advances a new reality and energizes new creations/new life for the Soul. (Rose)

FINAL DISPOSITOR

In traditional astrology there has been the idea of the 'final depositor' of a birth chart that then means that it operates like a 'bottom line' or 'foundation' upon which to understand and view the rest of the birth chart: that it conditions all other archetypes relative to that final depositor. Almost all charts have one or two planets that the rest of the birth chart comes to. In EA terms the obvious question is 'why' where the why correlates to the evolutionary necessity of having whatever planet(s) as the final depositor in the birth chart. (Rad)

HOUSE SYSTEM

Porphyry house system
The Porphyry house system is the preferred system for Evolutionary Astrology because it reflects the law of the trinity. The prime number in this system is '3.' It was developed by a Christian mystic named Porphyry in the 4th century. It is a system that assumes that the space/place of one's birth is equal. (Rad)

The recommended house system for EA is Porphyry. Porphyry is a very old house system that takes the space within each of the four quadrants and divides it into three equal sections. '3' is very important in EA, representing the trinity of past, present, and future, the essence of the Soul's evolutionary journey. (Steve)

As to why are there so many, like anything else in human life, people come up with the latest great idea that they think is superior to existing ideas. Some people sincerely think they have found something that is an improvement on existing methods, while others do something new trying to make a lasting name for themselves. Jeffrey Wolf Green shared with us that he had tried all of the house systems and to him the results he found with Porphyry correlated the closest with what he was experiencing in people's Souls. We are talking about Life, something that is real, breathing and alive, that was created with a set of rules or laws by its Creator. Thus it goes beyond someone having a new great idea. If a house system is going to be accurate it has to correlate with the natural laws of creation. Then it will produce accurate results. Most of the house systems use a quadrant system that divides the circle into 4 quadrants. Quoting from Wikipedia:

"There are many systems of house division. In most the ecliptic is divided into houses and the ascendant (eastern horizon) marks the cusp, or beginning, of the first house, and the descendant (western horizon) marks the cusp of the seventh house. Many systems of house division called quadrant house systems also use the midheaven (medium coeli) as the cusp of the tenth house and the nadir (imum coeli) as the cusp of the fourth house. Some house systems divide the celestial equator and the prime vertical instead of the ecliptic. Goals for a house system include ease of computation; agreement with the 'quadrant' concept (ascendant on the first house cusp, nadir on the fourth, descendant on the seventh, and midheaven on the tenth); defined and meaningful behaviour in the polar regions; acceptable handling of heavenly bodies of high latitude (a distinct problem from high-latitude locations on the Earth's surface); and symbolic value. It is impossible for any system to satisfy all the criteria completely, so each one represents a different compromise. The extremely popular Placidus and Koch systems, in particular, can generate undefined results in the polar circles. Research and debate on the merits of different house systems is ongoing."

Placidus is the most commonly used system. My understanding is this is because it was the first house system with a book of tables to determine house placements. This was before computerized charts, when it was a lot of work to cast a chart. Placidus made it easier so people adopted it. Personally I haven't found its results especially accurate. The main difference in quadrant systems is how the space within one quadrant is divided into 3. In Porphyry, the space is divided into 3 equal parts. Jeffrey felt this modelled the Natural Law of the Trinity that is seen throughout creation. We have cardinal, fixed, and mutable, and past, present, future. Thus 3 equally sized houses. For myself, when I started studying astrology people were asking me, "Where is your Scorpio?" because of the way I was, always seeking the bottom line and wanting to understand the Why of things. I have no planets in Scorpio in my natal chart. When I started learning EA and became aware of house systems, I discovered that in the Porphyry house system my

Pluto is in the last degree of the 8th house, while in most other systems it is in the 9th house. In EA, Pluto, 8th house and Scorpio correlate with the Soul. Thus with Pluto in 8th, the Soul itself is emanating its Scorpio nature. And in the last degree it means this placement is culminating within that Soul. That happened to correlate with exactly how I felt inside myself. This was not revealed in the other house systems I'd tried. Thus I received my own Scorpio proof based on my own case.

Since that time I have fairly often experienced the Porphyry chart shifting certain house positions in client charts that I've almost always felt made more sense than the natal chart they were used to seeing. To me this is an example of why Jeffrey recommended and used the Porphyry house system. I think every EA student should experiment with other house systems if they feel inclined to do so, and reach their own conclusion. The reason to use Porphyry is not because someone said it was better, or the one to use, but because the astrologer has experienced that for them, it is accurate and correlates with what they find within the client whose chart they are reading. That said, for people starting with EA who don't know much about house systems, we suggest using Porphyry. (Steve)

I feel called to clarify that Jeff Green never said that if you are not using Porphyry you are not doing E(A) Based on his own observations and correlations, he came to the conclusion that Porphyry is most accurate for this kind of astrology. Via our own correlation of various house systems to the observed inner Soul dynamics of other people we can certainly come to our own conclusions as long as we are being clear and honest that it is our own conclusion and not trying to convince others or prove others wrong etc. (Ari)

HOUSES AND CUSPS

Degree of a house cusp
The degree of a house cusp refers to the nature of the decans. The degrees within the decans that are within the signs correlates how far along in the evolutionary development the Soul is within the overall nature of the archetype of the sign itself. (Rad)

Planet one degree or less from a house cusp
[Example: Pluto within one degree of the 11th house cusp] Relative to orbs and house cusps: a planet, any planet, one degree or less from a house cusp means that an entire sequence of lives is culminating relative to the archetype of the house/sign that the Pluto, or any planet, is in. It's in essence mutating/evolving from one archetype to the next: the house on its immediate horizon. In this case that would be the 11th house. When a planet, any planet, is within one degree after a house cusp that means the culmination has basically been accomplished and that a brand new sequence of lives is beginning relative to the archetype of the house that that planet is in. (Rad)

When one has an accurate birth time, the natal chart is a map of the present evolutionary condition and intentions of that Soul. All planet locations in the chart are in essence selected by the Soul, Pluto, as they reflect (as in, indicate) where that Soul is at, where it left off in the previous life, where it intends to go in this life. When a planet is near the beginning or end of a house it means that a new phase of evolution, relative to the archetypes of that planet and house, is at hand. When it is near the beginning, that new phase has just begun. When it is near the end it is approaching. It all comes down to, we are where we are. We are not where we wish to be, no matter how strongly we desire or even believe we are there. We are where we are. And it is through accepting and embracing *where we are* that we best speed up the process of becoming what we wish to be. Again, being near the end of something is not the same as having completed it, no matter how much we yearn to be done with it and on with the next thing. The point to remember is *we are where we are*. That is what the birth chart indicates. Whether we want to believe what it is telling us is another matter altogether! (Steve)

Planet at 0 deg or 30 deg of a sign
Within any sign there of course are 30 degrees. When a symbol is at the zero degrees or within a degree or two of that, generally this correlates to a new evolutionary cycle of development relative to that symbol. Yet one must understand the entire EA paradigm, the whole chart, to know WHY that symbol is in a new evolutionary development. So too with a symbol at the end of that 30 degrees. This of course correlates to dynamics that are culminating. But, again, the need to know the entire EA paradigm and the rest of the chart is essential to know WHY that is. Within this to know why and what specifically is new or culminating is to know the entire EA context of any given Soul. Within this to know why and what specifically is new or culminating is to know the entire EA context of any given Soul. (Rad)

Decans – see DECANS above.

Signs on the houses

The signs on the houses correlate with how any given Soul's consciousness is orientated to phenomenal reality. So, for example, the 11th house correlates to specific archetypes within human consciousness, and any sign on that house then correlates to the archetypes, defined by that sign, of how any given Soul's consciousness is orientated to that 11th house. In essence, they are conditioning that 11th house for the evolutionary purposes of that Soul. The specific location of the planet that rules that sign, in this example Sagittarius which is ruled by Jupiter of course, then further conditions that orientation by its own house and sign placement. This in turn can be further conditioned by any aspects that it is making to other planets. The way JWG used to explain this is that the specific location of the planets within the birth chart correlate with the psychology within the consciousness of the individual Soul. (Rad)

"Culminating" archetype

In any chart, composite or otherwise, when Pluto, or any planet, is within a degree or two of the proceeding cusp this correlates, in evolutionary terms, to an evolutionary culmination of the whole archetype of the house of the actual Pluto, and relative to that culmination a new cycle of development is beginning – the proceeding house. (JWG)

There is always a long standing past. One of the core basics in life is that humans get attached to what they know. It comes to represent what feels safe and secure to us. That includes experiences that are quite dysfunctional – we get used to them and see them as normal, not dysfunctional, because they are the sorts of experiences many Souls have been having, over and over, for a long time. It takes much longer than one lifetime to learn all of the lessons of a single Pluto house. Jeffrey's words mean there have been a series of lives in which the Soul has been learning the lessons of that Pluto house. Thus those lessons, and that orientation to looking at life, have become very familiar. When Pluto is nearing the next house cusp, that whole series of lives is drawing to a close. That is what "culminating" means. It implies that all necessary things – lessons, endings of outmoded habits and ways of looking at life, etc. – need to come to completion before the Soul can move on. Usually we put off to the end the parts of things we like the least. When an archetype is culminating the Soul will force itself to deal with all of that, through the medium of "you" – the personality. At the same time, the Soul in some ways has gotten tired of the present lessons it has been engaged in for a series of lives. It feels, senses on the horizon, what is ahead. Something different and new. It experiences that promise as release and it will yearn for it. And yet, it is not there yet – it has to culminate what remains unfinished in the present Pluto house before it can truly move into that new. (Attempting to jump ahead prematurely can be one of the causes of skipped steps.) (Steve)

It IS CULMINATING, IS MUTATING. It does not say HAS CULMINATED, HAS MUTATED. When you are in the last month of your senior year in college you do not consider yourself graduated but as *imminently* graduating. It's not over until it's over, no matter how close "over" is. You would interpret yourself in that way – I'm graduating from college, almost there. The smell of the new is on the horizon – the next house – you can feel, sense, taste, smell it coming, you may be excited about it, you may be a little scared about it, but you are not there yet. That is how we'd see it ourself. It is the Pluto [or planet] with balsamic overtones. This is not balsamic in the classic EA sense of an aspect of conjunction prior to exact conjunction. But it has the *flavor* of balsamic, culmination. And the balsamic archetypes apply. It is possible during the course of this life that the planet enters the next house by progression – that is a symbol of the ongoing evolution. Yet the imprint of the natal chart remains throughout the present life, as the natal placements symbolize the underlying evolutionary causes of this present life. When those are fulfilled the person is leaving the present body as there's no longer any reason to sustain it. (Steve)

Planet conjunct a non-angular house cusp

The individual will exhibit psychological/behavioral dynamics of both of the archetypes. In the case where the planet is before the actual house cusp in question the bottom line in those dynamics will be the actual house that the planet is in while moving towards the archetypal dynamics of the house that it is moving towards. In the case where the planet is already in the house by one degree or less the bottom line dynamics will be that house with an 'overlay' of the dynamics/behaviors of the house that has just been left behind. (Rad)

Pluto, evolutionary progression through the houses

Pluto does NOT naturally evolve in progression through lifetimes from, example, the 10th house to an 11th house, then a 12th house, etc. (Rad)

Two signs in a house

The sign on that house cusp correlates with the archetypal orientation to that house. When another sign is within that house, and is then coming through that sign on the cusp, it is itself then 'conditioned' by that sign. Each sign has a natural trinity within it, ie Cancer has Cancer, Scorpio, and Pisces. All signs have their natural trinities. Thus, there is an evolution within the archetypes of all signs. Each sign has a natural division of 10 within it due to the natural trinity of three signs. Thus, the first ten degrees of any sign correlate with that sign. The next ten degrees incorporates that sign and the next within the trinity. And the last ten degrees the entire trinity that exists within any sign. So, following the Cancer example, the first 10 degrees would be pure Cancer, the next 10 would be Cancer and Scorpio, and the final 10 would be Cancer, Scorpio, and Pisces. So the actual degree of the sign on a cusp correlates to this natural evolution within a sign. And it is this degree of evolution that then 'conditions' the entire house that the sign is on the cusp of. So when there is another sign within that house that sign is thus conditioned by the evolutionary nature of the sign on the cusp as symbolized by the actual degree of that sign on the cusp. Both signs are considered because the sign on the cusp is the determinant of how that other sign in the house is being conditioned, and for what reasons from an EA point of view. Both signs are equally significant from an EA point of view. (Rad)

INTERCEPTED SIGNS

Generally speaking, when you find intercepted signs there are two reasons for it from an evolutionary point of view. The first is that these specific archetypes that are intercepted have been so thoroughly developed prior to the current life that the Soul does not need to develop those areas any further. If Aquarius is intercepted, yet the planetary ruler, Uranus is heavily aspected, or the Soul has a stacked 11th house, etc., then you can deduce that this case applies to that Soul. The second reason is that these archetypes have not been fully developed prior to the current life, again necessarily so, and that in this life the Soul is intended to develop those areas within consciousness. If there are no aspects to Uranus, or planets in the 11th house or Aquarius, then you could most likely determine this is the case for the Soul. These archetypes will become active through transit and progression of the natal chart for example. (Deva)

Intercepted sign in composite
Please read Pluto 2 (there is a section about intercepted signs) for guidelines as to how to determine "who is who." (Deva)
As far as EA methodology is concerned, you don't *have to* find the phases between anything. It's all completely optional. The whole point of the phases material in EA is, as was written in Pluto Vol. 2, that everything in creation is in a relationship with everything else in creation. Phases, and within them aspects, are indicators of where in their cycles the two planets (or points or bodies) are *in relationship to* each other. The sum total of all those relationships correlates to the sum total of the chart those relationships are appearing in. The issue is, there is way too much detail in all of that for almost anyone to be able to take in and assimilate. There are limits to what we can handle. Thus, Jeffrey laid out what he called "key planetary pairs." Those are the ones that he felt revealed the most to the EA astrologer. Thus I suggest concentrating on them, at least in the beginning of learning phases. This is not to be taken as some form of gospel – you don't have to do it this way. It's a suggested starting point, at least while learning the system. Each astrologer is going to find planetary combinations that are especially significant, or insignificant to them, and as they go along they should follow their intuition on this. The whole point of the cycle of phases and aspects, as opposed to the way typical astrology is taught most of the time, is that whether or not there is an aspect between two bodies, they are still in relationship to each other. The aspects represent gateway points, where either the past meeting the future tends to create stress, as it's a time when we are intended to move forward into yet another unknown, or, in the case of harmonious aspects like trines and sextiles, a point of fruition, where all the hard work we have been doing reaches a pinnacle and we get to experience the fruits from our labors for a while. (The ending of those fruition periods tends to be some of the more difficult periods to release from. Who wants to go from a time when things are almost magically working back into a time of stress and having to face more things?) The spaces between aspects are the times when we are simply in the evolutionary learning periods. This is akin to how the movement of the seasons from one day to the next is barely perceptible. Yet it is still going on, the proof being that it inevitably reaches the next seasonal change point. Those seasonal change points are the four squares in the chart, and the day to day movement towards them is like the times when two bodies in the chart are not within orb of an aspect. The shifting that is then going on between them is the necessary work/changes that lead to their next entrance into the orb of an aspect. (Steve)
In any given life the Soul chooses the lunar phase between the Sun and the Moon, as well as all other phases between planets, that it needs in order to continue with its ongoing evolutionary progression where the nature of that progression is then reflected in the exact phases between all the planets including the phase between the Sun and the Moon. In essence, it is the entire evolutionary context of any given Soul's prior lives that then dictate which specific phases between the planets to manifest. Once that entire evolutionary context is correctly understood then the 'why' of whatever the phases are between all the planets, including the Sun and the Moon, can be seen and understood. (Rad)

Intercepted sign within a house – Porphyry house system
An anonymous chart to demonstrate that an intercepted sign within a house is possible with the Porphyry house system. The houses within the quadrants are equal, but the quadrants themselves are not. (Linda)

KEY PLANETARY PAIRS (JWG)

Synthesizing the archetypes
These are the definitions of the key planetary pairs. Now you can place them in their phasal context and you will have some information in order to understand how they are operating archetypically. Then you add the next layer, the signs they are in, then the houses they are in, and then you synthesize, which is the art of the astrologer, the ability to synthesize archetypes, even if they are competing archetypes – that is the art of astrology, no longer a technical issue, but an art.

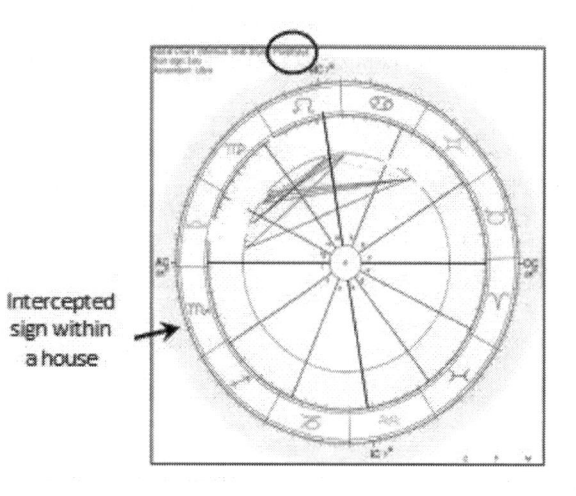

Sun/Moon phase
These correlate to the psychological notion of self-actualization, the need in all people to actualize their inherent purpose for their life on a day to day basis, to give that purpose a face and image, a way of personally identifying itself, Moon. It describes how the person continuously is integrating them self on a moment to moment, second to second, year to year basis. Now, the need to give it a self-image or a name equals the need to feel secure with it. The Moon, of itself, correlates to the nature, type and relative strength of one's ego, the phenomena of the ego itself. It is not possible to get rid of the ego. You cannot operate on the brain and remove the ego nor can you remove it psychologically. The issue, spiritually speaking, is to align that ego with the divine ego, that is what the true meaning of getting rid of the ego means. The ego is necessary because it is an individualizing agent. It gives a self-image. That self-image can be quite different, by the way, than how other people see you. There can be a discrepancy. What others see and what you see in the mirror is the Ascendant, how one instinctually projects oneself without forethought. It is pure instinct. So, the Sun/Moon describes this by phase. If it is new phase, this is not clearly described, from an evolutionary point of view, as how you go about actualizing yourself, your purpose in this life, comes under this new phase, instinctually. The Sun/Moon new phase has the instinctual need to initiate experience without encumbrance, without obligation, without commitment, without excessive apology or explanations. It is the need to have enough freedom in life to initiate enough experiences to gather the necessary reactions to find out about yourself and what that purpose is and, at a deeper level, to generate an egocentric structure which in a new phase is forever changing. When a new phase Sun/Moon gets frustrated or confused, it borrows from the full phase – the law of polarity.
Let's say we have Sun/Moon new phase, which is essentially an Arian vibration, and what if those two are in Capricorn, double Capricorn. Relative to the emergence of the new cycle, the new self, the new purpose, the new ego which is not formulated, it is obviously possible that this person is going to take his clues from the social system into which he is born and that from them. A classic illustration of this is Nixon. Nixon with a Sun in Capricorn and Moon in Aquarius, new phase, and yet a 10th house Pluto. He gravitated to powerful social identities, lawyer, EP, Senator, liar, that equaled his sense of personal identity and thus accepted all the prevailing social customs and norms as convenient props to use. This is why you had that weird body type. You have this Capricorn which is trying to contain the Aquarius which is trying to erupt; a person who doesn't know what they are. So you had all these herky-jerky movements, and all the sweat. Whole coats would be lost. Showering and airing wouldn't help. That is because of the high degree of inner compression equaling resistance.

Moon/Saturn
These correlate to your ability to integrate your ego, your personal identity, who you are within the context of the social systems and/or culture, Saturn, in which you find yourself. The ability to establish your own authority within the authority of the culture. Earlier, it is the social conditioning of family. Heritage, consensus values, lifestyles, beliefs, social class and sociological context – all these shape one's identity. This archetype perpetuates the status quo, the mainstream.
With a new phase Moon/Saturn, you are going to be highly susceptible to your family's imprint but, you are also going to find the instinct to define it, Saturn, yourself, Moon. This can create a clash with the parents and ultimately a cultural clash at some point. With the Moon/Saturn in Aries instead of Capricorn, parents who simply expect you to conform to their ways are going to be faced with a potential battle from day one. Contrast that with the Moon/Saturn being in Aries/Taurus still new phase. Now we would see cycles of collision, butting heads with cycles of stability, Taurus. Ultimately, the Moon/Saturn tells you how you are going to integrate into society.

Mars/Venus

How one completes oneself through relationships. The act of creation itself is a coupling, the coupling of the creator with its creation. The dynamic of relationship is pervasive and exists at all levels. It is also how one is relating to oneself and thus, how one is relating to another.

Mars/Venus in a crescent phase septile is an individual who is struggling to establish through introspection the uniqueness of her own needs and thus what she desires. The need to bulwark herself from the expectation, Venus, disseminating phase, of society. Throughout her life she will attract key people who will point out the right direction relative to the "y" in the road. This person will feel that she has a special, ie septile, mate to be with.

TABLE 11 – Key Planetary Pairs (JWG)

Sun/Moon	The need in all people to actualize the inherent purpose for their life on a day to day basis, to give that purpose a face and image, a way of personally identifying itself, Moon. It describes how the person continuously is integrating them self on a moment to moment, second to second, year to year basis.
Moon/Saturn	Your ability to integrate your ego, your personal identity, who you are within the context of the social systems and/or culture, Saturn, in which you find yourself. The ability to establish your own authority within the authority of the culture.
Mars/Venus	How one completes oneself through relationships.
Mercury/Jupiter	How one establishes her beliefs, her principles, her philosophies, and creates the necessary intellectual apparatus to explain them, to communicate them.
Jupiter/Saturn	Jupiter correlates to your beliefs and how they are in harmony or disharmony with the consensus belief patterns of the culture you are in thus, impacting your ability to economically survive. The economic issue relative to philosophy is obvious. The Jupiter/Saturn cycle has a 20 year life.
Saturn/Uranus	This is the most important cycle. It has a 48-year life and comes to maturity every 22 to 24 years after its conjunction. It establishes the social tone, structure, every 48 years. The new social impulse, order, structures.

Mercury/Jupiter

This is how one establishes her beliefs, her principles, her philosophies, and creates the necessary intellectual apparatus to explain them, to communicate them. As a result, it correlates to how the person goes about learning as a general dynamic throughout life. All the facts that one learns can ultimately be put together into a belief system.

Mercury/Jupiter in a first quarter square represents a person who instinctually resists or repels information, beliefs or philosophies that she, herself, has not decided upon. She is therefore, resistant to learning that which she does not want to learn. She may become combative or argumentative in conversations and communications of all kinds. She is considered to be strongly opinionated and yet by nature, she is destined to attract, based upon her inner vibration, people who are just as strongly opinionated, just as argument and confrontation prone. This could be a problem for a 71-year old who is now forced to go through the public education system. Let's put Mercury in Aquarius and Jupiter in Scorpio. As a form of rebellion, he would simply withdraw from the teacher. It would be covert, probably, but just as effective. So, in effect, this pair describes how you go about learning. In the new phase, this represents a person who challenges existing facts in order to determine new facts from such challenges. This would be different from a person who has Mercury/Jupiter in a disseminating trine. Here is a person who is tired from the battle, evolutionarily speaking.

Jupiter/Saturn

Again, Jupiter is correlating to your beliefs and how these beliefs are going to be linked or in harmony or disharmony with the consensus belief patterns of the culture in which you find yourself thus, impacting, ie beliefs do determine lifestyle, or your ability to economically survive. If one's beliefs are inherently antithetical to society's beliefs, one would have to create a lifestyle outside that society which impairs one's ability to earn a living, to make it financially.

Mercury in Pisces and Jupiter in Gemini in last quarter square would be confused about all kinds of ideas which come at them because they are susceptible to the prevailing ideas and would try to adopt them for themselves because they do not know what to think, Pisces. It is in a mutational state, crisis in consciousness, it is leaving behind that which has come before, but without conception, Pisces, and trying to compensate, Jupiter in Gemini, by adopting those Gemini ideas and calling them their own. But, because of the impulse of the last quarter, it will just throw out as it goes. It will adopt, apply for a while, throw out, adopt some more, throw out. So there will be cycles of clarity where some ideas will work for a while, then they will not work which sets in motion a pattern of collecting more information, etc.

The Jupiter/Saturn cycle has a 20-year life, from conjunction to conjunction and comes to a point of maturity at the opposition every 10 years. When they are in a new phase, you have the impulse of a new economic philosophy relative to political context which is now initiated by whoever happens to be holding power.

Saturn/Uranus
This is the most important cycle. It has a 48-year life from conjunction to conjunction and comes to maturity every 22 years to 24 years after the conjunction. It establishes the social tone, structure, every 48 years. The new social impulse, order, structures. For example, the last conjunction took place in 1942 in Taurus. The context at that time was WW2 and life was on the line. The instinct for survival of the human species is the archetype of Taurus. The revolutionary impulse of Uranus redefining the current structure, Saturn. The maturity in the late 60's was a radical revolution in values, Taurus, personal and human values. The effort was made to radically redefine society itself. The Jews' attitude in the concentration camps was that it was an act of revenge to survive and became a slogan amongst the Jews in the camps.

The original conjunction is now in a balsamic state with itself and is getting ready to form another conjunction next year [1988]. This next one is most important because it is going to be taking place in the center of our galaxy between 26-28 degrees Sagittarius. Sequentially, there is an inconjunction between the cycle that is now completing and the new one starting next year. Think about that in terms of necessary adjustments.

Mars/Venus phase in relationship
The Soul requires an external partner who is defined in the same way. Generally speaking, an individual who has a balsamic Mars/Venus phase can only really feel right with another in an intimate relationship who also has their Mars/Venus in a balsamic phase. (JWG)

What I think JWG must have meant is first that a Mars/Venus balsamic person can get along with just about anyone because of the balsamic phase, and, second, for such a Soul to feel really 'right' in an intimate relationship that another Soul either had to have their own balsamic Mars/Venus phase and/or other symbols that would correlate to such an inner orientation such as Venus or Mars being in Pisces or the 12th house, or possibly in some major aspect to Neptune. (Rad)

LAYERS

Layers – house, planet, sign, aspects, etc.
In EA we are taught to start with the house, this representing the deepest expression of the energies in that part of the chart. Example: the 10th house is inherently Saturnian so anything in the 10th house will operate in a Saturnian way. The sign on the house cusp represents the next level up. The art of EA is to synthesize how the natural house energy filtered through a layer of the sign on the cusp operates like. If Pluto is in that house, add in another layer – what does the natural house energy filtered through a layer of the sign on the cusp expressing itself in a Scorpionic (Pluto) way operate like? Starting with the evolutionary state, the social conditioning patterns, and the evolutionary signature (Pluto, nodes, nodal rulers), you quickly have a detailed picture of how that Soul/ego is structured, from the core out. (Steve)

LILITH TRINITY

> "The asteroids are symbolic transformers between two energy systems and point to the techniques by which the lower octave vibrations may be raised to a higher octave.
> The **Asteroid Lilith** describes the first stage in the mythical journey where she is suppressed, humiliated and flees in a fiery rage to the desolate wilderness.
> The **Dark Moon Lilith** depicts the pain of her exile where she plots and executes revenge.
> The **Black Moon Lilith** shows how she transmutes her distorted image back into its natural healthy expression." (Demetra George)

Asteroid Lilith indicates where our WOUND originated.
Dark Moon Lilith signifies how and where we experience the distorted aspects of Lilith in our lives
– her anguish, bitterness, betrayal, alienation, fear and hatred of sexuality, and revenge.
Black Moon Lilith shows how and where we cut away our pretensions, false roles, and delusions
and actualize who we essentially are. (Adina)

ASTEROID LILITH

Symbol: ⚴ Horizontal line with four little lines coming off it
Astrodienst: Listed as asteroid No. 1181

Asteroid Lilith is the only Lilith that is an actual, verifiable physical body.

"The asteroid Lilith shows how and where we experience the themes of suppression, resentment, explosive anger, rejection, and flight in our lives. She also indicates the ways in which we need to assert our own truths." (Demetra George)

Asteroid Lilith (4-5 year cycle) describes the original Lilith. We have all 'imprinted' in us the original, undistorted, female image, which is defined by the natal placement of an individual's asteroid Lilith. Where we feel free to move, act and speak our truth. This correlates in the current life to what our underlying ideal image is of a woman. The true and NATURAL expression of Lilith is that of pure, raw, feminine beauty. A woman that would chose freedom over just about anything. She is Pluto and she is also Mars. She was honored and praised for initiating and fully expressing her personal freedom and sexual passion. "In her original state, she is a symbol of true feminine power – complete unto herself and embodying her own brand of feminine self-containment, assertion and wholeness" (O'Donnell). Lilith is the octave transformer for Mars and Pluto! It serves as a bridge between the lower octave of Mars and the higher octave of Pluto. (Kristin)

Wherever the original Lilith (asteroid) shows up in a MAN'S CHART REFLECTS HIS IDEAL IMAGE OF A WOMAN. If the energy is blocked, the asteroid shows where we experience the themes of suppression, resentment, anger and flight in our lives. It orbits around the Sun along with many other asteroids in the belt between Mars and Jupiter. (JWG)

TABLE 9 – Lilith Trinity

	Symbol	Other names	astro.com	Appears in astro.com chart as	Actual or hypothetical
Asteroid Lilith	⚴	Natural Lilith	1181 in the Additional Asteroids list	Lilit	Asteroid Lilith is a real asteroid. It is the only Lilith that is an actual, verifiable physical body. In the main asteroid belt between Mars and Jupiter. Takes 4 years to orbit the Sun.
Black Moon Lilith (True)	⚸	Osculating Lunar Apogee, Apogee Lilith, True Osculating Lilith, "True" Lilith/Black Moon, Osc. Lilith, Osc. Apogee, Moon's Apogee, Osculating Lunar Apogee, Black Moon Osc., Resolution Lilith	h13	OSC. L	Not a solid object. It is a mathematical point of alignment, the apogee of the Moon's orbit, furthest away from the Earth. 9 year orbit. Spends 9 months in each sign. EA uses the True Apogee for Black Moon Lilith.
Black Moon Lilith (Mean)	⚸	Mean Lilith, Resolution Lilith	'Lilith' under Additional Objects	⚸ (white)	EA uses the True Apogee for Black Moon Lilith.
Dark Moon Lilith	⊘	Waldemath Dark Moon, DML New Moon, Waldemath's Moon, Waldemath Black Moon, Sepherial's Moon, Dark Moon, Ghost Moon	h58 hypothetical planet	Walde	Dark Moon Lilith is a real body in the sky, a 'hypothetical planet' resembling a dust cloud, or a second Moon of Earth. Takes 119 days to orbit the Earth. Spends 10 days in each sign.

BLACK MOON LILITH

Symbols: ⚸ Black Moon Lilith (True) ⚸ Black Moon Lilith (Mean)
Other names: Resolution Lilith, Apogee Lilith, True Osculating Lilith, Mean Lilith, Osc. Lilith, Osc. Apogee, Moon's Apogee, Osculating Lunar Apogee, Black Moon Osc.
Astro.com: Black Moon Lilith (True) listed as h13 – appears in chart as osc. L
Black Moon Lilith (Mean) listed under "Additional Objections" as "Lilith"
– appears in Astrodienst charts as a white version of this: ⚸

EA uses the True Apogee for Black Moon Lilith. (Jason)

The Black Moon Lilith is the resolution to the other two Liliths (the original women). Black Moon Lilith correlates to Hecate. (JWG) Black Moon Lilith shows how and where we cut away our pretensions, false roles, and delusions and actualize who we essentially are. The Black Moon Lilith (9 year cycle) is the resolution Lilith where one's distorted image may be transformed into a natural healthy expression. The dark Goddess's crescent shape knife cuts away all that is not authentic in our lives. The ENFORCED (I REPEAT ENFORCED) clarity of the Black Moon allows us to penetrate to the essence, eliminating all things that are unnecessary, false and impure. Wherever you find the resolution Lilith in your chart, represents an area where it will take tremendous COURAGE, where you can release the repressed anger from lifetimes and be set free. It is also an area of TRANSFORMATION – creative energy of the feminine GODDESS pours into you. Lilith is the NATURAL WILD WOMAN in the birth chart so the Moon and the Nodes must be incorporated in the interpretation as well as Venus. Stressful aspects between Black Moon Lilith and Mars, the planet that most clearly expresses the masculine power, may indicate that a woman's independence and confidence is threatened or met with opposition by men. Her own inner male is not strong. Women who have hard aspects from Black Moon Lilith to the Moon or in the 5th may have problems with pregnancy or childbirth, possible miscarriage, unwanted pregnancy, or a fear of motherhood. Often times transiting Black Moon Lilith can bring back feelings of emotional pain, but only if it is in the area where you have compromised your primal nature. Lilith forces us to look at ourselves with utter naked EMOTIONAL honesty. (Kristin)

DARK MOON LILITH

Symbol: ⦰ Circle with a line through it at an angle of about 1 pm and 7 pm. The line goes completely thru and extends beyond the line of the circle on each side.
Other names: Waldemath Dark Moon, Waldemath's Moon, Sepherial's Moon, Lunar Apogee, Dark Moon, Ghost Moon.
Astrodienst: Listed as hypothetical planet h58 – appears in chart as "Walde."

Dark Moon Lilith is a real body in the sky, a hypothetical planet such as a second moon or dust cloud.

"Some say there is a second moon circling the earth – a mysterious, dark moon, seen only rarely when the sky is dark and it is either in opposition to or crossing the suns face. It has a dusky presence that absorbs light rather than reflecting it. Observations by astronomers were recorded as long ago as 1618." – Kelley Hunter, Living Lilith, 2009

Dark Moon Lilith (119-177 day cycle) signifies how and where we experience the distorted aspects of Lilith in our lives – her anguish, bitterness, betrayal, alienation, fear and hatred of sexuality, and revenge. For centuries men and women have been conditioned by our patriarchal culture to suppress this feminine strength which has resulted in bitterness and resentment, inevitably leading to distortion and rage. How this distortion is played out is indicated by the natal placement of the Dark Moon Lilith. Dark Moon Lilith is the distorted Lilith representing Lilith's flee into a fiery rage of exile where she plots and executes her revenge. Find your Dark Moon Lilith placement and know that this area ***also creates a channel by which we can release the rage.*** (Kristin)

Unlike Black Moon Lilith, Dark Moon Lilith is a real body in the sky, a second Moon to the Earth that doesn't reflect light, hence the name Dark Moon. The glyph for Dark Moon Lilith is a zero with a forward slash running diagonally through it. There is some controversy over whether it is really there since it can only be seen as a spot moving across the Sun. However, there have been sightings since the 1600's as detailed in Delphine Jay's book, Interpreting Lilith, pages 1-6. Dr. Georges Waltemath, an astronomer, documented it in 1898 and came up with calculations which gave it an orbit of 119 days around the Earth. The astrologer Sepharial used the Waltemath calculations to come up with an ephemeris but he made errors which caused a difference of anywhere from about 2 to over 40 degrees. Delphine Jay, Ivy Goldstein-Jacobson, Mae Ludlum-Wilson and others copied Sepharial's calculations. The original Waltemath calculations can be found in Solar Fire software or Riyal freeware. Many astrologers use the Sepharial calculations with success, but the Waltemath calculations are more accurate. Dark Moon Lilith can be interpreted similarly to the other Liliths. Delphine Jay says Dark Moon Lilith is a place where you must operate impersonally because operating personally there will never be successful. (Lucius)

Our feminine principle and its evolution before, during and beyond the patriarchy. **Dark Moon Lilith** or Waldemath Dark Moon is a debated dark body/shadow revolving around the Earth. As it is debated it has more than one ephemeris. There is a 10-12 degree difference between the Solar Fire and Astrodienst ephemerides. The third symbol, **Black Moon Lilith**, is the ever moving focal point between the Moon and the Earth. This symbol is a point in space, an empty point which in essence symbolizes the midpoint on an invisible 'wire' between the Moon and the Earth. Today it comes up on the Astrodienst website within the most used asteroids window as 'Lilith' (Mean Lilith). However it is Black Moon Lilith, and its number is h13 (True Lilith). These three symbols in their totality correlating to our inner feminine principle contain a sequence hidden in them. They tell a threefold story of this aspect of our consciousness within our unique, individual Soul-history embracing past, present and future. Meaning, they unravel the mystery how our inner feminine principle has been affected, and how it operated before and during the patriarchy, while the symbolism also points out the way our feminine principle can be healed and how it can grow beyond the patriarchal distortion. These symbols can be applied to individual as well as to collective charts shedding light on the feminine principle and its evolution. These three symbols will be presented from the point of view how they correlate to our inner feminine principle, no matter which gender we incarnate.

Lilith the asteroid in any chart is an indicator of our original, individual feminine aspect, and how it was experienced within an equality-based matriarchal social setting. It will also correlate to how this aspect of our Soul reacted to the transition of the patriarchy when – relative to our own Soul history – it began to become a part of our experiences. We all have this essential feminine aspect within our Soul and of course this principle has been wounded and distorted in all of us via the takeover of the patriarchy – whether we know it consciously or not. How we encountered and then responded to the new patriarchal order will be signified by asteroid Lilith. This symbol sheds light on our individual history in this respect, via sign house and aspects. From there onward a progressive distortion occurred to our feminine nature in one way or another. This progressive distortion during and because of the patriarchy has a peak which is the greatest distortion of our feminine aspect caused by the insanity of the unnatural order within which we were all forced to live.

The symbol for this peak distortion is symbolized by **Dark Moon Lilith** or Waldemath Dark Moon. It's interesting to note the fact that today we have two different ephemeris's for this symbol: it's a kind of a shadow noted by only a few and debated by many. The two different ephemerides literally 'shadow' an area in our chart instead of giving a fixed point. Perhaps it is symbolic of the fact that the distortion is more than a point: it is an area in our consciousness through which the feminine in us has been most deeply affected by this peak distortion symbolism. It reflects the fact that the distortion is manifold impacting a whole area, and from there of course affecting our overall consciousness. The area that is between the two points (that the two different ephemerides give) is usually between 6-15 degrees. Thus it sometimes falls in one sign and house but sometimes affects another sign and house as well. The fact that it is debated, is unclear, and yet still used in different programs with different ephemerides appears as a perfectly fitting correlation: a feeling of uncertainty as it kind of goes into an unknown darkness. Unclear boundaries of an uncertain territory; the nature of the shadow.

The third symbol is **Black Moon Lilith**, the focal point between the Moon and Earth. This is the balancing/resolving symbol. It points out how to heal and recover our wounded, distorted feminine principle. This threefold symbolism clearly demonstrates what happened and how relative to our own Soul history (our whole chart) and relative to our own inner feminine principle (Lilith). This original feminine is what has been 'cast out' forcing it to sink into an 'unclear darkness' (Dark Moon Lilith) during the patriarchy – collectively as well as individually. For millennia women had to literally stop existing as they once were. This affected each one of us no matter what gender we were manifesting through. Our inner feminine principle was shattered inwardly and outwardly it became a shadow. Just as women had to literally become a shadow – a shadow of men as it was described to them –the only way for them to exist.

The resolution point, Black Moon Lilith, being the focal point between the Moon and the Earth has a deep symbolism. It is the center point, the balance point between the Earth and its water – moving, life giving, balancing, celestial body part – the Moon. According to current scientific research the formation of the Moon is what triggered a chemical and climatic chain reaction which resulted in life on Earth as we know it today. Black Moon Lilith is the symbol in our chart via which we can consciously heal, resolve and re-embrace our inner feminine principle. It points the way to how this cast-out, wounded part of us, diminished to a shadow, can be resolved to re-emerge intact again in our consciousness. Without the healing of the feminine no healthy life is possible for women and men. The imbalance of life caused by the patriarchy must be re-balanced and healed within us all. Black Moon Lilith is our own unique way which of course is connected to our original feminine principle and the specific wounds and distortions it went through. This focal point is like an invisible bridge between the Earth and its most immediate 'heavenly' partner, the Moon. Healing our inner feminine aspect leads to healing our emotions and our self-image. (Moon) The three Lilith symbols in the chart tell an interesting and complex story within our Soul-history, the story of our feminine principle. It embraces the past, present and the direction of the future from this particular point of view: the evolution of our feminine principle. The three Liliths can be applied to individual as well as collective charts: they always shed light as to what happened and how to the original feminine principle and how this principle can return to us as individuals or within a collective Soul. (Lia)

Lilith trinity and the chakras
We know that there are different planets that rule the chakras, but these Asteroid Goddesses can also be seen ruling each chakra. Original Lilith rules the ROOT chakra as she is the undistorted natural feminine, the unconditioned wild woman, independent, totally aligned with natural law, full unto herself. She is your primal feminine ROOT, and the Original Lilith placement for a woman reflects HOW YOU WERE DESIGNED BY GOD/DESS. In a man's chart the Original Lilith placement would reflect a man's ideal image of a

woman or how he most naturally actualizes the feminine within. The Resolution Lilith, otherwise known as the Black Moon (not to be confused with the Dark Moon Lilith which is where we have all gotten off course via our distortions), symbolized by the crescent Moon and cross below and most often seen in Solar Fire, symbolizes the way we get back to our ORIGINAL ROOT, hence the word Resolution. The Resolution Lilith lights the way back to our true feminine self, she shows you HOW to get back home to your unwavering center. Working with this Lilith trinity is a powerful exercise when you weave it into the Pluto paradigm, especially considering that Lilith is the octave transformer between Pluto and Mars. Once any Soul uncovers and remembers HOW they were originally designed, the Mars piece can be adjusted, as in choices made, that can now facilitate evolution. It works like a tuning fork, when any Soul is in harmony with their pure self, the weight of whatever has been collected will start flying off. (Kristin)

Octave transformers

The Asteroids act as octave transformers because they dwell BETWEEN the inner-conscious-rational-leftbrain-personal planets (Mercury, Venus, Mars) and the outer transpersonal-unconscious-rightbrain-spiritual planets (Uranus, Neptune, Pluto), and therefore are seen as "transformers in the archetypal circuitry" by raising lower octave vibrations to a higher octave. The role of the Asteroids is to re-awaken the FEMININE energy so that individuals and thus the collective become more whole. The incorporation of the conscious with the depths of the unconscious requires FEMININE perception, focus, insight, awareness, sensitivity, intuition, imagination, therefore the Asteroids form this necessary 'bridge.' A shift is occurring between the thinking-rational processes and becoming more in tune with the emotions. Individuals cannot give to the Collective a wholeness that they do not yet possess, therefore the Feminine needs to be fostered and nurtured in the evolution of consciousness as we come out of patriarchal conditioning. (Linda)

LOWER OCTAVE	OCTAVE TRANSFORMERS	HIGHER OCTAVE	PERSONAL DESIRE TO ACT FOR THE COLLECTIVE INTEREST
Mercury	**Pallas** *(feminine creative energy birthing new ideas)*	Uranus	Mercurial mind inspired and transformed by Uranian illuminations.
Venus	**Juno** *(sacred marriage, emotional truth)*	Neptune	Venus values and feelings raised by Neptunian compassion.
Mars	**Lilith** *(wisdom of the natural world, natural expression)*	Pluto	Mars personal desires acting for Plutonian individual/collective evolution.

MOTION OF THE NODES, MOON, PLANETS

Motion of the Nodes
The mean motion of the Lunar Nodes is retrograde in all charts, even if the Nodes are direct in a specific chart. In all cases the Nodes enter a sign at 29 degrees and exit at 0 degrees. (Steve)
There is a difference between Mean Nodes and Mean Motion. Mean Nodes is a mathematical abstraction that smoothes out the actual motion of the Nodes. This does not exist in reality, only in abstraction. Mean Motion means that, overall, the movement of the Nodes is retrograde, even though there are periods when the Nodes are direct and moving forward. (Steve)

Motion of the Moon
The planetary motions are not constant whereas the motion of the Moon relative to Earth is. (Steve)

Motion of the planets
The mean motion of EVERY PLANET is DIRECT, even the ones that are retrograde for almost 6 months a year. Even if a planet is retrograde in a chart, it entered a sign for the first time at zero degrees and exits after 29 degrees. There is no planet whose mean motion is backwards through the zodiac. (Steve)

MYSTIC RECTANGLE

According to Dane Rudhyar, "unlike the Grand Cross or Square, the Rectangle points in a certain direction and presents a challenge for a particular kind of integration. The rectangular shape was used in many temples and chambers of initiation, and the buildings themselves were built to symbolize the process of transition from one stage of personal-spiritual unfoldment to the next – the fulfillment of a great goal. Seen on the vertical plane, the rectangle becomes a DOOR, something to pass thru to enter a new realm" *(Astrological Aspects: A Process Oriented Approach)*. Dane Rudhyar came to call the Mystic Rectangle, the 'Harmonic Rectangle.' "One of the most practically constructive and spiritually harmonious possibilities of any rectangle is indicated when the two oppositions are linked by sextiles and trines." Where fully active, this 'Harmonic Rectangle' points to the potential development of a character strongly organized in an attempt to take an important step in personal growth and/or spiritual development. The configuration tends to bring the polarized elements symbolized by the oppositions into a unity, because a strong sense of organization (sextile) and a cohesive, purposeful vision (trine) are potential in the personality. Whatever tensions arise in the life or personality that are symbolized in the opposing planets (or opposition) don't necessarily 'go away.' But, they can be "laid on the altar," or channeled toward the concrete completion of a significant life-task," ibid. (Rad)

PLANETARY SPEEDS

TABLE 8A   Planetary Speeds
(from fastest to slowest)

Ascendant/Midheaven	Lucifer
Moon	Jupiter
Mercury	Moon's South and North Nodes
Venus	Saturn
Mars	Chiron
Vesta	Uranus
Juno	Neptune
Ceres	Pluto
Pallas	Sun

PROGRESSED CHART

(Q) Can we say that 'progressed' is like the 'inner' progress or evolution, and an aspect is like an 'outer' event that one faces? (Tory)
(A) No. All things in our life start from within ourselves first: the evolutionary and karmic 'script' of the Soul in any given life. Thus the progression of the planets, and the aspects that they are making, reflect this ongoing evolutionary script of the Soul at any point in time. (Rad)

RULERSHIPS

In EA Mars is the lower octave of Pluto, and is the natural ruler of Aries. Mercury is the natural ruler of Virgo. (Rad)
EA (and most modern astrology) sees Pluto as the ruler of Scorpio. Mars is the lower octave of Pluto, and would be considered a co-ruler, although in EA we tend to see Pluto as the ruler and rarely refer to Mars as a co-ruler. (Steve)

SABIAN SYMBOLS

One of the great astrologers of all time, Dane Rudhyar wrote a book on the specific meanings for each degree, in each sign called the Sabian Symbols. In this book Rudhyar creates metaphorical meanings for all the degrees within the all the signs in the zodiac. (Rad)
Sabian Symbols, Marc Jones: www.sabian.org/sabian_symbols.php

SECONDARY PROGRESSIONS

Secondary progressions are relevant in E(A) (Rad)

SOLAR ARCS

Solar arcs are relevant in E(A) (Rad)

SOLAR-LUNAR RETURNS

Comparison of Lunar Return, natal, transits, progressions
Knowing the natal chart and meaning of the Moon within the Pluto paradigm, only then through this lens look at the Progressed Moon and consider the current progressed sign of the Moon and see what natal house this activates, and aspects within the natal chart when placed there. Then, additionally, consider the house and aspects within the progressed chart itself. After understanding this to the best of your current ability, to add even more timing and detail, then look at the recent Lunar Return charts around any time period in question and apply all this back to understanding of the above. Within the Lunar Return chart interpretation itself, the Moon's house placement in the Lunar Return chart plus aspects at the moment of the Return to complete the timing of all issues stemming from and through the emotional body. Within this whole process, also keep in mind the meaning of the transiting Nodes thru the natal chart. (Bradley)

Solar-Lunar phase of a Solar Return chart – example
[Example: 2nd/8th natal Solar Return] It must be understood in the total context of the individual Soul and its ongoing evolutionary issues and dynamics in the current life. This would include the current transits to the natal chart, the current progressions to the natal chart, which are then referenced to the natal chart. In general, that signature [Full Moon] in the Solar Return chart correlates with the Soul's need to 'throw something off' of itself in order for evolution to proceed. The throwing off will correlate to some existing dynamics within the Soul that are blocking the evolution of the Soul. Circumstantially, these can appear as circumstances/people/situations that need to be opposed or thrown off for that ongoing evolution to occur. (Rad)

Solar Return – relocated chart
[Example: 2nd/8th natal Solar Return; 6th/12th relocated Solar Return] In the relocated Solar Return chart that 'throwing off' [see above] symbolized in the natal Solar Return in the 2nd/8th would then manifest as creating a variety of crises in the relocated Solar Return by way of the 6th/12th. Creating the necessary crises in the relocated chart would then lead to the question of 'why' relative to the natal Solar Return. In turn and combination this would then lead to the awareness, the information the Soul would need, in order to answer that core question in order to identify what needs to be thrown off in order for the Soul's evolution to proceed. All is ultimately related to the Pluto signatures in the Solar Return chart and the natal chart as the ultimate baseline that provides the core context for what is symbolized in the Solar Return charts. (Rad)

Solar Return – birth place and relocation
The place of birth is used to calculate the Solar Return chart. If the person has moved from there then it is also calculated for where they are but the place of birth Solar Return is used as the baseline to understand/interpret how that will then manifest in the current place of residence. (Rad)

TRUE NODES

EA astrologers have been taught to use True Nodes, as that is what actually exists in the sky. (Steve)

VERTEX AND ANTI-VERTEX

These points are not relevant in E(A) (Rad)

GOD/GODDESS – SPIRITUAL PRACTICE

Natural God

One of the most precious and profound teachings that Wolf has given is that of the imperfect Natural God. The notion that the Natural God is compassionate, loving, and forgiving has helped – you will finally receive the healing your Soul needs, and that God wants to give you. I can share with you, from direct personal experience, that God is indeed loving, compassionate, forgiving. God, as Creator of all, is the origin and source of the imperfection we personify and experience. Therefore, ultimately (Pisces/12th), there is nothing to forgive or be forgiven for. Judgment (a function of Saturn/10th house/Capricorn), especially unnecessary and excessive judgment, falls away very naturally when we find – first through intellectual concept, then as direct experience – that God Itself is an evolving force. Patriarchal religions (another function of Saturn/Capricorn/10th house) enforce the mistaken notion of a 'perfect' God that sits in judgment in a detached and punitive manner. The underlying human motive of power, control, and authority, is also reflected in that Capricorn archetype. All that happens or occurs through application of personal will always and only occurs within the broader context of Divine Will. Thus, we don't need to be saved or redeemed by some 'perfect' god in order to find healing and peace; we need only to redeem and save our concept/definition of God, in order to find the healing and peace that is our birthright. In the eyes of God, I believe, no one's mistakes are any worse than anyone else's – it is all for the sake of learning, growth, and evolution. Even with the mistakes made, it is a really beautiful path we walk to ever more knowledge and direct experience of God. (Lesley)

God (male and female simultaneously) itself is an evolving force. The very existence of evolution *implies* imperfection, for if God or we were perfect, what would we be evolving *towards*? And why would a perfect God create imperfect creations – what would be the point? (Granted, the answer to that is beyond knowing while in human form.) As others have said, the essence of the Natural God is the principles of giving, sharing, community, collective, tribe, mutual effort, the awareness that one cannot advance one's self at the expense of others, that the whole unit must work together, working through their differences for mutual survival and advancement. A chain is only as strong as its weakest link – create too many weak links in that chain and ultimately the chain breaks and is useless. This first requires the awareness to see that life is in fact a chain, with each of us a tiny link in the overall chain. Thus the fallacy and danger of an ego that can believe it is separate and superior to portions of the totality. (Steve)

Cycles of creation

God will continue in its own journey to its own perfection. In this beyond long journey what we call God expands and contracts over lengths of time that we cannot even imagine. This natural expansion and contraction corresponds with the collapse of the entire Creation which leads to yet another expansion manifesting as a new form of Creation. Thus the cycles of creation/evolution occur in this natural way. When the cycle of contraction occurs this is called the Natural Law of involution where all existing forms born in the expansion cycle are destroyed, and then reformulated energetically in yet another cycle of expansion and the forms of how creation looks like in each one. Intrinsic to Creation is CONSCIOUSNESS because of course what we call God is CONSCIOUS. The dimensions of each Creation called, in our terms, the Cosmos and Universes are so vast that we simply cannot comprehend from the limitation of the consciousness contained within the human form. And within that vastness all of the Natural Laws that God has SET IN MOTION in each cycle of Creation manifest in all kinds of different ways depending on Light, Gravity, Motion, Magnetism, Vibration, and Heat. Depending on CONDITIONS defined by these Natural Laws as they interact within themselves as found at various points throughout the vastness of the totality of the Creation Consciousness can take hold and root itself. This we call life.

Consciousness is born from what we call God. The root of consciousness is God. When consciousness becomes aware that it is conscious as manifested in different forms of life we then call this THE SOUL. Souls that are conscious that they are conscious. And because of this the Natural Laws of evolution of a Soul's evolution back to its Source, God, begins. Relative to the Natural Laws of contraction and expansion this is reflected in the Natural Laws of dual desires within the Soul: one is to separate from God, and one is to return to God. For a Soul's evolution to occur and continue to occur is not dependent of Earth. One day Earth will be no more, just as many other universes and planets will be no more. Wherever the CONDITIONS exist, at any moment in time, that facilitate the evolution of the Soul is where it will be born. Right now on this Earth it is in its own evolutionary journey starting from when it first formed. One day it will be burned up by the Sun. In between it has its own evolution that has been going on for roughly five or six billion years now.

The journey of what we call the 'human being' has been relatively brief on this planet as measured against that amount of time. Humans are of course part of the total Creation on this planet. And for most of that journey humans have been in a state of harmony with the totality of Creation on this planet. It has only been in fairly recent times that the human had begun to consider itself as superior to the totality of the Creation as manifested on this planet. Once that began it has led to where the planet is now. And it is through this perverted desire of separateness from the rest of the Creation on this planet, defined through the perversion of the Natural Laws of giving, inclusion, to and for others in order to NATURALLY SURVIVE, that the humans have now guaranteed their extinction. We must remember that 99.5 percent of all forms of life on this planet to date have led to extinction. Once that occurs then Consciousness/Souls will simply and naturally gravitate to other universes and planets in which the conditions exist that facilitate their own ongoing, individual, evolution back to their Source: God. (Rad)

God's Will
God's Will is symbolized through the natural water trinity of Pisces, Cancer, and Scorpio where Scorpio and Pluto correlates with the phenomena of will. Thus, via this natural water trinity we see the progressive transference in the center of gravity within consciousness wherein the Soul, Pluto, Scorpio, the 8th house becomes conscious and centered in its own Source: God/ess. Thus, the egocentric orientation of course changes: the Moon, Cancer and the 4th house evolving through the 8th, to the 12th, etc. In so doing the will of the Soul becomes progressively one with the will of God/ess. Thus, in the chart of Jesus, for example, we see his Neptune in Scorpio conjunct his South Node of the Moon. The rulers then become the Pluto conjunct his Mars. Acting out the will of God where his personal will is the will of God'ess. (Rad)

Imperfection of the Creator
The nature of the Creator, as Wolf taught in his lifetime, is in fact not perfect. The very origin of 'imperfection' is the Origin of Creation Itself. (Rad)

Source, the ultimate projector
The ultimate projector is the Source itself which is, of course, the origin of all things that have been Created and projected from within Itself. This phenomena, then, of projection is reflected in all that has been Created including the Soul that itself can project from within itself anything upon that Creation. (Rad)

Manifest and unmanifest creation
Pisces correlates with the totality of Creation that includes the manifested = known, and the unmanifested = unknown. Sagittarius correlates with the Natural Laws within the manifested Creation that can be understood by the Soul in human form as well as knowing what cannot be known: the unmanifested. God realization is limited to the manifested Creation. It can never be linked to the unmanifested = unknown because, after all, the unmanifested is not yet known because it is not manifested in the first place. What Souls in the human form can know is linked to the interfacing between the known = manifested and the unmanifested = unknown. That interfacing point between the manifested and the unmanifested is the point of Creation as Souls in human form can know it. This limitation is sustained until the Soul evolves beyond its causal body. At that evolutionary point in time, Capricorn, the Soul can then have a progressive knowledge of the unmanifested creation equaling the totality of what we call God/ess itself. (Rad)

Absolute totality of Truth
Pisces, Neptune, and the 12th house correlate to Ultimate and TOTAL truth. Yet consciousness in human form cannot know the absolute totality of the Truth: it is limited by the nature of the form. For example, what is the origin of God itself? And that Origin, and that Origin, and so on. Thus, the Soul and its consciousness within human form can only induce through its intuition a limited part of that total truth. And because it can only intuit through such induction limited truths of an ultimate nature this becomes the basis of what APPEARS to be conflicting truths. These conflicting truths of an apparent nature thus become the basis of conflicting ideas leading to a variety of philosophies and/or religions. In turn this becomes the basis of doubt due to the nature of these apparent conflicts. Doubt thus becomes the cause of asking ever more or deeper questions about the nature of the Creation in the first place. Sagittarius, the 9th house, and Jupiter attempts to synthesize via intuition the unity of these apparent conflicting truths, and the ideas that these various truths create. Yet, in the end, consciousness, embodied in human form that is called the Soul, can only realize, understand, or intuit via synthesis a limited amount of the Total Truth that is inductively sensed within the archetype of Pisces, Neptune, and the 12th house. This is why even within the idea systems we call astronomy, astrophysics, and the like that the greatest of the greats in those systems, like Einstein, Steven Hawkins, etc. come to the same conclusion about the nature and origins of the Creation. And they all call that God. (Rad)

Aligning with God/ess
Cancer is one of the archetypes of the subjective ego that the Soul creates in any given life, and is part of the natural trinity of Pisces and Scorpio. In combination these correlate to the evolution of the Soul in general, and how that evolution is reflected in the subjective ego, Cancer, in each life. In the end this is about remembering our origins: God/ess. And, thus, aligning, consciously, our Soul/will with that Origin. In so doing the subjective ego simply reflects that. So it's a matter of aligning our Soul, and the will within it, to the will of the Creator, the origin of the Soul in the first place. (Rad)

Seeking God first
The bottom line that JWG always went back to were the words of Jesus to seek God first, put God first, and what you need will be given to you. And that seeking needs to be sincere and consistent. Such a simple concept, and yet if we're honest with ourselves, it's much harder to pull off. But as JWG ALSO said many times, "The value is in the effort." (Adina)

How to be happy?
Demonstrate a very sincere wish to know God and the truth, do as much as possible to connect with a higher power in a direct experience. Then connect the personal wish with the power of the supreme will, develop the awareness of what that supreme power wants to create through the Soul, and just do it. This is happiness. (JWG)

How to Transcend Astrological Influences by Paramhansa Yogananda
Astrology is a very deep subject, but most people consider it a kind of superstitious guide to material progress. If you use astrology only for guidance in material matters, you will be doing its teachings an injustice. Astrology is too vast, both mathematically and philosophically, to be rightly grasped except by people of profound understanding. In ancient times, astrology was seen primarily as a guide to spiritual development. To use astrology for material purposes was considered a lower application of what is essentially a divine science. Astrology is the study of man's response to planetary stimuli. All parts of creation are linked together and interchange their influences. No matter what your environment, the surrounding rays of the earth and universe will have an impact upon you. Astrology was intended to assist you on your inner journey, by helping you become more aware of the interrelationships between the objective universe and the inner aspects of yourself. The relation of the stars to the human body and mind is very subtle. There is a correlation between the six centers (chakras) in the spine, which become twelve by polarity, and the twelve signs of the zodiac. Millions of volts of electrical current are lodged in these spinal centers. If your body and your mind are very strong, you will be impervious to the evil vibrations from the stars when they begin to shed their rays upon you. But if your body and mind are weak through transgressions of wrong eating, wrong thinking, bad character, and bad company, then the stellar rays will have the power to affect you.

How the stars affect us   The stars influence your life only in accordance with patterns that you yourself established in the past. A child is born on that day and at that hour when the celestial rays are in mathematical harmony with his individual karma (past actions). The astrological configurations serve only as symbols of karmic influences, which you have set into motion in the past. The stars and planets themselves can no more choose how they will affect you than you can select your own karmic destiny. The message boldly blazoned across the heavens at the moment of birth was not meant to emphasize fate, the result of past good and evil, but to arouse your will to escape from this universal bondage. What you have done, you can undo. You can overcome whatever effects are now prevalent in your life because you created them by your own actions in the first place, and because you have inner spiritual resources which are not subject to planetary pressure. The best way, therefore, to improve your lot is deliberately to act in such a way as to counteract the evil effects of past deeds. Especially if this course of action springs from inner attunement with God, or is adopted under the wise guidance of one who knows God, it will serve as an antidote to all baneful actions of the past.

Avoid passive dependence on astrology   Superstition means to seek guidance from effects, in ignorance of their causes. Many people look to the heavens for signs instead of choosing the wiser path of seeking guidance in their Souls, from God. Some people refuse to do anything for themselves until the planetary positions are favorable. While it is not unwise to initiate worthwhile undertakings at astrologically auspicious times, it merely affirms your passive dependence on fate to wait for a shift in the planets' positions before making important changes in your life. Anything you do with deep faith in God will blossom under better influences than you could hope to find by consulting the heavens for favorable aspects. Do not wait for changes in astrological influences to change your destiny. Look, rather, to Him who made the heavens and the earth and who alone can grant you eternal freedom. The lawful effects of your karma may seem irrevocable, but the effects of past actions can be changed by seeking God. Unless you remember that, you cannot spiritualize astrology.

How to spiritualize astrology   While studying astrology in a reasonable way, you must always remember that God's influence is the supreme influence. All human ills arise from some transgression of universal law. The scriptures point out that man must satisfy the laws of nature, while not discrediting the divine omnipotence. You should always say, "Lord, I trust in Thee, and know Thou canst help me, but I too will do my best to undo any wrong I have done." You have been given the free choice and intelligence, as a child of God, to surmount the difficulties of life. You are made in the image of God, not in the image of the stars. Strive unceasingly, from a center of inner calmness, to surmount every material, mental, and spiritual difficulty. Cooperate with His will by offering up to Him all the strength of your human will. If you can hold onto your happiness during all the difficulties in your life, then you will begin to rise above the influence of the stars. If you can retain your smile in spite of repeated challenges, that is a sign of the awakening of the consciousness of divinity within you. Through all such actions, you are changing your body and mind and how they are affecting the twelve centers in your spine. As a result of these changes, the stars will begin to smile upon you. By communing with God, you will reinforce the power of the twelve spinal centers, which will then act in cooperation with the twelve signs of the zodiac. The deeper your communion with God, the more you will automatically harmonize the influences of all planetary forces and transcend the evil effects of the powerful, but distant, planets. In these ways, you can spiritualize astrology. Seek help, therefore, not from the stars and planets, but from Almighty God. God is harmony; and if you attune yourself to Him, you will never perform any action amiss. Your activities will be correctly and naturally timed to accord with astrological law. After deep prayer and meditation you are in touch with His divine consciousness; there is no greater power than that inward protection. By plunging deeply into your own divine nature, you will discover those deeper levels within yourself that enable you to rise above all karmic realities.

The masters go beyond astrology Some people study astrology to ascertain the influence of their karma through the medium of planets, thus trying to counteract evil influences by astrological foreknowledge. But the great masters go beyond astrology. The man of realization does not choose any auspicious hour to perform noble deeds or initiate new wholesome ventures. He acts, moves, and sleeps under the one influence of God. He consults God instead of the stars for guidance. Although there is a certain vibratory influence of stars upon all human lives, a man of infinite will power tuned in with God, uses his free will to change his circumstances. He marches on, influenced only by the Sun of all Suns, the Almighty Spirit. To him, from the depths of his determination and faith, all things are possible. He burns the seeds of difficulties in the fire of wisdom, consults only God for guidance, and performs all of his actions according to divine guidance. Superstitious awe of astrology makes one an automaton, slavishly dependent on mechanical guidance. The wise man defeats his planets – which is to say, his past – by transferring his allegiance from the creation to the Creator. The more he realizes his unity with Spirit, the less he can be dominated by matter. The Soul is ever-free; it is deathless because birthless. It cannot be regimented by stars. If you live by astrology or anything else you will be bound by it. Depend wholly and solely on God. Live by God alone. Then nothing can hurt you.

Follow the way to inner freedom In karma's realm, karma rules supreme. Yet all human beings have the power to withdraw to another realm altogether. You cannot change the outer astrological influences, but you can do a great deal to change the way you receive them, inwardly. Instead of accepting fatalistically the decrees of karma, follow the inner way to freedom. Meditate daily. Commune deeply with God. Learn from Him, through the silent voice of intuition, the way out of Soul-degrading serfdom to bad habits. Ultimately, by ever deeper meditation, you will reach a point where you receive your influences from God alone.

God/Goddess enforcing evolution

The only "separate force outside that is enforcing the evolution" that can exist is what we humans call God/Goddess – that which created the individual Souls in the first place. When we talk of evolutionary intentions for a country or a planet, that is obviously beyond the sphere of the Souls of the individual humans, animals, etc. that inhabit a country/planet. In the broader picture the human, animal, plant Souls here are attracted to this particular planet because the evolutionary intentions for the planet as a whole align in some way with the evolutionary intentions of those individual Souls. It all comes down to the nature of the desires. (Steve)

Water trinity

The self-image (Cancer) of the Soul is very variable. It can range from a gross identification with the body and the total circumstances of its human life (ego linked with Saturn = identity that is defined by time and space: Consensus state). Or on the other extreme, the Soul can be fully aware of its oneness with Source (ego linked with Neptune = identity that is transcendent of time and space: Spiritual state). In both cases there exists a human form and a unique social background and conditioning (Saturn) however depending on the Soul's level of awareness, or God realization, it will identify more or less with that form. The Soul is that immutable consciousness that is on a journey of self-remembrance. The only thing that changes is the evolutionary state of the Soul. That evolutionary state manifests itself accordingly through what it is emotionally concerned with (ego). (Ari)

Ocean/wave analogy

Neptune can be both the Wave and the Ocean depending ON THE POINT OF VIEW of consciousness itself as encased in the human form. If we remember the natural trinity between Pisces/Neptune, Scorpio/Pluto, and Moon/Cancer – God, Soul, Ego – then of course it's possible for the ego within a given Soul to be 'intoxicated' – Neptune – with itself via the Ego that it creates. Thus, its relationship to itself is separative in nature relative to the totality of the Creation that it is inter-related with. Thus, from its point of view, it has become deluded – Neptune – within the wave: ego. Other Souls of course, relative to evolution, have their center of gravity – Saturn – within the ocean and know that their Soul and its ego are simply part of the totality of Creation itself that is co-equal in nature. Thus, their inner Neptune, is within the Ocean.

In the wave/ocean analogy the sense of identity depends on the evolutionary condition of the Soul. For most that identity lies in the wave: the ego that feels, perceives and thinks that it is separate from everything else. From the vantage point of the wave then everything else, the boats, ripples, whatever else correlates to the totality of its life circumstances become simply props in its personal play. For Souls who have evolved progressively into the Spiritual state the center of gravity within their consciousness progressively shifts from the ego to the Soul itself. As such their sense of identity is the Soul, the ocean, upon which the wave of its ego has been created for whatever ongoing evolutionary purposes it has. A Soul in that condition thus experiences simultaneously its distinct egocentric personal identity while at the same time its timeless Soul identity.

What it all comes down to is how something is perceived including our own sense of 'identity.' From the point of view of consciousness the issue, in the end, is where the center of gravity is within in. Gravity has a natural correlation to Saturn, Capricorn, and the 10th house. Saturn, etc., also correlates to the structural nature of anything. Thus, the structural nature of consciousness. It also has a natural correlation to the boundary of anything. Thus, it correlates to the natural boundary between our subjective awareness and the consciousness therein, and the progressive levels of the unconscious as in the individuated unconsciousness, Uranus, and the collective unconsciousness/consciousness which is Neptune. Deep within the unconscious is the Soul. Consciousness, as such, emanates from the primary brain. Within the subjective consciousness in all of us is the egocentric structure that the Soul creates in each life to facilitate its evolutionary intentions and progressions.

The ego is the Moon, Cancer, and the 4th house, and is, of course, the natural polarity of Capricorn, the 10th, and Saturn. For most individuals, given the natural evolutionary stages, the sense of identity is their own ego. Thus, the PERCEPTION of being separate from everything else. Thus, the WAVE on the ocean where the wave correlates to the subjective ego within the consciousness of the individual. So if the center of gravity within the individual is their ego then their sense of identity is then defined by the wave: their ego. Yet, as evolution proceeds, the center of gravity within an individual's consciousness shifts to the Soul itself: the OCEAN. The natural boundary of Saturn relative to the structural nature of consciousness dissolves in such a way that the PERCEPTION OF IDENTITY changes from the wave to the ocean. As a result the individual is then perceiving, is consciously aware of, its timeless identity called their individual Soul and the egocentric structures it creates from life to life AT THE SAME TIME. In other words the Soul is aware of and perceives the continuation of its ongoing lifetimes from life to life at the same time. The center of gravity is the Ocean, the Soul. As a result they do not perceive themselves as separate from anything, but, in fact, inter-related to everything. (Rad)

The third eye
From the point of view of evolution for all Souls the intent is to understand the Cause of Creation itself. Relative to the Moon, the 4th house, and Cancer it is part of the natural trinity, or triad, between Scorpio, 8th house, and Pluto, and Neptune, Pisces, and the 12th house. This natural triad correlates of course to the Source of Creation or God/ess, Neptune, Pisces, the 12th house, and the Souls that are created by this Source, the 8th house, Scorpio, and Pluto, and the egos that each Soul creates in each of its lives in order to facilitate its ongoing evolution BACK TO THE SOURCE ITSELF. So, in the end, ultimate evolution wherein progressively the Soul DESIRES TO RETURN TO ITS SOURCE. As such, in time, the Soul remembers that its Source is God/ess and, as it does so, it realizes that its identity, its ultimate identity, ego, is that Source. Very few folks realize that the Soul itself contains within itself its own 'self-image' or ego. And how that inner self-image or ego is then reflected through the subjective egocentric structures that it creates in each life for its evolution to proceed. But as it does so there will be a progressive shift within its consciousness, the center of gravity, gravity of course is Saturn, Capricorn, and the 10th house which is the natural polarity of Cancer, Moon, and the 4th, wherein that center of gravity will shift from the subjective ego and a 'separate identity' from the Source, to the Soul itself wherein it will then remember its own origins: God/ess.

When this begins to happen then the inner experience of the Soul's individuality, its own ego, is perceived and experienced as but an extension of that Source or God. As this occurs then the inner perception of what is called the third eye, the inner eye, is directly perceived and experienced. This, in fact, is actually hard wired into the brain: it is part of its structure of consciousness in human form. As the perception occurs the Soul, by birthright, REMEMBERS how to merge with that inner eye. As Jesus said when 'one's eyes are single, one's whole body is full of light.' The dual eyes reflect the Natural Law of duality, cause and effect. When one eye become single, the inner eye that is fused with, penetrated, moved THROUGH then one's whole being, or body, is full of Light. And that is the light of all the Natural Laws that the Source has set in motion at the moment of Creation. And these inner perceptions, gained in the natural way, finally lead the Soul to be able to directly inwardly experience, to know, to perceive, the interface between the MANIFESTED AND THE UN-MANIFESTED. And it is this interface that correlates to TIME AND TIMELESSNESS. In essence, the perception and direct experience OF CREATION ITSELF. This is the birth right of all Souls. And this is what the natural evolution of the Soul is about, in the end, as symbolized by the natural trinity of Pisces, Neptune, the 12th house, the 8th house, Pluto, Scorpio, and Cancer, the 4th house, and the Moon. (Rad)

Neptunian emotions
One of the core emotions that correlate with Neptune, Pisces, and the 12th house, and the Nodes of Neptune, and evolution is one of disillusionment. To be disillusioned means that the Soul had been creating a reality around 'something' in which a sense of ultimate meaning has been projected upon that something. In so projecting that sense of ultimate meaning into that 'something' when that something is not Goddess itself it means that that something has become a de facto Goddess. Thus, to be disillusioned

from that something holding such ultimate meaning is then to be faced with a deep inner void when the disillusioning is occurring. The Natural Law behind this is to make the Soul ask the question of what in fact constitutes the REAL ultimate meaning for its life. And that then is intended to lead right back to the Source of the Soul itself: Goddess. Of course most Souls don't do that even though it's the intention. Most Souls will then try to find another 'something' to project that ultimate meaning into all over again. So round and round the Soul goes in this way until the Soul finally realizes what that ultimate meaning for life is, and to commit to this.

The most intense and difficult Neptunian emotion that manifests relative to disillusionment is one of hysteria. Another natural emotion specific to Neptune, etc., is one of empathy where empathy allows us to truly understand the emotional realities and needs of others. And within this emotion the DESIRE to help others in the ways that we naturally can without any other motive or agenda attached to it: to give to others what they actually need in the best ways that we can. This then allows the Soul to evolve because it is one of the Natural Laws and 'commands' of the natural Goddess to do so. The deepest degree of this Natural Law and the emotion of it is to ALWAYS PUT OTHERS FIRST no matter what the consequences may be to oneself: think of Jesus here for example of an ultimate manifestation of this. And remember he did have six planets in Pisces, and Neptune conjunct his South Node. His South Node of Neptune was in Capricorn which is ruled by his Saturn in Pisces. When a Soul has committed through desire to reuniting itself with its own Source, and has inwardly realized that Source, then the natural Neptunian emotion of ECSTASY will permeate the Soul when that direct union with the Source takes place. Once any Soul has such an experience it will serve as the very basis and cause of its ongoing evolutionary journey back to the Source itself.

A pure emotion that correlates to Neptune, Pisces, and the 12th house that very, very few people understand or know about: the pure emotion of the psychological dynamics of feeling 'duped, naive, stupid' that can lead to that psychology is one wherein the Soul ASSUMES THAT ALL SOULS SIMPLY WANT TO DO THE RIGHT THING, ASSUMES THAT ALL PEOPLE ARE WHOM THEY APPEAR TO BE, ASSUMES THAT ALL OTHER SOULS DO NOT DO HARMFUL OR BAD THINGS TO ITS OWN SELF. This archetype here is one of EMOTIONAL ASSUMPTIONS. These kinds of emotional assumptions emanate from the natural psychological purity or innocence contained within the Pisces, Neptune, 12th house archetype. And it is this kind of emotion that can then lead to feeling stupid, duped, naive, disillusioned and so on. For evolution to take place through the emotions, *all three* types of emotions pertaining to the "water trinity" (Pisces, Scorpio, Cancer) are activated. (Rad)

Evolution through the emotional body

EA teaches that processing life experiences through the emotional body is evolutionary precisely because it enables the Soul to fully EXPERIENCE whatever experiences are the natural consequence of its desires and choices. If the Soul does not fully EXPERIENCE that which its choices have generated, then it will not truly know in a deep way the consequences of those desires and choices, and will not be able to integrate and learn from these experiences, and thus to make new choices and evolve. Evolution is a natural process of the universe – we can trust it to happen and we do not have to 'make' it happen, so much as let it happen. As Jeffrey taught, the Water Trinity shows involution in that Spirit/Neptune differentiates to Soul/Scorpio differentiates to Ego/Cancer; and also shows that evolution occurs naturally in the natural direction of the zodiac of the shift in conscious identification from Ego/Cancer to Soul/Scorpio to Spirit/Pisces. I find in my work that when people are able to experience their experience through the emotional body (Cancer/Moon), such a full experience naturally eventually leads them (over a period of minutes or lifetimes) to a desire to understand and transform the deeper unconscious patterns and/or Soul history (both Scorpio/Pluto) that has led to the given emotional experience. I don't need to try to push this inquiry in any way, it is the natural result of deeply experienced emotion, it is just what happens when we get out of the way and feel. And then I have also found that when people start to work at this deeper level, then also very naturally begin (again, whether in this lifetime or later) to experience their own encounters with Source (Pisces/Neptune), however this may manifest as appropriate to their perceptual capacities. The water naturally returns to the sea. So to me it is not so much about energy releasing or other particular things as much as it is about having a natural experience that leads to new understanding and choices (and thus new experiences) that eventually exhaust separating desires and leave only the desire to return to Source. In general bypassing the emotional body is essentially resisting evolution, which Souls at any stage in consciousness can do. (Jason)

Neptune and higher octave Venus

Neptune is the higher octave of Venus. Venus corresponds to the heart chakra. My intuition is that this does not mean that Neptune correlates to the heart chakra itself, but rather that the heart chakra and the crown have some sort of octave resonance to one another which is the manifestation of Source unity consciousness through the denser, interpersonal feeling center of the heart. (Ari)

A simple example: Neptune would correlate to unconditional love, whereas Venus would or can correlate to conditional love and the reasons for that conditional love. (Rad)

EA paradigm

EA and its paradigm symbolizes the individual journey of the Soul through time as it evolves back to its Source: God/ess. Even though Neptune symbolizes that Source it does not symbolize or reflect the individual journey of the Soul itself. EA is about understanding each individual Soul as it actually is: where it has been and why, where it is now and why, and where it is headed and why. The Soul correlates to Pluto. Neptune does not. (Rad)

Soul

The word Soul has been a word in almost every human language system that has ever been on Earth. So what is it? Can we open up the brain and find it? No, obviously we cannot. But we cannot open up the physical body and find emotion either for example. Yet we know we all have emotions. Can we open up the brain and find thought? No. Yet, we all know we at least have a thought or two in our heads. Can we open up the body and find sadness, or depression, or happiness, or love? No. Yet, we all know that these things exist within us. So obviously we are dealing with the nature of energy. The Soul is energy which is no different than the energy of consciousness itself. Again, we can't open the brain and find consciousness. Consciousness is one of the very greatest 'mysteries' of all to scientists for they cannot explain its origins or even how it came to be. Consciousness correlates astrologically to Neptune. This is exactly the starting point for what we call religion and philosophy: the human need to contemplate and consider, within the desire to know, where we come from and why. In turn this becomes the causative factor for 'beliefs' where beliefs are the result of the human pondering upon the origin of life itself.

But is there a difference between beliefs and actual knowing? Is there a way to know the answer to the big cosmic questions versus the need to believe in an answer? The happy news is that there is. For example by the sheer fact that there is a manifested Creation that exists as fact there must also be TRUTHS THAT INHERENTLY EXIST because of the fact of the manifested Creation in the first place. By the fact of its existence most of us can easily reason that there has to be something that is the origin of the Creation. In generic language we could call that something the Origin of All Things, or The Source, and in religious terminology it is called God or the Goddess. Consciousness is certainly part of the manifested Creation. It exists. That which is the origin of consciousness, of itself, must also be conscious. Thus the totality of consciousness emanates from this Source. As an observable fact we all know that consciousness is in all living things: all life forms. And all of these life forms have the appearance of being separate from all other life forms yet are simultaneously connected to them: two plants next to each other appear separate yet are simultaneously connected to one another by the sheer fact of being plants. So, on the one hand there is in fact the individualizing aspect of consciousness, yet, on the other, the universal aspect of consciousness which binds all the individual aspects of consciousness together.

Another way of illustrating this is the famous story of the wave and the ocean. Most of us would agree that it is the ocean that is the origin of the wave. Yet from the point of view of the wave, if the individualizing aspect of consciousness were centered there, the wave appears and seems separate. In other words if the center of gravity for consciousness were within the wave then from that center of gravity the wave appears, and is experienced, as something separate from its own source: the ocean. On the other hand if the center of gravity within consciousness were the wave itself then the ocean simultaneously experiences its totality while at the same time experiencing the individualizing aspects of itself as manifested in the waves that emanate from it. In the very same way then the Universal Consciousness which is the origin of all consciousness has created and manifested the totality of the manifested Creation which of course includes the human being and the consciousness within it. And within human consciousness there exists a natural individualizing aspect to it. This individualizing aspect to it occurs as a natural result of the human life form having distinct and individual forms relative to the its root: the human life form as a seed, so to speak, that produces many other branches that is no different than the ocean and the wave. Thus, each human life form has its own individualizing consciousness that is called the Soul.

The Soul, then, is an immutable consciousness, or energy, that is naturally part of the Universal Consciousness that has created it in the first place. Immutable here means that which cannot be destroyed. Why? Because energy can never be destroyed, it can only change form. To evolve. So how does the Soul evolve? What dynamics are inherent within it that are the cause of its own evolution? Within all human Souls there exists two antithetical desires where DESIRE IS THE DETERMINANT OF EVOLUTION. One desire is to RETURN to that which is the origin of us, of all of Creation, in the first place. And the other desire is to SEPARATE from that which is the Origin of All Things. This simple inner dynamic within the Soul is also the natural cause, or law, of free choice, or free will. The evolution of the Soul is simply based on a progressive elimination of all separating desires to the exclusion of only one desire that can remain: to return to the Origin of All Things. This does not require any belief system at all, or any religion that one must belong to. This simple truth, because it is a function of Natural Law, can be validated by anyone through their own life experience. Is it not true for example that any of us can have whatever separating desire that one can imagine. For example a desire for a new lover, or a new career post, the new possession, and so on. And we may have the ability to manifest that which we desire. And when we do there is in fact a sense of satisfaction of actualizing that which we have desired. But what soon replaces it? Is it not the sense of dissatisfaction, the sense of something more? It is precisely this sense of dissatisfaction, the sense of something more, that 'echoes' the ultimate desire to return to the Origin Of All Things, the only desire that will bring to us that ultimate satisfaction. All of us have this universal experience.

So how can we know, independent of belief systems, that there in fact exists an Ultimate Source? The human being knew long, long ago, before the manifestation of religions and complicated cosmologies, through inner contemplation, inner 'looking,' that when the breath in the body, inhale and exhale, became very, very shallow, even stopped, that there would then appear within the interior of their consciousness a LIGHT. This occurred as a natural function of the breath shallowing or stopping. Naturally. Much later in human history this was to be called the famous 'third eye.' And it is this very Light that symbolized and connected the individual consciousness reflected in the Soul to the Universal Consciousness that is the Origin Of All Things. The human being also learned long ago that by merging its own individual consciousness, or Soul, with that Light that its consciousness would then expand in such a way that the individual consciousness itself then became Universal and was then able to consciously experience that Ultimate Source Of All Things: the wave has returned to the ocean. The point here, again, is that any human being can know and validate these Natural Laws through their own actual experience that does not require belief systems of any kind. The key to do this, again, is to progressively shallow and stop the breath all together.

Anyone can do this. If you doubt this, or wonder how, simply try the following natural method to do so. On your inhaling breath simply mentally affirm the number one. On your exhaling breath simply mentally affirm the number two. The 'secret' here is to concentrate as hard as you can simply on the numbers one and two. It is this act of concentration intensified by desire manifesting as will that progressively your breath will in fact begin to shallow and even stop. Remember that consciousness is energy and cannot be destroyed. It can only change form. Thus, as some may think when the breath is stopped it does not mean that you have to die. Consciousness is NOT dependent on the human form. So when the breath is stopped the inner LIGHT which is intrinsic to consciousness will soon begin to appear. And as it does so simply move into it by the conscious act of surrender. Surrendering to it will then allow for a merging of your own consciousness with that Universal Consciousness as symbolized in the Light. ANYONE CAN DO THIS AND THEN KNOW FOR THEMSELVES THIS NATURAL TRUTH. It is this Natural Law of breath, when stopped or deeply shallowed, that allows for what all the great teachers of relatively recent centuries, when compared to how long the human being has actually been on the planet, have said including Jesus: "When thy eye is single ones whole body is full of light."

Symbolically speaking the two physical eyes that we have correlate to the two motions of breath: inhale and exhale. It is the inhaling and exhaling of the breath that keeps ones consciousness utterly involved and enmeshed in the duality, or polarity, of life itself. Likes and dislikes, happy and sad, love and hate, etc., etc., correlate to and demonstrate this Natural Law. The numbers one and two correlate to the Natural Law of finitude and duality: cause and effect. Yet between one and two there exists an interval or zero. The interval or zero correlates to the Universal Consciousness or infinity. Thus when the breath stops or becomes very, very shallow the interval is then perceived. And what is perceived in the single eye, or what has been called the 'third eye' that naturally exists within the interior of consciousness and can be accessed, merged with, with our Soul. When this occurs the law of duality ceases to exist. The ultimate 'satisfaction' is then realized. The Soul correlates astrologically to Pluto. From the point of view of Natural Laws it is interesting to note, historically speaking, that advanced mathematics like algebra, trigonometry, quantum physics, and so on could not have been realized unless there was an 'idea' or conception called zero. This occurred in the third century AD in India. It was the then Indian mathematicians that conceived of the number zero. And, of course, from the point of view of Indian cosmologies this occurred as a direct extension of their natural understanding of the origin of Creation: out of nothing, or zero, the manifested Creation occurred, the unmanifested/manifested, or the causeless cause. (Rad)

Stages of Samadhi

Samadhi is simply realization or oneness with God, and there are two main stages of samadhi: savikalpa samadhi and nirvikalpa samadhi. According to what Wolf taught, typically one has experienced the first stage of samadhi by the end of the 1st stage Spiritual, and the next three stages by the end of 2nd stage Spiritual, with the last three stages of samadhi occurring within the 3rd stage Spiritual. Savikalpa samadhi includes these first four stages of samadhi, and nirvikalpa samadhi includes the last three. As one's consciousness begins to expand, from the beginning of seeing the spiritual eye thru the first four stages of samadhi, the center of gravity of that consciousness is in the process of moving from ego to Soul. It is the movement from savikalpa samadhi to nirvikalpa samadhi that marks the evolution from 2nd stage Spiritual to 3rd stage Spiritual. When one reaches that 5th stage of samadhi, marking the entry into 3rd stage Spiritual, the center of gravity of one's consciousness is finally anchored in the Soul, rather than the ego.

When we meditate and withdraw our life force, our consciousness from the senses, we enter into one of the stages of savikalpa samadhi where the Soul is released from ego consciousness and becomes aware of Spirit beyond creation. During savikalpa samadhi, the Soul expands into spirit, but it doesn't lose its identity. One is in a kind of trance, an expanded awareness in which the consciousness is focused within, rather than being identified with the outside world. One cannot stay in savikalpa samadhi and go about their daily activities. This in itself, can be problematic. As one comes out of even the "small" ecstasy of the 1st samadhi back to this time/space reality, it produces a kind of depression for the "loss" of the experience of where it's just been, but also a longing to return. If we look at the first stage of savikalpa samadhi as a trip into deep space, but it's deep space withIN, so to speak, and the absolute peace and bliss of pure BEing, then maybe a simple way to put the progression is an expansion of that initial awareness, we can begin to experience – to really feel – the energy of each of the chakras as we go, the colors, the sounds, etc. associated with each.

In nirvikalpa samadhi, the Soul realizes that it's one with spirit, and can remain immersed in God while going about its daily activities. Again, the beginning stage of nirvikalpa is the point at which the center of gravity of the consciousness is anchored in the Soul, rather than the ego. There is more information/description of what happens during each of the seven stages of samadhi in Yogananda's translation and interpretation of the Bhagavad-Gita. These can be found in Ch. 6, v. 23 (p. 626–628). (Adina)

Guru/avatar assignments
The assignments of gurus or avatars would be proportionate to the Soul's evolutionary station. From what I understand, as the Soul evolves the assignments can become bigger and more difficult. Jesus had to speak the truth to the scribes and Pharisees. Yogananda tried to arrange a meeting with Hitler. The Dalai Lama has to negotiate with the Chinese government after they destroyed the entire culture of his people. Martin Luther King was not a guru or avatar, but look at what he had to do. (Steve)

Karma of an Avatar
All Souls have karma unless a Soul is in the most advanced states of Evolution such as an Avatar. First, we need to discriminate between the word 'karma' and the natural evolutionary process, intention and necessity that all Souls go through. In context of an Avatar there is no karma no matter what symbols you see in their charts. There are evolutionary intentions and necessities which of course are proved by the nature of their lives. Specifically, Avatars have no EARTHLY karma. Most still do have karma from the point of view of the Astral and Causal realms. In the case of an Avatar's chart, it is essential to understand the WHY in that chart in their CONTEXT. And the use of EA, properly understood and applied, does provide for that answer. No form of astrology, including EA, can say, of itself as in just looking at symbols in paper, who is and who is not an Avatar. (Rad)

Soul of Jesus
The Soul of Jesus is free from the necessity of coming back to this Earth. His Soul is within the Causal plane now. As any Soul whose Soul has evolved to a state where it's root plane of existence is within the Causal plane Jesus is 'overseeing' the developments of countless Souls in many, many places: not just Earth. (Rad)

Ramana Maharshi
Ramana has chosen a spiritual path in which God is conceived simultaneously as 'impersonal' and 'personal': Vedanta. The personal part means that the Soul who conceives of God in this way is then able to access the various agents of God, and to expand the consciousness through the third eye in such a way as to be able to perceive the interface of the unmanifested, thus beyond duality, and the manifested. When the Soul conceives of God in this way it is then inwardly experiencing these types of realizations and experiences through the emotional body relative to the consciousness inhabiting human forms. In this way the Soul then experiences the pure love of God through its agents, a state of inner ecstasy and rapture of that which is being perceived. This is what you then see exuding from his (or any other Soul who has evolved in this way) eyes and energy field in general. He is in the 3rd stage Spiritual, the middle of it. (Rad)

Yogananda
During some of the experiences I've had in preparation for my transition, I was blessed to really feel – truly experience – God's love through the inner presence of my guru, Yogananda, one of God's "agents." It was a really mind blowing experience, especially since I'm still a "recovering" masochist. When I had the experience, I remembered one of the things Yogananda taught about God's love, ie "If you knew how much God loves you, you would die for joy." And when my guru blessed me with that experience of God's love I realized why he had said what he did, because it's incredibly overwhelming, but in a "good" way. And even though that "small" experience was mind blowing for me, I finally began to understand why Master said what he did: we're given such experiences in small doses, so to speak, at the beginning because our systems aren't "wired" to process the full extent of God's love, so we get increasingly bigger "doses" as we evolve (kind of like Kundalini – one has to prepare the body for it). And at the beginning, even some of that smaller 'dose' of pure, unconditional love comes thru one's guru/teacher for similar reasons, and yet also according to our own evolutionary stage and needs. (Adina)

Even in the life of Yogananda he did not even 'believe' in the existence of evil, Lucifer, when he was a young man. At that point he thought or believed that evil was just a philosophical belief rather than an actual fact. All Souls on this Earth are not perfect, including his. All Souls are continuously learning and evolving even at the most advanced levels of evolution from the point of view of a consciousness/Soul on this Earth. Yogananda evolved and had to learn about the fact of evil even at his level of evolution. The later stages of his life are a testimony to this fact. (Rad)

Co-creation with the Divine
Correlates to the archetypes of the natural trinity of Neptune/12th house, Pluto/8th house, and the Moon/4th house. Co-creation of 'reality' occurs any time a consciousness has first evolved into a state of self-objectification where it realizes that it is a conscious

and individual identity. Once consciousness has evolved to this point it begins to 'co-create' reality in the form of the free choices that it makes relative to the nature of the phenomenal reality that it is existing within. By making free choices within that reality for itself it is thus creating reality due to those choices. In the time/space reality of Earth this then means that all human life forms, once consciousness is encased in that form, has the capacity to co-create reality by way of the choices that it makes. This is true for all humans, and is not a function of evolutionary status or specific astrological signatures. As the individual Soul within human consciousness evolves through great lengths of time it will progressively be aware that it is indeed a 'co-creator' of reality relative to the Source of itself: The Ultimate Creator. As any Soul is created by the Creator it becomes possible through its evolution to arrive at states of consciousness/awareness where it is literally possible to co-create reality in the form of being able to create anything, and to dissolve any form of that which it does create through the agency of its own Will. The highest manifestation of this is literally being able to create and destroy whole universes. This evolved capacity occurs when a Soul has evolved to a level within the total Creation called the Casual Universe. For a detailed teaching and explanation of all of this please see a book called The Holy Science by Sri Yukteswar which is available from SRF publications. (Rad)

Guru, teacher, shaman

The very nature of Natural Laws on this Earth correlates to the need for almost all Souls, at certain points in their own evolutionary journey, to have a guru or teacher that is more evolved than them self. This has been true since humans have been on this Earth. Long, long, ago when humans were living in small, nomadic groups there was always one who was considered to be the Shaman, the keeper of the spirit, that guided that small group. And certain Souls within those small groups would also become an apprentice to such a figure, such a Soul. So long, long ago even before there were such things as monasteries, formal religions, what came to be called gurus, there was this natural structure within which humans organized themselves. The function of a guru, or a shaman, etc., is to 'guide' the inner development, evolution, of the Souls who have formed a relationship to such a Soul. As a Soul evolves within by progressively expanding its consciousness to embrace the various spheres of the Universal there are many potential pitfalls that can occur that can destabilize the Soul, to cause confusion, because the very center of gravity within its consciousness changes from the immediacy of the ego, to the Soul itself. And it is this very transition of the center of gravity within a Soul's consciousness that the function and role of the guru, teacher, or shaman is for. And there are many different 'types' of gurus, shamans, and teachers to reflect the individual natures/needs of any given Soul. The birth chart of any Soul reflects their core natures: what types of Souls that they are. One of the beauties of EA is being able to determine the nature of any given Soul. (Rad) There are many types of guru, shaman, teachers who have mastered their discipline (for example martial arts, herbalism, hands on healing, counseling), and they are using this as an avenue to point the way home spiritually for their students. So generally speaking the teacher can take many forms but the intent is the same. (Heather)

TABLE 1   Seven Soul Types

Root	Saturn, Uranus, Pluto	physical, body, asanas	Hatha Yoga
Sacral	Jupiter, Neptune	sexuality, Daemon	Tantra Yoga
Solar Plexus, Navel	Mars, Pluto	warrior, natural need to lead, leadership	Hatha Yoga Kundalini Yoga
Heart	Venus	devotion	Bhakti Yoga
Throat	Mercury	prayer, chanting, mantra, service to others, healers	Karma Yoga
Brow, Third Eye, Medulla, Ajna	Sun, Moon	wisdom, teacher types	Jyana Yoga
Crown	Neptune	avatar, guru	Raja Yoga

Guru/discipline relationship

There is no Natural Law that correlates to the guru/shaman relationship and same gender. None. One of the core Natural Laws is to share, give, and include. Thus, to exclude based on gender would be a violation of Natural Laws. Any given Soul is NATURALLY drawn to another Soul who is at the evolutionary level of a guru or shaman. Whatever that gender is that such a Soul is drawn too, naturally, has its own reasons that are unique to the nature of that Soul. Of course, that can include gender switching dynamics as well as many, many other dynamics that are the determinants of these natural attractions to a Soul who is serving in the capacity of a guru, shaman, and are natural teachers. (Rad)

Authentic spiritual teaching can take place in ANY context. Literally, for GOD's sake, JWG did that with astrology – which until he came along, was not really available as a spiritual path (it was, for the most part, an individuated state science). Socrates in the book, "Way of the Peaceful Warrior," did that with ordinary living and gymnastics. (Ari)

Martial arts

(Q) Is martial arts mastery considered a spiritual path?
(A) It depends on where the teacher (and student) is inwardly oriented. If their inner motivation is using the martial art as a way to develop discipline in deepening their inner connection to the spiritual, then yes. If the orientation is more like becoming the most proficient, strongest, best, most concentrated etc. martial arts master or student that ever lived, then no. That is an egocentric orientation, not a spiritual one. An issue in modern times is people who come from the egocentric orientation have often learned all the language that goes with the spiritual orientation, and often have thoroughly convinced themselves that is where they are at. So an undiscerning student may hear the spiritual words and believe the teacher comes from a place other than where they actually come from. In those cases at times they will feel in their gut a disconnect between the teacher's words and how being around this teacher actually feels. (Some teachers genuinely desire to come from that place, they just are not there yet. And have convinced themselves they are further along than they really are.) Jeffrey said many times the true teacher only points the way home, never to themselves. That is one way to determine if the martial arts teacher is truly on a spiritual path. (Steve)

Guru/devotee crisis

The evolutionary path back to the Source is one of exhausting all separating desires. It is the same for both guru and devotee. Even though a Soul advances to guru status, that Soul can have separating desires that prevent true merging with the Source. It must be remembered that even a guru is in the process of evolving. As a Soul draws closer to the light, the more magnified the remaining impurities and ego attachments become. For some Souls who have reached this advanced state of merging, spiritual euphoria can translate into spiritual delusions of grandeur. A guru evolving at this midpoint in the spiritual journey can be one whose teachings attract many, but whose private life conflicts and contradicts, rather than reflects, their teachings. While the devotee can experience great disillusionment through the guru, it is imperative for the devotee to separate the individual from their teachings, and to continue to extract and validate the truth of the teachings for self. The guru is but a channel, vehicle or vessel, but they themselves are not the message. It is for the devotee to cup the teachings with the action of their own hands in order to quench spiritual thirst.

The guru's life is intertwined with those they serve, but the projections and expectations placed on the guru by the devotee are typically ones that are based in the conditionings of consciousness that have been groomed to ascribe to a hierarchal understanding of life and creation. It must be remembered that devotee and guru alike are equally divine creations and equal contributors/creators to the divine/master plan. All that is created is necessary to evolution. Our understanding of perfection has been largely manufactured by the conditionings of consciousness over time. In fact, God is an evolving force, and as such is also imperfect. The imperfect guru is a reflection of God seeking to expand its own divine consciousness. The guru that experiences the crisis of magnified personal exposure has reached a critical turning point and it is one that must be confronted in order for evolution to proceed.

The guru's fall from grace, and the devotee's crisis of faith are both necessary to their individualized evolutionary growth. Both have chosen to create in this manner in order to realign consciousness and to accelerate the evolutionary pace. The devotee that experiences disillusionment in the guru is learning another lesson in disengaging from personifying god in the human experience. Disillusionment, as painful as it is, and the loss of innocence that accompanies disillusionment, will ultimately serve as a catalyst to realign the devotee with the truth that is God. The guru's fall from grace and the devotee's crisis of disillusionment serves to cut the spiritual umbilical cord of co-dependency that is created between guru and devotee. It is a necessary severing in order to clear the pathway to unification with Universal Source/God. Light reveals shadow; shadow no longer exists when one stands bathed in the true center of light. Both guru and devotee are learning necessary lessons of discernment and detachment from the phenomenal realm of illusion, which includes the need to purge the philosophy of (spiritual) masochism – in other words, the acceptance of pain, punishment, and suffering, as the prelude to enlightenment. Choosing to live in crisis consciousness – in other words, utilizing crisis as a vehicle for growth – can serve to create an accelerated pathway to God, but it is but one of the roads to travel. (Rose)

Spiritual bypass

As I understand it, EA teaches that processing life experiences through the emotional body is evolutionary precisely because it enables the Soul to fully EXPERIENCE whatever experiences are the natural consequence of its desires and choices. If the Soul does not fully EXPERIENCE that which its choices have generated, then it will not truly know in a deep way the consequences of those desires and choices, and will not be able to integrate and learn from these experiences, and thus to make new choices and evolve. In some sense spiritual bypass is a kind of delaying tactic – the Soul resisting coming to terms with the natural consequences of its own desires and choices (though at the ego level this can simply look like a person avoiding painful emotions using Jesus or altered states or "ascension" or whatever). In this way the Soul keeps itself in a kind of evolutionary limbo in that it cannot truly exhaust separating desires since it is ever delayed from truly feeling what those desires have resulted in, and therefore must repeat them (in a sense wilfully failing to learn from history). You can see how this can correlate with skipped steps in some Souls.

Spiritual bypass to me also relates to the control orientation most of us carry and to the lack of trust in natural law that has been learned on this planet. Evolution is a natural process of the universe – we can trust it to happen and we do not have to "make" it happen, so much as let it happen. As Jeffrey taught, the Water Trinity shows involution in that Spirit/Neptune differentiates to Soul/Scorpio differentiates to Ego/Cancer; and also shows that evolution occurs naturally in the natural direction of the zodiac of the shift in conscious identification from Ego/Cancer to Soul/Scorpio to Spirit/Pisces. I find in my work that when people are able to experience their experience through the emotional body (Cancer/Moon), such a full experience naturally eventually leads them (over a period of minutes or lifetimes) to a desire to understand and transform the deeper unconscious patterns and/or Soul history (both Scorpio/Pluto) that has led to the given emotional experience. I don't need to try to push this inquiry in any way, it is the natural result of deeply experienced emotion, it is just what happens when we get out of the way and feel. And then I have also found that when people start to work at this deeper level, then also very naturally begin (again, whether in this lifetime or later) to experience their own encounters with Source (Pisces/Neptune), however this may manifest as appropriate to their perceptual capacities. The water naturally returns to the sea. So to me it is not so much about energy releasing or other particular things as much as it is about having a natural experience that leads to new understanding and choices (and thus new experiences) that eventually exhaust separating desires and leave only the desire to return to Source.

If we stay with the Water Trinity, then spiritual bypassing can be seen as an attempt to "bypass" the emotions (Cancer) and critically the step of self-confrontation and transformation (Scorpio) – after all that is really hard. But of course natural law doesn't work that way and what I would say is actually happening is that the Soul is actually going in the involutionary (clockwise) direction on the wheel, trying to escape to a regressive experience of preconsciousness rather like the womb (Pisces), so as not to feel the pain of emotion (Cancer). In therapy this is sometimes called the "flight into health." To me it exemplifies the issue of trines in that as Jeffrey taught they can make it "easy" to be conscious and cooperative with evolution but they can also make it "easy" to resist it.

Regarding evolutionary states and spiritual bypass, I have personally encountered bypass in all three of the main stages. At Consensus stages I often see it as "religious bypass" – people avoiding emotions by logging into pre-digested and pat religious answers (eg I don't want to feel grief about Sandy Hook, so I'll just blame it on schools not having Christian prayer every morning; or we don't want to feel the pain of Katrina so let's just blame it on the gays). At Individuated stages I often see it as "science bypass" or "political bypass" – people avoiding emotions by logging into political causes or sophisticated explanations of the aspects of experience they are avoiding. "Psychology bypass" also happens and a lot of insight-oriented psychotherapy does this, avoiding direct experience of emotions by explaining them. And then in the Spiritual stages and the later Individuated stages I often see it as the kind of "spiritual bypass" where people prefer to log in to particular states of consciousness or metaphysical frameworks and log out of the direct and lived experience of their emotions. But to me in general bypassing the emotional body is essentially resisting evolution, which Souls at any stage in consciousness can do.

Regarding whether the kind of mental/head-based quality that typifies the specific bypass (of preferring to dwell in primordial states), means that such individuals may be in the Individuated states vs Spiritual states, I would say that could be occurring in a Spiritual or an Individuated Soul. The difference would have to be discerned by understanding the nature of the Soul's motivation for its practice in the first place. I have seen some practitioners of these paths and techniques who are (mostly) seeking to reinforce their own sense of themselves and their specialness and ability to "achieve" and use spiritual practice as the vehicle for this (Individuated); and I have seen some who are (mostly) truly seeking to unite themselves with Source (Spiritual). And at both of these levels, I have seen Souls periodically fall into the trap of using these paths to dissociate from their emotions, or even live an entire lifetime in that kind of resistance.

Considering how to help Souls in this dynamic, as mentioned we are in the territory of Pisces/Neptune, and as EA teaches this archetype is about Source and spiritual realization, but at the same time also the process by which we "deify" all sorts of people and things and states of consciousness as if they themselves are Source or are spiritual realization, and then we experience eventual disillusionment when this turns out not to be true. In this context for me it has rarely worked to point out to people they that are in spiritual bypass; those rose-coloured glasses are pretty sticky and if you get Virgo/Mercury discerning and analytical they get even more Pisces/Neptune cloudy and ascending. Unless they are somehow really ready to hear it and to experience it as real, it is just a mental thing to say it, like telling an active addict that he or she has an addiction.

What I do find helpful in many situations is to assist the person in fully experiencing whatever they are experiencing, to feel what it is like to be where they are. In this case of bypass, to feel what it is like to view or use access to this primordial state as the "answer." What does that feel like, what is the impact of that in life? After all, the desire to prematurely transcend and resist the evolutionary process is itself also a desire that the Soul has created and wants to experience. Assisting the Soul to fully experience the full experience that is a consequence of that desire (whether it is the 'high' states, the frequent interpersonal isolation that results, the tendency to judge the 'unenlightened,' the pressure to maintain one's 'enlightenment,' whatever the full experience is), and eventually it will naturally include the experience of disillusionment, and the felt sense of disillusionment – feeling it, not just being told it by someone else – the disappointment, the grief, the anger – is what naturally leads the Soul to truly release the desire for bypass and move on to whatever is next for it. Just realizing it cognitively or because someone points it out typically means that although today's bypass strategy may be dropped, the desire will still exist in the Soul to do it and it will find another way to bypass (kind of like switching addictions from one substance/behavior to another when the deeper desires driving the addiction have not been addressed and released, only deferred). (Jason)

All that you [Jason] have said/shared about this is exactly right. We need to remember/understand that the Pisces, Cancer, Scorpio trinity, the Source, the Soul, and the ego it manifests, all emanate from the Water archetype. Water is of course pure emotion. The non-dual state, the desire for, is itself an emotional delusion that is impossible to achieve, or arrive at, relative to consciousness in the Soul in a human form. A Soul relative to certain 'spiritual' methodologies can indeed arrive at some sort of 'transcendental' state but that state always, cause and effect, snaps back to a 'normal' state of consciousness. Even in these naturally transcendental states or 'cosmic consciousness' the very essence of such a consciousness or state is EMOTIONAL: the emotion or feeling within that state of consciousness as it 'perceives' the various realities of those states. That perception leads to an emotional state as it 'reacts' to the nature of the perception itself. The need of all of our Souls to directly feel the nature of our emotions as they relate to any possible experience created by the Soul for its own evolutionary needs is the bottom line truth. For those who are able to create within themselves the various degrees of cosmic consciousness all of them will report being in a temporary state of ecstasy. Ecstasy of course is an experience of pure emotion.

When Souls align themselves with various religious and/or spiritual teachings that teach it is important, necessary even, to control or repress the emotions in order for 'x' spiritual state to be realized these Souls are reacting to the nature of their own emotional lives. In essence, they are running from those emotional lives for their own reasons but all reasons that lead to this running lead to repressing the very nature of the emotions themselves. In so doing they are repressing that which is NATURAL AND NECESSARY FOR THE SOUL TO EXPERIENCE for its own evolutionary reasons. If we accept that God/ess is the origin of all things then wherein lies the origin of emotions? And for what reasons? So for Souls who do orientate to these teachings that require repression, to 'transcend' them which means repressing them, the very act of repression then magnifies and distorts those natural emotions within the consciousness of those that do so. When anything that is natural is repressed for whatever reasons ANGER IS THE DIRECT RESULT: a natural inner anger. When this occurs all too often the Soul then feels itself to be a victim of life, a victim even to their own emotions which continue to live on, to exist, despite the repression. When this natural anger is then linked to the created consciousness of feeling to be a victim first to itself, then to others, this becomes the causative basis of lashing out at anyone the Souls feels 'victimized' by. In a 'religious' and/or 'spiritual' context this then is the cause of all the horror stories we are all too familiar with: the priest abusing boys, the 'guru' who is having intercourse with some devote, and so on.

As JWG and others have taught the liberation of the Soul does indeed take place through and because of the emotional body for the reasons that Jason [above] had correctly pointed out. A story that I just remembered about this is the story of one of Yogananda's chief disciples, a women who was essential for Yogananda and his work. She developed a terminal medical condition in which Yogananda interceded upon by way of asking God/ess to keep her alive because of the critical nature of her tasks helping his work. She lived ten years longer as a result. And upon her final transition, upon the moment of the very last breath, her final words were: "TOO MUCH JOY." (Rad)

The disciple that Rad is referencing in this post is Sri Gyanamata and the book is called "God Alone: Life and Letters of a Saint." This is a wonderful book which I highly recommend as it gives great perspective about how to emotionally heal and grow without any "spiritual bypass." (Deva)

Since deep emotional processing is the heart of the work I do, what I have found is that we simply cannot easily move through our own emotional defenses. Spiritual systems that are 'transcendent' in nature often collude with the already dissociative defence in place. Yes it is quite easy for already dissociated, fragmented psyches (ie all of us) to access "other/higher worlds" since so many of our parts already reside there!! The difficult part is unlocking the trauma that caused the fragmentation in the first place and then real Soul retrieval can happen. Re-living, ie descending into the original terror, wound, fear, horror, pain (fill in the blank) opens up not only the complex formed around such an event, but the defences that were crystallized also. These defences involved ALL levels of the being, etheric/physical body, emotional body, mental body and spiritual body. ALL these bodies need to become congruent in order for full integration to happen and each one can hold their own separate defence. One body is not superior to another despite what patriarchal bias tells us. Personally I trust the veracity and truth of emotion before I trust the machinations of head, my personal bias. Sharing a quote from R.D. Laing:

"When our personal worlds are rediscovered and allowed to reconstitute themselves, we first discover a shambles. Bodies half-dead; genitals dissociated from heart; heart severed from head; heads dissociated from genitals… Without inner unity, with just enough sense of continuity to clutch at identity: the current idolatry. Torn, body, mind and spirit, by inner contradictions, pulled in different directions, Man cut off from his own mind, cut off equally from his own body – a half-crazed creature in a mad world."

I perceive that we compensate for all these contradictions and dissociations largely with our mental prowess, using it to repress the true reality that lies underneath. This is why, collectively, we are so mentally defended because under those defences lies a much different, initially terrifying inner world, where our compensated identity is threatened to come apart, but when one has the courage to go there the reward is integration and coherence. (Patricia)

The non-dual state

We need to remember/understand that the Pisces, Cancer, Scorpio trinity, the Source, the Soul, and the ego it manifests, all emanate from the Water archetype. Water is of course pure emotion. The non-dual state, the desire for, is itself an emotional delusion that is impossible to achieve, or arrive at, relative to consciousness in the Soul in a human form. A Soul relative to certain 'spiritual' methodologies can indeed arrive at some sort of 'transcendental' state but that state always, cause and effect, snaps back to a 'normal' state of consciousness. Even in these naturally transcendental states or 'cosmic consciousness' the very essence of such a consciousness or state is EMOTIONAL: the emotion or feeling within that state of consciousness as it 'perceives' the various realities of those states. That perception leads to an emotional state as it 'reacts' to the nature of the perception itself. The need of all of our Souls to directly feel the nature of our emotions as they relate to any possible experience created by the Soul for its own evolutionary needs is the bottom line truth. For those who are able to create within themselves the various degrees of cosmic consciousness all of them will report being in a temporary state of ecstasy. Ecstasy of course is an experience of pure emotion.

When Souls align themselves with various religious and/or spiritual teachings that teach it is important, necessary even, to control or repress the emotions in order for 'x' spiritual state to be realized these Souls are reacting to the nature of their own emotional lives. In essence, they are running from those emotional lives for their own reasons but all reasons that lead to this running lead to repressing the very nature of the emotions themselves. In so doing they are repressing that which is NATURAL AND NECESSARY FOR THE SOUL TO EXPERIENCE for its own evolutionary reasons. If we accept that God/ess is the origin of all things then wherein lies the origin of emotions? And for what reasons? So for Souls who do orientate to these teachings that require repression, to 'transcend' them which means repressing them, the very act of repression then magnifies and distorts those natural emotions within the consciousness of those that do so. When anything that is natural is repressed for whatever reasons ANGER IS THE DIRECT RESULT: a natural inner anger. When this occurs all too often the Soul then feels itself to be a victim of life, a victim even to their own emotions which continue to live on, to exist, despite the repression. When this natural anger is then linked to the created consciousness of feeling to be a victim first to itself, then to others, this becomes the causative basis of lashing out at anyone the Souls feels 'victimized' by. In a 'religious' and/or 'spiritual' context this then is the cause of all the horror stories we are all too familiar with: the priest abusing boys, the 'guru' who is having intercourse with some devote, and so on. (Rad)

Practices to work with the emotional body

[Example: Various practices within Dzogchen and Tibetan Buddhism] These practices are not only unnecessary but in fact confuse those who try to practice them. They take what is inherently simple and complicates that. This happens because such practices are not in alignment with Natural Laws: they are essentially invented by individuals who have been conditioned by man-made laws, the patriarchy, that are then trying to harness the Natural Laws in unnatural ways. Personally, I won't have anything to do with them. To me the practices to be used are life itself. To have the knowledge of emotions is simply to experience them within a consciousness that becomes one with whatever emotion is existing relative to a cause that has ignited it in the first place. And, within this, to have a desire, conscious intention, to understand the nature of whatever emotion: its cause, and the reasons for that cause. Within this, the inherent knowledge that then exists in whatever emotion the consciousness becomes one with. Over time of course a state of total self-knowledge defined by the emotional body will take place. A book that came up that appears relevant to all this is "The Spiritual Anatomy of Emotion: How Feelings Link the Brain, the Body, and the Sixth Sense" [Paperback] by Michael (A) Jawer (Author), Marc S. Micozzi (Author), Larry Dossey (Foreword). (Rad)

Unconditional and conditional love

JWG does talk about Christ's love, and the power that unconditional love has to transform ourselves and others. He says that "Christ's love is so deep that you will never get to the bottom of it." He also talks about unconditional love, which is very different than conditional love, and when we experience unconditional love from the Divine and others it does have the power to transform our lives. The 12th house/Neptune/Pisces archetype reflects the dynamic of unconditional love/connecting to the Divine in this way (Divine Love). (Deva)

Unconditional love is reflected in the archetypes of the 12th house, Neptune, and of course Pisces. Unconditional love can be experienced and expressed at any evolutionary level or condition. Of course unconditional love is not a function of one's personal needs being met or unmet: it just is. Unconditional love has no expectations attached to it whatsoever whereas conditional love in fact does. It is those expectations associated with conditional love that manifest as projected needs upon another, and visa versa. When those projected needs associated with one's expectations are met then conditional love is in fact experienced. When they are not then what was once experienced as love can become something quite different.

Conditional love is time-based: finite. Unconditional love is timeless: infinite. Conditional love manifests as a function of evolutionary and karmic imperatives and necessities, unconditional love manifests as a function of the universal = timeless Natural Law of giving to others in whatever ways that any given Soul has within itself to give even if that giving is simply loving another for who and what they are without any expectation or need to be given back to in any way at all. The inner feeling we all have of 'love' for another when linked with conditional love occurs as a function of the physiology that is set in motion when we interface with another where that other, and visa versa, reflects what we need in our ongoing evolutionary journey through time: the inner psychological and emotional dynamics of any given Soul through time, and the reasons for those specific psychological and emotional dynamics. (Rad)

Natural law of free choice
All things, phenomena, have been set in motion by the Creator including the possibility of 'excess of will.' And that is due to the Natural Law of 'free choice' that the Creator is responsible for Creating in the first place. (Rad)

Deviation from Natural Law
Natural Law as set in motion by the Creator contains within it the possibility of 'deviation.' Thus, it is part of Natural Law. (Rad)

Dharma
Dharma means truth. The truth of one's being, one's natural truth as created by God/ess. To arrive at one's natural truth, how one has been created by God'ess, requires a progressive de-conditioning from external conditioning dynamics that any Soul is susceptible to. When one is in total harmony with how they have been naturally created by God AND ACT ACCORDINGLY THEN THERE IS NO KARMA CREATED. This is so because one's actions, rooted in desire, are in harmony with God's intentions for that Soul. To arrive at this state of evolution of course means that such a Soul is in the final stages of the 3rd stage Spiritual evolution, ie Jesus, Buddha, Yogananda, etc. (Rad)

Length of time it takes for liberation
It can take a really long time, longer than we like to think, to evolve through a single sub-stage. Yogananda taught that it is the natural evolutionary condition of nature that a human being will reach what some call enlightenment, naturally, over the course of a million years, without making any special effort at all. It's part of how human life was created. Yogananda taught that the Kriya yoga techniques that he taught (and there would be other techniques taught on other paths also, of course) are intended to speed up that natural process. In essence, that God had included as part of creation (Natural Law) ways that *those who so desired* (ie choose, voluntary) could accelerate the pace of the natural evolutionary process. These ways are built-in, thus they are also part of Natural Law. Most people who finally "achieve enlightenment" in some life have a desire nature firmly developed that has been concentrating on seeking that liberation for a series of lives, potentially a long series of lives. This creates an inner psychological nature, a character (the nature of the desire nature), that is pre-wired in any given birth to even more of that. In essence a process of elimination of separating desires has been occurring for a long time. That final release from the wheel has to occur in *some* life – when there are witnesses to someone breaking free, they see the before and after effects on that person. They don't see how many lives it took that person to get to the life in which they were finally liberated. (Steve)

How far can one evolve in one lifetime?
To me one of the key limiting factors in how far a Soul can go in a single life is how much the human can bear to take on in a single life. When we look at charts with 7, 8, 9 planets aspecting Pluto, and/or 4, 5, 6 retrograde planets, typically these people have had very intense lives. Lives most humans would say they would never wish on another, or want for themselves. Why? Why would a Soul take on a life like that? Because it accelerates the exhaustion of separating desires. They are literally ripped away, ready or not, over and over. Emotionally and humanly, many of these experiences are painful and difficult to integrate. They are taken on as part of accelerating the evolutionary process. PTSD boils down to more emotional voltage flowing down the nervous system wires than the wires are designed to handle. The wires literally burn or melt, creating permanent changes in the brain. It takes a tremendous amount of determination and focused desire to take all of that on, and there are limits to how much the circuits can handle. (Steve)

When Souls go back to Source
(Q) When all Souls finish their evolution and finally go back to God, is that the end of human beings? (Wei)
(A) EA does not specifically teach about that other than once the Soul is free from all separating desires, and has only one desire left which is to go home to its Source, God, then it will finally lead such a Soul back into a state of absolute union with its Source: God. In the end your question really refers to the nature of the manifested Creation in the first place, and the natural evolution that takes place within that manifested Creation. The deepest root of all within the manifested Creation is consciousness and intelligence within that consciousness. And of course the Source of the manifested Creation is that intelligence and the consciousness within it. From the point of view of consciousness/intelligence in 'human form' we must remember that is but one form among countless other forms that also contains consciousness and intelligence. What is the nature of those forms and the intelligent consciousness within them? Do they also have what we call Souls? Who can know the answers to this? Saying all this only to illustrate the complexity of the manifested Creation much of which is unknowable from the natural limitation of the human form. And because of that natural limitation humans thus create philosophies and beliefs that attempt to explain or answer the

types of questions you have brought up. Evolutionary Astrology is focused on the evolution of the Soul in human form, and the dual desires that are at its core, and how those desires directly correlate to the Soul's evolution through time and space. And, of course, those desires, like the Soul, emanate from the Source Of All Things. In the end, then, it's about the Soul reuniting with its Source by the elimination of all separating desires that keep it from such a reunion. The Soul in human form can then only know its Source by unifying its consciousness with the consciousness of the Source itself. Is that then the 'end of the human being?' To me the only way to answer this is that such a total union releases the Soul from being bound by the natural limitation of the human form. (Rad)

Death

An excellent book is *"On Death and Dying"* by Elisabeth Kubler-Ross. Of course Yogananda also explained in many of his teachings the actual transition from physical death of the body of the astral realm of the Soul. In his autobiography there is a chapter on the 'resurrection' of his own guru, Yukteswar, which could not be more graphic in actual detail. I also remember a chapter in Yukteswar's book, *"The Holy Science,"* where he describes step by step the transition of the Soul from physical death to the astral plane. (Rad)

'1, 2' meditation (Hong Sau), the way back home to the Creator

JWG says the key for the practice is to focus on the '1, 2' and not the breath. He says the key is concentration. If you just focus on the breath, the inhale and exhale, then you are remaining within the world of cause and effect, the world of duality that the inhale and exhale symbolize. To concentrate and focus on the '1, 2' is to create a third point, trinity, within the consciousness that allows for the breath to progressively shallow and then suspend itself. Without that concentration of the '1, 2' this transcendence from the world of duality cannot occur. To suspend the breath leads to the direct inner perception of the inner eye, the third eye: the third point, the trinity, linked to the two external eyes. Once this perception begins it will deepen over time and the Soul, by birth right, will remember how to unite with it, penetrate it. Once this begins the varying degrees or levels of cosmic consciousness begins. The 'secret' in meditation, like the '1, 2', is CONCENTRATION. As one concentrates on the '1, 2', inhale and exhale, and not the breath itself, then the concentration will lead to the progressive shallowing and suspension of the breath. The concentration that suspends the breath for a few seconds here and there is very temporary and at best does create a sense of the consciousness being expanded in some way. But this is very different than actually suspending the breath for a length of time beyond a few seconds here and there. Thus, the '1, 2' and/or any other meditation method that reduces all word possibilities to two words, ie hong and sau.

The pineal gland becomes increasingly stimulated as the breath begins to shallow. As it does so the pineal begins to generate higher levels of melatonin within the brain. Melatonin is very much part of the physiology, chemistry, within the brain that correlates with transcendent states of consciousness linked with the inner perception of the third eye. But it is not the third eye in and of itself. You can read about the nature of the pineal gland in many places. But it is not just the pineal that secretes various physiologic substances when the breath begins to shallow and then suspends itself. The hypothalamus, the pituitary, the entire limbic system deep in the brain, etc. all become activated and, in turn and in combination, secrete various physiologic substances that correlate to the perception of the third eye. The sustained suspension of breath, and the consequent unfolding of transcendent states of consciousness can occur to any Soul (in any evolutionary state) who so desires to return back to its origin: the Creator. It is 'hard wired' into the brain. It only takes desire to do so. It is appropriate for all Souls because it is the way back HOME for all Souls. And the Creator is the origin of that way, just as it is the origin of all Souls. Focus, concentrate with the will, upon the words themselves. In time this concentration will naturally lead to a shallowing and then suspension of the breath. As that begins the Soul does not even notice the breath anymore as it begins to shallow, and then stop. Two words are used because they correlate with the Natural Law of breathing, inhale and exhale, and the world of duality itself.

The root issue here is twofold: desire, and evolutionary conditions. God is indeed, or the Creator, is indeed the origin of all things. Since it is the origin of the Soul that means the Soul's ultimate home is in its Creator. Thus, there naturally exists a way back to that home which is no different that leaving where one currently lives, a house, street, city, state, and then coming back to that home via the relevant highways, streets, etc. So, in the same way, there exists an inner structure or map within consciousness that can bring the Soul back home to its Origin. And that natural way is what the '1, 2', or any combination of two words, is about. The very nature of the natural map thus correlates with the apparent world of duality that was set in motion by the Creator while, at the same time, correlates to non-duality: timelessness. This map is thus reflected in the two physical eyes, duality, and, at the same time, the 'third eye' within, that is perceived when the breath is shallowed and finally suspended. When this occurs the interfacing to time and timelessness occurs. The world of duality and non-duality is simultaneously perceived. This interfacing of the third eye with the two physical eyes is the basis of the Natural Law of the trinity. And it is through the third eye that the way Home is perceived and understood.

God is the origin of this Natural Law that EXISTS IN ALL FORMS OF CONSCIOUSNESS. It is a natural birthright because all things emanate from the Source, God. As such this natural way home exists for all. It only takes an active desire to go Home to ignite this natural inner map to go back to our Creator. And that is then the basis of evolution, and the natural evolutionary states for any given Soul/consciousness. Desire itself is the determinant of the evolution of the consciousness within any Soul that corresponds, in the end, to the degree of SELF-AWARENESS within any Soul. So even though the Soul 'is complete' from the moment that it is created by the Creator it takes a great amount of time, lifetimes, for the Soul to become self-aware of that fact. So, in potential, it is then possible for any Soul to access this natural inner map that takes the Soul back Home. Again, it is the Soul's birthright because the Soul has been created by the Creator. But it does require active and sustained desire. This natural fact, truth, was indeed the very basis of the enlightenment of the great Buddha under the Bodhi tree. So even though this potential exists for all Souls that potential is only actively desired as a Soul evolves through the duality of time and space manifesting as many, many lifetimes. This is that which then correlates to the Soul progressively exhausting all the separating desires that keep that inner map back Home in the shadows of our consciousness. And it is those shadows that correlate for so many to simply an inner darkness when the two physical eyes are closed. Yet, as those separating desires are exhausted, the Soul finally will desire to go back Home. As it does so it then aligns itself with the different paths that lead to that Home. That then becomes the basis of all the various religions and philosophies that have been created.

Yet the distillation of all of those comes down to one simple, natural, truth: the secret of the breath. And that secret requires no beliefs at all. It only requires a desire to know that secret. And when that desire to know that secret becomes realized then THE WAY BACK HOME IS REVEALED WITHIN THE INTERIOR OF ONE'S CONSCIOUSNESS. Where there was once darkness, there is now LIGHT. And as that Light becomes ever brighter THE WAY, THE INNER MAP, BACK HOME IS REVEALED. As Jesus taught: 'When one's eye is single, one's whole body is full of light.' The inherent 'completeness' of the Soul is then realized. There is no difference between this teaching and what Swami Kriyananda is teaching. As one concentrates on the Hong Sau linked with the inhaling-exhaling breath progressively the third eye will become perceived. When almost anyone first tries this natural method all they see within themself is darkness, not the third eye itself. Most will feel an energy complex/vortex where the third eye inherently is without actually seeing or perceiving it. Thus, to concentrate upon the hong-sau relative to the breath will progressively allow this perception to occur. As one begins to perceive it, concentrate upon it, this is in direct proportion to the breath naturally shallowing and, finally, suspending itself. At that point the Soul remembers, by birthright, how to merge with it. To merge with it means to move into it: consciousness expanding within as this merging occurs. From there the various levels of 'comic consciousness' occur. These words, Hong Sau or Sau Hong, translate into English as I am That – so it then either becomes That I am , or I am That – where That correlates with God/ess. Either way is fine. Any two words can be used but obviously it's best to use words that have natural correlations with the inner God/ess Head. NA MU would be words of that nature so they would be fine. The preliminary lights that most see before the appearance of the third eye begins in this mixture of purple/gold/blue/white is a variety of patterns within. This will evolve into the initial perception of the third eye. One of the colors that correlates with the third eye is blue, the other main color is gold that surrounds this blue in a sphere like fashion. Then, progressively, you will perceive the center of this which manifests as a five pointed white star. The allotment of time depends on the ability to concentrate on the two words. As a general 'rule' it's best to allow at least 45 minutes in the beginning so that the consciousness can settle within this concentration. Place your awareness within that area of the third eye. There is a natural vortex there as you will know. So feel and focus on that vortex. Keep the lids of the eyes either totally closed, or just slightly open in a Buddhist type way: which allows just a sliver of light to enter consciousness. The eyes will take care of themselves. When you actually perceive the third eye in total the eyes will then naturally 'look up' without you being aware of such. The issue is not to focus on the breath at all. It is to concentrate upon the two words as the breath naturally goes in and out relative to those two words. The above approach requires consciousness to be 'aware' of the breath which, in turn, distracts upon the total concentration of the two words. When there is total concentration on the two words that leads finally to the perception of the third eye in full, and the Soul then remembers by birth right how to merge, fuse, with it. Then the breath simply stops of itself without the Soul/consciousness even being aware of such.

The best time for you would be coming right out of sleep in the morning. The reason for this is that your consciousness, mind, will not yet be active. Also, there is still a lot of natural melatonin within the brain at that time. So in combination this is very conducive to deep mediation, and the very best way to start your day. Then around noon or so make this another time, and, finally just before you go to sleep. Do some yoga first at noon, and night time, then the meditations. The yoga creates a condition that facilitates the meditation. Within these daily routines, a natural trinity, practice using words like Hong Sau linked with the breath as much as you can. So driving in a car somewhere, sitting in a dentist office, etc. The more you prime the pump, the more water will gush forth. Using the words 1 and 2 is perfectly fine. Remember that it is essential that you consciously focus, concentrate, not only on the words, but the energy vortex between the eyebrows. That vortex, or chakra, has its own natural 'gravity' that when concentrated upon, relative to the 1 and 2, will progressively allow for an entire 'gravity shift' within your consciousness.

When this begins to occur the molecular density within the entire body system, all of its cells, will begin to shift. As that occurs it is then common for the person to inwardly experience and 'sense' that the external world is going into something like an earthquake feeling. The ground upon which you sit will seem to be moving around you. But if you opened your eyes in those moments you would then of course find that the external environment is in fact stable. What that sensation/feeling mirrors is the inner shift in the gravity mass within the body cells because of the pull of the gravity center within the vortex that exists between the eyebrows. One thing you might want to try that will allow for your consciousness to stay fixed, concentrated, upon that gravity vortex that is called the third eye is to do what many of the Buddhist meditation methods do: to keep the eyes slightly open that allows just a sliver of light to enter into your consciousness. The contrast of the light coming in through the eyes then 'highlights' the inner darkness relative to the energy vortex or chakra between the eyes. This helps the consciousness stay focused upon that chakra as a result. It also helps to keep the Soul/consciousness 'awake' instead of the tendency of the feeling of going to sleep.

We cannot open up the brain and find a physical tissue called the third eye like we could find dendrites for example. The nature of the third eye is ENERGY. Just as consciousness is energy. We can't open up the brain and find consciousness either. It is energy. We can't open up the body and find feelings or emotions either. They are energy. Yet we know we have feelings, emotions, and consciousness by the sheer fact of being alive in human form. When the breath shallows and is still the energy of the third eye is then perceived by consciousness, the Soul. Simply let the tongue be natural: no need to place it anywhere except where it is naturally. The location of the hands makes no difference at all, so whatever feels most natural for you.

The recommended return/grounding method is to allow another 10-15 minutes in which your consciousness can naturally integrate what has taken place during the meditation to the immediacy of the moment, and what requires to set your system 'back in motion.' The key is concentration. So if you are seeing the outer layers of the third eye, the well, simply concentrate ever more upon it WITHOUT ANY EXPECTATIONS. The increasing concentration over time will allow this initial perception to deepen into the full perception of the third eye. Every Soul is different and unique in its own way. For some this sense of the gravity shift creates the 'earthquake' feeling, and for others it does not. As in anything in the Soul's evolution all is dependent on DESIRE. So it takes an active and consistent desire to evolve the consciousness/Soul through these natural forms of meditation. So this kind of experience is dependent on desire and such desires typically do not occur to a Soul until it has entered the final stages of the 3rd stage Individuated and beyond.

The experience of the gravity shift manifesting as the 'earthquake' feeling typically occurs all at once. And it continues for some time where the time itself is relative to the nature of each Soul. Generally speaking, this sense does not last very long because it does correlate to an expansion of consciousness in such a way that the expansion itself, signaled by this kind of experience, moves rapidly into the other stages that occur after this effect is sensed. Thus, the consciousness is then focused on these other stages, not the gravity shift itself as experienced in the earthquake feeling. The perception of the third eye is perceived as a sphere within the forehead: between and just above the two physical eyes. The sphere has an outer ring of gold, the inner sphere is blue, and at its very center a five pointed white star. In time, after the perception occurs, the Soul remembers by birthright how to fuse, merge, or pierce this third eye. And when that occurs the perceptions within consciousness involves, progressively, the universal spheres, the cosmic spheres, in which the nature of Creation itself is perceived and understood. Within this state of consciousness the Soul can be in 'communion' with different 'divine' entities who have various and different messages or teachings for the Soul. As this state of consciousness evolves it can finally perceive where the Created and Uncreated meet: where the 'nothing' becomes 'one.'

Establish the habit for the Soul of meditating just after you get up in the morning, and just before you go to sleep, WHATEVER THOSE TIMES ARE, IRREGULAR OR NOT. It is the routine that the Soul gets 'used' to that becomes etched within its own memory banks. And the deeper that etch becomes, the more it will bear fruit. Of course meditating at sunrise is a very powerful time to do so, as is sunset. A good way to align with the Soul before the '1, 2' meditation is to do some simple yoga beforehand: the tree pose, the cobra, the spinal twist for example. Also coming out of sleep in the morning is conducive to this too because the consciousness is more or less in the Soul then, more than the ego. The '1, 2' is good to practice while walking, or doing anything really, because it gets the Soul ever more used to it. However, while walking, or doing anything else, is an 'action' that by its very nature requires the body to breathe. As a result, the perception of the third eye cannot occur because of the breath in the body: inhale/exhale. After the Soul has developed the capacity to perceive the third eye, and fuse with it, it is possible to perceive it even during physical activities. When that occurs then that means that the Soul has more or less shifted the center of gravity within its consciousness from the current life ego to the Soul itself at all times.

It is not advisable to take supplemental Melatonin because when the melatonin levels increase in this meditation that is a NATURAL RESPONSE because of the meditation. To ingest melatonin is not a natural response. And because it is not what would then happen is that the person would simply go to sleep, or become extremely drowsy. Certain transits can correlate to a NATURAL increase or decrease of the levels of melatonin. And when that happens, from an EA point of view, it is necessary to determine WHY. There is a reason for everything that exists. And anything that exists must be understood in the context that it exists within. It is the specific context of anything that is the determinant of how and why something exists in that context. No one size fits all. For example a person could have a Saturn transit on their natal Neptune that correlated, in their context of reality, to an increase in the production of melatonin. Yet, for another in a different context, is could correlate to a decrease of this production of melatonin. (Rad)

Kundalini and Kriya yoga

Kriya Yoga is very much rooted in Natural Laws that, in the end, is the natural knowledge/law of the breath. And, because of this, the practice of it allows for all the energy within consciousness to move up from the root chakra – through all the others – thus all the natural emotions/feelings that come from each one of them – each chakra – to be consciously awakened – self-knowledge – leading right back to where it all started for all of us: the Creator of us all. Within this the Kriya Yoga ignites the natural evolutionary energy called Kundalini. Kundalini now fused with the various emotions/feelings manifesting from each chakra that are unique to the nature of each chakra. Thus the evolution of them leading to a final liberation of the Soul through and because of the emotional body as a whole. (Rad)

Laya Yoga

Laya Yoga – Sounds specific to each chakra	
Root Chakra	the sound of bumble bees
Sacral Chakra	the sound of a flute
Naval Chakra	the sound of a harp-like instrument
Heart Chakra	the sound of a giant 'gong' or church bell-like sound
Throat Chakra	the sound of a wind like you would hear when picking up a conch shell and listening to the sound within that
Medulla/Ajana united with the Crown Chakra	the sound of OM, a continuous sound that is in essence the sound of the Creation itself: this can start with the sound of giant-like waterfalls, a roar of, that then morphs into the sound of OM

Another really neat natural yoga called Laya Yoga allows the Soul to hear the natural sounds that emanate from the various chakras. And each chakra correlates to specific knowledge/teachings that are specific to the nature of each chakra. When the Soul unites, fuses, totally with whatever sound it is hearing from whatever chakra is when that inherent knowledge occurs to consciousness. Each chakra correlates to a sphere or 'loka' that contains universal knowledge that is unique to the nature of each chakra/loka. For example, the heart chakra correlates to the entire nature of the truths that correlate with the nature of emotions in its fullest dimension. Each chakra has a natural sound that exists within them. The intent of Laya Yoga is to be able to have our consciousness/Soul tune into and hear these sounds. And, ultimately, to merge or fuse with the sound itself so that there is no more awareness of the 'listener.' When that occurs the consciousness of the Soul becomes aware of an entire universe within that chakra that correlates with the entire teaching or knowledge intrinsic to that chakra.

The way to do Laya Yoga is to sit very vertically and, if possible, on something made of cotton because cotton will cancel the negative magnetic vibration of the Earth field. While sitting vertically, raise up the arms in such a way as to place the thumbs over the appendage on the lower part of the ear to seal off external sound: press the thumbs inwardly upon it. Then allow the rest of each hand to rest upon the forehead/top part of the skull in such a way as to have the tips of the little finger of each hand to rest gently on the top of the eyelids at the very end: the end farthest away from the nose. Then allow the rest of the fingers to fall naturally upon the top of the forehead/skull. Allow the physical form to breath naturally, while at the same time concentrating the consciousness upon the natural vortex, chakra, third eye in the middle of the forehead. A natural sequence will then begin.

This sequence starts with the consciousness/Soul at first hearing the natural sound of the electrical system within the body form. This will sound something like standing underneath a high tension wire. Then this will give way to hearing the natural sound of the blood coursing through the body relative to the heart: pump, pump. Then, finally, this will evolve into being able to tune into the natural sounds of the chakras. What happens to most Souls at this point is that they will naturally tune into the chakras within them that are already most open. This will be different for each Soul. So if you at first hear the sound of the naval chakra, for example, to allow the consciousness to 'tune into' that sound ever more: to just go into it as much as possible.

In time, and with practice, there will come a point in which there is no more listener which will be simultaneous to the consciousness/Soul becoming aware of the entire universe/loka/sphere that is intrinsic to that chakra. The Soul/consciousness is then simply in a state of becoming aware of all the truths, Natural Laws, that are specific to that chakra. To practice this Laya Yoga over time will allow the Soul/consciousness to fully actualize and tune into each chakra. The knowledge gained is of course inwardly realized that correlates with universal, natural truths and laws of each of those chakras. Laya Yoga and the '1, 2' mediation can be used in conjunction with each other, one after the other, or as a 'stand-alone' relative to your own ongoing practices. (Rad)

The veil of maya

"Every human being is essentially a Soul, covered with a veil of maya. Through evolution and self-effort, each human makes a little hole in the veil; in time, one makes the hole bigger and bigger. As the opening enlarges, the consciousness expands; the soul becomes more manifest. When the veil is completely torn away, the Soul is fully manifest in him/her. That woman/man has become a master – master of their self and of maya." (Yogananda)

South Node of Neptune in Aquarius

(Q) In relation with the South Node of Neptune being in Aquarius (reflecting the original matriarchal roots of the current desires in all Souls to spiritualize consciousness), and the connection of natal Neptune with the Aquarius Age, in the context of the current transition between the Pisces Age into the next Aquarius Age, would imply that the root of these desires (ie the past of the Soul) is also symbolic of the future ways for the Souls to spiritualize consciousness (ie ways which will be in place for these Souls in the next Age). Is this correct? (Gonzalo)

(A) Yes. (Rad)
(Q) For me this is interesting to consider because it confirms that the current time frame is defined by a potential for accelerated evolution of Souls because it implies that the past is becoming the future now. Thus, the work on resolution of issues from past lifetimes related to the spiritual roots of the Soul and, at the same time, work on the resolution of issues pertaining to the future of the Soul – ie the past and the future are contained and concentrated within the current time. Is this correct?
(A) Yes. And what this will mean of course is if the original spiritual root will manifest again or not which itself is linked with the survival of the species. Within Aquarius is the triad of Libra and Gemini. Libra correlates with the Natural Law of giving, sharing, and inclusion. This is how humans were defined relative to groups of humans, Aquarius, for the balance of humans' existence on our planet. In relatively recent times this Natural Law of course has become perverted to self-interest and exclusion which then causes one group of humans, or one human, then trying to compete with other groups, or a human, relative to the survival instinct itself. In turn this leads to dominance and submission. If this is not corrected by going back to the original root, or past, and bringing that forwards into the future, then the extinction of the species is guaranteed.
(Q) So, in a sense, over lifetimes of evolution, as the "hole enlarges" or more veils are removed and more illusions dissolved (lots of disillusionment), from this perspective relative to Neptune's South Node, would it be sound understanding to correlate this symbol to what *has held* (past tense) ultimate meaning in the individualized consciousness relative to how much that consciousness has evolved? (Bradley)
(A) Yes. You can also include into this the natural planetary ruler of the South Node of Neptune which for all of us is Aquarius and its natural ruler Uranus. You can include the aspects to this Uranus as well as aspects to the South Node of Neptune itself. (Rad)
(Q) So, the Soul's journey has a past. The consciousness within the Soul journey, relative to the sense of an evolutionary past and future, has a past. This past may not be as we perceive linear time; however in the sense that the consciousness does has a past, along the journey it continues to evolve further into the fullest potential of consciousness within the human form. Would the South Node of Neptune then correlate to earlier in the Soul's evolutionary journey the ways which it spiritualized?
(A) Yes.
(Q) And then, relative to the Soul's individual past, what held ultimate meaning within that Soul's consciousness and thus still resonates as such, coming through the 'now' as a way to naturally spiritualize. And that which still holds a sense of ultimate meaning within the consciousness expressing outwardly relative to the stage at which the consciousness has evolved along the journey thus far (aka the evolutionary stage of the Soul)?
(A) Yes.

Natural Law that holds creation together
(Q) The glue or Natural Law that holds the creation together would have to be perfect. Is there anything at all that is PERFECT about God? (Linda)
(A) The 'glue' that holds the manifested Creation together, including all that which we call Natural Laws such gravity, is the Source of that glue itself. Your use of the word 'perfect' is indeed relative to any given moment in time yet 'time' itself is ever evolving so that what can appear to be 'perfect' at one point in time becomes 'imperfect' from the point of view of another point in time. It is indeed the interaction of what we can call perfect relatively speaking and imperfect that is the essence of evolution itself that leads to a 'timeless' perfect which is when what we call God/ess becomes perfect within Itself. (Rad)

JWG's method of eliminating LEARNED masochism
From my own personal experience, in relation to what JWG explained to me years ago, this technique helps eliminate LEARNED guilt, not natural guilt. Even in Natural Law we can experience natural guilt. But, at this point in our history we're just beginning to learn how to distinguish between natural guilt and the guilt we can feel by comparing ourselves to a "perfect" God. I think it boils down to a simple (Pisces) process of asking in any of these situations just WHAT the basis of the guilt is, ie whether it's rooted in man-made laws or Natural Laws. And as one asks that question more and more, I think we can start to weed out the source of any guilt. Even with the natural guilt, we need to remember that as Wolf used to put it, "God has goofed up, so why wouldn't WE goof up?" And another (Piscean) question: "How can anything perfect create something Imperfect?" It's really a shift in this understanding of "perfection" that I think helps in our understanding of Natural Law, and ultimately the forgiveness for both ourselves and others. (Adina)
This is a very simple technique, and it's absolutely free (except for the price of a cassette tape).
(1) Take a sheet of notebook paper and fold it down the middle. On the left side, list every negative message you've ever received from whatever person at any time. Take at least a week to do this – longer if necessary, AND use as many pieces of paper as necessary. (I think I had six pages, and I wrote on them front and back.) If you're like most of us who've done this, you'll find that many of the negative messages have been coming from yourself. Example: "Mary, you're just no good for anything."
(2) Once you're sure you've written down all the negative messages, then on the right side of the paper, across from each of the negative messages, write a positive, counteractive message. Example: Mary's response to above. "No. That's only their opinion of me. It's not a fact. I am good for lots of things, and can, in fact, do many things very well." (Notice that even if we start with a negative, the majority of the message is said in positive language.)

(3) Once you have all your positive/counteractive messages written down, take a 90-minute tape and record each of the messages in your own voice, saying them like you really MEAN them. You may find this difficult at first because the statements don't FEEL right to you. But be the best actor you can be and read each one with positive conviction. You need to fill only one side of the tape. Since you will be playing this as you go to sleep, if you have difficulty falling asleep right away, or the sound of voices keeps you awake, then leave about the first 20 minutes of the tape blank before you start to record your messages. The remaining 25 minutes of the tape will be more than enough to accomplish your purpose.

(4) Each night for the next four to six months (minimum of four) when you go to bed, try to place your tape recorder as close to your right side as possible, turn on your tape (if you sleep with a partner, use ear phones) and go to sleep. The messages will enter through your right ear and, thus, affect the left brain. (According to Jeffrey this is a shamanic technique.) This is different from saying affirmations when you're awake because when you're asleep the left brain can't argue or discount the information. It's absolutely CRUCIAL to do this EVERY NIGHT for the four to six months – do not skip even one night. If you miss a night, the "chain" of positive reinforcement in your brain is broken, and you have to start all over again.

Another thing to keep in mind is that since this simple practice radically changes your consciousness, freeing you from what can be thousands of years of guilt and not feeling ready enough or good enough, Lucifer will do its darnedest to make sure this shift doesn't happen. Incredibly stupid things can happen. It actually took me 16 months to get through a full six months without interruption. I don't want anyone to dwell on that part, but do be AWARE and take appropriate precautions. For example, make sure you have new batteries (if necessary) on a regular basis, etc. After a week or so, you'll start to notice that with each day you'll feel a little 'lighter,' a little bit stronger, and a little bit happier or more content. You'll start to feel empowered and like you ARE ready enough and/or good enough to take on something you want to do. Since there's strength in numbers, if you plan to do this and are open to sharing that you ARE doing it (no need to give details of the messages, etc.), then perhaps you could set up an email support group. This is an amazing technique to rid oneself of the learned masochism, and I wish any and all of you who try this the greatest success and a new lease on life. (Adina)

Jeffrey Wolf Green's Method of Eliminating LEARNED Masochism (for children)

To determine what behaviors indicate masochism in the child, read Pluto Vol. 2 in which Wolf went into detail about the sado-masochistic archetypes. In relation to children not being "steeped" in it yet, masochism will be reflected in a chart because it began BEFORE this lifetime, since the chart reflects the past, as experienced in the present, which leads to the future. When it's a young child, Wolf advocated the parents whispering the counteractive methods (for this and other conditions) in the child's right ear every night after the child had fallen asleep, and to do this for the four months, although sometimes the results start to appear much sooner. (Adina)

Archetypes correlating to the chakra system

The phenomenon of perception correlates with Scorpio, Pluto, and the 8th house. The Soul perceives the nature of phenomenal reality and then begins to give names and classifications to the nature of that phenomenal reality. Phenomenal reality is Jupiter which co-rules the sacral chakra with Neptune. The interpretation, Jupiter, of that phenomenal reality, Jupiter, that is perceived by the Soul, Pluto, is thus given order by way of organized linear thought that connects all the different shapes, forms, and the totality of the manifested Creation into a logical system of thought that is interconnected so as to make the Soul feel secure. Mercury is the natural polarity of Jupiter wherein lies the logical ordering of thoughts that correlate with the perception upon the nature of phenomenal reality. This then becomes the basis of all kinds of ways to organize phenomenal reality relative to the interpretation of what the phenomenal reality means. Thus the basis of that which is inherently true, Jupiter co-ruling with Neptune relative to the sacral chakra, and that which is not: delusive in nature. The Soul is given the God created right to perceive the nature of the phenomenal reality in any way that it so desires which includes knowing the truth, Jupiter/Neptune, of the manifested Creation.

With Uranus co-ruling the root chakra with Pluto, at its core, then Uranus, then Saturn on the outer layer, the Soul through evolutionary necessity will liberate, Uranus, from any perception of reality, the manifested Creation, that is not intrinsically rooted in the actual truth of that manifested Creation. Desires, Pluto, are of course the determinant through which the Soul chooses how to perceive the nature of anything, including the nature of the phenomenal manifested Creation. This includes the truth of one's own being, the truth of one's own Soul, at any moment in time. Mercury symbolizes and correlates to the nature of the conscious thoughts that the Soul has, and why. It correlates to how the Soul is 'thinking' about anything, and why. It correlates to how the Soul is mentally organizing the nature of its own phenomenal reality in any given life relative to its own unique, individual, evolutionary journey through time: Pluto combined with Saturn. Thus, as the Soul desires to 'liberate,' Uranus, from all temporal and finite forms of understanding itself, and the nature of the manifested Creation, this liberation will lead to that which is timeless, that which is the inherent truth of the manifested Creation set in motion by the Creator. In turn, this will correlate to the Soul's desire to understand its own inherent nature as Created by its Creator.

As this liberation unfolds, evolves, the Soul will now shift its center of gravity, Saturn, from the ego, Moon, it creates in each life, to the Soul itself. In so doing the Soul then realizes its individual Creation within the totality of all that has been Created: it has realized its timeless self that is not conditioned, Saturn, by anything other than the inherent truth of the phenomenal Creation, and the inherent truth of its own unique Soul. This progressive evolution is thus manifested through Mercury by way of the thoughts that exist within the consciousness of the Soul, and how those thoughts are related or communicated to anyone. Thus, it is the evolution taking place within the root chakra that is then reflected in the orientation of all the other chakras including the throat chakra: Mercury and Jupiter. The inherent function of Mercury is not more dense or differentiated than any other archetype of any of the planets. (Rad)

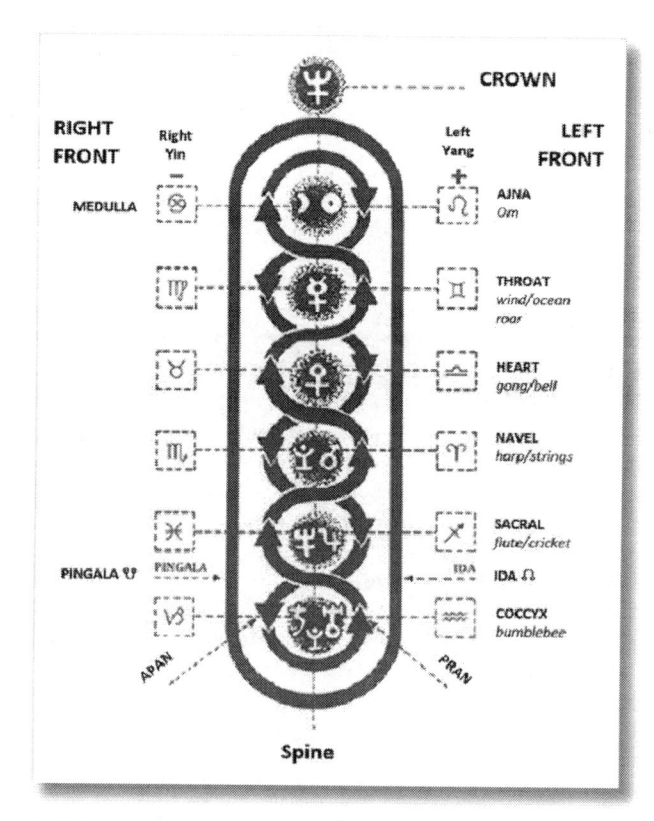

FIG 1 Chakra Correlations

They [the chakras] are meant to be understood according to what they mean, and correlate to. And they are meant to be integrated within the natural correlations of all the archetypes that apply to houses, signs, and planets. They go together. In the example of a heart-broken person, at a chakra level, would of course correlate to Venus. And Venus correlates relative to chakras with the heart region. Both the 2nd house and 7th house, Taurus and Libra, are ruled by Venus. Yet, for example, we could look into a birth chart and see heavy stress to the planet Venus no matter what house or sign that it is in. And, thus, from a chakra point of view we could see this entire chakra wounded, and needing to be healed. The systems go together is the point here. The 2nd house and Taurus are naturally correlated with sexual energy for this is the archetype of survival of the species: to procreate in order for the species to survive. It is inherent to all human beings. So it's not a matter of any planet or chakra 'activating' it. How the person relates to them self as a sexual being comes from this archetype, and the reasons for that. So the sign on that 2nd house, the location of its planetary ruler, the aspects to that planet, the location of the planet Venus by its own house and sign, the aspects to it, where the sign Taurus is located by house, all correlate to this, and the reasons for how a person relates to them sexually: their specific evolutionary and karmic signatures which starts with the underlying EA paradigm itself. All of these archetypes, correlate to any Soul's inner relationship to them self is, and how that inner relationship correlates to how any of us relates to others: the outer side of Venus which is then why it correlates to Libra, and the 7th house.

(Q) How would fundamental desires for creative self-actualization (Leo) translate by themselves into the activation of the third eye chakra?"

(A) It of course depends on the evolutionary condition of any given Soul. If a Soul is linking their desire for creative self-actualization with the Source of itself then this will lead to actualizing the Ajna chakra: the 3rd eye. On the other hand, if the Soul is solely identified with just itself as the source of its own self-actualization then this chakra will not be actualized or activated: it will remain dormant relative to the Soul that is glorifying itself through the egos that it creates from life to life: the natural polarity of the Ajna chakra of course is the Medulla which is ruled by the Moon: the egos created by the Soul in each life. (Rad)

Spiritual nature of water signs

Any kind of synthesis between water signs and houses emphasizes the underlying spiritual truth behind the human identity in the first place. Depending on evolutionary state that will be understood in different ways. Water points to the spiritual nature of the human being in the first place. Each water sign/house/planet points to the direct relationship between the totality of existence and each individual person. When we combine them in any way we are basically looking at a Soul that is asking the question, "Who am I?" The answer will only make sense in larger cosmological terms and yet will depend greatly on evolutionary state. Victimization, strong attachments, utter confusion, naïveté and all kinds of challenging psychological/emotional states can come up with these signatures – not just unconditional healing. Anyone with any chart can be more or less Soul/Source oriented. The emphasis on archetypes in the chart simply describes the specific karmic and evolutionary dynamics of that particular Soul. All Souls are, in the end, of the Source, and all Souls have the potential to desire that Source. (Ari)

Can putting God first be the cause of skipped steps?
I think the desire to put "God first" cannot, by its inherent nature, be the cause of skipped steps. Neither can the desire to know God cause skipped steps, whatever the evolutionary condition is. I think this is because the "nature" of God is radically different than that of anything existing within the manifested creation, and hence, the relation between the Soul and God is different by nature from any other relation; and further, because the purpose of the complete evolutionary journey is precisely to return to God. This is why God can be known (this knowledge is of course inherently limited) and can cause the desire to put God first, at any stage of evolution. What I think can cause skipped steps are dynamics linked with any idea about God, which in reality is different from God. (Gonzalo)

Disillusionment and doubt, a personal experience
(Q) I have been undergoing massive disillusionment within my own spiritual life and within my relationship to Spirit itself. I have noticed as a reaction to this, I have become extremely cautious and guarded about interpreting *anything* in directly spiritual terms anymore. It is as JWG frequently said, disillusionment can be one of the most bitter and difficult experiences that any of us can have, and I can say from direct experience that this is UTTERLY true. And because that experience is so hard and so painful, the last thing I personally want to do – and I'm sure the same is often true for others – is delude myself again and walk right back into it. This also connects to the Virgo archetype: transition. In my own case, I recognize that I am manifesting an extreme response to the disillusionment that has had to occur in myself – and one of the serious, unfortunate effects is that it has cut me off from my own lifeblood. That is something I just have to work out for myself, I know. But I do have this question correlating to disillusionment and doubt. How does one go through massive disillusionment and not get caught up in the debilitating psychology of doubt? If something has been regarded in one's heart of hearts as 'real' – and that something has also been providing the basis for ultimate meaning – it is a complete shock to consciousness when the illusions are exposed and the meaning within it is finally seen as an embellishment of one's own making. So the question becomes, how does one recover one's confidence in interpreting spiritual reality, ie what is a real manifestation of Spirit vs what is imagined or 'hoped,' following a major disillusioning of consciousness? – particularly when there is no immediate resource available to confirm or clarify the accuracy of one's interpretation? (Stacie)

(A) The actual archetype that specifically correlates with being disillusioned is Neptune, Pisces, 12th house, that can then trigger its natural polarity of the Virgo, 6th house, and Mercury that manifests as doubt. With Neptune now transiting Pisces, and it has been squaring the transiting nodal axis that was in Gemini/Sagittarius, this experience of disillusionment leading to doubt has been happening to many, many people. And necessarily so because the intention with Neptune in Pisces is to know or learn about that which is true, and that which is not. While those transiting Nodes were in Gemini/Sagittarius this then focuses on the difference between beliefs that are projected as ultimate meaning, that which is true from the point of view of pure beliefs, and that which is true from the point of view of INNER KNOWING. Inner knowing does not correlate with beliefs because what is known is experienced within the interior of the Soul itself as a by-product of desire to know that which is true, and that which is not. Inner knowing of that which is universally true occurs of course through various practices, Virgo, that are all aimed and shallowing or stopping the breath. As that occurs the Soul is then able to penetrate the inner realms of consciousness itself: Neptune correlates with the phenomena of consciousness. As it progressively penetrates these inner realms of consciousness a variety of natural truths that correlate with the nature and cause of consciousness itself become KNOWN. And this knowing, again, is not a function of beliefs because, as these inner truths are known, there is nothing to literally believe and everything to know. And because these inner truths are simply known there then becomes nothing to doubt. The knowing is a function of actual experience, and those experiences are universal to any Soul who so desires to know these inner truths that correlate with the nature of consciousness. Because they are in fact universal it then serves as a way of knowing that which is true, versus that which is make-believe.

When this is the baseline within the Soul's consciousness, the point of personal Soul knowing and integration, this then serves as the vehicle through which, and because of, the Soul then 'interprets' the nature of any given phenomenal reality. The dynamic or archetype of interpretation specially correlates to Sagittarius, Jupiter, and the 9th house. As the Soul interprets the nature of any external phenomenal reality relative to this inner baseline the MEANING of whatever external phenomenal reality is then projected upon that phenomenal reality. As the Soul does this it will then automatically create a way of intellectually organizing all of phenomenal reality that reflects the core inner baseline of the inner knowing of the nature of consciousness itself. This natural process of intellectually organizing phenomenal reality correlates to Gemini: how the nature of thoughts that occur as a function of the inner knowing are connected to create a larger whole that is organized. All of this then correlates to the nature of various 'spiritual' cosmologies that humans have manifested going back to its own origins on this Earth that are then called 'religions.' This is then exactly where the conflict between pure beliefs versus actual knowing can occur because many who do desire to know the Origin of all things, the Origin of consciousness itself, indeed the Origin of themselves, align themselves with whatever spiritual cosmology without actually doing what is necessary to know for themselves that which is true.

Thus, by attaching themselves to whatever cosmology then leads to their personal belief system that is of course used to interpret whatever phenomenal reality. When a Soul does this, without actually doing that which is necessary to inwardly know, these beliefs are then projected upon phenomenal reality so that when phenomenal reality manifests in ways that cause conflict with the projected beliefs the result is then doubt: doubting the nature of the projected beliefs themselves that have been born, again, from whatever spiritual cosmology they have latched onto relative to the pure desire to Know. This conflict caused by projected beliefs initially creates the disillusionment of those beliefs that then triggers the doubt. It should be said too that a Soul who does not do their own actual inner knowing but simply latches onto whatever spiritual cosmology can also create 'beliefs' about themselves and/or others that are also delusional or illusionary. Thus, when certain types of inner or outer events take place that defeat those projected inner beliefs about themselves or others that same experience of being disillusioned takes place that then leads to doubt: doubt about oneself, or doubt about another(s). In essence this correlates to self-deception, and/ or being deceived by others.

To recover one's confidence in interpreting phenomenal reality, or as you say 'spiritual' reality, is to go deeply within the interior of one's own consciousness with the pure desire to KNOW. To know the actual truth of anything. To do so always starts with some sort of natural practice that aims at stilling the breath, of shallowing it to the point that it NATURALLY STOPS. If one does this while at the same time holding the nature of whatever one is wanting to know about within their consciousness there will come a moment, a time, in which the answer simply OCCURS WITHIN CONSCIOUSNESS OF ITS OWN VOLITION: like a bubble manifesting from the depths of the sea onto the surface of the sea itself. And a Soul can do this repeatedly in such a way that the truth of what one is wanting to know about can be repeated as many times as the Soul needs it to be repeated so that the lingering doubt simply dissolves. The point here is that if that which is true relative to what one is asking about is indeed true it will repeat itself over and over for as many times that the Soul needs it to. In this way confidence is regained. (Rad)

How to deal with natural guilt

The best way to deal with it is to orientate to Soul to create conditions in its life that were the very causes that lead to the natural guilt in the first place, and then to do all that is possible to do the naturally right things in the face of those conditions. Everybody has natural guilt in varying degrees in their Soul. No Soul is 'perfect.' (Rad)

I was deeply struck when I first saw this, years ago in the movie Gandhi. More and more I understand why. It is such an example of this principle. During that fast, toward the end of the Gandhi movie, a devout Hindu came to Gandhi and said, "I am going to hell." Gandhi asked, "Why?" He said he had killed a Muslim boy during the violence that sprang up as the country was being divided into India and Pakistan. Gandhi replied, "I know a way out of hell. Find a child whose parents were killed in the violence and raise it. Only make sure it is a Muslim child and raise it as a Muslim." Think of the implications of a devout Hindu raising a child as a Muslim, and the effect that would have on the Hindu man's natural guilt, and also the effect on the child's Soul, whose parents had been murdered by Hindus. (Steve)

Another way one can make up for transgressions is, as one's life gradually changes, to remind other sincere Souls who struggle with a similar inner darkness that there is indeed a way out. This human life is often hard. But there is ALWAYS a path back to God/Goddess for sincere Souls ready to take the necessary steps, which start with owning where we have been. (Steve)

Awareness of transcendent truths

Sagittarius, Jupiter, and the 9th house correlate to our awareness that the Earth that we live upon is connected to a much larger whole that we call the universe. This awareness 'induces' realizations of a non-linear or abstract nature about the nature of the universe that the Earth is part of. This then includes what appears to be 'outside' of ourselves. This awareness thus induces how the whole of the universe, including Earth, is interconnected or related to one another. This then becomes the basis of understanding and knowing through intuition what we call the Natural Laws of the Creation that explains this interconnectedness: to understand the 'whole' truth. When this natural component of our consciousness is then linked with Pisces, Neptune, and the 12th house it then attempts to induce realizations as to the nature of the manifested Creation in the first place: that which is responsible for the Creation of the whole that we call the universe. Thus the 'transcendent' truths of Creation itself.

This awareness is then that which is responsible for desiring to KNOW those transcendent truths. In turn this desire to know these transcendent truths induces, through intuition, the natural truths or ways of doing so. To do so is then the basis or cause of intuitively knowing that such transcendent truths can only be known from WITHIN oneself: Pisces, Neptune, and the 12th house. This then becomes the basis and origin of natural methods or techniques that will allow for an 'induction' of that transcendent knowing. When those natural methods or techniques are employed by our consciousness this then leads to a 'transcendent state' within our consciousness in which the perception, knowing through direct perception, of the transcendent or comic laws of Creation occurs. And that knowing is 'induced' within our consciousness because of consciousness being in a cosmic or transcendent state. And this induction is based on what is perceived from WITHIN our consciousness that can then be applied to what we perceive by way of the Creation in its externalized forms: Earth, the universe itself. (Rad)

Natural Law of separation

The natural desire to separate was put in motion by the Creator itself. That's why it is natural. The intention within this as designed by the Creator was for all aspects of the Creation that had conscious awareness to realize, consciously realize, that in their APPARENT separateness that defined their sense of individuality, that their origins, where they came from, what their essence was/is, is the Creator itself. Within this core awareness is the awareness that all of the manifested Creation is thus interrelated and interdependent. All is part of the whole. It is a Natural Law. When humans lived in this way for the balance of its history until recent times, they were thus living in a reality that was defined by 'giving, sharing, and inclusion' which equaled their need for survival as individuals, and as groups of people. When this natural desire of separateness became perverted this Natural Law of giving, sharing, and inclusion changed to self-interest, and exclusion. Step back for a moment and imagine realities created by humans that were defined by the Natural Law of giving, sharing, and inclusion versus the realities that have been created by self-interest and exclusion. The stark relief created in this comparison should speak for itself.

A simple example: American Indians hunting for buffalo. Once the buffalo was killed the Indian would pray for the buffalo and thank it for providing food for the tribe in the understanding of how the WHOLE was interrelated, and how each part of that whole was dependent for survival on that whole. Now compare this to the White man, under the delusion of Manifest Destiny which itself manifested from their MAN-CREATED, not God-created, version of Christianity. And how the White man almost brought to extinction the entire buffalo species in its greed defined by self-interest and exclusion, ie the White man in its delusive self-importance and superiority to all that was NOT HIM having zero awareness of the WHOLE. Thus all other aspects of the Creation were to serve its own self-interest defined by others who threatened that self-interest. When the buffalo was killed it was left to rot on the ground that it was killed after its hide had been removed. This simple example of the perversion of the natural desire to separate could be exampled in literally thousands of ways. And it is because it can, the actual reality that has been created leading right up to the present moment, that humans have guaranteed their extinction. The Creator is also the origin of course of free choice. And it is through choice making that all of us are responsible for what we create. (Rad)

Exhausting separating desires

ANY DESIRE that is not rooted in the desire to reunite with our Source, God/ess, is a separating desire. All of us can be 'aware' of whatever desires we have that are separating in nature. That awareness does not automatically equal suddenly not having that desire(s) anymore. Countless Souls are aware of a variety of desires within the desire to know, to reunite, with God/ess. Very few Souls, at any given time on Earth, have only one desire left within them: the desire, the only one, to reunite with God/ess. Thus, most Souls who do have an active desire to know, reunite, with God/ess do so within the context of other, separating desires, that they feel must be acted out, or upon. Progressively these desires do become exhausted that leads to those Souls that have only one remaining desire: to reunite with God/ess. As desires become exhausted this leads to the awareness within a Soul that, 'I don't need this or that desire anymore. I am done with it.' When a previous desire(s) has reached that point of exhaustion, 'I don't desire this or that anymore,' they are then free from this or that desire. (Rad)

Profound discontent

Within the apparent dark clouds there is Light. And that Light is eternal for that Light is, indeed, God. When most Souls try to meditate, at first, they experience an inner darkness when they close their eyes: dark clouds. For any Soul, as the Soul's birthright, persists through the psychology of determination that inner darkness will turn into the inner Light that can be perceived within. And as that Light is perceived the Soul remembers how to merge, fuse, with It. And, as that merging itself evolves, the Soul remembers that natural path or way HOME. So even though Lucifer is now in Cancer, home, we must remember too that Lucifer also correlates with God: the bearer of Light. And that Light is meant to show us the way Home: Cancer. (Rad)

As it gets clearer and clearer to the remaining humans who are still sane that the wheels are increasingly coming off the bus, the strength of these feelings is going to grow. The more sensitive a person is the more they will emphatically pick up these emotions from the collective consciousness. (Steve)

Perfection

Through my own spiritual path and experience the ultimate nature of mind/awareness/source appears to be beyond what a human being can even label; beyond thought and language, yet inseparable from our experience of being. So if this is the case, then the very concept of what is perfect and what is not perfect becomes irrelevant since our ultimate nature is beyond this form of conceptualization. This ultimate nature as taught in EA, is represented by Neptune, which of course has an intangibility than cannot be defined. We also know through the teachings of EA that all the other archetypes are contained within Neptune/12th house, which again represents the inseparability of who we are. I speak about this because I sometimes feel that by saying we are not perfect, we actually create a psychology of masochism within a person. Holding an ideal to become perfect, when in fact, EA teaches that Source itself is not perfect, seems an impossible and fruitless task. How can striving towards an ideal of non-perfection not create a feeling of unworthiness and pointlessness? The humility comes in realizing this but I also feel that humility is a result of knowing that we are not separate from each other, and having compassion for the human condition which strives in great pain and conflict to be that which it already is.

I have heard teachers say that we *are* perfect, that there is nothing we need do but rest and recognize our true nature. I'm not saying I agree or believe this any more than the notion of non-perfection. I simply recognize in myself that I do not know. If there is no concept of perfection, then non-perfection itself is perfection. I've also struggled with the projected ideas of others that focusing on past lives/karma etc is an unnecessary indulgence to thoughts and emotions that really serve no purpose other than to keep us attached to a misguided idea of inseparability. Again, I neither agree nor disagree. However, what I feel I have grasped over the last year or so is a deeper understanding of the planetary functions of Jupiter and Neptune. All of what I am writing of course is my Jupiter speaking/intuiting despite what I am trying to convey, which is my Neptune. As EA teaches, the intuition of Jupiter can be the truth, and also the distortion of the truth. The transmission of Neptune is the ultimate truth – yet we can never really *know* Neptune (except for an experiential perception that cannot be defined). For me, this is where the humility comes from. My experience in resting my mind, which consequently rests my feelings, emotions, and body, gives me more access to a direct Neptunian transmission that comes via Jupiter. It feels like intuiting the next action in a way that has nothing to do with the me (ego) that is anything but pure Neptune (Source). Also, I feel that opening to Neptune in this way accelerates the exhaustion and dissolution of separating desires. This way I feel guided by Source and develop a trust that I will be provided with what I need, to do what I need to do. A pure Jupiterian intuition can be a purely egoic reaction which is not beneficial, or a result of, my ultimate nature.

What I have found helpful and liberating for myself and many people around me, is an understanding that all the archetypes that play out in our chart (Aries-Aquarius), are an inseparable part of our true nature (Source/Neptune). And since this is the case, there is nothing wrong with them! And more importantly, nothing needs to be changed or *perfected* about them! As astrologers we know there is no running away from the chart, but again as EA teaches, there are beneficial ways in which the archetypes play out, and distorted ways in which they play out. This to me emphasizes the beauty with which creation evolves, and the choices we make to liberate ourselves from any belief that we are perfect or not perfect. I mention all this as a typical Pluto in the 11th house among a group of people that on some level do not see the value in E(A) I of course do and am always thankful to Jeffrey from the bottom of my heart for sharing this teaching which has served as a true transmission to my Soul and path in life. I share these feelings about "we are not perfect" purely because I see them as a road block to my personal understanding of our true nature, and also because it becomes a belief that is a turn off to people that could gain a great deal from E(A) I feel the greatest way I can serve myself and those around me is to share EA in a way that is recognized as a path to the truth, rather than dismiss them or parts of the teaching due to clashing Jupiters. (Heidi)

One must be careful about using words like 'perfection.' "When I consider 1st stage Spiritual from reading the descriptions, I get a sense of perfection..." There is no perfection on this planet, and it's not even possible. Perfection cannot exist in a polarity reality whose basis is to evolve. The very principle of evolution is proof there is not perfection. There is nothing more to evolve to when one has reached perfection. And the principle of evolution, in every way, clearly underlies everything on this planet. The idea of perfection is the root principle in masochism, because we compare where we are to an ideal (Pisces) of perfection, which is an IDEAL, not a reality. In relation to the ideal (perfection) we can never measure up, for not one of the 7 billion humans does. This, in a masochist, then leads to a sense of guilt, for not being perfect enough, and a need to atone for what one has done that is less than one's definition of perfect. This becomes a repeating pattern of guilt and the need to atone, and attracting others who have guilt and rather than a need to atone for what they have done 'wrong,' a need to get back at, punish, those who have made them feel guilty, for they know they have done nothing wrong as it's all someone else's fault.

Such Souls have a need to punish, and masochists have a need to atone. Part of atoning is a sense of feeling inadequate or unworthy, which often creates a subconscious need to punish oneself, which can be actualized by drawing in external people with a need to punish others, who are quite happy to fill the masochist's need to be punished. The combined attraction leads to very dysfunctional interactions and relationships. The underlying basis of this dynamic is a belief that perfection is possible and indeed required, and a deep awareness that I am not at all perfect. It's extremely important to internalize that perfection in a body is never attainable. The standard to judge self against is not "Am I perfect?" but "Am I committed to making consistent ongoing progress (and taking the necessary ongoing steps/changes) even through inevitable temporary setbacks?" 1st stage Spiritual is NOT perfect. Neither is 3rd stage Spiritual. They represent *degrees of refinement* towards an ideal, the gradual exhaustion of separating desires. Realizing one is not going to be perfect in this life, while still holding an ideal to be that, is another source of increasing humility. (Steve)

To start, it's important that you (and anyone) follows the truth you know and find within yourself. As is implied in what you wrote about the nature of Neptune, all of our human truths are relative truths. One thing I found not addressed in what you wrote is you referred much to Source (Neptune) and also somewhat to personality (Cancer), but did not mention Soul/Pluto/Scorpio/8th house at all. I happen to have Pluto in the 8th house, and so am wired to be attuned to the reality of Soul. I'm not suggesting anything you said is wrong. I am just attempting to add a few pieces to what you wrote. The Soul is the *bridge* between the human and 'Neptune.' The Soul CREATES the human being, for its own evolutionary purposes, just as Neptune creates the Souls for *its* evolutionary purposes. That is why the focal point of everything in EA is Pluto, the Soul, and not Neptune, which is not really knowable in human form. Our work is to evolve our Souls, through the vehicle of our human natures. We CAN know our Soul, as opposed to knowing Neptune, and we are here as Steve and Heidi BECAUSE of our Souls – that is the point of our human evolutionary journey. In relation to Soul and the Soul's human journey, what I said about perfection and imperfection is quite relevant.

I have heard discussions about whether what EA calls imperfect is in the greater picture in fact perfect even though it is experienced as imperfect. I find these are discussions over the meaning of words. To me they miss the greater point that the words, limited as they must be, are trying to make. They are a *metaphor*. Day to day reality is very few (if any) humans are having an ongoing life they would describe as perfect. That is not debatable. And the patriarchal teachings of Divine Perfection cause many of these people to compare themselves to the unattainable patriarchal ideal of Divine Perfection vs their obvious human imperfection. As a result they judge themselves as inadequate, unworthy, less than, not good enough. And THAT is the cause of most of the masochistic patterns in people that I have encountered.

This begins with my own life history. My life changed radically after first encountering the EA perspective of God as an imperfect force seeking its own perfection. I felt more liberated and validated than I ever had in my life. And now that I am inwardly allowed to counsel others, somehow or other I attract many many people who have that issue (isn't that odd...). Almost everyone I have ever counselled on these issues, people with a similar conditioned orientation to feeling inadequate as a result of not measuring up to the ideal they'd been taught was the goal, has felt liberation on realizing what these words about imperfection vs perfection imply in their life. Why would a perfect God create imperfect creations – what is the point? How can I be more perfect than that which created me? Many times I have seen eyes light up – "You mean I am just okay as I am?" Patterns of many lifetimes begin cracking open before our eyes. That is both my personal experience, and the experience of many people I have counselled.

I also want to say that whether you call it imperfection or perfection, it's a METAPHOR, a *symbol*. If we are saying the same thing but using different words and tripping over each other's definitions of words, then please, throw my metaphor out and use whatever works for you and your clients. The metaphor's intent is to make people AWARE of the causes of their masochism, and to create a way to break those patterns. I have experienced it very effectively doing that. The last thing it's intended for is to create new masochism. If using that metaphor would create additional masochism for you or your clients, for God's sake, don't use it! (Steve)

Misconceptions about God

A subtle filter that is very common in the western world (if not all over this planet), that the natural intention of life is to be long and healthy, that if they really have it together spiritually and health wise, everyone should be able to heal all conditions and live long with good health. That is more of an ideal than a complete reality. Souls in 3rd stage Spiritual do get sick with incurable illnesses. The point of life is not to sustain an earthly body for the longest and healthiest possible length of time, but to fulfill the evolutionary intentions. In some cases the life plays out in the way we think we want it, long and healthy, while in others, not so. 3rd stage Spiritual Souls have surrendered their lives to doing the will of God/Goddess, whatever that involves for them. Why did Jesus have to die a horrible death? Logic would tell you such a great Soul would be brought up to heaven by adoring masses, yes? Yet it did not happen. Was it a mistake?

Wolf would tell you it's because of our misconceptions about God itself, that God itself is an imperfect force seeking its perfection, that we are here as part of that force seeking its perfection. And everything does not end rosy for all people at all times, the way we like to think it can. And much of that is not because the people did something wrong, but because it was intended or necessary, for various Soul learnings. In the case of 3rd stage Spiritual people, the learnings are around the need to totally surrender to being the vehicle or agent of divinity, no matter what that feels like on the human level. I suspect it's not an easy thing to learn at times. Someone here asked recently why a Soul entering 2nd stage Spiritual would even want to go there, why didn't they just stop evolving, knowing they were about to do things that might really screw people up. We could say the same thing about entering 3rd stage Spiritual – although they may be helping people more than hurting them, in some ways it's probably harder for the Soul than even 2nd stage Spiritual, because you can no longer hide out in spiritual ego grandiosity – your own Soul's desire nature continually pulls you forward into circumstances that are not fun at all from the human personality level, an ongoing personal sacrifice for the good of others, to carry out divine intent. (Steve)

Patriarchal standard of God-perfection

Every one of us has places we don't want to see or look at, feel like we are farther along than we really are, etc. These are universal human conditions. Wolf would say since all things originate from God, what does this say about the actual nature of God, when all people have these same traits. His answer is it points to the inherent imperfection in God itself. And we judge ourselves using a patriarchal standard of God-perfection which no human anywhere throughout time has ever lived up to. Thus the need to be very kind to ourselves, to recognize how difficult it is to walk this path. And to recommit to it again and again, no matter how many times we stray or fall down. To pick self back up and get back on the pathway, that is the way. In the end, however long it takes, mastery over self is assured. It's just that it takes a long time – that has to be accepted. (Steve)

Dominion over nature

Humans' separation from each other via distorted belief systems, as well as separation from other life forms on the planet not separated from God'dess includes the idea that humans are "superior" to other life forms, ie plants, animals, etc., instead of simply different from and interdependent. The idea of this kind of separateness – the DISTORTION of it – goes back to the Old Testament when humans were given "dominion over" nature. And that dominion over has created the destruction OF nature. Since the entire system IS interdependent, then we can see why humans' extinction is looming ahead of us. (Adina)

Violation of Natural Law

[The oil gush/spill] Events like this are not necessarily God's will. That perspective is too commonly used to excuse things that are flat out wrong, to avoid staring into the face of the consequences of human choices, behaviors. God gave us free will within certain ranges, to either align ourselves with Divine intent or to override and deny Divine intent and act in our selfish little ways (by "our" I mean by humans collectively). Just because something is within the realm of possibility does not mean people acting that out are actualizing God's will. Like the president of Goldman Sachs, a firm that has brought much of the world to its financial knees, who was quoted as saying that Goldman Sachs was doing God's work. Don't forget, God is the origin of the possibility of evil also. In that sense doing what is inherently wrong can be part of God's will, but is that really the part of God, the lower negative selfish possibilities, that you want to align yourself with, or make excuses for other humans and organizations who do that? "Violation of Natural Law" means acting in a way that puts self or self-interest or the interests of a few ahead of the greater interests of the whole, human and planet-wide. We don't HAVE to keep making the same sort of limited selfish stupid choices that inevitably wind up in wide scale loss and pain to all sorts of little people who never benefited from the vast fortunes made by the few in the first place (like oil companies). (Steve)

Inherent knowledge of right and wrong

As Jeffrey said many times, you don't need a religion to tell you it's wrong to put your baby out to play on the Autobahn – knowledge of the rightness and wrongness of things is simply inherent in all beings. The problem is we have been so conditioned with patriarchal distorted beliefs that we doubt our own perceptions, and too often feel guilt and shame while doing what is simply natural and right for us to do in a given moment, when that violates various social/cultural taboos. So the issue becomes whether one aligns self with Human Law or God/dess' Law also known as Natural Law. (Steve)

Archetype of judgment (Capricorn) manifesting through Pisces

What JWG taught is that judgment as an archetype in human consciousness is natural, and that the archetype of judgment in and of itself is Capricorn, the 10th house, and Saturn. He taught that the issue is not the right or wrongness of judgment as such, BUT THE CONTENT USED TO MAKE JUDGMENTS IN THE FIRST PLACE. Is that content rooted in Natural Laws, or is that content merely a collection of all kinds of man-made laws that have nothing to do with Natural Laws. When the archetype of judgment that emanates from the 10th house, Capricorn, or Saturn manifests through the 12th house, Neptune, or Pisces that then can correlate with the judgments made about spiritual disciplines, practices, the 'rights and wrongs' of spiritual life, of various gods and goddesses, and, of course, one's own relationship to all things spiritual. He taught a lot about all the artificial man-made rules and laws concerning spiritual life, all the 'should be's' so to speak. And how any Soul who enters spiritual life where the nature of that spiritual life has been created and defined by man-made laws that the judgments made either through one's own inner judgment of itself, or judgments made and projected upon others and oneself, that this commonly leads to not being good enough as measured against these man-made spiritual doctrines. This is why he talked and taught so much about the difference between these man-created, patriarchal, spiritual disciplines and their 'teachings' versus what natural spirituality is, what the Natural Laws are, and thus to change the very nature of the CONTENT used to make the judgments in the first place. (Rad)

A letter about the journey of human Souls – by Bradley Naragon

I say form a relationship with something transcendent; something beyond the illusion of this reality because that is the essence, at the bottom line, of what Libra in the 12th house is. I do not mean religion, because the limiting rules and restrictions of religion are more for Consensus stage Souls. Granted, some groups, like Unitarianism, are not so about conformity (Saturn). But, it is also clear that these spiritual groups do not 'feel' like religion. Jeffery would say, "Religion is for the Consensus." I did not specifically say spirituality because it can be confusing what that might look like or mean. From the teachings of Jeffery Wolf Green, he spoke of a time, prior to patriarchal 'sky god' religions, when Nature was the spiritual teacher for humans. [Thus, what you are already describing is a spiritual experience.] The essence of Pisces/12th/Neptune first is that it correlates to the phenomena of consciousness itself. When consciousness (Neptune) comes into form (Saturn), it then has the limits of the form it is in of how the consciousness (Pisces) will function (Saturn). Thus, all that exists in the phenomenal creation has the equal consciousness of Divine Spirit from which it came. So, that is why I do not just say 'spirituality.'

The trouble with human Souls on earth, once they evolve beyond Consensus, the Soul's desire is to 'individuate' (Uranus); thus to continually liberate (Uranus) from all pre-existing conditions (Saturn) until the Soul, in ego form (Moon – a lifetime in human form), then resonates with the core essential nature of the unique Soul that it is, no longer conditioned by the past, society, rules, beliefs, ways of living that are not what it essentially is. This process is challenging and means trauma for all Souls who have been doing this within the last 8,000+ years of patriarchal dominated cultures. But what often happens, is that the Soul becomes 'lost;' in the sense that they lose faith that there is a deeper ultimate intelligence and meaning to all of life. Some Souls stop believing in anything else at all, others are afraid to embrace one path. We come to the great 'WHY' of all of this? WHY? The fear to embrace one spiritual path is linked with the fear of losing the freedom of being who we really are, which we fought so hard to achieve for lifetimes, combined with the great disillusionment in the many false teachers and distorted religions, and the potential disbelief and scepticism that evolves over time. Even amongst 'spiritual lineages' today, we face and witness total bullshit at times.

Still, the transcendent impulse grows stronger and the search continues. In EA, this journey of the Soul is compared to a wave. When the wave is emerging out of the sea, growing larger, there is a momentum upward, away from the ocean. This, in EA, is the desire in the Soul to separate from the source from which it came (Divine Spirit – Pisces – the ocean in this example). At some point, it is natural for the wave to peak/crest – this is the end of the individuation process (Uranus), and as the wave crests, it begins to increasingly gain momentum to return to the sea (Spirit). This is the Soul's (Pluto/Scorpio) desire to transcend this reality (Saturn), the mayic illusion, and to return to the source from which it came. So, what happens is that there is a natural length of time this takes for a human Soul to reach this evolutionary final liberation. There is the place any Soul is at, which is natural and normal in the evolution of that Soul. It is the intention, as an evolutionary astrologer, to observe the evolutionary stage that a Soul is in. For example, if you were in the Consensus evolutionary stage, I would simply suggest forming a relationship to a religion which I intuitively felt drawn to speaking of and not have this discussion.

This is not you; your Soul has had many questions which it has not asked. From a past life point of view, why would, in other lifetimes, this pattern have started? What happens when we say that the emperor has no clothes? Exactly, everyone else around is invested in believing (Jupiter/Sagittarius) the illusion (Neptune/Pisces) of the reality (Saturn/Capricorn) around them. There becomes suppression (Saturn) of what is 'wrong' (Saturn) to speak (Mercury); there are social taboos (Pluto/Scorpio). "We don't talk about that, what is wrong with you for bringing that up" – there is nothing wrong with you – this is a pattern rooted in a past ego wound – it was only because of others' limited (Saturn) perception (Jupiter) and consciousness (Neptune) – which would mean others were unable to be secure (Moon/Cancer) enough to respond to your natural (Jupiter) instinctual (Mars) questions (Mercury) without feeling that it is threatening (Moon – ego insecurity) their version of reality (Saturn), right and wrong (Saturn). (Bradley)

KARMA

What is karma?

Karma is simply the Natural Law of each cause having an effect, every desire correlating to an action taken that creates an equal or proportionate reaction: cause and effect. All action is rooted in desire. Karma is the sum total of all of our actions in every possible way. JWG used to teach that all Souls are responsible for the lives that they create from life to life. From that point of view he would then say that 'there are no victims.' He would also teach the utter importance of working with clients who have felt victimized in the sense of not hammering them over the head with words like 'there are no victims, you are responsible for what you have felt victimized by.' He would also teach that everything is relative, even the feelings of being victimized. For example, say a woman gets brutally raped. And from the current life point of view that woman had done nothing that could be interpreted or perceived as her being responsible for the rape. So, from this life's point of view, this woman could easily and rightly be perceived as being a victim of that rape. Yet, if one could see the totality of that woman's prior lives, the reasons or causes for the current life could be seen. And those reasons are not just the simplistic stuff like she had raped someone in another life and, therefore, that's the reason that she created the rape in the current life: karma. That may, indeed, be one possible cause, but from the point of view of any given Soul's individual past life context, there can be an incredible amount of reasons or causes that have led to the current life rape.

The various evolutionary conditions have nothing to do with the idea and perception of victimization. This is a cultural/religious issue that spans all evolutionary conditions depending on the nature of the culture/religion that the Soul decided to be born into in any given life. And, thus, a function of conditioning depending on that culture/religion. In other words, there are, and have been, many other cultures/ways of understanding life that had no idea or conception of being a victim at all because, in those cultures/ways of understanding life, all Souls are responsible for what they create. This of course references the NATURAL LAW of cause and effect. Yet it is critical when working with clients, or ourselves, who have been victimized from the point of view of their, our, current life to exercise great compassion and understanding. One of the things that JWG taught when working with victimized clients is to ask them if they wanted to know the prior life causes that exist within them self that are in fact responsible for the current life circumstances that have led to the event in which they have felt victimized. And, if that answer is yes, then to gently do so. And, if not, to help that client deal with the effects of the event in which they have felt victimized by. (Rad)

Karma or evolutionary necessity?

Karma can be both difficult or negative and/or positive, reflecting a 'fruition' of what has come before. So many people in the west think of karma as something that is only negative or difficult. It can be very, very difficult to assess whether a particular dynamic or experience in a birth chart is a reflection of karma or evolutionary necessity until one has much experience under one's belt. The same signature, eg Mars square Moon, Moon square Uranus, with Mars and Uranus opposed, could be a karmic signature in one chart and a signature of evolutionary necessity in another. So how can one tell? Only through direct interaction and observation of the person. One must ask specific kinds of questions that deal with the signatures implicating these two dynamics, questions that can uncover the difference if one knows exactly the types of questions to ask. One can only gain this ability by working with many clients over time. (JWG)

These concepts (karmic causes/evolutionary necessity) are easy to misapply and can create a lot trouble and misunderstanding. I think it's important we don't lose sight of the fact that these ARE distinct dynamics, otherwise what reason would Wolf have for attempting to teach about their distinctions? Wolf has said that determining evolutionary necessity is simple to determine in the birth chart: it is reflected in every symbol that's connected to Pluto in the natal signature. He also made it clear that being able to determine karmic causes is NOT easy, and that there is no 'technique' that can be taught for making this determination. The issue I think, is that they are so CLOSELY linked, so non-linear, and so nuanced, that it takes an extremely developed capacity to be able to KNOW which is which. And even when karmic causes are accurately identified, one must have an absolute purity of intention and sensitivity/Soul attunement when attempting to communicate something like karmic causes to another, because the individual may not be ready on an inner basis to hear or resolve the content. To impose this kind of information upon someone who isn't actually ready to deal with it creates the risk of generating the exact *opposite* effect that EA was brought forth to serve, as does imposing this kind of information when it has not been correctly interpreted in the first place. As I understand it, those who have the developed capacity/clarity to accurately identify actual karmic causes from evolutionary necessity will convey it on the basis of receiving the specific inner direction to do just that. So when it comes to the practical application of EA for most of us, I agree that it's better to come from the simple standpoint of acknowledging that *any* emphasized dynamic in the Soul/birth chart simply reflects the outcome of experiences and choices made therein, relative to intention, relative to evolutionary capacity, and that the existing dynamics are exactly what the Soul needs for continuing on with its evolutionary growth. (Stacie)

Karmic signature
To become conscious of one's karmic signature (or evolutionary signature) – is to understand the signatures of the past, and the evolutionary intentions for this lifetime. For example, Pluto square Nodes evolutionary signature would be a significant part of that. Then we have to ACCEPT this signature – beyond understanding it intellectually, to emotionally embrace it. The point is, quite often there are parts of this we don't like, or wish would be other than they are – don't want to embrace, don't even want to admit to. The process starts speeding up as we accept, "Here is where I am, today, and here is where I'm intended to be heading." Then one makes an inner choice, decision, to *cooperate with* this unfolding process. Knowing that at times it's not going to feel comfortable, it's not going to feel like what we want to do or where we want to go – that is part of the process, comes with the territory. We have to accept that also. (Steve)

Karma in the birth chart
The Moon in Capricorn does not correlate with any implied karma by itself, neither does any isolated symbol in the birth chart imply a karma by itself. The Evolutionary Astrology paradigm does indeed allow one to know what type of "karma" is reflected in the birth chart, however, a complete analysis of the birth chart is necessary in order to know that, starting with the main evolutionary axis of the birth chart, ie Pluto, the Pluto polarity point, the nodal axis, and the planetary rulers of the lunar nodes. Then karma will always be reflected in Pluto, Scorpio, and the 8th house, the aspects to Pluto, the aspects to the Nodes, thus not one isolated symbol, but the complete birth chart needs to be understood in order to establish if and what type of karma exists, and how it has been created. As JWG said many times, "one size does not fit all." (Gonzalo)

Karma of skipped steps
Karma is simply the Natural Law of each cause having an effect, every desire correlating to an action taken that creates an equal or proportionate reaction: cause and effect. Throw a pebble in the pond and it creates ripples. Skipped steps do not happen by themselves. There is a Soul making choices that have effects to those choices. Thus, from this point of view the effects of the choices equaling skipped steps could be seen as the karmic consequence to those choices. Karma just is. How we 'judge' karma as 'good' or 'bad' karma is of course a subjective issue. It is, in fact, not possible to have planet(s) squaring the Nodes in the current life in which the prior life choices were not made symbolizing and indicating 'skipped steps.' (Rad)

Karma with parents
It is a combination of understanding the individual karmic dynamics with a person and the parents as symbolized in that person's individual chart. In combination with this are the synastry charts between the individual and each parent, and the composite chart of the person with each parent. (Rad)

Relationship karma
There is always a reason why any two Souls will be in relationship with each other. First the evolutionary and karmic dynamics of each particular Soul has to be understood – then based on that, we can move to the composite chart and the synastry in order to understand the nature of the relationship itself. In the end there can be any number of reasons why two Souls have come together in whatever way they have. As I understand it, most, if not all relationships have a past life story. It's the nature of a Soul's journey to be in constant relationship with everything. As it's progressively burning its separating desires, it's also engaging in relationship – thus creating karma with many other Souls based on what internal dynamics are being worked on. All Souls are doing this. (Ari)
It is highly recommended to read JWG's Pluto 2 book in full. And, there are, indeed, a variety of 'concrete' ways to understand the past life dynamics between people, and the reasons for those dynamics. One of the great dimensions of Evolutionary Astrology is to be able to answer the question WHY. So much of astrology is really a DESCRIPTIVE astrology without providing any insights into the why of anything. Describing something is very different than understanding something. The aspects between people do in fact correlate to existing dynamics between them that have been carried over from other lifetimes. So the underlying issue is to try to understand why those dynamics have occurred between them relative to their own individual evolutionary intentions. (Rad)

Karma through sexual exchange
[Example: Person A is the primary partner of person B; person B involves sexually with a person C, while maintaining the primary partner A, and sex with partner A]
Person A will osmose through person B the karma of person C because, after all, person C is now within partner B by the sheer fact of being sexual together – in essence partner B has taken in person C within them. The karma that is taken in by person A is not a 'direct' karma as it is with partner B being sexual with person C – it is much more oblique than direct – yet it is taken in nonetheless.

And by obliquely taking in the karma of person C through being sexual with partner B partner A will be able to feel it within them self in some way psychologically and/or emotionally. Partner A can then also feel like they have been invaded or contaminated in varying degrees DEPENDING ON HOW DEEPLY PARTNER B HAS TAKEN PERSON C INTO THEM. How much of the karma is obliquely taken to partner A via partner B's sexual union with person C is relative to how deeply partner B has taken in person C. In the case of absorbing the sexual fluids of person C that are within partner B because partner A is sexual with partner B after that partner had been sexual with person C then it can intensify this oblique absorption of the karma of person C. On the other hand, once partner B has taken in person C they have absorbed within them self the fluids of person C. So if partner A then becomes sexual with partner B after the fact those fluids are transferred anyway. (Rad)

Cleansing karma
The Agni ritual can cleanse karma but the absorption of the others' karma can also simply be 'thrown out or off' by the psychological act of recognizing what has been taken in: this is not mine. And then with an act of Soul/psychological will throwing it out: not allowing it to take hold, so to speak. The Agni ritual can be used to become clear and free between any two people, not just lovers. (Rad)

Agni ritual
This is a gig where she would first visualize a fire in her third eye, and then project whatever images of this ex-partner/creep to the fire, and to keep doing this until no more images appear – at the same time to project the thought 'I forgive you from the point of view of accepting the responsibility in my own actions.' When there is nothing left to project, at that point, she would have severed the karmic umbilical cord that has kept them connected – so next time around the person would appear as an acquaintance versus an intimate – also, whatever objects she may have left over from their connection, ie pictures, presents, whatever, should either be buried, tossed into salt water, the ocean, or burned by fire. (JWG)

Karmic relationships – Agni ritual
The very best thing to do is not to react at all and to involve oneself in the Agni ritual that will sever the karmic umbilical cord that has kept the two people going around in this karmic dance. (JWG)
JWG wrote that in the context of two people who could not stop going around and around with one another. If in fact the two people involved in such a dance mutually accept the responsibility in their own actions then the karmic past that has dictated the dance is over. (Rad)

Do Avatar's have karma?
All Souls have karma unless a Soul is in the most advanced states of evolution such as an Avatar. First, we need to discriminate between the word 'karma' and the natural evolutionary process, intention and necessity that all Souls go through. In context of an Avatar there is no karma no matter what symbols you see in their charts. There are evolutionary intentions and necessities which of course are proved by the nature of their lives. Specifically, Avatar's have no EARTHLY karma. Most still do have karma from the point of view of the Astral and Causal realms. In the case of an Avatar's chart, it is essential to understand the WHY of that chart in their CONTEXT. And the use of EA, properly understood and applied, does provide for that answer. In the cases of Avatars the only observation that can occur is the observation of the individual Soul itself. No form of astrology, including EA, can say, of itself as in just looking at symbols on paper, who is and who is not an Avatar. (Rad)

Yogananda
All of us need to be very, very careful in our use of the word karma and what it actually is or means. Relative to Yogananda and his 'lesson' of learning about 'evil' the only way I would use the word karma is if indeed he had made a prior life CHOICE, a willful choice, to not believe in or grasp the reality of evil. If that was the case then I would certainly use the word karma for what he then had to go through and endure in his life as Yogananda as it relates to evil being forcefully in his life in a variety of circumstances. On the other hand, if he had not made the prior life choice then I would understand his encounters with evil as a necessary ongoing evolutionary process, intention, for his Soul to continue to evolve. This is just how I try to approach this issue in order to effect some kind of discrimination in the use and application of the word karma, and the Natural Laws behind it. (Rad)

LOVE AND SEXUALITY

Love – conditional and unconditional
The phenomenon of love comes down to two types of love: conditional and unconditional. The correlation of Venus/Taurus/2nd Libra/7th, Mars/Aries/1st, Pluto/Scorpio/8th; and the planetary residents of and aspects to all of the above, calibrated to the Soul's evolutionary condition, equals all that is defined by conditional love where love is experienced or expressed as a function of having one's needs met by another. When those needs are not met then once that which was experienced as love with and for another, and visa versa, can change into something quite the opposite.

Unconditional love is reflected in the archetypes of the 12th house, Neptune, and of course Pisces. Unconditional love can be experienced and expressed at any evolutionary level or condition. Of course unconditional love is not a function of one's personal needs being met or unmet: it just is. Unconditional love has no expectations attached to it whatsoever whereas conditional love in fact does. It is those expectations associated with conditional love that manifest as projected needs upon another, and visa versa. When those projected needs associated with one's expectations are met then conditional love is in fact experienced. When they are not then what was once experienced as love can become something quite different.

Conditional love is time-based: finite. Unconditional love is timeless: infinite. Conditional love manifests as a function of evolutionary and karmic imperatives and necessities, unconditional love manifests as a function of the universal = timeless Natural Law of giving to others in whatever ways that any given Soul has within itself to give even if that giving is simply loving another for who and what they are without any expectation or need to be given back to in any way at all. The inner feeling we all have of 'love' for another when linked with conditional love occurs as a function of the physiology that is set in motion when we interface with another where that other, and visa versa, reflects what we need in our ongoing evolutionary journey through time: the inner psychological and emotional dynamics of any given Soul through time, and the reasons for those specific psychological and emotional dynamics.

In essence the feeling of 'love' that is ignited at the beginning of an attraction to another for these reasons IS TO DRAW THE SOULS TOGETHER SO THAT THE EVOLUTIONARY AND KARMIC REASONS that any given Soul has relative to its own ongoing evolutionary journey CAN BE MET. This is why JWG wrote his second Pluto book on relationships wherein one of those important chapters is called "So We Meet Again, Eh?" And as he said it takes more than one life with another who we draw into our lives through conditional love, as defined above, to be worked out. And when it is worked out we then move on to other Souls as our own evolutionary and karmic NEEDS change. This is exactly where, for example, John and Yoko found themselves in their own evolutionary journey together. And, of course, conditional love can in fact turn into unconditional love for some Souls. Thus, in the context of Souls who have been intimate where that intimacy has been defined by conditional love this will manifest as "I will always love you, but I no longer need you." (Rad)

Soul mates
It is also very possible for any two Souls to come together with a combination of unconditional love and conditional love at the same time. When this occurs such Souls have a simple and natural love for the inherent structure of the Souls of each, and unconditional love that binds them through the journey of time itself. Yet, because each also has their own specific evolutionary and karmic journeys this creates a situation and dynamic wherein they can come together in a series of lives in order to work out and through their individual evolutionary and karmic dynamics together, and also have other lives wherein they must work out their own evolutionary and karmic dynamics with others. Yet, because they started off with this core unconditional love for one another, wanting to give to each other unconditionally, of wanting to be together, desire, through time they will always circle back to one another as their own individual evolutionary journey continues through time. This is what JWG called and defined as Soul Mates. (Rad)

Loving feelings vs loving behaviors
The important distinction is between loving feelings, or feelings of attraction, and loving behaviors, or genuine love, in which one is willing to extend oneself for the sake of another, even at the expense of the ego's perception of its well-being. Often both of these exist together, but they can each also exist without the other. People have loving feelings all the time but do not act lovingly. People can also act lovingly without having particular personal feelings of love or attraction. To me feelings of love and attraction

are feelings which come and go, that can be stronger or weaker in their intensity in different situations for lots of reasons related to past karma or evolutionary intentions. Actions of love, genuine loving behaviors, are conscious choices, and one makes them, or chooses not to make them, from moment to moment. In the case of Yoko and John, I would offer that Yoko has definitely had loving feelings and feelings of attraction. Less so has she demonstrated loving behaviors, ie behaviors that are not motivated from her own egocentric desires to use the other person. After all, the neediness that motivated her Soul in a lot of this relationship over lifetimes and the desire to merge with power produces self-centered actions, not loving actions, no matter how lovey-dovey it all looks. Whereas in John's case, I see loving feelings and feelings of attraction as well, but also more instances of genuine love and loving behaviors – or better said, that he is more stabilized in a loving state, and therefore his behaviors have more often reflected that especially as he has transitioned into the Spiritual state. In terms of evolutionary conditions:

(1) Souls in all evolutionary conditions can experience loving feelings and attractions.
(2) Souls can have many motivations and evolutionary intentions for being drawn together, ie for creating loving feelings and magnetic attractions. These feelings can come from desires for separation as well as desires for union. The motivations and intentions could look like, for instance, creating security and success; having power (Yoko's, at least in the recent past, ie since at least the Scorpio sub-age); or being drawn into relationship to genuinely work stuff out (John's mommy stuff and his next step of gaining an objective awareness of where it has led him and what it has blinded him to in Yoko); among many other possible motives, some of which evolve the Soul and some of which don't.
(3) The motivations and intentions for attractions and loving feelings are described by Venus/Taurus/2nd/Libra/7th, Mars/Aries/1st, Pluto/Scorpio/8th; and the planetary residents of and aspects to all of the above; calibrated to the Soul's evolutionary condition.
(4) Souls in all evolutionary conditions can also genuinely love, ie practice loving behaviors, whether in the presence of loving feelings or not; for example, even in Consensus when consciousness is ego-identified and very concerned with itself and its own needs, people genuinely show up for one another without egocentric motivation from time to time (eg a mother placing herself in front of her child in a dangerous situation; I suppose one could look at this as somehow being about the consensus concern with survival, and that their ego has become so identified with the survival of the race or the lineage or whatever, that they do this, but to me this seems like evolutionary biologists' attempts to explain love without any actual understanding of it; though, I can also see the possibility that I am projecting my own reality of having had experiences of genuine love, onto others, out of a deep desire to see and feel more love in the world).
(5) However, the capacity and the orientation to *consistently* maintain this genuine loving, and loving behavior, is greater as a Soul moves through evolution, becoming less and less identified with the ego and therefore progressively able to transcend it, as genuine love requires. Souls in the earlier evolutionary conditions will more frequently revert to ego-based decision-making, eg desires to separate, even though they are capable of making loving choices from time to time, eg those emerging from desires for union. Of course this eclipsing of love by egoic concerns and wounding, happens at all states of evolution prior to 3rd Spiritual, but less and less frequently as the Soul progresses through the evolutionary levels.
(6) Loving feelings and feelings of attraction can arise from desires for separation as well as desires for union, therefore in some instances they will lead to evolution, and in some not. Loving behavior and genuine acts of love always arise from desires for union and always create evolutionary growth, and are also evidence of that growth.
(7) Loving feelings and feelings of attraction become progressively impersonal, eg as a Soul becomes more and more Spirit-identified and conscious of the unity of all Life as God/Goddess, it becomes more and more capable to experience love for all Life, and less concerned with specialized love objects such as primary partners, etc. – even though there may still be Souls with whom the Soul specifically connects to and has special relationships with for certain evolutionary purposes of one or the other or both. (Jason)

Love and control
(Q) Can real love can exist in a parallel sort of way with the simultaneous desire for power and control over another?
(A) The answer is yes relative to conditional love as long as the one that is being controlled is allowing him/herself to be controlled. If not, then that conditional love will turn into something quite different as in hate. (Rad)

Patriarchal sexual reality
What Wolf taught was that the sexual desires that emanate from the primary brain are the NATURAL sexual desires versus how all the natural sexual desires that emanate from it can also be distorted and perverted relative to either suppressing such desires and/or altering in a variety of ways due to the conditioning influence of the patriarchy. (Rad)
In the new book, "Essays on Evolutionary Astrology," JWG explains that 99.9 percent of everyone on earth is living under the influence of the patriarchal sexual reality. (Cat)

Primary brain, sexual desires
Sexual desires, naturally speaking, do emanate from the primary brain, Mars, Pluto, and the Moon, and through extension the Lunar Nodes and their rulers. Also, Mars and its planetary nodes and their rulers, and of course Pluto and its nodes, and their rulers. (Rad)

Suppression of sexual desires
When any given Soul suppresses their natural sexual desires in such a way that those desires then become distorted and can then manifest through many forms of behavior towards oneself and others. The distortion created by repression is thus a cause of rage manifesting in the behaviors towards themselves and others in various ways. Obviously most Souls on Earth are not suppressing their sexual desires in general. Most people are in fact sexual. When any given Soul has sexual desires that deviate from what is considered 'right' and 'wrong' from a patriarchal conditioning point of view then that Soul will typically feel 'guilty' because of the deviation. If that guilt then leads to suppression of their sexual desires THEN it will lead to rage and distortions manifesting in a variety of behaviors towards oneself and/or others. Some Souls, not very many, never allow themselves to be conditioned by anything other than Natural Laws which is to say they never allow themselves to be conditioned at all, no matter what the consequences may be when in lifetimes, places, in which artificial conditioning is taking place. (Rad)

Neptune and higher octave Venus
Neptune is the higher octave of Venus. Venus corresponds to the heart chakra. My intuition is that this does not mean that Neptune correlates to the heart chakra itself, but rather that the heart chakra and the crown have some sort of octave resonance to one another which is the manifestation of Source unity consciousness through the denser, interpersonal feeling center of the heart. (Ari)
A simple example: Neptune would correlate to unconditional love, whereas Venus would or can correlate to conditional love and the reasons for that conditional love. (Rad)

When sexuality is not a function of separating desires
(Q) Sexuality through the archetype of Taurus. Is it possible for two Souls that are not literally committing to each other to experience a form of sexuality that is rooted in a deep respect for the beauty of the body, of sensuality, of the growth and joy experienced through sharing sexuality, and that not being a function of separating desires?
(A) Yes.
(Q) In that state the two Souls seems to be elevating the sexual impulse to one of gratitude and joy and so long as this does not degrade into a pursuit of self-interest and indulgence, my intuition is that it is not a function of separating desires.
(A) Yes. (Rad)
Sex desire is not specifically a function of separating desires because the sexual instinct within all humans is necessary in order for the species to be sustained. The Soul's orientation to that natural sexual instinct is what needs to be examined. Whatever that orientation is may or may not be unconscious depending on the evolutionary condition or station of any given Soul, and the capacity of any given Soul to be self-reflective so as to consciously know what their orientation is, the reasons why, for any given sexual desire. Once any two Souls act upon their sexual desires for one another then a karma is established for them. (Rad)

Karma through sexual exchange
[Example: Person A is the primary partner of person B; person B involves sexually with a person C, while maintaining the primary partner A, and sex with partner A] Person A will osmose through person B the karma of person C because, after all, person C is now within partner B by the sheer fact of being sexual together – in essence partner B has taken in person C within them. The karma that is taken in by person A is not a 'direct' karma as it is with partner B being sexual with person C – it is much more oblique than direct – yet it is taken in nonetheless. And by obliquely taking in the karma of person C through being sexual with partner B partner A will be able to feel it within them self in some way psychologically and/or emotionally. Partner A can then also feel like they have been invaded or contaminated in varying degrees DEPENDING ON HOW DEEPLY PARTNER B HAS TAKEN PERSON C INTO THEM. How much of the karma is obliquely taken to partner A via partner B's sexual union with person C is relative to how deeply partner B has taken in person C. In the case of absorbing the sexual fluids of person C that are within partner B because partner A is sexual with partner B after that partner had been sexual with person C then it can intensify this oblique absorption of the karma of person C. On the other hand, once partner B has taken in person C they have absorbed within them self the fluids of person C. So if partner A then becomes sexual with partner B after the fact those fluids are transferred anyway. (Rad)

Sexual arousal with not actually having sex
Two Souls can certainly experience this taking in of each other's evolutionary history and karma without this exchange of sexual fluids BUT NOT TO THE EXTENT that occurs when those fluids are in fact exchanged. (Rad)

Agni ritual

The Agni ritual can cleanse that karma but the absorption of the others' karma can also simply be 'thrown out or off' by the psychological act of recognizing of what has been taken in: this is not mine. And then with an act of Soul/psychological will throwing it out: not allowing it to take hold, so to speak. The Agni ritual can be used to become clear and free between any two people, not just lovers. (Rad)

Agni ritual – this is a gig where she would first visualize a fire in her third eye, and then project whatever images of this ex-partner/creep to the fire, and to keep doing this until no more images appear – at the same time to project the thought, 'I forgive you from the point of view of accepting the responsibility in my own actions.' When there is nothing left to project, at that point, she would have severed the karmic umbilical cord that has kept them connected – so next time around the person would appear as an acquaintance versus an intimate – also, whatever objects she may have left over from their connection, ie pictures, presents, whatever, should either be buried, tossed into salt water, the ocean, or burned by fire. (JWG)

Understanding sexuality through the EA paradigm

To understand sexuality through the EA paradigm, to understand the sexual nature of a given Soul and particularly its sexual desires relative to the overall karmic past and evolutionary intentions of the Soul, beyond descriptions of sexual patterns, the question "why?" would be the focus: why this gender, this orientation, this sexual experience, and so on.

Sex and sexuality

(1) Mars/1st house/Aries/Nodes of Mars: Instinctual desire nature of the Soul;
(2) Venus/2nd house/Taurus/Nodes of Venus: Sexual needs, values, orientations;
(3) Pluto/8th house/Scorpio/Nodes of Pluto: Sexual encounters, experiences, and partners;
(4) The Pluto/Mars, Pluto/Venus, and Mars/Venus Cycles: Development of sexual themes across lifetimes; (5) The use of asteroids to flesh out particular sexual archetypes and patterns, such as the four goddess asteroids (Ceres, Pallas, Vesta, Juno), Persephone, Eros, Psyche, Cupido, Dionysus, Pan, Ganymede, Adonis, Lust, Sappho, Amor (these are useful, provided they are interpreted in the context of a correct understanding of the karmic and primary sexual axes of the chart).

Gender and gender identity

(1) Moon/4th house/Cancer/Nodes of Moon and Saturn/10th house/Capricorn/Nodes of Saturn: Relation to anima/animas, masculine/feminine dimensions of duality;
(2) Saturn/Moon Cycle: Development of gender identity in the context of the structuring of consciousness in a given evolutionary cycle of lifetimes. (Jason)

Gender switch

There are many different signatures correlating to gender switching. Among others, the following signatures can correlate to gender switch: Pluto or the Nodes in 4th house/10th house/Cancer/Capricorn; Moon/Saturn New Phase or Balsamic. (Rad)

There can be many possible signatures that correlate to gender switches, not just Pluto and the Nodes. But that does not mean that just any planet, by itself, in the 4th our 10th correlates to gender switching. It is common to find gender-switch signatures and homosexuality/bisexuality signatures in the same chart. (Rad)

There is no way astrologically, or otherwise, to determine gender switch. It's an entirely individual, each Soul, issue that is dependent on many, many factors and variables. (Rad)

Signatures correlating to homosexuality and bisexuality

Typical signatures of homosexuality include "Mars aspected to Neptune, Uranus, Pluto, Mars in Pisces or in the 12th. Venus also in these kinds of patterns, Neptune, Uranus, or Pluto in the 8th or 2nd, Neptune, Uranus, or Pluto in the 10th or 4th, Mars in the 10th or 4th, and so on." Libra can also connect to homosexuality and bisexuality "because of the natural connection to Gemini and Aquarius." Libra correlates to androgyny. Pisces correlates to homosexuality, ie "dissolving of gender distinction." (Gonzalo)

Gender switch, bisexuality, homosexuality, duplicity

Many times homosexuality originates in gender switch, either a recent gender switch or the Soul getting prepared for an upcoming gender switch. In turn, gender switch may originate in the nature of sexual desires of the Soul. Thus, sometimes homosexuality is not originated in gender switch, and sometimes gender switch is not caused by the nature of sexual desires, but because of other types of desires and needs. Gender switch will always be indicated in the birth chart. There are many different signatures correlating to gender switching. Among others, the following signatures can correlate to gender switch: Pluto or the Nodes in 4th house/10th house/Cancer/Capricorn; Moon/Saturn New Phase or Balsamic. Within consensus, individuals conform to their external sexual definition and expectations and roles thereof. Thus, they repress or suppress their inner sexual nature. During 1st stage Individuated, individuals may discover their true sexual orientation and desires, though they will still derive security from belonging to normalcy as defined by mainstream society. Hence, these individuals are most likely to create situations of concealment and duplicity. Concealment implies that they are having an awareness of inner desires and orientations that differ from social expectations, though, they don't feel capable to act out on these desires. This then leads to duplicity. Initially, it is duplicity between external reality of "normalcy" and their inner world. This translates into performing what they are supposed to be doing in their normal lives, though feeling inwardly alienated from that reality. Because of the vibration of the desires they are withholding, they will attract others who resonate with their desire nature, and will further create experiences reflecting their desire nature. At this stage duplicity will still manifest through maintaining an appearance of "normalcy," ie conformity to social expectations, including getting married with partners of the opposite sex, having children, etc., while creating a parallel life where they live out their inner sexual orientation. Concealment leads progressively to duplicity. And duplicity implies concealment in relation to one part of the individual's life, the part in which they are conforming. Conforming also involves creating a mask, a facade allowing that they keep appearing as "normal."

There can exist many different signatures correlating with concealment duplicity. Among many signatures, I wonder whether water signs or houses could correlate with concealment, ie these desires being conscious though not acted on; and mutable signs and houses, especially Gemini and Pisces, 3rd and 12th houses, and Neptune, could correlate to duplicity. Capricorn, 10th house and Saturn may also reflect the part of the life where the individual is hiding his true nature because of the need to conform, while other symbols at the same time correlate to other parts of the individual's life where the inner desires are being acted on. Further, there are several aspects that can correlate to these dynamics: crescent semisquare can correlate to the need to inwardly find out if the new desires or orientations are real; first quarter square can correlate to the need to adopt or define a form, ie sexual orientation to express through reflecting the new desires and orientations the Soul has been discovering; first quarter inconjunct can refer to not feeling prepared or capable to assume the Souls desires; gibbous opposition can reflect the need to socialize the new impulses and the fear of losing touch with those new desires because of socialization; full phase opposition can indicate the need and preparedness to openly assume one's sexual identity in relationships; the opposition may also indicate the need to integrate two different dynamics represented by the planets in opposition; disseminating sesquiquadrate can reflect the crisis created because of the conflict between how the individual is actualizing his/her new desires and orientations in (some) relationships and the social regulation and requirements of other relationships of the individual (if there is duplicity); last quarter square can indicate that, despite the existing social roles of the individual other desires and orientations are emerging in consciousness.

Duplicity could also be indicated through intercepted signs, ie dual house rulerships, where the sign on the house cusp and its ruler by house and sign serves to "mask" another set of desires or intentions reflected in the intercepted sign and its ruler. Many times duplicity creates trauma for the Soul and for others. Typically, this occurs because the double lives or parallel realities the individual has created are exposed at some time. This exposure of what was being hidden is an 8th house, Scorpio, experience. The resulting trauma will be reflected in signatures of trauma involving Aquarius, 11th house and Uranus. These symbols will also speak of the need of the individual to assume its inherent orientation and desires. Karmic consequences will also exist. Sometimes these karmic consequences can include the occurrence of events through which the individual's sexual type of desires are forced upon the individual, such as homosexual abuse or rape, sometimes happening in the family of birth.

At the 2nd stage Individuated, dynamics of duplicity and concealment would normally disappear, because the individual is openly embracing and de-conditioning his true inner nature. From 2nd sub-stage Individuated, the individual would be progressively discovering and assuming its own identity, including sexual identity, with independence of any social expectations of what this sexual identity should be. This will lead to a progressive integration of inherent male and female polarities. From 3rd stage Individuated onwards, the individual would be progressively relating to other people at Soul level, ie inherent male/femaleness. However, the Soul will or may switch genders even at the spiritual evolutionary condition. One purpose why homosexual desires can manifest is learning to shift the nature of sexual desires from the physical body to the Soul: that making love is making love to a Soul, not just a body. Gender switch occurs at the end of an evolutionary cycle in one gender, leading to a new evolutionary cycle in the other gender. It is a cardinal archetype. This means many lifetimes in one gender, then leading to a switch. Though, sometimes the Soul flip-flops between genders through a number of lifetimes, for certain reasons which relate to skipped steps. (Gonzalo)

Androgyny

Wolf taught, as well as many others, that all Souls are inherently androgynous. And this is because all Souls are reflections of the Creator who is the Origin of the male and female principles in the first place. Yet all Souls choose to be in one gender, preponderantly, over the other gender for their own reasons: a choice to be made by all Souls. Yet, at the same time, for evolutionary reasons all Souls must of course, at times, manifest themselves in the opposite gender in order for a very long evolutionary journey to occur which finally leads back to where all Souls started: their inherent androgyny. And, remember, that the 'ego' itself is but a reflection of the Soul: it does not, and cannot, exist of itself. The wave manifests from the ocean: it cannot exist of itself. So the ego of any Soul then reflects the gender of the Soul.

Example: the Soul of John Lennon preponderantly chose to be female most of the time in its prior lives due to the fact that his natal Pluto in his 4th and in opposition to his 10th house MOON. And, of course, his Pluto being conjunct his natal Vesta, with the North Node of Vesta also conjunct his natal Pluto, and Vesta itself. (Rad)

Another thing that has been taught here, is that as a Soul evolves further into the Spiritual stages gender switching becomes MORE commonplace as the Soul is itself androgynous. Progressively over many life times, the human ego, as it becomes more identified with the Soul itself, becomes less identified with the form of the body it inhabits. (Ari)

Dark Moon Lilith – fear and hatred of sexuality

Dark Moon Lilith signifies how and where we experience the distorted aspects of Lilith in our lives – her anguish, bitterness, betrayal, alienation, fear and hatred of sexuality, and revenge. For centuries men and women have been conditioned by our patriarchal culture to suppress this feminine strength which has resulted in bitterness and resentment, inevitably leading to distortion and rage. How this distortion is played out is indicated by the natal placement of the Dark Moon Lilith. DML is the distorted Lilith representing Lilith's flee into a fiery rage of exile where she plots and executes her revenge. Find your DML placement and know that this area ***also creates a channel by which we can release the rage.*** (Kristin)

LUCIFER

Lucifer – symbolizing God and Evil

We must remember that the asteroid Lucifer symbolizes both God and Evil within itself. The God part of course is ever calling us home, back to God, but also attempts to influence all Souls by way of their inherent natures to be what they are intended to be. As a result of these influences we become inwardly directed by way of inspirations, thoughts, impulses, and desires that reflect our ongoing evolutionary journey of our Souls. The nature of these inner desires, etc., can also manifest as key circumstances and people in our lives that attempt to point us in the right directions of our individual evolution. Lucifer of course will attempt to undermine and defeat any effort we make not only to come home back to God, but also the various inspirations, desires, etc. that if acted upon keeps us going in our individual evolutionary journey. It typically does this through negative thoughts and emotions that can also be reflected in our circumstantial reality and the people in those circumstances.

This dance is archetypal, all the time, for the planet, and each person on it. With the opposition now with Pluto and Lucifer, this natural dance becomes more intensified and pronounced. Literally Evil opposing all Souls who are attempting to evolve in the natural ways intended for each, at war with God and all that is good and right. Within this the duality of this war of Evil and God of course is also reflected in all the countries (Saturn) on Earth (Saturn). And the peoples in those countries. This then manifests as whole groupings of people that are doing the work of Evil, knowingly or not, and those trying to do the work of God, knowingly or not. Each country, as does each individual, has their own individual context of reality: Saturn. And in those individual contexts each country has its own natural evolutionary needs that reflect what is best for the whole of the peoples that live within them: the common good.

The groups of people that try to do God's work in this way then become opposed by the groups of people that are defined by the narrowness of self-interest, and what is best for the individual versus the common good. The key to defeating the influence of evil is to be conscious and mindful of how it manifests in all of our lives: by intensifying and magnifying any negative thought or emotion that is intrinsic to each of our natures in any given life that then has the effect of undermining, stopping, or blocking directions we are taking in our lives that we know to be right and correct no matter how radical those directions can seem at times. As Jesus himself said: "Satan, get behind me." In this way God wins, and each Soul that is victorious in this way not only comes home to God/ess, but stays focused and centered on its own natural evolutionary journey in each life. (Rad)

Evil

Evil itself – in a world of duality – is simply the opposite of "good"/God. Just as we have night/day, male/female, etc., so we also have good/evil, with evil represented in astrology by the asteroid Lucifer. Evil was part of the manifested creation from the beginning, as nothing can exist that does not come from God/Source, so evil, too, came from that same source. And because of the duality, we could not know God withOUT evil. We COULD characterize evil as anything that separates us from God, because it does happen to manifest through our separating desires. But it can take many forms. (Adina)

Adding a general rule of thumb: astrologically speaking apart from Lucifer's placement (which is the specific ways or weakest point for each of us to be influenced by evil) it is also Scorpio, Pluto and the 8th house which correlate to evil within the chart, the reason being that evil (of course) tries to entrap/enslave (Scorpio) the Soul (Pluto). So the Soul's natural desire nature is actually prone to evil, the Soul itself as an individualized consciousness subject to the duality of creation so subject to the influence of evil. This is true for each and every Soul NO EXCEPTION. (Lia)

Making or breaking a contract with evil

What Wolf meant by not being able to break the contract with evil for eternity is until God/dess itself reaches its own "perfection." Until there is no more need for the manifested creation. The bottom line reason that the contract canNOT be broken is that MOST of us would make that contract if it could be broken. We'd make it to get that "temporary fix"– whatever thing, relationship, or type of power we desired. We'd make it to get what we wanted, because we could later say, "OK, I'm done now." And, as Wolf pointed out on more than one occasion, it just doesn't work that way, for the reasons given. (Adina)

Making a contract with evil is a very different and kind of 'special' scenario and takes a conscious act to make that contract. The old saying, 'sold its Soul to the devil,' literally means just that, entering into a contract for something in return, that something is the power of evil. It's also important to know that it cannot be seen in a chart. In some cases it can be SUSPECTED but without the actual reality and the physical presence of the person it cannot be known. The only 'sign' is the eyes according to Jeffrey. Closely looking into the eyes, such eyes will try to 'shut' down as to prevent the observer to see what's behind them, so the pupils will become vertical like cat's eyes. According to Jeffrey only about 3-5% of the human population is in that irreversible condition, having made that horrible contract. Some unfortunately have great powers in our human world.

The contract cannot be broken within the infinity of creation. Deep inside all Souls know intuitively that the Source/God/Goddess is one side within the duality of the manifested creation and choosing the other side consciously and deliberately for whatever reason must happen from the depth of the Soul and must have the consequences also on that level, the depth of the Soul. One of the major themes about the archetype of Scorpio, Pluto and the 8th house is choice making, and that too is why it correlates to evil, the ultimate choice between good/God and evil. Temptation is also Scorpio/Pluto/8th house, and that's how evil works. Of course all this is based on our perception of being a separate entity from the rest of creation, and that too is Pluto. All this comes back in full circle. Evil can exist only as long as there is a belief/perception within human consciousness of separation from each other, from the rest of creation and from the Source, all of which is illusionary in effect. (Lia)

Contract with evil and the North Node/Pluto polarity point
(Q) I have a question regarding the general meaning of the evolutionary signatures in the chart of a Soul who has made a contract with evil. Since they are no longer evolving towards Source, what is the appropriate way to understand the general 'trinity of the future,' the North Node, its ruler, and the Pluto polarity point? Would it manifest in each life as perpetual, ingrained resistance to evolution, thus repeating, defending and strengthening the old karmic patterns and perpetually avoiding making decisions according to the evolutionary potential as indicated by the trinity of the future? (Ari)

(A) Once a Soul has made a contract with evil there does exist the Law of Evolution that leads such a Soul to ever greater 'powers' of a supernatural and evil nature. Just as a Soul who desires to know the Source Of All Things can evolve to the point of having its consciousness totally infused with that Source, ie Jesus, the great Yogananda, etc., so too a Soul who has made that contract can have its consciousness increasingly infused with evil itself: with the resulting 'capacity' to do the work of evil. To understand how the birth chart manifests when a Soul has made an actual contract with evil is to understand exactly the types of desires it has, relative to the natural EA paradigm, that will further take it towards that absolute identification with evil. So with Pluto conjunct the North Node this essentially means 'full steam ahead' relative to the house/sign placement of the natal Pluto conjunct the North Node which is facilitated by the location of the planetary ruler, by house/sign/aspects to it. (Rad)

So to clarify – in any chart of a Soul who has made such a contract the North Node can have a general signification for the evolutionary direction of that Soul as moving ever closer towards becoming 'self realized' within evil – as is the reality of evolution of that Soul according to the nature of its desires. (Ari)

Contract with evil – Hitler
(Q) Did Hitler make a contract before the life of Hitler? In his case, with his North Node in Cancer in the 9th, its ruler, the Moon on the South Node in Capricorn in the 3rd and Pluto in Gemini in the 8th, was the intention of his Soul, from the point of view of evil, to find ways to communicate his message in a way that can touch the heart of the entire culture (Cancer in the 9th) as to inspire a new national identity and thus actualize his desires, this leading to the Pluto polarity point of the 2nd house, having taken this all into his own hands? (Ari)

(A) Yes, and to magnify his relationship to himself, how he inwardly related to himself: the 2nd house polarity. And, in this context, to glorify himself as much as possible which is symbolized by the ruler of his South Node in Capricorn, which is conjunct the Moon, and Jupiter, in Leo in the 10th. He did this of course by manipulating the nature of the German belief systems wherein he simply found a scapegoat in the form of the Jews, the Gypsies, and all other 'undesirables.' The scapegoating is seen relative to his Pluto conjunct Neptune in Gemini in his 8th, and also symbolized by his Uranus in Libra in the 12th squaring his Nodal Axis. Thus, in this way, to create an extreme form of nationalism: the 10th house Saturn, the South Node in Capricorn with the Moon and Jupiter, the Uranus in Libra squaring the Nodes. His Lucifer of course is in Sagittarius in his 2nd and is the ruler of that Jupiter in Capricorn with the Moon on his South Node in Capricorn in the 3rd. So, in the end, it's all about puffing himself up into supernatural forms in such a way as to become the 'icon' for the German peoples who was meant to be a 'savior' for the Germans in general, and the Aryan race specifically. Thus using the 'power' of his oratory that is in union with Lucifer, evil, he managed to 'mesmerize' the German peoples to 'believe' that the Jews, etc., were the source of all their woes and problems starting with the destroyed economy of Germany at that time. (Rad)

(Q) Is it accurate to say that as a Soul progresses further towards evil that the Soul attracts into its life a natural polarization of circumstances to reflect its violation of Natural Law, ie coming into a life in which the Soul is subject to immense persecution/humiliation. And yet because of the contract, the Soul will catapult off the experience of persecution/humiliation via deepening their desires to take revenge/gain their power back etc. – thus evolving them even further within the domain of evil?

(A) This is true for some Souls who have made the contract, not others. Hitler is a perfect example of the point you are making.

(A) Another way of asking this is because God's law is the overarching principle of creation, the karma created from evil comes back to that Soul which will naturally have the effect of propelling them even further down the path of evil?
(A) Yes. The operational dynamic within such Souls is to feel 'victimized' by the karma they themselves are responsible for. Feeling victimized thus allows them to avoid accepting any responsibility in their own actions, and to always find some kind of scapegoat to project their victimization upon.
(Q) Since God's law is greater than evil, is there is a natural limit within creation to how much power can be granted to any Soul that has made a contract with evil? That at some point that Soul will be necessarily blocked from actualizing further desires for a number of subsequent lives, or that perhaps the Soul will be destroyed entirely?
(A) There is a natural limit to anything, and everything. The Soul, and Evil itself, will only be destroyed when the Manifested Creation, as it is now, itself is no longer: the natural retraction principle of the Manifested Creation.

Lucifer Rx
The retrograde Lucifer means that the Soul has the opportunity to redo, redefine, itself all the time. It also means repeating experiences in order for that type of questioning to take place. (Rad)

Profound discontent, dark clouds, violation of Natural Law
Relative to not feeling God, experiencing God within, at this time is an increasing 'plague' on our planet. And that is because of the choices humans are making that are rooted in violations of Natural Law. And of course we could example that a thousand different ways right now. And, because of this, those choices are allowing Lucifer to 'win,' relatively speaking. And because of this then creates an increasing 'pall,' like a dark cloud, all over this planet that permeates and invades the consciousness of all of us. So it's like trying to 'see' God through dark clouds that are becoming darker. And this is, indeed, intentional from Lucifer's point of view because the more that pall increases the more any Soul can feel an increasing sense of futility and self-defeat. As more and more humans feel this collectively the more Lucifer will continue to 'win,' and that 'winning' will correlate to increasing degrees and manifestations of all kinds of cataclysmic events on this planet. Thus, this can just keep compounding upon itself. The consequences of that become unspeakable in the end.
Yet God of course does exist, is still there for all of us. Even in the direst cataclysmic events we can still see God's hand at work in the form of humans trying to help other humans because of those events. And that, when it occurs, is the perfect example of the Natural Law or truth of 'giving, sharing, and inclusion.' On the other hand, it is tragic that it takes cataclysmic events to ignite this Natural Law in most humans at this time. Lucifer is now moving through the sign Cancer. And of course Cancer is part, archetypically, of our emotional bodies. As Wolf taught one of the main ways that evil operates is to magnify and distort negative emotions, like self-defeat or futility, to a state where we just want to give up because we feel powerless to change or alter anything. It can create the perception that the 'pall' or 'dark clouds' that seem to make God non-existent in our life even darker, and more impenetrable, than ever. This is intentional by Lucifer.
Within the apparent dark clouds there is Light. And that Light is eternal for that Light is, indeed, God. When most Souls try to meditate, at first, they experience an inner darkness when they close their eyes: dark clouds. For any Soul, as the Soul's birthright, that persists through the psychology of determination that inner darkness will turn into the inner Light that can be perceived within. And as that Light is perceived the Soul remembers how to merge, fuse, with It. And, as that merging itself evolves, the Soul remembers that natural path or way HOME. So even though Lucifer is now in Cancer, home, we must remember too that Lucifer also correlates with God: the bearer of Light. And that Light is meant to show us the way home: Cancer. (Rad)
As it gets clearer and clearer to the remaining humans who are still sane that the wheels are increasingly coming off the bus, the strength of these feelings [dark clouds etc.] is going to grow. The more sensitive a person is the more they will emphatically pick up these emotions from the collective consciousness. (Steve)

Anger
Of course anger could be part of the Lucifer effect. But the source of anger can be much more than that. Living in a patriarchal, unnatural reality as we do, anyone attuned to the natural is going to, at times, feel deep anger over the distortions that have occurred and continue occurring, due to the sense of the violations of Natural Law simply feeling "not right." Not to mention the personal pain and traumas we have experienced, as a result. Anger does exist within Natural Law – it has its natural purposes. Like everything else, it can get distorted and misapplied. (Steve)

Dreams – under attack, aggression, danger, sexual assault, attack by evil?
What you are sharing and describing here does not, of itself, correlate with dreams wherein the cause of such dreams is Lucifer/evil. For example, this sort of dream can also be a past life dream that reflects and symbolizes an intense trauma caused by extreme violence as in a war scenario. The sexual assault could also be linked with such a scenario as in being raped. The sense of suffocation can be the memory of the moment of death in such a life and/or linked with the act of the sexual violence as in being restrained or suffocated during the rape.

It could be, but it is much more likely that such dreams are rooted in some deep, unresolved, trauma that the Soul then relives in various ways in order to try to remove some of the pressure with the Soul caused by the intense repression of the trauma itself.

(Q) I notice people who have this experience truly believe in spirit – they are more close to God so evil wants to attack them? Why would evil attack a Soul through a dream? (Wei)

(A) This can be because Evil wants to take Souls away from God so can create dreams in order to scare the Soul: to get it to back off from its desire for God or spirit life. It is to scare them away, make them back off from the Spirit life and/or some very important inner realization that has the effect of accelerating the evolution of the Soul. (Rad)

(Q) Can evil chase the Soul life after life?

(A) Evil would not be the cause of the same kind of reoccurring dream. The reoccurring dream is almost always caused by unresolved trauma from prior lives.

(Q) If one meets and recognises someone as really evil whom they are terrified of, can the Soul warn them in a dream?

(A) This can be very true, yes. If this is the case such a dream will manifest very shortly after meeting such a person. When this is the case the face of the person who has been recently met will manifest within the dream that then morphs or changes into an evil image of some kind.

(Q) Is there any way to stop these dreams? Or is the point just to stay with God and not be afraid of these dreams?

(A) Once the Soul can objectify the nature of such dreams caused by Evil, thus detaching and distancing itself from the fear associated with such dreams, the 'power' that Evil has to cause such dreams is dramatically reduced if not eliminated altogether. Once objectified the Soul is thus self-empowered in such a way that there really is no reason to be afraid of these dreams. They are understood for what they are.

Lucifer – connection to Leo
Leo is connected with evil and the archetype of Lucifer, considering that the manifestation of evil is a consequence of free will acting upon the desire to create something which deviates from Natural Law and God's will. And that would be the reason or explanation for Lucifer itself. (Rad)

The weak point of Lucifer in Leo is one of an almost absolute sense of being special in such a way as to do whatever it feels it needs to do in order to gain favor to itself. (Rad)

Pluto transiting natal Lucifer
What's necessary first is to understand the meaning of your natal Lucifer in your chart. You can simply apply what you've come to learn about Lucifer within the EA paradigm. Start with Pluto and the Nodes, the nodal rulers, Pluto polarity point, aspects to all of the above. Through that, you can figure out why Lucifer is where it is in your chart. The key is to convert the temptation to give up, the fear that Lucifer tends to signify, into awareness and greater spiritual conviction. Then, transiting Pluto points to the Soul's intent, at this time in this incarnation, to evolve the natal dynamics of the chart in the way described by the transiting Pluto. Sometimes, or most of the time, we aren't capable of understanding why things are happening the way they are. If you're not familiar, check out the teachings of JWG on the various ways in which Pluto instigates evolution – he talks about it in the Pluto Vol. 1 book as well as some other places. One thing I can share from my own observation/personal experience with transits to Lucifer is that, in the style of the transiting planet, the intent is to turn towards the Light, and it is very important to remain devoted to that. Lucifer in Capricorn for example can develop a psychology of futility and defeatism – or become over-identified with its idea of success to the point of losing touch with its inner ethical compass. (Ari)

Transiting Lucifer/'Bearer of Light' archetype in Capricorn
[Example: Transiting Lucifer in Capricorn, January 2013] The transiting Lucifer is in Capricorn for the entire planet, all countries and groups of people everywhere, and of course for each individual. Both the individual and countries/groups of people everywhere have their own existing context of what REALITY is for them. Capricorn, Saturn, and the 10th house all correlate archetypically to the actual reality of anything. The reality of anything is a function of the choices that are made wherein the causative factor of those choices are existing dynamics that, by their very nature 'condition' the choices being made: determinants. Those existing dynamics, reality, of course have come to be because of prior choices that were made that lead to them, and those choices where themselves a function of those prior dynamics. Going backwards in time where time itself correlates to Capricorn, the 10th house, and Saturn, we now have the phenomena of his/herstory as individuals, and we have the his/herstory as countries/groups of people everywhere. One of the core archetypes of Capricorn, the 10th house, and Saturn is one of REFLECTION. To reflect on our reality, which means how it came to be in the first place: our existing dynamics that were caused by choices made relative to earlier dynamics that lead to those choices, and so on: his/herstory. The Soul's intention in reflection is to LEARN IN HINDSIGHT why we have made the choices that we have that are the determinants for the reality that we have created for ourselves: present and past. This necessary learning thus correlates to self-knowledge. This self-knowledge then that is learned in hindsight by way of reflection on the past that has led to the present is then intended, by the Soul, to be used in such a way as to bring to culmination any existing

dynamic that has created the reality that it has that no longer serves the ongoing evolutionary purpose of the Soul. At the same time this self-knowledge gained in hindsight by an active reflection on the present, and past, is also meant to be used by the Soul to sustain any dynamic that creates the reality for the Soul that it needs for its ongoing evolutionary needs and purposes.
While the transit of Lucifer manifests in Capricorn the 'bearer of Light' as a consciousness or impulse from on high, from God/ess, desires to make all of us as individuals aware of that which we need to be aware of by way of the dynamics within us that have been responsible for that which we have created for ourselves called REALITY. And this awareness occurs through reflection upon the past that has led to the present and, as a result, aware of new choices that we need to make that will culminate existing dynamics that we no longer need that have been responsible for our past reality that has lead us to the present, and, at the same time, aware of the dynamics that we desire to sustain because of reality that they create that we need for our ongoing evolutionary needs and purposes. Relative to the 'bearer of Light' this active reflection will seem to be occurring 'of itself.' In other words it just seems to be taking place whether our conscious egos like it or not. As this occurs of itself of course the Soul may recognize the value and needs in so doing and then consciously make choices to 'join hands' with the 'bearer of Light' so that which must be seen in this active reflection can be as thorough and complete as possible. If the Soul desires to resist, to attempt to block, this necessary active reflection the 'bearer of Light' will cause this reflection to happen anyway. Yet the totality that could be seen, the self-knowledge gained because of this active reflection, will not be as complete or thorough as it otherwise could be. Thus, the ability of the Soul to APPLY that necessary self-knowledge in order to make necessary new choices for its evolutionary needs can be impaired. In fact it can be repressed: Capricorn, Saturn, and the 10th house. The reasons that a Soul can resist this active reflection caused by the 'bearer of Light' is that the judgments made by the Soul to itself, the self-knowledge gained in hindsight, can be so painful and torturous that the Soul simply desires to suppress it. When this occurs then the Soul, unfortunately, is destine to repeat its past, Capricorn, the 10th house, Saturn over and over until it has no other choice but to allow the necessary self-knowledge to take place which implies becoming responsible for one's own actions. So with the Lucifer transit in Capricorn this has been taking place for all of us generally. By placing the transit in each specific horoscope by house we can then also see specific archetypal dynamics involved in this general process.
Another important archetype of Capricorn, the 10th house, and Saturn correlates to the structural nature of our individual and collective realities. The structural nature of reality correlates on a group basis to how any group of people judge and define phenomenal reality where phenomenal reality is simply the natural world of all the images within it. The Soul then makes necessary interpretations of this phenomenal reality is such a way that the nature of the interpretations, what things or images mean, will lead to a philosophical, cosmological, or religious whole. In turn this leads to how a group of people then organize themselves into a structural whole that is called a society wherein the nature of that structural organization is comprised of agreed upon, consensus, laws, rules, customs, taboos, moralities, and ethics. Within the consensus of any given society there is then an expectation that all members of that society conform to the structural nature of the society in which the individual is a member. All individuals within a society are then 'conditioned' by that society as to what is 'real:' what reality is according to the consensus of the society itself. In turn what is considered reality or real becomes the basis of judgments wherein the consensus of a society judge any member who is 'out of order,' or who is violating in some way the consensus expectation to conform. And because each member of a consensus society is conditioned by these judgments about what is right and wrong this becomes the basis of individual judgments as well. The totality of a consensus society expects all its members to individually integrate themselves within the consensus society according to the structural nature of the society itself. Thus all of us from birth in any given life are exposed to the very nature of the consensus society that serves progressively to 'condition' the very nature of the individual's consciousness relative to what is real and not real. Of what is expected of each individual by the consensus society. Any individual deviation from the consensus is met with judgments levelled at that individual who does so.
So from birth all of us are conditioned in this way which then leads all of us to integrating our inherent individuality into the society of birth ON ITS TERMS. So, as a result, the ego structure, Moon, with the Soul, Pluto, can then say things like, "I am a Romanian," "I am Chinese," "I ...." etc. Groups of people of course need to organize themselves into a structural whole in order for the stability of that group to occur. If not the result is simply anarchy. At any point in time relative to evolution the existing structural nature of any given society must make changes in order for that society to sustain itself. In the same way all of us as individual Souls must also, at any point in time, make changes to the structural nature of our individual reality in order to evolve. In order for the society or the individual to do this requires REFLECTION upon the existing nature of our individual and collective, societal, realities. The impulse or consciousness of the 'bearer of Light' while Lucifer transits Capricorn is to induce awareness within the individual and societal realities of that which needs to be structurally changed in order for the evolution of each to take place. Thus, what any of us needs to change in our existing reality in order for evolution to occur. Thus, what any given society needs to change in its existing reality in order for its own necessary evolution to take place in order to sustain itself. (Rad)

Transiting South Node of Lucifer/'Bearer of Light'
The meaning and intentions of the transiting South Node of Lucifer relative to the 'bearer of Light' archetype within it. The transiting South Node of anything of course correlate with the nature of one's past as it interfaces with the current moment in the life of the Soul: the 'now.' The nature of one's past is then helping to shape and define the nature of the moment as reflected in that past.

Relative to the nature of the 'bearer of Light' this would then correlate to something in the past history of the Soul that is being used by the Soul, with the 'unseen' help from the 'bearer of Light,' to shape and define the current moment of one's life. In essence something from the past that is intended to be brought not only into the current moment, but also to move forwards from that moment into the future in order for the evolution of the Soul to continue. (Rad)

Transiting Lucifer/Bearer of Light in Aquarius

[Example: Transiting Lucifer in Aquarius 2013] The transit of Lucifer has now moved into Aquarius for all people. Thus, it will have a collective as well as individual effect. Some simple correlations that apply to Aquarius, Uranus, and the 11th house, and how the 'bearer of Light' and the archetype of Evil manifests through them: One of the core archetypes I would like to discuss first is what JWG called in his book on Uranus the 'freedom from the known.' What he was talking about was the archetype of 'liberation' from the past that binds us to each moment in our lives, and how that binding past can act like a brake in a car to slow down and/or stop the ongoing evolutionary needs of the Soul. Thus, liberation, or freedom from the known, is to make choices that allow for a breaking free from that binding past. He also wrote that the archetype of the 'individuated unconscious' correlates to Uranus, Aquarius, and the 11th house. This is different than the 'collective unconscious' which applies to the entire species of humans. The individuated unconscious correlates to content within the Soul that is unique to that Soul. This content includes all the 'long term memories' that apply to not only this life, but the memories that correlate to the prior lifetimes that the Soul has lived that apply to the current life. The individuated unconscious also correlates to the evolutionary intentions of the Soul in the current life manifesting through this individuated unconscious. Those intentions correlate, so to speak, to a 'master blueprint' for the entire life. This master blueprint that correlates to the Soul's evolutionary intentions for the entire life manifests as 'thought forms' that percolate into the conscious awareness of the current life ego at key evolutionary stages of the Soul's development in the current life.

In combination this then creates an interfacing of all the long term memories of the Soul's past that serve to bind the Soul to its past in any given moment of the current life, and the thought forms that manifest from the Soul by way of the current life ego that serve to actualize the evolutionary intentions for the current life. Thus, for a Soul to act upon, actualize, those thought forms that correlate to the Soul's evolutionary intentions for the current life is to 'liberate' from the past that binds the Soul to its past: freedom from the known. This interfacing between these two archetypes of course occurs in the MOMENT: the past and the future interfacing in each moment of our lives. The past correlates for all humans to a known quantity. Thus familiarity and security. The future as manifested in these thought forms correlate to an unknown: thus insecurity. Most humans do not, cannot, psychologically embrace insecurity as a way of living their lives. Most make choices to recreate their pasts in various ways in order to maintain their sense of personal security. At key evolutionary junctures in the Soul's life in which the Soul intends to liberate from its past, to embrace and act upon the thought forms that correlate to its own master blueprint for the entire life, the Soul will then ignite these thought forms to the current life ego, conscious awareness, that have a repetitive nature to them. In essence these thought forms that correlate to the Soul's next evolutionary steps will repeat over and over in order to get the attention by way of the ego that the Soul has created in the current life. It is these repetitive messages that the Soul, by way of the ego created, needs to act upon in order to evolve: to liberate from the past that binds it. These repetitive messages are just that: repetitive versus thought forms, ideas, that appear at random and have no repetitive occurrence.

When the 'bearer of Light' archetype of Lucifer manifests through the archetypes of Uranus, Aquarius, and the 11th house this correlates to the impulse of God/ess, of the consciousness of God/ess, in our lives. It manifests as new thought forms that correlate to a freedom from the known, a liberation from the past that binds all of us to our pasts. These kinds of thought forms being stimulated by the 'bearer of Light' will seem to occur within all of our consciousnesses 'of themselves.' They just seem to appear all by themselves: not a product of conscious thinking. Yet as they manifest in this way it then of course ignites a process of conscious thinking about them: Mercury, the lower octave of Uranus. And that conscious thinking is necessary in order to understand the meaning of the messages themselves where that meaning occurs because of the individual pasts of each of us that are the very basis of the thought forms that correlate to our evolutionary next steps in order to break free from our pasts. The effect, and intent, of Lucifer transiting through Aquarius or the 11th house, or the Lucifer transit in any sign that makes aspects to our natal Uranus, or planets within our 11th house, is to create a 'boost assist' from God/ess in our lives that is intended to help all of us break from our pasts. (Rad)

LUNAR NODES

South Node

The South Node correlates to our past life habitual emotional patterns, created relative to the Soul's desire nature, brought into the present life. These reflect our *past choices*. Because of habit, fear, resistance, etc. we tend to repeat and repeat the same old choices. (Rad)

A frequent astrological misconception to clear up is we are not trying to leave the South Node behind and move exclusively to the North Node. There is no way to completely leave the South Node behind – it is too much a part of who I am, who I have been for a really long time. It is the South Node of the MOON, and the Moon represents my sense of self-image. What we are trying to do is not leave the South Node behind, but evolve how I perceive and live out the South Node. I take what is learned at the North Node back to the South Node, learning to do the South Node IN NEW WAYS. (Steve)

North Node

The North Node is as far away (180 degrees) from the South Node (the past, the known) as it can possibly be. In other words, evolving requires making choices that embrace stepping into an unknown, the exact opposite of what is known. What is known is what causes us to feel safe, secure, etc. even if what is known is dysfunctional. In stepping into an unknown, unconscious fears and insecurities arise, relative to past forgotten memories, which explains why moving into the unknown is so difficult at times for most of us. (Steve)

The North Node operates initially by the Soul creating a desire(s) that correlates with its ongoing evolutionary intentions as symbolized by the North Node itself. By acting on such desires the North Node then becomes actualized. (Rad)

North Node and Pluto polarity point

The North Node and the Pluto polarity point operate simultaneously, not independently. Planetary aspects to the North Node indicate that the North Node has been actualized to some extent, and this implies that the PPP has been actualized too. There will also be aspects within the natal chart, in most cases, to that PPP. This is exactly what JWG taught: that evolution is a very slow, ongoing process from one life to the next. (Rad)

Mean motion of the Nodes

The mean motion of the Lunar Nodes is retrograde in all charts, even if the Nodes are direct in a specific chart. In all cases the Nodes enter a sign at 29 degrees and exit at 0 degrees. (Steve)

There is a difference between Mean Nodes and Mean Motion. Mean Nodes is a mathematical abstraction that smoothes out the actual motion of the Nodes. This does not exist in reality, only in abstraction. Mean Motion means that, overall, the movement of the Nodes is retrograde, even though there are periods when the Nodes are direct and moving forward. (Steve)

True Nodes

EA astrologers have been taught to use True Nodes, as that is what actually exists in the sky. (Steve)

Nodes at 29 degrees

Remember that when we work with Nodes that their mean motion is retrograde. Thus, the 29 degrees would actually correlate to just coming into, like a new phase, the sign. (Rad)

Nodes at 0 degrees

This means an entire evolutionary cycle is culminating when the degrees are zero and a few minutes. The Soul is now preparing to begin an entire brand new cycle of evolutionary development as symbolized in the signs to come. Thus, this is a cycle of CULMINATION of many prior lives, and the dynamics that created those lives. This can create a sense of Soul frustration in many with these symbols because they can feel or sense what is ahead, of wanting to leap forwards, even as they must culminate all that has come before. (Rad)

Nodes at 1 degree
The natal symbols remain in the context of the current life. So with a North Node at 1 degree of Scorpio for example, that Node will remain in Scorpio for the entire life. The progression of it into the late degrees of Libra means that the dynamics of Libra will be evolved towards, yet INTEGRATED THROUGH THE NATAL NODE IN SCORPIO. (Rad)

Nodes – direct
Jeffrey wrote that in his experience, in general people with Nodes direct in their chart had a clearer idea earlier in life of their life direction than people with retrograde Nodes, however not in every case. I've discussed this in the past with other EA astrologers, and not everyone has experienced that correlation. It needs to be examined by each astrologer from their personal chart experiences. (Steve)

Nodes – stationary
A stationing anything, planet or node, is a magnifying force. (Rad)

Skipped steps – Planet t-square the Nodes
See chapter on SKIPPED STEPS.

Transiting Lunar Nodes, 'apparent' versus 'actual'
The 'apparent' versus the 'actual' issues of these transiting Nodes is that whatever house and sign the transiting Nodes are moving through correlates to the 'apparent' evolutionary issues that are linked to the natal Nodal Axis of the Moon, whereas the 'actual' evolutionary issues correlates to the NATAL PLACEMENT of the planets that rule these transiting Nodes. In essence, what is underneath those apparent issues, and why. The apparent issues are of course just as real as the actual issues: the difference, again, is what is underneath those apparent issues where what is underneath them is what those apparent issues are really about, and why. (Rad)

Transiting Lunar Nodes t-square natal planet
When this occurs through transit it symbolizes key evolutionary transitions between the existing past, and the future to come. If the Soul makes the choices necessary that allow these key transitions to take place all will be well for that Soul. On the other hand if the Soul does not make the necessary choices that reflect the intent of the evolutionary transition then this will lead to 'skipped steps' relative to those dynamics in a future life to come. (Rad)

Transiting Lunar Nodes t-square planet – in a death chart
(Q) If a person experiences the square of a transiting planet to the natal Lunar Nodes at the time of death, does it also create skipped steps? (Sherry)
(A) The answer is yes to your question about transiting planet(s) squaring the Nodes upon the physical death of a Soul. The nature of those skipped steps, the dynamics involved, will of course be symbolized by the nature of the entire skipped step paradigm in the death chart: the house the transiting planet is in, its sign, and of course the house/sign positions of the Nodes themselves. This will be true whether it is the transiting Nodes that are being squared by a transiting planet, or a transiting planet squaring the natal Nodes. It can be very useful to look backwards into the person's life when these kinds of transits occurred which in most cases they will have, to review exactly what the circumstances were at those times, and the choices the Soul made because of those circumstances. This can then provide a keen understanding and insight as to the specific nature of the skipped steps that took place at those times that then are symbolized at the moment of the Soul's physical death. And that then means that the Soul, in the very next life, will have that signature of the skipped steps symbolized in some way in that next life's birth chart. (Rad)

Transiting South Node of anything
The transiting South Node of anything of course correlates with the nature of one's past as it interfaces with the current moment in the life of the Soul: the 'now.' The nature of one's past is then helping to shape and define the nature of the moment as reflected in that past. (Rad)

Conscious/unconscious patterns
In terms of the Nodes, we are conscious of the pulls of the Nodes because they are part of our sense of self, self-image. That relates to the "familiar feels secure" principle. So we repeat old patterns and habits. Pluto's compulsions lie beneath that level of awareness, in the unconscious. Both are operative. (Steve)

Nodes – calculation of phasal relationship

For planets, we always start with the SLOWER moving planet of the two planets or points being considered. And then in a clockwise direction determine the degrees of separation between the two. When using the Nodes, because the mean motion is retrograde, the rule is reversed: using the slower moving point of the two you count in a counter-clockwise direction. When using the Sun, the Sun is always the first point of reference. (Rad)

Nodes in synastry – calculation of phasal relationship

Always use the natural zodiac as the frame of reference to calculate the phases of any two points. So in calculating the nodes in synastry that would mean to use the one person's node that preceded, naturally, the other person's node, ie South Node in Aries would precede the South Node in Cancer. Thus using that South Node in Aries as the baseline or start point. Yet, because the mean motion of the nodes is retrograde, we would then have to reverse the normal rules of the phases. If I had, say, Mars at 1 deg Aries, and another had their Mars at 1 deg Cancer, that would naturally be a first quarter square through natural progression of the signs. But the nodes are retrograde through mean motion. So even though we would still use the South Node of Aries as the baseline we would then see through the natural motion of the retrograde that the South Node of Cancer is MOVING TOWARDS that South Node in Aries. So it would then be a last quarter square or phase versus a first quarter square or phase if indeed the South Nodes were at 1 deg Aries and Cancer respectively. In this example that would then make the North Nodes at 1 deg Libra and 1 deg Capricorn. So, again, using the natural zodiac as our baseline we then see that Libra precedes Capricorn. With the mean motion of the nodes in mind that again means that the Capricorn node is moving towards the Libra node: another last quarter square or phase. (Rad)

Calculation of phasal relationship – nodes and planets, transiting and natal

- ✓ Natal Neptune is in a balsamic phase with the natal North Node.
- ✓ Transiting Mars is in a balsamic conjunction with the transiting North Node.
- ✓ Transiting North Node is in a new phase conjunction with the natal North Node (recent Nodal Return; new cycle).
- ✓ Transiting North Node is in a balsamic phase in relation to natal Neptune.
- ✓ Transiting Mars is in a balsamic conjunction with the natal North Node (a cycle ending, with a new cycle beginning soon).
- ✓ Transiting Mars is in a new phase relative to Natal Neptune.

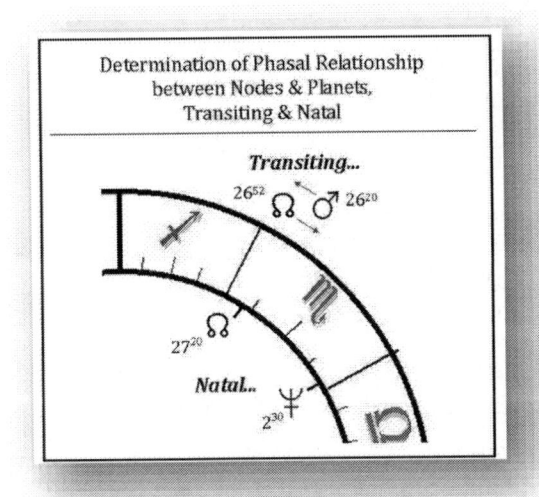

Nodal Axis, in the next life

The Nodal Axis, as well as the entire chart, correlate with dynamics, from life to life, that the Soul is evolving through relative to its core evolutionary intentions: dynamics that are necessary in order for that evolution to proceed. The Nodal Axis of course correlates with the types of egocentric structures that the Soul needs in order to accomplish its ongoing evolutionary intentions. When the Nodal Axis is symbolized by 29 or 0 degrees it does correlate to dynamics, the types of egocentric structures necessary for the Soul, that are either culminating, or just beginning. This does not mean that, for example, if the Nodes are at say 0 Virgo and Pisces that in the next life they will then still be in those signs. There are a variety of dynamics that correlate and contribute to the ongoing evolutionary needs of the Soul. Thus, for example, in the next life relative to those symbols in the current life, it would be entirely possible for the Nodal Axis to be in the 6th and 12th houses, but in totally different signs. It is possible to have the Nodal Axis in not only entirely different signs, but also houses. So we could have the ruler of one of the Nodes then in the 6th house, and the other in the 12th. And so on and so on. The combinations and possibilities are many. (Rad)

Shifts from South Node to North Node, and Pluto to Pluto polarity point

It's automatic. You can't separate the Nodes with Pluto and its polarity point because the ego (Nodes) are always a reflection of the Soul's desires (Pluto). The ego is never separate from the reason for why the ego exists in the first place. (Ari)

North Node Scorpio, ruled by Pluto

These symbols mean that such a Soul has been intensely resisting change/evolution in the most recent prior lives. The South Node being in Taurus would correlate to a 'frog in the well' in that the Soul has felt highly secure within the bottom of the well, and resisted jumping out of it in order to expose itself to the totality of the environment that surrounds the well. Jumping out of that well correlates to deep fears because it can no longer control its space or reality as defined in the bottom of the well. Thus, in these symbols the Soul will be continually confronted with its past, and the dynamics that are the cause of that past: the North Node in Scorpio ruled by the natal Pluto. The polarity point of the Pluto, the bottom line in the current life evolutionary intentions, will serve as a vehicle through which the Soul is given the opportunity to make new choices, changes, relative to re-experiencing its past, and the dynamics that correlate with that past.

The house placement of the North Node in Scorpio also serves to create opportunities of the Soul to make new choices relative to re-experiencing its past as symbolized not only in the house and sign of the natal Pluto, but, of course, the South Node by house, and the location of its planetary ruler by sign, house, and aspects to it. So you can see that the key here is indeed the polarity point of Pluto. The Soul has chosen to re-experience its past because it has felt secure within that past, and the dynamics that correlate to that past. That past is symbolized by not only the North Node, the South Node, and its planetary ruler, but also the natal Pluto by house and sign. And yet it is these very symbols that also correlate to evolving beyond that past by making new choices in the face of that past. And those new choices start with the polarity point of Pluto. By making those new choices in this way it then has the effect of evolving the North Node, South Node and its planetary ruler, but also of course the natal Pluto itself. (Rad)

South Node Scorpio, ruled by Pluto

The significance is that Souls who have this symbol have overly identified with their sense of security, emotional/ psychological/ sexual, in specific and fixed ways and that over-identification has caused the Soul to stop evolving due to the compulsiveness of it, the fixity of it. Thus, the Soul, by its own design, has created in most recent prior lives a series of lives of intense loss of those dynamics that have been overly identified with. This has been necessary in order for the Soul to continue with its evolution. Thus, the North Node being in Taurus and the total evolutionary change within the Soul in terms of its own inner relationship with itself. In so changing the Soul is thus changing its own inner magnetism, which, in turn, allows for an attraction of these exact types of circumstances (relative to both the dynamics that are symbolized by the South Node in Scorpio, and the North Node in Taurus) that allows the Soul to continue to grow and evolve. (Rad)

South or North Node in Cancer – on a personal level

The 'interpretation' of when the South/North Nodes of the Moon are in Cancer is totally dependent on the individual context, reality, of each Soul. The symbols of Cancer, the Moon, and the 4th house correlate to a total archetype within which there is a spectrum that symbolizes that total archetype. The evolutionary condition, the four natural stages of the Soul's evolution, must first be taken into consideration in order to begin to understand where any given Soul is at within that spectrum. Within that the nature of the country, society, or tribe in which the Soul chooses to be born must also be considered because they all correlate to the nature of the 'imprinting,' or conditioning of consciousness, that each type of society is defined by. Within this we much also consider the nature of the specific family structure that the Soul chooses to be born into that, of itself, influences wherein that total spectrum of the Cancer archetype is orientated to. Then, after these considerations, the specific nature of the Soul's past life history, dynamics, that are seen through the EA paradigm must be fully grasped in order to understand that Soul's individual context: their reality. When all of this is put together then the specific reasons as to why the Soul is choosing to have the North or South Nodes in Cancer can be rightly understood. In other words, there is no one 'cookbook' answer that fits all. (Rad)

South Node in Cancer, North Node in Capricorn – on a global level

On a global level with the South Node in Cancer, North Node in Capricorn, this correlates in general to the structural nature of our world at every level of reality that is rapidly changing. And, of course, how those structural changes are affecting every one of us on the planet: our individual reality, identity, sense of personal security, and of course our families. Each country, Capricorn, of course also has its own individual context defined by the nature of its governments, its economies, its demographics, and its laws. All of us of course live in whatever countries that we do. So the changing structural nature of reality in general at every level then affects each country relative to its own context. And within each country are all the individual citizens and their families that are then affected by the structural changes not only within their own country, but the world itself. For the millions of Souls that will be born while the transiting Nodal Axis is in Cancer/Capricorn they will be 'imprinted,' in general, by this high state of psychological/emotional anxiety based on the structural nature of the changes in the world as a whole, and their country of birth specifically. So the question then becomes from an EA point of view WHY? And each Soul will have their own unique answer. (Rad)

Planet conjunct South Node

With a planet on the North Node the Soul has an inner sense of moving towards something that has already been underway, whereas a planet on the South Node creates much more of a sense of being 'stuck' in something from the past that the Soul wants to move away from, but can't. With a planet on the South Node it means one of three possible evolutionary/ karmic conditions:

(1) a total re-live of past life conditions that have not been resolved or were avoided,
(2) a condition wherein that planet and South Node have been highly developed to the point of constituting a natural resource that is being brought forwards into the current life for the Soul's own karmic and evolutionary reasons, and
(3) a combination of both (1) and (2).

The rule about the second Saturn Return applies for planets on the South Node unless there are the mitigating factors (see Pluto conjunct South Node and second Saturn Return below). Other mitigating factors correlate to any planet forming an aspect to the North Node because that means that that North Node has been initially accessed prior to the current life. An aspect to the North Node of course means that there is also an aspect to the South Node. Thus, the linkage between the North/South Nodes before the current life. (Rad)

The three possible conditions of the South Node, and planets conjunct the South Node are re-live, fruition or combination of both. The particular condition of the South Node (ie relive, fruition, or mix), as well as the condition of planets conjunct the South Node, is a variable as it can only be assessed via observation of the Soul's life. (Ari)

Retrograde planet conjunct South Node

The internalization and introspection of the retrograde archetype manifests because of the planet being retrograde: it's an archetype that is essential to retrograde. Thus, when the Soul recreates for itself conditions that it has already lived prior to the existing life in the current life the intention is in fact to reflect, through internalization and introspection, exactly why it has done so. The answers realized because of this reliving thus serve the Soul's evolutionary purpose of self-knowledge that is meant to be applied to the Soul's evolutionary future that will be progressively individualized to reflect the individual design of its Soul. Any planet on the South Node correlates to that archetype being developed prior to the current life that is being relived through evolutionary necessity in order for evolution to proceed for the Soul. There are three karmic/evolutionary reasons for this: a total relive of the past that must be revisited in order for new choices to made relative to the circumstances created relative to the relive, a condition of total evolutionary fruition which means that archetypes have been highly developed, evolved, and is meant to be sustained in the current life in order for it to be helpful in the evolution of others' Souls, or a combination of both of those conditions that have the same evolutionary intentions. (Rad)

Planet conjunct North Node

When you see this situation, what you have is a Soul who is going to reflect the third of three karmic evolutionary conditions. In the third condition you have an element of past life dynamics being re-lived, and you also have what is called an element of karmic fruition. And when this is occurring, that releasing can occur at the first Saturn Return. Why? Because there is a planet on the North Node, meaning that Soul has already been trying to work, struggle free, break free – whatever that planet may be on the North Node. It shows you through that specific archetypal function and the house it is in, that they have been trying to break free, but it is not complete yet. So that is a combination of re-live and also fruition. What fruition means, karmic evolutionary fruition (when this is operative), is that the intentions and motivations have been sufficiently pure, because Pluto correlates with intentions, motivations, agendas, where I am coming from, desires that fuel it. Fruition here means that, relative to the conditions symbolized in the Pluto/South Node house, there has been a degree of evolution that has been pure enough, that they have some special quality or condition to bring into the life. So there can be this element of re-living from a positive, and a not so great point of view. (Steve)

Very simply, a planet conjunct the North Node means that that archetype has already been embraced by the Soul just previous to the current life in order to evolve, and is meant to continue that evolution in this life via the planet conjunct the North Node. With a planet on the North Node the Soul has an inner sense of moving towards something that has already been underway, whereas a planet on the South Node creates much more of a sense of being 'stuck' in something from the past that the Soul wants to move away from, but can't. Planets conjunct the North Node means that those archetypes have been worked upon prior to the current life: they are not brand new. And the intention of the Soul is to continue to work upon these archetypes as bottom line orientations to the current evolutionary intentions of the Soul. When planets are conjunct the North Node, it will be a feeling like when you are driving away from something in your car, and you look through the rear view mirror: the increasing sense of something being left behind (South Node). (Rad)

Retrograde planet conjunct North Node

With a planet on the North Node the Soul has an inner sense of moving towards something that has already been underway, whereas the South Node creates much more of a sense of being 'stuck' in something from the past that the Soul wants to move away from, but can't. With a planet retrograde on the North Node the Soul will continue to recreate circumstances, inner and outer, in which the operative principle will be one of individuation which, of itself, accelerates the evolution of the Soul. Thus recreating dynamics and circumstances that need to be repeated in order to move towards the Soul's evolutionary future in an increasingly individuated way that the Soul IS MOVING TOWARDS: what appears from the front window when driving versus what appears in the rear view mirror. (Rad)

A retrograde planet is not 'highly developed' but in the process of being developed which is serving as a 'lead point' in the ongoing evolution of the Soul. The retrograde archetype accelerates the evolution of the Soul because it naturally rebels from the consensus expectation of how that archetypal function defined by the planet itself is 'meant' to be actualized according to the consensus. Thus, there is a progressive 'individuation' of that archetype that reflects, in the end, the inherent individuality of that archetype according the original design of the Soul itself. A planet conjunct the North Node has been worked upon prior to the current life that reflects the evolutionary needs/desires of the Soul that serves as a lead point in the ongoing evolutionary journey of the Soul: this does not mean it is highly developed. It does mean that it is not brand new: the first life that involves this evolutionary intention. The retrograde archetype also means that any planet that is retrograde, on the North Node or not, is also recreating, re-experiencing, reliving dynamics from its past that must be relived in order for new choices to be made in order for the Soul's evolution to proceed. It can also correlate to karmic conditions, karmic issues, that also must be relived because they have yet to be dealt with and/or resolved. Thus the intention to do so in the retrograde symbol. And to accelerate the evolution of the Soul by rebelling or rejecting against the consensus of any given society's expectations of how that archetypal function is 'meant' to be actualized according to that consensus. (Rad)

A general [correct] example: Saturn retrograde on the North Node. If a Soul was overly conditioned by its responsibilities, then in this life there will be an evolutionary emphasis on liberating from that conditioning (Saturn retrograde) while continuing to actualize the role the structure is here to build (on the North Node). (Ari)

[Example: Neptune retrograde conjunct North Node 2nd] With the Neptune retrograde on the North Node all three of those retrograde archetypes will be experienced, just as they have been in the most previous past lives of that Soul. It should be clear that one of the dynamics/issues that the Soul is needing to deal with is the issue of personal delusions/illusions, Neptune, that the Soul EXPECTS, Neptune and its lower octave Venus, to occur as if by magic. As a result, this Soul has created a 'program' for itself in which various expectations that are projected into the life will be met with disillusionment, Neptune, so that the experience of disillusionment will be the causative factor of busting apart the very nature of the Soul's illusions and delusions. The intent in this of course is to re-orientate to actual reality because of the disillusionment. (Rad)

Moon conjunct South Node, ruler of North Node conjunct Pluto

[Limited information can be taken from these factors in isolation from the rest of the chart, but some basic guidelines are applicable.] With the Moon, or any other planet conjunct the South Node one of three evolutionary/karmic conditions exist as defined in Wolf's books:

(1) a total re-live of past life conditions that have not been resolved or were avoided,
(2) a condition wherein that planet and South Node have been highly developed to the point of constituting a natural resource that is being brought forwards into the current life for the Soul's own karmic and evolutionary reasons, and
(3) a combination of both (1) and (2). The nature of the planet, in this case, the Moon, correlates to what those conditions are: house, sign, and aspects to it, (and will be total re-live, total fruition or some partial re-live and partial fruition mixed).

With the planetary ruler of the North Node conjunct Pluto this will correlate to the fact that the evolutionary flow of the Soul symbolized by the North Node itself, in the person's chart by house and sign, has been moved towards just prior to the current life. Thus, it is not something 'brand new,' but relatively new. So the house, sign, of the North Node has been used by the Soul, just prior to the current life, to help move forwards, to evolve, the conditions symbolized by the Moon's conjunction to the South Node (re-live, fruition or both – of the Moon's sign/house/aspects). By having the ruler of the North Node conjunct Pluto itself symbolizes that the nature of the archetype of the planet that rules that North Node serves like a magnifying glass within the Soul to keep moving the evolution of the Moon/South Node conjunction forwards via the nature of that planet. The natural polarity point of Pluto, the bottom line in the Soul's current life evolutionary intent, will thus be consciously embraced by the Soul because it has been activated just prior to the current life. If the ruling planet of the North Node is in a balsamic conjunction to Pluto then this correlates to the Soul, via the Moon/South Node conjunction, recreating circumstances of the past in the current life in order to make NEW CHOICES in the face of those circumstantial triggers. If the conjunction is a new phase to Pluto then this means that that Soul has succeeded in beginning to making new choices relative to past dynamics triggered by circumstances just prior to this life, and will continue to do so. (Rad)

Moon conjunct South Node, example

[Example: South Node Capricorn 8th house conjunct the Moon in Capricorn, planetary ruler Saturn square Venus; North Node Cancer 2nd house] South Node conjunct the Moon in Capricorn/8th house symbolizes that the person's self-image (Moon) is a core or critical issue brought over from the past (conjunct the South Node). The Moon/South Node in Capricorn in the 8th reflects that a deep repression of the emotional body is trying to be unlocked, and a positive self-image is trying to manifest. In this way, a deepening and maturity within relationships can then be experienced (Saturn square Venus). The Capricorn archetype correlates with guilt (both conditioned and acquired guilt), and the need to emotionally mature by accepting responsibility in one's own actions. The North Node in Cancer in the 2nd house and also Saturn square Venus reflects that this person will experience, or has already experienced, being thrown back upon herself time and time again in order to learn the core issues of emotional self-reliance (North Node in Cancer/2nd house), and also learning how to emotionally nurture herself in the ways that she needs instead of projecting these needs within relationships. In this way, a state of internalized emotional security can be actualized, and she can transmute the limitations and repression of her old self-image, inner relationship to herself, and the types of relationships she attracted because of that self-image. Again, a deepening and maturity within relationships can be accomplished as she moves towards these life lessons (South Node in Capricorn/8th house conjunct the Moon, planetary ruler Saturn square Venus), then transmute to higher levels of expression. (Deva)

Pluto conjunct South Node, and second Saturn return
Pluto conjunct South Node will mean one of three karmic evolutionary conditions, the first two of which will be extreme, the third one will be common:

1. (extreme): A Soul who has utterly and completely avoided, denied the evolutionary intentions symbolized in the house and sign position of this conjunction. And because there has been a fundamental resistance to embracing those lessons, the Soul comes into this life karmically and evolutionarily determined to repeat those past life evolutionary intentions in this life. This can be very problematic on a psychological level. Why? They will sense the wistful promise of the North Node. And yet, based on karmic evolutionary determination, they are forced to remain within the conditions implied in the South Node/Pluto conjunction. Most people, when they come into a life, more or less do fulfil or live out the past life dynamics, up until around the first Saturn return. It goes right back to the principle of security, self-consistency, etc. Which is exactly why the first Saturn return, in terms of timing, is so problematic for most people. Why? They have done nothing to prepare for the current life purpose. And then the Saturn return happens, and all of a sudden they become aware psychologically that they are feeling stuck within the definitions of the reality which have been defined from the past. Generally speaking, the first Saturn return correlates with the opportunity to be released from those past conditions and to begin the actualization of the current life intentions. But when Pluto is conjunct South Node in this first extreme condition, those past life conditions cannot be released until the second Saturn return, the majority of the life span.

There can be mitigating conditions that modify this situation, specifically a planet conjunct North Node, which of course implies an opposition to Pluto. When you see this situation, what you have is a Soul who is going to reflect the third one of these three karmic evolutionary conditions. In the third condition you have an element of past life dynamics being relived, and you also have what is called an element of karmic fruition. And when this is occurring, that releasing can occur at the first Saturn return. Why? Because there is a planet on the North Node, meaning that Soul has already been trying to work, struggle free, break free – whatever that planet may be on the North Node. It shows you through that specific archetypal function and the house it is in, that they have been trying to break free, but it is not complete yet. So that is a combination of relive and also fruition. What fruition means, karmic evolutionary fruition (when this is operative), is that the intentions and motivations have been sufficiently pure, because Pluto correlates with intentions, motivations, agendas, where I am coming from, desires that fuel it. Fruition here means that, relative to the conditions symbolized in the Pluto/South Node house, there has been a degree of evolution that has been pure enough, that they have some special quality or condition to bring into the life. So there can be this element of reliving from a positive, and a not so great point of view.

2. (extreme): This can be a situation of absolute karmic fruition and evolutionary fruition, meaning again that the motives and intentions fuelled by desires have been sufficiently pure, that they bring in some special capacity or ability, a resource (Pluto) developed thoroughly from other lifetimes. And in this karmic evolutionary condition, the requirement is to disseminate or share that resource in some way with others. Now this also creates a high degree of frustration, even though it is a positive circumstantial condition in life. Why? Because the person has been doing it for so darned long. They want to do something else. And here again, unless you see a mitigating factor, the second Saturn return routine.

3. (the most common): Again having an element of reliving as well as of fruition. And unless you find a qualifying mitigating condition, ie a planet on North Node, here again, second Saturn return.

(Q) I don't understand the reason for such a set up in the first place. Is it because they have come into this world to fulfil a special purpose – sort of like an avatar – relative to that Pluto/South Node conjunction? (Ari)
(A) You will notice the word 'requirement' above. And that is what this is. And the reason for such a requirement will be different in each case. And, yes, Souls with this signature, requirement, has some special capacity or resource to share with others that will have a metamorphic effect once shared, whatever it may be. (Rad)
(Q) Meaning they are blocked from their North Node until the second Saturn Return specifically because they have chosen to assist others in some way?
(A) Yes, it's a requirement.
(Q) This would seemingly imply that it's not about that particular Soul?
(A) Why would it imply that? It doesn't. It is exactly about that particular Soul – a requirement that the Soul has to fulfil.

(Q) What metamorphosis can occur that enacts evolution for that Soul before the second Saturn return?
(A) The metamorphosis occurs through fulfilling the requirement itself. Beyond that, there will of course be other areas in the individual's life that will be evolving and metamorphosing. Pluto will be making aspects to other planets for example. There will of course be a sign on the 8th house cusp, and the location of its planetary ruler, that will be needing to be evolved. So too if there are planets in the natal 8th house and/or planets in Scorpio itself.
(Q) How is it possible for the desire nature of a natal Pluto by house and sign to express itself as relatively pure without awareness of its polarity point?
(A) There have been polarity points in other lives that have all lead to this karmic requirement of the Soul. This is why whatever the resource or capacity is that the Soul is required to give, to share, has reached this state of purity before the current life.
(Q) Does this rule about the second Saturn return apply for other planets on the South Node?
(A) Yes, unless there are the mitigating factors. Other mitigating factors correlate to any planet forming an aspect to the North Node because that means that that North Node has been initially accessed prior to the current life. An aspect to the North Node of course means that there is also an aspect to the South Node. Thus, the linkage between the North/South Nodes before the current life.

Pluto conjunct South Node

We must remember the three evolutionary/karmic possibilities with Pluto conjunct the South Node: (1) the Soul is in a condition of totally re-living prior life dynamics in this life because of an absolute resistance, prior choices, to acting upon the evolutionary intentions and necessities prior to the current life, (2) is a situation wherein the Soul has totally actualized those prior intentions in such a way as to develop unique abilities and capacities that are being brought forwards into the current life in order to benefit others because of those abilities and capacities, and (3) is a common condition in which elements of both the first two conditions exist. With a planet conjunct the South Node there is a requirement to disseminate or share a resource in some way with others. The reason for such a requirement will be different in each case. Souls with this Pluto conjunct South Node signature, requirement, have some special capacity or resource to share with others that will have a metamorphic effect once shared, whatever it may be. They are blocked from their North Node until the second Saturn Return specifically because they have chosen to assist others in some way. It's a requirement. Metamorphosis that enacts evolution before the second Saturn Return occurs through fulfilling the requirement itself. Beyond that, there will of course be other areas in the individual's life that will be evolving and metamorphosing. Pluto will be making aspects to other planets for example. There will of course be a sign on the 8th house cusp, and the location of its planetary ruler, that will be needing to be evolved. So too if there are planets in the natal 8th house and/or planets in Scorpio itself. The desire nature of the natal Pluto by house and sign expresses itself as relatively pure without awareness of its polarity point because there have been polarity points in other lives that have all lead to this karmic requirement of the Soul. This is why whatever the resource or capacity is that the Soul is required to give, to share, has reached this state of purity before the current life. (Rad)

Manifests as three possible conditions: re-live, fruition, or mixture of both. Pluto conjunct South Node will mean one of three karmic evolutionary conditions, the first two of which will be extreme, the third one will be common:

(1) (extreme) A Soul who has utterly and completely avoided, denied the evolutionary intentions symbolized in the house and sign position of this conjunction. And because there has been a fundamental resistance to embracing those lessons, the Soul comes into this life karmically and evolutionarily determined to repeat those past life evolutionary intentions in this life. This can be very problematic on a psychological level. Why? They will sense the wistful promise of the North Node. And yet, based on karmic evolutionary determination, they are forced to remain within the conditions implied in the South Node/Pluto conjunction. Most people, when they come into a life, more or less do fulfill or live out the past life dynamics, up until around the first Saturn Return. It goes right back to the principle of security, self-consistency, etc. Which is exactly why the first Saturn Return, in terms of timing, is so problematic for most people. Why? They have done nothing to prepare for the current life purpose. And then the Saturn Return happens, and all of a sudden they become aware psychologically that they are feeling stuck within the definitions of the reality which have been defined from the past. Generally speaking, the first Saturn Return correlates with the opportunity to be released from those past conditions and to begin the actualization of the current life intentions. But when Pluto is conjunct South Node in this first extreme condition, those past life conditions cannot be released until the second Saturn Return, the majority of the life span.

There can be mitigating conditions that modify this situation, specifically a planet conjunct North Node, which of course implies an opposition to Pluto. When you see this situation, what you have is a Soul who is going to reflect the third one of these three karmic evolutionary conditions. In the third condition you have an element of past life dynamics being re-lived, and you also have what is called an element of karmic fruition. And when this is occurring, that releasing can occur at the first Saturn Return. Why? Because there is a planet on the North Node, meaning that Soul has already been trying to work, struggle free, break free – whatever that planet may be on the North Node. It shows you through that specific archetypal function and the house it is in, that they have been trying to break free, but it is not complete yet. So that is a combination of re-live and also fruition. What fruition means, karmic evolutionary fruition (when this is operative), is that the intentions and motivations have been sufficiently pure, because Pluto correlates with intentions, motivations, agendas, where I am coming from, desires that fuel it. Fruition here means that, relative to the conditions symbolized in the Pluto/South Node house, there has been a degree of evolution that has been pure enough, that they have some special quality or condition to bring into the life. So there can be this element of re-living from a positive, and a not so great point of view.

(2) (extreme) This can be a situation of absolute karmic fruition and evolutionary fruition, meaning again that the motives and intentions fuelled by desires have been sufficiently pure, that they bring in some special capacity or ability, a resource (Pluto) developed thoroughly from other lifetimes. And in this karmic evolutionary condition, the requirement is to disseminate or share that resource in some way with others. Now this also creates a high degree of frustration, even though it is a positive circumstantial condition in life. Why? Because the person has been doing it for so darned long. They want to do something else. And here again, unless you see a mitigating factor, the second Saturn Return routine.

(3) (the most common) Again having an element of re-living as well as of fruition. And unless you find a qualifying mitigating condition, ie a planet on North Node, here again, second Saturn Return. (Steve)

Pluto conjunct South Node, balsamic

The South Node MOVING TOWARDS THAT PLUTO, due to retrograde motion, means many, many unresolved issues and dynamics that have been moving forwards from life to life with that Soul that remain unresolved, are starting to come to a head. Thus, the necessity of re-living over and over until they do, until new choices are made that allow the Soul to move forwards, to evolve. (Rad)

Pluto conjunct North Node, integrating the sign of the PPP

[Example: Pluto in Libra in the 3rd house conjunct the North Node] The sign that any planet is within naturally contains its opposite. The opposite house is simply coming through the lead point, the integration point, symbolized by the house/sign of Pluto's conjunction to the North Node of the Moon. The 9th house will come through that Pluto conjunct the North Node in Libra in the 3rd: it's not somehow dormant. It is simply coming through the lead point symbolized by the Pluto/North Node in Libra in the 3rd house. (Rad)

Pluto conjunct North Node – NO Pluto polarity point

When Pluto conjuncts the North Node it does indicate that the Soul has worked towards actualizing the evolutionary intentions symbolized by the house and sign position of the Pluto and the North Node that the Soul is meant to continue in that direction in this life. That is why Pluto's polarity point does not apply in that case. In other words, the Soul is meant to keep going in the direction symbolized by Pluto conjunct the North Node (full actualization of the evolutionary intentions described by the Pluto/North Node conjunction). If there are other planets forming aspects to the South Node then those planets will describe areas of potential stagnation and blocks towards actualizing the Pluto/North Node evolutionary intentions. (Deva)

In any chart that you see Pluto conjunct the North Node symbol it means that there is no polarity point for Pluto because the intention of the Soul is to continue its evolutionary development as symbolized by the house and sign of the Pluto/North Node conjunction which has already been underway prior to the current life. And in any chart that one sees this will always mean, of course, that the opposite sign of that Pluto/North Node conjunction has already been developed to the point of limiting the Soul's evolution if it remains focused on that alone. If so, then the Soul arrives at a place of Plutonian stagnation and non-growth. So when the EA astrologer sees Pluto conjunct the North Node in any chart it means that the entire chart, the entire evolutionary intent, is be focused upon and through that house and sign of the Pluto/North Node conjunction. That does not mean that the South Node in such charts does not evolve: it does. But it evolves through the focus upon the house and sign of the Pluto/North Node conjunction. (Rad)

That's a very unique evolutionary signature. When you find Pluto conjunct the north node it means in all cases, that that Soul has been working in that area of evolutionary development prior to the current life and is meant to completely focus on that area in the context of the current life. There is no polarity. (JWG)

Pluto conjunct North Node – what about the South Node?

In any chart that you see Pluto conjunct the North Node symbol it means that there is no polarity point for Pluto because the intention of the Soul is to continue its evolutionary development as symbolized by the house and sign of the Pluto/North Node conjunction which has already been underway prior to the current life. And in any chart that one sees this will always mean, of course, that the opposite sign of that Pluto/North Node conjunction has already been developed to the point of limiting the Soul's evolution if it remains focused on that alone. If so, then the Soul arrives at a place of Plutonian stagnation and non-growth. So when the EA astrologer sees Pluto conjunct the North Node in any chart it means that the entire chart, the entire evolutionary intent, is be focused upon and through that house and sign of the Pluto/North Node conjunction. That does not mean that the South Node in such charts does not evolve: it does. But it evolves through the focus upon the house and sign of the Pluto/North Node conjunction. (Rad)

Pluto conjunct North Node – and planet(s) aspecting South Node
When Pluto conjuncts the North Node it does indicate that the Soul has worked towards actualizing the evolutionary intentions symbolized by the house and sign position of the Pluto and the North Node that the Soul is meant to continue in that direction in this life. That is why Pluto's polarity point does not apply in that case. In other words, the Soul is meant to keep going in the direction symbolized by Pluto conjunct the North Node (full actualization of the evolutionary intentions described by the Pluto/North Node conjunction). If there are other planets forming aspects to the South Node then those planets will describe areas of potential stagnation and blocks towards actualizing the Pluto/North Node evolutionary intentions. (Deva)

Pluto conjunct North Node – amount of distance between Pluto and North Node
[Example: Pluto 7.48 deg Leo, North Node 6.50 deg Leo] When Pluto and the North Node are in the same house there is no polarity point because with the South Node in the house of what would be its natural polarity point this means that that has already been in operation prior to the current life. So the entire intent is then in the house/signs of the Pluto and North Node. You can actually measure how relatively new or old that intent is by determining if Pluto is before or after the conjunction to that North Node. In a new phase conjunction it is relatively new, and that relative newness can be determined by the amount of distance, degrees, from that North Node. The same rule is true for when Pluto is after that North Node. (Rad)
[Example: Pluto 7.48 deg Leo, North Node 6.50 deg Leo] It is a new phase by one degree which would then mean that the evolutionary intent has just come to a head in this life. (Lia)
[Example: Pluto 7.48 deg Leo, North Node 6.50 deg Leo] According to my understanding of how to determine phase of planets relative to the Moon's Nodes, this would be a new phase conjunction. Wolf taught that because the mean motion of the Lunar Nodes is retrograde, the normal rules for determining phase are reversed. (Stacie)

North Node in the same sign as, but not conjunct, Pluto – is there a Pluto polarity point?
[Example: North Node 3 deg Scorpio, Pluto 27 deg Scorpio.]
There is a polarity point for Pluto in this case. (Rad)

North Node in the same sign as, but not conjunct, Pluto, and in a different house to Pluto – is there a Pluto polarity point?
[Example: North Node 3 deg Scorpio in the 3rd house, Pluto 27 deg Scorpio in the 4th house.]
There is a polarity point for Pluto in this case. (Rad)

Ruler of North Node conjunct Pluto – is there a Pluto polarity point?
When the ruler of the North Node is conjunct Pluto, there is a polarity point for Pluto in this case. (Rad)

South Node Leo, ruled by the Sun
The desires and intentions reflected in the South Node in Leo have been actualized in past lives via its planetary ruler, ie the Sun, by house and sign. (Rad)

Sun conjunct North Node
When any planet conjuncts the North Node the evolutionary intent symbolized by the North Node will become more conscious than it otherwise would be. If the conjunction would take place via any other planet we could safely say that particular lessons regarding the North Node have already been worked on prior to the current life. With the Sun, this isn't necessarily the case regarding past lives, as the Sun is the current life's integration point. But it definitely symbolizes the Soul's intention to rapidly move "forward" in evolutionary terms, ie moving forward to the future symbolized by the North Node, and this movement starts from birth onward. The life purpose is directly connected to all the lessons that the North Node symbolizes. In itself this does not affect interpreting Pluto and its polarity point nor does it affect interpreting the South Node. The Sun being on the North Node will emphasize the need of moving away from the South Node. (Lia)

Sun square Nodes, and planets conjunct the North Node
With the Sun square the Nodes there is indeed a flip flopping that can take place between the Sun as an integrative principle relative to the current life purpose, and those Nodes: back and forth. Both Nodes need to be fully actualized relative to the Sun in order for the dynamic of skipped steps to not take place in a future life. [Example: two planets conjunct North Node] This means that the Soul has, prior to the current life, already been moving in the evolutionary direction symbolized by the North Node, and the planets that are conjunct it. The location of its planetary ruler would also have come into play prior to the current life. The Sun squaring both Nodes means that this evolutionary process of moving towards that North Node is not complete because of the resistance symbolized by the South Node, and the location of its planetary ruler. It is that existing resistance carried over from the recent prior

lives that now correlates to the Sun squaring the Nodes. This then means that if that resistance prevails again in the context of the current life it will then lead to the dynamic of skipped steps in the very next life. When there is a planet(s) conjunct the North Node that means that that North Node, and the location of its planetary ruler, has been in the evolutionary process and development of the Soul prior to the current life, and is intended to do so again in this life. (Rad)

Sun square Nodes, and NO planets conjunct the North Node
Without any planets conjunct the North Node, and the Sun is simply squaring the Nodal Axis, then there have not been any prior development of that North Node prior to the current life. (Rad)

Sun square Nodes, and nodal ruler conjunct the Sun
If either the planetary ruler of the South or North Nodes is conjunct the Sun that is squaring the Nodes that, of itself, is a symbol of 'skipped steps' prior to the current life. With the Sun now conjunct such a planetary ruler, in the current life, this then correlates to the Soul's core purposes for the current life which is to resolve those skipped steps. (Rad)

Sun square Nodes, nodal ruler conjunct the Sun – orbs
(Q) In the case that the Planetary ruler that is conjunct the Sun, is out of orb of a square to the nodal axis, would it still correlate directly to a skipped step? (Skywalker)
(A) First, we must be careful in establishing the 'range or orbs' to answer this question correctly. JWG taught, for the purposes of evolutionary astrology, that ten degrees is the range for squares. So if the planetary ruler of one of the Nodes is out of that range we then have two possible evolutionary issues linked with the phenomena of 'skipped steps.' The first issue is if the planetary ruler is coming TOWARDS the square aspect, and the second is if it is moving AWAY from the square aspect. In the first case this would mean that the Soul is right on the cusp, the recent prior lives leading to the current life, of creating the skipped steps if the current life choices, as demonstrated by the Sun itself being square the Nodal Axis, do not resolve the past lives build up defined by resistance in the current life. In the context of the current life if the Soul resolves that resistance by way of the choices it makes then the skipped step signature for the very next life will not take place. The second issue in one wherein the Soul has been successfully resolving the skipped step signature prior to the current life. With the planetary ruler of one of the Nodes now moving AWAY from the square this would then mean, relative to the Sun's square to those Nodes, that there are some residual issues that need to be addressed in the current life. If not, then the Soul will recreate the signature of skipped steps in the very next life. (Rad)

Sun square Nodes, and North Node ruler conjunct the Sun
If the planetary ruler of the North Node has come into play prior to the current life, it seems to make sense that by being conjunct the Sun, there is a need to continue to integrate the North Node lessons that were begun prior to the current life, whole heartedly, by creatively actualizing and giving conscious purpose (Sun) to the North Node ruler, thus integrating and expressing/developing the archetype of the planetary ruler conjunct the Sun. This will then help overcome the resistance as symbolized by the Sun square the Nodes, the South Node and its planetary ruler. (Skywalker)

North Node – and next life's Sun
In terms of the next life Sun being the sign of the present life North Node, it was stated [by JWG] that is often the case, but not always. Why Sun as past life North Node sign? The North Node is the future of our Moon, our personality, our sense of self. The Sun symbolizes actualization. This life's North Node, the evolutionary *potentials*, the direction to move in to break the hold of the past, would find expression in the next life as Sun, the intent being to directly *actualize* (Sun) those potentials, as life purpose (Sun). Thus the intention to turn potential into reality. (Steve)

Ruler of South Node conjunct Pluto
In that symbolism it is important to determine if that conjunction is a new phase conjunction, or a balsamic conjunction. In both conjunctions the past life dynamics of the Soul as symbolized by the house and sign of the South Node, and the location of its planetary ruler by house and sign, which of course is the natal house of the current life Pluto which is conjunct that South Node ruler, is being brought to a head so that the Soul can evolve beyond those existing dynamics. In a balsamic conjunction it means that the Soul is re-living the past, in the current life, that is specific to those dynamics as symbolized by the house and sign of the South Node, and the house and sign of natal Pluto conjunct the South Node ruler. It is those dynamics only versus the whole of one's life that is being re-lived in the current life.
The intention of the Soul in such a symbol is to gain the deepest inner insights possible as to the nature of those dynamics, and why they exist as they exist. It is this self-knowledge gained in such a re-live that then serves as the basis of being released from those dynamics. When that occurs it will lead to the new phase conjunction of the South Node ruler with the natal Pluto. In the new phase conjunction the experience is very different. This means that the Soul will indeed recreate dynamics, reflected through its

circumstantial life, that are of its past. Yet as those circumstances manifest that do symbolize the past, the Soul in this new phase conjunction is now giving itself the evolutionary challenge to make NEW CHOICES as those past life dynamics are repeated. The new choices thus allows the Soul to be finally freed from those past life dynamics. The awareness of those new choices occurs because of the active reflection that took place during the balsamic conjunction when the South Node ruler was conjunct natal Pluto. (Rad)

Ruler of South Node conjunct ruler of North Node (which is Pluto itself)
[Limited information can be taken from these factors in isolation from the rest of the chart, but some basic guidelines are applicable.] This would then mean that the North Node is Scorpio, and the South Node is Taurus. With the South Node being in Taurus this will correlate to a Soul that has been living in a kind of cocoon in the past: the frog in the well syndrome. The frog sees the sky above, but is afraid to embrace it for it makes the frog feel insecure from all that it cannot control. It can control the space that it inhabits in the bottom of the well. The South Node correlates to elements of our past evolutionary and past life background. With the South Node in Taurus the Soul desires to stay in the bottom of the well in order to feel secure. Pluto itself also correlates to our evolutionary past, and the desires that correlate to those past life dynamics. The North Node in Scorpio correlates with the Soul's evolutionary need to jump out of that well in order to expose it to the entire horizon of reality. Pluto of course also correlates to our evolutionary need to evolve from our past. Thus, it's natural polarity point in the birth chart. With the South Node ruler conjunct Pluto and the North Node this will be symbolized by deep inner and outer confrontations to the Soul whose intentions, the nature of the confrontations, is to force the Soul to evolve because of the limitations that have blocked the Soul from evolving in its most recent past lifetimes. (Rad)

Ruler of South Node conjunct ruler of North Node, and both also conjunct South Node
[Limited information can be taken from these factors in isolation from the rest of the chart, but some basic guidelines are applicable.] In Pluto Vol. 2, p.30, Jeffrey states that when the ruler of the North Node is conjunct the South Node then the same karmic conditions as for Pluto conjunct the South Node apply. And that the Polarity Point for Pluto will not be actualised until all the evolutionary conditions associated with the house/sign of the South Node, its ruler house/sign and ruler's aspects to other planets are all fulfilled first. (Upasika)
The Soul is recreating dynamics from the past in the current life in such a way that the current life will be almost identical to the Soul's most recent prior life(s). This then means a Soul has felt completely unresolved about what the past life(s) has been and needs to relive it in order to evolve beyond it. The nature of the planet ruling that North Node, house and sign, correlates to, points the way, of how to resolve and move beyond that past. (Rad)

Ruler of South Node conjunct ruler of North Node
[Limited information can be taken from these factors in isolation from the rest of the chart, but some basic guidelines are applicable.] In this scenario it depends on the nature of the conjunction. If it is balsamic, the ruler of the South Node balsamic to the ruler of the North Node, the Soul will feel that it is being blocked or prevented from actualizing new directions for itself: its evolutionary needs to evolve that will be symbolized by the house and sign of the North Node planetary ruler. And that feeling will exist because the Soul has yet to fully culminate or resolve conditions of its most recent prior lives that are defined by the house and sign of the planetary ruler. And, that is, indeed, the evolutionary intention of the Soul: to culminate that which must be culminated by way of reliving those prior life conditions in the context of the current life so that it's evolution can proceed. It creates the typical feeling within the Soul that says, 'I have done this before and I feel stuck by it. I want out, I want to do this in a new way.' And yet there are evolutionary and karmic reasons why this condition exists which typically involve necessary understandings and realizations that can only occur because of the need to relive those conditions and the dynamics that have caused those conditions. If the conjunction is a new phase one then it means that the Soul has just fulfilled those evolutionary requirements to complete those conditions defined by dynamics from the Soul's past, and is now in a life in which it, the Soul, will bring forwards elements of it's past, the house and sign of the South Node and the location of its planetary ruler, which will be actualized or manifested in brand new or expanded ways. To the Soul this will feel new while at the same time feeling old: 'I have done this before, but in other ways.' The new ways will be symbolized by not only the house/sign of the conjunction of the ruler of both Nodes, and the aspects to it by other planets, by also via the house/sign of the North Node itself, and planetary aspects to it. (Rad)

Ruler of South Node conjunct ruler of North Node, new phase
(Q) Is there still a tendency to experience that new phase conjunction as a gateway to the South Node?
(A) Not at as a 'gateway' as such. Much more about the natural gravity point being the South Node upon which the ruler of the North Node, by way of its new phase conjunction to the ruler of that South Node, is trying to pull away from. This is like a rocket ship being prepared to blast off into space, and the rocket ship is still tethered to the mast that holds it, then the straps of that tether come loose and the rocket begins to go into space. (Rad)

(Q) Is effort to activate the North Node still required, just not the necessity to relive past dynamics? Perhaps there is just an awareness of what needs to happen because the Soul has already been working towards the North Node (in Pluto)?
(A) There is no actual need to 'relive' the past life dynamics when this conjunction between the South Node ruler and the North Node ruler is new phase. That would be true if the conjunction was balsamic and the evolutionary need to CULMINATE the past. The recent past is used, like the rocket ship analogy, to be launched AWAY from. As just like the rocket ship that takes incredible power, effort, to move away from the launch pad where the launch pad symbolizes the recent past, it does take conscious effort to move towards brand new directions that the Soul needs in order to continue to evolve. The past is like a gravity point that wants to assert itself because there is familiarity in it. And that familiarity correlates to existing security within the Soul because it's a known quantity. So as the rocket ship moves off the launch pad, the past that is therein symbolized will initially shape and guide the new developments, dynamics, and directions that the Soul is taking. The further away the rocket gets from the launch pad the less that the launch pad, the familiar past, will have any hold on the Soul at all. (Rad)

Ruler of South Node conjunct South Node
[Limited information can be taken from these factors in isolation from the rest of the chart, but some basic guidelines are applicable.] When the ruler of the South Node is conjunct the South Node then one of three evolutionary /karmic conditions apply: (1) the planet and the aspects that it makes to other planets are in a total relive of the past because it has not been resolved or dealt with, (2) a condition of fruition wherein the archetypes involved have been totally developed to the point that they correlate as a natural resource that is being brought forwards into the current life relative to the Soul's evolutionary intent for the life, or (3) a combination of both of these archetypes: elements of the past that have not been resolved, and elements that have. (Rad)

Ruler of North Node conjunct North Node
[Limited information can be taken from these factors in isolation from the rest of the chart, but some basic guidelines are applicable.] When the ruler of the North Node is conjunct the North Node this correlates to an archetype, the planet on the North Node, that the Soul has begun to actualize, develop, prior to the current life in order to act upon the overall evolutionary intentions through this archetype. In the current life this archetype will be used by the Soul as the primary vehicle to continue its ongoing evolutionary intentions that are symbolized by the entire EA paradigm and birth chart. (Rad)

Ruler of North Node conjunct South Node, and both conjunct Pluto
[Limited information can be taken from these factors in isolation from the rest of the chart, but some basic guidelines are applicable.] When Pluto is conjunct the South Node one of three conditions apply that Wolf wrote about in his first Pluto book: (1) a total relive of the past in which the Soul is locked into, (2) a condition of total fruition relative to the house and sign that Pluto/South Node is in that is intended be brought forwards into the current life as a natural resource, and (3) a combination of both. If the ruler of the North Node is in a balsamic conjunction to the Pluto then a condition of totally needing to relive the past in order to finally culminate it is at hand. When the ruler of the North Node is in a new phase to that Pluto then it correlates to a condition of fruition that the Soul in bringing forwards into the current life and expressed, actualized, in a new way relative to the overall evolutionary intentions for the current life. (Rad)

Ruler of North Node conjunct South Node
In the scenario wherein the North Node ruler is conjunct the South Node this correlates with the Soul's future evolution being dependent on resolving past life issues and dynamics that have been brought forwards into this life. This resolution occurs by way of the Soul making new choices relative to old dynamics and issues that have been brought forwards into the current life. The nature of those new choices is symbolized by the house and sign of the North Node itself whereas the issues and dynamics of the past that are not resolved are symbolized by the house and sign of the South Node, and the planetary ruler of that North Node. If those new choices are then made in this way then there is a resolution of the South Node in such a way that an evolution of the Soul is then effected by recreating those past life issues and dynamics and making those new choices to deal with them. (Rad)

Role of the North Node when a planet is conjunct South Node
[Example: Venus conjunct South Node] Regarding the generic example, I understand that the Venus conjunct South Node symbolizes a specific karmic requirement that needs to be addressed in the current life (either unresolved karmic dynamics around relationship that need to be relived and resolved, and/or a special gift that is meant to be offered). The North Node still symbolizes the evolving egocentric structure that, along with its planetary ruler, activates the Pluto polarity point. Only in cases when there are no aspects to the North Node is the Soul required to FIRST work out the South Node (and the planets on the South Node) before the North Node and the Pluto polarity point can be developed. Jeff Green has taught that in such a case, the unresolved karma of the South Node and the planets on the South Node will only be released by the time of the second Saturn return. And even that is a matter of what kind of choices the Soul makes, ie it's not promised. The preliminary work has to be done first.

[Example: South Node and Venus 7th house, North Node 1st house] The 1st house kind of ego may be in process of being developed, thus evolution (Pluto polarity point) would in fact be activated to some extent. AND at the same time, that Venus/South Node symbolizes a karmic requirement that needs to be addressed as a part of the current life evolutionary requirement. However it's not a "South Node first, North Node second" kind of dynamic, unless of course there are no aspects to the North Node, as stated above. In the end, the South Node/planet on the South Node requirements are there to be worked out, so in the final analysis evolution will of course be *limited* if that is yet unresolved since the Soul's capacity to develop the North Node will be *limited* by the weight of the past. This will carry over in some way to the next life. (Ari)

[Example: Venus conjunct South Node] In essence with Venus on the South Node the fact of the Soul repeating all those Venus dynamics are true yet the North Node is that which is giving the opportunity of the Soul to make new choices relative to those existing and repeating dynamics. Thus, to make those correct choices that frees the Soul from the past is symbolized by the house, sign of the North Node, and the location of its planetary ruler by house, sign, and the aspects to it. This of course does not happen automatically. It requires conscious, deliberate, choice making. (Rad)

Nodal rulers in any non-conjunction aspect to each other

The specific nature of the aspect will correlate to how the Soul's past and future interact in each moment in order for the Soul's evolutionary intentions in total to be actualized. (Rad)

(Q) Would the phasal relationship between the nodal rulers be as significant for the non-conjunction as for the conjunction?

(A) No, it is not as significant. The archetype of whatever the phase is will correlate to how and why the interaction of the past and future, as experienced in each moment of the Soul's life will manifest. (Rad)

MATRIARCHY AND PATRIARCHY

Transition from matriarchy to patriarchy

The transition began right at the end of the Capricorn sub-age of the Cancer Age right around 6600 BCE. It took generally about 1,000 years for the full transition to take place. However, in various areas in the world there remained groups of people that sustained the matriarchy coming up to very recent times. For example there was a small matriarchal group of Sioux Indians, a 'splinter' group that lived in this natural way. There were also a group of archetypal women called Amazons that lived in various places on the globe for thousands of years after this transition began. And there are other examples of this also. But, in general, the patriarchal transition did take hold, in mass, all over the world from that transition forwards to now. There is of course no one 'chart' that correlates to this transition. When one studies history, ie 'HISstory,' the story of the patriarchy, one can discover how this transition took hold in different areas of the world, different cultures at different times. A great book that deals with this is called The Once and Future Goddess. And there are others of course. (Rad)

According to actual his/herstory itself the transition for the Natural Times that is called the matriarchy to what is called the patriarchy began at the very end of the Capricorn Sub-Age which was then ruled by Sagittarius: the change from Natural Laws that did not require 'beliefs' at all, to man-concocted beliefs that progressively turned the Natural Laws emanating from the Creator upside down, and inside out. There was no prior 'imbalance' that dictated that what we call the patriarchy to evolve at that time, until now. The primary cause, again, despite how odd it may seem now, is when men realized that they had an equal role in making babies with women. And this then lead to what it has led to, including the original formations of nuclear families where women were regarded as possessions of the men. The actual transition took about 1,000 years. And the his/herstory of those 1,000 years is incredible when remembered, or read about when stripped of the patriarchal rewriting of that time. It is that time frame that the origins of the 'sacred prostitute' began by the way. And remember that 'role' for 'women' was created by men, not women. The issue here is one of choice making, the Natural Law of free choice. So when men realized they had an equal role in making babies it is the choices they made then that has led to what it has led to from that time forwards. (Rad)

The transition from matriarchy to patriarchy was set in motion during the descending arc of the Treta Yuga. Note that the 1st Sandhi for Treta Yuga was from 6400–6700 BC.

Arcs within the Yugas		
Descending arc of Treta Yuga	6700 – 3100 BC	Yang
Descending arc of Dwarpara Yuga	3100 – 700 BC	Yang
Descending arc of Kali Yuga	700 – 500 AD	Yang
Ascending arc of Kali Yuga	500 – 1700 AD	Yin
Ascending arc of Dwarpara Yuga	1700 – 4100 AD	Yin

So we are now in the ascending arc of Dwarpara Yuga, and therefore it's up from here. And just to further clarify on the descending/ascending arcs within the cycle of yugas: the nature of the descending arc is YANG. The nature of the ascending arc is YIN. Also, each yuga correlates to a specific kind of spiritual knowledge, and that type of knowledge is reflected in the nature of each yuga's age. This is covered by Sri Yukteswar in The Holy Science. And by the way the spiritual knowledge correlating to the Treta Yuga = Divine magnetism. The Dwarpara Yuga correlates (in Sri Yukteswar's words) to "the knowledge of electricities and their attributes." (Stacie)

The word 'matriarchy' is really a symbol for how humans have lived on this planet for the vast majority of its her/history. Meaning living in accordance with Natural Laws, including the Natural Laws that correlate with the masculine and feminine principles as created by the Creator. Humans continued to live in accordance with Natural Laws right up and through the entire Cancer Age, and its sub-age Capricorn. Human life forms have been on the planet now for three to four million years: the beginning of them. And have evolved until this point in time, and are still evolving. So the vast majority of its her/history has lived in accordance with these Natural Laws. The last 8,000 years is very small compared to that vast amount of time. And yet look what has happened in that short amount of time once the violations to those Natural Laws began. It is at the very end of the Capricorn sub-age of the Cancer Age that this violation began. And that violation began as these Natural Laws and principles between the masculine and feminine laws happened, the natural relationship of men and women in every way, which, in turn, caused the Natural Laws of giving, sharing, and inclusion to also be violated. The choices that humans made at that time were not 'fated' or preordained in any way. Those choices occurred because of the Natural Law of free choice that was set in motion by the Creator Itself. Thus, humans are responsible for those choices, and the consequences to those choices. The reality that we on this planet are now living speaks for itself in terms of those consequences.

Since Cancer and Capricorn correlate astrologically to gender assignment, the Natural Laws of female and male, and the transition began at the Capricorn sub-age of the Cancer Age, the correlations to these signs to what we want to call the matriarchy and the patriarchy has occurred. Aquarius does not have a specific correlation to the 'matriarchal' or 'patriarchal' time at all. I am not sure where this correlation comes from, or even who made it. Whatever, it just does not apply. Aquarius, in this context, correlates to how people group themselves together, and the reasons for those groupings. Simple example: in Natural times, Natural Laws, people do not naturally group themselves according to caste, state, or any artificial hierarchy at all. Thus, there is no conception of inferior, or superior. All people in a group, living naturally, simply have natural functions on behalf of that group that are EQUAL within themselves. Once Natural Laws are violated, for the reasons that they were, then we have this perversion of those Natural Laws that then lead to that which is not natural. The transit of Pluto now in Capricorn, the Nodal axis of the Moon in Cancer/Capricorn, this is a time in which humans are being taught the responsibilities, and consequences, for all the choices that have been made prior to this time that have led to this time. And, within that, the consequences that will occur as we project from this time into the future, based on the choices that have been made from the past, and how those choices from the past continue to be made in the moment. (Rad)

Zarathustras

So then we have castes, classes of people, who is better or worse, artificial hierarchies, that lead to the perversion within some humans that we can call Zarathustras, and all the rest of what has occurred ever since this transition from natural times, 'matriarchy,' to what is in place now called the 'patriarchy' in which almost all the Natural Laws have been perverted, turned upside down. (Rad)

Planetary Nodes Capricorn/Cancer

The correlation to the Planetary Nodes in Capricorn/Cancer and the transition to the patriarchy from the matriarchy, is based on the Astrological Ages and their sub-ages. Thus the transition beginning at the very end of the Capricorn sub-age of the Cancer age. Thus the South Nodes of Pluto, Saturn, and Jupiter [currently] in the sign Capricorn. Because of the natural progression of the Astrological Ages through time. Thus, the alignment of the Capricorn sub-age within the Age of Cancer. That time frame, the actual his/herstory of the planet, correlates to that transition time between the matriarchy to the patriarchy. Cancer and Capricorn of course correlate to the male and female gender, and gender assignment issues within that. This is no different than, for example, Jesus who had Pluto in Virgo with his polarity point being Pisces. And he of course said he was here to usher in a New Age, the Pisces Age. (Rad)

Patriarchy, and evolutionary states

The patriarchal shift plays out for all Souls, in all evolutionary states, in the form of the incredible imbalance of the human life form on our planet relative to all other life forms: the totality of Nature. (Rad)

Modern culture vs indigenous culture

Capricorn/Saturn does not have to be a negative manifestation. That it is negative, and has been for quite a while now, is a result of human consciousness being relatively less open to Source – if I am understanding the Yugas, or cosmic cycles properly. In other Ages where human consciousness was relatively open to Spirit the consensus would be vastly different. I am thinking of this because of the Lakota consensus vs modern consensus child example – or I should say a kid in a store. The Lakota child would be consensus and adopting the prevailing social norms, beliefs, etc. without much thought. However, with room to evolve naturally and the social structure being in tune with Natural Law, would be a rather different situation than the child growing up in a high-chair in front of a movie they watch ten times a day, etc. I guess it's clear that if humans are to survive and the earth is to be healed consensus society needs to have Natural Law as its structure – seems a long way off though. I would add that in Natural Law, first there is natural 'democracy' and that spiritual elders are the leaders, not power-hungry, greedy know-nothings.

It's interesting to observe the different trajectories of European culture vs what we call indigenous or 'native.' Quote from 'Native American Healing' by Howard P. Bad Hand: "We have to know capability, ability, and how far we can stretch things, but we must also know how to define and discriminate the difference between good and evil. In the world, this is the backbone of people's behavior. The rules of conduct, the rules of behavior, morality. When you look out in the world, when you look at a tree, and you see its beauty, and you see its perfection as a living entity, when you wake up one day and realize that the beauty and perfection of that tree came about because of the boundaries that define what it is, you'll realize that life is not meant to be a path of unlimited possibilities. Unlimited possibilities for human kind would make human kind dissolve into the boundless. We attain free spirit when we surround ourselves with these boundaries, and by these boundaries, we determine for ourselves what our duty is. This leads to the proper relationship between you and the Spirit world, between you and the service you provide, and it allows people to know what to ask of you because your conduct, your behavior, will show them." (Lucius)

Matriarchal groups in recent times
In various areas in the world there remain groups of people that sustained the matriarchy coming up to very recent times. For example there was a small matriarchal group of Sioux Indians, a 'splinter' group that lived in this natural way. There were also a group of archetypal women called Amazons that lived in various places on the globe for thousands of years after this transition began. And there are other examples of this also. (Rad)

Natural Law, and the Sagittarius/Capricorn archetypes
The Sagittarius archetype correlates with the need to become aware of our connection to the universe in a metaphysical/cosmological context. This underlying need gives rise to the nature of all sorts of belief systems (and also religions) that attempt to explain our connection to the universe. This is where the issue of interpretation comes into play (our belief system is the determinate to how any of us will interpret life itself). The point within this is that, by the sheer fact that Creation exists, there must be intrinsic Natural Laws that govern and explain the nature of Creation (Natural Laws that are self-evident in nature). These Natural Laws, of course, have nothing to do with man-made religions and the laws that are taught in such religions. The intent within the Sagittarius archetype is to align with Natural Law in order to evolve and grow past limited beliefs that are based on man-made laws (the Sagittarius archetype also symbolizes growth and expansion). This is why the Sagittarius archetype correlates with Natural Law.

The Capricorn archetype, then, symbolizes how those beliefs will become crystallized, or given a structure to operate through. In other words, we feel the consequences, or effects, of our beliefs through the Capricorn archetype. Like my father so often taught, we do not need any religion to tell us it is wrong to put a baby on the freeway, we naturally know it is wrong to do so. In the archetype of Capricorn, then, we have the issue of judgments and also conditioned verses natural guilt. Man-made laws, in general, manifest distorted justifications for actions that inherently violate Natural Laws (there are both subtle and extreme forms of this), but on an inner level we all feel what is inherently right and wrong. In the Capricorn archetype we internalize the standard of behavior that is deemed "right and wrong" and we form judgments of ourselves and others accordingly. Again, this is based on the belief system we have formed/aligned with in the Sagittarius archetype. This describes, in a general sense, the interaction of the Sagittarius and Capricorn archetypes. (Deva)

From the point of view of Natural Law, we can say: In Sagittarius our core beliefs are the determinant for how we interpret life in the first place. If our beliefs are contrary to Natural Law, then we will interpret life according to the distortion of our beliefs. Based on those core beliefs and consequential interpretation of life, we establish and act upon various ethics and standards and rules that crystallize those beliefs into a social construct. If our beliefs (Sagittarius) are a distortion of Natural Law, then our behavior and the way we set up our lives (Capricorn) based on those beliefs will also reflect that distortion. (Ari)

What does undistorted Capricorn look like?
It looks like the natural structure of all Natural Laws inwardly realized, and applied. It looks like all humans living and being defined by those Natural Laws in terms of the reality that they live. This includes the natural roles between women and men. It includes natural parenting. It includes the vital principle of sharing, giving, and inclusion. It includes all knowledge being inwardly realized, versus having to 'believe' anything. It includes living in a STATE OF BALANCE WITHIN ALL OF CREATION AS MANIFESTED ON THIS EARTH: TO NOT DOMINATE OR CONTROL ANYTHING. (Rad)

Those people who were manifesting the natural Capricorn values within patriarchy (either as a person or as a group of people) have been most scapegoated, judged, oppressed and crashed. (Lia)

Extinction of the human race
To me the human race has made choices, and will continue to make choices, until it is too late, that will lead to its extinction. And the root of that cause, to me, is the utter delusion of self-interest equaling exclusion versus the Natural Laws of giving, sharing, and inclusion. This was, indeed, the cause of the patriarchy in the first place when men realized that they had an equal role in making babies with women. And what that then set in motion, which prevails to this day. Of course I hope I am completely wrong in my judgment that all will now lead to the extinction of the human species. Yet, it is what I feel in my bones. (Rad)

Biological parents
(Q) This is a question about the relevance of knowledge/information about the biological father. During natural times, before the patriarchal family existed, in the vast majority of cases who the biological father was of any born child was irrelevant. Even, most

men didn't know they contributed to children being born. And this was not relevant because parenting was communal. Patriarchy implied a big change in this, in that the nuclear family, biological fatherhood, virginity of the bride and monogamy of the woman became the basis of social structure. This implied many changes within relationships, like the meaning of commitment and the meaning of honesty, in relation with expectations of monogamy when they exist.

When the biological father is other than the 'apparent' father, ie the woman's couple, the woman's concealment of this fact would be reflected in the Yod pattern existing between Gemini (information, duplicity), Scorpio (genes, sex, secret) and Capricorn (family structure, patriarchy, society). This implies the potential for a crisis in the structure of the family. Some psychoanalysts speak of an instability generated within the psychic structure that has the potential to derive in psychosis. They say this instability, and potential psychosis, would exist either for the woman or for the next generation or two. My feeling is this type of consequence can exist in some cases, but not always.

The Yod between Gemini and Scorpio/Capricorn implies the potential for manipulations around the 'secret,' ie the Soul building protecting structures to prevent this critical piece of information to be known, by means of exclusions, further lies, or other means. Also, in most cases the dishonesty with the husband will create a fracture in the relationship, which will prevent true intimacy. These two dynamics can create some type of instability for the children. Beyond this, I don't feel there are any necessary consequences implied in such concealment, other than the karmic consequences for the mother. Is this correct? (Gonzalo)

(A) Yes. (Rad)

Patriarchal standard of God-perfection

Every one of us has places we don't want to see or look at, feel like we are farther along than we really are, etc. These are universal human conditions. Wolf would say since all things originate from God, what does this say about the actual nature of God, when all people have these same traits. His answer is it points to the inherent imperfection in God itself. And we judge ourselves using a patriarchal standard of God-perfection which no human anywhere throughout time has ever lived up to. Thus the need to be very kind to ourselves, to recognize how difficult it is to walk this path. And to recommit to it again and again, no matter how many times we stray or fall down. To pick self back up and get back on the pathway, that is the way. In the end, however long it takes, mastery over self is assured. It's just that it takes a long time – that has to be accepted. (Steve)

Patriarchal self-judgment

The natural principle of life is diversity – same source, myriad of outer forms. This is why EA talks a lot about Natural Law. In patriarchy, things are judged as good or bad relative to human-created standards of what is right and wrong and how things should be. That is the opposite of accepting diversity as it was created. Over lifetimes of rejection for being the way they are, Souls become wounded and come to have distorted self-images of who and what they are. Thus they come to internalize deep self-judgments based on internalizing experiences they've had within the patriarchal realities. They come to believe the distortions they have been subjected to are in fact real. Thus they hide away "unacceptable" parts of who they are, and adopt personas that try to conform to society's expectations of proper behavior, pretending (even to self) to be what they are not. That, right there, is the root of our individual issues. The way out is the path back to accepting self the way one was created by God, regardless of what anyone thinks about it. (It's a path that requires a lot of courage.) (Steve)

NATURAL LAW

Leadership within Natural Law

Aligned with Natural Law, there will simply be in most circumstances a natural leader for that circumstance, the person who is the "right one" to lead the way for that circumstance. They will not get attached to that role. In the next circumstance someone else may be the natural leader. Everyone involved would recognize and honor this natural principle. Those who were the more consistent "leaders" or elders or however they would be looked at, would have that position because they deserved it, due to their dedication to doing the right thing, their natural wisdom, the result of their level of evolution and their past with the same group of Souls. The basis of that leadership would be SERVICE, what I give back to the group, not the perks, privileges, benefits I get from being a leader. From what I have read, in the old days among the native people, if there was not enough food to go around, the chief did not eat. Everything was shared. There was not an entitled class who deserved more because of their leadership positions. These are what I would call natural hierarchies. They are self-evident, meaning it is clear why various people are in various roles – they have earned the right to be there, not bought or stolen or bribed their way into those positions. (Steve)

Natural Law of giving, sharing and inclusion

One thing I suggest reading is chapter 3 in Pluto Vol. 2, Social, Cultural, Parental, and Religious Imprinting. Think of the experiences – festivals, gatherings, workshops, etc. – you have attended, where people naturally cooperate and help each other rather than compete. (I used to go to events like that and wonder what would happen if everyone simply refused to go home – and started living that way all the time.) These are experiences in current times of Natural Law in action. Natural times were not utopian. Life was often hard. Food could be scarce. A tiger could eat your baby or your animals. Lightning could strike your hut. People lived in closer awareness of their dependency on nature for survival. That created a natural humility, and a sense of banding together as necessary for survival. We all lived through such times, and those memories are still within us. Some of it is finding the memories within, and paying attention to how they feel.

An important point is, Natural Law is Natural – we don't really have to learn how to live that way – it's the way we are actually wired, if only we stop listening to the distorted inner voices we've learned to let override how we naturally feel. Practicing listening to, and following, intuition is really important too. As is the work you are doing at getting to the root of the distorted patterns so you can begin releasing them. And remember, it took a long time to create the distorted patterns. The path back from distorted to natural can take less time than the path from natural to distorted, because it IS natural. But it does take time, because we have learned the distorted patterns very well. Practicing kindness and patience with self on the slow but steady journey back to natural is also really valuable. (Steve)

Knowledge vs belief

The operative word is BELIEFS. People can conjure up anything and make themselves believe it. Once they do that then the nature of whatever those 'beliefs' are become the determinant of how they interpret the nature of actual (natural) reality. They become the basis of what they come to value, and what they come to value then becomes the basis of the MEANING for their lives. In combination this then becomes the causative factor in judgments: internal and external. This is very important for all of us to understand for in NATURAL LAWS, the actual laws that have been set in motion by what we call God'ess, does not require BELIEFS whatsoever. It does require knowledge, TO KNOW, what has actually been created by what we call God'ess. To know is very different than believing anything. When Jesus said, for example, 'When thy eye is single one's whole body is full of light.' This does not require believing that. This natural truth or law can indeed be experienced within oneself by simply shallowing and suspending the breath. At that point the Soul KNOWS this truth. It does not believe it, because it knows it. (Rad)

Deviation – distortion – violation – perversion of Natural Law

Natural Law as set in motion by the Creator contains within it the possibility of 'deviation.' Thus, deviation from Natural Law is part of Natural Law. Natural Law as contained within manifested creation when it was set in motion was imperfect, and hence, Natural Law also needed to be changed (Sagittarius) by the Creator, as a consequence of the Creator's evolution. And that's because the nature of the Creator, as Wolf taught in his lifetime, is in fact not perfect. The very origin of 'imperfection' is the Origin of Creation Itself. (Rad)

As the patriarchy began, and has increased, there has been a progressive violation of all Natural Laws, the consequences of which all humans are being subjected to. As Wolf taught for so long, the term 'matriarchy' is really a word that symbolizes the vast majority of human her/history in which the human life form was living in accordance with all Natural Laws, and every other life form was. Thus, a state of balance on this Earth. And that, included, of course the Natural Laws of the masculine and feminine principles, laws, created by the Creator. The patriarchy is a word that thus symbolizes a progressive violation of these Natural Laws, and the consequences to that fact. The core Natural Law that has been violated in the Natural Law of 'giving, sharing, and inclusion' to 'self-interest' and 'exclusion.' That core violation has led to the totality of what we all are experiencing now. (Rad)

[The Oil gush/spill] Events like this are not necessarily God's will. That perspective is too commonly used to excuse things that are flat out wrong, to avoid staring into the face of the consequences of human choices, behaviors. God gave us free will within certain ranges, to either align ourselves with Divine intent or to override and deny Divine intent and act in our selfish little ways (by "our" I mean by humans collectively). Just because something is within the realm of possibility does not mean people acting that out are actualizing God's will. Like the president of Goldman Sachs, a firm that has brought much of the world to its financial knees, who was quoted as saying that Goldman Sachs was doing God's work. Don't forget, God is the origin of the possibility of evil also. In that sense doing what is inherently wrong can be part of God's will, but is that really the part of God, the lower negative selfish possibilities, that you want to align yourself with, or make excuses for other humans and organizations who do that? "Violation of Natural Law" means acting in a way that puts self or self-interest or the interests of a few ahead of the greater interests of the whole, human and planet-wide. We don't HAVE to keep making the same sort of limited selfish stupid choices that inevitably wind up in wide scale loss and pain to all sorts of little people who never benefited from the vast fortunes made by the few in the first place (like oil companies). (Steve)

In Natural Law Saturn, Capricorn, and the 10th house all correlate to the total structure of Natural Laws as manifesting in the time/space reality that we call Earth. On the other hand, they also correlate to the total perversion of those Natural Laws where those perversions have been caused by men through time. And, thus, what we call the patriarchy. So ever since the patriarchy began to emerge way back in the past this progressive perversion has in fact defined the vast majority, the Consensus evolutionary stage, right up until this moment in time. (Rad)

The essence of patriarchal distortion is that we have come to accept as normal what in fact is quite distorted. To the point that most people, when presented with what is actually natural, find it odd, primitive, strange, uncomfortable, not normal-feeling. Because next to nothing in modern life is natural. Natural is giving, sharing, inclusion, cooperation. Distortion is self-interest, domination/submission, hierarchy, superiority/inferiority, etc. (Steve)

Forces of evil

I don't feel what is playing out by way of the patriarchal extreme is due to another time of inequity from another time. And that's because there never was another time of inequity linked with the natural feminine principle: women. Previous to the time of the patriarchal transition the gender definitions of male and female were in fact NATURAL: natural feminine and natural masculine as reflected in their natural roles in every way. This perversion that the men/patriarchy has created leading to the utter imbalance that it has is due, to me, by the forces of evil. When we remember that evil, Lucifer, can only be sustained as long as delusions are in place within humans then we can see how evil manifests within humans in this way: the total dominance of one gender over another. How many folks realize, for example, that of all the property that is 'owned' in the world today that only one percent or less is 'owned' by women? And, to me, I do not ever see a time in the future in which this will change, to come back to a state of natural balance as defined by Natural Laws. (Rad)

Extinction of the human race

To me the human race has made choices, and will continue to make choices, until it is too late, that will lead to its extinction. And the root of that cause, to me, is the utter delusion of self-interest equaling exclusion versus the Natural Laws of giving, sharing, and inclusion. This was, indeed, the cause of the patriarchy in the first place when men realized that they had an equal role in making babies with women. And what that then set in motion, which prevails to this day. Of course I hope I am completely wrong in my judgment that all will now lead to the extinction of the human species. Yet, it is what I feel in my bones. (Rad)

Biological parents

(Q) This is a question about the relevance of knowledge/information about the biological father. During natural times, before the patriarchal family existed, in the vast majority of cases who the biological father was of any born child was irrelevant. Even, most men didn't know they contributed to children being born. And this was not relevant because parenting was communal. Patriarchy implied a big change in this, in that the nuclear family, biological fatherhood, virginity of the bride and monogamy of the woman became the basis of social structure. This implied many changes within relationships, like the meaning of commitment and the meaning of honesty, in relation with expectations of monogamy when they exist.

When the biological father is other than the 'apparent' father, ie the woman's couple, the woman's concealment of this fact would be reflected in the Yod pattern existing between Gemini (information, duplicity), Scorpio (genes, sex, secret) and Capricorn (family structure, patriarchy, society). This implies the potential for a crisis in the structure of the family. Some psychoanalysts speak of an instability generated within the psychic structure that has the potential to derive in psychosis. They say this instability, and potential psychosis, would exist either for the woman or for the next generation or two. My feeling is this type of consequence can exist in some cases, but not always.

The Yod between Gemini and Scorpio/Capricorn implies the potential for manipulations around the 'secret,' ie the Soul building protecting structures to prevent this critical piece of information to be known, by means of exclusions, further lies, or other means. Also, in most cases the dishonesty with the husband will create a fracture in the relationship, which will prevent true intimacy. These two dynamics can create some type of instability for the children. Beyond this, I don't feel there are any necessary consequences implied in such concealment, other than the karmic consequences for the mother. Is this correct? (Gonzalo)

(A) Yes. (Rad)

Natural Law of evolution of consciousness

The totality of Consciousness correlates with Neptune/Pisces, and the 12th house. And within that totality of Consciousness lies its total potential: of what can be realized. Virgo of course is the natural polarity of Pisces. That correlates, archetypically, to LACK where lack is in reference to the total potential that has yet to be realized. Immutable consciousness simply means energy, as Jeffrey pointed out, and that energy cannot be destroyed: it can only change form. It is inherently full of potential to be realized which is the causative factor for the evolution of the Soul: consciousness. Until that full potential of consciousness is realized the Soul necessarily experiences LACK because LACK infers or reflects THE DESIRE FOR MORE than we currently have. The desire for more infers DISSATISFACTION which is the evolutionary determinant for that which will correlate to total SATISFACTION. Total satisfaction correlates with the desire to return to the SOURCE of consciousness and/or the Soul which is held as potential within the Soul and the consciousness within it. Thus, the sense of lack IS ESSENTIAL FOR IT PROMOTES THE ONGOING EVOLUTION OF THE SOUL IN ORDER TO REALIZE IT'S TOTAL POTENTIAL WHICH, IN THE END, IS TO CONSCIOUSLY UNITE ITSELF WITH ITS SOURCE: GOD/ESS. (Rad)

Natural Law and command of the Natural Goddess

A natural emotion specific to Neptune, etc., is one of empathy where empathy allows us to truly understand the emotional realities and needs of others. And within this emotion the DESIRE to help others in the ways that we naturally can without any other motive or agenda attached to it: to give to others what they actually need in the best ways that we can. This then allows the Soul to evolve because it is one of the Natural Laws and 'commands' of the natural Goddess to do so. The deepest degree of this Natural Law and the emotion of it is to ALWAYS PUT OTHERS FIRST no matter what the consequences may be to oneself: think of Jesus here for example of an ultimate manifestation of this. (Rad)

Natural Law of the trinity

The Natural Law of the trinity does apply to E(A) Very simply when one combines with another one we have three. A simple example would be sperm and ovum. When they combine they produce a brand new organism. And of course the number three is the root number for all advanced math. It is in the union, combining, of the singular one's that then produces three. Union thus becomes the causative factor, or determinant, of evolution itself: genetic evolution through the RNA and DNA of all living organisms. Through this Natural Law we then can see, via the EA paradigm, and existing state of evolution as symbolized in the natal position of Pluto, its polarity point that is then united with, which in turn allows for an evolution of the existing state of evolution relative to the natal position of that Pluto. Same thing as applied to the existing South Node of the Moon, its North Node, that thus evolves the South Node itself. (Rad)

The natural evolutionary progression always involves the Natural Law of the trinity. The natal position of, for example, Pluto operates from birth relative to how the Soul comes into the current life from where it has been: there is a natural polarity point to this that symbolizes the core evolutionary intent. As the Soul moves, evolves, towards that intent it then simultaneously EVOLVES the orientation of the natal position of Pluto itself. Thus, the Natural Law of the trinity. We must remember that any house or sign is an entire archetype: a full spectrum within itself. As evolution proceeds within any archetype the various orientations within that spectrum are embraced as a result. (Rad)

Natural Law of involution

God will continue in its own journey to its own perfection. In this beyond long journey what we call God expands and contracts over lengths of time that we cannot even imagine. This natural expansion and contraction corresponds with the collapse of the entire Creation which leads to yet another expansion manifesting as a new form of Creation. Thus the cycles of creation/evolution occur in this natural way. When the cycle of contraction occurs this is called the Natural Law of involution where all existing forms born in the expansion cycle are destroyed, and then reformulated energetically in yet another cycle of expansion and the forms of how creation looks like in each one. (Rad)

Natural Laws of light, gravity, motion, magnetism, vibration, and heat

Intrinsic to Creation is CONSCIOUSNESS because of course what we call God is CONSCIOUS. The dimensions of each Creation called, in our terms, the Cosmos and Universes are so vast that we simply cannot comprehend from the limitation of the consciousness contained within the human form. And within that vastness all of the Natural Laws that God has SET IN MOTION in each cycle of Creation manifest in all kinds of different ways depending on Light, Gravity, Motion, Magnetism, Vibration, and Heat. Depending on CONDITIONS defined by these Natural Laws as they interact within themselves as found at various points throughout the vastness of the totality of the Creation Consciousness can take hold and root itself. This we call life. (Rad)

Natural Law of free choice

All things, phenomena, have been set in motion by the Creator including the possibility of 'excess of will.' And that is due to the Natural Law of 'free choice' that the Creator is responsible for Creating in the first place. (Rad)

The choices that humans have made, which has led to NOW, the reality of NOW, are that which is responsible for what the reality is that we are all living in NOW. The effect of the collective choices upon all individuals within that collective, even when certain percentages of humans have rebelled or disagreed with the vast majority of other humans who have made those choices. This has nothing to do with whether we are 'here' or 'not here.' It has everything to do with what the nature of 'here' is, now at this point in time. I am not saying it is 'negative' to be here at all. God/ess is the origin of all things, and is thus responsible for that fact. The fact of Creation, of creating anything, including the Natural Law of free choice. That law exists within all forms of the Creation, and those choices start with the evolutionary imperative to survive. It is because the human life form began to make choices 8,000 years ago now that started to violate all the Natural Laws, through the vehicle of free choice, that the survival of the species itself is now in question when projected into the future, based on the choices that have led to now: the past leading to the present. If humans had continued to make choices that we all in accordance with all the Natural Laws up until this moment in time then the very nature of the reality that we are all living now would be utterly different. And that difference would start with the human life form still being in a state of balance with the totality of the Creation, with the totality of all other living things on this planet. Humans would still be living a reality whose bottom line choices would revolve around 'giving, sharing, and inclusion.' Imagine – just imagine if that were true. (Rad)

Natural Law of separation

The natural desire to separate was put in motion by the Creator itself. That's why it is natural. The intention within this as designed by the Creator was for all aspects of the Creation that had conscious awareness to realize, consciously realize, that in their APPARENT separateness that defined their sense of individuality, that their origins, where they came from, what their essence was/is, is the Creator itself. Within this core awareness is the awareness that all of the manifested Creation is thus interrelated and interdependent. All is part of the whole. It is a Natural Law. When humans lived in this way for the balance of its history until recent times, they were thus living in a reality that was defined by 'giving, sharing, and inclusion' which equaled their need for survival as individuals, and as groups of people. When this natural desire of separateness became perverted this Natural Law of giving, sharing, and inclusion changed to self-interest, and exclusion. Step back for a moment and imagine realities created by humans that were defined by the Natural Law of giving, sharing, and inclusion versus the realities that have been created by self-interest and exclusion. The stark relief created in this comparison should speak for itself.

A simple example: American Indians hunting for buffalo. Once the buffalo was killed the Indian would pray for the buffalo and thank it for providing food for the tribe in the understanding of how the WHOLE was interrelated, and how each part of that whole was dependent for survival on that whole. Now compare this to the White man, under the delusion of Manifest Destiny which itself manifested from their MAN-CREATED, not God-created, version of Christianity. And how the White man almost brought to extinction the entire buffalo species in its greed defined by self-interest and exclusion, ie the White man in its delusive self-importance and superiority to all that was NOT HIM having zero awareness of the WHOLE. Thus all other aspects of the Creation were to serve its own self-interest defined by others who threatened that self-interest. When the buffalo was killed it was left to rot on the ground that it was killed after its hide had been removed. This simple example of the perversion of the natural desire to separate could be exampled in literally thousands of ways. And it is because it can, the actual reality that has been created leading right up to the present moment, that humans have guaranteed their extinction. The Creator is also the origin of course of free choice. And it is through choice making that all of us are responsible for what we create. (Rad)

Natural Law of elimination

The integration point between the dual nature of desires within all of our Souls is elimination. Eliminating, in the end, all separating desires to the exclusion of the only desire that can remain, and that desire of course is to reunite with that which is the Cause of Creation. The means for evolution to take place is based on this Natural Law of elimination within the Soul as reflected progressively in the egos that it creates from life to life. (Rad)

Natural Law of love

In the totality of creation, there are natural structures set in place by the creator. An example of this would be the spiritual reality of angels, devas, nature spirits, etc. Also all the various saints and spiritual guides that serve a unique function and role in creation, and this includes the natural wisdom of any Soul who has lived a full life in alignment with Natural Law. One thing that Capricorn teaches is the appropriateness of time and space. Different "rules" operate at different size scales. The only law that does not change is the Law of Love. Love is the guiding motivation of creation itself. I feel in essence, the Capricorn archetype reveals how we are meant to appropriately structure our existence in alignment with Natural Law, which is an expression of Love, as human beings here on earth. (Ari)

Natural Law of guilt

Natural guilt (no different than putting a baby on the autobahn) is just naturally wrong. And that creates the natural guilt as a result. Yet, unless that natural guilt is 'owned' or internalized the appropriate, natural, adjustment cannot be made. So these folks have a natural reaction or response that reflects this natural guilt yet, at the same time, DENY that guilt BECAUSE OF THE CONSEQUENCES of what owning that guilt would create and necessitate. A typical inner response to this would be something like "yes, I know this is true, but there is nothing I can really do about it. It's just too large of an issue for me to make any difference at all. It's just the way things are now. So I can only accept what is." It is precisely this kind of inner reaction within countless individuals in the face of all that is Naturally Wrong that, of course, allows all that is naturally wrong to be sustained. And that, of course, is how evil continues to 'win.' And the consequences of that 'winning,' then means the long term damage to the internal anatomy and physiology of all who consume food 'produced' in this way (inorganically). And what is the common dominator in this evil: money. Yet again. One form of that man-made teaching is the Christine doctrine called 'original sin' wherein somehow humans separated themselves from God. Or from a Jewish point of view the fact they were the 'chosen' people and, thus, must 'suffer' because of this 'fact.' And, from an Eastern point of view the total misuse of the word, and application of that word, 'karma.'

All of this crap is a total distortion of the Natural Laws, including the Natural Law of guilt. Natural guilt does indeed induce a 'feeling' that we did something wrong because of violating some Natural Law. And it is that feeling that then draws us inward to reflect on whatever our action or behavior was to induce that feeling. And then by going into that feeling it promotes realization, the realization of what Natural Law was violated. This is the natural way of learning induced by natural guilt. The person realizes it FROM WITHIN THEMSELVES. No one needs to be hammered over the head with harsh words about how 'bad' we are because we have 'violated' some man-made law. In fact when man-made laws have the effect of suppressing something that is natural, some natural behavior, that then becomes the basis of anger and rage. When anger and rage are induced because of this they, in turn, induce distortion: distorted behavior based on that which has been repressed because of the man-made law. (Rad)

Relative to the archetype of atonement linked with guilt each Soul reacts, and thus makes choices, differently. The natural process leading any Soul to finally be free of needing to atone for whatever guilt, natural or unnatural, is different for all Souls. And, of course, much depends on the very nature of the causative factors for the guilt in the first place: the extent and extremity of it. If any given Soul were responsible, say, for the deaths of a great many people due to its negligence how long would it take for such a Soul to stop atoning for this fact? If it were you, how long do you think that might be? If it were someone else, how long do you think it may take for that person to be free of atoning for such a guilt? There is just no way to know. Each Soul is different. The key issue here is whether the guilt is natural or not. (Rad)

When guilt occurs to a Soul that is natural then the very nature of that guilt, the events that have caused it, will stay within the Soul forever. It does this so that the Soul will never repeat the causes or actions that lead to the natural guilt. On the other hand, any guilt that is within the Soul that is not natural can and will be expelled from the Soul at some point. Thus when dealing with clients it is very important to understand this critical difference which then dictates how a client dealt with relative to a therapeutic approach. (Rad)

Learned guilt vs natural guilt

JWG made a critical distinction relative to the archetype of masochism because it can have two distinct causes. One cause is what he, and others, call spiritual masochism wherein the Soul is consciously and with intent 'sacrificing' its Soul for the benefit of others no matter what the personal cost to the Soul may be. The other cause is of course rooted in the need to atone for a sense of guilt because the Soul feels within itself that it has done something wrong which then necessitates the need to atone for that guilt. In both of these forms of masochism the 'wounding' that correlates with Chiron is thus based on the Soul having no boundaries or limits relative to the desire to help or heal others in the ways that are consistent with the evolutionary condition of the Soul: that which is possible because of the evolutionary condition or state of the Soul. When Chiron is manifesting itself though guilt and the need to atone for that guilt it is imperative, for those who are working with Chiron, to understand the difference between 'learned' guilt and natural guilt. Learned guilt occurs when a Soul is subjected to all kinds of projected judgments from others where the nature of those judgments are rooted in artificial or man-made laws that are temporal in nature. It can also occur by way of an inner self-judgment as the Soul measures or judges itself against these same man-made laws in which they forever come up short. In both cases this leads to the inner voice of 'there must be something wrong with me' in which the Soul then needs to 'atone' which then leads to the masochism inherent within Chiron. Natural guilt is a guilt that is rooted in that which is naturally right and wrong relative to all the Natural Laws that have been set in motion by the Creator in the first place. When a Soul transgresses these Natural Laws a state of natural guilt will occur. When this natural guilt manifests within the archetype of Chiron the need to atone for that natural guilt occurs. And that can then lead to the two forms of masochism that JWG taught. When working with those who are manifesting psychological or pathological masochism relative to their Chiron it is imperative to help them understand the difference between learned guilt versus natural guilt. Natural guilt will always remain in the Soul because that is how the Soul learns to do what is inherently right and wrong according the Natural Laws set in motion by the Creator. Learned guilt is that which can be jettisoned from the Soul because, after all, this type of guilt IS NOT NATURAL. In this way a healing of the wounds that correlate with Chiron can occur. It is also imperative that one understands the difference between pathological or psychological masochism versus what Green called 'spiritual masochism.' Spiritual masochism is a conscious choice by the Soul to sacrifice whatever wounds may occur to it by way of a pure giving to others ON THEIR BEHALF, ON GOD'S BEHALF. When this is the case it just is. There is nothing to heal or to change. JWG was the only one to my knowledge that taught that Chiron can also correlate to the wounding of others that then leads to a necessary guilt, and the need to atone for it NATURALLY. (Rad)

On the flip side, Chiron will also correlate to the possibility and often the past karma of a Soul creating such guilt and wounding for others. The nature of that would stem from a core denial of one's inner reality/condition by way of projecting that outwards towards others. This is how this would play out in patriarchal times where there are such strong distorted notions of absolute perfection and its implied polarity of fatal imperfection. The reality of having triggered wounding for others in the past can also be a cause for the Chiron guilt – and thus the psychological need to atone for that guilt. The integration of the Chiron archetype in a healthy way seems to entail a process of step by step healing which directly necessitates doing that which brings up the most pain while so doing it. In so doing, the Soul can receive the feedback/criticism of its environment and make necessary adjustments. Thus the Soul learns to bridge a higher spiritual purpose into this world by consciously integrating that purpose in a way that is pragmatic and focused – all rooted in deep self-acceptance. This produces in the end a great degree of compassion and ability to serve others, even in the midst of seemingly painful inner or outer circumstances. This can only be done through the vehicle of being willing and comfortable with one's own pain so that the Chiron work can evolve into selfless service without any martyrdom associated with it. (Ari)

This is essentially correct yet 'martyrdom' can also be a function of a Soul who has made a conscious choice to sacrifice itself on behalf of others no matter what the personal cost may be to the Soul who has made such a choice: spiritual masochism. (Rad)

Natural atonement – "I am sorry"

Natural atonement can be as simple as saying "I am sorry" to whatever the natural corrective action would be relative to the NATURE of the transgression of whatever Natural Law itself. If I steal something from you what would be the natural corrective action ? And so on. (Rad)

How to deal with natural guilt

The best way to deal with it is to orientate to Soul to create conditions in its life that were the very causes that lead to the natural guilt in the first place, and then to do all that is possible to do the naturally right things in the face of those conditions. Everybody has natural guilt in varying degrees in their Soul. No Soul is 'perfect.' (Rad)

I was deeply struck when I first saw this, years ago in the movie Gandhi. More and more I understand why. It is such an example of this principle. During that fast, toward the end of the Gandhi movie, a devout Hindu came to Gandhi and said, "I am going to hell." Gandhi asked, "Why?" He said he had killed a Muslim boy during the violence that sprang up as the country was being divided into India and Pakistan. Gandhi replied, "I know a way out of hell. Find a child whose parents were killed in the violence and raise it. Only make sure it is a Muslim child and raise it as a Muslim." Think of the implications of a devout Hindu raising a child as a Muslim, and the effect that would have on the Hindu man's natural guilt, and also the effect on the child's Soul, whose parents had been murdered by Hindus. (Steve)

Another way one can make up for transgressions is, as one's life gradually changes, to remind other sincere Souls who struggle with a similar inner darkness that there is indeed a way out. This human life is often hard. But there is ALWAYS a path back to God/Goddess for sincere Souls ready to take the necessary steps, which start with owning where we have been. (Steve)

Patriarchal standard of God-perfection

Every one of us has places we don't want to see or look at, feel like we are farther along than we really are, etc. These are universal human conditions. Wolf would say since all things originate from God, what does this say about the actual nature of God, when all people have these same traits. His answer is it points to the inherent imperfection in God itself. And we judge ourselves using a patriarchal standard of God-perfection which no human anywhere throughout time has ever lived up to. Thus the need to be very kind to ourselves, to recognize how difficult it is to walk this path. And to recommit to it again and again, no matter how many times we stray or fall down. To pick self back up and get back on the pathway, that is the way. In the end, however long it takes, mastery over self is assured. It's just that it takes a long time – that has to be accepted. (Steve)

Patriarchal self-judgment
The natural principle of life is diversity – same source, myriad of outer forms. This is why EA talks a lot about Natural Law. In patriarchy, things are judged as good or bad relative to human-created standards of what is right and wrong and how things should be. That is the opposite of accepting diversity as it was created. Over lifetimes of rejection for being the way they are, Souls become wounded and come to have distorted self-images of who and what they are. Thus they come to internalize deep self-judgments based on internalizing experiences they've had within the patriarchal realities. They come to believe the distortions they have been subjected to are in fact real. Thus they hide away "unacceptable" parts of who they are, and adopt personas that try to conform to society's expectations of proper behavior, pretending (even to self) to be what they are not. That right there is the root of our individual issues. The way out is the path back to accepting self the way one was created by God, regardless of what anyone thinks about it. (It's a path that requires a lot of courage.) (Steve)

Law of attraction – "The Secret"
The Secret wasn't any "secret" and, to me, it's just the New Age version of Christian guilt. You're not getting wealthy, healthy, the new job, whatever it is we want – because we don't BELIEVE enough – we don't PRAY hard enough. We don't envision already having what we want, or we don't use enough emotion, you're not TRYING HARD ENOUGH, etc., etc., etc., ad nauseum – just reinforcing the person's guilt and/or deep sadness because they haven't been able to manifest whatever it is they want. Think of what this does to the person whose karma/evolutionary necessity demand that they NOT have whatever it is they're trying to manifest – more guilt, more anger, more feelings of helplessness and hopelessness. The underlying premise that we need to and can change our thoughts to change our reality is valid, but it, too, somehow got distorted by tying it to man-made beliefs about what life is "supposed to look like/be." And again, it's getting back to the Natural God, the natural way of doing things, and the way things naturally are that will actually bring us to our own inner state of balance and grace. Sometimes we're going to get eaten by the lion, and sometimes we're going to be the one feasting on the filet. The bottom line that JWG always went back to were the words of Jesus to seek God first, put God first, and what you need will be given to you. And that seeking needs to be sincere and consistent. Such a simple concept, and yet if we're honest with ourselves, it's much harder to pull off. But as JWG also said many times, "The value is in the effort." (Adina)

Anger
Of course anger could be part of the Lucifer effect. But the source of anger can be much more than that. Living in a patriarchal, unnatural reality as we do, anyone attuned to the natural is going to, at times, feel deep anger over the distortions that have occurred and continue occurring, due to the sense of the violations of Natural Law simply feeling "not right." Not to mention the personal pain and traumas we have experienced, as a result. Anger does exist within Natural Law – it has its natural purposes. Like everything else, it can get distorted and misapplied. (Steve)

Hate
Hate correlates with Scorpio, the 8th house, and Pluto. It is a natural emotion. If the hate is being triggered because of conditions and/or events, there are many ways to deal with it, not just one way. All depends on the actual nature of such events and/or conditions. If such events and/or conditions are rooted in violations of Natural Laws then one can be pretty hard pressed to be free of it in meditation although, of course, it is possible. The guilt reaction to hate, itself, can be caused by many factors, not just one. It does not mean that things like rape, murder, etc. are natural at all. Hate is an emotion from within consciousness, the Soul that can be triggered by various external phenomena. What any given Soul does because of the emotion of hate, or anger which is another natural emotion, is up to that Soul. In patriarchal realities this can of course lead to things like murder and so on. Patriarchal realities are for the most part total distortions and perversions of Natural Laws. Thus, when a natural emotion like hate or anger is triggered within a Soul it can then manifest through these distorted realities in horrible ways like murder and so on. Hate is not a desire. It is an emotion that can be triggered by phenomenal events, or it can be triggered even as hate towards oneself by way of judging oneself against various standards that trigger the self-hate. One can see where the sign Scorpio is in any given chart, where Pluto is and/or Scorpio planets, and the sign on the 8th house cusp and the location of its planetary ruler by way of its own house, sign, and aspects to it that can all act as triggers for inner or outer hate. For example, if one had Gemini on the 8th house cusp one could feel 'jealous' of another's intellectual abilities that could then lead to 'hating' that person.
Nature is not human centered, indeed, and yet they are part of the totality of Nature. The fact that hatred can manifest in humans, as well as animals, has nothing to do whether a consciousness is distorted or not: the fact is it manifests and exists. Hatred does manifest in certain animals such as chimpanzees and other forms of the monkey kingdom for example. Humans are in fact part of the totality of Nature and humans have the emotion of hate within them which is simply an intensification of anger. Hate manifests from anger. It is a natural emotion, not one born simply of distortions. When hate is projected on another, humans or chimpanzees,

that other can then become an enemy. In humans and chimpanzees an enemy can be attacked and killed because of the hate. Chimpanzees can not only kill other chimpanzees because of being enemies, but they can also kill humans. They can even kill humans who want to own them as pets. When these things happen it has nothing to do with 'abstractions.' Ask any human when they are in the emotion of hate if they feel they are in an abstract state, or, in fact, in an emotional state. (Rad)

Fear of Natural Law
Where the person is trying to overturn the hold of the superstitious past, belief in religions and all the things that have held the race back, they have created science and technology as a new religion (although they rarely recognize that they have done this) that is going to save us from all the terrors and inequities of the past. Often people with those views are atheists, rebelling against the religious tyranny of the past. They have created Progress as a new religion. In essence they have thrown the baby out with the bath water. It's a phase necessary for those Souls to move through. They are seeing partial truth – they see the damaging hold that superstition and giving power away has had over much of humanity. And they rebel against that, rightfully so. The issue is, they have created a modern version of the same thing, yet another incomplete partial truth. But they are not yet in a place where they see the limitations of the perspectives they've adopted. Ultimately, somewhere along the line, they have to embrace a spiritual reality because that will represent the next step towards greater truth. But that can be a very long journey. Another thing the astrologer might consider is what unresolved hardships and traumatizations occurred to [her] the Soul during natural times and, even more so, during the transition into patriarchal times, that are the hidden memories that lead to her attitudes. "I don't want to go backwards!" is a very telling statement – it's an emotional statement. On a deeper level it is saying "I don't want to revisit the past". Why? Sometimes that is a tipoff to the forgotten, unresolved traumatic events from the past. If the Soul has to remember the past it knows it will have to deal with painful issues it's been avoiding forever.

One way to approach someone like that is to make it clear that revisiting the past does not mean we are going back to living in the jungle or in tipi's. Rather, ask her to consider if it's possible there might be anything at all of value from the past that has gotten lost with the transition into modern times that might be worth rediscovering. That she does not need to give up anything she now has to explore the past. Basically you are trying to find a place of receptivity to what lies beyond what she now knows, into an unknown. You can ask her what she fears she will lose by investigating – what is the potential cost? Fears are not rational, so if she responds with fear, ask her what she is afraid of. And if she states some fears, ask her why does she think she has those specific fears. Tell her what you are doing is the scientific method, to objectively examine and analyze what you find in her, to better understand it. And that this is the method that is used to develop the technology and science she believes in. You are applying that same methodology to objectively look into her inner emotional states. In other words, creating a frame that is aligned with her worldview that does not push her buttons. If you really want dialogue and to help her understand a bit more, you have to step into her worldview and accept it as she sees it. Then little by little perhaps you can help her expand from where she is now. (Steve)

Natural parenting
[The praise-punishment manner of raising children] is how the vast majority of children are being raised. Yet, we must also remember that the vast majority of people on this Earth do not have any conscious awareness of what is Natural, and what is not. Most humans have been so conditioned by all that is not natural that the very nature of that conditioning creates a reality in which that which is not natural is considered natural anyway. Thus, to be confronted with what is natural will then create a shock of recognition, because it is natural, then the guilt that comes from that recognition. And, yet, as JWG taught so often, the sense of psychological and emotional security for most humans is defined by the need to be self-consistent. So even when confronted by that which is natural, the shock of recognition that follows, there then is a typical defensiveness and denial because of the need to be self-consistent: the conditioning of what is 'normal' as defined by the consensus.

To admit that that which is natural would then require other admissions that would naturally lead to a state of awareness in most of how they have put phenomenal reality together is all wrong. All wrong. All of it. This would then in turn create a Soul angst, an existential anxiety of total insecurity. How many Souls are willing to go to that place? To literally start all over? Not too many. In fact I just read of a study in the USA that was born out of this incredible phenomena in that country of all these people who have made themselves 'believe' in an alternate reality that has nothing do with actual facts. The 'tea party' crowd is a perfect example of this, and those that still call themselves 'Republicans' in general as well. What these types of people have made themselves believe is total fiction, total delusion and illusions, that constitutes their actual reality. And when these people were then exposed to the actual facts that would of course defeat that alternate reality the typical reaction to those facts WAS TO DENY THOSE FACTS EVEN MORE, TO BECOME EVER MORE ENTRENCHED IN THEIR ALTERNATE REALITY AT ALL COSTS. This is the principle of self-consistency that JWG was teaching about for so long.

So of course, following all this, most parents have zero clue about what is natural, including NATURAL PARENTING. Most parents pass along their own conditioning to the kids of course, including how they themselves were raised. The function of natural guilt is to make us change whatever it is that we did to ignite the natural guilt in the first place. This is a NATURAL WAY OF LEARNING. It is a NATURAL WAY OF LEARNING DISCRIMINATION OF WHAT IS RIGHT AND WRONG. How many parents know this and then teach this to their children? Natural guilt is meant to make us feel 'bad' about ourselves. And yet how many parents use whatever it is that the child has done to create this guilt as a true teaching situation that allows the child to see what it has done is naturally wrong? To actually EMBRACE IT? And then to change their behavior naturally as a result? And when that behavior changes, based on the child's own recognition and desiring to change as a result, to extend to that child the type of LOVE that acknowledges the child's own recognition, and the change the child has made? The sad fact is that most parents pass along judgments to their children that reinforce man-made guilt rooted in the very nature of the conditioning patterns that define their reality: a reality that is not rooted in Natural Laws. It is this very fact that then causes the child to feel 'bad,' or that there is something 'wrong' with them, when they violate these man-made guilt associations. And that leads to the praise/punish syndrome. (Rad)

Natural roles for men and women
First, to me, there is no start point for the matriarchy. In fact what is called the matriarchy is a bit over-blown to me because all the people on Earth lived in a natural way, natural laws, that included the natural laws of men and women. Thus, the natural roles for women and men come from these natural laws. It is true that all issues relative to 'spiritual' matters were the domain of women who were typically regarded as the 'keeper of the flame.' Yet in those natural times there was no artificial God/ess that was ever conceived at all. All things in the natural world including spiritual issues were just that: natural. Thus the entire world of 'spirits' of all kinds is what the peoples of natural times understood, and lived by. Thus the role of the 'shaman' came from this time. Even all the 'shaman' until the patriarchy manifested were in fact women, not men: keepers of the flame. The first time a 'God' was conceived was exactly around the time of the transition from these natural times to the patriarchal times. The first actual conception for a Creator being that is called God/ess was in fact a feminine God: Namu. This was at the very beginning of the patriarchal time which of course gave way to all the patriarchal crap that followed that had the effect of completely distorting all things natural, including what we can call a Natural God/ess. (Rad)

It is important to understand the fact that the female produced the male in the first place for evolutionary reasons linked with necessary survival. JWG wrote quite a bit about this in his second book on Pluto that is all about relationships from an EA point of view that included a chapter on Pluto in Sagittarius wherein he talks about the natural laws that correlate to men and women. (Rad)

Male courting
Male courting is a result of patriarchal conditioning. JWG wrote an entire book on relationships: Pluto 2. In the Pluto in Sagittarius section there is quite a bit about the nature of the patriarchy/matriarchy in terms of what is natural, and what is not. (Rad)

Nature
Humans' separation from each other via distorted belief systems, as well as separation from other life forms on the planet includes the idea that humans are "superior" to other life forms, ie plants, animals, etc., instead of simply different from and interdependent. The idea of this kind of separateness – the DISTORTION of it – goes back to the Old Testament when humans were given "dominion over" nature. And that dominion over has created the destruction OF nature. Since the entire system IS interdependent, then we can see why humans' extinction is looming ahead of us. (Adina)

Daemon Soul
Daemon Souls, shamans, have evolved their state of consciousness to be in total unity within the consciousness of what many call Gaia: the total state, consciousness, of Nature manifesting in a variety of forms. In this unified consciousness the Daemon/Shaman Soul is thus aware of all the Natural Laws that exist in the time/space reality we call Earth. Being aligned and unified with these Natural Laws they are thus able to be in conscious relationships with the different states of consciousness as manifested in the various forms on Earth. The Daemon/Shaman Soul evolves, over time, into this total state of awareness. (Rad)

Consciousness of plants
(Q) Do some plants have a malevolent consciousness?

(A) No. All plants, as in any other form of life, have a natural instinct to survive and to reproduce in order for long term survival to occur. Thus, the 'strategies' that all forms of life, including plants, have learned by way of being in relationship to the totality of Creation itself on Earth are just that: learned strategies. How these strategies may be perceived and judged by humans has nothing to do with what the plants themselves are in fact doing in order to survive. (Rad)

Archetype of judgment (Capricorn) manifesting through Pisces
What JWG taught is that judgment as an archetype in human consciousness is natural, and that the archetype of judgment in and of itself is Capricorn, the 10th house, and Saturn. He taught that the issue is not the right or wrongness of judgment as such, BUT THE CONTENT USED TO MAKE JUDGMENTS IN THE FIRST PLACE. Is that content rooted in Natural Laws, or is that content merely a collection of all kinds of man-made laws that have nothing to do with Natural Laws. When the archetype of judgment that emanates

from the 10th house, Capricorn, or Saturn manifests through the 12th house, Neptune, or Pisces that then can correlate with the judgments made about spiritual disciplines, practices, the 'rights and wrongs' of spiritual life, of various gods and goddesses, and, of course, one's own relationship to all things spiritual. He taught a lot about all the artificial man-made rules and laws concerning spiritual life, all the 'should be's' so to speak. And how any Soul who enters spiritual life where the nature of that spiritual life has been created and defined by man-made laws that the judgments made either through one's own inner judgment of itself, or judgments made and projected upon others and oneself, that this commonly leads to not being good enough as measured against these man-made spiritual doctrines. This is why he talked and taught so much about the difference between these man-created, patriarchal, spiritual disciplines and their 'teachings' versus what natural spirituality is, what the Natural Laws are, and thus to change the very nature of the CONTENT used to make the judgments in the first place. (Rad)

PLANETARY NODES

Use and function of Planetary Nodes

Any natal planet will have its own North and South Nodes. The natal planets correlate to the current life of course. Yet each one of these planets has a past that has brought it to the current life. And that past is defined by not only the actual house and sign of the natal planet, but also its own South Node. Thus, the relationship between the natal planet by house, sign, and aspects correlates to the totality of its past that directly correlates to how and why it has come into the current life: the past that has led to the current moment, one's current life. So, in essence, the natal planet by house, sign, and aspect, relative to its South Node, is the totality of that past that has led to the current moment, the current life. This is no different than the South Node of the Moon, and the current natal Moon in one's birth chart. All the prior life egocentric structures created by the Soul that have correlated to prior life evolutionary dynamics that have led to the current life, the current egocentric structure that has been created because of the totality of the past. The current life Moon sign is the bridge between the past and the future, its North Node, as integrated and lived on a moment to moment basis in the context of the current life. Thus, the current life Moon by house, sign, and aspects, relative to its Nodes, and the planetary ruler of those Nodes by their own house and sign locations, the aspects to them, is the constant that evolves within itself as a reflection of this dynamic tension between the past and the future as integrated in each moment of our life.

This is exactly the same for all of our planets. They are in their own houses and signs, making whatever aspects to other planets, that have all contributed to the past life development of those planets that constitute the existing reality for any of us at the moment of birth. The South Nodes of these planets, like the South Node of the Moon, correlates to the history of those planets at different points in time. This correlates to the inner memories in any of our Souls that have all lead to the orientation of our Souls to the current life that we are living, the very reasons for the current life in all of its dimensions that must keep evolving, keep moving towards a future that is reflected in the ongoing evolutionary intentions for our Souls. All planets have their North Nodes, just as the Moon does. The North Node of these planets, like the Moon, correlates to the evolutionary progression and development of those planets. The natal position of the (whatever) planet, like the Moon, correlates to how the dynamic tension of our past and future is lived and integrated in each moment of our life. In essence, our past leads to the current moment, and that current moment is always moving towards a future. We can only know that there is in fact a future because we have had a past. The past leading to the moment is that which serves as the way any of us integrate, and move forwards into our future, where that future is the evolutionary intentions for our current life.

Thus, the North Nodes of the planets serve as the vehicles for the evolutionary future to manifest which is integrated in each moment by the natal position of those planets. The Nodes of Jupiter, Saturn, Uranus, Neptune, and Pluto move very, very slowly over great lengths of time. Thus, they have a generational as well as an individual application. Individual because they will be in each person's natal chart somewhere that is unique to that person. Yet generational because they are in the same sign for all of us. The South Nodes of Pluto, Jupiter, and Saturn are in Capricorn for all of us. The North Nodes of Pluto, Jupiter, and Saturn are in Cancer for all of us. Historically speaking, the South Nodes of these planets are in Capricorn, and that is the time frame in which the transition between the Matriarchy and the Patriarchy occurred. All Souls on Earth as a result are linked to that time whether they actually lived at that time or not. It is the COLLECTIVE MEMORY of that time that all Souls will draw upon as reflected in the current life they are living. So too with the South Node of Uranus which will be in Sagittarius for all of us, its North Node in Gemini. And the South Node of Neptune is in Aquarius for all of us, and its North Node in Leo. The North Nodes of all of these planets thus correlate to all peoples living on the planet now. They correlate to the evolutionary intentions for the entire species as that species, human beings, continue to evolve as a species. And, of course, the ongoing evolutionary intentions and necessities of the species can only be understood in direct relationship of the past of that species: the South Nodes.

Mars, Mercury, and Venus and their Nodes move through the signs much more quickly that the outer planets do. And these planets all correlate to that which is highly personal and unique to each Soul, its own individual reality that exists within the context of living with all the other humans that are living at the same time. The same principles of the past leading to the moment, and how that moment moves to the future, apply in these Nodes as well of course. The natal sign of these planets is that which is the constant, that which integrates the dynamic tension between the past and the future that is experienced in each moment. This then allows for an evolution to take place within the natal sign and house of these planets. (Rad)

SPREADSHEET – Annual Planetary Node Cycles Each Year Spreadsheet

For more detailed information, download the Annual Planetary Node Cycles Each Year Spreadsheet (by Bradley Naragon) from the message board of the School of Evolutionary Astrology website.

TABLE 4 Planetary Nodes for everyone

SOUTH NODES		NORTH NODES	
Pluto	19 — 22 Capricorn	Pluto	19 — 22 Cancer
Neptune	10 — 14 Aquarius	Neptune	10 — 14 Leo
Uranus	11 — 17 Sagittarius	Uranus	11 — 17 Gemini
Saturn	18 — 30 Capricorn	Saturn	17 — 30 Cancer
Jupiter	29 Sagittarius — 22 Capricorn	Jupiter	29 Gemini — 22 Cancer
Mars	9 Libra — 30 Sagittarius	Mars	8 Aries — 3 Cancer
Venus	Any sign	Venus	Any sign
Mercury	Any sign	Mercury	Any sign

Nothing is ever static. Everything evolves. In doing Evolutionary Astrology, as we can see, it is essential that we are able to see and deal with the various dimensions of time, and how those various dimensions of time, specific time frames, that correlate to specific lifetimes and the reasons for those lifetimes, interface and interact within themselves. It is this that correlates in each Soul's inner reality about the nature of its own evolution through time. It is this that correlates to the specific nature of each Soul: its own unique prior lifetimes, and the reasons for them that have been created through the vehicle of desires. It is this that allows us to understand the nature of the CURRENT LIFE, AND WHY THE CURRENT LIFE. And, it is this that allows us to understand the evolutionary intentions for any Soul, its own next steps as reflected in the North Nodes of the planets. When all of this is understood through the core evolutionary paradigm for all charts, the natal Pluto, its polarity point, the North and South Nodes of the Moon, the location of its planetary rulers, then a total understanding of any Soul's evolutionary journey can be understood. (Rad)

Pluto correlates to the Soul itself, and within that, the Natural Law of evolution. It correlates to what the desires of the Soul have been that has led to the current life, and the desires that correlate to its ongoing evolutionary needs. This is contained with Pluto, the Soul, itself. All the other planets in a current life birth chart are thus created by the Soul for its ongoing evolutionary needs that are reflected in its desires. The current life birth planets do have their own North and South Nodes. It is the South Nodes of these planets that do correlate to the past life dynamics that the Soul has created for itself that have led to the current life, and the position of whatever planet IN THIS LIFE that symbolizes the current life's evolutionary needs. The current life position brings the past forwards through it: the South Node coming through the current position of the planet itself. The North Node of the planet in turn correlates to the ongoing evolutionary journey of the Soul as it continues to evolve through each of the archetypes of all the planets. The cause of that evolution is the Soul, not any of the other planets themselves. The natural polarity point of the natal Pluto is the bottom line evolutionary intent for the Soul in each life. It is the primary cause that causes the North Nodes of all the other planets to actualize according to that primary evolutionary intention. The natal planet, in the current life, birth chart, serves to integrate the past and the future in each moment FOR THE ENTIRE LIFE. (Rad)

Understanding the Planetary Nodes is no different than understanding the Nodes of the Moon. As we all know all planets have a South and North Node. And, like the Nodes of the Moon, they all have a past and a future that is experienced in each moment of the current life, where that current moment is defined by the natal position of the planet in question. Thus, the past is always shaping that moment, the natal planet, and the future is also shaping that moment by way of the Soul's ongoing evolutionary development into the future. Thus, the moment is but a reflection, and caused by, the evolutionary forces of the past as they interface with the evolutionary forces of the future. That interface is what we then call the moment, the present moment. Every planet, or asteroid, having its own polarity point reflects an evolution of the sign that the planet is in at birth. The South Node of a planet, or asteroid, sets up the natal position in the current life: it leads to it. And that natal planet then has its polarity point as a core evolutionary dynamic within it that, in turn, is progressively actualized in the context of a lifetime through the North Node of the planet itself. Thus, the polarity point in combination with the North Node both serve to evolve the existing dynamics of the South Node, and the ongoing integration point defined by the natal planet itself. This all applies to the Moon as well. JWG did lecture on this at times, and there is a DVD available for sale too on the main site called From Karma to Dharma that reflects this. (Rad)

The North Node is the future that informs the moment just as the South Node is also informing that moment. Thus, the natal planet is the constant that allows for an integration for the past and the future in each moment. The combination of the past and the future in the moment then allows for an evolution to take place that is integrated by the natal planet throughout one's life.

Remember that the signs and houses contain within themselves a spectrum of archetypal correlations. And it is that totality within any sign or house, the spectrum of possibilities that is then evolved because of the evolutionary pull of the future as that future meets the past in each moment. (Rad)

Planetary Nodes – generational and individual context
The best way to understand this is to understand something that JWG wrote in his first Pluto book when he talked about how the dual desire nature of the Soul, the desires to separate and return, manifest with Pluto in any given sign. What sign that Pluto is in will correlate to, obviously, millions of people who have the same sign that Pluto is in. This is generational of course. And each generation has its own polarity point that symbolizes the ongoing evolutionary intentions for the planet as symbolized in the generations of Souls that share the same sign, and its polarity point. Yet, at the same time, the whole of a generation is comprised of individuals who all have their own evolutionary journey, and intentions, within the generation that they are born within. Relative to the dual desire nature of the Soul it is the generational context that then serves to ignite the desire to 'separate' from that generation that allows for the Soul's discovery of its own unique and individual nature, its own individual evolutionary journey.
For example, a Soul can have Pluto in Libra in the 5th house. Obviously millions of others also have Pluto in Libra. The individual Soul's natural polarity point of course is the 11th house, and Aries. So this would mean that all the other Souls who have Pluto in Libra would land, via synastry, in the individuals 5th house. Because of the dual desire nature within the Soul this then ignites or causes the individual with that 5th house Pluto in Libra to 'separate' from that generational context in order to actualize its own sense of individual identity. Thus, by igniting that desire to separate in this generational context it has the effect of stimulating the natural polarity point, the 11th house and Aries, for this Soul who has its natal Pluto in Libra in the 5th house. The Soul is born into this generational context that is shared by millions of other Souls. Obviously, the vast majority of all those Souls within the same generation have not known one another personally. On the other hand, we do of course make personal connections to others within our generational context. Astrological methods exist of course that inform us how to determine these personal connections within that generational context.
In the very same way this is how we need to understand the Planetary Nodes. Millions can have the South Node of Mars in Scorpio for example. This correlates, as do any of the signs that the Planetary Nodes can be in, to time frames in the past, the archetypal meanings of, that all those Souls who have the same signs, ie South Node of Mars in Scorpio share. And because of this there is a natural commonality between such Souls in general: the structure of their consciousness and why. As Wolf used to teach, it takes more than one Soul to accomplish the evolutionary intentions of the planet, the species. Yet, within this common sharing all Souls do make their own personal connections to others. To know whom we have made those prior life personal connections to, relative to the Planetary Nodes, like with Pluto in the signs, we must employ the astrological methods of synastry to know who they are. So it is then a combination of the generational context, and our individual relationships within that, that both have the effect and intent of igniting each individual Soul's ongoing evolutionary intentions. (Rad)

Motion of Planetary Nodes
There is a natural progressive cycle to the Planetary Nodes, meaning forwards through the zodiac. Yet they can also go in retrograde motion at different parts of the year, in the overall cycle of each Planetary Node. But the mean motion is forwards, not retrograde as in the Moon's Nodes. You can even have a situation, due to the irregular planetary motion of the planets where, for example, the South Node of Mars can be retrograde, yet its North Node is not. One needs to look into the tables for the Planetary Nodes in Solar Fire, for example, to see all this. There is a progressive movement of the Planetary Nodes through the zodiac at their mean motions. Of course they can go retrograde at times, yet the mean motion is progressive or forwards. (Rad)
The planetary motions are not constant whereas the motion of the Moon relative to Earth is. Thus when the various planets move above or below the elliptic of the Earth the Nodes that this then correlates to are not constant: they are irregular. (Rad)

Nodes of the Sun
The Nodes of the Sun are not used in Evolutionary Astrology. The present 'moment' only occurs because there is a past and future. Without a past or future there is no moment. (Rad)

Planetary South Node and North Node in the same sign
The reason that Mercury and Venus can have their Nodes in the same sign is because of their relative distances from the Sun. Mercury can be no further than 28 degrees away, and Venus can never be more than 45 degrees away from the Sun. As a result as these two planets move below or above the elliptic their Nodes can be in the same sign. Even though they can be in the same sign we must remember that each sign is evolved through. Each sign is the totality of an archetype. Thus, the Nodes can be in the same sign but there is an ongoing evolution within those signs that correlate to the ongoing evolutionary intentions of the Soul. (Rad)

Distinction between the North Node of Pluto and the Pluto polarity point

The North Node of Pluto reflects the ongoing evolutionary development of the Soul from within itself that is then actualized through the creation, projection, externalization of itself via the finite form it creates in each life. This is symbolized by the polarity point of Pluto in the current life birth chart. The Soul, from within itself, of course contains all the previous identities, singular life/finite forms, that it has ever lived. It also contains within itself all the different possibilities, future life/finite forms, that could occur. That which can occur is dependent on what the Soul, within itself, DESIRES. Those desires have been the prior life causes of what has already taken place. And in each of those lives the Soul created the necessity of subjective egocentric identities, finite life forms, for the desires to be actualized which of course has led to yet more desires to evolve that have led to yet another life. In each of these lives the Soul, from within itself, has had a North Node that has symbolized those ongoing evolutionary developmental desires. And in each life those desires are then actualized by way of the polarity point of Pluto in each life, in the individual birth chart. It's like, from within the Soul itself, it says, "I need or desire to evolve in the following way: its North Node, and in order to do this I will actualize it like this: the polarity point of Pluto in the individual life that it creates, in each life."

The Nodes of Pluto stay in signs, ie Cancer/Capricorn, or whatever signs, about 2,000 years. Most Souls of course will have more than one life within a span of 2,000 years. So the core evolutionary desires from within the Soul exist beyond the singularity of one finite life. In each of those singular lives the Soul continues to desire to evolve in this core archetypal way that is then actualized through each of the specific singular/finite lives that it lives. And in each of those singular lives that core evolutionary intent within the Soul is actualized by the polarity point of Pluto in those lives: the birth chart that symbolizes this entire process. Let's make a simple example of these dynamics. Let's say person X has in their current birth chart a 9th house Pluto in Leo, the South Node of Pluto being in Capricorn in the 2nd, which is ruled by Saturn in Leo in the 9th. The North Node of Pluto would be in Cancer in the 8th, and Pluto's polarity point would be in Aquarius in the 3rd. The Pluto in the 9th in Leo would correlate to a Soul that has desired to understand and actualize itself by way of understanding the nature of the cosmos, and the Natural Laws of Creation. It has spent many, many lives in relative isolation, the South Node of Pluto in Capricorn in the 2nd, in order to inwardly contemplate that nature of Creation in order to realize by way of that isolated contemplation the nature of these Natural Laws which thus become the very basis of the Soul's inner relationship to itself: the 2nd house. This, in turn would constitute the Soul's core sense of meaning for existence, of that which held the core meaning for life itself. The ruler of that South Node of Pluto is also in Leo in the 9th. This would restate the Soul actualizing these core desires within the context of Nature, living and being within Nature in order to inwardly know all the Natural Laws that are responsible for Creation, Leo, itself. In relation to the South Node of Pluto being in the 2nd these symbols put together correlate to a natural loner who has realized what it has desired in essential isolation in this way.

Yet, in this way, the Soul has reached an evolutionary limit, and needs to continue to evolve. The Soul, from within itself, realizes this which is then symbolized by its North Node being in Cancer in the 8th house: the desire and need to jump out of the well of its own isolation, and to then engage and help other Souls on their own evolutionary journey. In so doing the Soul will then necessarily interact with other Souls and THEIR REALITIES: the interaction of the South and North Nodes of Pluto where Capricorn correlates to the archetype of reality, the realities of Earth itself. In this interaction with others it thus causes the Soul from within itself to confront its own evolutionary limitations that then creates the ongoing awareness of what it needs to continue to evolve itself. This confrontation can then cause the Soul to feel insecure from within itself as it is required to evolve beyond where it was by way of its own understandings of the nature of reality on this Earth that are reflections of the Natural Laws of Creation. These confrontations are intended so that the Soul can evolve beyond where it has already been.

In order for these core Soul intentions to evolve it then creates a singular or finite life in which the polarity point of the natal Pluto is in Aquarius in the 3rd. This will manifest, in the context of the example we are using, by creating a life in which the very opposite of where it has been: living alone in relative isolation within Nature. The Soul now will create a life in which it will be totally involved with others who are living within the world, in their cities, wherever whole groups of people exist: Aquarius in the 3rd. And, in this way, purposefully engage the realities of countless others who have all kinds of ideas, opinions, points of views and philosophies from A to Z, so to speak. And all of this will then of course impact on the Soul's current state of understanding the nature of reality that it has already realized in its past. The Soul then has another choice to make: it can retreat back to where it has been in order to remain secure from within itself, or make a choice to continue to grow from within itself due to the confrontations to that existing reality through the diversity of ideas manifesting within these groups of people, other individuals. If it makes the choice to proceed in this way it will then of course continue to evolve which reflects the intention of Pluto's North Node in Cancer in the 8th. That North Node of Pluto in Cancer of course will be ruled by the current life Moon, its egocentric structure created in the current life. So the underlying dynamics within the Soul that we have been discussing will then be focused, like a lens in a movie projector that creates images on a screen, into a current life identity, the 'I' of the current life. This is the Natural Law of how a Soul externalizes or projects itself from life to life by creating an 'image' of itself that correlates to the entire 'movie' of that life. (Rad)

Planetary Nodes of Pluto in Capricorn/Cancer

Jeffrey said many times that the South Node of Pluto in Capricorn related back to the time period when the transition from matriarchy to patriarchy was already underway, and thus all Souls on Earth today have a natural connection to those times, or at least the energies of those times, even if they were not in human form on Earth at that time. Something interesting is that in 2018 transiting Pluto will be conjunct its own South Node of Pluto. We could consider what that means in terms of opening up the current version of the lessons from those times. Keeping in mind Cancer/Capricorn relate to gender role assignment, and the upcoming period we are entering is associated with the beginning of the return of the Goddess. Clearly the male-dominated present orientation is leading to the environmental devastation of the planet. Uranus enters Taurus in 2018/2019, and survival will necessitate radical change. Also, here in USA, we are having a US Pluto return in 2021/2022 at 27 degrees Capricorn. Capricorn squares Libra (extremes) and we will have pushed everything to the maximum extremes, being forced to change from no other options remaining. (Steve)

The correlation to the Planetary Nodes in Capricorn-Cancer and the transition to the patriarchy from the matriarchy, is based on the Astrological Ages and their sub-ages. Thus the transition beginning at the very end of the Capricorn sub-age of the Cancer age. Thus the South Nodes of Pluto, Saturn, and Jupiter [currently] in the sign Capricorn. Because of the natural progression of the Astrological Ages through time. Thus, the alignment of the Capricorn sub-age within the Age of Cancer. That time frame, the actual his/herstory of the planet, correlates to that transition time between the matriarchy to the patriarchy. Cancer and Capricorn of course correlate to the male and female gender, and gender assignment issues within that. This is no different than, for example, Jesus who had Pluto in Virgo with his polarity point being Pisces. And he of course said he was here to usher in a New Age, the Pisces Age. (Rad)

Nodes of Pluto

The Soul has its own unique identity as created by the Source, or God. As such, it has its own ego that creates an image in the Soul of that unique identity. The awareness of that unique Soul identity is a function of evolution itself which finally leads to being self-aware, and has the evolved capacity, at some point, to objectify itself. The South and North Nodes of Pluto correlate to this ongoing evolutionary development of the Soul from within itself. The natal position of the current life Pluto simultaneously correlates to what the desires have been within the Soul for its own development, thus where it left off in those lives that have led to the current life, and the evolutionary intent for the current life for its evolution to proceed: the natural polarity point of that natal Pluto. The South Node of Pluto, by its own house and sign location, aspects to it from other planets, and aspects to its natural planetary ruler, all correlates to archetypes and dynamics that the Soul has used to develop itself, evolve itself, relative to its core desires for its evolution that is symbolized in the natal position of Pluto itself. The North Node of Pluto correlates to how and why the Soul evolves itself from within itself: what it needs to continue in its evolution. Other planets that aspect this North Node are archetypes that correlate to this ongoing evolution of the Soul within itself.

In order for all these internal dynamics within the Soul itself that correlate to its own ongoing evolution it must project or externalize itself through the creation of forms: the human form. This Natural Law or principle is the same as what we call the Source of All Things, or God, projecting and externalizing itself in the form of what we call CREATION. What we call God does this in order to know itself in all of these forms in the totality of Creation. So too with the individual Soul. The Soul needs to project or externalize itself in order to know itself, to objectify itself. So the Soul projects and externalizes itself from life to life in the form of the lifetimes that it lives that are all finite. The Soul itself is infinite just as God itself is infinite. Each finite life that the Soul projects from within itself, just as God projects each individualized Soul from within itself, reflects and symbolizes the core desires from within the Soul that reflect its own ongoing evolutionary desires to evolve.

As a result of this projection from life to life we then have the birth charts for each of those lives that reflect the finite forms that the Soul creates in order to effect its ongoing evolution. In each of these finite forms that the Soul creates it thus creates a consciousness that has its own subjective self-awareness that we call the ego or 'I.' And of course that subjective ego, the egocentric structure, is a projection from the Soul itself in order to know itself relative to the finite form it has created in each life that reflects its ongoing evolutionary needs and requirements. The subjective 'I' or ego that is created in each life by the Soul of course is the archetype of the Moon. The evolutionary journey of the Soul through time is thus symbolized through all the different finite forms or lives that it creates that are determined by its evolutionary needs and desires. And it is each of these finite lives that the Soul creates that the birth chart correlates to. And in each of those lives the finite ego does indeed 'die,' just as the body dies. Yet the memories of each life are sustained and live on within the Soul itself. And it is these ongoing evolutionary experiences from life to life that are the ongoing determinant and cause for yet another life. In the end, the whole chart, in any given life, correlates with the inner identity or 'ego' of the Soul as it evolves through time and space. (Rad)

The Soul of course contains all the prior lives that it has ever lived. However, in any given life, the Soul does indeed only draw upon those prior lives which are directly linked to the current and ongoing evolutionary purposes that it has. So, no, the South Node of Pluto by house and sign does not correlate to ALL of the Soul's prior lives. A total and comprehensive understanding of the entire chart which would include the employment of geodetic equivalents which are linked to the Ages and their sub-ages would be necessary in order to understand where any given Soul was during [the patriarchal] transition.

(Q) Would the South Node of Pluto be the ultimate bottom line in which the house would correlate to a deeper level of unconscious security patterns than that of the natal Pluto?

(A) No. It would be equal to the natal Pluto itself. (Rad)

Nodes of Venus

Jeffrey was the first astrologer to teach about Venus' correlation to the inner relationship that all people have with themselves. He taught why Venus had a double rulership for the signs Libra and Taurus. He said that Taurus and the 2nd house correlated to the inner relationship we all have with ourselves, and that the 7th house and Libra correlated to the types of outer relationships that we form with other people and why. He taught that the planet Venus, of itself, symbolized both the inner and outer relationships within the archetype of Venus itself. A simple example: if a person has, let's say, Venus in Virgo and their inner relationship to themself is one of intense criticism, all the things that are wrong with them, that it shouldn't then be surprising that that person would then 'attract,' Venus, others who are then critical of them: the inner reflecting the outer. And that which we attract is a reflection of the inner vibration within us where that inner vibration is a reflection of our inner relationship to ourselves. Or, for another example, let's say that Venus in Virgo person was inwardly experiencing a high degree of 'lack' in their lives which then leads to a sense of being 'empty' from within. That inner relationship to themselves could then manifest outwardly as needing, Venus, many other people in their lives in order to 'fill them up,' and needing others to give to them that which they felt they were lacking.

He talked about the natural inconjunct between the 2nd house, Taurus, and the 7th house, Libra. He taught that this is the natural 'crisis' that exists in all of us that involves the need to be self-reliant and fulfilling our own needs, and how our needs can be projected onto others in such a way as to become dependent on others for the very needs that we need to satisfy within ourselves. And how our projected needs onto others correlate to 'expectations' that we can set up with other people. So what happens when our expectations that are projected onto others do not occur? For most some kind of crisis will occur where the intent of the crisis is to force the person back upon themselves so that self-reliance in some way can be developed when those expectations have reached a point of excessive dependency on others. He taught about the need for the EA astrologer to understand the totality of the Venus archetype. Thus, to not only understand the sign that Venus is in but all the aspects that it is making to other planets, the North and South Nodes of Venus in terms of what the past, present, and future of the evolving Venus archetype is in all charts, and to fully grasp the signs on the 2nd and 7th houses as they condition those natural archetypes, and the reasons for that conditioning relative to the ongoing evolutionary intentions of the Soul, and, lastly, the location of the planetary rulers of those signs and the aspects that they are making for the same reasons. (Rad)

Nodes of Mars

It takes 24,000 years for the Nodes of Pluto to go through the entire zodiac: one astrological age. What is really incredible when you start to think about it is that the Nodes of Mars also takes 24,000 years for them to move through all the signs in the zodiac. They spend about 4,000 years in three signs, then another three signs for another 4,000 years, etc. For example, the South Nodes of Mars since 500 AD have been in Libra, Scorpio and Sagittarius depending on the time of year, in any given year. And, the North Nodes are Aries, Taurus, and Gemini. This will remain in those signs until 4,300 AD. So there are two things to ponder in this. One is the fact that, as we know, the lower octave of Pluto is Mars of course. Pluto is the underlying Natural Law of evolution for all things, including humans. And Mars instinctually acts out those evolutionary imperatives through the various forms of life, including human. (Rad)

The South Node of Mars would indicate where the desires emanating from the Soul were left off relative to its desires to evolve. [Example, Aries on the 8th] would then symbolize the Soul's intention in this life to confront and evolve beyond those existing limitations: of where those desires were left off. The current life Mars will then, for the entire life, correlate to where and how this will be done, and the North Node of Mars will correlate to the new desires emanating from the Soul to how and where the desires symbolized by the natal Mars will evolve themselves which are relative to the Pluto's natal polarity point. (Rad)

Planet conjunct Planetary South Node

The three possible conditions (relieve, fruition or combination of both) apply to Planetary South Nodes and planets conjunct the Planetary South Nodes. (Rad)

Natal planets conjunct collective Nodes

All Souls have their unique evolutionary and karmic history that leads the Soul into each life. The collective Nodes all correlate to specific Astrological Ages and sub-ages in which all of us either have lived in those times and/or our consciousness is drawing from those times: the collective consciousness/unconsciousness. When natal planets conjunct those collective Nodes it means that the nature of those Astrological Ages and their sub-ages have been directly experienced by the Soul and is thus conditioning the Soul's consciousness in the current life. (Rad)

Planet square Planetary Nodes

The way that JWG taught it was that the phenomenon of skipped steps was specific to the Nodes of the Moon. Of course when one employs the use of all the Planetary Nodes, natal planets in the current birth chart can square those Nodes. Simple example: millions have Neptune in Libra, and that Neptune then squares the Nodes of Pluto, Saturn, Jupiter in most cases. So, obviously, all those millions of Souls are not all going to have 'skipped steps' relative to this signature. This is actually a subject that I never remember JWG discussing at all, or writing about. To me when we do see this kind of symbolism it does have generational applications as to its meaning, and the individual meaning within that as it is applied to each individual's birth chart: the houses that it would be in. Thus, the individual's interaction and relationship with the generation that it is born within, and how that relationship then serves the evolutionary intentions of the individual itself. (Rad)

Lunar Nodes square Planetary Nodes
Skipped steps would only be true if that actual planet of those Planetary Nodes is also square the Lunar Nodal Axis. In that case that planet would have to be conjunct either its own South Node, or its North Node. (Rad)
With only the Planetary Nodes squaring the Lunar Nodes this correlates to Soul stress around the dynamics symbolized, a stress that correlates with a necessary evolutionary leap. The natural archetypes relative to a first and last quarter square, or disseminating/crescent square, are that which is the cause of the evolutionary stress requiring a leap in the Soul's evolution. JWG wrote about these archetypes in his second Pluto book. There is a whole chapter dedicated to all the phases, from new through balsamic, and all the aspects that take place within these phases. (Rad)

Planet conjunct its own South Node, and both square the Nodal Axis
[Example: Venus in Capricorn conjunct South Node of Venus in Capricorn and both square the Nodal Axis]
(Q) Is it correct that skipped steps apply not only to Venus square the Nodal Axis, but also to the South Node of Venus square the Nodal Axis? That is, a natal planet conjunct *its own* Planetary Node? If so, is the interpretation based on TWO separate sets of skipped steps for Venus and its South Node, or a combination of both? If a combination of both, how would one interpret the skipped steps? (Linda)
(A) Since the Venus and South Node of Venus are conjunct and squaring the Nodal Axis this does in fact correlate to skipped steps wherein both symbols are implicated. This would in fact INTENSIFY the Soul's resistance to making the necessary choices that would allow it to continue to evolve. The actual houses in which the South Node of Venus, and natal Venus, occupy correlate to the dynamics within the Soul that are causing this resistance. Further, the location of the planet Saturn by its own house and sign, and aspects to it, will add to what those dynamics have been. The South Node of the Moon itself, with the location of its own planetary ruler by house, sign, and aspects correlate to the dynamics that have caused the Soul's resistance to making the choices necessary in order to evolve. The North Node by house, sign, and aspects to it in conjunction with the location of its own planetary ruler, and aspects to it, correlate to where, the dynamics involved, the Soul has attempted to leap ahead without addressing the ongoing dynamics that do not allow it to evolve until those dynamics are addressed with the attendant choices being made that will allow it in fact to continue to evolve. (Rad)

Planet conjunct the South Node of another planet, and both square the Nodal Axis
[Example: Venus in Capricorn conjunct South Node of Mercury in Capricorn and both square the Nodal Axis]
(Q) In this case, is it correct that there have been skipped steps with Venus square the Nodal Axis, but NO skipped steps correlating to the South Node of Mercury square the Nodal Axis? How does one interpret the skipped steps of Venus when it is conjunct the South Node of another planet, in this example Mercury?
(A) When a natal planet, in this example Venus, is conjunct a planetary South Node, in this case Mercury, this will symbolize and correlate to the archetypal dynamics of both Venus and Mercury being in a skipped step state relative to their squares to the Nodal Axis.

Sun conjunct another's Planetary South Node in synastry
The Sun in synastry will never correlate to prior life connections to anyone because the Sun, in EA, is about how the entire EA paradigm in the birth chart is integrated, actualized, and given a sense of purpose. In other words the Sun is specific to the current life. When it is conjunct another's South Node of Venus this would then mean that the Sun person would be triggering all the South Node of Venus dynamics in the other person's chart. So from an EA point of view the question then would become: why? At the same time the person who has that South Node of Venus, and all the past dynamics therein, would have their own impact on the person whose Sun is conjuncting that South Node of Venus. Again, why? Conversely, the Moon conjunct another's South Node of Venus can certainly correlate to the possibility of prior life connections in which there has been some relative high degree of proximity to one another. Yet we must be careful in working with the Planetary Nodes in this way. And that means we need to make sure that there are other symbols in the entire synastry contact charts that also indicate prior life connections to another. (Rad)

Planetary Nodes correlating to Astrological Ages
A Planetary Node [eg South Node Mars in Sagittarius] correlates to a Soul living or resonating with past lifetimes during the Ages of Aries and Sagittarius, and the Sub-Ages of Aries and Sagittarius. (Rad)

The Great Cycles

The 26,000 year time frame for the world cycle is based upon the current velocity of our Sun as it moves through the processional equinoctial cycle. According to Sri Yukteswar in "The Holy Science," the Indian sages mark the time of the world cycle to be about 24,000 years, making every degree 66.6 years long, and 2,000 years per zodiac age. Given this, there is reason to consider that our Sun's velocity is not constant, but changes during the cycle. If this were true, our Sun's speed is slower now, and will increase as we return back to our solar system's closest point to the galactic center in 10,500 years, or 12,500 AD. With respect to Pluto and Mars nodal cycles, Solar Fire only provides nodal data for the time period between roughly 4,500 BC to 4,500 AD. Everything else beyond that is based upon extrapolation, given nothing else to go on other than the known fact that there exists an apparent pattern to the order of the cosmos. The pattern of creation can be intuitively grasped based upon evolutionary principles under Natural Law. Pluto and Mars Nodes have different cycles. Pluto's Nodes spend about 2,000 years within every zodiac sign and its polarity. Moving in apparent harmony to our Sun as it shifts also every 2,000 years, based upon the 24k time frame. The Nodes of Mars however remain in three signs, with their polarity, for about 4,000 years. Then one sign with its polarity drops out of the trinity, and is replaced by the next sign in the sequence. For example, in 4,500 to 500 BC, the South Nodes for Mars are Virgo, Libra, and Scorpio. Its North Nodes are Pisces, Aries, Taurus. Then around 500 BC, the South Node of Virgo and North Node Pisces become phased out. They are replaced by the South Node Sagittarius, North Node Gemini. This pattern continues, the trinity of South Node in Libra, Scorpio, Sagittarius and North Node Aries, Taurus, Gemini, until about 4,300 AD. Then Mars South Node Libra, North Node Aries phases out and shifts to South Node Capricorn and North Node Cancer. Using this model, the Nodes of Mars complete one cycle every 24k years. When that cycle culminates, a new cycle begins, but what was the original sign for South Node of Mars (at the beginning of prior 24k cycle) shifts to become its North Node of Mars, and vice versa. Any given sign with its polarity that becomes active within the Mars cycle remains active for 12,000 years at

Using the above example for Mars Nodes at 4,500 BC, and extrapolating into the future at 24k Sun speed, in 19,500 AD (4,500 BC plus 24k) Mars South Node would be Pisces, Aries, Taurus and its North Node would be Virgo, Libra, Scorpio – the reverse. A whole new Mars cycle begins yet the Nodes are reversed. This is an example of the application of polarity upon an evolving consciousness as a gentle, yet provocative force. The 500 AD time is the point calculated by Sri Yukteswar which marks the halfway point in the world cycle. According to the Hindu model of the world cycle, called the Daiva Yugas, there are two halves or what are called by them Electric Couples (EC), each 12k years long. The switch from one Electric Couple to the other occurred in 500 AD. Relative to the patriarchy, it signals its culmination. The forces at work upon human consciousness which operated during the previous EC reflected the male creating principle, which is yang. They now lose their potency, so to speak, as they begin acceding to the female creating principle, which is yin in nature. In its wake will be a return to the Divine Mother and its attendant female creating principle, which will re-absorb (yin) all back into Herself, as a phenomenal experience relative to consciousness itself, which has been, heretofore, undergoing an individuating process during the prior EC for the prior 12K years, 11,500 BC to 500 AD.

Regarding the Roman empire, the Nodes of Mars actually shifted into Aries/Libra somewhere around 5,500 BC. This was, in fact, the time frame after the emergence of the patriarchy. Mars South Node in Libra, emphasizing giving, sharing and including, began much earlier in history, during the time when the Neolithic agricultural communities (Indus Valley, Nile Valley, and Tigris/Euphrates River Valleys to name the most well-known) were growing larger and larger before they became established cultural and trade centers, around 3,000 to 2,500 BC. By the way, the Nodes of Mars finally phase out of the Mars cycle around 4,300 AD, the end of their 12k life cycle. Replacing them are Mars South Node in Capricorn and North Node in Cancer – interestingly enough their natural squares. (Rad)

Transiting Planetary Nodes

To understand the transiting Planetary Nodes in any chart is first to understand the individual context for each Soul: the actual individual Soul reality. And that starts of course with an understanding of the natal position of Pluto as that is referenced to the South Node of the Moon by house and sign placement, and the location of its planetary ruler by its own house and sign, and aspects to it. Aspects to the South Node of the Moon, and aspects to that natal Pluto all correlate to the past context of the Soul: its desires for evolution. Within that we can then understand the actual context of the South Nodes of all the other planets as they all are linked to this underlying, core, evolutionary signature as symbolized by these points. In the same way, to understand the current evolutionary intent for the Soul is to understand Pluto's polarity point by house and sign, the location of the North Node of the Moon by house and sign, and the location of its planetary ruler by house and sign. And aspects to these points by other planets that all contribute to the current evolutionary intention of the Soul. The North Nodes of the other planets, once the individual context is understood, then all contribute to the actualization of this core evolutionary dynamic or intention by the location of their own houses and signs, and aspects to them by other planets. All of these symbols thus correlate to evolutionary dynamics of the Soul for its whole lifetime: the natal imprint.

The transiting South Nodes of the other planets simply means where the Soul is re-meeting its own past at any given moment relative to the archetypal meanings of each planet. Right now the transiting South Node of Venus is in Aquarius. So that will land somewhere in any of our birth charts. And the transiting North Node of Venus is in Taurus which will be somewhere in any of our charts. So first, of course, it is necessary to understand the total archetype of Venus. So, first, once we understand the natal evolutionary signature for any Soul, the core evolutionary dynamics symbolized by Pluto, its polarity point, the North and South Nodes of the Moon, and their planetary rulers, we can then look into any other of the Planetary Nodes to see how they all contributed to this core evolutionary signature. The South Nodes of all the other planets, by their own house and sign locations, other planets that may be aspecting them, have all contributed to the core evolutionary signature of the Soul's desires and intentions.

What kinds of relationships was the Soul forming and why?
What kinds of values did the Soul orientate to and why?
What constituted the sense of meaning and purpose for those lifetimes and why?
What kinds of inner relationships did the Soul have with itself and why?
How was it able to relate to others and why?

These are Venus things. So we do this with all the Planetary Nodes. It is just a matter of understanding the total archetypes of all the planets. What are the Mercury archetypes and how have they been orientated to in past lives and why? What are the Mars ones, Jupiter ones, etc. etc. Once we have this total grasp and understanding of all the past life dynamics and why, we can then understand where the Soul comes into life at: the past that has led to the current life. Once we know that total context then we can truly understand the nature of all the North Node symbols for all the other planets. It is through those North Nodes of all the other planets that not only do the archetypes of those planets evolve within the consciousness of the Soul, but they also correlate to how the Soul intends to fully develop the current evolutionary intentions for the life being lived as related to the core evolutionary signature in all charts: natal Pluto, its polarity point, the North and South Nodes of the Moon, the location of the planetary rulers of each.

Each planet has their own Nodal Axis. This is the Natural Law of the trinity that we can call the past, present, and future. The past of course are the South Nodes. The future are the North Nodes, and the present is the position of the natal planet as it relates to its nodal axis. The natal signature of all of these is a life signature that operates for the whole life: like a foundation upon which a house is built. The natal position of the planet relative to its own Nodes is the integration point relative to the past and the future for the past is always defining the moment as is the evolutionary pull of the future. The forces of the past and the future must have an integration point in the present. And that is the natal position of the planet itself. The transiting South Nodes of any planet, or the Moon, is where we are always meeting our past in some way so as to evolve it into the future which is the meaning of the transiting North Nodes of the planets and the Moon. Within this, of course, we also have the transit of the planets themselves at any moment in time with the transiting Nodes of those transiting planets. So, here again, we have the natural trinity: the transiting planet and its Nodes. The transiting planet relative to its Nodes is the integration point in the present for the issues that are manifesting relative to its Nodes: past and present. And this transiting trinity of a planet and its Nodes is then related to the underlying evolutionary signature for life as demonstrated in the natal positions of that planet and its Nodes. This is how to understand and use the Planetary Nodes in the individual's chart. Each Soul. Then of course there is the collective: the transiting positions at any moment in time for any planet, and its Nodes, and this affects and impacts on each of our individual lives. (Rad)

Transiting South Node of anything

The transiting South Node of anything of course correlates with the nature of one's past as it interfaces with the current moment in the life of the Soul: the 'now.' The nature of one's past is then helping to shape and define the nature of the moment as reflected in that past. (Rad)

South Node of Neptune in Aquarius

(Q) In relation with the South Node of Neptune being in Aquarius (reflecting the original matriarchal roots of the current desires in all Souls to spiritualize consciousness), and the connection of natal Neptune with the Aquarius Age, in the context of the current transition between the Pisces Age into the next Aquarius Age, would imply that the root of these desires (ie the past of the Soul) is also symbolic of the future ways for the Souls to spiritualize consciousness (ie ways which will be in place for these Souls in the next Age). Is this correct? (Gonzalo)

(A) Yes. (Rad)

(Q) For me this is interesting to consider because it confirms that the current time frame is defined by a potential for accelerated evolution of Souls because it implies that the past is becoming the future now. Thus, the work on resolution of issues from past lifetimes related to the spiritual roots of the Soul and, at the same time, work on the resolution of issues pertaining to the future of the Soul – ie the past and the future are contained and concentrated within the current time. Is this correct?

(A) Yes. And what this will mean of course is if the original spiritual root will manifest again or not which itself is linked with the survival of the species. Within Aquarius is the triad of Libra and Gemini. Libra correlates with the Natural Law of giving, sharing, and inclusion. This is how humans were defined relative to groups of humans, Aquarius, for the balance of humans' existence on our planet. In relatively recent times this Natural Law of course has become perverted to self-interest and exclusion which then causes one group of humans, or one human, then trying to compete with other groups, or a human, relative to the survival instinct itself. In turn this leads to dominance and submission. If this is not corrected by going back to the original root, or past, and bringing that forwards into the future, then the extinction of the species is guaranteed.

(Q) So, in a sense, over lifetimes of evolution, as the "hole enlarges" or more veils are removed and more illusions dissolved (lots of disillusionment), from this perspective relative to Neptune's South Node, would it be sound understanding to correlate this symbol to what *has held* (past tense) ultimate meaning in the individualized consciousness relative to how much that consciousness has evolved? (Bradley)

(A) Yes. You can also include into this the natural planetary ruler of the South Node of Neptune which for all of us is Aquarius and its natural ruler Uranus. You can include the aspects to this Uranus as well as aspects to the South Node of Neptune itself. (Rad)

(Q) So, the Soul's journey has a past. The consciousness within the Soul journey, relative to the sense of an evolutionary past and future, has a past. This past may not be as we perceive linear time; however in the sense that the consciousness does has a past, along the journey it continues to evolve further into the fullest potential of consciousness within the human form. Would the South Node of Neptune then correlate to earlier in the Soul's evolutionary journey the ways which it spiritualized?

(A) Yes.

(Q) And then, relative to the Soul's individual past, what held ultimate meaning within that Soul's consciousness and thus still resonates as such, coming through the 'now' as a way to naturally spiritualize. And that which still holds a sense of ultimate meaning within the consciousness expressing outwardly relative to the stage at which the consciousness has evolved along the journey thus far (aka the evolutionary stage of the Soul)?

(A) Yes.

PLUTO

Primary evolutionary/karmic axis, "the bottom line"
The entire EA paradigm of natal Pluto, the location of the South Node of the Moon, the location of its own planetary ruler by house, sign, and aspects to other planets, Pluto's polarity point, the location of the North Node of the Moon by its own house and sign, and the location of its planetary ruler by its own house, sign, and aspects to it correlates to the primary evolutionary/karmic axis, the bottom line, for the Soul's ongoing evolution from life to life for any of us. It's like a foundation upon which a house is built. Relative to that foundation the REST of the entire birth chart is then properly understood relative to THAT CONTEXT. Everything else is referred to that context, that primary evolutionary/karmic axis. (Rad)

Root structure of the chart
Pluto and its nodes, planetary rulers, aspects to these from other planets, correlate to the root structure within any birth chart. And from that root all else, the South Nodes of the Moon, their planetary rulers, aspects to these points, are 'birthed' from that root. It's like a tree that has branches where the root produces the trunk of the tree, and the trunk then produces branches with leaves. This core root and its branches within the birth chart are treated EQUALLY for it is the very structure of the chart itself. If we understand this root structure within the birth chart and relate it to the Natural Law of cause and effect then we can understand that core structure within the birth chart at once. It will, of itself, induce inductive logic. And from there we can then understand the origins and causes of all the specific leaves manifesting from the branches, ie why is this Mars in Gemini squaring Mercury in Pisces? (Rad)

Evolution is set in motion by Pluto, the Soul
Everything is set in motion by the Soul and the desires within it. Thus, the polarity point of Pluto only manifests by way of the desire within the Soul to do so. If that is done then the North Node of the Moon is simultaneously set in motion because of the desires emanating from the Soul. All evolution or motion within the birth chart, including the Nodes of the Moon, is set in motion, evolving, only because of the desires that emanate from the Soul: Pluto. In other words, the Moon, in and of itself, does not cause anything to happen: does not cause evolution to occur. All comes from the root of Pluto, the Soul. All combinations of planets and their nodes are created BY THE SOUL relative to its ongoing evolution over great lengths of time. Thus, all facilitate the Soul's evolution. But, again, it all starts from within the Soul itself. Without active desires, choices, to set all of these symbols in motion, to evolve, nothing will happen. It's like marking time. Once the Soul does make the choices by manifesting desires to do so then all of the symbols in the birth chart, the nodal axis of all planets, then facilitate that ongoing evolution of the Soul. (Rad)

Pluto paradigm
The underlying principle in all biological forms is to survive intact in the present form – that instinct is pre-wired. And we all have a need to feel secure. What makes us feel secure is what we already know. Thus we develop a self-image (Moon) of seeing "me" as a person who is and does whatever makes me feel secure. Over lives those repeated Moons become the basis of the South Node. The evolutionary impulse pulls us to the polarity – 180 degrees away from what makes us feel secure. This triggers our survival instincts – we don't feel safe 180 degrees away from what makes us feel secure, thus we resist. I don't feel the process is always linear from life to life. "Completing" 8th house Pluto, as from my chart would seem to be what this life is about for me, doesn't mean I necessarily start the next with Pluto at 0 degrees and 5 minutes into the 9th house. Astrology is symbolic not literal.
There are many placements that can create the Soul's desired lessons. For 8th house Pluto, for example, an 8th house South Node, or a Scorpio stellium, etc. In my chart, even in this life I have Sagittarius rising along with a very late 8th house Pluto. This I feel is seeding my Soul's long term evolutionary intentions. Everything always comes down to the Soul's dual desire nature. At a bottom line level that manifests as (1) the desire to survive and feel secure, which can ultimately lead to stagnation, and (2) the offsetting urge or instinct to grow and evolve – the impulse to the polarity. The one points to the past, the other to the future. We live in the present, between those two impulses. Most of us, until we change, keep compulsively and habitually repeating the past, BECAUSE we experience it as making us feel secure (even if the past is dysfunctional, it is what we know), even as we make occasional steps towards the future.

Everything comes down to free will/choice. When a Soul starts consciously embracing the intended future, the evolutionary intentions, things can start changing rapidly. That is because within itself that Soul gets off the fence and starts committing more deeply to one side of the dual desire nature. The pull to the past still exists and it still finds itself at times operating from the past knowns. But the center of gravity starts shifting from free will decisions, and the results of these inner decisions become increasingly apparent in the person's outer life. In other words, they progressively internalize and reduce resistance to the evolutionary intentions. No Soul is totally embracing the Pluto polarity in a lifetime. Even Jesus said something along the lines of, "Father, if you are willing, take this cup from me; yet not my will, but yours be done." To me that is because the aspirations of the Soul, being the long term view, go far beyond what any human being can possibly embrace in a single lifetime. The more you evolve the more the Soul wants to evolve. It is NEVER satisfied with what has been accomplished as there is always more. A mentor from my younger days used to describe this as "the itch you can't scratch." That is the desire nature of the Soul.

The natal position of Pluto correlates to the bottom line DESIRES, which are the root cause of everything else. And just as we humans have desire natures that shift around from time to time, I feel something similar occurs within the Soul too, although it seems there is always an underlying bottom line. So an emphasis could be on this in one lifetime and that in another lifetime. Yet the bottom line would be the same. My point is it's not like one achieves the aims of one life and then the Pluto point gets to move. The whole thing is a living, dynamic, moment by moment process. And free choice is the engine that can move us forward, or not. That is the whole point of following transits and progressions – they represent the natural unfolding of the timing of the evolutionary intentions for that lifetime. In this dimension they occur over time, not all at once. So although we have the same natal Pluto placement for a whole lifetime, within that placement, it evolves over time, through experiences and choices. We can only, at best, ever partially embrace anything new. By the time we fully embrace it, it's become what now makes us feel secure, which is the first sign that you are guaranteed that sooner or later it will be taken away, to be replaced with something else we resist that gradually becomes our new norm. That cycle goes on and on and on. The only thing we can truly count on for consistent security is within us. Everything else is temporary. Embracing that is not easy. But that IS our reality. (Steve)

Truth of the Pluto paradigm

You can know it for yourself by practice, and allowing your intuition to simply grasp the truth of the total EA paradigm. We all know, not believe, that we have a past because it's a known quantity: it exists. We also know that we have a future because we have had a past. And that knowing exists in each moment of our life: inhale and exhale. This is known. Does not require belief of any kind. The paradigm of EA perfectly reflects this simple, and natural truth. Thus, we have South Nodes, current life positions of planets, and North Nodes. It is the interweaving of the known past with the evolutionary pull of the future that manifests as desires that we act upon, and that action occurs in the moment. It's just that simple. The totality of the Soul's birth chart in each life symbolized in all of these symbols correlates to this Natural Law and truth. (Rad)

Layers – Pluto, nodes, rulers

Pluto is the deepest layer. The Nodes the next deepest layer. The rulers of the Nodes a layer above that. Most of us are more conscious of what is on the surface than what lies beneath it. So we act in certain ways habitually. This is going to relate at the top to the ruler, which is actualizing the intentions of the underlying Node, based on the planet, sign, house the ruler is located in. Similarly, the Node is actualizing the intentions of the underlying Pluto (for the South Node), or PPP (North Node). Pluto, or PPP, is always the baseline. The Nodes describe how Pluto has been carrying out (actualizing) its desire nature, the ruler how the patterns inherent in the Nodes have been actualized. The gist of it is, one can't really separate the PPP, the NORTH NODE, the NORTH NODE ruler – they are different layers or levels of the exact same thing, even though we may not consciously experience it that way. When you are focusing on the NORTH NODE, you ARE effecting and actualizing the intents of the PPP. (Steve)

Pluto, why it (and not other planets) represents the desires of the Soul

Pluto correlates to the Soul itself, and within that, the Natural Law of evolution. It correlates to what the desires of the Soul have been that has led to the current life, and the desires that correlate to its ongoing evolutionary needs. This is contained with Pluto, the Soul, itself. All the other planets in a current life birth chart are thus created by the Soul for its ongoing evolutionary needs that are reflected in its desires. The current life birth planets do have their own North and South Nodes. It is the South Nodes of these planets that do correlate to the past life dynamics that the Soul has created for itself that have led to the current life, and the position of whatever planet IN THIS LIFE that symbolizes the current life's evolutionary needs. The current life position brings the past forwards through it: the South Node coming through the current position of the planet itself. The North Node of the planet in turn correlates to the ongoing evolutionary journey of the Soul as it continues to evolve through each of the archetypes of all the planets. The cause of that evolution is the Soul, not any of the other planets themselves. The natural polarity point of the natal Pluto is the bottom line evolutionary intent for the Soul in each life. It is the primary cause that causes the North Nodes of all the other planets to actualize according to that primary evolutionary intention. The natal planet, in the current life, birth chart, serves to integrate the past and the future in each moment FOR THE ENTIRE LIFE. (Rad)

Step by step approach to understanding the evolutionary dynamics

In interpreting a chart, start with Pluto, the underlying evolutionary desires, before jumping further to the nodes and other factors. In order to have a foundation and a clear understanding it is best to follow these simple rules. So with Pluto, the Soul, what kind of desire nature led to the present, via the past? Then and only then can you consider how it was manifested via what kind of egocentric nature that the Soul created (this is the South Node). So how was this done? And from there the ruler of the South Node as the facilitator of that kind of egocentric consciousness via which the Soul operated. These are the steps to uncover the secret of the Soul – that's the miracle of EA – it is able to uncover that. Follow this order in chart interpretation and you'll get closer to the whole picture.

Then once you have determined at least the major evolutionary dynamics of the past – where the Soul actually comes from – you will understand more clearly the "whys" of the current evolutionary lessons, symbolized by Pluto's polarity point, the North Node and then the North Node's ruler. Only this way can you understand why, for example, any planet may conjunct the North Node and for what reason. The reason for any present condition always lies in the past. Without understanding that past we don't understand the present, and that may lead to misunderstanding and misinterpretation. The future of course is just as much connected to the present (and the choices the Soul makes) as the present is to the past. It is all continuous and interconnected – one step leads to the next. (Lia)

Pluto is the only mobilizer in the chart. The Soul (Pluto), having created the Sun, and other planets and their Nodes, has also created them in a way that they will all facilitate the evolution of the Soul itself, and as part of that process, the evolution of themselves too. And looking at the Nodes of those other planets (all except the Sun), we can see how the Soul has gone about facilitating itself in this way in the past, and also its intentions for doing so in the future. A natural tension arises between the past that's been and the future that is ahead of us, and this is felt and able to be integrated at the current placement of these planets. This tension is integrated by embracing the polar opposite realm of experience and understanding (polarity point) of each planet as consciously as possible. Conscious striving in this way towards our potential is what causes each area and aspect of ourselves (shown by the planets themselves in their current placements) to grow and evolve.

The relationship between the Soul (Pluto) and our subconscious identity (Moon – its egocentric structure) that is created each lifetime, reflects the core mechanism that we unconsciously create from within our Soul to enable a sense of self in our daily life, albeit usually a subconscious one. And we look at the Moon's Nodes to get information over time about this identity/facilitation process the Soul keeps creating for itself. This subconscious sense of identity is itself not a static position. It too is in a state of tension caused by the pull of the past and continuity (strengthening this sense of self) and the need to keep moving out of our comfort zone into a new unknown sense of self (Moon polarity point). It needs to do this to accommodate the inevitable changes that are brought about in our life as a result of the deep (and relatively unconscious) urge within us to evolve (Pluto) propelling us towards our deepest growth possible in this lifetime (Pluto's polarity point).

The relationship between Pluto, and Mars and its Nodes, reflects where the Soul is at within itself in regard to its creating desires to act on. The activation of these desires is what sets in motion all the other energies (all the remaining planets/asteroids with Nodes) in the chart, with their inbuilt role to play in facilitating the ongoing evolution of the Soul. We look at the Nodes of Mars and these other planets/asteroids, to get information about how these conscious desires and the particular roles of the other planets in the Soul's evolution, roles that have been created by the Soul in the first place, are all manifesting over time.

This whole process – starting in the relatively unconscious Soul (Pluto) manifesting as a subconscious awareness of identity and self which imparts a sense of continuity (Moon) – is initiated by the choice to evolve at the Soul level. This (relatively unconscious) choice to evolve, then manifests as multiple conscious desires that we are aware of in our lives. Both the Moon and the Sun register the urges, evolutionary intentions, from the Soul, Pluto, via Mars its lower octave; this whole process is integrated by our (relatively) much more conscious sense of being (the Sun) – in the realm of life shown by the Sun's house, with the disposition and needs of the sign the Sun is in. The conscious expression and integration of ourself (Sun) evolves within this realm (house) with more developed understanding (sign) as these desires emanating from our unconscious (Pluto) are acted upon and experienced over time (shown by all the Nodes). The resistance generated by the past (shown by the South Nodes) – to fulfilling the intentions arising from within our Soul (Pluto) and thus manifesting our future possibilities (North Nodes) – is broken down and dissolved when we choose out of free will to grow into the unknown (our polarity points). And in doing so, our future (shown by the North Nodes) then becomes actualized, and this consciousness through which we integrate everything that we are aware of (the Sun), then expands. In this way the Soul effects its evolution. (Upasika)

Pluto (sign/house); Pluto's nodes (sign/house); Pluto's nodal rulers (sign/house); aspects from all of the above to other planets (and their signs/houses – and if more info is required, also their nodes); are the fundamental root of any chart. From there, the sign/house of the Moon's nodes, Moon's nodal rulers, and Pluto's polarity point are brought in. Then aspects from all these to other planets (and their signs/houses). Also at this level a planet's nodes can be examined if more info was required. Then progression to examination of any other part of the chart that thus becomes implicated out of this. (Realizing of course that every part of the chart has a part in the whole person/event and so eventually needs to be included in a totally complete analysis.) (Upasika)

EA question, "Why?"

The EA question is, "Why did the Soul create the chart that way?" It always comes down to either past conditions, or evolutionary intentions, or both. Our work as EA astrologers is to do the detective work and try to understand the reasons for the chart. (Steve) The only reason why anyone would ever get sick is the same reason why anyone would ever be born, die, feel pain, laugh, etc. Sickness, dis-ease etc. only exist as a part of the maya of this reality that we created for our evolution. A Soul never gets sick – at the core, it is always, only in a state of DESIRE. The nature of that desire is what manifests the physical reality that it will experience. When a Soul experiences anything at all – it can ask, in neutrality, "why?" I feel that "why" can take a Soul as far as it wants to go. Now I get why JWG emphasizes that Pluto folks ask "why" about everything "why life, why death" – those are really good questions. (Ari)

Pluto paradigm analysis, an example

[Example: Pluto Sagittarius 8th, South Node Taurus 1st, Jupiter Scorpio 7th, 3rd stage Individuated] The Pluto in Sagittarius in the 8th, the river of the Soul, has desired to understand the WHY'S of life itself, the causes and effects of anything, human psychology in its fullest dimensions, its own psychology and the causes of it, and Natural Laws of Creation itself, how people in general interpret the phenomena of life in all of its forms and dimensions, what motivates people and why, and the sexual realities and the reasons for those realities in human nature, and so on. One of the tributary streams that feeds this Soul river, with Jupiter in Scorpio in the 7th, would correlate with the cultural anthropology of humans in diverse cultures, tribes, and societies that the Soul would contemplate in order to understand the core desires as manifesting in the 8th house Pluto. This contemplation would be fuelled by reading a variety of materials, travelling to many places, and observing the diversity of peoples. The South Node being in Taurus in the 1st creates and egocentric structure in which the Soul keeps itself distant and independent from people in general. This symbolism correlates to a banyan tree that remains rooted in one place for thousands of years while the panorama of time passes it by. The banyan tree, the egocentric structure, thus is secure within its own inner isolation as it observes and learns by all that which passes it by.

On a very selective basis the Soul through its 1st house Taurus egocentric structure would engage others in relationship, the tributary stream of the Jupiter in Scorpio in the 7th relative to Pluto in Sagittarius in the 8th house, that were inwardly evaluated to be of use by the Soul for its evolutionary intentions: needs. In turn, this would set in motion very intense and deep philosophical and psychological type discussions in which the core desires of the Soul were being met. In the above example this would then place the evolving egocentric structure, one of the core evolutionary intentions, in the 7th house: North Node in the 7th in Scorpio. This would then mean, that as a next step in the Soul's evolution, that it now must learn how to jump out of its cocoon of self-isolation: South Node in Taurus in the 1st. Rather than observing in such isolation in the ways that it has before, it must now learn how to FULLY ENGAGE, emotionally and psychologically, with others. The Soul intends to learn how to be in relationships with others in general in this way, and learn how to commit to being with a partner on a one to one basis. It is thus learning how to unite a core psychological and emotional paradox, the core paradox manifesting from the Soul. And that is the paradox of needing total independence and freedom relative to committing to others in general, and a partner specifically. (Rad)

Soul's desire nature – separating desires

The natural desire to separate was put in motion by the Creator itself. That's why it is natural. The intention within this as designed by the Creator was for all aspects of the Creation that had conscious awareness to realize, consciously realize, that in their APPARENT separateness that defined their sense of individuality, their origins, where they came from, what their essence was/is, is the Creator itself. Within this core awareness is the awareness that all of the manifested Creation is thus inter-related and interdependent. All is part of the whole. It is a Natural Law. When humans lived in this way for the balance of its history until recent times, they were thus living in a reality that was defined by 'giving, sharing, and inclusion' which equaled their need for survival as individuals, and as groups of people. When this natural desire of separateness became perverted this Natural Law of giving, sharing, and inclusion changed to self-interest and exclusion. Step back for a moment and imagine realities created by humans that were defined by the Natural Law of giving, sharing, and inclusion versus the realities that have been created by self-interest and exclusion. The stark relief created in this comparison should speak for itself. A simple example: American Indians hunting for buffalo. Once the buffalo was killed the Indian would pray for the buffalo and thank it for providing food for the tribe in the understanding of how the WHOLE was interrelated, and how each part of that whole was dependent for survival on that whole.

Now compare this to the white man, under the delusion of Manifest Destiny which itself manifested from their MAN-CREATED, not God-created, version of Christianity. And how the white man almost brought to extinction the entire buffalo species in its greed defined by self-interest and exclusion: ie the white man in its delusive self-importance and superiority to all that was NOT HIM having zero awareness of the WHOLE. Thus all other aspects of the Creation were to serve its own self-interest defined by others who threatened that self-interest. When the buffalo was killed it was left to rot on the ground that it was killed after its hide had been removed. This simple example of the perversion of the natural desire to separate could be exampled in literally thousands of ways. And it is because it can, the actual reality that has been created leading right up to the present moment, that humans have guaranteed their extinction. The Creator is also the origin of course of free choice. And it is through choice making that all of us are responsible for what we create. (Rad)

Pluto, by house and sign, correlates to the Soul's *desire nature*. The evolutionary intent is to change, to deepen, the Soul's desire nature. After repeated disappointments, disillusions, traumas, etc., eventually a Soul/Ego starts accepting that what it thought it knew no longer works, is no longer enough, and starts embracing the need to change, that is, the need to make different choices. Typically they don't know *how* to make any other choices. Most of us equate what I know with who I am. Thus a larger sense of who I am is being called for. (Steve)

It's really very simple. Diversity is the fundamental principle in our reality. Each human, cat, snowflake, grain of sand on beach, plant, microbe, is completely unique. Each Soul has its own interests and orientations. The range of separating desires is nearly infinite. There is no checklist of separating desires through which every Soul must pass. Through the principle of diversity we can explore and express as we please. (There are Natural Laws however, with natural consequences to our choices.) It comes down to, we do what we want to until we no longer want to. A Soul reaches a point in its journey where what it no longer wants is to chase the delusions and illusions we call separating desires. At that point it starts concentrating on God. Until then it doesn't. It's due to a change in what that Soul desires, not based on any kind of "should be's". (Steve)

Resistance and cooperation

The great gift with a chart heavily weighted towards growth is there is nothing you have to do to relinquish control. Life (Pluto) will simply make it impossible at key times for anything else to occur. Like good little humans we often resist until the bitter end, but in the end whatever is being resisted is removed from the life (Pluto) and the intention of relinquishing control is accomplished. And here you thought you were having a hard life – it's all been for your benefit, to accomplish the Soul's evolutionary intentions. That is why, once we realize this, we learn to try to cooperate with, rather than resist, the intentions, as they appear in our life as we move along. Even when they are difficult or painful. That helps accelerate the process of relinquishing control, once we have learned to trust that it is for our benefit, it is on our side, it is not there to try to mess up our lives no matter what it may feel like. (Steve)

On a practical level, the first step is to become conscious of one's karmic signature (or evolutionary signature) – to understand the signatures of the past, and the evolutionary intentions for this lifetime. For example, Pluto square Nodes evolutionary signature would be a significant part of that. Then we have to ACCEPT this signature – beyond understanding it intellectually, to emotionally embrace it. The point is, quite often there are parts of this we don't like, or wish would be other than they are – don't want to embrace, don't even want to admit to. The process starts speeding up as we accept, "Here is where I am, today, and here is where I'm intended to be heading." Then one makes an inner choice, decision, to *cooperate with* this unfolding process. Knowing that at times it's not going to feel comfortable, it's not going to feel like what we want to do or where we want to go – that is part of the process, comes with the territory. We have to accept that also. (Steve)

Evolution of natal Pluto itself

The natal Pluto is never left behind nor in any way does it become non-operational. The natural evolutionary progression always involves the Natural Law of the trinity. Thus, the natal position of Pluto operates from birth relative to how the Soul comes into the current life from where it has been. There is a natural polarity point to this, that symbolizes the core evolutionary intent. As the Soul moves, evolves, towards that intent it then simultaneously EVOLVES the orientation of the natal position of Pluto itself. Thus, the Natural Law of the trinity. We must remember that any house or sign is an entire archetype: a full spectrum within itself. As evolution proceeds within any archetype the various orientations within that spectrum are embraced as a result. (Rad)

Individualized context

To understand any one symbol in a birth chart one must understand the totality of that birth chart in order to understand the individual context that then allows for an understanding of any one symbol within it. One cannot make generalized statements about any one symbol that applies to all. The individual context is essential to understanding anything, and that starts with the EA paradigm itself, the evolutionary condition of the Soul, and the socio-cultural place of birth. (Rad)

Pluto, the sign of

The sign that Pluto is in, ie Leo, Virgo, etc. CONTAINS within itself the archetype of the planet that rules that sign and, thus, how the Soul desires to actualize itself. The actual house and sign of that planet that is the ruler of the sign that the Soul is in acts like a tributary stream that feeds the main river of the Soul. The river itself is Pluto by house and sign location, and its North and South Nodes with their respective planetary rulers. The tributary streams that flow into that river are the aspects by other planets to these Nodes, their planetary rulers, and Pluto itself. (Rad)

Pluto rulership

In EA Mars is the lower octave of Pluto, and is the natural ruler of Aries. (Rad)

EA (and most modern astrology) sees Pluto as the ruler of Scorpio. Mars is the lower octave of Pluto, and would be considered a co-ruler, although in EA we tend to see Pluto as the ruler and rarely refer to Mars as a co-ruler. (Steve)

In EA Mars is the ruler of Aries, Ascendant, and the 1st house. So when you see the Nodes in Scorpio that does not mean that Mars has a co-rulership with Pluto. Mars, the 1st house, and Aries all correlate to how the desires of the Soul get instinctually acted upon via the current life ego, Moon, and the subjective consciousness therein. (Rad)

Pluto and Mars

The current position, the natal position, of Mars correlates to how to move forwards in this life in order to evolve beyond where the Soul left off with the existing desires from past lifetimes. It is essential to remember that all desires emanate from the Soul. And that the root of such desires to evolve, the ongoing evolutionary journey of the Soul, is of course all symbolized by the natal position of Pluto, and its polarity point. Mars, as an archetype, is the lower octave of Pluto that instinctually acts out, acts upon, those desires emanating from the Soul itself. (Rad)

Mars is Aries energy, instinctual, and is the carrier, the vehicle, by which the Soul (Pluto) transmits its intentions, desires, into human awareness at an instinctual sub-conscious level – primal urges. (Steve)

[Mars is implicated with Pluto] when there are aspects to it from Pluto, or Mars aspects to the South Node, its planetary ruler, or aspects to that planetary ruler. (Rad)

Being a lower octave of Pluto, Mars will express on an ongoing external basis the dual desire nature of the Soul: the desire to separate and the desire to return to the Source. Aries, Mars, the 1st house, correlate with the desire and need to separate in order to create a sense of being a distinct individual, which in turn will induce a crisis because of the natural inconjunct between Aries and Scorpio – the Soul. This crisis is rooted in the dual desires of the Soul, which allows the ego perception (Cancer, 4th house, Moon) of being totally separate from anything else, yet needing to integrate back to where it emanated from – the Soul. Via Mars, the Soul will instinctively produce actions creating the experiences the Soul – Pluto – needs to actualize its intentions, to externally create what it desires. In turn, by means of actualizing its desires, and creating that which the Soul desires, the Soul will be able to discover what it is that it has desired: that which was unconscious will become apparent.

Thus, Mars will allow the Soul to evolve, because the externalization of desires, the surfacing of Soul desires through created experiences, is necessary for the process of exhausting and eliminating its separating desires. When Mars is in aspect to Pluto, the function of acting out desires is subject to metamorphic change: instinctual creation of experiences – Mars – strongly fueled by the desire nature of the Soul – Pluto. The individual will create experiences directly expressing its desires, be they desires of separation or desires to return. The individual will face its unconscious desire nature because he will have the power to externally or consciously create that which he desires: his desires will produce an effect. This effect will allow conscious awareness of the desire nature of the individual, and a metamorphosis of how the individual is acting out his desires. This dynamic exists in all people – it is the basis of evolution of human consciousness – whether or not Mars is in aspect to Pluto, though it will be emphasized when these aspects exist. (Gonzalo)

Pluto/Mars phase – primary/subsidiary lives

Primary lives exist when Pluto/Mars are in any of the following aspects: conjunction, semisquare, square, trine, sesquisquare, inconjunct or opposition. In primary lives the core evolutionary and karmic intentions are being directly worked on. (JWG)

It is all about the intention for the non-primary life which is simply continuing to actualize, evolve, whatever the original intentions are for the current evolutionary cycle that the Soul is living out. It takes many lives for this to happen. There can be any number of subsidiary lives working on the core evolutionary dynamics. (Rad)

Given there are 8 phases, the maximum number of primary lives for working on the same core evolutionary dynamics are 8 lives with many subsidiary lives along the way. The Soul does not move in a linear way through each of the 12 aspects relative to primary lives. It does not work that way. All depends on the individual dynamics within the Soul that then correlates to the TYPE OF ASPECT that it will have within one of 8 lunar phases that correlate with a primary life. So, in other words, it's not linear. There can of course be many subsidiary lives that take place within the 8 phases. (Rad)

Pluto and Mars indicating a primary lifetime means more evolutionary work is intended in that life. Since the end intention of evolutionary work is to deepen the awareness of self as Soul, to the extent the intended lessons are learned, that can deepen the knowing of self as Soul. It is more possible or probable in a primary life only because the intention of that life is to make that Soul do certain necessary work. Whether primary or secondary life, a Soul is still in the evolutionary station it is in. The issue is how much evolutionary advancement is intended. There are other indicators of that besides Mars/Pluto, including the number of aspects Pluto makes to other planets, number of planets in the birth chart that are retrograde. (Steve)

A primary lifetime is an evolutionary gateway lifetime. That is what the aspect between Pluto and Mars represents. That aspect is either culminating (balsamic qualities) like a crescent phase square, or beginning (new phase qualities) like a first quarter square. They are gateways into the next phase of that Soul's development. Because they relate to new orientations, in the case of stressful aspects at least, there is going to be inner tension and resistance to the intended changes. That resistance will be within the Soul itself, not just the personality. Thus it may take extra effort to move through the transition. Mars moves about half a degree a day. By progression, in an 80 year life Mars moves about 40 degrees, enough to move through any transitional gateway (unless it is retrograde for all or part of that period). Thus culminating aspects have the potential to complete within this life, if the evolutionary intentions are addressed. Jeffrey taught that it takes eight primary lifetimes to complete a Mars-Pluto cycle, which breaks down to one per phase. You can see by the progressions that 40 degrees in 80 years correlates to approx. one 45 degree phase of that cycle. (Steve)

The Mars/Pluto phase in a subsidiary life is a life in which the Soul is working out its intentions in a variety of indirect ways. (Cat) [Mars in aspect to other planets is the "variety of indirect ways" that the Soul is currently working out its desires through Mars...] This is analogous to entering a room and seeing another door on the opposite side of that room, yet to get to that door there is a variety of debris that must be removed before the door can be gotten to, and then walked through. In a primary life, it would mean entering that same room, seeing that door on the other side, and moving directly towards it without any debris being in that room to move through. (Rad)

I don't think JWG ever expanded much on the purpose of subsidiary (secondary) lifetimes. What fits for me is they are where we are completing and refining elements that were not quite finished in the primary lifetime. (It is our own Soul that determines if it is satisfied that completion was reached.) (Steve)

Pluto square Nodes – skipped steps   [*See* chapter SKIPPED STEPS]

It symbolizes that the Soul has skipped steps prior to the current life that must be recovered in the current life in order for personal growth to continue. The node that last formed a conjunction to Pluto is the "resolution node," or the node that will be used to integrate and resolve the skipped steps (if the South Node last formed a conjunction to Pluto then the South Node and its planetary ruler will be used to integrate the current evolutionary lessons symbolized by Pluto's polarity point and the North Node). In the case of Pluto square the nodal axis the Soul has not fully developed the lessons reflected by either of the nodes and so has skipped steps to resolve in both areas (North Node and South Node). The Soul has attempted to evade or escape these lessons by fluctuating back and forth between the behaviors of the South Node and the North Node (so neither area has been fully resolved or developed). In the current life then, the Soul must fully recover or resolve those skipped steps (it is a critical evolutionary juncture for any Soul that has this natal signature). (Deva)

In terms of integrating Pluto's polarity point when Pluto is square the Nodes, remember that it is about integrating the "resolution node" in a new way – breaking free from past habits through embracing Pluto's polarity point. Pluto's polarity point will be integrated through the resolution node, with its planetary ruler facilitating that process. In other words, the resolution node and its planetary ruler will become the bottom line upon which Pluto's polarity point will be integrated, and the skipped steps symbolized by Pluto square the nodal axis will be resolved. The point is that Pluto's polarity point must be embraced before these changes can happen, and the skipped steps resolved. In the context of Pluto's polarity point in the 4th, it emphasizes that one learn how to be in the world in a new way. (Deva)

[Example: Pluto 10th, PPP 4th] Pluto (or any planet) square the nodes are called skipped steps, which means the person has been flipping back and forth between the South and North Nodes without fully developing either. When Pluto squares the nodes, it means the Soul itself is directly doing this flipping. In essence it has gotten stuck in an m.o. that it unconsciously gravitates to at stressful points in the life, and it activates the flipping behavior to try to cope with the situation – it's a learned strategy. The problem is, the underlying issues can only be resolved when the work at one of the nodes is carried through to completion, rather than flipping to the other one at key stress points. The node that Pluto conjuncted last is called the resolution node. That is the one that needs to be developed/resolved, to break the flipping pattern. The Pluto polarity point (PPP) is just as important with Pluto squaring the nodes as in any other configuration. (The one exception to that rule is when Pluto conjuncts the North Node natally, there is no PPP. Other than that it applies in all cases.) Determining which node last conjuncted Pluto is a bit confusing because of the retrograde motion of the nodes. An EA astrologer came up with this method to quickly determine the resolution node. Picture yourself standing on the outer rim of the chart, facing the planet that squares the nodes (Pluto in this case). Point to the node on the left – that is the resolution node.

Sometimes the resolution node is the South Node, which on the surface doesn't make much sense – why would I need to develop the past habitual patterns? The meaning is, they need to be developed IN A NEW WAY. Developing the resolution node leads to untying the knots that are the root basis of the skipping pattern in the first place. As the new patterns develop, the Soul can break free from the habitual unconscious skipping pattern. When you have a skipped steps pattern with Pluto, when you have been consciously working on moving forward, ie developing the NORTH NODE, the tendency at stress points is going to be to want to dive back to the safety and known nature of the South Node. You have to become conscious of that tendency, to see how it plays out in your outer reality, to look at your life and see how you have actualized that tendency. There is where you look to the rulers. Typically what triggers skipping is having "bitten off more than you can chew," making a really big leap, "piece of cake, I can handle this," and finding overwhelm. Getting afraid or overloaded with the movement towards the NORTH NODE. Then finding all sorts of reasons why it's okay to go back to the known, the past, the familiar. The point is, just knowing that you do this does not in itself resolve it. But it's the beginning of resolving it – you become aware of, conscious of, what has always been going on that you did not realize previously was a pattern, a mode of behavior.

The first step in changing a behavior is becoming aware you are in it – because then when you find yourself going into that pattern again, you can say, "wait, here I am in this pattern again," and make a different choice. It literally is changing an old habit. Like changing any habit, it takes time, effort, determination. These habits go straight to the Soul, so they are even more entrenched. But the point is YOU CAN CHANGE THEM, you are not trapped, no matter how deep they appear to be. *Desire* is the root determinant – you make up your mind you are going to change. Even when you catch yourself making the same choice in a situation where you could have made a new choice, you do not get down on yourself, you simply reaffirm that you are in the process of changing a deep pattern, and you keep at it. Step by step, inch by inch. Through determination you move forward. Because it's aligned to the evolutionary intentions, there are a lot of unseen forces at work to assist your moving in these directions.

Another issue is, at times you simply are going to feel overwhelmed with change, and unable to move forward at that moment. This too is part of the process. Especially with [example] 10th house Pluto, there needs to be an honoring of your emotional states, and their limitations. You cannot force your way through the process, cannot have complete control over it. It takes on a life of its own, over time, becomes the basis of new habits, a new way of living and of looking at life. There are moments, times, when you NEED to go back to the safety of the known, if only for a short while, just to keep yourself sane. This is okay and necessary – just do it consciously, "I need to do this right now," and remain aware when it is time to get back to moving forward again.

In a sense this process is like growing a new baby in your womb (4th house PPP) that gradually takes on a life of its own. In this case that new baby will gradually replace your old existing sense of who you are altogether. It will integrate and incorporate these new perspectives, ways, into the totality of your own self-image (4th house). Words like organic, holistic, inclusive – it is a natural process that gradually engulfs you. Through this process the intentions of the PPP, the North Node, the North Node ruler simply unfold, because at the baseline you have inwardly committed yourself to the evolutionary intentions. You start the process by discerning what the chart symbols mean, what areas of life they reference, but as you increasingly move into that process as a way of life, it just unfolds by itself. This all starts by embracing the process in the first place and saying "yes" to it. The rest just happens. In all charts (except Pluto conjunct North Node) the intent is to activate the polarity point of Pluto. When Pluto (and thus its polarity point) is squaring the nodes, the question becomes how does one resolve the skipping – which node has to be worked on? When the North Node is the resolution node ("applying to"), the effort needs to go to developing the North Node.

"The ruler facilitating the process" applies to all nodes in all charts, not just this condition. Another description of facilitating the process is "actualizing itself through." In other words, these are like layers. Pluto is the deepest layer. The nodes the next deepest layer. The rulers of the nodes a layer above that. Most of us are more conscious of what is on the surface than what lies beneath it. So we act in certain ways habitually. This is going to relate at the top to the ruler, which is actualizing the intentions of the underlying node, based on the planet, sign, house the ruler is located in. Similarly, the node is actualizing the intentions of the underlying Pluto (for the South Node), or PPP (North Node). Pluto, or PPP, is always the baseline. The nodes describe how Pluto has been carrying out (actualizing) its desire nature, the ruler how the patterns inherent in the nodes have been actualized. The gist of it is, one can't really separate the PPP, the North Node, the North Node ruler – they are different layers or levels of the exact same thing, even though we may not consciously experience it that way. When you are focusing on the North Node, you ARE effecting and actualizing the intents of the PPP. To me, the idea of the North Node ruler is, if you focus your attempts at developing the North Node in the chart area represented by the North Node ruler by house, sign, planet (and aspects it makes to other planets by house and sign), you are concentrating/maximizing your efforts. And yet, since this is the underlying evolutionary intent in the first place, that naturally happens anyway. (Steve)

Pluto square Nodes 1st/7th houses – emotional paradox

Pluto square the nodal axis in the 7th/1st, or 1st/7th, is an underlying EMOTIONAL PARADOX that needs to be identified in order for the skipped steps, the Pluto square, to be resolved. The nature of that emotional paradox is one wherein the individual has two opposing emotional needs. One is for an almost absolute freedom, and the other is one of almost absolute relationship. Obviously these needs, desires, go in opposite directions. And because of this underlying emotional paradox the person then chooses partners in which only some of the core needs are met. It's like finding bits and pieces of the overall needs in each of these kinds of partners. This is an unconscious way of creating 'exit points' so that freedom, independence, can occur again. The way to resolve that is to identify all the core and essential needs and then making a relationship choice in that knowledge. (Rad)

Planet conjunct Pluto

(Q) Is there any special significance when a planet is conjunct Pluto beyond a general interpretation that what this planet symbolizes has been subjected to particularly strong evolutionary forces?
(A) No.
(Q) Does this circumstance indicate that a Soul on some level has been resisting growth as symbolized by the planet conjunct Pluto?
(A) These symbols alone do not indicate resistance or non-resistance to the evolutionary intentions so symbolized.
(Q) Does the relive/fruition/combination condition that applies to planets conjunct the South Node apply to this circumstance?
See Planet conjunct South Node
(A) Yes.
(Q) Presumably a New Phase conjunction would signal that this is a relatively new experience for the Soul. A balsamic conjunction would signal that the Soul has been working for this for a long time and is finishing up the process. The Soul with New Phase

conjunction would be likely to feel overwhelmed by the intensity. The Soul with a balsamic conjunction would be likely to feel more sure of itself?
(A) Yes. (Rad)

Sun conjunct Pluto
With the Sun conjunct Pluto one of three evolutionary/karmic conditions exist in which the current life purpose is integrated and actualized through. One is total reliving of prior life evolutionary/karmic conditions that have been denied and/or avoided at all costs. In order for evolution to proceed the Soul must therefore re-live these conditions through the intention of creating the current life purpose to do so. Two is a karmic/evolutionary condition of fruition in which the Soul has, previous to the current life, actualized some special capacity, ability, or resource that has had the effect of helping others change, transform, or evolve their own lives. The current life purpose as designed by the Soul is to recreate those same prior life conditions in the current life in order to continue in this way even as the Soul itself can already feel, prior to the current life, that it has done so and is thus desiring to move on. And three is a karmic/evolutionary condition that is a combination of both the first and second conditions. (Rad)

Sun conjunct Pluto, and South Node in Scorpio
The South Node in Scorpio, especially if the Pluto/Sun conjunction squares the South/North Nodes, correlates to a resistance to fulfilling the Soul intentions symbolized by the Pluto/Sun conjunction itself. It can also correlate and symbolize a Soul that is so fixated upon the past that the fixation itself is preventing the Soul from actualizing its current life intentions which is to resolve those prior life conditions so that evolution of the Soul can proceed. (Rad)

Sun opposite Pluto
The Sun correlates to how the Soul actualizes its evolutionary intentions in any given life, and how those intentions are then integrated within the Soul by way of the Sun. Thus, with the Sun conjunct the polarity point of Pluto, this simply means that the Soul is desiring from within itself that its intentions to evolve as symbolized by the polarity point will occur at all costs in one way or the other. Typically, but not always, when the EA astrologer observes this symbolism it correlates to a Soul who has been resisting, for whatever reasons, its ongoing evolutionary needs prior to the current life. That resistance, when that has been the case, is the determinant within the Soul itself that is saying to itself that it can no longer resist those evolutionary needs and intentions. In other cases this symbolism correlates to a Soul who is determined to evolve and actualize its evolutionary intentions as FAST AS IT POSSIBLY CAN. (Rad)

Sun opposite Pluto – gibbous and full phase
[Example: Individuated stage] The gibbous phase here would correlate to a Soul who is desiring to begin the evolutionary journey of throwing off all external conditioning so as to begin the journey of active self-discovery relative to its essential, non-conditioned, reality. In so doing this throwing off process correlates with being highly critical of all external conditioning no matter what the source of that conditioning may be. The Soul will also be hyper-aware, and self-critical, as to the nature of allowing itself to be conditioned by whatever source. This in turn creates a core feeling within the Soul of being quite alone, and inwardly empty, relative to the culture of birth. In the active process of throwing off any source of external conditioning is that which creates this inner sense of being empty, and alone. This occurs because in the process of throwing off the external conditioning the journey of self-discovery of its own essential nature has just begun. Thus, the process of refilling the Soul with circumstances including people that reflect its core or essential nature is quite new which is the basis of the feeling of inner emptiness, and of being alone.
The opposition phase [full phase] correlates to a Soul that has been in the process of discovering its essential nature as reflected in opposing the external conditioning sources, and is relatively 'full of itself' because of. In essence, the Soul has come to a point of inner strengthening by way of lives that have already been lived wherein the active process of throwing off the external conditioning has taken place. Thus, it has begun to actively recreate itself by way of desiring to actualize its essential nature. The oppositional phase thus correlates to opposing or stiff-arming anyone or anything that attempts to impose its will upon the Soul in such a way as to violate the ongoing inner discovery of its essential nature. In so doing the Soul can also then attempt to impose itself through the strength of its own will upon others in any kind of circumstance. When this occurs this then can attract 'opposing' forces to itself as others by way of such circumstances react to this imposing of the will upon them. When this occurs it is imperative, an evolutionary intention, that the Soul then re-examines itself in such a way as to inwardly oppose the existing dynamics that are causing this to occur. This then sets in evolutionary motion the next step for such a Soul: to actualize itself, its essential nature, in such a way that the circumstances that it creates for itself can receive, and accept, the Soul in non-confrontational ways. (Rad)

Pluto conjunct South Node, and second Saturn return
Pluto conjunct South Node will mean one of three karmic evolutionary conditions, the first two of which will be extreme, the third one will be common:

1. (extreme): A Soul who has utterly and completely avoided, denied the evolutionary intentions symbolized in the house and sign position of this conjunction. And because there has been a fundamental resistance to embracing those lessons, the Soul comes into this life karmically and evolutionarily determined to repeat those past life evolutionary intentions in this life. This can be very problematic on a psychological level. Why? They will sense the wistful promise of the North Node. And yet, based on karmic evolutionary determination, they are forced to remain within the conditions implied in the South Node/Pluto conjunction.

Most people, when they come into a life, more or less do fulfil or live out the past life dynamics, up until around the first Saturn return. It goes right back to the principle of security, self-consistency, etc. Which is exactly why the first Saturn return, in terms of timing, is so problematic for most people. Why? They have done nothing to prepare for the current life purpose. And then the Saturn return happens, and all of a sudden they become aware psychologically that they are feeling stuck within the definitions of the reality which have been defined from the past. Generally speaking, the first Saturn return correlates with the opportunity to be released from those past conditions and to begin the actualization of the current life intentions. But when Pluto is conjunct South Node in this first extreme condition, those past life conditions cannot be released until the second Saturn return, the majority of the life span.

There can be mitigating conditions that modify this situation, specifically a planet conjunct North Node, which of course implies an opposition to Pluto. When you see this situation, what you have is a Soul who is going to reflect the third one of these three karmic evolutionary conditions. In the third condition you have an element of past life dynamics being relived, and you also have what is called an element of karmic fruition. And when this is occurring, that releasing can occur at the first Saturn return. Why?

Because there is a planet on the North Node, meaning that Soul has already been trying to work, struggle free, break free – whatever that planet may be on the North Node. It shows you through that specific archetypal function and the house it is in, that they have been trying to break free, but it is not complete yet. So that is a combination of relive and also fruition. What fruition means, karmic evolutionary fruition (when this is operative), is that the intentions and motivations have been sufficiently pure, because Pluto correlates with intentions, motivations, agendas, where I am coming from, desires that fuel it. Fruition here means that, relative to the conditions symbolized in the Pluto/South Node house, there has been a degree of evolution that has been pure enough, that they have some special quality or condition to bring into the life. So there can be this element of reliving from a positive, and a not so great point of view.

2. (extreme): This can be a situation of absolute karmic fruition and evolutionary fruition, meaning again that the motives and intentions fuelled by desires have been sufficiently pure, that they bring in some special capacity or ability, a resource (Pluto) developed thoroughly from other lifetimes. And in this karmic evolutionary condition, the requirement is to disseminate or share that resource in some way with others. Now this also creates a high degree of frustration, even though it is a positive circumstantial condition in life. Why? Because the person has been doing it for so darned long. They want to do something else. And here again, unless you see a mitigating factor, the second Saturn return routine.

3. (the most common): Again having an element of reliving as well as of fruition. And unless you find a qualifying mitigating condition, ie a planet on North Node, here again, second Saturn return.

(Q) I don't understand the reason for such a set up in the first place. Is it because they have come into this world to fulfil a special purpose – sort of like an avatar – relative to that Pluto/South Node conjunction? (Ari)

(A) You will notice the word 'requirement' above. And that is what this is. And the reason for such a requirement will be different in each case. And, yes, Souls with this signature, requirement, has some special capacity or resource to share with others that will have a metamorphic effect once shared, whatever it may be. (Rad)

(Q) Meaning they are blocked from their North Node until the second Saturn Return specifically because they have chosen to assist others in some way?

(A) Yes, it's a requirement.

(Q) What metamorphosis can occur that enacts evolution for that Soul before the second Saturn return?

(A) The metamorphosis occurs through fulfilling the requirement itself. Beyond that, there will of course be other areas in the individual's life that will be evolving and metamorphosing. Pluto will be making aspects to other planets for example. There will of course be a sign on the 8th house cusp, and the location of its planetary ruler, that will be needing to be evolved. So too if there are planets in the natal 8th house and/or planets in Scorpio itself.

(Q) How is it possible for the desire nature of a natal Pluto by house and sign to express itself as relatively pure without awareness of its polarity point?

(A) There have been polarity points in other lives that have all lead to this karmic requirement of the Soul. This is why whatever the resource or capacity is that the Soul is required to give, to share, has reached this state of purity before the current life.

(Q) Does this rule about the second Saturn return apply for other planets on the South Node?

(A) Yes, unless there are the mitigating factors. Other mitigating factors correlate to any planet forming an aspect to the North Node because that means that that North Node has been initially accessed prior to the current life. An aspect to the North Node of course means that there is also an aspect to the South Node. Thus, the linkage between the North/South Nodes before the current life.

Pluto conjunct South Node
Manifests as three possible conditions: re-live, fruition, or mixture of both. Pluto conjunct South Node will mean one of three karmic evolutionary conditions, the first two of which will be extreme, the third one will be common:
(1) (extreme) A Soul who has utterly and completely avoided, denied the evolutionary intentions symbolized in the house and sign position of this conjunction. And because there has been a fundamental resistance to embracing those lessons, the Soul comes into this life karmically and evolutionarily determined to repeat those past life evolutionary intentions in this life. This can be very problematic on a psychological level. Why? They will sense the wistful promise of the North Node. And yet, based on karmic evolutionary determination, they are forced to remain within the conditions implied in the South Node/Pluto conjunction. Most people, when they come into a life, more or less do fulfill or live out the past life dynamics, up until around the first Saturn Return. It goes right back to the principle of security, self-consistency, etc. Which is exactly why the first Saturn Return, in terms of timing, is so problematic for most people. Why? They have done nothing to prepare for the current life purpose. And then the Saturn Return happens, and all of a sudden they become aware psychologically that they are feeling stuck within the definitions of the reality which have been defined from the past. Generally speaking, the first Saturn Return correlates with the opportunity to be released from those past conditions and to begin the actualization of the current life intentions. But when Pluto is conjunct South Node in this first extreme condition, those past life conditions cannot be released until the second Saturn Return, the majority of the life span.
There can be mitigating conditions that modify this situation, specifically a planet conjunct North Node, which of course implies an opposition to Pluto. When you see this situation, what you have is a Soul who is going to reflect the third one of these three karmic evolutionary conditions. In the third condition you have an element of past life dynamics being re-lived, and you also have what is called an element of karmic fruition. And when this is occurring, that releasing can occur at the first Saturn Return. Why? Because there is a planet on the North Node, meaning that Soul has already been trying to work, struggle free, break free – whatever that planet may be on the North Node. It shows you through that specific archetypal function and the house it is in, that they have been trying to break free, but it is not complete yet. So that is a combination of re-live and also fruition. What fruition means, karmic evolutionary fruition (when this is operative), is that the intentions and motivations have been sufficiently pure, because Pluto correlates with intentions, motivations, agendas, where I am coming from, desires that fuel it. Fruition here means that, relative to the conditions symbolized in the Pluto/South Node house, there has been a degree of evolution that has been pure enough, that they have some special quality or condition to bring into the life. So there can be this element of re-living from a positive, and a not so great point of view.
(2) (extreme) This can be a situation of absolute karmic fruition and evolutionary fruition, meaning again that the motives and intentions fuelled by desires have been sufficiently pure, that they bring in some special capacity or ability, a resource (Pluto) developed thoroughly from other lifetimes. And in this karmic evolutionary condition, the requirement is to disseminate or share that resource in some way with others. Now this also creates a high degree of frustration, even though it is a positive circumstantial condition in life. Why? Because the person has been doing it for so darned long. They want to do something else. And here again, unless you see a mitigating factor, the second Saturn Return routine.
(3) (the most common) Again having an element of re-living as well as of fruition. And unless you find a qualifying mitigating condition, ie a planet on North Node, here again, second Saturn Return. (Steve)

Pluto conjunct South Node ruler
In that symbolism it is important to determine if that conjunction is a new phase conjunction, or a balsamic conjunction. In both conjunctions the past life dynamics of the Soul as symbolized by the house and sign of the South Node, and the location of its planetary ruler by house and sign, which of course is the natal house of the current life Pluto which is conjunct that South Node ruler, is being brought to a head so that the Soul can evolve beyond those existing dynamics. In a balsamic conjunction it means that the Soul is re-living the past, in the current life, that is specific to those dynamics as symbolized by the house and sign of the South Node, and the house and sign of natal Pluto conjunct the South Node ruler. It is those dynamics only versus the whole of one's life that is being re-lived in the current life.
The intention of the Soul in such a symbol is to gain the deepest inner insights possible as to the nature of those dynamics, and why they exist as they exist. It is this self-knowledge gained in such a re-live that then serves as the basis of being released from those dynamics. When that occurs it will lead to the new phase conjunction of the South Node ruler with the natal Pluto. In the new phase conjunction the experience is very different. This means that the Soul will indeed recreate dynamics, reflected through its circumstantial life, that are of its past. Yet as those circumstances manifest that do symbolize the past the Soul in this new phase conjunction is now giving itself the evolutionary challenge to make NEW CHOICES as those past life dynamics are repeated. The new choices thus allow the Soul to be finally freed from those past life dynamics. The awareness of those new choices occurs because of the active reflection that took place during the balsamic conjunction when the South Node ruler was conjunct natal Pluto. (Rad)

Pluto conjunct North Node – NO Pluto polarity point
When Pluto conjuncts the North Node it does indicate that the Soul has worked towards actualizing the evolutionary intentions symbolized by the house and sign position of the Pluto and the North Node that the Soul is meant to continue in that direction in this life. That is why Pluto's polarity point does not apply in that case. In other words, the Soul is meant to keep going in the direction symbolized by Pluto conjunct the North Node (full actualization of the evolutionary intentions described by the Pluto/North Node conjunction). If there are other planets forming aspects to the South Node then those planets will describe areas of potential stagnation and blocks towards actualizing the Pluto/North Node evolutionary intentions. (Deva)

In any chart that you see Pluto conjunct the North Node symbol it means that there is no polarity point for Pluto because the intention of the Soul is to continue its evolutionary development as symbolized by the house and sign of the Pluto/North Node conjunction which has already been underway prior to the current life. And in any chart that one sees this will always mean, of course, that the opposite sign of that Pluto/North Node conjunction has already been developed to the point of limiting the Soul's evolution if it remains focused on that alone. If so, then the Soul arrives at a place of Plutonian stagnation and non-growth. So when the EA astrologer sees Pluto conjunct the North Node in any chart it means that the entire chart, the entire evolutionary intent, is be focused upon and through that house and sign of the Pluto/North Node conjunction. That does not mean that the South Node in such charts does not evolve: it does. But it evolves through the focus upon the house and sign of the Pluto/North Node conjunction. (Rad)

Pluto conjunct North Node – what about the South Node?
In any chart that you see Pluto conjunct the North Node symbol it means that there is no polarity point for Pluto because the intention of the Soul is to continue its evolutionary development as symbolized by the house and sign of the Pluto/North Node conjunction which has already been underway prior to the current life. And in any chart that one sees this will always mean, of course, that the opposite sign of that Pluto/North Node conjunction has already been developed to the point of limiting the Soul's evolution if it remains focused on that alone. If so, then the Soul arrives at a place of Plutonian stagnation and non-growth. So when the EA astrologer sees Pluto conjunct the North Node in any chart it means that the entire chart, the entire evolutionary intent, is be focused upon and through that house and sign of the Pluto/North Node conjunction. That does not mean that the South Node in such charts does not evolve: it does. But it evolves through the focus upon the house and sign of the Pluto/North Node conjunction. (Rad)

Pluto conjunct North Node – and planet(s) aspecting South Node
When Pluto conjuncts the North Node it does indicate that the Soul has worked towards actualizing the evolutionary intentions symbolized by the house and sign position of the Pluto and the North Node that the Soul is meant to continue in that direction in this life. That is why Pluto's polarity point does not apply in that case. In other words, the Soul is meant to keep going in the direction symbolized by Pluto conjunct the North Node (full actualization of the evolutionary intentions described by the Pluto/North Node conjunction). If there are other planets forming aspects to the South Node then those planets will describe areas of potential stagnation and blocks towards actualizing the Pluto/North Node evolutionary intentions. (Deva)

Pluto conjunct North Node – amount of distance between Pluto and North Node
[Example: Pluto 7.48 deg Leo, North Node 6.50 deg Leo] When Pluto and the North Node are in the same house there is no polarity point because with the South Node in the house of what would be its natural polarity point this means that that has already been in operation prior to the current life. So the entire intent is then in the house/signs of the Pluto and North Node. You can actually measure how relatively new or old that intent is by determining if Pluto is before or after the conjunction to that North Node. In a new phase conjunction it is relatively new, and that relative newness can be determined by the amount of distance, degrees, from that North Node. The same rule is true for when Pluto is after that North Node. (Rad)

[Example: Pluto 7.48 deg Leo, North Node 6.50 deg Leo] It is a new phase by one degree which would then mean that the evolutionary intent has just come to a head in this life. (Lia)

[Example: Pluto 7.48 deg Leo, North Node 6.50 deg Leo] According to my understanding of how to determine phase of planets relative to the Moon's Nodes, this would be a new phase conjunction. Wolf taught that because the mean motion of the Lunar Nodes is retrograde, the normal rules for determining phase are reversed. (Stacie)

North Node in the same sign as, but not conjunct, Pluto – is there a Pluto polarity point?
[Example: North Node 3 deg Scorpio, Pluto 27 deg Scorpio.]
There is a polarity point for Pluto in this case. (Rad)

North Node in the same sign as, but not conjunct, Pluto, and in a different house to Pluto – is there a Pluto polarity point?
[Example: North Node 3 deg Scorpio in the 3rd house, Pluto 27 deg Scorpio in the 4th house.]
There is a polarity point for Pluto in this case. (Rad)

Ruler of North Node conjunct Pluto – is there a Pluto polarity point?
When the ruler of the North Node is conjunct Pluto, there is a polarity point for Pluto in this case. (Rad)

Pluto, ruler of Scorpio SOUTH Node
The significance is that Souls who have this symbol have overly identified with their sense of security, emotional/ psychological/ sexual, in specific and fixed ways and that over-identification has caused the Soul to stop evolving due to the compulsiveness of it, the fixity of it. Thus, the Soul, by its own design, has created in most recent prior lives a series of lives of intense loss of those dynamics that have been overly identified with. This has been necessary in order for the Soul to continue with its evolution. Thus, the North Node being in Taurus and the total evolutionary change within the Soul in terms of its own inner relationship with itself. In so changing the Soul is thus changing its own inner magnetism, which, in turn, allows for an attraction of these exact types of circumstances (relative to both the dynamics that are symbolized by the South Node in Scorpio, and the North Node in Taurus) that allows the Soul to continue to grow and evolve. (Rad)

Pluto, ruler of Scorpio NORTH Node
These symbols mean that such a Soul has been intensely resisting change/evolution in the most recent prior lives. The South Node being in Taurus would correlate to a 'frog in the well' in that the Soul has felt highly secure within the bottom of the well, and resisted jumping out of it in order to expose itself to the totality of the environment that surrounds the well. Jumping out of that well correlates to deep fears because it can no longer control its space or reality as defined in the bottom of the well. Thus, in these symbols the Soul will be continually confronted with its past, and the dynamics that are the cause of that past: the North Node in Scorpio ruled by the natal Pluto. The polarity point of the Pluto, the bottom line in the current life evolutionary intentions, will serve as a vehicle through which the Soul is given the opportunity to make new choices, changes, relative to re-experiencing its past, and the dynamics that correlate with that past.
The house placement of the North Node in Scorpio also serves to create opportunities of the Soul to make new choices relative to re-experiencing its past as symbolized not only in the house and sign of the natal Pluto, but, of course, the South Node by house, and the location of its planetary ruler by sign, house, and aspects to it. So you can see that the key here is indeed the polarity point of Pluto. The Soul has chosen to re-experience its past because it has felt secure within that past, and the dynamics that correlate to that past. That past is symbolized by not only the North Node, the South Node, and its planetary ruler, but also the natal Pluto by house and sign. And yet it is these very symbols that also correlate to evolving beyond that past by making new choices in the face of that past. And those new choices start with the polarity point of Pluto. By making those new choices in this way it then has the effect of evolving the North Node, South Node and its planetary ruler, but also of course the natal Pluto itself. (Rad)

Shifts from South Node to North Node, and Pluto to Pluto polarity point
It's automatic. You can't separate the Nodes with Pluto and its polarity point because the ego (Nodes) are always a reflection of the Soul's desires (Pluto). The ego is never separate from the reason for why the ego exists in the first place. (Ari)

Pluto polarity point (PPP)
A good way to look at the Pluto polarity point is moving towards it *facilitating* the process of culminating the lessons in the current Pluto house. There are reasons we have not yet completed those lessons. They typically relate to getting bogged down, stuck, in familiar yet dysfunctional behaviors and patterns. Moving towards the PPP helps break down this resistance, brings new input into how we are "doing" the natal Pluto placement, allowing us to culminate and then move on. Everything in life contains evolutionary intentions and resistances to them. It is not linear in that only the North Node and PPP are where evolution occurs. Life is in constant movement. Its intentions are forward movement – growth. The North Node and PPP facilitate that forward movement – developing them will progressively untie the knots we have created, allowing the whole Soul and personality to more freely evolve with less resistance. But there is also movement within a house, from beginning to end, over time – that too is evolution. (Steve)

Pluto polarity point – ruler of
The ruler of the PPP is used in the Pluto paradigm. (Rad)
Although Wolf did not write about the planetary ruler of the polarity point for Pluto he did teach it for many years in his lectures. Just like the Nodes have their planetary rulers, by house and sign, that operate as the facilitators to the actualization of the Nodes themselves, so too with the location of the planetary ruler of Pluto's polarity point. (Rad)

Pluto polarity point – planetary phases
The PPP is 180 degrees away from Pluto, thus its phase will always be the polarity of the phase between Pluto and the reference planet. Thus, figure the phase between Pluto and that planet, and then the polarity of that phase is the phase between that planet and the PPP. If Pluto to planet is new phase, the PPP is full phase, etc. (Steve)

Pluto polarity point – Rx
If natal Pluto is Rx, this also comes into consideration for the PPP. (Rad)

Pluto polarity point – transiting
The transiting PPP is not taken into consideration. (Rad)

Is there a Pluto polarity point? – North Node in the same sign as, but not conjunct, Pluto
[Example: North Node 3 deg Scorpio, Pluto 27 deg Scorpio.]
There is a polarity point for Pluto in this case. (Rad)

Is there a Pluto polarity point? – North Node in the same house as, but not conjunct, Pluto
First, you want to determine if the North Node is balsamic or new phase relative to Pluto, which creates its own archetypical meaning. And then there used to be an old phrase in astrology (I am going to date myself now) but it used to be called in mundo, meaning conjunct by sign. But unless you have technically an absolute conjunction, then you have a different kind of meaning depending on the phasal relationship between Pluto and the North Node itself. (JWG)

Is there a Pluto polarity point? – North Node in the same sign as, but not conjunct, Pluto, and in a different house to Pluto
[Example: North Node 3 deg Scorpio in the 3rd house, Pluto 27 deg Scorpio in the 4th house.]
There is a polarity point for Pluto in this case. (Rad)

Is there a Pluto polarity point? – Ruler of North Node conjunct Pluto
When the ruler of the North Node is conjunct Pluto, there is a polarity point for Pluto in this case. (Rad)

Pluto polarity point – conjunct planet
Development of the planet conjunct the Pluto polarity point, by house and sign, is a crucial part of the Soul's ongoing evolutionary process. It's one of the most intense placements a planet can have. Review what Jeffrey had to say about Mars opposing Pluto and how extreme that is. Now substitute for the Mars archetypes that he described, the archetypes of the planet that is opposing Pluto. One thing that can often occur with this placement is people and events in the outer reality will occur in intense Plutonian ways. The person often sees this as external, as things that are happening to them. They have forgotten that everything that occurs externally is an out-picturing of the Soul's internal reality. Thus they can feel victimized, until they finally come to understand the evolutionary reasons these intense experiences have been necessary for the Soul's ongoing evolutionary needs. Then the lights start coming on. In the potential lack of awareness of external reality reflecting internal reality, the person may "own" one side of the opposition and project the other. That is one way it could play out. They would be projecting the parts they could not own. (Steve)

Pluto polarity point – conjunct Sun
The Sun correlates to how the Soul actualizes its evolutionary intentions in any given life, and how those intentions are then integrated within the Soul by way of the Sun. Thus, with the Sun conjunct the polarity point of Pluto, this simply means that the Soul is desiring from within itself that its intentions to evolve as symbolized by the polarity point will occur at all costs in one way or the other. Typically, but not always, when the EA astrologer observes this symbolism it correlates to a Soul who has been resisting, for whatever reasons, its ongoing evolutionary needs prior to the current life. That resistance, when that has been the case, is the determinant within the Soul itself that is saying to itself that it can no longer resist those evolutionary needs and intentions. In other cases this symbolism correlates to a Soul who is determined to evolve and actualize its evolutionary intentions as FAST AS IT POSSIBLY CAN. (Rad)

Pluto polarity point – conjunct Sun, gibbous and full phase
[Example: Individuated stage] The gibbous phase here would correlate to a Soul who is desiring to begin the evolutionary journey of throwing off all external conditioning so as to begin the journey of active self-discovery relative to its essential, non-conditioned, reality. In so doing this throwing off process correlates with being highly critical of all external conditioning no matter what the source of that conditioning may be. The Soul will also be hyper-aware, and self-critical, as to the nature of allowing itself to be conditioned by whatever source. This in turn creates a core feeling within the Soul of being quite alone, and inwardly empty, relative to the culture of birth. In the active process of throwing off any source of external conditioning is that which creates this inner sense of being empty, and alone. This occurs because in the process of throwing off the external conditioning the journey of self-discovery of its own essential nature has just begun. Thus, the process of refilling the Soul with circumstances including people that reflect its core or essential nature is quite new which is the basis of the feeling of inner emptiness, and of being alone.

The opposition phase [full phase] correlates to a Soul that has been in the process of discovering its essential nature as reflected in opposing the external conditioning sources, and is relatively 'full of itself' because of. In essence, the Soul has come to a point of inner strengthening by way of lives that have already been lived wherein the active process of throwing off the external conditioning has taken place. Thus, it has begun to actively recreate itself by way of desiring to actualize its essential nature. The oppositional phase thus correlates to opposing or stiff-arming anyone or anything that attempts to impose its will upon the Soul in such a way as to violate the ongoing inner discovery of its essential nature. In so doing the Soul can also then attempt to impose itself through the strength of its own will upon others in any kind of circumstance. When this occurs this then can attract 'opposing' forces to itself as others by way of such circumstances react to this imposing of the will upon them. When this occurs it is imperative, an evolutionary intention, that the Soul then re-examines itself in such a way as to inwardly oppose the existing dynamics that are causing this to occur. This then sets in evolutionary motion the next step for such a Soul: to actualize itself, its essential nature, in such a way that the circumstances that it creates for itself can receive, and accept, the Soul in non-confrontational ways. (Rad)

Pluto polarity point – square the Nodes
The Pluto Polarity Point (PPP) is just as important with Pluto squaring the Nodes as in any other configuration. The one exception to that rule is when Pluto conjuncts the North Node natally, there is no PPP. Other than that it applies in all cases. (Steve)

Pluto polarity point – conjunct Mars
The polarity point of Pluto in any chart correlates to the next step in the Soul's evolution that requires choices to be made by the Soul for that to happen. With Mars at this polarity point and in opposition to the natal Pluto this means that those desires that reflect the Soul's next evolutionary steps have been in place prior to the current life. The nature of the opposition means that the Soul has been, and is, in an evolutionary process of needing to 'throw off' existing dynamics within it that are blocking its next evolutionary steps. When those existing dynamics, whatever they are, are thrown off the Soul's next evolutionary steps, progression, can proceed. (Rad)

Pluto conjunct North Node, integrating the sign of the PPP
[Example: Pluto in Libra in the 3rd on the North Node] The sign that any planet is within naturally contains its opposite. The opposite house is simply coming through the lead point, the integration point, symbolized by the house/sign of Pluto's conjunction to the North Node of the Moon. The 9th house will come through that Pluto conjunct the North Node in Libra in the 3rd: it's not somehow dormant. It is simply coming through the lead point symbolized by the Pluto/North Node in Libra in the 3rd house. (Rad)

Pluto – retrograde and direct
Pluto retrograde (Rx) symbolizes that the Soul is "throwing off" or liberating from the mainstream or consensus conditioning patterns in general (not buying into the mainstream way of doing things). Thus, Pluto Rx serves to instigate personal and collective evolution. (Deva)

Pluto direct symbolizes that the Soul is not necessarily at an evolutionary juncture where the intense need to liberate in the ways described above is felt as in Pluto Rx. However, we must keep in mind the four natural evolutionary conditions of the Soul as well. In transit, in a general sense, when Pluto goes Rx it is a time to review the current life lessons we have been seeking to learn. When Pluto is direct we will be facing those lessons head on or "directly" in order to effect personal growth. (Deva)

Pluto retrograde (Rx) can occur at any evolutionary stage, however it is only an intention to liberate and de-condition. In other words, we all have a choice to cooperate with or resist the evolutionary intentions for our lives. Those in the Consensus state will typically suppress/repress and, thus, resist the evolutionary intentions symbolized by Pluto Rx through the act of emotionally withdrawing into him or herself but outwardly "going through the motions" so to speak because of the underlying need for conformity and social acceptance. For those in the Consensus it does create a higher degree of evolutionary pressure to move towards the Individuated state than those who have Pluto direct. (Deva)

[Example: Pluto retrograde in the 10th house] "Resisting being pigeonholed" illustrates the 10th house Pluto retrograde. The need to do it YOUR way (and necessarily so as Jeffrey used to say), and thus not fitting the 'mold,' so to speak, as defined BY society (10th house), and so being "blocked from playing a meaningful role in my society and culture," etc. The intent, of course, is in the PPP (Pluto polarity point) in the 4th house: to develop INNER security; to be independent FROM society; to draw strength and courage from within; to trust oneSELF, etc. There are also times, especially within the context of the society that we HAVE to follow the stupid 'rules' in ORDER to get to the position where one can DO what one wants within that society, but then doing it in ONE'S OWN WAY. It is important for the EA astrologer to know the specific evolutionary condition of each Soul. Anytime a Soul evolves beyond the Consensus the orientation to the 10th house Pluto is totally different than a Consensus defined Soul. (Rad)

Pluto Rx and PPP Rx
If natal Pluto is Rx, this also comes into consideration for the PPP. (Rad)

Nodes of Pluto

The Soul has its own unique identity as created by the Source, or God. As such, it has its own ego that creates an image in the Soul of that unique identity. The awareness of that unique Soul identity is a function of evolution itself which finally leads to being self-aware, and has the evolved capacity, at some point, to objectify itself. The South and North Nodes of Pluto correlate to this ongoing evolutionary development of the Soul from within itself. The natal position of the current life Pluto simultaneously correlates to what the desires have been within the Soul for its own development, thus where it left off in those lives that have led to the current life, and the evolutionary intent for the current life for its evolution to proceed: the natural polarity point of that natal Pluto. The South Node of Pluto, by its own house and sign location, aspects to it from other planets, and aspects to its natural planetary ruler, all correlates to archetypes and dynamics that the Soul has used to develop itself, evolve itself, relative to its core desires for its evolution that is symbolized in the natal position of Pluto itself. The North Node of Pluto correlates to how and why the Soul evolves itself from within itself: what it needs to continue in its evolution. Other planets that aspect this North Node are archetypes that correlate to this ongoing evolution of the Soul within itself.

In order for all these internal dynamics within the Soul itself that correlate to its own ongoing evolution it must project or externalize itself through the creation of forms: the human form. This Natural Law or principle is the same as what we call the Source of All Things, or God, projecting and externalizing itself in the form of what we call CREATION. What we call God does this in order to know itself in all of these forms in the totality of Creation. So too with the individual Soul. The Soul needs to project or externalize itself in order to know itself, to objectify itself. So the Soul projects and externalizes itself from life to life in the form of the lifetimes that it lives that are all finite. The Soul itself is infinite just as God itself is infinite. Each finite life that the Soul projects from within itself, just as God projects each individualized Soul from within itself, reflects and symbolizes the core desires from within the Soul that reflect its own ongoing evolutionary desires to evolve.

As a result of this projection from life to life we then have the birth charts for each of those lives that reflect the finite forms that the Soul creates in order to effect its ongoing evolution. In each of these finite forms that the Soul creates it thus creates a consciousness that has its own subjective self-awareness that we call the ego or 'I.' And of course that subjective ego, the egocentric structure, is a projection from the Soul itself in order to know itself relative to the finite form it has created in each life that reflects its ongoing evolutionary needs and requirements. The subjective 'I' or ego that is created in each life by the Soul of course is the archetype of the Moon. The evolutionary journey of the Soul through time is thus symbolized through all the different finite forms or lives that it creates that are determined by its evolutionary needs and desires. And it is each of these finite lives that the Soul creates that the birth chart correlates to. And in each of those lives the finite ego does indeed 'die,' just as the body dies. Yet the memories of each life are sustained and live on within the Soul itself. And it is these ongoing evolutionary experiences from life to life that are the ongoing determinant and cause for yet another life. In the end, the whole chart, in any given life, correlates with the inner identity or 'ego' of the Soul as it evolves through time and space. (Rad)

Distinction between the North Node of Pluto and the Pluto polarity point

The North Node of Pluto reflects the ongoing evolutionary development of the Soul from within itself that is then actualized through the creation, projection, externalization of itself via the finite form it creates in each life. This is symbolized by the polarity point of Pluto in the current life birth chart. The Soul, from within itself, of course contains all the previous identities, singular life/finite forms, that it has ever lived. It also contains within itself all the different possibilities, future life/finite forms, that could occur. That which can occur is dependent on what the Soul, within itself, DESIRES. Those desires have been the prior life causes of what has already taken place. And in each of those lives the Soul created the necessity of subjective egocentric identities, finite life forms, for the desires to be actualized which of course has led to yet more desires to evolve that have led to yet another life. In each of these lives the Soul, from within itself, has had a North Node that has symbolized those ongoing evolutionary developmental desires. And in each life those desires are then actualized by way of the polarity point of Pluto in each life, in the individual birth chart. It's like, from within the Soul itself, it says, "I need or desire to evolve in the following way: its North Node, and in order to do this I will actualize it like this: the polarity point of Pluto in the individual life that it creates, in each life."

The Nodes of Pluto stay in signs, ie Cancer/Capricorn, or whatever signs, about 2,000 years. Most Souls of course will have more than one life within a span of 2,000 years. So the core evolutionary desires from within the Soul exist beyond the singularity of one finite life. In each of those singular lives the Soul continues to desire to evolve in this core archetypal way that is then actualized through each of the specific singular/finite lives that it lives. And in each of those singular lives that core evolutionary intent within the Soul is actualized by the polarity point of Pluto in those lives: the birth chart that symbolizes this entire process. Let's make a simple example of these dynamics. Let's say person X has in their current birth chart a 9th house Pluto in Leo, the South Node of Pluto being in Capricorn in the 2nd, which is ruled by Saturn in Leo in the 9th. The North Node of Pluto would be in Cancer in the 8th, and Pluto's polarity point would be in Aquarius in the 3rd.

The Pluto in the 9th in Leo would correlate to a Soul that has desired to understand and actualize itself by way of understanding the nature of the cosmos, and the Natural Laws of Creation. It has spent many, many lives in relative isolation, the South Node of Pluto in Capricorn in the 2nd, in order to inwardly contemplate that nature of Creation in order to realize by way of that isolated contemplation the nature of these Natural Laws which thus become the very basis of the Soul's inner relationship to itself: the 2nd house. This, in turn would constitute the Soul's core sense of meaning for existence, of that which held the core meaning for life itself. The ruler of that South Node of Pluto is also in Leo in the 9th. This would restate the Soul actualizing these core desires within the context of Nature, living and being within Nature in order to inwardly know all the Natural Laws that are responsible for Creation, Leo, itself. In relation to the South Node of Pluto being in the 2nd these symbols put together correlate to a natural loner who has realized what it has desired in essential isolation in this way.

Yet, in this way, the Soul has reached an evolutionary limit, and needs to continue to evolve. The Soul, from within itself, realizes this which is then symbolized by its North Node being in Cancer in the 8th house: the desire and need to jump out of the well of its own isolation, and to then engage and help other Souls on their own evolutionary journey. In so doing the Soul will then necessarily interact with other Souls and THEIR REALITIES: the interaction of the South and North Nodes of Pluto where Capricorn correlates to the archetype of reality, the realities of Earth itself. In this interaction with others it thus causes the Soul from within itself to confront its own evolutionary limitations that then creates the ongoing awareness of what it needs to continue to evolve itself. This confrontation can then cause the Soul to feel insecure from within itself as it is required to evolve beyond where it was by way of its own understandings of the nature of reality on this Earth that are reflections of the Natural Laws of Creation. These confrontations are intended so that the Soul can evolve beyond where it has already been.

In order for these core Soul intentions to evolve it then creates a singular or finite life in which the polarity point of the natal Pluto is in Aquarius in the 3rd. This will manifest, in the context of the example we are using, by creating a life in which the very opposite of where it has been: living alone in relative isolation within Nature. The Soul now will create a life in which it will be totally involved with others who are living within the world, in their cities, wherever whole groups of people exist: Aquarius in the 3rd. And, in this way, purposefully engage the realities of countless others who have all kinds of ideas, opinions, points of views and philosophies from A to Z, so to speak. And all of this will then of course impact on the Soul's current state of understanding the nature of reality that it has already realized in its past. The Soul then has another choice to make: it can retreat back to where it has been in order to remain secure from within itself, or make a choice to continue to grow from within itself due to the confrontations to that existing reality through the diversity of ideas manifesting within these groups of people, other individuals. If it makes the choice to proceed in this way it will then of course continue to evolve which reflects the intention of Pluto's North Node in Cancer in the 8th. That North Node of Pluto in Cancer of course will be ruled by the current life Moon, its egocentric structure created in the current life. So the underlying dynamics within the Soul that we have been discussing will then be focused, like a lens in a movie projector that creates images on a screen, into a current life identity, the 'I' of the current life. This is the Natural Law of how a Soul externalizes or projects itself from life to life by creating an 'image' of itself that correlates to the entire 'movie' of that life. (Rad)

Pluto on the cusp
Relative to orbs and house cusps: a planet, any planet, one degree or less from a house cusp means that an entire sequence of lives is culminating relative to the archetype of the house/sign that the Pluto, or any planet, is in. It's in essence mutating/evolving from one archetype to the next: the house on its immediate horizon. When a planet, any planet, is within one degree after a house cusp that means the culmination has basically been accomplished and that a brand new sequence of lives is beginning relative to the archetype of the house that that planet is in. (Rad)

In any chart, composite or otherwise, when Pluto, or any planet, is within a degree or two of the proceeding cusp this correlates, in evolutionary terms, to an evolutionary culmination of the whole archetype of the house of the actual Pluto, and relative to that culmination a new cycle of development is beginning – the proceeding house. (JWG)

Pluto, culminating in a house
There is always a long standing past. One of the core basics in life is that humans get attached to what they know. It comes to represent what feels safe and secure to us. That includes experiences that are quite dysfunctional – we get used to them and see them as normal, not dysfunctional, because they are the sorts of experiences many Souls have been having, over and over, for a long time. It takes much longer than one lifetime to learn all of the lessons of a single Pluto house. Jeffrey's words mean there have been a series of lives in which the Soul has been learning the lessons of that Pluto house. Thus those lessons, and that orientation to looking at life, have become very familiar. When Pluto is nearing the next house cusp, that whole series of lives is drawing to a close. That is what "culminating" means. It implies that all necessary things – lessons, endings of outmoded habits and ways of looking at life, etc. – need to come to completion before the Soul can move on. Usually we put off to the end the parts of things we like the least. When an archetype is culminating the Soul will force itself to deal with all of that, through the medium of "you" – the personality. At the same time, the Soul in some ways has gotten tired of the present lessons as it has been engaged in for a series of lives. It feels, senses on the horizon, what is ahead. Something different and new. It experiences that promise as release and it will yearn for it. And yet, it is not there yet – it has to culminate what remains unfinished in the present Pluto house before it can truly move into that new. (Attempting to jump ahead prematurely can be one of the causes of skipped steps.) (Steve)

Pluto near a house cusp, and feeling that Pluto is in another house
[Example: Pluto's natal position is 28 deg Libra 1st house, and feeling that Pluto is in the 2nd house] The things to consider first are:
(1) Is your birth time accurate? The Ascendant changes one degree every four minutes. If your birth time was off by 30 or 40 minutes that could put your Pluto in a different house.
(2) You have to look at what the rest of your chart looks like. I see that when Pluto was at 28 deg Libra the Nodes were not in Taurus/Scorpio, but as a general rule you would consider that. If the individual has [for example] four Taurus planets, or three planets in the 2nd house squaring a bunch of other planets, any of those will give a Taurus feel to the whole chart. The issue is the Soul (Pluto) relates to the deepest part of our nature. Many people are not attuned to the deepest parts of their nature and thus could feel more at home in personality qualities of their nature. It is true that Pluto near a house cusp (within a few degrees) is going to pick up some of the flavor of the adjacent house, whether it is two degrees into a house (in which case the Soul has spent a lot of time with the archetype of the previous house in recent Soul memory, thus it will feel familiar) or if it is at the end of a house, it will start feeling the pull, the allure, of what is not yet at hand yet is coming on the horizon. We never, in EA, interpret a Pluto position as being in an adjacent house. The position of Pluto is the position of Pluto. In my own case, under Placidus I have Pluto in the 9th house. Under Porphyry I have Pluto 10 minutes (a sixth of one degree) before the 9th house cusp, in the 8th house. Anyone who knows me would likely see me as an 8th house Pluto even though I have Sagittarius tendencies (there are other 9th house and Sagittarius symbols in my chart that add to the Sagittarius effect).

The point is, the placement of Pluto is where it is, for the Soul's own reasons. And, you can't declare yourself in the next house just because you identify with it. It is what it is. You can't decide you are in the 6th grade when you are in the 5th grade, just because you want to be a 6th grader. If you go to the 6th grade class they will send you back to the 5th grade, because that is, at this time, where you naturally belong. Now if you still strongly identify with the 2nd house, and you don't have Taurus or 2nd house stelliums, I suggest you double check the possibility of your birth time being off. And if it turns out your birth time is accurate, you might ponder more deeply the 1st house Pluto archetypes and if you are repressing portions of your nature. (I will NEVER tell someone that because their chart says this, that you must be this way, and the fact that you don't feel that way means you are denying or repressing something. The way you feel is the bottom line reality for you. The issue is, EA is extremely accurate. So if you simply do not identify with 1st house Pluto and you feel you are not repressing aspects of your nature, I'd really consider the accuracy of your birth time). (Steve)

[Using the above example: Pluto's natal position is 28 deg Libra 1st house, and feeling that Pluto is in the 2nd house] Venus, the ruler of Pluto 28 deg Libra, naturally rules two signs: Libra and Taurus. Libra refers to relating to others in all our relationships that are "outside" of ourselves; while Taurus refers to our "inner" relationship to ourselves and to our inner needs. This could be one of the reasons why there is a resonation with the 2nd house to some degree. Another point to consider is that in this case the 2nd house cusp is Scorpio which is ruled by Pluto itself. So the 2nd house cusp is dynamically connected to the 1st house Pluto placement. So you would naturally resonate with both houses. (Linda)

Pluto in intercepted sign
Remember the house that a planet is in always comes first, then the sign on top of that. So with Pluto in a house and sign that is then intercepted means that the house that Pluto is in comes first, the core, that is then conditioned by the sign that it is in that in combination correlate to the core of the Soul's prior desires. When this core Pluto in the house within a sign that is then intercepted, or conditioned, by another sign on the house cusp, then further conditioning and adding to what types of desires, in total, the Soul has had that have correlated to its prior evolutionary desires. So it is then a matter of starting with the house position of Pluto and then adding onto it the sign that itself is in, and then adding onto that the sign on the house cusp where an interception is involved. Of course from an EA point of view, we need to determine why the Soul has created this situation for itself in the first place. (Rad)

Pluto, evolutionary progression through the houses
Pluto does NOT naturally evolve in progression through lifetimes from, example, the 10th house to an 11th house, then a 12th house, etc. (Rad)

Pluto in the 8th house
Any Soul with any house position of Pluto can become aware of cycles of karma, reincarnation, and separating desires. 8th house Pluto's always desire to know the 'why' of anything. They desire to penetrate to the bottom line of anything. This is one of the reasons that EA books speak to this fact of a preponderant amount of 8th house Pluto's are naturally drawn to things like EA and the way it presents and understands life. (Rad)

Significance of Scorpio and the 8th house in the Pluto paradigm
The zodiac, its houses and signs, correlate to the total structure of consciousness in human form. The planets within the zodiac correlate to bringing that consciousness to life, and thus setting in motion consciousness itself. The planets within the zodiac are

the unique structural nature of that consciousness from life to life. They are the gasoline within the tank. This is why we start with Pluto, the Nodes, the location of their planetary rulers, and all the aspects to other planets that they are making. This is the core and foundation upon which the Soul structure and its evolutionary background, and its evolutionary development, is understood. Wherever the sign Scorpio, by house, is will contribute to this foundation because the signs on the houses correlate to how consciousness is orientated to phenomenal reality. And that current life orientation to phenomenal reality reflects the evolutionary needs of the Soul in this life. Planets that are in Scorpio, or the 8th house, correlate to the Soul's intention, in this life, to metamorphose the existing development and limitations implied in the archetypes of the planets themselves. The sign on the 8th house is an archetype in which this same Soul intention to metamorphose the existing development of that archetype within consciousness exists. (Rad)

(Q) If however a Soul has Aries on the 8th with no planets in Aries, is it true to say that in this life, the intent for that Soul is to transform the pre-existing limitations and development from previous lives that are implied by natal Mars? (Ari)

(A) No. It would not be the natal Mars, but the South Node of Mars by sign, house, and aspects to it. The current position, the natal position, of Mars correlates to how to move forwards in this life in order to evolve beyond where the Soul left off with the existing desires from past lifetimes. It is essential to remember that all desires emanate from the Soul. And that the root of such desires to evolve, the ongoing evolutionary journey of the Soul, is of course all symbolized by the natal position of Pluto, and its polarity point. Mars, as an archetype, is the lower octave of Pluto that instinctually acts out, acts upon, those desires emanating from the Soul itself. The South Node of Mars would indicate where the desires emanating from the Soul was left off relative to its desires to evolve. Aries on the 8th would then symbolize the Soul's intention in this life to confront and evolve beyond those existing limitations: of where those desires were left off. The current life Mars will then, for the entire life, correlate to where and how this will be done, and the North Node of Mars will correlate with the new desires emanating from the Soul to how and where the desires symbolized by the natal Mars will evolve themselves which are relative to the Pluto's natal polarity point. (Rad)

(Q) Doesn't Mars in and of itself have Pluto implications?

(A) It does when there are aspects to it from Pluto, or aspects to the South Node, it's planetary ruler, or aspects to that planetary ruler.

(Q) When you say, "The natal position of Mars correlates to how to move forwards in this life in order to evolve beyond where the Soul left off with the existing desires (Pluto) from Pluto," does that really mean that one's natal Mars has no past life resonance?

(A) No, as above.

(Q) Does this mean we can only understand Mars in relation to its South Node, which itself can only be understood in relation to Pluto – WHICH ITSELF can only be understood in relation to the South Node of Pluto?

(A) Essentially yes, unless there are aspects that it forms as defined above. The current life Mars, is THE CURRENT LIFE MARS. If it is directly connected to the past, as above, it is still the current life Mars and operates in exactly the way that has been detailed above.

(Q) Do you have any meditation/guidance for how I can personally connect with this these facts, beyond the mind?

(A) You can know it for yourself by practice, and allowing your intuition to simply grasp the truth of the total EA paradigm. We all know, not believe, that we have a past because it's a known quantity: it exists. We also know that we have a future because we have had a past. And that knowing exists in each moment of our life: inhale and exhale. This is known. Does not require belief of any kind. The paradigm of EA perfectly reflects this simple, and natural truth. Thus, we have South Nodes, current life positions of planets, and North Nodes. It is the interweaving of the known past with the evolutionary pull of the future than manifests as desires that we act upon, and that action occurs in the moment. It's just that simple. The totality of the Soul's birth chart in each life symbolized in all of these symbols correlates to this natural law and truth.

Differences/nuances between Pluto 3rd house, Mercury in Scorpio, Scorpio ruling 3rd – an example

The way that the linear mind works, how it is put together, would be the same: Scorpio. The core issue and differences then would be based on the following: With Scorpio on the 3rd house cusp where then is the natal Pluto? What aspects to other planets is it making? With Mercury in Scorpio what natal house is it in? What aspects to other planets is it making? With Pluto in the 3rd house where is the sign Scorpio in the natal chart? And what aspects is that Pluto making to other planets? All of these differences of the various possibilities correlate then to what the actual CONTENT is within that Scorpio linear mind. Within these key differences the underlying issue, from the point of view of Evolutionary Astrology, is what is the evolutionary state of the Soul. Understanding that evolutionary state then is its own determinate of what that content is when we remember that a sign or a house correlates to a total spectrum within each archetype. The underlying evolutionary state of any given Soul then is the determinate of where within that total spectrum of an archetype that the Soul will be orientated to. From the point of view of Evolutionary Astrology it is very important to make these individual determinations for one size does indeed not fit all. The specific nature of the content within the linear mind defined by Scorpio in this example reflects the specific ongoing evolutionary needs of any given Soul. (Rad)

Pluto aspecting Sun

[The Sun in aspect to Pluto implying past life dynamics]….would be the one exception to the general rule about the Sun. Yet because the Sun does correlate to how the Soul gives the overall EA intentions for its life a purpose and way of integrating those intentions, the Sun, in this exception must then be understood in a two-fold way. One is that it does correlate to the prior modes of actualization of the Soul's intentions, South Node. This can then mean that the Soul can be stuck in its own past in the current life. If so, this of course would not allow for any evolution to occur for the Soul. Thus, the critical importance of the North Node, the location of its planetary ruler, and, of course Pluto's polarity point serve the Soul's intent to re-actualize that existing past in new ways so that the Soul can continue to evolve. (Rad)

Pluto/Uranus interface

A natal placement of some kind of connection between the Uranian and Plutonian archetypes is a life-long issue. There are reasons when the Soul is manifesting with that symbolism. Uranus in Scorpio or in the 8th house in itself (without any transit activation) is very intense. The Uranian archetype will have the Scorpionic intensity – trying to look for the bottom-line. Generally speaking, in one way or another, the liberation (inherent in the Uranian archetype) is directly intended to affect the deepest levels – the Soul level. This also signifies the fact that past traumas (Uranus) had already affected the Soul level in some way. The healing/liberation are intended to happen on that very level. Not only have deepest trust issues (Scorpio/8th house) been violated in general, but also very INTENSE deepest level shock and trauma have happened in ways that have blown apart the Soul's previous security base – the deepest Soul level security structure. Therefore there is an intention to heal that level. The previous limitation relates to those security structures which need to be reformulated in the most intense and most accelerated way. As for the repetitive messages and what to trust and what not to trust, the issue may correlate to the fact that on the deepest, unconscious level trust has been violated and that caused immense trauma in the past.

The Uranus/Pluto interface, in some ways, correlates to a HIGHLY traumatized SOUL. Keeping this symbolism in mind, the result is more than likely to manifest some level of GENERAL unconscious fear and distrust, even towards one's own perceptions from within, ie when the Soul trusted something or someone in the past the Soul experienced intense trauma (not an isolated experience). So for the Soul, it is natural to react to this unconscious content (Uranus) in a distrustful way (Scorpio). This can create some intense inner confusion and being stuck periodically. One of the evolutionary needs with this kind of symbol is to apply DETACHMENT and OBJECTIVITY instead of being lost in the intense inwardly experienced emotional turmoil. Can I trust something? What if I misread the signals from within? So whatever the issue may be, understanding the fact that the emotional body has been wounded in the DEEPEST POSSIBLE WAY is something that needs to be kept in mind.

In the higher evolutionary states another interesting phenomenon may occur: the content of the unconscious memories of the Soul can come to the surface of consciousness in a relatively easy way. And, together with the Uranian impulse, the Soul is simply able to "dump" the emotional content it carries onto the Uranian vehicle. Uranus also correlates to the subconscious which is just below our Saturnian current life egocentric consciousness. In a simplified symbolic way, Pluto/Scorpio is the core deep down, and the egocentric consciousness (Saturn) is high up and normally they are not directly connected. The Uranian archetype is the BRIDGE between them. The Uranian archetype does touch in some ways the Saturnian current life ego-level consciousness and at the same time is connected to the depth of the Soul.

So on that bridge, the content of the unconscious Soul – with all the imprints, including many many past lives, and all kinds of information, BOTH past and present, relatively speaking – can "connect" more easily between these two points (Soul and egocentric consciousness) than without this kind of symbolism. Of course all this is dependent upon many other factors: first of all the evolutionary state of the Soul's overall consciousness, then the whole chart which will then explain why that configuration and why the Soul needed it, what happened, what it intends to liberate from and how. There can be infinite scenarios of course. The above is a very general (and far from complete) description of the functions, archetypically speaking, which are connected in some ways within consciousness, when these two symbols are directly connected in a chart. (Lia)

Pluto/Neptune interface

For starters, Pluto relates to compulsion/repetition, the root of which is unconscious memories and desires within the Soul. An addiction is repetitive, so certainly there can be a Pluto component. Something is compulsive because the reasons for the attraction to it are below the threshold of awareness – emanating from the Soul, thus repeated and repeated seeking resolution, without understanding where the compulsion is coming from in the first place. Pisces/Neptune relates to delusion/escapism, and is definitely associated with addictions. If you take it deeper, the deepest craving in any of us is to return to Source, to experience Divinity, that which is the only thing that can truly fill all our desires and places of lack. Addictions are a counterfeit way, an attempt at a shortcut method, of fulfilling those desires – what we become addicted to makes us feel that very deep sense of pleasure and satisfaction, at least initially. The feelings themselves are real. The issue is we identify the source of what we are feeling as whatever it is that appears to be letting us feel that way, a drug, alcohol, or deep love of/from another person. That is a mis-identification, and that becomes the root of the addiction. Through the repetition complex (Pluto) we keep repeating the experience of taking the substance, or connecting with the person, hoping that this time we will once again feel the way it made us feel in the beginning. Somehow it never does. Yet we get in a loop and keep repeating the experience. (Steve)

Soul correlates to Pluto, not Neptune
EA and its paradigm symbolizes the individual journey of the Soul through time as it evolves back to its Source: God/ess. Even though Neptune symbolizes that Source it does not symbolize or reflect the individual journey of the Soul itself. EA is about understanding each individual Soul as it actually is: where it has been and why, where it is now and why, and where it is headed and why. The Soul correlates to Pluto. Neptune does not. (Rad)

Pluto sextile Neptune – collective evolution
The Pluto/Neptune aspect can serve as collective inspiration or collective delusion within any generation on a personal and collective level. (Deva)

When everyone on a planet shares an aspect, that is an example of intended collective evolution. Something shared by all humans, each in their own way of course, and generationally through the shifting of the signs the planets are in. When an aspect exists for a really long time, it indicates the necessity of learning important collective lessons. Also, consider that at times one or the other or both of those planets will be retrograde, further reinforcing the intention of really getting the evolutionary lessons. (Steve)

Pluto generations
Somewhere Jeffrey discussed that adjacent signs have a harder time seeing eye to eye, while two signs apart is the natural resonance of the sextile: thus Pluto in Leo and Pluto in Libra; Pluto in Cancer and Pluto in Virgo and Pluto in Scorpio – sextile and trine. This goes back to the cycle of phases aspects. Adjacent signs are semi-sextile, a stressful aspect. This pair represent yang-yin, energy going out and energy coming back, mirror images, thus a natural tension: Pluto in Cancer and Pluto in Leo, Pluto in Leo and Pluto in Virgo. Because of its elliptical orbit, Pluto was in Cancer and in Leo for many years. This stress symbolizes the "generation gap" boomers had with their parents. This can also symbolize a natural resonance between children and grandparents – Pluto's sextile. (Steve)

Transiting Pluto
Pluto in the birth chart represents the Soul's evolutionary intentions for this lifetime plus where that Soul has been prior to this lifetime. Transiting Pluto represents the timing of how those evolutionary intentions unfold. All Pluto transits in a birth chart are in relation to the location by sign and house of Pluto in the natal chart. Another way to say that is, transiting Pluto is in a cycle of phases and aspects with natal Pluto. This also occurs on the collective level. When we talk of the USA having an upcoming Pluto return, it takes 248 years for Pluto to return to the same place. (Steve)

Pluto transit – and the transiting Pluto polarity point
Whatever house transiting Pluto is in correlates to that house relative to the ongoing evolutionary journey of any given Soul. The transit of Pluto of course directly correlates to the natal EA paradigm itself as it evolves in the context of the Soul's current life. The transiting house of Pluto is the core of that transit wherein the natural polarity point in brought into of the house in which Pluto is transiting. (Rad)

(Q) If someone is having a Pluto transit to their 1st house, what I am sensing is that the Soul intention of that transit will be the 7th house themes – to open to others and to be more willing to see through the eyes of another. Embracing real partnership and cooperation with others – to really begin listening in to how reality occurs for others, to be open to the feedback from others instead of going it alone (where the impulse and instinct would be to do so [going it alone] for the time Pluto is transiting the 1st). (Dhyana)

(A) No. If Pluto is transiting the 1st house then the core archetypes of that house are the ones that serve as the bottom line for what that transit means. The natural polarity point is then brought into that core bottom line. In your example the transiting Pluto in the 1st house will correlate to a time in which the Soul is desiring and requiring many new directions in its life that require a separation from existing life circumstances that are no longer serving the evolutionary needs of the Soul. And that will be the core bottom line for this transit wherein the natural 7th house polarity manifests as the Soul perhaps asking others for their perspectives, ideas, feedback relative to what those new directions that the Soul needs to initiate. The individual context of the Soul's entire chart is necessary in order to understand the EA intent of any transiting or progressed planet to the natal chart. One size does not fit all. The simple example that I used was in reference to your own statements about Pluto transiting the 1st house in order to illustrate the correct way of understanding the Pluto transit. The Pluto transit is always in reference to the entire EA paradigm in any chart. Additionally, it also correlates the Nodal Axis of Pluto itself: where this is in the individual's chart. It will also reference the natal house upon which the sign Scorpio is found. All of this must be considered relative to the natal EA paradigm for any given Soul which also must include the evolutionary condition, and the cultural context of where a Soul lives. (Rad)

Pluto in Capricorn transit

One of its important functions is to remove structures of all sorts that have become crystallized (no longer serve a useful evolutionary function), frozen in place, through the principle that our sense of security is based on the known, on both the personal (Cancer/4th) and societal (Cap/10th) levels. In essence a dynamiting of hardened rock that is holding back evolutionary progress. This process is affecting everyone, 1st stage Consensus and 3rd stage Spiritual. It's sometimes not the most fun-filled feeling one has ever known. Long term, it quite effectively fulfils its intents. (Steve)

What I have noticed about transiting Pluto in Capricorn is that the intention to change/transform conditioning patterns of the past is very emphasized/intensely felt by the collective. The positive manifestation of this transit is that the very structure of our society can change due to deep levels of internal change within society as whole in the context of purging the previous conditioning patterns that are inhibiting growth/evolution. I have been noticing that there is a deep level of reflection in the collective relative to these issues that is coming to the surface right now. To me, the best way to approach this transit is to stay focused on the potentially positive outcome of personal/collective (social) transformation, and personally staying open to changing when necessary. (Deva)

Capricorn/Saturn, when implicated through transit/progression, always induces reflection on our prior choices that have created the present reality (Saturn/Capricorn) in which we currently live. The purpose of the reflection and introspection (which the West wants to label "depression" in many cases) is to acknowledge and take responsibility for all of the issues and dynamics within that have created what is now being experienced as our limits or blocks in life – the life circumstances that no longer fit, but now feel constraining or limiting (Saturn/Capricorn). Following reflection regarding what has not worked for us up to this point, the cardinal energy of Capricorn enables us to create a whole new reality based upon the new evolutionary cycle trying to be born. At this time, anything new that is initiated by the ego that is not relevant to the Soul's growth will be blocked in some way. It is Capricorn/Saturn's way of keeping us 'on course' for the next step, the next phase, in our lives and in our Soul's ongoing evolutionary path. It is the personal responsibility (Capricorn) taken for all prior actions and choices that enables an inner security (Cancer) while navigating the new evolutionary cycle that cardinal energy always ushers in. Once we see that we do in fact create our own reality, and all of our life circumstances, there is a tremendous sense of freedom (Aries square) that comes, and this makes available to the Soul a new and dynamic energy, so that it may begin to create again, and create anew.

Saturn, like all planets, absolutely correlates with spiritual evolution. As Saturn is about the nature and structure of our current reality at any given time, I believe that the task (Saturn!) regarding Saturn/Capricorn, for all of us 1st stage Spiritual Souls, is to deepen our spiritual reality, through disciplines (Saturn) like yoga, proper lifestyle (which means appropriate relationships, Libra; proper nourishment for the body, Cancer; proper understanding and directing of the desire nature, Aries). Like all planets, the way Saturn manifests in our lives can be evolved over the lifetime, based on a strengthening and deepening of the one desire to know God, and return Home. Saturn helps us manifest a spiritual reality on Earth within our own lives, when our desire nature (Aries) and emotional body (Cancer) are in alignment with that purpose, so that a Soul becomes a 'concrete' (Saturn!) example for others along the same path. (Yogananda was a Capricorn, with a 10th house Pluto/Neptune conjunction!) Development of natal Pluto's polarity point and the natal North Node, relative to any Pluto transit, is specific to each person, each evolutionary state/condition, etc. – but I believe that Saturn/Capricorn energy helps all of us become better creators, in the end, no matter where we fall on the spectrum. (Lesley)

Destruction? Population reduction? None of this is fated to occur. All will depend on the collective consciousness and collective choices made about the current imbalance between men and Gaia. The accuracy of prophecies such as Nostradamus' does not imply that they will necessarily come true. Their purpose is to induce an awareness of the potential consequences of human collective actions. JWG writes extensively about this time frame and also about Nostradamus in Pluto 2, Chapter 11, Pluto in Sagittarius. (Gonzalo)

The positive aspects of Pluto in Sagittarius were the foundation of new beliefs and cosmologies. That was followed by Pluto in Capricorn. Those new beliefs then have to be anchored and structured. Outer forms created then reflected those new beliefs. Yet we are caught in the struggle between the old and the new. Those who prospered under the old are using every trick to retain their control – a dark side of Pluto in Capricorn. The very systems and structures we have to live under are the problem itself (or at least a manifestation of the real problem, which is the very idea of me advancing myself at your expense). That is why those structures have to crumble. As structures crumble people experience real pain. And we are not exempt from experiencing some of that pain. Times of vast change are always uncertain and create insecurity. But they are also the only times during which great change CAN occur. So here we go again. Pluto in Capricorn also brings the Saturnian elements of facing reality, getting real, getting grounded, looking at our delusions and seeing them for what they are. It can bring on depression and futility too.

But the positive side of that is that when false hopes and beliefs are dashed on the rocks it opens the way for realistic hopes and beliefs to enter – what is POSSIBLE versus what I call magical thinking. We have to lower our grand ideals and deal with what is possible, rather than utopian dreams that are just not realistic given present context. Collectively we are in dire straits, and a lot of options that could have been possible if action had been taken decades ago when they were proposed are no longer possible. Pluto in Capricorn is also consequences – the consequences of our previous actions. So we are seeing that too. We are not going to get out of this with a story book ending. The best possible thing anyone can do is come to terms with that emotionally. That in itself can take time. Once you come to terms with that, what is possible, we can start acting in ways that are realistic and aligned with what is possible. A lot of that seems to be positioning self for personal survival through difficult times. Part of the intent of the discussions on these topics is to talk about what is possible, what can people realistically do, given the actual circumstances. (Steve) Since JWG wrote Chapter 11 in Pluto Vol. 2, many many collective choices have been made. What Gonzalo stated [above] is true, however human activities have affected Gaia to the point that some of the damage is no longer reversible. And, every time there is an international climate summit, the proposals for what will be done are about a quarter of the minimum needed to really change things, and instead of being put into place immediately, they are phased in for 10 to 20 years in the future. And by the time 10 to 20 years has gone by, next to nothing has actually changed, and another international conference is held, with the same basic results. Unfortunately the handwriting is now on the wall. Global temperatures and wind and precipitation patterns are rapidly shifting. This is going to affect the world's major food producing regions. The number of people on the planet is at an all-time high and rapidly growing. We will be seeing vast shortages of food and fresh water. This will be exacerbated by the new global corporate reality, which sees these scarcities as opportunities to reap vast new fortunes, at the expense of people's lives.

Look at what Wall Street is getting away with in the USA, for example. We are not entering a fun era on earth. In my opinion the only thing that is up to free choice at this point is the extent of the upcoming difficulties. There is no longer any way we will avoid all of it – we have gone too far. What we will see, as this unfolds, are the dual influences of patriarchy and matriarchy – those who want to advance their own interests through exploiting the suffering at the expense of others, and those who want to band together and help their fellow humans and other species through the hardships, as much as possible. These two approaches to human life will increasingly be colliding. People will be forced off the fence through circumstantial necessity. Everyone will have to choose their approach. We must wait and see to find which approach prevails. The answer to that is still up in the air. This is not intended to scare, but to suggest people look closely at what is going on, the directions things are going in, and start thinking about where and how to prepare for the coming changes. Again, not from a place of fear but from a place of awakeness. There will be many opportunities to evolve spiritually through the difficulties. (Steve)

One of the consequences of 'global warming,' caused by human activities that violate Natural Laws, is that the warming climate causes an acceleration of the Natural Law of mutation where mutation is a consequence of the survival instinct in all forms of life. Thus, the forms of life that are called bacteria, viruses, and fungus have begun this acceleration of mutations in order to survive. This will continue to accelerate at such a pace that humans' capacity to keep designing new drugs to counteract this will not be able to keep up with the accelerated pace of the evolving/mutating bacteria, viruses, and fungus. This will create, progressively, pan epidemics that will have the effect of killing a tremendous amount of people all over the globe. This in combination, as Steve pointed out, with increasing scarcity of fresh water sources, the dehydration of increasing amounts of land affecting food production, will cause cataclysmic circumstances for an ever increasing amount of human beings on this planet.

With Pluto in Capricorn, in the context of now, the EARTH REALITY of now, the very nature of the structural reality at every level will be metamorphosed through varying degrees of cataclysms. And those cataclysms will occur as a consequence of CHOICES THAT HAVE ALREADY BEEN MADE, AND WILL CONTINUE TO BE MADE IN OUR COLLECTIVE FUTURE. The essence of those choices comes down to the fact that the Natural Law, set in motion by the Creator, of 'giving, sharing, and inclusion' has been perversely altered to 'exclusion and self-interest.' It is this perversion, at a root level, that has been, and will remain to be, the cause of all kinds of cataclysmic events for whole groupings of people that has already occurred, and will be occurring. The transit of Pluto through Capricorn will move over its own South Node, as well as the South Nodes of Saturn and Jupiter. It is intended to create increasingly glaring and shocking events, events that can have cataclysmic consequences due to choices made, in order to get the attention of human beings so that other choices, choices in alignment with the Natural Laws of God/ess, can be made. And those choices either way will determine, Capricorn, how all of us will be able to live our personal lives, Cancer, on this planet: Earth. Our home. (Rad)

What is that Cancer Polarity? Reflections on Pluto in Capricorn – by Bradley Naragon

Yesterday, I considered how appropriate the word 'streamlining' is to describe the Pluto in Capricorn phenomena, especially in a capitalistic competitive society and economy. Seemingly, at every turn and stop, organizations, institutions, and businesses are 'tightening' up operations. Paper towels are now half the size they used to be and I think the toilet paper went from 2 ply to 1.5 ply. Seriously, with Mars in Capricorn and the recent conjunction to Pluto, now more than ever 'getting organized' is the aim and drive. Keeping the ducks in a row is not intrinsically a bad thing. As the South Node transits Taurus, the question of "Will this survive?" is more appropriate than ever. What is desired to survive is all based on one's values. Many people still greatly value the form capitalism exists in. Many people have gained their own wealth and survived and thrived because the current model is a patriarchal system set up for some to win and many to lose. As a result, I now see so clearly the compulsions of what it means to just "do the Pluto Capricorn" without its Cancer polarity. It's a funny phenomenon – more than ever we need every single 'i' dotted and 't' crossed or we risk not having access to what we need. The compulsion to create even more policies and create more 'red tape' and hoops to jump through is ever so real with Pluto in Capricorn. We are lucky when we actually get to talk to a human. Yet, when we do, will they be so restricted in their role that they only reflect back to us what we can and cannot do based on current policies? Where has the human gone? Cancer, oh, Cancer, under all these layers of armor we put on to survive in this work, there is a human being underneath there with emotions and feelings.

Recently, I was helping rewrite a returns policy for business. It really came down to going the 'hard ball route' and being really tight and limiting or creating what some called a 'wishy-washy' policy that supported actually allowing some room for the exceptions; to still allow wiggle room of being human. No room for exceptions is the shadow side of Pluto in Capricorn. This is Pluto Capricorn without its Cancer polarity. You either do or you don't meet criteria and then need to go through all the process to get what you want/need IF you can even access it. Recently, a friend was hit by a car. She had major medical surgery. The man who hit her was genuinely sincere and wished to do the right thing. Yet, she was strongly advised by others to get a lawyer to represent her case OR the insurance company would try to limit the amount they had to pay out. With Pluto in Capricorn, the need for the Cancer polarity is SO MUCH MORE OBVIOUS. Who are these people and how do they live with themselves – removing financial support in a time of personal crisis based on "what's the best business decision." Granted, much of this already has existed. The USA, beginning with the top down Capitalistic model (natal Pluto Capricorn), has always had such ruthless motives visibly and invisibly operative. Rad and Steve have shown us this correlation time again here on this message board. Now that we have Pluto in Capricorn, every product seems to be shrinking in size or offering, or going up in price. With the South Node [currently] in Taurus followed by Pluto in the "Taurus decan" of Capricorn, how will people survive? Will the decisions that we face embrace the empathetic nurturing principle?

What is the best business decision? To include the Cancer polarity means to value helping others over the bottom line equation of profit margin. Before that person hangs up the phone on you, do they step out of just being in the position of their job and acknowledge the reality you face? Even to hear someone say, "I'm sorry that is happening to you," would give some hope of this polarity expressing itself. Do we meet the former or do we hear, "That's the way it is and I cannot help you"? May our hearts remain open and full of compassion in these difficult times. (Bradley)

RELATIONSHIPS
SYNASTRY AND COMPOSITE

How to read synastry and composite charts

In order to accurately and comprehensively understand a composite chart you must look at the two natal charts, the synastry between both people, and then bring that understanding into the composite chart. The natal birth of each person, again, will give us a firm understanding of the core evolutionary dynamics/intentions for that individual, and we can then see how two people affect/impact one another through synastry analysis. If, through synastry, person A has Venus square Pluto, or the South Node conjunct a personal planet of the other person (Mars for example), then this is going to dramatically condition how we read the composite chart.

The composite chart reflects the two people as a single unit, or a combined person. In other words, the composite chart reflects the core evolutionary lessons that two people have desired to work on together as a couple, or unit (for example, in the composite chart the couple may have Venus square Pluto.) Synastry charts reflect the dynamics that exist between two people as separate beings, or between the two people as individuals. For example, person A might have Venus square person B's Mars. In this case person A will always manifest the Venus role, and person B will manifest the Mars role.

You cannot interpret the composite chart without first understanding each person's natal chart, and the synastry charts. You could apply the core meaning of Mars and Venus in the natal chart in the composite as long as you adjust that meaning to reflect that it symbolizes the couple's mutual desires (Mars) and relationship patterns (Venus) as a single unit so to speak. (Deva)

Venus and Mars in synastry – example

[Example: Mars/Venus square in synastry] Relative to the Mars/Venus square in a synastry chart where the one with the Venus is always the Venus person, and the other is always the Mars person, in composite if we see that Mars/Venus square then both can be the Mars/Venus depending on circumstances. It is imperative to understand each individual's birth chart and evolutionary background in total in order to understand the individual placements of all of their planets and the planetary Nodes. When that understanding is in place then one can make an accurate analysis of why any couple would have whatever planets in whatever signs and houses. So even though they may have a combined Mars in Capricorn, and the archetypes as spelled out in Wolf's Pluto 2 are what they are and they do apply to the COUPLE, it is essential to understand WHY the couple has chosen to have that Mars in Capricorn and every other planet/house placement in their composite chart. And we must remember too that, in the example of Mars in Capricorn, that it will also be in a house that then conditions the manifestation of that Mars in Capricorn as does the aspects that it is making to other planets. And, of course, the specific evolutionary condition/stage of the couple also qualifies and conditions the specific manifestation of it. (Rad)

Mars/Venus phase in relationship

The Soul requires an external partner who is defined in the same way. Generally speaking, an individual who has a balsamic Mars/Venus phase can only really feel right with another in an intimate relationship who also has their Mars/Venus in a balsamic phase. (JWG)

What I think JWG must have meant is first that a Mars/Venus balsamic person can get along with just about anyone because of the balsamic phase, and, second, for such a Soul to feel really 'right' in an intimate relationship that another Soul either had to have their own balsamic Mars/Venus phase and/or other symbols that would correlate to such an inner orientation such as Venus or Mars being in Pisces or the 12th house, or possibly in some major aspect to Neptune. (Rad)

Synastry – past life dynamics

In synastry charts, the location by house and sign of the planetary rulers of the South and North Nodes in one another's charts correlates with additional and specific past life dynamics (the South Node by house and sign, plus its planetary ruler by house and sign) that we may have shared with another that constitutes subconscious memory associations conditioning our response or reaction to that person, and the North Node by its house and sign location, plus its planetary ruler by house and sign location, that reflect how the next evolutionary step in this life is to be accomplished. The key aspects and dynamics to look for that will give a complete and total analysis involve the South Node, South Node ruler, North Node, North Node ruler, and Pluto. These are described in more detail on page 18, Pluto 2. (JWG)

Synastry – Pluto opposition by house
[Example: Pluto 2nd opposite Pluto 8th in synastry] Perhaps it simply is that the symbols in each individual birth chart, revealing how each Soul is defined, and oriented to life in general, and to relationships in general, that have needed to be understood individually before the synastry will determine, in the synastry, the different approach to the specific relationship, and the interaction between the individual energies – Souls – in the relationship, which would be symbolized by the archetypical relationship between the house positions, even if they are in the same signs. This may be quite obvious, and I don't think it would require another layer of analysis of the relationship, because this layer would be comprised in the analysis of the individual charts. If one Soul has a strong 2nd house emphasis, it may imply that the Soul has needed or desired to be very self-reliant, and that, as a consequence of such desire and need, has become limited by its pre-existing value associations, and the way it has defined itself. Thus, let's say, this Soul has withdrawn from meaningful relationships, or has resisted the evolutionary chances that have existed of growing beyond its limitations through meaningful relationships. Perhaps the Soul has even accepted relationships only to the extent the partners conform to the Soul's prior definitions, and otherwise, has chosen to maintain its limited value associations, and doing things on its own.

The other Soul, with a strong 8th house emphasis, has desired to depend on others as a source of security and power, and because of this dependency, has desired to manipulate others to secure the relationships. Now these two Souls meet, and, even though the planets in the synastry fall in each other's same emphasized houses, 2nd and 8th, their approach to the relationship will be quite different, ie opposed approaches (of course, this is an over-simplification): the 8th house emphasized Soul in the example would want to secure the relationship, and to manipulate the partner; though, the 2nd house emphasized Soul would very likely resist such approach, because it desires the relationship only to the extent that his/her own values are maintained within the relationship. However, because of the relationship, a push-pull could exist in which, because of the strong attraction (opposition-conjunction) and meaning and evolutionary possibilities for each Soul, both partners would have the chance to grow beyond their pre-existing limitations: thus, the 2nd house Soul would be able to embrace, to some extent, other values and orientations, and would very likely be exposed, through the manipulations, to larger frames of reference through which to understand itself. However, because of the resistance to being manipulated, he/she would be inducing the 8th house emphasized Soul to develop self-reliance. Thus, the relationship would be giving both Souls a chance to embrace their respective polarities, through the relationship, even though the other's planets fall in their same emphasized houses. (Gonzalo)

Synastry – how to calculate phasal relationship between the Nodes
Always use the natural zodiac as the frame of reference to calculate the phases of any two points. So in calculating the Nodes in synastry that would mean to use the one person's Nodes that preceded, naturally, the other person's Nodes, ie South Node in Aries would precede the South Node in Cancer. Thus using that South Node in Aries as the baseline or start point. Yet, because the mean motion of the Nodes is retrograde, we would then have to reverse the normal rules of the phases. If I had say Mars at 1 degree Aries, and another had their Mars at 1 degree Cancer, that would naturally be a first quarter square through natural progression of the signs. But the Nodes are retrograde through mean motion. So even though we would still use the South Node of Aries as the baseline we would then see through the natural motion of the retrograde that the South Node of Cancer is MOVING TOWARDS that South Node in Aries. So it would then be a last quarter square or phase versus a first quarter square or phase if indeed the South Nodes were at 1 degree Aries and Cancer respectively. In this example that would then make the North Node at 1 degree Libra and 1 degree Capricorn. So, again, using the natural zodiac as our baseline we then see that Libra precedes Capricorn. With the mean motion of the Nodes in mind that again means that the Capricorn Node is moving towards the Libra Node: another last quarter square or phase. (Rad)

Synastry – nodal opposition
My symbol for it is the one person is going where the other person habitually comes from. All humans resist movement towards our North Node. Thus picking a partner whose South Node conjuncts my North Node means where I am going is in my face through the vehicle of the partner all the time, the person literally being a mirror. It's not easy to live with. However, if they can both recognize what is going on and learn to embrace it, the potential for a lot of growth is high. It would take a commitment to understanding why they are together, and to sticking through it. That opposition also makes mutual projections an ongoing issue, as disowned shadow parts of each one are acted out by the other. Truly "in your face." (Steve)

Synastry – one person's planet square the other's Nodes
Relative to synastry charts alone 'skipped steps' are not symbolized when one person's planet or planets is squaring the Nodes in the other's chart. What this symbolizes are dynamics and issues that have created developmental stress between the two people

either in previous lives that has come forwards into the current life, or developmental stress that is occurring for the first time in their relationship: the current life. In previous lives such stress may have served to separate the two people, or they may have continued in their relationship with that developmental stress unresolved. In either case the relationship between the two cannot actually evolve until that developmental stress is identified and resolved. So too if it is the first lifetime in which that developmental stress is occurring. The person whose planet or planets is making the square to the other's Nodes is the causative factor creating the developmental stress for that other. When this other than reacts to the one causing this stress that reaction, of itself, will then create developmental stress within the one whose planet(s) are squaring that person's Nodes. This ongoing interaction of cause and effect, back and forth, is that which will create the ongoing developmental stress between the two people until the reasons for it are objectively identified and then resolved. Skipped steps between two people can only be symbolized in their composite chart together. If the two people try to go ahead in their relationship before resolving whatever the issues are, the developmental stress, symbolized by having one's planet(s) squaring the other's Nodes, will then lead to SKIPPED STEPS between them which will then be symbolized in their combined charts in the next life. (Rad)

Synastry – one person's Sun square the other's Nodes
The Sun in any chart correlates with how the entire EA paradigm, for any person, is given a current life purpose, and how that current life purpose relative to the EA paradigm is integrated. When a person's Sun squares the Nodes of another it's their own sense of current life purpose, and how that is integrated relative to the EA paradigm in their chart, that can then create the developmental stress for both people. This can occur because the Sun person may feel that their current life purpose is being held back by the other person relative to that person's own South Node: their own individual past. Conversely, the Sun person may also manifest in the other's life in order to help them actualize their future, their North Node, by encouraging them to move away from, evolve, their past. Thus, the Sun person creates a sense of developmental, evolutionary, stress for the Nodes person because of the Sun person's own sense of their current life purpose, and how to integrate it, causes the Nodes person to have a great deal of tension or developmental, evolutionary, stress around their own past and their future as experienced in each moment.
This can then create developmental stress in both the person whose Nodes are being squared by the other's Sun, and the Sun person them self, because the Sun person can feel that their own sense of current life purpose, and needing to fully actualize it, is being in some ways hamstrung because of this type of interaction with the Nodes person: being caught up in that person's own struggle to evolve from their past to their future. Everything depends on the nature and type of relationship involved of course. Is it a casual relationship? An intimate one? and so forth and so on. The type of relationship will of course determine each person's reaction to this type of developmental stress. And in each case the EA astrologer must be able to determine all the other connecting factors between the two people that have come before the current life in order to understand the exact WHY of having one's Sun square the other's Nodes. Once the core WHY is understood then a comprehensive understanding can take place in such a way as to know the correct way to understand this dynamic, and how to proceed because of it. On the other hand, there is always a first time for anything. (Rad)

Synastry – one person's Nodes square the other's Nodes
When one person's Nodes squares the other person's Nodes in synastry this will correlate to two Souls who have been in some kind of relationship in which various dynamics and issues between them has caused them to separate from one another previous to the current life. Those issues and dynamics will be symbolized by the houses and signs in which the squaring Nodes takes place within the chart of the one whose chart is receiving those squaring Nodes. Additionally, the placement of the planetary rulers of those Nodes, by their own house and sign placement, and the aspects they make to other planets within the chart of the one who is receiving these squaring Nodes, also add to what those dynamics and issues have been. Coming into this life with that signature correlates to the intentions of each of their Souls to 'pick up where it was left off' in order to continue to confront those issues so that the evolution together can continue in some way. (Rad)

Synastry, nodal square – person A Venus conjunct North Node, person B Venus conjunct South Node
This type of signature correlates to dynamics that have brought the two together in the past, Venus conjunct the South Node, and as that relationship was then developed around those dynamics they became limiting to the ongoing evolution of not only each individual, but also to the evolutionary growth of the relationship itself. Accordingly one of them then tried to evolve the relationship forwards, Venus conjunct the North Node, that then had the effect of creating resistance in the other person. This resistance over time then created a state of maximum polarization between them, the meaning of the Venus on the North Node from one to the other, and the Venus on the South Node from one to the other. Efforts would have been made by each to move towards the other relative to these polarized dynamics without either of them actually embracing those polarized dynamics that needed to be evolved. It is the trying to embrace the new dynamics that would allow the individuals, and thus the relationship, to evolve without actually being able to do so which then results in the skipped steps symbolized in the squaring Lunar Nodes. It would be like saying, "Let's agree to disagree," and then trying to keep the relationship going anyway. Evolutionarily, with this type of signature, the Soul's cannot just try to keep it going anyway because that has led to the skipped steps. (Rad)

Synastry – one person's planet conjunct the other's South Node
In synastry when one person has a planet on the other's South Node correlates to prior life dynamics as symbolized in the house and signs in each other's chart: the South Node of one lands in a house in the other's chart, and that other's planet that is conjuncting that South Node of course lands in the natal house wherein that South Node exists. In combination these dynamics between them correlate to past life dynamics that have brought them together before. (Rad)

Synastry – one person's planet conjunct the other's North Node
When a planet from one conjuncts the North Node in the other's chart this will correlate to a current life evolutionary intention of evolving the relationship forwards by way of the house and sign in which this takes place. (Rad)

Synastry – with famous people
The fact that two Souls are in relationship to one another is what provides the basis for any kind of astrology reading for them in the first place. We all have synastry with Obama, doesn't mean we have any particular past life connection with him. (Ari)

Composite – midpoint method
JWG says in the Pluto 2 book that the near midpoint composite chart is the relevant composite chart for EA work. (Gonzalo)

Composite and Progressed Composite charts
A Progressed Composite chart is based on the individual progressions for any two people. Those individual progressed charts can then be combined to correlate to a progressed chart for both of them/between them. Look at each natal chart individually, then the combined natal charts that then makes a Composite chart. In understanding Progressed Composite charts it is essential to have an understanding, first, of what the natal Composite chart means for any two people. Then the Progressed Composite chart is added to that as it symbolizes the 'progression' of the natal evolutionary intentions for two people in a relationship to one another. (Rad)

(Q) Can we say that 'progressed' is like the 'inner' progress or evolution, and an aspect is like an 'outer' event that one faces? (Tory)
(A) No. All things in our life start from within ourselves first: the evolutionary and karmic 'script' of the Soul in any given life. Thus the progression of the planets, and the aspects that they are making, reflect this ongoing evolutionary script of the Soul at any point in time. (Rad)

Composite – skipped steps between two people
Skipped steps between two people can only be symbolized in their composite chart together. (Rad)

Composite – transits, progressions and bi-wheel
The best way I have found to use progressions in composite charts is to do the current progressions for each person in the relationship, and then to make a composite chart based on those progressions. You can then relate that progressed composite to the natal composite of the relationship in question. And, of course, transiting planets to the composite. One thing that JWG used to teach too, although nothing in print on it, is that you can take the natal planets of each person in the relationship and then apply them to the composite chart of the couple. In other words a bi-wheel where the composite is the center chart, and the individual planets of each person can be put on the outer ring. This, according to JWG, then symbolized how each person in their relationship is 'relating' to the fact of their unique 'coupleness' – the composite. This is different than standard synastry charts that symbolize how each person relates to the other as individuals. This is about how each is relating to the coupleness itself. Very few astrologers know of this. Yet, when applied, it is a real eye opener. (Rad)

Composite South Node Scorpio, North Node Taurus
In a general sense composite South Node in Scorpio would correlate to a couple who are trying to transmute past limitations within the relationship, and also to penetrate each other psychologically. There are fears of abandonment, betrayal and loss that create an emotionally compulsive way of being together that creates a non-growth situation. The composite North Node in Taurus would then reflect the evolutionary intention to develop a state of internalized emotional security and self-reliance within the relationship, and as a couple, to support this type of growth together. (Deva)

Understanding the WHY in relationships
It is highly recommended that you read JWG's Pluto 2 book in full. And, there are, indeed, a variety of 'concrete' ways to understand the past life dynamics between people, and the reasons for those dynamics. One of the great dimensions of Evolutionary Astrology is to be able to answer the question WHY. So much of astrology is really a DESCRIPTIVE astrology without providing any insights into the why of anything. Describing something is very different than understanding something. The aspects between people do in

fact correlate to existing dynamics between them that have been carried over from other lifetimes. So the underlying issue is to try to understand why those dynamics have occurred between them relative to their own individual evolutionary intentions. (Rad)
There is always a reason why any two Souls will be in relationship with each other. First the evolutionary and karmic dynamics of each particular Soul has to be understood – then based on that, we can move to the composite chart and the synastry in order to understand the nature of the relationship itself. In the end there can be any number of reasons why two Souls have come together in whatever way they have. As I understand it, most, if not all relationships have a past life story. It's the nature of a Soul's journey to be in constant relationship with everything. As it progressively burning its separating desires, it's also engaging in relationship – thus creating karma with many other Souls based on what internal dynamics are being worked on. All Souls are doing this. (Ari)

Resolving relationship dynamics
The point of resolving relationship dynamics is not just to complete things with one specific person, but to gain insight into and release dysfunctions in one's overall relationship patterns. These same dynamics would show up in any relationship a person enters into as they are within the person. They are not exclusive to a relationship they have with one specific person. If the person can resolve those dynamics within self, or in a relationship with someone else, there may be no need for them to enter an intimate relationship with the original person when they meet again. (On the other hand, in some cases it may be within the Soul's intended program TO enter relationship with that person again.) At the same time, there can still be unfinished business between the two people. Perhaps the other person, on meeting in a new life, will desire that the relationship become intimate. Then it comes down to choice. Somewhere in Pluto Vol. 2 Jeffrey said many of the dynamics that need resolving between two people, when they meet again with that instinctual magnetic attraction, can be resolved over a cup of coffee. (Steve)

Shared affinities
Although he never wrote about it, Jeffrey mentioned on a few occasions something called "shared affinities." He mentioned that it is a very valid part of older astrology that has pretty much been forgotten in the present time. I can say from my experiences both personal and with clients I've seen a lot of validation of this principle. We are talking about Soul resonance, Souls who are constructed with similar, or complementary, natures. You can think of it as notes in a chord. Some naturally harmonize, others will always be dissonant. This goes well beyond past life contact. It's about vibrational frequency as God/dess created a Soul. That can never change; it's the way they are naturally created. It's far beyond conditioning, which only gets in the way of what is naturally there. (Steve)

Soul mates
JWG wrote in his second volume of Pluto, which is all about the evolutionary reasons and intentions for relationships, that Soul mates are as follows:
"Soul Mates are two people who have independently acted on their own desires a spiritual or transcendent reality and that the real purpose with the union of one another is to continue their individual spiritual development because of and through the relationship. In spiritual terms it is called the path of the householder in contrast to the path of the monastic. This does not mean that the two people are perfect. It does mean that both have embraced a transcendent or spiritual principle to guide both their individual lives, and their relationship. There is a common spiritual (philosophical) foundation upon which the relationship is built and based. As a result, there is a larger point of view to refer and defer to. This then allows for the unconditional love and support for one another as opposed to conditional love. Conditional love is one of the primary breeding grounds through which difficult karmic situations or conditions can be created. Unconditional love is one of the primary breeding grounds through which harmonious and or positive situations or conditions are created. Thus, true Soul Mates only have positive karma conditions or situations that are mutually supportive and beneficial to one another. The state of Soul Mates, evolutionarily speaking, is a condition that is evolved into from the most common of relationships: Karma Mates."
JWG also said in that book that relative to what he called 'relationship types' that true Soul Mates are also two Souls who have created an inner condition within themselves of being the self-reliant type. The self-reliant type of Soul is one who understands and actualizes their own needs within or upon themselves. Thus in a true Soul Mate relationship both are mutually self-reliant which then minimizes if not totally eliminates the 'projection' of need upon the other. The projection of needs is that which is one of the core dynamics in what he called Karma Mates. (Rad)

Determining past life gender of a couple
In combination with their individual charts, synastry charts, and composite charts this is possible. (Rad)

Love – conditional and unconditional
The phenomenon of love comes down to two types of love: conditional and unconditional. The correlation of Venus/Taurus/2nd Libra/7th, Mars/Aries/1st, Pluto/Scorpio/8th; and the planetary residents of and aspects to all of the above, calibrated to the Soul's

evolutionary condition, equals all that is defined by conditional love where love is experienced or expressed as a function of having one's needs met by another. When those needs are not met then once that which was experienced as love with and for another, and visa versa, can change into something quite the opposite.

Unconditional love is reflected in the archetypes of the 12th house, Neptune, and of course Pisces. Unconditional love can be experienced and expressed at any evolutionary level or condition. Of course unconditional love is not a function of one's personal needs being met or unmet: it just is. Unconditional love has no expectations attached to it whatsoever whereas conditional love in fact does. It is those expectations associated with conditional love that manifest as projected needs upon another, and visa versa. When those projected needs associated with one's expectations are met then conditional love is in fact experienced. When they are not then what was once experienced as love can become something quite different.

Conditional love is time-based: finite. Unconditional love is timeless: infinite. Conditional love manifests as a function of evolutionary and karmic imperatives and necessities, unconditional love manifests as a function of the universal = timeless Natural Law of giving to others in whatever ways that any given Soul has within itself to give even if that giving is simply loving another for who and what they are without any expectation or need to be given back to in any way at all. The inner feeling we all have of 'love' for another when linked with conditional love occurs as a function of the physiology that is set in motion when we interface with another where that other, and visa versa, reflects what we need in our ongoing evolutionary journey through time: the inner psychological and emotional dynamics of any given Soul through time, and the reasons for those specific psychological and emotional dynamics.

In essence the feeling of 'love' that is ignited at the beginning of an attraction to another for these reasons IS TO DRAW THE SOULS TOGETHER SO THAT THE EVOLUTIONARY AND KARMIC REASONS that any given Soul has relative to its own ongoing evolutionary journey CAN BE MET. This is why JWG wrote his second Pluto book on relationships wherein one of those important chapters is called "So We Meet Again, Eh?" And as he said it takes more than one life with another who we draw into our lives through conditional love, as defined above, to be worked out. And when it is worked out we then move on to other Souls as our own evolutionary and karmic NEEDS change. This is exactly where, for example, John and Yoko found themselves in their own evolutionary journey together. And, of course, conditional love can in fact turn into unconditional love for some Souls. Thus, in the context of Souls who have been intimate where that intimacy has been defined by conditional love this will manifest as "I will always love you, but I no longer need you." (Rad)

Culminating archetype in relationships

First, one can't tell from just the birth charts alone. One has to do the traditional astrology thing which is to observe and correlate the symbols to the observation. Thus, if I have a couple in front of me that feels from within themselves that their relationship is culminating, coming to an end, that they feel they have done all they can do with one another, this is the relevant observation to make based on their feedback. I then would look at their charts individually and combined (*see* Composite and Progressed Composite charts). If I then observed in so doing a lot of planetary phases that are indeed culminating, as in balsamic phases, I could then confirm to them their own observation/feelings. Conversely, if they made that observation about themselves and I looked into their charts and did not see a lot of planets in a balsamic phase then I would offer my view that I didn't feel that to be true. I would then explore with them why they felt this way and would point to the areas/dynamics within themselves as individuals, and how they came together in relationship, that still needed to be worked on together. If I did see planets in a balsamic relationship to one another I would also talk to them about the dynamics that are specific to those archetypes that are indeed culminating and why, and what the new seeds are for those dynamics to come: future lives. There is no one signature in EA that says, absolutely, that any relationship is totally over. (Rad)

Power dynamics in relationships

As far as giving up power in relationships, some of it comes down to better choice-making in picking potential partners, of looking deeper before getting overly involved, to see if the person has the capacity to go where you would like to go. Ideally that capacity is quite developed BEFORE entering the relationship. The old pattern would most likely be this is not the case, and the temptation to give in to temptation, yet again, would be quite strong. If one of your core issues is giving your power away, you want the kind of partner who won't let you do that, bottom line. That takes a pretty spiritually mature person who keeps pointing you back to yourself. (Steve)

Past life connection with historical figures

[Example: A Soul's birth chart with similarities to Joan of Arc] Using the birth charts alone to determine if someone was so and so in another life simply can't happen. How many other Souls on this planet will have that same, or very similar, birth chart? It is not UNCOMMON for a given Soul to relate to some historical figure in which their Soul has been, or is, the same or similar. (Rad)

Scorpio archetype – abandonment, betrayal, violation of trust

Remember, Pluto rules Scorpio. Core Scorpio archetypes/fears are abandonment, betrayal, and violation of emotional trust. These are going to appear wherever Pluto and Scorpio appear in the chart. Of course each person will experience them in their own way, based on their past and present. The nature of the fears is determined by the house and sign that Pluto is in. For example, if it's in the 5th, there could be fears of losing children. In the 8th, partners and/or money. In the 12th, fears of being abandoned by God/Goddess. In the 2nd of losing money/resources. (That is NOT a definitive list of all the possible fears that could occur by house – it's a short list to illustrate the flavor of what I mean.) In most cases the fears are based on actual events that have occurred in this and previous lives, often subconscious – forgotten – which explains the compulsive nature of Pluto/Scorpio. They are memories in the Soul, yet not consciously remembered. The significance of them causes the fears to repeat over and over – compulsion, fears or behaviors that seem to have no logical sense yet are completely logical when looked at from the Soul's long term memory of past events. Also take into account the number of aspects Pluto is making to other planets in the chart. Anything aspecting Pluto acquires Plutonian qualities. Also consider aspects made to the Pluto polarity point, and the South and North Nodes of Pluto.

As to the reasons for abandonment, I look at Pluto as a cosmic garbage collector – anything that has outlived its useful time as an agent of growth in a life, Pluto eventually takes away. We all have many things in our life we don't really want taken away. We sometimes hold onto them tightly. So experiences arise that force us to let go – abandonment, betrayal, violation of trust. In a strong Pluto chart – 8th house Pluto, 8th house stellium, stellium in Scorpio, lots of planets aspecting Pluto, etc., the person is so used to having things just disappear from their life, the experience becomes second nature. They come to expect that to occur, which can make it a self-fulfilling prophecy. Expecting it or not, it still hurts at times. It's easy to get sick of those experiences of loss and just try to hold on to something until the bitter end. Ultimately Pluto will win and whatever is being held onto will, once again, be removed. The root of this, in most cases, is the need to become self-reliant and self-contained – the polarity of Scorpio/8th is Taurus/2nd. To focus on the inner rather than getting overly immersed in relationship with others, the outer. Abandonment is a very effective tool towards those realizations, while certainly being a harsh teacher at times. (Steve)

Libra archetype – projection

Unless any reality is 'objectively' understood for what it is, whatever that reality is, then the Soul will project what they think that reality is into any situation that is not objectively understood. Projecting onto someone else what we think they need can be associated with Libra because Libra is naturally linked to Aquarius and Gemini through its own natural triad. (Rad)

Projections, delusions, expectations

Astrologically speaking, Aquarius is the archetype that correlates with projections (from our own unconscious). These projections can be based on past traumas (ie this reminds me of my ex-partner, old friend, parents, etc.) which are then cast onto the person who you are involved with now. These projections can also be based on the person's own unconscious inner dynamics/structure that are then cast onto others. In other words, the person projects what is inside themselves onto others. Aquarius correlates to the individuated unconscious and also to the dynamic of trauma. The projections that can surface within this archetype can be linked with the need to objectify and hopefully release what is stored/unresolved within the unconscious. [The situation you are describing] also sounds like dynamics that are linked with unconscious expectations that get projected upon others within relationships.

Astrologically speaking, expectations are linked with the archetype of Libra. Libra correlates with the nature of our expectations within relationships and our ability (or inability) to reach a balanced state of giving and receiving within relationships. Libra correlates with extremities, and the need to reach a state of balance relative to such extremities. Delusion/fantasy correlates with the archetype of Pisces. Pisces symbolizes the need for ultimate meaning, and to bring to closure an entire cycle of evolution in order to prepare for a new cycle which begins in the Aries archetype. When ultimate meaning is 'projected' externally within a relationship it is all too easy to fall into fantasies and delusions (infatuation) about the other person regardless of how much actual contact there has been.

The core point within this is that these types of projections and delusions are based on a need for ultimate meaning/fulfilment within life which we try to find in a variety of external sources. (There is a natural inconjunction between the Libra/Pisces archetypes which reflects the crisis of disillusionment that so many of us have experienced because of this dynamic in which our expectations/need for ultimate meaning are not met.) Pisces also correlates to the need to meet the need for ultimate meaning through creating a relationship with the Divine. Pluto Vol. 2 goes into a wonderful in-depth description of the connection between the Taurus, Libra, and Pisces archetypes and how these archetypes correlate with the need in all of us to progressively internalize (Taurus) our need for ultimate meaning through union with Spirit/the Divine (Pisces) and to reach a state of balance within our relationships (Libra). (Deva)

Projection, in general, correlates to Uranus, the 11th house, and Aquarius. Delusions, in general, correlate with Pisces, the 12th house, and Neptune. Delusions manifest from within the consciousness of any given Soul that can then be projected outwardly into the overall environment in such a way as to condition the very nature of that environment relative to the nature of the delusion itself. There are many possible causes including one's own essential needs within a relationship that the other seems to correlate to, past life connections in which something was not finished, resolved, or is intended to pick up again in the current life, the inner creation of 'fantasy' type ideas about the 'perfect' partner that the other seems to correlate to, etc. etc. etc. All of this correlates, obviously, to delusions if none of it is true: actual. The correlations are above, and those archetypes would be active relative to the transits or progressions at the time that this occurs. (Rad)

Libra archetype – de facto God or Goddess
The EA term is "making the partner the de facto God or Goddess." That is, we experience a taste of divinity THROUGH the partner. We become confused (Neptune) and think what we are feeling is coming from the partner, not realizing it is actually coming from within us. We then project (Libra) on the partner that they are the source of the good feelings we experience, when they are actually our own 12th house Return to Source yearnings. No human can ever consistently live up to these projections. As the interactions proceed we tend to start feeling let down by the partner's imperfections and tend to start criticizing the partner's faults as we start experiencing them more where they really are at, which is always less than the potential we saw within them. And yet, we also remember how wonderful we feel at those moments when we reach a momentary peak with that partner. All that becomes the root of co-dependence. In relationships EA describes this as the natural yod between the 12th, 2nd, and 7th houses. That brilliant material is covered in Pluto Vol. 2. (Steve)

Venus archetype – natural inconjunct between Taurus and Libra
Venus correlates with our inner relationship with ourselves, and also the external relationships we form as a reflection of our inner relationship. Venus is co-ruled by the signs of Taurus and Libra. Taurus reflects our inner relationship with ourselves, and the inner side, or inner nature, of Venus. Libra reflects the relationships we attract and initiate with other people (outer or external side of Venus). Venus correlates with our values which are a determinate to who we form relationships with and whom not, and also the needs we have within relationships. When we have not learned to meet our own needs they become projected onto our partner and others in general within relationships. There is a natural inconjunct between the Taurus and Libra archetypes which correlates with the crisis (inconjunct) that occurs when we project too many needs onto another within relationships and are then thrown back onto ourselves in order to learn self-reliance. Venus correlates with extremities, and how we will go about balancing or uniting discordant aspects of ourselves. Again, the need is to learn to identify what our specific needs are within relationships and meet those from within ourselves in order to attract relationships that are balanced, equal, and based on mutual independence. The natal placement of Venus in the birth chart correlates with the person's pre-existing relationship patterns, and the values and needs an individual will have within relationships. (Deva)

Jeffrey was the first astrologer to teach about Venus' correlation to the inner relationship that all people have with themselves. He taught why Venus had a double rulership for the signs Libra and Taurus. He said that Taurus and the 2nd house correlated to the inner relationship we all have with ourselves, and that the 7th house and Libra correlated to the types of outer relationships that we form with other people and why. He taught that the planet Venus, of itself, symbolized both the inner and outer relationships within the archetype of Venus itself. A simple example: if a person has, let's say, Venus in Virgo and their inner relationship to themself is one of intense criticism, all the things that are wrong with them, that it shouldn't then be surprising that that person would then 'attract,' Venus, others who are then critical of them: the inner reflecting the outer. And that which we attract is a reflection of the inner vibration within us where that inner vibration is a reflection of our inner relationship to ourselves. Or, for another example, let's say that Venus in Virgo person was inwardly experiencing a high degree of 'lack' in their lives which then leads to a sense of being 'empty' from within. That inner relationship to themselves could then manifest outwardly as needing, Venus, many other people in their lives in order to 'fill them up,' and needing others to give to them that which they felt they were lacking.

He talked about the natural inconjunct between the 2nd house, Taurus, and the 7th house, Libra. He taught that this is the natural 'crisis' that exists in all of us that involves the need to be self-reliant and fulfilling our own needs, and how our needs can be projected onto others in such a way as to become dependent on others for the very needs that we need to satisfy within ourselves. And how our projected needs onto others correlate to 'expectations' that we can set up with other people. So what happens when our expectations that are projected onto others do not occur? For most some kind of crisis will occur where the intent of the crisis is to force the person back upon themselves so that self-reliance in some way can be developed when those expectations have reached a point of excessive dependency on others. He taught about the need for the EA astrologer to understand the totality of the Venus archetype. Thus, to not only understand the sign that Venus is in but all the aspects that it is making to other planets, the North and South Nodes of Venus in terms of what the past, present, and future of the evolving Venus archetype is in all charts, and to fully grasp the signs on the 2nd and 7th houses as they condition those natural archetypes, and the reasons for that conditioning relative to the ongoing evolutionary intentions of the Soul, and, lastly, the location of the planetary rulers of those signs and the aspects that they are making for the same reasons. (Rad)

Venus archetype – the psychology of "listening"

Venus correlates to the nature of our "inner dialogue" with ourselves (Taurus side of Venus) and how we can all project this inner dialogue onto others. In other words, if I have Venus in Scorpio I will naturally be listening to others from a "bottom line" psychological standpoint ("where is this person coming from, can I relate to this or not?"). The Venus in Scorpio person may also come into relationships with unconscious fears of abandonment, betrayal, and loss, and unconsciously project these fears onto the other by listening to their partner in a defensive manner, and also project that the other person has ulterior motives or agendas which the other in fact does not have. Venus correlates with the psychology of listening (Libra side of Venus), and when we listen to others based on our own subjective inner dialogue we do not truly hear what they are communicating. Remember that the archetype of Libra correlates with the need to learn to listen to others from their reality, not our own, in order to truly understand what the other is communicating. (Deva)

Venus correlates to the psychology of listening. Via the Taurus side of Venus our inner dialogue with our self is all too often projected (Libra side of Venus) onto others in our relationships. Example, Venus in Virgo, the person could project the inner critical relationship/inner dialogue onto the other in the form of "hearing" the other criticize or undermine them when this is not the case (the other may be trying to give helpful advice for example). The point is that via the Libra side of Venus we must learn to objectively hear and listen to others from their reality so we do not project in this way, and truly hear what is being said. (Deva)

Since Pisces is the polarity of Virgo, the Soul with Venus in Virgo is always comparing themselves to perfection and often feeling the LACK to greater degrees. The Venus in Virgo can be so self-critical that this criticism can then be transferred to the partner, ie not just the self-judgment trips or hearing another incorrectly but also focusing on the partner's inadequacies versus their strengths, ie focusing on their lacks too. It is impossible to love another (7th house) unconditionally until and unless one can learn to love themselves (2nd house) unconditionally first, which is the evolutionary intent with a Venus in Virgo, ie the polarity of Virgo being PISCES (unconditional LOVE). (Kristin)

Venus archetype – past, present and future orientations

The present life Venus is conditioned by all the past "self and other" relationship tendencies and patterns that have preceded it. The South Node of Venus represents directly the way the Venus functions were handled in the past. The South Node of the Moon represents the Soul's past personality structures and emotional habits/patterns. Both of these are alive within the present life Venus function, subconsciously coloring it. Yet that Venus also contains the possibility of changing the past, in the present moment (the only moment in which anything can be changed). The intended directions for that Venus to evolve are indicated in the North Node of Venus, the Lunar North Node ruler, the Lunar North Node, and the Polarity Point of Pluto, in that order, from top to bottom. We try to mentally separate the past and the present and the future, to see them as different things. But in reality it's all the same, and it can't be separated.

That is why EA says you work the North Node, learn new ways of doing things, and then evolve your South Node function by integrating these new ways into your old ways of doing the South Node. The end result is the entire structure, Soul and personality, evolve. We can't really separate our internal Venus functions from our Mars functions, from our Moon functions, from our Saturn functions. We are complex beings that have all of these inner drives, desires, motivations, orientations. In reality they are all mixed together within us. We use astrology to gain objectivity by assigning this function to this planet and that function to that planet, but past a certain point those are constructs, not complete reality. In reality we are the sum total of all of them, and that includes our past and future also. EVERYTHING has something to do with the past. The imprint of the past is contained within the present Venus, and every other planet too. (Steve)

Venus retrograde

Venus retrograde indicates that the Soul is defined through the Taurus side of Venus (establishing a primary relationship within him or herself first) instead of the Libra side as most folks are (initiation of relationships with others which is the externalized side of Venus). (Deva)

When the planet Venus is retrograde in the sky, you may be able to feel the nature of this archetype intimately, especially the inner side of Venus as it works to help you reconnect with yourself and through extension Spirit. It is a time where your Soul is getting in touch with what holds the most meaning and value. A time to reflect about whether you are getting your essential needs (inner side of Venus) met and a time when your Soul is in the process of making changes to support those values.

[Example: Venus retrograde in Aries/Pisces] Venus is the lower octave of Neptune and Neptune is the ruler of Pisces, so as Venus slows down and slowly stations at the last degree of Pisces, many Souls are searching beyond what holds earthly meaning and to what holds ULTIMATE meaning, which can only really be found within – God/Goddess (Pisces/Neptune). This can also be a time when relationships (outer side of Venus) that are not matching what we need are ending, a time of culmination, Venus in Pisces; and also a time for healing the past, old wounds in relationships that have injured our inner relationship with ourselves, things being cleared. So when Venus moves direct and back into Aries, we can be stronger in our self and more clear about our desires and needs (Venus in Aries) and as a result how to move forward with others. As our inner relationship with our self changes, our vibration also shifts and this will then alter the nature of whom and what we attract. (Kristin)

Venus in Virgo
Since Pisces is the polarity of Virgo, the Soul with Venus in Virgo is always comparing themselves to perfection and often feeling the LACK to greater degrees. The Venus in Virgo can be so self-critical that this criticism can then be transferred to the partner, ie not just the self-judgment trips or hearing another incorrectly but also focusing on the partner's inadequacies versus their strengths, ie focusing on their lacks too. It is impossible to love another (7th house) unconditionally until and unless one can learn to love themselves (2nd house) unconditionally first, which is the evolutionary intent with a Venus in Virgo, ie the polarity of Virgo being PISCES (unconditional LOVE). (Kristin)

Higher octave of Venus – Neptune
Neptune is the higher octave of Venus. Venus corresponds to the heart chakra. My intuition is that this does not mean that Neptune correlates to the heart chakra itself, but rather that the heart chakra and the crown have some sort of octave resonance to one another which is the manifestation of Source unity consciousness through the denser, interpersonal feeling center of the heart. (Ari)

A simple example: Neptune would correlate to unconditional love, whereas Venus would or can correlate to conditional love and the reasons for that conditional love. (Rad)

Venus transit
Venus through transit reflects the ongoing evolution of our inner relationship with ourselves, and our outer relationships. The awareness of new and changing needs occurs through Venus transits. The transits of Venus also reflect the specific inner and outer relationship patterns we are working on at that moment in time relative to the house and sign it occupies in our natal chart. We can simply "outgrow" a current relationship we are in ("I do not feel I need this anymore"), or feel that it has reached a natural point of separation (no more growth is occurring for either person). We have all experienced times in our lives when we have exhausted the specific needs that were the basis of a relationship, and become aware of deeper aspects of ourselves that now need to be nourished, or nurtured, so to speak. In my view, it reflects that we are deepening our inner relationship with ourselves and this growth creates a natural evolution of our needs within relationships. We must then make the necessary inner and outer changes in our life to accommodate these changing needs. In general, Venus transits to the outer planets such as Jupiter, Uranus, Saturn, and Pluto will induce the deepest levels of change relative to the dynamics already described. (Deva)

Karmic relationships – Agni ritual
The very best thing to do is not to react at all and to involve oneself in the Agni ritual that will sever the karmic umbilical cord that has kept the two people going around in this karmic dance. (JWG)

JWG wrote that in the context of two people who could not stop going around and around with one another. If in fact the two people involved in such a dance mutually accept the responsibility in their own actions then the karmic past that has dictated the dance is over. (Rad)

Davison relationship chart
Jeffrey said somewhere in Pluto Vol. 2 that he'd found no validity in working with Davison composite charts. (Steve)

RETROGRADE ARCHETYPE

Accelerated evolution

Retrograde symbolizes that the specific areas within consciousness indicated by the house and sign position of the planet that is retrograde are being re-lived, or repeated, in order to be fully resolved. When the issues are resolved then the Soul can grow by leaps and bounds. The analogy that is used in the Pluto material is peeling away at the layers of an onion to arrive at its core. As such, those who resolve the necessary issues related to a planet that is retrograde will feel a deep sense of being released from those issues, coming into alignment with his or her natural individuality/identity in the context of "peeling away at the onion." The retrograde archetype accelerates a Soul's evolution no matter what evolutionary condition they have evolved to, even in the Consensus state, because the archetype of retrograde correlates to 'individuation' as Carl Jung used that word: to individuate from any external conditioning factor that attempts to define for an individual how any given phenomenon is 'meant' to be defined and lived out. The retrograde archetype is meant to induce a natural rebellion from those external conditioning pressures wherever they come from. And the intent of the rebellion is to arrive at a place of individuation. As a result it accelerates the evolutionary pace of the Soul by way of the planets that are retrograde in their birth charts. (Deva)

Individuation

Retrogrades accelerate the Soul's evolution because of the desire to question the consensus, status quo, expectation of how a planetary archetype is meant to actualize itself. Thus, the retrograde archetype is a naturally individualizing archetype. As a result, the retrograde archetype is a naturally questioning archetype that is desiring to recreate, or re-discover, itself in an individualizing way that reflects, ultimately, the individual nature of the Soul itself. Thus, the evolutionary need to recreate or re-live dynamics from the past of the Soul that by their very nature trigger the individualizing aspect of the retrograde archetype. (Rad)

In ALL Souls, not just those with retrogrades, individuation is necessary for evolution to continue. The process of evolution IS the progressive individuation of the Soul, until that Soul finally realizes in full who it truly is, not intellectually but experientially. Until then the individuation process is the progressive stripping away of all conditioned senses of "me" that have accumulated over many lifetimes, until finally all that's left is the experience of the true "me." That process takes many lives. The difference in a chart with retrogrades is the individuation process is heightened, emphasized – because there has been resistance to that process in the past. So the Soul through retrograde has set up conditions that will force it to emphasize its own individuation, as a way of overcoming its own conditioned resistance to that process. Other symbols emphasizing the individuation process include a lot of 11th house or Aquarius, Uranus aspecting many planets, etc. (Steve)

Retrograde is an archetype within itself. In other words, when any planet is retrograde it reflects a specific evolutionary/karmic dynamic within the Soul that conditions how that planetary function will be expressed/acted out. In the Pluto material it states that retrograde symbolizes that the specific areas within consciousness indicated by the house and sign position of the planet that is retrograde are being re-lived, or repeated, in order to be fully resolved. There is an individuated impulse reflected by the retrograde position. The planetary function must be given an individualized application and meaning independent of cultural/mainstream society. In other words, if I have Venus retrograde I must define FOR MYSELF the meaning and values that I have for any relationship. In fact, those who have Venus retrograde typically cannot relate to the traditional/mainstream types of relationships and tend to withdraw within themselves (Taurus co-rulership of Venus) in order to accomplish the individuation process that must occur from an evolutionary standpoint. They are defined through the Taurus side of Venus, not the Libra side (this is from Pluto Vol. 2). The point within this is that certain key situations must be re-lived, or re-experienced before they can be resolved. Most commonly the individuation process indicated by the retrograde planet has not been fully accomplished, and that is why the Soul will set up a life circumstance of re-living certain experiences. Those with Venus retrograde will attract key people with whom there is "unfinished business," for example, until the person resolves the necessary dynamics reflected by the house and sign of Venus retrograde. (Deva)

The intent of the retrograde as an archetype is to re-live, redo, repeat. And the intention within that, the reason for that, is to INDIVIDUATE. Any retrograde planet either by birth, or going retrograde in the context of a lifetime, is not only to repeat, re-live, and redo, which can have many reasons, but one of the core reasons is to individuate. It accelerates the evolutionary process of individuation. Thus the Soul desires to withdraw from ANY external circumstance or condition that is attempting to define, through expectations, how the archetype of the planet that is retrograde, at birth, progression, or transit, how that archetype (planet) is 'meant' to be actualized or lived out. And that is because the Soul is desiring to individuate its function which, in turn, allows for an acceleration of the Soul's development because of the effort to individuate. In its own way it ignites a deep feeling in the Soul that says, 'not this, not that, so what is it?' (Rad)

Resistance
Retrograde is a need to review/redo/renew because things need to change to allow evolution to proceed. Pluto symbolizes our Soul. Our Soul is the root principle/reason/cause/core of why we are all here in the first place. Pluto equates with resistance. This means, at our core every one of us has an inherent resistance. Anything that is at a core permeates through everything that manifests out of that core. The whole process is learning to accept that inherent resistance and not be completely limited and defined by it. (Steve)

The resistance to the forward movement will also still be present, thus there can be a real struggle within the Soul between its desire to evolve and its tendency to resist the evolutionary intentions. This can result in the feeling of painting self into a corner where there is no way out other than to do what is intended. The more retrograde planets in the chart, the more resistance has occurred in the past. Seven retrograde planets at times would not be a lot of fun as the two opposing forces to evolve and resistance to evolving would have quite a tug of war at times. The intention is to bust the pattern of resistance open once and for all, to release the log jam. If the person finally "gets it" and starts cooperating with the evolutionary intentions, as a result of this pressure/intensity, the progress can be rapid. If they continue with resistance as the primary response, the life may not be a lot of fun. The retrograde function adds a Uranian flavor to the planetary function – it is going to do what it does in its own unique way and not be so concerned with what others think about it. (Steve)

Dissatisfaction
The retrograde function is non-static, never rests, is in a perpetual, cyclical state of growing, is always dissatisfied. (JWG)

Dissatisfaction is a Plutonian experience, that facilitates evolutionary need. Retrograde emphasizes the sense of dissatisfaction, which then facilitates the evolutionary needs. When a person says, "There is something else possible." No matter what the evolutionary level is. If dissatisfaction is a Plutonian experience, and the retrograde function is always dissatisfied, doesn't that make the retrograde function inherently Plutonian? And Pluto does correlate with resistance. The more retrograde planets, the more resistance. That is why it is generally difficult for a retrograde personality (defined by Jeffrey as someone with four or more retrograde planets) to make the necessary changes, while at the same time there is a deep knowing of the NECESSITY of making those changes. The Soul has intentionally painted itself into a corner. (Steve)

Retrograde-type personality
Jeffrey's teaching was that those with four or more retrograde planets are a retrograde-type personality. Retrograde is the archetype of redo-review-renew. Normally the energies of a planet are focused outward. When retrograde, they are focused inward, back at the person, the gaze being inward. This creates an introspective nature (not necessarily introverted, but introspective). Pluto correlates with resistance. When there are four or more retrograde planets, this demonstrates there has been a lot of resistance within that Soul in the past towards fulfilling the evolutionary intentions. The Soul sometimes then comes in with a chart with a number of retrograde planets, as these force or accelerate the evolutionary intentions – the circumstances will appear in the life that will force that Soul forward. The resistance to the forward movement will also still be present, thus there can be a real struggle within the Soul between its desire to evolve and its tendency to resist the evolutionary intentions. This can result in the feeling of painting self into a corner where there is no way out other than to do what is intended. The more retrograde planets in the chart, the more resistance has occurred in the past. Seven retrograde planets at times would not be a lot of fun as the two opposing forces to evolve and resistance to evolving would have quite a tug of war at times. The intention is to bust the pattern of resistance open once and for all, to release the log jam. If the person finally "gets it" and starts cooperating with the evolutionary intentions, as a result of this pressure/intensity, the progress can be rapid. If they continue with resistance as the primary response, the life may not be a lot of fun. The retrograde function adds a Uranian flavor to the planetary function – it is going to do what it does in its own unique way and not be so concerned with what others think about it. (Steve)

Retrograde archetype, and evolutionary state
The retrograde archetype operates at all levels of evolution for all Souls. The individualizing aspect of it means that it operates in a Uranus-like way in that it progressively rejects or rebels against the external conditioning of how a given archetype, eg Venus, is expected to be actualized or lived. The rejection or rebellion is about uncovering, progressively, what the actual truth is about the inherent individuality of any given Soul relative to all the various archetypes that in total equals the consciousness of the Soul in human form. The rejection or rebellion of the retrograde archetype thus accelerates the natural evolutionary progression of the Soul because it withdraws from the external expectations equaling conditioning of the planet, archetype, that is retrograde. This individualizing aspect of the retrograde archetype applies to all levels of evolution. (Rad)

Retrograde archetype, and Consensus state

The retrograde archetype accelerates a Soul's evolution no matter what evolutionary condition they have evolved to, even in the Consensus state, because the archetype of retrograde correlates to 'individuation' as Carl Jung used that word: to individuate from any external conditioning factor that attempts to define for an individual how any given phenomena is 'meant' to be defined and lived out. The retrograde archetype is meant to induce a natural rebellion from those external conditioning pressures wherever they come from. And the intent of the rebellion is to arrive at a place of individuation. As a result it accelerates the evolutionary pace of the Soul by way of the planets that are retrograde in their birth charts. (Rad)

Retrograde archetype, and Spiritual state

In the Spiritual state, it means for each Soul to discover its own individual way of reuniting with its source: God/ess. (Rad)

Integrating the totality of a retrograde planet

To understand the totality of a retrograde planet or planets in terms of not only the individuation process that accelerates the Soul's evolution, but also in terms of that which is being re-lived for karmic and evolutionary reasons, which are themselves DETERMINED relative to the underlying primary evolutionary/karmic axis, one first focuses on the actual nature of the planet(s) that are retrograde, the sign and house location of that natal planet that is retrograde, the location by sign/house that that planet naturally rules (ie Venus naturally rules Libra and Taurus), aspects to that planet that is retrograde because those archetypal dynamics of other planets that are aspecting the retrograde planet all contribute to the total context of that which is being re-lived and individuated, and, lastly, the location by house and sign of the planetary nodes of the planet(s) that are retrograde. Understanding and integrating the totality of this will then lead the EA astrologer to a comprehensive understanding of the retrograde planet(s) for any Soul's individual context that is always established by understanding the main evolutionary/karmic foundation of each birth chart as symbolized by the EA paradigm of Pluto, its polarity point, the location of the North and South Nodes of the Moon, and the location of their planetary rulers. (Rad)

Phasal relationship between retrograde planets

[Example: Mars direct at 1 deg Aries, Mercury direct at 3 deg Aries] It could, for some reasons, be experienced somehow similar to a balsamic conjunction. While the new phase conjunction produces instinctual, unchecked action without egocentric awareness, the retrogradation of Mars will require the individual to listen to himself, his Soul or God, before taking action. This implies that action is required to operate not merely in an instinctual way. Mercury retrograde will require the Soul to discriminate about the type of information it collects from the environment in order to select information which serves its evolutionary intentions; otherwise, the Soul will be – as most likely has been in the past – mentally overwhelmed by indiscriminate information intake, and will experience confusion, leading to not knowing what to think, not knowing what to do. Thus, each planet in this new phase is requiring a deeper evolutionary response, which in turn is necessary because of what the prior response to each archetype has been – thus, a higher likelihood exists that the Soul may experience confusion in relation to these archetypes in the new cycle beginning – and also, they could serve as vehicles to grasp from within something deeper or more universal. (Gonzalo)

Retrograde planet conjunct South Node

The internalization and introspection of the retrograde archetype manifests because of the planet being retrograde: it's an archetype that is essential to retrograde. Thus, when the Soul recreates for itself conditions that it has already lived prior to the existing life in the current life the intention is in fact to reflect, through internalization and introspection, exactly why it has done so. The answers realized because of this reliving thus serve the Soul's evolutionary purpose of self-knowledge that is meant to be applied to the Soul's evolutionary future that will be progressively individualized to reflect the individual design of its Soul.

Any planet on the South Node correlates to that archetype being developed prior to the current life that is being relived through evolutionary necessity in order for evolution to proceed for the Soul. There are three karmic/evolutionary reasons for this: a total relive of the past that must be revisited in order for new choices to made relative to the circumstances created relative to the relive, a condition of total evolutionary fruition which means that archetypes have been highly developed, evolved, and is meant to be sustained in the current life in order for it to be helpful in the evolution of others' Souls, or a combination of both of those conditions that have the same evolutionary intentions. (Rad)

Retrograde planet conjunct North Node

A retrograde planet is not 'highly developed' but in the process of being developed which is serving as a 'lead point' in the ongoing evolution of the Soul. The retrograde archetype accelerates the evolution of the Soul because it naturally rebels from the consensus expectation of how that archetypal function defined by the planet itself is 'meant' to be actualized according to the consensus. Thus, there is a progressive 'individuation' of that archetype that reflects, in the end, the inherent individuality of that archetype according the original design of the Soul itself. A planet conjunct the North Node has been worked upon prior to the current life that reflects the evolutionary needs/desires of the Soul that serves as a lead point in the ongoing evolutionary journey of the Soul:

this does not mean it is highly developed. It does mean that it is not brand new: the first life that involves this evolutionary intention. The retrograde archetype also means that any planet that is retrograde, on the North Node or not, is also recreating, re-experiencing, reliving dynamics from its past that must be relived in order for new choices to be made in order for the Soul's evolution to proceed. It can also correlate to karmic conditions, karmic issues, that also must be relived because they have yet to be dealt with and/or resolved. Thus the intention to do so in the retrograde symbol. And to accelerate the evolution of the Soul by rebelling or rejecting against the consensus of any given society's expectations of how that archetypal function is 'meant' to be actualized according to that consensus. (Rad)

A general [correct] example: Saturn retrograde on the North Node. If a Soul was overly conditioned by its responsibilities, then in this life there will be an evolutionary emphasis on liberating from that conditioning (Saturn retrograde) while continuing to actualize the role the structure is here to build (on the North Node). (Ari)

[Example: Neptune retrograde conjunct North Node 2nd] With the Neptune retrograde on the North Node all three of those retrograde archetypes will be experienced, just as they have been in the most previous past lives of that Soul. It should be clear that one of the dynamics/issues that the Soul is needing to deal with is the issue of personal delusions/illusions, Neptune, that the Soul EXPECTS, Neptune and its lower octave Venus, to occur as if by magic. As a result, this Soul has created a 'program' for itself in which various expectations that are projected into the life will be met with disillusionment, Neptune, so that the experience of disillusionment will be the causative factor of busting apart the very nature of the Soul's illusions and delusions. The intent in this of course is to re-orientate to actual reality because of the disillusionment. (Rad)

Mars retrograde

Mars retrograde creates an internalization of the Mars function in general (ie slows down the process of initiation of actions in general). This is because, prior to the life, the Soul had acted upon many desires that were not relevant to his or her evolutionary intentions for the life, and may have had negative consequences, and so in this life the intent is for the individual to fully "think through" the desires that he or she acts upon in order to create an alignment with the current evolutionary intentions for this life. Mars retrograde creates an awareness of the nature of the Soul's desire nature in this way. (Deva)

Mercury retrograde

Mercury retrograde actually points to the Jupiter function (right brain leading the left brain). (Deva)

Mercury, when going retrograde, for a period of time in the Soul's life, GENERALLY means focusing on information that the Soul is interested in, and no more. (Rad)

Any planet retrograde inverts its normal function from outward to inward. The eyes turn inward. That is the intention. Natal Mercury retrograde is, lifelong, purging the buildup within the Soul of excessive information that is holding back the Soul's progress going forward. Jeffrey described it as they are only interested in that which has relevance to their intended life path. Thus they can have difficulty in school where rote memorization of unnecessary information is required. What would be true is natal Mercury retrograde people are more at home with the archetypes of Mercury retrograde [transit], since much of it is what their inner experience is like most of the time. A difference is when Mercury is direct they are somewhat alone in their orientation as it is a minority of people. When it's retrograde everyone is feeling it. Many non-retrograde people have not learned to traverse that retrograde terrain and may be having a difficult experience during that period. It's not so much the natal retrograde person has an easy time of it as they have more practice working with it. You also have to take into account everything in someone's chart. Some people's natal charts will show harmonious resonance with that natal Mercury retrograde while others will be in varying states of rebellion or disharmony. Also have to take into account aspects the transiting Mercury retrograde makes to the natal chart. If it's trining a lot of planets, for example, it could make for a smoother passage. That wouldn't be so with every Mercury retrograde. (Steve)

Venus retrograde

When the planet Venus is retrograde in the sky, you may be able to feel the nature of this archetype intimately, especially the inner side of Venus as it works to help you reconnect with yourself and through extension Spirit. It is a time where your Soul is getting in touch with what holds the most meaning and value. A time to reflect about whether you are getting your essential needs (inner side of Venus) met and a time when your Soul is in the process of making changes to support those values. (Kristin)

If I have Venus retrograde I must define FOR MYSELF the meaning and values that I have for any relationship. In fact, those who have Venus retrograde typically cannot relate to the traditional/mainstream types of relationships and tend to withdraw within themselves (Taurus co-rulership of Venus) in order to accomplish the individuation process that must occur from an evolutionary standpoint. They are defined through the Taurus side of Venus, not the Libra side (this is from Pluto Vol. 2). The point within this is that certain key situations must be re-lived, or re-experienced before they can be resolved. Most commonly the individuation process indicated by the retrograde planet has not been fully accomplished, and that is why the Soul will set up a life circumstance of re-living certain experiences. Those with Venus retrograde will attract key people with whom there is "unfinished business," for example, until the person resolves the necessary dynamics reflected by the house and sign of Venus retrograde. (Deva)

Venus retrograde, example
[Example: Venus retrograde into Pisces, Direct into Aries] Venus is the lower octave of Neptune and Neptune is the ruler of Pisces, so as Venus slows down and slowly stations at the last degree of Pisces, many Souls are searching beyond what holds earthly meaning and to what holds ULTIMATE meaning, which can only really be found within: God/Goddess (Pisces/Neptune). This can also be a time when relationships (outer side of Venus) that are not matching what we need are ending, a time of culmination (Venus in Pisces), and also a time for healing the past, old wounds in relationships that have injured our inner relationship with ourselves, things being cleared. So when Venus moves direct and back into Aries, we can be stronger in our self and more clear about our desires and needs (Venus in Aries) and as a result how to move forward with others. As our inner relationship with our self changes, our vibration also shifts and this will then alter the nature of whom and what we attract. (Kristin)

Saturn retrograde
When Saturn is retrograde the Soul will naturally rebel from anyone or anything telling it how to be, or what to do, or what to think, of what 'reality' is actually about as defined and assumed to be real by the consensus of the society that it is born into. It will rebel even from the parental authority if that authority is imposed for no other reason than to impose it. Saturn retrograde needs to determine its own reality, its own authority, and integrate itself into society in its own way that honors what it feels to be its inherent individuality. With Saturn retrograde and correlating to the structural nature of consciousness this then means that every other archetype, planet, within that consciousness is also being defined via this overall retrograde archetype even if other planets themselves are not retrograde. With Saturn retrograde it's like pointing an arrow towards Uranus. (Rad)

Neptune retrograde
When Neptune is retrograde it points to Pluto itself: our Soul. When Neptune is retrograde there is an accelerated evolutionary desire, need, to throw off all things that are of a delusive nature: that which is not actually 'real' yet what we have considered real before the delusion or illusion was finally understood. Thus, it emphasizes the process of disillusionment leading to that which is actually real from an ultimate point of view. Relative to uniting our consciousness, Soul, with that which has created us in the first place, the Neptune retrograde will necessarily do so in its own way. When Neptune is retrograde it does point to Pluto in that this symbolizes a Soul who intends to pierce the bubble of its own illusions, delusions, and all that has been given false meaning, an ultimate meaning in many ways, that has confused the Soul as to what the Ultimate Reality is really about: God/ess. (Rad)

Pluto retrograde, and evolutionary state
Pluto retrograde can occur at any evolutionary stage/condition, however it is only an intention to liberate and de-condition. In other words, we all have a choice to cooperate with or resist the evolutionary intentions for our lives. Those in the Consensus state will typically suppress/repress and, thus, resist the evolutionary intentions symbolized by Pluto retrograde through the act of emotionally withdrawing into him or herself but outwardly "going through the motions" so to speak because of the underlying need for conformity and social acceptance. For those in the consensus it does create a higher degree of evolutionary pressure to move towards the Individuated state than those who have Pluto direct. (Deva)

Pluto retrograde 10th house, example
"Resisting being pigeonholed" illustrates the 10th house Pluto retrograde. The need to do it YOUR way (and necessarily so as Jeffrey used to say), and thus not fitting the 'mold,' so to speak, as defined BY society (10th house), and so being "blocked from playing a meaningful role in my society and culture," etc. The intent, of course, is in the PPP (Pluto polarity point) in the 4th house: to develop INNER security; to be independent FROM society; to draw strength and courage from within; to trust oneSELF, etc. There are also times, especially within the context of the society that we HAVE to follow the stupid 'rules' in ORDER to get to the position where one can DO what one wants within that society, but then doing it in ONE'S OWN WAY. It is important for the EA astrologer to know the specific evolutionary condition of each Soul. Anytime a Soul evolves beyond the consensus the orientation to the 10th house Pluto is totally different than a consensus defined Soul. (Rad)

Transiting Pluto, retrograde and direct
Pluto retrograde symbolizes that the Soul is "throwing off" or liberating from the mainstream or consensus conditioning patterns in general (not buying into the mainstream way of doing things). Thus, Pluto retrograde serves to instigate personal, and collective, evolution. Pluto direct symbolizes that the Soul is not necessarily at an evolutionary juncture where the intense need to liberate in the ways described above is felt as in Pluto retrograde. However, we must keep in mind the four natural evolutionary conditions of the Soul as well. In transit, in a general sense, when Pluto goes retrograde it is a time to review the current life lessons we have been seeking to learn. When Pluto is direct we will be facing those lessons head on or "directly" in order to effect personal growth. (Deva)

Asteroid – retrograde
(Q) While it is an overall evolutionary impulse to reclaim/integrate the undistorted archetypes, if a person had many retrogrades natally or by progression of the asteroid goddesses, would it be even more incumbent for that person to reclaim the undistorted archetype in this lifetime? (Brenda)

(A) It depends on the evolutionary state of the Soul itself. From the Individuated state onwards the answer would be yes, yet the recovery would be an ongoing evolutionary process that could be finally realized within the 1st state Spiritual. (Rad)

(Q) For a person dealing with this, would they perhaps be confronted with many crises and induce a more inward internalization until this is achieved?

(A) This depends, again, on the evolutionary state of the person and other evolutionary factors. This would be one of the ways until internal realization was achieved.

Retrograde planet square the Nodes
The way we (EA astrologers) were taught is, regardless of the variations, the method of determining the Resolution Node is identical in all cases. The Nodes are retrograde 90% of the time, and that is the reason why. Their mean motion is always retrograde. And the mean motion of all planets is direct. Many people have had difficulty calculating which Node was the last to conjunct a planet, because of the nodal retrograde motion. Because of this a simpler method was developed for determining this. Looking at the chart, visualize yourself standing on the skipped step planet, on the outer periphery of the chart. The Node to the left of the planet is always the Resolution Node. This makes it all quite simple. (Steve)

It makes no difference according to EA [if a planet that squares the Nodes is retrograde]. The retrograde symbol can imply the need to re-live. Further, the skipped steps themselves imply the need to repeat, in order to resolve. (Gonzalo)

Retrograde planet conjunct North Node
With a planet on the North Node the Soul has an inner sense of moving towards something that has already been underway, whereas the South Node creates much more of a sense of being 'stuck' in something from the past that the Soul wants to move away from, but can't. With a planet retrograde on the North Node the Soul will continue to recreate circumstances, inner and outer, in which the operative principle will be one of individuation which, of itself, accelerates the evolution of the Soul. Thus recreating dynamics and circumstances that need to be repeated in order to move towards the Soul's evolutionary future in an increasingly individuated way that the Soul IS MOVING TOWARDS: what appears from the front window when driving versus what appears in the rear view mirror. (Rad)

Oblique retrograde (retrograde planet aspecting non-retrograde planet)
JWG taught the retrograde planet aspecting a non-retrograde planet correlates to an 'oblique' retrograde. So it's not like the non-retrograde planet is actually, directly, retrograde. It's an 'indirect' retrograde in that the retrograde planet itself that is impacting on the non-retrograde planet in this way causes that non-retrograde planet to obliquely act retrograde but only with respect to the actual planet that is retrograde and aspecting that non-retrograde planet. (Rad)

Retrograde archetype, and progressions
Retrograde is always the R words – redo, renew, review. A person could be born before Mars turns retrograde and it would be direct in natal and go retrograde by progression during their life. Or they could be born with Mars retrograde and Mars goes direct by progression during their life. Or they could be born with Mars retrograde by progression for the entire life. These are going to be distinct conditions for that Soul. Some of it undoubtedly relates to where that Soul was prior to the present life. (Steve)

Stationary planet or node
A stationing anything, planet or node, is a magnifying force. (Rad)

SKIPPED STEPS

Planet square Nodes – skipped steps

Planets squaring the Nodes are called skipped steps, which means the person has been flipping back and forth between the South and North Nodes without fully developing either. The evolutionary intent of course is to recover the skipped step(s). The Node that Pluto conjuncted last is called the Resolution Node. That is the one that needs to be developed/resolved, to break the flipping pattern. Determining which Node last conjuncted the skipped step planet is a bit confusing because of the retrograde motion of the Nodes. An EA astrologer came up with this method to quickly determine the Resolution Node. Picture yourself standing on the outer rim of the chart, facing the planet that squares the Nodes. Point to the Node on the left – that is the Resolution Node. Sometimes the Resolution Node is the South Node, which on the surface doesn't make much sense – why would I need to develop the past habitual patterns? The meaning is, they need to be developed IN A NEW WAY. Developing the Resolution Node leads to untying the knots that are the root basis of the skipping pattern in the first place. As the new patterns develop, the Soul can break free from the habitual unconscious skipping pattern. (Steve)

Any planet squaring the Nodes is a skipped step. The gist of it is, the person has been flip-flopping back and forth between the South Node and the North Node in the areas of life symbolized by the planet squaring the Nodes, its house and sign, and aspects it makes to other planets. It's not so much that the planet has had significant impact on past life nodal development as there are life lessons that have not been completed that must be worked on in the present life for evolution to proceed. The squaring of the Nodes indicates that the evolutionary intentions have been worked on in the past – the North Node's been partially developed. But there is more work that needs to be done. This is where the principle of the Resolution Node comes in, the Node (North or South) that needs to be developed to release the skipped step. (Steve)

The definition of a skipped step is the Soul has been skipping back and forth from the South Node to the North Node to the South Node to the North Node, completing neither of them. This has become a habitual behavior pattern. In order to break the habit pattern, one of the Nodes has to be developed to a completeness. How do you know which one? That is what the Resolution Node is. I visualize it as there are a series of knots that are jamming things up. The Resolution Node is the key knot that when untied allows all the other knots to be more easily released. Until it is released it's not possible to have consistent movement towards the North Node, which is the evolutionary intention. Another frequent astrological misconception to clear up is we are not trying to leave the South Node behind and move exclusively to the North Node. There is no way to completely leave the South Node behind – it is too much a part of who I am, who I have been for a really long time. It is the South Node of the MOON, and the Moon represents my sense of self-image. What we are trying to do is not leave the South Node behind, but evolve how I perceive and live out the South Node. When the North Node is the Resolution Node, I take what is learned at the North Node back to the South Node, learning to do the South Node IN NEW WAYS. When the South Node is the Resolution Node, I need to learn a new way to do the South Node AT THE South Node. Remember that skipped steps means effort has already been made at the North Node, so I have learned more. Perhaps the issue is I've not yet integrated what I've learned into the South Node – still doing it the same way. So I can integrate my new understandings into the South Node thus advancing my perceptions of it. The South Node contains our habitual emotional patterns. Changing it is just like changing any existing habit, to a new and improved one. (Steve)

Planet square Nodes, 10 degree orb

A maximum orb of 10 degrees for all planets squaring the Nodes. (Rad)

The tighter the orb, the greater the intensity of that planetary relationship. (Ari)

In those outer degrees, the correlation means that the Soul is giving itself the INITIAL opportunity to address and resolve what the skipped steps have been. As the degrees become closer to exact, this correlates to the fact that previous to those closer degrees the Soul has resisted the opportunity to resolve those skipped step issues. Thus, the closer degrees create a condition relative to the previous resistance wherein the nature of the skipped steps become ever more intense and focused, apparent, in the individual's life with the resulting intensity therein. So, the outer degrees correlate to the opportunity to resolve those skipped steps without the increasing compression that the resistance breeds to the necessity of resolving those skipped steps. It is all relative because of the Natural Law of free will/free choice. (JWG)

Planet (applying) just outside of orb of a square to the Nodes
The potential development of a skipped step in the future. (Rad)

Planet (separating) just outside of orb of a square to the Nodes
It means that the Soul has just finished recovering the skipped steps. (Rad)

Flip flopping
The flip flopping, the back and forth, would occur within the same lifetime(s). (Rad)
There is an equal flip flopping back and forth between the Nodes that takes place when the skipped steps are in place. This will continue to occur until such skipped steps are resolved in the ways that we have discussed many times now. (Rad)
The Resolution Node has been equally skipped, back and forth, as has the other Node. It's not a matter of being least developed. (Rad)

Rulers of the Nodes
"The ruler facilitating the process" applies to all Nodes in all charts, not just the condition of skipped steps. Another description of facilitating the process is "actualizing itself through." In other words, these are like layers. Pluto is the deepest layer. The Nodes the next deepest layer. The rulers of the Nodes a layer above that. (Steve)

Determining the Resolution Node
Determining which Node last conjuncted the skipped step planet is a bit confusing because of the retrograde motion of the Nodes. An EA astrologer came up with this method to quickly determine the Resolution Node. Picture yourself standing on the outer rim of the chart, facing the planet that squares the Nodes. Point to the Node on the left – that is the Resolution Node. (Steve)

Causes of skipped steps
The reasons for the skipped steps are within the nature of the symbols themselves that correlate to the skipped step signature. So, in essence, the solution is within the 'problem' itself. Not all Souls create skipped steps for themselves. (Rad)
A Soul can progress to a next stage of development without actually doing the work of the prior stage because there are many dynamics within any Soul. A Soul can evolve various dynamics while at the same time 'leaving behind' other dynamics that correlate to skipped steps. So when the birth chart in any given life symbolizes those skipped steps, and the intention to recover them, the evolution of the Soul, and all of its dynamics, are blocked until those skipped steps are indeed recovered. (Rad)
The skipped steps are not only symbolized by the planet that is squaring the Nodes, but also the South and North Nodes themselves, and the location of their planetary rulers, and all the aspects therein. The causative factor in the totality of the skipped steps is the actual planet squaring the Nodes by its house and sign locality, and the aspects to it. (Rad)
The causes of skipped steps are usually caused by traumas. But they can also be caused by guilt about something and the consequent 'need' to avoid or deny that guilt, and the reasons for it. This itself implies 'judgments' that the Soul has about itself that can be 'out-pictured' in the reality it creates: the circumstances of the life and the people in it. This can have the effect of reinforcing the guilt caused by such judgments. It then becomes important to understand the two causes of guilt: either man-made due to man-made rules, rights and wrongs, moralities, and the like, or natural guilt that is rooted in violations of Natural Laws. Avoidance and denial are the operative dynamics in skipped steps. So the EA astrologer has thus to play the role of 'detective' in order to understand what is causing that denial/avoidance. Those reasons will be contained within the symbols of the skipped step signature in all charts. Skipped steps can also occur as a function of 'spiritual' teachings that the Soul is attempting to embrace that has specific doctrines about what 'spiritual life' is all about, and meant to be. All too often such man-made doctrines attempt to inhibit or suppress natural human dynamics. This form of adherence to such doctrines can then cause 'skipped steps' relative to the natural human dynamics that are being repressed because of the nature of the spiritual doctrine being adhered to. (Rad)

Karma
Karma is simply the Natural Law of each cause having an effect, every desire correlating to an action taken that creates an equal or proportionate reaction: cause and effect. Throw a pebble in the pond and it creates ripples. Skipped steps do not happen by themselves. There is a Soul making choices that have effects to those choices. Thus, from this point of view the effects of the choices equaling skipped steps could be seen as the karmic consequence to those choices. Karma just is. How we 'judge' karma as 'good' or 'bad' karma is of course a subjective issue. (Rad)

Three reactions to evolutionary growth
There are three reactions/responses to our evolutionary growth needs:
(1) to totally resist (which is not common)
(2) to cooperate in some ways yet not in others (this is by far the most common choice)
(3) totally go for it (this is also not a common choice).

Somebody being in a total state of non-growth or resistance is rare. If the skipped steps are not worked on, growth cannot occur. (Deva)

Exactly what needs to be recovered?
What is needing to be recovered is symbolized by the entire signature for the skipped steps involving the house and sign of the planet that is squaring the Nodes, the houses/signs of the Nodes themselves, and the location of the planetary rulers of those Nodes. The planet squaring the Nodes is very much part of what the skipped steps is about. The entire signature of the skipped steps correlates to the main stream of what the skipped steps are about. The reasons for the skipped steps are within the nature of the symbols themselves that correlate to the skipped step signature. So, in essence, the solution is within the 'problem' itself. (Rad)

How to recover the skipped steps?
The WAY the skipped steps are recovered is to go back and DO what was missed at some prior time. In other words, you have to go backward before you can go forward. (Adina)

Skipped steps means that the Soul has been 'developing' both Nodes, and their planetary rulers, prior to the current life yet has been flip flopping back and forth between those Nodes and their rulers. Thus, skipped steps because neither has been fully actualized or developed. For the Soul's evolution to proceed these skipped steps need to be recovered. And as they are recovered it requires a way of consistently integrating those skipped steps. The way of consistently integrating those skipped steps is determined by the Node that the squaring planet is applying to, and its planetary ruler. The issue here is not developing 'new ways.' The issue is recovering the skipped steps. The only thing that would be 'new' is the fact of recovering those skipped steps that then allows the Soul to continue its ongoing evolutionary intentions. (Rad)

How to ascertain if the skipped steps have been resolved?
In terms of knowing if the skipped steps have been resolved you cannot tell by looking at the birth chart. The best thing to do is to ask the person questions regarding the skipped steps in the chart and determine how much work has been done to resolve them (and also determine the person's own understanding of what these skipped steps are about in general). (Rad)

What is the "done" point in skipped steps?
(Q) If the Resolution Node is the South Node, then is the path for the entire lifetime one of following the South Node and its ruler, or is there some point at which the person is "done" with that, and they can fully turn to the North Node? If there is a "done" point, how can this be recognized? How would you know the skipped step is resolved?

(A) No, the entire life is consistently integrated around that South Node, and the location of its planetary ruler. It's not a matter of 'turning' to the North Node for the North Node itself is being actualized consistently through the South Node itself: the baseline, like a foundation for a house. If the Soul does this for the entire life then the Soul is 'done' relative to resolving the skipped steps and is thus ready to proceed with its evolution. (Rad)

(Q) Is the person encouraged to focus on embodying and carrying out the functions and archetypes described by the Resolution Node and its ruler, but with some kind of tweak or modification relative to the skipped step?

(A) No. (Rad)

(Q) If the Resolution Node is the North Node, then what would be the difference between the path suggested to a person when the North Node is the Resolution Node for skipped steps vs the path suggested to a person who has the same nodal signature but without skipped steps? Would there be a difference?

(A) Yes, because for the Soul who does not have a planet(s) squaring the Lunar Nodes there is no previous experience to the North Node, and its ruler, at all. With a Soul that has the same Lunar Nodes with a planet(s) squaring the Lunar Axis it has in fact had previous experience relative to that North Node, and the location of its planetary ruler. It's the difference between that which is 'brand new' and that which is not. (Rad)

The resolution works by a Soul making a choice to recover the skipped steps. And that is done by consistently developing the Lunar Node that the squaring planet is applying to. This then becomes the consistent baseline upon which the entire chart, thus their life, is integrated. (Rad)

The person simply is encouraged to focus on embodying and carrying out the functions and archetypes described by the Resolution Node and its ruler. (Jason)

Making choices not to deal with skipped steps
When the Soul makes choices to not deal with the accumulated issues/dynamics from prior lives that is intended to do so, then this will lead to skipped steps in the current life that will then be symbolized again in the next life, and the next, etc. until the Soul does make those choices to do so. (Rad)

There are many possibilities that can correlate to developing skipped steps in any given life. The skipped steps would not be 'some future life:' they would be the very next life. And if they still didn't 'get it' it would then be the next life after that, etc., until they do 'get it.' The key in understanding skipped steps is the avoidance or denial of dealing with dynamics that are necessary to deal with in order for the Soul's evolution to proceed. Such denial and/or avoidance will precede planets aspecting the Nodes. When that avoidance/denial increases over some lifetimes it will then begin to manifest as the planets that correlate with the dynamics of the specific nature of that which is being avoided/denied aspecting the Lunar Nodes as non-stressful aspects. This is then like a 'warning bell' to the Soul that it needs to pay attention to those dynamics, to do something about them, so that the Soul's evolution can keep proceeding. If that denial/avoidance continues to be the choice that the Soul makes then this will then lead to a planet or planets squaring the Nodes where those planets correlate to the dynamics that are being avoided or in a state of denial. (Rad)

As long as the skipped step remains unresolved, there will be a deep tension in the consciousness of the Soul, back and forth, "sitting on the fence," "yes and no" to both Nodes, and the Soul will demonstrate a kind of flip-flopping behavior between the North Node and its ruler and the South Node and its ruler, back and forth, thus stagnating and unable to achieve the Soul's deepest evolutionary intentions as described by Pluto and its polarity point. This can last for lifetimes. (Jason)

Another way to understand it is that the Soul's evolution CANNOT PROCEED until the skipped steps are resolved. (Rad)

Appearance of earlier evolutionary stage
The WAY the skipped steps are recovered is to go back and DO what was missed at some prior time. In other words, you have to go backward before you can go forward. And when you do that, you can APPEAR to be in an earlier evolutionary stage than you actually are! And this could also explain flip-flopping for different reasons. The Soul going thru the recovery of skipped steps can, indeed, feel confused until they recover those skipped steps and "settle in" to their 'true' essence, so to speak. (Adina)

Given that the skipped step planet has not been adequately integrated by the Soul in previous lifetimes, if it remains unresolved or unintegrated in the current lifetime, the Soul will be unable to live consistently at the evolutionary stage it has actually attained overall, because when the skipped step is unresolved the Soul will still be acting out of the evolutionary stage at which the skipped step was skipped. In a sense the skipped step is the lowest common denominator in the chart and will be the default level of consciousness until it is resolved or in resolution. (Jason)

The skipped steps will always have occurred relative to the existing stage of evolutionary development UNLESS a Soul is on the cusp of just having evolved into a new stage of evolutionary development. In this case the Soul can have the 'appearance,' relative to the nature of those skipped steps, of the former state of evolutionary development. (Rad)

General themes
General themes will not manifest with a planet square the Nodes because the manifestation of any symbol in the birth chart will always depend on the overall signature of the birth chart, and the main evolutionary axis, relative to the evolutionary condition of the Soul. (Gonzalo)

Creating skipped steps in the current life
Anytime a Soul is embracing the next phase of their evolutionary journey by moving toward their Pluto polarity point and North Node, the risk will always be there for a skipped step to be created, depending on how the world responded to those steps and then how the Soul is affected by the response. (Kristin)

Skipped steps are the result of decisions made (or not made, which is just another form of making a decision, to decide to not do what was intended to be done, which choice is typically justified by large numbers of rational and logical sounding reasons that in actuality are just masking over what is actually going on). I've never heard this question before, and I feel it indicates a Soul that is looking at itself. My thought was, well if someone sees that they may be forming a future skipped step, it's possible to take it to the next step and objectify what is necessary to prevent the necessity of a future skipped step from even occurring, by making the changes NOW that would otherwise be required later to resolve the skipped step. Resolving a skipped step requires changes in behavior, attitude, beliefs, etc. to resolve. But it doesn't have to go to that extreme. Most of us don't change a lot until we are forced to, by things such as skipped steps.

Much of the beauty of EA is it helps us objectify our reality. If you can see that what you are doing is potentially creating a future skipped step, it then becomes wise to start making changes NOW that will begin breaking those patterns up, changing them, which potentially can even eliminate the necessity of that future skipped step. After all, they are only a reflection of a part of our own inner consciousness. If I change that consciousness then I break up the inner knots that create a skipped step. Thus I am not going to have a future skipped step because that is not what my inner consciousness will look like, so no skipped step will be reflecting that. The primary purpose of a skipped step is to force an issue. If I resolve the issue before a skipped step appears, there is no need for it.

[Example: Saturn opposite Pluto/Uranus, Saturn conjunct Pluto polarity point] This would be an important evolutionary lesson for the Soul – to deeply realize that it and it alone is responsible for the reality it has been experiencing, vs projecting (the opposition) responsibility for the life experiences onto the external characters and events it finds in the life. To emotionally realize they are the effect, not the cause. To thus progressively purge victimization from the Soul by taking responsibility for the reality it creates. To ask questions like, "Why have I been creating it the way I have?" and "What do I have to do, face, examine, to get to the root of this, to see how I can start breaking old patterns and forming new ones?" In that way the necessity of a future life skipped step can be reduced or possibly even eliminated.

It's NEVER 'too late,' because sooner or later we have to do it – some life, some place, some time. So as we realize that more and more, the thought arises, "Since we have to do it sooner or later, why not sooner?" Really, we have every opportunity right up to our last breath in (hopefully) old age, to change. No one is EVER too old to change, people only use that as an excuse to stay the same. No matter what we have done or not done in the past, somewhere, some place, some time we have to change. And we can CHOOSE to make that place and time 'NOW.' Or not. (Steve)

Planets, by transit, progression, or solar returns that square the Nodes can represent evolutionary forks in the road. How people react to the events signified by the square, can either lead to future growth (evolution) or to stagnation (skipped steps). (Shawn)
This [above] is exactly what JWG taught. (Rad)

[Example: transiting Lunar Nodes t-square natal planet] When this occurs through transit it symbolizes key evolutionary transitions between the existing past, and the future to come. If the Soul makes the choices necessary that allow these key transitions to take place all will be well for that Soul. On the other hand if the Soul does not make the necessary choices that reflect the intent of the evolutionary transition then this will lead to 'skipped steps' relative to those dynamics in a future life to come. (Rad)

Skipped steps, and the Pluto polarity point

The Pluto polarity point is active in any chart whether there are skipped steps or not: that's because Pluto, the Soul, is the causative factor for the whole chart/one's life. As a result it sets in motion the rest of the chart/life. When there are skipped steps the Soul ignites that Pluto polarity point yet because of the skipped steps is unable to fully actualize, move forwards in any kind of consistent way, until the skipped steps are resolved. This is of course intentional by the Soul in order to induce the awareness that something is amiss: skipped steps. When the Resolution Node is the South Node then the North Node comes through that Node. Remember when dealing with skipped steps that each Node has already been acted upon by the Soul, yet in inconsistent ways: only going so far then reverting back to the other Node for a while, then back to the other Node, like a ping pong ball. So when the South Node is the Resolution Node the North Node comes through the South Node that is now serving as the bottom line, the baseline, upon which the entire chart, life, is being integrated. (Rad)

The skipped steps must be actively resolved in order for the actualization of Pluto's polarity point and the North Node to manifest. The polarity point is in operation whether the person resolves the skipped steps or not. The issue is how it's in operation which means that this point will be used by the Soul as a vehicle to keep flip flopping back and forth between the Nodes, the skipped steps, until those skipped steps are recovered. Then the polarity point operates in a single minded focus versus the flip flopping. (Rad)

Two planets square Nodes

Two planets in conjunction squaring the Nodes are both skipped steps in their own right. (Upasika)

Two planets square the Nodes forming a grand cross

All skipped step signatures are worked upon equally. (Rad)

Multiple planets square Nodes

It is not COMMON to find such a pattern. In this case the core clue as to why that Soul has this pattern of skipped steps is deep, unresolved traumas that have been quite severe. If you can unravel what the nature of those traumas have been you will then be able to understand the nature of the skipped steps, and why. (Rad)

Multiple planets square Nodes, forming a grand cross

They will all square the Nodes so they are all skipped steps too. The skipped steps are all part of a compound skipped step situation. With many planets involved in a skipped step situation, each one will be contributing in its own way to the whole situation. It has become "compounded," and implies usually that the person has been avoiding something very essential over a long period of time (many lives) and that now the whole thing has got really out of hand. To determine the significance of each Node in the skipped step situation you need to see what Node each skipped step planet (skipped step planet and the planets conjunct it and opposing it) are "applying" to. The skipped step planet and conjuncting planet will be applying to one of the Nodes, and the planets opposing the skipped step planet will be applying to the other Node. It's the Node that each planet is applying to that must be embraced to "support" the resolution of the skipped steps. In this scenario, both Nodes will need to be fully embraced for the resolution to fully occur, but for different reasons. The reasons for embracing a Node will be related to the particular planets applying to that Node only. This is important because that Node will actually be detrimental to planets applying to the opposite Node. (Upasika)

The desire nature within Souls can be quite complex. That is indicated when multiple planets square the Nodes and the Resolution Node for some is the North Node and others the South Node. It is often tricky for the EA astrologer to grasp the nature of the conflicts and desires that led to these patterns. It takes practice. I can say from experience, once the nature of the paradox is intuitively grasped by the astrologer and related to the client you will start hearing in the client's own words the nature of their life-long back and forth flipping behaviors that will completely correlate to the symbols in the chart. As the astrologer starts grasping how this plays out in their clients' lives it gradually becomes easier to intuit the nature of what those symbols mean when seen in a new chart. Each person will play out the same themes in their own unique ways. But the core underlying complexes are always quite similar. (Steve)

It is a little tricky when the Resolution Node is the North Node for some planets and the South Node for other planets. It basically means they need to learn to do the South Node in new ways. Some of that will be through experiencing the South Node in new ways which lets them act out the North Node in new ways, and other parts from jumping into the North Node, learning new experiences there and bringing those back to the South Node. That assists in learning to do the South Node in new ways. A key concept in those cases in integration. Often the person will be almost split inside into at least two very different personality parts. They've had a hard time integrating the different sides of self. That is a key part of the work in such cases. To acknowledge the validity of ALL of their sides. To stop trying to deny or repress various parts of their nature. To realize they are all valid and are all expressions of their one Soul. Through the acceptance the integration process can proceed which leads to the ongoing resolution of the paradoxes in the desire nature. (Steve)

South Node resolution – why develop past habitual patterns?

(Q) If the Resolution Node is the South Node, which on the surface doesn't make much sense – why would I need to develop the past habitual patterns?

(A) The meaning is, they need to be developed IN A NEW WAY. Developing the Resolution Node leads to untying the knots that are the root basis of the skipping pattern in the first place. As the new patterns develop, the Soul can break free from the habitual unconscious skipping pattern. (Steve)

South Node resolution, and planets conjunct the South Node

When we have the skipped step signature in a birth chart, and the Node that last formed a conjunction to the planet(s) squaring the Nodes is the South Node, then the South Node is meant to be the integration point for the entire signature symbolized in the skipped steps. Also, when planets are conjunct the South Node those planets and the Node itself, and the house they take place in, will be archetypes within the Soul's consciousness, its prior lives, that are being brought forwards into the current life for ongoing evolutionary development and reasons. However, they are not meant to remain static within the Soul's ongoing evolution. These symbols will evolve by way of the North Node itself, and the location of its planetary ruler, relative to the bottom line evolutionary intent of the Soul: the opposite house and sign of the natal Pluto. (Rad)

North Node resolution, and planet conjunct South Node

First any planet conjunct the South Node correlates to one of three possible evolutionary/karmic conditions:

1. a situation of a total reliving of the past conditions in prior lives that is symbolized by the house and sign of this conjunction and the location of its planetary ruler by its own house and sign in which both points can have aspects to them from other planets/signs/and the houses that they are in,
2. a situation of karmic/evolutionary fruition wherein whatever the nature of that is also symbolized by all those point, and
3. a condition wherein both a relive of the past conditions are combined with some degree of fruition at the same time.

When the North Node is then the resolution node relative to the skipped steps signature, the South Node with a conjuncting planet is pulled forwards, into, that resolution node in such a way that all of those possible conditions symbolized by the South Node with a conjuncting planet evolve forwards because of that pull. In essence the pull of the resolution node, evolutionary pressure, creates new choices relative to the conditions being relived so that by making those new choices the Soul is thus evolving those relive conditions by the very nature of the new choices made. (Rad)

Pluto square Nodes

It symbolizes that the Soul has skipped steps prior to the current life that must be recovered in the current life in order for personal growth to continue. The Node that last formed a conjunction to Pluto is the "Resolution Node," or the Node that will be used to integrate and resolve the skipped steps (if the South Node last formed a conjunction to Pluto then the South Node and its planetary ruler will be used to integrate the current evolutionary lessons symbolized by Pluto's polarity point and the North Node). In the case of Pluto square the nodal axis the Soul has not fully developed the lessons reflected by either of the Nodes and so has skipped steps to resolve in both areas (North Node and South Node). The Soul has attempted to evade or escape these lessons by fluctuating back and forth between the behaviors of the South Node and the North Node (so neither area has been fully resolved or developed). In the current life then, the Soul must fully recover or resolve those skipped steps (it is a critical evolutionary juncture for any Soul that has this natal signature). (Deva)

In terms of integrating Pluto's polarity point when Pluto is square the Nodes, remember that it is about integrating the "Resolution Node" in a new way – breaking free from past habits through embracing Pluto's polarity point. Pluto's polarity point will be integrated through the Resolution Node, with its planetary ruler facilitating that process. In other words, the Resolution Node and its planetary ruler will become the bottom line upon which Pluto's polarity point will be integrated, and the skipped steps symbolized by Pluto square the nodal axis will be resolved. The point is that Pluto's polarity point must be embraced before these changes can happen, and the skipped steps resolved. In the context of Pluto's polarity point in the 4th, it emphasizes that one learn how to be in the world in a new way. (Deva)

[Example: Pluto 10th, PPP 4th] Pluto (or any planet) square the Nodes are called skipped steps, which means the person has been flipping back and forth between the South and North Nodes without fully developing either. When Pluto squares the Nodes, it means the Soul itself is directly doing this flipping. In essence it has gotten stuck in an m.o. that it unconsciously gravitates to at stressful points in the life, and it activates the flipping behavior to try to cope with the situation – it's a learned strategy. The problem is, the underlying issues can only be resolved when the work at one of the Nodes is carried through to completion, rather than flipping to the other one at key stress points. The Node that Pluto conjuncted last is called the Resolution Node. That is the one that needs to be developed/resolved, to break the flipping pattern. The Pluto polarity point (PPP) is just as important with Pluto squaring the Nodes as in any other configuration. (The one exception to that rule is when Pluto conjuncts the North Node natally, there is no PPP. Other than that it applies in all cases.) Determining which Node last conjuncted Pluto is a bit confusing because of the retrograde motion of the Nodes. An EA astrologer came up with this method to quickly determine the Resolution Node. Picture yourself standing on the outer rim of the chart, facing the planet that squares the Nodes (Pluto in this case). Point to the Node on the left – that is the Resolution Node.

Sometimes the Resolution Node is the South Node, which on the surface doesn't make much sense – why would I need to develop the past habitual patterns? The meaning is, they need to be developed IN A NEW WAY. Developing the Resolution Node leads to untying the knots that are the root basis of the skipping pattern in the first place. As the new patterns develop, the Soul can break free from the habitual unconscious skipping pattern. When you have a skipped steps pattern with Pluto, when you have been consciously working on moving forward, ie developing the NORTH NODE, the tendency at stress points is going to be to want to dive back to the safety and known nature of the South Node. You have to become conscious of that tendency, to see how it plays out in your outer reality, to look at your life and see how you have actualized that tendency. There is where you look to the rulers. Typically what triggers skipping is having "bitten off more than you can chew," making a really big leap, "piece of cake, I can handle this," and finding overwhelm. Getting afraid or overloaded with the movement towards the NORTH NODE. Then finding all sorts of reasons why it's okay to go back to the known, the past, the familiar. The point is, just knowing that you do this does not in itself resolve it. But it's the beginning of resolving it – you become aware of, conscious of, what has always been going on that you did not realize previously was a pattern, a mode of behavior.

The first step in changing a behavior is becoming aware you are in it – because then when you find yourself going into that pattern again, you can say, "wait, here I am in this pattern again," and make a different choice. It literally is changing an old habit. Like changing any habit, it takes time, effort, determination. These habits go straight to the Soul, so they are even more entrenched. But the point is YOU CAN CHANGE THEM, you are not trapped, no matter how deep they appear to be. *Desire* is the root determinant – you make up your mind you are going to change. Even when you catch yourself making the same choice in a situation where you could have made a new choice, you do not get down on yourself, you simply reaffirm that you are in the process of changing a deep pattern, and you keep at it. Step by step, inch by inch. Through determination you move forward. Because it's aligned to the evolutionary intentions, there are a lot of unseen forces at work to assist your moving in these directions. Another issue is, at times you simply are going to feel overwhelmed with change, and unable to move forward at that moment. This too is part of the process. Especially with [example] 10th house Pluto, there needs to be an honoring of your emotional states, and their limitations. You cannot force your way through the process, cannot have complete control over it. It takes on a life of its own, over time, becomes the basis of new habits, a new way of living and of looking at life. There are moments, times, when you NEED to go back to the safety of the known, if only for a short while, just to keep yourself sane. This is okay and necessary – just do it consciously, "I need to do this right now," and remain aware when it is time to get back to moving forward again.

In a sense this process is like growing a new baby in your womb (4th house PPP) that gradually takes on a life of its own. In this case that new baby will gradually replace your old existing sense of who you are altogether. It will integrate and incorporate these new perspectives, ways, into the totality of your own self-image (4th house). Words like organic, holistic, inclusive – it is a natural process that gradually engulfs you. Through this process the intentions of the PPP, the North Node, the North Node ruler simply unfold, because at the baseline you have inwardly committed yourself to the evolutionary intentions. You start the process by discerning what the chart symbols mean, what areas of life they reference, but as you increasingly move into that process as a way of life, it just unfolds by itself. This all starts by embracing the process in the first place and saying "yes" to it. The rest just happens. In all charts (except Pluto conjunct North Node) the intent is to activate the polarity point of Pluto. When Pluto (and thus its polarity point) is squaring the Nodes, the question becomes how does one resolve the skipping – which Node has to be worked on? When the North Node is the Resolution Node ("applying to"), the effort needs to go to developing the North Node.

"The ruler facilitating the process" applies to all Nodes in all charts, not just this condition. Another description of facilitating the process is "actualizing itself through." In other words, these are like layers. Pluto is the deepest layer. The Nodes the next deepest layer. The rulers of the Nodes a layer above that. Most of us are more conscious of what is on the surface than what lies beneath it. So we act in certain ways habitually. This is going to relate at the top to the ruler, which is actualizing the intentions of the underlying Node, based on the planet, sign, house the ruler is located in. Similarly, the Node is actualizing the intentions of the underlying Pluto (for the South Node), or PPP (North Node). Pluto, or PPP, is always the baseline. The Nodes describe how Pluto has been carrying out (actualizing) its desire nature, the ruler how the patterns inherent in the Nodes have been actualized. The gist of it is, one can't really separate the PPP, the North Node, the North Node ruler – they are different layers or levels of the exact same thing, even though we may not consciously experience it that way. When you are focusing on the North Node, you ARE effecting and actualizing the intents of the PPP. To me, the idea of the North Node ruler is, if you focus your attempts at developing the North Node in the chart area represented by the North Node ruler by house, sign, planet (and aspects it makes to other planets by house and sign), you are concentrating/maximizing your efforts. And yet, since this is the underlying evolutionary intent in the first place, that naturally happens anyway. (Steve)

Pluto square Nodes, and the Pluto polarity point
The polarity point of Pluto does apply when Pluto is square the Nodes. When the Resolution Node is the South Node this means that the entire life of the Soul must be consistently integrated through the South Node and its planetary ruler: by houses, signs, and aspects. The core issue is to create a 'bottom line' in which the Soul integrates not only the polarity point of Pluto, but also the North Node, and its planetary ruler. The North Node, and its planetary ruler, prior to the current life has been used by the Soul to 'jump ahead' of the total resolution of the dynamics symbolized by the South Node, and its planetary ruler as well as the totality of the dynamics and issues within the natal position of Pluto itself. Thus, the dynamics symbolized by the North Node and its planetary ruler are not 'new.' They have been inconsistently actualized prior to the current life. As a result, they will serve as a 'temptation' for the Soul to jump ahead, to skip steps, again. The natural polarity point of Pluto thus evolves the natal placement of Pluto and this core evolutionary step is thus integrated through the South Node, and its planetary ruler, and the natal position of Pluto itself. In essence the Soul will recreate prior life dynamics in the current life as symbolized by the natal Pluto, and the South Node and its planetary ruler. The polarity point of Pluto in combination with the North Node, and its planetary ruler, will thus create the opportunity for the Soul to make new choices relative to those repeating dynamics that come forwards from the Soul's past. By making those new choices relative to the bottom line of the South Node, its planetary ruler and the natal position of Pluto, the Soul not only recovers the skipped steps, but is evolving those dynamics that then allows the Soul to proceed in its evolutionary journey. (Rad)

Pluto polarity point square Nodes
The Pluto Polarity Point is just as important with Pluto squaring the Nodes as in any other configuration. The one exception to that rule is when Pluto conjuncts the North Node natally, there is no PPP. Other than that it applies in all cases. (Steve)

Pluto square Nodes – emotional paradox
Pluto square the Nodal Axis in the 7th/1st, or 1st/7th, is an underlying EMOTIONAL PARADOX that needs to be identified in order for the skipped steps, the Pluto square, to be resolved. The nature of that emotional paradox is one wherein the individual has two opposing emotional needs. One is for an almost absolute freedom, and the other is one of almost absolute relationship. Obviously these needs, desires, go in opposite directions. And because of this underlying emotional paradox the person then chooses partners in which only some of the core needs are met. It's like finding bits and pieces of the overall needs in each of these kinds of partners. This is an unconscious way of creating 'exit points' so that freedom, independence, can occur again. The way to resolve that is to identify all the core and essential needs and then making a relationship choice in that knowledge. (Rad)

Pluto square Nodes, South Node Scorpio, North Node Taurus
The underlying issue here is of course one of skipped steps. Thus, consistent with those skipped steps the Soul has been flip flopping back and forth between these two dynamics, the North and South Node, without fully developing either. So with that Resolution Node being the South Node that becomes the Node to consistently integrate the entire life around. With the North Node being in Taurus that is the evolutionary intent of the Soul that is in the ongoing process of totally metamorphosing its inner relationship to itself that finally leads to a state of deep inner security from within itself. This then changes the inner magnetism of the Soul in such a way that the dynamics of the South Node in Scorpio then also evolve. A simple example: this type of Soul will have had many prior life experiences in relationships in which they became compulsively dependent on another to the point of stopping their own individual growth because of the dependency. In order for the necessary growth to occur the Soul created experiences of intense loss of the ones in which that dependency was created upon them. The intent in this was to enforce the North Node in Taurus evolutionary next step: to learn a self-reliance. This would then create a cycle in which the Soul would find itself totally alone with the famous rug pulled out from under their feet. Yet for a series of lives that very aloneness would cause the Soul to compulsively try to recreate relationships with another in which the same dependency on that other would reoccur. So back and forth between these two dynamics the Soul would go for a series of lifetimes.

With the Resolution Node being the South Node this then means that such a Soul must learn fully how to develop its own inner relationship to itself that becomes the source of their own sustainment emotionally and psychologically. Yet, at the same time, learn how to do that in the context of relationships of every kind, including an intimate other. This is that which then changes the inner magnetism of the Soul that allows it to attract differently another to be in relationship with. That would then mean that the intimate other would ALSO HAVE TO BE ANOTHER SOUL WHO HAS ALSO LEARNED THIS LESSON OF TOTAL SELF-RELIANCE WITHIN THEM SELF. Thus, two Souls who are together in a deep and committed relationship in which each is psychologically and emotionally self-reliant. When this is accomplished the Soul has now successfully recovered its skipped steps. In this paradigm there is of course the polarity point to Pluto itself in the current life. This polarity point correlates to the core of the Soul's next evolutionary step. As such it provides for new content to enter into the consciousness of the Soul where the nature of that new content is symbolized by the opposite house and sign of the natal Pluto. As the Soul progressively expands its existing consciousness with this new content it then allows for an evolution of the natal Pluto itself: an expansion or evolution upon the existing consciousness of the natal Pluto from birth. This evolution, because of the expanded content of the consciousness within the Soul, thus allows for a new orientation to the nature of the skipped steps themselves relative to the squares of the North and South Nodes to the natal Pluto.

We must remember that those Nodes are also square the POLARITY POINT OF PLUTO ITSELF. Thus, the new orientation to the nature of the skipped steps creates the promise for the Soul to make NEW CHOICES relative to the nature of the skipped steps themselves. The key is for the Soul to focus on its own inherent resources, capacities and abilities and to fully develop them from within as the base line for its life. And to do so in the context of a committed relationship with another. I have seen many with this signature over the years in which such a Soul would spend lengths of time focused on some capacity such as being an artist which would require a relative isolation from their relationship with the committed other. Developing whatever the capacity or inherent resources are that the Soul has does require through that Resolution Node such periods of relative isolation. And that is intentional in order to resolve the skipped steps. It does lead the way to self-reliance in such a way that the prior compulsions defined by their projected needs upon another(s) is simply eliminated. Evolution then proceeds. (Rad)

Planet square Pluto
A square to Pluto, in and of itself, is not a skipped step. (Rad)

Sun square Nodes
Sun square Nodes does not indicate a skipped step since Sun applies to the present life. (Steve)
Very simply it means that there have been certain dynamics equaling circumstances in the Soul's prior lives that have not been successfully dealt with, and are now coming to a head in order to do so. If the Soul makes current life choices, the Sun square the Nodes, that do not allow for those past life dynamics to be dealt with then it will then lead to skipped steps in the next life, and beyond, until they are successfully dealt with and resolved. In essence, the Soul will be creating those skipped steps in the current life that will then be carried forwards. A final straw would occur in the current life that would result in skipped steps not only in the current life, but those to come until these dynamics equaling skipped steps is resolved. On the other hand, if the Soul chooses to make the choices to deal with those pre-existing issues in the current life that 'final straw' will allow for a resolution of those issues and, thus, no skipped steps: relative to those issues. (Rad)
Sun square Nodes does not correlate to 'skipped steps,' but to prior lives dynamics which have created an imbalance between the South and North Node archetypes, which the Soul needs to address in the current lifetime, in order not to create the situation of 'skipped steps.' (Gonzalo)
The said prior lives would be symbolized via the location of the planetary rulers of each of the Nodes, and the aspects to those two specific planets from other planets. In total this imbalance needs to be given a current life purpose, Sun, in order to make the choices leading to a balancing of those existing imbalances so that they do not become 'skipped steps' in the life(s) following the current life. (Rad)

Moon square Nodes
The Moon squaring Nodes can be a relevant dynamic within a larger signature that would correlate to dissociative behavior, but of itself it doesn't. There are many signatures that can correlate to dissociative behavior, too many to go through and list. As a very general example of what could combine with a Moon squaring Nodes to equal this kind of signature, you could find stressful aspects to Uranus, Neptune, Pluto, Saturn, implicating key signs like Gemini, Pisces, Aquarius, just to mention a few. But of course, it all depends on the individual chart signature as a whole. A Moon squaring Nodes of itself correlates more to a pattern where the ego (meaning one "I" / "me," not 2+ versions) oscillates between familiar emotional dynamics connecting with the Soul's past, and new dynamics. To whom the Soul is becoming. The ego goes back and forth, back and forth, not consistently integrating itself in either area. The oscillation is driven by a cyclic intense desire to feel secure (generating gravity toward the South Node – what's familiar), and the desire to grow beyond old dynamics, patterns, and ways that oneself has known, into new ways that are sensed but not yet consolidated in self-imagery that allows the ego to feel self-consistent. In a dissociative condition, the ego structure itself is in a condition of breaking down, dissolution, fragmentation, etc. for various reasons/causes, which implies a direct relationship to other functions in consciousness beyond the Moon. (Stacie)

It's also important to look at the planetary rulers of each of those Nodes: their house and sign location, and the aspect that each are making to other planets. The ego, Moon, has been going back and forth in recent prior lifetimes between each of these archetypes without fully developing either. Thus, the Soul and the ego it manifests will typically feel within itself this push/pull between these two archetypes: back and forth. The sense of personal identity and reality is switching back and forth, and, because of that, the effects of this to the emotional body of the individual. And one of those effects is what then constitutes security for the Soul. (Rad)

Jupiter square Nodes
In my view, Jupiter square the Nodes does not imply issues with honesty. It can correlate with issues of honesty, but not necessarily. The potential of involving issues with honesty comes from the Soul having identified its personal truth, or what is true for the Soul – Jupiter – within a conflict of self-identification (the Nodes alternating through this skipped steps planet). Thus, an aspect of reality that is being expanded because of Jupiter and which is given a larger meaning in the Soul's identity associations (Nodes), creating the irresolution of the identity process in the way it was unfolding, jumping to the other Node. Given that beliefs filter what the Soul considers as existing or real, despite they can only reflect a part of what exist, or a part of the Truth, Jupiter square the Nodes also contains the possibility of beliefs which reflect aspects of the self-identity that are not being acknowledged by the Soul, and that are being compensated – Jupiter – in the other aspects being emphasized. This implies the possibility of distortions of the self-image, based on what is "true" for the Soul, including exaggerations or distortions of the personal truth. This dynamic can also manifest externally through being attracted to belief systems (Jupiter) that will induce the crises (square) of the Soul's evolution implied in the square to the Nodes. This process also involves or leads to the possibility of the Soul not knowing what to believe, or not being able or willing to believe, or to attach to beliefs, including beliefs about itself or about life in general, because of the sense of security linked with the beliefs, that represent something which is familiar or known to the Soul's egocentric structures. There can exist other inner and outer manifestations of the archetypes, and variations or combinations of these dynamics. (Gonzalo)

Neptune square Nodes, example
[Example: Neptune in Sagittarius square North Node Virgo, South Node Pisces, Pluto Libra, PPP Aries] The South Node in Pisces correlates to the pre-existing focus of egocentric consciousness created by the Soul, that for many lifetimes has desired to embrace the totality of life, or the Source: to know the Unknown. The planetary ruler, Neptune, being in Sagittarius, indicates that the Soul, in order to know the totality of life, or the Source (Pisces), has desired to align itself with philosophical, cosmological, metaphysical or spiritual systems (Sagittarius), and to live a life, or lives, which reflect the truths (Sagittarius) contained in those philosophical, metaphysical or spiritual systems. Through these types of belief systems (Sagittarius) the Soul has desired not only to have beliefs, but to directly experience the Creator of All Things (Pisces, Neptune). Because Neptune is in Sagittarius, these symbols also imply prior lifetimes in which such expansion of consciousness that the Soul has desired have occurred in relation to nature, natural lives, and it also implies that the Soul has desired to align itself with Natural Law. Because Pisces correlates to ultimate ideals, and with the desire to merge with the totality of life in all its manifestations, and given that Neptune is square to the Nodal Axis, the Soul has created experiences of fundamental disillusionment. These experiences have occurred through false teachings (Neptune in Sagittarius squaring the Nodes), man-made beliefs implying distortions of Natural Law, and through teachers who have lacked honesty (Neptune in Sagittarius, squaring the Nodes from Pisces to Virgo). These experiences have produced massive crises involving not knowing what to believe, and how to live.

This has ignited the desire and need to discriminate (Virgo) in order to establish what is true, as contrasted to what is false. Also, because of the nature of these crises, and given the pre-existing desires to merge with the totality of life, the Soul has felt contaminated by the falsity of these teachings, and has desired to purify itself from all which the Soul perceives as false, or impure (Neptune squaring the North Node in Virgo). This has created a deep and constant self-analytical inner focus, a compulsive inner criticism (Virgo). This in turn has created other lifetimes for the Soul in which it has desired to align with man-made beliefs which sustain that human nature as essentially imperfect, and "fallen," and that it needs to suffer in order to advance spiritually (Virgo). In these lifetimes the Soul has desired to close itself to its spiritual awareness and its natural devotion, product of prior life efforts, because of the fears of spiritual contamination or dishonesty. These fears have been quite irrational (Neptune squaring the Nodes from Pisces to Virgo), because the Soul has not truly understood what the basis for these fears are, because it does not know how to interpret its feelings and desires, and what to believe (Neptune in Sagittarius): that they are rooted in experiences of fundamental disillusionment creating the feeling and fears of contamination.

Because in this configuration Pluto was in Libra, the Soul has also created desires to go on its own (Pluto polarity point in Aries), ie not to depend on external teachers. Given that the motion of the Nodes is retrograde, and the average motion of Neptune is direct, the last conjunction of Neptune with the Moon's Nodes occurred at the North Node in Virgo. Thus Neptune applies to Virgo, and Virgo is the Resolution Node for the skipped steps. This correlates to the ongoing need to discriminate, and to create a systematic approach to the inner experience and a conscious inner focus allowing an analysis, on a daily basis, of the contents emanating from the Soul, in order to linearly understand the inner experience of the Soul. It also correlates to the need of grounding and healing. Because Neptune is in Sagittarius, these symbols speak of the need to heal through direct contact with Nature, and, by means of

linearly understanding the nature of its irrational fears, progressively re-align with what is natural, as experienced from within (not external teachings, not teachers, but direct inner experience – both Pisces and Virgo are yin archetypes, ie consciousness moving back to the center).
Because the Resolution Node of the Neptune skipped steps is the North Node, this has to be accomplished by means of the polarity point of Pluto, ie Aries. This implies independent self-discovery, versus depending on external sources, this independent self-discovery being the natural way to validate from within that which is true and real in the Soul's inner experiences, and that which is not true, thus creating a progressive re-alignment with Natural Law (Sagittarius), and with the totality of life. The polarity point of Neptune being in Gemini indicates, though, the need to communicate with some others in order to linearly process the nature of the inner experience. The Resolution Node being in Virgo, also implies the need to work for those who are more needed than the Soul (karma yoga). (Gonzalo)
I think the desire to put "God first" cannot, by its inherent nature, be the cause of skipped steps. Neither can the desire to know God be the cause of skipped steps, whatever the evolutionary condition is. I think this is because the "nature" of God is radically different than that of anything existing within the manifested creation, and hence, the relation between the Soul and God is different by nature from any other relation. And further, because the purpose of the complete evolutionary journey is precisely to return to God. This is why God can be known (this knowledge is of course inherently limited) and can cause the desire to put God first, at any stage of evolution. What I think can cause skipped steps are dynamics linked with any idea about God, which in reality is different from God. (Gonzalo)
The integration of any birth chart, in total, is Pluto. The archetype of Neptune, skipped steps or not, is within the Soul: Pluto. It is not somehow outside of the Soul, thus cannot be integrated all by itself. The very context of the Neptune skipped step, or any other planet that correlates to a skipped step, indeed any other astrological symbol, are all within the context, the structure, of the Soul itself. The Soul is the determinant of all things. So in the case of Neptune applying to the South Node, relative to its square to the Nodal Axis, the resolution of those Neptune dynamics and issues is indeed that South Node, and the location of its planetary ruler. Yet that resolution is taking place within the total context of the Soul's evolutionary journey: past, present, and future. As such it is thus integrated within the total context of any given life that the Soul has, is, or will design. Pluto and its polarity point are involved in this. The Soul is the determinant of all things via the desires and the choices it makes. If the Soul does not make a choice to embrace its natural polarity point then the entire birth chart, the life of the Soul, will remain stagnant. Nothing will evolve. No resolution of skipped steps will occur. (Rad)

Planetary Nodes square Lunar Nodes
The perspective is the same as when the Nodes square a natal planet: skipped steps that are linked by the nature of the Nodes that are square. (Rad)
With only the Planetary Nodes squaring the Lunar Nodes this correlates to Soul stress around the dynamics symbolized, a stress that correlates with a necessary evolutionary leap. The natural archetypes relative to a first and last quarter square, or disseminating/crescent square, are that which is the cause of the evolutionary stress requiring a leap in the Soul's evolution. JWG wrote about these archetypes in his second Pluto book. There is a whole chapter dedicated to all the phases, from new through balsamic, and all the aspects that take place within these phases. Simple example: millions have Neptune in Libra, and that Neptune then squares the Nodes of Pluto, Saturn, Jupiter in most cases. So, obviously, all those millions of Souls are not all going to have 'skipped steps' relative to this signature. This is actually a subject that I never remember JWG discussing at all, or writing about. To me when we do see this kind of symbolism it does have generational applications as to its meaning, and the individual meaning within that as it is applied to each individual's birth chart: the houses that it would be in. Thus, the individual's interaction and relationship with the generation that it is born within, and how that relationship then serves the evolutionary intentions of the individual itself. (Rad)

Planet square Planetary Nodes (or square the midpoint of Planetary Nodes)
No, that does not indicate skipped steps. (Rad)

Outer planet square Planetary Nodes
The way that JWG taught it was that the phenomenon of skipped steps was specific to the Nodes of the Moon. Of course when one employs the use of all the Planetary Nodes, natal planets in the current birth chart can square those Nodes. Simple example: millions have Neptune in Libra, and that Neptune then squares the Nodes of Pluto, Saturn, Jupiter in most cases. So, obviously, all those millions of Souls are not all going to have 'skipped steps' relative to this signature. This is actually a subject that I never remember JWG discussing at all, or writing about. To me when we do see this kind of symbolism it does have generational applications as to its meaning, and the individual meaning within that as it is applied to each individual's birth chart: the houses that it would be in. Thus, the individual's interaction and relationship with the generation that it is born within, and how that relationship then serves the evolutionary intentions of the individual itself. (Rad)

Any planet square Planetary Nodes

The way that JWG taught it was that the phenomenon of skipped steps was specific to the Nodes of the Moon. Of course when one employs the use of all the Planetary Nodes, natal planets in the current birth chart can square those Nodes. Simple example: millions have Neptune in Libra, and that Neptune then squares the Nodes of Pluto, Saturn, Jupiter in most cases. So, obviously, all those millions of Souls are not all going to have 'skipped steps' relative to this signature. This is actually a subject that I never remember JWG discussing at all, or writing about. To me when we do see this kind of symbolism it does have generational applications as to its meaning, and the individual meaning within that as it is applied to each individual's birth chart: the houses that it would be in. Thus, the individual's interaction and relationship with the generation that it is born within, and how that relationship then serves the evolutionary intentions of the individual itself. (Rad)

Planet conjunct its own South Node, and both square the Nodal Axis

[Example: Venus in Capricorn conjunct South Node of Venus in Capricorn and both square the Nodal Axis]

(Q) Is it correct that skipped steps apply not only to Venus square the Nodal Axis, but also to the South Node of Venus square the Nodal Axis? That is, a natal planet conjunct *its own* Planetary Node? If so, is the interpretation based on TWO separate sets of skipped steps for Venus and its South Node, or a combination of both? If a combination of both, how would one interpret the skipped steps? (Linda)

(A) Since the Venus and South Node of Venus are conjunct and squaring the Nodal Axis this does in fact correlate to skipped steps wherein both symbols are implicated. This would in fact INTENSIFY the Soul's resistance to making the necessary choices that would allow it to continue to evolve. The actual houses in which the South Node of Venus, and natal Venus, occupy correlate to the dynamics within the Soul that are causing this resistance. Further, the location of the planet Saturn by its own house and sign, and aspects to it, will add to what those dynamics have been. The South Node of the Moon itself, with the location of its own planetary ruler by house, sign, and aspects correlate to the dynamics that have caused the Soul's resistance to making the choices necessary in order to evolve. The North Node by house, sign, and aspects to it in conjunction with the location of its own planetary ruler, and aspects to it, correlate to where, the dynamics involved, the Soul has attempted to leap ahead without addressing the ongoing dynamics that do not allow it to evolve until those dynamics are addressed with the attendant choices being made that will allow it in fact to continue to evolve. (Rad)

Planet conjunct the South Node of another planet, and both square the Nodal Axis

[Example: Venus in Capricorn conjunct South Node of Mercury in Capricorn and both square the Nodal Axis]

(Q) In this case, is it correct that there have been skipped steps with Venus square the Nodal Axis, but NO skipped steps correlating to the South Node of Mercury square the Nodal Axis? How does one interpret the skipped steps of Venus when it is conjunct the South Node of another planet, in this example Mercury?

(A) When a natal planet, in this example Venus, is conjunct a planetary South Node, in this case Mercury, this will symbolize and correlate to the archetypal dynamics of both Venus and Mercury being in a skipped step state relative to their squares to the Nodal Axis.

Angles square Nodes

Angular squares to the Nodes do not correlate to skipped steps because the MC, IC, AC and DC are CURRENT LIFE SYMBOLS DETERMINED BY THE MOMENT OF BIRTH that all correlate to the current evolutionary intentions of the Soul. Thus, when the Nodes square any of these points, there is a specific evolutionary reason for that. And if those reasons are not fulfilled THEN it will correlate to SKIPPED STEPS IN THE NEXT LIFE. So, for example, if this were the Nodes squaring the MC/IC axis this could show up in the next life as the Nodes squaring Saturn and/or the Moon. (Rad)

Angles square Nodes, example

[Example: AC/DC square Nodes; South Node in Sagittarius in the 3rd; North Node in Gemini in the 9th; both nodal rulers in Sagittarius in the 4th house] Ongoing evolutionary and karmic issue of absolute honesty at all costs to counteract lives of lying, misrepresentation, exaggeration, even making yourself actually 'believe' in your own lies to the point where the lies became your truth, has been in place for many lives now. It is not new. With your Ascendant and Descendent both squaring your Nodal Axis this means that it is this life that your Soul is making a choice to deal with this once and for all. These symbols mean that your Soul desires to bring to the forefront of your consciousness this very issue of long standing in this life. And to make choices that lead to being as honest as you can be at all times, and then letting the chips fall where they may. The underlying teaching is that honesty may hurt at times but it will always lead to exactly the right situation, the right resolution of any situation within or without. And, if you don't do this, then, yes, it will become the basis of skipped step next time around. (Rad)

Semisquare to the Nodes
Semisquares to the Nodes do not correlate with 'skipped steps.' The reason is that the nature of the archetypes, the evolutionary process therein, are different than squares. There is a section in Pluto II where JWG describes the nature of the 360 cycle and all the phases and aspects that take place within it from an evolutionary point of view. (Rad)

Retrograde planet square Nodes
It makes no difference according to EA if a retrograde planet squares the Nodes. The retrograde symbol can imply the need to re-live. Further, the skipped steps themselves imply the need to repeat, in order to resolve. (Gonzalo)

The way EA astrologers were taught is, regardless of the variations, the method of determining the Resolution Node is identical in all cases. The Nodes are retrograde 90% of the time, and that is the reason why. Their mean motion is always retrograde. And the mean motion of all planets is direct. Many people have had difficulty calculating which Node was the last to conjunct a planet, because of the nodal retrograde motion. Because of this a simpler method was developed for determining this. Looking at the chart, visualize yourself standing on the skipped step planet, on the outer periphery of the chart. The Node to the left of the planet is always the Resolution Node. This makes it all quite simple. (Steve)

Asteroids or Black Moon Lilith square Nodes
Any planet or asteroid squaring the Nodes correlates to a skipped step. Interpreting the nature of that skipped step depends entirely on the nature of the asteroid or, in the case of Chiron, comet. The reason is based on the nature of a square to the Nodes. Nodes correlate to the Soul's evolutionary journey including the past, and squares correlate to a crisis in action (first quarter) and crisis in consciousness (last quarter). A square leads to constructive integration. So based on that, anything creating such an aspect to the Nodes must imply that there are choices to be made in this life time in order for resolution to occur. (Ari)

The Resolution Node is always to the left with all bodies including asteroids. (Steve)

Wolf never taught about using anything other than the actual planets. And that's because there are so many asteroids. Which ones does one 'count' and 'not count.' (Rad)

Chiron square Nodes
Any planet squaring the Nodes indicates the necessity to continue specific resolving re that planet. Chiron's influence refers to the exceptional experiences of a person's life, all the key and critical ones – the most wounding and traumatizing, the most healing and gifted moments too (birth and death passages too). Chiron in aspect corresponds to the animation of peak cellular memories. When Chiron is square to the Nodes, what is revisited are the most dynamic, significant, traumatizing, defining, critical, turning point experiences. Cellular memory is particularly "juiced up and alive," and so whatever the imprint (and especially when found squaring the Nodes), it is highly sensitized and primed for karmic recall/replay. There is a strong sense/feel of the fated-ness of the life's key circumstances, experiences, and relationships. When Chiron is animated, the experiences are always beyond the usual, ordinary, or average – they are peak, special, exceptional, extraordinary, etc. When Chiron is emphasized, the memory imprints are vivid within cellular memory – they remain present/prevalent – which typically translates into a chronic condition or theme. Chiron correlates to homeopathic process, and creating an effective evolution for oneself. Chiron often translates into a chronic physical condition which forces concentrated attention and thus serves as a primary catalyst. Even birthmarks, scars, or physical handicaps can be echoes of the past life traumas – whether residues (minor) or wounds (major) they represent cellular memory imprints translated into the manifested/the physical. (Rose)

Chiron more often than not is highly active in the charts of those suffering from some sort of unresolved issues from past lives manifesting in THIS life as a chronic illness forcing the individual to face the underlying issues, however not always (but sometimes) able to heal the actual wounds/illnesses, but able to change the relationship the individual has to the past and thus heal the stigmata. (Sol)

Other planets aspecting a planet square Nodes
Other planets aspecting a planet square the Moon's Nodes, by any aspect, are indirectly involved in the skipped step shown by the planet squaring the Nodes. The nature of this indirect involvement is shown by the planet itself, along with the house and sign it's in, that is aspecting the skipped step planet, and also the aspect involved. Thus, even if the skipped step planet conjuncting Saturn isn't technically in a square to the Moon's Nodes (say using a 10 degree orb or less), the fact that it's conjunct Saturn means it's certainly indirectly involved, more rather than less as the aspect is a conjunction. The same for the planets opposing Saturn – even if they aren't strictly speaking square the Nodes, they will still be at least indirectly involved in the skipped step represented by Saturn, as they are in aspect to Saturn. However an opposition is a major aspect, like a conjunction, so it will be more involved rather than less. Some would say that the planet conjuncting Saturn and also those planets opposing it, are brought into a condition of actually directly squaring the Nodes too even if they are outside the orb of a square, by virtue of the fact they are conjuncting/opposing a planet that is in orb of a square to the Nodes. This rule of thumb certainly applies to a conjunction, and more often than not to an opposition, but not to other aspects. (Upasika)

Planets aspecting the planet that squares the Nodes give clues to the nature of the skipped step, how it has been actualized. Remember, it all goes back to the Soul's desire nature, the bottom line of why anything is in the first place. When you see planets opposing each other and squaring the Nodes this indicates deep conflicts in a Soul's desire nature. It has been going back and forth, back and forth between opposing desires. I describe it as wanting it to be day and night, summer and winter, at the same time. Which is obviously not possible. Over time the Soul gets confused and likely frustrated. Can't figure out how to resolve the paradox, goes back and forth, back and forth. Typically is unwilling to delve into the depths of what it would take to resolve the paradox. When it gets to a certain point and it starts getting difficult in ways that are all too familiar, it suddenly flips to acting out the opposite Node. That works for a while. Then the same thing happens at the other Node. It reaches a point where it's too hard, and makes what has by now become the familiar flip to the other Node, trying to get away from the pain or intensity. (Steve)

Planet conjunct South Node when the South Node is the Resolution Node
[Example: Planet conjunct the South Node in a condition of re-live, fruition or combination of both] In a 'fruition' condition where the Soul has already totally developed the dynamics that correlate with the nature of the planet, and the house it is in, in which there is an evolutionary requirement to keep living that dynamic because of the benefit to others in so doing, the Soul could resist this evolutionary requirement by making a choice to do so. This would then create its own kind of 'skipped step' that would require the Soul to go ahead and make that choice to resist, like it or not. (Rad)

Planet conjunct North Node when the South Node is the Resolution Node
It means that the Soul has used the dynamics that correlate with the archetypal nature of that planet as a way of avoiding/denying the archetypes of the planets and houses that correlate to the nature of the skipped steps in the first place. (Rad)

Planet square South Node, Pluto square North Node, example
The planet that is squaring the South Node is also in opposition to Pluto, and Pluto is then squaring the North Node. This means that the planet that is opposed to Pluto is also within the range of being conjunct Pluto's polarity point. All of that symbolism then means that all of those archetypes have been activated prior to the current life. And all of those archetypes are in a skipped step situation. So let's make a simple example to illustrate this, and the resolution of it. Let's say Pluto in the 4th, that Mercury is in the 10th and that this Mercury is squaring a 7th house South Node, and Pluto is squaring a 1st house North Node. The core intention of the 4th house Pluto is to develop a state of inner security. With the North Node in the 1st this would of course mean that the Soul has been desiring a state of almost total freedom and independence in order to actualize or act upon any experience that it feels drawn to do. And in so doing developing this state of inner security. Yet that Pluto is opposed the 10th house Mercury, which is square the 7th house South Node. This would correlate to the Soul 'thinking' that in order to feel emotionally secure that it needed to be in relationship to others in general, and an intimate other specifically. The reasons that the Soul would think that can be many including not feeling that it was nurtured or loved in the ways that it felt it needed to be by the parents of origin: 4th/10th house. So, in essence, the Soul is now conflicted within itself. This conflict would then manifest as cycles in which the Soul would desire to lose itself in the context of relationship: Mercury applying to the South Node in the 7th, in opposition to Pluto. By doing this the Soul is then defeating its core intention of learning an almost absolute state of inner emotional security. And the Soul, within itself, would know that because, after all, it is its own intention to do so.

Thus, this sets in motion the next cycle in which the Soul then tries to throw off, oppose, all relationships in order to be free, independent, in charge of its own life: Pluto in the 4th squaring the 1st house North Node. Yet in reacting in this way it then has led to the inner feeling of being totally alone and insecure. This would then lead the Soul to then go back to the other cycle of immersion in relationship in order to feel secure, and not alone. So back and forth the Soul goes within these two cycles without the archetypes of these dynamics being sufficiently developed: skipped steps. With Pluto applying to the North Node in the 1st, and the Mercury applying to the South Node in the 7th the resolution becomes this: The Soul must keep learning how to be secure within itself by actualizing a life that is determined from within itself: its own relationship to itself. Thus a life in which it can follow its own inner directions CONSISTENTLY wherever they may lead. And, at the same time, engage in relationships with others in general, and an intimate other specifically, in which the very nature of those others is also one of self-independence, and inner security. Others, by their very nature, help enforce the core lessons to this Soul: a state of inner security and independence in order to develop that inner security. Thus, the very nature of how others 'think' about relationships will be the same: the very nature of their psychological orientation to relationships will be the same. In this way the 'skipped steps' symbolized with Mercury applying to the South Node, and Pluto applying to the North Node will be resolved. (Rad)

Ruler of both Nodes in same sign and house
In this symbolism there are skipped steps involving dynamics and issues linked with the houses that the Nodes are in, and the house that the planetary rulers of each are within. In my experience this is a relatively unique situation and requires some real investigation as to determine exactly what the nature of those skipped steps are. Considerations to examine are these: Are the two

planetary rulers in a balsamic conjunction, or new? What other aspects are they making to other planets? Where is the natal Pluto, and what aspects is it making? Each case in unique to itself of course. (Rad)

When the ruler of the Resolution Node is the skipped step planet
This could occur of course. The way through it is to consciously be aware of what the resolutions/issues are and to then apply one's personal will so as to be able to stay focused upon them. In so doing, to make consistent choices that will allow that resolution to occur. (Rad)

Ruler of North Node conjunct South Node, South Node ruler square Nodal Axis (applying to the North Node)
Note: In the graphic below it appears Pluto is also SQUARE to the NN/SN axis, and therefore applying to NN, and while there is a "natural" square by sign, it's actually out of orb for a square in the person's chart (Plu 24Li, NNo 12 Cn). This is using a 10 deg orb for a square, as recommended by Jeffrey. (Upasika)

That there has been skipped steps in the past as symbolized, in this case, the South Node ruler squaring the Nodal Axis, and the intention is to recover those skipped steps in order to evolve. And that this intention of recovering those skipped steps has just preceded the current life being lived (symbolized by the North Node ruler conjunct the South Node). That means that the Soul has created, just before the current life, circumstances that serve to trigger old dynamics, these dynamics having previously kept the Soul bound to its past: fixed. The intention in this life is to make new choices, shown by the house and sign of the North Node, in the face of those circumstances (when they appear again in this life) that trigger the old, past, dynamics. This process is of course also emphasized by the South Node ruler applying to the North Node. If this is accomplished then the Soul will resolve the skipped steps. (Rad)

Mars/Pluto new conjunction square Nodes
[Example Mars/Pluto 7th, South Node 4th, North Node 10th] The new phase conjunction of Mars and Pluto does reflect that this is a primary life (a life wherein the core evolutionary dynamics within the chart are being directly worked on/confronted). The new phase conjunction reflects that a brand new evolutionary cycle is beginning, and the evolutionary intentions/impulse reflected by Mars/Pluto is brand new. The skipped step symbolized by the Pluto/Mars square to the Nodal Axis reflect that prior relationship patterns pertaining to the evolutionary past must be resolved in order for this new evolutionary cycle to be put into motion. In other words, the new cycle will require a necessary resolution of the skipped steps to occur in the areas/dynamics symbolized by Mars/Pluto and the Nodal Axis. New relationship patterns can then manifest as this resolution occurs which is a core evolutionary intention for this life. The specific nature of the new cycle that has just begun for the individual who has a Mars/Pluto new phase conjunction is symbolized by the South Node and its planetary ruler. The evolutionary intentions, as in all other charts, is reflected by Pluto's polarity point, the North Node, its planetary ruler. Issues pertaining to the evolutionary past (South Node and its ruler) must be resolved in order for the intended new cycle to begin. The new phase, in this case, will manifest as the individual makes the necessary efforts to resolve these issues, and deals with these unresolved issues in a "new way." (Remember, though, that skipped steps reflect unresolved issues/dynamics within both the areas indicated by the North and South Nodes). (Deva)

Skipped steps – different sign on house cusp
When there is a different sign on the house cusp than the planet within the house, this can be considered as part of the skipped steps in the sense of a tributary stream that is feeding the main stream itself. It contributes to the essence of what the skipped steps are about. (Rad)

Examples of Avatars with skipped steps
A perfect example is Jesus himself – Mercury squaring his Nodes – Mercury being in Aquarius. Another example is the great Ramakrishna – Uranus squaring his South Node in Scorpio, North Node Taurus. (Rad)

SOUL

Soul

The word Soul has been a word in almost every human language system that has ever been on Earth. So what is it? Can we open up the brain and find it? No, obviously we cannot. But we cannot open up the physical body and find emotion either for example. Yet we know we all have emotions. Can we open up the brain and find thought? No. Yet, we all know we at least have a thought or two in our heads. Can we open up the body and find sadness, or depression, or happiness, or love? No. Yet, we all know that these things exist within us. So obviously we are dealing with the nature of energy. The Soul is energy which is no different than the energy of consciousness itself. Again, we can't open the brain and find consciousness. Consciousness is one of the very greatest 'mysteries' of all to scientists for they cannot explain its origins or even how it came to be. Consciousness correlates astrologically to Neptune. This is exactly the starting point for what we call religion and philosophy: the human need to contemplate and consider, within the desire to know, where we come from and why. In turn this becomes the causative factor for 'beliefs' where beliefs are the result of the human pondering upon the origin of life itself.

But is there a difference between beliefs and actual knowing? Is there a way to know the answer to the big cosmic questions versus the need to believe in an answer? The happy news is that there is. For example by the sheer fact that there is a manifested Creation that exists as fact there must also be TRUTHS THAT INHERENTLY EXIST because of the fact of the manifested Creation in the first place. By the fact of its existence most of us can easily reason that there has to be something that is the origin of the Creation. In generic language we could call that something the Origin of All Things, or The Source, and in religious terminology it is called God or the Goddess. Consciousness is certainly part of the manifested Creation. It exists. That which is the origin of consciousness, of itself, must also be conscious. Thus the totality of consciousness emanates from this Source. As an observable fact we all know that consciousness is in all living things: all life forms. And all of these life forms have the appearance of being separate from all other life forms yet are simultaneously connected to them: two plants next to each other appear separate yet are simultaneously connected to one another by the sheer fact of being plants. So, on the one hand there is in fact the individualizing aspect of consciousness, yet, on the other, the universal aspect of consciousness which binds all the individual aspects of consciousness together.

Another way of illustrating this is the famous story of the wave and the ocean. Most of us would agree that it is the ocean that is the origin of the wave. Yet from the point of view of the wave, if the individualizing aspect of consciousness were centered there, the wave appears and seems separate. In other words if the center of gravity for consciousness were within the wave then from that center of gravity the wave appears, and is experienced, as something separate from its own source: the ocean. On the other hand if the center of gravity within consciousness were the wave itself then the ocean simultaneously experiences its totality while at the same time experiencing the individualizing aspects of itself as manifested in the waves that emanate from it. In the very same way then the Universal Consciousness which is the origin of all consciousness has created and manifested the totality of the manifested Creation which of course includes the human being and the consciousness within it. And within human consciousness there exists a natural individualizing aspect to it. This individualizing aspect to it occurs as a natural result of the human life form having distinct and individual forms relative to the its root: the human life form as a seed, so to speak, that produces many other branches that is no different than the ocean and the wave. Thus, each human life form has its own individualizing consciousness that is called the Soul.

The Soul, then, is an immutable consciousness, or energy, that is naturally part of the Universal Consciousness that has created it in the first place. Immutable here means that which cannot be destroyed. Why? Because energy can never be destroyed, it can only change form. To evolve. So how does the Soul evolve? What dynamics are inherent within it that are the cause of its own evolution? Within all human Souls there exist two antithetical desires where DESIRE IS THE DETERMINANT OF EVOLUTION. One desire is to RETURN to that which is the origin of us, of all of Creation, in the first place. And the other desire is to SEPARATE from that which is the Origin of All Things. This simple inner dynamic within the Soul is also the natural cause, or law, of free choice, or free will. The evolution of the Soul is simply based on a progressive elimination of all separating desires to the exclusion of only one desire that can remain: to return to the Origin of All Things. This does not require any belief system at all, or any religion that one must belong to. This simple truth, because it is a function of Natural Law, can be validated by anyone through their own life experience. Is it not true for example that any of us can have whatever separating desire that one can imagine. For example, a desire for a new lover, or a new career post, the new possession, and so on. And we may have the ability to manifest that which we desire. And when we do there is in fact a sense of satisfaction of actualizing that which we have desired. But what soon replaces it? Is it not the sense of dissatisfaction, the sense of something more? It is precisely this sense of dissatisfaction, the sense of something more, that 'echoes' the ultimate desire to return to the Origin Of All Things, the only desire that will bring to us that ultimate satisfaction. All of us have this universal experience.

So how can we know, independent of belief systems, that there in fact exists an Ultimate Source? The human being knew long, long ago, before the manifestation of religions and complicated cosmologies, through inner contemplation, inner 'looking,' that when the breath in the body, inhale and exhale, became very, very shallow, even stopped, that there would then appear within the interior of their consciousness a LIGHT. This occurred as a natural function of the breath shallowing or stopping. Naturally. Much later in human history this was to be called the famous 'third eye.' And it is this very Light that symbolized and connected the individual consciousness reflected in the Soul to the Universal Consciousness that is the Origin Of All Things. The human being also learned long ago that by merging its own individual consciousness, or Soul, with that Light that its consciousness would then expand in such a way that the individual consciousness itself then became Universal and was then able to consciously experience that Ultimate Source Of All Things: the wave has returned to the ocean. The point here, again, is that any human being can know and validate these Natural Laws through their own actual experience that does not require belief systems of any kind. The key to do this, again, is to progressively shallow and stop the breath all together.

Anyone can do this. If you doubt this, or wonder how, simply try the following natural method to do so. On your inhaling breath simply mentally affirm the number one. On your exhaling breath simply mentally affirm the number two. The 'secret' here is to concentrate as hard as you can simply on the numbers one and two. It is this act of concentration intensified by desire manifesting as will that progressively your breath will in fact begin to shallow and even stop. Remember that consciousness is energy and cannot be destroyed. It can only change form. Thus, as some may think when the breath is stopped it does not mean that you have to die. Consciousness is NOT dependent on the human form. So when the breath is stopped the inner LIGHT which is intrinsic to consciousness will soon begin to appear. And as it does so simply move into it by the conscious act of surrender. Surrendering to it will then allow for a merging of your own consciousness with that Universal Consciousness as symbolized in the Light. ANYONE CAN DO THIS AND THEN KNOW FOR THEMSELVES THIS NATURAL TRUTH. It is this Natural Law of breath, when stopped or deeply shallowed, that allows for what all the great teachers of relatively recent centuries, when compared to how long the human being has actually been on the planet, have said including Jesus: "When thy eye is single ones whole body is full of light."

Symbolically speaking the two physical eyes that we have correlate to the two motions of breath: inhale and exhale. It is the inhaling and exhaling of the breath that keeps ones consciousness utterly involved and enmeshed in the duality, or polarity, of life itself. Likes and dislikes, happy and sad, love and hate, etc., etc., correlate to and demonstrate this Natural Law. The numbers one and two correlate to the Natural Law of finitude and duality: cause and effect. Yet between one and two there exists an interval or zero. The interval or zero correlates to the Universal Consciousness or infinity. Thus when the breath stops or becomes very, very shallow the interval is then perceived. And what is perceived in the single eye, or what has been called the 'third eye' that naturally exists within the interior of consciousness and can be accessed, merged with, with our Soul. When this occurs the law of duality ceases to exist. The ultimate 'satisfaction' is then realized. The Soul correlates astrologically to Pluto. From the point of view of Natural Laws it is interesting to note, historically speaking, that advanced mathematics like algebra, trigonometry, quantum physics, and so on could not have been realized unless there was an 'idea' or conception called zero. This occurred in the third century AD in India. It was the then Indian mathematicians that conceived of the number zero. And, of course, from the point of view of Indian cosmologies this occurred as a direct extension of their natural understanding of the origin of Creation: out of nothing, or zero, the manifested Creation occurred, the unmanifested/manifested, or the causeless cause. (Rad)

EA paradigm – the evolutionary journey of the Soul

EA and its paradigm symbolizes the individual journey of the Soul through time as it evolves back to its Source: God/ess. Even though Neptune symbolizes that Source it does not symbolize or reflect the individual journey of the Soul itself. EA is about understanding each individual Soul as it actually is: where it has been and why, where it is now and why, and where it is headed and why. The Soul correlates to Pluto. Neptune does not. (Rad)

From the point of view of evolution for all Souls the intent is to understand the Cause of Creation itself. Relative to the Moon, the 4th house, Cancer it is part of the natural trinity, or triad, between Scorpio, 8th house, and Pluto, and Neptune, Pisces, and the 12th house. This natural triad correlates of course to the Source of Creation or God/ess, Neptune, Pisces, the 12th house, and the Souls that are created by this Source, the 8th house, Scorpio, and Pluto, and the egos that each Soul creates in each of its lives in order to facilitate its ongoing evolution BACK TO THE SOURCE ITSELF. So, in the end, ultimate evolution wherein progressively the Soul DESIRES TO RETURN TO ITS SOURCE. As such, in time, the Soul remembers that its Source is God/ess and, as it does so, it realizes that its identity, its ultimate identity, ego, is that Source. Very few folks realize that the Soul itself contains within itself its own 'self-image' or ego. And how that inner self-image or ego is then reflected through the subjective egocentric structures that it creates it each life for its evolution to proceed. But as it does so there will be a progressive shift within its consciousness, the center of gravity,

gravity of course is Saturn, Capricorn, and the 10th house which is the natural polarity of Cancer, Moon, and the 4th, wherein that center of gravity will shift from the subjective ego and a 'separate identity' from the Source, to the Soul itself wherein it will them remember its own origins: God/ess.

When this begins to happen then the inner experience of the Soul's individuality, its own ego, is perceived and experienced as but an extension of that Source or God. As this occurs then the inner perception of what is called the third eye, the inner eye, is directly perceived and experienced. This, in fact, is actually hard wired into the brain: it is part of its structure of consciousness in human form. As the perception occurs the Soul, by birthright, REMEMBERS how to merge with that inner eye. As Jesus said when 'one's eyes are single, one's whole body is full of light.' The dual eyes reflect the Natural Law of duality, cause and effect. When one eye become single, the inner eye that is fused with, penetrated, moved THROUGH then one's whole being, or body, is full of Light. And that is the light of all the Natural Laws that the Source has set in motion at the moment of Creation. And these inner perceptions, gained in the natural way, finally lead the Soul to be able to directly inwardly experience, to know, to perceive, the interface between the MANIFESTED AND THE UN-MANIFESTED. And it is this interface that correlates to TIME AND TIMELESSNESS. In essence, the perception and direct experience OF CREATION ITSELF. This is the birth right of all Souls. And this is what the natural evolution of the Soul is about, in the end, as symbolized the natural trinity of Pisces, Neptune, the 12th house, the 8th house, Pluto, Scorpio, and Cancer, the 4th house, and the Moon. (Rad)

Dual desires within the Soul

The Soul does evolve through purging separating desires. Separating desires are any desires that are not in harmony, or alignment with, the current evolutionary intentions for the life and rooted in the need to maintain the past (old patterns of behavior that are inhibiting further growth). We evolve through the evolutionary states as we exhaust our separating desires (it is a natural process). Pluto by house and sign in the natal chart will correlates to the specific past patterns of emotional security that must be transmuted in this life. Pluto's polarity point symbolizes the current evolutionary intentions for this life, and how to transmute the past patterns of behavior symbolized by Pluto. Remember that there are two coexisting, antithetical desires within the Soul – one to return and one to separate. We have a choice to cooperate or resist these evolutionary intentions. We can look at the natal chart and by using just Pluto and its polarity point we can determine how resistance or cooperation with the current evolutionary intentions will manifest.

For example, if a person has Pluto in the 5th house, and is compulsively acting upon desires that are rooted in the need to be recognized as special or important, that is excessively self-centered, and does not link the need for creative self-actualization in a way that reflects the need of others/humanity then resistance to the current evolutionary intentions symbolized by the 11th house polarity point is evident. Pluto itself symbolizes the dual desires within the Soul (one to return and one to separate). Mars is the lower octave of Pluto, and symbolizes how we will consciously act out the desires symbolized by Pluto. Mars symbolizes our conscious desire nature. The point within this is that Pluto in the birth chart will determine the core specific past patterns of behavior that are creating limitations and represent emotional security for the Soul. We will unconsciously resist growth by attempting to maintain these past patterns (separating desires). Pluto's polarity point symbolizes the current evolutionary intentions for the life, and the types of desires that the Soul will have to break free from the past patterns of behavior that are inhibiting further growth. Mars is the conscious desire nature we have that reflects how we will act out, or act upon, these desires symbolized by Pluto and to actualize the current evolutionary intentions for this life (Pluto's polarity point). (Deva)

Soul memories of prior lives

Most Souls do not have conscious access to the prior life memories for one reason, and that reason comes from the Creator itself. And that reason is this: if most Souls did have such access they would become so consumed in those prior lifetimes that they simply could not, or would not, get on with the business or intentions for the current life being lived. This is why those memories remain unconscious for most. There is no 'crisis' between the Soul and the subjective ego it creates in any given life because the Soul IS THE ORIGIN OF THAT EGO. The Soul structure itself may have a variety of crises within it, and the reasons for that, and that would then be reflected in the subjective egocentric structure it then created in whatever life. (Rad)

One must be careful in terms of what any given Soul thinks it can remember. Unless any given Soul has the actual capacity to see into prior lives, for itself and others, then very often such 'memories' get blurred and mixed up with other memories resident within the Soul itself. (Rad)

Past dynamics of the Soul

The past of the Soul becomes the determinant of the symbols in the current life, including the Moon. (Rad)
The prior lives of the Soul, the dynamics involved, can be ascertained by the entire chart, including the planetary nodes, minus the current life Sun. (Rad)
It's really important to keep in mind we have a mainly invisible incredibly long past that we project into every 'new' moment. And we are shaped by that past – our very conception of 'me' is mainly based on our individual past, filtered through the conditions and

experiences of the present lifetime. So even if the two people have a very similar evolutionary stage they're still going to breathe life into the very similar script in very different ways. We really are, every one of us, truly unique. That is simultaneously a great gift, and also the source of a lot of our human sense of aloneness. (Steve)

Past life memories and long term memories
The individual Soul contains all that correlates to the totality of its dynamics for all the lives it has ever lived which, of course, have all been caused by the nature of the dual desires within it. Thus, all the memories of all those lives exist within it. The consciousness within the Soul have different dynamics that allow for a knowledge of the Soul as manifested through the egocentric structure that the Soul creates from life to life. The dynamics that allow the egocentric structure within the Soul to know about its prior lives/memories correlate specifically to Uranus, the 11th house, and Aquarius. These archetypes correlate to the 'long term memories' that the egocentric structure within the Soul can access. In Jungian terms this is called the 'individuated' unconscious where individuated means memories that are unique to each individual. Long term memories exist with the current life of any Soul, and those memories also correlate to the past life memories of any Soul that can be accessed by the egocentric structure in a few ways. One of course is through hypnosis which can also create false memories as well as accurate ones. Another is simply based on the natural evolution of the Soul wherein at a certain point its past life memories can be accessed within itself relative to the egocentric structure created. Meditation is a good example of this process. (Rad)

Future dynamics of a Soul
Evolutionary Astrology does allow one to see the future dynamics of a Soul in lives to come that are dependent on the choices being made in the current life. So relative to the choices that the Soul made (eg resolving skipped steps), the EA astrologer can then look at the North Node by sign and house. (Rad)

Soul desires in the next lifetime
Every Soul is unique so there is no one answer to this question. In Einstein's case he left his body with an unfulfilled desire: the unifying principle of all of Creation. Thus, because that desire is unfulfilled that would of course correlate to the next life in which his Soul would incarnate in order to try to actualize that unfulfilled desire in some way. By way of comparison let's imagine that Einstein did in fact realize that desire before his physical death. In that case the desire had been realized which would then create a scenario in which his Soul would then act upon other desires in his next life. The current life birth chart of any Soul symbolizes all kinds of desires that have come forwards from other lives. In the current life the Soul will of course attempt to actualize those desires. Yet for most Souls it's not possible to exhaust all those desires in the context of one life. The desires that remain in the current life that have not been fulfilled then are taken forwards into the next life. Thus, it is very possible to see or understand what the next life of a Soul will be relative to those desires that have not yet been actualized or fulfilled. For example in the life of the great Yogananda he had one desire in that life that was not fulfilled. And that was the desire to live in isolated environments in the Himalayas as a monk. Before he left his body he said he would be reborn exactly two hundred years after the date of his physical death. When one calculates that chart for his next life it is in fact a perfect reflection of that one remaining desire. (Rad)

Conditioning patterns created by the Soul
The 'conditions' that any given Soul creates for its life, in any life, are the conditions that the Soul needs in order to further its own ongoing evolutionary intentions: whatever those conditions are. And those conditions of course affect the Soul: intentionally so. It is the very 'effect' of whatever those conditions are that serve to advance the Soul's evolutionary intentions. All Souls are 'affected' by the conditions of its lives. Even the most evolved of all Souls start off as children. And the conditions of their births that they have chosen 'affect' them as they would any child. For example the great Yogananda chose to come through a mother who loved him dearly, and he loved her dearly, yet she died when he was very young: four or five years of age. For him at that age this was total trauma. Yet, at that age, he determined within himself, since his earthly mother was no longer present, to find his 'Divine Mother.' And so at that age he took himself into an attic space in his home and sat there with the determination not to budge from that spot until the Divine Mother revealed herself to him from within. And She did. Yogananda had a 10th house Pluto conjunct Neptune which were both in opposition to his Venus in the 4th. The perfect symbolism for the 'conditions' of his childhood, and how those conditions affected his own ongoing evolutionary journey. (Rad)

Evolution comes from the root of Pluto, the Soul
Everything is set in motion by the Soul and the desires within it. Thus, the polarity point of Pluto only manifests by way of the desire within the Soul to do so. If that is done then the North Node of the Moon is simultaneously set in motion because of the desires emanating from the Soul. All evolution or motion within the birth chart, including the Nodes of the Moon, is set in motion, evolving, only because of the desires that emanate from the Soul: Pluto. In other words, the Moon, in and of itself, does not cause anything to happen: does not cause evolution to occur. All comes from the root of Pluto, the Soul. All combinations of planets and their Nodes are created BY THE SOUL relative to its ongoing evolution over great lengths of time. Thus, all facilitate the Soul's evolution.

But, again, it all starts from within the Soul itself. Without active desires, choices, to set all of these symbols in motion, to evolve, nothing will happen. It's like marking time. Once the Soul does make the choices by manifesting desires to do so then all of the symbols in the birth chart, the Nodal Axis of all planets, then facilitate that ongoing evolution of the Soul. (Rad)

Pluto, why it (and not other planets) represents the desires of the Soul

Pluto correlates to the Soul itself, and within that, the Natural Law of evolution. It correlates to what the desires of the Soul have been that has led to the current life, and the desires that correlate to its ongoing evolutionary needs. This is contained with Pluto, the Soul, itself. All the other planets in a current life birth chart are thus created by the Soul for its ongoing evolutionary needs that are reflected in its desires. The current life birth planets do have their own North and South Nodes. It is the South Nodes of these planets that do correlate to the past life dynamics that the Soul has created for itself that have led to the current life, and the position of whatever planet IN THIS LIFE that symbolizes the current life's evolutionary needs. The current life position brings the past forwards through it: the South Node coming through the current position of the planet itself. The North Node of the planet in turn correlates to the ongoing evolutionary journey of the Soul as it continues to evolve through each of the archetypes of all the planets. The cause of that evolution is the Soul, not any of the other planets themselves. The natural polarity point of the natal Pluto is the bottom line evolutionary intent for the Soul in each life. It is the primary cause that causes the North Nodes of all the other planets to actualize according to that primary evolutionary intention. The natal planet, in the current life, birth chart, serves to integrate the past and the future in each moment FOR THE ENTIRE LIFE. (Rad)

How the Soul effects its evolution

Pluto is the only mobilizer in the chart. The Soul (Pluto), having created the Sun, and other planets and their Nodes, has also created them in a way that they will all facilitate the evolution of the Soul itself, and as part of that process, the evolution of themselves too. And looking at the Nodes of those other planets (all except the Sun), we can see how the Soul has gone about facilitating itself in this way in the past, and also its intentions for doing so in the future. A natural tension arises between the past that's been and the future that is ahead of us, and this is felt and able to be integrated at the current placement of these planets. This tension is integrated by embracing the polar opposite realm of experience and understanding (polarity point) of each planet as consciously as possible. Conscious striving in this way towards our potential is what causes each area and aspect of ourselves (shown by the planets themselves in their current placements) to grow and evolve.

The relationship between the Soul (Pluto) and our subconscious identity (Moon – its egocentric structure) that is created each lifetime, reflects the core mechanism that we unconsciously create from within our Soul to enable a sense of self in our daily life, albeit usually a subconscious one. And we look at the Moon's Nodes to get information over time about this identity/facilitation process the Soul keeps creating for itself. This subconscious sense of identity is itself not a static position. It too is in a state of tension caused by the pull of the past and continuity (strengthening this sense of self) and the need to keep moving out of our comfort zone into a new unknown sense of self (Moon polarity point). It needs to do this to accommodate the inevitable changes that are brought about in our life as a result of the deep (and relatively unconscious) urge within us to evolve (Pluto) propelling us towards our deepest growth possible in this lifetime (Pluto's polarity point).

The relationship between Pluto, and Mars and its Nodes, reflects where the Soul is at within itself in regard to its creating desires to act on. The activation of these desires is what sets in motion all the other energies (all the remaining planets/asteroids with Nodes) in the chart, with their inbuilt role to play in facilitating the ongoing evolution of the Soul. We look at the Nodes of Mars and these other planets/asteroids, to get information about how these conscious desires and the particular roles of the other planets in the Soul's evolution, roles that have been created by the Soul in the first place, are all manifesting over time.

This whole process – starting in the relatively unconscious Soul (Pluto) manifesting as a subconscious awareness of identity and self which imparts a sense of continuity (Moon) – is initiated by the choice to evolve at the Soul level. This (relatively unconscious) choice to evolve, then manifests as multiple conscious desires that we are aware of in our lives. Both the Moon and the Sun register the urges, evolutionary intentions, from the Soul, Pluto, via Mars its lower octave; this whole process is integrated by our (relatively) much more conscious sense of being (the Sun) – in the realm of life shown by the Sun's house, with the disposition and needs of the sign the Sun is in. The conscious expression and integration of ourself (Sun) evolves within this realm (house) with more developed understanding (sign) as these desires emanating from our unconscious (Pluto) are acted upon and experienced over time (shown by all the Nodes). The resistance generated by the past (shown by the South Nodes) – to fulfilling the intentions arising from within our Soul (Pluto) and thus manifesting our future possibilities (North Nodes) – is broken down and dissolved when we choose out of free will to grow into the unknown (our polarity points). And in doing so, our future (shown by the North Nodes) then becomes actualized, and this consciousness through which we integrate everything that we are aware of (the Sun), then expands. In this way the Soul effects its evolution. (Upasika)

When Souls go back to Source

(Q) When all Souls finish their evolution and finally go back to God, is that the end of human beings? (Wei)
(A) EA does not specifically teach about that other than once the Soul is free from all separating desires, and has only one desire

left which is to go home to its Source, God, then it will finally lead such a Soul back into a state of absolute union with its Source: God. In the end your question really refers to the nature of the manifested Creation in the first place, and the natural evolution that takes place within that manifested Creation. The deepest root of all within the manifested Creation is consciousness and intelligence within that consciousness. And of course the Source of the manifested Creation is that intelligence and the consciousness within it. From the point of view of consciousness/intelligence in 'human form' we must remember that is but one form among countless other forms that also contains consciousness and intelligence. What is the nature of those forms and the intelligent consciousness within them? Do they also have what we call Souls? Who can know the answers to this? Saying all this only to illustrate the complexity of the manifested Creation much of which is unknowable from the natural limitation of the human form. And because of that natural limitation humans thus create philosophies and beliefs that attempt to explain or answer the types of questions you have brought up. Evolutionary Astrology is focused on the evolution of the Soul in human form, and the dual desires that are at its core, and how those desires directly correlate to the Soul's evolution through time and space. And, of course, those desires, like the Soul, emanate from the Source Of All Things. In the end, then, it's about the Soul reuniting with its Source by the elimination of all separating desires that keep it from such a reunion. The Soul in human form can then only know its Source by unifying its consciousness with the consciousness of the Source itself. Is that then the 'end of the human being?' To me the only way to answer this is that such a total union releases the Soul from being bound by the natural limitation of the human form. (Rad)

Frequency of incarnation
(Q) Are there any rules as to how frequent a Soul incarnates? (Henrik)
(A) There are no such 'rules.' Each Soul has its own evolutionary/karmic context which is then the determinant of when and why a given Soul incarnates. (Rad)

Karmic 'script' of the Soul
All things in our life start from within ourselves first: the evolutionary and karmic 'script' of the Soul in any given life. Thus the progression of the planets, and the aspects that they are making, reflect this ongoing evolutionary script of the Soul at any point in time. (Rad)

Ocean/wave analogy
Neptune can be both the Wave and the Ocean depending ON THE POINT OF VIEW of consciousness itself as encased in the human form. If we remember the natural trinity between Pisces/Neptune, Scorpio/Pluto, and Moon/Cancer – God, Soul, Ego – then of course it's possible for the ego within a given Soul to be 'intoxicated' – Neptune – with itself via the Ego that it creates. Thus, its relationship to itself is separative in nature relative to the totality of the Creation that it is inter-related with. Thus, from its point of view, it has become deluded – Neptune – within the wave: ego. Other Souls of course, relative to evolution, have their center of gravity – Saturn – within the ocean and know that their Soul and its ego are simply part of the totality of Creation itself that is co-equal in nature. Thus, their inner Neptune, is within the Ocean.

In the wave/ocean analogy the sense of identity depends on the evolutionary condition of the Soul. For most that identity lies in the wave: the ego that feels, perceives and thinks that it is separate from everything else. From the vantage point of the wave then everything else, the boats, ripples, whatever else correlates to the totality of its life circumstances become simply props in its personal play. For Souls who have evolved progressively into the Spiritual state the center of gravity within their consciousness progressively shifts from the ego to the Soul itself. As such their sense of identity is the Soul, the ocean, upon which the wave of its ego has been created for whatever ongoing evolutionary purposes it has. A Soul in that condition thus experiences simultaneously its distinct egocentric personal identity while at the same time its timeless Soul identity.
What it all comes down to is how something is perceived including our own sense of 'identity.' From the point of view of consciousness the issue, in the end, is where the center of gravity is within in. Gravity has a natural correlation to Saturn, Capricorn, and the 10th house. Saturn, etc., also correlates to the structural nature of anything. Thus, the structural nature of consciousness. It also has a natural correlation to the boundary of anything. Thus, it correlates to the natural boundary between our subjective awareness and the consciousness therein, and the progressive levels of the unconscious as in the individuated unconsciousness, Uranus, and the collective unconsciousness/consciousness which is Neptune. Deep within the unconscious is the Soul. Consciousness, as such, emanates from the primary brain. Within the subjective consciousness in all of us is the egocentric structure that the Soul creates in each life to facilitate its evolutionary intentions and progressions.
The ego is the Moon, Cancer, and the 4th house, and is, of course, the natural polarity of Capricorn, the 10th, and Saturn. For most individuals, given the natural evolutionary stages, the sense of identity is their own ego. Thus, the PERCEPTION of being separate from everything else. Thus, the WAVE on the ocean where the wave correlates to the subjective ego within the consciousness of the individual. So if the center of gravity within the individual is their ego then their sense of identity is then defined by the wave: their ego. Yet, as evolution proceeds, the center of gravity within an individual's consciousness shifts to the Soul itself: the OCEAN. The natural boundary of Saturn relative to the structural nature of consciousness dissolves in such a way that the PERCEPTION OF

IDENTITY changes from the wave to the ocean. As a result the individual is then perceiving, is consciously aware of, its timeless identity called their individual Soul and the egocentric structures it creates from life to life AT THE SAME TIME. In other words the Soul is aware of and perceives the continuation of its ongoing lifetimes from life to life at the same time. The center of gravity is the Ocean, the Soul. As a result they do not perceive themselves as separate from anything, but, in fact, inter-related to everything. (Rad)

Past life identity (name) of Soul
No kind of astrology, including EA, can determine for sure the specific name or identity of anyone. The dynamics of any Soul through time can of course be determined with incredible detail and accuracy. To determine this kind of information requires that an individual have 'other capacities' that can then be used and applied to E(A) (Rad)

Seven Soul types
The seven Soul types that Wolf talked about are reflected in the actual nature of each of the seven chakras. In other words, each chakra has a total nature that is specific to itself. (Rad)

The Soul types also correlate to the seven pathways to God. Since Neptune/Pisces represents the totality, the Universal, God, Goddess, etc., all paths, of course, astrologically speaking lead to Neptune/Pisces and in some way will involve the mutable grand cross of Gemini/Virgo/Sagittarius/Pisces. There can also be kind of a "sub-type," or secondary Soul type, ie, one primary LEADING to the secondary. As with the Daemon Soul, all the other Soul types can only be known through observation and correlation and then be backed up and/or revealed through the birth chart. The Chakra System itself has different correlations from the astrological ones. The correlations are rooted in the Hindu system of astrology. The astrological associations to the chakras correlate to the energy body, or the astral body. (Adina)

The paths – Bhakti, Jyana, Daemon, Raja, etc. are not "chosen" – their orientation resonates with the way the Soul is constructed, thus one is simply going to feel most at home in an orientation that closely resonates with that Soul's inherent nature. JWG said: "The reason to understand the chakra system, particularly with respect to medical diagnosis, is that it has a whole different astrological scheme of correlation, different from the traditional correlation of anatomy and physiology. It is a supplement or complement to that traditional analysis. It will reveal on a diagnostic level, information that you could not otherwise be able to determine in traditional methods of astro-medical diagnosis. When you combine the above with the chakra system, you will have a complete way of creating an absolutely correct diagnosis. For example, if you have a client with all kinds of problems in their stomach, and you are looking in that chart, the nature of the Moon and the planetary ruler of the 4th etc., and there does not seem to be any particular problem. But going to the chakra system you suddenly find the whole middle region of the body correlates with Mars and Pluto, and now if we re-look at that birth chart and see Mars and Pluto in opposition...! So basically this is a support system to the other system." (JWG)

TABLE 1 Seven Soul Types

Root	Saturn, Uranus, Pluto	*physical, body, asanas*	Hatha Yoga
Sacral	Jupiter, Neptune	*sexuality, Daemon*	Tantra Yoga
Solar Plexus, Navel	Mars, Pluto	*warrior, natural need to lead, leadership*	Hatha Yoga Kundalini Yoga
Heart	Venus	*devotion*	Bhakti Yoga
Throat	Mercury	*prayer, chanting, mantra, service to others, healers*	Karma Yoga
Brow, Third Eye, Medulla, Ajna	Sun, Moon	*wisdom, teacher types*	Jyana Yoga
Crown	Neptune	*avatar, guru*	Raja Yoga

Soul type example, Daemon Soul
It is important to remember that the Soul has not created itself. What we call God/ess is the origin of all things. Thus the origin of all Souls. And each Soul does have its own unique nature correlating with the seven Soul types that correlate to the time/space/gravitational reality of this Solar System: Earth. Thus, the inherent nature of the Soul created by God/ess is not something that can change. It is intrinsic. And, of course, it's also true that any given Soul type does and will experience all the other chakras along its progressive evolutionary journey. Yet it is the intrinsic orientation, as defined by its unique Soul type, that the Soul will be orientated to the nature of each of the chakras. A Daemon Soul is always a Daemon Soul that cannot change

because all Souls' unique nature has been created by God/ess, not itself. Thus, the Daemon Soul, or any other Soul Type, necessarily will experience all the other chakras – it's the orientation defined by the Soul's inherent typing that defines the orientation to those other chakras. (Rad)

Unique individuality of Soul
The entire birth chart reflects and symbolizes the unique individuality of all Souls, not just one symbol, but the entire chart. The beauty of EA, when rightly understood, offers just that. EA requires that one interface with the individual, to talk with them, observe them. The interface then between such interaction with the person and their birth chart generates the understanding of the uniqueness, the natural individuality, of their Soul. (Rad)

Soul's gender
Wolf taught, as well as many others, that all Souls are inherently androgynous. And this is because all Souls are reflections of the Creator who is the Origin of the male and female principles in the first place. Yet all Souls choose to be in one gender, preponderantly, over the other gender for their own reasons: a choice to be made by all Souls. Yet, at the same time, for evolutionary reasons all Souls must of course, at times, manifest themselves in the opposite gender in order for a very long evolutionary journey to occur which finally leads back to where all Souls started: their inherent androgyny. And, remember, that the 'ego' itself is but a reflection of the Soul: it does not, and cannot, exist of itself. The wave manifests from the ocean: it cannot exist of itself. So the ego of any Soul then reflects the gender of the Soul. Example: the Soul of John preponderantly chose to be female most of the time in its prior lives due to the fact that his natal Pluto in his 4th and in opposition to his 10th house MOON. And, of course, his Pluto being conjunct his natal Vesta, with the North Node of Vesta also conjunct his natal Pluto, and Vesta itself. (Rad)

Awareness of Soul

The Soul is that which is 'aware' in any of us. Without the Soul there can be no ego that reflects the individual Soul in the first place. The ego in each of us is of course aware, but that awareness is, relatively speaking, limited. The limitations themselves are relative to the degree of evolution within the Soul itself. (Rad)

Awareness of Soul is only going to begin in later 3rd stage Individuated, accelerating as the Spiritual stages are reached. The definition of Spiritual stage is increasing conscious awareness of the Soul, thus it's not possible for it to exist consciously in earlier evolutionary stages. "Knowing" something and living it consciously are two different things. There could be exceptions – evolved people with a spiritual mission involving the physical – perhaps Gandhi. In general, no. The more one is living in the Soul the deeper the sense of alienation from all orientations other than that. One increasingly feels things they used to consider really important no longer matter as much. Growing awareness in everything except the Soul is temporary. (Steve)
All life events manifest as a reflection of the inner dynamics within all Souls. A Soul is aware of the circumstances of their life of course because they are living their life. The issue of being inwardly aware so as to know the dynamics within themself that are causing these circumstances is of course a matter of evolution of the Soul. How the phases between planets is actualized, the specific manifestation, is dependent on the individual context, reality, of any given Soul. (Rad)

Ego of the Soul
The ego of the Soul is within itself: the Soul, thus Pluto. (Rad)
The Soul has its own unique identity as created by the Source, or God. As such, it has its own ego that creates an image in the Soul of that unique identity. The awareness of that unique Soul identity is a function of evolution itself which finally leads to being self-aware, and has the evolved capacity, at some point, to objectify itself. The South and North Nodes of Pluto correlate to this ongoing evolutionary development of the Soul from within itself. The natal position of the current life Pluto simultaneously correlates to what the desires have been within the Soul for its own development, thus where it left off in those lives that have led to the current life, and the evolutionary intent for the current life for its evolution to proceed: the natural polarity point of that natal Pluto. The South Node of Pluto, by its own house and sign location, aspects to it from other planets, and aspects to its natural planetary ruler, all correlates to archetypes and dynamics that the Soul has used to develop itself, evolve itself, relative to its core desires for its evolution that is symbolized in the natal position of Pluto itself. The North Node of Pluto correlates to how and why the Soul evolves itself from within itself: what it needs to continue in its evolution. Other planets that aspect this North Node are archetypes that correlate to this ongoing evolution of the Soul within itself.
In order for all these internal dynamics within the Soul itself that correlate to its own ongoing evolution it must project or externalize itself through the creation of forms: the human form. This Natural Law or principle is the same as what we call the Source of All Things, or God, projecting and externalizing itself in the form of what we call CREATION. What we call God does this in order to know itself in all of these forms in the totality of Creation. So too with the individual Soul. The Soul needs to project or externalize

itself in order to know itself, to objectify itself. So the Soul projects and externalizes itself from life to life in the form of the lifetimes that it lives that are all finite. The Soul itself is infinite just as God itself is infinite. Each finite life that the Soul projects from within itself, just as God projects each individualized Soul from within itself, reflects and symbolizes the core desires from within the Soul that reflect its own ongoing evolutionary desires to evolve.

As a result of this projection from life to life we then have the birth charts for each of those lives that reflect the finite forms that the Soul creates in order to effect its ongoing evolution. In each of these finite forms that the Soul creates it thus creates a consciousness that has its own subjective self-awareness that we call the ego or 'I.' And of course that subjective ego, the egocentric structure, is a projection from the Soul itself in order to know itself relative to the finite form it has created in each life that reflects its ongoing evolutionary needs and requirements. The subjective 'I' or ego that is created in each life by the Soul of course is the archetype of the Moon. The evolutionary journey of the Soul through time is thus symbolized through all the different finite forms or lives that it creates that are determined by its evolutionary needs and desires. And it is each of these finite lives that the Soul creates that the birth chart correlates too. And in each of those lives the finite ego does indeed 'die,' just as the body dies. Yet the memories of each life are sustained and live on within the Soul itself. And it is these ongoing evolutionary experiences from life to life that are the ongoing determinant and cause for yet another life. In the end, the whole chart, in any given life, correlates with the inner identity or 'ego' of the Soul as it evolves through time and space. (Rad)

FIG 1   Chakra Correlations diagram

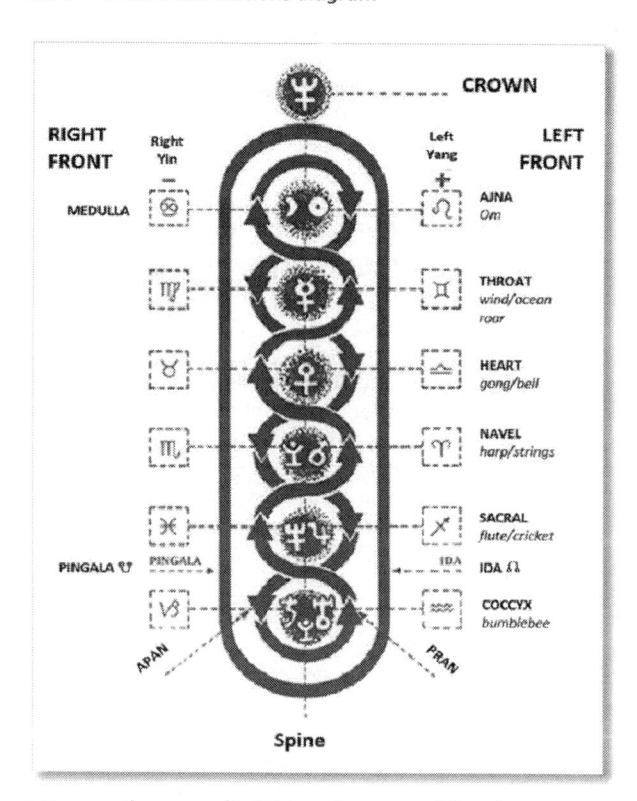

The Soul has its own 'identity,' or ego. This identity or 'ego' is not the same as the ego that the Soul creates in any given life on places like Earth. The ego of the Soul is one's 'eternal' identity. An easy way for any of us to understand this occurs when we dream. Obviously when we dream we are not identified with our subjective ego. After all we are 'asleep.' The subjective ego has temporarily 'dissolved' back into the Soul when we sleep. So the question becomes 'who and what is doing the dreaming?' Obviously it can only be the Soul, with its own ego that thus allows the Soul to know itself as a Soul that is eternal. Another way to validate the same thing occurs when we sometimes wake up from sleeping and cannot immediately 'remember' who we are: the current subjective ego, the "I," of this life. It takes some effort to actually remember the subjective I when this occurs. So, again, the question becomes "who and what must make the effort to remember the subjective 'I' of the current life?" Obviously it can only be our Soul. (Rad)

The Soul's orientation to the ego reflects the desire nature of that Soul – the experiences the Soul desires are reflected within the ego/personality. Most of us, most of the time, identify wholly as the personality, a personality that "has a Soul" – that's our frame. That is the source of the confusion since in reality I am a Soul who has created a personality/ego for a limited duration of time. It comes down to slowly and steadily breaking the hypnotized state of believing I am the ego – that I am the wave, not the Ocean. The more I come to experience myself as Ocean not wave, the more all of this makes sense. (Steve)

Let's look at the relationship between the 4th house and 8th house. 4th house is what we call the ego, the personality. In reality the ego is created by the Soul as part of its own evolutionary process. Many of us may know the fact that the ego is not what it appears to be, that it's actually a creation of the Soul and can't exist apart from the Soul. Very few of us live from an emotional reality where we perceive ourselves day to day as the Soul. Even though we know the intellectual fact we are, we operate emotionally from the reality of the 4th house, as if the ego is an ultimate reality. The ego of the Soul IS the Soul. It's not anything outside of that Soul. Here we look at the relationship between 12th house and 8th house, to parallel the relationship between 8th and 4th. 12th house is the ultimate reality, the source of all created realities. The Soul may know that as information, but very few Souls on earth live from a consistent emotional reality of that place, that ultimate oneness. The Soul's emotional reality, sense of self, is rooted in I am this Soul. In reality everything is unified and comes from The One – 12th house – and there is no separation between any two Souls. In actuality Souls experience themselves as separate and distinct from other Souls, even if they also see that all Souls are one, just as we see ourselves as separate and distinct from all other humans. That is the ego of the Soul – its sense of Who I Am as distinct from all other Souls. (Steve)

Ego identities created by the Soul
The ego is created by the Soul: it is not separate from it. The ego cannot ever 'get in the way' of the Soul because the Soul is the origin of the ego in the first place. If there are dysfunctional ways or issues, hanging on to insecurities, then these issues originate from within the Soul that is then reflected in the egocentric structures that it creates for itself. (Rad)

The ego does not exist of itself as something separate from the Soul. The ego in all of us is a reflection of what is going on within any of our Souls, so the issue is never one of bringing the ego in line with the Soul. (Rad)

The ego embodies the illusion of being separate and distinct from anything else, the wave as separated from the ocean – being such illusion maintained by the desire to separate – and that, then, the ego the Soul creates from life to life reflects the extent up to which this illusion and the desire that supports this illusion, are operating. (Gonzalo)

The Soul can use the ego to further its separating desires or as a way of returning to the source, but ultimately it is the desire (returning or separating) of the Soul that determines how the ego will be directed – the Soul is the driver so to speak, and the ego is the vehicle that follows what the Soul decides based on where it is at in its evolutionary journey, and as we evolve we decide to use our vehicle to go home. (Heather)

Like the vast majority of we humans, you [Jana] are looking at this from the perspective that "you" are the ego Jana, and that this Jana is distinct from all the other egos "your Soul" has ever created, and that Jana is also separate from the Soul who created Jana. Reality is who you are has never been Jana the ego. You have always been the Soul who created Jana the ego. Whether you experience that or not, it is still true. We can believe we are separate (and we do) but that doesn't make it so. It's not so much the ego "will identify increasingly more with Soul" as the ego will increasingly realize it never was who it thought it was in the first place, a separate ego. It will see that all along it has always been only the Soul. When the ego Jana identifies as Soul, it will realize it is one and the same as all the other egos that this Soul has ever created. They have all been steps along the way in the evolution of that Soul. Within that Soul all the memories from every ego/lifetime that Soul has ever experienced are stored. The metaphor of the wave and the ocean explains this. There are many waves on top of the ocean. Each wave separates from the ocean at some point, and ultimately "dies" when it crashes on a beach and rejoins the ocean. Jana believes she is a wave, distinct from all the other waves, when in reality she and all the other waves are only the ocean. The ocean represents the Soul, the waves represent the egos the Soul has created. As soon as a wave rejoins the ocean there is no issue of each individual wave having to remember it is the ocean – there is no more wave, only ocean. To match the metaphor, the ocean contains the memory of every wave it has ever created, and all that each wave ever experienced. (Steve)

Soul's memory of the ego
The memory of the ego is necessary for the Soul, for it is the memory of the ego that allows the Soul to not only review the life that has just been lived, but also serves as the basis for the next life to be lived, relative to the continuing evolution of the Soul itself. In each life we all pick up where we left off before. Thus, this memory of the ego in each life serves as the causative factor of what type of egocentric structure the Soul needs to create in the next life. In essence, it is the memory of the ego that the Soul draws upon, the 'images' contained therein, that serve as the basis of the next ego that the Soul needs to generate in each successive life to promote its ongoing evolution. Astrologically speaking, this is symbolized by Pluto (the Soul), and the South and North Nodes of the Moon. The South Node of the Moon correlates to the Soul's prior egocentric 'memories,' which determine the natal placement of the Moon in each life – the current ego. The North Node of the Moon correlates to the evolving ego of the Soul – the nature and types of inner and outer experiences that the Soul needs, desires, in order to facilitate its ongoing evolution. In turn this will then constitute the 'new' egocentric memories, images, that the Soul will draw upon when a life has been lived and terminated at physical 'death.' Most of us are aware that the Moon also correlates to one's family of origin in any given life. It should be clear then that upon the 'death' of the physical body, the Soul 'goes to' the astral plane, and meets again important family members and others close to the Soul. This is also why, for many Souls, we continue to meet again those family members upon rebirth into yet another physical life on places like Earth. It is the memory of the ego now combined with the memory of family that is the determinant in this phenomenon. And this phenomenon is sustained until there is no longer any evolutionary or karmic need to sustain such relationships. (JWG)

Soul's resistance to change
The Soul creates egocentric structures in each life that is orientated to phenomenal reality in such a way that reflects the ongoing evolutionary intentions, desires, of the Soul. The resistance to change is rooted in the need for security where security is a function of being self-consistent. Self-consistency is a function of the past that defines each present moment. The 'future' is an 'unknown' from the point of view of the past equaling the present 'moment.' As such it is inherently perceived by the Soul as something insecure because it is not a known fact. As a result of this most Souls then 'project' their past into the future in order to feel secure: self-consistent. As a result this is why most Soul's keep repeating their pasts over and over, making only minimal change in each life in order to grow at all: evolve. And yet all Souls must evolve. And they evolve as a function of desire for it is the dual desire nature of the Soul, as created by God/ess, that dictates this evolution. As a result we then have a 'future' because of the determinant of evolution: the dual desires inherent to all Souls. As Souls naturally evolve they do come to a place in which their sense of personal

identification is no longer within the egos that they create from life to life. Rather the Soul comes to a place where the sense of personal identification is that with which created the Souls in the first place: God/ess. Once this happens the entire sense of what constitutes security utterly changes. And it changes to being in the hands of its origin: God/ess. Once this happens then the 'resistance' to change, to evolve, simply ends. (Rad)

Souls blocking their inherent nature

In almost all of the cases (that I know of) in which this blocking of their consciousness, their natural natures, has happened from within the Soul itself it has been caused by a lifetime, or lifetimes, in which some major traumatic circumstance has happened BECAUSE OF THEIR INHERENT NATURES AND THE CONSCIOUSNESS THEREIN. And because of the nature of the trauma(s) this has caused the Soul such great fear in terms of being who they inherently are, their natures and consciousness, that they have then 'compensated' for their natures by 'hiding' from the world, the consensus world, who they actually are. And in that act of hiding trying to appear 'normal' from the point of view of the consensus world.

When this happens from the point of view of Evolution it is as if they come to a standstill, and are simply marking time. Psychologically speaking, they create the conditions for depression and the sense of simply going through the motions of life itself. Others will typically keep themselves overly busy with doing one thing after the other in order to avoid as best they can the deep inner pit of loneliness, and existential void, and no real sense of meaning or purpose of a lasting nature. Others can degenerate into a life of escapism in a variety of forms including drugs and alcohol. Compensation as a dynamic in astrology correlations is Jupiter, Sagittarius, and the 9th house. Trauma of course is Uranus, the 11th house, and Aquarius.

All Souls have karma unless a Soul is in the most advanced states of Evolution such as an Avatar. There is no way of being able to look at any birth chart and know if a person is 'fully awake' or not. One must do the traditional astrology thing which is to make observations of the person. Example, the archetypal embodiment of the skipped steps that have been caused by compensating for who they actually are due to past life traumas that have caused the Soul to hide. There are many possible astrological signatures that can correlate with this situation but the Sagittarius, 9th house, Jupiter, Uranus, 11th house, Aquarius archetypes will be implicated in all cases. (Rad)

Spiritual bypass

As I understand it, EA teaches that processing life experiences through the emotional body is evolutionary precisely because it enables the Soul to fully EXPERIENCE whatever experiences are the natural consequence of its desires and choices. If the Soul does not fully EXPERIENCE that which its choices have generated, then it will not truly know in a deep way the consequences of those desires and choices, and will not be able to integrate and learn from these experiences, and thus to make new choices and evolve. In some sense spiritual bypass is a kind of delaying tactic – the Soul resisting coming to terms with the natural consequences of its own desires and choices (though at the ego level this can simply look like a person avoiding painful emotions using Jesus or altered states or "ascension" or whatever). In this way the Soul keeps itself in a kind of evolutionary limbo in that it cannot truly exhaust separating desires since it is ever delayed from truly feeling what those desires have resulted in, and therefore must repeat them (in a sense wilfully failing to learn from history). You can see how this can correlate with skipped steps in some Souls.

Spiritual bypass to me also relates to the control orientation most of us carry and to the lack of trust in natural law that has been learned on this planet. Evolution is a natural process of the universe – we can trust it to happen and we do not have to "make" it happen, so much as let it happen. As Jeffrey taught, the Water Trinity shows involution in that Spirit/Neptune differentiates to Soul/Scorpio differentiates to Ego/Cancer; and also shows that evolution occurs naturally in the natural direction of the zodiac of the shift in conscious identification from Ego/Cancer to Soul/Scorpio to Spirit/Pisces. I find in my work that when people are able to experience their experience through the emotional body (Cancer/Moon), such a full experience naturally eventually leads them (over a period of minutes or lifetimes) to a desire to understand and transform the deeper unconscious patterns and/or Soul history (both Scorpio/Pluto) that has led to the given emotional experience. I don't need to try to push this inquiry in any way, it is the natural result of deeply experienced emotion, it is just what happens when we get out of the way and feel. And then I have also found that when people start to work at this deeper level, then also very naturally begin (again, whether in this lifetime or later) to experience their own encounters with Source (Pisces/Neptune), however this may manifest as appropriate to their perceptual capacities. The water naturally returns to the sea. So to me it is not so much about energy releasing or other particular things as much as it is about having a natural experience that leads to new understanding and choices (and thus new experiences) that eventually exhaust separating desires and leave only the desire to return to Source.

If we stay with the Water Trinity, then spiritual bypassing can be seen as an attempt to "bypass" the emotions (Cancer) and critically the step of self-confrontation and transformation (Scorpio) – after all that is really hard. But of course natural law doesn't work that way and what I would say is actually happening is that the Soul is actually going in the involutionary (clockwise) direction on the wheel, trying to escape to a regressive experience of preconsciousness rather like the womb (Pisces), so as not to feel the pain of emotion (Cancer). In therapy this is sometimes called the "flight into health." To me it exemplifies the issue of trines in that as Jeffrey taught they can make it "easy" to be conscious and cooperative with evolution but they can also make it "easy" to resist it. Regarding evolutionary states and spiritual bypass, I have personally encountered bypass in all three of the main stages. At

Consensus stages I often see it as "religious bypass" – people avoiding emotions by logging into pre-digested and pat religious answers (eg I don't want to feel grief about Sandy Hook, so I'll just blame it on schools not having Christian prayer every morning; or we don't want to feel the pain of Katrina so let's just blame it on the gays). At Individuated stages I often see it as "science bypass" or "political bypass" – people avoiding emotions by logging into political causes or sophisticated explanations of the aspects of experience they are avoiding. "Psychology bypass" also happens and a lot of insight-oriented psychotherapy does this, avoiding direct experience of emotions by explaining them. And then in the Spiritual stages and the later Individuated stages I often see it as the kind of "spiritual bypass" where people prefer to log in to particular states of consciousness or metaphysical frameworks and log out of the direct and lived experience of their emotions. But to me in general bypassing the emotional body is essentially resisting evolution, which Souls at any stage in consciousness can do.

Regarding whether the kind of mental/head-based quality that typifies the specific bypass (of preferring to dwell in primordial states), means that such individuals may be in the Individuated states vs Spiritual states, I would say that could be occurring in a Spiritual or an Individuated Soul. The difference would have to be discerned by understanding the nature of the Soul's motivation for its practice in the first place. I have seen some practitioners of these paths and techniques who are (mostly) seeking to reinforce their own sense of themselves and their specialness and ability to "achieve" and use spiritual practice as the vehicle for this (Individuated); and I have seen some who are (mostly) truly seeking to unite themselves with Source (Spiritual). And at both of these levels, I have seen Souls periodically fall into the trap of using these paths to dissociate from their emotions, or even live an entire lifetime in that kind of resistance.

Considering how to help Souls in this dynamic, as mentioned we are in the territory of Pisces/Neptune, and as EA teaches this archetype is about Source and spiritual realization, but at the same time also the process by which we "deify" all sorts of people and things and states of consciousness as if they themselves are Source or are spiritual realization, and then we experience eventual disillusionment when this turns out not to be true. In this context for me it has rarely worked to point out to people they that are in spiritual bypass; those rose-coloured glasses are pretty sticky and if you get Virgo/Mercury discerning and analytical they get even more Pisces/Neptune cloudy and ascending. Unless they are somehow really ready to hear it and to experience it as real, it is just a mental thing to say it, like telling an active addict that he or she has an addiction.

What I do find helpful in many situations is to assist the person in fully experiencing whatever they are experiencing, to feel what it is like to be where they are. In this case of bypass, to feel what it is like to view or use access to this primordial state as the "answer." What does that feel like, what is the impact of that in life? After all, the desire to prematurely transcend and resist the evolutionary process is itself also a desire that the Soul has created and wants to experience. Assisting the Soul to fully experience the full experience that is a consequence of that desire (whether it is the 'high' states, the frequent interpersonal isolation that results, the tendency to judge the 'unenlightened,' the pressure to maintain one's 'enlightenment,' whatever the full experience is), and eventually it will naturally include the experience of disillusionment, and the felt sense of disillusionment – feeling it, not just being told it by someone else – the disappointment, the grief, the anger – is what naturally leads the Soul to truly release the desire for bypass and move on to whatever is next for it. Just realizing it cognitively or because someone points it out typically means that although today's bypass strategy may be dropped, the desire will still exist in the Soul to do it and it will find another way to bypass (kind of like switching addictions from one substance/behavior to another when the deeper desires driving the addiction have not been addressed and released, only deferred). (Jason)

All that you [Jason] have said/shared about this is exactly right. We need to remember/understand that the Pisces, Cancer, Scorpio trinity, the Source, the Soul, and the ego it manifests, all emanate from the Water archetype. Water is of course pure emotion. The non-dual state, the desire for, is itself an emotional delusion that is impossible to achieve, or arrive at, relative to consciousness in the Soul in a human form. A Soul relative to certain 'spiritual' methodologies can indeed arrive at some sort of 'transcendental' state but that state always, cause and effect, snaps back to a 'normal' state of consciousness. Even in these naturally transcendental states or 'cosmic consciousness' the very essence of such a consciousness or state is EMOTIONAL: the emotion or feeling within that state of consciousness as it 'perceives' the various realities of those states. That perception leads to an emotional state as it 'reacts' to the nature of the perception itself. The need of all of our Souls to directly feel the nature of our emotions as they relate to any possible experience created by the Soul for its own evolutionary needs is the bottom line truth. For those who are able to create within themselves the various degrees of cosmic consciousness all of them will report being in a temporary state of ecstasy. Ecstasy of course is an experience of pure emotion.

When Souls align themselves with various religious and/or spiritual teachings that teach it is important, necessary even, to control or repress the emotions in order for 'x' spiritual state to be realized these Souls are reacting to the nature of their own emotional lives. In essence, they are running from those emotional lives for their own reasons but all reasons that lead to this running lead to repressing the very nature of the emotions themselves. In so doing they are repressing that which is NATURAL AND NECESSARY FOR THE SOUL TO EXPERIENCE for its own evolutionary reasons. If we accept that God/ess is the origin of all things then wherein lies the origin of emotions? And for what reasons? So for Souls who do orientate to these teachings that require repression, to 'transcend' them which means repressing them, the very act of repression then magnifies and distorts those natural emotions within the consciousness of those that do so. When anything that is natural is repressed for whatever reasons ANGER IS THE DIRECT RESULT: a natural inner anger. When this occurs all too often the Soul then feels itself to be a victim of life, a victim even to their own emotions which continue to live on, to exist, despite the repression. When this natural anger is then linked to the created consciousness of feeling to be a victim first to itself, then to others, this becomes the causative basis of lashing out at anyone the Souls feels 'victimized' by. In a 'religious' and/or 'spiritual' context this then is the cause of all the horror stories we are all too familiar with: the priest abusing boys, the 'guru' who is having intercourse with some devote, and so on.

As JWG and others have taught the liberation of the Soul does indeed take place through and because of the emotional body for the reasons that Jason [above] had correctly pointed out. A story that I just remembered about this is the story of one of Yogananda's chief disciples, a women who was essential for Yogananda and his work. She developed a terminal medical condition in which Yogananda interceded upon by way of asking God/ess to keep her alive because of the critical nature of her tasks helping his work. She lived ten years longer as a result. And upon her final transition, upon the moment of the very last breath, her final words were: "TOO MUCH JOY." (Rad)

The disciple that Rad is referencing in this post is Sri Gyanamata and the book is called "God Alone: Life and Letters of a Saint." This is a wonderful book which I highly recommend as it gives great perspective about how to emotionally heal and grow without any "spiritual bypass." (Deva)

Since deep emotional processing is the heart of the work I do, what I have found is that we simply cannot easily move through our own emotional defenses. Spiritual systems that are 'transcendent' in nature often collude with the already dissociative defence in place. Yes it is quite easy for already dissociated, fragmented psyches (ie all of us) to access "other/higher worlds" since so many of our parts already reside there!! The difficult part is unlocking the trauma that caused the fragmentation in the first place and then real Soul retrieval can happen. Re-living, ie descending into the original terror, wound, fear, horror, pain (fill in the blank) opens up not only the complex formed around such an event, but the defences that were crystallized also. These defences involved ALL levels of the being, etheric/physical body, emotional body, mental body and spiritual body. ALL these bodies need to become congruent in order for full integration to happen and each one can hold their own separate defence. One body is not superior to another despite what patriarchal bias tells us. Personally I trust the veracity and truth of emotion before I trust the machinations of head, my personal bias. Sharing a quote from R.D. Laing:

"When our personal worlds are rediscovered and allowed to reconstitute themselves, we first discover a shambles. Bodies half-dead; genitals dissociated from heart; heart severed from head; heads dissociated from genitals… Without inner unity, with just enough sense of continuity to clutch at identity: the current idolatry. Torn, body, mind and spirit, by inner contradictions, pulled in different directions, Man cut off from his own mind, cut off equally from his own body – a half-crazed creature in a mad world."

I perceive that we compensate for all these contradictions and dissociations largely with our mental prowess, using it to repress the true reality that lies underneath. This is why, collectively, we are so mentally defended because under those defences lies a much different, initially terrifying inner world, where our compensated identity is threatened to come apart, but when one has the courage to go there the reward is integration and coherence. (Patricia)

The non-dual state

We need to remember/understand that the Pisces, Cancer, Scorpio trinity, the Source, the Soul, and the ego it manifests, all emanate from the Water archetype. Water is of course pure emotion. The non-dual state, the desire for, is itself an emotional delusion that is impossible to achieve, or arrive at, relative to consciousness in the Soul in a human form. A Soul relative to certain 'spiritual' methodologies can indeed arrive at some sort of 'transcendental' state but that state always, cause and effect, snaps back to a 'normal' state of consciousness. Even in these naturally transcendental states or 'cosmic consciousness' the very essence of such a consciousness or state is EMOTIONAL: the emotion or feeling within that state of consciousness as it 'perceives' the various realities of those states. That perception leads to an emotional state as it 'reacts' to the nature of the perception itself. The need of all of our Souls to directly feel the nature of our emotions as they relate to any possible experience created by the Soul for its own evolutionary needs is the bottom line truth. For those who are able to create within themselves the various degrees of cosmic consciousness all of them will report being in a temporary state of ecstasy. Ecstasy of course is an experience of pure emotion.

When Souls align themselves with various religious and/or spiritual teachings that teach it is important, necessary even, to control or repress the emotions in order for 'x' spiritual state to be realized these Souls are reacting to the nature of their own emotional lives. In essence, they are running from those emotional lives for their own reasons but all reasons that lead to this running lead to repressing the very nature of the emotions themselves. In so doing they are repressing that which is NATURAL AND NECESSARY FOR THE SOUL TO EXPERIENCE for its own evolutionary reasons. If we accept that God/ess is the origin of all things then wherein lies the origin of emotions? And for what reasons? So for Souls who do orientate to these teachings that require repression, to 'transcend' them which means repressing them, the very act of repression then magnifies and distorts those natural emotions within the consciousness of those that do so. When anything that is natural is repressed for whatever reasons ANGER IS THE DIRECT RESULT: a natural inner anger. When this occurs all too often the Soul then feels itself to be a victim of life, a victim even to their own emotions which continue to live on, to exist, despite the repression. When this natural anger is then linked to the created consciousness of feeling to be a victim first to itself, then to others, this becomes the causative basis of lashing out at anyone the

Souls feels 'victimized' by. In a 'religious' and/or 'spiritual' context this then is the cause of all the horror stories we are all too familiar with: the priest abusing boys, the 'guru' who is having intercourse with some devote, and so on. (Rad)

Deepening the awareness of self as Soul
Pluto and Mars indicating a primary lifetime means more evolutionary work is intended in that life. Since the end intention of evolutionary work is to deepen the awareness of self as Soul, to the extent the intended lessons are learned, that can deepen the knowing of self as Soul. It is more possible or probable in a primary life only because the intention of that life is to make that Soul do certain necessary work. Whether primary or secondary life, a Soul is still in the evolutionary station it is in. The issue is how much evolutionary advancement is intended. There are other indicators of that besides Mars/Pluto, including the number of aspects Pluto makes to other planets, number of planets in the birth chart that are retrograde. (Steve)

Looking into the Souls of others
One of the reasons Wolf "got the job" to bring EA forth around the planet is because his Soul is of a level of evolution at which it sees directly into the Souls of others, discerning their actual natures, life lessons, past and future. He did not need a birth chart to see someone's evolutionary signature. He is not the only person with that capacity. But it is a very low percentage of humans (probably 5% or less). This is a potential capacity in all Souls, to see much more of the totality of what is in front of them. Unless the person reading the chart has the capacity to peer directly into the Soul, you cannot know with absolute certainty the actual nature of a physical condition. This person could then refine and tweak the system, to get the conclusions reached from the chart to match the conclusions reached from peering directly into a person's Soul.

A major point of the development of EA was to create a way that those of us who cannot directly see into the Soul (most of us) can see the workings and intentions of the Soul through the birth chart, by understanding the EA system. Wolf called this a gift to humanity from Yogananda's guru Sri Yukteswar, who he called a galactic astrologer. The Soul is beyond time and space. It's a matter of tuning in to the unique vibration of that particular Soul. Souls who have that capacity, those who have aligned themselves with doing God/Goddess intent, do not abuse that capability. They know by what feels right when they are "supposed to" look into a Soul, and when they are violating Natural Law by doing so. A pure impulse would be to simply desire to align self ever more with doing God/Goddess intent. Then that ability, the desire to be able to see into the past of the Souls in front of it, would either manifest over time, or not. The knowing would be, if it appears, a gift given to assist with the God/dess intended work. If it does not, it is simply not part of what is intended for the present time (or lifetime).

Another way this is explained in the east is "phenomena, phenomena, phenomena," which means, these powers, skills, abilities are not the end goal in themselves. When looked at in those ways, they become yet another separating desire that must be released from. The idea is to focus on the root, not the manifestation. The goal is to align the sense of self-identification with the Soul not personality. As that is progressively accomplished, possibly over thousands of years, the rest simply happens. You can't isolate it to specific practices in a single lifetime. If you are doing these practices with an end in mind, to attain an ability like past life viewing, you have an agenda, a desired outcome. What happens if you've done the practices intently for 60 years, your life is ending, and the ability has not appeared? We have to be prepared to spend 10, 20, 30 lifetimes if necessary. Not seeking an ability, but seeking to align ourselves ever more with Soul and divine intent. That is much closer to the way things really work. (Steve)

As I understand it, this capacity is really a function of evolution/expansion of consciousness itself, and one that is the development of intuition as Yogananda described it in the Gita. One can be "aligned with doing God/Goddess intent" and still not have that capacity. As far as Wolf originally explained it (and I understand it), this can BEGIN to happen sometime in 1st stage Spiritual, and then this increases as one's consciousness expands, to the point that someone like Krishna, Jesus, Yogananda, could see ALL the lifetimes of the Souls they helped. Within this, of course, effort must be made to expand one's consciousness, which results, then, in increasing degrees of this capacity; ie, from seeing one or two pertinent lifetimes, to being able to see all, but only, those lifetimes that are pertinent to the current life, to ALL lifetimes that the Avatars can see. Still, as always, the underlying "condition" for any capacity is simply to desire God first, to seek God first, then one develops/is given the capacities necessary for their own evolution and their particular "mission" on behalf of and as defined by God'dess. (Adina)

Special capacity to see past lives of any Soul
Unless any given Soul has the capacity, inner capacity, to actually see into and know about the history, past lives, of any Soul then those who project that this or that Soul has been so and so it remains to be a projection only. And, sadly, astrologers in general can 'make the case' using whatever astrological symbols necessary to make that case. Nonetheless making the case without actually inwardly knowing remains to be pure speculation and projection only. EA is much more about the ongoing evolutionary dynamics of any given Soul, and why those dynamics in order to understand the next steps in the Soul's journey. It is not really necessary to know 'who's who' in order to do that. At times on this message board I have done that only to help those who are learning EA through the various subjects/threads. At those rare times I have done that it has been for specific reasons that have helped the students understand those prior life dynamics that have 'set up' the current life being studied. [Example] The claim that the royal baby, George Alexander Louis, was Princess Diana is merely a projection. There is no basis in actual reality for this to be true. (Rad)

Soul projecting from within itself

The ultimate projector is the Source itself which is, of course, the origin of all things that have been Created and projected from within Itself. This phenomena, then, of projection is reflected in all that has been Created including the Soul that itself can project from within itself anything upon that Creation. (Rad)

Life purpose of the Soul

Every Soul, relative to its evolutionary conditions, has a true life purpose that is consistent with its ongoing evolutionary needs. The entire paradigm of the 10th, Saturn, Capricorn, 2nd, Taurus, Venus, the 6th, Mercury, and Virgo correlate to life purpose as expressed through the agency of one's work, or career. When the Soul begins to evolve into the Spiritual State then the Soul is inwardly and progressively attuned to the consciousness we call the Source, or God/ess. As such, these Souls will desire to do work that they feel inwardly called to do from that Source. The inner degree of awareness, evolution, within the Spiritual stage will correspond to not only the nature of what that is, but also that the nature of that work in every way is being consciously directed by that Source. The Souls who have reached the point in evolution in which the center of gravity has finally shifted from the subjective ego that the Soul creates to the Soul itself. At that point there no longer is any 'personal identification' with that work other than consciously cooperating with the inner directions from the Source to do that work. (Rad)

Soul evolving via polarity points of the planets

The nature of Life is that it evolves. It is ingrained. The way that life evolves is by going to its polarity point. It is not Pluto alone that has a polarity point. In his Pluto Volume 2 Relationships book, Jeffrey detailed in the chapters about Mars and Venus what moving towards the polarity of the sign that Mars and Venus are in looks like. The same principle applies to all the planets and symbols in our charts. It's just the way life works. If it makes more sense to you, you could visualize it as it is the polarity point that is moving forward through the zodiac over time in its evolutionary track. Since the planet must be 180 degrees apart from its polarity point, the planet is getting dragged forward by its advancing polarity point. This is also indicated in progressed charts, which show how the evolutionary intentions are unfolding OVER TIME. Thus the polarity point progresses also. It does come down to desire nature. At a certain point we get sick of something we previously loved. The feeling becomes "been there done that." This too is part of how life is constructed. (The EA material on the Cycles of Phases and Aspects is very relevant to this.) The Soul is not working on only one separating desire in a lifetime. The chart is a map of our desire nature. When you see grand crosses or a lot of squares or oppositions or a number of skipped steps, you are typically looking at the map of a Soul with conflicting simultaneous desires, wanting to go in multiple incompatible directions at the same time. The Pluto polarity point is the most significant polarity point as it tracks the evolution of the Soul itself. (Steve)

In NO conditions within the birth chart does any polarity point apply other than the polarity point of Pluto that needs to be consciously embraced, desire, for the evolution of the Soul to continue. And the one exception to that as Wolf taught is when the natal Pluto is conjunct the North Node. Even then there is a natural polarity within the sign that Pluto is in natally that NATURALLY is evolved towards via the Natural Law of polarities. And it is this natural polarity within the sign of a natal Pluto that then correlates to the evolution of an entire generation on Earth, and why any given generation is on Earth at any point in time. Every sign has a natural polarity within it that serves as the evolution within that sign because of its natural polarity. Thus, as the Soul evolves, makes a choice to evolve, which is symbolized by its opposite house and sign, and in the case of Pluto conjunct the North Node, by sign, and the location of the planetary ruler of that North Node, the aspects that it is making, this then CAUSES the rest of the entire birth chart to also evolve. It's automatic. So all those natural polarities that exist within the signs that the planets are in, in any birth chart, automatically are evolved towards. It is a function of evolution. The degree of evolution is dependent of course on the choices that the Soul makes in any given life relative to its core evolutionary signature which is symbolized by natal Pluto, the South Node and its planetary ruler, the polarity point of Pluto, and the North Node and its planetary ruler.

Every natal planet in a sign also has a natural polarity point by house, ie Mars in Scorpio in the 7th house would have a natural polarity of not only Taurus within Scorpio, but the 1st house as the polarity to the 7th. These natural polarity points by house are also automatically evolved towards once the Soul has made a choice to evolve which, again, is symbolized by the main EA paradigm. It is because these natural polarities within the signs and houses that naturally evolve, once the Soul has made a choice to evolve, that JWG never really taught about them. He did so because they do in fact naturally evolve in this way. He did this intentionally so as not to create such an overwhelming amount of evolutionary procedures that could potentially confuse students, but of course overwhelm any given client. It is enough to know the core EA paradigm, how it works, and how to apply it to one's life. The rest of these natural evolutionary points take care of themselves. Over his long career JWG only once, to my knowledge, taught about these other polarity points of the planets, and the houses they are in. And that is in a long workshop he held in Holland called "From Karma to Dharma." (Rad)

Split Soul – Same Soul – Twin Soul

Split Soul is also the same as 'Same Soul' which Wolf did write about in Pluto 2. Sometimes too this phenomenon can occur with what has been called 'Twin Souls' that Wolf also wrote about in Pluto 2. Another phenomenon that this can take place is through what in the East used to be called 'Bindu' yoga in which two people can sit face to face and penetrate each other's Souls through a continuous looking into each other's eyes: no looking away, constant penetration of one another through the eyes. For most this will reveal a variety of 'faces' that can reflect other lifetimes of each other's Souls. The problem here is that the various faces can begin to combine in such a way that the progressive images of the various faces become distorted, and can seem relatively frightening. And, lastly, this same type of 'yoga' can cause the phenomena when each of the two Souls have an evolved capacity to osmose other Souls within themselves, to absorb them within them self, in order to know that other Soul as the Soul knows itself. This occurs when such Souls have active desires to help other Souls with their life issues or problems. Thus, they can give to that other Soul exactly what they need because, in essence, by becoming an inner 'mirror' for that other Soul the Soul is then answering its own questions and/or issues through the other Soul that is serving as its mirror because of this evolved capacity. So when two Souls have this equal capacity, and have the same kind of desire nature to help other Souls, and they then face one another like in 'Bindu' yoga then this phenomena of mirroring one another can exist. A conscious choice by the Soul is made in the astral plane before the births occur on the Earth. (Rad)

Astrology, of itself, can never inform anyone about whether a Soul is a same Soul, or twin Soul. Only observation relative to the archetypal dynamics explained by JWG can make this determination. (Rad)

In answer to the question, is it possible that a mother and a child can be a Same Soul and a father and a son, the answer is yes. (Rad)

One cannot know if two people are the same Soul just from astrology alone. One must have other 'capacities' to know such things. (Rad)

It is never possible to determine from birth charts alone if they correlate to the Same Soul from life to life. It's just not possible. This can only be done through other means such as past life regressions if the Soul in question can actually remember their dates of birth, and more specifically, the actual time of birth. That's a big if. Other means can also include certain types of Souls who have the capacity to be able to see or determine such things. Some Souls also can remember within themselves their own prior lives independent of any means all together. In the two charts I had previously posted in another thread, this was a case of a family that I was very close to who had a child in which this determination was made. I am not at liberty of course to be able to go into very much detail because of the confidentiality of that family and their child. Second, the use of the geodetic astrological zones is used in conjunction with the cosmograms. Not just the cosmograms, or just the geodetic zones, but both. What has been presented on this message board about these methods is just the bare bones of them. In the case of chart 2 we can clearly see the direct correlation through the geodetic zones to the lives in that zone. It does not mean that because there is no actual cosmogram linked with the Ages and their sub-ages that that Soul did not have lives at that time in those zones. The actual cosmograms that can result from any birth chart linked with specific times and their respective astrological zones correlates to specific archetypes within the consciousness of the Soul that has been brought forwards into a current life for their own evolutionary needs and reasons. (Rad)

We were taught that in the higher evolutionary stages, starting in 1st stage Spiritual, that the Soul can split itself, have two incarnations going at the same time, to speed up its evolution. That each would be working with different elements of the Soul's desire nature. Lincoln was identified as being in 1st stage Spiritual. Yogananda said in the life prior to Lincoln, in fact, he was a yogi in India. So perhaps this explains the chronological overlap [with Obama]. (Steve)

Same Soul – Obama/Lindbergh

(Q) As JWG points out in Pluto 2, the essential reason for such Souls to 'split' is to facilitate and hasten its separating desires in its ultimate journey to reunite with source. The process of re-merging the disparate aspects of the Soul back into itself occurs at some point into a unified whole with one ego which can bridge its separate parts. There is a calling home, or Soul retrieval. In the case of Obama/Lincoln, the physical time/space reality is such that the two would never have a chance to meet. In the Obama/Lindberg case, although remote, there was a physical time/space overlap because Obama was about 12 when Lindbergh passed. Again, at some point the two must become one which means that one will have to release the desire for yet another separate body and the other must accept all into one, allowing the entirety of both to exist simultaneously. (Eric)

(A) No. The Soul is the determinant of this. It is not a matter of 'one' releasing its desire for another separate body/ego. When the Soul has no further evolutionary need for this split to occur then it will cease to manifest itself in different forms/egos that are existing in the same relative time/space continuum. (Rad)

(Q) So for the purpose of illustration, let's use the case of Obama again and progress the process to the point of initial reunification. Let's say that at some point in his life (maybe through meditation, a dream, indigenous ceremony, or some other event) the trumpets sound, the heavens part and so on, and the consciousness of his long lost separate identity reveals itself (apparently this is a possibility because by now the Soul has some familiarity in working beyond the perceived constraints of time/space). Having had this experience, must not the Soul seek to integrate the apparent separate identities into a composite whole? To move beyond its individual tracking in a way which allows the conditions for this merger to ripen?

(A) None of this is how the evolution of the Soul occurs when it splits itself into different egos/bodies in the relative same time/space continuum. It is not a matter of retrieving or recovering any long lost anything. The egos created by the Soul for the purposes of its accelerated evolution simply 'die' upon the death of the different bodies, no different than the ego dying when the Soul manifests itself in just one body from life to life. All the lessons learned relative to the ongoing evolutionary intent of the Soul by way of the ego(s) created reside within the Soul itself which then becomes the determinants of the next type of ego(s) that it will create in the next life or lives.

(Q) Since this hypothetical scenario is based on Obama and yet tied to the condition of same Souls, how about one more posit? Let's say that this Soul has Wolf as his personal astrologer (an interesting thought to consider). How would Wolf advise a Soul in this condition knowing the three individual charts? Certainly there exists a wealth of information tracking the past of the 'individuals.' And yet knowing the Souls intention to merge the separate parts, would his counsel towards the re-merging Souls evolution be based on the composite chart?

(A) The role of an EA astrologer when this phenomena occurs is to discuss with such a Soul why it has done this in the first place: its evolutionary reasons or necessities. And to do this only when it there is a necessary reason to do so in the first place. The composite charts have nothing to do with this at all.

(Q) Are you saying that it is not possible for this type of Soul (as one embodied aspect of itself) to have this type of Uranian infused experience (the memory of its 'other') at all? Or are you saying that the 'two' will typically not reunite into a new ego until both have croaked? Or possibilities exist?

(A) No, didn't say that at all. It is possible to have the memory of the 'other.' It's as possible for the 'two' to meet in any given life to not meeting at all with all kinds of relationship possibilities.

(Q) Specifically with the case of Lincoln/Obama, there is the fact of no time/space overlap. If Obama were to recognize himself as Lincoln, it could be internally (or externally) interpreted much the same as any Soul recognizing themself in a prior incarnation, without the split Soul phenomenon. On the other hand with the case of Lindbergh/Obama, if Obama were to recognize himself as Lindbergh, there would be the addition of the time/space overlap to contend with. This additional info would seem to inform and affect the Soul of the context of the relationship it has with itself. Would the composite of Lindbergh/Obama apply now in seeking to understand the relationship the Soul has with itself?

(A) Any given life of any Soul is simply an issue of actualizing whatever separating desires it has within itself that are all linked with the progressive evolution of the Soul. Thus, the 'relationship' the Soul has to itself is a function of the nature of whatever those separating desires have been, are, and will be. A variety of astrological methods from an EA point of view can then be used to understand this that all start with the natal charts in order to see the nature of those desires, and the reasons that they exist.

The knowing of who a Soul has been in other lifetimes cannot be determined by astrology, any kind of astrology, alone. One must have other capacities to be able to know these things. And when such a thing is known then, and only then, can the charts of various past life identities be compared through specifically Evolutionary Astrology. (Rad)

Same Soul – Romney/Greely, Paul Ryan/Hans Fritze

One thing I am called to offer is each life, and thus the natal chart that goes along with that life, is born as a result of where the Soul left off, ie its total desire nature. Each life is the next chapter in a series of many chapters. Therefore, once a past life connection is determined (through intuitive faculties, not astrology) the thing to examine would be the evolutionary purpose of the old lifetime and the kinds of choices that Soul made during that life. The total desire nature of the Soul leaving the last life is what then leads to the creation of the next life. For example: with Romney, it's abundantly clear that during the life of Greely that Soul only perpetuated a pre-existing karmic pattern (ie one that existed even before the life of Greely), thus deepening his separating desires. These desires were not exhausted; rather he made choices to further deepen these desires based on his resistance to growth. That has carried forth into the life of Romney whose chart reflects just that. (Ari)

Same Soul – phasal relationship from one life to the next

Greeley had an almost exact Moon/Saturn opposition in Gemini/Sagittarius and they both also square the Lunar Nodes. Romney comes into this life with Pluto in the 4th on the IC in opposition to Venus on the MC as well as Mars-Mercury in the 10th and Lucifer in the 4th squaring the Nodes involving the same exact archetypes of the Moon/Saturn squares to the Nodes of Greeley. Romney's Saturn lunar phase however is first quarter.

This is an indication as to how the phasal relationship between planets from life to life IS NOT A LITERAL continuation from one phase to the next (ie Greeley entering full phase Moon/Saturn, therefore Romney manifesting some phase after full), but rather a holistic representation of the ongoing phasal dynamics from life to life (as expressed in the above signatures). (Rad)

Two or more Souls – walk-in's – soul possession

EA does not deal with anything that is not true. Of course a Soul can be fragmented due to various traumatic causes but that does not correlate to having two or more Souls, or 'walk-ins.' If there were such a thing as 'walk-ins' human beings would have realized this long ago. The fact is this idea is a recent idea that came out somewhere in the 1980's if I remember right by I think someone called Ruth Montgomery. It's also true a Soul can be possessed but that does not correlate to 'walk-ins.' It does correlate with exactly what that means: Soul possession. (Rad)

Soul mates

JWG wrote in his second volume of Pluto, which is all about the evolutionary reasons and intentions for relationships, that Soul mates are as follows:

"Soul Mates are two people who have independently acted on their own desires a spiritual or transcendent reality and that the real purpose with the union of one another is to continue their individual spiritual development because of and through the relationship. In spiritual terms it is called the path of the householder in contrast to the path of the monastic. This does not mean that the two people are perfect. It does mean that both have embraced a transcendent or spiritual principle to guide both their individual lives, and their relationship. There is a common spiritual (philosophical) foundation upon which the relationship is built and based. As a result, there is a larger point of view to refer and defer to. This then allows for the unconditional love and support for one another as opposed to conditional love. Conditional love is one of the primary breeding grounds through which difficult karmic situations or conditions can be created. Unconditional love is one of the primary breeding grounds through which harmonious and or positive situations or conditions are created. Thus, true Soul Mates only have positive karma conditions or situations that are mutually supportive and beneficial to one another. The state of Soul Mates, evolutionarily speaking, is a condition that is evolved into from the most common of relationships: Karma Mates."

JWG also said in that book that relative to what he called 'relationship types' that true Soul Mates are also two Souls who have created an inner condition within themselves of being the self-reliant type. The self-reliant type of Soul is one who understands and actualizes their own needs within or upon themselves. Thus in a true Soul Mate relationship both are mutually self-reliant which then minimizes if not totally eliminates the 'projection' of need upon the other. The projection of needs is that which is one of the core dynamics in what he called Karma Mates. (Rad)

Soul – application of Uranus/Saturn to Pluto

The core role of the archetype of Uranus, relative to the Soul and Pluto, is to quicken or accelerate the evolution of the Soul itself. The archetype of Uranus correlates to the memories within the Soul that correlate to its prior lifetimes, as well as core blueprint, knowledge, that symbolizes its evolutionary future when that future is understood in the context of its past: Saturn. Thus, each Soul's history and future is unique to itself, yet, at the same time, all Souls of course share in the ultimate evolutionary future which is to return HOME to its origin: God, Neptune. The past is always defining the present moment as well as the future itself. The future and the past interface in each moment in time: the now. The Soul's evolutionary past is thus the determinant of its own unique moment, or life. In any given life of the Soul that past is familiar and known, thus secure. This is of course why most Souls evolve very slowly because that past is a known quantity. To move into any given moment that is completely free from that past is to create, for most Souls, a state of complete psychological and emotional insecurity. Thus, most Souls desire to stay connected to their past in order to feel psychologically secure and stable. Yet the Soul must evolve of course.

The next step in its evolution is symbolized by the EA paradigm that is the basis of the evolutionary journey of the Soul. Uranus correlates with the desire to quicken the evolutionary journey of the Soul, to accelerate it: 'to be free from the known.' To be free from the known is to emotionally and psychologically detach from the totality of all the lives that the Soul has lived which have brought it to its current lifetime. In this detachment the Soul is then able to observe itself in such a way as to be able to objectify all the inner dynamics within it that have been responsible for all that it has ever been and done. This objectification thus allows for a total knowledge of the Soul itself in such a way that the Soul by way of Uranus can then be free of that past because of the objectified knowledge of it. In this consciousness of detachment the Soul is then able by way of Uranus to determine what desires exist within it that it must act upon, desires to act upon, and the desires within it that no longer need to be acted upon: to liberate from them in this way. In this way the Soul is thus able to quicken or accelerate its evolution because it is no longer being conditioned by its past to the extent that that past is holding the Soul back from actualizing its next steps in evolution in the fastest or quickest way possible.

The polarity point of Pluto in any chart will be actualized to some extent by all Souls. Most Souls, as JWG taught, only make the most minimal efforts to do so because of the pull of their past: the familiar and the known. The natural first quarter square from the 8th and Scorpio to the 11th and Aquarius thus correlates to the 'crisis in action' relative to what paths to follow that allow for the quickest possible way for the Soul to evolve. The relationship of Uranus and Pluto is a generational one. It has a personal application in that the phase correlates to a variety of Uranian dynamics and archetypes that the Soul has been using for its ongoing evolutionary purposes that is then linked or understood in the context of the core EA paradigm, and how that core paradigm has been manifesting relative to the phase of Mars and Pluto. Freedom from the Known relative to Uranus correlates with the existing totality of any given Soul's reality: the entire past leading to the present life. It is a natural instinct, thus desire, within all of our Souls. As such it is operative in all Souls all the time. This is symbolized by Uranus. The totality of the Soul's reality, past and present, is of course Pluto itself.

Saturn correlates to the necessary structural reality of the Soul's consciousness in any given life where the nature of that structured consciousness is necessary so as to define the evolutionary impulse of the Soul from life to life in such a way that the Soul can then define the ongoing evolutionary impulse for itself in TIME. Thus, this structural definition of the evolutionary impulse by Saturn allows the Soul to integrate it in the context of the type of 'realities' that are necessary for that impulse to manifest in the way that the Soul so intends. The reality that the Soul thus creates relative to Saturn correlates with sequential lifetimes that all live: from life to life. And each life that the Soul creates through Saturn of course is given a subjective ego, Moon, the natural polarity of Saturn, so that the Soul can then focus itself as a subjective identity in each of these lives.

All of these lives in total, and as they are added to, correlates with the 'known' because they have been lived. Uranus is the archetype within our consciousness that desires to be 'free from the known:' to liberate from it. It is this archetypal desire, impulse, that then leads to Neptune and the root desire in all our Souls, Pluto, to go Home: to return back to the Origins Of All Things. All of this correlates to the inherent structure of consciousness in human form that we all share. Where Uranus is located by sign and house in any given chart, in any given life, correlates, among other things, to where, how, and why the 'quickening' evolutionary impulse that is rooted in the ultimate archetype of 'freedom from the known' is intended to manifest in any given life designed by the Soul itself. And this natural quickening impulse of course has its CONTEXT, the reasons for it, in all the lives that have preceded the current life. It is that preexisting context that thus correlates with the desire to 'be free from the known' where that known is the preexisting context itself. So, in essence, Uranus correlates with not only the ultimate impulse to be free, to go home to our Maker, but also the desire and impulse to accelerate our evolution in any given life relative to the preexisting context as defined or symbolized by the natal placement by house and sign of Uranus in any given life. (Rad)

As far as Uranus, I'd like to highlight a few other Uranian correlations – fracturing, trauma, and integration. One of the reasons we have such difficulty seeing the totality of this and trying to grasp the totality by reassembling the parts is because of the severe fracturing/fragmentation that has occurred in many many Souls. A major part of the de-conditioning process is realizing one's own fracturing, and going through the ongoing process of re-integrating self. It's like Humpty Dumpty who had a great fall and fractured into pieces that couldn't be put back together again. Except they can be put back together over time, step by step. And, the ongoing evolutionary process requires they must, little by little, over time through self-acceptance and patience. That is why we must de-condition, to see the greater totality of who we are and how we got to the place we now are. As that process proceeds, one finds the answers to the questions within self. You do see the parts. You don't quite know how to assemble them into a whole. That's because that's not something you do – it appears in flashes of intuition, of seeing the whole assembled, greater than its parts, beyond what can be perceived through left brain analysis. The value in pondering these questions is it keeps them active in your consciousness. That leads to the inevitable flashes of intuition. Those flashes are signs that the reintegration process is occurring. (Steve)

The nature of a question the Soul can ask

The nature of consciousness in human form desires, Soul, to know the 'why' of anything which starts with the nature of Creation itself. That root 'why' then sets in motion the desire to know everything about the nature of Creation, and everything within the totality of the manifested Creation. All questions that the Soul can ask all initially start within itself. The nature of a question, any question, involves a thought impulse within the brain: a causative action. This causative action in turn sets in motion a reaction to that action: the original impulse of a thought equaling a question is then reacted to by way of an answer to that thought. The nature of that answer of course is its own 'thought.' Thought by its very nature is defined by a word, or words. Whether those words are externally manifested or not does not matter because the internal process is what it is: thoughts that correlate to words. And this is of course necessary for all Souls in a time-based reality that is defined by inherent duality. This is how the consciousness in human form, Souls, comes to know and structurally organize the nature of the phenomenal reality that it finds itself within: the manifested Creation. (Rad)

Soul types, and religion

In terms of the time we live in now, the current yuga, there is no correlation between Soul types and religions. Religion as we understand that term now is for the consensus state. Religion in this sense, and time, correlates with 'belief.' Actual spirituality, naturally speaking, requires direct inner experience, thus 'knowing' versus believing anything. (Rad)

Soul worker

'....the true beauty of Evolutionary Astrology is.......to be a true SOUL WORKER, who desires to help any Soul understand their own unique, individual, evolutionary journey that ultimately takes them back to where they began: God.' (JWG)

Souls from other planets/star systems, eg Pleiades

Many Souls have other 'home planets' so to speak. And these types of Souls will NOT FEEL AT HOME ON EARTH. They feel a deep detachment and alienation from it. There are other 'home planets' from which they originally emanate, ie planets within the Pleiades like Hoova and the 'Dog Star.' It is important to know this for clients who are from other home planets so that they can understand the nature of their core alienation. (Rad)

The original home of the Daemon is the star system Sirius, in particular, Hoova. (Lucius)

Guilt within a Soul

The EA paradigm is only reflecting, symbolizing, life in its totality. Of itself it causes nothing. Each Soul is unique to itself. The choices each Soul makes, and the reasons for those choices, is also unique to each Soul. Relative to the archetype of atonement linked with guilt each Soul reacts, and thus makes choices, differently. The natural process leading any Soul to finally be free of needing to atone for whatever guilt, natural or unnatural, is different for all Souls. And, of course, much depends on the very nature of the causative factors for the guilt in the first place: the extent and extremity of it. If any given Soul were responsible, say, for the deaths of a great many people due to its negligence how long would it take for such a Soul to stop atoning for this fact? If it were you, how long do you think that might be? If it were someone else, how long do you think it may take for that person to be free of atoning for such a guilt? There is just no way to know. Each Soul is different. The key issue here is whether the guilt is natural or not. (Rad)

Natural guilt stays within the Soul forever

When guilt occurs to a Soul that is natural then the very nature of that guilt, the events that have caused it, will stay within the Soul forever. It does this so that the Soul will never repeat the causes or actions that lead to the natural guilt. On the other hand, any guilt that is within the Soul that is not natural can and will be expelled from the Soul at some point. Thus when dealing with clients it is very important to understand this critical difference which then dictates how a client dealt with relative to a therapeutic approach. (Rad)

Death, astral plane

When 'death' occurs in any given life, the ego that the Soul has created for a life then dissolves back into its origin: the Soul. Since both are energy, and energy cannot be destroyed, where does the Soul go upon the physical death of the body? In other words, where is it on an energetic level? Most of us have heard the words 'the astral plane,' or heaven and hell. Obviously, what these types of words refer to are other realities or planes of existence. There are in fact other energetic realities or planes of existence. Simply speaking, the astral plane is an energetic plane of existence that all Souls go to after the completion of a physical life on places like Earth. Energetically, this plane of existence is much less materially dense than places like Earth. After physical death the Soul 'goes to' the astral plane, in order to review the life that has just been lived, and to prepare for yet another birth on places like Earth. Upon the completion of a life on Earth, the 'ego' dissolves back into the Soul in such a way that the center of gravity within the consciousness, within the astral plane, is the Soul itself. For most folks living lives in the material plane we call Earth, the center of gravity of consciousness is the ego itself. This is why the vast majority of people living feel within themselves that they are 'separate' from everything else, the center of gravity being the egocentric "I." In the astral plane the center of gravity shifts to the Soul itself so that when death occurs in any given life the 'memory' of the ego of that life is sustained. (JWG)

Suicide

(Q) Do people who have taken their own life usually incarnate fairly soon after their death? I think I heard it on one of JWG's lecture tapes. (Henrik)
(A) Yes, that is what he taught, and also for those who have early life endings such a Soul will typically be reborn pretty quickly. (Rad)
(Q) Does the experience of "astral hell" leave an impression in the life that follows, for example, as having traumatic dreams or experiencing PTSD from birth? (JJ)
(A) It leaves an 'impression' within the Soul: a Soul memory. Upon returning into another life after this the resulting ego created by the Soul will not have a conscious memory of this in most cases. However, the memory within the Soul can manifest as specific types of dreams of that experience of being in the 'astral hell.' That same Soul memory can indeed create a form of PTSD relative to the ego created in the life following being in the astral hell. This is intentional so that the Soul does not commit suicide again. (Rad)
(Q) Does the act of unsuccessfully attempting suicide, one or more times, have an effect in the present life that makes it more difficult to move through what they are trying to avoid? I ask this because some times after someone tries to commit suicide, they may finally deal with the issue and move forward. Are there still negative consequences in this life or in the astral plane from making the attempt?
(A) This would depend on what you mean by 'negative consequences.' If you mean unsuccessful attempts lead to the 'astral hell' the answer is no. On the other hand the inner causes that have led to such attempts can create ongoing psychological difficulties if in fact the Soul has not made any efforts to resolve those existing causes: the reasons why, and then doing something constructive about them. An example of such psychological difficulties would be the degenerating psychology of futility that can permeate the Soul's entire reality. Or the psychology of a permeating sadness or grief that can impair the Soul in a variety of ways.
(Q) In the next life after a suicide, will suicidal thoughts tend to arise again when the Soul is faced with similar but intensified circumstances that they avoided in the life in which they committed suicide?
(A) Yes.

(Q) What is the purpose at a Soul level of having the circumstances be intensified in the next life? It seems like that could perpetuate the choice of suicide again in the next life.

(A) This is a karmic condition that the Soul itself is responsible for creating where the natural law of karma is ignited because of this natural law against suicide. The purpose of the intensified circumstances is to actually empower the Soul to make other choices that lead to its evolution BECAUSE OF THOSE INTENSIFIED CONDITIONS.

(Q) I am trying to check my understanding of the process of how the intensified conditions would empower the Soul to make other choices. Is it that the inner dynamics that created the conditions would become more clear to the Soul because the intensity of the conditions, and perhaps the consequent suffering, would provoke an inner questioning regarding "why these dynamics?" and also make it more difficult to avoid facing the dynamics?

(A) Yes. And remember that all Souls upon exiting any given life 'reviews' that life right after the life is exited. The intention in such a review of course is to learn in hindsight via the review many things related to that life. In the case of suicide this also applies BIG TIME. Thus, these types of 'lessons' are ingrained within the Soul upon its next birth in such a way that by recreating the conditions in its previous life in which the suicide took place this then has the effect of triggering those lessons learned in the review. Thus, acting upon those lessons relative to recreating those conditions empowers the Soul to evolve.

(Q) Of the four ways that Pluto effects evolution, in the case of a previous suicide, would the Soul come to understand the limiting dynamics most probably through cataclysm or stagnation, or could all of the ways that Pluto effects evolution be active in the discovery of limiting dynamics and the practical steps to take to move forwards? My understanding is that resistance to growth would be more likely to result in stagnation or cataclysm as a means of evolution; so until the Soul started to consciously desire and embrace their evolution, that would continue to be the primary means of evolution.

(A) Each Soul is unique to itself. Thus, the choices made by any given Soul reflect that individuality. Because of this all the four natural ways that Pluto effects its evolutionary necessities exits.

Soul and the veil of maya – Yogananda

"Every human being is essentially a Soul, covered with a veil of maya. Through evolution and self-effort, each human makes a little hole in the veil; in time, one makes the hole bigger and bigger. As the opening enlarges, the consciousness expands; the Soul becomes more manifest. When the veil is completely torn away, the Soul is fully manifest in him/her. That woman/man has become a master – master of their self and of maya." (Yogananda)

South Node of Neptune in Aquarius

(Q) In relation with the South Node of Neptune being in Aquarius (reflecting the original matriarchal roots of the current desires in all Souls to spiritualize consciousness), and the connection of natal Neptune with the Aquarius Age, in the context of the current transition between the Pisces Age into the next Aquarius Age, would imply that the root of these desires (ie the past of the Soul) is also symbolic of the future ways for the Souls to spiritualize consciousness (ie ways which will be in place for these Souls in the next Age). Is this correct? (Gonzalo)

(A) Yes. (Rad)

(Q) For me this is interesting to consider because it confirms that the current time frame is defined by a potential for accelerated evolution of Souls because it implies that the past is becoming the future now. Thus, the work on resolution of issues from past lifetimes related to the spiritual roots of the Soul and, at the same time, work on the resolution of issues pertaining to the future of the Soul – ie the past and the future are contained and concentrated within the current time. Is this correct?

(A) Yes. And what this will mean of course is if the original spiritual root will manifest again or not which itself is linked with the survival of the species. Within Aquarius is the triad of Libra and Gemini. Libra correlates with the Natural Law of giving, sharing, and inclusion. This is how humans were defined relative to groups of humans, Aquarius, for the balance of humans' existence on our planet. In relatively recent times this Natural Law of course has become perverted to self-interest and exclusion which then causes one group of humans, or one human, then trying to compete with other groups, or a human, relative to the survival instinct itself. In turn this leads to dominance and submission. If this is not corrected by going back to the original root, or past, and bringing that forwards into the future, then the extinction of the species is guaranteed.

(Q) So, in a sense, over lifetimes of evolution, as the "hole enlarges" or more veils are removed and more illusions dissolved (lots of disillusionment), from this perspective relative to Neptune's South Node, would it be sound understanding to correlate this symbol to what *has held* (past tense) ultimate meaning in the individualized consciousness relative to how much that consciousness has evolved? (Bradley)

(A) Yes. You can also include into this the natural planetary ruler of the South Node of Neptune which for all of us is Aquarius and its natural ruler Uranus. You can include the aspects to this Uranus as well as aspects to the South Node of Neptune itself. (Rad)

(Q) So, the Soul's journey has a past. The consciousness within the Soul journey, relative to the sense of an evolutionary past and future, has a past. This past may not be as we perceive linear time; however in the sense that the consciousness does has a past, along the journey it continues to evolve further into the fullest potential of consciousness within the human form. Would the South Node of Neptune then correlate to earlier in the Soul's evolutionary journey the ways which it spiritualized?

(A) Yes.
(Q) And then, relative to the Soul's individual past, what held ultimate meaning within that Soul's consciousness and thus still resonates as such, coming through the 'now' as a way to naturally spiritualize. And that which still holds a sense of ultimate meaning within the consciousness expressing outwardly relative to the stage at which the consciousness has evolved along the journey thus far (aka the evolutionary stage of the Soul)?
(A) Yes.

Natural Law that holds creation together
(Q) The glue or Natural Law that holds the creation together would have to be perfect.   Is there anything at all that is PERFECT about God? (Linda)
(A) The 'glue' that holds the manifested Creation together, including all that which we call Natural Laws such gravity, is the Source of that glue itself. Your use of the word 'perfect' is indeed relative to any given moment in time yet 'time' itself is ever evolving so that what can appear to be 'perfect' at one point in time becomes 'imperfect' from the point of view of another point in time. It is indeed the interaction of what we can call perfect relatively speaking and imperfect that is the essence of evolution itself that leads to a 'timeless' perfect which is when what we call God/ess becomes perfect within Itself. (Rad)

STAGES OF EVOLUTION

TABLE 2 Stages of Evolution

CONSENSUS	INDIVIDUATED	SPIRITUAL
1st stage Consensus	*1st stage Individuated*	*1st stage Spiritual*
– beginning – established – culminating	– beginning – established – culminating	– beginning – established – culminating
2nd stage Consensus	*2nd stage Individuated*	*2nd stage Spiritual*
– beginning – established – culminating	– beginning – established – culminating	– beginning – established – culminating
3rd stage Consensus	*3rd stage Individuated*	*3rd stage Spiritual*
– beginning – established – culminating	– beginning – established – culminating	– beginning – established – final liberation

Percentages in the evolutionary states

Dimly evolved – Roughly 3-4% of all Souls are in the 'Dimly Evolved' state. This means one of two things. Either Souls that are evolving into human consciousness from other forms of life such as animals and plants. Or Souls that are 'de-evolving' backwards into this condition due to 'karmic' causes.

Consensus – Souls that have evolved into what can be called the 'Consensus' state of evolution, which comprises roughly 70% of all Souls on the planet at this time.

Individuated – Where 'Individuated' is used in the Jungian sense of the word. This comprises roughly 20% of all Souls.

Spiritual – Comprises roughly 4-6% of all Souls on the planet.

Accurate determination of evolutionary stages

It is extremely important to understand no astrologer can determine which evolutionary condition exists for any Soul by simply looking at the birth chart alone. The astrologer must observe and interact with the client in order for this determination to be made. A good way to do this is in a counseling situation where a client has come to the astrologer, is to simply ask the client why they are there, and what questions do they have. Generally, the very nature of the questions that the client has will clue the astrologer as to what evolutionary condition exists for that client. For example, if one client asks, "When can I expect enlightenment," and another asks, "When will I have my new BMW," there clearly is an observed difference reflecting the level of evolutionary progression of the Soul. (Rad)

To accurately determine the evolutionary stage for any Soul one has to understand the totality of that Soul's reality. To isolate upon one dynamic, as in a desire to be 'seen,' will not, of itself be an indicator as to what the evolutionary stage is for any Soul. It is essential to know what any Soul's inner orientation to external reality is, what the bottom line within them is about as a core orientation to reality, to really know what the evolutionary stage is. The descriptions of the Four Evolutionary Stages, and their sub-stages, reflect what the core orientations to reality are for any possible Soul. The desire to be 'seen,' in and of itself, comes from the Leo archetype. And, by the way, by the time the Soul evolves to the beginning of the 3rd stage Spiritual there will no longer be any desire to be 'seen' from an egocentric point of view. Quite the opposite: an increasing desire to be unseen. (Rad)

The evolutionary stage is the evolutionary stage of the Soul, not of the personality. Without seeing the nature of the Soul you have no way to know the cause of the external phenomena you observe. You have to grasp the nature of the Soul. The externals, the personality, are EXPRESSIONS of the Soul. Each Soul will have its own reasons for having some external expression – unique to each Soul based on its past and the desire nature of that Soul. Without seeing the "why" behind the expression, you can't draw conclusions based on just the expression. In the chart we get clues to the nature of the Soul from the location of Pluto by house and sign, the location of Pluto's South Node by house and sign, the aspects Pluto is making to other planets by house and sign. Some of this may seem intangible. From my experience learning these things, if you keep working with it, gradually an inner light will turn on, an "aha" occurs, and you start grasping it from the inside out. (Steve)

The trick of learning the stages is to grasp the underlying psychological archetypes associated with a stage. Then you can begin to recognize that archetype playing out in various forms. 1st stage Individuated – are different, yet afraid to be different – pretend to be normal, are not. 2nd stage Individuated – look very different, have deep anger about the way things are, underneath, fear being pulled back into Consensus. 3rd stage Individuated – individuality fully formed – no way they can be pulled back to Consensus. They seek to reform, improve, transform the world for the better. 1st stage Spiritual – feel very small, desire to serve, spirituality of a devotional nature. (Steve)

When trying to discern the stage someone is in when they SEEM to be split between two stages. It could be said for someone in 3rd stage Individuated moving toward, or on the cusp of 1st stage Spiritual: they HAVE to do the same kinds of things the 1st stage Spiritual person would do in order to MOVE to that stage. (Adina)

I was hanging on to the last vestiges of "but surely if there is this or that signature it must have some reflection, even if indicating in the smallest of ways, that the person might be in evolutionary stage 'X'" etc. This was because I was new to EA, and still subconsciously coming from the traditional western astrology paradigm. Over the last while I've been forced to evaluate the evolutionary stage and sub-stage of several people I'm karmically connected with, in order to clarify my ongoing relationship to/with them. This has taken a lot of internal thought and contemplation. And it's made it totally clear to me, yet again, how the evolutionary stage of a person and their chart are totally completely different things. I have always operated on that basis since, but it's absolutely as clear as day now – it's become something I know now as my own experience at a core level. (Upasika)

What I have learned (and continue to learn) is EA works because it is aligned with, is a symbolic expression of, how life actually works. Beyond theory and intellectual constructs. Just, bottom line, how it actually is. So, as we increasingly see that, we see the principles EA expresses playing out in our lives. No astrology is required – they are simply there. To me one of the main gifts EA offers is it lets us objectify what we are experiencing – to step back from our subjective perspective and simply see what is going on without personal emotional investment. The way I look at it, a natal chart is a blueprint, a script. That script can be fleshed out in many ways – each Soul is going to play it out differently, based on its past, its desire nature, and its evolutionary station. So a 1st stage Consensus and a 1st stage Spiritual Soul could be born at the same moment. They have entirely different reasons for picking that moment and they are going to play that script out quite differently. And yet, there will be similarities. Jeffrey quoting Sri Yukteswar in the beginning of Pluto Vol. 1 – "A child is born on that day and at that hour when the celestial rays are in mathematical harmony with his individual karma." A friend of mine with interest in astrology has recently met someone on-line she doesn't know, who was born two minutes after her, same day and year, 700 miles apart in the US. They are having quite a time comparing notes. They are finding it's as I said above – they have uncanny similarities, yet they each have fleshed that script out in their own unique and different, yet similar, ways. (Steve)

Natural archetype of evolutionary stages

Regarding these being "natural archetypes," Wolf also taught that these were "natural archetypes, BUT ONLY from the standpoint that we all go thru stages of growth – expansion of consciousness, not in how they manifest. The way the stages are currently defined – how they manifest – is due to our still living in a patriarchal reality, ie only play out in a patriarchal setting; they would not manifest the same way when people are living by Natural Law. The stages themSELVES are natural, but how they are played out looks entirely different in a world of Natural Law, or one that is defined by giving, sharing and inclusion, rather than self-interest and exclusion. (Adina)

The problem is we live in a time of near-total patriarchy, so there aren't many around exhibiting the undistorted state. And people who do live from natural principles, regardless of evolutionary stage, tend to be very wounded from all they have been through in retaining their inner integrity. (Steve)

It is important to remember, again, that these are the natural evolutionary conditions that reflect the current reality of all peoples on Earth. For those who wish to use evolutionary astrology, it is essential that you make the necessary observations of any given person to determine their evolutionary state, and to then orient yourself to their natal chart accordingly. Again, one size does not fit all.

Evolutionary sub-sub-stages

Every evolutionary sub-stage also has three distinct inner stages within that sub-stage, ie within the 1st stage Spiritual there are three inner stages: those who just entered the 1st stage Spiritual, those who have been in it for a long while and have learned tremendous amounts of knowledge including discrimination and yet still on the way, and those who are culminating in this stage before entering the next stage, the 2nd stage Spiritual. (Lia)

Within all the states there are three subdivisions that we must account for, where each subdivision reflects the ongoing evolution of a Soul through the entire evolutionary state, which then leads to the next evolutionary state with its three subdivisions, until the final 'liberation' of a Soul occurs, relative to exhaustion of all separating desires, ultimately reflected in the third subdivision of the Spiritual state of evolution. (Rad)

Evolutionary stages – difference between appearance and reality

The answer to all such observations about people is always to be seen in each person's inner orientation to external reality. It is the inner orientation, how life is integrated because of, that is most important to ascertain in establishing where any given Soul is relative to its evolutionary condition. An example was the man who became the leader of SRF after Yogananda's passing. In his external life he was in fact a tycoon who was involved, as I recall, in the railroad industry of that time. Yet his inner orientation to 'reality' was one of God and God only. Thus, when he first met Yogananda he almost immediately remembered all his former lives that he dedicated to God. He attained the highest levels of cosmic consciousness in his current life due to his relationship with Yogananda.

In any life that we come into we are all exposed to whatever the conditions of 'reality' are as defined by one's parents, and, as we get older, the society of birth itself. And most Souls do not have past life recall at all which is a purposeful design by God. So of course this then allows and promotes being conditioned by the nature of our parents' reality and, as we get older, the conditioning of the current society of our birth. And for most Souls this then means 'wearing the clothes' of that conditioning. For those Souls who are only evolved somewhere within the Consensus stage this presents no problem at all. Their whole sense of personal identity is utterly bound up and defined by the conditions of their birth, parents, and the society of birth.

For Souls that have naturally evolved beyond the Consensus state the conditioning patterns reflected by the parents' reality, and the society of birth are progressively rebelled against unless those parents are themselves rebels against the Consensus. Even then the Soul in this condition will still desire to question everything and desire to design a life that looks like who they actually are as individuals. And so too for Souls who have naturally evolved into the Spiritual state. They will desire to find their own unique way spiritually speaking. As the Soul naturally evolves into the Spiritual state, progressively, the memories from other lifetimes do begin to occur in such a way as the Soul can actually know and understand the thread that connects all the lives, and the reasons for them. There can be a vast array of reasons why any Soul could be in this state and yet still find themselves as a 'businessman.' And that, indeed, is the beauty of Evolutionary Astrology for those who have the gift of truly understanding it: its totality. For those that do then the reasons for any condition or situation in anyone's life can be understood and explained to anyone who is desiring to know the 'why' of their life in every way. (Rad)

How evolution occurs through each evolutionary state

The way that evolution occurs through each state is by exhausting all the desires that are intrinsic to the nature of that evolutionary state or condition. (Rad)

Natural Law of the Trinity

The three evolutionary stages and the three sub-stages are related to the Natural Law of the Trinity. (Steve)

Shifts from South Node to North Node, and Pluto to Pluto polarity point

It's automatic. You can't separate the Nodes with Pluto and its polarity point because the ego (Nodes) are always a reflection of the Soul's desires (Pluto). The ego is never separate from the reason for why the ego exists in the first place. (Ari)

Dimly Evolved State

Souls that are evolving into human consciousness from other forms of life, typically animal and plant (animals and plants essentially have the same 'emotional' and 'nervous' systems as humans) are characterized by a very limited sense of self-awareness. This self-awareness is typically limited to the time and space that they personally occupy. When one looks into such Souls' eyes they typically express a 'density' within the pupils, like a film effect within the pupils. These Souls are typically very joyous; very, very innocent; and can bring great love to those who are close to them. Modern terminology that reflects these types of Souls are words like cretinism, very low IQ's, mongoloidism, mental retardation, and the like. The root desire within this evolutionary stage or state is the desire to be 'normal,' where normal means to be like most other people: the Consensus state. Conversely, it can occur, due to 'karmic' causes, that Souls can be de-evolved; which means that such Souls are forced back into this state. In terms of 'actual' reality such Souls are more evolved yet now limited through this apparent form of evolution due to karmic causes. This then becomes very problematic for such Souls, because they had previously evolved beyond this stage. Thus, such Souls now experience great and humiliating 'limitations' because of the de-evolution. As a result, these Souls are very, very angry, and some can go about creating great disturbances for other people. These Souls can also be 'classified' through the modern terminology as above. But the great difference is that when one looks into the pupil of these Souls' eyes, one will notice a great while light manifesting from the pupil: piercing like. And within that light one will inwardly experience the intense anger within such a Soul. (Rad)

CONSENSUS STATE

Astrologically speaking, this state correlates to Saturn, because of the underlying desire to conform to the Consensus of any society, culture, tribe or country. Thus such Souls' entire orientation to reality, including their values, the sense of meaning for life, moralities, customs, norms, taboos, what is right and wrong, and so on, are simply an extension of the prevailing Consensus of whatever society they are born into. In essence 'reality' for such Souls is merely an extension of the external conditioning that any Consensus group of people provides. They cannot step out of the box, so to speak. For example if a scientist claims that 'astrology is bogus,' then all those within the Consensus state will have the same opinion. Within the Consensus state, like all the other states, there are three subdivisions that we must account for, where each subdivision reflects the ongoing evolution of a Soul through the entire evolutionary state, which then leads to the next evolutionary state with its three subdivisions, until the final 'liberation' of a Soul occurs, relative to exhaustion of all separating desires, ultimately reflected in the third subdivision of the Spiritual state of evolution. The way that evolution occurs through each state is by exhausting all the desires that are intrinsic to the nature of that evolutionary state or condition. Within the Consensus state, the root desire that propels the evolution of the Soul forward, from the first subdivision through the third, is characterized by the desire to 'get ahead,' to get ahead of the 'system,' which of course means the Consensus society that they belong to. (Rad)

1st stage Consensus
Souls within the first subdivision of the Consensus state are characterized by a limited sense of self-awareness, essentially limited to the time and space that they occupy; a limited awareness of the dynamics of the community that they inhabit; an even more limited awareness of the dynamics of the country that they live within. And yet they are incredibly self-righteous relative to the values, moralities, Consensus religion of the existing society of birth, how life is 'interpreted' according to those beliefs, the judgments issued because of those beliefs, and so on. There simply is no ability to separate themselves from any of this. It is as if they are like social automatons. An apt analogy for these Souls is the worker bees in a bee hive. Typically, they are in the lowest social strata of the society of birth. (Rad)

2nd stage Consensus
As evolution proceeds for these Souls, relative to the desire to 'get ahead,' it will lead them into the second subdivision of the Consensus state, because that root desire means that they will want more from society than simply remaining in its lower strata. These Souls of course perceive from the point of view of the lower strata that there are others who have more than they have. This perception is more or less limited to others having more possessions of a grander nature than they have, social positions within society that they do not have, thus more social 'freedom' than they have, and so on. Yet that limited perception fuels the root desire to get ahead and have more. In order for this desire to be realized they must learn ever more how society and its dynamics work. It requires an expansion of their personal awareness for this learning to take place. It is the very fact of the evolutionary necessity to expand their awareness that propels the evolution of the Soul into the second Consensus state subdivision. There it becomes necessary for the Soul to learn ever more about the nature of society, to use the social system to its own evolutionary advantage – to get ahead. The 'reality' for such Souls is still totally defined by the Consensus of society: its values, moralities, religions, judgments, right and wrongs, and so on. Yet by desiring to get ahead, the Soul must expand its personal awareness of the nature of the dynamics of how the society it is a part of is put together: its rules, regulations, what is required for this or that ambition to be actualized, and so on. The Soul thus becomes ever more aware of 'others,' of the community that it is part of, and the country that it lives within. This expanding awareness also includes the beginning of becoming aware of other countries and the differences in values, moralities, religions, and so on, as reflected in other countries and societies. Thus personal awareness – self-awareness – expands, because of the heightened awareness of 'others' relative to the Soul's desire to get ahead. This evolutionary stage correlates to the 'middle strata' within the social order of any given society. (Rad)

3rd stage Consensus
As the Soul evolves through this state it increasingly becomes aware of the upper strata of society, of those that are in positions of power and leadership, of those that have great material abundance, and, as result, the desire to get ahead fuels the ongoing evolution of the Soul into the third subdivision within the Consensus state. For the Soul to evolve into the third subdivision within the Consensus state, an ever increasing awareness of how society 'works' in total is demanded. Because of this, personal awareness expands through evolutionary necessity, in order for the Soul's desires (defined by ambitions to get ahead) to be realized. The Soul's personal awareness has now expanded to the point that it is now very aware of the totality of the community and society that it belongs to, and of the country that it lives within. This also includes a progressive awareness of other countries, other cultures, and of the relativity of moralities, values, religions, and so on, as reflected in other countries and cultures. Even though

this awareness progressively expands, it does not mean the Soul in this third subdivision considers other countries, values, beliefs, and religions equal to its own society and country of birth. In fact, within this third subdivision, the self-righteousness born out of conformity (the underlying hallmark of the Consensus state in total) is sustained: we are right, and they are wrong. In total the Consensus state correlates to what is called 'nationalism'.

In this final subdivision within the Consensus state the Soul desires to be 'on top' of society; to have positions of social importance and relative power, prestige, and material abundance – the politicians, CEO's of corporations, important positions in the business world, mainstream religious leaders, and so on. As a result, these Souls constitute the 'upper strata' of society. As the Soul evolves through this last subdivision it will finally exhaust all the desires that are inherent within the Consensus state. As a result, the meaning to life itself will progressively be lost as those desires no longer hold any meaning. At the very end of the journey through this state the Soul will finally ask the question 'there must be more to life than this.' This very question implies an awakening alienation from the Consensus, from 'normal' life as defined by the Consensus. It is this awakening alienation from normalcy as defined by the Consensus of any society that now triggers the beginning of a new desire that will propel the Soul into the Individuated evolutionary state: the desire to liberate from all external conditioning that has previously defined the Soul's sense of reality in general, and its sense of personal identity, or individuality, specifically. (Rad)

Relative to desire natures, a person in 3rd stage Consensus is going to be focused on attaining positions of power and authority within which they can be seen as special. What Jeffrey called the Zarathustra class. The gist of it being, "I am among the elite, the ones who are beyond the rules, who make the rules for everyone," and those rules not applying to them. The *natural* archetype here would be to rule in service to the whole – to wield power wisely. The distorted inverted version, most common today, is, "I am special, all these peons can just serve me. I am the world shaker and mover." Within this today you can find not only CEO's but political leaders on all levels. (Steve)

Consensus, and Natural Laws

For the current Consensus to embrace the universal and timeless values from Natural Laws it would require massive cataclysmic events that had the effect of making those values the values lived by the Consensus because it would have no other choice but to do so because the nature of the cataclysms enforcing this would be so severe that the Consensus would have no other choice because survival itself would be on the line. If this did occur then such values would not be 'superficial' because life itself would be on the line. And, of course, 2012 will not correlate to a massive 'awakening' within the consciousness of the collective unless the intensity of the cataclysmic events just mentioned were so severe that such an awakening would occur because of those cataclysmic events. (Rad)

Consensus, and patriarchy

The Consensus exists within any group of people, at any point in time. It is not a function of the patriarchy of itself. What the nature of that Consensus is within any group, at any point in time, of course is different. (Rad)

Rates of evolution

(Q) Do some Souls simply evolve at different rates and this has nothing to do with resistance? So kind of like different flowers flowering at different times despite having been planted at the same time?
(A) Exactly. (Rad)
(Q) How to understand a Consensus Soul who had lived in matriarchal times?
(A) Souls in a Consensus state do not have 'memories' of living within matriarchal times. In terms of Uranus, unconscious stored memories, Souls relative to the Consensus stage of evolution would have no evolutionary capacity to know or remember such memories. The operative dynamic within such Souls has been, and is, TO CONFORM. (Rad)

Consensus, hating

As for sentiments concerning [hating] the Consensus state it is simply a matter of Aquarian detachment and objectification relative to knowing that they are simply where they are in their evolution, and cannot be any different than they actually are. Most are doing the best they can do with what they have to work with. (Rad)

Consensus state, and transcendental belief systems

Any belief system that is rooted in the cause and effect of Creation is a transcendent belief system. Consensus-based religions certainly are part of such transcendent belief systems. The archetype of the 12th house, Pisces and Neptune, in the end, correlates to what constitutes ultimate meaning for life itself. Any 12th house Pluto person is thus desiring what constitutes the ultimate meaning for their existence. For those in the Consensus state who are focused mainly on the material realm of existence this sense of ultimate meaning given to such a focus is destined to lead to a complete sense of disillusionment at some point. At that point the Soul is then confronted, internally, by exactly what will correlate to the ultimate meaning that they are actually desiring or seeking. At that point, relative to the Consensus state, Consensus-based religions then become the answer. (Rad)

Understanding the Sagittarius and Pisces archetypes within the Consensus state
(Q) Would you please help me understand the Sagittarius and Pisces archetypes within the Consensus state? Especially Souls who don't believe in any religion, and who are living in a society lacking in belief systems or metaphysical information. How would they evolve, generally speaking, if they are not into metaphysical, philosophical or religious information? (Wei)

(A) At first the EA astrologer must ask why such Souls choose to be born into such conditions in the first place. Every Soul has their own reasons of course, and those reasons are reflected/symbolized by the specific EA paradigm in each chart. Within the Consensus state any Soul will accept the Consensus beliefs and philosophical orientation of any culture, society, or tribe at birth. As a result it does not matter whether they are Sagittarius, Pisces, or any other sign. Remember the nature of the consensus state is to CONFORM. (Rad)

INDIVIDUATED STATE

Astrologically speaking, the Individuated state correlates to Uranus, because the Soul now desires to liberate or rebel against the Consensus state from which it is now evolving away from. Instead of the Soul being defined by the Consensus to shape its sense of reality in general, and its personal identity specifically, the Soul now desires to discover who and what it is, independent of such conditioning. Earlier it was stated that if a Soul were in the Consensus state and the scientist said 'astrology is bogus,' this would then be the automatic belief of those Souls who are within the Consensus state. If that same scientist said this to a Soul within the Individuated state, the response would be something like, 'no thank you, I will think for myself.' Souls in this evolutionary state inwardly feel 'different:' different than the majority of the society and country of birth. Because of the desire to liberate from the Consensus, the awareness of Souls in this state progressively expands to include ever larger wholes, or frames of reference. This expansion of awareness begins because the Soul no longer can identify with the Consensus of the society of birth. As a result the Soul now feels a progressive detachment from society: like standing on the outside and looking in. This then allows the Soul to 'objectify' itself, relative to personal awareness and self-perception. Rebelling against Consensus beliefs, values, moralities, what constitutes 'meaning' for life itself, and so on, the Soul now begins to question the assumptions that most people hold dear to their heart that correlate to what 'reality' is and is not. As a result, this Soul now begins to 'experiment,' by investigating other ways of looking at and understanding the nature of life itself. This is a reflection of the independent thinking that characterizes this evolutionary state. And it is through this independent thinking and investigating all kinds of different ways of understanding life, including ideas, beliefs, and philosophies from other lands and cultures, that allows for an ever-increasing expansion of their consciousness, and thus, their sense of personal awareness. As a result of this such Souls no longer feel at 'home' in their own land, in their country of birth. (Rad)

The Individuated stage is inherently a Uranian phase, the nature of the archetype, to throw off the Consensus (Saturn) need to conform (Saturn) – to de-condition in other words. Evolutionary stage is simply the result of millions of choices one has made. De-condition really means to change how one sees one's self – self-image = Moon. We are totally attached to images of who I am that are not at all who I am. De-conditioning means to release these limited perspectives. The process goes on and on. Emptying is a necessary precursor. But the natural outcome of emptying is a gradual refilling, into the next level, which we then perceive as so far beyond the previous one. But the day or lifetime will come when even the new "this is so far beyond where I was before" itself will have to be emptied as it too has become too limited. That process never ends as there is always more that we are than we believe we are. So it's a continual opening, integrating (also a Uranian function), and then eventual releasing. It's been described as peeling the layers off an onion. (Steve)

1st stage Individuated
In the first subdivision of the Individuated state, the Soul will typically try to 'compensate' for this inner feeling of being different, of not belonging to the Consensus, and the inner sense of alienation, by trying to appear normal. This compensation then causes the Soul to structure their outer reality much as Souls do in the Consensus state: normal kinds of work, normal kinds of friends, normal appearance, and so on. Yet inwardly they feel and know that they can no longer personally identify with that compensatory reality that they attempt to sustain. This compensation manifests in this subdivision because, after all, the Consensus is where the Soul has just been. Thus it constitutes a sense of security, relative to the inner feeling of being detached and different. We must remember that for most people, the sense of security in life is a function of constancy, self-consistency. And self-consistency is a function of the past. As a result, the compensation manifests as a reaction to this increasingly new feeling of being different, of not belonging anymore to the Consensus. This feeling creates a sense of insecurity in this first subdivision because is it brand new. The Soul has not been here before. Yet this act of compensation creates a very real state of 'living a lie.' Even as this compensatory behavior occurs, the Soul will nonetheless be questioning everything, deep within themselves, in the privacy of their inner life. Typically they will read all kinds of books that contain ideas that go way beyond the 'norm' as it is defined by the Consensus. Many, depending on cultural possibilities, will take classes or workshops that have these themes or intentions. Some will seek out 'alternative' environments to find and bond with others of like-mind – others who feel as they do. This compensatory behavior will progressively give way, involute, as the Soul evolves further in this subdivision. The Soul will progressively distance itself from the

Consensus and begin to form relationships with other alienated Souls just like itself. Because of the necessity of work or a job, most of these Souls will either do any kind of work just to get by, without identifying with such work in any way, or they will actualize a work that is individualistic and symbolic of their own individuality. (Rad)

2nd stage Individuated

In the second subdivision of the Individuated state, the underlying archetype of Uranus as it correlates to rebellion is at its highest. This rebellion is so extreme that the Soul has now 'thrown off' almost any idea or philosophy that has come before, at any level of reality. Such Souls end up in a kind of existential void, and typically hang out with other such alienated Souls, which has the effect of reinforcing the total state of rebellion from all of reality other than the reality they have now defined through the existential void. These Souls will exhibit a deep fear of integrating into society in any kind of way, for the fear suggests to them that if they do, that somehow that very same society or reality will absorb their hard won (at least to them) individuality, which is defined through the act of rebellion, in this stage. As a result, these Souls typically hang out in the avant-garde of society, hurling critical atom bombs at society, so as to reinforce their sense of personal righteousness, defined by their alienation from the Consensus. Because of the Natural Law of evolution (which is always preceded by an involution), these people at some point will realize that their fear of integrating into reality, into society, is just that: a fear only. Once this is realized, they then begin to make the effort to integrate back into society, but with their individuality intact. Once this is realized, the Soul will then evolve into the third subdivision. (Rad)

The underlying archetype/principle within the 2nd stage Individuated condition is absolute Uranus in the form of total rebellion against any expectation to conform to anything external to itself. Some may attempt to put on the 'clothes' of normalcy yet those clothes could never conceal or hide the inner vibrations within their Souls of absolute rebellion against any external pressure to be anything other than that which they are. So you could have one person in front of you who was indeed the 1st stage Individuated, and the other the 2nd stage Individuated, and both could have identical clothes on yet the vibrational nature of their Souls would quickly inform you as to who's who. (Rad)

Racist philosophy is something we would not typically find in a 2nd stage Individuated Soul. (Rad)

Transition from 2nd stage to 3rd stage Individuated

They are going to want to carry out their unique life purpose, on their own terms. For some Souls that will require playing a role that will put them operating within the mainstream. But they are not really reintegrating, because they are going to play that role out on their own terms. They will operate WITHIN society, but not as part of it. They are always maintaining allegiance to their unique inner vision. At the beginning of 3rd stage, that fundamental mistrust from 2nd is still going to be a strong archetype. That mistrust NEVER goes away. As they advance into 3rd stage, they simply become more accepting of its inevitability. It just becomes part of what is, something they have to accept to fulfill what they are here to do. Even though they are thoroughly alienated from the mainstream, they accept they have to operate within it anyway. Whereas second stage is less accepting of that. Once someone is in Individuated and beyond, the fundamental distrust of society is NEVER resolved. It is just accepted as a given. (Steve)

3rd stage Individuated

In the third subdivision of the Individuated state, the Soul will then begin to manifest within society or reality as a truly unique and gifted person, from the viewpoint of the Consensus. This means that such Souls will have in some way a unique gift, or capacity, to help the Consensus itself evolve, through integrating that capacity or gift within the Consensus. Yet these people will not inwardly feel identified with the Consensus: they stand inwardly very distant from it. The consciousness of these Souls has progressively expanded through the Individuated state in such a way that they are aware of the entire world and the relativity of beliefs, values, moralities, and so on. As a result they will feel within themselves to be 'world citizens' much more than being a singular citizen of the country of birth. The inner pondering of the very nature of existence, the nature of Creation, the nature of who they 'really' are, essentially defines the nature of their consciousness. Progressively, these people begin to really open up their consciousness to the universal, the cosmos, to God/ess. Not the God/ess defined through Consensus religions, but the real or natural God/ess. A perfect example in recent history of such a Soul is Albert Einstein. Another would be Howard Hughes. (Rad)

3rd stage Individuated examples

Beatles (except John Lennon); Krishnamurti; Ghandi.

3rd stage Individuated transition to 1st stage Spiritual

A generality may be that one who is new/just coming into 1st stage Spiritual – the precipice which they are standing on, the unknown dark abyss that lays ahead, is a letting go of this individual's sense of self (ego) and identity which defines the past (3rd stage Individuated) from which they are coming from (their past). In this archetypal crisis, to fall back to the light of the known past is to revert back to old ways/patterns/habits which were providing a sense of security to the individual they once were. So, for them to continue these past patterns which have outlived their evolutionary usefulness, is in effect to avoid evolution and growth. The crisis point, in this case, is seen by observing the nature of the old habits, patterns, lifestyle having their root in egocentric Individuated reality which leads to a further sense of inner emptiness and disorientation, even though this emptiness is also being avoided by the seeming fullness of what they were once so comforted by; at least the notion and idea of these ways has the allure of the same fulfillment it once did, but if acted out again and repeated simply does not. These old ways are clearly of an individual nature. Of course, one could have a hard time continuing the shift from ego to Soul at any point in the journey. In the Individuated stage one 'carves out' their own unique path and the transition to Spiritual is largely different in that the ego/Soul actually will orient to one Spiritual path/way of life that most resonates for them. This shift alone reflects a humbling of the ego because there is no longer this need to have individually created this 'way.' It is the shift to simply have one way that most resonates. (Bradley)

The 1st stage Spiritual has been described as Virgo-like. The Soul has gotten itself across the line between 3rd stage Individuated and stepped into 1st stage Spiritual. That process has required a great deal of humbling. Based on how I heard it once described, I have this mental picture of it. The Soul has spent countless lifetimes individuating itself from the consensus. It has been a hard-fought and hard-won attainment. There have been many scars and wounds, and that Soul has reached a point of feeling it knows itself. And yet, increasingly in 3rd stage Individuated there comes this sense of "there must be more than this" because all the great plans about how to reorganize society for the betterment of all are just not creating the changes the Soul was sure would happen when people saw how much better these new improvements would make things for everyone.

Any sort of major change like a shift from Individuated to Spiritual in general is initiated or triggered by some highly shocking or de-motivating (disillusioning) experiences. It's just not working the way I thought it would. Now what? This leads to some very deep Soul searching, where the Soul has to face it doesn't know how to do any more than what it has been doing – that is the humbling – and in a sense is brought to its knees. It sees that all of its hard-won individuality is not enough. And that is part of the resistance in early 1st stage Spiritual – it sees it has to surrender or give up what it's worked so hard to attain. Or at least it appears that way to that Soul at that time. There is inner knowing within that Soul of the direction it must head in, in order to evolve. And yet, resistance to that knowing based on the usual principle of familiarity equals security, and this change requires letting go of what has constituted security. It's the transition into that place where the outer work and behaviors have to progressively be aligned with that inner direction, and that requires having to release trying to control one's destiny – feeling I must provide for myself as no-one else is going to do it, which has been the evolutionary lesson of countless lives – the truth of that.

Suddenly now I am asked to let go of that and learn to trust that through following my natural inner impulses, God/Goddess somehow are going to provide for my needs (I of course have to act on the inner impulses of what I am supposed to be doing in place of spending all my time fending for my own survival – I can't just sit on the couch thinking about God, watching TV, thinking money and food are going to be left on my front porch because I am now so holy). It is scary to make that step – we have ample practical evidence it doesn't work that way. As we gradually start taking those steps we start seeing this very principle play out in the life, that it really truly does work when one stays aligned with inner intent. Then one gets a sense of how long they have been clueless that this even existed – the principle is universal truth. The Soul through its personas just has forgotten this and has lived in other ways. That too is humbling.

Awareness that one is one of 7 billion humans and billions of members of all other species on this planet, and that the planet itself, and even our whole galaxy, are microscopic in relation to the cosmos as a whole, and then we are talking only one dimension, a physical universe. Gradually one starts realizing the only thing that really makes any sense is to start living to serve the greater whole – everything else winds up feeling meaningless sooner or later. And then one sees how inconsistent one still is in their commitment to live to serve that greater whole, back and forth back and forth. And that further increases the sense of feeling very small – clueless even. And yet, as the inner commitment deepens, a feeling of deep sincerity strengthens – I may be clueless much of the time but at least I am sincere – and that counts for a lot.

One must be careful about using words like 'perfection.' "When I consider 1st stage Spiritual from reading the descriptions, I get a sense of perfection..." There is no perfection on this planet, and it's not even possible. Perfection cannot exist in a polarity reality whose basis is to evolve. The very principle of evolution is proof there is not perfection. There is nothing more to evolve to when one has reached perfection. And the principle of evolution, in every way, clearly underlies everything on this planet. The idea of perfection is the root principle in masochism, because we compare where we are to an ideal (Pisces) of perfection, which is an IDEAL, not a reality. In relation to the ideal (perfection) we can never measure up, for not one of the 7 billion humans does. This, in a masochist, then leads to a sense of guilt, for not being perfect enough, and a need to atone for what one has done that is less than one's definition of perfect. This becomes a repeating pattern of guilt and the need to atone, and attracting others who have guilt and rather than a need to atone for what they have done 'wrong,' a need to get back at, punish, those who have made them feel guilty, for they know they have done nothing wrong as it's all someone else's fault.

Such Souls have a need to punish, and masochists have a need to atone. Part of atoning is a sense of feeling inadequate or unworthy, which often creates a subconscious need to punish oneself, which can be actualized by drawing in external people with a need to punish others, who are quite happy to fill the masochist's need to be punished. The combined attraction leads to very dysfunctional interactions and relationships. The underlying basis of this dynamic is a belief that perfection is possible and indeed required, and a deep awareness that I am not at all perfect. It's extremely important to internalize that perfection in a body is never attainable. The standard to judge self against is not "Am I perfect?" but "Am I committed to making consistent ongoing progress (and taking the necessary ongoing steps/changes) even through inevitable temporary setbacks?"

1st stage Spiritual is NOT perfect. Neither is 3rd stage Spiritual. They represent *degrees of refinement* towards an ideal, the gradual exhaustion of separating desires. Realizing one is not going to be perfect in this life, while still holding an ideal to be that, is another source of increasing humility. (Steve)

Souls on the 'spiritual path' but not necessarily in the Spiritual state

(Q) I have some lingering questions in regard to those Souls that are very committed to being on the "spiritual path" but are not necessarily in the Spiritual state. I live in a place where being spiritual is the hip and 'in' thing, almost to the point of spiritual snobbery. I've noticed a large amount of serial seekers that are always involved with some kind of spiritual teaching, usually non-dual. These Souls seem to spend a great deal of time in intellectual debate about the teaching, the teacher, whether they agree, what is wrong with it, what is right with it, etc. I'm feeling that these Souls are largely 3rd Individuated? I ask this because of the intellectual approach, which is obviously very Uranian. What also strikes me is that these Souls appear to be doing this kind of seeking for their own growth and not for the service of others, it is like a lifestyle choice for them. Therefore, there is still an element of ego attached to their spiritualization. The part that is in constant debate appears to also be in doubt, unsure of what to trust or what the right path is for them. I feel that a Soul firmly planted in 1st Spiritual would experience their spirituality more from an inner emotional context, and therefore not feel the need to debate around the houses (or sound superior), and be more able to discern from an emotional and intuitive context what the right path is for them?

I am also curious about how the evolutionary states play out with the guru path. For instance, I know some Souls that have been involved with a guru but once they realized the relational dysfunction among the devotees, and the aggrandizement of guru which they no longer bought into, they left. I imagine these could be 3rd Individuated and possibly 1st Spiritual? There are others that notice the dysfunction and stay, and this is curious to me because I see different reasons for staying. Some seem to enjoy it, like a rebellion, for instance proclaiming that they don't identify with the worship of the guru, are not dependent or vulnerable, yet perfectly at home in some way. I'm assuming this is a 2nd Individuated Soul? Again, I can sense a lot of heart in many of these Souls but the devotional piece is clouded by an unsure ego. I know a few others that are fully aware of the dysfunction, aren't necessarily rebellious, but stay out of love and devotion because they feel that the guru somehow 'saved' them. However, I still feel that in these cases the devotion is somewhat misplaced because it is not being fully recognized as coming from within, but rather projected onto a guru that in some cases has taken advantage of the devotee. Would this be 3rd Individuated?

Finally, the EA teachings strongly emphasize the humility, desire to serve, and also seeking of spiritual self-improvement in 1st Spiritual Souls. If I am correct in my understanding, this type of Soul would primarily be seeking to evolve by following their own path of service, whatever that was to them, and trusting in and being guided by their own Soul. To me this could be anything and doesn't necessarily mean having a guru (which is more understood as coming from within), but at the same time it could also be about having a guru. However there would be a clear integration and recognition of the capacity in which the guru was serving the Soul. Any thoughts on this piece would be appreciated since I often feel that Souls are often perceived as being in the Spiritual state when they are devoted to a guru, yet most of the Souls I've come across that have one seem to be largely in the Individuated state. I also feel that since we are moving into the Aquarian Age, the traditional guru (Leo) path may be about to phase out as more and more Souls embrace equality. (Heidi)

(A) From all that you have observed and shared about those observations I feel that your estimation of these types of Souls being in the 3rd Individuated evolutionary state is exactly right. As I was reading through what you shared the memory of the Beatles came into my mind when they were off to India seeking out Maharishi, and what each as individuals then did with that. Seemed real similar to me, and each of those Souls in the Beatles was in the 3rd Individuated state with John right next moving into the 1st Spiritual state. (Rad)

Individuated, hiding signatures

The Soul who is in the Individuated state, and who is hiding, has created a 'double reality' in which their outer reality looks like the Consensus, and their inner reality will be totally different, or detached, from it. And they are in fact aware of this fact, this duality. This is typical of the 1st stage Individuated. In the 2nd stage there is no duality. In the 3rd stage Individuated, in general, their entire reality is a reflection of their inner reality, thus there is no hiding other than some emotional issues, affecting their personal lives, in which they are hiding from for a variety of possible reasons. (Rad)

Compensation

People in the beginnings of the 1st stage Individuated do in fact feel very different than the Consensus folks/state through which they have just evolved and yet because it is relatively new it of course creates a deep sense of insecurity and anxiety in terms of fully acting upon this individuating impulse. As a result of that fear such folks 'compensate' by way of trying to counteract this inner sense of insecurity and anxiety by creating the external appearance of normalcy including the very structures of their life, including many 'friends' that come out of that very consensus, 'normal' type jobs, etc., thus creating a living lie because of the act of compensation. All of us can 'compensate' in areas of our life relative to where we feel most insecure or powerless. (JWG)

Understanding the Sagittarius and Pisces archetypes within the Individuated state
(Q) Would you please help me understand the Sagittarius and Pisces archetypes within the Individuated state? Especially Souls who don't believe in any religion, and who are living in a society lacking in belief systems or metaphysical information. How would they evolve, generally speaking, if they are not into metaphysical, philosophical or religious information? (Wei)

(A) At first the EA astrologer must ask why such Souls choose to be born into such conditions in the first place. Every Soul has their own reasons of course, and those reasons are reflected/symbolized by the specific EA paradigm in each chart. In the Individuated state Sagittarius will inwardly experience a growing sense of alienation from the consensus of whatever society, tribe, or culture they are born into relative to the beliefs and philosophical orientation within them: the society at birth. Pisces will experience a fundamental sense of disillusionment relative to those beliefs, etc. Remember one of the core archetypes of Pisces is one of meaning, or ultimate meaning. Thus, the disillusionment is one of a sense of underlying meaninglessness relative to the society, etc., of birth. In the Individuated state itself these experiences of alienation and disillusionment do not automatically lead to seeking out replacement beliefs, philosophies, or cosmologies. In essence, such Souls can simply remain inwardly defined by this alienation and/or disillusionment without any replacement that would correlate to regaining a sense of meaning and/or not feeling as alienated. This would especially be so in the types of cultures or societies that do not offer any such replacements. Consequently such Souls can try to fill the inner void created by the alienation and disillusionment with any manner of external escapes in order to try to fill in that void. The manner/types of external escapes will be all the ways that exist within the structure of the culture, society, or tribe at birth. For some Souls in such conditions they will in fact desire, and make the effort, to understand exactly why they do feel this alienation and/or disillusionment. When this is the case they will do all that they can do, relative to the structure of the society, etc., of birth, in order to understand this inner question of why.

I remember a story that JWG shared with me long ago wherein he was invited to lecture in the country now called the Czech Republic. This was shortly after the big revolution there in which the people there kicked out the old Soviet Union from having total control of their culture. The old Soviet Union and those who ruled within it of course were all atheists who attempted to impose that atheism on the Czech culture. The Czech culture before the Soviet takeover of their country had a long tradition of religion and the spirituality within those religions. The Soviet control was such that no one was permitted to read anything along religious or spiritual lines. They could not take classes or attend any kind of lecture that was about this at all. So even within the consensus because of this Soviet imposition there was in fact a deep disillusionment and alienation from the atheistic philosophy being imposed because of the nature of the Czech culture: its long history before the Soviet invasion.

JWG was asked to lecture in Prague shortly after their revolution and kicking out the Soviets. His original book on Pluto somehow managed to go to many countries in the world including countries that were behind the Iron Curtain of those times. Thus, there were people in that country who knew of his work which, in the end, is about returning Home: the origins of all of our Souls. They could not offer him any money due to the hard economic times there at that time yet really sincerely asked him to come anyway. He could not say no. This little group that asked him to come was so poor that they could not even advertise his lectures. All they could do was put up hand-made posters around Prague advertising his lecture: The Evolutionary Journey of the Soul. As a result they did not expect very many to attend the lecture. Yet on the day of that lecture over 300 hundred people showed up in a 14th century library where the talk was held. No one knew English. Thus he spoke for hours, one sentence at a time that was being translated into Czech. It was the nature of the lecture that rang the inner bells of all those Souls that came to hear him, bells that were rung relative to their own long cultural history. This went on for hours, long after the allotted speaking time. Of all the places JWG lectured in his time he told me this was one of the most significant and meaningful experience of them all.

This reflects your questions, Wei. It is desire itself that is the determinant of anything the Soul creates for itself including being born into cultures, societies, or tribes whose existing consensus beliefs or philosophies are devoid of higher meaning. And it is desire that is the causative factor for any Soul to, no matter where they are born, that leads to the higher meaning, or ultimate understanding, of why we even have life in the first place: where did it all come from and why. There was one other part to that story that also demonstrates what a Soul can do when it so desires. The man who asked JWG to come to Prague desired to become a Catholic priest. Yet the Soviets repressed all religion. This man's desire was so strong that he would take himself deep underground into a specific building and shelter himself from making any sounds. Then he would read the Bible. (Rad)

SPIRITUAL STATE

Astrologically speaking, this evolutionary state correlates to Neptune, because now the root desire becomes to consciously KNOW, not just believe in, but to know and unite with the Source Of All Things: the universal, God/ess. Because of this root desire, the consciousness now progressively expands into the universal, the cosmos, in such a way that the very nature of the interior consciousness within the Soul becomes conscious of the living universe within: the wave within the ocean, and the ocean within the wave. Progressively, in this Spiritual state of evolution, the very center of gravity within the Soul's consciousness shifts from the subjective ego to the Soul itself. Once the center of gravity shifts to the Soul, then in the context of any given life the Soul is then able to simultaneously experience its specific individuality as reflected in the ego, while at the same time experiencing, being centered in, the Soul – the ocean that is aware of the waves that it manifests. The Soul contains within itself all the prior life memories from every life it has ever lived.

And the Soul has its own 'identity,' or ego. This identity or 'ego' is not the same as the ego that the Soul creates in any given life on places like Earth. The ego of the Soul is one's 'eternal' identity. An easy way for any of us to understand this occurs when we dream. Obviously when we dream we are not identified with our subjective ego. After all we are 'asleep.' The subjective ego has temporarily 'dissolved' back into the Soul when we sleep. So the question becomes 'who and what is doing the dreaming?' Obviously it can only be the Soul, with its own ego that thus allows the Soul to know itself as a Soul that is eternal. Another way to validate the same thing occurs when we sometimes wake up from sleeping and cannot immediately 'remember' who we are: the current subjective ego, the "I," of this life. It takes some effort to actually remember the subjective I when this occurs. So, again, the question becomes "who and what must make the effort to remember the subjective 'I' of the current life?" Obviously it can only be our Soul.

So, again, as evolution proceeds in this Spiritual state, there is a progressive shift in the center of gravity within the Soul's consciousness. When this shift firmly takes hold then the Soul, in any given life, is simultaneously experiencing its eternal 'self' or ego, while at the same time experiencing the subjective ego, and the individuality attendant to it, that it has created for its own ongoing evolutionary reasons and intentions. This is very similar to when we stand at the beach when the Sun goes down and at that moment when the Sun is equally half above and below the horizon. In this state of consciousness, the Soul is aware from within itself of all the prior lives that it has lived, and at the same time aware of the specific life, ego, that it is currently living. Progressively, as evolution proceeds in the Spiritual state of evolution, the Soul also becomes consciously aware of the Source Of All Things. This occurs as the consciousness of the Soul becomes truly universal: the inner experience of the entire universe within one's own consciousness. This state of 'cosmic consciousness' allows one to actually experience the very point of the manifested Creation itself: the interface between the unmanifested and the manifested. As this occurs, the Soul then also becomes aware of all the Natural Laws that govern and correlate to the very nature of Creation itself. In the most advanced states of evolution, the Soul, now being completely identified with these Natural Laws of Creation, is then able to harmonize with those laws in such a way as to use those laws at will in conjunction with the Will Of All Things: that which is the very origin of those Natural Laws. (Rad)

1st stage Spiritual

In the first subdivision in the Spiritual state, the Soul progressively becomes aware of just how 'small' it is, because of the increasing universal dimensions that are occurring within its consciousness. This is vastly different than being the center of one's own universe, as reflected in the Consensus state for example. Of itself, this has a naturally humbling effect on the Soul, and thus the current subjective ego, Moon, that it has created. It is exactly this naturally humbling archetype that progressively allows the center of gravity to shift within the Soul's consciousness from the subjective ego to the Soul itself, and ultimately to a conscious union with the Source Of All Things. As a result, the Soul desires to progressively commit itself to the desire to reunite with the Source. As this occurs, the Soul will progressively commit itself to devotional types of Spiritual practice in this subdivision. Within this, the Soul desires to commit itself to various forms of work that all correlate to being of service to the larger whole, of service to others in some way. Many will naturally want to orient to various forms of the healing arts or to start 'centers' in which the healing arts in some way are the focus.

The core issue here is that the Soul desires to do a work on behalf of the Source Of All Things, and to use the work as a vehicle through which The Source can be inwardly experienced because of the nature of the work. In the East this is called Karma Yoga. In this first subdivision, the Soul becomes progressively aware of all that it needs to improve upon within itself. A heightened state of awareness occurs that makes the Soul aware of all its imperfections and, as a result, the Soul can now become highly self-critical. Even though this is natural, it also creates a potential danger or trap to the Soul in that this heightened state of critical self-awareness can cause the Soul to not feel 'good enough' or 'ready' to do the task, or work, that it is being inwardly directed to do. This then sets in motion all kinds of excuse-making, always manifesting as perfectly rational arguments, of why the Soul will not do what it should do when it should do it. The way out of this trap is to realize that the path to 'perfection' occurs by taking one step at a time. As evolution progresses through this first subdivision, the Soul will increasingly have direct perception of the 'single eye,' or the third eye, which is inherent to consciousness. As a result, this perception allows the Soul to merge with that single eye in such a way that various types and states of cosmic consciousness will occur, which will lead into the second subdivision within the Spiritual state. (Rad)

1st stage Spiritual manifestations

In relation to how the 1st stage Spiritual condition can manifest, at the point where the Soul is preparing for direct Spiritual experience, ie experience of union with the Divine. In these patriarchally conditioned times, it is hard for the Soul to endure being at this stage, because of how patriarchy has distorted the natural life of the emotions. This distortion of the natural life of the emotions has produced weak egos, ie egos which are weak because the Soul has not been nurtured as it needs, and thus, the Soul, and the egos they create, are deeply permeated by a fundamental insecurity. No Soul or ego can feel safe within themselves if they have not experienced natural nurturing and caring, allowing to correctly identify themselves. This fundamental insecurity has created – to one degree or another – the desire to be powerful, or strong in some way. I assume such types of desires have been created in Souls because of patriarchal conditioning, because, if the Soul had been naturally nurtured and cared for, why should these desires to have power exist? These desires, in turn, have conditioned the misidentification of the Soul or the ego: thus, the

Soul believing or thinking or feeling it is something which it is not, or which is only a small part of what it really is. These weak egos, no matter how strong they can feel, reach this point where they begin to know that they are not what they thought, and that life itself is so much larger than all they have known before.

Here the Virgo purging desires begin to operate, in order to purify the prior identity associations, and the desire nature. The purging is necessary because the Soul is preparing to re-identify and re-experience itself in a new way. However, the weak egos are still hungry, so to speak, because the Souls have not been naturally nurtured and cared for, this being the causal factor for the weakness of the egos in first place – or its deluded sense of strength (which blossomed in the 3rd stage Individuated condition). Thus, the Soul, while in the process of purging and emptying itself from its prior associations and desires, begins to intensely desire the experience of union with the Divine, where it will find the Source of inner security it has lacked for so long (understanding this has been conditioned by the patriarchal ways of emotional relation to itself and others). The intensity of this desire to unite with the Divine is the origin of the 'hunger,' anxiety, and greed or avidity. At the same time, this desire is not totally pure: it is still mixed or contaminated with the pre-existing desire to have power or to be strong, its egocentric will and desires, etc. This is the reason why the Soul is purging, and will continue to purge until its desire nature becomes very pure: just the remaining desire to unite with the Divine, or the Source. At this point in the evolutionary journey, such purity has not been achieved. Such purity can only be achieved progressively, little by little.

However, the Soul, despite its impurity, can have an experience of such union with the Divine, and at some point this experience will necessarily begin to manifest. When this occurs, and because this experience is so fulfilling, and so nurturing, the Soul will want 'more,' and this desire for 'more' will be conditioned by the avidity, or hunger (or thirst). Because of this, the Soul can now be presented to, or come to face with, something which shows itself as the Divine, but in reality is not the Divine. Instead, it is a projection of the Soul's own desire nature, including separating desires. And this can present itself as being the Divine, and the Soul will be invited to unite with this, to enter in this spiritually deluded experience of wholeness. The need is to discriminate (Virgo) between God and evil, in that which is being presented to the Soul as Divine. In some cases this can be quite difficult, and it may be easier to discriminate between the nature of the Soul's desires and the different emotional states and emotional attitudes which are being combined within, in face of this 'temptation,' a temptation which may also include a 'temptation of not being tempted.' If the Soul, because of its separating desires, accepts to unite with this projected wholeness or mix of inner states and desires, it will gain a deluded sense of power, where its separating desires are indiscernible from the true Divine.

Thus, the Soul will experience itself as Divine, including the Soul's own separating desires, becoming spiritually 'intoxicated' with its own separating desires. This experience can manifest as being invited to enter back into Pardes, or Paradise, ie a state of consciousness pre-existing to duality, and the distinction between good and evil. And, of course, such state of consciousness exists, and the Soul is destined to 'return' to such state of consciousness. However, if the Soul does not honor its own inner created duality, which translates in discernment between good and evil as it manifests from within itself, it will become intoxicated. Why? Because such inner duality and inner distinction between good and evil – no matter how wrong or partial it may be – is a reflection of the Soul's separating desires, which needs to be consciously purged, step by step. Thus, the Virgo/Mercury needs to create an order within the inner experience, and discriminate between the different emotional states and desires, thus discerning what is pure, and what is not pure (ie paradoxically creating duality in order to purge duality). Only thus can the true 'Paradise' be entered into and known, progressively. If the Soul fails to continue with this ongoing purging of its desire nature, it will be identifying the Divine with a projection of itself, thus feeling full of an egocentric power of some kind. (Gonzalo)

The 1st stage Spiritual has been described as Virgo-like. The Soul has gotten itself across the line between 3rd stage Individuated and stepped into 1st stage Spiritual. That process has required a great deal of humbling. Based on how I heard it once described, I have this mental picture of it. The Soul has spent countless lifetimes individuating itself from the consensus. It has been a hard-fought and hard-won attainment. There have been many scars and wounds, and that Soul has reached a point of feeling it knows itself. And yet, increasingly in 3rd stage Individuated there comes this sense of "there must be more than this" because all the great plans about how to reorganize society for the betterment of all are just not creating the changes the Soul was sure would happen when people saw how much better these new improvements would make things for everyone.

Any sort of major change like a shift from Individuated to Spiritual in general is initiated or triggered by some highly shocking or de-motivating (disillusioning) experiences. It's just not working the way I thought it would. Now what? This leads to some very deep Soul searching, where the Soul has to face it doesn't know how to do any more than what it has been doing – that is the humbling – and in a sense is brought to its knees. It sees that all of its hard-won individuality is not enough. And that is part of the resistance in early 1st stage Spiritual – it sees it has to surrender or give up what it's worked so hard to attain. Or at least it appears that way to that Soul at that time. There is inner knowing within that Soul of the direction it must head in, in order to evolve. And yet, resistance to that knowing based on the usual principle of familiarity equals security, and this change requires letting go of what has constituted security. It's the transition into that place where the outer work and behaviors have to progressively be aligned with that inner direction, and that requires having to release trying to control one's destiny – feeling I must provide for myself as no-one else is going to do it, which has been the evolutionary lesson of countless lives – the truth of that.

Suddenly now I am asked to let go of that and learn to trust that through following my natural inner impulses, God/Goddess somehow are going to provide for my needs (I of course have to act on the inner impulses of what I am supposed to be doing in place of spending all my time fending for my own survival – I can't just sit on the couch thinking about God, watching TV, thinking money and food are going to be left on my front porch because I am now so holy). It is scary to make that step – we have ample practical evidence it doesn't work that way. As we gradually start taking those steps we start seeing this very principle play out in the life, that it really truly does work when one stays aligned with inner intent. Then one gets a sense of how long they have been clueless that this even existed – the principle is universal truth. The Soul through its personas just has forgotten this and has lived in other ways. That too is humbling.

Awareness that one is one of 7 billion humans and billions of members of all other species on this planet, and that the planet itself, and even our whole galaxy, are microscopic in relation to the cosmos as a whole, and then we are talking only one dimension, a physical universe. Gradually one starts realizing the only thing that really makes any sense is to start living to serve the greater whole – everything else winds up feeling meaningless sooner or later. And then one sees how inconsistent one still is in their commitment to live to serve that greater whole, back and forth back and forth. And that further increases the sense of feeling very small – clueless even. And yet, as the inner commitment deepens, a feeling of deep sincerity strengthens – I may be clueless much of the time but at least I am sincere – and that counts for a lot.

One must be careful about using words like 'perfection.' "When I consider 1st stage Spiritual from reading the descriptions, I get a sense of perfection..." There is no perfection on this planet, and it's not even possible. Perfection cannot exist in a polarity reality whose basis is to evolve. The very principle of evolution is proof there is not perfection. There is nothing more to evolve to when one has reached perfection. And the principle of evolution, in every way, clearly underlies everything on this planet. The idea of perfection is the root principle in masochism, because we compare where we are to an ideal (Pisces) of perfection, which is an IDEAL, not a reality. In relation to the ideal (perfection) we can never measure up, for not one of the 7 billion humans does. This, in a masochist, then leads to a sense of guilt, for not being perfect enough, and a need to atone for what one has done that is less than one's definition of perfect. This becomes a repeating pattern of guilt and the need to atone, and attracting others who have guilt and rather than a need to atone for what they have done 'wrong,' a need to get back at, punish, those who have made them feel guilty, for they know they have done nothing wrong as it's all someone else's fault.

Such Souls have a need to punish, and masochists have a need to atone. Part of atoning is a sense of feeling inadequate or unworthy, which often creates a subconscious need to punish oneself, which can be actualized by drawing in external people with a need to punish others, who are quite happy to fill the masochist's need to be punished. The combined attraction leads to very dysfunctional interactions and relationships. The underlying basis of this dynamic is a belief that perfection is possible and indeed required, and a deep awareness that I am not at all perfect. It's extremely important to internalize that perfection in a body is never attainable. The standard to judge self against is not "Am I perfect?" but "Am I committed to making consistent ongoing progress (and taking the necessary ongoing steps/changes) even through inevitable temporary setbacks?"

1st stage Spiritual is NOT perfect. Neither is 3rd stage Spiritual. They represent *degrees of refinement* towards an ideal, the gradual exhaustion of separating desires. Realizing one is not going to be perfect in this life, while still holding an ideal to be that, is another source of increasing humility. (Steve)

1st stage Spiritual examples

Eckhart Tolle exhibits none of the signs of Spiritual arrogance, thus is not 2nd stage Spiritual. He is 1st stage Spiritual. He speaks in what people consider great wisdom. Jeffrey identified Dane Rudhyar as 1st stage Spiritual. (Steve)

2nd stage Spiritual

The second subdivision within the Spiritual state: As the Soul evolves into this state, it has already had various kinds of inner cosmic or universal kinds of experiences within its consciousness. Yet in this state the final shift in the center of gravity within consciousness from the subjective ego to the Soul itself has yet to occur. In this state the shift manifests more like a rubber band, wherein the gravity point keeps going back and forth from the subjective ego to the Soul. The problem that this generates is that the progressive inner experiences within consciousness of the universal, the cosmic, of the Source fuels the subjective ego in such a way that the Soul feels more evolved than it actually is. This can then set in motion in varying degrees of intensity 'Spiritual delusions of grandeur' from an egocentric and Soul point of view. When this occurs, such Souls will then feel that they have a Spiritual 'mission' to fulfill on behalf of others, of the world itself. It is important to remember in trying to understand this subdivision that as the Soul gets ever closer to the Source, The Light, that whatever egocentric impurities remain within the Soul must be purged. As a result, as the Soul draws closer to re-uniting with its own Origin, these impurities will manifest thru the current life subjective ego that the Soul's own ego contains.

These impurities can be many things, depending on the specific nature of each Soul, but all Souls in this subdivision will share one common impurity: the 'ego' of the Soul that is still identifying itself as somehow 'separate' from that which has created it. This ongoing delusion is thus reflected in the subjective ego that the Soul creates. This common impurity will then be exhibited in specific psychological behaviors that essentially boil down to such Souls pointing the way to themselves as the vehicle of 'salvation,' or to know God/ess; while at the same time, pretending that they are not. In other words, they are extremely good salespeople that peddle God/ess as the hook, in order to have themselves revered as the way to actually know God/ess. There is always a hidden or secret egocentric agenda within these Souls, that is masked by the overlay of whatever Spiritual or religious teaching they are representing. Examples of this, in recent modern history, would be Bhagwan Rajneesh, Clare Prophet, JZ Knight (Ramtha), Da Free John, Rasputin, and the like. As the Soul evolves through this subdivision, it finally realizes the nature of this root impurity. As a result, it experiences a 'natural' guilt. This guilt is then used by the Soul to create its own downfall, in order to 'atone' for that guilt. The downfall can occur in many different ways, depending on the specific nature of the circumstantial life that the Soul has generated. This downfall, caused by guilt and the need to atone for that guilt, thus serves as the final evolutionary development that allows the Soul to evolve into the third subdivision within the Spiritual state. (Rad)

The nature of the 2nd stage Spiritual evolutionary condition is one of core egocentric purification relative to Spiritual awareness which has been realized in the evolutionary journey. The Spiritual state itself is a Neptunian condition – the 2nd stage has Leonian emphasis within that. Before the Soul can evolve into the 3rd stage Spiritual, the ego has to go through a necessary purging, where all the egocentrically identified impurity can be purified and culminated. It can thus be a problematic stage. (Stacie)

To further clarify, the nature of 2nd stage Spiritual PRODUCES individuals who would be described as "a bit sketchy" AT BEST. These individuals "feel they have a unique toehold on the truth that no one else has ever had before." They HAVE in fact, by that point, had *real* Spiritual experiences, and that is the basis by which others are attracted to these folks. What you get is a mixture of truth and falseness. There IS truth in their teachings, and it is mixed with a bunch of self-oriented stuff. They are not fully living out their own teachings. Underlying it all is a deep permeating sense of Spiritual arrogance. Sometimes you can't see this at all until you get really close to the person. In one case, the person had been identified as being close to 3rd stage Spiritual but still in 2nd. There was tremendous truth in much of what they taught. In that particular case, the person did not manifest the possible extremes of 2nd stage Spiritual. They were not in huge power grabs, in fact were revolted by all that. Yet the issues manifested anyway, subtly, among those gathered around this individual. There was a core underlying arrogance that permeated through the words they spoke, while on the outside they lived a most humble life and not wanting to be idolized or put on a pedestal reality at all. And yet, there was this underlying state that had been there all along.

This is a natural archetype. The Spiritual state is a Neptune phenomenon. The 1st stage Spiritual is Virgo-like; the 2nd is Leo-like. Thus there is an explosion of a Spiritual ego. The words from the Pluto books are something like, the person at some point is destined to experience a major downfall, out of which that Spiritual ego pops, and they then begin the entry to 3rd stage Spiritual for real. It's been said it's possible for the 2nd stage Spiritual to be navigated in ways that are less harmful to others than some of the well-known extreme cases have turned into. These stages take a lot longer to pass through than we like to think they do, as in most cases, many many lifetimes for even a small amount of advancement. Yogananda said the typical person changes very little from lifetime to lifetime. To give evolutionary perspective, typically 2nd stage people are surrounded by followers or believers. As the 2nd stage person goes through their downfalls, these people also go through a downfall of sorts – the disillusioning of their hopes, dreams, beliefs, as the actual reality of the person they believed in and committed parts of their lives to becomes apparent. In other words, they are thrown back on themselves.

Many go into a complete victim state when this occurs, "I was blameless, I was taken advantage of, I was abused, I did nothing, all I did was give my all to the effort," etc. The gist of it is, it is part of the "believer's" evolutionary journey TO have these experiences with the 2nd stage person – often the necessary lesson is to stop looking outside of self for one's answers, to stop putting anyone on a pedestal and holding them up as better. And it is just as difficult for many of the believers to own that lesson, to look at their "mistakes," as it is for the 2nd stage Spiritual person to own their own lessons. They need each other, to learn, to grow. So it once again comes back to all concerned taking responsibility for the reality they have created and not blaming or being a victim. There are plenty of examples of true abuse occurring in such situations, from sexual predators, pedophiles, con artists, etc. and the wounds some experience from those types of realities are very deep and difficult.

There are always inner reasons an experience is necessary in someone's life, as difficult as it may be. The Pluto course transcript says, on how to recognize such people, "there is a fundamental discrepancy between how they are conducting their personal life and the nature of their teachings." (That of course applies to a whole range of modern day religious people and Senators, who are not 2nd stage Spiritual.) At times these people are indeed able to tap a place of deep Spiritual truth/wisdom that few among us can experience, but it's inconsistently applied. There are always exceptions to the rules, and because of their pumped-up self-declared state of evolution, they are exempt from the normal rules. The 2nd stage Spiritual section of Pluto Vol. 2 says, "truly God-realized Souls only point the way home, not to themselves." When you combine the Leonian tendency in 2nd stage Spiritual to feel one's own special brilliance with that statement, it makes it easier to identify those in 2nd stage Spiritual. They also feel an inner destiny/need to teach, so there are plenty of them around. And because so many people feel desperate and lost, there is no shortage of students. (Steve)

Generally speaking, there are seven levels of Samadhi realization, and typically, one has made it through the first four by the end of 2nd stage Spiritual. (Adina)

It is that total refusal to acknowledge and accept other perfectly valid paths to God (diversity itself is a Natural Law!) that is a hallmark of this evolutionary condition. That, and pointing to self as the path back to God, instead of pointing to God'dess and encouraging each individual to embrace his/her own natural way to spiritualize. (Lesley)

The 2nd stage Spiritual although indeed Leo-like, is actually Jupiter manifesting in this way – a personal identification with the 'truth' – as all Souls have different unique natures it plays out differently. The 2nd stage cannot be completed unless it reaches its Jupiterian peak. So at the end it will be a blow because the Soul BELIEVES (Jupiter) IN ITS OWN MERGING WITH THE TRUTHS – it simply can't help it – and will cause disillusionment to others. But this comes in stages – there are many life times BEFORE and AFTER the peak within the 2nd stage. (Lia)

I spent ten years in a community founded by someone I'd now call 2nd stage Spiritual (I didn't know of such terms at the time). I did not experience so much a single premise. I experienced a combination of truth (very much so truth) intermixed with b.s., the whole package presented as truth. The hook for us young folks was there was clearly much truth in parts of what was presented. So if those parts were true, other parts that seemed more questionable, they must be true also, because how could someone who knows all of that true stuff be doing other things that seem so off base. So maybe they aren't off base. But in fact they were. Even that however doesn't negate the parts that were true. Everything has to be put in perspective. That is the Virgo element, the need to learn to discriminate what is true from what is false, and to learn to trust one's own perceptions, no matter how unpopular they may be within the context of your sub-group. (Steve)

2nd stage Spiritual examples

Bhagwan Shree Rajneesh, Clare Prophet, Ramtha, David Koresh (Waco), Elijah Muhammad, Adi Da (Da Free John), JZ Knight (Ramtha), Grigori Rasputin.

3rd stage Spiritual

The third subdivision within the Spiritual state: In the final subdivision within the Spiritual state the Soul is now finally and firmly identified with that which has created it: The Source Of All Things. The center of gravity within consciousness has finally centered within the Soul, not on the subjective ego created by the Soul. At this point in the evolution of the Soul, all subsequent evolution through this final subdivision will be focused on the elimination of any separating desires that the Soul still has. Because of this final shift within consciousness to the Soul itself, the Soul is inwardly attuned to the Source Of All Things in such a way that it perceives itself as but a singular manifestation of the Source. Simultaneously, the Soul perceives all others, all of Creation, as manifestations of that Source. Thus the Soul's inner and outer responses to life itself, how life is understood and interpreted, how it comes to understand the nature of the life it is currently living, how it understands the purpose for the current life, and how it comes to make decisions relative to the life being lived, are all based on this inner attunement and alignment with that which has Created it.

As evolution begins in this final subdivision the Soul inwardly feels and knows that it is here to serve The Source in some way. It knows that it cannot just live for itself. It knows that it has some kind of work to do on behalf of the Source. The consciousness of the Soul at this point is entirely structured to give to others, and to give purely without any ulterior agenda or motive involved. The nature of the work will always involve the theme of teaching or healing in some way. Because the Soul is now consciously identified with the Source, the very nature of the Souls own vibration radiates in such a way that many others are drawn to it like a magnet. Many other Souls are drawn magnetically to these Souls, because they also reflect and radiate a fundamental wisdom of life, of a deep compassion at the 'human condition.' This occurs because, after all, these Souls have traveled a very long evolutionary journey, which has taken them through almost every kind of life experience imaginable.

Such Souls are naturally very unassuming, naturally humble, and have no desire whatsoever for any kind of acclaim to their ego. Quite the opposite: they shy away from such things and always remind anyone who tries to give them acclaim of any kind for that which they do, that all things come from God, or the Source. They only point the way 'Home,' and never to themselves. Conversely, these Souls can also attract to themselves others who project onto them all manner of judgments, projection of motives, intentions, of 'who they really are,' and wholesale persecution. The reason this occurs is because the very nature of these Souls is fundamentally pure, and full of the inner Light of the Source. As a result, their own inner light has the effect of 'exposing' the impurities in others, of the actual reality of others, versus the persona created by others; of others' actual intentions and motives for anything. Accordingly, those who do this kind of projection and so on feel threatened by these types of Souls, for they know they themselves are fundamentally dishonest, and that they are invested in having others believe in the persona they are creating to hide their actual reality/agendas. Feeling threatened thus causes these types of people to manifest this type of behavior (projections) with these Souls.

In the beginning of this third subdivision, the nature of the work that the Soul does, the number of people it is destined to help in some way through the vehicle of teaching or healing, is relatively small and limited to the immediate area of the community in which they live. Progressively this evolves from a limited application to increasingly larger circles, in which the nature of the work on behalf of the Source increases. In the end this increasing circle will include the entire world. And at the very end of evolution in this subdivision, the Soul will be remembered by countless others long after the physical life of the Soul is over – the nature of their life, and the teachings they represented. Examples of these types of Souls are 'individuals' like Jesus, Yogananda, Lao-Tzu, Buddha, Mohammed, Saint Teresa, and so on. (Rad)

Soul/ego from 3rd stage Spiritual perspective, what does it look like?

Imagine that you are underneath the water, in the ocean, and from there you perceive various waves upon the surface of that ocean that are of course manifesting from that ocean. And within the ocean, your awareness of being there, and perceiving those waves, is your Soul that is perceiving the various egos/personalities of many, many lifetimes: the waves. So on the one hand the center of your consciousness, your awareness, is your Soul, and, on the other, you are aware from that center of the different lifetimes that your Soul has created for its own purposes: the evolutionary intentions of your Soul, and KNOWING the reasons why for each of those lifetimes. And from within your Soul, ocean, you are of course aware of the current wave, the current ego/personality, of the life that is being lived now. This awareness creates a conscious knowing of all those lives that have led to the present life simultaneously: all at once. On the one hand this creates a real sense of stability within the Soul because of this, and, on the other, it can create a sense of instability in the sense of 'remembering' which wave, the current life, to SURFACE THROUGH.

The experience of this center of gravity in the Soul is very, very analogous to standing on a beach at sundown where the Sun is equally below the horizon, and above it. So the person is aware of their Soul because that is the center of gravity of their consciousness, and all the lives that have led to this one, the current moment, current life, and at the same time being aware of the moment of this life. This is an ongoing double awareness all the time for such a Soul. Thus, how it understands and perceives reality, the reality of itself, and the reality of everything else, is totally different than those who are not in this state of consciousness. Such a Soul is aware of the past OF EVERYTHING THAT HAD LEAD TO THE CURRENT MOMENT, AT ANY MOMENT. And that includes the past of other Souls. Imagine carrying a consciousness like that ALL THE TIME. Thus, how everything is understood, perceived, and interpreted with the corresponding behavior and actions of such a Soul is totally different than for those Souls who have not evolved to this state of consciousness. (Rad)

Spiritual state, and Saturn

Saturn, like all planets, absolutely correlates with Spiritual evolution. As Saturn is about the nature and structure of our current reality at any given time, I believe that the task (Saturn!) regarding Saturn/Capricorn, for all of us 1st stage Spiritual Souls, is to deepen our Spiritual reality, through disciplines (Saturn) like yoga, proper lifestyle (which means appropriate relationships, Libra; proper nourishment for the body, Cancer; proper understanding and directing of the desire nature, Aries). Like all planets, the way Saturn manifests in our lives can be evolved over the lifetime, based on a strengthening and deepening of the one desire to know God, and return Home. Saturn helps us manifest a Spiritual reality on Earth within our own lives, when our desire nature (Aries) and emotional body (Cancer) are in alignment with that purpose, so that a Soul becomes a 'concrete' (Saturn!) example for others along the same path. (Yogananda was a Capricorn, with a 10th house Pluto/Neptune conjunction!) Saturn/Capricorn energy helps all of us become better creators, in the end, no matter where we fall on the spectrum. (Lesley)

Karmic 'script' of the Soul

All things in our life start from within ourselves first: the evolutionary and karmic 'script' of the Soul in any given life. Thus the progression of the planets, and the aspects that they are making, reflect this ongoing evolutionary script of the Soul at any point in time. (Rad)

Ocean/wave analogy

Neptune can be both the Wave and the Ocean depending ON THE POINT OF VIEW of consciousness itself as encased in the human form. If we remember the natural trinity between Pisces/Neptune, Scorpio/Pluto, and Moon/Cancer – God, Soul, Ego – then of course it's possible for the ego within a given Soul to be 'intoxicated' – Neptune – with itself via the Ego that it creates. Thus, its relationship to itself is separative in nature relative to the totality of the Creation that it is inter-related with. Thus, from its point of view, it has become deluded – Neptune – within the wave: ego. Other Souls of course, relative to evolution, have their center of gravity – Saturn – within the ocean and know that their Soul and its ego are simply part of the totality of Creation itself that is co-equal in nature. Thus, their inner Neptune, is within the Ocean.

In the wave/ocean analogy the sense of identity depends on the evolutionary condition of the Soul. For most that identity lies in the wave: the ego that feels, perceives and thinks that it is separate from everything else. From the vantage point of the wave then everything else, the boats, ripples, whatever else correlates to the totality of its life circumstances become simply props in its personal play. For Souls who have evolved progressively into the Spiritual state the center of gravity within their consciousness progressively shifts from the ego to the Soul itself. As such their sense of identity is the Soul, the ocean, upon which the wave of its ego has been created for whatever ongoing evolutionary purposes it has. A Soul in that condition thus experiences simultaneously its distinct egocentric personal identity while at the same time its timeless Soul identity.

What it all comes down to is how something is perceived including our own sense of 'identity.' From the point of view of consciousness the issue, in the end, is where the center of gravity is within in. Gravity has a natural correlation to Saturn, Capricorn, and the 10th house. Saturn, etc., also correlates to the structural nature of anything. Thus, the structural nature of consciousness. It also has a natural correlation to the boundary of anything. Thus, it correlates to the natural boundary between our subjective awareness and the consciousness therein, and the progressive levels of the unconscious as in the individuated unconsciousness, Uranus, and the collective unconsciousness/consciousness which is Neptune. Deep within the unconscious is the Soul. Consciousness, as such, emanates from the primary brain. Within the subjective consciousness in all of us is the egocentric structure that the Soul creates in each life to facilitate its evolutionary intentions and progressions.

The ego is the Moon, Cancer, and the 4th house, and is, of course, the natural polarity of Capricorn, the 10th, and Saturn. For most individuals, given the natural evolutionary stages, the sense of identity is their own ego. Thus, the PERCEPTION of being separate from everything else. Thus, the WAVE on the ocean where the wave correlates to the subjective ego within the consciousness of the individual. So if the center of gravity within the individual is their ego then their sense of identity is then defined by the wave: their ego. Yet, as evolution proceeds, the center of gravity within an individual's consciousness shifts to the Soul itself: the OCEAN. The natural boundary of Saturn relative to the structural nature of consciousness dissolves in such a way that the PERCEPTION OF IDENTITY changes from the wave to the ocean. As a result the individual is then perceiving, is consciously aware of, its timeless identity called their individual Soul and the egocentric structures it creates from life to life AT THE SAME TIME. In other words the Soul is aware of and perceives the continuation of its ongoing lifetimes from life to life at the same time. The center of gravity is the Ocean, the Soul. As a result they do not perceive themselves as separate from anything, but, in fact, inter-related to everything. (Rad)

Sense of aloneness and alienation in the Spiritual state

The percentage of people on earth in the Spiritual state is between 2% and 10%. In other words, what you know as reality within yourself can never be grasped by 90%–98% of those around you, at this point in time. This in itself creates an intense sense of aloneness. There IS no way you can integrate, or even accept, the mainstream Consensus on its own terms. The approach one must learn to adopt is to realize you can be (or, may have to be) IN it, but it has nothing to do with who you are. It's like, that is your CAREER (10th house), but it is not who you are and in itself will never complete you. That just has to be accepted. It comes with the territory. All the frustration, aloneness, and the rest, point you back to yourself, to realize ever more deeply your actual nature, who you truly are. You also have to remember, you are not the Doer – the real work simply comes through you. You have a deep inner yearning to do what you feel you have come here to do, but also have to remember, past a certain point the timing is not up to you. All you can do is show up, inwardly say, "I am ready," and at times when appropriate it will happen. It's not so much about you getting to use your gifts that would help others as it is about serving the needs of those God sends your way, whether two or twenty thousand.

If you are putting forth all your efforts and they are not appearing, this is not a mistake, nor does it mean you are doing something wrong. It would come down to timing, and patience. And acceptance of What Is at this time. As far as having to work in the mainstream, this too is likely temporary. You are not supposed to "like" it or feel at home there, you will not fit in (ever), and it has little to do with who you are. Really accepting that, deeply, helps. It's not uncommon that even within situations like that, you wind up being of service to others, as you wind up in conversations with people who start revealing things they normally don't discuss, and then you have insight that helps them, eases their mind, gives them new approaches to consider. They would not normally have access to this, in the lives they have created. And then you are fulfilling a function that God has placed you there to do, helping others in the most mundane setting. The point is, in such circumstances you are always thrown back on yourself, to your baseline sense of who you are – out of that aloneness and alienation, you gradually become increasingly aware of greater depth within. Inner resolve strengthens, and you realize ever more that even though you may be stationed within the mainstream, it has nothing to do with who you are. (Steve)

It has something to do with the principle of self-honesty. Since we live in a 70% Consensus world, the more I insist on being my unique self, the fewer people are going to be able to relate to me, and vice versa. By the time 1st stage Spiritual is reached the Soul has begun to recognize to some extent it's never going to find ANYTHING in this world it can relate to or feel at home in. That may not be the friendliest news someone has ever received – they are not yet in true communion with the Soul. It creates an increasing sense of aloneness and alienation. On the deepest levels the intention is to force it inward, to learn to build that inner connection. Often times that impulse is resisted for all it's worth. I believe I recall Jeffrey having written once that, coming up through the Individuated stages, the Soul has finally won its "hard-won individuality." And now the inner nature is changing and it seems to be getting asked to surrender even this hard won individuality. And the obvious initial response is resistance and, "I don't think so." So it's a back and forth struggle. This is the reason for inconsistent practice if moving towards Divinity in the early stages of 1st stage Spiritual, back and forth, back and forth. It's a hard thing to accept, that you are fundamentally going to feel alienated from 95% of everything you encounter and everyone you meet. (Steve)

What makes you think a 1st stage Spiritual person doesn't feel as different on the inside as a 1st stage Individuated person? I'd say they may feel even more different. One difference between the two would be in general the 1st stage Spiritual will have better come to terms with accepting their inherent difference – they may not like it, but they have come to terms with it. (Remember, they have passed through 3rd stage Individuated in which they have fully realized they can never again be pulled back into the collective.) So even while hiding they would still on some level know who they are. They are just trying to keep others from finding out, wanting to avoid repetition of painful consequences of being seen that they have subconscious memories of. (Steve)

Discrimination in the Spiritual state
Discrimination does indeed occur in the Spiritual stage starting within the 1st stage. It is indeed an evolutionary imperative to do so throughout the totality of the Spiritual stage. As Wolf taught the Spiritual stage as a whole correlates to the sign Pisces. The natural polarity of Pisces of course is Virgo: discrimination. (Rad)

The 1st stage Spiritual can buy into illusions from time to time and will necessarily experience some disillusionment in order to proceed with its evolution to get closer to the "whole truth." The Soul starts to learn to think for itself from 1st stage Individuated onwards. It can discriminate between true and false statements or teachings from this time onward relative to its own understanding, awareness and individual Soul structure. 1st stage Spiritual needs quite a good Spiritual framework to buy into something. Of course that still can be and from time to time will be an illusion in essence, but that's not because the 1st stage Spiritual cannot discern or discriminate at all (Consensus state is when a Soul can't) it is because the nature of illusion (Neptune) is always based on the APPEARANCE of reality. In other words something that appears real is actually an illusion in the end. The illusions that the 1st stage Spiritual tend to buy into always resonates with some inner IDEALS that the 1st stage Spiritual Soul has. That's the key. So because of those ideals and the resulting wish that it would be true may lead the Soul to believe/follow something that is actually NOT what it appeared/presented/stated it was/is. Part of this comes from the inner humility which translates to self-doubt. The 1st stage Spiritual tends to question itself and easily considers others (who present themselves "spiritually") as more knowledgeable than itself. This too adds to the tendency to fall prey to false teachers, but the point being: those who don't have the inner cycles of doubt/belief/clarity/confusion but follow something without discrimination are Consensus even if it is an alternative religion, while there are those who have followed or follow a mainstream religion and yet inwardly experience the above cycles with great inner intensity, are likely to be in the 1st stage Spiritual. These details depend on the individual circumstances of each Soul within each given life.

Any Soul's actual reality is defined from within, and not by the outer circumstances, ie just because somebody may be following a mainstream religion doesn't necessarily mean they are in the Consensus state, and in the same way just because somebody is part of a New Age or whatever Spiritual movement doesn't necessarily mean they are 1st Spiritual. A closer look at the individual's actual reality is what counts. Each major evolutionary state and their three sub-states have a spectrum wherein, in other words there is room for continuous evolution within any evolutionary stage. None of the stages are one or two life times. Far far more than that! So for example, within the 1st stage Spiritual there is an INCREDIBLE AMOUNT OF DISCRIMINATION intended to be learned for each Soul in their own unique way. Let's say 10 lifetimes after a Soul entered the 1st Spiritual, would they display the same Spiritual gullibility than 10 lifetimes before? There will be no evolution if that would be true, and yet the Soul is still in the 1st Spiritual. (Lia)

Emotional complexes in the Spiritual state
Being in the Spiritual state of evolution does not necessarily mean that co-dependent dynamics or other emotional complexes such as alienation etc. do not happen. They just happen with more conscious awareness (eventually), with the underlying intention of bringing about a deeper relationship with the divine within, which then naturally flows to service and healing. In the Consensus, they are played out but with NO awareness, and it takes a lot more work (or several hundred more lifetimes) to become aware. (Patricia)

Awareness of Soul in the Spiritual state
Awareness of Soul is only going to begin in later 3rd stage Individuated, accelerating as the Spiritual stages are reached. The definition of Spiritual stage is increasing conscious awareness of the Soul, thus it's not possible for it to exist consciously in earlier evolutionary stages. "Knowing" something and living it consciously are two different things. There could be exceptions – evolved people with a Spiritual mission involving the physical – perhaps Gandhi. In general, no. The more one is living in the Soul the deeper the sense of alienation from all orientations other than that. One increasingly feels things they used to consider really important no longer matter as much. Growing awareness in everything except the Soul is temporary. (Steve)

Advancing one's own evolution in the Spiritual state
A Spiritual state individual's burning desire to know the Divine will accelerate their evolutionary journey. If you find yourself on a large boat that appears to be sinking: even if you feel you may eventually drown, you still do everything you possibly can to try to help. Reality is accepting the boat may still sink. But you do all you can anyway, because it's the right thing to do. That is what EA means when it says the value is in the effort, not in the outcome. You are one Soul out of seven billion humans on this planet. So to the extent one Soul out of seven billion affects the human collective, yes you are advancing the collective evolution with your burning desire to know the Divine. But the point of your burning desire is not to advance the collective evolution but to advance

your own evolution. Advancing the collective is something that just happens from your personal efforts. Of course you have the desire to help. But the only person you can really change is yourself. You can support others in their evolutionary journey, but it's up to them to take the steps. (Steve)

Evolutionary stage – baby and parents
Generally, any given Soul born into the evolutionary stages of its parents will either reflect that stage, be just beyond it, or just behind it. This is not always true of course, but generally true. Since the very essence of astrology, all of it, is rooted in the natural science of observation and correlation this then means it will take some time to specifically know the EA of any incarnating Soul in the form of a baby. In other words, one can't know until enough time has been spent in such observation/correlation of the baby unless certain Souls have the inner capacity to know such things independent of observation/correlation. (Rad)

Evolutionary state of children
Children come into life in a specific evolutionary state, and specific conditioning patterns set in later in life (as children grow up) that are not there as a small child. This tends to start happening at the first Saturn square (at about 7 years of age) because we start to become aware of the nature of the society/culture we are growing up in, and what that society expects from us in terms of conformity to it (Saturn). Of course, this is also true of the family environment (Saturn correlates to the authority figure in our life that tends to be the father, and the father will act as the parent who determines the accepted behavior that must be conformed to). So, this conditioning happens on a societal/cultural level and within the family (Cancer polarity point to Capricorn/Saturn). The way to determine the evolutionary state of a child is the same as an adult – observe the child's natural orientation and "bottom line." Some children are much more interested in art/poetry/individualist areas, than others who are mainly focused on material possessions and more "traditional" areas of life. Also, within the Individuated state you feel that the child is alienated from the rest of the group, and will hopefully seek out support for this in one way or another. (Deva)

In general, children are either in the same evolutionary condition as the parents, or sometimes a little ahead. But this is in general, not an absolute. (Rad)

If you want to get metaphysical about it, "children" (in reality, Souls inhabiting small bodies) are coming here straight out of the astral, where every thought/desire manifests right before your eyes. Is it any wonder they expect "instant gratification?" They are not yet (once again) *used to* earth reality, where the law of Time is present, where desires are not instantly fulfilled. To me the reaction of a child wanting "instant gratification" is not so much a function of a level of Spiritual evolution, it is part of an adjustment process that all Souls must go through. A difference between more evolved "Souls as children" and Consensus "Souls as children" is the more evolved Souls would be more conscious of the nature of this reality from past experience, and thus have more context/perspective, thus be able to more rapidly adapt and accept the inherent limitations of life in a three dimensional child body. Not too many Souls are excited about the opportunity of entering yet another body where they can feel limited and constricted – that's not too hard to grasp! It comes down to the capacity to accept the limitations, to realize WHY they are being imposed – to further that Soul's evolution, and hopefully that, along the way, also serves others. The more evolved Souls will inherently remember this and thus their behaviors may be more tempered than the more typical 3 year olds.

We also live in a consumer culture that feeds the immediate gratification impulse in children, on purpose, to create life-long patterns of consuming (feel bad? go shopping), to sustain our economic system. So children "get used to" that impulse being immediately fulfilled, and then they start to expect it as a right. Behaviors that are pretty common in adults too. That is an example of societal conditioning, of creating values that are not natural, that ultimately have an ulterior motive – to benefit someone else at the expense of the individual so conditioned. The hallmark of 1st stage Individuated is a feeling of being different and not wanting to be different, trying to hide the differences, compensating by acting "normal" (ie how everyone else does). Typically the true "normal" people can see there is something different about that person anyway. If the person is of a masochistic temperament they could blame self for their sense of alienation, "What is wrong with me? Why can't I be like everyone else?" whereas others would blame external forces, victimization (a Pisces attribute).

As the Soul evolves into the higher forms of the Individuated stage it learns that feeling alienated is part of the price it must pay for being an individual, since at least 70% of people (Consensus) are not individuals (don't think for themselves). To a person who follows the herd, a person who thinks for self is perceived as threatening. People follow the herd because they believe that brings security – acceptance by the mass of the group. The Individuated person has begun to notice that this acceptance is dependent on conforming to the collective's (conditioned) beliefs/values, that when one's views are contrary, the acceptance disappears. Thus that is not real security at all. The ultimate lesson is that the only true security is within. Most of us have been conditioned to look without for security. That becomes the source of the alienation – "so few see things as I do." At first it feels lonely and limiting. Through following that path one becomes increasingly aware of their own uniqueness – which becomes increasingly liberating. Thus the price of alienation is balanced by increased self-awareness. Souls making the transition from Consensus to Individuated don't yet have that increased self-awareness. Thus they may experience more of the detrimental aspects of that process, and so resist it.

To tie this back to the evolutionary condition of children, when you see signs in a child of a capacity to be an individual, to not let the need for approval from others limit its forms of self-expression, who seems to understand in some deep way some essential things about the nature of life, is described by others as being wise beyond their years, these are signs of a Soul that is in a more advanced evolutionary state. Signs of this can be seen from early childhood. They are going to FEEL all that alienation – it does not go away in the Spiritual state – if anything it intensifies – but it can be better accepted in the Spiritual state – the Soul has come to take it as a given. Whether they LIKE it is another issue altogether – acceptance is required. The same sort of questions or signs you would look for in an adult in terms of determining evolutionary stage can be applied to a child – they are just going to express these words or attitudes in ways aligned with the way a child will think. They are still a child, even if the Soul is very highly evolved. The working of these things is what EA calls Natural Law – it is the way that life is, that life actually works, regardless of what I think about those ways. It's simply What Is, self-evident. (Steve)

There is no one explanation for it [Consensus child of Spiritual parents] as all evolutionary and karmic conditions are unique and specific to each Soul including the parents who would have such a child. It is not common for parents who themselves have evolved to the Spiritual condition to have children in the Consensus. I don't think I would use the word 'rare' to describe this, but simply not common. It can be quite difficult to know the evolutionary condition of a child when very young. As ever it does come down to observation and correlation but that normally requires some time to assess correctly. There are no magic techniques to employ: only observation over an amount of time can lead to the right understanding. (Rad)

Confusing the natural innocence of children with their level of Spiritual evolution: they are not the same thing. It takes many lifetimes to move along the evolutionary scale, even a small amount in the great majority of cases. This measures the evolutionary stage of the Soul itself, not the personality. To the Soul each new lifetime is just one more opportunity to advance itself at least to a small extent. The basic nature of a Soul is pure, and we see this reflection in early childhood. But soon enough we start seeing the places within that Soul, brought in from the past, appearing. Because that is the actual nature of that Soul, operating in its actual state of self-awareness – after all, evolutionary stages represent degrees of self-awareness vs externally defined expectations of who one is and is supposed to be. I don't see it as Souls "diminish" into an Individuated state. If you think about it, 70% of Souls haven't even reached the Individuated state. Thus how can they diminish into something they don't even know in the first place? We are born here, and as we fully enter the body in the first years of childhood, we find ourselves operating from the same m.o., the same self-reality, self-identity we left with, perhaps in old-age, in the last go round. In other words, we start exactly where we left off, literally. Which explains the so-called rebellious child, who simply is more evolved than its parents.

It's a pretty strange feeling to be 3 years old and realizing you understand way more than your parents do. Whereas other children, perhaps even siblings, are quite content to simply accept the reality put forth by the parents. Nothing is inherently stated that a Soul in an Individuated state is not going to have the same desires for immediate gratification that other humans have. It comes with the territory. I would say the difference is, as a Soul evolves, the nature of its relationship with the desire for immediate gratification changes – it becomes more okay with the reality that it's not going to get everything it wants when it wants it. It matures in that way – more inherent acceptance of the laws that define human life in a body. Again, a child starts where it left off. An Individuated child is going to display a sense of alienation from an early age. It will feel different. In some cases it will be born into a family that cannot relate to that child's reality at all, which has the effect of throwing that child back on itself, to further deepen and develop that necessary individuating process. In other cases the child will be born into a family that itself is in an individuating process, or beyond, that will validate that child's natural ways and teach it that what is right for that child is what that child knows is right for itself, no matter anyone else's opinions on that matter.

It is unique for each child/Soul – there are no generic rules. It's all dependent on the nature of that Soul's past, and the nature of the life lessons that Soul has planned for itself in the new incarnation. A principle that in EA is called Evolutionary Necessity – certain experiences are simply necessary to bring about the desired growth. In some cases those experiences can feel painful, lonely, and difficult, in others more inclusive nurturing and warm. It all depends on what that Soul has decided is the most effective method for bringing forth the insights it wants to develop in the present life. In terms of a child exhibiting signs of both 3rd stage Consensus and 1st stage Individuated, that is what would be described as at the cusp of a change in evolutionary stage, which itself can take several lifetimes to really settle into the new stage. The person will go back and forth, exhibiting signs of both. Yet they will be predominantly in one or the other, which reflects the place of actual evolutionary stage. At some point the actual crossover occurs, and then it progressively shifts forward from there. This phenomena is quite similar to having Pluto at the exact cusp between two houses. One archetype is culminating, a new one is being birthed. Prior to the actual conjunction to the cusp, the dominant archetype is the old one. Once the conjunction to the cusp has occurred the dominant archetype is the new one – in that case there will still be traces of the old exhibited at times, as it is familiar and has been the prevailing m.o. for a long time. Over time the imprint of the old progressively weakens and the archetype of the new progressively strengthens. We can't measure the shifting in evolutionary stage by looking at a two dimensional birth chart, as we can to chart the oncoming conjunction of Pluto and a house cusp, but the phenomena is basically the same – the old is slowly yet progressively replaced with the new. The issue is, new always feels insecure, unknown and uncertain, old feels safe, known, familiar, comfortable. Thus our tendency to stay with what we know. But it becomes like a child whose growing foot no longer fits comfortably in a favorite sneaker – it's becomes too small to contain the foot, so ultimately it must be released and move forward into a new pair of shoes, shoes that need to be broken in, gotten used to, made my own so to speak. Which does gradually occur.

The Soul comes to whatever family can provide a chance to learn the appropriate lessons for that Soul's evolution. Every possible combination [of evolutionary states of family members] can occur, as necessary for the evolution of the Souls involved. Remember, it's not just the evolution of the child – the Souls of the parents have their own evolutionary intentions. When an "advanced" child is born into a Consensus family, something within the Souls of those parents has also desired this situation, as it will result, at some point, in their own evolutionary advancement, even if they strongly resist it. The work of the EA astrologer is to look at the overall dynamics of all concerned and try to discern why these experiences have been necessary for both the child and the parents. I seem to remember however (not positive) Jeffrey saying that in the majority of cases the evolutionary stage of the parents will be close to the evolutionary stage of the children, as in the same or one stage higher or lower – 1st stage Individuated and 3rd stage Consensus, etc. The parents' stage can be more advanced than the child's, which has its own reasons for being. Every possible combination occurs. (Steve)

Evolutionary state of twins

Perhaps in the 'identical twin' cases, where even the houses are probably almost identical too, the evolutionary stage would be sometimes the only or major point of difference (assuming they were different Souls, not twin Souls etc. which would probably be a pretty low likelihood)? (Upasika)

A difference in evolutionary stage would certainly be a point of difference. But it's really important to keep in mind we have a mainly invisible incredibly long past that we project into every 'new' moment. And we are shaped by that past – our very conception of 'me' is mainly based on our individual past, filtered through the conditions and experiences of the present lifetime. So even if the two people have a very similar evolutionary stage they're still going to breathe life into the very similar script in very different ways. We really are, every one of us, truly unique. That is simultaneously a great gift, and also the source of a lot of our human sense of aloneness. (Steve)

In that light I suppose it couldn't be any other way, could it. I've never been involved with identical twins but if I ever had to read their charts I'd now look for those differences on the subtle and also deeper levels – I'd have a keener sense of what I was looking for, and then hopefully be able to see how exactly the same chart was working differently in each case. (Upasika)

Kristin Fontana has a (fraternal) twin sister. She contributed a chapter on twins to the book edited by Rose Marcus, "Insights into Evolutionary Astrology" which is very much about what you just said. She didn't say so in the book but the example charts she used are her own case. (Steve)

Hiding signature

A phenomena called masking or hiding – a Soul that creates an outer reality in which it operates, and has itself convinced it is, at a level below its actual state of Spiritual evolution. (This is often associated with the Pisces archetype – hiding.) Reasons for this can vary but quite commonly include intense traumas that have occurred in past lives relative to its actual state of Spiritual awareness, it being perceived as different, outside the mainstream, challenging or threatening to the existing order. And in the present life that Soul says to itself, "who needs more of that? I'm just going to act like I'm 'supposed to,' and convince myself that I'm not really as different as I feel I am." And it will live that way, perhaps for a really long time. Such Souls are identified when doing readings for them because on the outside they are living very conventional lives, yet the degree of depth and insight they exhibit goes well beyond the nature of the outer life, even the physical appearance – dress, manner of speaking, etc., they have adopted. (Steve)

Compensation

Compensation can show up in someone in any evolutionary stage where the person is not operating fully aligned with Natural Law. The gist of compensation is (as an example) if a person feels inadequate and bad about themselves inside (Virgo-like) they may cultivate an outer persona that seems really self-confident and almost full of self (Leo-like). It works the other way around also, a person with a big ego presenting themselves as humble and serving. Compensation is a form of AVOIDING rebalancing. Because it comes out of denial, where the person believes (Jupiter) that the way they are showing up IS the truth, when in fact it is a way of avoiding looking at (Virgo, denial) the actual reality, and pretending to be something other than what they really are. That is not my definition of rebalancing. If they OWNED the underlying condition and then practiced coming from a polarity to work towards balancing it, that I'd describe as rebalancing. Denial can never be a path to equilibrium. I'm not sure I'd call compensation a natural phenomenon. It's more like a survival mechanism. A person feels so wounded inside they can't show up as what and where they really are – they pretend (fooling themselves) to be more than or less than what they actually are. That is to survive. If aligned with Natural Law, a person would just accept wherever they found themselves to be – why would they need to compensate? There's a big difference between being aware you feel highly inadequate, accepting that you do and showing up anyway with acceptance of your inadequacies (humility), and showing up acting like you are confident and self-assured, an adopted persona, when that is not at all where the person is within themselves. In other words, compensation is more making a condition even more out of balance than it is rebalancing a condition. The thought is one that Jeffrey used to say, that where Jupiter is transiting it has gifts to bring you. But you have to be willing to give something up before you can receive the gifts. The "something" is not some random something that you pick out yourself. Rather it is something that has become outmoded in the life and needs to be let go of. I'd say it's not a conscious process – Jupiter is intuition – one would just know what the something needs to be. No letting go, no gifts. (Steve)

Evolutionary state and the retrograde archetype
The retrograde archetype operates at all levels of evolution for all Souls. The individualizing aspect of it means that it operates in a Uranus-like way in that it progressively rejects or rebels against the external conditioning of how a given archetype, eg Venus, is expected to be actualized or lived. The rejection or rebellion is about uncovering, progressively, what the actual truth is about the inherent individuality of any given Soul relative to all the various archetypes that in total equals the consciousness of the Soul in human form. The rejection or rebellion of the retrograde archetype thus accelerates the natural evolutionary progression of the Soul because it withdraws from the external expectations equaling conditioning of the planet, archetype, that is retrograde. This individualizing aspect of the retrograde archetype applies to all levels of evolution. In the Spiritual state, for example, it means for each Soul to discover their own individual way of reuniting with its source: God/ess. (Rad)

In ALL Souls, not just those with retrogrades, individuation is necessary for evolution to continue. The process of evolution IS the progressive individuation of the Soul, until that Soul finally realizes in full who it truly is, not intellectually but experientially. Until then the individuation process is the progressive stripping away of all conditioned senses of "me" that have accumulated over many lifetimes, until finally all that's left is the experience of the true "me." That process takes many lives. The difference in a chart with retrogrades is the individuation process is heightened, emphasized – because there has been resistance to that process in the past. So the Soul through retrograde has set up conditions that will force it to emphasize its own individuation, as a way of overcoming its own conditioned resistance to that process. Other symbols emphasizing the individuation process include a lot of 11th house or Aquarius, Uranus aspecting many planets, etc. (Steve)

Evolutionary state and Pluto retrograde
Pluto Rx can occur at any evolutionary stage/condition, however it is only an intention to liberate and de-condition. In other words, we all have a choice to cooperate with or resist the evolutionary intentions for our lives. Those in the Consensus state will typically suppress/repress and, thus, resist the evolutionary intentions symbolized by Pluto Rx through the act of emotionally withdrawing into him or herself but outwardly "going through the motions" so to speak because of the underlying need for conformity and social acceptance. For those in the Consensus it does create a higher degree of evolutionary pressure to move towards the Individuated state than those who have Pluto direct. (Deva)

Client readings, adjust for evolutionary stage
In terms of how to best use language during readings, it is very important to determine, of course, what is most important to the client (why the reading in the first place?), and take note of the kind of language they use, and adjust to whatever level (stage of evolution) of reality the client is at. Another good technique I use that is taught by my father is to look at Pluto's polarity point in the natal chart, and to use simple language that reflects the core evolutionary intentions for that Soul based on the understanding of what the polarity point symbolizes (guide the person in that direction). My main point is that based on the interaction with the client and understanding core dynamics within the chart, we can adjust our own language and approach to the reading to reflect the client's level of reality and orientation. (Deva)

How a planet, eg Mercury, manifests in each evolutionary stage – by Gonzalo Romero
[The examples are just examples, and don't intend to be exhaustive or comprehensive of all possible manifestations. This methodology can be further refined.]

First, we know the evolutionary stages are conditioned by archetypes. Consensus is conditioned by Saturn, Individuated is conditioned by Uranus, and Spiritual is conditioned by Neptune. That is, Capricorn, Aquarius, and Pisces within the natural zodiac. We just have to apply this to each archetype, first in general terms, let's say, Mercury, and then in an individual case, let's say Mercury in the 2nd house Virgo. In general terms, each archetype, eg Mercury, is conditioned in each evolutionary stage by Saturn/Capricorn, Uranus/Aquarius, and Neptune/Pisces.

Thus, within Consensus, Mercury is conditioned by the relationships within the zodiac of Gemini with Capricorn. Further, it is conditioned by the relationship between Virgo and Capricorn. Within the zodiac, an inherent inconjunct exists between Gemini and Capricorn. Very simply, this aspect reflects that, within Consensus, the thought and language forms are required to adjust – inconjunct – to the prevailing intellectual orientations defining the consensus of society. If the individual's thought forms fail to adjust to such requirement, a crisis – inconjunct – will be delivered upon the individual, a crisis of validation of these thought orientations, etc. At the same time, thought forms that are validated by Consensus, and that support Consensus, will be integrated within social functioning. Thus, the thought forms at this evolutionary stage need to support, be submissive, and serve, or be an extension of the intellectual constructions of Consensus – Virgo trine Capricorn. The individual thought orientation is expected to serve established authority from a position of inferiority, and if such position is assumed, the though forms of the individual will be accepted, validated and supported by social authority.

Now the same Mercury within the Individuated state. A natural trine exists between Gemini and Aquarius. Here we can see the tremendous development of neuronal connections required for people to start thinking in their own, personal ways, ie beyond Consensus, and the role within Individuation of transcultural thought forms, revolutionary ideologies, etc. Further, we can see the role of group associations with like-minded individuals that will support and encourage the emerging thought forms that allow the separation from Consensus, and then becoming a minority. With Virgo being inconjunct Aquarius, the thought forms intend to change society or to help society improve or become better, and the individual will experience diverse crises of alienation, exclusion, or persecution, because the new thought forms are at odds with Consensus.

Within the Spiritual state, that Gemini is square Pisces. Thus, an inherent crisis in consciousness/action because the individual desires to know the Whole, not just a part, the individual wants to experience the Unknown, instead of dealing with the known, and wants to relate to the unconditioned, absolute and timeless, instead of referring to the relative, time/space conditioned reality. Thus, the desire to de-condition thought forms, and define new thought forms that reflect the new purpose at the intellectual level. With Virgo being naturally opposite Pisces, the intellect is humbled because of the Soul's desire to know the Unknown, and because of the dynamic of contrast and comparison (opposition) with something so much larger. The individual will desire and need to define – Gemini square Pisces – new thought forms that serve to relate to a reality that is perceived in a new way, and that are adequate to be of service to the Source.

These are general archetypes that condition the Mercury function at each stage. Then we apply the archetypes to the individual Mercury in the birth chart, ie Mercury in 2nd house Virgo, keeping in mind the general archetypes.

Within Consensus, the trine between Virgo and Capricorn correlates with thought forms that intend to serve society in society's terms, or that are submissive to authority, or that are approved or validated by authority, etc. The natural trine between 2nd house and 10th house correlates to thought forms that support Consensus value associations, and that serve Consensus to survive, and to expand. These thought orientations will allow the individual to make money in an easy way (this is a possibility among others). In some cases, if the individual at this stage is more focused on serving society and helping society to survive, versus its own self-interest, some individuals with Mercury in Virgo in the 2nd may be able to only survive, or not to survive, through their intellectual function. We can see this as a manifestation of the trine between Virgo and Capricorn, and further, as a manifestation of the Gemini/Capricorn inconjunct: groups in power are not interested in the survival of all society, but instead are merely concerned in their own self-interest. Thus, the helping professions within Consensus don't make much money unless they also serve wealthy people to become more wealthy, or sustain the existing power structures or ideologies. As an example, we can see the difference between the authoritative role of a medical doctor within the health system, versus the role of a nursing assistant which is more focused on providing regular care.

Within Individuated, the intellectual isolation will first create crisis (2nd house square 11th house, Virgo inconjunct Aquarius) because the individual will tend to be slow to change its way of thinking. Duplicity, if it exists, will be exposed. Further along the road, isolation will serve the individual to define thought forms that are highly personal and highly elaborate in nature, which embrace increasing connections with overall reality, even if this will be occurring from a personal point of view. Thus, a very systematic and consistent approach to understanding reality, which, though, will be difficult to integrate socially, or beyond the scope of like-minded Souls. In some cases, the individual's intellectual orientation will evolve through independent thinking, ie withdrawing almost totally from social interaction. In other cases, the individual will indeed develop deep intellectual connections with groups of like-minded individuals (the 2nd house/11th house square, and the Gemini/Aquarius trine). The ideas of the individual may serve to support or define the intellectual framework of groups rebelling against Consensus. Crises in survival or sustainment can also occur because of intellectual isolation. Also, because the individual can be perceived by Consensus as an embodiment of revolutionary ideas which threaten the existing order (the 2nd house/11th house square, and the 2nd house/10th house trine).

Within the Spiritual state, the 2nd house sextile to the 12th house, and the Virgo/Pisces opposition, in relation with the Gemini/Pisces square, reflects a crisis in intellectual organization because of a transition between perception of the conditioned and the unconditioned. This impacts in how the individual relates to self, other people, and overall reality. This can be seen in Mercury being Mercury in the 2nd house Virgo, but also reflects the interface between the last quarter sextile, versus the crescent phase sextile, both between Gemini and Pisces. On the one hand, a need to withdraw from interaction in order to discover from within the new thought forms reflecting new value associations rooted in progressive perception of the Spiritual. On the other hand, the need to have this new orientation applied through new roles at a social level. (Gonzalo)

Illness and personal sacrifice

A subtle filter that is very common in the western world (if not all over this planet), that the natural intention of life is to be long and healthy, that if they really have it together spiritually and health wise, everyone should be able to heal all conditions and live long with good health. That is more of an ideal than a complete reality. Souls in 3rd stage Spiritual do get sick with incurable illnesses. The point of life is not to sustain an earthly body for the longest and healthiest possible length of time, but to fulfill the evolutionary intentions. In some cases the life plays out in the way we think we want it, long and healthy, while in others, not so. 3rd stage Spiritual Souls have surrendered their lives to doing the will of God/Goddess, whatever that involves for them. Why did Jesus have to die a horrible death? Logic would tell you such a great Soul would be brought up to heaven by adoring masses, yes? Yet it did not happen. Was it a mistake? Wolf would tell you it's because of our misconceptions about God itself, that God itself is an imperfect force seeking its perfection, that we are here as part of that force seeking its perfection. And everything does not end rosy for all people at all times, the way we like to think it can. And much of that is not because the people did something wrong, but because it was intended or necessary, for various Soul learnings. In the case of 3rd stage Spiritual people, the learnings are around the need to totally surrender to being the vehicle or agent of divinity, no matter what that feels like on the human level. I suspect it's not an easy thing to learn at times. Someone here asked recently why a Soul entering 2nd stage Spiritual would even want to go there, why didn't they just stop evolving, knowing they were about to do things that might really screw people up. We could say the same thing about entering 3rd stage Spiritual – although they may be helping people more than hurting them, in some ways it's probably harder for the Soul than even 2nd stage Spiritual, because you can no longer hide out in Spiritual ego grandiosity – your own Soul's desire nature continually pulls you forward into circumstances that are not fun at all from the human personality level, an ongoing personal sacrifice for the good of others, to carry out divine intent. (Steve)

Countries
The very paradigm of a 'country' itself is a Consensus paradigm. There is always a 'Consensus' reality on this Earth any time humans forms groups, tribes, or societies to co-exist within. (Rad)

Advancement of evolutionary stages – exhaustion of separating desires
Evolutionary stages cannot be approached from an overly linear/mathematical perspective. Everything in life proceeds from DESIRE. It's basically a matter of yearning for or believing in something that seems to be what I want. I then go out and work to bring it into form, and eventually experience it. Over eons of time I gradually discover what I thought I wanted does not create the feelings I thought it would. This brings on crises in loss of meaning and disillusionment. Then questions start arising within, "there has to be more than this," which leads to Soul searching, which eventually leads to daring to try something new. The EA term is "exhaustion of separating desires." There are myriads of separating desires, thus it takes a long time. Changes from stage to stage ultimately occur because of shifts in the Soul's desire nature. And what sort of experiences bring about those shifts? How do they feel on the human level? How easy is it to change those ingrained patterns, habits, ways of perceiving reality? It takes a long time and a lot of discouraging events, to move forward on the evolutionary journey. Out of all of that is born compassion, tender understanding of how difficult all this is, which is a signature quality of the highly evolved. They know from personal experience how hard this is. Out of love and caring they come around and help us understand, slowly, by example, by encouraging us when we are discouraged. As we learn these deeper lessons, we are slowly yet inevitably progressing on that scale of evolutionary Soul stages. The advancement is all based on desire and personal effort. (Steve)

Evolutionary states, changes in percentages
Jeffrey did say in the last Pluto school he taught that there were more aware Souls being born in the Pluto in Sagittarius generation that the percentage of Spiritual state Souls could now be as much as 10%, up from the 3-5% he originally wrote about. That number is still low. This is an ongoing issue with EA people. It comes from self-segregation or natural attraction. People who are in 3rd stage Individuated or 1st stage Spiritual tend to associate with others who are in 3rd stage Individuated/1st stage Spiritual. Since that is who is predominantly in their lives there is a strong tendency to believe that more and more people are becoming more and more like that. To a small extent there is some truth in it, but not as much as we would like to believe, and not enough really to turn around the impending collective consequences that humanity has been creating for itself. At the same time we can also acknowledge that the consciousness of Consensus itself evolves over time. Many things are accepted as normal today that were considered strange when I was young. But that evolution is slower than we hope for and want to believe is possible. We humans are very set in our ways. The principles of the four evolutionary states are part of Natural Law – there will always be the largest percentage of Souls in the Consensus state. What happens over the passage of time is the definition of Consensus itself evolves. There will always be Souls who are ahead of the curve, who are bringing in the new and showing by example the possibilities inherent in the human form. That is part of how physical reality here was constructed. Those Souls will always carry the price that comes with being part of the curve. They are here as part of their own evolutionary journey. Alienation and aloneness come with that territory. (Steve)

Evolutionary state, and the survival instinct
The "survival instinct" (especially as it relates to money-food) applies to every evolutionary stage. Everyone on this planet in a body needs to eat and needs a roof of some sort over their head. For most of us those require money. The more evolved a Soul, the less able to fit into Consensus jobs and career the person is. That in itself can trigger insecurity, crisis and trauma around survival. Ultimately, it's pushing us to realize God/dess is the actual source of our survival needs, not *from* our personal effort but *through* our personal effort. But not many of us live in that place 100% of the time. So of course you experience insecurity around money

and food. That does not mean you are in the Consensus state. The difference is the *relationship* a Consensus person has with survival issues vs the relationship an Individuated or Spiritual state person will have with survival issues. Their perspectives on survival are entirely different. You must look at the perspective to determine the evolutionary state. (Steve)

TRANSITS

Understanding transits

To understand any planetary transit, is to understand what the issues and dynamics are for the natal planet in question. Within that to understand the planet's relationship to the rest of the birth chart from an evolutionary point of view. Why is the planet in this or that house, this or that sign, this or that aspect, etc? In this understanding make sure to include the natal Planetary Nodes of the planet you are considering. Once the totality of this understanding from a natal point of view is understood then the current position of the transit of that planet correlates to how all those issues and dynamics are being worked through by the house and sign that the planet in question is moving through. (Rad)

Transits symbolize critical times from an evolutionary point of view where the core lessons in the natal chart are emphasized to be resolved, and growth is intended to occur in an accelerated/intensified manner. The specific transit will of course reflect the core dynamics to be worked upon. (Deva)

Karmic 'script' of the Soul

All things in our life start from within ourselves first: the evolutionary and karmic 'script' of the Soul in any given life. Thus the progression of the planets, and the aspects that they are making, reflect this ongoing evolutionary script of the Soul at any point in time. (Rad)

Phasal relationships – transiting to natal

There are phasal relationships via transiting planets to natal ones. The natal one, whatever planet it is, is used as the baseline to determine the phase relative to transiting planets. For example, if the Moon is at 5 Gemini, and transiting Saturn is at 2 Gemini, then this would be a balsamic phase. If the transiting Saturn were at 8 then it would be a new phase. (Rad)

Comparing transits to the natal chart

The natal chart itself and the transits are two different things and correlate to a different schemes of things. The natal chart refers to the entire life span, the whole life, versus transits, which only refer to chapters within that life time. That's why they are on a different scale. An analogy, the natal chart is like a study plan for an entire "course" so to speak, let's say a 4 year degree course as an example. So within that course there will be many steps, many milestones to be passed, and those steps will then culminate: these are the transits. They are the "tests" and the "exams" within the "course." Of course, without passing them, one can't finish the course, so they are important in their own right, but not to be mixed up with the entire "course." Every chapter in our lives has lessons. These lessons have a beginning, culmination, and end, and then another new chapter begins. These are the natural cycles in our lives which are signified by the transits. Whatever the transit aspects may be, they only relate to that chapter of life. Some cycles are a few years long, others maybe 10 or 20 years – they are the details within the whole – the whole is the natal chart. Transits need to be compared to the natal chart. The natal chart is the bigger picture, and transits relate to the details within that. When considering transits we always use the natal chart and all of its symbols as the base line simply because that's the natal chart. As such, it simply DOESN'T move, it is fixed. Even 50 years from now natal chart placements will be the same, so all transits are compared to the natal chart. All planets within the natal chart are fixed points. (Lia)

Transits, activating other planets in the chart

[Example: Pluto in Capricorn] And how those intentions, through time, become activated as symbolized by its transit. The [current] Saturn transit in Libra will of course correlate to the natal house that is transiting for any of us, and it will also refer to where the sign Capricorn is by natal house, and because of Libra's natural rulership of Venus, the house, sign, and natal aspects to your Venus will also be activated. (Rad)

Transit creating a temporary planetary configuration, eg yod

[Example: Transiting yod configuration – Saturn, Pluto, and Jupiter at the apex] It is important to understand the archetypal meaning of the phase first. The various aspects within the totality of a phase correlate to the evolutionary progression through the phases.

Firstly, by understanding the nature of the phases: the full phase relative to Jupiter and Saturn, and the gibbous phase relative to Pluto and Jupiter. Then the meaning of the archetypes of the inconjunct within the phasal context. Then add onto that the archetypes of the signs involved: Gemini, Scorpio, and Pluto. You can then apply this understanding to the collective as well as each individual: where this is taking place in their chart. (Rad)

Difficult transits

Quite frequently when we make major changes all our fears rush to the surface, because shaking the roots of what is secure to us is scary!! Feeling very vulnerable is normal. For example, Jupiter/Uranus opposite Saturn is exactly that kind of transit. Most of the time when we make big changes, it is our Soul prompting us to do so and answering the Soul's call can feel threatening to our 'small' selves. Your energy is better spent praying/talking to the universe asking for clarity and support during your transition. (Patricia)

No astrologer who knows what they are doing will predict based on symbols in a chart your plane will crash. Nothing in astrology is that specific. Archetypes are symbols. Symbols manifest symbolically, not literally. There are thousands of ways that a Jupiter/Uranus conjunction opposed Saturn could manifest. That is why specific predictions are wrong 90% of the time. A good way to approach this is to remember that your motivation and desire is to follow your Soul's intentions. Thus, anything that happens, including a plane crash, is part of your Soul's intentions, and ultimately brings you closer to God/Goddess. So there is nothing to fear, including death. You will not die until you are intended to die, and you are not going to avoid dying when it is your moment to die no matter what you do. Those are the parameters we live in while encased in human form, like it or not. Accepting them makes the whole process smoother. (Steve)

Making predictions

Most of our life is about free choice relative to the 'parameters' of one's life where those parameters are defined by the nature of the EA paradigm in each chart: individual context. And of course those parameters are reflections of choices/desires that the Soul has already made in prior lives, relative to past life evolutionary intentions. And that in turn has set up the parameters/intentions for the current life, and the choices to be made. Once one understands those parameters, and the intention for the whole life within them, then one can 'predict' when various issues, dynamics, and circumstances will occur in the future of one's life. And that of course is determined by the nature of the transits and progressions in one's life at any point in time. One cannot 'predict' the choices any Soul will make in the face of those future circumstances, dynamics, and issues because of the Natural Law of free choice. Yet an EA astrologer can understand what the natural tendencies are for any given Soul given their prior life choices, or the choices made in the current life. One of the best things for any EA astrologer to do when working with clients, and the future for them, is to point out the WHY of future circumstances, dynamics, and issues and then to provide the insight as to what the consequences would be given this or that choice. The consequences of the choices can be rightly 'predicted.' (Rad)

Mars transit

Mars is the leading edge of evolutionary growth, or change. It gives the evolutionary dynamics in the chart a constant forward motion, or momentum. It is the lower octave of Pluto, or how we consciously act out the desires that emanate from Pluto. Mars correlates with the beginning of a brand new evolutionary cycle, and the need to initiate, or put into motion, actions that will allow this new cycle to begin. Mars transits symbolize the need to put into motion necessary life changes relative to the beginning of a new part or cycle within our life that will allow the current evolutionary/karmic dynamics to be actualized. Mars correlates with instinctual behavior, and learns on an action-reaction basis. When experiencing Mars transits there will be an increasing need for freedom and independence to initiate the necessary actions, or direction, that will allow the new evolutionary cycle to move forward. It is important to understand that the new evolutionary cycle is not consciously known, or understood by the individual because it is so new.

In other words, Mars/Aries/1st house correlates with the process of self-discovery, and again, the need for freedom and independence to discover what the new evolutionary cycle is about. Mars also correlates with anger. Anger can be linked with many things, but one critical dynamic that is linked with anger is not wanting to have personal freedom restricted in any way. When experiencing Mars transits, anger at personal limitations or any external restrictions to initiating the new cycle that the individual feels is necessary at that time of the transit can manifest. It is important to understand that anger can be projected into external situations that are perceived as the cause of the limitations instead of understanding that the increasing desire to change existing life circumstances is a reflection of the desire to create forward momentum in evolutionary growth, and to use anger in a constructive way to create the necessary changes that must be made at this time. A Pluto, Saturn, Jupiter or Uranus transit to Mars will have a deeper impact than transiting Mars to these planets because of the length of the transit itself (Mars moves fast in the sky).

The natal Mars/Pluto phase and of course house and sign position correlates to how the evolutionary intentions within the birth chart will be acted upon in a consistent manner. Mars transits/progressions reflect critical times in the Soul's journey that trigger, or ignite, these core dynamics relative to the specific nature of the transit/progression. (Deva)

Mars transit – anger

My main point about Mars and anger is that anger that is projected upon others, or the environment as the source of personal limitations typically creates a negative and destructive outcome (personal degeneration) during Mars transits because the person does not understand that the limitations/restrictions are actually a reflection of the need to move forward in life, and that it is an inner limitation that is creating the restriction towards further growth. When this anger is used constructively, or in a positive way, the person can respond to a Mars transit in a way to grow past whatever personal limitation is creating a block towards putting into motion a new evolutionary cycle. Anger that is triggered at this time that is linked with not wanting personal freedom or independence to be limited can be used to create a new way of responding to external circumstances that are limited, or confining in some way to change those situations instead of just blowing up on another person, or blaming the outer circumstance. Anger can be used to initiate the new cycle of becoming that correlates with Mars instead of creating situations of personal degeneration or self-implosion. Just as a simple example: I recently had a Mars return (natal Mars in Cap/9th house), and I found myself feeling so much repressed anger coming to the surface that needed to be released that I become very impatient and also intolerant in ways that were inappropriate. The point within this is that there was also a desire to release this kind of anger, and to use it in a way to be free from my own inner dynamics of emotional repression that were the cause of my intense anger at that time. I had to learn to respond to certain situations that triggered this anger in a new way that allowed personal growth to occur (not reacting in an instinctual way to the triggers of the past that created personal degeneration). Mars also correlates with fears of all sorts, and during these transits our fears can come to the surface. Mars transits offer an opportunity to break free from these fears. (Deva)

Mars transit – example

When interpreting any transit we must be able to put it in the individual context of the natal chart. To fully understand Mars transits, then, we must understand the meaning of natal Mars in the individual chart. The event that occurred for the woman who had a significant Mars transit is that a wild fire burned down her house. She was left with nothing but a few possessions (her cherished guitar being one of those few possessions). Thankfully, the community reached out to her and others who had lost their house. She also had a significant Pluto transit which reflects the intensity of this event that occurred. This woman is in 1st stage Spiritual condition, and grew up in the lower economic class. She grew up with a disabled mother and several older brothers who had to help take care of the mother at an early age. In her natal chart she has Pluto in the 11th house forming a balsamic conjunction to Mars/Sun/Uranus. The South Node is in Taurus/8th house ruled by Venus in Virgo/12th house, North Node in Scorpio in the 2nd house conjunct the Moon. The need to liberate/de-condition from pre-existing emotional patterns that are based on a negative self-image/self-worth and the need to transform dependencies upon others within relationships that are based on the need for positive feedback (Pluto in Leo in the 11th house balsamic conjunction to Mars/Sun/Uranus).

The need to re-empower herself from within based on validating her own inner capacities, and to re-claim her own "inner power" or strength is reflected in this natal signature. A fundamental self-reliance can be developed as she learns to validate herself from within, and her self-image and inner relationship will progressively turn from negative to positive (South Node in Taurus in the 8th house, North Node in Scorpio in the 2nd house conjunct the Moon). In this example, Mars is in a balsamic conjunction to Pluto in Leo/11th house, and Pluto is conjunct Uranus and the Sun also in a balsamic phase. This correlates with the need to culminate an entire evolutionary cycle relative to how she has acted upon the desires reflected by Pluto, and to align her personal will and desires towards actualizing the current evolutionary intentions for the life. In this context, the need to put into motion actualizing her desires of a spiritual nature that allow personal transformation and continual evolution to manifest is reflected in these symbols. As mentioned before, attracting relationships where she gave away, or lost, her power and ability to be self-reliant created situations of being trapped or consumed by these relationships. The dynamic of guilt and the need to atone for the guilt can be seen by planetary ruler of the South Node, Venus in Virgo/12th house conjunct Mercury. Pluto/Mars in a balsamic phase, and Virgo in the 12th house correlate with the need to act upon the need to spiritually develop and merge with the Divine, and in so doing bring to resolution the emotional/psychological patterns of the past that have already been described.

At the time of the fire, Mars was in Aries in her 7th house making a trine to her natal Uranus in Leo/11th house which makes the aspects already mentioned. Pluto was also making an exact conjunction to her Moon/North Node conjunction (quite a graphic symbol of a house burning down!). At the time of the fire, she was experiencing intense difficulties in her current relationship (transiting Mars in Aries/7th house), and was feeling an increasing desire to be free from the limitations of these kinds of relationships in general (transiting Pluto conjunct North Node/Moon conjunction), and start a new cycle of evolutionary becoming through liberating from the emotional patterns already described (Mars trine Uranus in Leo in the 11th house). Her own experience of this very intense and traumatic event was that she felt, on an inner level, that the fire was symbolic (Pluto transit) of the new cycle that she wanted to initiate, and she also felt a sense of relief that the old cycle was coming to a close. She was able to objectify the inner dynamics that were creating these types of life circumstances, and to create the necessary inner changes with speed and amazing courage. In other words, in this case the Mars trine to her Uranus reflects that she was ready to initiate the necessary inner changes to allow the new evolutionary cycle to begin. She was able to use the very stressful traumatic event that occurred in a way that created forward movement and personal growth (transiting Mars trine Uranus). With Pluto conjunct Mars she is able to accomplish a lot of growth very quickly! (Deva)

Venus transit

Venus through transit reflects the ongoing evolution of our inner relationship with ourselves, and our outer relationships. The awareness of new and changing needs occurs through Venus transits. The transits of Venus also reflect the specific inner and outer relationship patterns we are working on at that moment in time relative to the house and sign it occupies in our natal chart. We can simply "outgrow" a current relationship we are in ("I do not feel I need this anymore"), or feel that it has reached a natural point of separation (no more growth is occurring for either person). We have all experienced times in our lives when we have exhausted the specific needs that were the basis of a relationship, and become aware of deeper aspects of ourselves that now need to be nourished, or nurtured, so to speak. In my view, it reflects that we are deepening our inner relationship with ourselves and this growth creates a natural evolution of our needs within relationships. We must then make the necessary inner and outer changes in our life to accommodate these changing needs. In general, Venus transits to the outer planets such as Jupiter, Uranus, Saturn, and Pluto will induce the deepest levels of change relative to the dynamics already described. (Deva)

Uranus transit

The Uranian archetype/function in consciousness being activated by important TRANSITS, produces repetitive abstract thoughts/awareness which are relevant to the nature of one's approaching future. These awarenesses occur spontaneously, of themselves, and NOT the result of effort or premeditated thought. And this, combined with sustained repetition over a length of time, are the indicators of the content being credible and appropriate to act upon when the time to act arrives, versus delusional thoughts for instance, which can manifest in a similar way, but will not demonstrate the sustained repetition over time. For this reason it is necessary to observe these kinds of Uranian thought patterns in as detached a way as possible over a period of time, and take action only when the natural rhythm of the archetypal pattern indicates it is right to do so, ie when the time to act arrives, the repeating messages/thoughts will occur (again, of themselves) with progressively brief intervals between them – more frequently – like a drumbeat – and though often seemingly disjointed or disconnected from the existing reality, will contain the specific information needed with respect to preparing for the abstract future which approaches. (Stacie)

Pluto transit – retrograde and direct

Transiting Pluto Retrograde symbolizes that the Soul is "throwing off" or liberating from the mainstream or consensus conditioning patterns in general (not buying into the mainstream way of doing things). Thus, Pluto Rx serves to instigate personal, and collective, evolution. Pluto Direct symbolizes that the Soul is not necessarily at an evolutionary juncture where the intense need to liberate in the ways described above is felt as in Pluto Rx. However, we must keep in mind the four natural evolutionary conditions of the Soul as well. In transit, in a general sense, when Pluto goes Rx it is a time to review the current life lessons we have been seeking to learn. When Pluto is Direct we will be facing those lessons head on "or directly" in order to effect personal growth. (Deva)

Pluto in the birth chart represents the Soul's evolutionary intentions for this lifetime plus where that Soul has been prior to this lifetime. Transiting Pluto represents the timing of how those evolutionary intentions unfold. All Pluto transits in a birth chart are in relation to the location by sign and house of Pluto in the natal chart. Another way to say that is, transiting Pluto is in a cycle of phases and aspects with natal Pluto. This also occurs on the collective level. When we talk of the USA having an upcoming Pluto return, it takes 248 years for Pluto to return to the same place. (Steve)

Transiting Pluto polarity point

The transiting PPP is not taken into consideration. (Rad)

Chiron transit

If the person has done their inner work prior to this point in time, an inner work that has allowed them to become aware of the dynamics that have caused the previous wounding relative to the natal Chiron, and then applied that awareness, for example, to a new intimate possibility, then these sorts of transits can in fact correlate to a healing of those wounds relative to the person who has now come into their life. If not, then of course these same transits can create a scenario in which those pre-existing wounds manifest in even deeper ways relative to the new person coming into their life. If so, the intention of course is to create a circumstance in which those pre-existing wounds are finally addressed. I would be talking to them [the client] about the nature of the wounds as symbolized in the natal chart/Chiron. Why they came about and the dynamics involved. Then I would ask them if they were aware of all that, and, if so, if they had already made some choices that correlated to addressing those dynamics so that the wounds would not repeat themselves. This of course would include being able to be aware when those old dynamics were being stimulated relative to the nature of a new person/attraction coming into their life. And, if so, being able to talk about those wounds/dynamics with the new person in such a way as to objectively gauge whether that new person, by way of their own responses, was coming into the life to help heal those old wounds and/or if that person has come into their life to recreate those wounds so that they could finally be addressed. So I would be sharing with the client this type of information and empowering them to be able to know what is what. (Rad)

A Chiron transit will manifest based on prior choices and advances one has made. Of course usually it is a mix, in the wounding experience comes opportunity for healing, in the healing experience comes some relinquishing, acquiescing, or bittersweet recognition – it is a homeopathic experience. (Rose)

Transiting Lunar Nodes, 'apparent' and 'actual'
The 'apparent' versus the 'actual' issues of these transiting Nodes is that whatever house and sign the transiting Nodes are moving through correlates to the 'apparent' evolutionary issues that are linked to the natal Nodal Axis of the Moon, whereas the 'actual' evolutionary issues correlates to the NATAL PLACEMENT of the planets that rule these transiting Nodes. In essence, what is underneath those apparent issues, and why. The apparent issues are of course just as real as the actual issues: the difference, again, is what is underneath those apparent issues where what is underneath them is what those apparent issues are really about, and why. (Rad)

Transiting Lunar Nodes t-square natal planet
When this occurs through transit it symbolizes key evolutionary transitions between the existing past, and the future to come. If the Soul makes the choices necessary that allow these key transitions to take place all will be well for that Soul. On the other hand if the Soul does not make the necessary choices that reflect the intent of the evolutionary transition then this will lead to 'skipped steps' relative to those dynamics in a future life to come. (Rad)
Planets, by transit, progression, or solar returns that square the Nodes can represent evolutionary forks in the road. How people react to the events signified by the square, can either lead to future growth (evolution) or to stagnation (skipped steps). (Shawn)
This [above] is exactly what JWG taught. (Rad)

Transiting Lunar Nodes t-square planet – in a death chart
(Q) If a person experiences the square of a transiting planet to the natal Lunar Nodes at the time of death, does it also create skipped steps? (Sherry)
(A) The answer is yes to your question about transiting planet(s) squaring the Nodes upon the physical death of a Soul. The nature of those skipped steps, the dynamics involved, will of course be symbolized by the nature of the entire skipped step paradigm in the death chart: the house the transiting planet is in, its sign, and of course the house/sign positions of the Nodes themselves. This will be true whether it is the transiting Nodes that are being squared by a transiting planet, or a transiting planet squaring the natal Nodes. It can be very useful to look backwards into the person's life when these kinds of transits occurred which in most cases they will have, to review exactly what the circumstances were at those times, and the choices the Soul made because of those circumstances. This can then provide a keen understanding and insight as to the specific nature of the skipped steps that took place at those times that then are symbolized at the moment of the Soul's physical death. And that then means that the Soul, in the very next life, will have that signature of the skipped steps symbolized in some way in that next life's birth chart. (Rad)

Transiting Planetary Nodes
To understand the transiting Planetary Nodes in any chart is first to understand the individual context for each Soul: the actual individual Soul reality. And that starts of course with an understanding of the natal position of Pluto as that is referenced to the South Node of the Moon by house and sign placement, and the location of its planetary ruler by its own house and sign, and aspects to it. Aspects to the South Node of the Moon, and aspects to that natal Pluto all correlate to the past context of the Soul: its desires for evolution. Within that we can then understand the actual context of the South Nodes of all the other planets as they all are linked to this underlying, core, evolutionary signature as symbolized by these points. In the same way, to understand the current evolutionary intent for the Soul is to understand Pluto's polarity point by house and sign, the location of the North Node of the Moon by house and sign, and the location of its planetary ruler by house and sign. And aspects to these points by other planets that all contribute to the current evolutionary intention of the Soul. The North Nodes of the other planets, once the individual context is understood, then all contribute to the actualization of this core evolutionary dynamic or intention by the location of them by their own houses and signs, and aspects to them by other planets. All of these symbols thus correlate to evolutionary dynamics of the Soul for its whole lifetime: the natal imprint.
The transiting South Nodes of the other planets simply means where the Soul is re-meeting its own past at any given moment relative to the archetypal meanings of each planet. Right now the transiting South Node of Venus is in Aquarius. So that will land somewhere in any of our birth charts. And the transiting North Node of Venus is in Taurus which will be somewhere in any of our charts. So first, of course, it is necessary to understand the total archetype of Venus. So, first, once we understand the natal evolutionary signature for any Soul, the core evolutionary dynamics symbolized by Pluto, its polarity point, the North and South Nodes of the Moon, and their planetary rulers, we can then look into any other of the Planetary Nodes to see how they all contributed to this core evolutionary signature. The South Nodes of all the other planets, by their own house and sign locations, other planets that may be aspecting them, have all contributed to the core evolutionary signature of the Soul's desires and intentions. What kinds of relationships was the Soul forming and why? What kinds of values did the Soul orientate to and why?

What constituted the sense of meaning and purpose for those lifetimes and why? What kinds of inner relationships did the Soul have with itself and why? How was it able to relate to others and why? These are Venus things. So we do this with all the Planetary Nodes. It is just a matter of understanding the total archetypes of all the planets. What are the Mercury archetypes and how have they been orientated to in past lives and why? What are the Mars ones, Jupiter ones, etc. etc. Once we have this total grasp and understanding of all the past life dynamics and why, we can then understand where the Soul comes into life at: the past that has led to the current life.

Once we know that total context then we can truly understand the nature of all the North Node symbols for all the other planets. It is through those North Nodes of all the other planets that not only do the archetypes of those planets evolve within the consciousness of the Soul, but they also correlate to how the Soul intends to fully develop the current evolutionary intentions for the life being lived as related to the core evolutionary signature in all charts: natal Pluto, its polarity point, the North and South Nodes of the Moon, the location of the planetary rulers of each. Each planet has its own Nodal Axis. This is the Natural Law of the trinity that we can call the past, present, and future. The past of course are the South Nodes. The future are the North Nodes, and the present is the position of the natal planet as it relates to its Nodal Axis. The natal signature of all of these is a life signature that operates for the whole life: like a foundation upon which a house is built.

The natal position of the planet relative to its own Nodes is the integration point relative to the past and the future for the past is always defining the moment as is the evolutionary pull of the future. The forces of the past and the future must have an integration point in the present. And that is the natal position of the planet itself. The transiting South Nodes of any planet, or the Moon, is where we are always meeting our past in some way so as to evolve it into the future which is the meaning of the transiting North Nodes of the planets and the Moon. Within this, of course, we also have the transit of the planets themselves at any moment in time with the transiting Nodes of those transiting planets. So, here again, we have the natural trinity: the transiting planet and its Nodes. The transiting planet relative to its Nodes is the integration point in the present for the issues that are manifesting relative to its Nodes: past and present. And this transiting trinity of a planet and its Nodes is then related to the underlying evolutionary signature for life as demonstrated in the natal positions of that planet and its Nodes. This is how to understand and use the Planetary Nodes in the individual's chart. Each Soul. Then of course there is the collective: the transiting positions at any moment in time for any planet, and its Nodes, and this affects and impacts on each of our individual lives. (Rad)

Saturn Return

A major part of Saturn Returns to me is a maturation factor. They naturally divide a lifetime into segments. Saturn also represents Time itself, and maturation is a timing process. The first is childhood and the transition into adulthood. The second is the transition from adulthood into what we might call elderhood, if the person has been paying attention. The focus becomes more reflective (Saturn) and inward, tying all the pieces of a lifetime together. The start of a winding down process. A desire to give something back for all one has received is common. Some make it to the third Saturn Return. There from my understanding the focus increasingly moves to planning the next lifetime. As always, the great majority of us have a lot of resistance to these natural transitions. My experience is most don't really start growing up until 32 or 33, when life no longer tolerates their acting like children. Thus the period from 28/29 to 32/33 is a transition time. Similarly for the mid-life crisis which is Uranus opposition to itself followed by Saturn's opposition to itself in the midpoint of the first Saturn Return period. Another adjustment that is frequently resisted for a period of years. On the other hand, for those who have been paying attention the Saturn Return can be another Saturn archetype, fruition, the natural timing of release. Jeffrey used to talk of how he got his first astrology job on the very day of his first Saturn Return. One way I visualize it is, an act in the play is ending. A natural time to move on. (Steve)

JWG used to teach that the majority of Souls come into any given life by acting out their past in a variety of ways where that past is not only the past of the current life leading to the first Saturn Return, but the past history of the Soul itself which of course is symbolized by the EA paradigm in any chart. Because of this most Souls do not make the choices early in their life that reflect the core EA intentions for the life being lived. This is why the first Saturn Return for most can be such a difficult time because many Souls begin to realize that their life to date, the choices made, have not been in accordance with the underlying intentions for the current life. Thus, the first Saturn Return gives the Soul the opportunity to make the necessary adjustments that will reflect the underlying intentions for the current life. The keyword here is 'opportunity.' Even though such an opportunity exists at that time many Souls do not make those choices to adjust their life anyway because of the nature of their existing 'reality,' Saturn, at that time: the structural nature of the reality that has been created to date.

For those that do make the necessary adjustments to their reality that do honor the underlying intentions for the current life then this can lead to an acceleration of those Souls' ongoing evolution through time. For those that don't, the evolutionary intentions will be actualized in a very slow, minimal way in a variety of ways. This can occur through the internalization of the Soul's consciousness via that common frustration that Souls feel at the time of the Saturn Return: "If I had only done this or that, or gee I would really like to be doing that,' and so on. These internalizations of the consciousness at that time that leads to these sorts of inner realizations do serve as 'seed thoughts,' desires, that will become active at some time in the future for such Souls. For the Souls who have made the choices earlier in their life, prior to the first Saturn Return, that reflects the EA intentions for the life, then the first Saturn Return can serve as the timing for actualizing what the Soul has been preparing itself for. JWG was informed at 24, his second Jupiter return, as to the nature of the life he was to lead. And that included becoming an astrologer. From 24 right up to the time of his first Saturn Return he did learn astrology in his own way, and did charts for free so as to learn as much as he could through observation and correlation. To the very day his Saturn Return occurred he was offered a job as being an astrologer for a brand new astrology bookstore in Seattle, W(A) (Rad)

Mid-life transits
The purpose in these transits is not so much 'karmic' as their correlations to what can be called evolutionary transitions: the need to move beyond, or evolve, some existing reality in our lives that has been created by inner dynamics to a new form of reality that requires new dynamics in order for that to occur. Everyone has their individual contexts. Thus, how these mid-life transits are experienced will reflect that individual context. The archetypal themes of these transits occur and manifest relative to that individual context. Karma is a reflection or reaction to actions taken where those actions occur due to choices being made by the Soul. Understood in this way all Souls are creating 'karma' for themselves throughout their lives. Relative to these mid-life transits, which do correlate to evolutionary 'turnstiles,' the karma that is created is a result of the choices being made at those times. We must remember that 'karma' is not just some 'negative' thing which is how most Western people have come to understand it. Karma again is simply a reflection of choices equaling actions where every action has a proportionate reaction. Thus, 'karma' can and is also a very 'positive' thing when the choices made by any given Soul reflect the evolutionary intentions of that Soul. (Rad)

Uranus opposite Uranus
The Uranus transit in opposition to itself transits from a gibbous phase opposition to a new phase opposition. This is the transit that most identify as the 'mid-life crisis.' This transit correlates with the Soul's need to 'throw off' any part of its reality that is no longer serving the Soul's ongoing need to evolve. In the gibbous phase it creates the awareness of parts of our life that seem empty and outmoded. As it moves toward the full phase this correlates with the Soul sending 'messages' to our conscious ego that correlate with all kinds of future possibilities for the Soul. The challenge for the Soul as this occurs is to inwardly monitor the messages that become repetitious versus those that only appear once or twice. It is the messages that become repetitious, over and over, that will reflect the next three to five years of the Soul's life. The challenge of course is to take action upon those messages no matter how 'radical' some may seem from the point of view of the Soul's existing reality. (Rad)

Neptune square Neptune
The Neptune square Neptune has the same archetype of moving from a crescent phase square to a first quarter square. This will correlate to what the underlying sense of meaning is for our current life. Thus, what has been meaningful loses its meaning, and the Soul desires, needs, new directions in order for a new sense of meaning to occur. A sense of disillusionment with certain parts of our life can precede this 'crisis of action' as the Soul initiates new directions in order to discover new forms that generate meaning for its life. (Rad)

Pluto square Pluto
The Pluto square Pluto will always be a crescent phase square that transits into a first quarter square: the Soul needing to create new directions for itself relative to what has already been established as its reality. This can then create a 'crisis in action' for the Soul. (Rad)
[Example: Natal Pluto 4th, transiting Pluto 7th] If someone has a karmically strong 4th house, and there is Pluto activity taking place by transit in the 7th house, even if aspects aren't involved, Pluto is still in some sort of phase to the planets in the 4th house and that phase is being played out by way of its transit through the 7th house, which as an archetype is naturally square the 4th house. So there will be crescent phase or first quarter phase inner experiences going on involving the 4th and 7th houses even if the square aspect itself isn't occurring. (Ari)

Pluto crossing the Ascendant
[Example: Capricorn ascendant] You can expect that the life that you have known up until that point, the person you have seen yourself as, will end. Seriously. I have Ascendant in early Sagittarius. I've been through this. That may sound scary. And it will feel that way at times. But I suggest to people having this transit that, as best they can, look at it as an exciting adventure. Because the natural time for a very long past is coming to an end. One is forced by life circumstance to break free from much of that past. Many things that used to work will simply stop working. With the Ascendant being in Capricorn, major changes to the structure of life will require adjustment. The more one is able to co-operate with this process, the more at peace with it they will feel. It is definitely an adjustment. The intention is for major changes in the life of that Soul, over time a whole new reality, directions, orientations forming. Jeffrey Wolf Green taught that the maximum pressure or difficulty in the life of a person with that transit occurs 18 to 20 months ahead of the exact aspect. (Note to others reading this: that statement was made only about Pluto crossing the Ascendant, not about other Pluto aspects and not about other planets crossing the ascendant.) If you happen to have Jeffrey's book Pluto Vol. 1, read the section towards the back of the book on Pluto transiting through the 1st house. Read the long section Pluto in the 1st

house natally, towards the front of the book. Although you don't have Pluto in the 1st house natally, the 15 years (plus or minus) that Pluto will be transiting through your 1st house will have you feeling and driven very much like what you will read about Pluto in the 1st. The difference is that because it is not your natal signature, it will be an overlay ON TOP OF your natal Pluto/Nodes signature rather than being your core itself. You will be feeling Aries-like much of the time. And you are SUPPOSED to feel that way – that is the point of the transit. (Steve)

How you might feel about the process will be determined to an extent by the condition of Pluto in the natal chart. If you have many aspects from Pluto to other planets in your chart, especially to personal planets, you will be more used to Pluto type energy/experiences as a result, than if you have a lightly aspected Pluto. Also if Pluto and Mars in the natal chart are in a major or hard aspect (conjunction, opposition, trine, square, semisquare, sesquiquadrate, inconjunct, sextile) then you will also have probably had strong evolutionary type experiences in your life before as a result from this too. All this would add up to being a person who knows through previous experience the turmoil and often deep gut level, very disturbing effect Pluto energy can have on themselves when it is activated in one's life. So if this were the case, with Pluto crossing your Ascendant you might feel more prepared (internally) for the approaching tsunami in your life. In fact if all the above were true for you, and you are a positively inclined person, as the process unfolds and these deep changes start taking place, you may recognize the great blessing that this transit can be – it will bring a huge rollercoaster of energy into your life that makes great personal and world changes now possible. You might come to feel that, without this energy now available to you, you would otherwise never be able to make such changes and benefit from such profound and rapid growth.

There could be a feeling that the energy this transit brings into your life is a great gift, and not a drop of it is to be wasted, as once it's gone you will be left with only your "normal" energy and power, and there'll never be the exact same opportunity again, not one involving the conjunction to your Ascendant anyway. But if the natal chart is not a strong Pluto type chart, and you haven't had any major Pluto transits up to now, then this transit may be a very new and eye-opening time for you, where, for the first time you come up against the full impact of the evolutionary force of Pluto. If that is the case, hang on to your hat, take many deep breaths and be prepared to learn a huge amount about how Pluto energy renders the past ways of being and doing things, approaches to situations, inoperable and recreates something new in its place. Again if viewed positively, you'll probably come to view these changes as invaluable, although it may be much later in the piece that this really becomes apparent. Either way, big changes are inevitable. Also, as Pluto will be conjuncting your Ascendant at the same time it will be opposing your Descendant. Some of these changes are highly likely to affect all your relationships, some of them directly. (Upasika)

It is true that Pluto crossing any angle or entering any house or changing signs or conjuncting, squaring or opposing a "personal planet" is going to have a profound effect on a person's life. But Pluto crossing the Ascendant is, to me, a unique case. (Perhaps Pluto conjunct the Moon would be something similar in nature.) That said, the nature of Pluto is death-rebirth. Some of what we hang onto for security reasons that no longer serves our evolutionary intentions is simply removed from the life, with or without our cooperation. One learns that whether or not I cooperate it happens anyway. And that it's easier to get through the changes by accepting them. It's still uncomfortable at times however. That is the main reason I see TO cooperate. From the human perspective, other than that it doesn't make a lot of sense some of the time. (Steve)

Pluto transit – and the transiting Pluto polarity point

Whatever house transiting Pluto is in correlates to that house relative to the ongoing evolutionary journey of any given Soul. The transit of Pluto of course directly correlates to the natal EA paradigm itself as it evolves in the context of the Soul's current life. The transiting house of Pluto is the core of that transit wherein the natural polarity point in brought into of the house in which Pluto is transiting. (Rad)

(Q) If someone is having a Pluto transit to their 1st house, what I am sensing is that the Soul intention of that transit will be the 7th house themes – to open to others and to be more willing to see through the eyes of another. Embracing real partnership and cooperation with others – to really begin listening in to how reality occurs for others, to be open to the feedback from others instead of going it alone (where the impulse and instinct would be to do so [going it alone] for the time Pluto is transiting the 1st). (Dhyana)

(A) No. If Pluto is transiting the 1st house then the core archetypes of that house are the ones that serve as the bottom line for what that transit means. The natural polarity point is then brought into that core bottom line. In your example the transiting Pluto in the 1st house will correlate to a time in which the Soul is desiring and requiring many new directions in its life that require a separation from existing life circumstances that are no longer serving the evolutionary needs of the Soul. And that will be the core bottom line for this transit wherein the natural 7th house polarity manifests as the Soul perhaps asking others for their perspectives, ideas, feedback relative to what those new directions that the Soul needs to initiate. The individual context of the Soul's entire chart is necessary in order to understand the EA intent of any transiting or progressed planet to the natal chart. One size does not fit all. The simple example that I used was in reference to your own statements about Pluto transiting the 1st house in order to illustrate the correct way of understanding the Pluto transit. The Pluto transit is always in reference to the entire EA paradigm in any chart. Additionally, it also correlates the Nodal Axis of Pluto itself: where this is in the individual's chart. It will also reference the natal house upon which the sign Scorpio is found. All of this must be considered relative to the natal EA paradigm for any given Soul which also must include the evolutionary condition, and the cultural context of where a Soul lives. (Rad)

Pluto in Capricorn transit

Capricorn/Saturn, when implicated through transit/progression, always induce reflection on our prior choices that have created the present reality (Saturn/Capricorn) in which we currently live. The purpose of the reflection and introspection (which the West wants to label "depression" in many cases) is to acknowledge and take responsibility for all of the issues and dynamics within that have created what is now being experienced as our limits or blocks in life – the life circumstances that no longer fit, but now feel constraining or limiting (Saturn/Capricorn). Following reflection regarding what has not worked for us up to this point, the cardinal energy of Capricorn enables us to create a whole new reality based upon the new evolutionary cycle trying to be born. At this time, anything new that is initiated by the ego that is not relevant to the Soul's growth will be blocked in some way. It is Capricorn/Saturn's way of keeping us 'on course' for the next step, the next phase, in our lives and in our Soul's ongoing evolutionary path. It is the personal responsibility (Capricorn) taken for all prior actions and choices that enables an inner security (Cancer) while navigating the new evolutionary cycle that cardinal energy always ushers in.

Once we see that we do in fact create our own reality, and all of our life circumstances, there is a tremendous sense of freedom (Aries square) that comes, and this makes available to the Soul a new and dynamic energy, so that it may begin to create again, and create anew. Libra factoring in is that new people will be brought into the life/reality as new choices and decisions are made and acted upon. Libra correlates with trial-and-error: a process of elimination that helps us ultimately arrive at a reality (Capricorn) that is relevant to and reflective of our inherent and true identity (Cancer). Libra brings so many options, and at a time of transition, the ego is easily confused about which way to go, how to proceed. Cardinal energy is so instinctive, so the Soul may, at a time like this, 'cast a wide net,' trying to see what fits (Libra), and the blocks we experience thus help us narrow down our options so as to lead us in the appropriate direction. (Lesley)

One of its important functions is to remove structures of all sorts that have become crystallized (no longer serve a useful evolutionary function), frozen in place, through the principle that our sense of security is based on the known, on both the personal (Cancer/4th) and societal (Capricorn/10th) levels. In essence a dynamiting of hardened rock that is holding back evolutionary progress. This process is affecting everyone, 1st stage Consensus and 3rd stage Spiritual. It's sometimes not the most fun-filled feeling one has ever known. Long term, it quite effectively fulfils its intents. (Steve)

What I have noticed about transiting Pluto in Capricorn is that the intention to change/transform conditioning patterns of the past is very emphasized/intensely felt by the collective. The positive manifestation of this transit is that the very structure of our society can change due to deep levels of internal change within society as whole in the context of purging the previous conditioning patterns that are inhibiting growth/evolution. I have been noticing that there is a deep level of reflection in the collective relative to these issues that is coming to the surface right now. To me, the best way to approach this transit is to stay focused on the potentially positive outcome of personal/collective (social) transformation, and personally staying open to changing when necessary. (Deva)

Destruction/population reduction? None of this is fated to occur. All will depend on the collective consciousness and collective choices made about the current imbalance between men and Gaia. The accuracy of prophecies such as Nostradamus does not imply that they will necessarily come true. Their purpose is to induce an awareness of the potential consequences of human collective actions. JWG writes extensively about this time frame and also about Nostradamus in Pluto 2, Chapter 11 – Pluto in Sagittarius. (Gonzalo)

Since JWG wrote Chapter 11 in Pluto Vol. 2, many many collective choices have been made. Human activities have affected Gaia to the point that some of the damage is no longer reversible. And, every time there is an international climate summit, the proposals for what will be done are about a quarter of the minimum needed to really change things, and instead of being put into place immediately, they are phased in for 10 to 20 years in the future. And by the time 10 to 20 years has gone by, next to nothing has actually changed, and another international conference is held, with the same basic results. Unfortunately the handwriting is now on the wall. Global temperatures, and wind and precipitation patterns are rapidly shifting. This is going to affect the world's major food producing regions. The number of people on the planet is at an all-time high and rapidly growing. We will be seeing vast shortages of food and fresh water. This will be exacerbated by the new global corporate reality, which sees these scarcities as opportunities to reap vast new fortunes, at the expense of people's lives. Look at what Wall Street is getting away with in the USA, for example.

We are not entering a fun era on earth. In my opinion the only thing that is up to free choice at this point is the extent of the upcoming difficulties. There is no longer a way we will avoid all of it – we have gone too far. What we will see, as this unfolds, are the dual influences of patriarchy and matriarchy – those who want to advance their own interests through exploiting the suffering at the expense of others, and those who want to band together and help their fellow humans and other species through the hardships, as much as possible. These two approaches to human life will increasingly be colliding. People will be forced off the fence through circumstantial necessity. Everyone will have to choose their approach. We must wait and see to find which approach prevails. The answer to that is still up in the air. This is not intended to scare, but to suggest people look closely at what is going on, the directions things are going in, and start thinking about where and how to prepare for the coming changes. Again, not from a place of fear but from a place of awakeness. There will be many opportunities to evolve spiritually through the difficulties. (Steve) One of the consequences of 'global warming,' caused by human activities that violate Natural Laws, is that the warming climate causes an acceleration of the Natural Law of mutation where mutation is a consequence of the survival instinct in all forms of life. Thus, the forms of life that are called bacteria, viruses, and fungus have begun this acceleration of mutations in order to survive. This will continue to accelerate at such a pace that the humans' capacity to keep designing new drugs to counteract this will not be able to keep up with the accelerated pace of the evolving/ mutating viruses, bacteria, and fungus. This will create, progressively, pan epidemics that will have the effect of killing a tremendous amount of people all over the globe. This in combination, as Steve pointed out, with increasing scarcity of fresh water sources, the dehydration of increasing amounts of land affecting food production, will cause cataclysmic circumstances for an ever increasing amount of human beings on this planet. With Pluto in Capricorn, in the context of now, the EARTH REALITY of now, the very nature of the structural reality at every level will be metamorphosed through varying degrees of cataclysms. And those cataclysms will occur as a consequence of CHOICES THAT HAVE ALREADY BEEN MADE, AND WILL CONTINUE TO BE MADE IN OUR COLLECTIVE FUTURE. The essence of those choices comes down to the fact that the Natural Law, set in motion by the Creator, of 'giving, sharing, and inclusion' has been perversely altered to 'exclusion and self-interest.' It is this perversion, at a root level, that has been, and will remain to be, the cause of all kinds of cataclysmic events for whole groupings of people that has already occurred, and will be occurring. The transit of Pluto through Capricorn will move over its own South Node, as well as the South Nodes of Saturn and Jupiter. It is intended to create increasingly glaring and shocking events, events that can have cataclysmic consequences due to choices made, in order to get the attention of human beings so that other choices, choices in alignment with the Natural Laws of God/ess, can be made. And those choices either way will determine, Capricorn, how all of us will be able to live our personal lives, Cancer, on this planet: Earth. Our home. (Rad) Pluto now in Capricorn correlates to the nature of 'races' of people on Earth, nationalities with skin colors within that that degenerates into finding 'scapegoats,' the collisions of the different 'status' of peoples in life: the poor, the rich, the middle class, the powerful versus those with no power, all will now be confronted in an accelerated way. We must remember to consider the natural squares from Capricorn to Libra and Aries that correlates to the undercurrents within all of this: the need for balance and equality so that a new way can be discovered for the whole of the human race which of course will necessitate an entirely new self-image for the entire race: Cancer the natural polarity of Capricorn. Failing all this, what will be the consequences? (Rad)

What is that Cancer Polarity? Reflections on Pluto in Capricorn – by Bradley Naragon
Yesterday, I considered how appropriate the word 'streamlining' is to describe the Pluto in Capricorn phenomena, especially in a capitalistic competitive society and economy. Seemingly, at every turn and stop, organizations, institutions, and businesses are 'tightening' up operations. Paper towels are now half the size they used to be and I think the toilet paper went from 2 ply to 1.5 ply. Seriously, with Mars in Capricorn and the recent conjunction to Pluto, now more than ever 'getting organized' is the aim and drive. Keeping the ducks in a row is not intrinsically a bad thing. As the South Node transits Taurus, the question of "Will this survive?" is more appropriate than ever. What is desired to survive is all based on one's values. Many people still greatly value the form capitalism exists in. Many people have gained their own wealth and survived and thrived because the current model is a patriarchal system set up for some to win and many to lose. As a result, I now see so clearly the compulsions of what it means to just "do the Pluto Capricorn" without its Cancer polarity. It's a funny phenomenon – more than ever we need every single 'i' dotted and 't' crossed or we risk not having access to what we need. The compulsion to create even more policies and create more 'red tape' and hoops to jump through is ever so real with Pluto in Capricorn. We are lucky when we actually get to talk to a human. Yet, when we do, will they be so restricted in their role that they only reflect back to us what we can and cannot do based on current policies? Where has the human gone? Cancer, oh, Cancer, under all these layers of armor we put on to survive in this work, there is a human being underneath there with emotions and feelings.

Recently, I was helping rewrite a returns policy for business. It really came down to going the 'hard ball route' and being really tight and limiting or creating what some called a 'wishy-washy' policy that supported actually allowing some room for the exceptions; to still allow wiggle room of being human. No room for exceptions is the shadow side of Pluto in Capricorn. This is Pluto Capricorn without its Cancer polarity. You either do or you don't meet criteria and then need to go through all the process to get what you want/need IF you can even access it. Recently, a friend was hit by a car. She had major medical surgery. The man who hit her was genuinely sincere and wished to do the right thing. Yet, she was strongly advised by others to get a lawyer to represent her case OR the insurance company would try to limit the amount they had to pay out. With Pluto in Capricorn, the need for the Cancer polarity is SO MUCH MORE OBVIOUS. Who are these people and how do they live with themselves – removing financial support in a time of personal crisis based on "what's the best business decision." Granted, much of this already has existed. The USA, beginning with the top down Capitalistic model (natal Pluto Capricorn), has always had such ruthless motives visibly and invisibly operative. Rad and Steve have shown us this correlation time again here on this message board. Now that we have Pluto in Capricorn, every product seems to be shrinking in size or offering, or going up in price. With the South Node [currently] in Taurus followed by Pluto in the "Taurus decan" of Capricorn, how will people survive? Will the decisions that we face embrace the empathetic nurturing principle?

What is the best business decision? To include the Cancer polarity means to value helping others over the bottom line equation of profit margin. Before that person hangs up the phone on you, do they step out of just being in the position of their job and acknowledge the reality you face? Even to hear someone say, "I'm sorry that is happening to you," would give some hope of this polarity expressing itself. Do we meet the former or do we hear, "That's the way it is and I cannot help you"? May our hearts remain open and full of compassion in these difficult times. (Bradley)

Original conjunction of Uranus/Pluto 1965
The seed point of intention of a new cycle is always at the original conjunction. Thus you go back to the most recent conjunction of the two planets, the moment at which their relationship became new phase. That is the seed point of the upcoming cycle – very much like the New Moon (which is the monthly conjunction of Sun and Moon) where we are told one plants (or realizes) the intentions of the upcoming month. The original intention/purpose of the new phase between those two planets, as indicated by the house and sign of the conjunction, the aspects made to other planets, and the meaning of those planets in relation to the natal evolutionary signature – Pluto and polarity, Nodes, rulers of Nodes. For a relevant current example, the essence of the 1960's was the conjunction of Pluto and Uranus in 1965. Life has been all over the place since then. Now with Uranus increasingly squaring Pluto it is going to pull us back to the evolutionary intent released in 1965 at the point of the original conjunction. Life's intentions will be to eliminate everything that has gotten in the way. The degree to which people open to that intention will determine the outer results that occur. (Steve)

Transit event charts – original conjunction, 1st quarter square, etc.
[Example: Transiting Uranus square transiting Pluto] The specific 'rules' are these: upon the first conjunction this sets in motion the archetypal intention for the first Uranus/Pluto square. The second conjunction takes place while one or both are retrograde which is a time to reflect upon what the first conjunction has set in motion. And then upon the third conjunction the archetypal intent is to take action, real action, upon what the first conjunctions intent was/is that is deeply revealed upon the second conjunction. In the context of world events there is of course the general archetypal intentions for the entire world that is then made specific to the individualized context of each country/society. (Rad)

The specific rules [above] are also applied to the 1st quarter square as well as subsequent phasal aspects between the two transiting planets. (Linda)

[Example: Pluto transit through Capricorn] Event charts start with an understanding of the existing reality of any given country and/or society upon which the evolutionary intentions of evolving that reality is reflected, symbolized, by the transiting planets being considered. From an EA point of view this should always start with the transiting position of Pluto because this correlates to the natural law of evolution itself. Thus, the two primary ways in which the evolutionary intentions and/or necessity manifests: either through cataclysmic events or slow yet progressive change. As we have learned from JWG the determinant in how the evolutionary intentions is the degree of resistance to that evolutionary intention. When resistance reaches a point of preventing the EA intention this then manifests as cataclysmic events. So it is then necessary to understand the evolutionary intention of what Pluto transiting, now, Capricorn correlates to which, in essence, boils down to the existing structural nature of any country, indeed the world, that are the determinants of the 'reality' that each country, and the world, is currently experiencing.

The bottom line intention of the Pluto transit through Capricorn is to evolve any existing structure within the reality of any given country that is thwarting or preventing the necessary evolutionary needs of that country. Within this bottom line we then look to the other planets that correlate with a collective of people: Uranus, Neptune, and Saturn. The archetypes that each planet is energizing relative to the signs that they are transiting is then linked or added to the bottom line of the sign that Pluto is transiting. Within this to incorporate the signs that the transiting Lunar Nodes are moving through that symbolize the archetypes that the collective in any country is experiencing by way of the 'lead points' within that collective consciousness that serve as the specific triggers to events that are all part of the larger evolutionary intentions as symbolized by the outer planets starting with Pluto.

An example of all this is reflected in the Rio Tinto Mine in Australia. Here is a statement that reflects all the above: "Australia is riding an unprecedented wave of resources investment due to booming demand from Asia, with hundreds of billions of dollars' worth of resource projects in the pipeline." Here you see the leading edge of the Lunar Nodes in Taurus/Scorpio: an unprecedented wave of resources, Taurus, because of the booming demand, Scorpio, from Asia that will lead to all the money returned to Australia based on that investment. And, of course, all the competing interests of the various groups, Uranus in Aries, within Australia that have led to the confrontations with the Australian government, Pluto in Capricorn, that reflects the existing structural reality, that have and are impacting on what the Australian government perceives as its evolutionary needs in order to grow. Within these groups of competing interests the Neptune transit in Pisces manifests and that can range from utter disillusionment and bitter outrage to a kind of euphoria for those that this investment will benefit. And, of course, the underlying archetype of the Neptune in Pisces is whether all the reasons that have been used by the Australian government to justify this are delusional or inspired by actual reality. Saturn in Scorpio is currently conjunct the transiting North Node which then correlates with the specific timing, Saturn, correlating with time as does Capricorn, to this decision that lead to the various confrontations within the competing groups that are defined by their own structural reality. (Rad)

Cardinal Grand Cross (2011 onwards)
The entire structures of reality, the past that has brought us to this point in time, are and will be radically changing. The Saturn transit in Libra correlates to the increasing extremity between those that have power, and those that do not, and the 'reality' that this is and will be creating. Libra of course is the archetype within Natural Law of 'giving, sharing, and inclusion.' Capricorn and Cancer naturally square Libra of course, and Aries opposes it. The original self-image of humans was rooted in this Natural Law. Yet in these 'modern' times that very Natural Law has become almost a 'slur' word in much of the world where it is now called 'socialism:' with a sneer. And, of course, this Natural Law has been perverted manifesting as 'self-interest and exclusion.' It is this root perversion of the Natural Law of giving, sharing, and inclusion that is the very cause of the absolute distortions of just about every element and form of 'reality' today. And if that root cause of the distortions does not revert back to its Natural Law then the acceleration of all the existing distortions will occur. (Rad)

TABLE 1 Seven Soul Types

Root	Saturn, Uranus, Pluto	*physical, body, asanas*	Hatha Yoga
Sacral	Jupiter, Neptune	*sexuality, Daemon*	Tantra Yoga
Solar Plexus, Navel	Mars, Pluto	*warrior, natural need to lead, leadership*	Hatha Yoga Kundalini Yoga
Heart	Venus	*devotion*	Bhakti Yoga
Throat	Mercury	*prayer, chanting, mantra, service to others, healers*	Karma Yoga
Brow, Third Eye, Medulla, Ajna	Sun, Moon	*wisdom, teacher types*	Jyana Yoga
Crown	Neptune	*avatar, guru*	Raja Yoga

TABLE 2 Stages of Evolution

CONSENSUS	INDIVIDUATED	SPIRITUAL
1st stage Consensus	*1st stage Individuated*	*1st stage Spiritual*
– beginning – established – culminating	– beginning – established – culminating	– beginning – established – culminating
2nd stage Consensus	*2nd stage Individuated*	*2nd stage Spiritual*
– beginning – established – culminating	– beginning – established – culminating	– beginning – established – culminating
3rd stage Consensus	*3rd stage Individuated*	*3rd stage Spiritual*
– beginning – established – culminating	– beginning – established – culminating	– beginning – established – final liberation

TABLE 3 Chart Rectification – Questions to Ask by Pluto House

House	Questions
1st	Do you feel you have a special destiny to achieve, meaning something out of the ordinary? The related question, Do you have an inner resistance to completing yourself in relationship? (Why? There has been a whole prior life background of essential independence.) You could also ask the Pluto polarity point questions.
2nd	Do you feel that you are fundamentally self-contained? Do you feel that you are fundamentally able to identify and meet your own needs?
3rd	Do you feel that you have a fundamental curiosity to understand the nature of life, that curiosity primarily manifesting at an intellectual level? As an example, Do you feel you have a compulsion to read many, many books, and yet your tendency being to read three or four pages in each book and not the whole book? Do you feel that your mind is simply a roller coaster brain of competing perspectives, the roller coaster or roll x-carts generating competing perspectives? The polarity point question would be, Do you feel that you are trying to find that one philosophical system that puts it all together for you?
4th	Do you feel that you are born with fundamental insecurity at a compulsive level? Do you feel that you had parents that were unable to understand the nature of your emotional needs, and therefore the nature of nurturing accordingly? Do you feel that you have a problem identifying with traditional gender role assignment? Do you feel in your intimate relationships that at times you have problems with what we can call pathological jealousy that is quite different than normal jealousy? Pathological jealousy is demonstrated in O.J. Simpson, meaning a person that can never let go.
5th	Do you feel that you are the center of your own universe? Do you unconsciously expect all things to revolve around you? Do you feel you have a bottomless pit in terms of the need to receive positive feedback for whatever your efforts may be?
6th	Do you feel that you have a problem with a core feeling of fundamental inadequacy? An inner feeling that you are not good enough to do what your higher mind suggests is possible to do? This becomes the basis of compulsive excuse-making, which sounds like rational reasons. Do you feel you have a problem with priority confusions? Do you feel you have a compulsion to make crisis out of thin air? Do you feel the emphasis in your consciousness is left brain analytical thought processes? Do you feel that you are plagued by personal doubt? Do you feel that you are your own worst enemy?
7th	Do you have a compulsive need to be needed? Do you feel you have a lesson in terms of learning when to give and when not to give, and more importantly, how to receive? Do you feel you have problems in co-dependency in relationship? Do you feel you have problems in projection in relationship? (either one or both partners compulsively projecting their subjective reality on one another)
8th	Do you feel you are born with fundamental emotional fears of betrayal, emotional fears of loss, emotional fears of abandonment, impacting on your ability to trust? Do you feel that you crawled out of the womb asking "why?" ie do you feel that you psychoanalyze yourself to the point of tears, and psychoanalyze everyone else to the point of tears? Do you feel that you are an inherently suspicious person? Do you feel that you have an awareness of larger forces in the universe that you cannot control?
9th	Do you feel that you have been asking giant questions for lifetimes, why life, why death, how do I fit into the cosmos? Do you have an element in your consciousness that just knows what it knows without knowing how it knows it? Meaning, do you feel the strength of your Soul is intuitive? Are you born with a fundamental restlessness? For an Individuated or Spiritual person the question becomes, Do you feel that you have a core alienation from society? Do you feel that you have a need to understand yourself in cosmological terms?
10th	Do you feel that you are born with a core sense of guilt that you can no longer define? Do you feel that you have a tremendous standard of inner judgment, which equals becoming your own worst enemy? Do you feel you have a fundamental fear of losing control? Do you have a need to be recognized by society? A related question in the Individuated and Spiritual state, Are you having problems in gender assignment (consensusly defined)? Was there a power problem with one or both parents?
11th	Were you born with a fundamental feeling of being inherently different than most other people? A related question, Not knowing quite where to fit, in society's terms? Do you feel you are born with an inherent capacity to innovate? Do you feel you are born with major lessons in terms of who is a friend and who is not? Do you have a consciousness that is naturally constructed to promote social orders that are more equitable for all concerned, meaning natural humanitarian? That will exist even in the consensus state. Lyndon Johnson had an 11th house Pluto, Bill Clinton has an 11th house Pluto.
12th	Fundamental question, Is your deepest fear falling into the great, great inner abyss? Do you feel you are born with a core of ideals that are continually frustrated? Were you born with no clear sense of boundaries between where you start and something else starts around you? Do you have a fundamental fear of going crazy or insane? Do you have an inner feeling of being in a prison, in which there is no way out?

TABLE 4   Planetary Nodes for everyone

SOUTH NODES		NORTH NODES	
Pluto	19 — 22 Capricorn	Pluto	19 — 22 Cancer
Neptune	10 — 14 Aquarius	Neptune	10 — 14 Leo
Uranus	11 — 17 Sagittarius	Uranus	11 — 17 Gemini
Saturn	18 — 30 Capricorn	Saturn	17 — 30 Cancer
Jupiter	29 Sagittarius — 22 Capricorn	Jupiter	29 Gemini — 22 Cancer
Mars	9 Libra — 30 Sagittarius	Mars	8 Aries — 3 Cancer
Venus	Any sign	Venus	Any sign
Mercury	Any sign	Mercury	Any sign

TABLE 5   EA Phases and Zodiacal Correlations

Phase	Sign / Polarity	Keywords	Description
NEW PHASE	Aries / Yang	INITIATION BEGINNING	The beginning of a cycle. Action is instinctual. Absolute freedom is required. The question is, "Who am I?" The actions one takes brings feedback.
CRESCENT	Taurus / Yin	INTERNALIZATION OF NEW PHASE, WITHDRAWAL, STRUGGLE	The feedback has been obtained. The need is to withdraw and to come to an understanding of who one is.
FIRST QUARTER	Gemini / Yang	CHOICES TO BE MADE CRISIS IN ACTION	One now has an understanding of who one is. Now the question is, "What specific form do I take?" A time of intense activity. Building one's foundations in terms of who one is.
GIBBOUS	Virgo / Yin	HUMBLING AND ADJUSTING	The old (egocentric) ways are no longer working. The need to re-evaluate. The realization that it is not about "me" anymore.
FULL PHASE	Libra / Yang	ENTERING THE SOCIAL SPHERE, SOCIALIZATION	The dilemma is now in the full light of day. This is me vs what is required of me in the social sphere. Comparing and contrasting self to everyone else. The necessary feedback from significant others in one's life to begin the process of integrating oneself/one's sense of purpose into the social sphere.
DISSEMINATING	Capricorn / Yin	TOTALITY OF SOCIETY, INTEGRATION OF PURPOSE	Fully integrating oneself/one's sense of purpose into the social sphere. What has been learned enters the mainstream.
LAST QUARTER	Aquarius / Yang	BREAKING FREE, REBELLING FROM ALL THAT HAS COME BEFORE IN CYCLE, CRISIS IN BELIEF	Questioning the underlying beliefs that have underpinned all prior actions. Detaching from what one has created and the social sphere in which one has participated.
BALSAMIC	Pisces / Yin	CULMINATION OF THE ENTIRE CYCLE, IT DISSOLVES BACK INTO FROM WHENCE IT CAME	Attunement to the Divine. Understanding oneself in the context of the Divine and the corresponding expansion of consciousness. Letting go of all that has come before that hinders this attunement. The beginnings of new imaginings for a new cycle.

TABLE 6

Astrological Ages and Sub-Ages

Leo Age: 10,900 BC – 8740 BC
10,900 – 10,810 Leo
10,810 – 10,720 Virgo
10,720 – 10,630 Libra
10,630 – 10,540 Scorpio
10,540 – 10,450 Sagittarius
10,450 – 10,360 Capricorn
10,360 – 10,270 Aquarius
10,270 – 10,180 Pisces
10,180 – 10,090 Aries
10,090 – 10,000 Taurus
10,000 – 9,910 Gemini
9,910 – 9,820 Cancer

Aquarius Sub-Age of the Leo Age: 9,820 – 8,740 BC
9,820 – 9,730 Aquarius
9,730 – 9,640 Pisces
9,640 – 9,550 Aries
9,550 – 9,460 Taurus
9,460 – 9,370 Gemini
9,370 – 9,280 Cancer
9,280 – 9,190 Leo
9,190 – 9,100 Virgo
9,100 – 9,010 Libra
9,010 – 8,920 Scorpio
8,920 – 8,830 Sagittarius
8,830 – 8,740 Capricorn

Cancer Age: 8,740 – 6,580 BC
8,740 – 8,650 Cancer
8,650 – 8,560 Leo
8,560 – 8,470 Virgo
8,470 – 8,380 Libra
8,380 – 8,290 Scorpio
8,290 – 8,200 Sagittarius
8,200 – 8,110 Capricorn
8,110 – 8,020 Aquarius
8,020 – 7,930 Pisces
7,930 – 7,840 Aries
7,840 – 7,750 Taurus
7,750 – 7,660 Gemini

Capricorn Sub-Age of the Cancer Age: 7,660 – 6,580 BC
7,660 – 7,570 Capricorn
7,570 – 7,480 Aquarius
7,480 – 7,390 Pisces
7,390 – 7,300 Aries
7,300 – 7,210 Taurus
7,210 – 7,120 Gemini
7,120 – 7,030 Cancer
7,030 – 6,940 Leo
6,940 – 6,850 Virgo
6,850 – 6,760 Libra
6,760 – 6,670 Scorpio
6,670 – 6,580 Sagittarius

Gemini Age: 6,580 – 4,420 BC
6,580 – 6,490 Gemini
6,490 – 6,400 Cancer
6,400 – 6,310 Leo
6,310 – 6,220 Virgo
6,220 – 6,130 Libra
6,130 – 6,040 Scorpio
6,040 – 5,950 Sagittarius
5,950 – 5,860 Capricorn
5,860 – 5,770 Aquarius
5,770 – 5,680 Pisces
5,680 – 5,590 Aries
5,590 – 5,500 Taurus

Sagittarius Sub-Age of the Gemini Age: 5,500 – 4,420 BC
5,500 – 5,410 Sagittarius
5,410 – 5,320 Capricorn
5,320 – 5,230 Aquarius
5,230 – 5,140 Pisces
5,140 – 5,050 Aries
5,050 – 4,960 Taurus
4,960 – 4,870 Gemini
4,870 – 4,780 Cancer
4,780 – 4,690 Leo
4,690 – 4,600 Virgo
4,600 – 4,510 Libra
4,510 – 4,420 Scorpio

Taurus Age: 4,420 – 2,260 BC
4,420 – 4,330 Taurus
4,330 – 4,240 Gemini
4,240 – 4,150 Cancer
4,150 – 4,060 Leo
4,060 – 3,970 Virgo
3,970 – 3,880 Libra
3,880 – 3,790 Scorpio
3,790 – 3,700 Sagittarius
3,700 – 3,610 Capricorn
3,610 – 3,520 Aquarius
3,520 – 3,430 Pisces
3,430 – 3,340 Aries

Scorpio Sub-Age of the Taurus Age: 3,340 – 2,260 BC
3,340 – 3,250 Scorpio
3,250 – 3,160 Sagittarius
3,160 – 3,070 Capricorn
3,070 – 2,980 Aquarius
2,980 – 2,890 Pisces
2,890 – 2,800 Aries
2,800 – 2,710 Taurus
2,710 – 2,620 Gemini
2,620 – 2,530 Cancer
2,530 – 2,440 Leo
2,440 – 2,350 Virgo
2,350 – 2,260 Libra

Aries Age: 2,260 – 100 BC
2,260 – 2,170 Aries
2,170 – 2,080 Taurus
2,080 – 1,990 Gemini
1,990 – 1,900 Cancer
1,900 – 1,810 Leo
1,810 – 1,720 Virgo
1,720 – 1,630 Libra
1,630 – 1,540 Scorpio
1,340 – 1,450 Sagittarius
1,450 – 1,360 Capricorn
1,360 – 1,270 Aquarius
1,270 – 1,180 Pisces

Libra Sub-Age of the Aries Age: 1,180–100 BC
1,180 – 1,090 Libra
1,090 – 1,000 Scorpio
1,000 – 910 Sagittarius
910 – 820 Capricorn
820 – 730 Aquarius
730 – 640 Pisces
640 – 550 Aries
550 – 460 Taurus
460 – 370 Gemini
370 – 280 Cancer
280 – 190 Leo
190 – 100 Virgo

Pisces Age: 100 BC – 2060 AD
100 BC – 10 BC Pisces
10 BC – 80 AD Aries
80 – 170 Taurus
170 – 260 Gemini
260 – 350 Cancer
350 – 440 Leo
440 – 530 Virgo
530 – 620 Libra
620 – 710 Scorpio
710 – 800 Sagittarius
800 – 890 Capricorn
890 – 980 Aquarius

Virgo Sub-Age of the Pisces Age: 980 – 2060 AD
980 – 1070 Virgo
1070 – 1160 Libra
1160 – 1250 Scorpio
1250 – 1340 Sagittarius
1340 – 1430 Capricorn
1430 – 1520 Aquarius
1520 – 1610 Pisces
1610 – 1700 Aries
1700 – 1790 Taurus
1790 – 1880 Gemini
1880 – 1970 Cancer
1970 – 2060 Leo

TABLE 7   EA Phases, Aspects & Degrees

New	Conjunction	0	**Full**	Opposition	180
	Semi-Sextile	30		Tri-Septile	206
	Novile	40		Inconjunct	210
Crescent	Semisquare	45	**Disseminating**	Bi-Quintile	216
	Septile	51.25		Sesquiquadrate	225
	Sextile	60		Trine	240
	Quintile	72		Bi-Septile	257
First Quarter	Square	90	**Last Quarter**	Square	270
	Bi-Septile	102.5		Quintile	288
	Trine	120		Sextile	300
				Septile	308
Gibbous	Sesquiquadrate	135	**Balsamic**	Semisquare	315
	Bi-Quintile	144		Novile	320
	Inconjunct	150		Semi-Sextile	330
	Tri-septile	154		Conjunction	360

TABLE 8A   Planetary Speeds
(from fastest to slowest)

Ascendant/Midheaven	Lucifer
Moon	Jupiter
Mercury	Moon's South and North Nodes
Venus	Saturn
Mars	Chiron
Vesta	Uranus
Juno	Neptune
Ceres	Pluto
Pallas	Sun

TABLE 8B   Asteroid Speeds
from fastest to slowest (with orbital periods)

Mars	
Vesta	3.63 years
Asteroid Lilith (not Black Moon Lilith or Dark Moon Lilith)	4.36 years
Juno	4.37 years
Kassandra	4.38 years
Pandora	4.58 years
Ceres	4.6 years
Pallas	4.62 years
Lucifer	4.93 years
Amazone, Persephone	5.34 years
Jupiter	

TABLE 9 Lilith Trinity

	Symbol	Other names	astro.com	Appears in astro.com chart as	Actual or hypothetical
Asteroid Lilith	⚸	Natural Lilith	1181 in the Additional Asteroids list	Lilit	Asteroid Lilith is a real asteroid. It is the only Lilith that is an actual, verifiable physical body. In the main asteroid belt between Mars and Jupiter. Takes 4 years to orbit the Sun.
Black Moon Lilith (True)	⚸	Osculating Lunar Apogee, Apogee Lilith, True Osculating Lilith, "True" Lilith/Black Moon, Osc. Lilith, Osc. Apogee, Moon's Apogee, Osculating Lunar Apogee, Black Moon Osc., Resolution Lilith	h13	OSC. L	Not a solid object. It is a mathematical point of alignment, the apogee of the Moon's orbit, furthest away from the Earth. 9 year orbit. Spends 9 months in each sign. EA uses the True Apogee for Black Moon Lilith.
Black Moon Lilith (Mean)	⚸	Mean Lilith, Resolution Lilith	'Lilith' under Additional Objects	⚸ (white)	EA uses the True Apogee for Black Moon Lilith.
Dark Moon Lilith	⌀	Waldemath Dark Moon, DML New Moon, Waldemath's Moon, Waldemath Black Moon, Sepherial's Moon, Dark Moon, Ghost Moon	h58 hypothetical planet	Walde	Dark Moon Lilith is a real body in the sky, a 'hypothetical planet' resembling a dust cloud, or a second Moon of Earth. Takes 119 days to orbit the Earth. Spends 10 days in each sign.

TABLE 10 EA General Orbs

Conjunction	10 degrees	Sextile	4 degrees
Opposition	10 degrees	Square	10 degrees
Inconjunct/Quincunx	5 degrees	Trine	10 degrees
Quintile	3 degrees	Bi-septile	2 degrees
Sesquiquadrate	5 degrees	Novile	2 degrees
Semi-sextile	3 degrees	Bi-quintile	3 degrees
Semisquare	3 degrees	Tri-septile	2 degrees
Septile	2 degrees		

TABLE 11 Key Planetary Pairs (JWG)

Sun/Moon	The need in all people to actualize the inherent purpose for their life on a day to day basis, to give that purpose a face and image, a way of personally identifying itself, Moon. It describes how the person continuously is integrating them self on a moment to moment, second to second, year to year basis.
Moon/Saturn	Your ability to integrate your ego, your personal identity, who you are within the context of the social systems and/or culture, Saturn, in which you find yourself. The ability to establish your own authority within the authority of the culture.
Mars/Venus	How one completes oneself through relationships.
Mercury/Jupiter	How one establishes her beliefs, her principles, her philosophies, and creates the necessary intellectual apparatus to explain them, to communicate them.
Jupiter/Saturn	Jupiter correlates to your beliefs and how they are in harmony or disharmony with the consensus belief patterns of the culture you are in thus, impacting your ability to economically survive. The economic issue relative to philosophy is obvious. The Jupiter/Saturn cycle has a 20 year life.
Saturn/Uranus	This is the most important cycle. It has a 48-year life and comes to maturity every 22 to 24 years after its conjunction. It establishes the social tone, structure, every 48 years. The new social impulse, order, structures.

TABLE 12 EA Archetypes

Aries keywords

Separation	War	Primal	Narcissism
Anxiety of separation	Loner	Spontaneous enthusiasm	Self-interest
Anger / Rage	Self	Initiative	Warrior
Desires	Violence	Initiation	Pioneer
Desire nature	Sexual instinct	Expression of will	Sexual violence
Identity	Impatience (anger at limitations)	Super-human	Destroyer
Freedom	Intolerance for weakness	Zarathustra	Paranoia
Independence	Instinct	Special destiny	

Taurus keywords

Survival	Self-sufficiency	Starvation	Cautious
Fertility	Security	Poverty	Literal
Procreation	Isolated	Give up	Materialist
Preservation	Withdrawal	Suppress emotions	Possessions
Self as Resource	Stagnation	Shut down	Landowner
Inner resources	Personal worth	Stubborn	Farmer
Values	Personal value	Hoarding	Thief
Beauty	Self-esteem	The Body	Carpenter
Prostitution	Patience	Pleasure	Shepherd

Gemini keywords

Communication	Scattered	Short-term memory	Instability
Learning	Superficial	Fluctuating viewpoint	Ever changing
Writing	Literal	Rationalization	Teacher
Speaking	Cynic	Siblings / Twins	Scribe
Thinking / Left Brain	Liar / Lies	Relatives	Short journeys
Information	Trickster	Logic	Trader / Merchant
Duality	Opinion	Intellectual doubt	

Cancer keywords

Ego	Security	Inner	Emotions
Womb	Protection	Nurturing	Self-image
Childhood Environment	Mother	Protection	Touchy
Children	Family	Neglect	Subjective
Home	Clan	Helpless	Gender Roles
Roots	Ancestors	Needs	Housewife/husband

Leo keywords

Creative Self-Actualization	Grandiose	Being noticed	Gambler
Ruler King/Queen	Subjective awareness	Special recognition	Actor/ress
Power	Artist	Fame	Risk taker
Arts	Inflation – positive/negative	Romance	Affairs – Adultery
Drama	Involvement	Creativity	Mistress
Integration	Approval	Child Prodigy	Children
Purpose	Exhibitionism	Artist	Inner Child
Full of self	Applause		

Virgo keywords

Inferiority	Discipline	Lack	Healing
Service	Shame	Self-improvement	Craftsman
Servant / Slave	Perfection	Health	Reality
Apprentice	Place in Society	Critical	Discernment
Humility – Humiliation	Self-Improvement	Guilt	Nun
Victim	Existential Void	Masochism	Virgin
Persecuted	Aloneness	Crisis	Sadomasochism
Self-Sacrifice / Martyr	Inadequacy	Nurse / Medicine	

Libra keywords

The "other"	Listening	Choices	Damaged trust
Social	Extremes	Flirt	Intimacy
Objective awareness	Polarity	Beauty	Casanova
Relationships	Denial	Surface – Shallow	Philanderer
Comparison	Mask	Half-truths	Idealism
Others' needs	Relativity	Boundary-less	Appearance
Projection	Relatedness	Social grace	
Pleasing others	Co-dependency	Partner	

Scorpio keywords

Commitment	Shared resources	Metamorphosis	Priest / Priestess
Fear of entrapment	Resourcefulness	Alchemy	Egypt
Spy	Power – Powerlessness	Taboo	Intensity
Betrayal	Magic – Curses	Covert	Fascination
Compulsions	Corrupt power	Secret	Macabre
Obsessions	Manipulation	Darkness	Psychological
Fear of Vulnerability	Loss	Sexual violence	Violence
Fear of Intimacy	Abandonment	Phobia	Evil
Sex	Merging	Paranoia	Destruction

Sagittarius keywords

Adaptability	Intuition	Explorer	Half-truth
Beliefs	Honesty	Inspiration	Silver-tongue devil
Dogmatic	Long Journeys	Restless	Charmer
Philosophy	Pilgrimage	Wanderlust	Guru
Wisdom	Multicultural	Zealous faith	Teacher
Meaning	Foreigners	Missionary	Natural Law
Expansion	Immigrants	Priest	Shaman
Trust	Ideals / Ideas	Convert	Alienation
Faith	Nomad	Sales	
Truth	Homeless	Freedom	

Capricorn keywords

Social position	Punishment	Man-made law	Patriotism
Authority	Discipline	Ancestral	Politics
Judgment	Totalitarian	Tradition	Responsibility
Judge	Fear	Guilt	Depression
Maturity	Rigid	Self-defeat	Burden
Old age	Paralysis	Futility	"Fall from Grace"
Repression	Conformity	Boundaries	Conditioning by family/society
Oppression	Suicide	Structure / Form	
Grief	Isolation	Nationalism	

Aquarius keywords

Liberation from conditioning	Alienation	Trauma	Prometheus
Individuality	Hopes / Ideals	Mass trauma	Revolutionary
Individuation	Long-term memory	Splitting	Ostracized
Rebellion	Anarchist	Unique	Cast out
Like-minded groups	Tribe	Shocking	Astral plane
Group hysteria	Community	Projection	Telepathic
Secret societies	Fragmentation	Hyper-activity	Objective awareness

Pisces keywords

Disillusionment	Psychic	Wounded	Musician
Victim	Astral glamour	Suffering	Loss / erosion
Persecuted	Addiction	Innocence	Isolation
Martyr	Escape	The Fool	Confusion
Savior	Hopeless	Suicide	Dreamer
Illusions	Helpless	Lost identity	Dissociation
Priest	Weak boundaries	Masochist	Disbelief
Alcoholism	Surrender	Fantasy	Drugs
Mystic	Subconscious	Naïve	Guilt (individual)
Medium	Transcendence	Poet	Guilt (collective)

FIG 1   Chakra Correlations

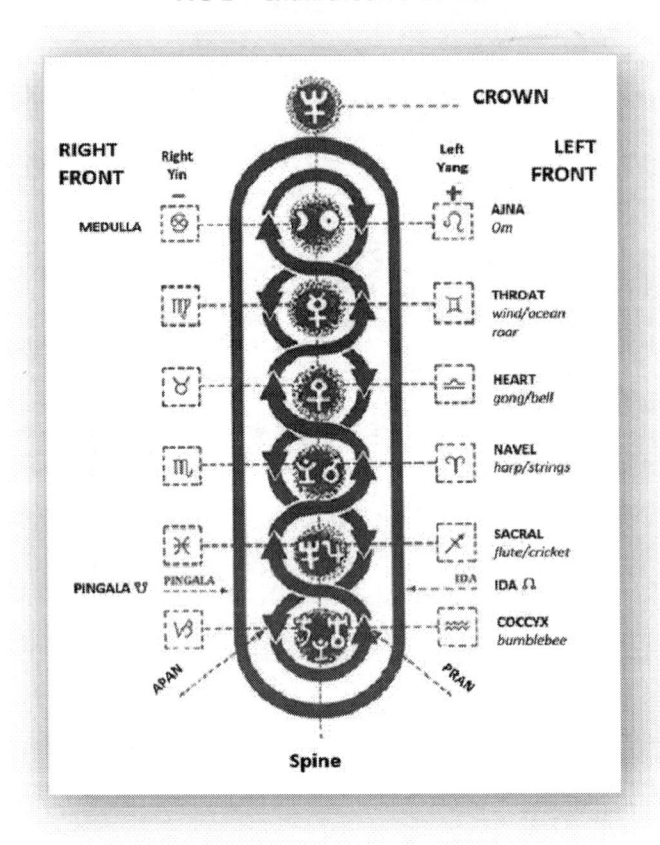

FIG 2   EA Aspects, Phases and Degrees Chart

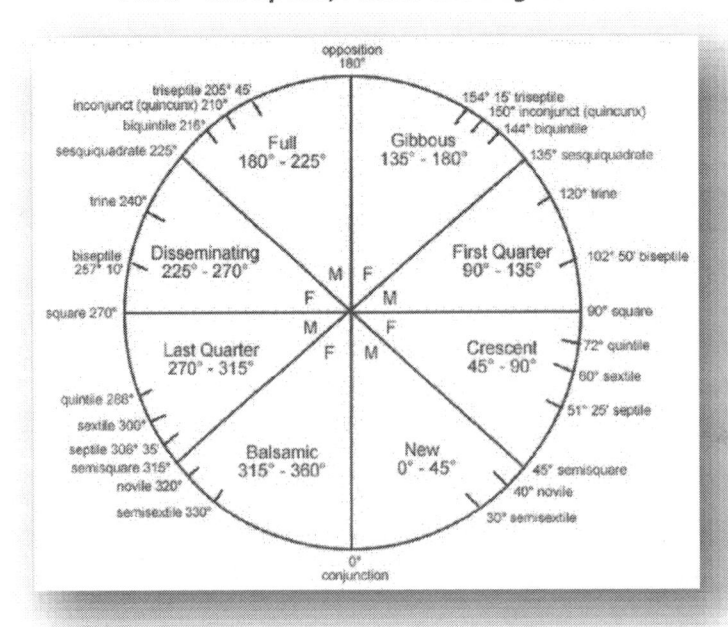

Made in the USA
Lexington, KY
20 June 2015